HANDBOOK OF BILINGUALISM

Handbook of Bilingualism

Psycholinguistic Approaches

EDITED BY
JUDITH F. KROLL
ANNETTE M. B. DE GROOT

OXFORD
UNIVERSITY PRESS

Oxford University Press, Inc., publishes works that further
Oxford University's objective of excellence
in research, scholarship, and education.

Oxford   New York
Auckland   Cape Town   Dar es Salaam   Hong Kong   Karachi
Kuala Lumpur   Madrid   Melbourne   Mexico City   Nairobi
New Delhi   Shanghai   Taipei   Toronto

With offices in
Argentina   Austria   Brazil   Chile   Czech Republic   France   Greece
Guatemala   Hungary   Italy   Japan   Poland   Portugal   Singapore
South Korea   Switzerland   Thailand   Turkey   Ukraine   Vietnam

Copyright © 2005 by Oxford University Press, Inc.

Published by Oxford University Press, Inc.
198 Madison Avenue, New York, New York 10016

www.oup.com

First issued as an Oxford University Press paperback, 2009

Oxford is a registered trademark of Oxford University Press

Library of Congress Cataloging-in-Publication Data
Handbook of bilingualism : psycholinguistic approaches /
edited by Judith F. Kroll,
    Annette M.B. De Groot.
        p. cm.
    Includes bibliographical references and index.
    ISBN: 978-0-19-537365-3 (pbk.)
    1. Bilingualism—Psychological aspects. 2. Language acquisition. I. Groot, A. M. B. de.
    II. Title.

P115.4.K76 2008
404´.2019—dc22   2008039711

9 8 7 6 5 4 3 2

Printed in the United States of America
on acid-free paper

Preface and Acknowledgments

As recently as 10 years ago, the topic of bilingualism was somewhat outside the mainstream of experimental cognitive psychology. There were many studies on disparate topics, but no systematic body of research that could be identified as constituting a clear focus within the field. In the time since, activity in this field has accelerated at a dizzying pace. There are now journals, a variety of books, international meetings, and cross-disciplinary graduate programs in psychology, linguistics, applied linguistics, and education, all dedicated to second language acquisition and bilingualism. In 1997, we edited a book, *Tutorials in Bilingualism* (Erlbaum), to provide students and researchers with overviews of the topics that we considered central to the emerging psycholinguistics of bilingualism. At the time, we could not possibly anticipate the rapid developments in this field that have occurred.

As we try to understand why interest in cognitive approaches to bilingualism has grown, we can point to the global economy, to the increasing multilingual presence in the United States and elsewhere where monolingualism was once the accepted norm, to debates regarding bilingual education, and to the introduction of exciting new methods for revealing brain activity during language processing. But, what we really believe is the main reason for this increased interest is that cognitive scientists have come to appreciate that learning and using more than one language is a natural circumstance of cognition. Not only does research on second language learning and bilingualism provide crucial evidence regarding the universality of cognitive principles, but it also provides an important tool for revealing constraints within the cognitive architecture.

The chapters in this book represent what we take to be the essence of the new psycholinguistics of bilingualism, one that is informed by developments in linguistics and neuroscience and that builds on the rigor of experimental cognitive science. As in any young field, there are some topics that garner more attention than others and some questions that historically have been underrepresented. It is our hope that the chapters in this volume will satisfy the interest of students who wish to learn about psycholinguistic approaches to bilingualism and at the same time encourage researchers across a range of fields to see that there are still many important questions yet to be answered.

We have had the good fortune of being colleagues and collaborators for 15 years. During this time, we have exchanged ideas and students, we have co-taught a course, visited each other's labs, and shared a special friendship. This book, like our previous edited volume, is a full and equal collaboration between us.

There are many people we wish to thank for their support in the process of compiling this volume. At the top of the list are the contributors; they were generous with their time, patient with us in the process of assembling a handbook of this length, and wrote outstanding reviews of the research in their respective areas. We thank Catharine Carlin, our editor at Oxford, who was extremely encouraging, incredibly patient, responsive to all of our questions; she made us feel throughout that the project was as exciting in the thick of revisions as on the first day it was proposed.

We have been fortunate to work with a wonderful group of students, visitors, and colleagues who spent time in our labs during this period and enriched our lives both professionally and personally. They include Teresa Bajo, Susan Bobb, Susanne Borgwaldt, Kate Cheng, Ingrid Christoffels, Philip Delmaar, Sara Hasson, Noriko Hoshino, Cristina Izura, April Jacobs, Nan Jiang, Rineke Keijzer, Martin van Leerdam, Jared Linck, Lorella Lotto, Pedro Macizo, Erica Michael, Natasha Miller, Maya Misra, Pilar Pinar, Petra Poelmans, Rik Poot, Carmen Ruiz, Mikel Santesteban, Béryl Schulpen, Ana Schwartz, Bianca Sumutka, Gretchen Sunderman, Natasha Tokowicz, Rosanne van den Brink, Ellen van den Eijnden, and Zofia Wodniecka.

The quality of our intellectual lives has also been supported by a fantastic group of colleagues on both sides of the Atlantic; they made discussions about bilingualism a vibrant source of stimulation that has led to enduring collaborations. We especially thank Dorothee Chwilla, Albert Costa, Ton Dijkstra, Giuli Dussias, Chip Gerfen, David Green, Jan Hulstijn, Wido La Heij, Jaap Murre, Scott Payne, Nuria Sagarra, Janet van Hell, Vincent van Heuven, and Dan Weiss.

Finally, each us of would like to thank some special people in our lives. Judy would like to thank her parents, Ruth Kroll and Sol Kroll, who have always been a source of support; her twin daughters, Nora Kroll-Rosenbaum and Sarah Kroll-Rosenbaum, who know what it means to be on the team and how to make jokes about psycholinguistic models that might never occur to anyone else in the field; her sister Elise Kroll, who is the only real bilingual in the immediate family; and especially David Rosenbaum, her partner of 28 years, who understands that for a couple to have two careers is a bit like having two languages—they are always active to a high level, they compete, and somehow they manage to speak in a single voice that sustains them both. It is to them that she dedicates this effort.

Annette would like to thank her father, Johan de Groot, who at a very respectable age is still closely monitoring the well-being of each member of his large family; her son Jan, just for being the nice young man he is; her sisters Francis de Groot, Monique de Groot, Birgitte van den Elzen, and especially Marion de Groot, who over the years gradually filled the void that was left following the death of Annette's twin sister, Jeannette de Groot. It is to the memory of Jeannette and of her mother, Cher de Groot, that she dedicates this effort.

Contents

Contributors

Dr. Jubin Abutalebi
Centre for Cognitive Neuroscience
Vita Salute San Raffaele University
Via Olgettina, 58
I-20132 Milan
Italy
E-mail: abutalebi.jubin@hsr.it

Dr. Ellen Bialystok
Department of Psychology
York University
Toronto, Ontario M3J 1P3
Canada
E-mail: ellenb@yorku.ca

Dr. David Birdsong
Department of French and Italian
University of Texas at Austin
1 University Station B7600
Austin, TX 78712
USA
E-mail: birdsong@ccwf.cc.utexas.edu

Dr. Laura Bosch
Parc Científic and
Departament Psicologia Bàsica
Universitat de Barcelona
P. de la Vall d'Hebron, 171
08035 Barcelona
Spain
E-mail: laurabosch@ub.edu

Dr. Stefano F. Cappa
Department of Neuroscience
Vita Salute San Raffaele University
Via Olgettina, 58
I-20132 Milan
Italy
E-mail: cappa.stefano@hsr.it

Dr. Ingrid K. Christoffels
Department of Neurocognition
Faculty of Psychology
Maastricht University
P.O. Box 616
6200 MD Maastricht
The Netherlands
E-mail: i.christoffels@psychology.
  unimaas.nl

Dr. Albert Costa
Parc Científic and
Departament Psicologia Bàsica
Universitat de Barcelona
P. de la Vall d'Hebron, 171
08035 Barcelona
Spain
E-mail: acosta@ub.edu

Dr. Annick De Houwer
UIA-PSW
University of Antwerp
Universiteitsplein 1
B2610-Antwerpen
Belgium
E-mail: annick.dehouwer@ua.ac.be

Dr. Robert DeKeyser
Department of Linguistics
University of Pittsburgh
Pittsburgh, PA 15260
USA
E-mail: rdk1+@pitt.edu

Dr. Bruno Di Biase
Building A Bankstown Campus
University of Western Sydney
Locked Bag 1797

Penrith South DC NSW 1797
Australia
E-mail: B.DiBiase@uws.edu.au

Dr. Ton Dijkstra
Nijmegen Institute for Cognition
    and Information
Radboud University of Nijmegen
P.O. Box 9104
NL-6500 HE Nijmegen
The Netherlands
E-mail: t.dijkstra@nici.ru.nl

Dr. Nick C. Ellis
English Language Institute
University of Michigan
3134 TCF Building
401 East Liberty Street, Suite 350
Ann Arbor, MI 48104-2298
USA
E-mail: ncellis@umich.edu

Dr. Wendy S. Francis
Department of Psychology
University of Texas at El Paso
500 West University Avenue
El Paso, TX 79968
USA
E-mail: wfrancis@utep.edu

Dr. Cheryl Frenck-Mestre
Laboratoire Parole et Langage
CNRS and Université de Provence
29 avenue Robert Schuman
13621 Aix-en-Provence France
France
E-mail: Frenck@univ-aix.fr or
    frenck@romarin.univ-aix.fr

Dr. José E. García-Albea
Departament de Psicologia
Facultat de Ciències de l'Educació i
    Psicologia
Universitat Rovira i Virgili
Carretera de Valls s/n
Tarragona 43007
Spain

Dr. Tamar H. Gollan
Department of Psychiatry

University of California, San Diego
9500 Gilman Drive
La Jolla, CA 92093-9151-B
USA
E-mail: tgollan@ucsd.edu

Dr. David W. Green
Department of Psychology
University College London
Gower Street
London WC1E 6BT
United Kingdom
E-mail: d.w.green@ucl.ac.uk

Dr. Annette M. B. de Groot
University of Amsterdam
Spui 21
1012 WX Amsterdam
The Netherlands
E-mail: A.M.B.deGroot@uva.nl

Dr. Gisela Håkansson
Department of Linguistics
Lund University
Helgonabacken 12
S-223 62 Lund
Sweden
E-mail: Gisela.Hakansson@ling.lu.se

Dr. Rachel Hull
Department of Psychology MS-25
Rice University
Houston TX 77251
USA
E-mail: rhull@rice.edu

Dr. Jan Hulstijn
Department of Second Language
    Acquisition
University of Amsterdam
Spuistraat 134
1012 VB Amsterdam
The Netherlands
E-mail: hulstijn@hum.uva.nl

Dr. Satomi Kawaguchi
Building A Bankstown Campus
University of Western Sydney
Locked Bag 1797
Penrith South DC NSW 1797

Australia
E-mail: s.kawaguchi@uws.edu.au

Dr. Judith F. Kroll
Department of Psychology
641 Moore Building
Pennsylvania State University
University Park, PA 16802
USA
E-mail: jfk7@psu.edu

Dr. Wido La Heij
Cognitive Psychology Unit
Leiden University
P.O. Box 9555
2300 RB Leiden
The Netherlands
E-mail: laheij@fsw.leidenuniv.nl

Dr. Jenifer Larson-Hall
Department of English, Linguistics
    Division
University of North Texas
P.O. Box 311307
Denton, TX 76203
USA
E-mail: jenifer@unt.edu

Dr. Brian MacWhinney
Department of Psychology
Carnegie Mellon University
5000 Forbes Avenue
Pittsburgh, PA 15213
USA
E-mail: macw@cmu.edu

Dr. Renata F. I. Meuter
School of Psychology and Counselling
Queensland University of Technology
Carseldine Campus, Beams Road
Carseldine, QLD 4034
Australia
E-mail: r.meuter@qut.edu.au

Dr. Erica B. Michael
Department of Psychology
Carnegie Mellon University
Pittsburgh, PA 15213
USA
E-mail: emichael@andrew.cmu.edu

Dr. Jaap M. J. Murre
Department of Psychology
University of Amsterdam
Roetersstraat 15
1018 WB
Amsterdam
The Netherlands
E-mail: pn_murre@macmail.psy.uva.nl

Dr. Carol Myers-Scotton
Linguistics Program
University of South Carolina
Columbia, SC 29208
USA
E-mail: CarolMS@gwm.sc.edu

Dr. Michel Paradis
Department of Linguistics
McGill University
1085 Dr. Penfield Avenue
Montreal, Quebec H3A 1A7
Canada
E-mail: michel.paradis@mcgill.ca

Dr. Aneta Pavlenko
Department of Curriculum, Instruction,
    and Technology in Education
Temple University
College of Education
457 Ritter Hall (003-00)
Philadelphia, PA 19122
USA
E-mail: apavlenk@astro.temple.edu

Dr. Daniela Perani
Department of Neuroscience
Vita Salute San Raffaele University
Via Olgettina, 58
I-20132 Milan
Italy
E-mail: daniela.perani@hsr.it

Dr. Charles A. Perfetti
Learning Research and
    Development Center
3939 O'Hara Street
University of Pittsburgh
Pittsburgh, PA 15260
USA
E-mail: Perfetti@pitt.edu

Dr. Manfred Pienemann
Department of Linguistics
University of Paderborn
Warburger Str. 100
Gebäude H, Raum 341
D-33100 Paderborn
Germany

and

The University of Newcastle Upon Tyne
Tyne, United Kingdom
E-mail: Pienemann@zitmail.upb.de

Dr. Rosa Sánchez-Casas
Facultat de Ciències de
   l'Educació i Psicologia
Universitat Rovira i Virgili
Carretera de Valls s/n
Tarragona 43007
Spain
E-mail: rscp@fcep.urv.es

Dr. Herbert Schriefers
Nijmegen Institute for Cognition
   and Information (NICI)
Radboud University of Nijmegen
P.O. Box 9104
NL-6500 HE Nijmegen
The Netherlands
E-mail: schriefers@nici.ru.nl

Dr. Núria Sebastián-Gallés
Parc Científic and
Departament Psicologia Bàsica
Universitat de Barcelona
P. de la Vall d'Hebron, 171
08035 Barcelona
Spain
E-mail: nsebastian@ub.edu

Dr. Norman Segalowitz
Department of Psychology
Concordia University
7141 Sherbrooke Street West

Montréal, Québec H4B 1R6
Canada
E-mail: norman.segalowitz@concordia.ca

Dr. Michael S. C. Thomas
School of Psychology
Birkbeck College, University of London
Malet Street
London WC1E 7HX
United Kingdom
E-mail: m.thomas@psychology.bbk.ac.uk

Dr. Natasha Tokowicz
Learning Research and Development
   Center
3939 O'Hara Street
University of Pittsburgh
Pittsburgh, PA 15260
USA
E-mail: tokowicz@pitt.edu

Dr. Jyotsna Vaid
Department of Psychology
Texas A&M University
College Station, TX 77843-4235
USA
E-mail: jxv@psyc.tamu.edu

Dr. Janet G. van Hell
Department of Special Education
Radboud University Nijmegen
Montessorilaan 3
6525 HR Nijmegen
The Netherlands
E-mail: j.vanhell@pwo.ru.nl

Dr. Walter J. B. van Heuven
Nijmegen Institute for Cognition
   and Information
Radboud University Nijmegen
P.O. Box 9104
6500 HE Nijmegen
The Netherlands
E-mail: w.vanheuven@nici.ru.nl

PART I

ACQUISITION

Nick C. Ellis

Introduction to Part I
Acquisition

How we acquire our native language is a question fundamental to humankind. It pervades the long history of our inquiries, yet it is an interesting and difficult enough issue to have escaped a consensual answer to date. Indeed, never has there been so much debate as there currently is concerning the mechanisms of first language (L1) acquisition. Simple arithmetic might suggest that the question of bilingual acquisition, then, would be doubly worthwhile. But the chapters that follow here belie this calculation, with the second language (L2) equals two times the L1 sum falling far short of the real interest mark.

Factors such as language transfer, typological distance and interaction, and the much wider possible ranges of L2 social environments, ages of acquisition, levels of learner cognitive and brain development, motivations, educational environments, and language exposure conspire in multiple factorial interactions to make bilingualism and second language acquisition (SLA) far more complex and fascinating than the mere sum of two first language acquisition (L1A) parts. And, multilingualism is humankind's norm. With perhaps 6,000 languages of the world, far more than the 200 or so countries, an equally rough-and-ready calculation suggests that human beings are more likely than not to be able to speak more than one language.

This part on acquisition provides tutorials on what is currently known about how these diverse factors make SLA so rich and interesting. In what follows here, I briefly introduce these reviews and pull out some of the key themes, generalities, and differences—some summary and sums. A number of the chapters cover areas that reflect traditional boundaries in linguistics: vocabulary, syntax, phonology, grammar, and processing. Others review work done within an approach: the Competition Model, processability theory, or connectionism. Others still focus on factors that moderate the degree to which SLA resembles L1A: age and transfer.

As you read these chapters, bear ever in mind the scope for complexity in SLA and avoid over-ready generalizations. Despite their likenesses, the sum L1A = SLA is as much an oversimplification as is the assumption of identity even within bilingual acquisition itself: Acquiring two languages from birth (bilingual first language acquisition, BFLA) is quite a different thing from acquiring a second language in later life, BFLA ≠ SLA. Moderating variables such as age have differential effects on the degrees to which L1A ≈ SLA in phonology, lexicon, syntax, morphology, and pragmatics. Effects that pertain in one representational domain need not apply in another; for example, transfer pervades phonology, but may be more circumscribed in intermediate and higher levels of syntactic generation.

Vocabulary

In chapter 1, De Groot and Van Hell consider the learning of foreign language vocabulary. The starting point of SLA is words and lexicalized phrases, and vocabulary acquisition continues as a constant throughout our experience of language: However proficient we are, most days provide us the experience of new words. The richness of learners' vocabulary is a major determinant of both their communicative efficiency and their understanding of their second language, and vocabulary breadth fuels the acquisition of other language representations too, with a sufficient mass of exemplars providing the database from which the regularities of phonology, morphology, and syntax can be abstracted.

De Groot and Van Hell focus on direct methods of learning vocabulary because a vocabulary of the 3,000 most frequent word families provides around 95% of the coverage of written texts. They review keyword, rote-rehearsal, word association, and picture association methods for learning foreign language vocabulary, and they evaluate their effects on receptive and productive learning, speed of access, and resistance to forgetting. Words vary on various dimensions, such as their concreteness; their morphological, phonological, and orthographic complexity; their frequency; and their cognate status. De Groot and Van Hell show that all of these factors affect the ease of learning a word and its eventual representation. Concrete words are easier to learn than abstract words, a result of their greater information content, richer representation, and greater opportunity for anchoring and retrieval. Word forms that are phonologically familiar to the learner are easier than those that sound more foreign. These two factors compound in making cognate words particularly easy to learn. De Groot and Van Hell analyze these effects in terms of their implications for the structure of the bilingual lexicon, that is, whether it is compound, coordinate, or subordinate, an issue considered in parts II and III of this volume as it applies to proficient bilingual representation.

Whatever the structure of the bilingual lexicon at fluency, at which point thousands of hours of contextualized L2 vocabulary use have ground direct connections between the L2 forms and their meanings, the evidence here suggests a word association organization of the low-proficiency learner by which the processing of L2 is mediated via the L1. Early L2 vocabulary acquisition is parasitic on L1 phonological representations, L1 conceptual representations, and L1 word-concept mappings; L2–L1 independence only comes as a result of considerable L2 experience.

Syntax

In chapter 2, De Houwer focuses on early bilingual acquisition of morphosyntax. In acquiring two languages from birth with parents who accord to the "one person, one language" principle, a situation referred to as BFLA, do children undergo a double acquisition process in which the two morphosyntactic systems are acquired in parallel as fundamentally independent closed systems (the Separate Development Hypothesis, SDH)? Alternatively, does BFLA produce a single hybrid, a "Mish-Mash" that results from systematic morphosyntactic influence of each language on the other? Research in the 1970s suggested the single-system hypothesis held, with children systematically applying the same syntactic rules to both languages.

De Houwer corrects this misapprehension. She begins with a clear methodological analysis of the types of evidence required to test the SDH, particularly that separate development must be evident for most of the comparable morphosyntactic structures in the child's speech that reflect differences in the input languages. She then reviews the majority of the longitudinal studies published in the last 15 years that have looked at morphosyntactic development in BFLA children. Her analysis of the speech productions of these 29 children between the ages of 1 and nearly 6 years, who together acquired 12 languages in 13 different combinations, showed that no child produced the sort of language repertoire that would be predicted to develop in bilingual children in line with a transfer theory. Young bilingual children reflect the structural possibilities of both languages of exposure and are able to produce utterances that are clearly relatable to each of their different languages; from very early on, the morphosyntactic development of the one language does not have any fundamental effect on the morphosyntactic development of the other.

In general, BFLA children's language-specific development within one language differs little from that of monolingual acquisition, except of course that bilingual children do it for two languages at a time. Equally, like adult bilinguals, young BFLA children are able to switch between languages very easily, either at utterance boundaries or within utterances. De Houwer also claims that there is no evidence that hearing two languages from birth leads to language delay. Empirical confirmation of the SDH entails that young bilingual children are keenly attuned to the specific linguistic environments in which they find themselves.

In chapter 3, MacWhinney considers SLA. In contrast to infant (B)FLA, L2 learners already know a great deal about the world, their brains are committed and entrenched in their L1, and they cannot rely on an intense system of social support from their caregivers. These differences have led some researchers to propose that SLA requires a totally separate understanding from L1A. Yet the many similarities of microprocess in first and second language acquisition and the fact that L2 learning is influenced by transfer from L1 mean that a model of SLA must take into account the acquisition and structure of L1.

For these reasons MacWhinney sketches the plan of a new unified model in which the mechanisms of L1 learning are seen as a subset of the mechanisms of L2 learning. This unified account builds on his earlier Competition Model, which maintains that the learner's task is to learn the forms of language that serve as the most reliable cues to interpretation—in essence, trying to learn the probability distribution $P_{(interpretation|cue, context)}$, a mapping from form to meaning conditioned by context, with the different interpretations competing for realization in any particular context according to their cue strength. All language processing can be viewed thus as a set of competitive interactions driven by either auditory and formal cues in comprehension or functional cues in production.

The unified model supports this theory of cue validity by extending it here with additional theoretical constructs for dealing with cue cost and cue support. Cue cost relates to the salience of formal cues, particularly the forms that are not salient to the learner because of their expectations that have developed from their first language experience: These are aspects of learned selective attention resulting from transfer. To acquire these low-salience cues properly, L2 learners can support their implicit learning with additional cognitive mechanisms, such as combinatorial learning, chunking, and use of analogy in the acquisition of new linguistic constructions, mnemonics, and other metalinguistic knowledge and the use of social support strategies.

The unified model incorporates a grounded cognition, functional explanation of grammar as a set of devices that marks the flow of perspective across five cognitive domains: direct perception, space–time deixis, causal action, social roles, and belief systems. In these ways, MacWhinney links research in bilingualism to mainstream cognitive psychology and to cognitive and functional linguistics. All of these areas predict that there will be considerable transfer in SLA: Connectionism predicts it, spreading activation predicts it, the notion of "thinking for speaking" predicts it, and perceptual learning and interference theory predict it. MacWhinney reviews the factors that promote, and those that protect against, language transfer in phonology, lexicon, syntax, morphology, and pragmatics.

Phonology and Bilingualism

In chapter 4, Sebastián-Gallés and Bosch consider bilingual acquisition of phonology. In the first year of life, it is almost guaranteed that monolingual children will acquire the ability to process the sound system of their native language. Yet, when L2 learners later in life try to acquire these same abilities, most of them do not succeed; their speech is betrayed by their nonnative accent; in listening, they often fail to perceive foreign sounds correctly.

Sebastián-Gallés and Bosch consider L1A, BFLA, and adult SLA of the range of systems of phonological representation. At 4.5 months of age, bilingual infants can separate their languages, recognizing when there is a switch from one to the other, even if they are rhythmically very similar. By 6 months old, monolingual infants show maternal language-specific phoneme perception behavior, and their sensitivity to nonnative phonetic contrasts declines during the first year of life.

Thus, acquisition reflects processes of perceptual reorganization that result from linguistic experience, with monolingual children's phonological system becoming perceptually tuned to categorize their native language optimally. For bilingual children, the outcome of these perceptual reorganization processes should result in two sound systems that correspond to the two languages of their experience. It does, but their perceptual learning takes longer: It is only by 14–21 months of age that bilinguals show evidence of categorizing stimuli in each of their two languages as do monolinguals.

If these discrimination capacities of BFLA children are temporarily delayed in comparison to monolinguals, this is nothing compared to the difficulties of second language learners when processing nonnative phonemes. Sebastián-Gallés and Bosch review theories of why is it so difficult to perceive some foreign contrasts and why these difficulties are not "universal," but depend on the first language of the listener: The ease or difficulty with which two phonemes will be discriminated depends on the similarities and differences between L1 and L2 phoneme systems. They then ask these same questions for bilingual acquisition of the perception of stress, phonotactics, and receptive and productive lexicons. The lexical activation studies addressed in this volume in chapters concerning adult bilingual comprehension, production, and control persuasively demonstrate that, even when placed in a totally monolingual mode, phonological input activates both of the bilingual's auditory lexicons. The acquisition and processing of phonology is riddled with transfer effects.

Biological Bases

Chapters 5 and 6 provide a balanced perspective on issues relating to age and critical periods for SLA. It is an incontrovertible fact that ultimate second language attainment is less successful in older than younger learners. Both chapters agree on this. There is a large body of empirical evidence showing that age of acquisition (AoA) is strongly negatively correlated with ultimate second language proficiency, for grammar as well as for pronunciation. But, close scrutiny of this effect reveals a range of different interpretations, the implications of which are currently under debate in the literature.

In chapter 5, DeKeyser and Larson-Hall present a detailed review of the published results relating AoA and proficiency. These studies have tested speakers of a wide variety of languages and used a wide variety of testing formats and dependent variables, albeit with grammaticality judgments as the most common measure of morphosyntax and global pronunciation ratings the most common index of phonological proficiency. The large majority of these studies demonstrated substantial child–adult differences or strong correlations between AoA and L2 proficiency. L2 learners' performance in morphosyntax varied as a function of age more when grammaticality items were presented in oral rather than written form, and not all areas of the target language grammar were equally susceptible to age effects.

Despite these variations, DeKeyser and Larson-Hall argue that the evidence is doubtful that any person has learned a second language perfectly in adulthood, claiming that four studies showing overlap between adult and native acquirers for morphosyntax can be explained to result from methodological factors, and that the rare observations that some learners can achieve very high levels of nativelike pronunciation are limited to performance on constrained rather than spontaneous production tasks. Their subsequent analysis considers whether the age effect may be caused by confounded variables such as quantity and quality of input, amount of practice, level of motivation, and other social variables differentiating child and adult learners, but they discount the role of these confounds because these variables play a limited role when the effect of AoA is removed statistically; AoA maintains a large and significant role when the social and environmental variables are removed.

Despite their clear conclusion that there is a maturational decline in second language learning capacity during childhood, DeKeyser and Larson-Hall caution that it is important not to overinterpret the implications of this finding for educational practice. The observation that "earlier is better" only applies to certain kinds of naturalistic learning,

which schools typically cannot provide. The implication of this research for education is that instruction should be adapted to the age of the learner, not that learners should necessarily be taught at a young age. If early language teaching is needed, it should be based on communicative input and interaction, whereas adolescents and adults need additional focus on form to aid explicit learning mechanisms, which at least some of them can substitute for implicit learning with a satisfactory degree of success.

In chapter 6, Birdsong subjects many of these same studies relating age and SLA to an equally admirable methodological scrutiny. He cautions that there is a constant need to assess independently the effects of length of residence (and consequent amount of L2 exposure) and AoA. But, his major critique concerns not the effect of age per se, but rather whether the reported relationships between AoA and attainment conform to a strict notion of a critical period. The orthodox conception of a critical period hypothesis is that there is a circumscribed developmental period before adulthood during which SLA is essentially guaranteed and after which mastery of an L2 is not attainable. Accordingly, there should be discontinuities in the function relating age and ultimate attainment. In particular, there should be an offset that coincides with the point at which full neurocognitive maturation is reached and after which no further age effects are predicted.

Birdsong's analysis of end-state SLA research reveals little congruence with these geometric and temporal features of critical periods. The geometry of the age function (its slope and any discontinuities), and temporal features of the age function (the points at which AoA begins to, and ceases to, correlate significantly with outcomes) vary from study to study, depending on such factors as the linguistic feature tested, amount of L2 use, and L1-L2 pairing. The general conclusion is that there is no apparent period within which age effects are observed, but rather that they persist indefinitely.

Birdsong also reviews these studies to determine whether there are any cases of nativelike attainment in late bilinguals. He concludes that this is possible in rare but nonnegligible frequencies, and that the 5% or greater incidence of nativelikeness in late bilinguals, which is roughly as predicted from the slope of the age function, is a substantial enough incidence to warrant rejection of a strong critical period hypothesis for SLA.

The Human Language Processor, Grammar, Transfer, and Acquisition

In chapter 7, Pienemann, Di Biase, Håkansson, and Kawaguchi describe processability theory (PT), a psycholinguistic analysis of the human language processor and its operation according to linguistic analyses using lexical-functional grammar, a unification grammar attractive in its typological and psychological plausibility. The basic logic underlying PT is that structural options are produced in the learner's interlanguage only if the necessary processing procedures are available. Language acquisition routes are thus constrained by the architecture of the human language processor because, for linguistic hypotheses to transform into executable processing skills, the processor needs to have the capacity for processing the structures relating to those hypotheses.

PT can be applied cross-linguistically to investigate the nature of the computational mechanisms involved in the processing and acquisition of different L1s. PT can also be used to analyze the interplay between L1 transfer and psycholinguistic constraints on L2 processability: It assumes that the initial state of the L2 does not necessarily equal the final state of the L1 because there is no guarantee that a given L1 structure is processable by the underdeveloped L2 parser. In other words, L1 transfer is constrained by the capacity of the language processor of the L2 learner irrespective of the typological distance between the two languages.

Pienemann et al. present a cross-linguistic survey of L1 transfer effects in SLA and demonstrate (a) that learners of closely related languages do not necessarily transfer grammatical features at the initial state even if these features are contained in both L1 and L2, providing the features are located higher up the processability hierarchy; (b) that such features are transferred when the interlanguage has developed the necessary processing prerequisites; and (c) that typological distance and differences in grammatical marking need not constitute a barrier to learning if the feature to be learned is processable at the given point in time. These findings strongly qualify theories that emphasize extensive L1 transfer at the initial state, and they demonstrate the ways that processability moderates L1 transfer.

Computational Simulation

In chapter 8, Murre reviews computational models of monolingual and bilingual acquisition. As is abundantly clear from the chapters preceding it, the ways by which exposure to tens of hundreds of hours of language input results in the mental representation of language are hugely complex. There are too many variables to hold in mind for a properly considered complete theory. Therefore, language researchers take recourse to computer modeling by which the test of the simulation is whether competences emerge that parallel those of human language learners exposed to similar input. In this way, the debate between deductive and inductive approaches to language acquisition is being rephrased in terms of well-articulated models and real-world data.

Murre reviews computational simulation research into language acquisition using subsymbolic–inductive connectionist approaches. Such research demonstrates that, despite being very noisy and inconsistent, the nature of language input is nevertheless sufficient to support inductive mechanisms by which seemingly rulelike behavior emerges from a data-driven learning process. Examples are given from a variety of language domains (including stress assignment, phonology, past tense formation, localization, and certain aspects of semantics) using a variety of exemplar-based and connectionist architectures (including feedforward networks, simple recurrent networks, Hopfield nets, and Kohonen self-organizing maps for monolingual perceptual and semantic representation and a Self-Organizing Connectionist Model of Bilingual Processing) and a variety of theoretical frameworks (including latent semantic analysis, the Competition Model, the Interactive Activation Model and its bilingual extensions Bilingual Interactive Activation and Bilingual Model of Lexical Access, and the Bilingual Speech Learning Model).

Different aspects of language are best modeled using different architectures, a finding that accords well with the individualities outlined at the beginning of this introduction. Murre concludes that, compared to the thriving field of computational psycholinguistics and the developing subfields of models of language acquisition or models of bilingual processing, there are still very few models of bilingual language acquisition. Murre suggests a number of areas of bilingual acquisition ripe for simulation research.

Summary

As each of these chapters shows, we have come a long way in our understanding of these complex issues. The most telling insight, which only be-comes apparent from the compendium of a hand-book like this, is what is seen from the alignment and comparison of what is currently known about these issues when taken together. It is clear that a true understanding can only come from the synthe-sis of these different questions and approaches. Three themes stand out in my mind in illustration.

The first is the age factor and how it engages aspects of interaction and contexts of acquisition, education, transfer, and brain. Although DeKeyser and Larson-Hall and Birdsong might disagree over continuity/discontinuity in the AoA/SLA end-state function and about the possibility of nativelike at-tainment in late bilinguals, they are in clear accord that SLA is less successful in older learners. There follows the question of why this should be, a single question that begs considerable further research. What are the brain mechanisms that underpin such loss of plasticity? Are they a function of age or increasing L1 entrenchment? What is the role of linguistic variables in determining the timing and shape features of the age function? What are the cognitive developmental factors relating to these differences, particularly those relating to implicit and explicit learning potential in adults and chil-dren? What are the implications for the promotion of multilingualism?

The second is second language processing (Pie-nemann et al.). We require a psycholinguistically plausible account of grammar, one with processing stages that are clearly specified, and one that can be applied to different languages in a principled way. We need a well-specified theory of the architecture of the human language processor. We need to un-derstand how this processor develops and how new routines are acquired as a result of exposure to the linguistic evidence available from the input. We need to understand language typology and distance. We need to understand the interplay between lan-guage transfer and language-specific growth.

The third is transfer itself. These chapters clearly demonstrate linguistic transfer, most reli-ably regarding the acquisition of L2 phonology (Sebastián-Gallés and Bosch; De Groot and Van Hell), but with examples spanning lexicon, or-thography, syntax, and pragmatics. Hence, Mac-Whinney's general Competition Model dictum that "everything that can transfer will." But, there are situations that also seem to protect against transfer.

BFLA seems to promote rapid language-specific morphosyntax acquisition to the standards ex-pected of monolinguals, not some messy Mish-Mash. To what extent is it the FLA aspect of this equation that allows this success or the clear envi-ronmental cuing that comes from "one person, one language"? Is the acquisition of two separate syntactic systems really as rapid as the acquisition of just one? If so, why is this true for syntax (De Houwer), whereas the BFLA of phonology is some-what delayed in comparison to monolingual acqui-sition (Sebastián-Gallés and Bosch)?

Pienemann et al. similarly provide evidence of lack of transfer in L2 sentence production. Is it the case that transfer has its effects via selective atten-tion, the way learners perceive the L2 input, and the hypotheses they generate about the second lan-guage, whereas the processing of the L2 rapidly becomes L2-content driven, with the modularity of the eventual L2 grammar driven by the combinato-rial possibilities of L2 lexical forms and construc-tions and unsullied by cross-linguistic influence? Modular systems are implicit, the sorts of system that are well simulated by connectionist models (Murre). They are automatic in their inhibition of cross-linguistic competitors. How is this selective interference of a multilingual's other languages controlled? Consciousness unites, with the potential to pull together everything we know. To what extent is transfer an implicit learning phenomenon, and to what extent is it determined by explicit learning under attentional control? What are the cues that multilingual individuals use to determine which language is spoken, how are these mentally re-presented, and how do they function in language processing?

We have to know all of these things. The be-ginnings of answers to some of these questions are to be found elsewhere in this handbook, but in sum, only some. The further concerted efforts of individuals in cognitive neuroscience, linguistics, psychology, and education are required to fully appreciate the complex nature of bilingualism. It has been claimed that binary variables have prop-erties of all other scales: In a paradoxical way, the two values meet requirements of nominal, ordinal, interval, and ratio scales. The evidence of this part shows that it is less of a stretch to claim that bi-lingual language acquisition has properties of first language acquisition and much more besides.

Annette M. B. de Groot
Janet G. van Hell

1

The Learning of Foreign Language Vocabulary

ABSTRACT   This chapter reviews experimental research into learning foreign language (FL) vocabulary, focusing on direct methods of teaching, such as keyword mnemonics, paired association learning (including rote rehearsal), and picture association learning. We discuss the relative effectiveness of these methods, the constraints in using them, and the way they interact with other factors, most notably the amount of experience a learner has had with learning foreign languages. We review research that shows that some types of words are easier to learn than others and discuss the reasons why this might be so. We also discuss the important role that good phonological skills play in successful FL vocabulary learning and review preliminary research that suggests that background music may be beneficial for some FL learners but detrimental for others. Finally, acknowledging the fact that FL learning via one of the direct methods discussed only provides the starting point for FL word learning, we discuss more advanced stages of the full-fledged learning process.

Learning a language, native or foreign/second,[1] involves the learning of a number of language subsystems, including the language's grammar, phonology, and vocabulary. Although vocabulary is obviously of crucial importance to the language learner, foreign language (FL) teachers as well as FL researchers have until recently treated vocabulary as less central to FL learning than grammar and phonology. (See Boyd Zimmerman, 1997, who provides a historical overview of instruction methods for FL teaching, starting at the end of the 18th century, and explains why vocabulary was often neglected in these methods.) Yet, it has been claimed "that native speakers can better understand ungrammatical utterances with accurate vocabulary than those with accurate grammar and inaccurate vocabulary" (Widdowson, 1978, in Boyd Zimmerman, 1997, p. 13). A corollary of this claim is that the chances of getting one's basic needs fulfilled in an FL environment are substantially larger if the FL learner possesses some well-chosen basic vocabulary in that language than when he or she masters the language's grammar flawlessly, a fact that presumably all FL learners who have tried

to make themselves understood in an FL environment are willing to accept (and that is acknowledged by publishers of travel guides, which almost without exception include a carefully selected vocabulary of the language spoken in the country to be visited).

The pivotal role of vocabulary in FL use is also demonstrated in studies that have looked at the relation between FL reading comprehension and FL vocabulary knowledge (e.g., Laufer, 1992, 1997; Nation, 1993). These studies have shown that FL vocabulary knowledge is a good predictor of success in reading in the FL, a finding that echoes the strong relation that has long been known to exist between native language vocabulary knowledge and vocabulary skills (including fast, automatic access of word knowledge in memory) on the one hand and reading in one's native language on the other hand. This relationship has formed the basis of a number of influential models of reading and reading disability (e.g., Perfetti & Roth, 1981; Stanovich, 1980).

The core assumption of these models, supported by a wealth of data, is that fast and automatic access to the words stored in the reader's mental lexicon is a prerequisite of fluent reading. If word recognition fails (because the word encountered is unknown to the reader or because it is known but cannot be accessed rapidly or automatically), reading comprehension breaks down. The reason is that, in the case of laborious, nonautomatic word recognition, precious attentional capacity (precious because only a limited amount of attentional capacity is available at any moment in time) has to be allocated to figuring out the word and its meaning, leaving too little of the remaining attentional capacity to be allocated to higher level processes, such as finding the antecedent for a pronoun.

On acknowledging the importance of vocabulary knowledge and fast access to and retrieval of this knowledge for fluent FL use, teachers and FL learners appear to face an immense and daunting task. A language contains many tens of thousands of words, far too many to teach and learn via a method of direct teaching. Moreover, for each word, ultimately seven types of information have to be learned: phonological and orthographic, syntactic, morphological, pragmatic, articulatory, idiomatic, and semantic information (Schreuder, 1987).

The majority of these words have multiple meanings. It has been suggested that the number of meanings per word amounts to 15 to 20, none of which—contrary to what is often thought—can be singled out as the word's "basic" or "real" meaning (Fries, 1945, in Boyd Zimmerman, 1997). Add to this the fact that word meanings are not stable but instead, just as a language's phonology, develop gradually over time (see Pavlenko, chapter 21, this volume), and it can easily be imagined that the teaching and learning of a full-fledged FL vocabulary is an impossible task that may discourage both teachers and learners of FL and direct their efforts to more manageable components of FL knowledge instead.

However, several studies indicated that familiarity with a relatively small, carefully selected, number of words suffices for adult language comprehension (Laufer, 1992; Nation, 1993; see Hazenberg & Hulstijn, 1996, for a review). Nation argued that a vocabulary of the 3,000 most frequent word families (about 5,000 lexical items; but see Bogaards, 2001) provides around 95% coverage of written texts in English, which should enable an adequate level of comprehension of these texts (but see Hazenberg & Hulstijn, 1996). This point of view has clear implications for FL learning: If the FL learner needs to attain an initial vocabulary of "only" a few thousand words, direct (explicit) vo-

cabulary instruction becomes a feasible means of instruction. The remaining vocabulary can subsequently be learned implicitly, similar to the way native speakers and early bilinguals acquire vocabulary from an early age (e.g., Ellis, 1995) and through extensive reading in the FL.

This chapter focuses on research that has employed direct methods of FL vocabulary teaching (or, from the learner's viewpoint, on direct methods of FL vocabulary *learning*) in (primarily) experimental settings. The first section discusses the various methods used and their effectiveness and constraints. The next two sections focus on the differential learning effects that have been obtained with different types of words. A description of these word-type effects precedes a discussion of plausible theoretical explanations of their occurrence.

A considerable amount of recent research points at the importance of good phonological skills in vocabulary learning. This work constitutes the topic discussed in the next part of this chapter. It is followed by a section that shows that much more is involved in FL vocabulary learning than just storing the FL word's name in memory. The final two sections discuss, first, a topic of obvious pedagogical importance, namely, the beneficial or detrimental effects that background music may have on FL vocabulary learning and, second, a number of the causes of the large differences in FL vocabulary learning outcomes and learning ability that exist across studies and between groups of FL learners and individual FL learners.

Direct Methods of Learning Foreign Language Vocabulary

Keyword Mnemonics

A well-known, imagery-based instruction method for the learning of novel vocabulary, including FL vocabulary, is the keyword method. The keyword method is a mnemonic technique in which learning is divided into two steps. In the first step, one learns to associate the novel word (e.g., *mariposa*) to a keyword (e.g., *marinade*). A keyword is a word in the native language that looks or sounds like the novel word that must be learned. In the second step, the learner creates a mental image in which both the keyword and the first language (L1) translation (here "butterfly") of the novel word interact (e.g., a butterfly swimming in the marinade). The keyword mnemonic thus establishes both a form and a semantic connection (by means of the interactive image) between the novel word and its L1 translation. After learning, presentation of the novel FL word will elicit the keyword, which in turn will evoke the interactive image between the keyword and the novel word, after which the learner can produce the L1 translation.

The keyword method may seem a rather laborious procedure for learning FL vocabulary. Many studies have found, however, that the keyword method facilitates foreign vocabulary learning and enhances recall in comparison to rote rehearsal (in which the novel word and its L1 translation are subvocally repeated) and unstructured learning (in which learners may choose their own strategy; for reviews, see Cohen, 1987; Hulstijn, 1997; Pressley, Levin, & Delaney, 1982). Beneficial effects of the keyword method on learning and immediate recall of FL vocabulary have been obtained in a wide variety of languages, including Chinese (Wang & Thomas, 1992), English (Elhelou, 1994; Rodríguez & Sadoski, 2000), German (e.g., Desrochers, Wieland, & Coté, 1991), Russian (Atkinson & Raugh, 1975), and Tagalog (e.g., Wang, Thomas, & Ouellette, 1992).

The keyword method has been successful in a wide variety of settings, including laboratory experiments (as in Atkinson & Raugh, 1975) and studies in more natural settings, often a classroom (Levin, Pressley, McCormick, Miller, & Shriberg, 1979; Rodríguez & Sadoski, 2000). The method benefited FL vocabulary learning and recall of learners of various ages, ranging from children (e.g., Elhelou, 1994; Pressley, Levin, & Miller, 1981) to elderly learners (Gruneberg & Pascoe, 1996).

The keyword method's success can be illustrated by the classical study of Atkinson and Raugh (1975), which instigated a wealth of studies on keyword mnemonics. These authors had university students learn 120 Russian words on three consecutive days (40 words a day). The learners, all native speakers of English with no prior knowledge of Russian, received instructions to follow the keyword method or were instructed to use any learning method they wished. Atkinson and Raugh found that keyword learners outperformed the own-strategy learners on all recall tests.

A second striking example concerns a study by Beaton, Gruneberg, and Ellis (1995), who studied the 10-year retention of a FL vocabulary of 350 words learned by a 47-year-old university lecturer via the Linkword Italian course. In this course, subsequently published by Gruneberg (1987, in Beaton et al., 1995), the keyword method of vo-

cabulary learning is integrated with basic grammar. After 10 years, without any use of Italian, this person remembered 35% of the previously learned FL vocabulary, and after 10 minutes of relearning, added an additional 93 words to the list of recalled words. Although the learner's performance in acquiring Italian could have been facilitated by his knowledge of other languages, including French, Spanish, German, and Greek, and long-term retention with other instruction methods has not been evaluated, the amount of vocabulary retained after so long is still remarkable.

Theoretical explanations of the benefits of the keyword method point toward an important role of imagery. According to the dual-coding theory of Paivio and colleagues (e.g., Paivio, 1986; Paivio & Desrochers, 1981), the keyword method enhances learning and recall because the method uses both the verbal system and the image system in human memory. During learning, both a verbal and an image code are encoded in memory. Assuming that these codes have additive effects, retrieval of the FL word is facilitated because there are two memory codes for the learning event, either of which can support recall. An alternative explanation was proposed by Marschark and his colleagues, who suggested that imaginal processing facilitates recall by increasing the relative relational value and distinctiveness of the information generated during learning (Marschark, Richman, Yuille, & Hunt, 1987; Marschark & Surian, 1989).

Although many studies reported positive effects of the use of keyword mnemonics in FL vocabulary learning, the findings of other studies suggested that the method may not be effective under all conditions. Questions that have been raised pertain to the long-term benefits of the keyword method and intentional versus incidental learning conditions, its usefulness for certain word types, the effects on retrieval speed, the benefits for experienced learners, and its usefulness for receptive and productive learning and recall. These findings potentially constrain and qualify the general applicability of this method. We discuss each of these topics next.

Durability of Memory Traces   In the majority of studies reporting long-term benefits of the keyword method, the delay interval between learning and testing is typically manipulated within subjects: Each subject is tested both on the immediate test and on subsequent delayed tests. In a series of studies, Wang and Thomas questioned the viability of this approach for measuring long-term effects of the keyword method because the immediate test potentially provides an additional learning trial or allows testing the adequacy of retrieval paths (Wang & Thomas, 1992, 1995; Wang, Thomas, & Ouellette, 1992). They examined the long-term effectiveness of the keyword method by treating the delay interval as a between-subjects variable, testing some learners immediately after study and others only after a delay of several days. Their manipulation also changed the learning set from intentional learning instructions (in which the learners know in advance that their newly acquired knowledge will be tested after learning) to incidental learning instructions. Wang and Thomas convincingly showed that, under these conditions, long-term forgetting is greater for keyword learners than for rote learners (Wang et al., 1992; Wang & Thomas, 1992, 1995; but see Gruneberg, 1998). The poorer retention for keyword learners observed by Wang and Thomas may have surfaced because of the between-subjects manipulation, which prevented additional learning or retrieval rehearsal on the immediate test.

The Role of Word Type   A second potential constraint on the applicability of the keyword method concerns the diversity of the words presented in these studies. In most keyword studies, the FL vocabulary items are concrete words, referring to easily imaginable concepts. This sample of words does not represent adult vocabulary knowledge and language usage faithfully. Moreover, the exclusive use of concrete words may have overestimated the merits of the keyword method: Creating an interactive image between the keyword and the L1 equivalent of the novel FL word, a crucial step in the keyword method, is likely to be easier for concrete words (e.g., *butterfly*) than for abstract words (e.g., *duty*). Ellis (1995) even conjectured that the keyword method would be of little use in learning abstract vocabulary.

However, the few studies that explicitly tested the applicability of the keyword method to words that varied in imageability or concreteness did not seem to substantiate this idea (Delaney, 1978; Pressley et al., 1981; Van Hell & Candia Mahn, 1997; cf. Ellis & Beaton, 1993a). For example, Van Hell and Candia Mahn presented abstract and concrete FL words to keyword learners and rote learners. They found that concrete words were learned and remembered better than abstract words under rote rehearsal instructions (as is commonly found; see the word-type effects discussed in the next part of this section). However, the advantage of

concrete words over abstract words was not notably larger under keyword instructions.

Another type of FL words that may be less suitable for learning via the keyword method is cognates. Remember that the keyword is an L1 word that looks or sounds like the to-be-learned FL word. In learning cognates, for instance, for the Spanish word *rosa*, the most obvious keyword would be its translation, here *rose*. The keyword method thus seems an unnecessarily laborious and ineffective method for learning cognates, particularly considering the large advantage that cognates have over noncognates in the more straightforward learning methods of word association and picture association learning (see the detailed discussion of the role of word type in FL vocabulary learning).

Retrieval Speed   In the keyword literature, the benefits of learning are typically expressed in terms of the percentage or proportion of correctly recalled words, often measured in a cued recall task. In the cued recall task, one of the elements in a pair (the cue) is presented during testing, and the participant is asked to come up with the other element of the pair. In the cross-language variant of the cued recall task, as frequently applied in FL vocabulary learning studies, the cue is a word in one language, and the element to come up with is its translation in the other language; the cross-language version of the cued recall task is thus essentially a word translation task. The cued recall retrieval measure expressed as percentage of correctly recalled words is assumed to reflect the items successfully encoded in long-term memory during learning. However, as discussed in this chapter, fluent language use is determined not only by retrieval accuracy, but also by the speed with which a word can be retrieved from memory. Nearly three decades ago, Atkinson (1975) raised a similar point. He assumed that FL learning via the keyword method would not slow subsequent retrieval of the learned FL words as compared to methods in which word retrieval is less complex, like rote rehearsal.

Remarkably few studies, however, have examined the effect of keyword instruction on FL word retrieval speed (see Van Hell & Candia Mahn, 1997, and Wang & Thomas, 1999, for exceptions). In two experiments, Van Hell and Candia Mahn examined retrieval speed by comparing retrieval times of keyword and rote learners for newly learned FL words in a timed cued recall task. Performance was assessed in three tests: immediately after the learning phase, after a 1-week delay, and after a 2-week delay. In all tests, they observed considerably shorter retrieval times for rote learners than for keyword learners (with the differences ranging between 452 and 966 ms). The faster retrieval times for rote learners were not compromised by poor recall performance. Rather, the proportion of correctly recalled words of rote learners was higher than (Experiment 1) or equal to (Experiment 2) that of the keyword learners. Wang and Thomas (1999) corroborated these results by measuring response times via a timed recognition task (treating the delay interval as a between-subjects factor).

Together, these findings showed that keyword learners need more time to retrieve the newly learned words from memory than rote learners do, suggesting that the retrieval of newly learned words may be slowed by the use of keyword mnemonics. Moreover, it appears that the keyword does not become superfluous, but is still used as a retrieval cue well after learning (cf. Atkinson, 1975). This may impede an important goal of FL learning, namely, the attainment of verbal fluency.

The Role of Experience in Foreign Language Learning   A fourth factor that may constrain the applicability and suitability of the keyword method concerns the learner's amount of FL learning experience. In the majority of keyword studies, the participants were inexperienced FL learners. Studies using more advanced learners suggested that these learners may benefit less from keyword mnemonics than inexperienced learners do. Levin et al. (1979), Moore and Surber (1992), and Hogben and Lawson (1994) used learners who had followed FL classes for at least a year and observed that the typical beneficial effects of keyword mnemonics were less robust with more advanced learners of the target language. These findings were extended by Van Hell and Candia Mahn (1997) to another group of experienced learners, namely, multilingual language users with a considerable amount of experience in learning FL vocabulary (i.e., in English, French, and German), but who had no prior knowledge of the target language, Spanish. In these learners, keyword instructions were less effective than rote rehearsal instructions in both immediate and delayed recall.

These studies suggested that keyword mnemonics are relatively ineffective in experienced FL learners, both advanced learners of the target language and inexperienced learners of the target language who had experience with learning a number of other FLs. Apparently, there is no single most effective way of FL vocabulary learning, but a particular type of learner benefits most from a particular learning method. (Another experimental result that substantiates this claim is presented in the section The Effect of Background Music on Learning Foreign Language Vocabulary.)

Direction of Testing   Another factor that may qualify the benefits of the keyword method concerns the direction of recall. Most keyword studies have used a "receptive" cued recall task in which the newly learned FL word is presented and the L1 translation must be produced; this task corresponds to "backward" word translation (see, e.g., De Groot, Dannenburg, & Van Hell, 1994). The reverse task, "productive" cued recall (or "forward" translation), is used less frequently. Ellis and Beaton (1993a) found that keyword mnemonics are effective for receptive recall, but less so than rote rehearsal instructions for productive recall.

In conclusion, numerous studies reported the beneficial effect of using keyword mnemonics in FL vocabulary learning. Yet, a drawback of the method is that it seems to impede word retrieval after learning, and that its success is constrained by a number of factors, including the learners' experience with FL learning and the type of words to be learned. One of the learning methods discussed in the next section, the word association method, does not suffer from these constraints.

Paired Associate Learning

Two other common methods used in FL vocabulary learning studies are versions of a general learning method that has been used in verbal learning and memory research for decades, namely, the so-called paired associate paradigm. In studies employing this method, pairs of stimuli are presented during learning. At testing, the cued recall task is often employed; one of the elements in a pair (the cue) is presented, and the participant is asked to come up with the second element of the pair. Alternatively, whole pairs are presented at testing that were or were not presented as such during learning, and the participants are asked to indicate whether the presented stimulus pair is "old" (presented during learning) or "new" (not presented during learning; "recognition"). The stimuli as complete pairs, and the separate elements within a pair, may vary on many dimensions, such as the modality of presentation (e.g., auditory or visual) and the nature of the stimuli. Line drawings of common objects or the objects themselves, nonsense shapes, words of various grammatical categories, nonsense combinations of letters, single letters, numerals, and, indeed, foreign words have been used as stimulus materials in paired associate studies (see Runquist, 1966, for an early description of the essentials of the method).

The two versions of this general paradigm that have often been used in FL vocabulary learning research are the word association and picture association methods. In the word association method, the paired associates presented during learning are two words, one a native language word and the second its translation in the target FL. The FL words to be learned may be actual words in a natural language or invented, artificial words that do not occur as such in any natural language. In the latter case, the FL word to be learned may be a letter sequence that is formed according to the orthographic and phonological systems of the learner's native language but that carries no meaning (a "pseudoword") or an orthographically or phonologically "illegal" letter string that does not follow the orthographic or phonological rule systems of the learner's native language (a "nonword"). In the picture association method, one of the elements in the study pairs is the targeted FL word and the second is a picture (or a line drawing) depicting the referent of this word. Typically, in both these methods the words are presented visually, but in word association (and for the FL words in the picture association condition), auditory presentation is a feasible alternative as well and may indeed sometimes be the only option (when the learners are illiterate).

The term *word association method* is used here to stress the fact that, in this method, two words are paired in each learning trial. The term is neutral with respect to the exact learning strategy the participants actually use. Often, no specific instructions regarding which strategy to adopt are given to the participants, a learning setting that is also referred to as *unstructured learning*. Under these circumstances, learners report the use of various learning strategies (e.g., associating the two words in the pair; rehearsing them silently; detecting similarities between the words in a pair; forming mental images of the words; constructing sentences containing the words in the pair; inventing memory aids; De Groot & Van den Brink, 2004); different participants in the same experiment may use different strategies, but individual participants may also replace a strategy employed early in the learning episode with a new strategy. In other studies, the

instructions are somewhat more specific. For instance, in studies employing the rote learning technique, the participants are instructed to rehearse and memorize the presented materials silently (this is how the term was employed above).[2]

Of the two paired associate learning methods, the word association technique can be applied more widely than the picture–word association method. As pointed out, the success and applicability of the keyword method, although effective in many circumstances, is constrained by a number of factors. One of these is the fact that the method is not optimally suited for the learning of abstract words and is unsuitable for learning cognates. The picture association technique suffers from one of these constraints as well and to an even larger extent than the keyword method: Whereas with some effort it is possible to employ the keyword method in learning abstract words (Van Hell & Candia Mahn, 1997), it is virtually impossible to depict abstract words, which by definition cannot be experienced by the senses, including the eye. (Unlike the keyword method, there is no restriction to limit the picture association method to noncognates.)

The word association method does not suffer from any of these constraints; it can be used, and indeed has been used, to study the learning of concrete and abstract words and cognates and noncognates (and frequent and infrequent words, but this variable also does not constitute a constraint for the picture association and keyword methods). The pertinent studies and the effects found are discussed in the section on word type effects.

Why then, if its applicability is restricted to the study of only a subset of words in a language, is the picture association method used at all? An important reason presumably is that it lends itself rather naturally to study vocabulary learning in young children because the method closely resembles a common form of L1 vocabulary acquisition in these children, namely, the association of a word with the corresponding object in the child's environment. Experimental data collected by Wimer and Lambert (1959) suggested that this association of the to-be-learned FL word with environmental objects and events is a relatively effective FL vocabulary learning method for adult learners as well, but a more recent study (Lotto & De Groot, 1998) refuted this claim (see the section Individual Differences in Learning Foreign Language Vocabulary for details).

When the picture–word association method is used with very young children, it can only be exploited in an auditory form (presenting a picture with the spoken form of its FL name) because these children will typically still be illiterate. Whereas visual presentation of the FL word is an option for young children who have just passed the very initial stages of learning to read, it is not a recommended mode of presentation for this learner group either. The reason is that, for these children, word reading has not been automatized yet and therefore coming up with the correct sound structure of the visually presented words (via the written forms) often constitutes a real challenge to them. This cognitive limitation cannot be ignored in studies of vocabulary acquisition because it is a well-established fact that generating the phonological forms of visually presented words by means of overt or subvocal speech is an essential component of successful vocabulary acquisition (see The Role of Phonology in Foreign Language Vocabulary Learning section).

Learning Words in Context

In the FL vocabulary learning methods discussed above (i.e., keyword learning, rote rehearsal, word association learning, and picture association learning), the newly learned words are presented in highly impoverished contexts. Language users, including FL learners, typically perform in contextually richer situations. This evokes the idea that an FL word may be better learned in a larger, more meaningful linguistic context like a sentence. In the field of FL vocabulary learning studies using direct instruction methods, the question whether such learning is more effective using restrictive contexts, as in the studies discussed above, or using a larger linguistic context has received relatively little empirical attention (but see, e.g., Moore & Surber, 1992; Prince, 1996). One prerequisite of learning FL vocabulary in an FL sentence context is that the FL learners have a basic level knowledge of the FL language that should be at least sufficient to understand the sentence context.

Prince (1996) examined more advanced FL learners who had studied the FL (English) for 5 to 8 years and instructed them to learn new FL words in either a sentence context condition or a word association condition. He found that more words were recalled with word association than with sentence context instructions. It should be noted, however, that recall of the relatively weak learners (but not of the more advanced learners) in the word association condition was notably poorer when measured via a sentence completion task than via a cued recall task. This finding suggests that FL learners may differ in the extent to which they can successfully transfer new vocabulary learned via contextually restricted methods (here via word association) to more meaningful and contextually richer FL situations.

Word-Type Effects

Word-Type Effects on Learning

Words vary on a number of dimensions. For instance, words may refer to concrete objects or to abstract entities (the variable concreteness); they may share (a large part of their) visual or auditory form with their translation in another language (cognate status); they may be used often or rather sparsely in speech and writing (frequency); they may be morphologically simple or complex (morphological complexity) or may differ in structural complexity for other reasons (e.g., they may contain more or less-complex consonant clusters).

The effect of some of these variables, most notably concreteness, cognate status, and word frequency, has been studied frequently in bilingual representation studies, which focus on the way translation pairs are represented in bilingual memory (e.g., as "compound," "coordinate," or "subordinate" structures in the words of Weinreich, 1953/1974, or as "word-association" or "concept-mediation" structures in the terminology of Potter, So, Von Eckardt, and Feldman, 1984; see De Groot, 1993; Kroll, 1993; and Kroll & Tokowicz, chapter 26, this volume, for reviews). The tasks most commonly employed in these studies are word translation (e.g., De Groot et al., 1994), word association (e.g., Kolers, 1963; Van Hell & De Groot, 1998a), and semantic priming across languages (e.g., De Groot & Nas, 1991; Keatley, Spinks, & De Gelder, 1994).

In contrast to the bilingual representation studies, relatively few FL vocabulary learning studies have manipulated word-type variables, even though doing so is likely to provide relevant information on the learning process and the ensuing memory representations. Furthermore, results of such studies may inform FL curricula, especially the sequencing of the vocabulary to be learned by the students (e.g., Meara, 1993).

A plausible reason why only a few of these learning studies varied word type is that typically the word set presented for learning in these studies consisted of rather few words, too few to contain a sufficiently large number of each type (e.g., concrete noncognates) to obtain reliable effects of the variables concerned. For instance, studies by Cheung (1996), Papagno, Valentine, and Baddeley (1991), and Wimer and Lambert (1959) presented only three, eight, and nine words, respectively, for which an FL word was to be learned.

As the representation studies, the few FL vocabulary learning studies that manipulated word type showed reliable effects of two of the above variables: word concreteness (De Groot & Keijzer, 2000; De Groot & Van den Brink, 2004; Ellis & Beaton, 1993b; Service & Craik, 1993; Van Hell & Candia Mahn, 1997) and cognate status (De Groot & Keijzer, 2000; Ellis & Beaton, 1993b; Kroll, Michael, & Sankaranarayanan, 1998; Lotto & De Groot, 1998). For some of these studies, namely, those that have employed an orthogonal (not a correlational) design, it is possible to determine the actual size of the effects. These analyses show that the effects are substantial: Across the relevant studies, the magnitude of the concreteness effects varies between 11% and 27%, meaning that the recall scores are from 11% to 27% higher for concrete words than for abstract words (De Groot & Keijzer, 2000; De Groot & Van den Brink, 2004; Van Hell & Candia Mahn, 1997). Similarly, the magnitude of the effect of cognate status varies between 15% and 19% when highly experienced FL learners were the participants in the vocabulary learning studies (De Groot & Keijzer, 2000; Lotto & De Groot, 1998). When less-experienced FL learners served as participants, the cognate effect even appears to be substantially larger (about 25% in a receptive testing condition and about 50% in a productive testing condition; Kroll et al., 1998, p. 383).

Acknowledging the fact that fluent use of a FL not only requires that FL knowledge (here, the knowledge of FL vocabulary) is stored in memory, but also that this knowledge is accessed and retrieved rapidly (see also the section on keyword mnemonics), the five studies that employed an orthogonal design measured retrieval times as well. The results of these analyses generally converged with the analyses on the recall scores, although fewer of the effects were statistically significant. But, whenever a significant effect occurred, its direction strengthened the conclusions drawn from the analyses of the recall scores. That is, responses to concrete words and cognates were generally faster than those to abstract words and noncognates, respectively.

A third variable that has been manipulated in some of the above studies is word frequency.

Compared to the effects of word concreteness and cognate status, the effect of this variable is not robust. If it occurs at all in a particular study, it is rather small (effects of 3% to 7% in De Groot & Keijzer, 2000; De Groot & Van den Brink, 2004; and Lotto & De Groot, 1998), and in two of these studies (De Groot & Keijzer, 2000; De Groot & Van den Brink, 2004), this small effect (with better performance for high-frequency words than for low-frequency words) was attributable to a subset of the items only.

The FL vocabulary learning studies discussed in this section employed different methods of FL learning. As mentioned, Van Hell and Candia Mahn (1997) contrasted the keyword method and rote rehearsal; De Groot and Keijzer (2000) and De Groot and Van den Brink (2004) used the word association technique; and Kroll et al. (1998) and Lotto and De Groot (1998) contrasted the word association and picture association methods. Maybe the most noteworthy word-type effect reported in these studies combined is the finding by Kroll et al. and Lotto and De Groot that an effect of cognate status not only materialized in the word association condition, but also in the picture association condition. What is more, the cognate effect was equally large in these two conditions. The reason to qualify this finding as noteworthy is that it is generally assumed that the form relation between translation equivalent terms underlies the effects of cognate status in both representation and learning studies. But of course, a word and a picture representing this word do not share any form similarity.

The effect of cognate status in the picture-learning condition thus suggested that the presentation of a picture activates the corresponding L1 word form (Lotto & De Groot, 1998, pp. 58–59), and that the learner then recognizes the similarity between the generated L1 word form and the to-be-learned FL word form accompanying the picture. This awareness then somehow (see the section Cognate Status for more detail) facilitates the learning of the new form. In theory, the form concerned could be phonological, orthographic, or both because the two elements within the cognate pairs used in these studies are typically similar both in spelling and in phonology, and the learner's recognition of either type of relationship might facilitate learning. Lotto and De Groot, however, argued that the forms involved presumably are the phonological forms (see the original reference for details). Furthermore, they noted that such a conclusion fits in nicely with the results of a number of related studies that all suggested an important role for phonology in learning FL vocabulary, even when the learning materials are presented visually (e.g., Baddeley, Papagno, & Vallar, 1988; Papagno et al., 1991; Van Hell & Candia Mahn, 1997; see The Role of Phonology in Foreign Language Vocabulary Learning section for a more detailed discussion).

Word-Type Dependent Forgetting

The goal of FL vocabulary learning is to install durable, not transient, representations in memory. At least two studies suggested that this goal is not met equally often for all types of words, but that instead more forgetting occurs for the types of words that are the most difficult to learn (De Groot & Keijzer, 2000; De Groot & Van den Brink, 2004). When the participants of these studies where retested about a week after initial learning (without further learning), it turned out that more forgetting had occurred for abstract words than for concrete words, and that more forgetting had occurred for noncognates than for cognates. These results converged with the findings of Bahrick and Phelps (1987), who showed (at a global level, without examining the performance for different types of words) that, 8 years after learning, retention was best for words that had required the fewest learning trials to obtain criterion performance during learning.

Note that this does not imply that manipulations that increase the difficulty of a learning task lead to more forgetting. In a FL vocabulary learning study using the word association method, Schneider, Healy, and Bourne (2002) found that increasing the difficulty of learning during the initial phase (i.e., through learning procedures involving the more difficult L1-FL direction rather than the reverse direction, mixing rather than blocking semantic categories, or no pretraining of FL words) leads to poorer learning and immediate retention, but not to inferior delayed retention, transfer, and relearning. Importantly, in Schneider et al.'s study, the difficulty of the learning conditions pertained to the difficulty of learning procedures rather than of the FL materials to be learned, as in the work of De Groot and Keijzer (2000) and De Groot and Van den Brink (2004). In other words, concrete words and cognates may be better retained than abstract words and noncognates, respectively, but FL words learned under difficult learning procedures may be better retained than those same words when learned under easy learning conditions.

Explaining the Word-Type Effects

Concreteness

Effects of concreteness are ubiquitous in studies on first and second/foreign language learning and language processing. For instance, the concreteness effect observed in the FL vocabulary learning studies discussed above has a parallel in L1 acquisition, in which concrete words are acquired earlier than abstract words (e.g., Brown, 1957; Schwanenflugel, 1991). The questions remain what causes these effects and whether all effects of this variable, both in L1 acquisition and in FL learning and both in language acquisition/learning and in language processing, can be parsimoniously attributed to the same source or whether different causes underlie the various manifestations of the effect.

For instance, a likely cause of the concreteness effect in L1 acquisition is that acquiring concrete words is often supported by the tangible, visible, audible, or palpable presence of the corresponding objects in the child's surroundings, whereas this sensory information is by definition missing for abstract words. If this explanation holds, a different explanation of the concreteness effect in FL vocabulary learning has to be provided because, in none of the pertinent studies discussed, the entities to which the to-be-learned concrete words referred were present in the learning environment (although these objects may have been imagined by the participants, a process that may have caused or contributed to the effect).

De Groot and Keijzer (2000) suggested two possible causes of the concreteness effect in FL vocabulary learning; both attribute the effect to differences between the memory representations of concrete and abstract words. Both explanations assign a critical role to the amount of information concerning the L1 word that is stored in memory: The more information that is stored, the more opportunity the learner has to anchor the to-be-learned FL word form onto it and therefore the more successful learning is. One of these explanations is in terms of dual-coding theory (see also the section on keyword mnemonics), which assumes two memory representations for concrete words, one in the verbal system and one in the image system, whereas only one, stored in the verbal system, is assumed for abstract words. Note that this state of affairs implies that dual-coding theory assumes qualitatively different memory representations for concrete and abstract words.

The second explanation is in terms of the differential informational density of memory representations for concrete and abstract words within an amodal, monolithic memory system (De Groot, 1989; Kieras, 1978; Van Hell & De Groot, 1998b; Van Hell & Sjarbaini, 2004). Within this framework, the memory representations of concrete and abstract words are only assumed to differ quantitatively, not qualitatively: Those of concrete words are assumed to contain more information elements than those of abstract words (see De Groot, 1989, for experimental support). Again, this allows more anchoring opportunities in the case of learning a FL word form for concrete L1 words. Lotto and De Groot (1998) proposed this same explanation for the (relatively small) frequency effect in FL vocabulary learning that has sometimes (but not reliably) been obtained.

This explanation of the concreteness effects in FL vocabulary learning cannot account for the analogous effects in L1 vocabulary acquisition by toddlers. The reason is that the former effects result from differences in memory structures for concrete and abstract words that presumably reflect the outcome, not the beginning, of the L1 acquisition process. At the onset of L1 vocabulary acquisition, representations are not likely to exist in memory for either concrete words or abstract words; in other words, at that stage concrete and abstract words do not differ with respect to their memory representations; the buildup of memory information for both types of words presumably starts from scratch. A plausible explanation for the concreteness effect in L1 vocabulary acquisition was already provided above: Only the acquisition of concrete words, not that of abstract words, is supported by the perceptual presence of these words' referents in the child's environment.

Cognate Status

Lotto and De Groot (1998) and De Groot and Keijzer (2000) suggested three possible sources for the superior FL vocabulary learning performance for cognates, considering both the learning stage (storage) and the testing stage (retrieval) as possible loci of the effect. The first explanation extends a view of bilingual memory representation that assumes shared representations for cognates, but language-specific representations for noncognates (Kirsner, Lalor, & Hird, 1993; Sánchez-Casas, Davis, & García-Albea, 1992; see also Sánchez-Casas & García-Albea, chapter 11, this

volume). In fact, a cognate relation between two words is considered a special case of a morphological relation that may exist between words within the same language and that is reflected in the joint storage of morphologically related words in memory. According to this view, bilingual memory, just as monolingual memory, is organized by morphology, not by language. For instance, a French-English bilingual has one memory representation containing both the English words *marry*, *marriage*, and *married* and the French words *marier* and *mariage* (Kirsner et al., 1993). If true, the learning of a FL word that shares a noncognate relation with the corresponding L1 word involves creating a new entry in memory, whereas learning a cognate word may only involve adding new information to, or adapting, a representation already stored there prior to the learning episode. The latter process may be less demanding than the former, causing the learning advantage of cognates over noncognates.

A second possible cause for the cognate advantage is that in the case of learning a FL cognate, which shares form with its translation, less has to be learned than when a noncognate FL word has to be learned. Finally, because of the form overlap between cognate translations and the absence of such overlap in the case of noncognates, when a cognate is presented as the testing stimulus, it will constitute a strong cue for the retrieval of its translation equivalent in the target language. These three suggested causes of the effects of cognate status do not have to be mutually exclusive, but may all contribute to the effect.

Word-Type Dependent Effects on Forgetting

The differential forgetting of concrete words and cognates on the one hand and abstract words and noncognates on the other suggests that, in terms of Atkinson (1972), immediately after training abstract words and noncognates are in a T (for temporal) state relatively often. This means that the newly learned word is only known temporarily, and that subsequent learning of other words will cause interference, causing forgetting of the previously known word. The second state Atkinson distinguishes is a P (permanent) state for newly learned words that have gained a permanent status in memory immediately after training. The data suggest that concrete words and cognates have reached a P state relatively often at the conclusion of the training phase. A third possible state that words presented for learning can be in, and that abstract words and noncognates are in relatively often immediately after training, is the *U* (unknown) state. Of course, distinguishing between these three retention states only concerns a rephrasal of the effects obtained, not an explanation. A true explanation may ultimately be provided in terms, again, of differential memory representations for different types of words (e.g., being embedded in a denser representation and, as such, being linked to a relatively large number of information elements in memory might render a newly learned FL word relatively immune to forgetting).

The Role of Phonology in Foreign Language Vocabulary Learning

The cognate effect observed in the picture association learning condition in the work of Lotto and De Groot (1998) and Kroll et al. (1998) suggested that participants generated the names of the presented pictures during learning (see Word-Type Effects on Learning). This was regarded as support for the view that phonology plays an important role in FL vocabulary learning. Gathercole and Thorn (1998) reviewed the relevant literature and provided overwhelming support from various sources for this view.

For instance, Papagno et al. (1991) showed that an experimental technique called *articulatory suppression* disrupts the learning of FL vocabulary (although suppression had little effect on meaningful paired-associate learning in L1). The articulatory suppression technique involves the repeated uttering of a sound (e.g., *bla*) while learning the paired associates consisting of, say, an L1 word and its FL translation. Suppression interferes with the phonological recoding of visually presented items, thus preventing their short-term phonological storage. Furthermore, suppression interferes with "subvocal" rehearsal, a process that is deemed necessary for transfer from short-term memory into long-term memory.

Service (1992), in a 3-year longitudinal study of Finnish children learning English as a FL, showed a close relationship between the children's ability at the start of the program to repeat presented pseudowords and their grades in English at the end of the program. Subsequent work (Service & Kohonen, 1995) suggested that this relationship was mediated by English vocabulary knowledge. Pseudoword repetition is assumed to involve phonological memory, and the level of accuracy at which the task is performed is thought to reflect phonological-memory skills and capacity. Therefore, these data also suggest a relation between phonological memory and FL vocabulary learning. This conclusion is strengthened further by neuropsychological evidence: Baddeley et al. (1988) showed that their patient P. V., who had a reduced phonological store capacity, was unable to repeat back pseudowords longer than three syllables and to learn auditorily presented pseudowords paired with real words.

The important role of phonology in FL vocabulary learning is further supported by studies using experienced FL learners. Papagno and Vallar (1995) observed that polyglots performed better than nonpolyglots in phonological memory tasks and in FL paired associate learning, suggesting a relation between phonological-memory capacity and FL vocabulary learning.

Van Hell and Candia Mahn (1997) observed that experienced FL language learners benefited more from rote rehearsal learning than from keyword learning. They proposed that subvocal rehearsal of the FL word and its translation activates phonological codes, and that experienced learners in particular benefit from using phonological information in learning novel FL words. Specifically, experienced FL learners not only may have better phonological memory skills (as suggested by Papagno and Vallar's 1995 study), but also may possess more refined long-term knowledge of phonological structures. For example, the experienced FL learners in Van Hell and Candia Mahn's study had all learned the subtle, yet important, differences in the pronunciation of the cognate *hotel* across the Dutch, English, French, and German languages. This fine-grained and broad repertoire of phonological knowledge, along with better phonological memory skills, may make experienced FL learners more receptive to the phonological information novel FL vocabulary contains and may thus guide and facilitate the learning of novel FL words.

Finally, the "typicality" of the FL words to be learned affects their learning; that is, if the sound structure of the to-be-learned words conforms to the phonotactic rules of the learner's native language, learning is more successful than when phonotactically alien FL words are presented for learning. Gathercole, Martin, and Hitch (in Gathercole & Thorn, 1998) varied the nonwords in word–nonword pairs on "wordlikeness" (in terms of sound structure) and demonstrated that more wordlike nonwords than non-wordlike nonwords were learned. Similarly, immediately after learning,

De Groot and Van den Brink (2004) obtained recall scores that were 14% higher for phonotactically typical nonwords than for phonotactically atypical nonwords. Furthermore, a week after learning, more forgetting had occurred for the latter. (This is yet another demonstration of the earlier finding of De Groot and Keijzer, 2000, that words hard to learn are more easily forgotten than words relatively easy to learn.) All these findings converge on the conclusion that, during the learning of FL vocabulary, phonological codes are generated and used to support the learning process: The typicality effect is likely to arise from the fact that the generation of phonological codes is easier for phonotactically typical words than for atypical such words.

Baddeley, Gathercole, and Papagno (1998) proposed a model of the phonological loop that accommodates the findings of the studies discussed above (and those of many other studies; see Baddeley et al., 1998; Gathercole & Thorn, 1998). The phonological loop, a component of the multicomponent model of working memory, is specialized in the retention of verbal information over short periods of time. The phonological loop includes a phonological store (which holds information in phonological form) and a rehearsal process (which serves to preserve decaying representations in the phonological store).

The primary function of the phonological loop is to mediate language learning by providing a temporary storage of unfamiliar phonological forms (novel words) while more permanent memory representations are constructed. It is proposed that the phonological loop and long-term knowledge of the language operate in an interactive manner. Relevant for FL vocabulary learning is the assumption that the phonological loop function in FL learning is enhanced by instructions that emphasize subvocal rehearsal, as in rote rehearsal (e.g., Ellis & Beaton, 1993a; Van Hell & Candia Mahn, 1997), and is disrupted by articulatory suppression (e.g., Ellis & Sinclair, 1996; Papagno et al., 1991).

Baddeley et al. (1998) proposed that the phonological loop function may vary across individuals. Specifically, the natural talent of polyglots, or gifted language learners in general, for learning language may arise from an excellent phonological loop function. (See also Michael and Gollan, chapter 19, this volume, for a discussion of other aspects of working memory, such as working memory capacity, that may play pivotal roles in becoming proficient FL users.)

Freeing and Fine-Tuning the Newly Learned Foreign Language Words

The storage of durable representations for the newly learned FL word forms in memory by means of any of the learning methods discussed above—keyword mnemonics, rote rehearsal, word association learning, or picture association learning—is only a first step toward establishing an FL word representation that resembles a native speaker's representation of this same word and that enables the access (in comprehension) and retrieval (in production) of this representation in a way that resembles these processes in a native speaker. So far, the new representation consists of little more than an extra element—the FL word label—attached to (or embedded in) the representation for the corresponding native language word. At this learning stage, when this new word form is encountered by the FL learner in actual FL speech or writing, he or she can only come to grips with it by assigning it the meaning of the corresponding L1 word.

There is evidence to suggest that, during the very initial stages of learning, this process of L1 meaning assignment proceeds indirectly via the L1 word form (Chen & Leung, 1989; Kroll & Curley, 1988; Kroll & Sholl, 1992; Kroll & Stewart, 1994; Sholl, Sankaranarayanan, & Kroll, 1995; cf. Weinreich's 1953/1974 subordinate type of bilingualism; see also Kroll & Tokowicz, chapter 26, this volume). Similarly, during FL language production, the retrieval of the FL word form is assumed to start with the activation of the meaning representation of its translation in L1 and then to "pass through" the L1 form representation before the FL form is retrieved and produced. Soon after, with increasing FL experience, the FL word form starts to become functionally detached from the corresponding L1 word form representation and to access meaning as directly as the corresponding L1 word does.

A number of studies have suggested that such "freeing" of the FL word form from the L1 word form starts very early on in the FL learning process for this word (Altarriba & Mathis, 1997; De Groot & Poot, 1997; Potter et al., 1984). Ultimately, retrieval of this word form in FL will no longer exploit the L1 word-form representation at all (cf. Weinreich's, 1953/1974, "coordinate" bilingualism).

Assigning FL words the meaning of the corresponding L1 words, either indirectly via the L1 word forms or, later, directly would imply the use of a strong "semantic accent"; the reason is that translation "equivalents" seldom share all aspects of their meaning: The meaning aspects specific to the word in L1 would be implied when using its L2 (second language) equivalent (see MacWhinney, chapter 3, this volume, for other types of L1 transfer in FL learning). Highly technical words possibly constitute the only exception to the apparent rule that the meanings of a word and its closest translation do not overlap perfectly (Fries, 1945, in Boyd Zimmerman, 1997, p. 11), although for particular classes of words (concrete words) the overlap in meaning between the two languages is larger than for other classes (abstract words; emotion words).

For this reason, De Groot (1992; see also Van Hell & De Groot, 1998a) proposed the "distributed feature" model of bilingual lexical representation as an alternative to the more common "localist" models. In this model, word meaning is represented in memory as a set of semantic features, some of which are shared between a pair of translations, whereas others are unique to either the L1 word or the FL word. Translations of concrete words share more of these semantic features than translations of abstract words (see Kroll & Tokowicz, chapter 26, this volume, for further details).

Furthermore, assigning a FL word the meaning of "its" translation equivalent entails the flawed assumption that a word has only one meaning, whereas the truth is that words typically have many different meanings (some claim from 15 to 20 in English; Fries, 1945, in Boyd Zimmerman, 1997, p. 11), some of which are related, but others apparently are unique. Which of a word's many meanings should be assigned to it when it is encountered in speech or reading depends on the context of use.

This plethora of meanings and shades of meaning words may have and the context dependence of word meaning have frustrated the attempts by many to obtain exact definitions of words and have led others to accept the view that "word meanings cannot be pinned down, as if they were dead insects. Instead, they flutter around elusively like live butterflies. Or perhaps they should be likened to fish which slither out of one's grasp" (Aitchison, 1987, p. 40). Or, in the words of Labov (1973, in Aitchison, 1987): "Words have often been called slippery customers, and many scholars have been distressed by their tendency to shift their meanings and slide out from under any single definition" (p. 40). In keyword mnemonics, word association learning, and picture association learning, only one of this plethora of meanings is singled out (either by the

stimulus itself, e.g., the picture of a mug, or by the learner), leaving all remaining meanings of the FL word yet to be learned through other means.

Insight into learning the meaning of words in more advanced FL vocabulary learning was provided by Bogaards (2001). He studied the learning of new meanings for known words and for combinations of known words in learners of French, all native Dutch speakers, who were in their fourth year of learning this FL in high school. The results of this study (see the original reference for details) suggest that both previously learned word forms and word meanings may promote the learning of new meanings for familiar forms and expressions comprised of familiar forms.

In sum, for ultimate use of a FL word in a nativelike way, the FL word form must provide access to meaning and be retrieved from conceptual representations directly, bypassing the form representation of its L1 translation. The meaning that is initially associated with the FL word (the meaning of its L1 translation) must gradually be narrowed (to get rid of the unique L1 meaning parts), extended (to also cover the unique L2 meaning parts or be used in multiword expressions) and refined such that it covers all of its FL meanings and captures the specific connotations of each.

Needless to say, gaining such a detailed level of FL vocabulary knowledge requires extensive practice of the FL words in contexts varied enough to acquaint the learner with the finesse of all their meanings. Apart from extended immersion in an environment in which the FL is the dominant language, only extensive reading in that language is likely to provide that outcome. The initial, flimsy representations set up via the direct instruction methods discussed here provide no more than the means to bootstrap into this time-consuming learning process, but as such are extremely valuable.

The Effect of Background Music on Learning Foreign Language Vocabulary

When performing cognitively demanding tasks, some people prefer a quiet environment, claiming to be hindered by noise, including music, whereas others seem not to be bothered by a certain noise level or even prefer (a particular type of) background music while performing the task, claiming to perform better under those circumstances. This observation, if confirmed and understood in rigorous research, has obvious pedagogical implications as it might, for instance, inform teachers about how to create the optimal learning environment in the classroom and advise students with respect to the most effective circumstances to do their homework. Of course, the potential impact of well-controlled studies into this topic reaches far beyond the classroom because cognition is involved in the majority (if not all) tasks to be performed by humans, even tasks performed automatically most of the time.

Acknowledging its potential importance, the effect of background music (and other types of noise ignored in the present discussion) on task performance has been a topic of study by several groups of researchers, most notably applied psychologists, cognitive psychologists, and personality psychologists. The applied psychologists among these researchers primarily tried to find out whether music affects workers' satisfaction and morale or their productivity at work. The cognitive psychologists' goal was to look at ways in which music affects attention and processing in various tasks. The personality psychologists' focus was on the way music and different musical styles interact with individual differences in personality. See Furnham and Allass (1999) and Furnham and Bradley (1997) for a historical overview of this work.

The role of background music in learning has also received the attention of teachers and educators with an interest in a field of study carrying the esoteric name of Suggestopedia, a name based on a teaching method thus dubbed and introduced in Bulgaria by Lozanov (1978, in Felix, 1993). The innovative element this learning method introduced in the classroom was the systematic use of music in the instruction process. Especially, classical baroque music was thought to support the learning process. Felix (1993) reviewed the pertinent studies and concluded that positive effects of music played during learning have been reported for vocabulary learning and reading performance; that effects of music played during testing do not consistently occur; and that playing the same music during both learning and testing leads to the best achievement. The latter finding exemplifies the well-known phenomenon of "context-dependent" memory, that is, that test performance is better the more similar the circumstances under which testing occurs are to the circumstances present while learning (e.g., Godden & Baddeley, 1975).

De Groot and Van den Brink (2004) looked at the effect of background music on learning "FL words" (which in fact were pronounceable and nonpronounceable nonwords) for a set of Dutch words. The participants were all drawn from the same population of relatively experienced FL learners. Half of them learned the FL words in silence; the other half learned them while part of the Brandenburg Concerto by J. S. Bach was playing in the background. During testing, no music was played to either group of participants. The results were promising, but not in all respects conclusive: The recall scores were higher (by 8.7%) in the music condition than in the silent condition, but this effect only generalized over items, not over participants. This finding suggests that only a subset of the participants in the music condition benefited from the presence of background music. It also suggests that the remaining participants in this condition also were not hindered by it because otherwise an overall null effect of the music manipulation might have been expected.

Studies by Furnham and Bradley (1997) and Furnham and Allass (1999) hinted at an exciting explanation of why the effect of the music manipulation did not generalize over participants. Inspired by Eysenck's (1967) theory that introverts and extraverts differ in their levels of cortical arousal, they predicted that background music might have a detrimental effect on cognitive task performance in introverts, but a beneficial effect on such performance in extraverts. Manipulating this personality trait, Furnham and Allass observed that introverts performed substantially better in the silent condition than in the (pop) music condition in a reading comprehension task and a recall task, whereas for extraverts exactly the opposite pattern of results was obtained. The detrimental effect of music for the introverts was larger in a condition in which the music played was complex than in a condition in which it was simpler. Again, this pattern reversed for the extraverts.

Furnham and Bradley (1997) also demonstrated an interaction between the introvert/extravert variable and the music variable on two cognitive tests, one a reading comprehension test and the second a memory test, and Daoussis and McKelvie (1986) showed a similar interaction in a study looking at reading comprehension. The results of the last two studies differed from those of Furnham and Allass (1999) in that music had a detrimental effect on the cognitive performance of introverts, whereas extraverts appeared immune to the effects of the music manipulation. But, all three studies converge on the same conclusion: The introvert/extravert personality trait plays an important role in the effects of background music on cognitive performance.

The authors of the three studies just discussed all turned to Eysenck (1967) to account for this intriguing interaction between the introvert/extravert personality trait and the presentation of music during learning. Eysenck posited that introverts have a lower neurological threshold of arousal and therefore experience greater arousal in response to lower-intensity stimulation than extraverts; this results in introverts' satisfaction at relatively low levels of stimulation. It was posited that in introverts optimum performance is reached at moderate levels of arousal. In contrast, extraverts require relatively high levels of arousal for optimal performance (Furnham & Allass, 1999, pp. 28–29). Presumably without awareness of this alleged underlying physiological cause, introverts and extraverts are apparently aware of the effect of background music on their study success because extraverts claim to play background music more often while studying than introverts (Daoussis & McKelvie, 1986; Furnham & Bradley, 1997).

This account of music effects on learning provides a possible explanation for the above finding by De Groot and Van den Brink (2004) that the effect of the music manipulation did not generalize over all participants. In that study, the introvert/extravert personality trait was not taken into account, and the participant sample most likely included both introverts and extraverts. The extraverts may have benefited from background music, causing the overall higher recall scores in this condition. The fact that a net positive effect of background music was obtained suggests that the introverts were neither helped nor hindered by background music.

The role of a number of other factors that may affect music's effect on learning success, such as music preference (see Etaugh & Michals, 1975, who studied the effect of this variable on reading comprehension), vocal versus nonvocal music (Belsham & Harman, 1977), and musical styles (e.g., classical, jazz, and popular; Sogin, 1988), is still largely unknown. The evident pedagogical implications of filling this knowledge gap on creating optimal learning environments warrant increased research efforts devoted to unraveling the relevant variables and their interactions.

Individual Differences in Learning Foreign Language Vocabulary

At various points in the preceding sections, we alluded to the existence of individual differences in the learning of FL vocabulary, both differences between learner groups and differences within groups of learners. For instance, it was pointed out that advanced (experienced) learners of a particular target language benefit less from keyword mnemonics than less-advanced (inexperienced) learners of that language do (e.g., Moore & Surber, 1992), and that for multilingual language users, who have considerable experience with learning FLs, rote rehearsal is a more effective learning method than keyword mnemonics is (Van Hell & Candia Mahn, 1997). Lotto and De Groot (1998) obtained a similar result: They showed that multilingual language users, sampled from the same population as the participants in Van Hell and Candia Mahn's study, learned more FL vocabulary when a word association method was used than when the picture association method was employed.

In contrast, Wimer and Lambert (1959), comparing word association learning with object association learning (in which the word to be learned is paired with an object rather than a picture of that object), obtained better recall performance with object association than with word association. They concluded that "environmental events are more effective stimuli for the acquisition of foreign-language responses than are native-language equivalents for the new words, at least for the learning of a simple, basic vocabulary" (p. 35). The results of Lotto and De Groot (1997) and (if imaging objects plays the same role in learning as actual objects or pictures of actual objects do) those of Moore and Surber (1992) and Van Hell and Candia Mahn (1997) suggest that this conclusion does not hold for all groups of learners. Possibly, the participants in Wimer and Lambert's study were relatively inexperienced FL learners. If so, this combined set of studies would suggest that learner group and learning method interact such that, for experienced FL learners, the word association technique (or rote rehearsal, as one particular implementation of this technique) is more effective than learning techniques that employ the visual (imagined or actual) analogues of the FL words to be learned, and that for less-experienced learners the opposite holds.

The results of Kroll et al. (1998; Experiment 1) that, just as Lotto and De Groot (1998) contrasted word association and picture association learning, provide some direct support for this suggestion: Whereas Lotto and De Groot, testing experienced FL learners, obtained better results overall with word association learning than with picture association learning (82% correct for word association learning vs. 77% correct for picture association learning; only productive testing was employed), Kroll et al., who tested less-experienced language learners, obtained the opposite pattern of results (78.5% and 39.5% correct for word association learning in receptive and productive testing conditions, respectively, vs. 82% and 42% for these testing conditions, respectively, following picture association learning; all data collapsed across a test condition that tested with picture stimuli and one that tested with word stimuli). That the participants in Kroll et al.'s study were less-experienced learners than those of Lotto and De Groot is strongly suggested by the far lower learning scores in the productive testing condition in the work of Kroll et al. than in that of Lotto and De Groot. Furthermore, to achieve an overall recognition accuracy of 70% in the (relatively easy) receptive testing condition, the data of only half of the participants (45 of 99) could be included in the analyses (see Kroll et al., 1998, pp. 379 and 381). In Lotto and De Groot (1998), to achieve at least 60% accuracy in the (relatively hard) productive testing condition (the only condition that they tested), only 8 of the 64 participants tested had to be removed from the analyses (p. 43).

The amount of FL learning experience is unlikely to be the only variable that interacts with the specifics of the learning environment. That other factors may be relevant as well was implicit in our discussion of the effect of background music on learning FL words. As shown, the relevant literature suggests that the personality trait introversion/extraversion interacts with a role of background music. We hypothesized that the pattern of results obtained by De Groot and Van den Brink (2004), who tested experienced FL learners exclusively, emerged from an interaction between this personality trait and the music manipulation. If that analysis is correct, the results of that study indicate that FL learning experience is only one of the factors that determine what the optimal learning circumstances are. In other words, the effects of FL learning experience and background music both suggest that there is no single optimal procedure of learning FL vocabulary, but that instead the optimal procedure depends on learner characteristics. Different learners may benefit most from different circumstances, and the same learner may benefit most from different circumstances at different stages of learning.

Differences in phonological knowledge and processes and other aspects of working memory, such as working memory capacity, were mentioned as yet another source of individual differences in FL vocabulary learning (Baddeley et al., 1998; Papagno & Vallar, 1995; see also Michael & Gollan, chapter 19, this volume). As we have seen, phonological coding appears to play an important role in transferring newly learned words from transient memory stores into permanent memory, and the presence of fine-grained phonological knowledge in long-term memory may increase the learner's receptiveness to subtle phonological differences in the learning material.

Baddeley et al. (1998) suggested that the phonological loop function differs between individuals, and that gifted language learners are characterized by an excellent such function. The amount and subtlety of phonological information in memory is obviously a function of the amount of language experience, native and foreign, a learner has, so that ultimately language learning experience may underlie (a substantial part of) the effects of phonological skills on FL language learning. It remains to be seen whether, if all other things (such as language learning experience) are equal, a thing such as "talent" for learning FLs can still be identified.

Conclusion

This review of studies on FL vocabulary learning has highlighted some of the factors that need to be taken into account to gain a complete understanding of successful learning performance; it has only briefly touched on, or even completely ignored, other factors. For instance, much attention was devoted to contrasting the various direct FL vocabulary learning methods and pointing out their limitations and the ways they interact with learner characteristics such as FL learning experience and phonological skills. Similarly, the fact that various word characteristics determine the success of learning FL equivalents for L1 words and the way these effects can be explained were discussed at length.

We also reviewed at some level of detail the research that tries to resolve the dispute regarding the role that background music may play in FL vocabulary learning. Finally, some discussion was devoted to the later stages of FL vocabulary acquisition, in which the newly learned FL words are functionally detached from their L1 counterparts, and their meaning representations gradually develop toward those of L1 users of the FL concerned.

Other aspects of FL vocabulary learning received little or no attention, for instance, the role of proximity of the to-be-learned FL to the learner's L1. This issue was only briefly touched on in the discussion of the effect of word typicality on learning performance. The larger the distance between L1 and the FL to be learned, the more FL word forms to be learned will be atypical for the learner, the more alien the meanings of the FL words will be to the learner, and the more mapping problems between elements in the L1 and the FL the FL learner will encounter. FL vocabulary learning studies that test a FL similar to the learner's L1 (or that test the learning of pseudowords, which by definition have phonological forms akin to the learner's L1) may overestimate learning performance as compared to testing more distant FLs. Such effects of language proximity/distance warrant a more thorough discussion than received here.

A further neglected topic concerns the large difference in performance that is typically obtained between productive and receptive testing conditions, with receptive testing producing better results. Mention was made of these two ways of testing newly learned FL vocabulary, but without providing theoretical accounts of this effect (see De Groot & Keijzer, 2000, pp. 43–45, for a discussion).

Finally, hardly anything has been said on the crucial differences between late FL vocabulary learning, which, albeit implicitly, was the topic of the present discussion, and early bilingual vocabulary acquisition (see De Houwer, chapter 2, this volume). These learning processes differ crucially because, in early bilingual vocabulary acquisition, as in L1 vocabulary acquisition, the acquisition of word form and word meaning proceed in parallel, whereas in late FL vocabulary learning, a meaning for the new word to be learned is already in place (although it requires adjustment; see the section Freeing and Fine-Tuning the Newly Learned Foreign Language Words). Future reviews of studies on FL vocabulary learning might shift the focus to these and other issues neglected here.

Notes

1. A *foreign language* is a language that is not a native language in a country. In North America, *foreign language* and *second language* are often used interchangeably in this sense. In British usage, a distinction between the two is often made, such that a *foreign language* is a language taught in school but not used as a medium of instruction in school, nor is it a language of communication within a country (e.g., English in France). In contrast, a second language is a language that is not a native language in the country, but is widely used as a medium of communication (e.g., in education and government) and is used alongside another language or languages (e.g., English in Nigeria). In both Britain and North America, the term *second language* describes the native language in a country as learned by immigrants who have another first language (*Longman Dictionary of Language Teaching and Applied Linguistics*). In this chapter, we consistently use the term foreign language (FL) to cover all these usages, although most of the studies described concern the learning of a FL in experimental settings by learners whose native language is the dominant (and only official) language in the country where they live.

2. Note that the term *word association learning* should not be confused with the word association technique often employed in semantic memory research, in which the structure of semantic memory is revealed by presenting participants with words they know, and they are asked to provide the first word they think of after they are given a stimulus word.

References

Aitchison, J. (1987). *Words in the mind: An introduction to the mental lexicon*. Oxford, UK: Basil Blackwell.

Altarriba, J., & Mathis, K. M. (1997). Conceptual and lexical development in second language acquisition. *Journal of Memory and Language, 36*, 550–568.

Atkinson, R. C. (1972). Optimizing the learning of a second-language vocabulary. *Journal of Experimental Psychology, 96*, 124–129.

Atkinson, R. C. (1975). Mnemotechnics in second-language learning. *American Psychologist, 30*, 821–828.

Atkinson, R. C., & Raugh, M. R. (1975). An application of the mnemonic keyword method to the acquisition of a Russian vocabulary. *Journal of Experimental Psychology: Human Learning and Memory, 104*, 126–133.

Baddeley, A. D., Gathercole, S., & Papagno, C. (1998). The phonological loop as a language learning device. *Psychological Review, 105*, 158–173.

Baddeley, A. D., Papagno, C., & Vallar, G. (1988). When long-term learning depends on short-term storage. *Journal of Memory and Language, 27*, 586–595.

Bahrick, H. P., & Phelps, E. (1987). Retention of Spanish vocabulary over 8 years. *Journal of Experimental Psychology: Learning, Memory, and Cognition, 13*, 344–349.

Beaton, A., Gruneberg, M., & Ellis, N. (1995). Retention of foreign vocabulary learned using the keyword method: A 10-year follow-up. *Second Language Research, 11*, 112–120.

Belsham, R. L., & Harman, D. W. (1977). Effect of vocal versus non-vocal music on visual recall. *Perceptual and Motor Skills, 44,* 857–858.

Bogaards, P. (2001). Lexical units and the learning of foreign language vocabulary. *Studies in Second Language Acquisition, 23,* 321–343.

Boyd Zimmerman, C. (1997). Historical trends in second language vocabulary instruction. In J. Coady & T. Huckin (Eds.), *Second language vocabulary acquisition* (pp. 5–19). Cambridge, England: Cambridge University Press.

Brown, R. W. (1957). Linguistic determinism and the part of speech. *Journal of Abnormal and Social Psychology, 55,* 1–5.

Chen, H.-C., & Leung, Y.-S. (1989). Patterns of lexical processing in a nonnative language. *Journal of Experimental Psychology: Learning, Memory, and Cognition, 15,* 316–325.

Cheung, H. (1996). Nonword span as a unique predictor of second-language vocabulary learning. *Developmental Psychology, 32,* 867–873.

Cohen, A. D. (1987). The use of verbal and imagery mnemonics in second-language vocabulary learning. *Studies in Second Language Acquisition, 9,* 43–62.

Daoussis, L., & McKelvie, S. J. (1986). Musical preferences and effects of music on a reading comprehension test for extraverts and introverts. *Perceptual and Motor Skills, 62,* 283–289.

De Groot, A. M. B. (1989). Representational aspects of word imageability and word frequency as assessed through word association. *Journal of Experimental Psychology: Learning, Memory, and Cognition, 15,* 824–845.

De Groot, A. M. B. (1992). Bilingual lexical representation: A closer look at conceptual representations. In R. Frost & L. Katz (Eds.), *Orthography, phonology, morphology, and meaning* (pp. 389–412). Amsterdam: Elsevier Science.

De Groot, A. M. B. (1993). Word-type effects in bilingual processing tasks: Support for a mixed-representational system. In R. Schreuder & B. Weltens (Eds.), *The bilingual lexicon* (pp. 27–51). Amsterdam: Benjamins.

De Groot, A. M. B., Dannenburg, L., & Van Hell, J. G. (1994). Forward and backward word translation by bilinguals. *Journal of Memory and Language, 33,* 600–629.

De Groot, A. M. B., & Keijzer, R. (2000). What is hard to learn is easy to forget: The roles of word concreteness, cognate status, and word frequency in foreign language vocabulary learning and forgetting. *Language Learning, 50,* 1–56.

De Groot, A. M. B., & Nas, G. L. J. (1991). Lexical representation of cognates and noncognates in compound bilinguals. *Journal of Memory and Language, 30,* 90–123.

De Groot, A. M. B., & Poot, R. (1997). Word translation at three levels of proficiency in a second language: The ubiquitous involvement of conceptual memory. *Language Learning, 47,* 215–264.

De Groot, A. M. B., & Van den Brink, R. (2004). Effects of background music, word concreteness, word frequency, and word typicality on learning foreign language vocabulary. Manuscript in preparation.

Delaney, H. D. (1978). Interaction of individual differences with visual and verbal elaboration instructions. *Journal of Educational Psychology, 70,* 306–318.

Desrochers, A., Wieland, L. D., & Coté, M. (1991). Instructional effects in the use of the mnemonic keyword method for learning German nouns and their grammatical gender. *Applied Cognitive Psychology, 5,* 19–36.

Elhelou, M. W. A. (1994). Arab children's use of the keyword method to learn English vocabulary words. *Educational Research, 36,* 295–302.

Ellis, N. C. (1995). The psychology of foreign language vocabulary acquisition: Implications for CALL. *Computer Assisted Language Learning, 8,* 103–128.

Ellis, N., & Beaton, A. (1993a). Factors affecting the learning of foreign language vocabulary: Imagery keyword mediators and phonological short-term memory. *Quarterly Journal of Experimental Psychology, 46A,* 533–558.

Ellis, N. C., & Beaton, A. (1993b). Psycholinguistic determinants of foreign language vocabulary learning. *Language Learning, 43,* 559–617.

Ellis, N. C., & Sinclair, S. G. (1996). Working memory in the acquisition of vocabulary and syntax: Putting language in good order. *Quarterly Journal of Experimental Psychology, 49A,* 234–250.

Etaugh, C., & Michals, D. (1975). Effects on reading comprehension of preferred music and frequency of studying to music. *Perceptual and Motor Skills, 41,* 553–554.

Eysenck, H. (1967). *The biological basis of personality.* Springfield, IL: Thomas.

Felix, U. (1993). The contribution of background music to the enhancement of learning in suggestopedia: A critical review of the literature. *Journal of the Society for Accelerative Learning and Teaching, 18,* 277–303.

Furnham, A., & Allass, K. (1999). The influence of musical distraction of varying complexity on the cognitive performance of extraverts and introverts. *European Journal of Personality, 13,* 27–38.

Furnham, A., & Bradley, A. (1997). Music while you work: The differential distraction of background music on the cognitive test performance of introverts and extraverts. *Applied Cognitive Psychology, 11,* 445–455.

Gathercole, S. E., & Thorn, A. S. C. (1998). Phonological short-term memory and foreign language learning. In A. F. Healy & L. E. Bourne (Eds.), *Foreign language learning: Psycholinguistic studies on training and retention* (pp. 141–158). Mahwah, NJ: Erlbaum.

Godden, D., & Baddeley, A. D. (1975). Context-dependent memory in two natural environments: On land and under water. *British Journal of Psychology, 66,* 325–331.

Gruneberg, M. M. (1998). A commentary on criticism of the keyword method of learning foreign languages. *Applied Cognitive Psychology, 12,* 529–532.

Gruneberg, M. M., & Pascoe, K. (1996). The effectiveness of the keyword method for receptive and productive foreign vocabulary learning in the elderly. *Contemporary Educational Psychology, 21,* 102–109.

Hazenberg, S., & Hulstijn, J. H. (1996). Defining a minimal receptive second-language vocabulary for non-native university students: An empirical investigation. *Applied Linguistics, 17,* 145–163.

Hogben, D., & Lawson, M. J. (1994). Keyword and multiple elaboration strategies for vocabulary acquisition in foreign language learning. *Contemporary Educational Psychology, 19,* 367–376.

Hulstijn, J. (1997). Mnemonic methods in foreign vocabulary learning: Theoretical considerations and pedagogical implications. In J. Coady & T. Huckin (Eds.), *Second language vocabulary acquisition* (pp. 203–224). Cambridge, England: Cambridge University Press.

Keatley, C., Spinks, J., & De Gelder, B. (1994). Asymmetric semantic facilitation between languages. *Memory and Cognition, 22,* 70–84.

Kieras, D. (1978). Beyond pictures and words: Alternative information-processing models for imagery effects in verbal memory. *Psychological Bulletin, 85,* 532–554.

Kirsner, K., Lalor, E., & Hird, K. (1993). The bilingual lexicon: Exercise, meaning and morphology. In R. Schreuder & B. Weltens (Eds.), *The bilingual lexicon* (pp. 215–248). Amsterdam: Benjamins.

Kolers, P. A. (1963). Interlingual word associations. *Journal of Verbal Learning and Verbal Behavior, 2,* 291–300.

Kroll, J. F. (1993). Accessing conceptual representation for words in a second language. In R. Schreuder & B. Weltens (Eds.), *The bilingual lexicon* (pp. 53–81). Amsterdam: Benjamins.

Kroll, J. F., & Curley, J. (1988). Lexical memory in novice bilinguals: The role of concepts in retrieving second language words. In M. M. Gruneberg, P. E. Morris, & R. N. Sykes (Eds.), *Practical aspects of memory: Current research and issues* (pp. 389–395). New York: Wiley.

Kroll, J. F., Michael, E., & Sankaranarayanan, A. (1998). A model of bilingual representation and its implications for second language acquisition. In A. F. Healy & L. E. Bourne (Eds.), *Foreign language learning: Psycholinguistic studies on training and retention* (pp. 365–395). Mahwah, NJ: Erlbaum.

Kroll, J. F., & Sholl, A. (1992). Lexical and conceptual memory in fluent and nonfluent bilinguals. In R. J. Harris (Ed.), *Cognitive processing in bilinguals* (pp. 191–204). Amsterdam: North-Holland.

Kroll, J. F., & Stewart, E. (1994). Category interference in translation and picture naming. Evidence for asymmetric connections between bilingual memory representations. *Journal of Memory and Language, 33,* 149–174.

Laufer, B. (1992). How much lexis is necessary for reading comprehension? In P. J. L. Arnaud & H. Béjoint (Eds.), *Vocabulary and applied linguistics* (pp. 126–132). Basingstoke: Macmillan.

Laufer, B. (1997). The lexical plight in second language reading: Words you don't know, words you think you know, and words you can't guess. In J. Coady & T. Huckin (Eds.), *Second language vocabulary acquisition* (pp. 20–34). Cambridge, England: Cambridge University Press.

Levin, J. R., Pressley, M., McCormick, C. B., Miller, G. E., & Shriberg, L. K. (1979). Assessing the classroom potential of the keyword method. *Journal of Educational Psychology, 71,* 583–594.

Lotto, L., & De Groot, A. M. B. (1998). Effects of learning method and word type on acquiring vocabulary in an unfamiliar language. *Language Learning, 48,* 31–69.

Marschark, M., Richman, C. L., Yuille, J. C., & Hunt, R. R. (1987). The role of imagery in memory: On shared and distinctive information. *Psychological Bulletin, 102,* 28–41.

Marschark, M., & Surian, L. (1989). Why does imagery improve memory? *European Journal of Cognitive Psychology, 1,* 251–263.

Meara, P. (1993). The bilingual lexicon and the teaching of vocabulary. In R. Schreuder &

B. Weltens (Eds.), *The bilingual lexicon* (pp. 279–297). Amsterdam: Benjamins.

Moore, J. C., & Surber, J. R. (1992). Effects of context and keyword methods on second language vocabulary acquisition. *Contemporary Educational Psychology, 17,* 286–292.

Nation, P. (1993). Vocabulary size, growth, and use. In R. Schreuder & B. Weltens (Eds.), *The bilingual lexicon* (pp. 115–134). Amsterdam: Benjamins.

Paivio, A. (1986). *Mental representations: A dual coding approach.* New York: Oxford University Press.

Paivio, A., & Desrochers, A. (1981). Mnemonic techniques in second-language learning. *Journal of Educational Psychology, 73,* 780–795.

Papagno, C., Valentine, T., & Baddeley, A. D. (1991). Phonological short-term memory and foreign-language vocabulary learning. *Journal of Memory and Language, 30,* 331–347.

Papagno, C., & Vallar, G. (1995). Verbal short-term memory and vocabulary learning in polyglots. *Quarterly Journal of Experimental Psychology, 48A,* 98–107.

Perfetti, C. A., & Roth, S. (1981). Some of the interactive processes in reading and their role in reading skill. In A. M. Lesgold & C. A. Perfetti (Eds.), *Interactive processes in reading* (pp. 269–297). Hillsdale, NJ: Erlbaum.

Potter, M. C., So, K.-F., Von Eckardt, B., & Feldman, L. B. (1984). Lexical and conceptual representation in beginning and proficient bilinguals. *Journal of Verbal Learning and Verbal Behavior, 23,* 23–38.

Pressley, M., Levin, J. R., & Delaney, H. D. (1982). The mnemonic keyword method. *Review of Educational Research, 52,* 61–91.

Pressley, M., Levin, J. R., & Miller, G. E. (1981). The keyword method and children's learning of foreign vocabulary with abstract meanings. *Canadian Journal of Psychology, 35,* 283–287.

Prince, P. (1996). Second language vocabulary learning: The role of context versus translations as a function of proficiency. *The Modern Language Journal, 80,* 478–493.

Rodríguez, M., & Sadoski, M. (2000). Effects of rote, context, keyword, and context/keyword methods on retention of vocabulary in EFL classrooms. *Language Learning, 50,* 385–412.

Runquist, W. N. (1966). Verbal behavior. In J. B. Sidowski (Ed.), *Experimental methods and instrumentation in psychology* (pp. 487–540). New York: McGraw-Hill.

Sánchez-Casas, R. M., Davis, C. W., & García-Albea, J. E. (1992). Bilingual lexical processing: Exploring the cognate/non-cognate distinction. *European Journal of Cognitive Psychology, 4,* 293–310.

Schneider, V. I., Healy, A. F., & Bourne, L. E., Jr. (2002). What is learned under difficult conditions is hard to forget: Contextual interference effects in foreign vocabulary acquisition, retention, and transfer. *Journal of Memory and Language, 46,* 419–440.

Schreuder, R. (1987). *Het mentale lexicon* (The mental lexicon), Inaugural address, University of Nijmegen, The Netherlands.

Schwanenflugel, P. J. (1991). Why are abstract concepts hard to understand? In P. J. Schwanenflugel (Ed.), *The psychology of word meanings* (pp. 223–250). Hillsdale, NJ: Erlbaum.

Service, E. (1992). Phonology, working memory, and foreign-language learning. *Quarterly Journal of Experimental Psychology, 45A,* 21–50.

Service, E., & Craik, F. I. M. (1993). Differences between young and older adults in learning a foreign vocabulary. *Journal of Memory and Language, 32,* 608–623.

Service, E., & Kohonen, V. (1995). Is the relation between phonological memory and foreign-language learning accounted for by vocabulary acquisition? *Applied Psycholinguistics, 16,* 155–172.

Sholl, A., Sankaranarayanan, A., & Kroll, J. F. (1995). Transfer between picture naming and translation: A test of asymmetries in bilingual memory. *Psychological Science, 6,* 45–49.

Sogin, D. W. (1988). Effects of three different musical styles of background music on coding by college-age students. *Perceptual and Motor Skills, 67,* 275–280.

Stanovich, K. E. (1980). Toward an interactive-compensatory model of individual differences in the development of reading fluency. *Reading Research Quarterly, 16,* 32–71.

Van Hell, J. G., & Candia Mahn, A. (1997). Keyword mnemonics versus rote rehearsal: Learning concrete and abstract foreign words by experienced and inexperienced learners. *Language Learning, 47,* 507–546.

Van Hell, J. G., & De Groot, A. M. B. (1998a). Conceptual representation in bilingual memory: Effects of concreteness and cognate status in word association. *Bilingualism: Language and Cognition, 1,* 193–211.

Van Hell, J. G., & De Groot, A. M. B. (1998b). Disentangling context availability and concreteness in lexical decision and word translation. *Quarterly Journal of Experimental Psychology, 51A,* 41–63.

Van Hell, J. G., & Sjarbaini, L. (2004). Concreteness effects in foreign language vocabulary learning. Manuscript in preparation.

Wang, A. Y., & Thomas, M. H. (1992). The effect of imagery-based mnemonics on the long-term retention of Chinese characters. *Language Learning, 42,* 359–376.

Wang, A. Y., & Thomas, M. H. (1995). Effect of keywords on long-term retention: Help or hindrance? *Journal of Educational Psychology, 87,* 468–475.

Wang, A. Y., & Thomas, M. H. (1999). In defence of keyword experiments: A reply to Gruneberg's commentary. *Applied Cognitive Psychology, 13,* 283–287.

Wang, A. Y., Thomas, M. H., & Ouellette, J. A. (1992). Keyword mnemonic and retention of second-language vocabulary words. *Journal of Educational Psychology, 84,* 520–528.

Weinreich, U. (1974). *Languages in contact: Findings and problems.* The Hague, The Netherlands: Mouton. (Original work published 1953)

Wimer, C. C., & Lambert, W. E. (1959). The differential effects of word and object stimuli on the learning of paired associates. *Journal of Experimental Psychology, 57,* 31–36.

Annick De Houwer

2

Early Bilingual Acquisition
Focus on Morphosyntax and the
Separate Development Hypothesis

ABSTRACT   This chapter discusses morphosyntactic development in bilingual children under age 6 years. The primary focus is on the relationship between children's two languages in production. The available empirical evidence so far from children acquiring 13 different language combinations strongly supports the Separate Development Hypothesis (SDH), which states that in learning to speak, children raised with two separate languages from birth approach their languages as two distinct, closed sets. The SDH can only be meaningfully addressed, however, after taking into consideration some basic methodological and analytical steps. A second point of focus is a comparison of monolingual and bilingual acquisition. Apart from the fact that bilingual children can communicate in two languages and monolingual children just in one, the acquisition process appears to be very similar in the two populations. A final issue is the structure of mixed utterances. Young bilingual children's mixed utterances do not differ much from those of adult bilinguals, albeit that they appear to be less varied in nature. The majority of young bilingual children's lexically mixed utterances consist of noun insertions from one language into an utterance in another language. Given the robust nature of the findings supporting the SDH, the real challenge for the field of bilingual acquisition now is to explain how separate morphosyntactic development is possible.

The last 15 years have seen a great increase in publications reporting on the language use and development of young children exposed to more than one language from a very early age. Prior to the mid-1980s, however, empirical studies of how young children become bilingual were few. However, what the field of bilingual acquisition used to lack in volume is well compensated by its long history: The first empirical study of bilingual development dates from 1913, written by the French linguist Jules Ronjat. Aside from being the first book-length publication on early bilingual acquisition, this monograph was also the very first volume to present an empirical study of bilingual behavior and should receive a place of honor in any bilingualism scholar's library.

Before the mid-1980s, there were only three other data-based monographs published on the process of early bilingual acquisition (the book by García, 1983, does concern bilingual children, but

does not offer a developmental perspective). Of these, the monumental work by yet another linguist, Werner Leopold, is by far the most famous and the most insightful. His four volumes appeared in several installments between 1939 and 1949 and were reprinted in 1970.

The most recent of the four early monographs is the much criticized volume by the psychologist Traute Taeschner (1983); it elaborates on earlier work published in the very influential, but also heavily criticized, article that Taeschner wrote with Virginia Volterra (Volterra & Taeschner, 1978). I briefly outline these criticisms in the section on the relationship between a child's two languages.

Less well known is the study on the acquisition of French and Serbian ("le serbe") by the psychologist Millivoïe Pavlovitch (1920). This study differs from the other three in that it dealt with the very early acquisition of a second language (L2). The studies by Ronjat, Leopold, and Taeschner, in contrast, were concerned with the acquisition of two first languages (L1s), as it were, that is, with cases for which the children in the study heard two languages from birth (and continued to do so at least until the time of study).

The present overview chapter also focuses on the acquisition of two languages from birth. Children who hear two languages from birth are undergoing a process of what Meisel (1989) called bilingual first language acquisition (BFLA; see also De Houwer, 1990). In BFLA, there is no "second" language in the chronological sense. It thus makes no sense to speak of an L1 or an L2. To refer to the two languages that play a role in BFLA, I use the terms language A and language Alpha (terminology borrowed from Wölck, 1984). This does not necessarily imply that both these languages need be on the same footing; that is, they need not be used in equal proportion or with equal frequency or regularity. Rather, the terms here refer to the input languages and specify that both input languages start to be used in regular communication with the child at the same time in development (viz., from birth or very soon afterward).

This chapter, then, reviews recent studies of children under the age of 6 years exposed to two spoken languages from birth who continued to hear these languages fairly regularly and frequently until the time of data collection (for a rare study that focused on the bilingual development of a signed and a spoken language in young children, see van den Bogaerde & Baker, 2002). Studies of children who have been regularly addressed in three or even more languages from birth do not feature in this review: So far, none appear to have been published (see Quay, 2001). There are, however, studies of children acquiring two languages from birth who start hearing a third language regularly once they are just a little older (see, e.g., Quay, 2001; Widdicombe, 1997).

I define *bilingual input* as dual-language input consisting mainly of substantial numbers of utterances that both lexically and structurally belong to one language only. Mixed utterances (i.e., utterances containing morphemes and/or lexemes from two languages) may account for some of the input as well. Even if the people in the child's environment address the child mainly in either of two languages and thus follow the "one person, one language" strategy (Ronjat, 1913), they will occasionally use mixed utterances. However, if a child hears nothing but mixed utterances, as might be the case in some so-called bilingual communities, I would argue that the child is not exposed to two languages from birth, but rather to one. After all, all the people interacting with the child would be using the same types of utterances, regardless of whether linguists could describe these as consisting of elements from two languages (cf. mixed languages in the sense of, e.g., Bakker, 1992). Bilingual input as understood here involves variation between strictly unilingual utterances in at least two languages, but will in most cases include mixed utterances as well.

I only refer to children acquiring varieties of what are commonly seen as distinct languages rather than a standard language and a regional variety of that same language, although the actual formal differences between them may in fact be similar to those between two different languages. The overview focuses on aspects of language production as it can be observed and recorded in naturalistic interactional settings. All studies mentioned here concern children growing up without any known handicaps or language learning problems.

A Frame of Reference for Studying Morphosyntactic Development in Young Bilinguals

In modern studies of monolingual acquisition, morphosyntactic development continues to be the most frequently investigated area of research. The same is true for recent work on bilingual acquisition. For instance, in an article giving an overview of many different aspects of BFLA published since 1985 (De Houwer, 1999b), 35 of the 64 original research articles or book chapters cited concerned morphosyntax; the 29 remaining texts were spread out over six other major research topics (i.e., the role of the input, the lexicon, phonological development, the use of mixed utterances, and language choice; I discuss all these aspects, in addition to morphosyntactic development, in De Houwer, 1995b, as well).

As the field of bilingual acquisition research grows and flourishes (see, e.g., the volume edited by Cenoz & Genesee, 2001), more and more different topics are under investigation. Nevertheless, more is currently known about morphosyntactic development in bilingual children than about any other area of language functioning. This justifies the primary focus here on morphosyntactic issues in early bilingual development.

In the field of language acquisition research, there have for a long time been divergent views regarding the role and status of morphosyntactic categories in early language development and when it makes sense to use morphosyntactic categories for describing children's early language productions. The controversies focus mainly on what is commonly termed the two-word stage (compare, e.g., Lieven, Pine, & Baldwin, 1997, and Vihman, 1999). New lines of research in developmental psycholinguistics that focus on transitions and connections between different kinds of knowledge (phonological, lexical, morphological, and syntactic) hold great promise for greater insight into the roots of morphosyntactic development (see the contributions in Weissenborn & Höhle, 2001).

For the purposes of the discussion in this chapter, I consider morphosyntactic development in production to be evident once a child growing up bilingually has begun to produce utterances containing at least three clause constituents or two-word utterances containing at least one bound morpheme, whichever comes first. This is not to imply that from this point on children have an awareness or abstract knowledge of the morphosyntactic categories they are using, and I do not mean to imply that no such knowledge is available prior to this (as, e.g., Golinkoff, Hirsh-Pasek, & Schweisguth, 2001, have suggested, it is quite possible that children as young as 18 months have a representation of some morphological categories well before they use these categories in production).

Space does not permit an extensive explanation, but I believe that the fairly conservative position taken here strikes a reasonable balance between overestimating and underestimating a child's grammatical skills. At the same time, it takes into consideration the huge typological differences between different languages as far as their reliance on constituent order versus bound morphology is concerned. Clearly, my position here excludes the one-word stage as a relevant focus of interest for a discussion of morphosyntactic development. This corresponds to what appears to be a consensus in the field of language acquisition in general: Morphosyntactic analyses of single-word utterances when children are still in the one-word stage are conspicuous by their absence (it is acknowledged, however, that at the one-word stage, precursors of bound morphology may be already present; see, e.g., Peters, 1983).

For the so-called two-word stage (which may be very drawn out or so brief it is hardly noticeable), there is less consensus (see above), but my proposal for bilingual data here is in line both with Meisel's (1994) reluctance to see children's early two-word utterances as exhibiting syntactic properties and

Deuchar and Quay's (2000, pp. 82–83) view that later two-word utterances that show morphological markings are in principle analyzable in morphosyntactic terms. Once children produce a large proportion of multiword utterances, child language researchers seem to agree that it is fully appropriate to describe their language use in morphosyntactic terms.

The Relationship Between a Child's Two Developing Languages: The Status of the Separate Development Hypothesis

Ronjat (1913) was not only the first to publish an empirical study on a bilingual individual's language use, but was also the first to formulate generalizations regarding the relationship between a young bilingual child's two languages. In addition, Ronjat was the first to address, based on empirical data, the issue of the relationship between a bilingual speaker's two languages.

It is this relationship between bilingual children's two languages that continues to be in the limelight in bilingual acquisition studies today. Basically, the question is to what extent and at what point in overall development a bilingual child's two separate input languages are processed as two independent systems. As researchers develop more sophisticated tools to investigate bilingual infants' perceptual capabilities and earliest vocalizations (see, e.g., Bosch & Sebastián-Gallés, 2001; Poulin-Dubois & Goodz, 2001), this question may finally have a chance of being answered. However, both the methodological and the analytical problems are quite formidable and have led some researchers to question whether in fact it will be possible to address fully the issue for children's very earliest stages of linguistic development. In particular, determining whether bilingual children's early phonologies develop as separate systems or not is quite a daunting task (Johnson & Lancaster, 1998; cf. also Deuchar & Quay, 2000, p. 111).

Earlier publications strongly defended either the Independent Development Hypothesis (e.g., Bergman, 1976), which claims that from the very beginning of language development infants who were hearing two languages from birth develop two independent systems, or, alternatively, they strongly supported the one hybrid system interpretation (e.g., Leopold, 1939–1949/1970, Vol. 2, p. 206; Volterra & Taeschner, 1978, p. 312), which posits an initial processing of two input languages as one hybrid system. Both these opposing points of view made their claims regarding all basic levels of language functioning (i.e., phonology, lexicon, morphosyntax). Within the hybrid system view, it then became crucial to try to explain just how children did in fact eventually manage to "differentiate" between their languages (see, e.g., Arnberg & Arnberg, 1992). Today, researchers are fortunately much more aware of the methodological and theoretical complexities involved in explaining the very earliest stages of bilingual development and understandably reluctant to make definitive claims.

For the development of morphosyntax in production, however, the issue of the extent to which bilingual children speak like the people acting as models for their two input languages is in principle much more amenable to investigation. Once children start showing clear signs of morphosyntactic development in production, which typically occurs around their second birthday (cf. the previous section outlining a frame of reference for studying morphosyntactic development), their phonologies tend to be more stable, and the huge problems of identifying language sources for children's vocalizations start to decrease steadily. It comes as no surprise, then, that many studies of language development in toddlers who grow up with two languages from birth have given a lot of attention to the relationship between children's developing morphosyntactic systems.

On the basis of an in-depth case study of a Dutch-English bilingual child, Kate, I proposed the Separate Development Hypothesis (SDH), which states that children regularly exposed to two languages from birth according to the one person, one language principle develop two distinct morphosyntactic systems in that "the morphosyntactic development of the one language does not have any fundamental effect on the morphosyntactic development of the other" (De Houwer, 1990, p. 66). At the time, there were only a few published studies that provided empirical support for the SDH (or the Differentiation Hypothesis, as Meisel, 2001, termed it), and the Kate study was the first to address the issue based on a very wide variety of morphosyntactic phenomena as present in the speech of one and the same child.

The 1990s saw an explosion of other studies providing additional support for the SDH. The fact that there is also a study (Deuchar & Quay, 2000) that supports the SDH even though the subject of this study did not quite hear her languages according to the one person, one language principle suggests that the input condition that is part of my original formulation of the SDH may in fact not be necessary. However, more studies are needed to investigate this issue. Also, I know of no studies that have explored young children's language development under mainly "mixed" conditions (i.e., when children heard most of the people in their environment speak two languages to them).

Because of the potentially very large role of input conditions, it is too early, then, to generalize the SDH to all children growing up with two languages from birth (see also De Houwer, 1990). At the same time, I know of no study that clearly shows evidence against the SDH. There appears to be a broad consensus among researchers today that the Separate Development Hypothesis accurately characterizes the basic process of morphosyntactic development in young bilingual children (see also Meisel, 2001, p. 16).

In the conclusion to my 1990 monograph, I speculated on the reasons that make separate development possible. One basic reason must be that young children pay very close attention to the variable nature of the input. Without at least this, it would appear impossible for young bilingual children to produce utterances that are clearly relatable to each of their input languages.

Given the existence of widely available earlier and in-depth reviews (Meisel, 1989; De Houwer, 1990, pp. 36–47, and 1995b; Lanza, 1997b; Deuchar & Quay, 2000), I only briefly mention a few of the many criticisms that have over the years been leveled at earlier claims concerning the initial stages of morphosyntactic development in bilingual children. These claims were part of the general "single-system" hypothesis (cf. the discussion in the third paragraph of this section). For early morphosyntactic development, they posited that children systematically apply "the same syntactic rules to both languages" (Volterra & Taeschner, 1978, p. 312), thus implying that very young bilingual children do not follow the ways of speaking of the people around them. In this view, bilingual children are seen as unable to keep two grammatical systems separate (Meisel, 1989), a process that has been called *fusion* in the bilingualism literature (Wölck, 1984). The authors making these claims do not refer to input conditions, but all the data supposedly supporting the claims come from children growing up according to the one person, one language principle.

A first basic problem is that the nature of the empirical support offered by Volterra and Taeschner (1978) and later by Taeschner (1983) is very unclear, and that the few analyses given showed internal inconsistencies and were often inaccurate (see, e.g., Mills, 1986; Meisel & Mahlau, 1988).

A more analytical problem is that Volterra and Taeschner, like Leopold (1939–1949/1970, Vol. 1, p. 179, and Vol. 3, p. 186) interpreted the use of lexically mixed utterances as evidence for a fused system. As I have argued (De Houwer, 1990, p. 39), the use of utterances that contain lexical items from two languages is not necessarily a reflection of one underlying language system. If so, all bilingual speakers would necessarily be operating with one fused system since all bilingual speakers at least occasionally use lexically mixed utterances. Rather, young bilingual children's lexically mixed utterances first and foremost need a sociolinguistic explanation: It needs to be investigated under which sociolinguistic conditions they do and do not appear and whether children are socialized in an environment that encourages their use or not (see also Lanza, 1997b). Once this is clear, psycholinguistic models can be constructed to explain the occurrence of mixed utterances and their form.

Volterra and Taeschner (1978) also discussed instances of lexically unilingual utterances that they claimed showed interference between their subjects' two languages. They considered such utterances to be evidence for their single-system hypothesis. As Meisel (1989) pointed out, the notion of "interference" requires the existence of two systems that can exert influence on each other. This is very different from positing, as Volterra and Taeschner (1978) and Taeschner (1983) did, one single rule system that gives rise to an "undifferentiated" language that by implication has as its output a type of language production that differs substantially from each input system.

The single-system or "Mish-Mash" hypothesis (a term used by Bergman, 1976) is not incompatible with the strong version of what I have termed a transfer theory of bilingual development (De Houwer, 1987, pp. 138–140, and 1990, p. 66). In its stronger version, such a theory assumes that "any morphosyntactic device belonging to input system A will be used in the child's speech production in utterances containing only lexical items from language B and vice versa" (De Houwer, 1990, p. 66). Stated in these empirically testable terms, support for the theory would consist of a quantitatively much higher proportion of utterances with lexical items from language A, but structural features of language Alpha than of utterances with lexical items and structural features from the same language (De Houwer, 1987, p. 138, and 1990, p. 66).

Following Slobin (1973), a weaker version of the transfer theory that is based on a kind of continuous comparison procedure between structures in both input languages, predicts transfer only if a particular morphosyntactic feature of input system A is less complex than a functionally equivalent feature of input system Alpha. Other proponents of this weaker version, such as Arnberg (1987, p. 68), however, tend to refer only to differences in formal complexity and ignore a crucial aspect in Slobin's original proposal: functional equivalence. The weaker version of the transfer theory is less easily testable since it is very difficult, if not impossible, to compare levels of formal complexity across languages (cf. De Houwer, 1987, pp. 138–139, and 1990, pp. 56–58).

Neither version of the transfer theory explains how children eventually do become able to combine lexical items from language Alpha with morphosyntactic features of the same language. Note also that the transfer theory presupposes a very great deal of creative tenacity in the young bilingual child that manifests itself even in the face of continuous contradictory and nonsupporting evidence as provided in the dual-language input.

So far, no studies have empirically shown the actual existence of the kinds of language repertoires predicted by the transfer theory in children with bilingual input from birth. For children undergoing a process of early L2 acquisition, though, clear and frequent signs of transfer may appear in one of their languages once children are beyond the silent stage (Ervin-Tripp, 1974; Tabors, 1987) and the formulaic stage (Wong-Fillmore, 1979). Preschool-aged children who start out hearing only one language from birth and who start regularly hearing an L2 on top of that at, say, age 3, may produce quite a few utterances with lexical items from L2 but structural features mainly from L1 (Fantini, 1985; Ekmekçi, 1994; Pfaff, 1994). The proportion of these kinds of utterances in relation to the child's overall production in L2 is not known, but they appear to be quite common.

The characteristics of children's L2 speech production are quite different from what is generally reported for young children with bilingual exposure from birth. These children's language production shows on the whole very little evidence of morphosyntactic transfer from one input system to the other (see also the section on studies of BFLA that offer support for the SDH). Rather, most of young bilingual learners' utterances with words from language A have morphosyntactic features that are relatable to the same input language. The same goes for language Alpha as well. This is precisely what the SDH predicts.

In the next section, I discuss in more detail the basis for concluding whether there is separate development. First, though, it needs to be emphasized that, to be able to interpret the morphosyntactic features of their two input languages, bilingual children must have processing mechanisms that are able to approach each input language as a morphosyntactically closed set. So far, there have been no reports that bilingual toddlers or preschoolers are somehow slow or have difficulty in real-time comprehension of their input languages or switches between them, whether utterance-internal or not. However, this issue has to my knowledge not been explicitly addressed as yet. Since in young children language comprehension generally precedes and paves the way for language production (see, e.g., Bates, Dale, & Thal, 1995), it is not unlikely that separate development in comprehension is partly what makes separate development in production possible.

Methodological Requirements for Addressing the Separate Development Hypothesis

Once children with bilingual input from birth start to use morphosyntactic elements in their utterances, they use three types of utterances: (a) lexically unilingual utterances in language A, (b) lexically unilingual utterances in language Alpha, and (c) mixed utterances, which contain lexical items or bound morphemes from languages A and Alpha. These are also the types of utterances that older bilingual speakers produce and that will be present in the child's bilingual input.

The basic question to be answered is whether a child with bilingual input from birth follows a target-language-like developmental path in two languages (cf. the third section). Thus, it needs to be investigated to what extent the child's lexically unilingual utterances in language A use morphosyntactic features from language A and to what extent the child's lexically unilingual utterances in language Alpha use morphosyntactic features from language Alpha. The answer to this question will show the extent to which young bilingual children's lexically unilingual utterances resemble those used by the people around them and thus to what extent the SDH is an accurate descriptive generalization of early bilingual development. The SDH thus depends on analyses of lexically unilingual utterances only (De Houwer, 1990, p. 69, and 1994, 1998, p. 256; De Houwer & Meisel, 1996). Of course, should a child's repertoire consist mainly of mixed utterances, it becomes impossible to investigate the SDH (or its counterpart, the transfer theory). As it turns out, though, most of young bilingual children's utterances are lexically unilingual and thus offer ample opportunity for investigating the extent to which these unilingual utterances resemble target structures present in each of the input languages.

In principle, the SDH should be addressed on the basis of children's acquisition of aspects of morphosyntax that clearly differ between the child's two input languages but that are comparable in that they fulfill more or less the same function (cf. De Houwer, 1990; Meisel, 1989; for a particularly penetrating argumentation explaining this need, see Serratrice, 2002). After all, when both input systems use different morphosyntactic means for expressing a particular function, there are different expectations for their use in the child's language A than in language Alpha. When both input systems closely resemble each other for a particular feature, the child could not be expected to use different features.

An example will help clarify this point: In English yes-no questions involving lexical verbs, there is use of do-support as in "Do you want some tea?" In contrast, Dutch yes-no questions involving lexical verbs do not use do-support ("*Wil je thee?*" literally, "Want you tea?"). The SDH would predict do-support only in the child's lexically English questions and would not expect any do-support in the child's lexically Dutch questions. The transfer theory would expect either no do-support in English or do-support in Dutch. On the other hand, English and Dutch yes-no questions involving the copula have exactly the same structure: "Is that tea?" or "*Is dat thee?*" (literally, "Is that tea?"). Application of the Dutch rule to English or the English rule to Dutch gives the same result. Hence, English and Dutch yes-no questions with a copula are not constructions that can provide insight into whether children transfer rules from one language to the other.

Children may not always agree with linguists regarding what should count as a particular structure. Getting back to the example of the yes-no questions, it is quite possible that, for English, a bilingual child has not yet learned that questions with a copula are structured differently from questions with a lexical verb. The child might use do-support for all English questions, including those with a copula. As long as the child does not use do-support in Dutch questions, though, there is no evidence of transfer. Rather, the child's overuse of do-support in English even lends stronger evidence for the SDH than if the child was producing do-support only when required.

But, what if the child does not use any do-support? The fact that she or he fails to use it when English requires it is not necessarily a result of transfer since English questions with a copula provide evidence that in English do-support is not necessary in all questions. The child may be overgeneralizing in English on the basis of English input evidence, and the child's lack of do-support may have nothing to do with influence from Dutch. The child's lack of do-support in English, then, cannot be interpreted. It is not support or lack of support for either the transfer theory or the SDH.

As I suggested elsewhere (De Houwer, 1994, p. 45), one way of getting around this interpretative problem might be to look at data from monolingual acquisition: If the bilingual child uses forms similar to those used in the same language by a monolingual peer, there is a possibility that the forms are intralinguistically determined. However, such a comparative approach can never entirely settle the issue since a similarity of form does not necessarily indicate a similarity in processing. Hence, intrinsically ambiguous forms in the bilingual data will often have to remain just that.

Clear evidence for the SDH, then, consists of the child using comparable structures that differ across both input languages in utterances with lexical items from the appropriate language. Although evidence for the SDH is not expected to be noticeable when both input systems closely resemble each other for a particular feature, such evidence might in fact occur if, at the same age, the child does use this particular feature, but only in one language. An example of this can be found in a study by Almgren and Idiazabal (2001). Their Basque-Spanish bilingual subject, Mikel, started using imperfective pasts to refer to imaginary events in Spanish 9 months before he did this in Basque. Yet, imperfective pasts can be used to refer to imaginary events in both Spanish and Basque.

To be able to conclude that one particular child is developing two separate morphosyntactic systems, a wide spectrum of morphosyntactic features must be studied. After all, it is possible that separate development holds in some areas of morphosyntactic functioning, but not in others.

For the SDH to be confirmed, then, separate development must be evident for most of the morphosyntactic structures in the child's speech that reflect differences in the input languages. Occasional instances of apparent transfer in lexically unilingual utterances of features that differ across the input languages do not detract from the validity of the SDH, but should of course only be very occasional (see further discussion in this section). They should occur in no more than a few percent of the relevant cases within a brief time frame (say, in all the recordings made in a month's time). Structures that appear to push the two systems apart even more than necessary are obviously additional evidence for the SDH (cf. the theoretically possible example above for which do-support is used in English yes-no questions with a copular verb). Morphosyntactic features that appear in both input languages as well as in the child's unilingual utterances are neutral to the SDH.

Analyzing all or most of the morphosyntactic features used by a bilingual child is highly time consuming. Most child language researchers therefore prefer to limit their analyses to specific subparts of children's language production. When these different analyses are combined, though, we actually get a random sample of a variety of structures used by different children living in different parts of the world and acquiring different language pairs. If the SDH is not valid, such a database should reveal this fairly easily. However, as I show in the next section, quite the contrary is the case.

Studies of Bilingual First Language Acquisition That Offer Support for the Separate Development Hypothesis

In this section, I give an overview of a large portion of the empirical studies published in the last 15 years that have looked at morphosyntactic development in children growing up with two languages from birth. All these studies show evidence of the separate development of morphosyntax, whether this was made explicit by the authors or not (Table 2.1). The analyses of the data in the studies listed in Table 2.1 that provide support for the SDH all refer to children's unilingual utterances and to aspects of morphosyntax that clearly differ across the two languages investigated.

Table 2.1 Empirical Studies on Bilingual Acquisition that Confirm the Separate Development Hypothesis

Child	Languages	Age(s)*	Study/Studies
Natalie	Slovak/English	1;3–5;7	Stefánik, 1995, 1997
Andreu	Catalan/English	1;3–4;2	Juan-Garau and Pérez-Vidal, 2000
Jean	French/Swedish	1;10–3;9	Schlyter, 1995
Mimi	French/Swedish	2;0–4;2	Schlyter, 1995
Anne	French/Swedish	2;3–4;4	Schlyter, 1995
Olivier	French/English	1;11–2;10	Paradis and Genesee, 1996
Gene	French/English	1;11–3;1	Paradis and Genesee, 1996
William	French/English	2;2–3;3	Paradis and Genesee, 1996
Mathieu	French/English	1;9–2;11	Paradis and Genesee, 1997
Yann	French/English	1;11–3;0	Paradis and Genesee, 1997
Odessa	French/English	2;7–2;9	Jisa, 1995
Anouk	French/Dutch	2;3–3;4	Hulk and Van der Linden, 1996
Kate	Dutch/English	2;7–3;4	De Houwer, 1990, 1997
Ivar	French/German	1;4–2;9	Meisel, 1990
		1;5–3;0	Müller, 1994a
		1;5–4;3	Meisel and Müller, 1992; Müller, 1990b
		1;5–5;0	Koehn, 1994
		1;5–5;10	Müller, 1994b
		1;10–3;0	Kaiser, 1994
		1;10–3;5	Schlyter, 1990a; Müller, 1993
		2;0–2;8	Meisel, 1994
		2;2–3;5	Klinge, 1990
		2;2–2;6	Köppe, 1994b
		2;4–3;5	Müller, Crysmann, and Kaiser, 1996
Pascal	French/German	1;5–4;0	Meisel and Müller, 1992; Müller, 1990b
		1;5–4;7	Müller, 1994b
		1;8–4;10	Stenzel, 1994
		1;9–2;11	Kaiser, 1994
		1;10–2;5	Köppe, 1994b
		1;10–3;5	Müller, 1993
		2;4–4;7	Stenzel, 1996
Annika	French/German	2;0–3;11	Stenzel, 1994
Caroline	French/German	1;0–3;6	Meisel, 1985
		1;0–3;1	Meisel, 1990
		1;6–3;0	Müller, 1995
		1;6–5;0	Meisel and Müller, 1992, Müller, 1990a, 1994a, 1994b
		1;10–3;10	Meisel, 1986, 1989
		1;11–2;8	Meisel, 1994
		1;11–4;6	Klinge, 1990
Christoph	French/German	1;1–3;8	Parodi, 1990
		1;11–3;5	Schlyter, 1990a
		2;3–3;8	Klinge, 1990
François	French/German	2;4–3;4	Schlyter, 1990a
Pierre	French/German	1;0–3;6	Meisel, 1985
		1;0–4;0	Meisel, 1990
		2;6–4;0	Meisel, 1989
		2;7–3;3	Meisel, 1994
		2;7–3;8	Meisel, 1986
Zevio	Spanish/English	0;11–4;6	Krasinski, 1995
Manuela	Spanish/English	1;7–2;3	Deuchar and Quay, 1998
		1;7–3;2	Deuchar, 1992
		1;8–2;2	Deuchar and Quay, 2000, pp. 82–87

(continued)

Table 2.1 (*Contd.*)

Child	Languages	Age(s)*	Study/Studies
Sonja	German/English	2;0–2;6	Sinka and Schelleter, 1998
Maija	Latvian/English	1;2–1;11	Sinka and Schelleter, 1998
Peru	Spanish/Basque	1;11–3;2	Idiazabal, 1988, 1991
		1;11–4;0	Barreña, 2001
Mikel	Spanish/Basque	1;6–3;0	Almgren and Barreña, 2000
		1;6–3;6	Barreña, 1997
		1;6–4;0	Barreña, 2001
		1;7–4;0	Almgren and Idiazabal, 2001; Ezeizabarrena and Larrañaga, 1996
Rie	Japanese/English	2;4–2;10	Mishina-Mori, 2002
Ken	Japanese/English	2;8–3;2	Mishina-Mori, 2002
Carlo	Italian/English	1;10–3;2	Serratrice, 2001, 2002

[a]Ages are indicated in years;months (months have been rounded up to the next month for children who were at least 20 days into the next month); a dash between ages means from age X to age Y.

In the field of child language research, several quite different methods are used to collect data. It is still the case, however, that data based on natural, spontaneous interaction are the most desirable when little is known about the developmental course of a particular language or pair of languages. Given the very scant knowledge about early bilingual acquisition up until about 15 years ago, it will come as no surprise that most of the studies reviewed here are longitudinal case studies that used spontaneous speech as their main database. For this reason, Table 2.1 is organized as a function of the children studied. This has the advantage of giving a clear picture of the current database on which present-day knowledge of morphosyntactic development in young bilinguals is based. Aside from listing the language combination acquired, Table 2.1 also shows the age ranges from which data were drawn in the studies reporting on a particular child's speech.

As Table 2.1 shows, the current database for studies that support the SDH consists of the speech productions of 29 children (17 boys, 12 girls) between the ages of 1 and nearly 6 years, who together are acquiring 12 languages in 13 different combinations. All but 2 of those 12 languages belong to the group of Indo-European languages (Catalan, Dutch, English, French, German, Italian, Latvian, Slovak, Spanish, and Swedish). The 2 non–Indo-European languages that have been studied in publications addressing the SDH are Basque and Japanese. As in child language acquisition research involving monolingual children, English is much more heavily represented than any other language: Of the total of 13 different language combinations listed in Table 2.1, 9 include English. Four of the combinations include French. The more language combinations show support for the SDH, the less likely the chance that evidence for the SDH is somehow a result of the specific languages investigated and the more likely the chance that the SDH indeed captures an important aspect of the bilingual acquisition process in general (see also De Houwer, 1994, p. 45).

It is often claimed that bilingual children reported on in the literature are primarily children of (psycho-)linguists (see, e.g., Romaine, 1999). Whereas this might have been the case in the past, it certainly no longer is today: Only 6 of the 29 children in Table 2.1 (viz., Andreu, Manuela, Natalie, Odessa, Sonja, and Zevio) are children of linguists or psychologists (viz., correspondingly, Pérez-Vidal, Deuchar, Stefánik, Jisa, Schelleter, and Krasinski). As in most studies of child language in general, the children studied primarily live in a middle class environment that, on the whole, is fairly common in the Western world (most of the children studied live in Western Europe and North America).

Most of the children listed in Table 2.1 have been exposed to their two languages according to the one person, one language principle. As discussed here, the SDH was originally formulated to apply only to children growing up in these circumstances. However, at least one child in Table 2.1 (Deuchar's daughter Manuela) quite clearly was not raised according to the one person, one language principle. Instead, Manuela's bilingual parents spoke English to her when there were other English speakers present and Spanish in all other circumstances. She heard English from monolingual English speakers.

Yet, she developed her two languages along two separate morphosyntactic paths as well.

Many studies listed in Table 2.1 analyzed data from the same children, but investigated different subtopics in morphosyntactic development (see below). Also, they do not always use data from the same age period, even though they may concern the same child. Most notable here are the many studies published by Meisel and his collaborators in the framework of the Hamburg DUFDE project (*Deutsch und Französisch—Doppelter Erstsprach-erwerb* [German and French—Double First Language Acquisition]; for overviews, see Köppe, 1994a, and Schlyter, 1990b). The children Annika, Caroline, Christoph, François, Ivar, Pascal, and Pierre were all studied in the framework of this influential project.

The studies in Table 2.1 investigated a wide variety of morphosyntactic subtopics. These subtopics are listed in Table 2.2 together with the studies that have a particular topic as their main focus. When studies concern more than one subtopic, they appear more than once in the table.

As discussed in the previous section, it is important to investigate all or most of the morphosyntactic elements used by a particular bilingual child in order to have firm evidence for the SDH. If the information from Tables 2.1 and 2.2 is combined, it is clear that for quite a few children in Table 2.1 many different morphosyntactic aspects have been investigated. This is particularly the case for the children Andreu, Caroline, Christoph, Kate, Ivar, Maija, Manuela, Mikel, Pascal, Pierre, Sonja, and Carlo (see also Serratrice, 1999, besides the publications listed in Tables 2.1 and 2.2). These children, then, were definitely approaching their two languages as fundamentally closed morphosyntactic sets. Whether the same can be said for the other children is yet to be determined; in any case, the

Table 2.2 Morphosyntactic Topics Investigated in Empirical Studies of Bilingual First Language Acquisition Confirming the Separate Development Hypothesis

Topic	Study/Studies
Morphology of the nominal constituent	Almgren and Barreña, 2000; Barreña, 1997; De Houwer, 1990; Ezeizabarrena and Larrañaga, 1996; Idiazabal, 1988, 1991; Koehn, 1994; Meisel, 1986; Müller, 1995; Parodi, 1990; Sinka and Schelleter, 1998; Stefánik, 1995, 1997; Stenzel, 1994, 1996
Syntactic gender	De Houwer, 1990; Müller, 1990a, 1994, 1995; Sinka and Schelleter, 1998; Stefánik, 1995, 1997
Pronouns/clitics	Almgren and Barreña, 2000; De Houwer, 1990; Kaiser, 1994; Müller et al., 1996; Serratrice, 2002
Determiners	Barreña, 1997; De Houwer, 1990; Müller, 1994; Paradis and Genesee, 1997
Pluralization	Barreña, 1997; De Houwer, 1990; Deuchar and Quay, 1998; Müller, 1994; Sinka and Schelleter, 1998
Verb morphology	Almgren and Barreña, 2000; Almgren and Idiazabal, 2001; De Houwer, 1990; Deuchar, 1992; Ezeizabarrena and Larrañaga, 1996; Jisa, 1995; Meisel, 1996; Meisel and Müller, 1992; Müller, 1990b; Paradis and Genesee, 1997; Serratrice, 2001; Sinka and Schelleter, 1998
Aspect and/or time markings	Almgren and Barreña, 2000; Almgren and Idiazabal, 2001; De Houwer, 1990, 1997; Jisa, 1995; Krasinski, 1995; Meisel, 1985, 1994; Mishina-Mori, 2002; Serratrice, 2001; Schlyter, 1990a, 1995
Congruence/agreement	Almgren and Barreña, 2000; De Houwer, 1990; Deuchar, 1992; Meisel, 1989, 1990, 1994; Meisel and Müller, 1992; Müller, 1990b; Paradis and Genesee, 1996; Serratrice, 2002; Sinka and Schelleter, 1998
Negation	Mishina-Mori, 2002; Paradis and Genesee, 1996, 1997
Syntactic word order	Almgren and Barreña, 2000; De Houwer, 1990; Hulk and Van der Linden, 1996; Köppe, 1994b; Meisel, 1986, 1989; Meisel and Müller, 1992; Müller, 1990b, 1993; Parodi, 1990; Sinka and Schelleter, 1998
Complex sentences	Barreña, 2001; De Houwer, 1990; Müller, 1993, 1994b
Subject realization	Juan-Garau and Pérez-Vidal, 2000; Serratrice, 2002
General development	De Houwer, 1990; Juan-Garau and Pérez-Vidal, 2000

remaining children show no signs of interlinguistically determined development in any of the areas that happen to have been investigated.

The fact that young, actively bilingual children essentially develop their two morphosyntactic systems separately from each other implies that one language may be further developed than the other. The children studied by Jisa (1995), Juan-Garau and Pérez-Vidal (2000), Schlyter (1995), and Stefánik (1995, 1997) (viz. Odessa, Andreu, Jean, Mimi, Anne, and Natalie), for instance, showed quite different language abilities for at least some time during the period they were studied. Most of the other children were at roughly the same level of development in each of their languages at the time of data collection (that is, if it is accepted that levels of development can in fact be meaningfully compared across languages, a point I am not so sure of unless the differences are blatantly obvious; see De Houwer, 1998).

Given the general lack of relevant data that could speak to this issue of uneven (but still separate) development, however, it is not clear what the range of possibilities here is: For instance, it is theoretically possible that a bilingual child produces complex sentences in one language while in the other language only two-word utterances appear. But are there any children growing up bilingual from birth who exhibit these sorts of patterns? So far, reports showing these kinds of divergent paths in skilled child speakers are lacking. The few studies that do show very differing levels of language ability across bilingual children's two languages (cf. above) happen to concern very young children who are just entering the multiword stage in one of their languages. Also, it remains to be investigated which factors determine gross differences across bilingual children's abilities in either language. In any case, it is a common observation that young bilingual children who have been regularly addressed in two languages from birth do not necessarily speak their two languages equally well.

Interlinguistic Influence in Unilingual Utterances

As suggested, even if a child is found to develop two morphosyntactic systems as fundamentally closed sets, occasionally the child may use unilingual utterances in language A that could well be explained as drawing on structural features of language Alpha. Such utterances will be nonadultlike, except when they are in fact modeled in the actual input to which the child is exposed (in which case the use by the child of structurally similar utterances is to be expected and as such not surprising or in need of special analytic treatment).

An example of such an utterance that might be a result of interlinguistic influence is "I want another," produced by my Dutch-English bilingual subject, Kate, at age 3 years (cf. also De Houwer, 1995b, p. 236). The pronominalizer "one" would have been expected here from an adult's perspective. Its nonrealization could be a result of simply insufficient, immature knowledge of the English system (i.e., a developmental explanation); after all, children often sound unlike adults because they omit a particular word or phrase. As it happens, Kate often used the pronominalizer one at around the same age in other (and similar) sentences, so this explanation might be less likely.

It should be noted, though, that it is typical for young children to show variability in their language use: For instance, at the same point of development, Dutch-speaking monolingual 3-year-olds may correctly say "*ik heb*" ("I have") and incorrectly *"ik heeft"* ("I has") (De Houwer & Gillis, 1998). Alternatively, the utterance "I want another" might be considered a speech error. Or, the utterance might be explained by reference to Dutch (i.e., by influence from one language on another one), in which saying "I want another" but with Dutch words as in "*Ik* (I) *wil* (want) *een ander* (another)" is perfectly fine. Often, it will be impossible to choose between these three explanatory possibilities.

If potentially interlinguistically generated utterances of a similar nature are very rare on the whole, they are of little theoretical consequence: It will usually be impossible to verify their exact status with any degree of certainty, and because they are so rare, they will hardly be able to exert any lasting effects on the rest of the child's developing systems. So far, there has to my knowledge only been one study that has expressly looked at possibly interlinguistically generated utterances within a corpus of bilingual child speech, and that has published precise quantitative data regarding the frequency of occurrence of such utterances: Sinka (2000, p. 171) reported that in the corpus for her Latvian-English subject Mara, spanning nearly 1 year of data collection, only 2 (which is less than a tenth of a percent) of a total of 5,275 unilingual utterances were possibly cases showing interlinguistic influence on the syntactic level; for her second Latvian-English subject Maija, there were 13 (or less than a quarter of a percent) such utterances of a total of

5,537 utterances recorded in a year (Sinka noted that these utterances might in fact be performance errors). Clearly, with such small numbers, further analyses are quite pointless.

Bilingual and Monolingual Acquisition Compared

Already in the very first study of bilingual acquisition by Ronjat (1913), the question was raised how bilingual development compares to monolingual development (see also my summary of Ronjat's views in De Houwer, 1990, pp. 51–52). Ronjat complained that in effect he could not really address this issue in any detail since there simply were no sources for monolingual comparisons available. Since 1913, the situation has improved, although some of Ronjat's problems are still with us today (see below). The interest in comparing bilingual and monolingual development, however, has not changed.

Children who have been regularly and frequently exposed to two languages from birth and who actually speak those languages (not all bilingual exposure results in active bilingualism; see, e.g., De Houwer, 1999a) are no different from children growing up with just one language as far as the general course of morphosyntactic development is concerned. The main distinction between actively bilingual children on the one hand and monolingual children on the other is that the former are able to make themselves understood in two languages whereas the latter are not. Apart from this, there are no major differences. Both bilingual and monolingual children start off their conventionally meaningful language production using single-word sentences or *holophrases*. They then go on to produce two-word sentences, and after producing multiword sentences for a while, they start to use complex sentences as well.

On the morphological level, depending on the language that is acquired, both bilingual and monolingual children may use a number of bound morphemes at a very early stage in development. From the two-word stage onward, both monolingual and bilingual children speak a clearly identifiable language (for a critique of earlier theories that implicitly denied this as far as bilingual children are concerned, see De Houwer, 1995b).

Although young bilingual and monolingual children clearly speak a particular language from a very early age onward, they still differ quite dramatically from how the adults in their environment speak that language. Both bilingual and monolingual preschool children make morphological and syntactic errors, and they both produce only a fraction of the range of morphosyntactic devices available to mature speakers.

Further global similarities between bilingual and monolingual children concern the timing of a number of important milestones in language development. Except for the huge range of normal individual variation that exists between monolingual children (and which also exists among bilingual children), there are no systematic differences between normally developing bilingual and monolingual children in the ages at which basic language skills are acquired. Just like his or her monolingual friend, a bilingual 2-year-old can be expected to be able to carry on a brief, but largely comprehensible, conversation with a familiar adult using an occasional two-word utterance. A great deal more can be expected from a bilingual 3-year-old (just as can be expected of a 3-year-old monolingual): The child should be able to produce utterances containing three or four words and should be quite comprehensible to strangers.

There is as yet no empirical basis for the claim that, as a group, bilingual children develop their languages more slowly than monolingual children.

Finally, there are quite detailed similarities to be noted for bilingual and monolingual children concerning the developmental course of one specific language. In other words, if comparisons are made, for instance, of the English language use of a bilingual child and that of a monolingual child of approximately the same age, the similarities are quite striking. It is impossible to say on the basis of a corpus of English utterances by a 3-year-old whether they were produced by a bilingual or a monolingual child. Monolingual and bilingual children acquiring the same language from birth use that language in very similar ways: They produce the same sorts of utterances (some studies even reported identical utterances; see, e.g., De Houwer, 1990) with similar types of errors and characteristics.

Detailed comparisons between bilingual and monolingual children so far have been undertaken for Basque, Dutch, English, French, German, and Spanish. Obviously, it must not be forgotten that, in comparisons between bilingual and monolingual children acquiring a common language, there may be a great deal of variation between individual children. That individual variation makes it quite difficult in some cases to determine whether a small point of difference is relatable to the fact that the bilingual child is simultaneously acquiring another language or not.

Future studies will have to show to what extent the minimal differences that do crop up here and there in very detailed comparisons are to be explained in terms of individual variation or other factors. One problem here is that often there is little material available for monolingual acquisition that could be used as a dependable basis for comparison (this problem sometimes occurs even for English, the most frequently researched language in acquisition studies). Another problem is that studies of spontaneous child speech often have few quantitative data, so that it is impossible to decide the extent of quantitative differences between monolingual and bilingual children in the frequency of occurrence of particular types of linguistic structures (for a more in-depth comparison of monolingual and bilingual acquisition, see De Houwer, 2002).

So far, I have mainly emphasized the similarities between the morphosyntactic development of bilingual and monolingual children. Those similarities highlight the robust nature of the primary language development process, which seems immune to whether a child is growing up learning two languages or just one. Note, however, that I have so far discussed bilingual children's morphosyntactic development only on the basis of a portion of their speech production (viz. on the basis of lexically and morphologically unilingual utterances). All young bilingual children, however, also produce lexically and morphologically mixed utterances (which, by definition, monolingual children cannot). It is these to which I turn next.

Structural Aspects of Bilingual Children's Mixed Utterances

Mixed utterances in bilingual speech are here defined as utterances with surface realization that clearly includes lexical items or bound morphemes (or both) from two languages (I leave aside the theoretical issue of the extent to which mixed utterances can be seen as instances of code switching or code mixing; for an in-depth discussion of this regarding young bilingual children, see, e.g., Lanza, 1997a). The very youngest of bilingual speakers use mixed utterances from the first stages of morphosyntactic development. The use of mixed utterances, then, is an integral part of early bilingual development, although on the whole, children's use of lexically or morphologically mixed utterances is rather infrequent in comparison with their use of lexically unilingual utterances (that is, for those children for whom we have data).

Switching between different types of utterances is apparently not a problem: To my knowledge, there have been no reports of bilingual children who had trouble switching between unilingual utterances from languages A and Alpha or vice versa or between unilingual utterances and mixed utterances. The use of far more hesitations in one language than another, though, might give rise to less-fluent transitions from one type of utterance to another. In my study, the only one I am aware of that counted a bilingual child's (Kate's) hesitations and analyzed their use in both languages (De Houwer, 1990, pp. 96, 331), I found no differences between the languages. In the absence of evidence to the contrary, fluent switching between different types of utterances seems to be part and parcel of early bilingual production in children raised with two languages from birth.

Parents in bilingual families are sometimes surprised to hear their young children use mixed utterances, especially when they see themselves as not using mixed utterances (however, as Goodz (1989) has shown, for instance, there may be quite a difference between self-reported and actual language use in bilingual situations). Often, parents (and in the past, researchers as well) see the use of mixed utterances by their young bilingual children as evidence of language confusion. As Lanza (1997b) admirably demonstrated, young bilingual children's early use of mixed utterances cannot be seen as a result of "language confusion," but can be explained by the language socialization practices in the family and children's sensitivity to them. Young bilingual children are in general very responsive vis-à-vis the sociolinguistic norms that exist in their environment regarding language choice (see, e.g., De Houwer, 1990; Deuchar & Quay, 2000). Also, the use of mixed utterances can be explained in terms of this sensitivity: Children will use more mixed utterances, and will continue to use them, the more tolerance there is for them in their environment. The use of mixed utterances, then, is in most cases not reducible to a lack of language skill.

There have been only a few studies of bilingual children's morphosyntactic development that have both looked in detail at lexically unilingual and mixed utterances produced by the same child and have tried to draw comparisons between them (De Houwer, 1990; Sinka, 2000). The general picture gained from these studies is that the structure of mixed utterances tends to reflect the overall structure of lexically unilingual utterances produced by the bilingual child at the same age: Both the global length and linguistic complexity of mixed utterances resemble those of the unilingual utterances the child is producing at the time.

There have been rather more studies of bilingual children's mixed utterances per se, although again the number of studies focusing on their morphosyntactic characteristics is limited. Because young bilingual children are still quite immature speakers, they will often produce very short utterances consisting of just two words. For these, it will be impossible to investigate which elements are mixed into what (cf. De Houwer, 1990, 1995a; but see Lanza, 1997b, for an alternative view). For longer mixed utterances, it may be possible to identify the consistency of the mixed elements.

The empirical data available so far, regardless of the particular language combination studied (see, e.g., De Houwer, 1990, 1995a; Saunders, 1988; Sinka, 2000; Wanner, 1996) show that, in utterances that clearly are utterances in language A with one or more elements inserted from language Alpha (or vice versa), the insertions from language Alpha mainly consist of single nouns when children are under age 4 years (at a somewhat later age, insertions mainly consist of noun phrases in addition to single nouns; cf. Bentahila & Davies, 1994). Also, in bilingual adults, noun insertions are the most commonly inserted category in mixed utterances (see, e.g., Romaine, 1995).

In De Houwer (1995a), I applied an analytical method based on utterance length and guest and host language status to mixed utterances produced by 11 preschool children acquiring five language combinations. The data for this study were drawn from the spoken language corpora archive CHILDES (MacWhinney, 1991) as well as from several published sources. The main finding was that, regardless of the actual language pair involved, children's mixed multiword utterances consisted mainly of free morpheme insertions of the guest languages into the host language. These free morpheme insertions were most often nouns.

More analyses that apply one specific method for cross comparisons are needed, however, to obtain a clearer picture of the main characteristics of young bilingual children's mixed utterances.

Conclusion

In acquiring two languages from birth, children are undergoing a sort of "double" acquisition process

in which two morphosyntactic systems are acquired as fundamentally separate and closed systems. This does not imply, of course, that structural influence from one language on the other is not possible, but until now no evidence has been found of systematic morphosyntactic influence from one language on the other in children who have been regularly and frequently exposed to two languages from birth. Young bilingual children reflect the structural possibilities of both languages to which they have been exposed and are able to produce utterances that are clearly relatable to each of their different languages from very early. This would not be possible without very close attention to the variable nature of the input (De Houwer, 1990).

In general, bilingual children's language-specific development within one language differs little from that of monolingual acquisition, except of course that bilingual children do it for two languages at a time. There is no evidence that hearing two languages from birth leads to language delay.

In being able to produce unilingual utterances in two languages, bilingual children closely resemble bilingual adults. In addition, just like adult bilinguals, young bilingual children are able to switch between languages very easily, either at utterance boundaries or within utterances. Utterances in which lexical or morphological switching occurs are an integral mark of bilingual functioning both in young child bilinguals and in more mature bilingual speakers. In mixed utterances produced by either child or adult bilinguals, noun insertions are a common feature. Naturally, though, in both mixed and unilingual utterances, child bilinguals do not yet exhibit the full wealth and breadth of the sorts of structures of which adult bilinguals are capable.

As they acquire two separate linguistic systems, young bilingual children learn from a very tender age which norms for language choice exist in their environment, and in general they are able to apply those norms in their own language production. The use of mixed utterances is to be seen as one of the language choice possibilities within the socialization patterns present in bilingual children's linguistic environments rather than as a sign of insufficient linguistic skill.

It is clear, then, that young bilingual children are very much attuned to the specific linguistic environment in which they find themselves, and that they are very much influenced by this environment. The real challenge for explaining bilingual development is to discover the precise links between that environment and bilingual child language use.

Acknowledgments

Many thanks to the editors and to Wolfgang Wölck of the State University of New York, Buffalo, for very helpful feedback on a draft version of this chapter. I also thank Hugo Baetens Beardsmore for confirming that Ronjat's (1913) study was the first empirical study on bilingual behavior.

References

Almgren, M., & Barreña, A. (2000). Bilingual acquisition and separation of linguistic codes: ergativity in Basque versus accusativity in Spanish. In K. Nelson, A. Aksu-Koç, & C. Johnson (Eds.), *Children's language* (Vol. 11, pp. 1–35). Mahwah, NJ: Erlbaum.

Almgren, M., & Idiazabal, I. (2001). Past tense verb forms, discourse context and input features in bilingual and monolingual acquisition of Basque and Spanish. In J. Cenoz & F. Genesee (Eds.), *Trends in bilingual acquisition* (pp. 107–130). Amsterdam: Benjamins.

Arnberg, L. (1987). *Raising children bilingually: The pre-school years.* Clevedon, U.K.: Multilingual Matters.

Arnberg, L., & Arnberg, P. (1992). Language awareness and language separation in the young bilingual child. In R. Harris (Ed.), *Cognitive processing in bilinguals* (pp. 475–500). Amsterdam: Elsevier.

Bakker, P. (1992). *A language of our own. The mixed Cree-French language of the Canadian Métis.* Amsterdam: University of Amsterdam.

Barreña, A. (1997). Desarrollo diferenciado de sistemas gramaticales en un niño vasco-español bilingüe. In A. Pérez-Leroux & W. Glass (Eds.), *Contemporary perspectives on the acquisition of Spanish. Volume 1: Developing grammars* (pp. 55–74). Somerville, MA: Cascadilla Press.

Barreña, A. (2001). Grammar differentiation in early bilingual acquisition: Subordination structures in Spanish and Basque. In M. Almgren, A. Barreña, M. J. Ezeizabarrena, I. Idiazabal, & B. MacWhinney (Eds.), *Research on child language acquisition. Proceedings of the Eighth Conference of the International Association for the Study of Child Language* (pp. 78–94). Somerville, MA: Cascadilla Press.

Bates, E., Dale, P., & Thal, D. (1995). Individual differences and their implications for theories of language development. In P. Fletcher & B. MacWhinney (Eds.), *Handbook of child language* (pp. 96–151). London: Blackwell.

Bentahila, A., & Davies, E. (1994). Two languages, three varieties: A look at some bilingual children's code-switching. In G. Extra & L. Verhoeven (Eds.), *The cross-linguistic study of bilingual development* (pp. 113–128). Amsterdam: North-Holland.

Bergman, C. (1976). Interference versus independent development in infant bilingualism. In G. D. Keller, R. V. Teschner, & S. Viera (Eds.), *Bilingualism in the bicentennial and beyond* (pp. 86–96). New York: Bilingual Press/Editorial Bilingüe.

Bosch, L., & Sebastián-Gallés, N. (2001). Early language differentiation in bilingual infants. In J. Cenoz & F. Genesee (Eds.), *Trends in bilingual acquisition* (pp. 71–94). Amsterdam: Benjamins.

Cenoz, J., & Genesee, F. (Eds.). (2001). *Trends in bilingual acquisition.* Amsterdam: Benjamins.

De Houwer, A. (1987). *Two at a time: An exploration of how children acquire two languages from birth.* Unpublished doctoral dissertation. Brussels, Belgium: Vrije Universiteit Brussel.

De Houwer, A. (1990). *The acquisition of two languages from birth: A case study.* Cambridge, U.K.: Cambridge University Press.

De Houwer, A. (1994). The separate development hypothesis: Method and implications. In G. Extra & L. Verhoeven (Eds.), *The cross-linguistic study of bilingual development* (pp. 39–50). Amsterdam: North-Holland.

De Houwer, A. (1995a). Alternance codique intra-phrastique chez des jeunes enfants bilingues. *AILE (Acquisition et Interaction en Langue Etrangère), 6,* 39–64.

De Houwer, A. (1995b). Bilingual language acquisition. In P. Fletcher & B. MacWhinney (Eds.), *Handbook of child language* (pp. 219–250). London: Blackwell.

De Houwer, A. (1997). The role of input in the acquisition of past verb forms in English and Dutch: Evidence from a bilingual child. In E. Clark (Ed.), *Proceedings of the 28th Stanford Child Language Research Forum* (pp. 153–162). Stanford, CA: CSLI.

De Houwer, A. (1998). By way of introduction: Methods in studies of bilingual first language acquisition. *International Journal of Bilingualism, 2,* 249–264.

De Houwer, A. (1999a). Environmental factors in early bilingual development: The role of parental beliefs and attitudes. In G. Extra & L. Verhoeven (Eds.), *Bilingualism and migration* (pp. 75–95). Berlin, Germany: Mouton de Gruyter.

De Houwer, A. (1999b). Language acquisition in children raised with two languages from birth: An update. *Revue Parole, 9–10,* 63–88.

De Houwer, A. (2002). Comparing monolingual and bilingual acquisition. *Alkalmazott*

Nyelvtudomány (Hungarian Journal of Applied Linguistics), 2(1), 5–19.

De Houwer, A., & Gillis, S. (1998). Dutch child language: An overview. In S. Gillis & A. De Houwer (Eds.), *The acquisition of Dutch* (pp. 1–100). Amsterdam: Benjamins.

De Houwer, A., & Meisel, J. (1996, June). *Analyzing the relationship between two developing languages in bilingual first language acquisition: methodology, data, findings.* Paper presented at the Workshop on Language Contact: Linking Different Levels of Analysis, Wassenaar, The Netherlands, Netherlands Institute for Advanced Study.

Deuchar, M. (1992). Can government and binding theory account for language acquisition? In R. Vide (Ed.), *Lenguajes Naturales y Lenguajes Formales VIII* (pp. 273–279). Barcelona, Spain: Universitat de Barcelona.

Deuchar, M., & Quay, S. (1998). One vs. two systems in early bilingual syntax: Two versions of the question. *Bilingualism: Language and Cognition, 1,* 231–243.

Deuchar, M., & Quay, S. (2000). *Bilingual acquisition: Theoretical implications of a case study.* Oxford, U.K.: Oxford University Press.

Ekmekçi, Ö. (1994). Bilingual development of English preschool children in Turkey. In G. Extra & L. Verhoeven (Eds.), *The cross-linguistic study of bilingualism* (pp. 99–112). Amsterdam: North-Holland.

Ervin-Tripp, S. (1974). Is second language learning like the first? *TESOL Quarterly, 1974,* 111–127.

Ezeizabarrena, M., & Larrañaga, M. (1996). Ergativity in Basque: A problem for language acquisition? *Linguistics, 34,* 955–991.

Fantini, A. (1985). *Language acquisition of a bilingual child: a sociolinguistic perspective (to age 10).* Clevedon, U.K.: Multilingual Matters.

García, E. (1983). *Early childhood bilingualism.* Albuquerque: University of New Mexico Press.

Golinkoff, R., Hirsh-Pasek, K., & Schweisguth, M. (2001). A reappraisal of young children's knowledge of grammatical morphemes. In J. Weissenborn & B. Höhle (Eds.), *Approaches to bootstrapping* (pp. 167–188). Amsterdam: Benjamins.

Goodz, N. (1989). Parental language mixing in bilingual families. *Infant Mental Health Journal, 10,* 25–44.

Hulk, A., & Van der Linden, E. (1996). Language mixing in a French-Dutch bilingual child. *Toegepaste Taalwetenschap in Artikelen, 2,* 89–101.

Idiazabal, I. (1988). *First verbal productions of a bilingual child learning Basque and Spanish simultaneously. Analysis of the noun phrase.* Unpublished manuscript.

Idiazabal, I. (1991, November). *Evolución de la determinación nominal en un niño bilingüe vasco-hispanofono.* Paper presented at the First International Conference on Spanish in Contact With Other Languages, University of Southern California, Los Angeles.

Jisa, H. (1995). L'utilisation du morphème *be* en anglais langue faible. *AILE (Acquisition et Interaction en Langue Etrangère), 6,* 101–127.

Johnson, C., & Lancaster, P. (1998). The development of more than one phonology: A case study of a Norwegian-English bilingual child. *International Journal of Bilingualism, 2,* 265–300.

Juan-Garau, M., & Pérez-Vidal, C. (2000). Subject realization in the syntactic development of a bilingual child. *Bilingualism: Language and Cognition, 3,* 173–191.

Kaiser, G. (1994). More about INFL-ection and agreement: the acquisition of clitic pronouns in French. In J. Meisel (Ed.), *Bilingual first language acquisition. French and German grammatical development* (pp. 131–160). Amsterdam: Benjamins.

Klinge, S. (1990). Prepositions in bilingual language acquisition. In J. Meisel (Ed.), *Two first languages. Early grammatical development in bilingual children* (pp. 123–156). Dordrecht, The Netherlands: Foris.

Koehn, C. (1994). The acquisition of gender and number morphology within NP. In J. Meisel (Ed.), *Bilingual first language acquisition. French and German grammatical development* (pp. 29–51). Amsterdam: Benjamins.

Köppe, R. (1994a). The DUFDE project. In J. Meisel (Ed.), *Bilingual first language acquisition. French and German grammatical development* (pp. 15–27). Amsterdam: Benjamins.

Köppe, R. (1994b). NP-movement and subject raising. In J. Meisel (Ed.), *Bilingual first language acquisition. French and German grammatical development* (pp. 209–234). Amsterdam: Benjamins.

Krasinski, E. (1995). The development of past marking in a bilingual child and the punctual-nonpunctual distinction. *First Language, 15,* 277–300.

Lanza, E. (1997a). Language contact in bilingual 2-year-olds and code-switching: Language encounters of a different kind? *International Journal of Bilingualism, 1,* 135–162.

Lanza, E. (1997b). *Language mixing in infant bilingualism. A sociolinguistic perspective.* Oxford, U.K.: Clarendon Press.

Leopold, W. (1970). *Speech development of a bilingual child. A linguist's record.* New York: AMS Press. (Original work published 1939–1949)

Lieven, E., Pine, J., & Baldwin, G. (1997). Lexically-based learning and early grammatical development. *Journal of Child Language, 24,* 187–219.

MacWhinney, B. (1991). *The CHILDES project: Tools for analyzing talk.* Hillsdale, NJ: Erlbaum.

Meisel, J. (1985). Les phases initiales du développement de notions temporelles, aspectuelles et de modes d'action. Étude basée sur le langage d'enfants bilingues français-allemand. *Lingua, 66,* 321–374.

Meisel, J. (1986). Word order and case marking in early child language. Evidence from simultaneous acquisition of two first languages: French and German. *Linguistics, 24,* 123–183.

Meisel, J. (1989). Early differentiation of languages in bilingual children. In K. Hyltenstam & L. Obler (Eds.), *Bilingualism across the lifespan. Aspects of acquisition, maturity and loss* (pp. 13–40). Cambridge, U.K.: Cambridge University Press.

Meisel, J. (1990). INFL-ection: Subjects and subject-verb agreement. In J. Meisel (Ed.), *Two first languages. Early grammatical development in bilingual children* (pp. 237–298). Dordrecht, The Netherlands: Foris.

Meisel, J. (1994). Getting FAT: Finiteness, agreement and tense in early grammars. In J. Meisel (Ed.), *Bilingual first language acquisition. French and German grammatical development* (pp. 89–130). Amsterdam: Benjamins.

Meisel, J. (2001). The simultaneous acquisition of two first languages. Early differentiation and subsequent development of grammars. In J. Cenoz & F. Genesee (Eds.), *Trends in bilingual acquisition* (pp. 11–41). Amsterdam: Benjamins.

Meisel, J., & Mahlau, A. (1988). La adquisición simultanea de dos primeras lenguas. Discusión general e implicaciones para el estudio del bilingüismo en euzkadi. In *Actas del II Congreso Mundial Vasco: Congreso sobre la Lengua Vasca* (Vol. 3). Vitoria, Spain: Servicio de publicaciones del Gobierno Vasco.

Meisel, J., & Müller, N. (1992). Finiteness and verb placement in early child grammars. Evidence from simultaneous acquisition of two first languages: French and German. In J. Meisel (Ed.), *The acquisition of verb placement. Functional categories and V2 phenomena in language acquisition* (pp. 109–138). Dordrecht, The Netherlands: Kluwer.

Mills, A. (1986). Review of T. Taeschner's *The Sun Is Feminine. Linguistics, 24,* 825–833.

Mishina-Mori, S. (2002). Language differentiation of the two languages in early bilingual development: A case study of Japanese/English bilingual children. *International Review of Applied Linguistics, 40,* 211–233.

Müller, N. (1990a). Developing two gender assignment systems simultaneously. In J. Meisel (Ed.), *Two first languages. Early grammatical development in bilingual children* (pp. 193–236), Dordrecht, The Netherlands: Foris.

Müller, N. (1990b). Erwerb der Wortstellung im Französischen und Deutschen. Zur Distribution von Finitheitsmerkmalen in der Grammatik bilingualer Kinder. In M. Rothweiler (Ed.), *Spracherwerb und Grammatik. Linguistische Untersuchungen zum Erwerb von Syntax und Morphologie* (pp. 127–151). Opladen, Germany: Westdeutscher Verlag.

Müller, N. (1993). *Komplexe Sätze. Der Erwerb von COMP und von Wortstellungsmustern bei bilingualen Kindern (Französisch/Deutsch).* Tübingen, Germany: Gunter Narr Verlag.

Müller, N. (1994a). Gender and number agreement within DP. In J. Meisel (Ed.), *Bilingual first language acquisition. French and German grammatical development* (pp. 53–88). Amsterdam: Benjamins.

Müller, N. (1994b). Parameters cannot be reset: evidence from the development of COMP. In J. Meisel (Ed.), *Bilingual first language acquisition. French and German grammatical development* (pp. 235–270). Amsterdam: Benjamins.

Müller, N. (1995). L'acquisition du genre et du nombre chez des enfants bilingues (Français-Allemand). *AILE (Acquisition et Interaction en Langue Etrangère), 6,* 65–99.

Müller, N., Crysmann, B., & Kaiser, G. (1996). Interactions between the acquisition of French Object drop and the development of the C-system. *Language Acquisition, 5(1),* 35–63.

Paradis, J., & Genesee, F. (1996). Syntactic acquisition in bilingual children: Autonomous or interdependent? *Studies in Second Language Acquisition, 18,* 1–25.

Paradis, J., & Genesee, F. (1997). On continuity and the emergence of functional categories in bilingual first-language acquisition. *Language Acquisition, 6(2),* 91–124.

Parodi, T. (1990). The acquisition of word order regularities and case morphology. In J. Meisel (Ed.), *Two first languages. Early grammatical development in bilingual children* (pp. 157–192). Dordrecht, The Netherlands: Foris.

Pavlovitch, M. (1920). *Le langage enfantin. Acquisition du serbe et du français.* Paris: Champion.

Peters, A. (1983). *The units of language acquisition.* Cambridge, U.K.: Cambridge University Press.

Pfaff, C. (1994). Early bilingual development of Turkish children in Berlin. In G. Extra & L. Verhoeven (Eds.), *The cross-linguistic study of bilingualism* (pp. 75–97). Amsterdam: North-Holland.

Poulin-Dubois, D., & Goodz, N. (2001). Language differentiation in bilingual infants: Evidence from babbling. In J. Cenoz & F. Genesee (Eds.), *Trends in bilingual acquisition* (pp. 95–106). Amsterdam: Benjamins.

Quay, S. (2001). Managing linguistic boundaries in early trilingual development. In J. Cenoz & F. Genesee (Eds.), *Trends in bilingual acquisition* (pp. 149–200). Amsterdam: Benjamins.

Romaine, S. (1995). *Bilingualism* (2nd ed.). Oxford, U.K.: Blackwell.

Romaine, S. (1999). Early bilingual development: from elite to folk. In G. Extra & L. Verhoeven (Eds.), *Bilingualism and migration* (pp. 61–73). Berlin: Mouton de Gruyter.

Ronjat, J. (1913). *Le développement du langage observé chez un enfant bilingue.* Paris: Champion.

Saunders, G. (1988). *Bilingual children: From birth to teens.* Clevedon, U.K.: Multilingual Matters.

Schlyter, S. (1990a). The acquisition of tense and aspect. In J. Meisel (Ed.), *Two first languages. Early grammatical development in bilingual children* (pp. 87–122). Dordrecht, The Netherlands: Foris.

Schlyter, S. (1990b). Introducing the DUFDE project. In J. Meisel (Ed.), *Two first languages. Early grammatical development in bilingual children* (pp. 73–86). Dordrecht, The Netherlands: Foris.

Schlyter, S. (1995). Formes verbales du passé dans des interactions en langue forte et en langue faible. *AILE (Acquisition et Interaction en Langue Etrangère),* 6, 129–152.

Serratrice, L. (1999). *The emergence of functional categories in bilingual first language acquisition.* Unpublished doctoral dissertation, University of Edinburgh, U.K.

Serratrice, L. (2001). The emergence of verbal morphology and the lead-lag pattern issue in bilingual acquisition. In J. Cenoz & F. Genesee (Eds.), *Trends in bilingual acquisition* (pp. 43–70). Amsterdam: Benjamins.

Serratrice, L. (2002). Overt subjects in English: evidence for the marking of person in an English-Italian bilingual child. *Journal of Child Language, 29(2),* 1–29.

Sinka, I. (2000). The search for cross-linguistic influences in the language of young Latvian-English bilinguals. In S. Döpke (Ed.), *Cross-linguistic structures in simultaneous bilingualism* (pp. 149–174). Amsterdam: Benjamins.

Sinka, I., & Schelleter, C. (1998). Morphosyntactic development in bilingual children. *International Journal of Bilingualism, 2,* 301–326.

Slobin, D. (1973). Cognitive prerequisites for the development of grammar. In C. Ferguson & D. Slobin (Eds.), *Studies of child language development* (pp. 175–208). New York: Holt, Rinehart, and Winston.

Stefánik, J. (1995). Grammatical category of gender in Slovak-English and English-Slovak bilinguals. *Journal of East European Studies, 4,* 155–164.

Stefánik, J. (1997). A study of English-Slovak bilingualism in a child. *Journal, 30,* 721–734.

Stenzel, A. (1994). Case assignment and functional categories in bilingual children. In J. Meisel (Ed.), *Bilingual first language acquisition. French and German grammatical development* (pp. 161–208). Amsterdam: Benjamins.

Stenzel, A. (1996). Development of prepositional case in a bilingual child. *Linguistics, 34,* 1029–1058.

Tabors, P. (1987). *The development of communicative competence by second language learners in a nursery school classroom: An ethnolinguistic study.* Unpublished doctoral dissertation, Harvard University, Boston, MA.

Taeschner, T. (1983). *The sun is feminine: A study on language acquisition in bilingual children.* Berlin: Springer Verlag.

Van den Bogaerde, B., & Baker, A. (2002). Are young deaf children bilingual? In G. Morgan & B. Woll (Eds.), *Directions in sign language acquisition* (pp. 183–206). Amsterdam: Benjamins.

Vihman, M. (1999). The transition to grammar in a bilingual child: Positional patterns, model learning, and relational words. *International Journal of Bilingualism, 3,* 267–301.

Volterra, V., & Taeschner, T. (1978). The acquisition and development of language by bilingual children. *Journal of Child Language, 5,* 311–326.

Wanner, P. (1996). A study of the initial codeswitching stage in the linguistic development of an English-Japanese bilingual child. *Japan Journal of Multilingualism and Multiculturalism, 2,* 20–40.

Weissenborn, J., & Höhle, B. (Eds.). (2001). *Approaches to bootstrapping* (Vols. 1 and 2). Amsterdam: Benjamins.

Widdicombe, S. (1997). *Code-switching, coining and interference in trilingual first language acquisition: A case study*. Unpublished master of science dissertation, Aston University, Birmingham, U.K.

Wölck, W. (1984). Komplementierung und Fusion: Prozesse natürlicher Zweisprachigkeit. In E. Oksaar (Ed.), *Spracherwerb— Sprachkontakt—Sprachkonflikt* (pp. 107– 128). Berlin, Germany: de Gruyter.

Wong-Fillmore, L. (1979). Individual differences in second language acquisition. In C. Fillmore, D. Kempler, & Y. Wang (Eds.), *Individual differences in language ability and language behavior* (pp. 203–228). New York: Academic Press.

3

A Unified Model of Language Acquisition

ABSTRACT   This chapter presents an extended formulation of the Competition Model. The extended model is designed to account for a large range of phenomena in first and second language acquisition, including bilingualism. As in the classic version of the Competition Model, competition is at the core of a set of nonmodular interacting forces. However, now the various inputs to competition are described in terms of six additional subcomponents: arenas, cues, chunking, storage, codes, and resonance. Learning is viewed as a resonant process that relies on storage, chunking, and support to acquire new mappings.

First language (L1) acquisition differs from second language (L2) acquisition in several fundamental ways. First, infants who are learning language are also engaged in learning about how the world works. In comparison, L2 learners already know a great deal about the world. Second, infants are able to rely on a highly malleable brain that has not yet been committed to other tasks (MacWhinney, Feldman, Sacco, & Valdes-Perez, 2000). Third, infants can rely on an intense system of social support from their caregivers (Snow, 1999).

Together, these three differences might suggest that it would make little sense to try to develop a unified model of L1 and L2 acquisition. In fact, many researchers have decided that the two processes are so different that they account for them with totally separate theories. For example, Krashen (1994) sees L1 learning as involving "acquisition" and L2 learning as based instead on "learning." Others (Bley-Vroman, Felix, & Ioup, 1988; Clahsen & Muysken, 1986) argue that universal grammar is available to children up to some critical age, but not to older learners of L2.

Even those researchers who emphasize the differences between L1 and L2 acquisition recognize the fact that these two processes are intimately interwoven in actual language learning (Felix & Wode, 1983). For example, the method we use for

learning new word forms in an L2 is basically an extension of the methods we used for learning words in our L1. Similarly, when we come to combining L2 words into sentences, we use many of the same strategies we used as children when learning our L1. Furthermore, the fact that L2 learning is so heavily influenced by transfer from L1 means that it would be impossible to construct a model of L2 learning that did not take into account the structure of the L1.

Thus, rather than attempting to build two separate models of L1 and L2 learning, it makes more sense to consider the shape of a unified model in which the mechanisms of L1 learning are seen as a subset of the mechanisms of L2 learning. Although these L1 learning mechanisms are less powerful in the L2 learner, they are still partially accessible (Flynn, 1996). Therefore, it is conceptually simpler to formulate a unified model.

This same logic can be used to motivate the extension of a unified model to the study of both childhood and adult multilingualism. In the case of childhood multilingualism, there is now an emerging consensus (De Houwer, chapter 2, this volume) that children acquire multiple languages as separate entities. However, there is also good evidence that multiple languages interact in children through processes of transfer and code switching (Myers-Scotton, chapter 16, this volume) much as they do in adults. These processes are best understood within the context of a unified acquisitional model. Similarly, current theories of adult bilingualism have tended to emphasize bilingual competence as a steady state with minimal developmental inputs (La Heij, chapter 14, this volume). However, this view fails to consider how dynamic aspects of code switching and interference (Meuter, chapter 17, this volume) arise from years of interaction between the languages during the child's development. Furthermore, adult multilinguals continue to develop competence in particular domains, such as the skill of simultaneous interpretation (Christoffels & De Groot, chapter 22, this volume). These acquisitions depend on many of the same learning mechanisms we see operative in the earliest stages of L1 acquisition, as well as other mechanisms evidenced in L2 learners.

These initial considerations suggest that we need to consider what it might mean to construct a unified model for L1 acquisition, childhood multilingualism, L2 acquisition, and adult multilingualism. This chapter outlines the first stages of this attempt. It relies on the Competition Model (Bates & MacWhinney, 1982; MacWhinney, 1987a) as the starting point for this new unified model. Although the Competition Model was not originally designed to account for all aspects of L2 learning and multilingualism, it has certain concepts that fit in well with a broader, fuller account. In particular, we can build on the core Competition Model insight that cue strength in the adult speaker is a direct function of cue validity. However, the unified account needs to supplement the theory of cue validity with additional theoretical constructs for dealing with cue cost and cue support. Figure 3.1 represents the overall shape of the model that I develop here. This figure is not to be interpreted as a processing model. Rather, it is a logical decomposition of the general problem of language learning into a series of smaller, but interrelated, structural and processing components.

Earlier versions of the Competition Model included the core concept of competition, as well as the three components of arenas, mappings, and storage at the top the figure. The new aspects of the Unified Competition Model include the components of chunking, codes, and resonance given at the bottom of the figure. Before examining the operation of the new model, its seven components are defined briefly.

1. *Competition.* At the core of the model is a processing system that selects between various options or cues on the basis of their relative cue

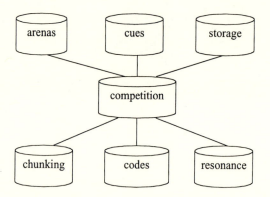

Figure 3.1 The seven components of the Unified Competition Model.

strength. In the classic version of the model, competition was based on cue summation and interactive activation. In the unified model, competition is viewed as based on resonance as well as cue summation.

2. *Arenas.* The linguistic arenas within which competition occurs are the four traditional levels recognized in most psycholinguistic processing models: phonology, lexicon, morphosyntax, and conceptualization. In production, these arenas involve message formulation, lexical activation, morphosyntactic arrangement, and articulatory planning. In comprehension, the competitive arenas include auditory processing, lexical activation, grammatical role decoding, and meaningful interpretation. Processing in each of these different arenas is subserved by a different combination of neuronal pathways. In addition to the eight competitive arenas listed, older learners also make use of two arenas of orthographic competition, one for reading and one for writing.

3. *Cues.* At the core of the Competition Model—in both its classical form and the newer unified form—is a notion of the linguistic sign as a mapping between form and function. The theory of mappings is similar in many ways to the theory of linguistic options articulated in Halliday's systemic grammar. In these mappings, forms serve as cues to functions during comprehension, and functions serve as cues to forms during production. In other words, in production, forms compete to express underlying intentions or functions. In comprehension, functions or interpretations compete on the basis of cues from surface forms. The outcome of these competitions is determined by the relative strength of the relevant cues.

For example, in English, the positioning of the subject before the verb is a form that expresses the function of marking the perspective or agent. Or, to give another example, the pronoun "him" is a form that expresses the functions of masculine gender and the role of the object of the verb. The Competition Model focuses primarily on the use of forms as cues to role assignment, coreference, and argument attachment as outlined in MacWhinney (1987a). Mappings are social conventions that must be learned for each of the eight linguistic arenas, including lexicon, phonology, morpho-syntax, and mental models.

4. *Storage.* The learning of new mappings relies on storage in both short-term and long-term memory. Gupta and MacWhinney (1997) developed an account of the role of short-term memory in the construction of memories for the phonological forms of words and the mapping of these forms into meaningful lexical items. Short-term memory is also crucially involved in the online processing of specific syntactic structures (Gibson, Pearlmutter, Canseco-Gonzalez, & Hickok, 1996; MacWhinney & Pléh, 1988). MacWhinney (1999) examined how the processes of perspective switching and referent identification can place demands on verbal memory processes during mental model construction. The operation of these memory systems constrains the role of cue validity during both processing and acquisition. For example, the processing of subject-verb agreement for inverted word orders in Italian is not fully learned until about age 8 years (Devescovi, D'Amico, Smith, Mimica, & Bates, 1998) despite its high cue validity and high cue strength in adult speakers.

5. *Chunking.* The size of particular mappings depends on the operation of processes of chunking. Work in L1 acquisition has shown that children rely on both combinatorial processing and chunking to build up syllables, words, and sentences. For example, a child may treat "what's this" as a single unit or chunk, but will compose phrases such as "more cookie" and "more milk" by combination of "more" with a following argument. MacWhinney (1978, 1982) and Stemberger and MacWhinney (1986) showed how large rote chunks compete with smaller analytic chunks in both children and adult learners.

6. *Codes.* When modeling bilingualism and L2 acquisition, it is important to have a clear theory of code activation. The Competition Model distinguishes two components of the theory of code competition. The first component is the theory of transfer. This theory has been articulated in some detail in Competition Model work in terms of predictions for both positive and negative transfer in the various linguistic arenas. The second component is the theory of code interaction, which determines code selection, switching, and mixing. The Competition Model relies on the notion of resonance, discussed next, to account for coactivation processes in both L2 learners and bilinguals. The choice of a particular code at a particular moment during lexicalization depends on factors such as activation from previous lexical items, the influence of lexical gaps, expression of sociolinguistic options (Ervin-Tripp, 1968), and conversational cues produced by the listener.

7. *Resonance.* Perhaps the most important area of new theoretical development in the Unified Competition Model is the theory of resonance. This theory seeks to relate the Competition Model to research in the area of embodied or embedded cognition, as well as newer models of processing in neural networks.

The seven-component model sketched out here includes no separate component for learning. This is because learning is seen as an interaction between each of the various subcomponents during the processes of competition and resonance. Each of the seven components of the model is now explored in more detail.

Competition

The basic notion of competition is fundamental to most information-processing models in cognitive psychology. In the unified model, competition takes on slightly different forms in each of the eight competitive arenas. These arenas are not thought of as encapsulated modules, but as playing fields that can readily accept input from other arenas when that input is made available. In the course of work on the core model and related mechanisms, my colleagues and I have formulated working computational models for most of these competitive arenas.

1. In the auditory arena, competition involves the processing of cues to lexical forms based on both bottom-up features and activation from lexical forms. Models of this process include those that emphasize top-down activation (Elman & McClelland, 1988) and those that exclude it (Norris, 1994). In the Competition Model, bottom-up activation is primary, but top-down activation will occur

in natural conditions and in those experimental tasks that promote resonance.

2. In the lexical arena, competition occurs within topological maps (Li, Farkas, & MacWhinney, 2004) in which words are organized by semantic and lexical type.

3. In the morphosyntactic arena, there is an item-based competition between word orders and grammatical markings centered on valence relations (MacDonald, Pearlmutter, & Seidenberg, 1994; MacWhinney, 1987b).

4. In the interpretive arena, there is a competition between fragments of mental models as the listener seeks to construct a unified mental model (MacWhinney, 1989) that can be encoded in long-term memory (Hausser, 1999).

5. In the arena of message formulation, there is a competition between communicative goals. Winning goals are typically initialized and topicalized.

6. In the arena of expressive lexicalization, there is a competition between words for the packaging and conflation of chunks of messages (Langacker, 1989).

7. In the arena of sentence planning, there is a competition of phrases for initial position and a competition between arguments for attachment to slots generated by predicates (Dell, Juliano, & Govindjee, 1993).

8. In the arena of articulatory planning, there is a competition between syllables for insertion into a rhythmic phrasal output pattern (Dell et al., 1993).

Cues

Experimental work in the Competition Model tradition has focused on measurement, using a simple sentence interpretation procedure, of the relative strength of various cues to the selection of the agent. Subjects listen to a sentence with two nouns and a verb and are asked to say who was the actor. In a few studies, the task involved direct object identification (Sokolov, 1988, 1989), relative clause processing (MacWhinney & Pléh, 1988), or pronominal assignment (MacDonald & MacWhinney, 1990; McDonald & MacWhinney, 1995); usually, the task was agent identification. Sometimes, the sentences were well-formed grammatical sentences, such as "The cat is chasing the duck." Sometimes, they involved competitions between cues, as in the ungrammatical sentence *"The duck the cat is chasing." Depending on the language involved, the cues in these studies included word order, subject-verb agreement, object-verb agreement, case marking, prepositional case marking, stress, topicalization, animacy, omission, and pronominalization. These cues were varied in a standard orthogonalized analysis of variance design with three or four sentences per cell to increase statistical reliability. The basic questions were always the same: What is the relative order of cue strength in the given language, and how do these cue strengths interact?

In English, the dominant cue for subject identification is preverbal positioning. For example, in the English sentence "The eraser hits the cat," it is assumed that the eraser is the agent. However, a parallel sentence in Italian or Spanish would have the cat as the agent. This is because the word order cue is not as strong in Italian or Spanish as it is in English. In Spanish, the prepositional object marker *a* is a clear cue to the object, and the subject is the noun that is not the object. An example of this is the sentence "*El toro mató al torero*" ("The bull killed to the bullfighter"). No such prepositional cue exists in English.

In German, case marking on the definite article is a powerful cue to the subject. In a sentence such as "*Der Lehrer liebt die Witwe*" ("The teacher loves the widow"), the presence of the nominative masculine article *der* is a sure cue to identification of the subject. In Russian, the subject often has a case suffix. In Arabic, the subject is the noun that agrees with the verb in number and gender, and this cue is stronger than the case marking cue. In French, Spanish, and Italian, when an object pronoun is present, it can help identify the noun that is not the subject.

Thus, we see that Indo-European languages can vary markedly in their use of cues to mark case roles. When we go outside Indo-European languages to languages like Navajo, Hungarian, or Japanese, the variation becomes even more extreme.

To measure cue strength, Competition Model experiments rely on sentences with conflicting cues. For example, in "The eraser push the dogs," the cues of animacy and subject-verb agreement favor "the dogs" as agent. However, the stronger cue of preverbal positioning favors "the eraser" as agent. As a result, English-speaking adult subjects strongly favor the eraser even in a competition sentence of this type. However, about 20% of the participants will choose the dogs in this case. To measure the validity of cues in the various languages studied, we rely on text counts in which we list the cues in favor of each noun and track the relative availability and reliability of each cue. *Cue availability* is defined as the presence of the cue in some contrastive form. For example, if both of the nouns in a sentence are animate, then the animacy cue is not contrastively available.

By looking at how children, adult monolinguals, and adult bilinguals speaking about 18 different languages process these various types of sentences, the following conclusions regarding sentence comprehension have been reached:

1. When given enough time during sentence comprehension to make a careful choice, adults assign the role of agency to the nominal with the highest cue strength.
2. When there is a competition between cues, the levels of choice in a group of adult subjects will closely reflect the relative strengths of the competing cues.
3. When adult subjects are asked to respond immediately, even before the end of the sentence is reached, they will tend to base their decisions primarily on the strongest cue in the language.
4. When the strongest cue is neutralized, the next strongest cue will dominate.
5. The fastest decisions occur when all cues agree, and there is no competition. The slowest decisions occur when strong cues compete.
6. Children begin learning to comprehend sentences by first focusing on the strongest cue in their language.
7. As children get older, the strength of all cues increases to match the adult pattern with the most valid cue growing most in strength.
8. As children get older, their reaction times gradually get faster in accord with the adult pattern.
9. Compared to adults, children are relatively more influenced by cue availability as opposed to cue reliability.
10. Cue strength in adults and older children (8–10 years) is not related to cue availability (because all cues have been heavily encountered by this time), but rather to cue reliability. In particular, it is a function of conflict reliability, which measures the reliability of a cue when it conflicts directly with other cues.

This list of findings from Competition Model research underscores the heuristic value of the concept of cue strength.

Storage

One of the core findings of Competition Model research has been that, when adult subjects are given plenty of time to make a decision, their choices are direct reflections of the cumulative validity of all the relevant cues. In this sense, we can say that offline decisions are optimal reflections of the structure of the language. However, when subjects are asked to make decisions online, then their ability to sample all relevant cues is restricted. In such cases, we say that "cue cost" factors limit the application of cue validity. These cue cost factors can involve various aspects of processing. However, the most important factors are those that require listeners to maintain the shape cues in working memory.

Theories of the neural basis of verbal memory view this storage as involving a functional neural circuit that coordinates inputs from Broca's area, lexical storage in the temporal lobe, and additional structures that support phonological memory. Unlike local lexical maps, which are neurologically stable, this functional circuit is easily disrupted and relies heavily on access to a variety of cognitive resources.

At the core of syntactic processing is the learning and use of item-based constructions (MacWhinney, 1975). Item-based constructions open up slots for arguments that may occur in specific positions or that must receive specific morphological markings. Although item-based constructions are encoded in local maps, they specify combinations that must be processed through functional circuits. The importance of item-based constructions has been reemphasized in a new line of research reviewed by Tomasello (2000). The account of MacWhinney (1982) held that children first learn that a verb like throw takes three arguments (thrower, object thrown, recipient). Then, by comparing groups of these item-based patterns through analogy, children can extract broader class-based patterns. In this case, they would extract a pattern that matches the set of transfer verbs that take the double-object construction as in "John threw Bill the ball." By the end of the third year, these new constructions (Goldberg, 1999) begin to provide the child with the ability to produce increasingly fluent discourse. L2 learners go through a similar process, sometimes supported by pattern drills.

By maintaining words and constructions in short-term sentence memory, learners can facilitate a wide range of additional learning and processing mechanisms. Perhaps the most remarkable of these processes is the learning of the skill of simultaneous translation (Christoffels & De Groot, chapter 22, this volume). Practitioners of this art are able to listen in one language and speak in the other in parallel while performing a complex mapping of the message of the input language to the very different syntax of the output language. The very existence of simultaneous translation underscores the extent to which two languages can be coactivated (Spivey & Marian, 1999) for long periods of time (Meuter, chapter 17, this volume).

The problems involved in simultaneous translation nicely illustrate how language can place a heavy load on functional neural circuits. Let us take a simple case to illustrate the problem. Consider a German sentence with a verb in final position. If the German sentence is short, the interpreter will have little problem converting the German SOV (subject-object-verb) order to English SVO (subject-verb-object) order. For example, a sentence like "*Johannes hat den Mann mit dem dunkelen Mantel noch nicht kennengelernt*" ("John has not yet met the man with the dark coat") will cause few problems because the interpreter can lag behind the speaker enough to take in the whole utterance along with the verb before starting to speak. The interpreter prepares an utterance with a subject and object already in final form. When the verb comes along, it is simply a matter of translating it to the English equivalent, dropping it into the prepared slot, and starting articulatory output. However, if there is additional material piled up before the verb, the problem can get worse. Typically, simultaneous interpreters try not to lag more than a few words behind the input. To avoid this, one solution would be to store away the short subject and dump out the large object as the head of a passive as in, "The man with the dark coat has not yet been met by John." Another, rather unhappy, solution is topicalization, as in "John, in regard to the man with the dark coat, he hasn't seen him yet." Similar problems can arise when translating from relative clauses in languages with VSO (verb-subject-object) order, such as Tagalog or Arabic. Studies of Hungarian (MacWhinney & Pléh, 1988) and Japanese (Hakuta, 1981) show that the stacking up of unlinked noun phrases can be even worse in SOV languages.

If interpreters had access to an unlimited verbal memory capacity, there would be little worry about storing long chunks of verbal material. However, we know that our raw memory for strings of words is not nearly large enough to accommodate the simultaneous interpretation task. In fact, the conventional estimate of the number of items that can be stored in short-term memory is about four. The interpreter's task is made even more difficult by the fact that they must continue to build mental models of incoming material (MacWhinney, 1999) while using previously constructed mental models as the basis for ongoing articulation. To do this successfully, the interpreter must be able to delineate chunks of comprehended material that are sufficient to motivate full independent output productions. In effect, the interpreter must maintain two separate conceptual foci centered about two separate points in conceptual space. The first attentional focus continues to take in new material from the speaker in terms of new valence and conceptual relations. The second attentional focus works on the comprehended structure to convert it to a production structure. The location of the production focus is always lagged after that of the comprehended structure, so the interpreter always has a split in conceptual attention. As a result of the load imposed by this attentional split and ongoing activity in two channels, interpreters often find that they cannot continue this line of work past the age of 45 years or so.

Interpreters are not the only speakers who are subject to load on their use of functional neural circuits. It is easy to interfere with normal language processing by imposing additional loads on the listener or speaker. Working within a standard Competition Model experimental framework, Kilborn (1989) has shown that even fully competent bilinguals tend to process sentences more slowly than monolinguals. However, when monolinguals are asked to listen to sentences under conditions of white noise, their reaction times are identical to those of the bilinguals. Similarly, Blackwell and Bates (1995) and Miyake, Carpenter, and Just (1994) have shown that, when subjected to conditions of noise, normal individuals process sentences much like aphasics. Gerver (1974) and Seleskovitch (1976) reported parallel results for the effects of noise on simultaneous interpretation.

Chunking

The component of chunking is a recent addition to the Competition Model. However, this idea is certainly not a new one for models of language learning. Chunking operates to take two or more items that frequently occur together and combine them into a single automatic chunk. Chunking is the basic learning mechanism in Newell's general cognitive model (Newell, 1990), as well as in many neural network models. MacWhinney and Anderson (1986) showed how the child can use chunking processes to build up larger grammatical structures and complex lexical forms. Ellis (1994) has shown how chunking can help us understand the growth of fluency in L2 learning. Gupta and MacWhinney (1997) showed how chunking can also apply to the learning of the phonological shape of individual words for both L1 and L2.

Chunking plays a particularly interesting role in the acquisition of grammar. For L2 learners, mastering a complex set of inflectional patterns is a particularly daunting challenge. These problems are a result of the tendency of L2 learners to fail to pick up large enough phrasal chunks. For example, if learners of German not only would pick up that *Mann* means "man," but also would learn phrases such as *der alte Mann*, *meines Mannes*, *den jungen Männern*, and *ein guter Mann*, then they not only would know the gender of the noun, but also would have a good basis for acquiring the declensional paradigm for both the noun and its modifiers. However, if they analyze a phrase like *der alte Mann* into the literal string "the + old + man" and throw away all of the details of the inflections on *der* and *alte*, then they will lose an opportunity to induce the grammar from implicit generalization across stored chunks. If, on the other hand, the learner stores larger chunks of this type, then the rules of grammar can emerge from analogic processing of the stored chunks.

Chunking also leads to improvements in fluency (Segalowitz & Hulstijn, chapter 18, this volume). For example, in Spanish, L2 learners can chunk together the plan for *buenos* with the plan for *días* to produce *buenos días*. They can then combine this chunk with *muy* to produce *muy buenos días* (very good morning). Chunking (Ellis, 1994) allows the learner to get around problems with Spanish noun pluralization, gender marking, and agreement that would otherwise have to be reasoned out in detail for each combination. Although the learner understands the meanings of the three words in this phrase, the unit can function as a chunk, thereby speeding production.

Codes and Transfer

Any general model of L2 learning must be able to account for interlanguage phenomena such as transfer and code switching. In addition, it must offer an account of age-related learning effects that have been discussed in terms of critical periods and fossilization. Because of space limitations, I will not include a discussion of code-switching theory here and focus instead on the theory of transfer and its impact on age-related effects.

The basic claim is that whatever can transfer will. This claim is theoretically important for at least two reasons. First, because the Competition Model emphasizes the interactive nature of cognitive processing, it must assume that, unless the interactions between languages are controlled and coordinated, there would be a large amount of transfer. Second, the model needs to rely on transfer to account for age-related declines in L2 learning ability without invoking the expiration of a genetically programmed critical period (Birdsong, chapter 6, this volume; DeKeyser and Larson-Hall, chapter 5, this volume).

For simultaneous bilingual acquisition (De Houwer, chapter 2, this volume), the model predicts code blending in young children only when parents encourage this or when there are gaps in one language that can be filled by "borrowing" from the other. This prediction follows from the role of resonance in blocking transfer. When the child's two languages are roughly similar in dominance or strength, each system generates enough system-internal resonance to block excessive transfer. However, if one of the languages is markedly weaker (Döpke, 2000), then it will not have enough internal resonance to block occasional transfer. The situation is very different for L2 learners because the balance between the languages is then tipped so extremely in favor of L1. To permit the growth of resonance in L2, learners must apply additional learning strategies that would not have been needed for children. These strategies focus primarily on optimization of input, promotion of L2 resonance, and avoidance of processes that destroy input chunks.

In the next sections, the evidence for transfer from L1 to L2 is briefly reviewed. There is clear evidence for massive transfer in audition, articulation, lexicon, sentence interpretation, and pragmatics. In the area of morphosyntax and sentence production, transfer is not as massive, largely because it is more difficult to construct the relations between L1 and L2 forms in these areas. Pienemann, Di Biase, Kawaguchi, and Håkansson (chapter 7, this volume) have argued that transfer in these areas is less general than postulated by the Competition Model. However, their analysis underestimates transfer effects in their own data.

Transfer in Audition

Phonological learning involves two very different processes. Auditory acquisition is primary and begins even before birth (Moon, Cooper, & Fifer, 1993). It relies on inherent properties of the mammalian ear (Moon et al., 1993) and early pattern detection through statistical learning. This same statistical learning mechanism is operative in children, adults, and cotton-top tamarins (Hauser, Newport, & Aslin, 2001).

Research on early auditory processing (Sebastián-Gallés & Bosch, chapter 4, this volume) yielded three major findings. First, it appears that children begin to separate prosodically distinct languages from the first months. This means, for example, that children who are growing up in a home where Swedish and Portuguese are spoken will have perhaps 16 months of experience in distinguishing these two languages by the time they say their first words. The fact that these languages are separated in audition so early makes findings of early separation in production (De Houwer, chapter 2, this volume) less surprising and more clearly understandable in Competition Model terms.

Research (Werker, 1995) has also shown that children begin to "lock in" the sounds of their L1(s) by the end of the first year and become relatively insensitive to distinctions in other languages. This commitment to the sounds of L1 can be reversed through childhood. However, for at least some sounds, it is difficult to obtain nativelike contrast detection during adulthood. The classic example of this is the difficulty that Japanese adults have in distinguishing /l/ and /r/ in English (Lively, Pisoni, & Logan, 1990). Examples of this type demonstrate the basic claim for generalized transfer effects in the Competition Model. But, note that what is transferring here from Japanese is not a contrast, but the L1 tendency to block out a contrast. At the same time, there are other non-L1 distinctions that can easily be perceived by adults. It appears that a full account of which contrasts can be learned and which will be blocked will need to be grounded on a dynamic model of auditory perception that is not yet available.

Finally, work on early audition has shown that children are picking up the auditory shapes of words well before they have their own productive vocabulary. Moreover, they are making the first steps toward classifying words into phrases and combinations on the auditory level even before they understand their meanings. These same mechanisms play an important role in L2 learning, as suggested by the input hypothesis. Through exposure to large amounts of auditory input in L2 that echo in a resonant way on the auditory level, L2 learners can also begin acquisition even before they demonstrate much in the way of independent productive ability.

Transfer in Articulation

The major challenge facing the L1 learner is not the acquisition of perceptual patterns, but the development of articulatory methods for reproducing these patterns (Menn & Stoel-Gammon, 1995). The coordination of motor mechanisms for speech output is a relatively late evolutionary emergence (MacWhinney, 2002), and it is not surprising that it is a relatively difficult skill for the child to control. However, by age 5 years, most children have achieved control over articulatory processes.

For the adult L2 learner and the older child, the situation is much different. For them, learning begins with massive transfer of L1 articulatory patterns to L2 (Flege & Davidian, 1984; Hancin-Bhatt, 1994). This transfer is at first successful in the sense that it allows a reasonable level of communication. However, it is eventually counterproductive because it embeds L1 phonology into the emergent L2 lexicon. In effect, the learner treats new words in L2 as if they were composed of strings of L1 articulatory units. This method of learning leads to short-term gains at the expense of long-term difficulties in correcting erroneous phonological transfer.

Older children acquiring an L2 can rely on their greater neuronal flexibility to escape these negative transfer effects quickly. In doing so, they are relying on the same types of adolescent motor abilities that allow adolescents to become proficient acrobats, gymnasts, dancers, and golfers. Adults have a reduced ability to rewire motor productions on this basic level. However, even the most difficult cases of negative transfer in adulthood can be corrected through careful training and rehearsal (Flege, Takagi, & Mann, 1995). To do this, adults must rely on resonance, selective attention, and learning strategies to reinvigorate a motor learning process that runs much more naturally in children and adolescents.

Transfer in Lexical Learning

In the arena of lexical processing, the L2 learner can achieve rapid initial progress by simply transferring the L1 conceptual world en masse to L2. Young bilinguals can also benefit from this conceptual transfer. When learners first acquire a new L2 form, such as *silla* in Spanish, they treat this form as simply another way of saying "chair." This means that initially the L2 system has no separate conceptual structure, and that its formal structure relies on the structure of L1. Kroll and Tokowicz (chapter 26, this volume) review models of the lexicon that emphasize the extent to which L2 relies on L1 forms to access meaning rather than accessing meaning directly. In this sense, we can say that L2 is parasitic on L1 because of the extensive amount of transfer from L1 to L2. The learner's goal is to reduce this parasitism by building up L2 representations as a separate system. They do this by strengthening the direct linkage between new L2 forms and conceptual representations.

Given the fact that connectionism predicts such massive transfer for L1 knowledge to L2, it might be asked why more transfer error in L2 lexical forms is not seen. There are three reasons for this:

First, a great deal of transfer occurs smoothly and directly without producing error. Consider a word like "chair" in English. When the native English speaker begins to learn Spanish, it is easy to use the concept underlying chair to serve as the meaning for the new word *silla* in Spanish. The closer the conceptual, material, and linguistic worlds of the two languages are, the more successful this sort of positive transfer will be. Transfer only works smoothly when there is close conceptual match. For example, Ijaz (1986) showed how difficult transfer can be for Korean learners of English in semantic domains involving transfer verbs, such as "take" or "put." Similarly, if the source language has a two-color system (Berlin & Kay, 1969), as in Dani, acquisition of an eight-color system, as in Hungarian, will be difficult. These effects underscore the extent to which L2 lexical items are parasitic on L1 forms.

Second, learners are able to suppress some types of incorrect transfer. For example, when a learner tries to translate the English noun "soap" into Spanish by using a cognate, the result is *sopa* (soup). Misunderstandings created by "false friend" transfers such as this will be quickly detected and corrected. Similarly, an attempt to translate the English form "competence" into Spanish as *competencia* will run into problems because *competencia* means competition. Dijkstra (chapter 9, this volume) notes that, in laboratory settings, the suppression of these incorrect form relatives is incomplete, even in highly proficient bilinguals. However,

this persistent transfer effect is probably less marked in nonlaboratory contexts.

Third, error is minimized when two words in L1 map onto a single word in L2. For example, it is easy for an L1 Spanish speaker to map the meanings underlying *saber* and *conocer* (Stockwell, Bowen, & Martin, 1965) onto the L2 English form "know." Dropping the distinction between these forms requires little in the way of cognitive reorganization. It is difficult for the L1 English speaker to acquire this new distinction when learning Spanish. To control this distinction correctly, the learner must restructure the concept underlying know into two new related structures. In the area of lexical learning, these cases should cause the greatest transfer-produced errors.

Transfer in Sentence Comprehension

Transfer is also pervasive in the arena of sentence interpretation. There are now over a dozen Competition Model studies that have demonstrated the transfer of a "syntactic accent" in sentence interpretation (Bates & MacWhinney, 1981; De Bot & Van Montfort, 1988; Gass, 1987; Harrington, 1987; Kilborn, 1989; Kilborn & Cooreman, 1987; Kilborn & Ito, 1989; Liu, Bates, & Li, 1992; McDonald, 1987a, 1987b; McDonald & Heilenman, 1991; McDonald & MacWhinney, 1989). Frenck-Mestre (chapter 13, this volume) presents a particularly elegant design demonstrating this type of effect during online processing. These studies have shown that the learning of sentence processing cues in an L2 is a gradual process. The process begins with L2 cue weight settings that are close to those for L1. Over time, these settings change in the direction of the native speakers' settings for L2.

This pattern of results is perhaps most clearly documented in McDonald's studies of English-Dutch and Dutch-English L2 learning (McDonald, 1987b). This pattern shows the decline in the strength of the use of word order by English learners of Dutch over increased levels of competence. In Fig. 3.2, the monolingual cue usage pattern for English is given on the left and the monolingual Dutch pattern is given on the right. Between these two patterns, we see a declining use of word order and an increasing use of case inflection across three increasing levels of learning of Dutch. In Fig. 3.3, we see exactly the opposite pattern for Dutch learners of English. These results and others like them constitute strong support for

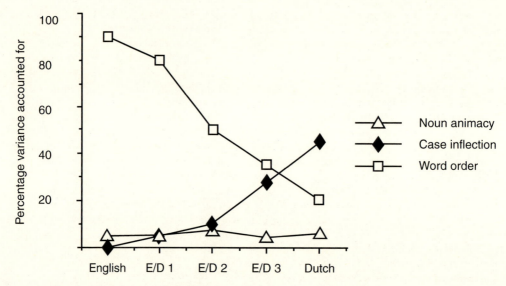

Figure 3.2 Changes in cue strength as English speakers learn Dutch (McDonald, 1987b). E/D 1, E/D 2, E/D 3 indicate English-Dutch learning levels.

the Competition Model view of L2 learning as the gradual growth of cue strength.

The Competition Model view of the two languages as interacting in a variety of ways is further supported by evidence of effects from L2 back to L1. Sentence processing studies by Liu et al. (1992) and Dussias (2001) have demonstrated the presence of just such effects. Although the Competition Model requires that the strongest transfer effects should be from L1 to L2, the view of competition as interactive leads us to expect some weaker amount of transfer from L2 back to L1.

Transfer in Pragmatics

The acquisition of pragmatic patterns is also heavily influenced by L1 transfer. When we first begin to use an L2, we may extend our L1 ideas about the proper form of greetings, questions, offers, promises, expectations, turn taking, topic expansion, face-saving, honorifics, presuppositions, and implications. If the two cultures are relatively similar, much of this transfer will be successful. However, there will inevitably be some gaps. In many cases, the L2 learner eventually will need to reconstruct the entire system of pragmatic patterns in the way they were learned by the child acquiring L1.

Much of this learning is based on specific phrases and forms. For example, the L1 learners' understanding of greetings is tightly linked to use

of specific phrases such as "*Guten Morgen*" or "Bye-bye." Learning about how and when to use specific speech acts is linked to learning about forms such as "Could you?" "Listen," and "Why not?" Learning these forms in a concrete context is important for both L1 and L2 learners.

However, pragmatics involves much more than simple speech act units or pairs. We also need to learn larger frames for narratives, argumentation, and polite chatting. By following the flow of perspectives and topics in conversations (Mac-Whinney, 1999), models of how discourse represents reality in both L1 and L2 can eventually be internalized.

Transfer in Morphology

Learning of the morphological marking or inflections of an L2 is very different from learning of the other areas we have discussed. This is because, in morphosyntax, it is typically impossible to transfer from L1 to L2. For example, an English learner of German cannot use the English noun gender system as a basis for learning the German noun gender system. This is because English does not have a fully elaborated noun gender system. Of course, English does distinguish between genders in the pronouns ("he" vs. "she"), and this distinction is of some help in learning to mark German nouns that have natural gender such as *der Vater* (the-masc

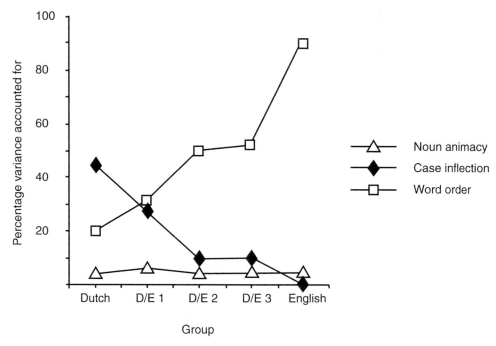

Figure 3.3 Changes in cue strength as Dutch speakers learn English (McDonald, 1987b). D/E 1, D/E 2, D/E 3 indicate Dutch-English learning levels.

father) and *die Mutter* (the-fem mother). However, one really does not need to rely on cues from English "he" and "she" to realize that fathers are masculine and mothers are feminine. On the other hand, there can be some real transfer effects to German from other languages that have full nominal gender systems. For example, a Spanish speaker might well want to refer to the moon as feminine on the basis of *la luna* in Spanish and produce the erroneous form *die Mond* in German rather than the correct masculine form *der Mond*.

Similarly, a Spanish learner of Chinese cannot use L1 knowledge to acquire the system of noun classifiers because Spanish has no noun classifiers. Chinese learners of English cannot use their L1 forms to learn the English contrast among definite, indefinite, and zero articles. This is because Chinese makes no overt distinctions in this area, leaving the issue of definiteness to be marked in other ways, if at all.

The fact that morphosyntax is not subject to transfer is a reflection of the general Competition Model dictum that "everything that can transfer will." In the areas of phonology, lexicon, orthography, syntax, and pragmatics, there are attempts to transfer. However, in morphology there is no

transfer because there is no basis for transfer. The exception here is between structurally mapable features, as in the example of gender transfer from Spanish to German.

Although there is no transfer of the exact forms of morphosyntax and little transfer of secondary mappings such as thinking that the moon is feminine, there is important positive and negative transfer of the underlying functions expressed by morphological devices. Concepts such as the instrumental, locatives, or benefactives often have positive transfer between languages. For example, many languages merge the instrumental "with" and the comitative "with." If L1 has this merger, it is easy to transfer the merged concept to L2. Similarly, semantically grounded grammatical distinctions such as movement toward and movement from can easily be transferred across languages. However, in other areas, transfer is less positive. One remarkable area of difficulty is in the learning of article marking in English by speakers of Chinese, Japanese, or Korean. These languages have no separate category of definiteness, instead using classifiers and plurals to express some of the functions marked by the English definite. Moreover, the complexity of the subcomponents of definiteness in

English stands as a major barrier for speakers of these languages.

Transfer in Sentence Production

Pienemann et al. (chapter 7, this volume) present evidence that the Competition Model claim that everything that can transfer will does not hold in the area of L2 sentence production. Instead, they suggest that "only those linguistic forms that the learner can process can be transferred to the L2." Their analysis of this issue is exceptionally detailed, and the additional evidence they bring to bear is bound to lead to very helpful sharpening of the issues at stake.

Pienemann et al. (chapter 7, this volume) present the case of the learning of the German V2 rule by speakers of L1 Swedish. The V2 rules in Swedish and German allow speakers to front adverbs like "today" or "now" as long as the verb immediately follows in "V2" position. This rule produces sentences such as "Today likes Peter milk." The surprising finding is that Swedes do not produce this order from the beginning, starting instead with "Today Peter likes milk." This finding is only surprising if one believes that what learners transfer are whole syntactic frames for whole sentences.

However, the Competition Model holds that the basic unit of both L1 and L2 acquisition is the item-based pattern. In this case, learners first learn to place the subject before the verb, as in "Peter likes milk." Later, they add the adverb to produce "Peter likes milk today." Only in the final stages of learning do they then pick up the item-based frame that allows adverbs to take the initial slot. The important point here is that, in this part of sentence production, much as in morphology, the mapping from L1 to L2 is low level and conservative. Thus, the failure to see a transfer of the V2 rule from Swedish to German is based on the fact that Swedes are learning German from item-based patterns, not by picking up whole sentence frames at a time. The emphasis on learning from item-based patterns should hold for all beginning L2 learners. For example, early transfer to Italian of the English cleft structure would not be expected, although the structure is present in both languages, and learners will eventually make the mapping. The problem is that during the first stages of learning, learners are just not working on the sentence level.

The opposite side of this coin is that, when L2 structures can be learned early on as item-based patterns, this learning can block transfer from L1.

Pienemann et al. (chapter 7, this volume) present the example of learning of Japanese SOV order by speakers of L1 English. These learners almost never generalize English SVO to Japanese. Of course, the input to L2 learners consistently emphasizes SOV order and seldom presents any VO sequences, although these do occur in colloquial Japanese.

This learning is best understood in terms of the account of MacWhinney (1982, 1987a). Learners acquire a few initial Japanese verbs as item-based constructions with slots for objects in preverbal position marked by the postposition "o" and topics in initial position marked by the postpositions "wa" or "ga." After learning a few such items, they generalize to the "feature-based" construction of SOV. This is positive learning based on consistent input in L2. If L1 were to have a transfer effect at this point, it would be extremely brief because L2 is so consistent, and these item-based constructions are in the focus of the learner's attention.

What these two examples illustrate is that L1 transfer in the areas of sentence production and morphosyntax is limited by the fact that morphosyntax is the most language-specific part of a target language. Because the mappings are hard to make, transfer in this area is minimized. Once relations between the two languages can be constructed, as in the case of the transfer of the English cleft to Spanish, some positive transfer can be expected. However, we should not expect to see consistent early transfer in this particular area. Thus, the analyses of Pienemann et al. (chapter 7, this volume) are remarkably close to those found in the Competition Model once the importance of item-based patterns is recognized.

Resonance

As mentioned, the Unified Competition Model includes three new components that were not found in the classic model. These are chunking, codes, and resonance. The theory of chunking is certainly not new and could well have been included in the model many years ago. The theory of code relations is also not entirely new because it incorporates and extends ideas about transfer that have been in development within the Competition Model for nearly 15 years. The component of resonance, on the other hand, is new to the theory. Despite this newness to the model, it plays an important central role in understanding code separation, age-related effects, and the microprocesses of learning and processing.

It is fairly easy to get an intuitive grasp of what resonance means in L1 and L2 learning. Resonance occurs most clearly during covert inner speech. Vygotsky (1962) observed that young children would often give themselves instructions overtly. For example, a 2-year-old might say "pick it up" while picking up a block. At this age, the verbalization tends to guide and control the action. By producing a verbalization that describes an action, the child sets up a resonant connection between vocalization and action. Later, Vygotsky argues, these overt instructions become inner speech and continue to guide our cognition. The L2 learners go through a process much like that of the child. At first, they use the language only with others. Then, they begin to talk to themselves in the new language and start to "think in the second language." At this point, the L2 begins to assume the same resonant status that the child attains for the L1.

Once a process of inner speech is set into motion, it can also be used to process new input and relate new forms to other forms paradigmatically. For example, if I hear the phrase "*ins Mittelalter*" in German, I can think to myself that this means that the stem *Alter* must be *das Alter*. This means that the dative must take the form *in welchem Alter* or *in meinem Alter*. These resonant form-related exercises can be conducted in parallel with more expressive resonant exercises in which I simply try to talk to myself about things around me in German or whatever language I happen to be learning.

On a mechanistic level, resonance is based on the repeated coactivation of reciprocal connections. As the set of resonant connections grows, the possibilities for cross associations and mutual activations grow, and the language starts to form a coherent coactivating neural circuit. Although this idea of resonance seems basic and perhaps obvious, it is important to note that modern connectionist models (Murre, chapter 8, this volume; Thomas & Van Heuven, chapter 10, this volume) have provided virtually no place for learning in resonant models. This is because current popular neural network models, such as backpropagation, work in only a feedforward fashion, so resonant links cannot be established or utilized. Self-organizing maps such as the DisLex model of Li et al. (in press) can provide local resonance between sound and meaning, but have not yet been able to model resonance on the syntactic level. Grossberg's (1987) adaptive resonance theory would seem to be one account that should capture at least some ideas about resonance. However, the resonant connections in that model only capture the role of

attentional shifts in motivating the recruitment of additional computational elements.

Perhaps the model that comes closest to expressing the core notion of resonance is the interactive activation model of the early 1980s. Interactive activation models such as the bilingual interactive activation model and the bilingual interactive model of lexical access (Thomas & Van Heuven, chapter 10, this volume) have succeeded in accounting for important aspects of bilingual lexical processing. Although these models have not explicitly examined the role of resonance, they are at least compatible with the concept.

We can also use resonance as a way of understanding certain dynamic multilingual processes. For example, variations in the delays involved in code switching in both natural and laboratory tasks can be interpreted in terms of the processes that maintain language-internal resonant activations. If a particular language is repeatedly accessed, it will be in a highly resonant state. Although another language will be passively accessible, it may take a second or two before the resonant activation of that language can be triggered by a task. Thus, a speaker may not immediately recognize a sentence in a language that has not been spoken in the recent context. On the other hand, a simultaneous interpreter will maintain both languages in continual receptive activation while trying to minimize resonant activations in the output system of the source language.

Like La Heij (chapter 14, this volume), I would argue that multilingual processing relies more on activation and resonance than on inhibition (Green, 1998). Of course, it is known that the brain makes massive use of inhibitory connections. However, these are typically local connections that sharpen local competitions. Inhibition is also important in providing overt inhibitory control of motor output, as in speech monitoring. However, inhibition by itself cannot produce new learning, coactivation, and inner speech. For these types of processing, resonant activation is more effective.

The cognitive psychology of the 1970s (Atkinson, 1975) placed much emphasis on the role of strategic resonance during learning. More recently, the emphasis has been more on automatic processes of resonance, often within the context of theories of verbal memory. The role of resonance in L1 learning is an area of particular current importance. It is known that children can learn new words with only one or two exposures to the new sounds. For this to work successfully, children must resonantly activate the phonological store for that word. In the model of Gupta and MacWhinney (1997), this resonance will involve keeping the phonological form active in short-term memory long enough for it to be reliably encoded into the central lexical network (Li et al., in press). This preservation of the auditory form in the phonological buffer is one form of resonant processing.

Resonance can facilitate the sharpening of contrasts between forms. Both L1 and L2 learners may have trouble encoding new phonological forms that are close to words they already know. Children can have trouble learning the two new forms *pif* and *bif* because of their confusability, although they can learn *pif* when it occurs along with *wug* (Stager & Werker, 1997).

This same phonological confusability effect can have an impact on L2 learners. For example, when I came to learn Cantonese, I needed to learn to pay careful attention to marking with tones so I would not confuse *mother, measles, linen, horse,* and *scold* as various forms of /ma/. Once a learner has the tonal features right, it is still important to pay attention to each part of a word. For example, when I was learning the Cantonese phrase for "pivoting your foot inward," I initially encoded it as *kau geu* instead of the correct form *kau geuk*. This is because there is a tendency in Cantonese to reduce final /k/. However, the reduced final /k/ is not totally absent and has an effect on the quality of the preceding vowel. At first, I did not attend to this additional component or cue. However, after my encoding for *kau geu* became automated, my attentional focusing was then freed enough so that I could notice the presence of the final /k/. This expansion of selective attention during learning is a very general process.

Once the auditory form is captured, the learner needs to establish some pathway between the sound and its meaning. Because few words encode any stable conventional phonological symbolism, pathways of this type must be constructed anew by each language learner. It has been proposed that activation of the hippocampus (McClelland, McNaughton, & O'Reilly, 1995) is sufficient to encode arbitrary relations of this sort. If this were true, L2 learners would have virtually no problem picking up long lists of new vocabulary items. Although the hippocampus certainly plays a role in maintaining a temporary resonance between sound and meaning, it is up to the learner to extract additional cues that can facilitate the formation of the sound-meaning linkage.

Resonant mappings can rely on synesthesia (Ramachandran & Hubbard, 2001), onomatopoeia,

sound symbolism, postural associations (Paget, 1930), lexical analysis, or a host of other provisional relations. It is not necessary that this symbolism be in accord with any established linguistic pattern. Instead, each learner is free to discover a different pattern of associations. This nonconventional nature of resonant connections means that it will be difficult to demonstrate the use of specific resonant connections in group studies of lexical learning.

However, it is known that constructive mnemonics provided by the experimenter (Atkinson, 1975) greatly facilitate learning. For example, when learning the German word *Wasser*, the sound of water running out of a faucet can be imagined and associated with the /s/ of *Wasser*. For this word, the sound of the German word can also be associated to the sound of the English word *water*. At the same time, we can associate *Wasser* with collocations such as *Wasser trinken*, which themselves resonate with *Bier trinken* and others. Together, these resonant associations among collocations, sounds, and other words help to link the German word *Wasser* into the developing German lexicon.

It is likely that children also use these mechanisms to encode the relations between sounds and meanings. Children are less inhibited than adults in their ability to create ad hoc symbolic links between sounds and meanings. The child learning German as an L1 might associate the shimmering qualities of *Wasser* with a shimmering aspect of the sibilant; or the child might imagine the sound as plunging downward in tone in the way that water comes over a waterfall. The child may link the concept of *Wasser* tightly to a scene in which someone pours *ein Glas Wasser*, and then the association between the sound of *Wasser* and the image of the glass and the pouring are primary. For the L1 learner, these resonant links are woven together with the entire nature of experience and the growing concept of the world.

A major dimension of resonant connections is between words and our internal image of the human body. For example, Bailey, Chang, Feldman, and Narayanan (1998) characterize the meaning of the verb *stumble* in terms of the physical motion of the limbs during walking, the encountering of a physical object, and the breaking of gait and posture. As Tomasello (1992) noted, each new verb learned by the child can be mapped onto a physical or cognitive frame of this type. In this way, verbs and other predicates can support the emergence of a grounded mental model for sentences. Workers in L2 (Asher, 1977) have often emphasized the importance of action for the grounding of new meanings, and this new literature in cognitive grammar provides good theoretical support for that approach. Item-based patterns are theoretically central in this discussion because they provide a powerful link between the earlier Competition Model's emphasis on processing and cue validity and the newer theories of grounded cognition (MacWhinney, 1999).

Resonance can make use of analogies between stored chunks, as described in the theories for storage and chunking. Gentner and Markman (1997), Hofstadter (1997), and others have formulated models of analogical reasoning that have interesting implications for language acquisition models. Analogies can be helpful in working out the first examples of a pattern. For example, a child learning German may compare *steh auf!* (stand up!) with *er muß aufstehen* (He must get up). The child can see that the two sentences express the same activity, but that the verbal prefix is moved in one. Using this pattern as the basis for further resonant connections, the child can then begin to acquire a general understanding of verbal prefix placement in German.

The adult L2 learner tends to rely on rather less-imaginative and more structured resonant linkages. One important set of links available to the adult is orthography. When an L2 learner of German learns the word *Wasser,* it is easy to map the sounds of the word directly to the image of the letters. Because German has highly regular mappings from orthography to pronunciation, calling up the image of the spelling of *Wasser* is an extremely good way of activating its sound. When the L2 learner is illiterate or when the L2 orthography is unlike the L1 orthography, this backup system for resonance will not be available. The L2 learning of Chinese by speakers of languages with Roman scripts illustrates this problem. In some signs and books in mainland China, Chinese characters are accompanied by romanized pinyin spellings. This allows the L2 learner a method for establishing resonant connections among new words, their pronunciation, and their representations in Chinese orthography. However, in Taiwan and Hong Kong, characters are seldom written out in pinyin in either books or public notices. As a result, learners cannot learn from these materials. To make use of resonant connections from orthography, learners must then focus on the learning of the complex Chinese script. This learning itself requires a large investment in resonant associations because the Chinese writing system is based largely on radical elements that have multiple resonant associations with the sounds and meanings of words.

Resonance can also play an important role in the resolution of errors. For example, I recently noted that I had wrongly coded the stress on the Spanish word *abanico* (fan) on the second syllable, as in *abánico*. To correct this error, I spent time both rehearsing the correct stress pattern a few times and then visualizing the word as spelled without the stress mark or with the stress on the second syllable, which is normally not written in Spanish spelling. I also tried to associate this pattern in my mind with the verb *abanicar* (fan) and even the first person singular of this verb that has the form *abanico*. Having rehearsed this form in these various ways and having established these resonant connections, the tendency to produce the only incorrect form was somewhat reduced, although it will take time to banish fully the traces of the incorrect pattern.

Age-Related Effects

It may be helpful to review here how the Unified Competition Model accounts for age-related changes in language learning ability. As Dekeyser and Larson-Hall (chapter 5, this volume) note, the default account in this area has been the critical period hypothesis, which holds that, after some time in late childhood or puberty, L2s can no longer be acquired by the innate language acquisition device, but must be learned painfully and incompletely through explicit instruction.

Following the work of Birdsong (chapter 6, this volume), the Unified Competition Model attributes the observed facts about age-related changes to very different sources. The model emphasizes the extent to which repeated use of L1 leads to its ongoing entrenchment. This entrenchment operates differentially across linguistic areas, with the strongest entrenchment occurring in output phonology and the least entrenchment in the area of lexicon, for which new learning continues to occur in L1 in any case. To overcome entrenchment, learners must rely on resonant processes that allow the fledgling L2 to resist the intrusions of L1, particularly in phonology (Colomé, 2001; Dijkstra, Grainger, & Van Heuven, 1999). For languages with familiar orthographies, resonance connections can be formed among writing, sound, meaning, and phrasal units. For languages with unfamiliar orthographies, the domain of resonant connections will be more constrained. This problem has a severe impact on older learners because they have become increasingly reliant on resonant connections between sound and orthography.

Because learning through resonant connections is highly strategic, L2 learners will vary markedly in the constructions they can control or that are missing or incorrectly transferred (Birdsong, chapter 6, this volume). In addition to the basic forces of entrenchment, transfer, and strategic resonant learning, older learners will be affected by problems with restricted social contacts, commitments to ongoing L1 interactions, and declining cognitive abilities. None of these changes predict a sharp drop at a certain age in L2 learning abilities. Instead, they predict a gradual decline across the life span.

Conclusion

This concludes the examination of the Unified Competition Model. Many of the pieces of this model have already been worked out in some detail. For example, there is a good model of cue competition in syntax for both L1 and L2. There are good models of L1 lexical acquisition. There are good data on phonological and lexical transfer in L2. There are clear data on the ways in which processing load has an impact on sentence processing in working memory. We are even learning about the neuronal bases of this load (Booth et al., 2001). Other areas provide targets for future work. But, the central contribution of the unified model is not in terms of accounting for specific empirical findings. Rather, the unified model provides a high-level road map of a very large territory that can now be filled out in greater detail.

References

Asher, J. (1977). Children learning another language: A developmental hypothesis. *Child Development, 48,* 1040–1048.

Atkinson, R. (1975). Mnemotechnics in second-language learning. *American Psychologist, 30,* 821–828.

Bailey, D., Chang, N., Feldman, J., & Narayanan, S. (1998). Extending embodied lexical development. *Proceedings of the 20th Annual Meeting of the Cognitive Science Society,* 64–69.

Bates, E., & MacWhinney, B. (1981). Second language acquisition from a functionalist perspective: Pragmatic, semantic and perceptual strategies. In H. Winitz (Ed.), *Annals of the New York Academy of Sciences Conference on Native and Foreign Language Acquisition* (pp. 190–214). New York: New York Academy of Sciences.

Bates, E., & MacWhinney, B. (1982). Functionalist approaches to grammar. In E. Wanner & L. Gleitman (Eds.), *Language acquisition: The state of the art* (pp. 173–218). New York: Cambridge University Press.

Berlin, B., & Kay, P. (1969). *Basic color terms: Their universality and evolution.* Berkeley: University of California Press.

Blackwell, A., & Bates, E. (1995). Inducing agrammatic profiles in normals: Evidence for the selective vulnerability of morphology under cognitive resource limitation. *Journal of Cognitive Neuroscience, 7,* 228–257.

Bley-Vroman, R., Felix, S., & Ioup, G. (1988). The accessibility of universal grammar in adult language learning. *Second Language Research, 4,* 1–32.

Booth, J. R., MacWhinney, B., Thulborn, K. R., Sacco, K., Voyvodic, J. T., & Feldman, H. M. (2001). Developmental and lesion effects during brain activation for sentence comprehension and mental rotation. *Developmental Neuropsychology, 18,* 139–169.

Clahsen, H., & Muysken, P. (1986). The availability of UG to adult and child learners: A study of the acquisition of German word order. *Second Language Research, 2,* 93–119.

Colomé, À. (2001). Lexical activation in bilinguals' speech production: Language specific or language independent. *Journal of Memory and Language, 45,* 721–736.

De Bot, K., & Van Montfort, R. (1988). "Cue-validity" in het Nederlands als eerste en tweede taal. *Interdisciplinair Tijdschrift voor Taal en Tekstwetenschap, 8,* 111–120.

Dell, G., Juliano, C., & Govindjee, A. (1993). Structure and content in language production: A theory of frame constraints in phonological speech errors. *Cognitive Science, 17,* 149–195.

Devescovi, A., D'Amico, S., Smith, S., Mimica, I., & Bates, E. (1998). The development of sentence comprehension in Italian and Serbo-Croatian: Local versus distributed cues. In D. Hillert (Ed.), *Syntax and semantics: Vol. 31. Sentence processing: A cross-linguistic perspective* (pp. 345–377). San Diego, CA: Academic Press.

Dijkstra, A., Grainger, J., & Van Heuven, W. J. B. (1999). Recognizing cognates and interlingual homographs: The neglected role of phonology. *Journal of Memory and Language, 41,* 496–518.

Döpke, S. (2000). Generation of and retraction from cross-linguistically motivated structure in bilingual first language acquisition. *Bilingualism: Language, and Cognition, 3,* 209–226.

Dussias, P. E. (2001). Bilingual sentence parsing. In J. L. Nicol (Ed.), *One mind, two languages: Bilingual sentence processing* (pp. 159–176). Cambridge, MA: Blackwell.

Ellis, R. (1994). A theory of instructed second language acquisition. In N. C. Ellis (Ed.), *Implicit and explicit learning of language* (pp. 79–114). San Diego, CA: Academic Press.

Elman, J. L., & McClelland, J. L. (1988). Cognitive penetration of the mechanisms of perception: Compensation for coarticulation of lexically restored phonemes. *Journal of Memory and Language, 27,* 143–165.

Ervin-Tripp, S. M. (1968). Sociolinguistics. In L. Berkowitz (Ed.), *Advances in experimental social psychology* (Vol. 4, pp. 91–165). New York: Academic Press.

Felix, S., & Wode, H. (Eds.). (1983). *Language development at the crossroads.* Tübingen, Germany: Gunter Narr.

Flege, J., & Davidian, R. (1984). Transfer and developmental processes in adult foreign language speech production. *Applied Psycholinguistics, 5,* 323–347.

Flege, J., Takagi, J., & Mann, V. (1995). Japanese adults can learn to produce English "r" and "l" accurately. *Language Learning, 39,* 23–32.

Flynn, S. (1996). A parameter-setting approach to second language acquisition. In W. C. Ritchie & T. K. Bhatia (Eds.), *Handbook of second language acquisition* (pp. 121–158). San Diego, CA: Academic Press.

Gass, S. (1987). The resolution of conflicts among competing systems: A bidirectional perspective. *Applied Psycholinguistics, 8,* 329–350.

Gentner, D., & Markman, A. (1997). Structure mapping in analogy and similarity. *American Psychologist, 52,* 45–56.

Gerver, D. (1974). The effects of noise on the performance of simultaneous interpreters: Accuracy of performance. *Acta Psychologica, 38,* 159–167.

Gibson, E., Pearlmutter, N., Canseco-Gonzalez, E., & Hickok, G. (1996). Recency preference in the human sentence processing mechanism. *Cognition, 59,* 23–59.

Goldberg, A. E. (1999). The emergence of the semantics of argument structure constructions. In B. MacWhinney (Ed.), *The emergence of language* (pp. 197–213). Mahwah, NJ: Erlbaum.

Green, D. M. (1998). Mental control of the bilingual lexico-semantic system. *Bilingualism: Language and Cognition, 1,* 67–81.

Grossberg, S. (1987). Competitive learning: From interactive activation to adaptive resonance. *Cognitive Science, 11,* 23–63.

Gupta, P., & MacWhinney, B. (1997). Vocabulary acquisition and verbal short-term memory: Computational and neural bases. *Brain and Language, 59,* 267–333.

Hakuta, K. (1981). Grammatical description versus configurational arrangement in language acquisition: The case of relative clauses in Japanese. *Cognition, 9,* 197–236.

Hancin-Bhatt, B. (1994). Segment transfer: A consequence of a dynamic system. *Second Language Research, 10,* 241–269.

Harrington, M. (1987). Processing transfer: language-specific strategies as a source of interlanguage variation. *Applied Psycholinguistics, 8,* 351–378.

Hauser, M., Newport, E., & Aslin, R. (2001). Segmentation of the speech stream in a non-human primate: statistical learning in cotton-top tamarins. *Cognition, 78,* B53–B64.

Hausser, R. (1999). *Foundations of computational linguistics: Man-machine communication in natural language.* Berlin: Springer.

Hofstädter, D. (1997). *Fluid concepts and creative analogies: Computer models of the fundamental mechanisms of thought.* London: Allen Lane.

Ijaz, H. (1986). Linguistic and cognitive determinants of lexical acquisition in a second language. *Language Learning, 36,* 401–451.

Kilborn, K. (1989). Sentence processing in a second language: The timing of transfer. *Language and Speech, 32,* 1–23.

Kilborn, K., & Cooreman, A. (1987). Sentence interpretation strategies in adult Dutch-English bilinguals. *Applied Psycholinguistics, 8,* 415–431.

Kilborn, K., & Ito, T. (1989). Sentence processing in Japanese-English and Dutch-English bilinguals. In B. MacWhinney & E. Bates (Eds.), *The crosslinguistic study of sentence processing* (pp. 257–291). New York: Cambridge University Press.

Krashen, S. (1994). The input hypothesis and its rivals. In N. C. Ellis (Ed.), *Implicit and explicit learning of languages* (pp. 45–78). San Diego, CA: Academic.

Langacker, R. (1989). *Foundations of cognitive grammar. Vol. 2: Applications.* Stanford, CA: Stanford University Press.

Li, P., Farkas, I., & MacWhinney, B. (2004). Early lexical development in a self-organizing neural network. *Neural Networks, 17,* 1345–1362.

Liu, H., Bates, E., & Li, P. (1992). Sentence interpretation in bilingual speakers of English and Chinese. *Applied Psycholinguistics, 13,* 451–484.

Lively, S., Pisoni, D., & Logan, J. (1990). Some effects of training Japanese listeners to identify English /r/ and /l/. In Y. Tohkura (Ed.), *Speech perception, production and linguistic structure* (pp. 46–55). Tokyo: OHM.

MacDonald, M. C., & MacWhinney, B. (1990). Measuring inhibition and facilitation from pronouns. *Journal of Memory and Language, 29,* 469–492.

MacDonald, M. C., Pearlmutter, N. J., & Seidenberg, M. S. (1994). Lexical nature of syntactic ambiguity resolution. *Psychological Review, 101,* 676–703.

MacWhinney, B. (1975). Pragmatic patterns in child syntax. *Stanford Papers and Reports on Child Language Development, 10,* 153–165.

MacWhinney, B. (1978). The acquisition of morphophonology. *Monographs of the Society for Research in Child Development, 43*(1).

MacWhinney, B. (1982). Basic syntactic processes. In S. Kuczaj (Ed.), *Language acquisition: Vol. 1. Syntax and semantics* (pp. 73–136). Hillsdale, NJ: Erlbaum.

MacWhinney, B. (1987a). The Competition Model. In B. MacWhinney (Ed.), *Mechanisms of language acquisition* (pp. 249–308). Hillsdale, NJ: Erlbaum.

MacWhinney, B. (1987b). Toward a psycho-linguistically plausible parser. In S. Thomason (Ed.), *Proceedings of the Eastern States Conference on Linguistics*. Columbus: Ohio State University.

MacWhinney, B. (1989). Competition and lexical categorization. In R. Corrigan, F. Eckman, & M. Noonan (Eds.), *Linguistic categorization* (pp. 195–242). Philadelphia: Benjamins.

MacWhinney, B. (1999). The emergence of language from embodiment. In B. MacWhinney (Ed.), *The emergence of language* (pp. 213–256). Mahwah, NJ: Erlbaum.

MacWhinney, B. (2002). The gradual emergence of language. In T. Givón & B. F. Malle (Eds.), *The evolution of language out of pre-language* (pp. 231–263). Philadelphia: Benjamins.

MacWhinney, B., & Anderson, J. (1986). The acquisition of grammar. In I. Gopnik & M. Gopnik (Eds.), *From models to modules* (pp. 3–25). Norwood, NJ: Ablex.

MacWhinney, B., Feldman, H. M., Sacco, K., & Valdes-Perez, R. (2000). Online measures of basic language skills in children with early focal brain lesions. *Brain and Language, 71,* 400–431.

MacWhinney, B., & Pléh, C. (1988). The processing of restrictive relative clauses in Hungarian. *Cognition, 29,* 95–141.

McClelland, J. L., McNaughton, B. L., & O'Reilly, R. C. (1995). Why there are complementary learning systems in the hippocampus and neocortex: Insights from the successes and failures of connectionist models of learning and memory. *Psychological Review, 102,* 419–457.

McDonald, J. L. (1987a). Assigning linguistic roles: The influence of conflicting cues. *Journal of Memory and Language, 26,* 100–117.

McDonald, J. L. (1987b). Sentence interpretation in bilingual speakers of English and Dutch. *Applied Psycholinguistics, 8,* 379–414.

McDonald, J. L., & Heilenman, K. (1991). Determinants of cue strength in adult first and second language speakers of French. *Applied Psycholinguistics, 12,* 313–348.

McDonald, J. L., & MacWhinney, B. (1989). Maximum likelihood models for sentence processing research. In B. MacWhinney & E. Bates (Eds.), *The crosslinguistic study of sentence processing* (pp. 397–421). New York: Cambridge University Press.

McDonald, J. L., & MacWhinney, B. J. (1995). The time course of anaphor resolution: Effects of implicit verb causality and gender. *Journal of Memory and Language, 34,* 543–566.

Menn, L., & Stoel-Gammon, C. (1995). Phonological development. In P. Fletcher & B. MacWhinney (Eds.), *The handbook of child language* (pp. 335–360). Oxford, U.K.: Blackwell.

Miyake, A., Carpenter, P., & Just, M. (1994). A capacity approach to syntactic comprehension disorders: Making normal adults perform like aphasic patients. *Cognitive Neuropsychology, 11,* 671–717.

Moon, C., Cooper, R. P., & Fifer, W. P. (1993). Two-day infants prefer their native language. *Infant Behavior and Development, 16,* 495–500.

Newell, A. (1990). *A unified theory of cognition.* Cambridge, MA: Harvard University Press.

Norris, D. (1994). Shortlist: A connectionist model of continuous speech recognition. *Cognition, 52,* 189–234.

Paget, R. (1930). *Human speech.* New York: Harcourt Brace.

Ramachandran, V. S., & Hubbard, E. M. (2001). Synaesthesia: A window into perception, thought and language. *Journal of Consciousness Studies, 8,* 3–34.

Seleskovitch, D. (1976). Interpretation: A psychological approach to translating. In R. W. Brislin (Ed.), *Translation: Application and research* (pp. 113–134). New York: Gardner.

Snow, C. E. (1999). Social perspectives on the emergence of language. In B. MacWhinney (Ed.), *The emergence of language* (pp. 257–276). Mahwah, NJ: Erlbaum.

Sokolov, J. L. (1988). Cue validity in Hebrew sentence comprehension. *Journal of Child Language, 15,* 129–156.

Sokolov, J. L. (1989). The development of role assignment in Hebrew. In B. MacWhinney & E. Bates (Eds.), *The crosslinguistic study of sentence processing* (pp. 158–184). New York: Cambridge University Press.

Spivey, M., & Marian, V. (1999). Cross talk between native and second language: Partial activation of an irrelevant lexicon. *Psychological Science, 10,* 281–284.

Stager, C. L., & Werker, J. F. (1997). Infants listen for more phonetic detail in speech perception than in word learning tasks. *Nature, 388,* 381–382.

Stemberger, J., & MacWhinney, B. (1986). Frequency and the lexical storage of regularly inflected forms. *Memory and Cognition, 14,* 17–26.

Stockwell, R., Bowen, J., & Martin, J. (1965). *The grammatical structures of English and Spanish.* Chicago: University of Chicago Press.

Tomasello, M. (1992). *First verbs: A case study of early grammatical development.* Cambridge, U.K.: Cambridge University Press.

Tomasello, M. (2000). The item-based nature of children's early syntactic development. *Trends in Cognitive Sciences, 4,* 156–163.

Vygotsky, L. (1962). *Thought and language.* Cambridge, MA: MIT Press.

Werker, J. F. (1995). Exploring developmental changes in cross-language speech perception. In L. Gleitman & M. Liberman (Eds.), *An invitation to cognitive science: Language, Volume 1* (pp. 87–106). Cambridge, MA: MIT Press.

Núria Sebastián-Gallés
Laura Bosch

4

Phonology and Bilingualism

ABSTRACT In this chapter, research about phonological processing in bilinguals is reviewed. Different domains within phonological processing are considered. We approach the different domains within phonology following the developmental sequence that infant research has proposed for early linguistic development. First, the question of when bilingual infants are able to distinguish between the two languages of exposure is addressed. This issue is approached from the perspective of the rhythmic hypothesis, and its consequences on adult speech processing are also discussed. Next, the acquisition of two sound systems is analyzed. In doing so, research in the acquisition of segmental, suprasegmental (stress), and phonotactic knowledge is presented. Data about auditory word recognition are also included, and relevant work on the relationship between phonology and lexical representation is reviewed. Finally, some considerations about age of acquisition effects and individual differences are discussed.

During the first year of life, human beings acquire a remarkable ability to process the sound system of their maternal language. This ability, which will be refined in the following years, will allow them to be identified as native members of a particular language community. Quite exceptional circumstances must concur for this not to happen. On the contrary, when human beings later in life try, sometimes very hard, to acquire these very same abilities, most will not succeed, and they will be betrayed by their nonnative accent. This nonnative accent not only will be restricted to the domain of speech production, but also will be observed in speech perception; nonnative listeners often fail to perceive foreign sounds correctly.

Why is it so difficult to master the sound system of a second language (L2)? This is a quite complex question, and in trying to answer it, other questions arise: Why is it that some people succeed in this task, and others do not? Why is it that some, but not all, sounds of a foreign language are more difficult, sometimes impossible, to be learned than others? Both questions refer to core issues in the domain of the acquisition and processing of a nonnative phonology. The first one deals with the topic of individual differences. Although it is a

central issue, it is not addressed in this review (see Michael & Gollan, chapter 19, this volume). The second question tackles the issue of the relationship between native and nonnative sound systems. A third critical question in trying to understand the difficulties of learning a nonnative phonology is the issue of plasticity of the speech learning system.

It is undeniable that there are two major determinants of the level of proficiency attained in an L2. Everybody knows not only that "the earlier, the better," but also that "the more experience, the better"—that is, time and amount. These two aspects are the principal variables underlying brain development and change. At the beginning of life, brains are highly plastic; thus, relatively small amounts of a particular exposure may have long and important consequences. But, our brains are also living structures, always changing and adapting to the demands of the environment; thus, provided sufficiently extended exposure, significant changes can be induced. It also has to be considered that not all brain areas mature at the same pace; for instance, although we are technically blind at birth, our auditory system is operating at an excellent level. Learning an L2 in general and its sound system in particular requires the collaboration of different brain areas, some of them already functional at birth; others may take several months, perhaps years, to be fully developed (Posner, Rothbart, Farah, & Bruer, 2001).

In this scenario, the meaning of early or late exposure to a language may differ according to which brain areas are recruited in a particular process. We are just beginning to understand the neural substrate of most of our mind, and we are even more at the beginning of understanding how the brain develops.[1] Our knowledge of how speech is processed in the brain is also not very profound. Nevertheless, at least for some particular domains, our knowledge about the functioning of the speech processing system is quite robust. Behavioral research done in the past years to understand the basic mechanisms of acquisition and processing of nonnative languages has provided insightful results, solid bases, and hypotheses to be tested.

In this chapter, we review different aspects of the processing of the sound systems in bilinguals. Although we cover a wide range of phonological domains, we do not address in an exhaustive way relatively well-known areas (like, for instance, the processing of nonnative phonemes) for which other reviews already exist. We also restrict our review to oral languages, and bilingualism in written and sign languages is not addressed (basically because almost nothing exists for the domain of phonological processing).

The organization of this chapter follows a developmental sequence in describing the different phonological subsystems. We start by what is known about newborns' speech processing capacities, and we subsequently review data of older infants, from their second semester of life up to the age when they have already begun to build a receptive vocabulary and can easily associate word labels to novel objects, as in the classical word-learning task experiments. This approach helps stress the importance we give to the developmental pattern.[2]

Becoming a Bilingual: The Discovery of the Existence of Different Sound Systems

One of the first prerequisites to become a bilingual is to be able to distinguish the existence of two different sound systems spoken in the environment. Data of monolingual newborn infants show that they can differentiate between some pairs of languages, but not between any language pair. For instance, newborns can distinguish between Spanish

and English and between English and Japanese, but not between Dutch and English or between Spanish and Italian. That is, newborns can distinguish between languages that differ fundamentally with respect to their rhythmic or prosodic structure (Abercrombie, 1967), but not between languages that belong to the same rhythmic category (Mehler et al., 1988; Nazzi, Bertoncini, & Mehler, 1998). This ability is not specific to human beings because it can be traced back in other mammals, like tamarin monkeys (Ramus, Hauser, Miller, Morris, & Mehler, 2000) and rats (Toro, Trobalón, & Sebastián-Gallés, 2003). However, independent of the phylogenetic origins of this capacity, the early acquaintance with the prosodic structure of the language of exposure has been considered the core of the prosodic bootstrapping hypothesis for the lexical and syntactic acquisition by different researchers (Guasti, Nespor, Christophe, & Van Ooyen, 2001).

It has been suggested that the prosody of speech may provide infants with crucial information to start acquiring the language. For instance, it has been hypothesized that some major syntactic parameters, such as the direction of recursivity, might be set at a prelexical stage based on the prosodic prominence of whole utterances to which the infant is exposed early in life (Christophe, Guasti, Nespor, Dupoux, & Van Ooyen, 1997). For infants in bilingual environments, prosody could also be initially helpful in setting the languages apart after a short period of exposure, possibly just a few months. Prosodic information could facilitate the discovery of two different language systems and perhaps help infants start the building of this information in two separate systems before they reach the lexical stage in their language development.

Although no data are available on language discrimination capacities in newborns or very young infants (up to 4 months of age) growing up in bilingual environments, it is reasonable to say that, at least theoretically, newborns simultaneously exposed to languages belonging to different rhythmic categories should be able to tell apart both sound systems at an early age; newborns exposed to languages with more similar prosodic structures would face a rather different starting point, with perhaps a later differentiation.[3]

How long does it take these bilingual infants to separate both systems? Research in our laboratory with infants exposed from birth to Catalan and Spanish (two Romance languages belonging to the same rhythmic group; Ramus, Nespor, & Mehler, 1999) has shown that as early as 4.5 months of age, bilingual infants can separate both languages. In that research, infants were familiarized to six different sentences in their maternal language (that is, the language predominantly spoken by their mother, Catalan or Spanish; thus, there were two different groups of bilingual infants in the study). After 2 minutes of familiarization, they were tested on their attention time to novel utterances for eight test trials, half in the same language of the familiarization phase and half with a switch in the language (always the same female speaker with a motherese style). Both groups of infants showed significant mean attention time differences to the switch and same trials, with longer listening time to trials with a switch in the language (Bosch & Sebastián-Gallés, 2001b). Similar results were obtained with two parallel groups of infants from monolingual environments, thus indicating that these two Romance languages can be differentiated rather early in life independent of the level of exposure. The crucial point to be stressed here is the fact that simultaneous bilingual exposure was not creating any specific trouble in the process of language differentiation for this pair of languages, a case for which a later differentiation had been predicted (Mehler, Dupoux, Nazzi, & Dehaene-Lambertz, 1996).

Thus, the possibility of separating both languages, even if they are rhythmically very similar, would already be present in the first half of the first year of life, before any language-specific behavior has been observed (the first one is vowel perception; see the next section). Interestingly, other studies with monolingual infants have also shown that by 5 months of age they are already able to make some discriminations within rhythmic group for stress-based languages, provided that the languages in the test belong to the native rhythmic class.

For instance, Jusczyk and collaborators found that 5-month-old American monolingual infants can discriminate between British English and Dutch (both stress based) and between two English dialects (British English and American English); however, they cannot distinguish between Dutch and German, again two stress-based languages (Nazzi, Jusczyk, & Johnson, 2000). This result is interesting because it indicates, as suggested by the authors, that the ability to make within-category discriminations emerges as a consequence of infants' gradual learning of the specific rhythmic features of the native language, and this ability is related to how similar the languages are when compared to the native language or native dialect. This discrimination capacity thus seems to be tied

to the specific characteristics of the native language representation, which gradually includes fine-grained details on the specific rhythmic and prosodic information of the language.

Parallel experiments have been done in our laboratory with syllable-based languages to assess further this perceptual refinement that seems to take place approximately from 2 to 5 months of age. Infants from monolingual Spanish and monolingual Catalan families have been analyzed in their capacities to discriminate between Catalan, Spanish, and Italian at 4.5 months of age (Bosch & Sebastián-Gallés, 2000b). These monolingual infants can distinguish not only Spanish from Catalan (see previous discussion in this section), but also Italian from Catalan; however, they cannot distinguish between Spanish and Italian. These particular results are interpreted not in terms of prosodic differences (which seem to be minimal, as data from low-pass-filtered materials with adult participants have suggested; Bosch & Sebastián-Gallés, 2002), but as a function of the specific frequency and distribution of vowels in the fluent speech of these three languages: Italian and Spanish would show a more similar distribution of vowel sounds than Catalan, a language in which central vowels /a/ and schwa count for more than half of the total number of vowels present in fluent speech.

These results emphasize the importance of distributional cues, segmental rather than prosodic, to help reach finer discriminations between the native language and a nonfamiliar one. This hypothesis is currently under exploration with the contrast between Spanish and Basque, a non-Indo-European language with a subject-object-verb (SOV) basic order. This pair of languages shows similar vowel repertoires and distributional properties of the segments; rhythmic and syntactic differences are notorious.[4]

Even though all these results have been obtained with monolingual infants, they are relevant in identifying the specific acoustic cues in the speech signal that are useful to discriminate languages and to start creating a native language representation that, through extended exposure, will become more and more refined. As for the bilinguals, the only studies in which a native language (one of them, the one spoken by the mother) has been contrasted with a nonfamiliar language have been developed in our laboratory.

Some evidence exists showing that 4.5- as well as 6-month-old bilingual infants do discriminate between their maternal language and English (syllable-based vs. stress-based languages), although their pattern of results is in clear contrast to the one obtained with monolingual infants (Bosch & Sebastián-Gallés, 1997, 2001a). Moreover, a language differentiation has also been observed between the maternal language and Italian, a within-category distinction not yet available for monolinguals at 4.5 months of age when Spanish and Italian are contrasted (Bosch & Sebastián-Gallés, 1997).

Altogether, the results seem to suggest that, in bilingual exposure, attention to specific prosodic and distributional cues of syllabic or segmental units in the speech signal may help the infant reach an early differentiation between the languages, although the specific mechanisms involved may vary for different pairs of different languages, and possible delays in differentiation might be observed even for languages quite different in prosodic terms. Refinement in the specification of the types of cues available must wait until new data are gathered from bilingual language acquisition studies.

It has been proposed (Cutler & Mehler, 1993; Mehler et al., 1996; Mehler & Christophe, 2000) that learning a particular language belonging to a specific rhythmic group in infancy has lasting consequences in the way adults perceive speech. According to these authors, individuals exposed to *stress* languages (like English or Dutch) would perceive the speech signal in a different way than speakers of *syllabic* languages (like French or Spanish). Different studies have made use of this cross-linguistic difference to analyze how bilinguals perceive their languages. But, let us see first what it means to perceive a language in a "syllable way."

It has been observed that, when performing a syllable detection task, native French listeners are faster when the target to detect coincides with the initial syllable of the carrier word. For example, when asked to detect the sequence /ba/ at the beginning of a French word like *balance* or *balcon,* French speakers are faster in the former case. Reaction times are reversed when the syllable to be detected is "bal" (Mehler, Dommergues, Frauenfelder, & Segui, 1981). In contrast, when English native listeners are asked to perform an equivalent task with stimuli like the English words *balance* and *balcony*, they do not show a syllable advantage effect; in fact, in several studies using this technique, English natives have failed to show any syllabic trace (Bradley, Sánchez-Casas, & García Albea, 1993; Cutler, Mehler, Norris, & Segui, 1983, 1986).

Cutler and colleagues also studied highly balanced French-English simultaneous bilinguals performing this task, both in English and in French (Cutler, Mehler, Norris, & Seguí, 1989, 1992). The results showed a complex configuration of results; basically, two different patterns were observed: Either participants behaved like English monolinguals (no syllabic effect in French and in English) or they showed a syllabic effect for French, but not for English materials. The authors concluded that the results were more consistent with the notion that, even for simultaneous bilinguals, there is a dominance of one language over the other (in their sample, the dominant language was most often the language of the mother).[5]

The consequences of these different parsing strategies of the speech signal caused by rhythmic differences across languages have also been observed in other experimental situations. It seems that the ability to adapt to time-compressed speech is also mediated by the rhythmic properties of the maternal language. In a series of experiments (Altmann & Young, 1993; Dupoux & Green, 1997; Mehler et al., 1993; Pallier, Sebastián-Gallés, Dupoux, Christophe, & Mehler, 1998; Sebastián-Gallés, Dupoux, Costa, & Mehler, 2000), it was shown that listeners can adapt to highly time-compressed sentences rather rapidly. In these experiments, participants are presented highly compressed utterances in a particular language (or condition), and they are asked either to listen passively to them or to try to transcribe as much as they can. After the habituation phase, participants are presented with a set of target sentences (in their maternal language), and they are asked to write them down (there can also be a control situation in which participants are not presented with any habituation sentences, and they are just asked to try to write down the test sentences).

Sebastian-Gallés et al. (2000) observed that transfer of adaptation occurred within rhythmic group languages, but not across rhythmic group languages; that is, listening to time-compressed Catalan, Italian, or Greek (three syllabic languages) helped Spanish natives better perceive the target Spanish time-compressed sentences than listening to time-compressed English or Japanese, languages not belonging to the syllabic group.[6] Pallier et al. (1998) reported no transfer for monolingual English speakers from adapting to time-compressed French, and they showed intermediate transfer (compared with habituation to English) with Dutch sentences.

In this last study, Pallier et al. (1998) also studied different groups of bilinguals. They studied two groups of Catalan-Spanish and English-French bilinguals (highly proficient in both languages, although they had learned the L2 in early child-hood, not from birth). The results showed that, even in the case of highly proficient bilinguals, transfer across rhythmic groups did not occur. That is, Spanish-Catalan bilinguals showed benefits from exposure to time-compressed Catalan when tested with time-compressed Spanish (and vice-versa). But, French-English bilinguals did not benefit from habituation to French and then tested in English and vice-versa.

The Discovery of the Building Blocks (Phonemes)

Monolingual infant research has shown that, as early as 6 months of age, infants show maternal language-specific phoneme perception behavior. Several studies have addressed the issue of the developmental changes in the perception of vowel and consonant contrasts. The pioneering work by Werker and Tees (1984) showed a decline in infants' sensitivity to nonnative phonetic contrasts during the first year of life. Canadian infants from English-speaking families were tested with an operant head-turn procedure on three different contrasts, one native (ba-da), and two nonnative (the Hindi retroflex/dental stop contrast and the Salish velar/uvular contrast). Although younger infants were all able to discriminate these three contrasts, by 8 to 10 months only some of the infants showed a sensitivity for the nonnative contrasts, and by 10–12 months of age infants were no longer able to discriminate any of the two nonnative contrasts; sensitivity remained only for the native contrast. These results were also subsequently replicated in a longitudinal study with fewer subjects, but the tendency was confirmed. Moreover, infants exposed to Hindi and Salish showed sensitivity to these contrasts by 12 months of age.

Other studies have also shown the same decline in sensitivity for consonants by the end of the first year of life in what has been called perceptual reorganization processes that result from linguistic experience (Best, 1994; Werker & Lalonde, 1988). In a different study, Best and collaborators tested different groups of infants with the apical/lateral Zulu click contrast; in this case, discrimination could be observed in infants of all age groups (and in adults) for these sounds that do not occur in English (Best, McRoberts, & Sithole, 1988). Thus, linguistic experience was not the only factor to take into account to explain these perceptual changes in the discrimination of consonant sounds. The specific properties of the sounds to be contrasted with respect to the frequently experienced sounds in the language of exposure make discrimination easily available because they cannot be assimilated to the native sounds, and they are possibly treated as "noises."

Similar perceptual reorganization processes have been identified for vowel sounds and at an earlier time in development. Work by Kuhl and collaborators showed language-specific effects on vowel perception by 6 months of age (Kuhl, Williams, Lacerda, Stevens, & Lindblom, 1992). American and Swedish infants performed differently in a discrimination task involving either the American /i/ or the Swedish /y/ as the background stimulus contrasted with different variants of these two prototypical exemplars. Discrimination was reduced for exemplars around the prototypical vowel of the native language (/i/ for American infants and /y/ for Swedish infants), thus indicating that linguistic experience was already playing a role in the building of the first native language vowel categories. The native language magnet model fully accounts for these language-specific perceptual biases that reflect the role of language exposure (Kuhl, 1998, 2000). A different study has also addressed the issue of infants' vowel perception changes; in general terms, the results are congruent with the notion of an earlier decline for vowels (by 6–8 months of age) than for most of the consonants (Polka & Werker, 1994; but see Polka & Bohn, 1996, for a controversial result).

Support for these language-specific changes in vowel and consonantal perception has been obtained by electrophysiological studies. The study of electric brain responses to selected vowel stimuli offers evidence of age-related changes in mismatch negativity (MMN)[7] amplitude measures that are interpreted as a consequence of the phonemic status certain sounds gradually acquire during the second semester of life (Cheour et al., 1998). Other research has addressed the analysis of the processing steps involved in the discrimination of phonemes (mainly consonants by means of syllable presentation), showing at least two processing stages corresponding to an increasingly refined analysis of the auditory input in the temporal lobes where phonetic changes are detected (Dehaene-Lambertz & Dehaene, 1994).

The study of perceptual reorganization processes and the development of language-specific sound categories in bilinguals have been addressed in our laboratory. For bilingual children, the outcome of these perceptual reorganization processes should be compatible with the existence of two sound systems corresponding to the two languages in their environment. If the attunement to the phonetic contrasts in the native language takes place during the second semester of life, earlier for vowel sounds than for consonants, and if we agree that in many bilingual situations a general language differentiation can be reached before 6 months of age, then no great differences would be expected when exploring the sound discrimination capacities in monolingual and bilingual infants.

However, first results in our laboratory revealed a specific developmental pattern in the bilingual group not found in the monolingual population (Bosch & Sebastián-Gallés, 2003b).

Infants at 4 and 8 months old from monolingual (Spanish or Catalan) and bilingual (Spanish-Catalan) environments were tested with a familiarization-preference procedure on a vowel contrast present only in Catalan: /e/–/ɛ/ (/ˈdedi/ vs. /ˈdɛdi/). Not surprisingly, younger infants were all able to perceive this contrast, independent of the language of exposure, because at that young age they respond in an acoustic rather than a phonemic way. However, by 8 months, only infants from Catalan monolingual environments succeeded, and although a decline in sensitivity was expected for the monolingual Spanish group, the bilingual results were clearly unexpected because Catalan was one of the ambient languages. An additional group of bilingual infants, by now 12 months of age, was also tested to analyze the stability and time course of this particular pattern of response. Results from this additional experiment at 12 months of age indicated that bilinguals finally achieved discrimination, and their behavior was similar to that found in monolinguals 4 months younger (Bosch & Sebastián-Gallés, 2003b).

These results challenge the view that mere exposure is enough to maintain the capacity to perceive a contrast and suggest specific perceptual reorganization processes and a different time course in infants who have to cope with the building of two separate systems. It is possible to argue that the specific Catalan contrast tested was particularly problematic because it partially overlaps with the single midfront vowel /e/ of the Spanish system. Thus, it might be argued that discrimination cannot be easily reached in this case, as if the infants were judging the stimuli as tokens of the same "word," in the same way as Spanish infants were responding to this experiment. (However, there was nothing in the test situation that might suggest to the infant that the stimuli belonged to one specific language, so an interpretation of the results based on infants having adopted a "Spanish perceptual way of listening" to the material cannot be a priori supported.)

A simpler interpretation can derive from a distributional account. Infants exposed to Catalan and Spanish hear an increased number of Spanish /e/ vowel tokens compared to the two Catalan midfront vowels (Bosch & Sebastián-Gallés, 2003b), altogether forming a unimodal distribution that reduces discrimination, as suggested by the work of Maye, Werker, and Gerken (2002). Consequently, discrimination cannot be initially reached until some mechanism triggers differentiation; one possible candidate is the gains in lexical knowledge usually observed by the end of the first year of life. If this is correct, then similar processes should be observed for other vowel contrasts, especially those that are infrequent or that do not perfectly overlap when both systems are compared. More recent data in our laboratory exploring the discrimination capacities for other vowel contrasts suggest that this explanation may be right, with infants showing the same reduced discrimination pattern by 8 months and reaching the contrastive categories by 12 months of age (Bosch & Sebastián-Gallés, 2003a).

A similar trend has been observed in work by Werker and collaborators (Burns, Werker, & McVie, 2002). In a series of experiments, they investigated the developmental time course and nature of infant phonetic representations relative to the phonetic category boundaries for [b], [p], and [pʰ]. When comparing monolingual and bilingual infants, differences arose by 10–12 months of age, when monolinguals had already placed the category boundary in the appropriate location for their native language, and bilinguals still did not show a categorization compatible with either one or both of their native languages. However, later in time, that is, by 14–21 months of age, bilinguals showed evidence of either categorizing the stimuli as monolinguals in one of their two languages or finally having the boundaries that correspond to both of the languages of exposure (French and English). The parallelism between this study and our work with vowel discrimination in bilinguals lies in the fact that, at a certain age (8 months in the vowel study and 10–12 months in the consonant boundary study), infants from bilingual environments seemed to be still in the process of organizing (or reorganizing) their phonetic representations, and their discrimination capacities thus were, temporarily, delayed compared with monolinguals.

If tuning the phoneme system to the maternal language occurs very rapidly and with a reduced amount of exposure (it takes place within a few months), this does not seem to be the case for adults when learning new sound categories. Probably the most explored domain within phonological processing in bilinguals and L2 learners is that of the processing of nonnative phonemes. There are two different groups of questions that need to be addressed in this field. First, it must be explained why it is so difficult to perceive some foreign contrasts and why difficulties are not "universal," but depend on the first language (L1) of the listener. These questions relate to the "static" aspects of the relationship between an already-existing phonetic system and the one to be acquired. Second, what is the impact of the age of exposure (and the amount of exposure) on the adult level of competence in the L2, and what are the consequences of the acquisition of a second sound system on the already-existing one? These last questions refer to the dynamics of the learning process.

Two different models have been developed to address these questions, the perceptual assimilation model of Best and Strange (Best, 1994, 1995; Best & Strange, 1992) and the speech learning model (SLM) of Flege (1992, 1995, 2003). Although the first model exclusively deals with the first set of problems, the second model stresses the importance of the dynamic factors. Basically, both models make similar predictions when referring to the particular relationships between L1 and L2 (static aspects), although from quite different theoretical perspectives. Summarizing their proposals, both models assume that the ease or difficulty with which two phonemes will be discriminated will depend on the similarities and differences between L1 and L2 phonemes.

In particular, Best's model proposes three types of perceptual assimilations: (a) the new L2 sound will be assimilated to an already existing (L1) category as a more or less good realization; (b) it will be perceived as a new sound; or (c) it can be perceived as a nonlinguistic sound (like when listeners of English or Spanish hear the Zulu clicks). According to this model, when two contrastive L2 sounds are assimilated to a single L1 category, but are equally deviant (or equally acceptable) from the L1 sound, they will be very hard to distinguish (as happens with the popular example of the difficulties of Japanese listeners in perceiving the English /r–l/ contrast).

The SLM adds to this level of explanation the dynamic aspects that address the issues of the impact of the age of acquisition of the L2 and the amount of use of the L1. One important characteristic of this model is that, for Flege, the capacity to acquire new phonemes remains intact all life long; therefore, at least theoretically, it should be possible, at any moment in life, to learn any new L2 sound. It would justify a whole chapter (and a book) to cover in a minimally comprehensive way the literature existing in this domain. Instead, we concentrate on an apparent paradox that exists when some behavioral and neurophysiological measures are compared.

Recent research, mostly using electrophysiological measures, has shown that the human auditory system keeps a high degree of plasticity to learn new speech sounds. One first group of studies refers to the comparison of event-related potential (ERP) signatures (in particular, MMN) to maternal and foreign languages. Different studies (Näätänen et al., 1997; Phillips et al., 1995; Rivera-Gaxiola, Csibra, Johnson, & Karmiloff-Smith, 2000; Sharma & Dorman, 2000; Winkler et al., 1999) have shown that the MMN for a deviant that crosses a phonemic boundary (which is categorized as a distinct linguistic unit) is larger than the MMN for a deviant that falls within a phonemic boundary (which is categorized as a different token of the same phoneme as the standard). That is, MMNs are larger for between-category contrasts and smaller for within-category ones. Unfortunately, these studies have never been done, to our knowledge, with either early (and highly proficient bilinguals) or simultaneous bilinguals, so it is unknown if, with extended exposure (and learning), nonnative contrasts can elicit MMN of the same amplitude as native ones.

Although the dynamics of extended exposure have never been addressed, several studies have analyzed the impact of short-term training. In these studies, monolingual individuals were trained with difficult L2 contrasts (nonexisting in their own language). ERP signatures were measured before and after training and after each training phase. Tremblay and coworkers (Tremblay, Kraus, Carrell, & McGee, 1997; Tremblay, Kraus, & McGee, 1998) observed that training resulted in a significant increase in the amplitude of the MMN (a characteristic that the studies reviewed in the preceding paragraph have shown to distinguish between native and foreign contrasts). Importantly, these changes were lateralized to the left, and they generalized to new, nontrained contrasts, indicating that they were not restricted just to the trained sounds.

Taken together, these data indicate that, as the SLM model postulates, the auditory system of adults keeps a high degree of plasticity. Then, the question that remains is to understand why with natural stimuli and with very early and extensive exposure many bilinguals fail to acquire new phonetic categories. The feeling that most bilinguals and L2 learners have is that acquiring new phonetic categories is not an easy task; on the contrary, both everyday experience and behavioral research seem to point just in the opposite direction.

Several studies performed in our laboratory with highly skilled Spanish-Catalan bilinguals raised as monolinguals for the first 3–6 years of their lives, but who from this age on had been exposed to both languages intensively and who received all their education in a bilingual system, have shown that a large percentage of this population totally fails in learning a nonnative contrast. In particular, we have extensively tested the perception of the Catalan-specific contrast /e–ɛ/ by Spanish-dominant bilinguals (Spanish only has one /e/ vowel falling roughly between Catalan /e–ɛ/). Using a wide variety of tasks (categorical perception, gating, odd-ball discrimination, among others), both with synthesized and natural tokens, presented in isolation or within word contexts, Spanish-dominant bilinguals systematically failed to perceive the contrast (Bosch, Costa, & Sebastian-Gallés, 2000; Pallier, Bosch, & Sebastián, 1997; Pallier, Colomé, & Sebastián-Gallés, 2001; Sebastián-Gallés & Soto-Faraco, 1999).[8] Results pointing in the same direction have been obtained in other studies (Mack, 1989) with French-English bilinguals and a consonantal contrast. That is, these results show that, for those difficult contrasts, as predicted by both Best's perceptual assimilation model and Flege's SLM model, the influence of the first exposure is not easily overcome.

One possible explanation could be that, once the window of opportunity is gone, only laboratory training in highly controlled situations may help in these circumstances (but see Takagi, 2002; Takagi trained monolingual Japanese listeners to identify English /r/ and /l/ in a quite intensive way and concluded that "truly native like identification of /r/ and /l/ may never be achieved by adult Japanese learners of English," p. 2887).

In research in our laboratory, Echeverría (2002) indicated that this is not the case. Echeverría trained Spanish-dominant Spanish-Catalan bilinguals (who had acquired Catalan before the age of 4 years and who were highly proficient in both languages) both with synthesized and natural stimuli, using two different training techniques: the *fading technique* (Jamieson & Morosan, 1986) with synthesized

materials, similar to the one used in the Tremblay et al. (1997, 1998) studies, and the *high variability* procedure developed by Lively and coworkers (Lively, Logan, & Pisoni, 1993; Lively, Pisoni, Yamada, Tohkura, & Yamada, 1994; Logan, Lively, & Pisoni, 1991) with natural tokens.

In both techniques, participants are asked to identify stimuli as belonging to one category or the other. One interesting characteristic of Echeverría's study is that, contrary to previous studies, the evaluation of the perceptual capacities of the bilinguals was not restricted to the stimuli or tasks used in the training phases. Indeed, bilingual perceptual competence was also assessed using several tasks: gating, identification, discrimination, and lexical decision. Tasks were classified either as directly related with the training (i.e., the task to be performed was an identification task, the same as the one used in the training) or as indirectly related with the training (i.e., discrimination, gating, and lexical decision).

The results showed that Spanish-dominant bilinguals increased their perceptual capacities in the posttest in a percentage similar to those previously observed with the same techniques and materials. However, the improvement was restricted to the tests directly related to the training. No trace of improvement was observed in the posttest for the tasks indirectly related with the training. Furthermore, the improvement faded away for almost all of the tasks when participants were retested 6 months later. This fact is particularly relevant because, contrary to most training studies (in particular, Lively et al., 1993, 1994; Logan et al., 1991; Tremblay et al., 1997), the individuals were trained in a contrast that was produced in their environment, and thus they had all the opportunities after training was completed to use the acquired contrast in their ordinary life.

Getting Stress: Some Suprasegmentals

It has been suggested that, in the same way that nonnatives may show great difficulties in perceiving contrasting phonemes not existing in the maternal language, this may apply to other speech dimensions. One aspect that has been particularly analyzed and for which data on bilinguals have been gathered is that of the perception of stress.

Languages differ not only in their phonemic inventory, but also in the presence or absence of lexical stress. English and Spanish are languages that have "contrastive stress"; that is, pairs of stimuli just differing in the position of their stress (*forbear–forebear* in English and *sábana–sabána* in Spanish) can be found. On the contrary, French is a "fixed-stress" language in that all content words bear stress on the last syllable. Although the ability to perceive differences between pairs of syllables just differing in one phoneme seems to be present at birth (at least for a vast majority of the phonemes), the empirical evidence that newborns can discriminate stimuli on the basis of stress is not conclusive.

Newborns (French) have been shown to be sensitive to changes in stress when tested with the high-amplitude sucking paradigm on disyllabic phonetically unvaried words (['mama] vs. [ma'ma]), on trisyllabic consonant-varied words (['takala] vs. [ta'kala]), and on two sets of disyllabic words varied in consonants but keeping the same vowel [a] in all syllables (Sansavini, Bertoncini, & Giovanelli, 1997). So, newborns' processing of stress does not seem to be affected by consonant variations, but no published work has reported the same ability for stimuli in which the vowel sounds are changed. On the contrary, it has been suggested that vowel variations might affect the processing of stress patterns, because of the perceptual saliency of vowels (Sansavini, 1994).

Although no concluding data exist on newborns and very young infants, several studies have shown the preference for certain stress patterns and the usefulness of stress cues in word segmentation tasks in older infants. Monolingual data, mainly from English-learning infants, just indicated that by 9 months of age, but not earlier, they showed a "trochaic bias" in their listening preferences; that is, they preferred to listen to lists of words with a strong–weak pattern over lists consisting of words with a iambic or weak–strong pattern (Jusczyk, Friederici, Wessels, Svenkerud, & Jusczyk, 1993). Echols, Crowhurst, and Childers (1997) also replicated the trochaic preferences in 9-month-olds but not in younger infants, and they showed the easiness of segmenting trochaic sequences over iambic ones at this age.

Research by Morgan and Saffran (Morgan, 1994; Morgan & Saffran, 1995) also examined the role of rhythm in grouping syllabic units in the input and showed how a trochaic pattern seems to produce greater cohesiveness in the perception of disyllables at 8 and 9 months of age. In general, the failure to observe a preference for a specific rhythmic pattern in younger infants of 6–7 months of age has been interpreted as an indication that it

may result from experience with the language because in English the disyllabic trochee is a frequent word type. Preference studies with infants learning languages with words that do not predominantly follow the trochee would shed light on this issue.

The question still remains whether stress discrimination follows a developmental pattern similar to the one found in the contrastive sound category formation, that is, with an initial period of a general sensitivity to perceive stress changes in any direction followed by a language-specific attunement that should determine perceptual differences between native speakers of languages with a fixed stress and speakers of languages with contrastive stress. Less is even known at present about the specific time course and nature of the stress discrimination abilities in the case of bilingual infants.

In contrast to this lack of concluding evidence from the developmental studies, adult research has shown parallel results in the perception of stress with those observed in the domain of segment perception. Dupoux, Christophe, Sebastian-Gallés, and Mehler (1997) observed that Spanish and French natives showed contrasting results in performing an ABX task with nonwords that contrasted in the position of the stressed syllables. In this experiment, participants were presented with pairs of CVCVCV strings (uttered by Dutch natives, so they sounded "foreign" for all subjects), and then they were asked to decide if a third stimulus sounded like the first or the second one. Stimuli pairs differed either in the position of stress (/'tamido/ vs. /ta'mido/) or in one phoneme (/tamido–pamido/). In the latter case, the contrast existed in both languages, and thus both populations were expected to perform equally well. However, if French participants had difficulties in perceiving the position of stress, they should perform worse than the Spanish ones. This is indeed what was found. French participants were significantly worse than Spanish ones, but just in the stress condition and not in the phoneme condition.

These data have been confirmed by Dupoux, Peperkamp, and Sebastián-Gallés (2001), who used a short-term memory task. In this task, participants were asked to memorize and repeat sequences of different length (from 2 to 6) composed of random alternations of members of minimal pairs. Pairs were dissyllabic nonwords differing in either one phoneme or in the position of the stress (/tuku–tupu/ and /'mipa–mi'pa/). This task totally separated French and Spanish participants in that there was no overlap between the scores obtained by native

French and native Spanish participants (scores were estimated by calculating the percentage of stress errors minus the percentage of phoneme errors). Because of this sharp contrast between the performance of both types of populations, this task seemed particularly suited to study the perception of stress in French-Spanish bilinguals.

Peperkamp, Dupoux, and Sebastián-Gallés (2002) studied two groups of French-Spanish bilinguals with this technique (although with different materials and only sequences of four tokens). One of the groups was composed of native-simultaneous bilinguals; individuals in this group had one parent who spoke French, and the other spoke Spanish; thus, they had learned both languages at the same time from birth. The other group of participants was composed of late learners, native French speakers who had learned Spanish after the age of 10 years. Preliminary data showed that the late learners displayed the same pattern as the French monolinguals not exposed to Spanish. In fact, Peperkamp et al. analyzed separately the results of a group of late learners who had a very high command of Spanish (but who nonetheless did learn it after the age of 10), and they also failed to perceive stress in a comparable way as French monolinguals. More interesting, the data of the French-Spanish simultaneous bilinguals indicated that only about 60% of them were similarly competent in performing the phoneme and the stress conditions (the "native Spanish" pattern). That is, in spite of exposure to Spanish from birth, about 40% of the simultaneous bilinguals were "stress deaf" in a similar way as French monolinguals.

To summarize, although the developmental pattern of the acquisition of some suprasegmental information, specifically stress, is not conclusive, adult research is showing similarities in the processing difficulties observed in nonnative and bilingual individuals. It is not possible at present to give an explanation of either the developmental or adult results (but see Peperkamp & Dupoux, 2002, for a proposal). Models developed to account for adult segment perception cannot be applied in a straightforward manner to the domain of stress processing. For instance, in explaining why some phonemes are particularly difficult for speakers of a specific language to learn, the relative distance of the segments of the maternal language plays a crucial role. Because of the very nature of stress, it is not possible to postulate difficulties in terms of "stress distance," at least not in the same way as for phonemes.

Building the Lexicon: Phonotactics

During the second half of the first year of life, infants acquire different types of phonological knowledge, most of which will be used to segment words in the speech stream. One particular type of knowledge concerns the sequencing of segments occurring within words (and between words). That is, they will compute the transitional probabilities of segments within and across word boundaries (Friederici & Wessels, 1993; Jusczyk, Luce, & Charles-Luce, 1994). Prosodic cues initially, but also phonotactic and allophonic sources of information later, can be reliably used in conjunction to segment words correctly from fluent speech from 10.5 months of age (Jusczyk, Hohne, & Bauman, 1999; Myers et al., 1996).

Because all these different sources of information are language specific (for instance, the prototypical stress value of English words is on the initial syllable; the prototypical stress value of Spanish words is on the penultimate syllable), bilingual infants should compute two different sets of statistics for each language to segment the speech signal properly into words and develop appropriate lexicons for each of their languages. Thus, beyond prosodic information cues that may offer an initial and rudimentary way of segmenting speech in word units (for infants exposed to languages prosodically similar, this cue may not be very informative as a way to separate the two lexicons), building separate phonotactic knowledge for each language could be considered an important step into constructing the lexicon.

To our knowledge, only one study has addressed this issue, comparing monolingual and bilingual infants in a head-turn preference procedure with lists of nonwords that were phonotactically either legal or illegal in just one of the languages of exposure for the bilingual infants (Sebastián-Gallés & Bosch, 2002). The infants tested were 10-month-old Spanish monolinguals, Catalan monolinguals, and Spanish-Catalan bilinguals (half of them Catalan dominant and the other half Spanish dominant). The stimuli were CVCC nonwords, some of them legal in Catalan and some of them illegal in Catalan (because Spanish does not allow for final word complex codas, all stimuli were illegal in this language). Following previous results by Friederici and Wessels (1993) and Jusczyk et al. (1994) that had shown 9-month-old infants' sensitivity to legal and to frequent phonotactic patterns in the speech they hear, the aim of this study was to analyze the building of phonotactic knowledge in bilingual infants exposed to two languages with similar prosodic structure, but with a few differing phonotactic patterns.

It is reasonable to think that infants exposed to two languages during the first year of their lives have less exposure to each language than monolingual infants. Thus, it could be the case that bilingual infants are less sensitive to certain phonotactic patterns of their environmental languages because they have fewer chances to observe them. It is also plausible to hypothesize that sensitivity is developed toward the common sound patterns in both languages, even if the languages can be distinguished. On the other hand, the opposite tendency could be observed: Attending to differential sound patterns would become a strategy to exploit because this could help infants increase the perceptual distance between the languages of exposure. Consequently, two different outcomes were possible, one suggesting a delay in bilinguals and the other suggesting a similar developmental trend for bilinguals and monolinguals. Furthermore, as there were two groups of bilinguals in this study, classified according to the language more frequently spoken by their mother, a third possibility also existed, with bilinguals showing a language dominance already at this early age. In this case, only the Catalan-dominant group would behave similarly to the Catalan monolingual group of infants.

The results obtained fit better with this last possibility: Spanish monolingual infants showed no preference for either type of stimuli. Catalan monolingual and Catalan-dominant bilingual infants showed a similar pattern of preference for legal over illegal sequences, although Spanish-dominant bilingual infants showed an ambiguous pattern halfway between the Catalan and the Spanish monolingual groups. Thus, the results are more consistent with the notion of an early language dominance in infants raised in a bilingual environment, although complete support for this hypothesis would require further research in which Spanish-dominant bilinguals would also show a pattern of preference for some language-specific structure present only in Spanish.

In this same study, adult Spanish-Catalan bilinguals were also examined. The participants, although highly proficient bilinguals (of the same type as those described above) were not exposed from birth to both languages (Catalan-dominant bilinguals had only been exposed to Catalan during early childhood, in the same way as Spanish-dominant bilinguals had only been exposed to Spanish early in life). Using a subset of the same materials as those in the infant studies, two different tasks were employed: a phoneme-monitoring task and a modified gating task (in the version employed in the experiment, participants were given two alternatives, and they had to chose one of them). The rationale behind these experiments was that, if Spanish-dominant bilinguals had not properly acquired Catalan phonotactics, they would perform equally with both types of materials (both in monitoring the consonants and in doing the gating task). In contrast, Catalan-dominant bilinguals should take advantage of the restrictions imposed by the phonology of their maternal language in what can constitute a final word complex coda and perform better with legal than with illegal stimuli.

The results partially supported this hypothesis. Catalan-dominant bilinguals performed better: They were more accurate in rejecting consonants in illegal than in legal nonwords in the phoneme-monitoring task, and they identified earlier the legal stimuli in the gating task. But, Spanish-dominant bilinguals also showed this pattern of results. However, in both tasks the advantage of legal over illegal stimuli was larger for the Catalan-dominant than for the Spanish-dominant bilinguals, indicating that although both groups of participants had acquired the Catalan phonotactic constraints, those individuals who had been exposed to this language in the first years of their lives still showed an advantage over those who had been exposed to it in their early childhood.

Weber (2002) also addressed the question of the processing of phonotactic information, although in the context of lexical access. Weber (2000, 2002) studied the recognition of English words by native listeners and skilled nonnative listeners (German L1). It has been shown that the fact that some phoneme sequences never occur at the beginning of a word in a particular language is used as a reliable cue to signal a potential word onset; in particular, the fact that some phonemes never co-occur within a syllable would signal a potential word boundary between those phonemes.

For instance, McQueen (1998) observed that Dutch natives found it more difficult to detect the word *rok* (skirt) when it appeared in the sequence /fi.drok/ than in the sequence /fim.rok/. Weber used analogous materials and tasks to compare English natives and German-English late bilinguals. She observed that English natives found it easier to spot "lunch" embedded in *moyshlunch* than in *moycelunch* because no English word starts or ends in "shl": *Moyshlunch* will activate no competitors overlapping with "lunch," and it will be relatively easily detected. In contrast, many English words begin with "sl"; thus, *moycelunch* will activate many potential competitors, making recognition slower (as compared with *moyslunch*). However, in German the sequence probabilities are reversed. No German words begin or end with "sl," but many begin with "shl-." German natives showed the opposite pattern from the English natives. One explanation would be that the native vocabulary is activated by the nonnative input. This leads us to the last group of studies addressing the question of the representation and processing of phonology in bilinguals.

Building-up One or Two Lexicons? The Representation of Words

It is surprising that, although there is extensive literature on morphosyntax (see De Houwer, chapter 2, this volume, for a review) and on the development of the productive lexicon in bilingual infants, data on the development of the receptive lexicon are very sparse. As we show next, the same situation appears to hold for studies of auditory lexical access: There is a large number of studies on visual lexical access in adult bilinguals, but the data on the auditory modality are scarce.

Jusczyk and Aslin (1995) showed that the ability to segment words from fluent speech was present by 7.5 months of age, and that this ability involved rather detailed phonetic knowledge because, when words were modified by just one feature in their initial consonant (cup → tup) they were no longer recognized. This ability was explored in bilingual infants from French/English environments (Polka, Sundara, & Blue, 2002). Initial results indicated that there is no delay in this ability when bilinguals are compared to monolinguals (infants in both groups were 7.5 months old), and that the bilinguals are able to segment disyllabic words in both of the languages of exposure, in this case, rhythmically different languages with different stress patterns in words (trochaic in English and iambic in French). If the tendency observed in a small sample is eventually confirmed, then it will be necessary to analyze further whether bilinguals are developing separate strategies for segmenting words in each of the languages of exposure (behaving as monolinguals in each of the languages) or whether they rely on particular types of segmentation cues that could be useful in both languages, thus relying on strategies rather different from the ones found in monolinguals.

What kind of information do infants use to recognize a word? Most models of adult word recognition (see discussion further in this section) consider that adults are highly sensitive to fine-grained phonetic detail (potential word candidates are "penalized"—in ways that differ depending on the model—when subphonemic mismatches between the speech input and the lexical representation occur). How fine is the phonetic information that infants use to recognize words? Considering the reduced size of infant vocabularies, it could be the case that no such fine-grained detail is needed (at least not until a certain vocabulary size is reached).

There is now an extended body of work, mainly developed by Werker and colleagues, that shows the continuity between the prelexical phonetic categories developed during the second semester of life and the use of these categories in the functional representations of words once the child has started to develop a receptive lexicon. Also, spoken word recognition studies with 18- to 23-month-olds suggested that children's representations of familiar words are phonetically well specified (Swingley & Aslin, 2002). However, some controversial results were obtained (Stager & Werker, 1997) that showed an inefficient use of language-specific sensitivities when mapping sound onto meaning. That is, infants of 14 months of age failed to map two novel words forming a minimal pair (/bih–dih/) to two different objects, although able to perceive the contrast when the words were not linked to objects. Then, in a series of follow-up experiments, it was shown that this inability was no longer present at 17 and 20 months of age. A possible explanation for this temporary deficit was that it was the consequence of the computational demands of the word-learning situation. It was further suggested that more expert word learners (either older children or children with a bigger productive vocabulary size) should be better able to pick up fine phonetic detail, and this hypothesis was confirmed (Werker & Fennell, 2004).

Werker and colleagues also explored the behavior of bilingual children in this word-learning task. According to their hypothesis of a resource limitation that interferes with the ability to learn minimal pairs, the bilingual population seems suitable to explore this hypothesis further, especially if considering the increasing demands of having to acquire two lexical systems simultaneously. Results indicated that they not only showed a similar difficulty by 14 months of age, but also were still experiencing the same difficulty by 17 months of age, when most monolinguals were already able to learn the minimally different words correctly (Fennell & Werker, 2000). So, despite having to deal with two different language systems, the bilingual children did not use more phonetic detail in learning phonetically similar object labels. Access to phonological detail seems to be reached later in bilinguals than in monolinguals, at least in this word-learning task. Further research with a different methodological approach is required before firmly establishing this position.

As stated, the data on auditory lexical access in adults is not very extensive. Although different models for (monolingual) auditory word recognition have been postulated (Gaskell & Marslen-Wilson, 1997; Luce & Pisoni, 1998; McClelland & Elman, 1986; Norris, 1994), to our knowledge, there is no operating model for bilingual auditory word recognition. Until very recently, the only existing works were the pioneering studies of François Grosjean that resulted in the proposal of the bilingual interactive model of lexical access (Grosjean, 1988; Léwy & Grosjean, 1996, 1999). This model is based on the architecture proposed by McClelland and Elman in the TRACE model. It assumes the existence of two separate language networks, independent but interconnected at the same time. Although developed to account for bilingual lexical access in general, the arguments for both assumptions rely on arguments about language selection and code-switching situations. For Grosjean and Léwy, both networks needed to be independent because bilinguals are able to speak just one language without any effort. Also, networks need to be interconnected because bilinguals can easily switch from one language to the other. Although the model makes interesting assumptions about the way phonology is represented (it assumes a single feature level, but separate phoneme levels, duplicating common phonemes), we do not review it here because its central goals fall out of the scope of this chapter (see Thomas & Van Heuven, chapter 10, this volume, for further details).

Different studies have addressed questions that tackle in a more specific way the relationship between phonology and lexical representation. Pallier et al. (2003) used a repetition priming technique to study the representation of minimal pairs in L2 in Spanish-Catalan bilinguals. As said here, most Spanish-dominant Spanish-Catalan bilinguals have

difficulties in perceiving some Catalan-specific contrasts. The question Pallier et al. addressed was whether Catalan minimal pairs like /per[ə]–pɛr[ə]/ (meaning "pear" and "Peter") could be represented as homophones.

Alternatively, it could be the case that lexical entries would also represent the acoustic information present in the signal, as has been postulated by episodic models (Goldinger, 1996) and by the work of Tremblay et al. (1998) mentioned above, which suggests that no conscious awareness would be needed to perceive nonnative contrasts. In this way, /per[ə]–pɛr[ə]/ could constitute separate phonological lexical entries even for those Spanish-dominant Spanish-Catalan bilinguals. If Spanish-dominant bilinguals had shared lexical phonological entries for the words of Catalan minimal pairs like /per[ə]–pɛr[ə]/, in a repetition priming paradigm they should show equivalent repetition savings when one member of the pair was preceded by itself or by the other member of the pair; that is, the amount of facilitation of /per[ə]/ preceded by /per[ə]/ or by /pɛr[ə]/ should be the same. But, if they had separate entries, there should be no repetition savings when the other member of the pair was presented before; this pattern of results should not differ from that of Catalan-dominant bilinguals, who do perceive the contrast. This is indeed what was found. Spanish-dominant bilinguals showed equivalent repetition effects with exact repetitions and with minimal pairs, but Catalan-dominant bilinguals only showed repetition effects when the same word was presented twice.

Another relevant line of research is that initiated by Spivey and Marian (1999), who analyzed auditory lexical access in Russian-English (late) bilinguals. In this study, participants were simultaneously presented with four objects; following auditory instructions, they were asked to pick up one of them (the target) and place it at a specific location while eye movements were recorded. Critically, in one condition, one of the distractor objects had a translation that shared initial phonetic features with the target word (the interlingual distractor); for instance, if participants were instructed in Russian to pick up the stamp (*marku* in Russian), one of the distractors was a marker. The results showed that bilinguals looked briefly to the interlingual distractor object more often than to a control object bearing no phonetic relationship to either the target word or its translation. These results indicated that, in spite of a totally monolingual mode, bilinguals activate both auditory lexicons.

Marian, Spivey, and Hirsch (2003) replicated and extended their results measuring both eye tracking and brain activation with functional magnetic resonance imaging. Weber and Cutler (Weber, 2002; Weber & Cutler, 2004) also used a procedure similar to Spivey and Marian's, obtaining parallel results with (late) Dutch-English bilinguals. Weber and Cutler also made use of this procedure to explore if nonnatives were restrictive (as natives are) in using fine phonetic information to access words in their nondominant language. In this second series of experiments, they presented figures containing, for instance, a parrot, a pirate, a strawberry, and a duck. After hearing "Click on the pa..." the percentage of gazes to pirate, strawberry, and duck were equivalent, indicating that the mismatch between the acoustic input "pa" and the beginning of "pirate" had been enough to discard this object as a potential candidate. In another condition, the target object and one of the competitors constituted a vowel pair that is usually difficult to be discriminated by Dutch listeners, for instance, the initial vowels of the words "paddle" and "pedal." In this case, after listening to "Click on the pa...," the number of gazes to both objects were equivalent, indicating that the vowel mismatch had not been enough to discard the distractor object.

The experiments of Pallier et al. (2003) and Weber and Cutler (Weber, 2002; Weber & Cutler, 2004) revealed that skilled and less-skilled bilinguals, because of insufficiently precise phonetic discrimination, activate the L2 lexicon in a less-restrictive way than native listeners. Therefore, delayed recognition for nonnative words should be expected because of the existence of more competitors (or homophones) for the L2. Although Weber and Cutler concluded from their data the existence of this less-efficient lexical selection for L2, the results of Pallier et al. indicated that there were no differences in the lexical decision times between Spanish-dominant and Catalan-dominant bilinguals. There are several possibilities to account for this apparent paradox. One possibility would be that the bilinguals studied in both studies were not equivalent in their proficiency: It is quite likely that the Spanish-Catalan bilinguals are more proficient in their L2 than the Dutch-English bilinguals of the study of Weber and Cutler. Another possibility would be that the lexical decision task includes a decision stage not present in the eye-monitoring paradigm, and that the small disadvantage observed by Weber and Cutler was not detectable in the lexical decision task.

Conclusion

In this chapter, a review of the research on phonological processing in bilinguals has been presented. In doing so, many important questions, some of them mentioned in the introduction, have been left out. Before concluding, we briefly comment on some of these "neglected" topics.

One neglected domain has been that of individual differences. Yet, a striking feature of learning an L2 is the sharp contrast between individuals who seem to master their different languages in an equivalent and nativelike way and those individuals who, even if exposed to their L2 very early and very intensively, keep on having great difficulties with it all of their lives. Different proposals have been advanced, ranging from motivational aspects to personality differences (see Shehan, 1989, and Michael & Gollan, chapter 19, this volume, for a review). Golestani, Paus, and Zatorre (2002), using voxel-based morphometry, have uncovered structural brain differences between good and poor phoneme learners. Although we are far from understanding what determines these differences, the use of these new imaging techniques opens new windows to explore their causes.

But, the results of imaging experiments are not always easy to accommodate within the existing knowledge of speech processing in bilinguals. Research with both behavioral and electrophysiological measures has shown that important differences exist in the way bilinguals process their two languages; however, these differences have not been easily observed with imaging data. Perani et al. (1996, 1998; see also Abutalebi et al., chapter 24, this volume) have argued that proficiency—at the moment of test—and not age of acquisition is the most relevant factor affecting the bilingual language system at the level of the neural substrate.

It is surprising that imaging techniques have failed to capture the important differences that behavioral and electrophysiological research have uncovered, particularly in the domain of phonological processes, as a function of the maternal language. One possible source of this failure is that the time resolution of imaging studies may be insufficient at this stage to show these differences because images correspond to the activation obtained in several seconds (sometimes over 1 minute), but most phonological processes take place within milliseconds.

Another possibility is that what these studies show is related to changes in brain organization as a consequence of the automatization of different processes. That is, as in any other cognitive domain, less-skilled bilinguals have to devote more effort to process their L2 than more skilled bilinguals. Research with brain imaging techniques in other cognitive domains (for instance, the work of Raichle et al., 1994, with a verbal task) has shown that when a new task becomes automatic, it is not just performed more rapidly in the same brain structures, but that a real transfer to other brain areas occurs; thus, important reorganization takes place.

A last possibility is that proficiency and age of acquisition may be affecting different processes involved in language processing. It may be that more "core" linguistic knowledge, like different aspects of phonology and grammar, are more sensitive to age of acquisition differences. For instance, Wartenburger and colleagues (2003), studying grammatical processing of Italian-German bilinguals, found that it was age of acquisition and not proficiency that determined how L1 and L2 were represented in the brain.

Brain imaging techniques undoubtedly enable new and interesting ways to investigate language acquisition and processing, but careful attention needs to be paid to the kinds of linguistic knowledge that are in every moment under study.

Finally, the importance of the early exposure followed by an "interruption" of this exposure has been addressed in two studies. In the first one, Pallier et al. (2003) studied forgetting the maternal language in a group of adult Koreans who were adopted by French families in childhood and who never again were exposed to Korean. The data of this study showed that there were no remaining signs of Korean in either behavioral tests (language identification and word recognition) and imaging data (listening to sentences in four different languages while performing a fragment detection task). The only observed difference between French natives and the adopted Koreans was obtained in the imaging task, when the activation patterns to French sentences in both populations were compared: The activation covered a larger brain area in the native French subjects than in the adopted ones. The authors interpreted this difference as indicating that, although an L1 can be forgotten and a L2 thus replace the first, this replacement is not complete.

The other study was reported by Au, Knightly, Jun, and Oh (2002), who analyzed the effects of exposure to an L2 during early childhood (and subsequently not again for a long period of time) on (re)learning this L2. In this study, two different linguistic domains were explored: phonology and morphosyntax. Savings of early exposure were observed, but only for phonological aspects of language processing and not for morphosyntax. The particular interests of this study are that it indicated that the language system cannot be considered as a whole, and that the impact of early (and continued) exposure on its different subsystems, because of the specific brain areas involved, may vary.

To summarize, in this chapter we reviewed various pieces of work that give evidence of the adaptation of the human brain to handle two sound systems. The impact of this bilingual exposure has been shown at different levels of phonological processing. However, the precise nature of the way the bilingual brain deals with this exposure needs further research to be understood fully.

Acknowledgments

Preparation of this chapter was facilitated by a grant from the James S. McDonnell Foundation (Bridging Brain, Mind, and Behavior Program), by BSO2001-3492-C04-01 grant from the Spanish Ministerio de Ciencia y Tecnología and by a grant from the Catalan Government (2001SGR00034).

Notes

1. There is an ongoing debate about the existence of critical periods in L2 learning (see, for instance, Birdsong, chapter 6, this volume, and DeKeyser & Larson-Hall, chapter 5, this volume). The interesting research from the domain of biology under development in this area (see Knudsen, 2003) should not be neglected.

2. Before starting, let us say a few words about what will be understood as "a bilingual" and the different subtypes. We do not focus our presentation on L2 learners with a relatively poor competence in their L2. Ideally, we would have liked just to consider individuals extremely proficient in both languages, that is, individuals who use both languages in an equivalent way in all aspects of their lives. Then, within this group, we would distinguish between simultaneous and successive bilinguals. However, the data in some aspects of phonology are quite scarce, and less-proficient bilinguals will be considered when necessary.

3. To our knowledge, the precise consequences of an early versus late differentiation have not been thoroughly analyzed, and the implications in terms of the unfolding of the first steps in the language acquisition processes remain still unclear.

4. Preliminary data indicated that discrimination cannot be reached, neither at 4 months nor at 6 months of age, using different experimental procedures. If these data are confirmed, the hypothetical use of the language discrimination capacities in newborns and infants in helping to establish some syntactic knowledge should be revised.

5. The authors proposed an explanation in terms of markedness. They suggested that syllable segmentation is a marked speech-processing routine, and that it would develop only "when the language which encourages use of the marked routine dominates the language which encourages use of the unmarked routine" (Cutler et al., 1989, p. 160).

6. French, a syllabic language, gave an intermediate pattern of results, falling between English and the other syllabic languages.

7. The MMN is an event-related potential (ERP) component that is elicited when a "different" stimulus (the deviant) is presented in the context of a repeated series of particular stimuli (the standard). One particularly interesting property of this measure for the research in L2 phonological processes is that it does not require consciousness.

8. This is not to say that no Spanish-dominant bilingual perceived the contrast, but that as a group they did not. Depending on the task, between 10% and 25% of Spanish-dominant bilinguals fell within the range of the Catalan-dominant group.

References

Abercrombie, D. (1967). *Elements of general phonetics*. Edinburgh, U.K.: Edinburgh University Press.

Altmann, G. T. M., & Young, D. (1993, September). *Factors affecting adaptation to time-compressed speech*. Paper presented at the Eurospeech '93, Berlin, Germany.

Au, T. K., Knightly, L. M., Jun, S., & Oh, J. S. (2002). Over hearing a language during childhood. *Psychological Science, 13*, 238–243.

Best, C. T. (1994). The emergence of native-language phonological influence in infants: A perceptual assimilation model. In J. C. Goodman & H. C. Nusbaum (Eds.), *The development of speech perception: The transition from speech sounds to spoken words* (pp. 167–224). Cambridge, MA: MIT Press.

Best, C. T. (1995). A direct realist view of cross-language speech perception. In W. Strange (Ed.), *Speech perception and linguistic experience* (pp. 171–206). Baltimore: York Press.

Best, C. T., McRoberts, G. W., & Sithole, N. N. (1988). The phonological basis of perceptual loss for non-native contrasts: maintenance of discrimination among Zulu clicks by English-speaking adults and infants. *Journal of Experimental Psychology: Human Perception and Performance, 14*, 345–360.

Best, C. T., & Strange, W. (1992). Effects of language-specific phonological and phonetic factors on cross-language perception of approximants. *Journal of Phonetics, 20*, 305–330.

Bosch, L., Costa, A., & Sebastián-Gallés, N. (2000). First and second language vowel perception in early bilinguals. *European Journal of Cognitive Psychology, 12*, 189–222.

Bosch, L., & Sebastián-Gallés, N. (1997). Native-language recognition abilities in four-month-old infants from monolingual and bilingual environments. *Cognition, 65*, 33–69.

Bosch, L., & Sebastián-Gallés, N. (2000a, July). *Coping with two languages: Early differentiation and beyond*. Paper presented at the International Workshop on Speech Perception Development in Early Infancy: Behavioural, Neural-Modelling and Brain Imaging Data, Barcelona, Spain.

Bosch, L., & Sebastián-Gallés, N. (2000b, July 19–20). *Exploring 4-month-old infants' abilities to discriminate languages from the same rhythmic class*. Paper presented at the International Conference on Infant Studies, Brighton, UK.

Bosch, L., & Sebastián-Gallés, N. (2001a). Early language differentiation in bilingual infants. In J. Cenoz & F. Genesee (Eds.), *Trends in bilingual acquisition* (pp. 71–93). Amsterdam: Benjamins.

Bosch, L., & Sebastián-Gallés, N. (2001b). Evidence of early language discrimination abilities in infants from bilingual environments. *Infancy, 2*, 29–49.

Bosch, L., & Sebastián-Gallés, N. (2003a, April 30–May 3). *Developmental changes in the discrimination of vowel contrasts in bilingual infants*. Paper presented at the Fourth International Symposium on Bilingualism, Arizona State University, Tempe.

Bosch, L., & Sebastián-Gallés, N. (2003b). Simultaneous bilingualism and the perception of a language specific vowel contrast in the first year of life. *Language and Speech, 46*, 217–243.

Bradley, D. C., Sánchez-Casas, R., & García-Albea, J. E. (1993). The status of the syllable in the perception of Spanish and English. *Language and Cognitive Processes, 8*, 197–233.

Burns, T. C., Werker, J. F., & McVie, K. (2002, November). *Development of phonetic categories in infants raised in bilingual and monolingual environments*. Paper presented at the Boston University Conference on Language Development, Boston, MA.

Cheour, M., Ceponiene, R., Lehtokoski, A., Luuk, A., Allik, J., Alho, K., et al. (1998). Development of language-specific phoneme representations in the infant brain. *Nature Neuroscience, 1*, 351–353.

Christophe, A., Guasti, M. T., Nespor, M., Dupoux, E., & Van Ooyen, B. (1997). Reflections on phonological bootstrapping: its role for lexical and syntactic acquisition. *Language and Cognitive Processes, 12*, 585–612.

Cutler, A., & Mehler, J. (1993). The periodicity bias. *Journal of Phonetics, 21*, 103–108.

Cutler, A., Mehler, J., Norris, D., & Seguí, J. (1983). A language-specific comprehension strategy. *Nature, 304*, 159–160.

Cutler, A., Mehler, J., Norris, D., & Segui, J. (1986). The syllable's differing role in the segmentation of French and English. *Journal of Memory and Language, 25*, 385–400.

Cutler, A., Mehler, J., Norris, D., & Seguí, J. (1989). Limits on bilingualism. *Nature, 320*, 229–230.

Cutler, A., Mehler, J., Norris, D. G., & Segui, J. (1992). The monolingual nature of speech segmentation by bilinguals. *Cognitive Psychology, 24*, 381–410.

Dehaene-Lambertz, G., & Dehaene, S. (1994). Speed and cerebral correlates of syllable discrimination in infants. *Nature, 370*, 292–295.

Dupoux, E., Christophe, A., Sebastián-Gallés, N., & Mehler, J. (1997). A distressing deafness in French. *Journal of Memory and Language, 36*, 406–421.

Dupoux, E., & Green, K. (1997). Perceptual adjustment to highly compressed speech: Effects of talker and rate changes. *Journal of Experimental Psychology: Human Perception and Performance, 23*, 914–927.

Dupoux, E., Peperkamp, S., & Sebastián-Gallés, N. (2001). A robust method to study stress "deafness." *Journal of the Acoustical Society of America, 110*, 1606–1618.

Echeverría, S. (2002). *El aprendizaje de contrastes fonéticos no nativos: Límites y reversibilidad.* Unpublished doctoral thesis, Universitat de Barcelona, Spain.

Echols, C. H., Crowhurst, M. J., & Childers, J. B. (1997). The perception of rhythmic units in speech by infants and adults. *Journal of Memory and Language, 36*, 202–225.

Fennell, C. T., & Werker, J. F. (2000, July). *Does bilingual exposure affect infants' use of phonetic detail in a word learning task?* Poster presented at the ICIS 2000 meeting, Brighton, U.K.

Flege, J. E. (1992). Speech learning in a second language. In C. A. Ferguson, L. Menn, & C. Stoel-Gammon (Eds.), *Phonological development: Models, research and implications* (pp. 565–604). Timonium, MD: York.

Flege, J. E. (1995). Second language speech learning: Theory, findings and problems. In W. Strange (Ed.), *Speech perception and linguistic experience* (pp. 233–272). Baltimore: York.

Flege, J. E. (2003). Assessing constraints on second-language segmental production and perception. In N. Schiller & A. Meyer (Eds.), *Phonetics and phonology in language comprehension and production* (pp. 319–355). Berlin, Germany: Mouton de Gruyter.

Friederici, A. D., & Wessels, J. M. I. (1993). Phonotactic knowledge and its use in infant speech perception. *Perception & Psychophysics, 54*, 287–295.

Gaskell, M. G., & Marslen-Wilson, W. (1997). Integrating form and meaning: A distributed model of speech perception. *Language and Cognitive Processes, 12*, 613–656.

Goldinger, D. S. (1996). Words and voices: Episodic traces in spoken word identification and recognition memory. *Journal of Experimental Psychology: Learning, Memory, and Cognition, 22*, 1166–1183.

Golestani, N., Paus, T., & Zatorre, R. J. (2002). Anatomical correlates of learning novel speech sounds. *Neuron, 35*, 997–1010.

Grosjean, F. (1988). Exploring the recognition of guest words in bilingual speech. *Language and Cognitive Processes, 3*, 233–274.

Guasti, M. T., Nespor, M., Christophe, A., & Van Ooyen, B. (2001). Pre-lexical setting of the head-complement parameter through prosody. In J. Weissenborn & B. Hoehle (Eds.), *How to get into language: Approaches to bootstrapping early language development* (pp. 231–248). New York: Benjamin.

Jamieson, D. G., & Morosan, D. E. (1986). Training non-native speech contrasts in adults: Acquisition of English /q/–/ð/ contrast by francophones. *Perception and Psychophysics, 40*, 205–215.

Jusczyk, P. W., & Aslin, R. N. (1995). Infants' detection of sound patterns of words in fluent speech. *Cognitive Psychology, 29*, 1–23.

Jusczyk, P. W., Friederici, A. D., Wessels, J., Svenkerud, V. Y., & Jusczyk, A. M. (1993). Infants' sensitivity to the sound patterns of native language words. *Journal of Memory and Language, 32*, 402–420.

Jusczyk, P. W., Hohne, E. A., & Bauman, A. (1999). Infants' sensitivity to allophonic cues for word segmentation. *Perception and Psychophysics, 61*, 1465–1476.

Jusczyk, P. W., Luce, P. A., & Charles-Luce, J. (1994). Infants' sensitivity to phonotactic patterns in the native language. *Journal of Memory and Language, 33,* 630–645.

Knudsen, E. I. (2003). Early experience and critical periods. In L. R. Squire, F. E. Bloom, S. K. McConnell, J. L. Roberts, N. C. Spitzer, & M. J. Zigmond (Eds.), *Fundamental neuroscience* (2nd ed., pp. 555–573). New York: Academic Press.

Kuhl, P. (1998). The development of speech and language. In T. J. Carew, R. Menzel, & C. J. Shatz (Eds.), *Mechanistic relationships between development and learning* (pp. 53–73). New York: Wiley.

Kuhl, P. (2000). Language, mind, and brain: Experience alters perception. In M. S. Gazzaniga (Ed.), *The new cognitive neurosciences* (2nd ed., pp. 99–115). Cambridge, MA: MIT Press.

Kuhl, P. K., Williams, K. A., Lacerda, F., Stevens, K. N., & Lindblom, B. (1992). Linguistic experience alters phonetic perception in infants by 6 months of age. *Science, 255,* 606–608.

Léwy, N., & Grosjean, F. (1996). *A computational model of bilingual lexical access.* Unpublished manuscript, Neuchâtel University, Switzerland.

Léwy, N., & Grosjean, F. (1999, April). *BIMOLA: A computational model of bilingual spoken word recognition.* Paper presented at the Second International Symposium on Bilingualism, University of Newcastle upon Tyne, Newcastle, U.K.

Lively, S. E., Logan, J. S., & Pisoni, D. B. (1993). Training Japanese listeners to identify English /r/ and /l/. II. The role of phonetic environment and talker variability in learning new phonetic categories. *Journal of the Acoustic Society of America, 94,* 1242–1255.

Lively, S. E., Pisoni, D. B., Yamada, R. A., Tohkura, Y., & Yamada, T. (1994). Training Japanese listeners to identify English /r/ and /l/ III. Long-term retention of new phonetic categories. *Journal of the Acoustic Society of America, 96,* 2076–2087.

Logan, J. S., Lively, S. E., & Pisoni, D. B. (1991). Training Japanese listeners to identify English /r/ and /l/: A first report. *Journal of the Acoustic Society of America, 89,* 874–886.

Luce, P. A., & Pisoni, D. B. (1998). Recognizing spoken words: The neighborhood activation model. *Ear and Hearing, 19,* 1–36.

Mack, M. (1989). Consonant and vowel perception and production: Early English-French bilinguals and English monolinguals. *Perception and Psychophysics, 46,* 189–200.

Marian, V., Spivey, M., & Hirsch, J. (2003). Shared and separate systems in bilingual language processing: Converging evidence from eyetracking and brain imaging. *Brain and Language, 86,* 70–82.

Maye, J., Werker, J. F., & Gerken, L. A. (2002). Infant sensitivity to distributional information can affect phonetic discrimination. *Cognition, 82,* B101–B111.

McClelland, J. L., & Elman, J. L. (1986). The TRACE model of speech perception. *Cognitive Psychology, 18,* 1–86.

McQueen, J. (1998). Segmentation of continuous speech using phonotactics. *Journal of Memory and Language, 39,* 21–46.

Mehler, J., & Christophe, A. (2000). Acquisition of Languages: Infant and adult data. In M. S. Gazzaniga (Ed.), *The new cognitive neurosciences* (pp. 897–908). Cambridge, MA: MIT Press.

Mehler, J., Dommergues, J. Y., Frauenfelder, U., & Segui, J. (1981). The syllable's role in speech segmentation. *Journal of Verbal Learning and Verbal Behavior, 20,* 298–305.

Mehler, J., Dupoux, E., Nazzi, T., & Dehaene-Lambertz, G. (1996). Coping with linguistic diversity: the infant's viewpoint. In J. L. Morgan & K. Demuth (Eds.), *Signal to syntax* (pp. 101–116). Mahwah, NJ: Erlbaum.

Mehler, J., Jusczyk, P. W., Lambertz, G., Halsted, G., Bertoncini, J., & Amiel-Tison, C. (1988). A precursor of language acquisition in young infants. *Cognition, 29,* 143–178.

Mehler, J., Sebastián-Gallés, N., Altmann, G., Dupoux, E., Christophe, A., & Pallier, P. (1993). Understanding compressed sentences: The role of rhythm and meaning. *Annals of the New York Academy of Sciences* (Vol. 682, pp. 272–282). New York: New York Academy of Sciences.

Morgan, J. L. (1994). Converging measures of speech segmentation in preverbal infants. *Infant Behavior and Development, 17,* 389–403.

Morgan, J. L., & Saffran, J. R. (1995). Emerging integration of sequential and suprasegmental information in preverbal speech segmentation. *Child Development, 66,* 911–936.

Myers, J., Jusczyk, P. W., Kemler-Nelson, D. G., Charles Luce, J., Woodward, A., & Hirsh-Pasek, K. (1996). Infants' sensitivity to word boundaries in fluent speech. *Journal of Child Language, 23,* 1–30.

Näätänen, R., Lehtokoski, A., Lennes, M., Cheour, M., Huotilainen, M., Livonen, A., et al. (1997). Language-specific phoneme representations revealed by electric and magnetic brain responses. *Nature, 385,* 432–434.

Nazzi, T., Bertoncini, J., & Mehler, J. (1998). Language discrimination by newborns: towards an understanding of the role of rhythm. *Journal of Experimental Psychology: Human Perception and Performance, 24,* 756–766.

Nazzi, T., Jusczyk, P. W., & Johnson, E. K. (2000). Language discrimination by English-learning 5-month-olds: Effects of rhythm and familiarity. *Journal of Memory and Language, 43,* 1–19.

Norris, D. (1994). Shortlist: A connectionist model of continuous speech recognition. *Cognition, 52,* 189–234.

Pallier, C., Bosch, L., & Sebastián, N. (1997). A limit on behavioral plasticity in vowel acquisition. *Cognition, 64,* B9–B17.

Pallier, C., Colomé, À., & Sebastián-Gallés, N. (2001). The influence of native-language phonology on lexical access: Exemplar-based vs. abstract lexical entries. *Psychological Science, 12,* 445–449.

Pallier, C., Dehaene, S., Poline, J.-B., LeBihan, D., Argenti, A.-M., Dupoux, E., et al. (2003). Brain imaging of language plasticity in adopted adults: Can a second language replace the first? *Cerebral Cortex, 13,* 155–161.

Pallier, C., Sebastián-Gallés, N., Dupoux, E., Christophe, A., & Mehler, J. (1998). Perceptual adjustment to time-compressed speech: A cross-linguistic study. *Memory and Cognition, 26,* 844–851.

Peperkamp, S., & Dupoux, E. (2002). A typological study of stress "deafness." In C. Gussenhoven & N. Warner (Eds.), *Papers in laboratory phonology 7* (pp. 203–240). Berlin, Germany: Mouton de Gruyter.

Peperkamp, S., Dupoux, E., & Sebastián-Gallés, N. (2002, October). *Stress "deafness" in early and late French-Spanish bilinguals.* Paper presented at the Structure of Learner Language, Kolymbari, Greece.

Perani, D., Dehaene, S., Grassi, F., Cohen, L., Cappa, S., Dupoux, E., et al. (1996). Brain processing of native and foreign languages. *NeuroReport, 7,* 2439–2444.

Perani, D., Paulesu, E., Sebastián-Gallés, N., Dupoux, E., Dehaene, S., Bettinardi, V., et al. (1998). The bilingual brain: Proficiency and age of acquisition of the second language. *Brain, 121,* 1841–1852.

Phillips, C., Marantz, A., McGinnis, M., Pesetsky, D., Wexler, K., Yellin, A., et al. (1995). Brain mechanisms of speech perception: A preliminary report. *MIT Working Papers in Linguistics, 26,* 125–163.

Polka, L., & Bohn, O. S. (1996). A cross-language comparison of vowel perception in English-learning and German-learning infants. *Journal of the Acoustic Society of America, 100,* 577–592.

Polka, L., Sundara, M., & Blue, S. (2002, June). *The impact of language experience on word recognition.* Paper presented at the 143rd meeting of the Acoustic Society of America, Pittsburgh, PA.

Polka, L., & Werker, J. F. (1994). Developmental changes in perception of non-native vowel contrasts. *Journal of Experimental Psychology: Human Perception and Performance, 20,* 421–435.

Posner, M., Rothbart, M., Farah, M., & Bruer, J. (Eds.). (2001). The developing human brain [Special issue]. *Developmental Science, 4*(3).

Raichle, M. E., Fiez, J. A., Videen, T. O., Ma-cLeod, A. M. K., Pardo, J. V., Fox, P. T., et al. (1994). Practice-related changes in human brain functional anatomy during nonmotor learning. *Cerebral Cortex, 4,* 8–26.

Ramus, F., Hauser, M. D., Miller, C., Morris, D., & Mehler, J. (2000). Language discrimination by human newborns and by cotton-top tamarin monkeys. *Science, 288,* 349–351.

Ramus, F., Nespor, M., & Mehler, J. (1999). Correlates of linguistic rhythm in the speech signal. *Cognition, 73,* 265–292.

Rivera-Gaxiola, M., Csibra, G., Johnson, M., & Karmiloff-Smith, A. (2000). Electrophysiological correlates of cross-linguistic speech perception in native English speakers. *Behavioural Brain Research, 111,* 13–23.

Sansavini, A. (1994). *Percezione della prosodia del linguagio nei primi giorni di vita* [Perception of the prosody in the first days of life]. Unpublished doctoral thesis, Università di Bologna, Italy.

Sansavini, A., Bertoncini, J., & Giovanelli, G. (1997). Newborns discriminate the rhythm of multisyllabic stressed words. *Developmental Psychology, 33,* 3–11.

Sebastián-Gallés, N., & Bosch, L. (2002). The building of phonotactic knowledge in bilinguals: The role of early exposure. *Journal of Experimental Psychology: Human Perception and Performance, 28,* 974–989.

Sebastián-Gallés, N., Dupoux, E., Costa, A., & Mehler, J. (2000). Adaptation to time-compressed speech: Phonological determinants. *Perception and Psychophysics, 62,* 834–842.

Sebastián-Gallés, N., & Soto-Faraco, S. (1999). On-line processing of native and non-native phonemic contrasts in early bilinguals. *Cognition, 72,* 112–123.

Sharma, A., & Dorman, M. F. (2000). Neurophysiologic correlates of cross-language phonetic perception. *Journal of the Acoustical Society of America, 107,* 2697–2703.

Shehan, P. (1989). *Individual differences in second-language learning.* London: Arnold.

Spivey, M. J., & Marian, V. (1999). Cross talk between native and second languages: Partial activation of an irrelevant lexicon. *Psychological Science, 10*, 281–284.

Stager, C. L., & Werker, J. F. (1997). Infants listen for more phonetic detail in speech perception than in word-learning tasks. *Nature, 388*, 381–382.

Swingley, D., & Aslin, R. N. (2002). Lexical neighborhoods and the word-form representations of 14-month-olds. *Psychological Science, 13*, 480–484.

Takagi, N. (2002). The limits of training Japanese listeners to identify English /r/ and /l/: Eight case studies. *Journal of the Acoustic Society of America, 111*, 2887–2896.

Toro, J. M., Trobalón, J. B., & Sebastián-Gallés, N. (2003). The use of prosodic cues in language discrimination tasks by rats. *Animal Cognition, 6*, 131–136.

Tremblay, K., Kraus, N., Carrell, T., & McGee, T. (1997). Central auditory system plasticity: Generalization to novel stimuli following listening training. *Journal of the Acoustical Society of America, 6*, 3762–3773.

Tremblay, K., Kraus, N., & McGee, T. (1998). The time course of auditory perceptual learning: neurophysiological changes during speech-sound training. *NeuroReport, 9*, 3557–3560.

Wartenburger, I., Heekeren, H. R., Abutalebi, J., Cappa, S. F., Villringer, A., & Perani, D. (2003), Early setting of grammatical processing in the bilingual brain, *Neuron, 37*, 159–170.

Weber, A. (2000, May). *The role of phonotactics in the segmentation of native and non-native continuous speech.* Paper presented at the Workshop on Spoken Access Processes, Max Planck Institute for Psycholinguistics, Nijmegen, The Netherlands.

Weber, A. (2002). *Language-specific listening: The case of phonetic sequences.* Unpublished doctoral thesis, Katholieke Universiteit Nijmegen, The Netherlands.

Weber, A., & Cutler, A. (2004). Lexical competition in non-native spoken-word recognition. *Journal of Memory and Language, 50*, 1–25.

Werker, J. F., & Fennell, C. T. (2004). Listening to sounds versus listening to words: Early steps in word learning. In D. G. Hall & S. Waxman (Eds.), *Weaving a lexicon* (pp. 79–111). Cambridge, MA: MIT Press.

Werker, J. F., & Lalonde, C. E. (1988). Cross-language speech perception: Initial capabilities and developmental change. *Developmental Psychology, 24*, 672–683.

Werker, J. F., & Tees, R. C. (1984). Cross-language speech perception: Evidence for perceptual re-organization during the first year of life. *Infant Behavior and Development, 7*, 49–63.

Winkler, I., Lehtoksoki, A., Alku, P., Vainio, M., Czugler, I., Csepe, V., et al. (1999). Pre-attentive detection of vowel contrasts utilizes both phonetic and auditory memory representations. *Cognitive Brain Research, 7*, 357–369.

Robert DeKeyser
Jenifer Larson-Hall

5

What Does the Critical Period Really Mean?

ABSTRACT   A large amount of empirical evidence shows that age of acquisition is strongly negatively correlated with ultimate second language proficiency for grammar as well as for pronunciation. It is even doubtful that any evidence exists at this point of any person having learned a second language perfectly in adulthood. Some researchers have rightly pointed out that correlation is not causation, and that the age effect may be caused by confounded variables such as quantity and quality of input, amount of practice, level of motivation, and other social variables. Many studies, however, have shown that these variables play a very limited role when the effect of age of acquisition is removed statistically, but age of acquisition keeps playing a large role when the social and environmental variables are removed. Other researchers have objected to a "critical period" interpretation of such age effects because these do not show the discontinuities that would be expected under the critical period hypothesis. We argue here, however, that quite a few studies have documented discontinuities, and that their absence in some studies may be because of a variety of confounding variables and other methodological problems. Assuming there is indeed a maturational decline in second language learning capacity during childhood, then there is a need to investigate whether this decline affects competence, performance, or both and what the ultimate cause of this decline is. Increasingly, evidence points toward fundamental maturational changes in certain aspects of memory. The challenge for critical period researchers is to tie such changes to both specific neurological antecedents and specific psycholinguistic corollaries. Regardless of one's view of the critical period, it is important not to overinterpret its implications for educational practice. The observation that "earlier is better" only applies to certain kinds of learning, which schools typically cannot provide. Therefore, the implication of critical period research seems to be that instruction should be adapted to the age of the learner, *not* that learners should necessarily be taught at a young age.

If there is anything about second language (L2) acquisition with which the average layperson is familiar, it is probably the "younger is better" phenomenon, both because of the personal experience of countless immigrants and their families and because of the institutional push in certain quarters for either early immersion or foreign language in the elementary school. Yet, an explanation of this phenomenon continues to elude the experts. In the last few years, some have engaged in spirited debates about it (e.g., Marinova-Todd, Marshall, & Snow, 2000, 2001, vs. Hyltenstam & Abrahamsson, 2001;

or DeKeyser, 2000, vs. Bialystok, 2002); others have been extremely cautious in their literature reviews (see especially Scovel, 2000; Singleton, 2001).

The reason why age of acquisition (AoA) differences and their implications continue to arouse so much interest among L2 acquisition researchers and applied linguists is probably that they are seen as central to both practical and theoretical concerns. In the practical realm, the younger is better argument has been both used and abused, both refuted and misunderstood by advocates of early intervention from the very beginnings of formal immersion education to this day (Marinova-Todd et al., 2000; Patkowski, 1994; Penfield & Roberts, 1959; see especially Scovel, 1988). The younger is better phenomenon has also been given a number of far-reaching theoretical interpretations, stretching from cognitive psychology (see, e.g., Newport 1990), to neurology (e.g., Long, 1990; Pinker, 1995; Pulvermüller & Schumann, 1994; Scovel, 1988; Ullman, 2001; Walsh & Diller, 1981), to evolutionary theory (e.g., Hurford, 1991; Hurford & Kirby, 1999).

The origins of the modern debate[1] about AoA in L2 learning are usually traced back to Penfield's epilogue on "the learning of languages" in Penfield and Roberts's (1959) book *Speech and Brain-Mechanisms*. In the 1950s and 1960s, the neurologist Penfield was a staunch advocate of early immersion education (see Scovel, 1988), but the researcher whose name became most strongly associated with the issue of age in language learning is Lenneberg, whose 1967 book *Biological Foundations of Language* contains the first use of the term *critical period* (CP) in the context of language acquisition (p. 158, pp. 175 ff.). A number of authors have suggested that this term has too absolute a ring to it, and that *optimal* or *sensitive* would be a better term than critical, but the term critical has stuck and is the only one we use in what follows, without necessarily implying an absolute end point for all language acquisition. See Oyama (1978) and Schachter (1996) for more discussion of the terms *critical* and *sensitive* and Scovel (1988) for further discussion of the history of the CP debate in the 20th century.

Terminological squabbles aside, it is important to be clear about what we mean by CP. Far too often, in our opinion, the idea of a CP is rejected because of specific interpretations of it, rather than because of the core idea. In particular, a number of authors seem to think that the term should be rejected if no clear cause for the younger is better phenomenon can be found in what is known about neurological development (e.g., Flege, 1987; Snow, 1987) or if processing rather than representation is at issue (e.g., McDonald, 2000). We adhere to a broader interpretation of the term, which does not prejudge its causes and is more in line with Lenneberg's (1967) definition: It is "automatic acquisition from mere exposure" that "seems to disappear after this age" (p. 176), regardless of the exact nature of the underlying maturational causes. As Oyama (1978) put it:

It is a developmental phenomenon not in that it is "determined by the genes" in some rigid or

direct way, but rather insofar as it reflects an intricate sequence of interactions between the developing phenotype and the environment, which is sufficiently typical of the species that it appears despite individual differences and widely varying experiences. (p. 10)

More specifically, we use the term *critical period hypothesis* (CPH) in this chapter to designate the idea that language acquisition from mere exposure (i.e., implicit learning), the only mechanism available to the young child, is severely limited in older adolescents and adults.

The hypothesis applies to both first language (L1) acquisition and SLA. Evidence from L1 acquisition not only is the most dramatic, but also—fortunately—is limited in quantity. Until fairly recently, it consisted of hard-to-interpret findings about "feral" children, who had largely failed to acquire language at an older age having been deprived of normal input during the CP. The best-documented cases are Victor, the "wild boy of Aveyron" (Lane, 1976), Genie (Curtiss, 1977), and Chelsea (Curtiss, 1988), but even in these cases, it was impossible to determine to what extent extreme social deprivation, maybe even food deprivation or sensory deprivation, may have been confounded with language input deprivation. In the last 15 years or so, more systematic research with deaf children born to hearing parents, and therefore deprived of good signed input until grade school or later, has demonstrated the strength of the AoA effect when lack of input was not confounded with extreme forms of social deprivation: The older the age of first exposure to American Sign Language is, the worse the ultimate attainment is (Emmorey, Bellugi, Friederici, & Horn, 1995; Grimshaw, Adelstein, Bryden, & MacKinnon, 1998; Mayberry, 1993; Mayberry & Eichen, 1991; Newport, 1990). Evidence about how the hypothesis applies to ultimate attainment in SLA is discussed in detail in the remainder of this chapter.

The hypothesis does not apply, however, to rate of acquisition. Since Krashen, Long, and Scarcella (1979) stressed the difference between rate of learning and ultimate attainment, this distinction has been generally accepted. The fact that adults or adolescents seem faster or at least no slower in the initial stages of acquisition compared to children (for morphosyntax, Slavoff & Johnson, 1995, and Snow & Hoefnagel-Höhle, 1978; for phonology, Ekstrand, 1976; Fathman, 1975; Harley, 1986; Loewenthal & Bull, 1984; Morris & Gertsman, 1986; Olson & Samuels, 1973; and Thogmartin,

1982) has no direct bearing on the CPH, even though ultimately the two phenomena (i.e., faster initial acquisition but more limited ultimate attainment by older learners) may be due to the same underlying cause, as is argued below.

In what follows, then, we largely restrict the discussion to ultimate attainment in SLA. We first present a fairly detailed and systematic summary of empirical findings and then discuss possible interpretations.

Empirical Findings on Age of Acquisition and Second Language Acquisition

The Basic Argument: Age of Acquisition–Proficiency Correlations

Evidence From Oral Grammaticality Judgment Tests Since the late 1970s, studies have been accumulating that document a strong negative correlation between AoA and L2 proficiency. A variety of techniques have been used to assess L2 proficiency in this kind of research, but the most commonly used instrument has been grammaticality judgments of auditorily presented stimulus sentences. In part, this is because of the visibility of Johnson and Newport's (1989) study, which led to a number of replications or semireplications. Johnson and Newport (1989) had a sample of Chinese or Korean speakers listen to 276 short English sentences and judge them as correct or incorrect. The sentences were designed to represent 12 basic grammar structures of English. Johnson and Newport found a correlation of $-.77$ between AoA and L2 proficiency ($-.87$ for AoA below 16 and $-.16$ for AoA above 16).

Other studies have found correlations that were not as high, but similar (see Table 5.1), not only with native speakers of Korean and Chinese, but also with speakers of Vietnamese, Spanish, Hungarian, and Russian. Although most studies used the number of items correct (or the error rate) on the grammaticality judgment test (GJT) as the only outcome variable, three others also documented the reaction time (RT; R. Kim, 1993; McDonald, 2000; Shim, 1993). All found negative correlations between AoA and test score and positive correlations with error rate or RT. A number of studies also presented correlations of length of residence (LoR) with proficiency or correlations of AoA with

proficiency after LoR was partialed out. They typically found that AoA is a much better predictor than LoR—DeKeyser (2000) even found a zero correlation for LoR and proficiency—with the one exception of proficiency in terms of error rate in the work of Shim (1993), for which LoR was a better predictor than AoA.

In conclusion, all the studies that used grammaticality judgments of auditory stimuli found a moderate to very strong negative correlation between AoA and L2 proficiency. In most cases, there was a strong decline up to a certain age and a leveling off for adults or a strong decline around puberty with little age differentiation within the child and adult groups. The studies of Bialystok and Miller (1999) and Birdsong and Molis (2001) were the only ones that found a strong AoA effect within the adult group. In the former study, this may have been because of the very low LoR of some members of the adult group, which means their test results were not representative of ultimate attainment. In the latter study, the correlation appears to be largely because of two outliers (two of the five oldest members of the group had extremely low scores).[2] The majority of studies, then, clearly documented a decline (of considerably varying degree) during childhood, followed by a low to zero correlation through adulthood.

Evidence From Other Tests of Morphosyntax Written GJTs have tended to yield lower, but still significant, AoA–proficiency correlations (see Table 5.2). Especially interesting are the correlations obtained with the oral and written presentation of the same stimuli. Johnson (1992), with the same stimuli as in Johnson and Newport (1989) and the same subjects tested a year later, found an AoA-GJT correlation of $-.54$ for the group as a whole and $-.73$ for AoA less than 15 (as opposed to $-.77$ and $-.87$, respectively, for oral presentation). Jia (1998) found an AoA-GJT correlation of $-.35$ for written presentation (as opposed to $-.68$ for oral presentation). Bialystok and Miller (1999), however, found no significant correlation with AoA for written presentation (the actual r was not reported).

A couple of studies used written grammaticality judgments only and did not calculate correlations between AoA and GJT scores, but simply compared the mean scores for different AoA groups: Coppieters (1987) and Sorace (1993) found significant differences between natives and adult acquirers (in Coppieters's case, there was even no overlap between natives and nonnatives), in spite of the fact

Table 5.1 Correlations Between Age of Acquisition (AoA) and Second Language (L2) Proficiency as Measured by Oral Grammaticality Judgment Tests

Study	L1	L2	LoR Range	n	AoA Range	r Between AoA and L2	Remarks
Johnson and Newport, 1989	Chinese + Korean	English	3–26	46	5–39	−.77 −.87 −.16	For all learners For AoA < 16 For AoA > 16
Johnson and Newport, 1991	Chinese	English	5–15	21	4–16	−.63	All AoA < 16
R. Kim, 1993	Korean	English	Minimum 3	30	3–35	.66 .55	For error rate For reaction time
Shim, 1993	Korean	English	5–21	60	0–29	.45 .71	For error rate For reaction time
Jia, 1998	Various	English	5–32	105	3–34	−.68	
Flege, Yeni-Komshian, and Liu, 1999	Korean	English	Minimum 8	240	1–23	−.71 −.23	For AoA < 15 For AoA > 15
Bialystok and Miller, 1999	Chinese	English	1–18	33	1–32	−.82 −.57	For AoA < 15 For AoA > 15
	Spanish	English	2–23	28	3–41	−.68 −.51	For AoA < 15 For AoA > 15
DeKeyser, 2000	Hungarian	English	Minimum 10 Mean 34	57	1–40	−.63 −.26 −.04	For all learners For AoA < 16 For AoA > 16
McDonald, 2000	Spanish	English	3–24	28	0–20	−.61	For test score; for RT, late acquirers differ from all others
	Vietnamese	English	9–23	24	0–10	−.59	For test score; for RT, all L2 acquirers differ from L1 acquirers
Birdsong and Molis, 2001	Spanish	English	Minimum 10	61	3–44	−.24 −.69	For AoA < 16 For AoA > 16

L1, first language; LoR, length of residence; RT, reaction time.

that participants in both studies were considered nativelike.

Some researchers have used other kinds of passive testing (not requiring production). Lee and Schachter (1997) used a picture/sentence matching task, and Oyama (1978) used a listening comprehension test with varying levels of masking with white noise.

Several other studies were based on production data. Hyltenstam (1992) administered oral and written production tasks; Ball (1996) used the Bilingual Syntax Measure; and Patkowski (1980, see also 1990) had native-speaking judges give global syntactic proficiency ratings on the basis of written transcriptions of 5-minute audio recordings.

The pattern for these various types of morphosyntactic outcome variables is very much the same as for the oral GJTs discussed above: strong negative correlations between AoA and morphosyntactic score, no overlap between native-speaking and non-native-speaking groups, or at the very least a significant difference between native and adult acquirers.

Evidence From Phonological Measures   Almost no research has been conducted to test any specific area of phonological acquisition comparing child and adult L2 learners. A rare exception is Ioup and Tansomboon's (1987) small-scale experiment on the acquisition of Thai tone by L1 English

Table 5.2 Correlations Between Age of Acquisition (AoA) and Second Language (L2) Proficiency as Measured by Other Tests of Morphosyntax

Study	L1	L2	LoR Range	n	AoA Range	r Between AoA and L2	Remarks
Johnson, 1992	Chinese + Korean	English	4–27	46	5–39	−.54 −.73	For all learners For AoA < 15
Jia, 1998	Various	English	5–72	105	3–34	−.35	
Bialystok and Miller, 1999	Chinese Spanish	English	1–18 2–23	33 28	1–32 3–41	ns	Exact r not reported
Coppieters, 1987	Various	French	Minimum 5.5 Mean 17.4	21	Minimum 18	Not reported	No overlap with NS group
Sorace, 1993	English French	Italian	5–15	24 20	18–27	Not reported	Significant difference with NS group
Lee and Schachter, 1997	Korean	English	2.2–4.6	76	3–24	Not reported	AoA >15 worst AoA 11–15 best
Oyama, 1978	Italian	English	5–20	60	6–20	−.57	r is for AoA-L2 with LoR removed
Hyltenstam, 1992	Finnish Spanish	Swedish	No information (sound native)	24	<15	Not reported	No overlap with NS group
Ball, 1996	Greek	English	10–72	102	1–40	−.62[a]	Marked decline for AoA >16
Patkowski, 1980	Various, mostly Indo-European	English	6–61	67	5–5	−.74	

L1, first language; LoR, length of residence; NS, native speaker.
[a]See note 3.

speakers. Their child SL learners did well on measures of tone; among adult learners, even the most advanced performed poorly.

In contrast, many studies have examined the pronunciation of individuals with differing ages of first exposure to L2 through global measures of phonological competence, such as ratings of sentence reading or free production tasks (see Table 5.3). These ratings were based on production, not perception. Judges usually rated the learners on a scale of accentedness, for which one end of the scale indicated "native speaker" and the other end indicated "strong foreign accent." This means that judges were taking many kinds of phonological evidence into account in their ratings, including segments, syllable structure, stress, intonation, and rhythm. Thus, it may be said that studies in this area measured global pronunciation ability and not necessarily underlying phonological abilities. In general, the longer and less constrained the speech sample to be judged was, the more sharply foreign accents were noted by judges (cf. Neufeld, 1988, for an example). In addition, being found "accent free" in an L2 does not seem to be guaranteed for any AoA, but has been found statistically more probable for earlier AoA.

The first large-scale study that examined the pronunciation of immigrants whose AoA varied from child to adult seems to be that done by Oyama (1976), who tested Italian immigrants to the United States and who had AoA from 6 to 20 years. Both a reading task and a sample of spontaneous speech showed less accent than paragraph readings; pronunciation ratings correlated highly with AoA when LoR was partialed out. Subsequent measures of pronunciation ability have tended to follow the same format as that of Oyama (1976).

Patkowski (1980) included a replication of Oyama's (1976) work with 67 immigrants of various backgrounds on a spontaneous speech task. Bongaerts, Planken, and Schils (1995) reexamined Patkowski's data and noted that 15 of the 33 subjects with AoA less than 15 obtained a perfect accent rating; none with a higher AoA received as high a score. Thompson (1991) tested Russian-speaking immigrants to the United States on sentence and passage reading and on a spontaneous speech task. Asher and García (1969) had Spanish-speaking immigrants read four sentences. In the work of Tahta, Wood, and Loewenthal (1981), immigrants to the United Kingdom read paragraphs that were judged on a 0–2 scale (*no foreign accent* to *marked accent*).

Several more recent studies have upheld the findings of these earlier studies, but have avoided some of their problems by consistently including controls, having a wider range of AoA, and reporting scores by AoA, not just at a certain predetermined cutoff point, such as above and below 15. Flege, Munro, and MacKay (1995) tested sentence production by Italian immigrants to Canada. Any bilinguals who received a mean rating that fell within two standard deviations of the mean native speaker rating were considered to have native accents. Flege, Yeni-Komshian, and Liu (1999) evaluated the performance of Korean immigrants to the United States in a similar way.

As can be seen in Table 5.3, all the studies that have used global accent ratings on sentences or paragraphs that were read or spontaneous speech have found that degree of accent increases as AoA increases. Many studies have found that even learners with AoA less than 6 cannot achieve the same ratings as native speakers. This may be a result of the postponement of onset of true exposure to the L2 until age 5–6 years even when AoA was earlier, however. At this point, the studies indicated that earlier is better as far as the probability of achieving accent-free L2 speech is concerned. In studies that conducted multiple regression analyses, AoA accounted for at least 50% of the variance in accent scores, with other factors such as sex, length of residence, motivation, identification with L2 culture, or self-confidence either not significant or adding only 5% or less to the total variance (see sections on input and social-psychological variables for more detail).

Evidence From Other Dependent Measures   A few studies used global self-assessments of proficiency rather than a test. Bialystok and Hakuta (1999) obtained data from the 1990 U.S. population census and used proficiency self-assessments on a 5-point scale from the Spanish and Chinese speakers in the state of New York with LoR less than 10. This yielded a sample of 38,787 for L1 Spanish and 24,903 for L1 Chinese. AoA–proficiency correlations for these two groups were −.52 and −.44, respectively.

Stevens (1999) also used the 1990 census data, but restricted her sample to subjects who were between 18 and 40 years old at the time of the census and did not exclude subjects with limited LoR. She did not report raw correlation coefficients, but graphically presented curvilinear relationships; AoA appeared to be a much stronger predictor of proficiency than LoR, at least for individuals with LoR greater than 5.

Table 5.3 Correlations Between Age of Acquisition (AoA) and Second Language (L2) Proficiency as Measured by Global Phonological Ratings

Study	L1	L2	LoR Range	n	AoA Range	r Between AoA and L2	Remarks
Oyama, 1976	Italian	English	5–20	60	6–20	.69 (stories) .83 (paragraph)	For error rate; LoR partialed out
Patkowski, 1980	Various	English	6–61	67	5–50	−.76	
Thompson, 1991	Russian	English	Not given	36	4–42	.81	For error rate
Asher and Garcia, 1969	Spanish	English	Mean 5	71	1–19	Not reported	For AoA > 12: only 7% near native
Tahta et al., 1981	Various	English	Minimum 2	109	Minimum 6	.66	For error rate; AoA < 6: all perfect
Flege, Munro, et al., 1995	Italian	English	15–44	240	2–23	Not reported	AoA accounts for 60% of variance; AoA > 16: none native-like
Flege et al., 1999	Korean	English	Minimum 8	240	1–23	−.62 −.5	For AoA < 12 For AoA > 12
Yeni-Komshian, Flege, and Liu, 2000	Korean	English	Minimum 8	240	1–23	−.85	Significant difference between NS and all Koreans
Yeni-Komshian, Robbins, and Flege, 2001	Korean	English	Minimum 8	192	6–23	.31 (Consonants) .69 (Vowels)	For error rate

L1, first language; LoR, length of residence; NS, native speaker.

Seliger, Krashen, and Ladefoged (1975) sampled 394 immigrants to the United States and Israel to obtain self-reports on pronunciation. The researchers asked the participants if they thought their English/Hebrew would be viewed as nativelike by the native speakers of the country where they resided. Of the participants who arrived in the country before age 10 years, 85% believed they would be taken for native speakers; only 7% of those who arrived at 16 years or older claimed the same.

Finally, a few researchers have used neurological rather than linguistic measures as dependent variables in a morphosyntactic task. K. H. S. Kim, Relkin, Lee, and Hirsch (1997) had 12 highly proficient English L2 speakers of various L1 backgrounds engage in a silent narration task and measured activity in narrowly defined segments of Broca's and Wernicke's areas. Comparing subjects exposed to L2 in infancy and in early adulthood, functional magnetic resonance imaging revealed a significant difference in the location of strongest activity within Broca's area.

Weber-Fox and Neville (1996) used event-related potentials to compare the brain activity of Chinese-English bilinguals with AoA varying from 0 to 16+. They found significant differences compared with natives for semantic processing tasks in speakers with AoA above 11 and for syntactic processing tasks in speakers with AoA above 4. The same researchers also documented accuracy differences in the same group of bilinguals for AoA above 16 in semantic judgments and AoA above 4 in syntactic judgments (even for AoA > 1 in the case of subjacency violations). Also using ERP, Hahne (2001) found similar effects for Russian-German bilinguals with AoA greater than 10, with small differences in semantic processing, but clear qualitative differences for syntactic processing. For a discussion of these and other findings in neuroanatomical terms, see the work of Ullman (2001).

Some Counterevidence   A few studies are often cited as having documented equivalence of native speakers and adult acquirers: Bialystok (1997), Ioup, Boustagui, El Tigi, and Moselle (1994), Birdsong (1992), White and Genesee (1996) for morphosyntax, and Ioup et al. (1994) and work by Bongaerts and colleagues for phonology. Bialystok (1997) reported on two studies that actually showed an advantage for adults over children. This very result, however, along with the fact that no minimal LoR was reported, leads one to suspect that what was at issue here was a rate advantage of adults in early stages of learning (adults are known to acquire faster initially; see above).

In terms of morphosyntax, Ioup et al. (1994) merely documented that two adult learners of Arabic as an L2—and language teachers themselves—did very well, not that they were completely indistinguishable from natives. Birdsong (1992) showed substantial overlap between a group of adult learners and a group of native speakers, but this may have been because of the high degree of variability within the native speaker group. Typically, CP studies are conducted on the acquisition of basic structures, for which native speakers obtain virtually perfect scores; this was not the case here.

White and Genesee (1996) showed that proficiency among a group of near-native English L2 speakers was not correlated with AoA, but not much correlation with any variable can be expected in a group that, by definition, can show almost no variation. Furthermore, the researchers acknowledged that the similarity of L2 to the L1 of many near-natives may have played a role (most members of the near-native category spoke a Germanic or Romance language, especially French).

Studies of exceptional learners in the realm of phonology by Bongaerts and his associates (Bongaerts, 1999; Bongaerts et al., 1995; Bongaerts, Mennen, & Van der Slik, 2000; Bongaerts, Van Summeren, Planken, & Schils, 1997) have shown that some learners who sound very nativelike in ordinary conversation can obtain accent ratings in the native speaker range when they read sentences. Bongaerts and colleagues tested participants who learned L2 Dutch and L2 French in both naturalistic and instructed settings. Bongaerts et al. (1997) claimed that passing for a native speaker in a sentence-reading task is a feat that can only be accomplished if the learner has a nativelike underlying competence, but we would like to see such feats accomplished on passages of constrained free speech (like those found in the work of Ioup et al., 1994) before such a claim could be definitively accepted, especially when some researchers claim that Bongaerts et al.'s findings show that nonnative speakers can "speak the L2 without a detectable foreign accent" (Flege & Liu, 2001, pp. 549–550).

Conclusion   A large number of studies have documented large child-adult differences or strong correlations between AoA and L2 proficiency. These studies have used a wide variety of testing formats and dependent variables (even though grammaticality judgments are the most common for morphosyntax, and global pronunciation ratings are the most common for phonology) with speakers of a wide variety of languages (even though Chinese and Korean speakers are most strongly represented for morphosyntax). Only four studies have found substantial overlap between adult and native acquirers for morphosyntax, and in all four, the contradictory results could probably be explained by conceptual problems or methodological issues. Those studies cited for phonology have shown that some learners can achieve very high levels of nativelike pronunciation in mostly constrained tasks, but have yet to show that late learners can achieve the same level of phonology as native speakers in spontaneous production.

Counterarguments: Reinterpreting the Age of Acquisition Effect

A number of subtler counterarguments against the CPH have been raised. Although few researchers doubt anymore that there is a strong effect of AoA on ultimate L2 attainment, many question the maturational interpretation of this effect, arguing that AoA is confounded with a number of environmental variables that are the true cause of the decline in ultimate attainment. Others do believe the cause of the AoA-related decline is to be found within the individual, but they question whether the shape of the AoA–proficiency function is compatible with the traditional concept of a CP coming to an end around puberty.

Input and Practice   One of the oldest counterarguments concerns the role of environmental input. Adults are likely to receive input that is quantitatively and qualitatively different from that which children obtain from their caregivers. Strongly simplified language aimed at improving comprehension, and often believed to contribute to acquisition, is probably often avoided in interaction with adults for fear it may cause offense. On the other hand, many adults do not receive input with a variety of social functions, as would be the case for a child, because the use of L2 in their professional lives is limited to impoverished, almost stereotyped interactions, such as initial meetings and shopping scenarios. Although this argument cannot be rejected for some individual learners, it is clear that many adults fossilize at a level high enough to make highly simplified input irrelevant. Many others marry native speakers of the L2, yet fail to reach native levels, even after decades of using the L2 most of the time in their social lives.

The AoA effects are too pervasive to be explained completely by lack of high-quality input and interaction.

If amount of practice could explain the AoA–L2 correlation, then why would there be no correlation between L2 proficiency and LoR in many studies of morphosyntax? In virtually every study cited above, LoR was a nonsignificant predictor of L2 after the effect of AoA was removed; in some other studies, even the raw correlation was nonsignificant, and in the work of DeKeyser (2000), it was exactly zero. Flege et al. (1999) looked at LoR–L2 relationships for specific structures and found that LoR was the best predictor for lexically based items, but not rules.

For phonology, correlations of accent ratings with LoR were not significant in some of the studies cited above (Oyama, 1976; Tahta et al., 1981); others found a correlation that did not add significantly or only very little ($<5\%$) to variance in a multiple regression (Flege, Munro, et al., 1995, 1999; Thompson, 1991).

However, some significant correlations have been found in studies, such as those of Asher and García (1969), Snow and Hoefnagel-Höhle (1978), Suter (1976), and Purcell and Suter 1980. Snow and Hoefnagel- Höhle only looked at acquisition in the first year of naturalistic exposure; Asher and Garcia were apparently testing young children who were probably still enjoying the beneficial effects of a CP. Suter (1976) and Purcell and Suter (1980) found significant effects for LoR, but the range of LoR and AoA of the participants was unspecified. Flege, Takagi, and Mann (1995) found significant LoR effects for adult L2 learners, but a replication of this study by Larson-Hall (2001) could not duplicate Flege, Takagi, et al.'s results. Flege and Liu (2001) found a significant and positive partial correlation with LoR and results on a phonological identification task by Chinese learners who were students, but the nonstudents with shorter LoR scored just as highly initially as the students with longer LoR. Thus, it is not clear whether LoR or input was the real factor leading to these L2 speakers' proficiency.

In addition, even if a correlation between LoR and L2 proficiency could be solidly established, correlation is not causation, just like the correlation between AoA and L2 proficiency does not *automatically* imply causation. Even more important, the practice argument is hard to use in the case of immigrants who have used the L2 almost exclusively for 30 or 40 years. By then, they may have had twice as much practice in L2 as a monolingual college student in L1.

More recently, however, the input-and-interaction argument has taken a new direction and led to more quantifiable hypotheses. Bialystok and Miller (1999), Jia (1998), and McDonald (2000) all documented a strong relationship between individuals' knowledge or use of L1 and their proficiency in L2 morphosyntax. Jia (1998) found a correlation of .61 between AoA and L1 proficiency, the inverse of and almost as strong as the correlation of −.68, which she found for AoA and L2. Bialystok and Miller (1999) found a correlation of −.63 between L1 and L2 proficiency, but only for the Chinese, not the Spanish, sample in their study and only for oral, not written, grammaticality judgments.

Such findings about the influence of the use of L1 also exist for phonology. Earlier studies such as that of Tahta, Wood, and Loewenthal (1981) found that the factor of "use of English at home" accounted for 9% of variance in a multiple regression analysis. Flege, Frieda, and Nozawa (1997) found that, within AoA groupings, Italian immigrants to Canada differed in scores on sentence accent depending on whether they reported high or low use of Italian, with those reporting lower use of the L1 scoring better. Yeni-Komshian, Flege, and Liu (2000) found that there was a significant negative correlation ($r = −.65$) between L1 and L2 pronunciation scores for Korean immigrants to the United States. This inverse relationship was only significant, however, for the groups with AoA 1–11 and not for adult learners. These findings are important, and the hypothesis that a high level of proficiency in any language requires an enormous amount of practice, and that therefore bilinguals must show a trade-off between L1 and L2 proficiency, is certainly a plausible one (cf. Grosjean, 1998), but again the correlation with use does not explain the very robust AoA effects documented.

Social-Psychological Variables It is well known that variables such as integrative motivation, risk taking, self-consciousness, attitude toward the L2 community, and identification with the L2 culture are significant predictors of success in L2, particularly in naturalistic contexts (see, e.g., Gardner, 1985; Krashen, 1981; Skehan, 1989, 1998; Spolsky, 1989, 2000). Therefore, early discussions of the CPH often include the hypothesis that the reason for the AoA–L2 correlation is to be found in social-psychological factors. Older learners tend to be more self-conscious, tend to have less of a need to integrate fully into the L2 community, and tend to

identify less fully with the L2 culture; therefore, they would be expected to be less successful in L2. Again, however, just as for the input variable, these correlations do not explain the fact that the AoA effect is so pervasive, even for people who seem to give off sparks of enthusiasm for the L2, its community, and its culture. Moreover, every single study on AoA and L2 morphosyntax that includes stepwise regressions, or partial correlations for social-psychological variables with the effect of AoA partialed out, has found these variables not to be significant (Jia, 1998; Johnson & Newport, 1989; Oyama, 1978). For phonology, in studies that have compared both younger and older learners, such variables have contributed either not at all (Oyama, 1976; Thompson, 1991; Yeni-Komshian et al., 2000) or very little (Flege, Munro, et al., 1995; Flege et al., 1999). One exception was the work of Moyer (1999), but this study only included speakers with AoA above 11, which means there was little room left for variation as a function of AoA.

Maturation Without a Critical Period Inherent in the idea of a CP is the concept of an end point, a point beyond which learning becomes difficult or impossible. This very idea of an end point implies that by then maturation has taken its course, and not much further decline for the same maturational reasons can be expected. Therefore, a litmus test for the CPH seems to be whether there is a discontinuity in the AoA–proficiency. If ultimate attainment kept declining as a function of AoA at more or less the same rate, even for immigrants who arrived in the L2 environment well into adulthood, then this would constitute a serious challenge to the CPH function (see, e.g., Birdsong, chapter 6, this volume).

Bialystok and Hakuta (1999) and Stevens (1999) both documented a significant decline through adulthood when L2 proficiency was operationalized as self-assessment on the 5-point scale used by the 1990 U.S. Census. There are two reasons, however, to be very cautious in interpreting their figures. First, the validity of self-assessments is particularly problematic in this research context. The idea that younger is better for L2 learning is widespread in the population, but the idea of a sharp decline at a very specific AoA is not. Therefore, subject expectancy is a serious problem when using this particular instrument for this particular research question: The older immigrants were when they arrived, the lower their expectations for L2 proficiency. Moreover, the particular scale used by the U.S. Census has a strange quirk. The 5 points on the scale are labeled as "not at all," "not well," "well," "very well," and "speak only English." It is clear that being monolingual in English does not necessarily mean speaking better than a bilingual, yet this is what this scale seems to imply. (And even if only the percentage of respondents who say "very well" as a function of age was analyzed, that would still be in part a function of how many people said "speak only English" because younger immigrants who have become monolingual cannot say "very well.")

Birdsong and Molis (2001) also found a significant decline through adulthood, even though they used the same grammatically judgment items as Johnson and Newport (1989) and several other studies. In fact, they found a much stronger decline through adulthood than through childhood and early adolescence. As argued here, however, the strong AoA–L2 correlation for adults in this study appears to be largely because of the effect of outliers. (Note also that this study did find a discontinuity around AoA 15–18, even though in the opposite direction compared to Johnson and Newport.) Finally, Bialystok and Miller (1999) found a continuing decline in early adulthood, but only for Chinese learners, for whom the LoR (from 1 to 6 years) makes it clear that the scores do not reflect ultimate attainment.

Some studies in phonology have found that the highest probability of being judged as having a nativelike accent is found for speakers with an AoA lower than 6 (Flege et al., 1999; Oyama, 1976; Thompson, 1991), but because others have reported their data based on predetermined groupings (such as before and after AoA 15 in the work of Patkowski, 1980), it is not always easy to see where discontinuities might appear within those groups. For further comments on the shape of the regression line, see the section on Methodology.

Lack of Qualitative Differences   If the effect of AoA on ultimate attainment does not reflect mere differences in input or use, it must reflect differences in learning mechanisms. Therefore, as Hakuta (2001) stated, it is important for proponents of the CPH to show different patterns of acquisition in adults and children. Hakuta (2001) argued that such differences have not been found in studies on the role of L1 in L2, studies of the role of universal grammar (UG), and studies on acquisition orders. Although this may be largely true, almost no research has been carried out to establish such differences (even among the many studies on acquisition orders, for instance, very few make any child–adult comparisons, with the 1987 work of Pak a rare study that did), and many other possible qualitative differences have not been researched at all.

On the other hand, the couple of studies that have tried to assess qualitative differences indirectly by assessing which aptitude factors played the biggest role for younger and older learners did find significant differences. DeKeyser (2000) showed that verbal aptitude was a significant predictor for adults, but not for children (or conversely, that there was no significant AoA effect for high-aptitude learners, but there was for the others). Harley and Hart (1997) showed that aptitude was the best predictor for older learners; memory was the best predictor for young children. The claim that no qualitative differences in L2 learning exist between children and adults appears premature, to say the least.

Conclusion   A number of important questions have been raised about the shape of the AoA–proficiency function and its interpretation. It appears that a number of factors, such as differences in input, use of L1 and L2, and a variety of social-psychological factors may reinforce the AoA effect, but they far from fully explain it. Nor is there sufficient evidence at this point of a continuous decline through childhood and adulthood, which would threaten the CP interpretation of the AoA–proficiency correlation. Many studies, on the other hand, have documented the kind of discontinuity in the AoA function that is expected under the CPH.

Interpreting the Findings

Even if the arguments above allow us to reject nonmaturational explanations for the AoA effects documented, that still leaves us with a lot of unanswered questions. What exactly is the nature of the developmental changes that underlie the younger is better phenomenon? To understand them better, the data certainly must be examined more closely. What kinds of L2 structures are affected the most? Do the same differences appear with different testing formats? Are AoA differences reflected equally in accuracy and RT? And, what does all of that tell us about the qualitative nature of the CP?

What Kinds of Structures Are Most Sensitive to Age of Acquisition?

A handful of studies have tried to assess the differential sensitivity to AoA of different elements of L2. The findings of Ioup and Tansomboon (1987) seemed to indicate that lexical tone may be much more troublesome for L2 learners than segmental difficulties in phonology. Weber-Fox and Neville (1996) found a later discontinuity for semantic than for syntactic violations. Patkowski (1980, 1990) found about the same effects for phonology and morphosyntax. Flege et al. (1999) found that phonology was more sensitive to AoA, rule-based syntactic knowledge to level of education, and item-based syntactic knowledge to LoR. Birdsong (1992) found no difference between structures assumed to be part of UG and non-UG structures. Johnson and Newport found essentially the same effects for structures assumed to be UG in their 1991 study and for non-UG structures in their 1989 study. Within the non-UG group, however, the AoA effect varied widely from structure to structure. Similar results were obtained by De-Keyser (2000) and McDonald (2000).

Basic word order always seems to be acquired, regardless of AoA and L1. Both subject-verb inversion and do-support in yes-no questions also seem highly impervious to AoA effects. On the other hand, articles, plurals, and some subcategorization phenomena show strong AoA effects, whether L1 is Korean, Chinese, Hungarian, Spanish, or Vietnamese and for accuracy as well as RT.

Interpretations for these varying levels of sensitivity to AoA varied, however. Johnson and Newport (1989) made a vague reference to "universal factors in learnability" (p. 92); DeKeyser (2000) argued for the role of salience; and McDonald (2000) hypothesized the explanation is to be sought in processing difficulties. One argument for the last interpretation is that nonnative speakers have accuracy problems for those items for which native speakers show a slow RT.

What Kinds of Tasks Are Most Sensitive to Age of Acquisition?

Processing difficulties have also been invoked by other researchers on the basis of different arguments. Juffs and Harrington (1995) showed that Chinese learners of English differed from native speakers in RT, but not in accuracy, and concluded that older learners have processing rather than

competence problems. Hyltenstam (1992) argued, on the basis of the distribution of errors in oral and written production tasks, that many errors were an issue of control rather than competence.

Bialystok and Miller (1999) seemed to question that the AoA effects found were a matter of competence because different results were obtained for oral and written presentation of the same items to nonnative speakers, both in their own study and in comparing the oral presentation in the work of Johnson and Newport (1989) with the written presentation in the work of Johnson (1992).

Finally, if the need for accuracy and the need for speed are seen as different "tasks," one more study needs to be cited here: Shim (1993) found different AoA functions for accuracy and RT and even posited a CP for processing speed that ends earlier than the one for accuracy.

Conclusion: Competence or Performance?

Clearly, the AoA effects found for different tasks and different outcome variables are not the same. The AoA effects for RT tend to be stronger and show up earlier than those for accuracy. The AoA effects for oral tasks also tend to be stronger than for written tasks. These differences, however, may very well be nothing but method effects, with natives and young learners at ceiling for accuracy but not for RT, or conscious monitoring playing an especially strong role in written tests. Therefore, it seems premature at this point to draw any broad psycholinguistic conclusions in terms of competence versus performance or control. Most important, as argued in the introduction, the concept of CP refers to a discontinuous maturational AoA effect regardless of whether its locus is in processing or representation. Whether the changes are in processing efficiency or at the representational level, they require a deeper explanation of why they show a specific AoA-dependent function.

Deeper Causes

We have argued so far that the negative correlation between AoA and ultimate attainment, documented in a wide variety of studies, is not caused by different amounts of input and practice, social–psychological variables, or general maturational issues affecting the whole lifespan. Instead, there appears to be a qualitative change in language learning capacities somewhere between ages 4 and 18 years. That still leaves the question of how this qualitative change should be characterized.

Bley-Vroman (1988) argued that there is a fundamental change in the sense that children use domain-specific learning procedures and adults general problem-solving systems. DeKeyser (2000), on the basis of the different role aptitude plays at different AoAs (as documented in his study and in the work of Harley and Hart, 1997), further interpreted this difference in terms of children as largely limited to implicit learning and adults largely limited to explicit learning. Ullman (2001), on the basis of neurolinguistic evidence, came to a similar conclusion about implicit/procedural versus explicit/declarative learning as a function of AoA.

Whether these interpretations are correct, they still beg the question of why such qualitative differences would obtain. Several strands of research, however, provided some intriguing suggestions, mostly along the lines of age differences in the size of working memory, referred to variously as the "less-is-more" hypothesis (Newport, 1990, 1991), the advantage of "starting small" (Elman, 1993), or the consequences of learning through a "narrow window" (Kareev, 1995).

Newport first argued that "language learning declines over maturation precisely because cognitive abilities increase" (1990, p. 22). The reasoning behind this claim is that reduced storage of language input because of memory limitations actually simplifies the computation of basic form–meaning relationships at the morpheme level and thereby avoids or reduces formulaic learning, which initially speeds up acquisition, but turns out to be a developmental dead end. Goldowsky and Newport (1993) provided evidence for this view in the form of mathematical modeling.

Cochran, McDonald, and Parault (1999) showed that adults who were given instructions to practice American Sign Language strings holistically or who had to perform under dual-task conditions learned sign language structure better than adults under normal conditions. In the same vein, Kersten and Earles (2001) found that adults learned the morphology of a miniature linguistic system better when they were initially presented with only small segments of the language. Elman (1993) showed that training neural networks to process complex sentences succeeded only when working memory was limited in initial stages of learning and argued in some detail why such findings could be seen to follow logically from various characteristics of neural networks.

Kareev and his associates made a slightly different argument. Capacity limitations are beneficial not only because of their input-filtering effect, but also because they act as an amplifier for correlation patterns in the data. Theoretical analyses of this phenomenon were provided in the work of Kareev (1995, 2000), and empirical corroboration through experimental data from adults with different working memory capacities and exposed to samples of different sizes can be found in the study of Kareev, Lieberman, and Lev (1997).

In spite of this variety of theoretical and empirical arguments, however, there are reasons to remain skeptical. First, there is no direct proof that memory limitations are the cause of children's initially slower, but ultimately more successful, learning; there is only an indirect chain of reasoning in the sense that children have been shown to have limited memory capacities, and that limited memory capacities have been shown to be advantageous in adult language learning and in various forms of mathematical and computational modeling. Second, some empirical research on neural networks has failed to replicate Elman's results (Rohde & Plaut, 1999). Finally, the formulaic language learning that supposedly helps to speed up learning initially, but is detrimental for ultimate analysis, has been documented repeatedly in L2 learning by young children (e.g., Wong-Fillmore, 1976; Peters, 1983). Thus, it seems to characterize child L2 learning at least as much as adult L2 learning and can therefore not be attributed to a disadvantage in the area of language learning brought about by general cognitive maturation.

Whether the less-is-more hypothesis or any other cognitive explanation of an ontogenetic nature is accepted, it is obvious that the cognitive changes postulated will have to be represented somehow in the brain. We reported above on a number of studies that have documented differences in neurological representation between language acquirers of different AoAs. There, of course, the documented neurological differences are the result, not the cause, of the different ages of exposure.

But, is there any evidence of the opposite, that is, maturationally determined differences in the brain that lead to differences in level (and mechanism) of acquisition? Lenneberg (1967), Long (1990), Penfield and Roberts (1959), Pinker (1995), Pulvermüller and Schumann (1994), Scovel (1988), and innumerable others have pointed to various aspects of neurological maturation that take place between birth and puberty. To this day, however, nobody has even hypothesized, let alone proven, a correlation between the development or decline of a specific neurophysiological mechanism and the incomplete acquisition of specific elements of language that is so characteristic of late learners.

This is not to say that such a link cannot be found. Perhaps there is a way in which specific aspects of neurological maturation lead to a serious reduction in the capacity for implicit learning of linguistic structures, for instance (which may affect different structures differently depending on their salience and corollary ease of explicit learning), but any such explanation remains highly speculative. Clearly, just about everything develops between birth and puberty, so that causal interpretations of correlations are even more suspicious here than they are in general.

Practical Implications

Although the ultimate causes of the CP are still a matter of speculation, few issues in SLA theory have had as much practical impact as the CPH. From Canadian-style immersion programs in the early 1960s to foreign language in the elementary school (FLES) programs designed and implemented in various countries at this point in time, many administrators have justified the very existence of their curricula with references to the literature that shows younger is better. As a result, opponents of the CPH, such as Hakuta (2001) and Marinova-Todd et al. (2000), argued that the CPH has had a very questionable impact on practice.

In reality, however, the correctness of the CPH is largely irrelevant to arguments for or against formal language teaching at an early age. FLES programs (and probably form-focused partial immersion programs) do not capitalize on the implicit learning skills of the child because of their focus on form and, more important, because of the limited time involved. Implicit learning works slowly and requires many years of massive input and interaction, which even 12 years in an early immersion program apparently cannot provide in sufficient quantity to lead to near-native proficiency (cf., e.g., Swain, 1985). Therefore, even if the CPH is correct, one cannot expect any substantial proficiency after several years of FLES (typically less than an hour a day), as many parents have come to realize. Patkowski (1994) already pointed this out, but has often been ignored.

On the other hand, some college students become discouraged when they hear about the CPH

because they think it implies adolescents and adults can no longer learn a foreign language well. This inference clearly also is not justified given that many CP studies have documented a number of highly successful (if imperfect) adult learners.

Both misunderstandings stem from a superficial interpretation of younger is better. As was pointed out in the introduction, younger learners are not faster. Nor are they any better at understanding rules of grammar, just the contrary. Whatever may be thought of the various tentative explanations for the CP mentioned here, the fact remains that what children are good at is ultimate attainment as a result of prolonged intensive exposure. What many adults, especially the more verbally gifted, are good at is relatively quick grasping of certain abstract patterns that can easily be made explicit.

DeKeyser (2000) and Harley and Hart (1997) showed that SLA success among children depends more on memory and success among adults more on analytical skill. Robinson (2002) showed that analytical skill plays a big role in explicit, not implicit/incidental learning, and that (working) memory plays a bigger role in incidental learning. Taken together, these results strongly suggest that children and adults use different mechanisms for learning, which draw on different aptitudes, and that these different aptitudes play a different role depending on the instructional approach.

Further confirmation of this hypothesis came from more pedagogically oriented studies, such as that of von Elek and Oskarsson (1973), which showed that, with an implicit method, children learned better than adults; with an explicit method, adults learned more than children. Muñoz (2001) documented that older learners (starting at age 11 years) performed better on a variety of tests than younger learners (starting at age 8 years) after the same number of hours of (relatively form-focused) English as a foreign language (EFL) classroom instruction. Curriculum designers and program administrators should take these differential strengths and weaknesses into account for learners of all ages.

The main practical implication of the CP literature, then, is not to call for early programs of any kind, but to adapt programs very thoroughly to the age of the learner. Children can learn very little explicitly; adults can learn very little implicitly. Therefore, if early language teaching is needed, it should rely on large doses of communicative input and interaction; adolescents and adults need focus on form to boost the explicit learning mechanisms, which at least some of them can substitute for implicit learning with a satisfactory degree of success.

Methodological Recommendations

The literature review in this chapter makes it clear that a very large percentage of CP studies have relied on the same kinds of instruments, both in phonology and morphosyntax. This is especially obvious in the morphosyntax area, for which many researchers have used largely the same items as Johnson and Newport (1989), usually in a listening format. Although this approach is advantageous from the point of view of comparability of results, it also entails the danger of introducing a method effect, that is, an artifact in the form of an AoA effect caused by the peculiarities of the instrument. Therefore, the use of different structures, different items, and different testing formats is certainly advisable.

Another consequence of the attention drawn by Johnson and Newport (1989) is the high percentage of studies that have worked with Chinese or Korean immigrants. This also is a bit of a threat to generalizability because it is known that L1 plays a large role in many aspects of language learning, and there is no reason to assume it would not be reflected in AoA effects. It does seem advisable, however, to keep conducting research with speakers from one specific L1 background in a given study to avoid noise in the analysis. It is better to strive for generalizability by conducting a number of studies with different L1s than to try to generalize from one study with many L1s, which would sacrifice internal to external validity. L1–L2 pairings of various kinds should be useful here as long as the pattern is not obscured by including structures for which the particular L1–L2 pairing poses no learning problem at all.

A related point is the desirability of a careful qualitative analysis of the specific learning problems posed by a given L2 structure (e.g., adverb placement) for a given L1 (e.g., L1 French, L2 English). This analysis can be linguistic, psycholinguistic, or cognitive-psychological in nature, showing how the structures with a specific AoA effect can be characterized in terms of salience, markedness, prototypicality, semantic complexity, form-meaning transparency, UG status, processing difficulty, and so on. Several studies have shown that the strength of the AoA effect varies dramatically depending on the structure; a qualitative

analysis of this pattern is indispensable if the CPH is to have explanatory adequacy (cf. Hyltenstam & Abrahamsson, 2003). The processing issue can be seen as one particular example of this problem.

It is important to pursue work along the lines of Bialystok and Miller (1999), Juffs and Harrington (1995), or McDonald (2000) in order to find out to what extent AoA effects are due to increased processing problems, not necessarily to argue for or against the CPH, but to give AoA effects their proper interpretation, thus refining the concept rather than debating it. Different forms of data collection (oral and written, with and without time pressure, and with focused RT measurements) will be necessary to that end. Both Juffs and Harrington and McDonald provided very useful methodological suggestions for such work.

The crux of the CP debate, however, seems to be the shape of the AoA–proficiency function. A number of vague hypotheses about the biological reasons for the CP have led various researchers to hypothesize boundaries at certain AoAs (for instance, AoA 15 because of puberty or AoA 5 because of putative end of lateralization). However, the testing of premature hypotheses about underlying causes should not be confused with the hypothesis itself that there is a maturationally defined CP; in other words, turning discontinuities at certain predetermined AoAs into a litmus test for the CPH seems beside the point. Empirical establishment of discontinuities is needed before interpretation of them.

This is easier said than done, however, for several reasons. First, several authors have argued that there may be different CPs for different broad areas, such as phonology or morphosyntax (Eubank & Gregg, 1999; Schachter, 1996; Seliger, 1978), or even more specifically for narrowly defined structures (see especially Lee & Schachter, 1997; Weber-Fox & Neville, 1996). If these hypotheses were found to be correct, this alone would preclude a "boundaries test." Even for a very specific structure, it must be taken into account that data are necessarily averaged over individuals, which will lead to a smoothing out of discontinuities because of interindividual differences. And, even for a given individual and a specific L2 structure, acquisition mechanisms presumably are not switched off overnight.

As a result, establishing the exact shape of various AoA functions will require data for narrowly defined (groups of) structures from large numbers of individuals with the same L1 or at least L1s that are equivalent in terms of the structure at issue.

The only CP study so far that has met even this elementary requirement with real test data is that of Flege et al. (1999).

The next problem is that of statistical analysis. Many studies have presented correlation coefficients for AoA and L2 proficiency, shown linear regression lines, or both. Obviously, these techniques are not ideal if there are reasons to suspect the AoA function may not be linear. Other researchers have basically let their computers find a regression line of any kind, whether linear or polynomial (cubic, quadratic, etc.). Such an analysis, of course, is extremely sensitive to even slight outliers, especially with the CP rather small samples typically used. The very least that should be done in such cases is to test whether the regression equation that provides the best fit is significantly better than the others. The study that comes closest to meeting this requirement is probably that of Birdsong and Molis (2001).

A related problem is the issue of hypothesized discontinuities and cutoff points. Here is the very heart of the problem. On the one hand, if there are good reasons to hypothesize such a point of discontinuity, one can try to fit different functions to different segments of the AoA continuum, but we stated that these cutoff points should be considered an empirical matter at this point. On the other hand, if there is a polynomial function that is significantly better than any other, then this is a great help in positing a point of discontinuity within a narrow confidence interval, but this only increases the pressure on the statistical analysis to identify every bend in the slope, no more, no less, and to peg it to a precise AoA. Neither situation is ideal, but it seems to us that, at least with large and otherwise homogeneous samples, this latter, inductive, approach is likely to be most fruitful at this point. Otherwise, the risk is too big that testing a broader hypothesis becomes confounded with testing poorly justified values for some of its parameters.

Difficult as these issues may be, there is yet a further complication. Even if there is such a thing as a CP for SLA, this does not automatically imply that this CP is the only maturational age effect that plays a role. Clearly, individuals go through gradual physical and psychological changes of all kinds throughout their lifespan, and there is no reason to believe these changes in visual/auditory acuity, attention, memory, analytical ability, and so on play no role in SLA. In other words, such changes may be superimposed on the CP phenomenon and add an extra layer of difficulty to the analysis. The

AoA–proficiency curve may reflect a variety of influences, and the challenge is neither to equate all of them with the CP nor to reject the CP because it cannot explain all AoA-dependent variation. Ultimately, what is needed for the understanding of these AoA-related functions is an equivalent of Fourier analysis in acoustics (which analyzes complex sound waves into their underlying sinus waves).

Finally, researchers should take great care to avoid both ceiling and floor effects. An inverted S shape of the kind that has been found in some CP studies (no significant change up to a certain AoA, gradual change for a certain AoA range, and then no additional significant change) could be caused by the combination of a ceiling effect affecting the youngest learners and a floor effect affecting the oldest learners (cf. Hyltenstam & Abrahamsson, 2003; Jia, 1998). Different tests may be needed for the youngest and oldest arrivals to establish early and late discontinuities; testing formats other than yes-no grammaticality judgments may also help to avoid ceiling and floor effects.

Conclusion

Evidence from numerous studies has shown that, although adults may be faster than children in initial stages of L2 learning, their ultimate attainment is most likely to fall short of native speaker standards. This may seem paradoxical to some (e.g., Harley & Wang, 1997). In our view, however, the two phenomena can both be explained by the same underlying difference in learning mechanisms: Children necessarily learn implicitly; adults necessarily learn largely explicitly. As a result, adults show an initial advantage because of the shortcuts provided by the explicit learning of structure, but falter in those areas in which explicit learning is ineffective, that is, where rules are too complex or probabilistic in nature to be apprehended fully with explicit rules. Children, on the other hand, cannot use shortcuts to the representation of structure, but eventually reach full native speaker competence through long-term implicit learning from massive input. This long-term effect of age of onset is most obvious to the casual observer in pronunciation, but on closer inspection appears to be no less robust in the domain of grammar.

Such widely documented AoA effects should not make one jump to the conclusion that they are maturational in nature. It is certainly logically possible that they are caused by environmental and other variables that tend to correlate strongly with AoA, and several such variables have been investigated. The preponderance of the evidence suggests, however, that they cannot explain away the very robust effects of AoA. On the other hand, researchers are still far away from providing complete explanatory adequacy for the CP concept.

What is it about maturation that causes a decline in the ability to learn specific aspects of language? Clearly, to answer this question continuing research in SLA will be needed, as will advances in the explanatory capabilities of developmental neuropsychology as it relates to language acquisition. Until that is accomplished, however, we see no reason to reject the concept of a CP. In doing so, a robust empirical finding would be confounded with some of its fledgling explanations.

Notes

1. The idea that children are somehow better at language learning and should therefore be immersed in a language at a very tender age goes back much further and was discussed quite explicitly by renaissance authors such as de Montaigne and Comenius.

2. Footnote 2 in Birdsong and Molis (2001) mentioned that, with the three latest arrivals removed, the correlation was just marginally significant ($r = -.36$; $p = .05$). The fifth latest arrival, however, constituted the most extreme outlier. If the five oldest arrivals were removed (or simply the three lowest scores rather than the three latest arrivals), then a $p > .05$ would result, given that a p value of exactly .05 was found with removal of less-extreme scores.

3. We derive this from the R^2 of 37.8 given in Ball's (1996) Table 4.2.

References

Asher, J. J., & García, R. (1969). The optimal age to learn a foreign language. *The Modern Language Journal, 53*, 334–341.

Ball, J. (1996). *Age and natural order in second language acquisition*. Unpublished doctoral dissertation, University of Rochester, New York.

Bialystok, E. (1997). The structure of age: in search of barriers to second language acquisition. *Second Language Research, 13*, 116–137.

Bialystok, E. (2002). On the reliability of robustness: A reply to DeKeyser. *Studies in Second Language Acquisition, 24*, 481–488.

Bialystok, E., & Hakuta, K. (1999). Confounded age: linguistic and cognitive factors in age differences for second language acquisition. In D. Birdsong (Ed.), *Second language acquisition and the critical period hypothesis* (pp. 161–181). Mahwah, NJ: Erlbaum.

Bialystok, E., & Miller, B. (1999). The problem of age in second-language acquisition: Influences from language, structure, and task. *Bilingualism: Language and Cognition, 2*(2), 127–145.

Birdsong, D. (1992). Ultimate attainment in second language acquisition. *Language, 68*, 706–755.

Birdsong, D., & Molis, M. (2001). On the evidence for maturational constraints in second-language acquisition. *Journal of Memory and Language, 44*, 235–249.

Bley-Vroman, R. (1988). The fundamental character of foreign language learning. In W. Rutherford & M. Sharwood Smith (Eds.), *Grammar and second language teaching: A book of readings* (pp. 19–30). New York: Newbury House.

Bongaerts, T. (1999). Ultimate attainment in L2 pronunciation: the case of very advanced late L2 learners. In D. Birdsong (Ed.), *Second language acquisition and the critical period hypothesis* (pp. 133–159). Mahwah, NJ: Erlbaum.

Bongaerts, T., Mennen, S., & Van der Slik, F. (2000). Authenticity of pronunciation in naturalistic second language acquisition: The case of very advanced late learners of Dutch as a second language. *Studia Linguistica, 54*, 298–308.

Bongaerts, T., Planken, B., & Schils, E. (1995). Can late learners attain a native accent in a foreign language? A test of the critical period hypothesis. In D. Singleton & Z. Lengyel (Eds.), *The age factor in second language acquisition* (pp. 30–50). Clevedon, U.K.: Multilingual Matters.

Bongaerts, T., Van Summeren, C., Planken, B., & Schils, E. (1997). Age and ultimate attainment in the pronunciation of a foreign language. *Studies in Second Language Acquisition, 19*, 447–465.

Cochran, B. P., McDonald, J. L., & Parault, S. J. (1999). Too smart for their own good: The disadvantage of a superior processing capacity for adult language learners. *Journal of Memory and Language, 41*, 30–58.

Coppieters, R. (1987). Competence differences between native and near-native speakers. *Language, 63*, 544–573.

Curtiss, S. R. (1977). *Genie: A linguistic study of a modern day "wild child."* New York: Academic Press.

Curtiss, S. R. (1988). Abnormal language acquisition and the modularity of language.

In F. J. Newmeyer (Ed.), *Linguistics: The Cambridge survey* (pp. 96–116). Cambridge, U.K.: Cambridge University Press.

DeKeyser, R. M. (2000). The robustness of critical period effects in second language acquisition. *Studies in Second Language Acquisition, 22*, 499–533.

Ekstrand, L. H. (1976). Age and length of residence as variables related to the adjustment of migrant children, with special reference to second language learning. In G. Nickel (Ed.), *Proceedings of the fourth International congress of applied linguistics* (pp. 179–196). Stuttgart, Germany: Hochschul Verlag.

Elman, J. L. (1993). Learning and development in neural networks: The importance of starting small. *Cognition, 48*, 71–99.

Emmorey, K., Bellugi, U., Friederici, A., & Horn, P. (1995). Effects of age of acquisition on grammatical sensitivity: Evidence from on-line and off-line tasks. *Applied Psycholinguistics, 16*, 1–23.

Eubank, L., & Gregg, K. R. (1999). Critical periods and (second) language acquisition: Divide et impera. In D. Birdsong (Ed.), *Second language acquisition and the critical period hypothesis* (pp. 65–99). Mahwah, NJ: Erlbaum.

Fathman, A. (1975). The relationship between age and second language productive ability. *Language Learning, 25*, 245–253.

Flege, J. E. (1987). A critical period for learning to pronounce foreign languages? *Applied Linguistics, 8*, 162–177.

Flege, J. E., Frieda, E. M., & Nozawa, T. (1997). Amount of native-language (L1) use affects the pronunciation of an L2. *Journal of Phonetics, 25*, 169–186.

Flege, J. E., & Liu, S. (2001). The effect of experience on adults' acquisition of a second language. *Studies in Second Language Acquisition, 23*, 527–552.

Flege, J. E., Munro, M. J., & MacKay, I. R. (1995). Factors affecting strength of perceived foreign accent in a second language. *Journal of the Acoustical Society of America, 97*, 3125–3138.

Flege, J. E., Takagi, N., & Mann, V. A. (1995). Japanese adults can learn to produce English /r/ and /l/ accurately. *Language and Speech, 38*, 25–55.

Flege, J. E., Yeni-Komshian, G. H., & Liu, S. (1999). Age constraints on second-language acquisition. *Journal of Memory and Language, 41*, 78–104.

Gardner, R. C. (1985). *Social psychology and second language learning: The role of attitude and motivation.* London: Arnold.

Goldowsky, B. N., & Newport, E. L. (1993). Modeling the effects of processing limitations on the acquisition of morphology: The less is more hypothesis. In E. Clark (Ed.), *The proceedings of the 24th Annual Child Language Research Forum* (pp. 124–138). Stanford, CA: CSLI.

Grimshaw, G. M., Adelstein, A., Bryden, M. P., & MacKinnon, G. E. (1998). First-language acquisition in adolescence: evidence for a critical period for verbal language development. *Brain and Language, 63*, 237–255.

Grosjean, F. (1998). Studying bilinguals: Methodological and conceptual issues. *Bilingualism: Language and Cognition, 1*, 131–149.

Hahne, A. (2001). What's different in second-language processing? Evidence from event-related brain potentials. *Journal of Psycholinguistic Research, 30*, 251–266.

Hakuta, K. (2001). A critical period for second language acquisition? In D. Bailey, J. Bruer, F. Symons, & J. Lichtman (Eds.), *Critical thinking about critical periods* (pp. 193–205). Baltimore, MD: Brookes.

Harley, B. (1986). *Age in second language acquisition.* Clevedon, U.K.: Multilingual Matters.

Harley, B., & Hart, D. (1997). Language aptitude and second language proficiency in classroom learners of different starting ages. *Studies in Second Language Acquisition, 19*, 379–400.

Harley, B., & Wang, W. (1997). The critical period hypothesis: Where are we now? In A. M. B. de Groot & J. F. Kroll (Eds.), *Tutorials in bilingualism. Psycholinguistic perspectives* (pp. 19–51). Mahwah, NJ: Erlbaum.

Hurford, J. R. (1991). The evolution of the critical period for language acquisition. *Cognition, 40*, 159–201.

Hurford, J. R., & Kirby, S. (1999). Co-evolution of language size and the critical period. In D. Birdsong (Ed.), *Second language acquisition and the critical period hypothesis* (pp. 39–63). Mahwah, NJ: Erlbaum.

Hyltenstam, K. (1992). Non-native features of near-native speakers: On the ultimate attainment of childhood L2 learners. In R. J. Harris (Ed.), *Cognitive processing in bilinguals* (pp. 351–368). New York: Elsevier.

Hyltenstam, K., & Abrahamsson, N. (2001). Age and L2 learning: the hazards of matching practical "implications" with theoretical "facts." *TESOL Quarterly, 35*, 151–170.

Hyltenstam, K., & Abrahamsson, N. (2003). Maturational constraints in second language acquisition. In C. Doughty & M. Long (Eds.), *Handbook of second language acquisition* (pp. 539–588). Oxford, U.K.: Blackwell.

Ioup, G., Boustagui, E., El Tigi, M., & Moselle, M. (1994). Reexamining the critical period hypothesis: A case study of successful adult SLA in a naturalistic environment. *Studies in Second Language Acquisition, 16,* 73–98.

Ioup, G., & Tansomboon, A. (1987). The acquisition of tone: a maturational perspective. In G. Ioup & S. H. Weinberger (Eds.), *Interlanguage phonology* (pp. 333–349). Cambridge, MA: Newbury House.

Jia, G. X. (1998). *Beyond brain maturation: The critical period hypothesis in second language acquisition revisited.* Unpublished doctoral dissertation, New York University, New York.

Johnson, J. S. (1992). Critical period effects in second language acquisition: The effect of written versus auditory materials on the assessment of grammatical competence. *Language Learning, 42,* 217–248.

Johnson, J. S., & Newport, E. L. (1989). Critical period effects in second language learning: The influence of maturational state on the acquisition of English as a second language. *Cognitive Psychology, 21,* 60–99.

Johnson, J. S., & Newport, E. L. (1991). Critical period effects on universal properties of language: The status of subjacency in the acquisition of a second language. *Cognition, 39,* 215–258.

Juffs, A., & Harrington, M. (1995). Parsing effects in second language sentence processing: Subject and object asymmetries in wh-extraction. *Studies in Second Language Acquisition, 17,* 483–516.

Kareev, Y. (1995). Through a narrow window: Working memory capacity and the detection of covariation. *Cognition, 56,* 263–269.

Kareev, Y. (2000). Seven (indeed, plus or minus two) and the detection of correlations. *Psychological Review, 107,* 397–402.

Kareev, Y., Lieberman, I., & Lev, M. (1997). Through a narrow window: Sample size and the perception of correlation. *Journal of Experimental Psychology: General, 126,* 278–287.

Kersten, A. W., & Earles, J. L. (2001). Less really is more for adults learning a miniature artificial language. *Journal of Memory and Language, 44,* 250–273.

Kim, K. H. S., Relkin, N. R., Lee, K.-M., & Hirsch, J. (1997). Distinct cortical areas associated with native and second languages. *Nature, 388,* 171–174.

Kim, R. (1993). A sensitive period for second language acquisition: A reaction-time grammaticality judgment task with Korean-English bilinguals. *IDEAL, 6,* 15–27.

Krashen, S. D. (1981). Aptitude and attitude in relation to second language acquisition and learning. In K. C. Diller (Ed.), *Individual differences and universals in language learning aptitude* (pp. 155–175). Rowley, MA: Newbury House.

Krashen, S. D., Long, M. A., & Scarcella, R. C. (1979). Age, rate, and eventual attainment in second language acquisition. *TESOL Quarterly, 13,* 573–582.

Lane, H. (1976). *The wild boy of Aveyron.* Cambridge, MA: Harvard University Press.

Larson-Hall, J. (2001). *Language acquisition by Japanese speakers: Explaining the why, how, and when of adult segmental success.* Unpublished doctoral dissertation, University of Pittsburgh, Pennsylvania.

Lee, D., & Schachter, J. (1997). Sensitive period effects in binding theory. *Language acquisition, 6,* 333–362.

Lenneberg, E. H. (1967). *Biological foundations of language.* New York: Wiley.

Loewenthal, K., & Bull, D. (1984). Imitation of foreign sounds: What is the effect of age? *Language and Speech, 27,* 95–97.

Long, M. (1990). Maturational constraints on language development. *Studies in Second Language Acquisition, 12,* 251–285.

Marinova-Todd, S. H., Marshall, D. B., & Snow, C. E. (2000). Three misconceptions about age and L2 learning. *TESOL Quarterly, 34,* 9–34.

Marinova-Todd, S. H., Marshall, D. B., & Snow, C. E. (2001). Missing the point: A response to Hyltenstam and Abrahamsson. *TESOL Quarterly, 35,* 171–176.

Mayberry, R. I. (1993). First-language acquisition after childhood differs from second language acquisition: The case of American sign language. *Journal of Speech and Hearing Research, 36,* 1258–1270.

Mayberry, R. I., & Eichen, E. B. (1991). The long-lasting advantage of learning sign language in childhood: Another look at the critical period for language acquisition. *Journal of Memory and Language, 30,* 486–512.

McDonald, J. L. (2000). Grammaticality judgments in a second language: Influences of age of acquisition and native language. *Applied Psycholinguistics, 21,* 395–423.

Morris, B. S. K., & Gertsman, L. J. (1986). Age contrasts in the learning of language-relevant materials: Some challenges to critical period hypotheses. *Language Learning, 36,* 311–352.

Moyer, A. (1999). Ultimate attainment in L2 phonology: The critical factors of age, motivation and instruction. *Studies in Second Language Acquisition, 21,* 81–108.

Muñoz, C. (2001). Factores escolares e individuales en el aprendizaje formal de un idioma extranjero. In S. Pastor Cesteros & V. Salazar García (Eds.), *Tendencias y líneas de investigación en adquisición de segundas lenguas* (*Estudios de Lingüística, Anexo 1*) (pp. 249–270). Alicante, Spain: Universidad de Alicante.

Neufeld, G. G. (1988). Phonological asymmetry in second-language learning and performance. *Language Learning, 38,* 531–559.

Newport, E. (1990). Maturational constraints on language learning. *Cognitive Science, 14,* 11–28.

Newport, E. L. (1991). Contrasting conceptions of the critical period for language. In S. Carey & R. Gelman (Eds.), *The epigenesis of mind: Essays on biology and cognition* (pp. 111–130). Hillsdale, NJ: Erlbaum.

Olson, L., & Samuels, S. (1973). The relationship between age and accuracy of foreign language pronunciation. *Journal of Educational Research, 66,* 263–267.

Oyama, S. (1976). A sensitive period for the acquisition of a nonnative phonological system. *Journal of Psycholinguistic Research, 5,* 261–283.

Oyama, S. (1978). The sensitive period and comprehension of speech. *Working Papers in Bilingualism, 16,* 1–17.

Pak, Y. (1987). *Age differences in morpheme acquisition among Korean ESL learners: Acquisition order and acquisition rate.* Unpublished doctoral dissertation, University of Texas at Austin.

Patkowski, M. S. (1980). The sensitive period for the acquisition of syntax in a second language. *Language Learning, 30,* 449–472.

Patkowski, M. S. (1990). Age and accent in a second language: A reply to James Emil Flege. *Applied Linguistics, 11,* 73–89.

Patkowski, M. S. (1994). The critical age hypothesis and interlanguage phonology. In M. Yavas (Ed.), *First and second language phonology* (pp. 205–221). San Diego, CA: Singular.

Penfield, W., & Roberts, L. (1959). *Speech and brain-mechanisms.* Princeton, NJ: Princeton University Press.

Peters, A. M. (1983). *The units of language acquisition.* New York: Cambridge University Press.

Pinker, S. (1995). *The language instinct.* New York: HarperCollins.

Pulvermüller, F., & Schumann, J. H. (1994). Neurobiological mechanisms of language acquisition. *Language Learning, 44,* 681–734.

Purcell, E. T., & Suter, R. W. (1980). Predictors of pronunciation accuracy: A reexamination. *Language Learning, 30,* 271–287.

Robinson, P. (2002). Effects of individual differences in intelligence, aptitude, and working memory on incidental SLA: A replication and extension of Reber, Walkenfield, and Hernstadt (1991). In P. Robinson (Ed.), *Individual differences and instructed language learning* (pp. 211–266). Amsterdam: Benjamins.

Rohde, D. L. T., & Plaut, D. C. (1999). Language acquisition in the absence of explicit negative evidence: how important is starting small? *Cognition, 72,* 67–109.

Schachter, J. (1996). Maturation and universal grammar. In W. C. Ritchie & T. K. Bhatia (Eds.), *Handbook of second language acquisition* (pp. 159–193). San Diego, CA: Academic Press.

Scovel, T. (1988). *A time to speak. A psycholinguistic inquiry into the critical period for human speech.* Rowley, MA: Newbury House.

Scovel, T. (2000). A critical review of the critical period research. *Annual Review of Applied Linguistics, 20,* 213–223.

Seliger, H. W. (1978). Implications of a multiple critical periods hypothesis for second language learning. In W. C. Ritchie (Ed.), *Second language acquisition research: Issues and implications* (pp. 11–19). New York: Academic Press.

Seliger, H. W., Krashen, S. D., & Ladefoged, P. (1975). Maturational constraints in the acquisition of second language accent. *Language Science, 36,* 20–22.

Shim, R. J. (1993). Sensitive periods for second language acquisition: A reaction-time study of Korean-English bilinguals. *IDEAL, 6,* 43–64.

Singleton, D. (2001). Age and second language acquisition. *Annual Review of Applied Linguistics, 21,* 77–89.

Skehan, P. (1989). *Individual differences in second language learning.* London: Edward Arnold.

Skehan, P. (1998). *A cognitive approach to language learning.* Oxford, UK: Oxford University Press.

Slavoff, G. R., & Johnson, J. S. (1995). The effects of age on the rate of learning a second language. *Studies in Second Language Acquisition, 17,* 1–16.

Snow, C. E. (1987). Relevance of the notion of a critical period to language acquisition. In M. Bernstein (Ed.), *Sensitive periods in development: An interdisciplinary perspective* (pp. 183–209). Hillsdale, NJ: Erlbaum.

Snow, C. E., & Hoefnagel-Höhle, M. (1978). The critical period for language acquisition: Evidence from second language learning. *Child Development, 49,* 1114–1128.

Sorace, A. (1993). Incomplete vs. divergent representations of unaccusativity in non-native grammars of Italian. *Second Language Research, 9,* 22–47.

Spolsky, B. (1989). *Conditions for second language learning*. Oxford, UK: Oxford University Press.

Spolsky, B. (2000). Language motivation revisited. *Applied Linguistics, 21*, 157–169.

Stevens, G. (1999). Age at immigration and second language proficiency among foreign-born adults. *Language in Society, 28*, 555–578.

Suter, R. W. (1976). Predictors of pronunciation accuracy in second language learning. *Language Learning, 26*, 233–253.

Swain, M. (1985). Communicative competence: some roles of comprehensible input and comprehensible output in its development. In S. M. Gass & C. G. Madden (Eds.), *Input in second language acquisition* (pp. 235–253). Rowley, MA: Newbury House.

Tahta, S., Wood, M., & Loewenthal, K. (1981). Foreign accents: Factors relating to transfer of accent from the first language to a second language. *Language and Speech, 24*, 265–272.

Thogmartin, C. (1982). Age, individual differences in musical and verbal aptitude, and pronunciation achievement by elementary school children learning a foreign language. *IRAL—International Review of Applied Linguistics, 41*, 66–72.

Thompson, I. (1991). Foreign accents revisited: the English pronunciation of Russian immigrants. *Language Learning, 41*, 177–204.

Ullman, M. T. (2001). The neural basis of lexicon and grammar in first and second language: The declarative/procedural model. *Bilingualism: Language and Cognition, 4*, 105–122.

Von Elek, T., & Oskarsson, M. (1973). *A replication study in teaching foreign language grammar to adults* (Research Bulletin No. 16). Gothenburg School of Education, Gothenburg, Sweden.

Walsh, T. M., & Diller, K. C. (1981). Neurolinguistic considerations on the optimal age for second language learning. In K. C. Diller (Ed.), *Individual differences and universals in language learning aptitude* (pp. 3–21). Rowley, MA: Newbury House.

Weber-Fox, C. M., & Neville, H. J. (1996). Maturational constraints on functional specializations for language processing: ERP evidence in bilingual speakers. *Journal of Cognitive Neuroscience, 8*, 231–256.

White, L., & Genesee, F. (1996). How native is near-native? The issue of ultimate attainment in adult second language acquisition. *Second Language Research, 12*, 233–365.

Wong-Fillmore (1976). *The second time around: Cognitive and social strategies in second language acquisition.* Unpublished doctoral Dissertation, Stanford University, California.

Yeni-Komshian, G., Flege, J. E., & Liu, S. (2000). Pronunciation proficiency in the first and second languages of Korean-English bilinguals. *Bilingualism: Language and Cognition, 3*, 131–149.

Yeni-Komshian, G., Robbins, M., & Flege, J. E. (2001). Effects of word class differences on L2 pronunciation accuracy. *Applied Psycholinguistics, 22*, 283–299.

David Birdsong

6

Interpreting Age Effects in Second Language Acquisition

ABSTRACT   Age effects in second language acquisition (SLA) are often construed as evidence for a maturationally based critical period. However, an analysis of end-state SLA research reveals little congruence with geometric and temporal features of critical periods. In particular, there is no apparent period within which age effects are observed; rather, they persist indefinitely. We see that not only are maturation and aging distinct biological processes, but also their behavioral effects are not realized in comparable ways. Our understanding of age effects in SLA must also take into account the significant incidence of nativelike attainment among late learners. This incidence can be roughly predicted from the slope of the age function. The chapter concludes with a discussion of factors that influence the slope of the age function.

On even a casual consideration of bilingualism, one is struck by the negative correlation between the age at which acquisition begins and level of attainment in the second language (L2). Popular wisdom would have it that there is a circumscribed developmental period before adulthood during which second language acquisition (SLA) results in nativelike attainment and after which complete mastery of an L2 is not possible.

This is a plausible hypothesis because critical periods are observed in the development of many species. For example, Marler (1991) described the innately determined timetables of song learning in several species of birds. Similarly, for vision to develop fully in cats, Hubel and Wiesel (1965) demonstrated the necessity of receiving stimuli to the visual cortex before 3 months of age. In our species, researchers have documented pathologically low levels of grammatical development among individuals whose acquisition of the first language (L1) is delayed (e.g., Curtiss, 1977). For most researchers, the deficits appear compatible with a maturationally determined timetable. However, there is much less of a consensus on the appropriateness of the critical period hypothesis (CPH) as it applies to SLA (CPH/SLA). There are acknowledged age effects, but not all researchers agree that

the effects are consistent with the notion of a critical period. A collection of papers is illustrative of both sides of this debate (Birdsong, 1999b).

It is against this backdrop of ongoing controversy that this chapter presents several perspectives on the interpretation of age effects in SLA. After an orientation to typical methodologies and evidence in SLA age-related research, I consider the temporal and geometric features of maturationally determined critical periods and contrast these with functions that fail to exemplify one or more of these features. From this, a more focused discussion of the types of age effects that are observed in SLA is presented. In the next section, a number of behavioral studies of age effects in SLA are reviewed, with the preponderance of the evidence converging on the generalization that the construct of a critical period is a poor fit for SLA age effect data. Following this, the question of nativelike performance in experimental SLA studies is addressed, beginning with its relevance to the CPH/SLA and moving to the relation of the incidence of nativelikeness to the slope of the age function. In the final section, the role of intervening factors in determining the shape of the age function is examined, and the need for granularity in future study of age effects in SLA is stressed.

A Brief Orientation to the Age Question in Second Language Acquisition Research

Consistent with most research on age effects in SLA, the age variable considered in this chapter is the learner's age of arrival in the L2-speaking country or community. In the typical instance, age of arrival is the age of immigration, which is followed by long-term immersion in the L2. As is the case with L1 acquisition, SLA begins in earnest with immersion.

Researchers who investigate age of arrival in SLA are careful to partial out or control for the factor of length of residence (LoR), which often covaries with age of arrival. For some individuals, there may be incidental exposure to the L2 prior to definitive immigration, whether through schooling, dealings with L2-speaking relatives, or in the course of brief visits to the target country. Like LoR, the early exposure variable is usually taken into account in the design of the study and properly handled with statistical methods (for a study of the effects of early exposure, see Au, Knightly, Jun, & Oh, 2002). In studies of L2 end-state performance, it has been shown repeatedly that the strongest biographical predictor variable (strongest in the sense of accounting for the most variance in performance) is age of arrival, not early exposure or LoR. Other variables affecting level of L2 attainment are discussed in this chapter.

The effects of age of arrival on L2 attainment can be examined from two orthogonal perspectives: the rate of acquisition and the upper limits of acquisition. This chapter is concerned with the latter (for discussion of studies of rate of acquisition, see Long, 1990; Marinova-Todd, Marshall, & Snow, 2000). When considering how age-related factors might constrain the upper limits of SLA, the relevant data come from studies of learners at asymptote.

Other terms relating to the asymptote are end state, final state, and ultimate attainment. These terms, particularly the last, are sometimes misunderstood as implying nativelikeness or near-nativelikeness, when in fact they simply refer to the outcome of acquisition, however nativelike or nonnativelike this outcome may be. Deciding when the end state has been reached is often a matter of thoughtful estimation. In stipulating a generous LoR requirement for participation (10 years or more in some studies), researchers are comfortably assured that subjects are at or very close to the SLA end state. Needless to say, the chosen LoR criterion is applied commonsensically. Thus, for example, a 10-year resident of the target country who is socially isolated from L2 speakers could not reasonably be expected to have reached full potential for attainment and thus would not be considered for participation in a study of the end state.

Research on SLA often purports to determine the effect of age of arrival on attained L2 proficiency or L2 competence. More precisely, what is typically studied is how age of arrival predicts performance on an experimental linguistic task. For example, subjects of varying ages of arrival may be asked to make judgments of grammaticality for L2 sentences, with accuracy and response latency as dependent variables. In studies of L2 pronunciation, participants may be asked to read aloud words from lists; subsequent instrumental analyses involve comparisons with natives' performance on the task, targeting such variables as voice onset time in consonants, vowel formant frequencies, and vowel length and stability. Pronunciation studies may also examine suprasegmental features of sentences read aloud. In these instances, raters blind to the linguistic backgrounds of the participants assess the accentedness of both learners and natives, with assessments of the native controls serving as benchmarks against which the performance of learners is compared. Some research has also looked at the correlation of age of arrival with self-reported proficiency in the L2. Summaries of research on age effects in SLA may be found in the work of Birdsong (1999a), DeKeyser and Larson-Hall (chapter 5, this volume), Long (1990), and Marinova-Todd et al. (2000).

The study of age effects in SLA thus covers a broad range of linguistic features and experimental methodologies. Not unexpectedly, age of arrival effects are not monolithic. We know, for example, that modality of experimental presentation makes a difference. Bialystok and Miller (1999) and Johnson (1992) observed that L2 learners' performance in morphosyntax varies as a function of whether the items are presented in oral or written form. Similarly, not all areas of the target language grammar are equally susceptible to age of arrival effects (e.g., Bialystok & Miller, 1999; Birdsong & Flege, 2001; see also the Age and Other Factors section of this chapter). In addition, the geometry of the age function (its slope and any "elbows" or discontinuities), as well as temporal features of the age function (the points at which age of arrival begins to, and ceases to, correlate significantly with outcomes) may vary from study to study, depending on such factors as the linguistic feature tested, amount of L2 use, and L1-L2 pairing (see Flege, Yeni-Komshian, & Liu, 1999; Moyer, 1999; Scovel, 1988; Seliger, 1978; as well as further sections of this chapter). Transcending these assorted variabilities, however, a simple generalization emerges, as is shown in this chapter: Observed age effects in SLA are not confined to a temporally bounded period, but persist over the age of arrival spectrum.

A number of studies have examined neurological dimensions of language processing and representation among late versus early L2 learners and high- versus low-proficiency L2 learners. The evidence in these studies comes most often from event-related brain potentials, functional magnetic resonance imaging, and positron emission tomography. These methods are applied as subjects perform such tasks as passive listening to stories, cued word production, and reactions to syntactic and semantic anomalies. Because the focus of this chapter is on behavioral evidence for age effects in SLA, a review of the neurological evidence is beyond its scope; for overviews, see the work of Abutalebi, Cappa, and Perani (2001, and chapter 24, this volume), Birdsong (in press-b), and Ullman (2001a).

However, note in passing a provocative issue raised in this research: Do polyglots engage distinct neurological substrates in processing/representing each language? Results vary somewhat as a function of task and method, but a good deal of evidence converges on the generalization that high levels of L2 proficiency are associated with a common neurofunctional organization for the L1 and the L2. (Although L2 proficiency normally correlates negatively with age of arrival, the separate effects of these two factors can be teased out by varying them independently in the experimental design or by statistical factoring and partialing techniques.) That is, if high levels of proficiency are attained, late SLA does not entail loss of plasticity or massive functional reorganization, with broad recruitment of neural circuitry outside areas subserving the L1. Further discussion of age of arrival and neurofunctional organization in SLA may be found in the work of Brovetto (2002) and in further sections of this chapter.

Geometric and Temporal Features of Critical Periods

Generically, a critical period is considered the temporal span during which an organism displays a heightened sensitivity to certain environmental stimuli, the presence of which is required to trigger a developmental event. Typically, there is an abrupt onset or increase of sensitivity, a plateau of peak sensitivity, followed by a gradual offset or decline, with subsequent flattening of the degree of sensitivity.

As Bornstein (1989, p. 183) observed, it is sometimes assumed that the degree of sensitivity remains constant over the course of the critical period. By a strict understanding of this assumption, any increase in sensitivity would take place prior to the critical period per se, and any decrease in sensitivity would be a phenomenon occurring after the critical period. This view is represented in Fig. 6.1A. Taking as given that level of attainment is derivable from level of sensitivity, in Fig. 6.1A and in subsequent figures the vertical axis represents both sensitivity and attainment. Newport (1991, p. 114) specified the mathematical relationship between sensitivity and attainment.

Under the conception of the critical period given in Fig. 6.1A, the highest level of attainment is possible only during the temporal span of the critical period. It is this notion, apparently, that Towell and Hawkins (1994) had in mind when they maintained that, in SLA, "parameter values become progressively resistant to resetting with age, following the critical period" (p. 126). This view, although not incompatible with the sensible notion that full attainment is possible only during a specified "window of opportunity," does not incorporate the transitions that lead up to and follow the highest level of sensitivity, that is, the onset and the offset, respectively. As Bornstein (1989) noted, "By definition, the sensitive period endures within the confines of its onset and offset" (p. 182). Accordingly, the span of a critical period is properly understood as beginning at the moment when sensitivity starts to increase and ending at the point at which sensitivity is at its lowest level. Thus, as opposed to a brief plateau of peak sensitivity (Fig. 6.1A), the critical period extends from the beginning of the onset to the end of the offset; Fig. 6.1B represents this orthodox conception of a critical period.

Consistent with the representation in Fig. 6.1B, henceforth we consider a critical period to include all heightened sensitivity, the transitions as well as the uppermost level. (Note that it is of no consequence if one or both of the transitional phases is extremely abrupt or even absent. The idea here is to incorporate the transitions if they *are* present, in contrast to their exclusion under the conception represented in Fig. 6.1A.) As for behavioral outcomes, the degree of attainment that is reached

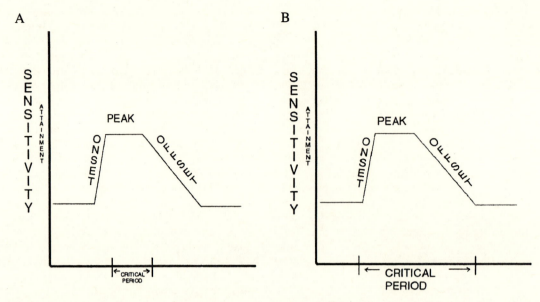

Figure 6.1 (A) Unconventional representation of a critical period as coextensive with the term of peak sensitivity; (B) orthodox representation of a critical period that includes transitional and peak sensitivities.

when learning begins within a critical period is not limited to full attainment, but includes lower levels as well.

A further potential confusion to confront is terminological in nature. Some researchers use *sensitive period* in place of critical period to emphasize the gradual nature of the phenomenon and to suggest interindividual differences in the timing of onset and offset. In other instances, such as in the quotation from Bornstein in this section, sensitive period is understood more neutrally, that is, in reference to the bounded duration of enhanced sensitivity to relevant environmental input. In the present contribution, I refrain from use of sensitive period to avert possible misconstruals of the term. My use of critical period is consonant with the generic characterization given at the beginning of this section and incorporates the dimensions of gradualness and interindividual variability.

Let us now consider the characteristics of a putative critical period for language acquisition. Various studies have shown that sensitivity to sounds found in natural languages, such as the ability to distinguish [ba] from [pa], is present among newborns only a few hours old (Eimas, Siqueland, Jusczyk, & Vigorito, 1971). Although this and other sensitivities essential to language learning may become more acute in the months immediately following birth, for practical purposes

it can be argued that the highest level of sensitivity is effectively at birth or so close to it that the slope of the onset would be extremely steep. By most accounts, language learning (first and second) to full adult competence is possible if begun as late as 4 to 7 years. It is at this point that the beginning of the offset of the critical period could be roughly located. As for the end of the offset, and thus the end of the critical period, Johnson and Newport (1989) argued that critical period effects relating to language acquisition should cease at the point of complete neurocognitive maturation, roughly in the mid- to late teens.

As shown in Fig. 6.2, the prototypical geometric features of a hypothesized critical period for language acquisition form what may be called a *stretched* Z. Regarding the hypothesized temporal features, the period of maximal sensitivity to linguistic input, with full attainment of grammatical competence assured, extends through early childhood (to simplify the image, no onset is represented in Fig. 6.2 and figures that follow). At this juncture, the beginning of the offset of the critical period is observed. The end of the offset coincides with the point at which full neurocognitive maturation is reached. After this point, no further age effects are predicted. Note the addition of a horizontal leg extending rightward past the end of the critical period per se. This flat function represents a floor of

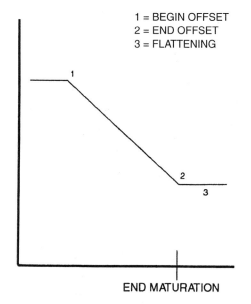

1 = BEGIN OFFSET
2 = END OFFSET
3 = FLATTENING

END MATURATION

Figure 6.2 The stretched Z: geometric features of a prototypical critical period for language acquisition.

sensitivity and parallels the ceiling of sensitivity associated with full attainment. As discussed further here, this ongoing stabilization of sensitivity at its lowest level has been identified as a necessary feature of the critical period function. With the understanding that the particular slope of the decline in Fig. 6.2 as well as the placement of discontinuities (the beginnings and ends of onset and offset) are for illustrative purposes, the stretched Z

representation serves as a basis for contrasts with other age functions that do *not* exemplify features of a critical period.

Consider now the age function given in Figs. 6.3A–6.3C. Figure 6.3A represents what might at first blush be taken as a critical period. There are two anomalous features, however. First, the offset begins at the point at which maturation has ceased. Thus, this is clearly an age function, but it is not maturational in nature. Second, there is no end point for the offset; that is, there is no end to the sensitivity decline, no bounding of the putative critical period.

Relatedly, consider Fig. 6.3B. This graphically illustrates an offset that begins prematurationally. However, as in Fig. 6.3A, the age effect continues ad infinitum: There is no "period" to which age effects are confined.

Finally, consider Fig. 6.3C. Like Figs. 6.2, 6.3A, and 6.3B, Fig. 6.3C represents sensitivity that is at its highest point at or near birth; however, there is no point of inflection representing either the beginning or end of the offset of sensitivity. Without such discontinuities, Fig. 6.3C lacks necessary features of a critical period. The age effect illustrated here reflects a linear, monotonic decline of learning over the age of arrival spectrum, with age effects continuing past the point at which maturation has ceased.

In the next two sections, these various functions are related to formulations of the CPH in the SLA context and to age-related behaviors observed in the SLA literature.

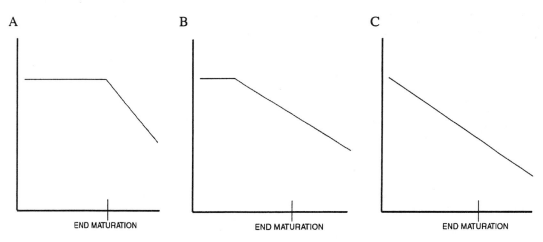

Figure 6.3 Unbounded age functions with (A) postmaturational offset, (B) prematurational offset, and (C) linear decline.

The Critical Period Hypothesis in the Context of Second Language Acquisition

There are multiple formulations of the CPH as it is applied to SLA. These include variations on the notion that increasing age entails decreasing neural plasticity in the relevant cortical areas (e.g., Lenneberg, 1967; Pulvermüller & Schumann, 1994); loss of access to the language learning faculty or universal grammar (e.g., Eubank & Gregg, 1999); a gain in information processing capacity that might be ill-suited to the task of language acquisition (Newport, 1991); dismantling of relevant cortical circuitry (Pinker, 1994); loss of function of mediating mental faculties from lack of use (Bever, 1981); and the inhibition of learning by entrenched L1 knowledge (Marchman, 1993). For further discussion, see Birdsong (1999a).

All of these proposed mechanisms are reasonable accounts of constraints on L2 learning in the sense that their predictions align with the generalization that attained levels of L2 proficiency correlate negatively with age of arrival. However, only the account developed by Pinker (1994) can be construed as consistent with the necessary temporal and geometric features of a critical period for language acquisition as laid out here and illustrated in Fig. 6.2.

Pinker (1994) described the age effect in language acquisition and its underlying causes as follows:

> [A]cquisition of a normal language is guaranteed for children up to the age of six, is steadily compromised from then until shortly after puberty, and is rare thereafter. Maturational changes in the brain, such as the decline in metabolic rate and the number of neurons during early school-age years, and the bottoming out of the number of synapses and metabolic rate around puberty, are plausible causes. (p. 293)

To elaborate briefly on the relationship of metabolic rate to cortical function, an increase in metabolic rate in a given neurological structure is understood as signaling the emergence of its corresponding function. A return to stable levels suggests that the relevant functional development is complete. Pinker (1994), proposing what could be termed a "use it, then lose it" version of the loss of language learning ability, noted: "Language-acquisition circuitry is not needed once it has been used; it should be dismantled if keeping it around incurs any [metabolic] costs. And it probably does incur costs" (p. 294).

Restating Pinker's (1994) description in terms of the temporal features of a critical period, there is a plateau of maximal sensitivity that goes on until age six, at which time the offset (decline) of sensitivity begins. The offset ends after puberty, after which there is a flattening of the function that coincides with a neurological and metabolic "bottoming out." Pinker's formulation nicely meshes with the stretched Z geometric features of a critical period shown in Fig. 6.2, and each feature is ascribed to a biological (maturational) cause. Note especially that the description relates to a limited developmental span and as such does not suggest ongoing declines past puberty.

Similar geometric and temporal features were suggested by Johnson and Newport (1989). Although they did not invoke the same set of neural and metabolic mechanisms as Pinker (1994), Johnson and Newport made it clear that a maturationally based critical period for language acquisition should be bounded, emphasizing the biologically determined point at which sensitivity (and thus attainment) reaches its lowest point, then levels off.

> If the explanation for late learners' poorer performance relates to maturation, performance should not continue to decline over age because presumably there are not many important maturational differences between, for example, the brain of a 17-year-old and the brain of a 27-year-old. Instead, there should be a consistent decline in performance over age for those exposed to the language before puberty, but no systematic relationship to age of exposure, and a leveling off of ultimate performance among those exposed to the language after puberty. (p. 79)

(In this context, "age" and "age of exposure" are understood to refer to age of arrival.)

Unlike Pinker (1994) and Johnson and Newport (1989), the other accounts of age effects mentioned do not specify limitations on the declining levels of sensitivity and hence attainment. In other words, these are not accounts of a circumscribed period of sensitivity. This does not mean these accounts are misguided. Indeed, the age-related constraints on learning to which they refer are empirically grounded. What is more, they are a good fit for the data. As seen in the remainder of this chapter, the most commonly observed age effects in SLA are straight-line decrements over the entire age of arrival spectrum and later-starting declines that persist beyond the end of maturation. In neither instance do the effects of age appear finite.

An Analysis of Age Effects in Second Language Acquisition Behavioral Data

A general class of argument invoked by critics of the CPH/SLA is the failure of observed age effects in SLA to display necessary features of a critical period as discussed above. Specifically, age effects do not appear to be bounded; there is no *period* of sensitivity. Relatedly, in terms of geometry, observed age functions in SLA are often not characterized by discontinuities suggestive of nonlinear variations in sensitivity. And, when discontinuities are observed, they often do not coincide with maturational milestones. In this section, a number of recent studies of SLA age effects are analyzed with an eye to departures from presumed temporal and geometric features of critical periods.

Straight-Line Age Effects

Flege (1999) discussed shortcomings of the CPH/SLA in a retrospective consideration of data from Flege, Munro, and MacKay (1995). In this study the L2 English pronunciation of 240 Italian natives, all with a minimum of 15 years of residence in English-speaking Ontario, Canada, was rated by English native speakers from that area. As shown in Fig. 6.4, age of arrival in Ontario systematically predicted accent ratings. Flege's analysis (Flege, 1999) of these ratings revealed no discontinuity in ratings at any age of arrival. The linearity of the function is suggested by the fact that the straight-line fit to the accentedness ratings accounted for more than 71% of the variance, with an additional 15% of the variance accounted for by amount of English use. Flege (1999) noted that similar evidence for the linear relationship of accent and age of arrival was reported by Yeni-Komshian, Flege, and Liu (1997) for 240 Koreans learning English. As with the Flege et al. (1995) data, there was no evidence of nonlinearity that would suggest the beginning of the offset of sensitivity, and in neither study did the data reveal a flattening out of the function marking the end of a period of sensitivity.

Hakuta, Bialystok, and Wiley (2001) examined 1990 U.S. Census results that included self-reported English oral proficiency ratings by Chinese ($n = $ 324,444) and Spanish ($n = 2,016,317$) immigrants to the United States. In this instance, mathematical modeling of regression discontinuities (Neter, Kutner, Nachtsheim, & Wasserman, 1996) was applied to the data. Under this model, a discontinuous

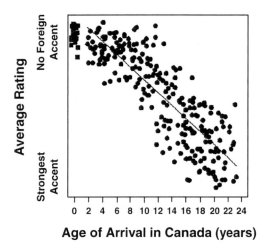

Age of Arrival in Canada (years)

Figure 6.4 Average foreign accent ratings for 240 native speakers of Italian who arrived between the ages of 2 and 23 years (filled circles) and 24 native English controls (filled squares) in English-speaking Canada. Data are from Flege et al. (1995), reproduced in Flege (1999, p. 103). Reprinted from Flege (1999, p. 103), copyright 1999, with permission of Lawrence Erlbaum Associates.

function is defined as a change of slope, a change of mean, or both. Performing analyses with early–late cutoffs at two different ages of immigration, 15 and 20 years, Hakuta et al. found no significant discontinuity in the proficiency ratings. A subsequent analysis, using a local regression model, likewise failed to reveal a discontinuity in the function. For additional statistical analyses of these data, see the work of Stevens (1999).

Bialystok and Hakuta (1999) examined self-assessed English L2 oral proficiency ratings from a subset of the Chinese ($n = 24,903$) and Spanish ($n = 38,787$) immigrants who had lengths of residency of 10 years or longer and whose age of arrival in the United States ranged from 0 to 60 years. Once again, statistical analyses revealed a linear trend in the data, which can be observed in Fig. 6.5A (Chinese respondents) and Fig. 6.5B (Spanish respondents). As with the Flege data (Fig. 6.4), visual inspection of Figs. 6.5A and 6.5B suggests that a bounded period is not an appropriate construct to apply to the data, as neither a beginning of decline from peak sensitivity, nor flattening of sensitivity, is indicated by an articulation near the end the function.

In their analysis of English pronunciation data from 240 Korean immigrants to the United States, Flege et al. (1999) likewise failed to find evidence

A

B

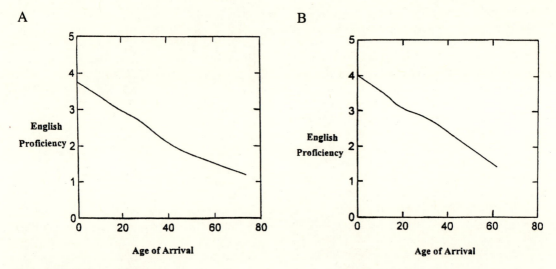

Figure 6.5 Self-rated English L2 oral proficiency by age of arrival for (A) Chinese native speakers and (B) Spanish native speakers living in the United States. Reprinted from Bialystok and Hakuta (1999, pp. 174–175), copyright 1999, with permission of Lawrence Erlbaum Associates.

of discontinuity in the regression of accent ratings against age of arrival. However, for the same group of subjects, the researchers noted a slight discontinuity in the function relating age of arrival to scores on a 144-item test of knowledge of English morphosyntax adapted from Johnson and Newport (1989). This inflection point occurred at age of arrival of approximately 12 years. Flege et al. point out, however, that age effects persisted for the late-arriving participants. Separate analyses were performed for age of arrival >12 years and age of arrival >15 years; significant correlations in both cases were reported, suggesting an ongoing decline in sensitivity.

In studies such as those in this section, data from early-arriving and late-arriving subjects are pooled into a single linear regression analysis; in these cases, the negative correlation of attainment level and age of arrival typically reaches significance. Indeed, this generalization holds even with data that have been presented as evidence for the CPH/SLA. For example, testing for knowledge of L2 English morphosyntax, DeKeyser (2000) obtained $r = -.63$, $p < .001$, and Johnson and Newport (1989) found $r = -.77$, $p < .01$ in their correlations of grammaticality judgment scores with age of arrival for all subjects.

Patkowski (1990) reported significant negative correlations of accuracy of L2 English pronunciation with age of arrival for all subjects ($r = -.76$,

$p < .0001$). For two separate measures of degree of nonnativelike accent, Oyama (1976) obtained significant positive correlations with age of arrival ($r = .83$, $p < .001$, and $r = .69$, $p < .001$; partial correlations, removing LoR). The observation of effects across the spectrum of age of arrival clashes with the notion that the effects should be bounded within a maturationally dictated temporal span.

Disaggregation Analyses

Different—and sometimes contradictory—pictures emerge when early-arriving and late-arriving subjects are segregated for separate analysis. In some cases, results suggest discontinuities in the sensitivity function over age of arrival. For example, in Patkowski's (1990) reanalysis of English L2 pronunciation data from his dissertation (1980), the researcher disaggregated the sample into early learner (age of arrival younger than 15, $n = 33$) and late learner (age of arrival older than 15, $n = 34$) subgroups. As noted, the pooled data for all 76 subjects had suggested a strong age effect over the span of age of arrival (range = 5–50 years). In contrast, the analyses for subgroups suggested different distributions of accentedness among early versus late learners. Separate analyses revealed that the slope of the early arrivals' regression line was a fairly steep .052, whereas the regression line for the late arrivals had a less-pronounced slope of .028. Patkowski (1990) reported that these results are in line with syntactic proficiency data from the same sample of subjects (Patkowski, 1980) and viewed these findings as evidence for a discontinuity in the age of arrival function. (However, no statistical significance for the slope differences is reported.) It should be noted that the data do not strongly suggest a termination of declining sensitivity because the age effect among the late learners approaches significance ($r = -.288$, $p = .098$). What is also curious about these results is that the correlation of age of arrival and performance was not significant ($r = -.245$, $p = .169$) among early learners, that is, for just those subjects whose ages of arrival (5–15 years) represented the temporal span during which, by the CPH/SLA, sensitivity should be predictably declining.

The disaggregation methodology was also employed in the landmark study of Johnson and Newport (1989). Participants were 46 Korean and Chinese learners of English, all of whom had lived in the United States for 5 years or more. Half the sample were early learners, having arrived in the United States at age 15 years or younger; the others were late learners who had immigrated between the ages of 17 and 39 years. Participants were asked to provide grammaticality judgments for 276 English sentences presented on an audiotape. Separate linear correlations of age of arrival with test scores were performed for early and late arrivals. Consistent with the idea that age effects should be observed early, there was a strong age effect among the early-arriving subjects ($r = -.87$, $p < .01$); moreover, the correlation of age of arrival with performance for late arrivals was not significant ($r = -.16$, $p > .05$).

As noted, Johnson and Newport (1989, p. 79) explicitly related these results to their understanding of the CPH/SLA, emphasizing that for post-maturational age of arrival "performance should not continue to decline over age," and that, with increasing age of arrival among late learners, there should be no change up or down in level of attained proficiency. Johnson and Newport (1989, p. 79) stated that this was exactly the pattern of results they observed. To bolster this conclusion, Newport (1991, pp. 122–123) took the late and early learners' scores from Johnson and Newport (1989) and plotted the mean performance of seven respondent subgroups: natives and ages of arrival 3–7, 8–10, 11–15, 17–22, 23–28, and 31–39 years. Lines connecting the subgroup means produced an image

conforming precisely to the stretched Z geometry illustrated in Fig. 6.2 (Newport, 1991, p. 123).

However, this image is an artifact of graphing means as points without regard to intragroup variance. The illusion of a roughly flat and tidy function (i.e., the right tail of the stretched Z graphic in Newport, 1991) is achieved by connecting the points that represent the mean scores of the ages of arrival 17–22, 23–28, and 31–39 years subgroups. Consider Fig. 6.6, which displays the actual scores of these subjects (from Birdsong & Molis, 2001, adapted from Johnson & Newport, 1989). Plainly, the 23 individual late learners' scores are not distributed in an orderly manner parallel to the x axis. This essentially random distribution of scores does not license the conclusion that "through adulthood the function is low and flat" or the corresponding interpretation that "the shape of the function thus supports the claim that the effects of age of acquisition are effects of the maturational state of the learner" (Newport, 1991, pp. 122–123).

To expand on this observation, note that a best-fit regression line will be visibly flat and the correlation coefficient will approach 0 under two conditions: when the distribution of points is

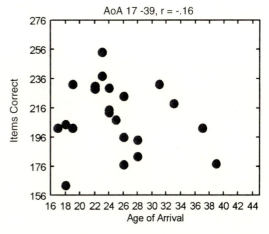

Figure 6.6 Plot of L2 English grammaticality judgment scores from late-arriving Korean and Chinese participants. Data are from Johnson and Newport (1989), reproduced in Birdsong and Molis (2001). AoA, age of arrival. Reprinted from *Journal of Memory and Language, 44*, D. Birdsong and M. Molis, On the evidence for maturational effects in second language acquisition, pp. 235–249, Copyright 2001, with permission from Elsevier Science.

random and when the points are distributed horizontally. However, it is only in the latter case that it can be concluded that sensitivity has stabilized. Recall that, for their late learners, Johnson and Newport (1989) reported a correlation of age of arrival and scores with a coefficient close to 0 ($r = -.16$). This result reflected the near-random distribution of scores. It is properly interpreted as indicative of "no systematic relationship [of performance] to age of exposure" and definitely is not a "leveling off of ultimate performance among those exposed to the language after puberty" (Johnson & Newport, 1989, p. 79).

Related studies that employed the disaggregation analysis have likewise produced ambiguous results. In DeKeyser (2000), Hungarian learners of English were tested with a shortened version of the Johnson and Newport (1989) instrument. For all subjects, the correlation of judgment accuracy and age of arrival was significant ($r = -.63$, $p > .001$). However, for neither the late arrival subgroup ($n = 42$) nor the early arrivals (age of arrival younger than 16 years, $n = 15$) did the correlation reach significance. Although the results are viewed

as consonant with those of Johnson and Newport (1989) and as evidence of the "robustness" of critical period effects, the absence of an age effect among early learners, along with the significant age effect over the spectrum of age of arrival, call this interpretation into question.

Separate analyses for the groups of early and late ages of arrival were also carried out by Birdsong and Molis (2001) in a strict replication of the Johnson and Newport (1989) study. Participants were Spanish natives ($n = 29$ early arrivals, $n = 32$ late arrivals). Early arrivals (age of arrival = 16 years) performed at or near ceiling ($r = -.24$, $p = .22$), producing a nearly flat function. In contrast, the performance of late arrivals (age of arrival = 17 years) was strongly predicted by age of arrival ($r = -.69$, $p < .0001$). As in other studies discussed here, age of arrival was predictive of performance over all subjects ($r = -.77$, $p < .0001$).

The disparate results obtained by Birdsong and Molis (2001) and Johnson and Newport (1989) may be viewed in Fig. 6.7. Visually, the two pairs of regressions are very different. In the Johnson and Newport data, there was a sharp decline for early

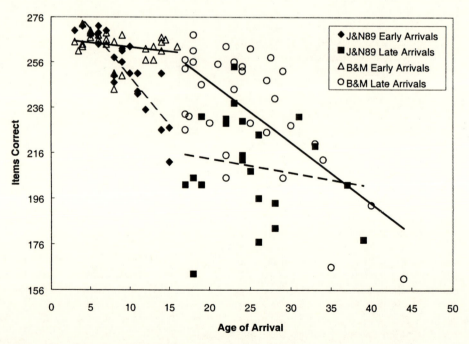

Figure 6.7 Number of items correct as a function of age of arrival. Solid regression lines are fit to the Birdsong and Molis, 2001 (B&M), data; dashed lines are fit to the Johnson and Newport, 1989 (J&N89), data. Division of late and early age of arrival groups equals 16 years. Reprinted from *Journal of Memory and Language, 44*, D. Birdsong and M. Molis, On the evidence for maturational effects in second language acquisition, pp. 235–249, Copyright 2001, with permission from Elsevier Science.

arrivals and a less-steep function for late arrivals; in the Birdsong and Molis results, essentially the obverse pattern was seen. To determine if these differences are statistically significant, Birdsong and Molis carried out numerous post hoc comparisons of their data with those of Johnson and Newport and used various cutoff points for early- versus late-arriving subjects. The two sets of results differed with respect to the regression slopes over all subjects and for the early and late age of arrival subgroups.

Returning to the question of discontinuity, analyses of the disaggregated samples in the work of both Johnson and Newport (1989) and Birdsong and Molis (2001) indicated that there are separable linear functions. However, as noted, these functions are not comparable in terms of their slopes. In the Birdsong and Molis study, the nearly flat function at ceiling for the early arrivals was followed by a steep decline for late arrivals; thus, unlike the Johnson and Newport results, the age effect came into play *after* the end of the putative critical period. Moreover, a series of analyses that placed the cutoff point for early versus late arrivals at various ages of arrival between 15 and 27.5 years consistently showed a significant age effect for late arrivals. To see if the age effect for late arrivals was an artifact of scores at the low end of performance, Birdsong and Molis performed additional regression analyses, removing the lowest two and lowest three scores; resulting values were still significant.

Interestingly, Bialystok and Hakuta's (1994) reanalysis of the Johnson and Newport (1989) results revealed that, by moving the early arrival/late arrival group cutoff point to an age of arrival of 20 years, the resulting linear correlation for late arrivals increased to statistical significance ($r = -.50$, $p < .05$). (In a separate analysis of the Johnson and Newport data, Bialystok and Hakuta demonstrated that the best-fitting linear functions were obtained with a cutoff at age of arrival 20 years.)

Finally, consistent with this emergent picture of age effects among late arrivals (DeKeyser, 2000, is the exception), Birdsong's (1992) study of Anglophone late learners of French (age of arrival 11.5–28 years) showed a significant decline in performance on a grammaticality judgment task with increasing age of arrival ($r = -.51$, $p = .02$).

Summary

Reviewing the analyses reported in this section, the following are observed:

1. For pooled early and late learners, analyses of age of arrival effects on linguistic performance revealed little evidence of nonlinearity suggestive of the beginning of a sensitivity decline.

2. In all cases of pooled early and late learners, age of arrival effects persisted indefinitely, with no flattening of the function signaling the end of a sensitivity decline and subsequent stabilization of sensitivity level.

3. In disaggregated samples, there was inconsistent evidence of significant age of arrival effects for early learners, which would indicate prematurational decline in sensitivity.

4. In disaggregated samples, most of the surveyed evidence showed significant age of arrival effects for late learners, indicating postmaturational decline in sensitivity.

5. In disaggregated samples, there was no evidence that the performance of late learners flattened out with increasing age of arrival, which would suggest stabilization of sensitivity at its lowest level.

These conclusions may be summarized by recalling the age functions for language acquisition illustrated in Figs. 6.2 and 6.3A–6.3C. Results from pooled samples tended to conform to Fig. 6.3C. Data from disaggregated samples resembled either Fig. 6.3A or Fig. 6.3B. None of the results matched up with the stretched Z features of a critical period for SLA given in Fig. 6.2. (The results also did not resemble a stretched L, a figure representing the possibility that the sensitivity decline begins close to birth. Like the stretched Z, the stretched L image captures the eventual stabilization of sensitivity at low levels.) In particular, the Johnson and Newport (1989) data did not pattern with critical period geometry; the random dispersion of their late arrivals' scores was not consistent with a floor effect in the sensitivity function. Moreover, Bialystok and Hakuta's (1994) reanalysis of the Johnson and Newport data revealed that declines of performance with increasing age of arrival persisted among subjects with age of arrival of 20 years.

Thus, the available behavioral evidence suggests that age effects in SLA do not operate within a well-defined temporal period. Further, the occasional nonlinearities in the age function do not reliably map onto predicted developmental and geometric patterns of declining sensitivity under the CPH/SLA.

What these results do suggest is an effect that persists over the span of age of arrival. To what can this ongoing decline be attributed? In the Age and Other Factors section of this chapter, a speculative account is considered that relates to neurocognitive aging. Alternatively, one might try to salvage maturation as a causal mechanism and couple it with other factors. That is, multiple mechanisms could be invoked that underlie the generation of a single linear function. For example, under such a view maturational effects might take their toll on language learning ability up through the midteens, then general age effects would be responsible for subsequent declines. Likewise, limits on attainment arising from a synergistic blend of biology and linguistic representation could be imagined. Perhaps maturation is an early constraining factor; as L1 representations become progressively entrenched (both during and beyond the maturational period), they inhibit the establishment of competing linguistic representations.

It is not the purpose of this chapter to evaluate such multimechanism formulations, although it must be said that they do not have parsimony to recommend them. However, it is again emphasized that maturational effects and age effects are not synonymous. The *Merck Manual of Geriatrics* (Beers & Berkow, 2000) explains that maturation is a circumscribed phase within the biological process of aging. This relationship is played out in quite different predictions—and behavioral evidence—for age effects and maturational effects in L2 learning.

Nativelike Attainment

Interpreting the Incidence of Nativelike Attainment Among Late Learners

Nativelikeness is defined in the experimental context as L2 learners' performance that falls within the range of native control subjects (some studies employ stricter criteria, such as performance within a standard deviation above or below natives' means). The attainment of nativelikeness in late SLA has been viewed as evidence for falsification of the CPH/SLA. Under the criterion proposed by Long (1990), "a single learner who began learning after the [critical period] closed and yet whose underlying linguistic knowledge . . . was shown to be indistinguishable from that of a monolingual native speaker would serve to refute the [CPH]" (p. 255). (Here, with reference to the discussion of the geometric features of a critical period, it is assumed that Long's reference to the closure of the

critical period relates to the point at which sensitivity has bottomed out, i.e., the end, not the beginning, of the offset.)

At the time Long (1990) set forth his Popperian criterion, there was little evidence of nativelikeness to threaten the CPH/SLA. For example, with respect to pronunciation, none of the roughly 20 subjects with age of arrival of 12 years in Oyama's (1976) study and only one of Patkowski's (1980) 34 subjects with age of arrival older than 15 years performed within the range of native controls. In the area of morphosyntax, none of Coppieters's (1987) 21 adult learners of French (ages of arrival not specified) and none of Johnson and Newport's (1989) 23 late learners of English (age of arrival of 17 years) performed within the range of natives. (For additional discussion of nonnativelike outcomes, see Hyltenstam, 1992; Hyltenstam & Abrahamsson, 2000; Long, 1990.)

However, several experimental studies have demonstrated that nativelike attainment is not an impossibility for late learners of SLA. A sample of research in which nativelikeness was observed includes the work of Birdsong (1992, 2003); Bongaerts (1999); Cranshaw (1997); Ioup, Boustagui, El Tigi, and Moselle (1994); Juffs and Harrington (1995); Mayberry (1993); Montrul and Slabakova (2001); Van Wuijtswinkel (1994); and White and Genesee (1996). These studies dealt with a variety of target and L1s (including American Sign Language) and covered a range of grammatical features, including wh-movement and tense/aspect distinctions, as well as pronunciation. In most of these studies, the incidence of nativelike attainment ranged from 5% of the sample to 15% or above. For a summary of evidence for nativelikeness, see Birdsong (1999a).

Some evidence relating to nativelikeness in late SLA is ambiguous. For example, 6% of the late-arriving participants in the study of Flege et al. (1995) performed with nativelike pronunciation, but all had ages of arrival younger than 16 years. The late learners in the work of Birdsong and Molis (2001) obtained scores well above those in Johnson and Newport's (1989) study, but only 1 subject of 32 late arrivals had a score in the native range, and this subject's age of arrival was a relatively young 18 years. However, within this group, 13 participants achieved 92% or higher accuracy scores, and 3 of these scores were above 95%.

Evidence of nativelike attainment in late SLA and its relevance to the CPH/SLA must be considered with due caution. For example, if valid comparisons with native controls are to be made, the learner sample should not differ from the sample of natives in terms of education level and chronological age. Care must also be taken not to overestimate the incidence of nativelikeness by basing the estimate on a sample of "the cream of the crop," that is, learners screened for high levels of attainment prior to experimentation, as was the case in the work of Montrul and Slabakova (2001) and White and Genesee (1996).

Normally, the success rate is based on a random sample of participants who meet a residency requirement, often an LoR of 10 years or longer. As noted, this is a methodological move intended to ensure that subjects are at their end state of SLA—not to ensure high levels of proficiency—with the result that varying degrees of nativelikeness are represented in the sample. With this range of outcomes, researchers are able to carry out informative correlations with various biographical factors, such as amount of L2 use. Further, the use of unscreened samples allows for safer generalization of observed incidences of nativelikeness to broader populations (Birdsong, 2004).

Similarly, an understatement of the rate of nativelikeness can be an artifact of sampling procedures. To target individuals who are at or near their SLA end state, and thus who have reached their limits of attainment, the bilingual sample should consist of those subjected to benign exogenous conditions such as extended residence and interaction with natives. Irrelevant to determining the incidence of nativelikeness are individuals who have had occasional naturalistic exposure to an L2 or whose exposure was limited to foreign language course work.

As a way to imagine the relatively small size of the appropriate L2 population from which to sample, consider the input conditions of L1 acquisition. To be ecologically comparable to L1 learners in the first 5 years of life, each of the individuals representing the L2 population should have had more than 6 million target language utterances directed to him or her by native speakers (Birdsong, 1999a). It is likely that statements about the insignificant rate of success in SLA—below 5% according to Bley-Vroman (1989) and Selinker (1972)—are based on consideration of individuals with considerably less input than this. That is, the low estimates may have been pegged to a much larger and less-relevant population.

What is to be made of a 5% or greater rate of nativelikeness in a sample of a relevant population of late bilinguals? Certainly, such an incidence exceeds Long's (1990) criterion for rejection of the CPH/SLA. Further, viewed as parameters within a normal distribution, such numbers clearly occupy a meaningful area under the bell curve, moving outward from a point less than two standard deviations away from the mean. In this sense, they are not "outliers" to be treated dismissively. Moreover, a 5% or greater incidence of nativelikeness would imply that there are substantial numbers of late learners who have attained near-nativelike proficiency. Age in SLA is not so constraining a factor that it prevents late learners from making remarkable strides toward nativelikeness, a fact recognized by Lenneberg (1967, p. 176).

Some researchers argued, however, that referencing of attainment to a monolingual standard is inappropriate for research in bilingualism (see Cook, 1997; Grosjean, 1989). Bilinguals are not "two monolinguals in one" in any social, psycholinguistic, or cognitive neurofunctional sense. From this perspective, it is of questionable methodological value to quantify bilinguals' linguistic attainment as a proportion of monolinguals' attainment, with those bilinguals reaching 100% levels of attainment considered nativelike. However, as Mack (1997) and Birdsong and Molis (2001) pointed out, demonstrations of nativelike performance by late bilinguals are at least of heuristic utility because they constitute a challenge to received views that the upper limits of late SLA are inevitably inferior to those of L1 acquisition.

Nativelike Attainment and the Age Function

Let us now reconsider the finding by Birdsong and Molis (2001) and Flege et al. (1995) that nativelikeness in the late age of arrival samples is observed among learners with relatively early ages of arrival, that is, those with ages of arrival in the late teens. First, note that further empirical study needs to be carried out to determine if the incidence of nativelikeness is indeed confined to "early" late learners. If this does turn out to be a valid generalization, how may it be interpreted?

On the one hand, advocates of the CPH/SLA could argue that their position is not threatened if the only apparent exceptions are those learners with ages of arrival on the fringe of a period with approximative temporal milestones. A contrasting interpretation is subtler. Recall the premise that the midteen years roughly mark the end of the offset of sensitivity, after which sensitivity should not continue to decline, but should level off. By this account, individuals with ages of arrival of 15 years and beyond cannot be differentiated in terms of sensitivity level; therefore, among late learners the incidence of nativelikeness should not be expected to be confined to just those with ages of arrival in the late teens and early 20s. In contrast, if sensitivity continues to decline indefinitely, then the probability of nativelike attainment should steadily decline with all ages of arrival past the period of peak sensitivity. Thus, among late L2 learners, a decreased incidence of nativelikeness with advancing age of arrival would suggest that the function is not in fact characterized by a flattening out of sensitivity.

This section concludes by putting a fine point on the notion that the later the age of arrival is, the lower the incidence of nativelike performance will be. To understand this logical entailment fully, the slope of the function must be considered. If the slope of the age-related decline in performance is shallow, then at a given age of arrival the incidence of nativelikeness will be greater than if the slope is steep (this comparison assumes that both functions are linear, and that their declines begin at the same age of arrival). This rather self-evident relationship is illustrated in Figs. 6.8A and 6.8B. For illustrative purposes, an age of arrival of 25 years was chosen. For both the relatively shallow age function in Fig. 6.8A and the steeper function in Fig. 6.8B, let us assume a normal distribution of scores at this age of arrival and similar kurtosis of the bell curves. Let us further assume that the regression lines in both cases intersect with the central point (mean, median, mode) of the distributions of scores at that age

of arrival. Plainly, for the distribution illustrated in Fig. 6.8A, the incidence of scores falling within the range of native controls' performance is greater than in Fig. 6.8B. Thus, it can be seen that, from a shallow slope, the incidence of nativelikeness can be predicted to exceed the rate of nativelikeness associated with a steeper slope.

In the next section, various factors are considered that may affect the slope of the age function. As this slope and the rate of nativelikeness have been shown to covary, it can be predicted that these factors likewise influence the probability that nativelikeness will be observed at a given age of arrival.

Age and Other Factors

It is frequently noted in the SLA literature that age effects are moderated by other variables. For example, with respect to self-reported English proficiency of Chinese and Spanish immigrants, Bialystok and Hakuta (1999) found that varying years of education were associated with different slopes of the age function. Flege and colleagues (e.g., Flege et al., 1999; Flege, Frieda, & Nozawa, 1997) showed that greater use of the L2 is associated with less-accented L2 pronunciation across various ages of arrival. The contrasting slopes seen in Fig. 6.7 are arguably a consequence of the different native language backgrounds of the subjects (Chinese and Korean for Johnson & Newport, 1989; Spanish for Birdsong & Molis, 2001).

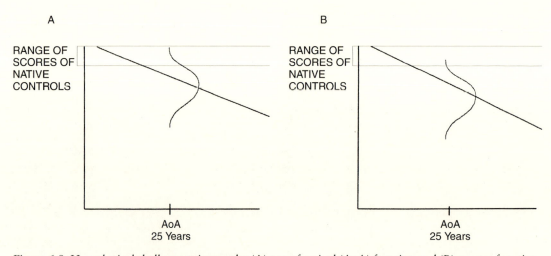

Figure 6.8. Hypothetical shallow attainment by (A) age of arrival (AoA) function and (B) steeper function, with superimposed distribution of attainment values at AoA = 25 years.

A variety of other cognitive, task-related, attitudinal, experiential, demographic, aptitude, and training variables may affect the slope of the age function and, as discussed, the rate of nativelikeness at a given age of arrival. For further consideration of these factors, see Bialystok and Miller (1999); Klein (1995); Marinova-Todd et al. (2000); Moyer (1999; 2001); Pulvermüller and Schumann (1994); Singleton (1989, 2001); Skehan (1989); and Stevens (1999).

Of particular theoretical interest is the role of linguistic variables in determining the timing and shape features of the age function in SLA. As noted by Eubank and Gregg (1999), Flege et al. (1999), Flynn and Manuel (1991), Seliger (1978), and others, the effect of age of arrival is not uniform for all aspects of L2 knowledge.

A study by Birdsong and Flege (2001) illustrated the heuristic potential of investigating possible interactions of age of arrival and linguistic variables, specifically a theorized distinction between regulars and irregulars. Pinker (1999, inter alia) argued that computation of regular inflectional morphology in verb pasts (e.g., *talk-ed*) and noun plurals (e.g., *pen-s*) involves processing of the compositional features stem plus affix, which are represented symbolically. In contrast to this rule-based computation, irregulars (e.g., *bought* and *geese*) are accessed as units from lexical (associative) memory. Ullman (2001b) reviewed an array of behavioral and neurofunctional evidence that pointed to the dissociability of rule-based and lexical knowledge and proposed that different types of memory and different neural substrates are involved in processing regulars versus irregulars. (Crucial details of the dual-mechanism model and challenges to it are beyond the scope here; see McClelland & Patterson, 2002; Pinker & Ullman, 2002.)

For the SLA context, Flege et al. (1999) had noted that, with increasing age of arrival, Korean learners of English were less accurate in their judgments of items exemplifying arbitrary features of English than for items that exemplified predictable regularities. My 2001 study with Flege was designed to pursue further this interaction of age of arrival by regularity. We recruited L2 English subjects who were Spanish ($n = 30$) and Korean ($n = 30$) natives with LoRs between 10 and 16 years; thus, they were at or near SLA asymptote. For each native language, groups of 10 participants represented ages of arrival of 6–10, 11–15, and 16–20 years. To disconfound somewhat the factors of age at testing and age of arrival, subjects' chronological age ranges overlapped the ranges of age of arrival. Thus, age at

testing for the group with an age of arrival of 6–10 years ranged from 16 to 26 years; for the group with an age of arrival of 11–15 years, the chronological age was 21–31 years, and participants in the group with an age of arrival of 16–20 years were between 26 and 36 years of age at testing.

We (Birdsong & Flege, 2001) presented 80 sentences containing regular and irregular English verb pasts and noun plurals in a multiple-choice format on a laptop computer, and subjects were asked to indicate which of five options was the correct inflected form of the verb or noun. Within each class of regulars and irregulars, equal numbers of high- and low-frequency nouns and verbs were represented. (An additional 20 sentences contained phrasal verbs, e.g., *look in on*, which are understood to be a class of irregular or idiosyncratic features of the lexicon.) Response latencies and accuracies were analyzed. Among both Korean and Spanish subjects, we observed strong frequency effects for irregulars, but only weak ones for regulars, a result consonant with the basic premises of the dual-mechanism model. Age effects were also asymmetrical: For regulars, increasing age of arrival had little effect on either response times or accuracy, whereas for irregulars, response times increased and accuracy decreased with advancing age of arrival. Fig. 6.9 represents approximate

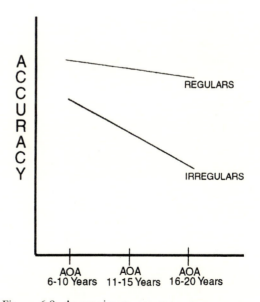

Figure 6.9. Approximate accuracy scores on regular versus irregular items, by age of arrival (AoA) group, for Korean and Spanish participants in the study of Birdsong and Flege (2001).

accuracy values for pooled Spanish and Korean subjects. Details of the accuracy data underscore the interaction of age of arrival and the linguistic variable in question. Among Spanish natives, proportions correct by increasing age of arrival group were .94, .89, and .92 for regulars and .71, .68, and .51 for irregulars. Corresponding values for Koreans were .98, .95, and .93 for regulars and .87, .74, and .69 for irregulars. Brovetto (2002) suggested that regular–irregular dissociations can be observed among higher proficiency L2 learners (thus mirroring the organization observed at the L1 acquisition end state), but not among learners at lower levels of L2 proficiency.

This behavioral dissociation is an example of a research finding that speaks to the need for finer-grained perspectives on the SLA age question than the simple "earlier is better" rule of thumb. In addition, it opens the door to new speculation on the possible mechanisms underlying age effects. Ullman (2001b) argued that declarative memory is involved in learning and storing assorted facts, whereas computations of regular forms and other symbolic or rule-based knowledge are coordinated by the procedural memory system.

I suggested (Birdsong, 2004) that declarative memory and its associated neuroanatomy are discrepantly affected by aging. For example, cortisol levels increase with age, leading to atrophy of the hippocampal area and impairing learning and declarative memory function (Lupien, Lecours, Lussier, Schwartz, Nair, & Meaney, 1994; Lupien et al., 1998). In addition, starting as early as 30 years of age, neurofibrillary tangles and neuritic plaques develop in the normal brain. These degenerative histological features are most prevalent in the neural regions that subserve declarative memory, specifically the hippocampus and temporal-associative cortex (Scheibel, 1996). Starting at age 20 years, normal aging is associated with declines in dopamine D_2 receptors in the hippocampus and frontal cortex areas (Li, Lindenberger, & Sikström, 2001). However, such declines are also found in the basal ganglia, anterior cingulate cortex, and amygdala, leading to an important clarification: The associative areas of the brain are not the only ones affected by aging, but age-related declines may be more severe in the associative areas than in other areas. Consistent with this idea is the general observation that declarative memory abilities decline dramatically more with age than procedural memory functions.

To sum this line of speculation, the neural substrates underlying the learning and processing of declarative information may be more negatively impacted by aging than other brain areas, particularly more so than those implicated in coordinating activities in real time (i.e., the combinatorial operations involved in regular affixation). Note that this putative deficit is not thought to affect the ability to accumulate new lexical items—for example, as we age we add neologisms like "e-mail" and "blogger" to our vocabulary—but impairs the retrieval of prescribed (irregular) phonological forms.

This avenue of investigation lends itself to the formulation of several falsifiable hypotheses:

1. With respect to linguistic features, age effects in SLA are not indiscriminate, because they disrupt the learning and retrieval of idiosyncratic, irregular forms (which are usually ascribed to the lexicon) more than abstract elements of the grammar.
2. The slopes of the age functions associated with knowledge of regulars and irregulars are distinct.
3. The age functions for both regulars and irregulars are not characterized by discontinuities or bottoming out, but by linear, unbounded performance decrements.
4. The class of irregulars may include not only irregular inflections on nouns and verbs, but also other idiosyncratic linguistic facts, such as the choice and placement of particles and prepositions in phrasal verbs.
5. In terms of neurofunctional anatomy, there are distinct loci of age effects in SLA that are relatable to the regular–irregular distinction.
6. Cognitively, SLA age effects are most apparent in a declarative memory system that is not dedicated uniquely to facts of language.
7. Declining linguistic performance is not related specifically to maturation, but to the aging process more generally.

Conclusion

The objective of the preceding section was not to propose a research agenda, but to illustrate how the understanding of SLA age effects might benefit from principled, granular investigations of linguistic variables that may interact with the age factor. Similarly, the other sections of the chapter were intended to suggest ways that age effects in SLA can be interpreted without being bound to ill-suited constructs such as the CPH/SLA and to received notions such as an insignificant incidence of nativelikeness.

The observed patterns of linguistic behavior reviewed in this chapter suggest that the "use it, then lose it" characterization of SLA age effects is imprecise on several counts. First, the decline in attained L2 proficiency is not linked to maturational milestones, but persists over the age spectrum; this is progressive loss, not decisive loss. At the same time, any number of exogenous and endogenous variables may come into play that can flatten the slope of the decline and result in significant numbers of nativelike attainers. Not everybody is "losing it" to the same degree. Finally, the "it" of the characterization suggests a single monolithic learning faculty. However, it is likely that L2 learning involves distinct cognitive and neural components with differential susceptibilities to the effects of age.

References

Abutalebi, J., Cappa, S. F., & Perani, D. (2001). The bilingual brain as revealed by functional neuroimaging. Bilingualism: *Language and Cognition, 4,* 179–190.

Au, T. K.-F., Knightly, L. M., Jun, S.-A., & Oh, J. S. (2002). Overhearing a language during childhood. *Psychological Science, 13,* 238–243.

Beers, M. H., & Berkow, R. (Eds.). (2000). *The Merck manual of geriatrics.* Whitehouse Station, NJ: Merck.

Bever, T. G. (1981). Normal acquisition processes explain the critical period for language learning. In K. C. Diller (Ed.), *Individual differences and universals in language learning aptitude* (pp. 176–198). Rowley, MA: Newbury House.

Bialystok, E., & Hakuta, K. (1994). *In other words: The science and psychology of second-language acquisition.* New York: Basic Books.

Bialystok, E., & Hakuta, K. (1999). Confounded age: Linguistic and cognitive factors in age differences for second language acquisition. In D. Birdsong (Ed.), *Second language acquisition and the critical period hypothesis* (pp. 161–181). Mahwah, NJ: Erlbaum.

Bialystok, E., & Miller, B. (1999). The problem of age in second language acquisition: Influences from language, task, and structure. *Bilingualism: Language and Cognition, 2,* 127–145.

Birdsong, D. (1992). Ultimate attainment in second language acquisition. *Language, 68,* 706–755.

Birdsong, D. (1999a). Introduction: Whys and why nots of the critical period hypothesis. In D. Birdsong (Ed.), *Second language acquisition and the critical period hypothesis* (pp. 1–22). Mahwah, NJ: Erlbaum.

Birdsong, D. (Ed.). (1999b). *Second language acquisition and the critical period hypothesis.* Mahwah, NJ: Erlbaum.

Birdsong, D. (2003). Authenticité de prononciation en français L2 chez des apprenants tardifs anglophones: Analyses segmentales et globales. *Acquisition et Interaction en Langue Étrangère, 18,* 17–36.

Birdsong, D. (2004). Second language acquisition and ultimate attainment. In A. Davies and C. Elder (Eds.), *The handbook of applied linguistics* (pp. 82–105). London: Blackwell.

Birdsong, D., & Flege, J. E. (2001). Regular-irregular dissociations in the acquisition of English as a second language. In A. H.-J. Do, L. Domínguez, & A. Johansen (Eds.), *BUCLD 25: Proceedings of the 25th Annual Boston University Conference on Language Development* (pp. 123–132). Boston: Cascadilla Press.

Birdsong, D., & Molis, M. (2001). On the evidence for maturational effects in second language acquisition. *Journal of Memory and Language, 44,* 235–249.

Bley-Vroman, R. (1989). What is the logical problem of foreign language learning? In S. Gass & J. Schachter (Eds.), *Linguistic perspectives on second language acquisition* (pp. 41–68). Cambridge, U.K.: Cambridge University Press.

Bongaerts, T. (1999). Ultimate attainment in foreign language pronunciation: The case of very advanced late foreign language learners. In D. Birdsong (Ed.), *Second language acquisition and the critical period hypothesis* (pp. 133–159). Mahwah, NJ: Erlbaum.

Bornstein, M. H. (1989). Sensitive periods in development: Structural characteristics and causal interpretations. *Psychological Bulletin, 105,* 179–197.

Brovetto, C. (2002). *The representation and processing of verbal morphology in the first and second language.* Unpublished doctoral dissertation, Georgetown University, Washington, DC.

Cook, V. J. (1997). Monolingual bias in second language acquisition research. *Revista Canaria de Estudios Ingleses, 34,* 35–49.

Coppieters, R. (1987). Competence differences between native and near-native speakers. *Language, 63,* 544–573.

Cranshaw, A. (1997). *A study of Anglophone native and near-native linguistic and meta-linguistic performance.* Unpublished doctoral dissertation, Université de Montréal, Canada.

Curtiss, S. R. (1977). *Genie: A linguistic study of a modern day "wild child."* New York: Academic Press.

DeKeyser, R. M. (2000). The robustness of critical period effects in second language acquisition. *Studies in Second Language Acquisition, 22,* 499–533.

Eimas, P. D., Siqueland, E. R., Jusczyk, P. W., & Vigorito, J. (1971). Speech perception in infants. *Science, 171,* 303–306.

Eubank, L., & Gregg, K. R. (1999). Critical periods and (second) language acquisition: Divide et impera. In D. Birdsong (Ed.), *Second language acquisition and the critical period hypothesis* (pp. 65–99). Mahwah, NJ: Erlbaum.

Flege, J. E. (1999). Age of learning and second-language speech. In D. Birdsong (Ed.), *Second language acquisition and the critical period hypothesis* (pp. 101–131). Mahwah, NJ: Erlbaum.

Flege, J. E., Frieda, A. M., & Nozawa, T. (1997). Amount of native-language (L1) use affects the pronunciation of an L2. *Journal of Phonetics, 25,* 169–186.

Flege, J. E., Munro, M. J., & MacKay, I. R. A. (1995). Factors affecting strength of perceived foreign accent in a second language. *Journal of the Acoustical Society of America, 97,* 3125–3134.

Flege, J. E., Yeni-Komshian, G. H., & Liu, S. (1999). Age constraints on second-language acquisition. *Journal of Memory and Language, 41,* 78–104.

Flynn, S., & Manuel, S. (1991). Age-dependent effects in language acquisition: "Critical period" hypotheses. In L. Eubank (Ed.), *Point-counterpoint: Universal grammar in the second language* (pp. 117–145). Amsterdam: Benjamins.

Grosjean, F. (1989). Studying bilinguals: Methodological and conceptual issues. *Bilingualism: Language and Cognition, 1,* 131–149.

Hakuta, K., Bialystok, E., & Wiley, E. (2001). *Critical evidence: A test of the critical period hypothesis for second language acquisition.* Unpublished manuscript, Stanford University, California.

Hubel, D. H., & Wiesel, T. N. (1965). Binocular interaction in the striate cortex of kittens reared with artificial squint. *Journal of Neurophysiology, 21,* 1041–1059.

Hyltenstam, K. (1992). Non-native features of near-native speakers: On the ultimate attainment of childhood L2 learners. In R. Harris (Ed.), *Cognitive processing in bilinguals* (pp. 351–368). Amsterdam: Elsevier.

Hyltenstam, K., & Abrahamsson, N. (2000). Who can become native-like in a second language? All, some, or none? On the maturational constraints controversy in second language acquisition. *Studia Linguistica, 54,* 250–166.

Ioup, G., Boustagui, E., El Tigi, M., & Moselle, M. (1994). Reexamining the critical period hypothesis: A case study of successful adult SLA in a naturalistic environment. *Studies in Second Language Acquisition, 10,* 303–337.

Johnson, J. (1992). Critical period effects in second language acquisition: The effect of written versus auditory materials on the assessment of grammatical competence. *Language Learning, 42,* 217–248.

Johnson, J., & Newport, E. L. (1989). Critical period effects in second language learning: The influence of maturational state on the acquisition of English as a second language. *Cognitive Psychology, 21,* 60–99.

Juffs, A., & Harrington, M. (1995). Parsing effects in second language sentence processing: Subject and object asymmetries in wh-extraction. *Studies in Second Language Acquisition, 17,* 483–516.

Klein, W. (1995). Language acquisition at different ages. In D. Magnusson (Ed.), *The lifespan development of individuals: Behavioral, neurobiological, and psychosocial perspectives. A synthesis* (pp. 244–264). Cambridge, U.K.: Cambridge University Press.

Lenneberg, E. H. (1967). *Biological foundations of language.* New York: Wiley.

Li, S.-C., Lindenberger, U., & Sikström, S. (2001). Aging cognition: From neuromodulation to representation. *Trends in Cognitive Sciences, 5,* 479–486.

Long, M. H. (1990). Maturational constraints on language development. *Studies in Second Language Acquisition, 12,* 251–285.

Lupien, S., DeLeon, M., DeSanti, S., Convit, A., Tarshish, C., Nair, N. P. V., et al. (1998). Longitudinal increase in cortisol during human aging predicts hippocampal atrophy and memory deficits. *Nature Neuroscience, 1,* 69–73.

Lupien, S., Lecours, A. R., Lussier, I., Schwartz, G., Nair, N. P. V., & Meaney, M. J. (1994). Basal cortisol levels and cognitive deficits in human aging. *The Journal of Neuroscience, 14,* 2893–2903.

Mack, M. (1997). The monolingual native speaker: Not a norm, but still a necessity. *Studies in the Linguistic Sciences, 27,* 113–146.

Marchman, V. A. (1993). Constraints on plasticity in a connectionist model of the English past tense. *Journal of Cognitive Neuroscience, 5,* 215–234.

Marinova-Todd, S. H., Marshall, D. B., & Snow, C. E. (2000). Three misconceptions about age and L2 learning. *TESOL Quarterly, 34,* 9–34.

Marler, P. (1991). The instinct to learn. In S. Carey & R. Gelman (Eds.), *The epigenesis of mind: Essays on biology and cognition* (pp. 37–66). Hillsdale, NJ: Erlbaum.

Mayberry, R. (1993). First-language acquisition after childhood differs from second-language acquisition: The case of American Sign Language. *Journal of Speech and Hearing Research, 36*, 1258–1270.

McClelland, J. L., & Patterson, K. (2002). Rules or connections in past-tense inflections: What does the evidence rule out? *Trends in Cognitive Sciences, 6*, 465–472.

Montrul, S., & Slabakova, R. (2001). Is native-like competence possible in L2 acquisition? In A. H.-J. Do, L. Domínguez, & A. Johansen (Eds.), *BUCLD 25: Proceedings of the 25th Annual Boston University Conference on Language Development* (pp. 522–533). Boston: Cascadilla Press.

Moyer, A. (1999). Ultimate attainment in L2 phonology. *Studies in Second Language Acquisition, 21*, 81–108.

Moyer, A. (2001). *Beyond "ultimate attainment": Contextualizing language acquisition inquiry for a multicultural Germany.* Unpublished manuscript, University of Maryland, College Park.

Neter, J., Kutner, M., Nachtsheim, C., & Wasserman, W. (1996). *Applied linear statistical models.* Chicago: Irwin.

Newport, E. L. (1991). Contrasting conceptions of the critical period for language. In S. Carey & R. Gelman (Eds.), *The epigenesis of mind* (pp. 111–130). Hillsdale, NJ: Erlbaum.

Oyama, S. (1976). A sensitive period for the acquisition of a nonnative phonological system. *Journal of Psycholinguistic Research, 5*, 261–283.

Patkowski, M. S. (1980). The sensitive period for the acquisition of syntax in a second language. *Language Learning, 30*, 449–472.

Patkowski, M. S. (1990). Age and accent in a second language: A reply to James Emil Flege. *Applied Linguistics, 11*, 73–89.

Pinker, S. (1994). *The language instinct: How the mind creates language.* New York: Morrow.

Pinker, S. (1999). *Words and rules.* New York: Basic Books.

Pinker, S., & Ullman, M. (2002). The past and future of the past tense. *Trends in Cognitive Sciences, 6*, 456–463.

Pulvermüller, F., & Schumann, J. H. (1994). Neurobiological mechanisms of language acquisition. *Language Learning, 44*, 681–734.

Scheibel, A. B. (1996). Structural and functional changes in the aging brain. In J. E. Birren & K. W. Schaie (Eds.), *Handbook of the psychology of aging* (4th ed.) (pp. 105–128). San Diego, CA: Academic Press.

Scovel, T. (1988). *A time to speak: A psycholinguistic inquiry into the critical period for human speech.* Rowley, MA: Newbury House.

Seliger, H. W. (1978). Implications of a multiple critical periods hypothesis for second language learning. In W. Ritchie (Ed.), *Second language acquisition research: Issues and implications* (pp. 11–19). New York: Academic Press.

Selinker, L. (1972). Interlanguage. *International Review of Applied Linguistics, 10*, 209–231.

Singleton, D. (1989). *Language acquisition: the age factor.* Clevedon, U.K.: Multilingual Matters.

Singleton, D. (2001). Age and second language acquisition. *Annual Review of Applied Linguistics, 21*, 77–89.

Skehan, P. (1989). *Individual differences in second-language learning.* London: Arnold.

Stevens, G. (1999). Age at immigration and second language proficiency among foreign-born adults. *Language in Society, 28*, 555–578.

Towell, R., & Hawkins, R. (1994). *Approaches to second language acquisition.* Clevedon, U.K.: Multilingual Matters.

Ullman, M. T. (2001a). The neural basis of lexicon and grammar in first and second language: The declarative/procedural model. *Bilingualism: Language and Cognition, 4*, 105–122.

Ullman, M. T. (2001b). A neurocognitive perspective on language: The declarative/procedural model. *Nature Reviews Neuroscience, 2*, 717–727.

Van Wuijtswinkel, K. (1994). *Critical period effects on the acquisition of grammatical competence in a second language.* Unpublished thesis, Katholieke Universiteit, Nijmegen, The Netherlands.

White, L., & Genesee, F. (1996). How native is near-native? The issue of ultimate attainment in adult second language acquisition. *Second Language Research, 12*, 238–265.

Yeni-Komshian, G., Flege, J. E., & Liu, S. (1997). Pronunciation proficiency in L1 and L2 among Korean-English bilinguals: The effect of age of arrival in the U.S. *Journal of the Acoustical Society of America, 102*(A), 3138.

Manfred Pienemann
Bruno Di Biase
Satomi Kawaguchi
Gisela Håkansson

7

Processing Constraints on L1 Transfer

ABSTRACT   This chapter focuses on the interplay between first language (L1) transfer and psycholinguistic constraints on second language (L2) processability. The theoretical assumptions underlying this chapter are those made in processability theory (PT) (Pienemann, 1998), which include, in particular, the following two hypotheses: (a) that L1 transfer is constrained by the processability of the given structure, and (b) that the initial state of the L2 does not necessarily equal the final state of the L1 because there is no guarantee that the given L1 structure is processable by the underdeveloped L2 parser. In other words, it is assumed that L1 transfer is constrained by the capacity of the language processor of the L2 learner (or bilingual speaker) irrespective of the typological distance between the two languages. Using the PT hierarchy as a comparative matrix, we demonstrate on the basis of empirical studies of L2 acquisition that learners of closely related languages do not necessarily transfer grammatical features at the initial state even if these features are contained in L1 *and* L2, providing the features are located higher up the processability hierarchy. We further demonstrate that such features *will* be transferred when the interlanguage has developed the necessary processing prerequisites. In addition, we demonstrate that typological distance and differences in grammatical marking need not constitute a barrier to learning if the feature to be learned is processable at the given point in time. All of this demonstrates that processability is a key variable in L1 transfer.

This chapter focuses on the interplay between first language (L1) transfer and psycholinguistic constraints on second language (L2) processability. The basic thesis of this chapter is that L1 transfer is constrained by the capacity of the language processor of the L2 learner (or bilingual speaker) irrespective of the typological distance between the two languages.

Before we lay out our argument, it may be useful to characterize briefly the nature of the various competing approaches to L1 transfer and their theoretical basis. In the study of language contact, bilingualism, and L2 acquisition, cross-linguistic influence appears to be one of the key phenomena that has caught the attention of scholars for over 100 years. For instance, Sweet (1899) and Palmer (1917/1968) both discussed L1 transfer in relation to what would now be termed *typological distance*. Weinreich (1953/1974), in his seminal treatment of transfer in language contact, placed great emphasis

on operationalizing this concept in the context of the overall "linguistic system" as conceptualized in the structuralist theory of communication of his time. And, in his review of research on the study of transfer in bilingualism, he complained that "all these studies suffer... from a lack of linguistic advise" (p. 12). Indeed, his review contained many examples of anecdotal approaches.

One of Weinreich's achievements was to place the notion of transfer in the context of the overall design of structuralist linguistics. In other words, L1 influence was not considered an accidental or irregular accumulation of L1 "borrowings" in an individual bilingual, but was placed firmly within the overall system of the source and the target languages. Other scholars established a theoretical link between behaviorist theories of learning and the notion of L1 transfer (e.g., Lado, 1957), thereby establishing an influential paradigm that was ultimately damaged by the rationalists' critique of behaviorist concepts of language learning.

By the 1970s, the outlook on L1 transfer had changed under the influence of the newly emerging discipline of second language acquisition research, which was fueled initially in particular by the idea that learners construct their own linguistic systems that may be quite independent of the L1 and L2. With the new emphasis on the "creative construction process" (e.g., Dulay & Burt, 1974) in L2 acquisition, the notion of L1 transfer appeared a less attractive explanatory concept. It became clear that specific L2 acquisition theories were needed that would be able to predict the exact conditions for creative construction on the one hand and for L1 transfer on the other hand because these explanations compete with each other.

In this context, Felix (1980) argued that the role of L1 transfer can be determined in empirical studies only if the null hypothesis is tested in a typological manner. This requires a systematic typological comparison of the given linguistic feature in L1 and L2 and in the interlanguage (i.e., the learner language) in the following constellation:

	First language	Second language	Interlanguage
Feature x	+	−	+
Feature x	−	−	−

Felix (1980) argued as follows: When the interlanguage contains an L2 deviation that is structurally similar to the L1, it can be assumed that this structure has been transferred from the L1 only if this structure does not appear in the interlanguages of other learners of the same L2 whose L1 does not contain the feature in question. Using this matrix in empirical studies, Felix demonstrated, however, that in the above constellation features are often assigned as follows:

	First language	Second language	Interlanguage
Feature x	+	−	+
Feature x	−	−	+

Felix (1980) illustrated this with the distinction between *why* and *because*, which is made in English and German (*warum*, *weil*), but not in spoken Italian. He showed that, despite this linguistic contrast (in their L1), both Italian learners of German and German learners of English fail to observe this distinction in their interlanguage at a certain stage. In

other words, looking at the Italian-German contrast by itself, there appears to be a case for transfer. However, once the contrast inherent in the German-English constellation is included, it can be seen that the lack of a why–because distinction appears in the interlanguage independent from the typological contrast between L1 and L2. In such cases, the transfer hypothesis has to be rejected. Instead, it has to be concluded that this is a genuine interlanguage feature. Unfortunately, this logic has not always been adhered to in later research. However, in making a case for developmental constraints on L1 transfer, we apply exactly this logic in evaluating the significance of empirical evidence for or against competing theoretical positions, including our own.

Another example of an interlanguage feature that may, at first glance, be taken as an instance of L1 transfer appeared in the acquisition of English question formation. Lightbown and Spada (1999) found that French learners of English made a distinction between subject-verb inversion with pronominal and referential subjects (containing a noun). Lightbown and Spada claimed that the preference of the French learners of English for pronominal subjects was caused by influence from the L1 because French requires inversion only with pronouns, not with referential subjects. However, when the same task was given to a group of Swedish learners of English (Ewehag & Järnum, 2001), the same pattern was found. Again, inversion was preferred with pronominal subjects. Given that Swedish does not make a distinction between pronominal and referential subjects, the preference shown by the Swedish learners cannot be attributed to transfer.

A key factor in evaluating research on L1 transfer is its underlying theoretical basis. As Weinreich (1953/1974) pointed out, a great deal of research before his time was inexplicit or even prescientific in its theoretical foundation. The majority of studies that were conducted in the two decades following Weinreich were associated with behaviorist ideas that, in the view of many L2 acquisition researchers, were discredited by the above-mentioned rationalist critique. This may be one reason why in the past three decades a great deal of research on L1 transfer has been carried out within a largely rationalist paradigm that makes two key assumptions: (a) the modularity of mind and (b) the existence of a "universal grammar" to which learners may or may not have access. To describe more clearly the research carried out in this tradition, it may be useful to sketch the background of these two assumptions.

In the rationalist tradition, learnability analyses have been based on four components that must be specified in any learnability theory (e.g., Pinker, 1979; Wexler & Culicover, 1980): (a) the target grammar, (b) the data input to the learner, (c) the learning device that must acquire that grammar, and (d) the initial state.

The rationale for assuming these components is rooted in the way in which learnability theory has been formulated in response to the "logical problem" in language acquisition (cf. Wexler, 1982). The logical problem basically describes the following paradox: Children acquire the basic principles of their native language in a relatively short period of time and on the basis of limited linguistic input. Many of these principles are said to be impossible to infer from the observations made by the learner.

In other words, the rationalist approach proposed by Wexler (1982) characterizes a theory of language learnability as a solely linguistic problem of the relationship between the representation of linguistic knowledge and the acquisition of that knowledge. This is why the four components of such a theory are described as (a) *the target grammar*, which describes linguistic knowledge; (b) *linguistic input*; and (c) *the learning device*, which has to acquire the target grammar given a certain set of knowledge contained in the (d) *initial state*.

These assumptions go hand in hand with the assumed *autonomy of syntax*. Chomsky (1990) claimed that natural languages display properties learnable only if the principles underlying these properties do not have to be acquired explicitly but can be inferred from the structure of an innate cognitive system (spelled out in universal grammar, which contains universal principles and parameters[1]). Fodor (1981) argued that such principles cannot be reduced to principles of other domains of cognition, and that therefore it must be assumed that they are specific to the linguistic domain of cognition, which is similar in its specificity to the visual domain of cognition. This assumption is known as the *modularity hypothesis* and forms the basis for limiting the components of a theory of language learnability to the above four components: If there is an independent linguistic module of cognition, then it is possible to study it in isolation. This does not exclude interaction with other cognitive systems, but it justifies the reductionism present in Wexler's (1982) assumption.

Scholars who accept that universal grammar plays a role in L2 acquisition attribute different roles to it. These roles vary according to the degree to which L2 learners are thought to have access to universal grammar and according to the degree to which L1 knowledge is transferred to the L2.

The most radical position is that of Schwartz and Sprouse (1994, 1996), who proposed the full transfer/full access model. These authors assumed that "the initial state of L2 acquisition is the final state of L1 acquisition" (Schwartz & Sprouse, 1996, p. 40). Schwartz and Sprouse assumed that L2 learners have full access to universal grammar. However, they believed that parameters are already set as in the L1. In this perspective, L2 acquisition is seen as the process of restructuring the existing system of grammatical knowledge. In keeping with this, if positive evidence in the input is needed to restructure aspects of L1 knowledge, and this evidence is not available or "obscure," then this can lead to fossilization. The last process is thought to explain why, contrary to child language, in L2 acquisition "convergence with the TL [Target Language] grammar is not guaranteed" (Schwartz & Sprouse, 1996, p. 42).

The full transfer/full access model has also been assumed in research within a nonparametric framework (LaFond, Hayes, & Bhatt, 2001) based on optimality theory (Tesar & Smolensky, 1998). In this context, universal grammar is seen as the basis of innately specified grammatical knowledge, and optimality theory is used as the learning mechanism that allows the learner to restructure the L1 constraint hierarchies to conform with the hierarchies found in the L2. Unfortunately, alternative models of access to universal grammar were not evaluated in this research.

The position of Vainikka and Young-Scholten (1994, 1996) differed from that of Schwartz and Sprouse's (1996) full access/full transfer position in the amount of transfer assumed to occur from the L1 to the L2 setting of parameters. For Vainikka and Young-Scholten, transfer is limited to lexical categories; they assumed that the L2 initial state contains only lexical categories and their projections (including the directionality of their heads). However, functional categories are not transferred from the L1. They therefore described their position as the "minimal tree" position, which in effect includes the assumption that L1 word order is transferred.

A further position was proposed by Eubank (1993), who hypothesized that lexical and functional categories can be transferred to the L2, but that the feature strength associated with functional categories is not transferred. Eubank argued that the feature strength of the inflection will not be transferred because the affixes themselves may be fundamentally different from language to language.

Platzack (1996) proposed a universal "initial hypothesis of syntax" based on the Minimalist Program. His study focused on the acquisition of Swedish word order, and he demonstrated that word order constellations can be captured by the weak/strong distinction in functional heads.[2] He assumed that the default value of functional heads is "weak." If all functional heads are weak in a sentence, a universal default word order subject-verb-complement' will be generated. Only if a functional head is strong can the position of grammatical functions change.

Platzack (1996) claimed that "the initial syntactic hypothesis of the child must be that all syntactic features are weak" (p. 375). He further claimed that "the child has access to the full range of functional categories already at the time of first sentence-like utterances" (p. 377). In other words, he claimed that "every human being is expected to assume from the outset that any unknown language s/he is exposed to, including the first language, has the word order subject-verb-complement: this is the order obtained if there are no strong features at all" (p. 378). Regarding L2 acquisition, he claimed that "we initially go back to...[the initial hypothesis of syntax] when trying to come to grips with a second language" (p. 380).

The above views all have in common that L2 learners are believed to have full access to universal grammar. However, several scholars hold other views. Felix (1984), Clahsen (1986), and Meisel (1983, 1991) all developed models in which L2 learners have limited or indirect access to universal grammar. This assumption is congruent with the observation that L2 acquirers do not necessarily become native speakers of the L2. Given that the limited availability of universal grammar creates an explanatory void, these authors all made proposals for a more general cognitive substitute that can account for the somewhat deficient process present in L2 acquisition.

The competition model (Bates & MacWhinney, 1981, 1982, 1987; MacWhinney, chapter 3, this volume) represents a fundamentally different approach to language acquisition from the rationalist tradition. It is a functionalist approach that is based on the assumption that linguistic behavior is constrained, among other things, by general cognition (rather than a language-specific cognitive module) and communicative needs. In keeping with the functionalist tradition, Bates and MacWhinney (1981) assumed that "the surface con-

ventions of natural languages are created, governed, constrained, acquired, and used in the service of communicative functions" (p. 192).

The competition model has been applied to child language, language processing, and L2 acquisition. According to this model, it is the task of the language learner to discover the specific relationship between the linguistic forms of a given language and their communicative functions. The linguistic forms used to mark grammatical and semantic roles differ from language to language. For instance, agreement marking, word order, and animacy play different roles in the marking of subjecthood and agency in different languages. Linguistic forms are seen as "cues" for semantic interpretation in online comprehension and production, and different cues may compete, as in the above case of the marking of subjecthood, hence the name *competition model.*

In the competition model, the process of learning linguistic forms is driven by the frequency and complexity of form–function relationships in the input. In this context, the majority of L2 learning problems are modeled in connectionist terms. MacWhinney (1987) exemplified this with the preverbal positioning of a linguistic form as a (processing) cue for the semantic actor role. He stated that the strength of this cue "can be viewed as the weight on the connection between the preverbal positioning node (an input node) and the actor role (an output node). If the preverbal positioning node is activated, it then sends activation to the actor node in proportion to the weight on the connection" (p. 320).

The competition model has formed the conceptual basis of experiments on bilingual sentence processing (e.g., Gass, 1987; Harrington, 1987; Kilborn & Ito, 1989; McDonald & Heilenman, 1991; Sasaki, 1991). In these studies, bilingual speakers of different languages need to identify the function of different cues in L1 and L2. The input material is designed to reflect the coordination and competition of cues. For instance, Harrington (1987) studied the (competing) effect of word order, animacy, and stress on the comprehension of Japanese and English sentences by native speakers and nonnative speakers of the two languages who were all speakers of both languages. Obviously, the three cues have different weights in the two target languages concerned. The results showed that L2 learners transferred their L1 processing strategies (i.e., weighting of cues) when interpreting L2 sentences. This overall result was predicted by the competition model because, within this framework, processing cues are not initially separated by languages, and it is therefore to be expected that their weighting is transferred.

MacWhinney (chapter 3, this volume) also attributes a key role to L1 transfer in the acquisition (as opposed to the processing) of an L2. This is motivated mainly by the stark contrast in learning outcomes in L1 and L2 acquisition that has also been noted by many rationalist researchers (e.g., Bley-Vroman, 1990; Clahsen & Muysken, 1989; Meisel, 1991). The logic behind this is straightforward: Both L1 and L2 learners rely on cue strength in acquisition. The reason the outcomes are different is because, in the case of L2 learners, L1 patterns interfere with L2 learning. On the basis of the above assumptions, MacWhinney developed (1997) a strong view on L1 transfer that is in effect similar to the full transfer/full access hypothesis of Schwartz and Sprouse (1996), despite their fundamentally different theoretical orientation:

[T]he early second language learner should experience a massive amount of transfer from L1 to L2. Because connectionist models place such a strong emphasis on analogy and other types of pattern generalization, they predict that all aspects of the first language that can possibly transfer to L2 will transfer. This is an extremely strong and highly falsifiable prediction. (p. 119)

MacWhinney (1997) illustrated his point about structurally "impossible transfer" using German and English as an example. German nouns are implicitly marked for grammatical gender, whereas English nouns are not. He concluded that German learners therefore have no basis for transferring the German gender system to English. Therefore, this set of features is not included in the list of things that will be transferred.

Our own approach to cross-linguistic influences in L2 acquisition does not take the initial state or general learning mechanisms as its point of departure, but instead argues in terms of processing constraints (e.g., Håkansson, Pienemann, & Sayehli, 2002; Pienemann, 1998). As mentioned, the theoretical assumptions underlying our approach are those made in processability theory (PT; Pienemann, 1998), which include, in particular, the following hypotheses: (a) that L1 transfer is constrained by the processability of the given structure and (b) that the initial state of the L2 does not necessarily equal the final state of the L1 (contrary to the assumption made by Schwartz and Sprouse, 1996) because there is no guarantee that the given

L1 structure is processable by the underdeveloped L2 parser.

The key assumption of the processing perspective in L2 acquisition is that L2 learners can produce only those linguistic forms for which they have acquired the necessary processing prerequisites (Pienemann, 1998). Therefore, PT predicts that, regardless of linguistic typology, only those linguistic forms that the learner can process can be transferred to the L2. These claims are operationalized in PT by embedding in a coherent theoretical framework of L2 processing. To illustrate this operationalization, we give a summary of PT and characterize the lexical and hence language-specific nature of the processing of key morphosyntactic features within this framework.

The assumption that L1 transfer may be developmentally constrained is not new in L2 acquisition research. Wode (1976, 1978) demonstrated such constraints for the acquisition of negation and interrogatives. He showed that German learners of English produce certain forms that exist in the L1 and the L2 only after they have developed the structural prerequisites in the L2. Zobl (1980) observed similar phenomena, as did Kellerman (1983). What PT (Pienemann, 1998) adds to the concept of developmental constraints on transfer is an explicit formal framework for specifying these constraints. This framework is described in the following sections before testing it in sets of data to allow us to test the null hypothesis for transfer in typological "minimal pairs."

A Sketch of Processability Theory

The basic logic underlying PT is this: Structural options that may be formally possible will be produced by the language learner only if the necessary processing procedures are available. In this perspective, the language processor is seen, in agreement with Kaplan and Bresnan (1982), as the computational mechanisms that operate on (but are separate from) the native speaker's linguistic knowledge. PT primarily deals with the nature of those computational mechanisms and the way in which they are acquired.

The fundamental point behind PT is that recourse needs to be made to key psychological aspects of human language processing to account for the developmental problem[3] because describable developmental routes are at least partly caused by the architecture of the human language processor. For linguistic hypotheses to transform into executable *procedural knowledge* (i.e., a certain processing skill), the processor needs to have the capacity for processing the structures relating to those hypotheses.

Processability theory is based on a universal hierarchy of processing procedures that is derived from the general architecture of the language processor. This hierarchy is related to the requirements of the specific procedural skills needed for the target language. In this way, predictions that can be tested empirically can be made for language development.

The view of language production followed in PT is largely that described by Levelt (1989). It also overlaps to some extent with the computational model of Kempen and Hoenkamp (1987), which emulates much of Garrett's work (e.g., Garrett, 1976, 1980, 1982). The basic premises of that view are the following:

> *Premise 1.* Processing components, such as procedures to build NPs (noun phrases) and the like, are relatively autonomous specialists that operate largely automatically. Levelt (1989) described such grammatical procedures as "stupid" because their capacity is strictly limited to the very narrow but highly efficient handling of extremely specific processing tasks (e.g., NP procedures and verb phrase [VP] procedures). The automaticity of these procedures implies that their execution is not normally subject to conscious control.
>
> *Premise 2.* Processing is incremental. This means that surface lexico-grammatical form is gradually constructed while conceptualization is still ongoing. One key implication of incremental language processing is the need for grammatical memory. For the next processor to be able to work on still-incomplete output of the current processor and for all of this to result in coherent surface forms, some of the incomplete intermediate output has to be held in memory.
>
> *Premise 3.* The output of the processor is linear, even though it may not be mapped onto the underlying meaning in a linear way. This is known as the *linearization problem* (Levelt, 1981), which applies both to the mapping of conceptual structure onto linguistic form and to the generation of morphosyntactic structures. One example of this is subject-verb agreement, as illustrated in the sentence, "She gives him a book." The affixation of the agreement marker to the verb depends,

among other things, on the storage of information about the grammatical subject (namely, number and person), which is created before the verb is retrieved from the lexicon.

> *Premise 4.* Grammatical processing has access to a grammatical memory store. The need for a grammatical memory store derives from the linearization problem and the automatic and incremental nature of language generation. Levelt (1989) assumed that grammatical information is held temporarily in a grammatical memory store that is highly task specific and in which specialized grammatical processors can deposit information of a specific nature (e.g., the value of diacritic features, such as the values for "person" and "number"). In Kempen and Hoenkamp's (1987) Incremental Procedural Grammar, the specialized procedures that process NPs, VPs, and the like are assumed to be the locus of the grammatical buffer. Pienemann (1998) presented evidence from online experiments and aphasia in support of these assumptions (e.g., Cooper & Zurif, 1983; Engelkamp, 1974; Paradis, 1994; Zurif, Swinney, Prather, & Love, 1994).

The process of incremental language generation as envisaged by Levelt (1989) and Kempen and Hoenkamp (1987) is exemplified in Fig. 7.1, which illustrates some of the key processes involved in the generation of the example sentence "a child gave the mother the cat." The concepts underlying this sentence are produced in the Conceptualizer. The conceptual material produced first activates the lemma CHILD in the lexicon. This activation starts from within the lexicalization system, a subsystem of the grammatical encoder. The lemma contains the category information N, which calls the categorial procedure NP. This procedure can build the phrasal category in which N is head, that is, NP. The categorial procedure inspects the conceptual material of the current iteration (the material currently being processed) for possible complements and specifiers and provides values for diacritic features. Given certain conceptual specifications, the lemma "A" is activated, and the NP procedure attaches the branch Det to NP.

During this process, the diacritic features of Det and N are checked against each other. This implies that the grammatical information "singular" is extracted from each of the two lemmas at the time of their activation and is then stored in NP until the

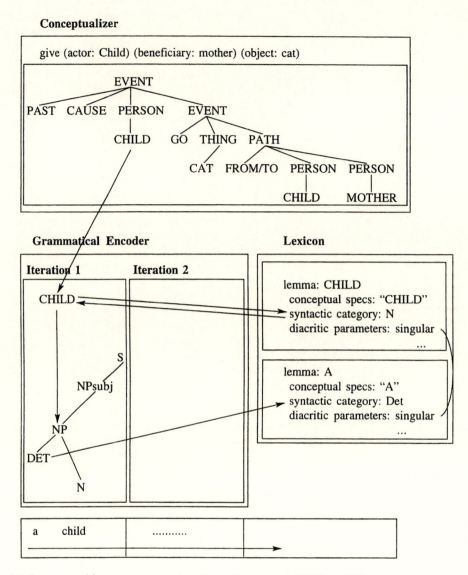

Figure 7.1 Incremental language generation. (From Pienemann, 1998, p. 68.)

head of the phrase is produced. This process of exchange of grammatical information is a key feature of language production. Below, we utilize Lexical-Functional Grammar (cf. Bresnan, 1982, 2001), which has the capacity to model the exchange of grammatical information by feature unification.

The production process has now proceeded to the point at which the structure of a phrase has been created, and the associated lemmata are activated. What is missing to make this the beginning of a continuous and fluent utterance is the establishment of a relation between the phrase and the rest of the intended message. This is accomplished by assigning a grammatical function to the newly created phrase.

Although the process was still ongoing, the next conceptual fragment would have been processed in parallel, and the output of the Formulator[4] would have been delivered to the Articulator. This means that new conceptualization occurs while the conceptual structure of the previous iteration is produced. The whole process then moves from iteration to iteration.

Kempen and Hoenkamp's (1987) research implied that, in the process of incremental language generation, the following processing procedures and routines are activated in the following sequence:

1. Lemma access
2. The category procedure
3. The phrasal procedure
4. The S procedure
5. The subordinate clause procedure, if applicable

Pienemann (1998) hypothesized that these key grammatical encoding procedures are arranged according to their sequence of activation in the language generation process, and that this sequence follows an implicational pattern in which each procedure is a necessary prerequisite for the following procedures. The basic thesis of PT is that, in the acquisition of language processing procedures, the assembly of the component parts will follow the above-mentioned implicational sequence. The key to predicting which grammatical structures are processable and in which sequence is based on a matrix of information transfer that determines which pieces of grammatical information can be exchanged between which constituents given the availability of the different procedures and their storage capacity. Pienemann pointed out that these processing procedures are operational only in mature users of a language, not in language learners:

> While even beginning second language learners can make recourse to the same *general* cognitive resources as mature native language users, they have to create language-specific processing routines. In this context it is important to ensure that Levelt's model (and Kempen and Hoenkamp's specific section of it) can, in principle, account for language processing in bilinguals, since second language acquisition will lead to a bilingual language processor. (1998, p. 73)

Processability theory utilizes, among other things, De Bot's (1992) work to apply the processability hierarchy to bilingual language production. De Bot (1992) adapted Levelt's model to language production in bilinguals. Based on work by Paradis (1987), he argued that information about the specific language to be used is present in each part of the preverbal message, and this subsequently informs the selection of language-specific lexical items and of the language-specific routines in the formulator. The key assumption of De Bot's work for L2 processing is that, in all cases for which the L2 is not closely related to the L1, different (language-specific) procedures have to be assumed. Pienemann (1998, p. 78) therefore concluded that most of the processing procedures discussed in this section have to be acquired by the L2 learner. He cited diacritic features such as "tense," "number," "gender," and "case," which vary between languages, as obvious examples of cross-linguistic differences in the lexical prerequisites for language processing.

Recall that it is hypothesized by PT that the time course in the activation of grammatical encoding procedures determines the sequence in which these procedures are acquired by L2 learners. The reader may wonder how language can be produced when a given learner has not developed a specific encoding procedure. This is in fact the case for every stage of acquisition before mastery of the target language. All of the grammatical forms not yet developed are caused by the absence of specific processing procedures. PT assumes that the hierarchy of processing procedures will be cut off in the procedural grammar of the learner at the point of the missing processing procedure. The rest of the hierarchy will be replaced by a direct mapping of conceptual structures onto surface form as long as there are lemmata that match the conceptually instigated searches of the lexicon. In other words, it is hypothesized by PT that the processing procedures and the capacity for the exchange of grammatical information will be acquired in their implicational sequence as depicted in Table 7.1, where t_1, t_2, and so on refer to different points in the course of language development.

Memory Stores in Language Processing

In characterizing some of the key psychological constraints on language production, we repeatedly made reference to the storage of linguistic information. It is therefore useful to clarify to some extent the role of the storage of grammatical information in the process of language production.[5] There are several factors that necessitate the storage of linguistic information in language production. At various points in the production process, propositional or grammatical information has to be held in memory. One factor is the *linearization problem* (Levelt, 1981): When conceptualization and articulation are not temporally aligned,

Table 7.1 Hypothetical Hierarchy of Processing Procedures

	t_1	t_2	t_3	t_4	t_5
S′ procedure (embedded S)	—	—	—	—	+
S procedure	—	Simplified	Simplified	Interphrasal information exchange	Interphrasal information exchange
Phrasal procedure (head)	—	—	Phrasal information exchange	Phrasal information exchange	Phrasal information exchange
Category procedure (lexical category)	—	Lexical morphemes	Lexical morphemes	Lexical morphemes	Lexical morphemes
Word/lemma	+	+	+	+	+

Source: From Pienemann (1998, p. 79).

processed material has to be held in memory until it can be used by the articulator. What is needed here is a store with fast access time.

The information generated by the formulator is specifically syntactic in nature and therefore has to be deposited in a store that is suited to handle this type of information, and attention to it (conscious or non-conscious) is not necessary for this operation. For instance, one does not need to be aware of, or control, the fact that the information concerning "person" and "number" matches the lexical entries of the verb and the grammatical subject. In fact, it is possible to attend to only a small number of such processes. Otherwise, with the normal speed of language generation, attentional memory resources would get "clogged up." On the other hand, attention must be focused on the propositional content because it reflects the conceptualization the speaker wants to express. Propositional information is therefore temporarily stored in working memory, which functions as the resource for temporary attentive processes[6] that include conceptualizing and monitoring (Baddeley, 1990; Broadbent, 1975).

Levelt (1989) assumed that grammatical information is held temporarily in a syntactic buffer, a memory store which is highly task specific and non-attentive. Specialized grammatical processors can deposit information of a specific nature in the syntactic buffer, which is needed to synchronize the availability of surface structure fragments for phonological encoding because surface structure fragments may be available before they need to be produced.

Specialized "ultra-short-term" stores are also known in other cognitive fields, for instance, in

vision, for which Gough (1972) argued on the basis of experimental evidence that letters are taken out of the visual buffer at the rate of about 15 ms per letter.

The lexicon is stored in permanent memory and is at least partly open to conscious processing. It is therefore a store of declarative knowledge that can be activated for language production.

In other words, there is a fundamental division between procedural (implicit) and declarative (explicit) memory stores that is crucial to the architecture of the Formulator. Overwhelming empirical evidence supporting the dissociation of procedural and declarative knowledge was amassed by Paradis (1994). He summarized the available clinical evidence as follows:

Lesions in the hippocampal and amygdalar system as well as in parietal-temporal-occipital and frontal association cortices compromise recognition and recall, and cause selective anterograde impairment of declarative memory while preserving procedural memory such as the acquisition and execution of complex skills. On the other hand, lesions of the basic ganglia, cerebellum, and other non-limbic-diencephalic sites, as well as circumscribed neocortical lesions, selectively affect learning and memory for skilled, automatised functions (Mayes, 1988) such as language (aphasia) and well practised voluntary movements (apraxia). (p. 396)

Paradis (1994, p. 396) cited a wealth of studies demonstrating the dissociation of procedural and declarative knowledge in patients with Alzheimer's disease, alcoholic Korsakoff's syndrome, antero-grade amnesia, Parkinson's disease, as well as in aphasia and apraxia and in relation to anesthetic techniques. He summarized these findings as follows:

> Patients with Alzheimer's Disease, Korsakoff's syndrome, or amnesia have impaired explicit memory but intact implicit memory; patients with Parkinson's Disease demonstrate a selective impairment of procedural memory.... An Anaesthesia with isoflorane/oxygen spares implicit memory..., but not with sufentanil/nitrous oxide. (p. 396)

Further, he quoted Cohen (1984, 1992), who argued that procedural and declarative memory "are subserved by neuroanatomically distinct systems. While declarative memory depends on the integrity of the hippocampal system and is stored over large areas of tertiary cortex, procedural memory is linked to the cortical processors through which it was acquired" (p. 396).

Other psychological aspects of language processing are also supported by neurophysiological evidence. In particular, Levelt's model represents the Conceptualizer and the Formulator as two entirely distinct components—to the extent that the Conceptualizer is not capable of processing the type of information contained in the Formulator. Empirical evidence for the different nature of the processing of propositional content and grammatical information comes, among other things, from the study of aphasia and amnesia.

Cooper and Zurif (1983), for instance, showed that in Broca's and, to a lesser extent, in Wernicke's aphasia, lexical retrieval and semantic representation are functional, and grammatical information cannot be processed. This is true for production as well as for comprehension. Tests carried out by the authors showed that patients suffering from Broca's aphasia were able to construct semantic relations on the basis of pragmatic principles; the same is not possible using only grammatical markers. This means that the capacity to use grammatical markers can be located in the region which is affected in Broca's patients, but not in Wernicke's. Zurif et al. (1994) went a step further and linked a specific set of syntactic procedures to changes in cortically localized processing procedures. They demonstrated that Wernicke's patients can link the elements of dependency relations in the same way as neurologically intact subjects; Broca's patients cannot.

Applying Processability Theory to Specific Languages

Given that PT is based on general principles of language generation, it can serve as a cross-linguistic matrix for the measurement of linguistic development. However, before it can serve this function, it needs to be interpretable in relation to grammatical structures of individual languages. This is achieved by interpreting the processability hierarchy through a theory of grammar that is typologically and psychologically plausible. The theory of grammar used for this purpose in PT is Lexical-Functional Grammar (cf. Bresnan, 1982, 2001; Kaplan & Bresnan, 1982). The reason for this choice is that every level of the hierarchy of processing procedures can be captured through feature unification[7] in Lexical-Functional Grammar. This grammatical theory also shares three key features with Kempen and Hoenkamp's (1987) procedural account of language generation, namely (a) the assumption that grammars are lexically driven, (b) the functional annotations of phrases (e.g., "subject of"), and (c) the reliance on lexical feature unification as a key process of sentence generation. In other words, a Lexical-Functional Grammar description of the structure to be learned affords an analysis of the psycholinguistic process of grammatical information exchange, and the latter is the key component of the processability hierarchy. As Bialystok (1997) suggested (cf. Frenck-Mestre, chapter 13, this volume), the role linguistic theory plays in a theory of L2 acquisition needs to be clear and consistent. It is for this reason that we are describing the linguistic theory adopted by PT in some detail as well as explicating the relationship between the two theories.

A Brief Sketch of Lexical-Functional Grammar

Before we demonstrate how the processability hierarchy is implemented into a description of a target language (and the developing interlanguage) in Lexical-Functional Grammar, we give a brief outline of this theory of grammar. Lexical-Functional Grammar is a unification grammar; its most prominent characteristic is the unification of features. Put simply, the process of feature unification ensures that the different parts that constitute a sentence do actually fit together.

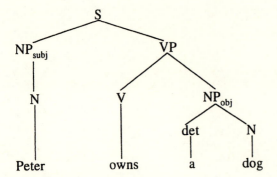

Figure 7.2 Constituent structure example.

$$
\begin{aligned}
S &\rightarrow NP_{subj}\ VP \\
NP &\rightarrow (det)\ N \\
VP &\rightarrow V\ (NP_{obj}).
\end{aligned}
$$

Figure 7.3 Annotated constituent structure rules.

Lexical-Functional Grammar consists of three parts: (a) a constituent structure component that generates "surface structure" constituents and constituent structure relationships, (b) a lexicon with entries that contain syntactic and other information relevant to the generation of sentences, and (c) a functional component that compiles for every sentence all the grammatical information needed to interpret the sentence semantically.

All constituent structures are generated directly by phrase structure rules without any intervening transformations. Hence, the mapping of predicate–argument structures onto surface forms is achieved without any intervening levels of representation. Grammatical functions assume the role of grammatical primitives, and major constituents are annotated for their grammatical function. The constituent structure of the sentence "Peter owns a dog," for instance, is shown in Fig. 7.2. This

structure can be generated by the annotated phrase structure rules shown in Fig. 7.3. A simplified account of the lexical entries relating to Fig. 7.2 is given in Fig. 7.4. As is obvious from these simplified examples, lexical entries specify a number of syntactic and other properties of lexical items by assigning values to features (e.g., NUM[BER] = singular [SG]). In most cases such equations define the value of features. In some cases, they may also "demand" certain values elsewhere in the functional description of a sentence. Such demands are expressed through constraining equations. One example for such a constraining equation would be $WH =_c +$. This equation stipulates that the phrase to which the equation is attached must be a wh- word.

The functional structure (or *f-structure*) of a sentence is a list of those pieces of grammatical information needed to interpret the sentence semantically. It is generated by the interaction between constituent structure and the lexicon. The functional structure of the sentence in Fig. 7.2 is given in Fig. 7.5. The predicate entry [PRED "own" (SUBJ, OBJ)] is taken from the lexical entry of the verb. Listing the stem of the verb in quotation marks ("own") is simply a shorthand convention for a semantic representation of the word.

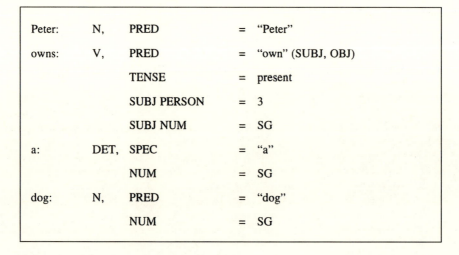

Figure 7.4 Lexical entries.

PRED	"own" (SUBJ, OBJ)	
TENSE	present	
SUBJ	PRED	"Peter"
OBJ	SPEC "a"	
	NUM SG	
	PRED	"dog"

Figure 7.5 Functional structure.

Table 7.2 Lexical Entries for "A Man Owns Many Dogs"

a:	DET,	SPEC = 'A' NUM = SG
man:	N,	PRED = 'MAN' NUM = SG PERS = 3
owns:	V,	PRED = 'OWN' (SUBJ)(OBJ) SUBJ NUM = SG SUBJ PERS = 3 TENSE = PRESENT
many:	DET,	SPEC = 'MANY' NUM = PL
dogs:	N,	PRED = 'DOG' NUM = PL

The slots to the right of the verb that are filled by SUBJ[ECT] and OBJ[ECT] in Fig. 7.5 list the arguments of the predicate: first the owner, then the item owned.

The PRED entry of the f-structure therefore makes it possible to relate the different constituents to the *roles* (actor, patient, etc.) described by the sentence. This forms the link between the syntactic form and its underlying predicate–argument relations.

As mentioned, feature unification is one of the key concepts that relates Lexical-Functional Grammar to the psycholinguistic model of language generation presented in the work of Levelt (1989). Therefore, it may be useful to have this key notion illustrated in light of the sketch of Lexical-Functional Grammar. In the context of this chapter, this may best be achieved with reference to morphological structures.

In Lexical-Functional Grammar, the morphological component operates on the basis of a functional description of the sentence. The sentence "A man owns many dogs" may illustrate this. Note that lexical entries contain information that is relevant here. The relevant pieces of information are listed in Table 7.2. The well-formedness of sentences is guaranteed, among other things, by ensuring that functional descriptions of the sentence and lexical entries match, that is, the phrase "a man" is functionally well formed because—among other things—the value for NUM[BER] is SG (i.e., singular) in the subsidiary function NUM = SG under SUBJ as well as in the lexical entry for "man." In the same way, the noun phrase "many dogs" is well formed because of a match of the feature NUM in "many" and "dogs." The actual structure of the morphological component is not crucial to the present line of argument. The central point here is that feature unification entails the matching of feature values (such as NUM[BER]) within and across constituents.

Implementing a Processing Hierarchy Into Lexical-Functional Grammar

The implementation of the processability hierarchy into a description of a given language based on Lexical-Functional Grammar affords a prediction of the stages in which the language can develop in L2 learners. The main point of the implementation is to demonstrate the flow of grammatical information in the production of linguistic structures. We demonstrate this with the example of three morphological rules and two word order rules, both relating to English.

The brief discussion of feature unification in the previous section may serve as a useful basis for an illustration of the flow of grammatical information in morphological structures. Considering the unification of the feature NUM[BER] in the noun phrase "a man" (i.e., matching the values of this feature for "a" and "man"), one can see that the unification of the NUM value in noun phrases is an operation that is restricted entirely to the noun phrase. In fact, the noun phrase procedure is the locus of this operation. In PT, an affixation resulting from feature unification within a phrase is called *phrasal* because it occurs inside phrase boundaries (cf. Pienemann, 1998). This operation relies on the capacity of phrasal procedures to store and unify the feature values of their constituents.

In contrast, some morphological regularities rely merely on category procedures. An example is English or German tense marking (-ed or -te), the information for which can be read off the lexical entry of the verb without any further exchange of lexical information within the phrase, as can be seen in

Table 7.1. In PT, an affix resulting from the use of a category procedure is called a *lexical* morpheme.

Subject-verb agreement, in contrast, involves the matching of features in two distinct constituents, namely NP_{subj} and VP. The insertion of the -s affix for subject-verb agreement marking requires the following grammatical information:

-s Vaffix	TENSE	=	present
	SUBJ NUMBER	=	sg
	SUBJ PERSON	=	3

The value of the first equation (the one relating to tense) is read off the functional description of sentences as illustrated in Fig. 7.5. The values for NUMBER and PERSON must be identical in the functional structure of SUBJ and the lexical entry of V. Hence, this information from inside both constituents has to be matched across constituent boundaries. This process may be described informally as follows:

[A man]$_{NP_{subj}}$ [{owns} . . .]$_{VP}$ (Present, imperfective)

PERSON = 3   PERSON   = 3
NUM   = sg   NUM   = sg

From a processing point of view, the two morphological processes, plural agreement in noun phrases and subject-verb agreement, have a different status. Whereas the first occurs exclusively inside one major constituent, the second requires that grammatical information be exchanged across constituent boundaries. This type of morphological process is referred to as *interphrasal affixation*. This operation relies on the capacity of the sentence procedure to store and unify the feature values of sentence constituents.

The basic point to bear in mind for the discussion of word order within the framework of Lexical-Functional Grammar is the fact that word order is defined through constituent structure. This is because this theory of grammar contains only one level of constituent structure, and no intervening representations occur. In other words, no actual linguistic material is assumed to be "moved" from one place to another, as proposed in transformational grammar. Instead, in Bresnan's (1982) and Pinker's (1984) account of English word order, constituent structure allows a range of different word order constellations. To achieve the correct constellation in a given context, these

authors made constituent structure dependent on control equations as in Rule 1, which stipulate constituents to be filled by certain lexical classes.

$$S'' \to (XP) \qquad\qquad S'$$
$$\left\{ \begin{array}{l} wh = {}_c+ \\ adv = {}_c+ \\ SENT\ MOOD = INV \end{array} \right\}$$
(Rule 1)

Rule 1 describes the occurrence of wh-words and adverbs in focus position as in "yesterday he went home." Note that this position (= XP) can only be filled by wh-words and adverbs because this is defined in the constraint equations.

English "inversion" can be accounted for by Rule 2:

$$S' \to (V) \qquad\qquad S$$
$$\left\{ \begin{array}{l} aux = {}_c+ \\ ROOT = {}_c+ \\ SENT\ MOOD = {}_c Inv \end{array} \right\}$$
(Rule 2)

It is the interaction of Rule 1 and Rule 2 that creates the correct word order (for instance, "Where has he been?"). A lexical redundancy rule for wh-words ensures that the filling of the focus position creates the information "MOOD = inv" (inversion). This information then feeds into the equation in Rule 2, which licenses an auxiliary verb in a position left of NP_{subj}. In other words, grammatical information is created through the processing of one constituent, and that information is utilized during the processing of another constituent. In terms of exchange of information, then, *inversion* is an example of exchange of grammatical information at the level of the sentence procedure (cf. Table 7.1) because the information "MOOD = inv" present in XP and in Aux is matched in the sentence procedure.

The second word order example is canonical word order, which in Lexical-Functional Grammar is expressed simply through constituent structure rules:

$$S \to NP_{subj} V (NP_{obj1}) (NP_{obj2}) \qquad (Rule\ 3)$$

$$S \to NP_{subj} (NP_{obj1}) (NP_{obj2}) V \qquad (Rule\ 4)$$

Rule 3 accounts for a subject-verb-object (SVO) language, whereas Rule 4 accounts for a subject-object-verb (SOV) language. Because grammatical functions are assigned at the level of constituent structure, a strict canonical order obviously does not

Table 7.3 Processing Procedures Applied to English

Processing Procedure	L2 Process	Morphology	Syntax
5 Subordinate clause procedure	Main and subordinate clauses		Cancel INV
4 S-procedure	Interphrasal information	*SV agreement*	Do2nd, *Inversion*, 3sg − s
3 Phrasal procedure	Phrasal information	*NP agreement*	ADV, Do-Front, Topi, Neg +V
2 Category procedure	Lexical morphology	*Plural*	*Canonical order*
1 Word/lemma	"Words"	Invariant forms	Single constituent

involve the unification of any features across major constituent boundaries. In other words, no information on lexical features has to be transferred between constituents. It is quite possible to produce canonical sentence schemata without phrasal categories by using a flat constituent structure and by mapping semantic roles directly onto c-structure in the initial stage of syntactic development.

However, canonical word order is not the only possible organization principle of early syntax. A parallel type of organization principle is based on the morphological marking of semantic roles. This would involve an affixation process driven directly by the conceptual structure and based merely on the lexical class of the lexical material. Such affixes could be inferred directly from constituent structure and would not involve any agreement marking. Slobin (1982) supplied evidence in support of this prediction. His data showed that, in the acquisition of Turkish, a nonconfigurational[8] language, children acquired morphological markers of grammatical functions at the same developmental point in time as fixed word order was acquired in configurational languages.

We are now in a position to locate five English morphosyntactic phenomena within the hierarchy of processability. The structures discussed here are highlighted in Table 7.3, which includes lexical, phrasal, and interphrasal morphemes as well as canonical word order and inversion. The table also lists a number of further structures and their position within the hierarchy. However, because of limited space, a full exposition of English as a second language development within PT is not possible here (for further details, cf. Pienemann, 1998).

The Interface of Lexical-Functional Grammar and Processability Theory

Given the key role that Lexical-Functional Grammar plays in PT, it may be useful for the coherence of this chapter to highlight briefly the relationship of this theory of grammar to language production and to sketch out additional constraints that the architecture of the Formulator imposes on Lexical-Functional Grammar. At the most general level, the language processor is seen, in the PT perspective, concurrent with Kaplan and Bresnan (1982) as the computational routines that operate on but are separate from the native speaker's linguistic knowledge. We pointed out that feature unification, which is one of the main characteristics of Lexical-Functional Grammar, captures a psychologically plausible process that involves (a) the identification of grammatical information in the lexical entry, (b) the temporary storage of that information, and (c) its utilization at another point in the constituent structure. Pienemann (1998) also demonstrated that feature unification is one of the key processes in morphology and word order. Every level of the hierarchy of processing procedures can be represented through feature unification. In other words, the essence of that hierarchy can be captured through feature unification in Lexical-Functional Grammar.[9]

The main proviso on this made by Pienemann (1998) is that the procedures that underlie Lexical-Functional Grammar cannot be understood to represent psychological procedures themselves. Instead, they can be considered a shorthand notation that contains all the necessary elements to relate structures to a hierarchy of processability. The formalism of Lexical-Functional Grammar is designed to be highly noncommittal about when unifications are performed. They can be done incrementally, as each phrase is built, or at the end, when an entire constituent structure has been constructed (see Maxwell & Kaplan, 1995, for some discussion on this point). Because PT assumes strict limits on grammatical memory, it would follow that unifications ought to be done as soon as possible (cf. Pienemann, 1998).

These limitations on memory are relevant to a further feature of Lexical-Functional Grammar, which is that the theory in its present form imposes no limitations on the amount or nature of information that can be transferred between constituents by unification. For example, arbitrarily complex substructures can be built in different constituents and checked for consistency. This possibility has been shown to lead to the possibility of writing Lexical-Functional Grammars for highly unnatural kinds of languages (Berwick & Weinberg, 1984, pp. 107–114) and to computational intractability (Barton, Berwick, & Ristad, 1987, pp. 103–114). In PT, rather than having an unlimited and unconstrained ability to unify information from different constituents, learners are assumed initially to have no such ability, but to acquire it gradually. This argues that Lexical-Functional Grammar should be modified so that information flow between constituents is inherently restricted. Pienemann (1998) used the system of Lexical-Functional Grammar with the informal assumption that unification occurs at the lowest node shared by the two constituents between which information needs to be unified.

In short, Lexical-Functional Grammar affords a valid application of Pienemann's (1998) hierarchy of processing procedures; it is also readily available, compatible with Levelt's model, and attractive from a typological point of view.

Processing Constraints on First Language Transfer

The internal mechanics of PT imply processing constraints on L1 transfer for the following reason. Given the architecture of the language generator, there is no guarantee that one can simply utilize L1 procedures for the L2. Pienemann (1998) argued that such "bulk transfer" would lead to internal problems:

> because all of the above processing procedures need to be orchestrated in a language-specific way. If any one of them is missing or incompatible with the rest, the Formulator is inoperable. If, for instance, the lexical category information is missing, category and phrasal procedures cannot be called. If diacritic features are missing or have no values or values which are not compatible with those listed in agreeing phrases or if they are incompatible with the Functorisation Rules, then the processor will be inoperable. (p. 80)

PT does not imply, however, that the learner will never attempt to form diacritic features and functorization rules that reflect L1 regularities. Instead, the theory does imply processing constraints on L1 transfer:

> "[B]ulk-transfer" of the L1 Formulator would lead to very unwieldy hypotheses. German learners of English, for instance, would have to invent large sets of diacritic features for nouns, verbs and adjectives without any evidence of their existence in the L2, since German definite determiners express a complex set of diacritic features of the noun (three genders and two numbers). Since English nouns do not contain these diacritic features the complex system of definite determiners presented in Table 7.4 corresponds to merely one English grammatical morpheme ("the"). (p. 81)

> In this case the simplest structural solution would be to abandon the L1 diacritic features altogether. This would in fact reproduce a situation which is close to the English determiner system. However, the relationship between L1 and L2 diacritic features may be more complex than in the above example, with two intersecting sets of diacritic features and different form-function relationships in L1 and L2. In other words, there is potentially a multitude of L1 features only some of which are applicable to the L2. (p. 81)

In essence, the lack of psychological plausibility present in the bulk transfer approach forms a logical argument in favor of processing constraints on L1 transfer, the position assumed by PT:

> I hypothesize that the L1 Formulator will not be "bulk-transferred." Instead, the learner will reconstruct the Formulator of the L2. This would

Table 7.4 The German Definite Article

	masculine		feminine		neuter	
	sgl	pl	sgl	pl	sgl	pl
Nominative	der	die	die	die	das	die
Genitive	des	der	der	der	des	der
Dative	dem	den	der	den	dem	den
Accusative	den	die	die	die	das	die

pl, plural; sgl, singular.

not exclude that in the course of this process L1 procedures be utilized. However, I hypothesize that such L1 transfer always occurs as part of the overall reconstruction process. (pp. 81–82)

The case of constraints on the transfer of morphological and lexical regularities is relatively straightforward, as the example of the determiner illustrates. Similar constraints are operational on word order. This point has been illustrated by Pienemann (1998, pp. 99–102) with the acquisition of German separable verbs, but is not repeated here for reasons of space. Suffice it to say that word order phenomena depend crucially on the correct annotation of lexical entries that differ in their diacritic features even between related languages.

In other words, according to PT, both the construction of the L2 from "square one" and developmental constraints on L1 transfer follow from the hierarchical nature of the learning task. In this scenario, there is no other logical point of departure for this L2 construction process than the beginning of the processability hierarchy because the hierarchy at this point is stripped off all language-specific lexical features and syntactic routines. It would therefore be logical for this L2 construction process to follow the path described in the processability hierarchy and for L1 knowledge and skills to become accessible once they are processable in the developing system.

To sum, PT implies the hypothesis that the L1 Formulator will not be bulk transferred because the processing of syntax is lexically driven, and the processor relies on highly language-specific lexical features. Instead, the learner will construct the Formulator of the L2 from scratch. This would not exclude that, in the course of this process, L1 procedures will be utilized. However, it is hypothesized that such cases of L1 transfer occur as part of the overall L2 construction process. This means that L1 transfer is developmentally moderated and will occur only when the structure to be transferred is processable within the developing L2 system.

Typological Proximity Without an Advantage

The notion of *developmentally moderated transfer* basically implies that certain grammatical structures identical in L1 and L2 nevertheless require the development of certain processing prerequisites before the L1 procedures can be utilized in the L2. In this section, we review a number of key studies in support of this hypothesis. What these studies have in common is that they all focus on L1 transfer in the context of typological proximity. In other words, we provide empirical evidence to show that typological proximity does not guarantee L2 learners ready access to L1 knowledge or to L1 processing skills.

Håkansson et al. (2002) provided empirical evidence to demonstrate that L1 transfer is developmentally moderated as predicted by PT. The study focuses on the acquisition of German by Swedish school children. The L1 and the L2 share the following word order regularities in affirmative main clauses:

SVO
  Peter mag Milch
  Peter gillar mjölk
  (Peter likes milk[10])
Adverb fronting (ADV)
  *Heute Peter mag Milch
  *Idag Peter gillar mjölk
  (Today Peter likes milk)
Subject-verb inversion (INV) after ADV
  Heute mag Peter Milch
  Idag gillar Peter mjölk
  (Today likes Peter milk)

To place this developmental sequence in the overall context of the processability hierarchy, an overview of the implementation of key morphosyntactic features of German and Swedish is provided in Tables 7.5 and 7.6. For a full exposition of this implementation process and supporting empirical

Table 7.5 Processing Procedures Applied to German Word Order and Morphology

Stage	Exchange of Information	Procedures	Word Order	Morphology
5		Subclause procedure	V-final	
4	Interphrasal	S-procedure	INV	SV agreement
3	Phrasal	Phrasal procedure	ADV	Plural agreement
2	None	Lexical categories	SVO	Past – te, etc.
1	None			"Words"

Table 7.6 Processing Procedures Applied to Swedish Word Order and Morphology

Stage	Exchange of Information	Procedures	Word Order	Morphology
5		Subclause procedure	Neg V_f	
4	Interphrasal	S-procedure	INV	Predicative agr.
3	Phrasal	Phrasal procedure	ADV	Attributive agr.
2	None	Lexical categories	SVO	Past., etc.
1	None			"Words"

evidence, refer to the studies of Pienemann (1998) and Pienemann and Håkansson (1999).

The results of the study by Håkansson et al. (2002) are summarized in Table 7.7, which treats all learner samples as parts of a cross-sectional study. Therefore, Table 7.7 represents an implicational scale[11] (cf. Hatch & Farhady, 1982) of the data, which demonstrates that the learners follow the sequence (a) SVO, (b) ADV, and (c) INV. In other words, ADV and INV are not transferred from the L1 at the initial state even though these rules are contained in the L1 and the L2. This implies that, for a period of time, learners produce the constituent order

*adverb + S + V + O

Table 7.7 Implicational Scale Based on All Learners in the Study by Häkansson et al. (2002)

Name	SVO	ADV	INV
Gelika (Year 1)	+	−	−
Emily (Year 1)	+	−	−
Robin (Year 1)	+	−	−
Kennet (Year 1)	+	−	−
Mats (Year 2)	+	−	−
Camilla (Year 2)	+	−	−
Johann (Year 1)	+	+	−
Cecilia (Year 1)	+	+	−
Eduard (Year 1)	+	+	−
Anna (Year 1)	+	+	−
Sandra (Year 1)	+	+	−
Erika (Year 1)	+	+	−
Mateus (Year 2)	+	+	−
Karolin (Year 2)	+	+	−
Ceci (Year 2)	+	+	−
Peter (Year 2)	+	+	−
Johan (Year 2)	+	+	+
Zandra (Year 2)	+	+	+
Zofie (Year 2)	+	+	+
Caro (Year 2)	+	+	+

ADV, adverb fronting; INV, subject-verb inversion; SVO, subject-verb-object.

which is ungrammatical in the L1 as well as in the L2 (e.g., *Heute Peter mag Milch).

Håkansson et al. (2002) argued on the basis of PT that the L2 system can utilize L1 production mechanisms only when the L2 system has developed the necessary prerequisites to process the L1 forms, and that therefore the INV procedure of the L1 cannot be utilized before the full S-procedure has been developed in the L2.

Given that, in this study, German was in fact the third language of the informants and that English was the second, it may be easy to conclude that the nonapplication of INV (or V2) was caused by transfer from English. In fact, this explanation is popular among Swedish schoolteachers of German and has also been suggested by Ruin (1996) and Naumann (1997). Many Swedish teachers of German disrespectfully termed this phenomenon the "English illness."

However, such a proposal is far from conclusive. In the study discussed in this section, ADV did not appear at the early stage, although it is also part of English grammar and could therefore be transferred. In other words, for the proposal to be conclusive, one would need to consider how the transfer-from-L2 hypothesis would be testable. Logically, the hypothesis would have to predict that all L2 word order constraints would be transferred or at least all those that are shared by the L1, the L2, and the L3. Otherwise, the transfer hypothesis would have no predictive power and could not be falsified unless one added a separate theory predicting which items are to be transferred and which are not.

In the absence of such a theory, one can only test the transfer-all hypothesis. To follow this line of argument, it is important to remember that the data from the study showed a strictly implicational development. It is evident from this analysis (see Table 7.7) that 6 of the 20 learners produced SVO only and no ADV. If one follows the transfer-from-L2 view, they would appear to have transferred selectively only one word order pattern known from their L2 (English). This clearly falsifies the transfer-all hypothesis and leaves the selective-transfer-from-L2 hypothesis with the problem of making no testable prediction about when transfer will take place.

Further evidence supporting the hypothesis that L1 transfer is developmentally constrained comes from Johnston's study of the acquisition of English by learners of Polish and Vietnamese. Johnston's study consisted of a total of 16 samples from Polish and Vietnamese adult immigrants in Australia and focused on the acquisition of L2 grammatical rules. The full distributional analysis of this study is available in the work of Johnston (1997) and is also partly reported in the work of Pienemann, Johnston, and Brindley (1988), for instance. Polish uses subject-verb agreement marking, Vietnamese does not. According to the full transfer/full access hypothesis, AGR[EEMENT] ought to be transferred from Polish to English. This would mean that Polish learners should have an advantage over the Vietnamese learners concerning this structure. However, a separate implicational analysis of the two groups revealed that both groups followed the same pattern, and in both groups AGR[EEMENT] was acquired late.

Typological Proximity With an Advantage

The proposal made in the preceding section was the following: Typological proximity does not guarantee L2 learners ready access to L1 knowledge or to L1 processing skills. In this section, we show that typological proximity *may* have an advantage—if it entails that the L1–L2 similarity is based on a structure that is located low in the processability hierarchy.

Haberzettl (2000) studied the acquisition of German word order by Russian and Turkish learners. Turkish is an agglutinative language with SOV as the preferred word order, whereas Russian has postverbal objects and basically follows an SVO pattern. Haberzettl focused on the acquisition of the German split-verb position, which creates an SVXV pattern with the inflected verb in second position and the uninflected verb in the final position, as in the following example:

er <u>hat</u> ein Bier <u>getrunken</u>
he has a beer drunk
"He has drunk/drank a beer."

Haberzettl (2000) carried out a longitudinal study of four child learners of German aged 6 to 8 years over a period of 2 to 4 years based on monthly sessions 20–60 min long. The key finding in the present context is that the Russian learners acquired the split-verb position gradually over several months, whereas the Turkish learners acquired it categorically and with nativelike correctness once the structure emerged. Haberzettl concluded from these findings that the Turkish learners benefited from the structural overlap in word order constellations in German and Turkish. This conclusion is fully compatible with the predictions that can be made on the basis of the processability hierarchy and the notion of developmentally moderated transfer. As the discussion here has shown, the split-verb construction is in fact associated with Level 4 of the hierarchy, and both types of learners followed the predicted sequence. However, the Turkish learners could take advantage of their L1 processing skills once their interlanguage developed to the point at which they could be integrated into the L2 processor. In other words, this type of study constitutes evidence in support of the productive nature of developmentally moderated transfer; the studies reviewed in the preceding section demonstrated the constraining nature of the same notion.

Typological Distance Without a Disadvantage

We reviewed studies carried out in the context of typological proximity and demonstrated that typological proximity does not guarantee L2 learners ready access to L1 knowledge or to L1 processing skills. In this section, we reverse the typological constellation and review studies in the context of typological distance. We demonstrate that typological distance does not necessarily imply a learning barrier. In other words, L2 structures that are absent from the L1 may nevertheless be positioned at the bottom of the processability hierarchy and may therefore be readily learnable.

Kawaguchi (1999, 2002, in preparation) studied the acquisition of Japanese syntax by native speakers of English. One aspect she studied was the acquisition of word order by Australian university students of Japanese. The study examined a typological contrast in which native speakers of a highly configurational, head-first language with SVO word order (English) acquired a less configurational, head-last language (Japanese; cf. Shibatani, 1990) with preferred SOV word order.

Kawaguchi's study constituted a prime test case for the full transfer/full access model (Schwartz & Sprouse, 1994, 1996) as well as for the competition model (MacWhinney, chapter 3, this volume), which would both predict the Australian learners of Japanese to transfer English SVO word. However, this prediction was clearly falsified by Kawaguchi's study.

The results of Kawaguchi's study for the initial word order hypothesis are displayed in Table 7.8, which is based on a longitudinal corpus collected from two informants without any previous exposure to the target language. The informants were interviewed four times in their first year of learning Japanese as an L2 starting at the very beginning of the learning process.

Table 7.8 affords a distributional analysis of the corpus in relation to the positioning of the verb in clauses. The first line in the body of Table 7.8 lists the number of target-like occurrences of the verb in clause-final position, and the second line lists the number of occurrences of the verb in nontarget positions. It is easy to see from this analysis that from the very beginning of their acquisition of Japanese, neither of the learners ever produced verbs in a nonfinal position, and this was without exception,[12] despite the fact that this is in stark contrast to the structure of their L1.

To summarize, we found that all learners of Japanese studied longitudinally by Kawaguchi started with SOV word order and with subject omission although their L1s followed an SVO pattern and one of the L1s does not permit subject omission. Obviously, these findings falsified the hypothesis that L1 features are transferred to the L2 at the initial state.

This raises the question of why L2 learners would start out with a structure that is typologically rather distant from their L1. The answer is implied in PT and, more specifically, in the developmentally moderated transfer hypothesis advocated in this chapter. In relation to the initial hypothesis for word order, PT predicts the use of a canonical word order pattern. Japanese follows a canonical SOV word order, which requires no exchange of grammatical information within the sentence as it can rely on direct mapping of semantic roles onto surface structure (cf. our discussion above). In other words, because of the low demands on processability, this word order pattern can be processed at the initial stage of clause development despite the typological distance between the L1 and the L2 (for a more detailed and formal account of information distribution in Japanese syntax, see Kawaguchi, in preparation, and Di Biase and Kawaguchi, 2002).

This analysis of the initial word order in the acquisition of Japanese as an L2 also highlights a key difference between Clahsen's (1984) strategies and the processability approach. As Vainikka and Young-Scholten (1994) and Towell and Hawkins (1994) pointed out, Clahsen's strategies would predict that the initial hypothesis in L2 acquisition is formed on the perceptual array "actor, action, acted upon," thus producing universal SVO patterns for all L2s. No such assumption is made in PT. The only stipulation that exists at this level is that no grammatical information be exchanged within the sentence. This constrains the language processor to produce only structures that can be processed without such information exchange. SVO and SOV both satisfy this condition.

Di Biase (in preparation) studied another typological constellation of the same kind as Kawaguchi. In his study, he focused on the acquisition of a "pro-drop" language[13] (Italian) as L2 by speakers of a non-pro-drop language (English). According to White's (1989, p. 87) analysis, this type of learner has to learn two things: the fact that null subjects are permitted and the circumstances in which the language makes use of null subjects. These assumptions were derived from the more general assumption that L2 learners transfer the setting of the L1 parameter to the L2.

Di Biase (in preparation) carried out a longitudinal study with two Australian informants over a 1-year period. Both informants were university students of Italian. One informant (Ernie) was

Table 7.8 The Position of the Verb in Main Clauses by Second Language Learners of Japanese (Jaz and Lou)

	t_1		t_2		t_3		t_4	
	Jaz	Lou	Jaz	Lou	Jaz	Lou	Jaz	Lou
Verb in clause final position	3	10	12	19	17	12	28	27
Verb not in clause final position	0	0	0	0	0	0	0	0

Table 7.9 Realization of Grammatical Subject with Lexical Verbs in Percentage

	t_1	t_2	t_3	t_4
Ernie				
Null	54	64	67	84
Pronominal	4	24	4	2
Referential	43	12	29	14
Lisa				
Null	71	52	59	79
Pronominal	24	45	30	11
Referential	6	3	11	13

a beginning learner who had had no previous exposure to the language. The first set of data ($= t_1$) was collected as soon as the learner started producing utterances with more than one constituent. The second informant (Lisa) was an intermediate student when the first set of data was collected.

Table 7.9 compares the three different types of realization of grammatical subjects (null, pronominal, and referential) for both informants. It is easy to see that, contrary to White's (1989) prediction, both learners started with a high level of null realizations of grammatical subjects. In fact, the level of null subject realizations found in these data is not unlike that found by Bates (1976) in her study of Italian L1 acquisition, namely, about 70%.

In terms of the processability hierarchy, null subjects are placed at the same level as pronominal subjects because both are directly derived from constituent structure (for a detailed analysis of information distribution in these structures, see Di Biase and Kawaguchi, 2002). Therefore, Di Biase's finding supports the prediction that the acquisition of a typologically distant L2 does not necessarily cause a learning barrier as long as the structure in question is located at the lower end of the processability hierarchy—even if it does not exist in the L1.

This finding was supported by other studies with the same typological constellation as in the work of Di Biase (in preparation). For instance, Phinney (1987) studied the acquisition of null subjects in English learners of Spanish (i.e., L1 = −pro-drop, L2 = +pro-drop) and found an early appearance of null subjects. Liceras and Diaz (1999) studied the acquisition of L2 Spanish (+pro-drop) by speakers of Chinese, English, French, German, and Japanese (i.e., speakers of both types of languages) and found a consistent early appearance of null subjects in all informants.

Conclusion

In this chapter, we proposed that L1 transfer is developmentally moderated. This hypothesis follows from the internal design of PT, which provides a framework for relating specific L1 and L2 structures to a universal hierarchy of processability based on grammatical information transfer in the production process. This overall framework predicts which processing procedures are required for the processing of specific L2 structures. This is the basis for the general prediction that L1 knowledge and skills can be utilized for L2 processing only if the necessary processing resources have developed.

Our developmentally moderated-transfer hypothesis was tested empirically in the context of both typological proximity and typological distance. We demonstrated that, in both types of context, transfer may or may not occur. The key predictive factor is always processability. In other words, processability acts as a constraint on L2 transfer and may override typological distance. In addition to this constraining effect, processability also has a facilitating effect that sets in (given structural L1-L2 overlap) once the L2 has developed to the point at which the L1 structure is processable. This is evident in the advantage of Turkish learners of German over Russian learners of the same L2 with respect to word order (cf. Haberzettl, 2000).

The empirical studies discussed in this chapter also shed light on the validity of the set of competing approaches to L1 transfer discussed here. We can now state that the full access/full transfer hypothesis of Schwartz and Sprouse (1994) is strongly falsified by all cases of nontransfer reported above because the authors assumed that the final state of the L1 is the initial state of the L2. The falsification of this assumption was particularly obvious in the study by Håkansson et al. (2002), which showed that Swedish learners of German did not transfer verb-second although both languages contain this structure.

The so-called minimal tree hypothesis predicts that L1 word order is transferred to L2. This is falsified by Kawaguchi's (in preparation) observation that Australian learners of Japanese start with an initial SOV hypothesis. This observation and the study of Swedes learning German both also falsified the transfer hypothesis implied in the competition model (cf. MacWhinney, chapter 3, this volume), according to which all transferable structures will be transferred at an early stage. The above studies showed that this prediction was not borne out by empirical data. Swedish learners of German did not transfer V2 to German (which would yield a correct result), and Australian learners of Japanese did not transfer SVO to Japanese (which would yield an incorrect result).

The strong initial transfer assumption inherent in MacWhinney's (1997, and chapter 3, this volume) competition model also produces predictions that were falsified by empirical data, particularly by the Swedish-German study (Håkansson et al., 2002), which showed that verb-second is not transferred from Swedish to German even though this structure exists in the L1 and in the L2. All other cases of nontransfer discussed above proved the same point.

In addition, it may be useful to consider the explanatory parsimony of MacWhinney's (1997) assumption that "all aspects of the first language that can possibly transfer to L2 will transfer" (p. 119). Recall that MacWhinney (1997) illustrated his point about structurally "impossible transfer" using German and English as an example. German nouns are implicitly marked for grammatical gender, whereas English nouns are not. He concluded that German learners therefore have no basis for transferring the German gender system to English. Consequently, this set of features was not included in his list of things that will be transferred.

Our point is the following. Whereas L1-L2 contrasts are transparent to the linguist, the question remains regarding how the learner recognizes these differences. Recall that at the beginning of this chapter we argued that the relationship between German and English diacritic features (of nouns) is not obvious to the learner, and that a full transfer hypothesis would lead to unwieldy hypotheses. Conversely, it is precisely this lack of transparency in the relationship between L1 and L2 that makes a radical no-transfer hypothesis equally unlikely.

Assuming a lexically driven model of language production such as the one proposed by Levelt (1989), gender is one of several diacritic features residing in the lexical entry for (German) nouns, and the learner will have to discover for all lexical classes (such as noun, verb, etc.) which of the L1 diacritic features are also marked in the L2, using known or unknown linguistic means, and which additional diacritic features are marked using which linguistic means. This is a monumental learning task. Assuming that diacritic features such as gender are not transferable for structural reasons would amount to a classical conditioning assumption within the competition model that would

assume a strictly linear relationship between input and output, following the motto "if it is not in the input, it cannot occur in the output." As noted, empirical data falsify such an assumption. This is also illustrated by the well-attested example of overgeneralization in English regular past marking, such as in Cazden's "She holded the baby rabbits" (1972, p. 96).

As these examples show, the assumption of a strictly linear relationship between input and output and a rich transfer assumption produce predictions that are falsified by empirical data—at least for the domain of morphosyntax.

A rich transfer assumption also is not supported in the area of bilingual L1 acquisition. According to De Houwer (chapter 2, this volume) no studies have empirically backed up the existence of the sort of language repertoires that would be predicted to develop in bilingual children in line with a transfer theory. Indeed, she maintains that the interpretation of morphosyntactic features of the two input languages would assume that processing mechanisms in bilingual children would enable them to "approach each input language as a morphosyntactically closed set."

The gist of the cross-linguistic survey of L1 transfer presented in this chapter can be summed in two fundamental trends: (a) Structures higher up the processability hierarchy are never transferred at the initial state—regardless of typological constellation; (b) initial word order may vary as long as the flow of grammatical information is restricted to the initial stage of processability.

These trends clearly contradict any theory that places emphasis on extensive L1 transfer at the initial state and support a view on transfer that is sensitive to the developmental state of the learner's language.

Acknowledgments

We would like to thank the editors of this volume for their thoughtful and detailed comments on an earlier version of this chapter. We would also like to express our gratitude to MARCS Auditory Laboratories, University of Western Sydney, Australia, for financial assistance to create an opportunity for us to meet in Sydney and discuss the research presented in this chapter. We also want to thank Simone Duxbury for her careful editorial work on the manuscript. The research published in this chapter was funded in part by a grant by the State Department of Higher Education of North Rhine Westfalia, Germany, to Manfred Pienemann.

Notes

1. Principles and parameters are abstract notions that are specific to the formal aspect of language. Often, parameters apply to several structural domains. An example is the "head position parameter," which determines the headedness of a language in all types of phrases (i.e., NPs, VPs, PPs [prepositional phrases], etc.). A parameter has different settings (e.g., "left" or "right" in the case of the headedness parameter). Another example is the pro-drop parameter, which relates to a cluster of superficially unrelated phenomena, such as overt subjects, inversion, and agreement (cf. Meisel, 1995, p. 12).

2. In the preminimalist as well as in the minimalist framework, a distinction is made between lexical and functional heads. Lexical heads are heads of one of the four lexical phrases VP, AP (adjective phrase), NP, or PP. Functional heads are heads of functional phrases such as IP (inflectional phrase) or CP (complementizer phrase). Functional phrases may contain lexical material, such as affixes, but are not required to do so (cf. Cook & Newson, 1996, pp. 136 ff.).

3. The *developmental problem* (cf. Clahsen, 1992) refers to the fact that all learners of L2s follow a describable developmental trajectory. This is a fact that has to be accounted for by a theory of L2 acquisition, hence the term *problem*.

4. In Levelt's (1989) model, the Grammatical Encoder and the Phonological Encoder made up the Formulator.

5. This section does not deal with the constraints of working memory on language processing or language learning. The volume by Harris (1992) contains a number of chapters on those issues.

6. Baddeley (1990) assumed that an executive control level of working memory is the locus of attended processing.

7. This term refers to a process during sentence generation in which, for instance, a lexical feature of a noun (e.g., number = singular) and a determiner (e.g., number = singular) are matched (i.e., unified). This is part of a procedure that ensures that the resulting noun phrase is grammatically well formed.

8. A configurational language is a language that marks underlying semantic roles such as "agent" or grammatical functions such as "subject" by means of word order. English is an example of a configurational language. The vast majority of English affirmative sentences follow a strict SVO pattern.

9. In Pienemann's (1998) use of a modified and somewhat simplified Lexical-Functional Grammar formalism, the focus is on the implementation of the processability hierarchy in morphology and word order. It is not claimed that all other formal aspects of Llexical-Functional Grammar are related

in a similar way to the processes modeled in Incremental Procedural Grammar. In particular, psychological plausibility is at present attributed only to the unification of lexical features, not unification generally. It may well be that other adjustments will have to be made to the formalism at a later stage.

10. The English transliteration is a word-by-word gloss that follows the same word order as the German and Swedish example sentences.

11. The implicational scaling technique was developed by Guttman (1944) and applied to linguistic dynamics by DeCamp (1973) and to dynamics in L2 acquisition by Meisel, Clahsen, and Pienemann (1981) (for further information, see also Pienemann, 1998).

12. Note that the informants hardly ever omit the verb (cf. Kawaguchi, in preparation, for further detail).

13. A language in which the co-referential grammatical subject does not need to be pronominalized.

References

Baddeley, A. (1990). *Human memory: Theory and practice.* Hillsdale, NJ: Erlbaum.

Barton, G. E., Berwick, R. C., & Ristad, E. S. (1987). *Computational complexity and natural language.* Cambridge, MA: MIT Press.

Bates, E. (1976). *Language and context: The acquisition of pragmatics.* New York: Academic Press.

Bates, E., & MacWhinney, B. (1981). Second-language acquisition from a functionalist perspective: Pragmatic, semantic, and perceptual strategies. In H. Winity (Ed.), *Native language and foreign language acquisition* (pp. 190–214). New York: Annals of the New York Academy of Sciences.

Bates, E., & MacWhinney, B. (1982). Functionalist approaches to grammar. In E. Wanner & L. R. Gleitman (Eds.), *Language acquisition: The state of the art* (pp. 173–218). Cambridge, England: Cambridge University Press.

Bates, E., & MacWhinney, B. (1987). Competition, variation and language learning. In B. MacWhinney (Ed.), *Mechanisms of language acquisition* (pp. 157–193). Hillsdale, NJ: Erlbaum.

Berwick, R., & Weinberg, A. (1984). *The grammatical basis of linguistic performance: Language use and language acquisition.* Cambridge, MA: MIT Press.

Bialystok, E. (1997). Why we need grammar: Confessions of a cognitive generalist. In L. Eubank, L. Selinker, & M. Sharwood Smith

(Eds.), *The current state of interlanguage* (pp. 55–61). Amsterdam: Benjamins.

Bley-Vroman, R. (1990). The logical problem of second language learning. *Linguistic Analysis, 20,* 3–49.

Bresnan, J. (Ed.). (1982). *The mental representation of grammatical relations.* Cambridge, MA: MIT Press.

Bresnan, J. (2001). *Lexical-functional syntax.* Oxford, England: Blackwell.

Broadbent, D. E. (1975). The magic number seven after 15 years. In A. Kennedy & A. Wilkes (Eds.), *Studies in long term memory* (pp. 3–18). London: Wiley.

Cazden, C. (1972). *Child language and education.* New York: Holt, Reinhart, and Winston.

Chomsky, N. (1990). On the nature, use and acquisition of language. In W. G. Lycan (Ed.), *Mind and cognition. A reader* (pp. 627–646). Cambridge, MA: Blackwell.

Clahsen, H. (1984). The acquisition of German word order: A test case for cognitive approaches to L2 development. In R. W. Andersen (Ed.), *Second languages: A cross-linguistic perspective* (pp. 219–242). Rowley, MA: Newbury House.

Clahsen, H. (1986). Connecting theories of language processing and (second) language acquisition. In C. W. Pfaff (Ed.), *First and second language acquisition processes* (pp. 103–116). Cambridge, MA: Newbury House.

Clahsen, H. (1992). Learnability theory and the problem of development in language acquisition. In J. Weissenborn, H. Goodluck, & T. Roeper (Eds.), *Theoretical issues in language acquisition: Continuity and change* (pp. 53–76). Hillsdale, NJ: Erlbaum.

Clahsen, H., & Muysken, P. (1989). The UG paradox in L2 acquisition. *Second Language Research, 2,* 1–29.

Cohen, N. (1984). Preserved learning capacity in amnesia: Evidence for multiple memory systems. In L. R. Squire & N. Butters (Eds.), *The neuropsychology of human memory* (pp. 83–103). New York: Guilford Press,

Cohen, N. (1992, November). *Memory, amnesia and the hippocampal system.* Paper presented at the Cognitive and Neuro Science Colloquium, McGill University, Montreal, Quebec, Canada.

Cook, V. J., & Newson, M. (1996). *Chomsky's universal grammar. An introduction* (2nd ed.). Oxford, England: Blackwell.

Cooper, W. E., & Zurif, E. B. (1983). Aphasia: Information-processing in language production and reception. In B. Butterworth (Ed.), *Language production* (Vol. 2, pp. 225–256). London: Academic Press.

De Bot, K. (1992). A bilingual production model: Levelt's "speaking" model adapted. *Applied Linguistics, 13,* 1–24.

DeCamp, D. (1973). Implicational scales and sociolinguistic linearity. *Linguistics, 73,* 30–43.

Di Biase, B. (in preparation) Processability and subject-verb agreement in a pro-drop language. In M. Pienemann (Ed.), *Cross-linguistic aspects of processability theory.* Amsterdam: Benjamins.

Di Biase, B., & Kawaguchi, S. (2002). Exploring the typological plausibility of processability theory: Language development in Italian second language and Japanese second language. *Second Language Research, 18,* 272–300.

Dulay, H., & Burt, M. (1974). Natural sequences in child second language acquisition. *Language Learning, 24,* 37–53.

Engelkamp, J. (1974). *Psycholinguistik.* Munich, Germany: Ullstein.

Eubank, L. (1993). On the transfer of parametric values in L2 development. *Language Acquisition, 3,* 183–208.

Ewehag, R., & Järnum, H. (2001). *Förstaspråkets inverkan på andraspråket* [First language influence on the second language]. Unpublished manuscript, Department of Linguistics, Lund University, Sweden.

Felix, S. W. (1980). Interference, interlanguage and related issues. In S. W. Felix (Ed.), *Second language development. Trends and issues* (pp. 93–107). Tübingen, Germany: Narr.

Felix, S. W. (1984). Maturational aspects of universal grammar. In A. Davies, C. Criper, & A. Howatt (Eds.), *Interlanguage* (pp. 133–161). Edinburgh, Scotland: Edinburgh University Press.

Fodor, J. (1981). Fixation of belief and concept acquisition. In M. Piatelli-Palmarini (Ed.), *Language and learning. The debate between Jean Piaget and Noam Chomsky* (2nd ed., pp. 143–149). Cambridge, MA: Harvard University Press.

Garrett, M. F. (1976). Syntactic processes in sentence production. In R. Wales & E. Walker (Eds.), *New approaches to language mechanism* (pp. 231–256). Amsterdam: North-Holland.

Garrett, M. F. (1980). Levels of processing in language production. In B. Butterworth (Ed.), *Language production, Vol. 1, Speech and Talk* (pp. 170–220). London: Academic Press.

Garrett, M. F. (1982). Production of speech: Observations from normal and pathological language use. In A. W. Ellis (Ed.), *Normality and pathology in cognitive functions.* London: Academic Press.

Gass, S. M. (1987). The resolution of conflicts among competing systems: A bidirectional perspective. *Applied Psycholinguistics, 8,* 329–350.

Gough, P. B. (1972). One second of reading. In J. F. Kavanagh & I. G. Mattingly (Eds.), *Language by ear and by eye* (pp. 331–358). Cambridge, MA: MIT Press.

Guttman, L. (1944). A basis for scaling qualitative data. *American Sociological Review, 9,* 139–150.

Haberzettl, S. (2000). *Der Erwerb der Verbstallung in der Zweisprache Deutsch durch Kinder mit typologisch verschiedenen Muttersprachen. Eine Auseinandersetzung mit Theorien zum Syntaxerwerb anhand von vier Fallstudien.* Doctoral dissertation, Potsdam University, Potsdam, Germany.

Håkansson, G., Pienemann, M., & Sayehli, S. (2002). Transfer and typological proximity in the context of L2 processing. *Second Language Research, 18,* 250–273.

Harrington, M. (1987). Processing transfer: Language-specific processing strategies as a source of interlanguage variation. *Applied Psycholinguistics, 8,* 351–377.

Harris, R. J. (Ed.), (1992). *Cognitive processing in bilinguals.* New York: Elsevier Science.

Hatch, E., & Farhady, H. (1982). *Research design and statistics for applied linguistics.* Rowley, MA: Newbury House.

Johnston, M. (1997). *Development and variation in learner language.* Doctoral thesis, Australian National University, Canberra, Australia.

Kaplan, R., & Bresnan, J. (1982). Lexical-functional grammar: A formal system for grammatical representation. In J. Bresnan (Ed.), *The mental representation of grammatical relations* (pp. 173–281). Cambridge, MA: MIT Press.

Kawaguchi, S. (1999). The acquisition of syntax and nominal ellipsis in JSL discourse. In P. Robinson (Ed.), *Representation and process: Proceedings of the Third Pacific Second Language Research Forum* (Vol. 1, pp. 85–93). Tokyo: Pacific Second Language Research Forum.

Kawaguchi, S. (2002). Grammatical development in learners of Japanese as a second language. In B. Di Biase (Ed.), *Developing a second language* (pp. 17–28). Melbourne: Language Australia.

Kawaguchi, S. (in preparation). Syntactic development in Japanese as a second language. In M. Pienemann (Ed.), *Cross-linguistic aspects of processability theory.* Amsterdam: Benjamins.

Kellerman, E. (1983). Now you see it, now you don't. In S. Gass & L. Selinker (Eds.),

Language transfer in language learning (pp. 112–134). Rowley, MA: Newbury House.

Kempen, G., & Hoenkamp, E. (1987). An incremental procedural grammar for sentence formulation. *Cognitive Science, 11,* 201–258.

Kilborn, K., & Ito, T. (1989). Sentence processing in a second language: The timing of transfer. *Language and Speech, 32,* 1–23.

Lado, R. (1957). *Linguistics across cultures: Applied linguistics for language teachers.* Ann Arbor, MI: University of Michigan.

LaFond, L., Hayes, R., & Bhatt, R. (2001). Constraint demotion and null-subjects in Spanish L2 acquisition. In J. Camps & C. R. Wiltshire (Eds.), *Romance syntax, semantics and L2 acquisition* (pp. 121–136). Amsterdam: Benjamins.

Levelt, W. J. M. (1981). The speaker's linearisation problem. *Philosophical Transactions, Royal Society London, B295,* 305–315.

Levelt, W. J. M. (1989). *Speaking. From intention to articulation.* Cambridge, MA: MIT Press.

Liceras, J. M., & Diaz, L. (1999). Topic-drop versus pro-drop: Null subjects and pronominal subjects in the Spanish L2 of Chinese, English, French, German and Japanese speakers. *Second Language Research, 15,* 1–40.

Lightbown, P., & Spada, N. (1999). *How languages are learned.* Oxford, England: Oxford University Press.

MacWhinney, B. (1987). Applying the competition model to bilingualism. *Applied Psycholinguistics, 8,* 315–327

MacWhinney, B. (1997). Second language acquisition and the competition model. In A. M. B. de Groot & J. F. Kroll (Eds.), *Tutorials in bilingualism* (pp. 113–142). Mahwah, NJ: Erlbaum.

Maxwell, J. T., & Kaplan, R. M. (1995). The interface between phrasal and functional constraints. In M. Dalrymple, R. M. Kaplan, J. T. Maxwell, & A. Zaenen (Eds.), *Formal issues in lexical-functional grammar* (pp. 571–590). Stanford, CA: CSLI.

Mayes, A. R. (1988). *Human organic memory disorders.* Cambridge, England: Cambridge University Press.

McDonald, L. J., & Heilenman, L. K. (1991). Determinants of cue strength in adult first and second language speakers of French. *Applied Psycholinguistics, 12,* 313–348.

Meisel, J. M. (1983). Strategies of second language acquisition: More than one kind of simplification. In R. W. Anderson (Ed.), *Pidginisation and creolisation as language acquisition* (pp. 120–157). Rowley, MA: Newbury House.

Meisel, J. M. (1991). Principles of universal grammar and strategies of language use: On some similarities and differences between first and second language acquisition. In L. Eubank (Ed.), *Point-counterpoint. Universal grammar in the second language* (pp. 231–276). Amsterdam: Benjamins.

Meisel, J. M. (1995). Parameters in acquisition. In P. Fletcher & B. MacWhinney (Eds.), *The handbook of child language* (pp. 10–35). Cambridge, MA: Blackwell.

Meisel, J. M., Clahsen, H., & Pienemann, M. (1981). On determining developmental stages in natural second language acquisition. *Studies in Second Language Acquisition, 3*, 109–135.

Naumann, K. (1997). Svenska som främmande språk i Schweiz [Swedish as a foreign language in Switzerland]. In G. Håkansson, L. Lötmarker, L. Santesson, J. Svensson, & Å. Viberg (Eds.), *Svenskans beskrivning* (Vol. 22, pp. 318–334). Lund, Sweden: Studentlitteratur.

Palmer, H. (1968) *The scientific study and teaching of language*. Language and Language Learning Series. London: Oxford University Press. (Original work published 1917)

Paradis, M. (1987). *The assessment of bilingual aphasia*. Hillsdale, NJ: Erlbaum.

Paradis, M. (1994). Neurolinguistic aspects of implicit and explicit memory: Implications for bilingualism and SLA. In N. Ellis (Ed.), *Implicit and explicit learning of languages* (pp. 393–419). London: Academic Press.

Phinney, M. (1987). The pro-drop parameter in second language acquisition. In T. Roeper & E. Williams (Eds.), *Parameter setting* (pp. 221–238). Dordrecht, The Netherlands: Reidel.

Pienemann, M. (1998). *Language processing and second language development: Processability theory*. Amsterdam: Benjamins.

Pienemann, M., & Håkansson, G. (1999). A unified approach towards the development of Swedish as L2: A processability account. *Studies in Second Language Acquisition, 21*, 383–420.

Pienemann, M., Johnston, M., & Brindley, G. (1988). Constructing an acquisition-based procedure for second language assessment. *Studies in Second Language Acquisition, 10*, 217–224.

Pinker, S. (1979). Formal models of language learning. *Cognition, 7*, 217–283.

Pinker, S. (1984). *Language learnability and language development*. Cambridge, MA: Harvard University Press.

Platzack, C. (1996). The initial hypothesis of syntax: A minimalist perspective on language acquisition and attrition. In H. Clahsen (Ed.),

Generative perspectives on language acquisition (pp. 369–414). Amsterdam: Benjamins.

Ruin, I. (1996). *Grammar and the advanced learner: On learning and teaching a second language*. Stockholm: Almqvist and Wiksell.

Sasaki, Y. (1991). English and Japanese interlanguage comprehension strategies: An analysis based on the competition model. *Applied Psycholinguistics, 6*, 190–204.

Schwartz, B. D., & Sprouse, R. A. (1994). Word order and nominative case in non-native language acquisition. A longitudinal study of (L1 Turkish) German interlanguage. In T. Hoekstra & B. D. Schwartz (Eds.), *Language acquisition studies in generative grammar: Papers in honour of Kenneth Wexler from the 1991 GLOW workshops* (pp. 317–368). Philadelphia: Benjamins.

Schwartz, B. D., & Sprouse, R. A. (1996). L2 cognitive states and the full transfer/full access model. *Second Language Research, 12*, 40–72.

Shibatani, M. (1990). *The languages of Japan*. Cambridge, England: Cambridge University Press.

Slobin, D. I. (1982). Universal and particular in the acquisition of language. In E. Wanner & L. R. Gleitman (Eds.), *Language acquisition. The state of the art* (pp. 128–172). Cambridge, England: Cambridge University Press.

Sweet, H. (1899, 1964). *The practical study of languages*. Language and Language Learning Series. London: Oxford University Press.

Tesar, B., & Smolensky, P. (1998). Learnability in optimality theory. *Linguistic Inquiry, 29*, 229–268.

Towell, R., & Hawkins, R. (1994). *Approaches to second language acquisition*. Clevedon, England: Multilingual Matters.

Vainikka, A., & Young-Scholten, M. (1994). Direct access to X'-theory: Evidence from Korean and Turkish adults learning German. In T. Hoekstra & B. D. Schwartz (Eds.), *Language acquisition studies in generative grammar: Papers in honour of Kenneth Wexler from the 1991 GLOW workshops* (pp. 7–39). Philadelphia: Benjamins.

Vainikka, A., & Young-Scholten, M. (1996). Gradual development of L2 phrase structure. *Second Language Research, 12*, 7–39.

Weinreich, U. (1953, 1974). *Languages in contact. Findings and problems*. The Hague, The Netherlands: Mouton.

Wexler, K. (1982). A principle theory for language acquisition. In E. Wanner & L. R. Gleitman (Eds.), *Language acquisition: The state of the art* (pp. 288–315). Cambridge, England: Cambridge University Press.

Wexler, K., & Culicover, P. (1980). *Formal principles of language acquisition.* Cambridge, MA: MIT Press.

White, L. (1989). *Universal grammar and second language acquisition.* Amsterdam: Benjamins.

Wode, H. (1976). Developmental sequences in naturalistic L2 acquisition. *Working Papers on Bilingualism, 11,* 1–12.

Wode, H. (1978). The L1 versus L2 acquisition of English negation. *Working Papers on Bilingualism, 15,* 37–57.

Zobl, H. (1980). The formal and developmental selectivity of L1 influence on L2 acquisition. *Language Learning, 30,* 43–57.

Zurif, E., Swinney, D., Prather, P., & Love, T. (1994). Functional localization in the brain with respect to syntactic processing. *Journal of Psycholinguistic Research, 23,* 487–497.

Jaap M. J. Murre

8

Models of Monolingual and Bilingual Language Acquisition

ABSTRACT   Children learn language despite the very impoverished nature of the input. Since the 1960s, the symbolic-deductive paradigm has explained this with reference to an innate mental language system. For about two decades, an alternative to symbolic accounts of language and language acquisition has been offered by connectionism, which can be viewed as one of the main subsymbolic-inductive paradigms. The recent models in this paradigm test detailed models against large databases of utterances. A general conclusion from this research is that, despite being very noisy and inconsistent, the nature of language input is nevertheless sufficient to support inductive mechanisms by which seemingly rulelike behavior emerges from a data-driven learning process. Constraints on the learning process are imposed by the architectures of the models. Several models within the symbolic-deductive paradigm have now also been worked out in much more detail, and a lively discussion between proponents of the two paradigms is currently taking place. We review some of the prominent models in both paradigms, with an emphasis on the connectionist models. In particular, we look at models of the acquisition of stress assignment, phonology, past tense formation, pluralization, and certain aspects of semantics.

How language is acquired has been at the heart of linguistic theorizing since the well-known debate between Chomsky and Skinner in the 1950s. Although Skinner proposed an inductive learning scheme, Chomsky argued that the verbal input children receive is far too impoverished to acquire language, and that an innate learning facility is necessary that is largely prestructured for language processing. Chomsky's arguments convinced the majority of the linguistic community, and his symbolic-deductive theoretical framework of language acquisition is among the most successful theories in social science. With the rebirth of connectionism in the 1980s and the exponential increase in computer processing speed and storage capacity, the debate has received a new impulse. As discussed in this chapter, large-scale models are currently under development that are often fed with real-world data, comparable to what a child will hear. Perhaps surprisingly, many of these systems are able to induce aspects of language with little or no "inborn" structure in the model. Neo-Chomskians have responded with elaborate criticism that is often couched in the form of countermodels. Thus, it is observed that the debate between deductive and inductive approaches to language acquisition is being rephrased in terms of well-articulated models and real-world data (Broeder & Murre, 1999, 2000).

In this chapter, I review a number of models of language acquisition, focusing most on first language (L1) acquisition. Very few models for bilingual or second language (L2) acquisition have been developed, so we are forced to look at what might be rather than at what is currently available. Before discussing the various models, I review some of the principal modeling formalisms. Some of the key concepts commonly found in the modeling literature are also discussed.

Modeling Formalisms

There are many different languages for formulating language acquisition models, but in general two main approaches can be distinguished. One approach uses deduction to prove various theorems. The other principal approach consists of computational models, which rely mainly on simulation because their structure and functioning are too complex to tackle through analysis. This review concentrates on the latter type of models because this area has seen most progress recently. Computational models themselves comprise a wide variety of formalisms, of which three are briefly reviewed: structural, remember-all, and connectionist models.

Structural Models

One of the oldest approaches to the study of language acquisition is mathematical linguistics (see Partee, Ter Meulen, & Wall, 1994, for an introduction), which includes many models that use a combination of discrete mathematics, algorithmic analysis, and statistics to model various forms of grammatical induction. An example is stochastic grammars, for which the linguistic production rules have a certain probability of application during sentence generation. Such a grammar assigns to each sentence in the language a probability of generation. Given a set of production rules and a set of sentences (e.g., produced by young children), it is sometimes possible to estimate the probabilities of production rule application (Fu, 1974; Gonzalez & Thomason, 1978). Finding the production rules themselves through induction is not computationally feasible for context-free grammars in general, but the problem of grammar acquisition can to some extent be modeled by stochastic context-free grammars.

A restricted form of context-free stochastic grammars is known as Hidden Markov Models (Rabiner & Juang, 1986). Although the more general class of stochastic context-free grammars is more powerful (Allerhand, 1987), Hidden Markov Models exhibit considerable capacity to learn or induce the phonetics in a certain language domain, and they are applied routinely in automatic speech perception software.

Remember-All Models

One approach to modeling behavior is to store and remember all instances of behavior ever encountered. An instance here typically includes a command or stimulus (input) and a consequence (output). When a new stimulus is encountered, it is compared to all stored ones, and the closest match is selected. Similarly, when behavior must be initiated to reach a given target output, the closest match is retrieved, and the corresponding command (input) is selected and executed. Although this approach seems simpleminded, it is often surprisingly successful, and the "learned" behavior may generalize well to new instances (e.g., Atkeson, Moore, & Schaal, 1997).

An obvious criticism of the remember-all approach is that it may rapidly exhaust the brain's memory capacity. However, the storage capacity of the brain is large, with human cortex alone containing about 10,000 times 10 billion (i.e., 10^{14}) nerve cell-to-cell connections, called *synapses* (Murre & Sturdy, 1995), each capable of storing roughly 1 byte worth of information. So, if the instances are not too large, 10 terabytes goes a long way.

Another objection might be that memory is associative and may form prototypes and schemata of prevalent categories encountered. This objection can be countered by arguing that, in the memory and categorization literature, many models based on storage of all instances are found. These instance-based models are nonetheless able to exhibit behavior suggestive of prototype formation (even though they do not form prototypes; they appear as a side effect of the instance matching rules when a response is generated). This class of models includes some of the most-cited ones, such as the generalized context model of categorization and identification by Nosofsky (1986, 1990), the Search of Associated Memory (SAM) and Retrieving Efficiently from Memory (REM) models by Raaijmakers, Shiffrin, and Seyvers (Raaijmakers & Shiffrin, 1981; Shiffrin & Steyvers, 1997) and the model of recognition memory by McClelland and Chappell (1998).

Connectionist Models

Connectionism has its roots in the work of William James, which was inspired by associationism and early insights into neural processing. Hebb (1949) rekindled the connectionist spirit, formulating James's associationist learning principle in terms of a neural learning rule that can be paraphrased as "nerve cells that fire together, wire together." In the 1950s, early computers were used to implement Hebb's ideas in actual learning systems. At the end of the 1950s, Rosenblatt (1958, 1962) invented the Perceptron, the first learning neural network, which enjoyed very wide popularity and seemed to have wide applicability. He also provided some important proofs that guaranteed correct learning behavior of the Perceptron. This started the first wave of widespread interest in connectionism.

Neural networks, as foreseen by Hebb (1949) and developed by Rosenblatt and many others after him, are based on the metaphor of networks of interconnected nerve cells (neurons) that exchange simple signals, called *activations*, over connections. What such a network can do depends on how it is wired, on which nerve cells are connected, and on how strong or efficient the connections are. Learning is achieved by adjusting the efficiency (*weight*) of each connection in such a way that the behavior of the network is slowly molded into desired or target behavior. This target behavior may be provided by the modeler in the form of teaching or target signals, in which case error-correcting learning is discussed. Sometimes, neural networks are able to extract regularities from the stimuli to which they are exposed without being told their aim. They achieve this regularity learning by creating and updating internal category structures.

Thus, it is seen that network models vary in the extent to which they need to be supervised. First or second language learning will probably have elements of both unsupervised and supervised learning. Using neural networks, it is possible to study just how much supervision is necessary to achieve a certain learning performance. In some cases, the model is not given a specific target to produce, but it is merely informed how close it was to the target. This is called *reinforcement learning*. An often-used example is balancing a broom on one's hand or on a computer-controlled car. The broom is observed continuously, and adjustments are made to the position of the hand or car until the broom finally falls down. The reinforcing signal in this case is of the form 1, 1, 1, ... (as long as the broom stays up), ..., 1, 1, −1 (when it finally falls down).

An interesting class of learning models that also falls somewhere between the two extremes of fully supervised learning and reinforcement learning is *imitation learning*. It involves a babbling stage in which the network learns how it must control its own effectors (e.g., muscles) to achieve a certain goal. A good example is the robot arm by Kuperstein (1988). Before any goal-directed tasks are attempted, the robot first spends a period exploring its own movements by setting the joint angles of its arm to random values. Its two eyes observe the effects of this *motor babbling*, and the internal network connections between the visual image and the arm position are adjusted so that they become more synchronous as time goes by. After a prolonged phase of such imitation learning, the robot is able to relate the joint angles of the arm to the visual image. The robot is now able to go from an envisioned goal position to a set of joint angle values; it can move its hand to grab an object it sees.

Imitation learning may also play a role in the development of speech. During the babbling stage, an infant makes random movements with the speech organs while at same time hearing the sounds caused by these movements. In the next stage, the infant is able to echo the sounds of his or her caretakers. During the final stage, the babbling becomes less random and drifts toward the phoneme inventory of the caretakers.

Backpropagation

The most popular form of error-correcting learning for neural networks is *backpropagation* (Rumelhart, Hinton, & Williams, 1986). One of its earliest applications illustrates the power of this learning algorithm. Sejnowksi and Rosenberg (1987) trained a network to pronounce text by presenting it with samples of text with a phonetic transcription. The network was capable of learning the task and showed generalization of its behavior. When new texts to which it had not been exposed were presented, it correctly pronounced the majority of the words. With the advent of backpropagation and the concurrent publication of a comprehensive collection of articles on neural network models and principles, the so-called PDP (Parallel Distributed Processing) volumes (McClelland & Rumelhart, 1986; Rumelhart & McClelland, 1986b), a second wave of popularity started for connectionism (see, e.g., Bechtel & Abrahamsen, 2002, for a recent introduction to connectionism).

The underlying learning mechanism of backpropagation is based on the Perceptron learning rule pioneered by Rosenblatt. The perceptron is limited to input and output values of 0 and 1 (i.e., no graded values are allowed). For each output node, a target signal (also 0 or 1) is available. The network has to learn to produce these target signals given the input pattern. An output node's activation becomes 1 if its net input is higher than some threshold (usually 0) and is 0 otherwise.

The Perceptron learning rule works with a very simple principle: If some input contributes toward an error (mismatch between spontaneous and target activation) in the output, adjust the weights from those inputs. Or, more precisely, if the output is already equal to the output target, the weight is left unchanged. Otherwise, if the target activation is higher than the spontaneous output, the weights to the output node are increased by some small amount, and if the target is lower, the weights are decreased by a small amount. Weights from nodes with activation value 0 are never changed. When a pattern (input-target pair) is presented, the learning rule is applied to all weights in the network. An entire training set, consisting of many patterns, usually has to be presented several times during the training procedure while small adjustments are made to the weights. This typically continues until no further improvement in the performance is observed.

The Perceptron is a two-layer network. It has no middle layers (called *hidden* layers), so it cannot do any internal processing. Minsky and Papert (1969) proved that two-layer networks cannot represent certain important logical relationships between input and output, including the exclusive-or function. Their analysis implied that there are many interesting pattern sets for which there exist no weight values that allow it to produce an error-free output for every input pattern. Nonetheless, if a solution does exist, the Perceptron learning rule is guaranteed to find it (Rosenblatt, 1958).

The backpropagation algorithm by Rumelhart et al. (1986) remedied the shortcomings of the perceptron algorithm because (a) it can be used in networks with one or more hidden layers (therefore, it is sometimes known as *multilayer perceptron*), and (b) it can be used with networks that have graded inputs and outputs. Widrow and Hoff (1960) had published a learning rule that could be used with some types of graded activation rules: the delta rule. The backpropagation rule can be seen as a generalization of this learning rule and is, therefore, often called the *generalized delta rule*.

The backpropagation learning rule is very similar to the perceptron rule when applied to the weights from the hidden units to the output units; for weights from the input layers to the hidden layers (for which no explicit target output is given), the errors are backpropagated from the output layers. The local error values in the output and hidden nodes are used similar to the perceptron rule.

Backpropagation will not always find an optimal solution in the form of a set of weights that maximizes the performance, but it will typically deliver at least a "good" solution. For many interesting learning problems, it can be proven that it is not feasible to find the globally optimal solution within a reasonable amount of time, so for these problems we must make do with a good but suboptimal solution.

Standard backpropagation works with feedforward networks only. This means that higher layers cannot be connected to lower layers (i.e., those closer to the input). This limits their use to input–output associations and makes it hard to apply them to time-varying signals, such as language utterances. In such cases, the system must retain an internal state that reflects the history of the signal thus far. This state may be compared to the stack necessary to parse context-free languages. Generalizations to backpropagation networks with recurrent connections were presented in the work of Rumelhart et al. (1986).

A simplified version of a backpropagation network that is able to learn time-varying signals is the Simple Recurrent Network by Elman (1990), which is also able to learn simple grammars. This network uses a buffer into which the hidden layer activations are copied after each learning cycle (see Fig. 8.1). The buffer enables the network to keep track of the history of past patterns encountered. One of the problems with these networks is that they are hard to train. Elman had to use a special procedure, called combined subset training, by which the network was first trained on a small set

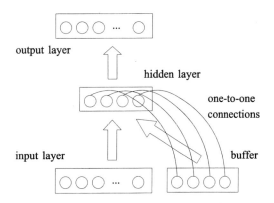

Figure 8.1 Simple Recurrent Network (Elman, 1990). After each learning cycle, the contents of the hidden layer are copied to the buffer and held during the next cycle. In this way, new patterns are processed together with some trace of past patterns. These networks are therefore able to learn series of patterns and simple grammars.

of examples. Throughout the training, this set was gradually extended to the final set. This procedure may broadly be compared to grammar learning by infants, starting with a small set of simple utterances before a larger range is acquired. Unfortunately, as discussed in the Models section, the suitability of Simple Recurrent Networks as psychological models of grammar acquisition is very limited (Sharkey, Sharkey, & Jackson, 2000).

Hebbian Learning and Categorization

One of the main features of a neural network is usually its insensitivity to small perturbations in the input patterns. Some networks are connected such that they can store patterns. When noisy versions of these patterns are presented, they are able to correct the small mistakes in the input, a feat often dubbed *pattern completion* or *content-addressable memory*.

Hopfield (1982) showed that this behavior can be obtained with Hebbian learning and a simple activation rule. Interesting and nontrivial comparisons with certain complex systems in physics can be made, by which the concept of attractor is linked with that of *energy*. With this approach, an attractor becomes an activation state with low energy, and under the influence of activation updates, the activation state migrates toward a low-energy state. When analyzing the pattern completion behavior, it thus appears that distortions of a pattern are attracted toward the original pattern. A stored representation in a Hopfield network is therefore an *attractor*.

Hebbian learning is often used to extract regularities from the set of input patterns. For example, if the input was speech, a network could be used to find the phonemes automatically. A key ingredient in nearly all of these algorithms is a form of competition between the nodes: Only one node (or a few nodes) can be active in a layer. The node with the highest net input usually wins the competition.

The principle of competitive learning is illustrated in Fig. 8.2. The network has three input nodes, which only serve to hold the input pattern. In this case the input nodes represent the letters *i*, *n*, and *o*, so that the words *in* and *no* can be formed. The network also has two uncommitted representation nodes U_1 and U_2. Initially, they do not represent any specific pattern. One of the main goals of a competitive learning procedure is to have these nodes represent specific input patterns or categories

of related input patterns. In Fig. 8.2, it is shown how first the word *in* is learned and then the word *no*.

Learning proceeds in two stages: First, a process of competition among the representation nodes takes place; as a result, a single "winning" node remains activated (in this case, Node U_2). Second, the connections to this node are adjusted. Using the Hebb rule, a weight from node *i* to node *j* is increased if (and only if) both nodes are activated. Typically, the weight is decreased if node *j* is activated but node *i* is not. After having been exposed to in and no, pattern in will always activate the in node and pattern no will activate the no node. In this way, we could produce a word recognizer that learns in an unsupervised manner: Simply by presenting many words to the system, it will develop word recognition nodes.

Modularity and Innate Knowledge

The value of unsupervised learning lies in that it is possible to discover regularities in the input patterns and to form categories or other higher-level units in an autonomous fashion. It is very likely that such processes play a crucial role in the acquisition of cognitive skills. Moreover, networks such as shown in Fig. 8.2 can serve as modules in larger networks. For example, there could be lower-level modules that recognize letters on the basis of handwritten patterns. On top of the letter modules, then could be positioned one or more word modules. It would suffice to provide such a model with enough handwritten words to allow it to discover both letter units and word units (see Murre, 1992, or Murre, Phaf, & Wolters, 1992, for an example of such a simulation). If it were trained with Russian input patterns, it would develop nodes recognizing Cyrillic letters and Russian words. The outcome of the learning process thus is strongly determined by the input patterns.

The above learning scheme might seem to be an example of pure induction, with little room for innate knowledge. This is not true, however, because the modular architecture of such a model has to be taken into account. How many modules does it have? How large are they? How are they connected? This overall structure provides an important constraint on what can and cannot be learned. It is, therefore, the second determinant of the outcome of the learning process, and it can be regarded as one of the points at which innate knowledge shapes the learning process.

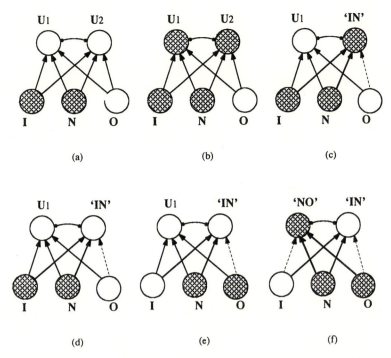

Figure 8.2 Schematic overview of competitive learning. The connections with circles at the end indicate inhibitory connections; arrowheads indicate excitatory connections. (a) Letters "I" and "N" of the word "IN" have been presented. (b) Uncommitted representation nodes U_1 and U_2 are competing. Assume that the weights are initially equally strong with small random variations. (c) Node U_2 has won the competition process because its connections were a little bit stronger. After resolution of the competition process, the connections from letter nodes I and N to node U_2 are strengthened (Hebbian learning); the connection from O to U_2 is weakened (anti-Hebbian learning). (d) When the word IN is presented again, the IN node will very rapidly become activated. (e) When the word "NO" is presented, however, the other node will become activated. (f) Hebbian learning further establishes the previously uncommitted node U_1 as the NO node.

When many different networks are generated in a process of simulated evolution, certain types of modular architectures are selected as "highly fit" in that they are particularly efficient at solving a given learning task. The models studied by Happel and Murre (1994), for example, evolved modular architectures that were particularly suitable for learning handwritten numerals on the basis of examples. Such processes could provide pointers to how inborn or "native" knowledge interacts with patterns encountered in the world around us. An efficient modular architecture—which is "innate"—will lead to very rapid discovery of the crucial units of processing, such as speech sounds and words. Innateness in these models means a predisposition towards learning certain aspects of the world.

Self-Organizing Maps

A variant on competitive learning is the Kohonen map or self-organizing map (Kohonen, 1989, 1990). Here, the nodes are arranged in a spatial structure, typically in a two-dimensional rectangle. When a pattern is presented, one of the nodes will be activated most and is the winner. With competitive learning, the weights to the winner would be increased (and perhaps those of neighbors decreased). With the Kohonen map, however, the weights to the winner are moved in the direction of the input pattern, and the weights of the nodes in the neighborhood are moved toward the pattern. If the pattern has the values (0.5, 0.3, 0.9) and the weights of the winner were (0.2, 0.0, 1.0), then after adjusting it, the latter values may have changed, respectively, into (0.3, 0.1, 0.9). The weights of the neighbors would also be shifted toward the input pattern. Exactly how large the neighborhood is varies, and generally it shrinks in the course of the learning process. Initially, it may incorporate half the network, whereas toward the end of learning, it may include only the winner itself.

The self-organizing map is interesting because it offers a model for the acquisition and emergence of similar maps found in the brain. Such topological maps are found, for example, in the auditory areas of the temporal cortex, where neurons that are sensitive to well-defined pitches are neatly arranged from high to low in a tonotopic map. Many other examples have been documented, including the visual areas and somatosensory areas of the brain.

Kohonen maps have been applied to areas relevant for language processing, such as learning of phonemes and speech recognition (the "phonetic typewriter" by Kohonen, 1988); of handwritten graphemes, including those of cursive writing (Schomaker, 1991); and of the semantics and broad lexical class as in the semantotopic maps by Ritter and Kohonen (1990). In the last, a Kohonen map was trained on simple three-word sentences of the type {*John, Mary*} {*walks, runs*} {*slowly, fast*}, such as "John walks slowly" or "Mary runs slowly." Many small sets of related words and many possible set-sequences were used. In the resulting semantotopic map, nouns, verbs, and adverbs occupied consecutive positions, covering three different areas of the map. Within these areas, related words were positioned on nodes that were close together. The semantic similarity was thus reflected in the two-dimensional layout of the map.

Based on these types of maps, and with addition of several other modules and learning algorithms, Miikkulainen (1993; also see Miikkulainen & Dyer, 1991) constructed an impressive system that can answer questions about stories and can parse and paraphrase them. Semantotopic maps have not yet been found in the brain, although there is good evidence for at least an overall organization into people, animals, and tools on the temporal cortex (Gazzaniga, Ivry, & Mangun, 2002).

The vocabulary and grammar used by Ritter and Kohonen (1990) were very small compared to real language, making it a toy problem. Using advanced techniques from matrix algebra, however, it has proven to be possible to "harvest" semantics from raw texts (Landauer & Dumais, 1997). The approach has much in common with that of Ritter and Kohonen (1990). For example, they also used the heuristic that words that occur in a similar neighborhood are semantically related. This approach to semantics is explored further in the section Harvesting Semantics From Texts. In the following section, a selection of models of language acquisition is reviewed, and a small selection of models of L2 acquisition is examined in the next section. A more general and more complete overview of computational psycholinguistic models can be found in the work of Dijkstra and De Smedt (1996), and a recent collection of models of (first) language acquisition can be found in the book by Broeder and Murre (2000).

Models of First Language Acquisition

When reviewing a certain area of modeling in psychology or cognitive neuroscience, different levels of maturity in the approach can be distinguished. In relatively new or difficult areas, the models are often merely aimed at *existence proofs*, attempting to show that something is indeed possible. Thus, Sejnowski and Rosenberg's (1987) NetTalk demonstrated that it is indeed possible to achieve industry standard text-to-speech conversion with a highly automated method based on learning from examples. Although their text and phoneme transcriptions were aligned manually, no rules or other information entered into the learning process. A competing model, DECTalk, had been developed through laborious encoding of the pronunciation rules of English with its many exceptions. Yet, despite the fact that more explicit information was used in creating DECTalk, NetTalk achieved a comparable generalization of performance on untrained texts. Once there is such an existence proof, more sophisticated research questions may be asked, delving into the psychological plausibility of the approach and perhaps even into the biological plausibility. With connectionist models, there is often the implicit promise that similar processes may go on in the brain, although the class of models for which this claim is substantiated is still quite small.

One aspect that many models such as NetTalk have in common is that they exhibit rulelike behavior, yet rules are not explicitly represented, and no symbols are passed around in the network. There is only the flow of activation signals from input to output. The output activation pattern must be interpreted to arrive at a phonetic transcription, for example, by selecting the output node with the highest activation value. The total output of the network is thus richer than the single phoneme it produces because it also produces a host of "second guesses." When the final output is very similar to that of rule-based systems, we still say that the network has discovered the rules of pronunciation. A set of rules in such a case can be considered a compact description of a much richer domain.

Once the existence proofs have been established, more advanced questions may be asked. In the case of language acquisition, the focus could be questions like the following: Is the model scalable? In other words, is it able to deal with large, real-world training sets that have not been extensively preprocessed? Does the system acquire the pronunciations or other task aspects modeled in roughly the same order as human subjects? What are the difficult cases? Do humans frequently falter on these as well? Is the method of training comparable to the way humans acquire the task (e.g., considering the number of training trials)? Can stages in the learning process be discerned? If the network is damaged, will the errors resemble those of human subjects with certain types of brain damage? Can anything be learned from the internal representations that have been formed during the learning process? Is there a relationship between the overall model architecture and theories of cognitive processing? Is there any such relationship with the gross anatomy of the brain? As more and more such questions are answered in a satisfactory manner, the models become more sophisticated.

During this process, there is usually a simultaneous demand for more detailed and more extensive collections of data, as can indeed be observed for the case of language acquisition. With the development of very fast personal computers, it is now feasible to model real-world data sets. Moreover, their collection, administration, and distribution are greatly boosted by the Internet. An example is the CHILDES (Child Language Data Exchange System) database at http://childes.psy. cmu.edu/, created by Brian MacWhinney (MacWhinney & Snow, 1985).

Remember-All Models of Prosody

Like many other language domains, prosody can be modeled through explicit rules and through other subsymbolic or nonsymbolic approaches. Children may learn correct stress assignment, for example, through the development of explicit rules. Alternatively, they could simply memorize the stress

pattern of each individual word with the rest of the word's structure.

Gillis, Daelemans, and Durieux (2000) described a remember-all model that uses "lazy learning" to acquire stress assignment. The system is fed with words with stress assigned. All instances are stored and remembered. When a new word is encountered, its stress pattern can be determined by finding the words in long-term memory that resemble it. In remember-all schemes, it is usually necessary to calculate similarity between remembered instances and newly encountered ones, and much of the work done on this type of model is invested in the study of similarity metrics. Their approach is based on that by Aha, Kibler, and Albert (1991), with some extensions. Suppose, for example, that the system encounters a new Dutch word *politie* (/po:li:si:/, police). It will attempt to assign one of a limited number of stress patterns by comparing it with all words in the database (long-term memory).

Words are matched in a syllable grid, and the number of attribute value coincidences is counted. For example, /po:li:si:/ and /po:li:o:/ (*polio*, polio) give a high match, whereas /po:li:si:/ and /a:Grɛssi:/ (*agressie*, aggression) give a low match. This approach can be refined, as Gillis et al. (2000, Table 5.1) showed, because not all attributes give the same amount of information. In fact, most of the information necessary for stress assignment is carried by the nucleus (middle) and coda (end) of the final syllable. They therefore weighed each attribute (entry in the grid) by its importance. Using this revised scheme, the match between /po:li:si:/ and /po:li:o:/ becomes lower because the final syllable does not match. The match between /po:li:si:/ and /a:Grɛssi:/ becomes much higher, and the system decides to assign the latter's stress pattern to *politie*, which is correct (penultimate syllable). Using that of *polio* would have led to an incorrect assignment of the antepenultimate syllable.

Differential weighing of attributes also forms the cornerstone of Nosofsky's (1986) Generalized Context Model, which is instance based as well. Attributes that are important for category distinctions receive a higher weight compared to those attributes that categories tend to have in common. Intuitively, this makes sense; if animals have to be categorized as either cats or dogs, it helps very little to know that the animal to be categorized has four legs, two eyes, two ears, and a tail. Although there are four attribute values, they convey no differential information, and they would each receive a weight of 0.

The Overregularization Debate

Some of the most interesting debates about the inductive or deductive nature of language acquisition have focused on overregularization phenomena. Many languages have inflections and genders that follow complicated rules with many exceptions. Proponents of the Chomskian deductive paradigm have argued that connectionist systems cannot explain these; in particular, the exceptions will throw the learning algorithms off track, causing either faulty generalization or inadvertent neglect of the exceptions.

The model of past-tense acquisition by Rumelhart and McClelland (1986) spawned the first debates in this area. They presented a model based on backpropagation learning that exhibited similar phases as children when they acquire the past-tense system of English. Very young speakers will generally use the correct forms for both regular (*added*, *asked*) and irregular words (*did*, *went*) and so will advanced speakers. Between the very early and the proficient phases, however, there is a phase in which children will frequently make overregularization errors (**doed*, **goed*).

Rumelhart and McClelland (1986) argued and demonstrated through simulation with a backpropagation network that this behavior emerges through the general acquisition of the regularities. The first examples are simply memorized. Then, the central regularities are extracted, and they may temporarily become dominant, leading to overregularization. As learning progresses, exceptions will be learned without disturbing the central trends.

Pinker and Prince (1988) and other critics did not agree with this account of the simulations by Rumelhart and McClelland (1986). They argued that the behavior of the model is not in accordance with that of children, and that for example, the amount of overregularization is not related in the same manner to the number and type of encountered words in children.

As an elaboration of the viewpoint by Pinker and colleagues, Marcus (e.g., 2000) formulated a theory by which resemblance to stored exemplars is used for irregular verbs (*sing–sang*, *ring–rang*) and a rule (add *-ed*) for regular forms. He called this the rule-and-memory model and argued that rules and more statistical approaches are complementary in modeling aspects of cognition.

One of the main criticisms of the general approach by Rumelhart and McClelland (1986) was that the method works only because the regular inflections of the past tense also happen to be highly frequent in English. Low-frequency but regular inflections might not generalize well, for example, because they are learned as individual exemplars without extraction of the central trend.

Goebel and Indefrey (2000) demonstrated that this is not necessarily true. They studied the acquisition of the German -s plural, which can be called an "infrequent default." Subjects preferred to use the -s plural to a degree that cannot be predicted from its frequency. A connectionist model trained on a representative set of inputs indicated that the correct generalization may be obtained even with low-frequency examples.

Simple Recurrent Networks and the Acquisition of Grammar

Grammars are typically considered rule-based systems that manipulate symbols and produce terminal structures such as strings of words or phonemes. The order in which the rules are applied is often seen as a representation of the hierarchical structure of a sentence, if not as a reflection of the actual production process. Connectionist models never use explicit symbol passing, and most connectionist paradigms are ill suited to the production or recognition of strings of patterns. As a consequence, connectionist models are not great models of grammatical processing, at least not if rule-based grammars are considered the standard.

It is not the case, however, that connectionist systems are in principle unable to implement (e.g., through manual wiring) the necessary logic underlying rule-based processing. In 1943, McCulloch and Pitts showed that connectionist systems can be hardwired to implement a wide range of logical circuits, fully comparable, for example, to those that drive a modern-day personal computer. Since then, many studies have demonstrated how neural networks can be hardwired directly for grammatical processing.

Here, we are interested in models that not only produce or recognize grammatical strings of patterns, but also are able to learn the underlying grammar on the basis of a limited number of examples. Such grammatical acquisition (often called *induction*) is also difficult for traditional grammars, and in its general form, it has been proven computationally unfeasible even for certain very simple types of grammars. Thus, it can be concluded that at the moment neither traditional grammars nor connectionist systems provide an adequate answer to the acquisition of grammar problems.

One of the most popular approaches to grammar learning is the simple recurrent network of Elman (1988, 1991), which is a special case of backpropagation through time as formulated by Rumelhart et al. (1986). The simple recurrent network is able to acquire (i.e., induce) simple phrase structure grammars so that, when given a grammatically correct sentence fragment, it is able to produce a legitimate next word. Several other studies have been carried out, all indicating that the networks are indeed able to capture grammatical regularities from an input set (e.g., Cleeremans, 1993). Servan-Schreiber, Cleeremans, and McClelland (1991) showed that their simple recurrent network could be trained to be a perfect recognizer for a finite-state grammar. So, there seem to be good possibilities for at least one class of neural network models.

Sharkey et al. (2000), however, analyzed the behavior of the simple recurrent network and pointed out several difficulties that severely limit its applicability as a psychological model of grammar acquisition. One of the problems mentioned by Sharkey et al. concerns the low maximum level of embedding that can be handled. This problem is sidestepped here because it could be argued that human working memory has severe limitations as well.

One of the other problems addressed by Sharkey et al. (2000) is the extreme difficulty of training a simple recurrent network to be a grammar recognizer. In one study, only 2 of 90 simulations yielded a successful performance. Several other problems were signaled, including one that plagues all backpropagation networks, namely, catastrophic interference (e.g., French, 1999). In this case, it would be predicted that children would have to relearn a substantial fraction of the already-learned examples each time they came across novel grammatical structures. If no relearning takes place on old patterns when novel ones are learned, the backpropagation network (including simple recurrent networks) rapidly forgets everything it has learned. Sharkey et al. (2000) did not explore remedies that have been proposed to alleviate this catastrophic forgetting (French, 1999; Murre, 1992). Once these are applied, some of the negative conclusions by Sharkey et al. (2000) may be lifted.

Harvesting Semantics From Texts

How meaning is represented in mind and brain and how it is acquired are important topics that have generated a staggering number of theories and philosophies. Compared to these, the contributions of computational models have been modest. These are nonetheless interesting because they illustrate how rough but useful semantic associations between words can be derived even from raw, unpreprocessed texts.

The semantotopic maps by Ritter and Kohonen (1990) illustrated the principle using a small-scale database. Recent techniques have used very large corpora, exceeding in some cases even the size of those to which a single human is exposed during a lifetime. The basic premise of most of this research is that words that tend to appear in the same context must be semantically related. As a first approach, all words encountered could be placed in a huge list, and a count of all words observed in the context could be kept behind each word. Context could be defined arbitrarily as, say, within 10 words to the left and 10 to the right, or some linguistic or textual unit such as the sentence or paragraph could be chosen. If any two words are selected from the list, the match can be looked at in context to gain a rough estimate of their semantic relatedness. This approach was used by several authors.

Landauer and Dumais (1997), for example, defined a "feature vector" for each word encountered in a text, for which the features consisted of those words found in the neighborhood. These vectors may become very large as the number of lexical types may approach 100,000. Therefore, they used methods from matrix algebra (Singular Value Decomposition, a form of generalized factor analysis) to reduce this vector and shrink it to about 80 features. Landauer and Dumais showed that this not only results in a more manageable long-term memory size, but also gives better performance (also see the material at http://lsa.colorado.edu/). Their method, called *Latent Semantic Analysis*, amplifies underlying semantic factors and filters out some of the noise.

A similar approach was followed by Griffiths and Steyvers (2004). Instead of dimension reduction, they used a topic-finding approach. Each word occurs in the context of certain topics. Selection of one or more topics gives a distribution of words that are likely to occur. Their topic-based system was able to successfully classify abstracts of articles published in the *Proceedings of the National Academy of Sciences*. An extension of their model also included word order statistics, based on Hidden Markov Models (Griffiths & Steyvers, 2003), and is able to generate pseudoabstracts after topic selection.

Although these methods have clear practical applications, they have at this point to my knowledge not been studied as models of human semantic acquisition. One step toward this would be to study the gradual pattern of acquisition rather than to process a large batch of text at once.

Children not only have to learn how words relate to each other, but also have to ground their meaning by relating them to aspects of the nonlinguistic environment. Siskind (1996, 2000) pointed out that this is a nontrivial problem because many words may be presented simultaneously with many possible aspects of the nonlinguistic context. He presents a lexical acquisition method for "bootstrapping" the cross-domain semantics using an online method, rejecting a remember-all approach. Although his simulations used artificial examples, he did consider the effect noise might have.

Models of Multilanguage Acquisition

Although the field of bilingualism is developing rapidly, computational modeling of multilanguage acquisition lags far behind. Some advances, however, suggest that important contributions can be expected in this area. Most models focus on the learning process of an L2 after an L1 has already been mastered. This distinction between L1 and L2 is itself subject to theorizing. How much later must L2 be learned to be considered an L2? What are the criteria?

Ullman (2001) addressed this issue in the context of his declarative/procedural model. He argued that learners at a greater age of exposure change their learning strategy of grammar from procedural to declarative, from implicit habit formation to explicit memorization of instances and schoolbook rules. The L2 thus is acquired in a fundamentally different manner. The use of rules here is quite different from the rulelike behavior that emerges in the models discussed in the preceding section. These often lack internal rules, but are able to show regularities in processing that are hard to distinguish from true rule-based processing. Ullman stressed the explicit, conscious use of rules in late L2 learning as the main mechanism.

A general approach to modeling language acquisition, the Competition Model (Bates & Mac-Whinney, 1982; MacWhinney, 1987) has been extended to L2 acquisition (MacWhinney, in press; also see MacWhinney, chapter 3, this volume). The model is comprehensive and addresses most areas in language processing and acquisition: phonology, lexicon, morphosyntax, and conceptualization (Levelt, 1989). The Extended Competition Model emphasizes competition between various options as the main mechanism that operates during production and comprehension. Different possibilities, such as word orders or choices of lexical items, compete. Levels may—but need not—influence each other, which is called *resonance*. MacWhinney (in press) argued that models of L2 learning must always take into account L1 learning because of transfer effects and common learning mechanisms. The Extended Competition Model provides a basis for implementation in a series of computational models, but this has not been accomplished yet.

Bilingual Lexicon

The two leading connectionist models of the bilingual lexicon are the Bilingual Interactive Activation (BIA) model (Dijkstra & Van Heuven, 1998; Grainger, 1993; also see chapter 10 by Thomas and Van Heuven in this volume) and the Bilingual Interactive Model of Lexical Access (BIMOLA; Grosjean, 1988, 1997), both building on the work of James McClelland and colleagues. Although neither models the acquisition process, they form an important benchmark against which acquisition models of bilingual lexicons should be tested.

The BIA model is an extension of the interactive activation model by McClelland and Rumelhart (1981), which was developed to account for context effects in letter recognition. It has three levels: letter features, letters, and words. Only four-letter words can be represented. Important in the model are the recurrent connections from the word level down to the letter level. A partially recognized word is able to help disambiguate a letter, so that a B in *beer* will be recognized faster than in *bxxx*, as is the case in humans. The BIA model adds a fourth level: language nodes. Activating a particular language node allows selection of words in that language while inhibiting words in the other languages. The words from different languages are represented in an integrated lexicon at the word level. During recognition, all word nodes that become activated through a particular language node will be strongly favored in the recognition process.

The BIMOLA is an extension of the TRACE model of McClelland and Elman (1986) and as such focuses on spoken word recognition. It has no language level, but has distinct modules for different languages at the phoneme and word levels. Both the BIA model and BIMOLA have been applied to cross-modal priming, recognition of cognates and homographs, semantic effects, and other phenomena. Many of these are reviewed in chapter 10 by Thomas and Van Heuven in this volume.

Meara (1999) also studied the bilingual lexicon, using Random Autonomous Boolean (RAB) networks (Kauffman, 1993), which resemble somewhat the model by Hopfield (1982). RAB networks also have recurrent connections as well as attractor states. The basic idea of Meara's model is that L1 and L2 both form an attractor state, and that the network is in either of the two states. When the network is in L1, more and more lexical units from L2 may be recruited, for example, because the system is suddenly exposed to many words from L2. In that case, the attractor will rapidly shift to L2, which will then become the dominant lexical process. This model aims to explain aspects of language shifting, although it has not been systematically compared with experimental data.

Neither the BIA model nor the BIMOLA models the acquisition phase; their connections are hardwired. Two models that specifically aim to model acquisition are by French (1998) and by Li and Farkas (2002).

French (1998) applied a simple recurrent network to modeling the lexicon in bilingual memory. His basic simulation uses a "grammar" with only subject-verb-object (SVO) sentences and with two minivocabularies with four words per category (e.g., subject nouns in language Alpha are *boy*, *girl*, *man*, *woman* and in language Beta are *garçon*, *fille*, *homme*, and *femme*; French also mentioned a scaled-up version with 256 words per category). Sentences are generated as a continuous stream with a very small chance of switching from Alpha to Beta (never within a SVO sentence): *boy lifts toy man sees pen man touches book...boy pushes book femme souleve stylo fille prend stylo*, and so on. A 300,000-word training sequence was fed into a single recurrent network with a hidden layer of 32 nodes. With backpropagation, distributed representations are expected to develop in the hidden layer, with strong overlap between learned items.

French (1998) analyzed these representations and founds that they were neatly clustered, first into the two languages and within these into the three grammatical categories. It is interesting that there was single hidden node, Node 22, that had a very strong influence on which language was processed. When a random subset of the nodes was lesioned (deactivated), the overall characteristics of the clustering did not change, but when Node 22 was lesioned, the separation between the two languages was severely disrupted. French compared this finding to that of bilinguals with diffuse brain damage, who do not usually mix languages, and contrasted it with that of rare cases for whom a small lesion caused a loss of separation between languages (e.g., Albert & Obler, 1978).

Li and Farkas (2002) presented a self-organizing model of bilingual processing (SOMBIP) that is similar in spirit to French's model but takes a quite different approach. Its architecture is based on two coupled self-organizing maps, one of which is a semantotopic map (Miikkulainen, 1993; Ritter & Kohonen, 1990); the other represents the phonology (a phonotopic map). The system was trained on realistic bilingual speech input from the CHILDES corpus: conversations between a child (1–3 years old) and the child's native English-speaking father and native Cantonese-speaking mother. The input was analyzed for lexical co-occurrence statistics with a new technique that automatically generates a meaningful semantic representation in a way comparable to Latent Semantic Analysis (see Harvesting Semantics From Texts section): Related words have more similar representations than unrelated words. When a word is encountered, the semantotopic map is presented with its semantic representation (derived earlier); simultaneously, the phonotopic map is presented with its phonological representation. Hebbian learning associates corresponding representations in the two maps while these are still emerging. Even though English and Cantonese were presented intermittently and without explicit language labeling, both the semantics and the phonology self-organized into separate regions of the maps, forming language-specific lexicons in a single integrated network. Lexical categories, such as nouns, verbs, and prepositions, organized themselves into separate regions within the language areas of the maps. The system also showed evidence of cross-language priming and interference, but the simulations were not fitted to human data.

Bilingual Phonology and Speech Perception

Hancin-Bhatt and Govindjee (1999) developed an L2 model of phonology. They used a network to explain when and why L2 learners have trouble acquiring a particular L2 phonology. They were interested in the pattern of substitutions that takes place when, for example, German speakers of English substitute a continuant /s,z/ for the English interdentals /θ,ð/ and speakers of Hindi and Turkish use a stop /t/, for example. Their network takes into account frequency of occurrence, and it has both a perception and a production part, so that it can be used to explain both aspects of language processing. It was trained on the L1 phonology in Hindi and Japanese and then tested on the L2 phonology of English interdentals. The pattern of errors approximated that of experimental subjects. One of their conclusions was that L1 speakers are biased in their perception of L2, and that this is the main determinant in, possibly inaccurate, feature selection.

A model of the acquisition of speech sounds in a foreign language is that of Keidel, Zevin, Kluender, and Seidenberg (2003). Their approach can be seen as an implementation of Flege's Speech Learning Model (Flege, 1995) and Best's Perceptual Assimilation Model (Best, McRoberts, & Goodell, 2001). In the Speech Learning Model, L2 speech sounds are perceived relative to existing L1 prototypes. The model predicts, among others, that L2 speech sounds are easier to acquire if they differ phonetically from those in L1. The Perceptual Assimilation Model bears many similarities to this model, but assumes that speech perception occurs by direct perception of gestural information.

Keidel et al. (2003) presented a large number of digitized English and isiZulu CV syllables, recorded from native speakers, to a network model. The network was trained on the English speech with a generalized recurrent backpropagation algorithm (Pearlmutter, 1995), of which the Simple Recurrent Network discussed in a separate previous section is a special case. The system learned to recognize and generalize the English speech sounds well. When presented with the Zulu stimuli, these were assimilated to English phonemes in accordance with human English speakers when exposed to Zulu. Models such as this are able to make specific predictions when complex phonetic systems interact and contrastive analysis may be difficult or inconclusive.

Current and Future Developments

Compared to the thriving field of computational psycholinguistics (e.g., Dijkstra & De Smedt, 1996) and the developing subfields of models of language acquisition (Broeder & Murre, 2000) or models of

bilingual processing (see Thomas & Van Heuven, chapter 10, this volume), there are still very few models of bilingual language acquisition. Considering the progress that has been made, where such models could be developed can be sketched. The work on latent semantic analysis by Landauer and Dumais (1997), for example, seems very promising as a basis for a model of the bilingual lexicon, possibly using neural networks as an implementation (cf. Ritter & Kohonen, 1990) rather than matrix algebra.

Dumais, Letsche, Littman, and Landauer (1997) have already shown that their approach is able to handle multilanguage semantics. The system was trained on aligned French and English texts (i.e., translations). The language's semantic spaces were moved into proper alignment through forced placement of selected words that were assumed to be semantically identical in both languages (e.g., names of countries). In the next training stage, texts in one language only were added to the system ("folded-in"). The system was tested on cross-language retrieval: Queries in, say, English successfully retrieved texts in both English and French, including French texts that had not been presented with an aligned English translation. It will be clear that this scenario resembles semantic acquisition and translation, and it would be interesting to study the models from that perspective.

Another area in which computational models will undoubtedly contribute is the critical period debate (see chapters 2, 5, and 6, this volume). Models such as that of Keidel et al. (2003), discussed in the preceding section, may be used to elucidate the extent that already-formed speech categories influence the acquisition of new ones. Is (biologically constrained) plasticity of the system the all-important factor, or does a firmly converged set of prototypes by itself hamper new acquisition? Can these insights be used to forge new representations, for example, by presenting synthetically exaggerated speech sounds to L2 learners, as was done by McClelland, Fiez, and McCandliss (2002)? These authors made practical use of the insights gleaned from modeling in the teaching of an L2.

In the future, the development of more of these models can tell us how to increase the acquisition speed when learning another language. Because computational models are fed with real-world data, it is even feasible to build such models into computer-assisted language learning programs, such that the learning process will be optimized for individual students. Models of bilingual language acquisition are rapidly becoming more sophisticated, providing new battlegrounds for theory and practice.

Acknowledgment

Writing of this chapter was supported by a grant by the Netherlands Organisation for Scientific Research.

References

Aha, D., Kibler, D., & Albert, M. (1991). Instance-based learning algorithms. *Machine Learning, 6,* 37–66.

Albert, M., & Obler, L. K. (1978). *The bilingual brain: Neuropsychological and neurolinguistic aspects of bilingualism.* New York: Academic Press.

Allerhand, M. (1987). *Knowledge-based speech pattern recognition.* London: Kogan Page.

Atkeson, C. G., Moore, A. W., & Schaal, S. (1997). Locally weighted learning. *Artificial Intelligence Review, 11,* 11–73.

Bates, E., & MacWhinney B. (1982). Functionalist approaches to grammar. In E. Wanner & L. Gleitman (Eds.), *Language acquisition: The state of the art* (pp. 173–218). New York: Cambridge University Press.

Bechtel, W., & Abrahamsen, A. (2002). *Connectionism and the mind: Parallel processing, dynamics, and evolution in networks* (2nd ed.). Oxford, U.K.: Blackwell.

Best, C. T., McRoberts, G. W., & Goodell, E. (2001). Discrimination of non-native consonant contrasts varying in perceptual assimilation to the listener's native system. *Journal of the Acoustic Society of America, 109,* 775–794.

Broeder, P., & Murre, J. M. J. (Eds.) (1999). *Language and thought in development: Cross-linguistic studies.* Tübingen, Germany: Gunter Narr Verlag.

Broeder, P., & Murre, J. M. J. (Eds.). (2000). *Models of language acquisition: Inductive and deductive approaches.* Oxford, U.K.: Oxford University Press.

Cleeremans, A. (1993). *Mechanisms of implicit learning: Connectionist models of sequence processing.* London: MIT Press.

Dumais, S. T., Letsche, T. A., Littman, M. L., & Landauer, T. K. (1997). Automatic cross-language retrieval using Latent Semantic Indexing. In *AAAI-97 Spring Symposium on Cross-Language Text and Speech Retrieval* (pp. 18–24). March 24–26, Stanford University, California.

Dijkstra, A., & De Smedt, K. (Eds.) (1996). *Computational psycholinguistics: Symbolic and subsymbolic models of language processing.* London: Taylor and Francis.

Dijkstra, A., & Van Heuven, W. (1998). The BIA model and bilingual word recognition. In J. Grainger & A. M. Jacobs (Eds.), *Localist connectionist approaches to human cognition* (pp. 189–225). Mahwah, NJ: Erlbaum.

Elman, J. L. (1988). *Finding structure in time* (Technical Report No. 8801). San Diego: University of California, Center for Research in Language.

Elman, J. L. (1990). Finding structure in time. *Cognitive Science, 14,* 179–211.

Elman, J. L. (1991). Distributed representations, simple recurrent networks and grammatical structure. *Machine Learning, 7,* 195–225.

Flege, J. E. (1995). Second-language speech learning: Theory, findings, and problems. In W. Strange (Ed.), *Speech perception and linguistic experience: Theoretical and methodological issues* (pp. 229–273). Timonium, MD: York Press.

French, R. M. (1998). A simple recurrent network model of bilingual memory. In *Proceedings of the 20th Annual Cognitive Science Society Conference* (pp. 368–373). Hillsdale, NJ: Erlbaum.

French, R. M. (1999). Catastrophic forgetting in connectionist networks. *Trends in Cognitive Sciences, 3,* 128–135.

Fu, K. S. (1974). *Syntactic methods in pattern recognition.* New York: Academic Press.

Gazzaniga, M. S., Ivry, R., & Mangun, G. R. (2002). *Fundamentals of cognitive neuroscience* (2nd ed.). New York: Norton.

Gillis, S., Daelemans, W., & Durieux, G. (2000). "Lazy learning": Natural and machine learning of word stress. In P. Broeder & J. M. J. Murre (Eds.), *Models of language acquisition: Inductive and deductive approaches* (pp. 76–99). Oxford, U.K.: Oxford University Press.

Goebel, R., & Indefrey, P. (2000). A recurrent network with short-term memory capacity learning the German -s plural. In P. Broeder & J. M. J. Murre (Eds.), *Models of language acquisition: Inductive and deductive approaches* (pp. 177–200). Oxford, U.K.: Oxford University Press.

Gonzalez, R. C., & Thomason, M. G. (1978). *An introduction to stochastic pattern recognition.* Reading, MA: Addison-Wesley.

Grainger, J. (1993). Visual word recognition in bilinguals. In R. Schreuder & B. Weltens (Eds.), *The bilingual lexicon* (pp. 11–26). Amsterdam: Benjamins.

Griffiths, T. L., & Steyvers, M. (2003). Prediction and semantic association. In J. Becker, S. Thrun, & K. Obermayer (Eds.), *Advances in Neural Information Processing Systems* (p. 15). Cambridge, MA: MIT Press.

Griffiths, T. L., & Steyvers, M. (2004). Finding scientific topics. *Proceedings of the National*

Academy of Sciences, 101(Suppl. 1), 5228–5235.

Grosjean, F. (1988). Exploring the recognition of guest words in bilingual speech. *Language and Cognitive Processes, 3*, 233–274.

Grosjean, F. (1997). Processing mixed languages: Issues, findings, and models. In A. M. B. de Groot & J. F. Kroll (Eds.), *Tutorials in bilingualism: Psycholinguistic perspectives* (pp. 225–254). Mahwah, NJ: Erlbaum.

Hancin-Bhatt, B., & Govindjee, A. (1999). A computational model of feature competition in L2 phonology. In P. Broeder & J. M. J. Murre (Eds.), *Language and thought in development: Cross-linguistic studies* (pp. 145–161). Tübingen, Germany: Gunter Narr Verlag.

Happel, B. L. M., & Murre, J. M. J. (1994). The design and evolution of modular neural network architectures. *Neural Networks, 7*, 985–1004.

Hebb, D. O. (1949). *The organization of behavior.* New York: Wiley.

Hopfield, J. J. (1982). Neural networks and physical systems with emergent collective computational abilities. *Proceedings of the National Academy of Sciences USA, 79*, 2554–2558.

Kauffman, S. (1993). *The origins of order.* Oxford, U.K.: Oxford University Press.

Keidel, J. L., Zevin, J. D., Kluender, K. R., & Seidenberg, M. S. (2003). Modeling the role of native language knowledge in perceiving nonnative speech contrasts. In M. J. Salé, D. Recasens, & J. Romero (Eds.), *Proceedings of the 15th International Congress of Phonetic Sciences* (pp. 2221–2224). Barcelona, Spain: Causal Productions.

Kohonen, T. (1988, March). The "neural" phonetic typewriter. *IEEE Computer*, pp. 11–22.

Kohonen, T. (1989). *Self-organization and associative memory* (3rd ed.). Berlin, Germany: Springer-Verlag.

Kohonen, T. (1990). The self-organizing map. *Proceedings of the IEEE, 78*, 1464–1480.

Kuperstein, M. (1988). Neural model of adaptive hand-eye coordination for single postures. *Science, 239*, 1308–1311.

Landauer, T. K., & Dumais, S. T. (1997). A solution to Plato's problem: The latent semantic analysis theory of the acquisition, induction, and representation of knowledge. *Psychological Review, 104*, 211–240.

Levelt, W. J. M. (1989). *Speaking: From intention to articulation.* Cambridge, MA: MIT Press.

Li, P., & Farkas, I. (2002). A self-organizing connectionist model of bilingual processing. In R. Heredia & J. Altarriba (Eds.), *Bilingual sentence processing* (pp. 59–85). North-Holland, The Netherlands: Elsevier Science.

MacWhinney, B. (1987). The competition model. In B. MacWhinney (Ed.), *Mechanisms of language acquisition* (pp. 249–308). Hillsdale, NJ: Erlbaum.

MacWhinney, B. (in press). Extending the Competition Model. *International Journal of Bilingualism.*

MacWhinney, B., & Snow, C. (1985). The Child Language Data Exchange System. *Journal of Child Language, 12*, 271–296.

Marcus, G. (2000). Children's overregularization and its implications for cognition. In P. Broeder & J. M. J. Murre (Eds.), *Models of language acquisition: Inductive and deductive approaches* (pp. 154–176). Oxford, U.K.: Oxford University Press.

McClelland, J. L., & Chappell, M. (1998). Familiarity breeds differentiation: A Bayesian approach to the effects of experience in recognition memory. *Psychological Review, 105*, 724–760.

McClelland, J. L., & Elman, J. (1986). Interactive processes in speech perception: The TRACE model. In J. L. McClelland, D. E. Rumelhart, & the PDP research group (Eds.), *Parallel distributed processing: Explorations in the microstructure of cognition* (Vol. 2, pp. 58–121). Cambridge, MA: MIT Press.

McClelland, J. L., Fiez, J. A., & McCandliss, B. D. (2002). Teaching the /r/-/l/ discrimination to Japanese adults: Behavioral and neural aspects. *Physiology and Behavior, 77*, 657–662.

McClelland, J. L., & Rumelhart, D. E. (1981). An interactive activation model of context effects in letter perception. Part 1: An account of basic findings. *Psychological Review, 88*, 375–405.

McClelland, J. L., & Rumelhart, D. E. (Eds.) (1986). *Parallel distributed processing: Explorations in the microstructure of cognition. Volume 2: Psychological and biological models.* Cambridge, MA: MIT Press.

McCulloch, W. S., & Pitts, W. (1943). A logical calculus of the ideas immanent in nervous activity. *Bulletin of Mathematical Biophysics, 9*, 127–147.

Meara, P. (1999). Self-organization in bilingual lexicons. In P. Broeder & J. M. J. Murre (Eds.), *Language and thought in development: Cross-linguistic studies* (pp. 127–144). Tübingen, Germany: Gunter Narr Verlag.

Miikkulainen, R. (1993). *Subsymbolic natural language processing: An integrated model of scripts, lexicon, and memory.* Cambridge, MA: MIT Press.

Miikkulainen, R., & Dyer, M. (1991). Natural language processing with modular PDP networks and distributed lexicon. *Cognitive Science, 15,* 343–399.

Minsky, M. L., & Papert, S. A. (1969). *Perceptrons.* Cambridge, MA: MIT Press.

Murre, J. M. J. (1992). *Categorization and learning in modular neural networks.* Hemel Hempstead: Harvester Wheatsheaf, and Hillsdale NJ: Lawrence Erlbaum.

Murre, J. M. J., Phaf, R. H., & Wolters, G. (1992). CALM: Categorization and Learning Module. *Neural Networks, 5,* 55–82.

Murre, J. M. J., & Sturdy, D. P. F. (1995). The connectivity of the brain: Multi-level quantitative analysis. *Biological Cybernetics, 73,* 529–545.

Nosofsky, R. M., (1986). Attention, similarity, and the identification-categorization relationship. *Journal of Experimental Psychology: General, 115,* 39–57.

Nosofsky, R. M. (1990). Relations between exemplar-similarity and likelihood models of classification. *Journal of Mathematical Psychology, 34,* 393–418.

Partee, B. H., Ter Meulen, A. G., & Wall, R. (1994). *Mathematical methods in linguistics, corrected second printing of the first edition.* Dordrecht, The Netherlands: Kluwer Academic.

Pearlmutter, B. A. (1995). Gradient calculations for dynamic recurrent neural networks: A survey. *IEEE Transactions on Neural Networks, 6,* 1212–1228.

Pinker, S., & Prince, A. (1988). On language and connectionism: Analysis of a parallel distributed processing model of language acquisition. *Cognition, 28,* 73–193.

Raaijmakers, J. G. W., & Shiffrin, R. M. (1981). Search of associative memory. *Psychological Review, 88,* 93–134.

Rabiner, L. R., & Juang, B. H. (1986, January). An introduction to hidden Markov models. *IEEE ASSP Magazine,* 4–16.

Ritter, H., & Kohonen, T. (1990). Learning "semantotopic maps" from context. *Proceedings of the International Joint Conference on Neural Networks, Washington DC* (Vol. 1, pp. 23–26). Hillsdale, NJ: Erlbaum.

Rosenblatt, F. (1958). The perceptron: A probabilistic model for information storage and organization in the brain. *Psychological Review, 65,* 386–408.

Rosenblatt, F. (1962). *Principles of neurodynamics.* Washington, DC: Spartan Books.

Rumelhart, D. E., Hinton, G. E., & Williams, R. J. (1986). Learning internal representations by error propagation. In D. E. Rumelhart & J. L. McClelland (Eds.), *Parallel distributed processing: Explorations in the microstructure of cognition. Volume 1: Foundations* (pp. 318–362). Cambridge, MA: MIT Press.

Rumelhart, D. E., & McClelland, J. L. (1986a). On learning the past tenses of English verbs. Implicit rules or parallel distributed processing. In J. L. McClelland & D. E. Rumelhart (Eds.), *Parallel distributed processing: Explorations in the microstructure of cognition. Volume 2: Psychological and biological models* (pp. 216–271). Cambridge, MA: MIT Press.

Rumelhart, D. E., & McClelland, J. L. (Eds.). (1986b). *Parallel distributed processing: Explorations in the microstructure of cognition. Volume 1: Foundations.* Cambridge, MA: MIT Press.

Schomaker, L. R. B (1991). *Simulation and recognition of handwriting movements.* Doctoral dissertation, Technical Report NICI 91-03, Nijmegen University, The Netherlands.

Sejnowski, T. J., & Rosenberg, C. R. (1987). Parallel networks that learn to pronounce English text. *Complex Systems, 1,* 145–168.

Servan-Schreiber, D., Cleeremans, A., & McClelland, J. L. (1991). Graded state machines: The representation of temporal contingencies in simple recurrent networks. *Machine Learning, 7,* 161–193.

Sharkey, N., Sharkey, A., & Jackson, S. (2000). Are SRNs sufficient for modelling language acquisition? In P. Broeder & J. M. J. Murre (Eds.), *Models of language acquisition: Inductive and deductive approaches* (pp. 33–54). Oxford, U.K.: Oxford University Press.

Shiffrin, R. M., & Steyvers, M. (1997). A model for recognition memory: REM: Retrieving effectively from memory. *Psychonomic Bulletin and Review, 4,* 145–166.

Siskind, J. (1996). A computational study of cross-situational techniques for learning word-to-meaning mappings. *Cognition, 61,* 39–91.

Siskind, J. (2000). Learning word-to-meaning mappings. In P. Broeder & J. M. J. Murre (Eds.), *Models of language acquisition: Inductive and deductive approaches* (pp. 121–153). Oxford, U.K.: Oxford University Press.

Ullman, M. T. (2001). The neural basis of lexicon and grammar in first and second language: The declarative/procedural mode. *Bilingualism: Language and Cognition, 4,* 105–122.

Widrow, B., & Hoff, M. E. (1960). Adaptive switching circuits. *1960 IRE WESCON Convention Record, Part 4,* 96–104.

PART II

COMPREHENSION

Natasha Tokowicz
Charles A. Perfetti

Introduction to Part II
Comprehension

The goal for many aspiring bilinguals is successful communication in their second language (L2), including becoming able to comprehend spoken and written messages. Language comprehension is complex from a scientific point of view. For a competent speaker, however, comprehension is "a piece of cake." All the lexical, semantic, syntactic, and textual processes that compete for attention and memory resources (and fill up diagrams in models of comprehension) are executed with ease and without notice. Such may not be the case for the learner of an L2 or perhaps even for the moderately skilled bilingual. On the other hand, for the skilled bilingual, as for the monolingual, the machinery of comprehension may be so skillfully engaged that only the most clever of experimental designs can expose any confusion or difficulty.

For the bilingual, which factors influence the success of L2 comprehension? The chapters in this part provide an overview of the research on some of the levels of bilingual comprehension. To introduce the issues seen in the study of bilingual comprehension, we first outline a general framework for comprehension processes. This framework reflects a body of research largely undertaken without the slightest notice that some comprehenders might be able to engage more than one language. That is, it reflects the consensus view of comprehension from the perspective of research in monolingual contexts. We then describe some of the relevant research conducted on bilinguals for each aspect of comprehension. Our review is far from comprehensive, focusing on only a few major issues in each area and pointing to the chapters of this section for more detailed reviews.

The Processes of Comprehension

The component processes of language comprehension and the ways they are interconnected provide a platform to view problems of bilingual comprehension. Reviews of spoken language comprehension and written language comprehension by Cutler and Clifton (1999) and Perfetti (1999), respectively, provide frameworks for the key component processes of comprehension and their interrelationships. Here, we simply provide an outlined description of some of the key components. Ignoring the physical properties of speech and print, no small matter, simplifies the problem of comprehension so that what we need to account for is merely the following:

1. Word identification: How words are identified such that their context-appropriate meanings are selected.
2. Parsing: How words and morphemes are configured into phrasal units that govern interpretation.
3. Semantic-syntactic representations: How the meanings of words and the grammar of the language combine to provide the meaning of clauses and sentences.
4. Text representation: How the meanings of clauses and sentences are integrated into a coherent representation of an extended discourse.
5. Understanding: How all the above function to yield actual comprehension, a more-or-less veridical representation of a token discourse.

Finally, in all of these processes, there can be individual differences that produce variability in comprehension skill.

These processes can serve as a starting point for the study of bilingual comprehension. Of course, an L2 brings added complexity to an already rather complex problem. This may be part of the reason for an unevenness seen in the extent to which component processes and their relationships have been addressed in bilingual research. In particular, there is much more to say about bilingual word-level processes than higher-level comprehension processes.

Word Identification

Word identification entails lexical access through phonological and printed inputs. It is axiomatic that these inputs are linguistically specific. One hears a word with Dutch phonology or with French phonology, and a comprehender with the required language skill identifies the word accordingly. From this point, however, the details become interesting. Two of the chapters in this part relate to the study of bilingual word identification. Although it seems intuitively reasonable to skilled bilinguals that they can effectively "turn off" or attenuate one of their languages, the research by now suggests that this seldom happens. Perhaps one language can be "turned down," but not quite turned off. As Dijkstra (chapter 9) demonstrates, bottom-up factors such as stimulus list composition and task demands make a difference for bilingual word recognition. Furthermore, top-down information, such as the knowledge that only one of your languages is needed for a given task is not sufficient and can be overridden by the bottom-up information (see also MacWhinney, chapter 3).

A classic question is whether word form information for the two languages is stored together or separately. Given the above results and others, we may conclude that word form information is most likely stored in a shared way (or at least in a way that allows sufficient cross talk between the two languages; see Francis, chapter 12). As mentioned, task demands will influence whether there appears to be selective or nonselective access of word forms in the two languages.

The critical issue of how words are recognized by bilinguals recently has received much attention because of the precision available in mathematical models. Thomas and Van Heuven (chapter 10) provide a review of the two major types of computational models used in this area, localist and distributed models. Their review includes a summary of the issues that have been tackled with models; these issues include neighborhood effects, priming, and homograph/cognate effects. Although we are far from a complete model of bilingual comprehension, progress in computational modeling comes from models designed for specific problems rather than for general purposes. Bilingual word recognition has made great advances in the recent past as a result of the available models. Thomas and Van Heuven suggest that joining localist and distributed models will further our understanding of bilingual comprehension. Beyond the representational details of models, however, is the value of building competing models that address the same problems. This competition exposes basic assumptions about language processes that can be hidden when each model addresses a different problem.

Parsing

Listeners and readers must do something with the words they hear and see to construct messages. Building phrasal units from strings of words and connecting these units with each other in the way allowed by the grammar of the language is a large part of this process. How to explain parsing in the first language (L1) has proved to be difficult and contentious. How do comprehenders decide, on a word-by-word basis, how to attach a word to the current representation of a sentence? Theories that stress basic principles of simplicity and theories that stress more complex multiple constraints offer rather different solutions to this question. In the case of an L2, the question becomes even more difficult. The grammar of the L2 is not as well represented as that of the L1 in most cases. So, how does a learner of a second language go about deciding how to attach a word to a current sentence representation?

Frenck-Mestre (chapter 13) reviews some of the recent research on bilingual parsing. In particular, she considers the evidence that bilinguals use information from their L1 to process their L2. Thus, a person's L1 can indicate which particular syntactic structures will be difficult to comprehend in L2. A similar conclusion was reached by Fender (2003), who showed that Japanese and Arabic speakers of English as a second language have opposite difficulties in processing English as a result of different native language structures. The dominance of L1 syntactic structures in L2 comprehension was also evident in research by Tokowicz and MacWhinney (2002), who showed that native English speakers learning Spanish had difficulty rejecting Spanish sentences with grammatical errors when the word-by-word translation mapped directly to an acceptable English structure. Also, Tokowicz and MacWhinney (in press) found that these learners showed brain responses (measured by event-related potentials) that indicated more sensitivity to grammatical violations in their L2 (Spanish) when the constructions were formed similarly, rather than differently, in L1 and L2. This was true despite the participants' inability to distinguish grammatically acceptable and unacceptable sentences overtly. Finally, evidence shows that nonproficient bilinguals initially comprehend L2 through an L1 lens. McDonald (1987) showed that English learners of Dutch declined in their use of word order (a valid English cue) and increased in their use of case inflection (a valid Dutch cue) to comprehend L2 sentences as their Dutch competence increased.

Semantic-Syntactic Representations

Representing meaning is central to comprehension at all levels. Word identification brings access to word meanings and their associated concepts, and parsing builds groupings of words and morphemes into phrasal units that provide both reference and semantic relationships. The result of these word identification and syntactic processes is a representation of meaning at the clausal and sentence levels. This meaning representation, corresponding to a proposition in theories of comprehension (Kinstsch, 1988), can be considered the basic unit of relational meaning in a text, spoken or written.

It is our impression that there is little in bilingual research that corresponds fully to this level of analysis, although several chapters in this section focus on parts of it. For example, how words are represented in the memory of a bilingual has been a major question. Are words from the two languages stored separately in their own language or connected together by their meaning similarity? Do translation equivalents activate identical meaning representations? Are cognate translations stored differently from noncognate translations? Each of these issues is addressed in this section.

The basic answer to the first of these questions is, well, it depends. A single pool of semantic features most likely comprises the meanings of translation equivalents. Whether translation equivalents activate exactly the same meaning may depend on the manner in which L2 was learned (e.g., in the classroom or abroad; see De Groot, 1992). However, as always, there are caveats. Generally, it seems that the differences in meaning are few and far between. For the most part, translations are just that, words that have the same meaning across languages (see Guasch, 2001; Sánchez-Casas, Suárez-Buratti, & Igoa, 1992; Tokowicz, 2000;

and Tokowicz, Kroll, De Groot, & Van Hell, 2002, for more information about the consequences of imprecise meaning overlap across languages).

In answer to the question of whether cognates are stored in a special way relative to noncognates, Sánchez-Casas and García-Albea (chapter 11) conclude that there is preliminary evidence to support a special status for cognate representations. They argue that cognates are treated as morphologically related words within a language and demonstrate that they follow the same priming pattern as such words. Interestingly, Francis (chapter 12) provides evidence that translation equivalents in general are not treated as within-language synonyms.

Another factor that has been shown to influence meaning representation is age of acquisition (AoA). Izura and Ellis (2002, 2004) showed that regardless of L1 AoA, L2 words learned earlier are processed more rapidly than L2 words learned later. This pattern has been observed in several tasks, including translation recognition, lexical decision, and object naming. Thus, the age at which an L2 word is learned has an impact on the word form-to-meaning connection that is the foundation of L2 comprehension.

Text Representation and Integration (and Understanding)

Text representation and integration is an area that has received relatively little attention in the psycholinguistic literature on bilingualism and is not represented in the chapters in this part. This is true also for the level of real understanding (fifth in our list of comprehension processes), so we comment on these two together. We suspect that the neglect results from the natural focus on word- and, to a lesser extent, syntactic-level processes that are the building blocks of comprehension. In the long run, we would expect to see increased attention at least to the consequences for text representation of the lexical and syntactic processes that have been studied. Presumably, a parsing problem in reading a sentence in L2 must lead to one of two consequences—a breakdown in comprehension such that both the current sentence and subsequent sentences are misunderstood or a reflective repair that slows the comprehension process, but keeps the representation coherent. Both of these outcomes place comprehension at risk. Similarly, at the word level, does it matter "downstream" in the representation of sentence and clause meaning that a word read in L2 has also activated an L1 word representation for a few milliseconds? Moreover, does sustained reading or listening to an L2 text build up some protection from this word-level interference?

Beyond these basic questions about how text-level processes might interact with lexical and parsing processes is the application of text comprehension research tools to bilingual processing. For example, computational models of comprehension (e.g., Kintsch, 1988; Van den Broek, Young, Tzeng, & Linderholm, 1999) can be sensitive to limitations in working memory, readers' knowledge and goals, and other factors that would apply to L2 comprehension as well as L1.

Individual Differences

Comprehension processes in L1 show wide-ranging individual differences in adults and children; these differences arise from such components as we reviewed above, plus others (Perfetti, 1999). Similarly, there are many individual difference that are likely to affect how one learns and processes an L2, and some of these appear to lie in L1 abilities. Michael and Gollan (chapter 19), in part III on language production and control, provide an overview of research on the effects of L1 processing skill (e.g., working memory capacity and suppression) on L2 processing. Furthermore, motivational factors can also have an impact on an individual's success in L2 learning and, ultimately, comprehension.

With recent applications of neuroimaging and electrophysiological techniques to the study of language processing, such as functional magnetic resonance imaging, positron emission tomography, and event-related potentials, we have even more methods to study bilingual comprehension. Having these added techniques, along with the advances in mathematical modeling, will undoubtedly enhance the already-rich picture of what happens during bilingual language processing. These advances will allow researchers to pose questions other than those already asked. The converging evidence from this set of increasingly diverse methods is likely to encourage the development of models of bilingual comprehension that are more complete and, at the same time, better capture the implications for general models of language comprehension that in the past have focused on monolingual experience alone.

References

Cutler, A., & Clifton, C. E. (1999). Comprehending spoken language: A blueprint of the listener. In C. M. Brown & P. Hagoort (Eds.), *The neurocognition of language* (pp. 123–166). Oxford, England: Oxford University Press.

De Groot, A. M. B. (1992). Determinants of word translation. *Journal of Experimental Psychology: Learning, Memory, and Cognition, 18,* 1001–1018.

Fender, M. (2003). English word recognition and word integration skills of native Arabic- and Japanese-speaking learners of English as a second language. *Applied Psycholinguistics, 24,* 289–315.

Guasch, M. (2001). *Forma y significado en el procesamiento léxico de bilingües del castellano y del catalán.* Unpublished master's thesis, Universitat Rovira i Virgili, Tarragona, Spain.

Izura, C. & Ellis, A. W. (2002). Age of acquisition effects in word recognition and production in first and second languages. *Psicológica, 23,* 245–281.

Izura, C. & Ellis, A. W. (2004). Age of acquisition effects in translation judgment tasks. *Journal of Memory and Language, 50,* 165–181.

Kintsch, W. (1988). The role of knowledge in discourse processing: A construction-integration model. *Psychological Review, 95,* 163–182.

McDonald, J. L. (1987). Sentence interpretation in bilingual speakers of English and Dutch. *Applied Psycholinguistics, 8,* 379–414.

Perfetti, C. A. (1999). Comprehending written language: A blueprint of the reader. In C. Brown & P. Hagoort (Eds.), *The neurocognition of language* (pp. 167–208). Oxford, England: Oxford University Press.

Sánchez-Casas, R., Suárez-Buratti, B., & Igoa, J. M. (1992, September). *Are bilingual lexical representations interconnected.* Paper presented at the Fifth Conference of the European Society for Cognitive Psychology, Paris.

Tokowicz, N. (2000). *Meaning representation within and across languages.* Unpublished doctoral dissertation, The Pennsylvania State University, University Park.

Tokowicz, N., Kroll, J. F., De Groot, A. M. B., & Van Hell, J. G. (2002). Number-of-translation norms for Dutch-English translation pairs: A new tool for examining language production. *Behavior Research Methods, Instruments, and Computers, 34,* 435–451.

Tokowicz, N., & MacWhinney, B. (2002, April). *Judging grammatical acceptability in L2: Competing grammatical systems in the second language learner.* Paper presented at the Forty-Seventh Annual Meeting of the International Linguistic Association, Toronto, Canada.

Tokowicz, N., & MacWhinney, B. (in press). Implicit and explicit measures of sensitivity to violations in second language grammar: An event-related potential investigation [Special issue]. *Studies in Second Language Learning.*

Van den Broek, P., Young, M., Tzeng, Y., & Linderholm, T. (1999). The landscape model of reading: Inferences and the on-line construction of a memory representation. In H. van Oostendorp & S. R. Goldman (Eds.), *The construction of mental representations during reading* (pp. 71–98). Mahwah, NJ: Erlbaum.

Ton Dijkstra

9

Bilingual Visual Word Recognition and Lexical Access

ABSTRACT   In spite of the intuition of many bilinguals, a review of empirical studies indicates that during reading under many circumstances, possible words from different languages temporarily become active. Such evidence for "language nonselective lexical access" is found using stimulus materials of various kinds: interlingual homographs (words that are identical in orthography between languages, such as the English-Dutch word *brand*, meaning "fire" in Dutch), cognates (words that have an orthography and a meaning that are similar or identical across languages, such as *tomato* in English and *tomaat* in Dutch), and interlingual neighbors (words from two languages that differ in only one letter position, such as *steak* and *sterk*, meaning "strong" in Dutch). However, although there is parallel lexical activation in both languages during bilingual word recognition, the actually observed result patterns also appear to be task dependent. A distinction must therefore be made between factors affecting the word identification system directly (such as sentence context) and factors affecting the task/decision system (nonlinguistic context and task demands). Recent models of bilingual word recognition are discussed with respect to these two types of factors.

Many readers of this chapter will be bilinguals whose native language is not English but, for instance, Spanish or Dutch. When they read these lines, does only their English lexicon play a role in the recognition of the words of which the sentences consist, or does their native language lexicon also become activated? I asked someone who is not a language researcher what he thought about this issue. His reasoning was as follows. "When bilinguals speak, they select the language they want to use, so they must be able to do the same when they read. Thus, when bilinguals read an English book, they will select only English words as possible candidates for recognition because they are aware that the language of the preceding sentences is English. Besides, when they read, only English words enter their awareness. Therefore, reading must surely be a language-selective process."

However, this reasoning may be based on some unwarranted arguments. First, notice that although speakers can determine the language to be spoken, readers are dependent on the language of the text they are facing. This might make a difference to the mental processes involved in speaking and reading. Furthermore, introspection (looking inside one's consciousness) has proven to be a very unreliable research tool. It is well known, for instance, that in monolingual word recognition many possible words initially become active on the presentation of a letter string, and the reader is usually not aware of them; only the word that is eventually recognized becomes available to awareness. Thus, the question whether access to the bilingual mental lexicon is restricted to one language (language-selective access) or not (language-nonselective access) must be resolved by experiments rather than by intuitive reasoning.

This chapter examines the available empirical evidence and theoretical viewpoints pertaining to the process of bilingual word recognition, and I argue that in fact this process is completely different from what the above-mentioned intuition tells us. Bilingual word recognition appears to be basically language nonselective, automatic (i.e., not under control of the reader), and—although task dependent—its first processing stages might remain unaffected by nonlinguistic contextual factors.

Word Recognition and Lexical Access

Lexical access is the process of entering the mental lexicon to retrieve information about words. The *mental lexicon* is the database containing all words in the mind of the language user. Lexical information can be, for instance, orthographic (spelling), phonological (sound), or semantic (meaning) in kind. Word recognition can then be defined as the process of retrieving these word characteristics on the basis of the input letter string. Although these different characteristics might become active under many circumstances (for instance, phonological codes may become available automatically), particular tasks may require specific kinds of lexical information to be performed.

For instance, if one needs to decide whether a particular letter string is a word in the target language or a nonword (lexical decision), orthographic, phonological, and semantic information could in principle all be used. However, if one must name a presented word, the retrieval of its phonological information is indispensable to access the word's articulatory code. Finally, if asked to semantically categorize the object represented by the word (e.g., Is a *hammer* a tool?), the word's meaning information must be found before a response can be initiated.

Retrieving information from the mental lexicon about these characteristics of a word takes time. It may take a few hundreds of milliseconds to retrieve a word's meaning information. Furthermore, research in the monolingual domain indicates that the presentation of a letter string initially leads to the activation of several possible orthographic word candidates in relatively close correspondence to the input signal. For instance, it appears that all words that differ from the presented input string in only one letter position become noticeably active. Such words are called "neighbors" (e.g., *cork* is a neighbor of *work*).

In subsequent stages of word recognition, a more and more careful analysis of the input signal is performed, leading to a reduction of the number of possible lexical candidates and finally to the recognition of the presented word. In localist connectionist network models (see Thomas & Van Heuven, chapter 10, this volume), this viewpoint is often represented in terms of an activation process. On presentation of a letter string, a number of word candidates are initially activated, one of them the intended target word. A subsequent lateral inhibition process between word candidates leads to a reduction of the activation of nontarget candidates. Finally, the target word becomes activated the most, and it is recognized when it surpasses a recognition threshold.

Relative to the monolingual domain, two unique questions can be posed with respect to the bilingual word recognition process. The first question is whether lexical candidates from different languages that share their script are activated when a letter string is presented. For instance, is the Dutch word VORK activated on presentation of the English word PORK? The answer to this question may be "no" (implying language specific lexical access), "yes" (implying language nonselective access), or "it depends." This last option suggests that lexical access can be selective or nonselective depending on the circumstances.

Particular tasks or experimental circumstances might induce language-specific access, for instance, by modulating the activation of representations that are or are not required for responding. The complete nonselective access view and the context-dependent nonselective access view agree in that the underlying word recognition architecture should allow language-nonselective lexical access under at least some circumstances, but they differ in their interpretation of task-dependent results.

The second question that is unique to the bilingual domain is whether language information can be used to speed up the processing of presented words. Language information could be provided by the nonlinguistic or linguistic context in which the item is presented (e.g., the instruction or stimulus list composition in an experiment or the language of a book) or by the item itself (e.g., its language membership). If information about language is provided by the context, the question is whether the word identification system can use it to reduce the number of items in the candidate set (e.g., by suppressing the activation of items from the irrelevant language). If information about language is provided by the item itself, the question is whether it is available in time to affect word recognition or arrives only after the word has already been recognized.

In the first part of this chapter, I review the empirical evidence with respect to these two issues and follow with a brief discussion of earlier models that specifically focused on the language selective versus nonselective access issue in the domains of reading and listening. In the second part of the chapter, I consider empirical evidence on how task demands and context factors affect the bilingual word recognition process. This part includes a discussion of more recent models and viewpoints that not only account for bilingual word recognition, but also consider its task and context dependence.

Empirical Studies: Language-Selective Access of Interlingual Homographs and Cognates

Studies that examined whether lexical candidates from different languages are activated during bilingual word recognition basically made use of two types of stimulus materials: words that are identical or very similar in meaning or form between two languages (so-called cognates and interlingual homographs), and words that exist only in one language but vary with respect to the number of similar words in the other language (interlingual neighborhood density variations). An overview of studies involving these two types of test words is presented.

Interlingual homographs are words that are identical with respect to their orthography, but not their meaning (or, most often, their phonology). Other terms used are *interlexical homographs* or *false friends*. An example is the Dutch-English word *room*, meaning "cream" in Dutch. *Cognates* are words from two languages that are identical (or very similar) in orthographic form and largely overlap in meaning. A Dutch-English example is *film*. Researchers have used these types of items in their research to determine if they are read by bilinguals in a different way than matched control words that occur in only one language. If reaction time (RT) differences between the two item types arise, this is probably because of their existence in two languages rather than one. Such RT differences therefore provide evidence in favor of language-nonselective access; their absence supports language-selective access.

In a number of early studies, no clear RT differences were observed between test items and controls (Caramazza & Brones, 1979; Macnamara & Kushnir, 1971; Soares & Grosjean, 1984). For instance, in a study by Gerard and Scarborough (1989), English monolinguals and Spanish-English bilinguals performed a lexical decision experiment with interlingual homographs and cognates. Stimulus words included cognates, homographic noncognates, and nonhomographic control items. Cognates and controls were either high frequency or low frequency in both English and Spanish. Homographic noncognates were high frequency in English and low frequency in Spanish or vice versa. The findings generally supported the language-selective access hypothesis. Although a significant main effect of word type was found, this was mainly caused by slow responses to homographic noncognates that were of low frequency in the target language. Word latencies varied primarily with the frequency of usage in the target language; the frequency of the word forms in the nontarget language did not affect the latencies. Finally, no significant latency differences were found between the bilinguals and monolinguals, suggesting that they were all effectively operating in a language-selective manner. In sum, this study suggested that lexical access in bilingual word recognition was restricted to only one language.

Several later studies replicated the null results under comparable experimental circumstances (De Groot, Delmaar, & Lupker, 2000, Experiment 2; De Moor, 1998; Dijkstra, Van Jaarsveld, & Ten Brinke, 1998, Experiment 1). In the first experiment from Dijkstra, Van Jaarsveld, et al. (1998), Dutch-English bilinguals performed an English lexical decision task on a list of words that included English-Dutch homographs and cognates, as well as exclusively English control words. Analogous to the earlier findings by Gerard and Scarborough for Spanish-English bilinguals, the experiment did not result in any significant RT differences for interlingual homographs relative to exclusively English control words. Although that finding again appeared to support selective access, a puzzling result was that cognates, in contrast to the homographs, *did* induce a significant facilitation effect. This finding was in accordance with language-nonselective access and interpreted as such by Dijkstra, Van Jaarsveld, et al. (1998). De Groot et al. (2000, Experiment 2) replicated the null results for homographs observed in Experiment 1 by Dijkstra, Van Jaarsveld, et al. with a different set of English stimulus materials and for a different sample of Dutch-English bilinguals.

However, problematic to the language-selective access view, more and more studies following Gerard and Scarborough's work reported evidence in support of language-nonselective access, even under the experimental conditions investigated by these authors. For instance, Von Studnitz and Green (2002) found significant inhibition effects for homographs in a similar German-English experiment and suggested that a different focus of the participants on speed and accuracy or on the "wordlikeness" of the stimuli underlay this result. Font (2001) performed a Spanish lexical decision study involving French-Spanish bilinguals and found facilitatory effects for French-Spanish interlexical homographs that had little phonological similarity across languages.

The only way to save the selective access account, therefore, would be to assume that the evidence showing cross-language differences between interlexical homographs and control items was somehow flawed, for instance, because the item types were not really comparable or were not matched properly. However, this explanation is impossible to defend, not only because the available studies appeared to be conducted properly, but also because many other studies observed RT differences for interlingual homographs and cognates under different experimental conditions. Moreover, yet other studies observed cross-linguistic effects using different stimulus materials (see the studies on between-language neighborhood effects discussed below).

How then may the null results observed by Gerard and Scarborough (1989) and Dijkstra, Van Jaarsveld, et al. (1998) be reconciled with a language nonselective access hypothesis? First, the null results could be a consequence of a particular combination of stimulus characteristics, stimulus list composition, and task demands. Of course, this view requires a specification of the mechanism that induced the null results.

Several proposals to this end have been made. Dijkstra, Van Jaarsveld, et al. (1998) and Grosjean (2001) interpreted the null results in terms of relative English/Dutch language activation. They noted that the experiments in question contained only purely English words and test words for which the English reading was relevant. At the same time, Dutch was the stronger native language of the participants. As a consequence, Dutch may have been activated only to a limited degree, sufficiently to induce a difference between control words and cognates, but not sufficiently to lead to a difference between controls and interlingual homographs.

Whereas the accounts by Dijkstra, Van Jaarsveld, et al. (1998) and Grosjean (2001) referred to relative language activation, De Groot et al. (2000) proposed an account that is strategic in nature. Participants would not always follow the instruction in the task ("Say yes to an English word") to the letter. On some trials, they would explicitly check the language membership of the target item to make sure that they responded to an English item ("language-specific processing strategy"). This would induce slower responses to homographs than to matched controls because, in a nonselective access system, not only the target reading, but also the nontarget language reading of a homograph would be activated, leading to lexical competition and slower responses. On other trials, they would not check the language membership of the item and would respond "yes" to any word they encountered. Thus, in this "language-neutral" processing mode the response to a homograph would be based on the availability of any reading, irrespective of language, and homographs could then be responded to faster than controls. This mixture of two processing modes would lead to a mixture of facilitation and inhibition effects for homographs, yielding an overall null result. I return to this issue in the discussion of the task dependence of bilingual word recognition studies.

Empirical Studies: Language Nonselective Access of Interlingual Homographs and Cognates

Recent studies have demonstrated that, in spite of the observed null results for interlingual homographs, language-nonselective access indeed took place. De Moor (1998) repeated the English lexical decision study by Dijkstra, Van Jaarsveld, et al. (1998) and showed that the meaning of the Dutch reading of the interlingual homographs was apparently activated as well. She first replicated the finding of similar RTs to interlingual homographs and controls under the circumstances of Dijkstra et al.'s study. Next, on the trial after the interlingual homograph appeared, De Moor presented the English translation of the Dutch reading of the homograph. For instance, the interlingual homograph *brand* was followed by *fire*, which is the English translation of the Dutch word *brand*. A small but reliable translation priming effect of 11 ms was found. In a replication of this experiment with different stimulus materials, Van Heste (1999) observed a reliable 35-ms difference between translation and control trials. These findings indicate that the Dutch word form had been activated, even though it did not affect the lexical decision latency to the homograph on the previous trial.

Furthermore, cross-linguistic effects of orthographic and semantic overlap between the different readings of cognates and interlingual homographs have been reported by many studies. Several of such studies used experimental paradigms involving unmasked and masked primes. For instance, Beauvillain and Grainger (1987) had French-English bilinguals make English lexical decisions on target strings preceded by French prime words. With respect to their English reading, the homographic primes were either semantically related to the target (e.g., *coin–money*, where *coin* means *corner* in French) or unrelated. The RTs to target words were shorter for the related condition than for the unrelated condition when prime words were presented for a duration of 150 ms. Thus, although the participants knew the prime word always belonged to the French language and was (strictly spoken) irrelevant to the target decision, they were still affected by the English reading of the homographic prime.

In a Spanish-English priming study, Cristoffanini, Kirsner, and Milech (1986) compared the amount of priming that was observed when the prime was either a cognate's counterpart from the other language (*obediencia*, followed by *obedience*) or the cognate itself (*obedience–obedience*). Priming effects were qualitatively and quantitatively similar to those observed for inflections and derivations, suggesting that morphology and not language was the feature governing lexical organization and access (see also Sánchez-Casas and García-Albea, chapter 11, this volume). Furthermore, the effects decreased as a function of orthographic similarity.

More recent studies have masked the briefly presented primes to avoid conscious participant strategies (e.g., Bijeljac-Babic, Biardeau, & Grainger, 1997; De Groot & Nas, 1991; Sánchez-Casas, Davis, & García-Albea, 1992). In the study by Sánchez-Casas et al. (1992), Spanish-English bilinguals performed a semantic categorization task on target words preceded by masked primes with a duration of 60 ms. Prime–target pairs involved identical cognates or noncognates (*rico–rico*; *pato–pato*), translations of cognates or noncognates (*rich–rico* vs. *duck–pato*); or nonword primes combined with cognates or noncognates as targets (control condition: *rict–rico* vs. *wuck–pato*). Faster responses were obtained to targets in the identity condition

than in the control condition. More important, responses to cognate translations were as fast as in the identity condition, but noncognate translations were as slow as in the control condition.

Yet other studies have shown that language-nonselective access occurs not only with respect to orthographic codes, but also for phonological codes (e.g., Brysbaert, Van Dyck, & Van de Poel, 1999; Doctor & Klein, 1992; Jared & Kroll, 2001; Jared & Szucs, 2002; Nas, 1983). Nas asked Dutch-English participants to perform an English lexical decision experiment in which half of the nonwords were cross-language pseudohomophones that "looked like" English, but "sounded like" Dutch words (according to the English spelling-to-sound rules). An example is the pseudohomophone SNAY, which sounds like the Dutch words SNEE (pronounced [snay]). The bilinguals rejected the pseudohomophones more slowly and with more errors than standard nonwords (such as PRUSK). Apparently, the language-nonselective lexical access to the internal lexicon of a bilingual seems to proceed at least in part via nonselective phonological mediation.

Brysbaert et al. (1999) found that there is a parallel application of spelling-to-sound rules of two languages to stimulus input. In a masked priming paradigm, Dutch-French bilinguals and French monolinguals identified briefly presented French target items preceded by briefly presented and masked prime words or nonwords. The primes were French nonwords or Dutch words. French nonword primes were pseudohomophonic with the target and different in only one letter (e.g., *fain–faim*), pseudohomophonic with only one letter in common (*fint–faim*), or nonhomophonic graphemic controls (*faic–faim*). If the prime was a Dutch word, it was either homophonic to the French target (*paar–part*), a graphemic control (*paal–part*), or unrelated to the target (*hoog–part*). For the French prime–French target stimuli, the bilinguals identified fewer target words than the monolinguals, but the two groups displayed similar orthographic and phonological priming effects for the three types of nonwords. For the Dutch prime–French target stimuli, the effects of orthographic prime–target overlap were also comparable across the two groups of participants. However, with respect to phonological overlap, a different pattern emerged for bilinguals and monolinguals. Significant interlingual phonological priming effects were observed for bilinguals, but not for monolinguals.

In a study by Dijkstra, Grainger, and Van Heuven (1999), Dutch-English bilinguals performed an

English lexical decision task with English words varying in their degree of orthographic (O), phonological (P), and semantic (S) overlap with Dutch words. Their six different test conditions are exemplified by the following items: "hotel" (overlap in S, O, and P codes), "type" (SO), "news" (SP), "step" (OP), "stage" (O), and "note" (P). The first two conditions (SOP and SO conditions) consist of what are usually called cognates; the last three conditions contain interlingual homographs (OP and O conditions) or interlingual homophones (P condition). Lexical decisions were facilitated by cross-linguistic orthographic and semantic similarity relative to control words that belonged only to English. In contrast, phonological overlap led to inhibitory effects. A control experiment with American English monolinguals did not lead to systematic differences between test and control items. Because the items in this study were comparable to those in Dijkstra, Van Jaarsveld, et al. (1998), they provide a new explanation for the occurrence of null effects in the earlier study. The null effects may have been caused by mixing of two types of items (O and OP items), leading to a cancellation of O facilitation effects by P inhibition effects.

Lemhöfer and Dijkstra (2004) showed that the pattern of results varied in a systematic way when the task was changed from English lexical decision to generalized Dutch-English lexical decision. The generalized lexical decision task is a *language-neutral* or *global* variant of the lexical decision task in which bilingual participants press a "yes" button if a presented item is a word in at least one of their languages (e.g., English or Dutch) and a "no" button if it is a nonword in either language. When Dutch-English bilinguals performed this task, interlingual homographs were processed faster than English control words, but about as fast as Dutch controls. Cross-linguistic phonological overlap did not affect the RTs, suggesting that participants responded primarily on the basis of the fastest available orthographic codes.

The difference between these results and those of Dijkstra et al. (1999) for the same interlingual homographs can be understood as a consequence of differences in the time-course of activation of words of the native first language (L1) and nonnative second language (L2) and the demands of the two types of lexical decision task. First, note that native language words are generally activated faster than nonnative language words. Because in the generalized lexical decision task the response could be based on the first available code, the participants

probably responded mostly to the Dutch readings of the interlingual homographs. This explains why the RTs to interlingual homographs were similar to those for Dutch (L1) controls and faster than those to English (L2) controls. In the English lexical decision task, however, the target language was English, and the participant could only respond safely after verifying that the language of the presented item was English. Under these task conditions, the early available Dutch (L1) codes had time to affect the response based on the English (L2) codes. This accounts for the overlap effects (orthographic facilitation and phonological inhibition) that Dijkstra et al. (1999) observed for the interlingual homographs.

Interestingly, Lemhöfer and Dijkstra (2004) further found that cognates *were* recognized faster than the matched English and Dutch controls. Because at the same time the homographs (having an identical orthographic form across languages) did not show any effects (relative to Dutch controls), the effect for cognates appears to depend at least on their overlap in meaning across languages. In other words, there must have been coactivation of the cognates' semantics in both languages. In fact, it may be that cognates are represented in a special way, with a strong link between orthographic and semantic representations.

In these last two studies, the orthographic representation of cognates was identical in the two languages (e.g., *film*). What happens if cognates are presented that are nonidentical in the language pair the bilingual knows? For instance, are Dutch-English bilinguals affected in their recognition of the Dutch word *bakker* by its similarity (but nonidentity) to the English word *baker*? Van Hell and Dijkstra (2002) had trilinguals with Dutch as their native language, English as their L2, and French as their third language perform a word association task or a lexical decision task in their L1. Stimulus words were (mostly) nonidentical cognates such as *bakker* or noncognates. Shorter association and lexical decision times were observed for Dutch-English cognates than for noncognates. For trilinguals with a higher proficiency in French, faster responses in lexical decision were found for both Dutch-English and Dutch-French cognates. In other words, even when their orthographic and phonological overlap across languages is incomplete, cognates may be recognized faster than noncognates.

In a lexical decision study with French-Spanish bilinguals, Font (2001) found that cognates differing in one letter between languages (called neighbor cognates by Font) were still facilitated but significantly less so than identical cognates. Furthermore, the amount of facilitation depended on the position of the deviating letter in the word. Neighbor cognates with the different letter at the end of the word (e.g., French *texte*–Spanish *texto*) were facilitated more than neighbor cognates with the different letter inside (e.g., French *usuel*–Spanish *usual*). In fact, facilitatory effects for the latter type of cognate disappeared, and effects tended toward inhibition when such cognates were of low frequency in both languages. Similar patterns of results were found in L1 and L2 processing.

These results make it likely that the size of RT effects observed for cognates and interlingual homographs depends on their degree of cross-linguistic overlap (also cf. Cristoffanini et al., 1986). Note that it follows logically that across-language pairs that do not share orthography (e.g., Chinese and English), no "orthographically similar" word candidates can be activated, but effects of phonological similarity and semantic overlap might still occur (Bowers, Mimouni, & Arguin, 2000; Gollan, Forster, & Frost, 1997).

Other studies showed that, in tasks with L1 target words, effects of L2 competitors can be obtained as well in mixed stimulus lists (Dijkstra, Timmermans, & Schriefers, 2000) and even in completely blocked (L1) lists (Van Hell & Dijkstra, 2002). Observed effects of L2 on L1 are often smaller than those of L1 on L2, but this appears to be because of the relative strength of the two languages and is therefore also dependent on L2 proficiency (cf. Jared & Kroll, 2001). To conclude, many studies support the language-nonselective access hypothesis with respect to form (orthographic and phonological) as well as semantic representations.

Empirical Studies: Orthographic and Phonological Neighborhood Effects

Perhaps the strongest results in favor of nonselective access concern experiments that used so-called neighbors as stimulus materials. As indicated in the Introduction, an orthographic neighbor is any word differing by a single letter from the target word with respect to length and letter position (Coltheart, Davelaar, Jonasson, & Besner, 1977). For instance, *work* and *cord* are both neighbors of *cork*. Monolingual word identification and word naming have been shown to be sensitive to the number of orthographic neighbors (neighborhood density) of the target words and to the frequency of

such orthographically similar words (neighborhood frequency). In bilingual studies, effects of number of orthographic neighbors were used as indexes of the relative influence of nontarget language words on target word recognition in different experimental tasks and conditions. Target words themselves belonged only to one language (i.e., there were no interlingual homographs, homophones, or cognates in the stimulus list).

In an English lexical decision task performed by Dutch-English bilinguals, Grainger and Dijkstra (1992) found that English words with many neighbors in Dutch (the nontarget language) were harder to recognize than neutral words with approximately the same number of neighbors in two languages, which were in turn harder to recognize than English words with more neighbors in their own language. Thus, RTs to items existing exclusively in one language were affected by the number of similar words from another language.

Van Heuven, Dijkstra, and Grainger (1998) manipulated the number of orthographic neighbors of the target words in the same and the other language of the bilinguals in a series of progressive demasking and lexical decision experiments involving Dutch-English bilinguals. Increasing the number of Dutch orthographic neighbors systematically slowed RTs to English target words. Within the target language itself, an increase in neighbors consistently produced inhibitory effects for Dutch target words and facilitatory effects for English target words. Monolingual English readers also showed facilitation because of English neighbors, but no effects of Dutch neighbors.

Simulations with a computer model of bilingual word recognition (the bilingual interactive activation [BIA] model; see Thomas & Van Heuven, chapter 10, this volume) suggest that the opposite effects of English (facilitation) and Dutch (inhibition) neighbors may be caused by differences in the specific organization of the English and Dutch lexicons. Whatever the correct explanation may be, the most important point is that neighbors from both the same and the other language are activated during the presentation of a target word. This provides evidence that, with respect to orthographic codes, the lexicon of bilinguals is integrated and nonselective in nature.

Jared and Kroll (2001) showed that the same conclusions hold for the phonological part of the bilingual lexicon. In a word naming study, they observed cross-linguistic effects of phonological word body neighbors, effects that could only have arisen during the word identification process. Word body neighbors are words that share their medial vowels plus final consonants (word body) with the target word. For example, *save* and *wave* are body neighbors. In four experiments involving English-French and French-English bilinguals, Jared and Kroll tested if word naming in the target language (e.g., *bait* in English) was slowed by the existence of word body neighbors with different pronunciations in the nontarget language (e.g., *fait* in French). Participants named blocks of English test words that preceded and followed blocks of French filler words. For the first-presented English words, cross-language interference effects were obtained in French-English bilinguals, for whom French was a more dominant language than English. Such effects were not observed for English-French participants, whose L1 was English. For them, nontarget language spelling-to-sound correspondences were apparently more weakly activated than the target language spelling-to-sound correspondences. After a switch from naming in another language (French), spelling-to-sound correspondences from both the bilingual's languages appeared to be activated across blocks, depending on language fluency. Less-fluent English-French participants showed effects of French spelling-to-sound rules in English naming afterward if they had been presented with the enemies themselves, but not with other items having the same word bodies.

These neighborhood studies, involving target words that occur exclusively in one language, indicate that the bilingual lexicon is integrated in nature for language pairs such as Dutch-English and French-English that have a common script. At the same time, they also show that word candidates from both languages of the bilingual are activated in parallel and therefore also support a language-nonselective access hypothesis.

To conclude, the studies reviewed in the present and the previous sections provide an answer to the first question posed in the Introduction, whether lexical candidates from different languages sharing their scripts are activated when a letter string is presented. The answer appears to be an unqualified "yes." In the next section, the second question posed in the Introduction is considered: Can language information be used to speed up the processing of presented words?

Language Information and Bilingual Word Recognition

Bilinguals know, of course, to which language a particular word belongs. This kind of information must be stored in the bilingual's mental lexicon for each word. It has been referred to as a *language tag* or a *language node*. Very little is known about such tags or nodes. Two representational possibilities are that the language information pertaining to an item is retrieved via the form (orthographic or phonological) representation of an item or via its lemma, a more abstract syntactic/semantic representation. Possibly, each word has its own separate language tag; alternatively, all words of one language may share their language tag.

An interesting question is at which moment in time language information becomes available relative to word identification. If such information is available soon enough, it might help to speed up word recognition by excluding lexical candidates from the nontarget language. For instance, if the task is to respond to English words, all word candidates that are not English could be excluded from consideration. Furthermore, if language information from the context is able to affect the speed of word recognition, then bilinguals might be slower to recognize a target word if it is preceded by an item of a different language relative to an item of the same language as the target.

Dijkstra, Timmermans, et al. (2000) examined the role of language information contained in the item itself. In three experiments, each with a different instruction, bilingual participants processed the same set of homographs embedded in identical mixed-language lists. Homographs of three types were used: high frequency in English and low frequency in Dutch; low frequency in English and high frequency in Dutch; and low frequency in both languages. In the first experiment (involving language decision), one button was pressed when an English word was presented, and another button was pressed for a Dutch word. In the second and third experiments, participants reacted only when they identified either an English word (English go/no go) or a Dutch word (Dutch go/no go), but they did not respond if a word of the nontarget language (Dutch or English, respectively) was presented. The overall results in the three experiments were similar to those obtained by Dijkstra, Van Jaarsveld, et al. (1998, Experiment 2) for lexical decision. In all three tasks, inhibition effects arose for homographs relative to one-language controls. Even in the Dutch go/no go task for Dutch-English bilinguals performing in their native language, participants were unable to completely exclude effects from the nontarget language on homograph identification.

More important for the present discussion, however, is the finding that target language homographs were often "overlooked," especially if the frequency of their other language competitor was high. In the Dutch go/no go task, participants did not respond to low-frequency items belonging to their native language in about 25% of the cases. Inspection of cumulative distributions showed that if they did not respond after about 1,500–1,600 ms, they did not respond anymore within the time window of 2 s. The observed flattening of the cumulative distribution toward an asymptotic value suggests that recognition of the homograph reading from the nontarget language in some way "prohibited" the subsequent recognition of the target language reading (e.g., after recognition, all other lexical candidates may be suppressed). Thus, selection of one of the readings of the interlexical homographs takes place rather late during processing.

It is clear that the system must at some time arrive at a selection of one lexical item only, but apparently the role played by the language of that item in aiding selection is only minor. In fact, determination of the language of the item may depend on lexical selection having taken place. In addition, it does not seem possible to discard the homograph reading from the nontarget language and focus on the target reading only on the basis of the instruction that just the target language needs a response. One reason for this may be a tendency that the word, rather than its language label, triggers the response.

A number of studies have investigated whether the language of the previous item in a list can affect the recognition of a target word (e.g., Kolers, 1966; Macnamara & Kushnir, 1971). Such list effects could arise in two ways. First, after a target item in a list is recognized, it might leave behind a "trace of activation" of the language that it belongs to until the subsequent trial, thereby affecting the processing of the next item. For instance, a language switching effect would arise if on trial t an English word activates the English language tag, and on trial $t + 1$, this language tag feeds back activation to all English words or if it then inhibits all words from the Dutch lexicon.

Second, a switch effect could be observed if the decision process on the target item would be slightly changed because of the language of the previous trial or because a task switch occurred between trials as well. In line with the first view, Von Studnitz and Green (1997) found that bilinguals' RTs on switch trials were a significant 17 ms slower than on nonswitch trials in a (German-English) generalized lexical decision task. Furthermore, in

a generalized lexical decision experiment by Van Heuven et al. (1998), significant language switching effects (on the order of 30–35 ms) occurred as well.

However, other research by Von Studnitz and Green (1997, 2002) and by Thomas and Allport (2000) indicated that task/decision switches generally may be much larger in size than language switches. Indeed, in a combined event-related potential and RT study involving a generalized lexical decision task on triplets of items, De Bruijn, Dijkstra, Chwilla, and Schriefers (2001) did not find any effects of prime language on the activation of the two readings of interlingual homographs. These results suggest that context language as such does not operate as a very effective factor for lexical selection in stimulus lists.

The relationship between lexical selection and language selection might be different for items for which the language membership could in principle already be determined before recognition because of the presence of "language cues" in the items themselves. The items could contain, for instance, language-specific bigrams or diacritical markers. In such cases, lexical search might be limited to the relevant target language from the very beginning. On the basis of earlier-presented evidence (the neighborhood studies), it is assumed that information contained in the signal is an important early determiner of the set of lexical candidates that is initially activated. Thus, it seems likely that language-specific bigrams or diacritical markers are critical in this respect, and that because of their presence, the initial set of lexical candidates activated may indeed become restricted to one language (see Mathey & Zagar, 2000, p. 200, for relevant monolingual data). However, I deem it unlikely that, for words that are well known by the bilingual, this kind of information is often used in a top-down way (i.e., the bilingual notices a particular bigram that is unique to a language and then uses this information for his or her language decision) because the automatized bottom-up recognition process will usually be much faster. (Note that the presence of cross-linguistic phonological effects in Chinese-English bilinguals indicates that they are not using script differences as a language cue to restrict their lexical selection process.)

To conclude, the empirical evidence collected so far suggests that language information associated with the presented lexical item or provided by the list context cannot be used to any great extent to speed up the processing of the target item.

Models of Bilingual Memory and Bilingual Word Recognition

Ever since the first empirical studies on bilingual word recognition appeared, researchers have attempted to formulate models to account for the available evidence. It is therefore no wonder that the most early models often assumed the bilingual lexical access was selective in nature, and that the two languages of a bilingual were stored independently (cf. the study by Gerard & Scarborough, 1989, discussed in the section on language-selective access of interlingual homographs and cognates). In the following section, some classical models of bilingual word processing that focused on how words are stored in and retrieved from the bilingual lexicon are discussed. More recent models then are discussed that also take into account task demands and context dependence of processing. Table 9.1 provides a summary of some major model characteristics. For figures and more detailed discussion of implemented models, refer to Thomas and Van Heuven's chapter 10 of this volume.

Classical Models of Bilingual Representation and Translation

As early as 1953, Weinreich (1968) proposed that there might be three types of bilingualism: coordinative, compound, and subordinative. In coordinate bilinguals, the words of their two languages would be kept completely separate, leading to a specific word form and meaning representation for each item. For instance, the word *book* in English and its Russian equivalent *kniga* would have their own, distinct form and meaning. In contrast, compound bilinguals would distinguish the word forms *book* and *kniga*, but they would have only one shared meaning. Finally, subordinate bilinguals would interpret the words of their weaker language (usually L2) through the words of the stronger language (usually L1). For instance, an English-Russian bilingual would recognize the word *kniga* because it evokes the English word *book* and subsequently its meaning.

In later models, the distinction (especially between compound and subordinative types) was used

---

Table 9.1 Characteristics of Current Bilingual Word Recognition Models

---

Bilingual interactive activation model (BIA; Dijkstra & Van Heuven, 1998)
- Resting level activation of words reflects the state of language activation as well as proficiency
- Stimulus list composition (previous items) affects activation state of word forms
- Participant expectations do not exert strong effects on the activation state of words
- Top-down inhibition effects on the non-target language arise via language nodes
- Identification and decision levels interact

Inhibitory control model (Green, 1986, 1998)
- Language task schemas (specifying how a task is performed) can compete and cooperate
- Schemas can alter the activation level of lexical representations (lemmas)
- Stimulus list composition (previous items) affects activation state of lemmas
- Participant intentions can affect the activation state of items
- Reactive top-down inhibition effects operate on lemmas, not on word forms
- Identification and decision levels interact

Language mode framework (Grosjean, 1997, 2001)
- Relative activation state of languages (language mode) is continuous and sensitive to many factors
- Stimulus list composition (previous items) affects language activation state
- Participant intentions/expectations and instruction affect language activation state
- Context-sensitivity of language mode is partially caused by such top-down effects
- Identification and decision levels interact

BIA + model (Dijkstra & Van Heuven, 2002)
- Resting level activation of words reflects the state of language activation as well as proficiency
- Stimulus list composition (previous items) affects task/decision system
- Participant expectations may affect task/decision system
- No top-down effects from task/decision system on identification system (bottom-up activation of lexemes)
- Identification-decision: purely bottom-up information flow
- Nonlinguistic context affects task/decision system; linguistic context affects activation of lexemes

---

as a characterization, not of bilingual participants, but of items in the bilingual's mental lexicon that are more or less well known (cf. De Groot & Comijs, 1995). This led to the suggestion that there might be two ways in which the equivalent of a word in another language could be determined: via concept mediation or via word association. Take, for instance, the Russian word *kniga*. On presentation of the Cyrillian letter string corresponding to this word, an orthographic representation might be activated that itself would activate the corresponding meaning representation. In the next step, this meaning activation could activate the English word form *book*. This translation procedure would be called *concept mediation*. However, a second possibility would be that the Russian word form *kniga* would directly activate the English word form *book* either via a direct orthographic connection (between scripts) or through a phonological connection. This translation route would be referred to as *word association*.

Potter, So, Von Eckardt, and Feldman (1984) contrasted the two routes experimentally by comparing bilingual performance in word translation and in picture naming. For picture naming, they assumed that access to the meaning representation on the basis of the picture was necessary before the name of the picture became available. A model assuming that the word association route is always followed predicts that translation from L1 to L2 will be faster than picture naming in L2. This is because translation can be done through a direct L1-L2 connection (one step), but the picture needs to be turned into a concept and then into the L2 word (two steps). In contrast, a pure concept mediation model predicts that the translation into L2 and picture naming in L2 will take about equally long because both tasks require a retrieval of the concept before the L2 word form can be retrieved (two steps in both routes; in a sense, the word form could be considered as a picture). In a group of highly fluent Chinese-English bilinguals, clear evidence was found in favor of the concept mediation model. Picture naming and translation in L2 led to comparable results (if anything, picture naming was faster rather than slower than translation). The same result held for a less-proficient group of English-French bilinguals.

In a number of later studies, Kroll and colleagues found evidence that early (novice) bilinguals appeared to use the word association link; more proficient bilinguals showed more evidence in favor of concept mediation. As one example, Kroll and Curley (1988) replicated Potter's study with more

varied groups of bilinguals. Participants who had studied the L2 for less than 2 years showed results in correspondence with the word association model; participants with more language experience behaved in line with the concept mediation model.

On the basis of this study and others, Kroll and Stewart (1994) proposed the revised hierarchical asymmetric model, which combines the two translation routes in an elegant way. According to this model, translation from L1 into L2 requires concept mediation, in other words, two processing steps: L1 → C, C → L2. As a consequence, it takes more time than the translation from L2 into L1, which is lexically mediated and proceeds via word association (one direct link from L2 to L1). Research with respect to the revised hierarchical model has focused on the extent of asymmetry in the connections between L1 and L2 and on the degree of L2 proficiency needed to obtain a gradual shift from word association to concept mediation (because of an increasingly strong link of L2 word forms to concepts through L2 use).

More recent evidence with respect to these issues has not always been consistent, suggesting that additional factors may play a role (e.g., the nature of the mapping between the languages). For instance, although Sholl, Sankaranarayanan, and Kroll (1995) presented evidence from picture naming and translation in support of asymmetric effects, some other studies reported symmetric effects (De Groot & Poot, 1997; La Heij, Kerling, & Van der Velden, 1996). Furthermore, Kroll, Michael, Tokowicz, and Dufour (2002) found that translation from L1 to L2 (assumed to be conceptually mediated) changed more in the course of acquisition than translation in the other direction. At the same time, other studies obtained evidence supporting the presence of conceptual mediation in early bilinguals (Altarriba & Mathis, 1997; Van Hell & Candia Mahn, 1997). See also Kroll and Tokowicz's chapter 26 of this volume for additional discussion of these issues.

The Bilingual Interactive Activation Model and Bilingual Visual Word Recognition

The BIA model (Dijkstra & Van Heuven, 1998; Van Heuven et al., 1998) is an implemented localist-connectionist model of bilingual visual word recognition. Here, it is discussed only in general terms (for more details on the BIA model, including a visualization, see Thomas & Van Heuven, chapter 10, this volume). The language-nonselective access model distinguishes four hierarchically organized levels of different linguistic representations: letter features, letters, words, and language tags (or language nodes). When a word is presented to the model, first the features of its constituent letters are registered (activated). Next, letter features activate the letters of which they are part for each letter position in the presented word. These letters in turn activate the words of which they are part in any language. Word candidates activate the language tag to which they are connected and simultaneously feed activation back to the letter level. Word candidates and letters also inhibit other word candidates and letters, respectively (lateral inhibition). Language nodes inhibit the activation of word candidates from another language (e.g., the English language node reduces the activation of Dutch word candidates). After a complex interactive process of activation and inhibition, the lexical candidate corresponding to the presented word becomes the most active word unit.

The BIA model assumes that the resting level activation of words from different languages reflects the subjective frequency of the words, that is, the number of times that the language user has encountered or used them. This level is therefore dependent on the L1 and L2 proficiency of the bilingual. In addition, the resting level activation of words depends on their recency of use. If a word has not been used for a while, its resting level activation may slowly decrease further.

The language nodes provide a potential mechanism in the BIA model through which (list and sentence) context effects can operate (Dijkstra, Van Heuven, & Grainger, 1998). If context would affect the relative activation of the language nodes, the subsequent suppression by these nodes of words from another language may change the relative activation state of words from different languages. For instance, in an English language context, activation of Dutch words could be inhibited or partially suppressed.

Although in the BIA model only orthographic representations are implemented, the model has been shown to account for a variety of empirical effects in the domain of word recognition: neighborhood density effects within and between languages, shifting neighborhood effects across an experiment, masked priming effects in bilinguals (Bijeljac-Babic et al., 1997), L2 proficiency differences in masked priming with bilinguals, effects for interlingual homographs in a go/no go task (Dijkstra et al., 1998a), and (verbally) language of

previous item effects (Dijkstra, Van Jaarsveld, et al., 1998). In spite of this list, there are many aspects of bilingual word recognition that are not fully accounted for by the model. For instance, there are no phonological or semantic representations in the model, the representation of interlingual homographs and cognates is underspecified, the language node concept is not without problems, and task and context effects are not described in any detail (the BIA+ model, discussed separately, fills in some of these theoretical gaps).

The Bilingual Interactive Model of Lexical Access and Bilingual Auditory Word Recognition

With respect to spoken word recognition by bilinguals, Léwy and Grosjean (1997) have proposed a model that at first sight is rather similar to the BIA model, but nevertheless makes a number of different assumptions. This model, the bilingual interactive model of lexical access (BIMOLA), is also a localist-connectionist model. A visualization of the model is given by Thomas and Van Heuven in chapter 10 of this volume.

Similar to BIA and the monolingual TRACE model for auditory word recognition (McClelland & Elman, 1986), BIMOLA consists of three levels of nodes. First, an auditory input word activates phonological *features*, which are shared by the two languages. Second, features activate associated *phonemes*, which are organized to some extent in independent subsets for each language, but are part of a larger system. Within the phoneme level, there is subset activation and lateral inhibition. Subset activation implies that when a phoneme in a given language is activated, it sends a small positive signal to other phonemes in the language subset (indicating that the language in question is probably relevant to the situation at hand). At the same time, phonemes exert an inhibitory influence on other phonemes of the same language (lateral inhibition within the subset). Finally, phonemes activate *words* of which they are part. The word level is organized similar to the phoneme level, allowing subset activation and lateral inhibition. Between levels, units can be activated from both the bottom up and the top down. Furthermore, the word level receives top-down preactivation from external information, for example, reflecting the language mode (activation state of the two languages) of the bilingual and higher linguistic information from syntactic or semantic sources.

A comparison of BIMOLA to the BIA model reveals some important differences between the two models. First, in contrast to the BIA model, BIMOLA assumes the presence of subset activation, making it possible that word candidates of one language (the "base language") become active before words from the other language. This allows the auditory word identification system to function rather language selectively under certain circumstances. Second, BIMOLA assumes there can be top-down effects from higher-level information sources on word activation.

If these assumptions are correct, the processes and mechanisms underlying bilingual auditory and visual word recognition would operate somewhat differently. However, although undoubtedly differences in input and modality characteristics must have their consequences for processing, the abstract organization of the processing systems for the two modalities may be more similar than expected (e.g., Schulpen, Dijkstra, Schriefers, & Hasper, 2003). In other words, some of the mentioned differences may arise from researcher disagreement rather than from actual processing.

Task Dependence of Bilingual Word Recognition Results

The empirical studies and models reviewed above are in support of the view that lexical access is nonselective under many circumstances. However, in the introduction the possibility was suggested that even if access to the identification system is basically nonselective in nature, particular circumstances might allow it to operate in a language-selective way. It is therefore important to consider the extent to which the result patterns observed in different experimental situations are task dependent and how such context dependence comes about.

There is clear evidence in the literature that task demands can affect bilingual performance to a considerable extent (e.g., De Groot et al., 2000; Dijkstra, Timmermans, et al., 2000; Dijkstra, Van Jaarsveld, et al., 1998; Thomas & Allport, 2000). Dijkstra and Van Heuven (1998) compared the results of a number of different tasks and found that some of these tasks showed *functional overlap*, that is, they led to similar result patterns, whereas others were more different. For instance, when the same stimulus materials were used, lexical decision and progressive demasking results were often highly correlated, but language decision sometimes

led to a much lower correlation with these other tasks. To clarify the nature of the cross-task comparison in this study, progressive demasking is a task in which the target stimulus gradually becomes visible because the duration of a mask is reduced and that of the target increased. In language decision, in contrast, bilingual participants press one button if a visually presented word belongs to one target language (e.g., English) and another one if it belongs to the other target language (e.g., Dutch).

De Groot, Borgwaldt, Bos, and Van den Eijnden (2002) investigated in more detail what may be the common and different mental processes underlying different tasks such as (delayed) word naming, lexical decision, and perceptual identification in L1 and L2. An important conclusion based on these studies is that it may be inappropriate to talk about bilingual word recognition in general (i.e., without specifying the precise task and experimental circumstances under which it takes place) because performance is so task and context dependent.

In a series of closely related experiments, Dijkstra, Van Jaarsveld, et al. (1998) examined the effects of task demands and stimulus list composition on bilingual word recognition in some detail. In the section on language-selective access, the first experiment of this study was described. In an English lexical decision task including English-Dutch homographs and cognates as well as exclusively English control words, Dutch-English bilinguals responded about equally fast to interlingual homographs and exclusively English control words (and faster to cognates). In the second experiment of this study, exclusively Dutch words were added to the stimulus list, but the task remained English lexical decision. Participants had to respond "no" to these items because they were not real English words. In this experiment, strong inhibition effects arose for interlingual homographs relative to control items, especially for homographs that were low frequency in English and high frequency in Dutch. Dijkstra et al. explained the inhibition effects in Experiment 2 as the result of a frequency-dependent competition between the two readings of the homographs for which the participants could not ignore the nontarget language reading of the interlingual homograph.

If there was a race to recognition between the two readings, the inhibitory effects should be able to turn into facilitation effects using the appropriate task instructions. This hypothesis was tested in a generalized lexical decision task (Dijkstra, Van Jaarsveld, et al., 1998, Experiment 3). Here, participants responded as soon as either of the two readings of a homograph became available. As the result of a "race" between the two readings of the homograph, a facilitation effect of homographs relative to their matched monolingual controls should arise. In addition, the degree of facilitation observed should be a function of the frequency of both the English and the Dutch readings of the homograph. The largest benefit to the RT relative to matched English controls should now be observed for the homographs with low-frequency English and high-frequency Dutch readings. This was indeed what happened. Given the instruction "Say yes to English and/or Dutch words," participants were able to use either reading of an interlingual homograph to speed up their decision process. Furthermore, the presence of both English and Dutch word frequency effects suggests that participants reacted on the basis of the first available reading of the homograph. Therefore, the homographs that benefited most from the change in instruction in Experiment 3 were those that suffered most in Experiment 2: homographs with a low-frequency English reading and a high-frequency Dutch reading.

Figure 9.1 shows the differences between homographs and matched controls for the different frequency categories in the three experiments. It will be clear to the reader that the result patterns change across experiments in a systematic yet complex way. The result patterns obtained in experiments are not necessarily direct reflections of the underlying identification system, but depend on a complex interaction among this system, the requirements of the task to be performed, and stimulus list composition. The presence of strong inhibition effects when stimulus list composition was changed from exclusively English to mixed English-Dutch (Dijkstra, Van Jaarsveld, et al., 1998, Experiment 2) indicates that task demands (top-down sources) could not easily reduce the parallel activation of words from the two languages (bottom-up sources, Experiment 1). Otherwise, participants would have "switched off" the Dutch lexicon because it hindered task performance. At the same time, the change from inhibition to facilitation effects when the task changed from English lexical decision to generalized lexical decision indicates that participants could exploit such parallel activation to speed up their response (Experiment 3).

Dijkstra, De Bruijn, Schriefers, and Ten Brinke (2000) performed an English lexical decision experiment that combined features of Experiments 1 and 2 by Dijkstra, Van Jaarsveld, et al. (1998). Prior to the experiment, the participants were

explicitly instructed that they would encounter Dutch words requiring a "no" response, but such items were presented only in the second part of the experiment. No significant RT differences were found between the interlingual homographs and matched English control items in the first part of the experiment. However, strong inhibitory effects for interlingual homographs relative to control words were observed in the second part. Examination of the transition from part 1 to part 2 showed that, as soon as Dutch items started to come in, the RTs to interlingual homographs were considerably slowed compared to control words. The results in the two parts of the experiment mimicked Experiments 1 and 2 in the study by Dijkstra et al. In contrast to earlier experiments, the instruction of the present experiment clearly indicated that Dutch words requiring a "no" response might appear. Nevertheless, no inhibition for interlingual homographs was obtained in part 1. Apparently, the participants' performance was not affected by whether the instruction did or did not mention the possibility that Dutch words would be presented.

These results not only show quite clearly that participants are sensitive to the demands of the task, but also suggest that various tasks affect the *process* of word recognition itself only to a limited extent. In the next section, it is suggested that the output of the identification system is used as input to a task/decision system.

How a Dutch-English Bilingual Recognizes an Interlexical Homograph in English Lexical Decision

On the basis of the empirical evidence discussed in the previous sections, now I present a detailed illustration of the bilingual word recognition process as it takes place in a specific task context. Assume that Dutch-English bilinguals perform the English lexical decision experiment by Dijkstra, De Bruijn, et al. (2000), discussed in the section on task dependence. The participants are instructed to respond "yes" to all words that had an English reading (including homographs) and "no" to Dutch words and to nonwords. To give the correct response, the participant must somehow relate (or "bind") the "yes" response (e.g., pressing the right button) to English words and the "no" response to Dutch words and nonwords.

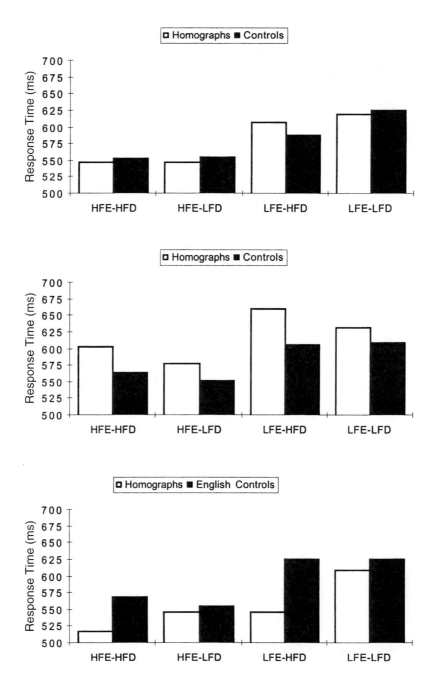

Figure 9.1 Result pattern of Experiments 1–3 in the work of Dijkstra, Van Jaarsveld, and Ten Brinke (1998). Experiment 1: English lexical decision without exclusively Dutch words; Experiment 2: English lexical decision including exclusively Dutch words; Experiment 3: generalized lexical decision (including exclusively Dutch words). HFE-HFD, high-frequency English–high-frequency Dutch; HFE-LFD, high-frequency English–low-frequency Dutch; LFE-HFD, low-frequency English–high-frequency Dutch; LFE-LFD, low-frequency English–low-frequency Dutch.

The upper part of Fig. 9.2 shows how this may be done in the initial phase of the experiment. For a clear presentation, the figure does not make a distinction among orthographic, phonological, and semantic codes for words, but as this review has indicated, different codes do play a role in recognition. Further, note that the "no" response to Dutch words involves a different decision process than that to nonwords (not indicated). Dutch words will generate considerable activity in the mental lexicon, and the "no" response can only be given after the language membership of the words is retrieved. In contrast, nonwords will induce much less activity in the lexicon than words, and the "no" response will be initiated when no word has been recognized after a temporal deadline has passed.

In the first half of the experiment, no exclusively Dutch words are presented to the participants. In other words, the response binding of Dutch words to the "no" response is not strengthened. As a consequence, participants will respond to interlexical homographs about as quickly as to monolingual English words because the English reading of the homograph elicits the "yes" response. The only effects that will be observed are those arising from interactions between representations in the lexicon (cf. the study by Dijkstra et al., 1999). Because the Dutch reading is not strongly connected to the "no" response, by itself it contributes little to the response. Note that the participants may respond to the presence of a word rather than to the presence of an *English* word. Indeed, the information that the word that is recognized is English might come in only after the response has already been initiated. If the language check is done only after response initiation or execution, the response will still always be correct. It may be that the participants notice that, in fact, they responded to the *wrong* reading of an interlexical homograph, namely, the Dutch reading. This might not only speed up the response in the trial in question (relative to controls), but also would make the participants more careful during the next time a homograph was presented, perhaps slowing them at that time relative to controls.

In the second half of the experiment, Dutch words are interspersed in the stimulus list. If the first word is presented, participants are often too late to check the language membership of the target item, so they respond "yes" to the Dutch word and make an error. They realize this as soon as they have retrieved the language membership of the item and then become more careful in subsequent trials.

In fact, they now strengthen the relationship between the Dutch word and the "no" response, or they slow down to make sure their decision is also based on language membership information (for evidence that such modulation is possible, see Von Studnitz & Green, 2002).

Because the response to English controls remains relatively constant across the two parts of the experiment, the first option seems to be the more likely one. The lower part of Fig. 9.2 represents this option graphically. The strengthening of the stimulus–response binding for Dutch words has severe consequences for the interlingual homographs. When an interlingual homograph is presented, the Dutch reading now interferes strongly with the English reading because both the "no" response and the "yes" response are activated. In other words, response competition leads to much slower RTs to interlingual homographs than to controls (of course, there may be other reasons for such results as well).

Task and Context Effects in Bilingual Word Recognition Models

The previous sections have shown that bilingual word processing depends on the task that must be performed and the nonlinguistic and linguistic contexts in which it is performed. A number of more recent bilingual word recognition models incorporate the distinction between the actual word identification system and a task/decision system that I argued for on the basis of the empirical evidence. These models are discussed in the remainder of the chapter. Some of their basic characteristics are summarized in Table 9.1.

The Inhibitory Control Model and the Task/Decision System

Green (1986, 1998) developed a model that is to a large extent compatible with and complementary to the BIA model and the revised hierarchical model (also see chapters 17, 22, and 25, this volume). Rather than on the process of item identification itself, this inhibitory control (IC) model focuses on the importance of the demands posed by different tasks and the control (regulation) that language users can exert on their language processing by modifying levels of activation of (items in) language networks (Green, 1998, p. 68). A key

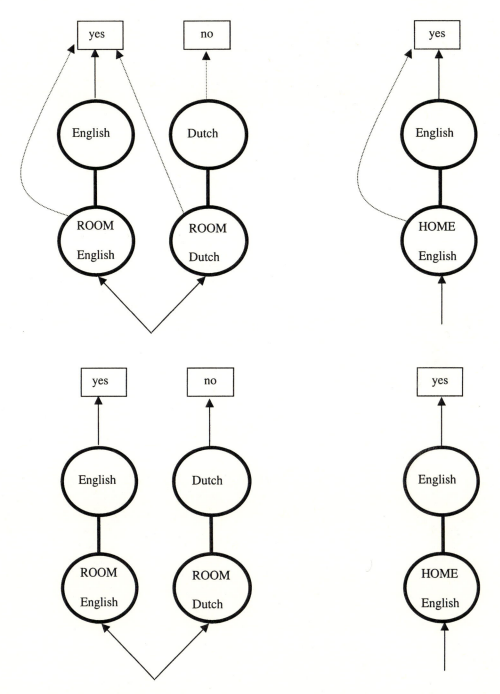

Figure 9.2 Stimulus–response bindings in the English lexical decision experiment by Dijkstra, De Bruijn, Schriefers, and Ten Brinke (2000). On the left side, simplified word and language membership representations are presented for the interlexical homograph ROOM; on the right side, they are for the matched English control word HOME. In the first part of the experiment (top), no Dutch words were included; therefore, the binding of Dutch words (including the Dutch reading of the interlexical homographs) to the "no" response was weak. In the second part (bottom), the presence of Dutch words led to stronger binding. The possibility that participants responded whenever a word was triggered (checking language membership information only later) is indicated by the shortcut from word level to response.

concept in this model is the *language task schema* that specifies the mental processing steps (or *action sequences*) that a language user takes to perform a particular language task. A language task schema regulates the output from the word identification system by altering the activation levels of representations within that system and by inhibiting outputs from the system (Green, 1998, p. 69). For instance, when a bilingual switches from one language to another in translation, a change in the language schema that is applied must take place. When an English word must be translated into French, this requires the language users to switch from the input language of the item, English, to the output language, French. Otherwise, the presented English word would be repeated (read out loud) instead of translated. Thus, the task schema for translation must actively suppress the word representations (or *lemmas*) with an English language tag (membership) at the stage of output selection. Because this suppression can take place only after the (lemma) representations are activated, inhibition is called *reactive*. However, the exerted inhibition of English words needs to be overcome later if such words are presented on the next trial. In sum, language changes require overcoming the inhibition of the previous language tags.

Irrespective of whether the details of this approach turn out to be correct, the IC model makes the important point that bilingual language processing is a process that always takes place within a particular task context and with certain goals in mind. In other words, it is not very informative to talk about bilingual word recognition in general without providing more information about the conditions under which it takes place and the goal that needs to be achieved.

The Language Mode Framework and Nonlinguistic Context Effects

Both the IC and the BIA models assume that the relative activation of languages can be affected to some extent by stimulus context via top-down inhibition of lexical representations. More generally, task context can affect the activation state of the word recognition system. There is yet another theoretical approach that assumes that the relative activation state of words and languages is context sensitive. In the language mode framework proposed by Grosjean (1997, 1998, 2001), language processing mechanisms and languages as a whole can be active to different extents. This relative

activation state of languages is called *language mode*, and it is continuous and sensitive to many factors. Examples of such factors in interactions are, for instance, the person spoken or listened to, the language user's language proficiency, the user's attitude toward language mixing, and the content and function of the ongoing discourse. Listeners and readers can be in a *bilingual mode* if they are talking to other bilinguals or are reading a text about which they know that there are possibly elements from another language (Grosjean, 1998, p. 137). However, if a bilingual listens to someone who is obviously monolingual, the activation state of the bilingual's languages would switch more to a *monolingual mode*, in which only or mainly the context-relevant language is active. According to Grosjean, the bilingual's language mode affects perception and the speed of access to one or two lexicons, and the language mode itself is affected both by the language user's expectations and by language intermixing (whether there are words of one or more languages embedded in the stimulus list).

If this view is evaluated in terms of the presently available data on the recognition of isolated visually presented words, it appears that only the second part of this view can be correct. For instance, the role played by the readers' expectations seems to be limited. Under various circumstances, word candidates of different languages are activated if they are close enough in terms of their characteristics to the input letter string (parallel activation of word candidates also seems to take place in the auditory domain). Bilingual lexical access seems to be profoundly language nonselective, and top-down factors such as expectation do not seem to be able to change that. At the same time, Grosjean seems to be correct in asserting that stimulus list composition (language intermixing) is an important factor affecting bilingual word recognition performance. Similar comments hold with respect to the BIA and IC models: The assumption that nonlinguistic context may affect the activation state of individual presented words does not seem to be warranted.

However, note that in daily life words are usually recognized in the linguistic context of a sentence, not as isolated items in stimulus lists. The language mode hypothesis has been formulated especially for language use in such natural contexts. In the following section, the BIA+ model is considered; it proposes that the effects of nonlinguistic and linguistic context may come about through different mechanisms.

The BIA+ Model and Linguistic Context Effects

The BIA+ model (Dijkstra & Van Heuven, 2002) is an extension and adaptation of the BIA model (see Fig. 9.3). The BIA+ model contains not only orthographic representations and language nodes, but also phonological and semantic repre-sentations. All these representations are assumed to be part of a word identification system that provides output to a task/decision system. The information flow in bilingual lexical processing proceeds exclusively from the word identification system toward a task/decision system without any influence of this task/decision system on the activation state of words.

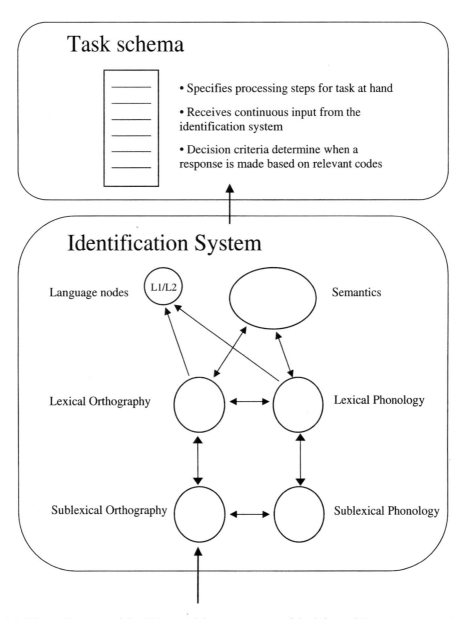

Figure 9.3 The architecture of the BIA+ model (an extension of the bilingual interactive activation [BIA] model) (Dijkstra & Van Heuven, 2002). L1, first language; L2, second language.

In this framework, nonlinguistic context effects can affect the word recognition process only indirectly, via the task/decision system. Nonlinguistic context effects arising from instruction or participant expectancies can affect the way information from the word identification system is used, but not the activation state of word candidates. In contrast, linguistic context (such as a preceding sentence) can interact directly with the word recognition system. In other words, semantic and syntactic aspects of the sentence context can modulate the activation of lexical candidates (of course, both nonlinguistic and linguistic context effects may operate at the same time).

The few studies that have so far investigated bilingual word recognition in sentence context (e.g., Altarriba, Kroll, Sholl, & Rayner, 1996; Li, 1996) suggest that semantic and syntactic aspects of sentence context may indeed modulate the bilingual word recognition process. For instance, Altarriba et al. recorded the eye movements of Spanish-English bilinguals who were reading English (L2) sentences that contained either an English (L2) or a Spanish (L1) target word (Experiment 1). Sentences provided either high or low semantic constraints on the target words. An example sentence of the high constraint and Spanish target condition is "He wanted to deposit all his *dinero* at the credit union," for which *dinero* is Spanish for "money." An interaction arose between the frequency of the target word and degree of sentence constraint for Spanish target words with respect to the first fixation duration, but not for English target words. Thus, when the Spanish target words were of high frequency and appeared in highly constrained sentences, the participants apparently experienced interference. This result suggests that sentence constraint influences not only the generation of semantic feature restrictions for upcoming words, but also that of lexical features. The high-frequency Spanish word matched the generated set of semantic features, but not the expected lexical features when the word appeared in the alternate language (Altarriba et al., p. 483). Note that word frequency (a lexical information source) and not language membership interacted with the sentence constraint. This suggests that (just as for isolated words) lexical characteristics are more important than language characteristics in the determination of word recognition in sentences.

On the basis of a review of the available studies of the processing of words in sentence context, Kroll and Dussias (2004) drew some important conclusions. First, they concluded that sentence processing in both languages is affected by the acquisition and use of more than one language. This suggests that nonselective access holds not only with respect to lexical aspects of processing, but also with respect to semantics and syntax. This conclusion leads to a number of interesting predictions. One prediction is that syntactic priming might arise between languages (e.g., the Dutch dative construction "*De man voerde de hond een kluif*" ["The man fed the dog a bone"] might prime the analogous English construction in "The woman gave the child a book"). Another prediction is that bilinguals should differ from monolinguals in certain switching tasks because bilinguals possess such well-developed cognitive skills for controlling cross-language competition. With respect to the interactions of L1 and L2 during sentence processing, Kroll and Dussias concluded that bilinguals resemble monolinguals in the semantic domain of sentence processing, but that they clearly process language differently in the syntactic domain. For instance, similar event-related brain potentials were found for L1 and L2 speakers in several studies for semantic processing, but not for syntactic processing (e.g., Hahne, 2001; Hahne & Friederici, 2001; Weber-Fox & Neville, 1996).

In sum, although the BIA+ model makes some basic assumptions to allow the development of an account for the recognition of words in sentence context, a detailed account is not available. Considerable research efforts are necessary before the contours of such an account will become visible.

Conclusion

The empirical data reviewed in this chapter indicate that the recognition process of isolated words is basically language nonselective in nature. This means that word candidates from different languages initially become active on the presentation of a letter string. This nonselectivity seems to hold for all representations that characterize words (e.g., orthographic, phonological, and semantic codes). Bilingual word recognition also seems to be automatic in the sense that the process takes place relatively unaffected by nonlinguistic contextual factors. This applies not just to words from the native language (L1), but also to words from the L2. At the same time, when words are processed in sentence context, their processing seems to be sensitive to the semantic and syntactic aspects of the sentence.

Word recognition models have aptly described the bilingual word recognition process by means of the activation metaphor. This metaphor is useful to describe how, on the basis of stimulus characteristics such as word frequency and different degrees of similarity between input and lexical representation, lexical candidates can be activated to various degrees. Attempts have been made to apply the activation metaphor to the level of languages as a whole as well, but it remains to be determined what it means to say that languages can be activated to different degrees (Dijkstra & Van Hell, 2003).

Available models differ considerably in their views about how different tasks and contextual factors such as instruction and participant expectations affect the bilingual word recognition process. Some approaches assume considerable context sensitivity of the L1/L2 activation state in the mental lexicon; others explain context effects at strategy-sensitive decision levels rather than at the level of the word recognition system.

To conclude, an increasing amount of research in the last decade has led to important insights, for instance, that bilingual word recognition appears to be subserved by a language-nonselective access system that is sensitive to task demands and context aspects. Future research must investigate how different sorts of contextual factors affect the word recognition process and to what extent bilinguals can exert cognitive control over the different components of the language processing system. Research is also needed to disentangle lexical, syntactic, and semantic effects on words processed in sentences with various task goals in mind.

References

Altarriba, J., Kroll, J. F., Sholl, A., & Rayner, K. (1996). The influence of lexical and conceptual constraints on reading mixed-language sentences: Evidence from eye-fixation and naming times. *Memory and Cognition*, 24, 477–492.

Altarriba, J., & Mathis, K. M. (1997). Conceptual and lexical development in second language acquisition. *Journal of Memory and Language*, 36, 550–568.

Beauvillain, C., & Grainger, J. (1987). Accessing interlexical homographs: Some limitations of a language-selective access. *Journal of Memory and Language*, 26, 658–672.

Bijeljac-Babic, R., Biardeau, A., & Grainger, J. (1997). Masked orthographic priming in bilingual word recognition. *Memory and Cognition*, 25, 447–457.

Bowers, J. S., Mimouni, Z., & Arguin, M. (2000). Orthography plays a critical role in cognate priming: Evidence from French/English and Arabic/French cognates. *Memory and Cognition*, 28, 1289–1296.

Brysbaert, M., Van Dyck, G., & Van de Poel, M. (1999). Visual word recognition in bilinguals: Evidence from masked phonological priming. *Journal of Experimental Psychology: Human Perception and Performance*, 25, 137–148.

Caramazza, A., & Brones, I. (1979). Lexical access in bilinguals. *Bulletin of the Psychonomic Society*, 13, 212–214.

Coltheart, M., Davelaar, E., Jonasson, J. T., & Besner, D. (1977). Access to the internal lexicon. In S. Dornic (Ed.), *Attention and performance VI* (pp. 535–555). New York: Academic Press.

Cristoffanini, P., Kirsner, K., & Milech, D. (1986). Bilingual lexical representation: The status of Spanish-English cognates. *Quarterly Journal of Experimental Psychology*, 38A, 367–393.

De Bruijn, E. R. A., Dijkstra, A., Chwilla, D. J., & Schriefers, H. J. (2001). Language context effects on interlingual homograph recognition: Evidence from event-related potentials and response times in semantic priming. *Bilingualism: Language and Cognition*, 4, 155–168.

De Groot, A. M. B., Borgwaldt, S., Bos, M., & Van den Eijnden, E. (2002). Lexical decision and word naming in bilinguals: Language effects and task effects. *Journal of Memory and Language*, 47, 91–124.

De Groot, A. M. B., & Comijs, H. (1995). Translation recognition and translation production: Comparing a new and an old tool in the study of bilingualism. Language Learning, 45, 467–509.

De Groot, A. M. B., Delmaar, P., & Lupker, S. J. (2000). The processing of interlexical homographs in a bilingual and a monolingual task: Support for nonselective access to bilingual memory. *Quarterly Journal of Experimental Psychology*, 53, 397–428.

De Groot, A. M. B., & Nas, G. (1991). Lexical representation of cognates and noncognates in compound bilinguals. *Journal of Memory and Language*, 30, 90–123.

De Groot, A. M. B., & Poot, R. (1997). Word translation at three levels of proficiency in a second language: The ubiquitous involvement of conceptual memory. *Language Learning*, 47, 215–264.

De Moor, W. (1998). *Visuele woordherkenning bij tweetalige personen* [Visual word recognition in bilinguals]. Unpublished master's thesis, University of Ghent, Belgium.

Dijkstra, A., De Bruijn, E., Schriefers, H. J., & Ten Brinke, S. (2000). More on interlingual homograph recognition: Language intermixing versus explicitness of instruction.

Bilingualism: Language and Cognition,
3, 69–78.

Dijkstra, A., Grainger, J., & Van Heuven, W. J. B.
(1999). Recognition of cognates and
interlingual homographs: The neglected role
of phonology. *Journal of Memory and
Language, 41*, 496–518.

Dijkstra, A., Timmermans, M. & Schriefers, H.
(2000). Cross-language effects on bilingual
homograph recognition. *Journal of Memory
and Language, 42*, 445–464.

Dijkstra, A., & Van Hell, J. (2003). Testing the
language mode hypothesis using trilinguals.
*International Journal of Bilingual Education
and Bilingualism, 6*, 2–16.

Dijkstra, A., & Van Heuven, W. J. B. (1998). The
BIA model and bilingual word recognition. In
J. Grainger & A. M. Jacobs (Eds.), *Localist
connectionist approaches to human cognition*
(pp. 189–225). Mahwah, NJ: Erlbaum.

Dijkstra, A., & Van Heuven, W. J. B. (2002). The
architecture of the bilingual word recognition
system: From identification to decision.
Bilingualism: Language and Cognition, 5,
175–197.

Dijkstra, A., Van Heuven, W. J. B., & Grainger,
J. (1998). Simulating competitor effects with
the bilingual interactive activation model.
Psychologica Belgica, 38, 177–196.

Dijkstra, A., Van Jaarsveld, H., & Ten Brinke, S.
(1998). Interlingual homograph recognition:
Effects of task demands and language
intermixing. *Bilingualism: Language and
Cognition, 1*, 51–66.

Doctor, E. A., & Klein, D. (1992). Phonological
processing in bilingual word recognition. In
R. J. Harris (Ed.), *Cognitive processing in
bilinguals* (pp. 237–252). Amsterdam:
Elsevier.

Font, N. (2001). *Rôle de la langue dans l'accès
au lexique chez les bilingues: Influence de la
proximité orthographique et sémantique
interlangue sur la reconnaissance visuelle de
mots.* Unpublished doctoral thesis, Université
Paul Valery, Montpellier, France.

Gerard, L. D., & Scarborough, D. L. (1989).
Language-specific lexical access of
homographs by bilinguals. *Journal of
Experimental Psychology: Learning,
Memory and Cognition, 15*, 305–313.

Gollan, T., Forster, K. I., & Frost, R. (1997).
Translation priming with different scripts:
Masked priming with cognates and non-
cognates in Hebrew-English bilinguals. *Jour-
nal of Experimental Psychology: Learning,
Memory, and Cognition, 23*, 1122–1139.

Grainger, J., & Dijkstra, A. (1992). On the representation and use of language information
in bilinguals. In R. J. Harris (Ed.), *Cognitive

processing in bilinguals* (pp. 207–220).
Amsterdam: Elsevier.

Green, D. W. (1986). Control, activation, and
resource: A framework and a model for the
control of speech in bilinguals. *Brain and
Language, 27*, 210–223.

Green, D. W. (1998). Mental control of the
bilingual lexico-semantic system. *Bilingualism:
Language and Cognition, 1*, 67–81.

Grosjean, F. (1997). Processing mixed language:
Issues, findings and models. In A. M. B. de
Groot & J. F. Kroll (Eds.), *Tutorials in
bilingualism: Psycholinguistic perspectives*
(pp. 225–254). Hillsdale, NJ: Erlbaum.

Grosjean, F. (1998). Studying bilinguals:
Methodological and conceptual issues.
*Bilingualism: Language and Cognition,
1*, 131–149.

Grosjean, F. (2001). The bilingual's language
modes. In J. L. Nicol (Eds.), *One mind, two
languages: Bilingual language processing*
(pp. 1–22). Oxford, England: Blackwell.

Hahne, A. (2001). What's different in second-
language processing? Evidence from event-
related brain potentials. *Journal of
Psycholinguistic Research, 30*, 251–266.

Hahne, A., & Friederici, A. (2001). Processing a
second language: Late learners' comprehension mechanisms as revealed by event-related
brain potentials. *Bilingualism: Language and
Cognition, 4*, 123–141.

Jared, D., & Kroll, J. (2001). Do bilinguals activate
phonological representations in one or both of
their languages when naming words? *Journal
of Memory and Language, 44*, 2–31.

Jared, D., & Szucs, C. (2002). Phonological activation in bilinguals: Evidence from interlingual homograph naming. *Bilingualism:
Language and Cognition, 5*, 225–239.

Kolers, P. A. (1966). Reading and talking
bilingually. *American Journal of Psychology,
79*, 357–376.

Kroll, J. F., & Curley, J. (1988). Lexical memory
in novice bilinguals: The role of concepts
in retrieving second language words. In
M. Gruneberg, P. Morris, & R. Sykes (Eds.),
Practical aspects of memory (Vol. 2,
pp. 389–395). London: Wiley.

Kroll, J. F., & Dussias, P. E. (2004). The
comprehension of words and sentences in
two languages. In T. Bhatia & W. Ritchie
(Eds.), *Handbook of bilingualism*
(pp. 169–200). Cambridge, MA: Blackwell.

Kroll, J. F., Michael, E., Tokowicz, N., &
Dufour, R. (2002). The development of
lexical fluency in a second language. *Second
Language Research, 18*, 137–171.

Kroll, J. F., & Stewart, E. (1994). Category
interference in translation and picture

naming: Evidence for asymmetric connections between bilingual memory representations. *Journal of Memory and Language, 33,* 149–174.

La Heij, W., Kerling, R., & Van der Velden, E. (1996). Nonverbal context effects in forward and backward translation: Evidence for concept mediation. *Journal of Memory and Language, 35,* 648–665.

Lemhöfer, K., & Dijkstra, A. (2004). Recognizing cognates and interlingual homographs: Effects of code similarity in language specific and generalized lexical decision. *Memory and Cognition, 32,* 533–550.

Léwy, N., & Grosjean, F. (1997). *A computational model of bilingual lexical access.* Manuscript in preparation, Neuchâtel University, Switzerland.

Li, P. (1996). Spoken word recognition of code-switched words by Chinese-English bilinguals. *Journal of Memory and Language, 35,* 757–774.

Macnamara, J., & Kushnir, S. (1971). Linguistic independence of bilinguals: The input switch. *Journal of Verbal Learning and Verbal Behavior, 10,* 480–487.

Mathey, S., & Zagar, D. (2000). The neighborhood distribution effect in visual word recognition: Words with single and twin neighbors. *Journal of Experimental Psychology: Human Perception and Performance, 26,* 184–205.

McClelland, J. L., & Elman, J. L. (1986). The TRACE model of speech perception. *Cognitive Psychology, 18,* 1–86.

Nas, G. (1983). Visual word recognition in bilinguals: Evidence for a cooperation between visual and sound based codes during access to a common lexical store. *Journal of Verbal Learning and Verbal Behavior, 22,* 526–534.

Potter, M. C., So, K.-F., Von Eckardt, B., & Feldman, L. B. (1984). Lexical and conceptual representation in beginning and proficient bilinguals. *Journal of Verbal Learning and Verbal Behavior, 23,* 23–38.

Sánchez-Casas, R., Davis, C. W., & García-Albea, J. E. (1992). Bilingual lexical processing: Exploring the cognate/non-cognate distinction. *European Journal of Cognitive Psychology, 4,* 311–322.

Schulpen, B., Dijkstra, A., Schriefers, H. J., & Hasper, M. (2003). Recognition of interlingual homophones in bilingual auditory word recognition. *Journal of Experimental Psychology: Human Perception and Performance, 29,* 1155–1178.

Sholl, A., Sankaranarayanan, A., & Kroll, J. F. (1995). Transfer between picture naming and translation: A test of asymmetries in bilingual memory. *Psychological Science, 6,* 45–49.

Soares, C., & Grosjean, F. (1984). Bilinguals in a monolingual and bilingual speech mode: The effect on lexical access. *Memory and Cognition, 12,* 380–386.

Thomas, M. S. C., & Allport, A. (2000). Language switching costs in bilingual visual word recognition. *Journal of Memory and Language, 43,* 44–66.

Van Hell, J. G., & Candia Mahn, A. (1997). Keyword mnemonics versus rote rehearsal: Learning concrete and abstract foreign words by experienced and inexperienced learners. *Language Learning, 47,* 507–546.

Van Hell, J. G., & Dijkstra, A. (2002). Foreign language knowledge can influence native language performance in exclusively native contexts. *Psychonomic Bulletin and Review, 9,* 780–789.

Van Heste, T. (1999). *Visuele woordherkenning bij tweetaligen* [Visual word recognition in bilinguals]. Unpublished master's thesis, University of Leuven, Belgium.

Van Heuven, W. J. B., Dijkstra, A., & Grainger, J. (1998). Orthographic neighborhood effects in bilingual word recognition. *Journal of Memory and Language, 39,* 458–483.

Von Studnitz, R. E., & Green, D. W. (1997). Lexical decision and language switching. *International Journal of Bilingualism, 1,* 3–24.

Von Studnitz, R. E., & Green, D. (2002). Interlingual homograph interference in German-English bilinguals: Its modulation and locus of control. *Bilingualism: Language and Cognition, 5,* 1–23.

Weber-Fox, C. M., & Neville, H. J. (1996). Maturational constraints on functional specializations for language processing: ERP and behavioral evidence in bilingual speakers. *Journal of Cognitive Neuroscience, 8,* 231–256.

Weinreich, U. (1968). *Languages in contact.* The Hague, The Netherlands: Mouton.

Michael S. C. Thomas
Walter J. B. van Heuven

10

Computational Models of Bilingual Comprehension

ABSTRACT This chapter reviews current computational models of bilingual word recognition. It begins with a discussion of the role of computational modeling in advancing psychological theories, highlighting the way in which the choice of modeling paradigm can influence the type of empirical phenomena to which the model is applied. The chapter then introduces two principal types of connectionist model that have been employed in the bilingual domain: localist and distributed architectures. Two main sections then assess each of these approaches. Localist models are predominantly addressed toward explaining the processing structures in the adult bilingual. Here, we evaluate several models, including the Bilingual Interactive Activation model, the Bilingual Interactive Model of Lexical Access, and the Semantic, Orthographic, and Phonological Interactive Activation model. Distributed models are predominantly addressed toward explaining issues of language acquisition and language loss. This section includes discussion of the Bilingual Single Network model, the Bilingual Simple Recurrent Network model, and the Self-Organizing Model of Bilingual Processing. Overall, the aim of current computational models is to account for the circumstances under which the bilingual's two languages appear to interfere with each other during recognition (for better or worse) and those circumstances under which the languages appear to operate independently. Based on the range of models available in the unilingual literature, our conclusion is that computational models have great potential in advancing our understanding of the principal issues in bilingualism, but that thus far only a few of these models have seen extension to the bilingual domain.

In this chapter, we review the use of computational models in formulating theories of bilingual language comprehension, focusing particularly on connectionist (or artificial neural network) models. Over the last 20 years, a huge amount of research has been generated by the use of connectionist models to study processes of unilingual comprehension and production. Models have been put forward to capture the final adult language system and to capture the developmental processes that lead to this system. Within psycholinguistics, computer models have emerged as an essential tool for advancing theories because of the way they force clear specification of those theories, test their coherence, and generate new testable predictions.

In the following sections, we compare and contrast two types of model that have been applied to bilingual word recognition. These are the localist interactive activation adult state models of Van Heuven, Dijkstra, Grainger, Grosjean, and Lewy (e.g., the Bilingual Interactive Activation [BIA] model; the Semantic, Orthographic, and Phonological Interactive Activation [SOPHIA] model; the Bilingual Interactive Model of Lexical Access [BIMOLA]), and the distributed developmental models of Thomas, French, Li, and Farkaš (e.g., Bilingual Single Network [BSN], the Bilingual Simple Recurrent Network [BSRN], the Self-Organizing Model of Bilingual Processing [SOMBIP]). We explore how these models have accounted for empirical data from bilingual word recognition, including cross-language priming, similarity, and interference effects. We then evaluate the respective strengths and weaknesses of each type of model before concluding with a discussion of future directions in the modeling of bilingual language comprehension.

Early Views of the Word Recognition System

Historically, theories of unilingual word recognition have always appealed to metaphors of one kind or another to characterize the cognitive processes involved. For example, one theory of the 1970s appealed either to the metaphor of a "list" of words that would be searched in serial order to identify the candidate most consistent with the perceptual input while another appealed to the metaphor of a set of word "detectors" that would compete to collect evidence that their word was present in the input (e.g., Forster, 1976; Morton, 1969). The limitation of such theories was that they were often little more than verbal descriptions. There was no precision in the specification of how these recognition systems would work. As a result, it was not always possible to be sure that the theories were truly viable or to derive specific testable hypotheses that might falsify them.

Early models of bilingual word recognition shared this general character, for instance, focusing on whether the bilingual system might have a single list combining words from both languages or separate lists for each language (in which case, the question would be whether the lists would be searched in parallel or one after the other). Theories of lexical organization speculated on whether bilingual "memories" would be segregated or integrated across languages and what "links" might exist between translation equivalents in each language or between semantically related words in each language (see, e.g., Grainger & Dijkstra, 1992; Meyer & Ruddy, 1974; Potter, So, Von Eckardt, & Feldman, 1984; and Francis, chapter 12, this volume, for a review).

The advent of widespread computational modeling has changed the nature of theorizing within the field of bilingual language processing, to the extent that such models are now an essential component of most theoretical approaches. The consequence has been an advance in the precision and rigor of theories of bilingual language comprehension.

Use of Computational Models

Computational models force clarity on theories because they require previously vague descriptive notions to be specified sufficiently for implementation to be possible. The implemented model can then serve as a test of the viability of the original theory via quantitative comparisons of the model's output against empirical data. This is a particular advantage when the implications of a theory's assumptions are difficult to anticipate, for instance, if behavior relies on complex interactions within the model. Models also allow the generation of new testable hypotheses and permit manipulations that are not possible in normal experimentation, such as the investigation of systems under various states of damage. There are more subtle implications of using computational models that bear consideration, however.

First, although computational models are evaluated by their ability to simulate patterns of empirical data, simulation alone is insufficient. Models serve the role of scaffolding theory development, and as such it is essential that the modeler understands why a model behaves in the way that it does. This means understanding which aspects of the design and function of the model are responsible for its success when it succeeds in capturing data and which aspects are responsible for its failure when it does not.

Second, different types of model embody different assumptions. Sometimes, those assumptions are explicit because they derive from the theory being implemented. For example, in a bilingual system, word detectors might be separated into two pools, one for each language, as an implementation of the theory that lexical representations are language specific. However, sometimes assumptions can be implicit, tied up in the particular processing structures chosen by the modeler. Such choices can make the model appropriate to address some sorts of empirical phenomena but not others. The particular processing structure chosen may also influence the theoretical hypotheses subsequently considered. For example, let us say that a bilingual model is constructed that implements a system of discrete word detectors, and moreover that the modeler must now decide how to include words that have the same form but different meaning in the bilingual's two languages (interlingual homographs). By virtue of plumping for discrete detectors, the modeler is forced into a binary theoretical choice: Either both languages share a single detector or each language employs a separate detector.

In the following sections, therefore, it is worth considering that the choice of model type can affect both the phenomena that are examined and the types of hypothesis that are considered within its framework.

Two Modeling Approaches

Most computational models of bilingual word comprehension have worked within the connectionist tradition, that is, they are computational models inspired by principles of neurocomputation. Although these are high-level cognitive models, they seek to embody characteristics of neural processing based on two beliefs. The first is the belief that the functional processes and representations found in the cognitive system are likely to be constrained by the sorts of computations that the neural substrate can readily achieve. The second is the belief that models employing "brain-style" processing are more likely to allow us to build a bridge between different levels of description (i.e., to connect behavioral data and data gained from functional brain imaging). However, the appropriate level of biological plausibility of a model's computational assumptions is still a matter of debate. By definition, models contain simplifications. Necessarily, they will not incorporate all characteristics of the biological substrate, but instead appeal to a more abstract notion of neurocomputation.

Bilingual researchers have appealed to two different types of connectionist models in studying processes of comprehension: localist and distributed. Both types share the neural principle that computations will be achieved by simple processing units (analogous to neurons) connected into networks. Units have a level of activation (analogous to a firing rate), and each unit affects the activity level of the other units depending on the strength of the connections between them. The models differ in the extent to which they emphasize changing the connection strengths as a function of experience and whether individual units in the network are to be assigned prior identities (e.g., as corresponding to a particular word, letter, or phoneme). Note that neither approach claims a direct relationship between the simple processing units contained in the models and actual neurons in the brain. Rather, the attempt is to capture a style of computation.

Localist Models

Localist models tend to assign discrete identities to individual units, for instance, by splitting networks into layers of units corresponding to letter features, letters, and words. Localist models also tend not to focus on changes in the model through learning. Instead, connection strengths are set in advance by the modeler as a direct implementation of his or her theory. These models can be seen as direct descendants of the original word detector models proposed in the 1970s. Each simple processing unit corresponds to the detector for the existence of a given entity in the input, and a *network* comprises a set of linked detectors. Because these models do not incorporate change according to experience, their focus within bilingual research has been to investigate the static structure of the word recognition system in the adult bilingual (or the child at a single point in time). Their main advantage is that all network states are readily comprehensible because activity on every unit has a straightforward interpretation. Although localist models seem simple, their behavior can be quite complex through the interaction between units within and between layers.

Distributed Models

In contrast, distributed models tend to represent individual entities (like words) as patterns of activity spread over sets of units. The entity represented by a network cannot therefore be identified by looking at a single unit, but only as a code over several units. Second, distributed models tend to focus on experience-driven change, specifically on learning to map between codes for different types of information (such as a word's spoken form and its meaning). Connection strengths in such a network are initially randomized, and a learning rule is allowed to modify the connection strengths so that, over time, the system learns to relate each word to its meaning. In addition, these networks can contain banks of "hidden" processing units that, during learning, can develop internal representations mediating the complex relationship between input and output. Because these models incorporate changes according to experience, they can be applied more readily to issues of language acquisition and change in language dominance over time. However, patterns of activity over hidden units are less readily interpreted, and these models are sometimes thought of as more theoretically opaque.

The Relationship Between the Models

The relationship between these two types of model is a complex and controversial one (see, e.g., Page, 2000, and Seidenberg, 1993, for arguments in favor of each type of model). In the previous sections, we outlined the ways in which each type of model has commonly been used. However, these usages do not represent the *necessary* features of their design. Ultimately, the distinction between the localist and distributed models is not a dichotomous one, but a continuum, and it depends on the degree of overlap between the representations of individual entities within the model, that is, the extent to which processing units are involved in representing more than one entity. Aside from emphasizing the different ways in which these models have been used, two points are worth making for current purposes.

First, although their details are different, the model types are closely related in that they explain behavior by appealing to the distribution of information in the problem domain. In localist models, this pattern is hardwired into the structure of the model. In distributed models, it is "imprinted" onto the structure of the model by a learning process. To illustrate, let us say that one language has a higher frequency of doubled vowels (or some other statistical difference) than another language. A localist model built to recognize the first language (L1) will show superior ability in recognizing doubled vowels because its structure incorporates many word units that contain doubled vowels, each poised to encourage detection of this pattern in the input. A distributed model trained to recognize L1 will show a similar superior ability because during learning, by virtue of more frequent exposure to doubled vowels, it will have developed stronger weights linking input codes containing doubled vowels to its output units representing word meaning or pronunciation. In either case, the explanation for the superior performance is the distributional properties of the language that the system is recognizing, in this example the high frequency of doubled vowels.

Second, although localist and distributed models have different advantages for studying various phenomena of bilingual language processing, the characteristics of these models must eventually be combined. A final model must reflect both how the bilingual system is acquired as well as details of its processing dynamics in the adult state.

Issues to be Addressed in the Modeling of Bilingual Language Processing

Before turning to the specific empirical data from bilingual language comprehension that computational models have sought to capture, it is worth considering the general issues pertaining to bilingual language processing that appear throughout this book so that we may evaluate the potential of both current and future connectionist models to address them. The following are some of the most salient issues:

- Do bilinguals have a single language processing system, different processing systems, or partially overlapping systems for their two languages?
- How is the language status of lexical items encoded in the system?
- What interference patterns result from having two languages in a cognitive system?
- How can language context be manipulated within the system in terms of inhibiting/facilitating one or other language during comprehension or production (the language "switch") or in terms of gaining or countering automaticity of a more dominant language?
- How is each language acquired? To what extent are there critical period effects or age of acquisition effects in the acquisition of an L2? To what extent are there transfer effects between an L1 and an L2? How is an L2 best acquired: by initial association to an existing L1 or by a strategy that encourages direct contact with semantics (such as picture naming)?
- How is each language maintained in terms of ongoing patterns of relative dominance or proficiency?
- To what extent are the characteristics of bilingualism (such as dominance) modality specific (i.e., differential across spoken and written language, comprehension, and production)?
- How is each language lost: in terms of aphasia after brain damage in bilinguals or in terms of the natural attrition of a disused language? How may languages be recovered?

We contend that, between them, localist and distributed models have the potential to inform every one of these issues. However, we begin by a consideration of the current status of models of bilingual word comprehension.

Localist Approaches

In psycholinguistic research, localist models of monolingual language processing have been used since the beginning of the 1980s. In 1981, McClelland and Rumelhart (1981; Rumelhart & McClelland, 1982) used a simple localist connectionist model to simulate word superiority effects. This Interactive Activation (IA) model has since been used to simulate orthographic processing in visual word recognition. The model has been extended with decision components by Grainger and Jacobs (1996) to account for wide variety of empirical data on orthographic processing.

The IA models were used to simulate word recognition in a variety of languages (e.g., English, Dutch, French), but in each case within a monolingual framework. Dijkstra and colleagues (Dijkstra & Van Heuven, 1998; Van Heuven, Dijkstra, & Grainger, 1998) subsequently extended the IA model to the bilingual domain. They called this new model the Bilingual Interactive Activation (BIA) model. Both the IA and BIA models are restricted to the orthographic processing aspect of visual word recognition, encoding information about letters and visual word forms in their structure.

In the following sections, we focus on the BIA model and examine how this model can or cannot account for empirical findings on cross-language neighborhood effects, language context effects, homograph recognition, inhibitory effects of masked priming, and the influence of language proficiency. We end this section with a short discussion of a localist model of bilingual speech perception (BIMOLA) and a new localist bilingual model based on the theoretical BIA+ model (Dijkstra & Van Heuven, 2002), which integrates orthographic, phonological, and semantic representations (SOPHIA).

The Bilingual Interactive Activation Model

Structure   The BIA model is depicted in Fig. 10.1. It consists of four layers of nodes. It shares with the IA model the same lower-level layers of feature and letter nodes, by which the features and letters are coded for each position of a 4-letter word. There are 14 visual features and 26 letters for each position. The two top layers in the BIA model differ from the IA model. The BIA model has a word layer of all Dutch and English 4-letter words. Furthermore, the BIA model has a language node layer, assigning a single node to each language. Visual input in the model is coded as the absence or presence of letter features. At each position, letters are excited when they are consistent with a feature and inhibited when they are not consistent with a visual feature (in Fig. 10.1, arrows with triangular heads represent excitatory sets of connections, and those with circular heads represent inhibitory sets of connections). Each letter activates words that have that letter at the same position and inhibits words that do not have that letter at that position.

An important aspect of the BIA (and the IA) model is that all nodes at the word level are interconnected; they can mutually inhibit each other's activation. This is called *lateral inhibition*. Furthermore, activated words feed activation back to their constituent letters. The parameters that regulate these interactions in the BIA model are identical to the ones used in the original IA model (McClelland & Rumelhart, 1981). Because words of both languages are fully connected to each other, the BIA model implements the assumption of an integrated lexicon. In addition, because the letters at the letter layer activate words of both languages simultaneously, the model implements the assumption of nonselective access. However, lateral connections allow the words of the two languages to compete and inhibit each other.

Moreover, this competition can be biased. Apart from the incorporation of two lexicons, the BIA model is special in its inclusion of language nodes, in this case one for English and one for Dutch. The language nodes collect activation of all words from one lexicon and, once activated, can suppress the word units of the other language. The parameter that controls this inhibition is important to the behavior of the model (Dijkstra & Van Heuven, 1998). In the summary of simulation results with the BIA model, we discuss the role of this top-down inhibition.

Processing   The behavior of the BIA model in response to an input is determined by a combination of excitatory and inhibitory influences that cycle around the network. Three components contribute to this interaction. First, activation flows up the network, from feature, to letter, to word, to

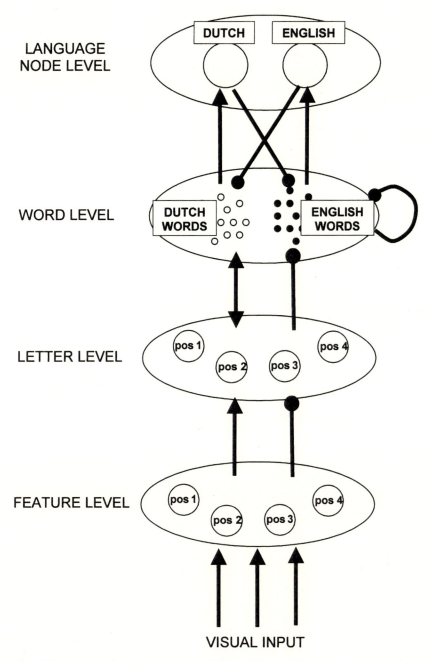

Figure 10.1 The Bilingual Interactive Activation (BIA) model. Excitatory connections are indicated by arrows (with arrowheads pointing in the direction of activation spread), inhibitory connections by lines with closed circles (pos, position). Note that although two pools of word units are depicted, one for each language, during processing all words compete with all other words via inhibitory lateral connections, representing an integrated lexicon.

language nodes. In each case, the higher nodes with which the input is consistent are activated, and those with which the input is inconsistent are inhibited. Second, at the word level, words (from both languages) compete with each other to be the most active. Third, activation also flows back down the network. Word units reinforce the letters of which they are comprised, and language units inhibit words of the opposing language. Letters and words are therefore not processed in isolation, but in the context of the words that contain these letters and of the languages of which words are members.

Each time step (cycle), activation flows between the layers, and the new activation of each node is calculated. After a few cycles, letters and words that are similar or identical to the input are activated. Thus, the word node that best matches the input string will reach the recognition threshold. The number of cycles it takes to reach this threshold can then be compared with human response latencies. The threshold can be at a fixed word activation level, or it can vary around a mean (Jacobs & Grainger, 1992).

Modeling Second Language Proficiency in the Bilingual Interactive Activation Model

An important aspect of the BIA model is that differences in word frequency are reflected in the resting-level activation of the words. High-frequency words have a higher resting-level activation than low-frequency words. Therefore, high-frequency words are activated more quickly and reach the recognition threshold earlier than low-frequency words.

Word frequencies of Dutch and English taken from the CELEX database (Baayen, Piepenbrock, & Van Rijn, 1993) are converted into resting-level activations in the BIA model. These word frequencies reflect frequencies from a perfectly balanced bilingual. Most studies with bilinguals, however, use participants who acquired their L2 later in life ("late bilinguals") and who are less proficient in their L2. One consequence is that, for these participants, the (subjective) word frequencies of their L2 are lower than the frequencies of their L1 (especially for high-frequency L2 words). In the BIA model, this can be implemented by varying the resting-level activation range of the L2. This is not to assume that differences in proficiency can be explained solely in terms of frequency effects. For instance, greater knowledge of L2 grammar might result in relatively high L2 proficiency as well. However, the manipulation of resting activation nevertheless captures the empirical fact that L2 words tend to be comprehended and produced more slowly and less accurately than their comparable L1 translation equivalents in unbalanced bilinguals.

Language Nodes   Dijkstra and Van Heuven (1998) described several functions of the language nodes in the BIA model. For example, the language nodes represent a language tag that is activated during word identification and that indicates the language to which the word belongs. In addition, language nodes can inhibit words of the other language to reflect a "stronger" representation of, for example, the L1 language compared to the L2 language. As a result, L1 words will inhibit L2 words more strongly during recognition because of extra top-down inhibition from the language node. As indicated by Dijkstra, Van Heuven, and Grainger (1998), the BIA model would probably produce a similar functional behavior without top-down inhibition from the language nodes, when lateral inhibition at the word level is asymmetric between words of different languages (e.g., L1 words inhibit L2 words more than vice versa).

Furthermore, top-down inhibition from the language nodes can be used to simulate context effects in word recognition. Thus, the correct reading of an interlingual homograph depends on language context, an effect that the language nodes could implement. However, this function of the language might also be replaced by a decision mechanism because results obtained with homographs suggest that bilinguals are not able to suppress nontarget language candidates even in the context of explicit instructions to do so (Dijkstra, De Bruijn, Schriefers, & Ten Brinke, 2000).

Finally, language nodes collect activation from the word level and therefore serve as an indicator of the total activation of all the word nodes in their respective languages. Summed activation is an important notion in, for example, the multiple readout model (MROM) of Grainger and Jacobs (1996). A large value, representing lots of word node activity, implies that the input must be fairly wordlike. Summed activation is used as a criterion to make a "yes" response in the lexical decision task. Furthermore, summed activation is used to adjust the deadline of the "no" response (if the input is very wordlike, give the word nodes more time for one of them to reach threshold before deciding the input is actually a nonword). Although the MROM does not explicitly implement this summed activation as a representation in the model, the language nodes of the BIA model can be seen as an explicit implementation of this notion.

Bilingual Interactive Activation Model Simulations

Neighborhood Effects   An interesting aspect of the BIA model is that it incorporates the IA model as part of its structure. Therefore, the behavior of the IA model inside and outside of the BIA structure can be compared. Indeed, examining two IA models, one for each language, would constitute a particular theory of bilingual word recognition (one in which there was selective access of the input to each language and no top-down inhibition from the language nodes). Thus, the BIA model permits a detailed comparison of a selective access model with a nonselective access model.

In this way, Dijkstra and Van Heuven (1998) were able to compare three models of bilingual visual word recognition, each implementing a different theory: (a) a selective access model, simulated with the monolingual IA model; (b) the BIA model with top-down inhibition; (c) the BIA model without top-down inhibition. In addition, they changed the frequencies of the English words in the model by changing the resting-level range to reflect the fact that the target empirical data for the models were collected from participants who were not balanced bilinguals. All other parameter settings were identical in the three models. The performance of each model was compared with the empirical results of Van Heuven et al. (1998), who demonstrated that the presence of neighbors (words that can be constructed by changing a single letter of a target word) in the nontarget language slowed word recognition in both Dutch and English. The presence of within-language neighbors accelerated recognition times in English, but had an inhibitory effect on Dutch word recognition.

The correlation of the simulation data with the English word data showed that, irrespective of the assumed frequency range, the BIA model that included asymmetric top-down inhibition (from the Dutch language node to English words) produced better simulation results than the other models. In contrast to the English results, for Dutch, high correlations were obtained with the selective access model that incorporated only the Dutch lexicon.

However, combining the results over both languages, the highest correlations over all experiments were obtained with a BIA model variant involving only top-down inhibition from the Dutch language node to active English words and a reduced English

frequency range. Simulations showed that this model was able to capture several effects. For Dutch targets, it replicated the inhibitory effect of Dutch and English neighbors. For English targets, it replicated the inhibition effect of Dutch neighbors and the facilitation effect of English neighbors. Thus, the model correctly simulated the different effects of within-language neighbors in Dutch and English.

Here, an important exploratory role of computational modeling is demonstrated. Detailed comparison of the model's performance against empirical data allows the evaluation of different theoretical assumptions once implemented in the model.

Priming Effects   Effects of nontarget language neighbors have been also obtained in masked priming experiments (Bijeljac-Babic, Biardeau, & Grainger, 1997, for French and English). The BIA model can be used to simulate masked priming using the simulation technique described by Jacobs and Grainger (1992). This technique simulates masked priming by presenting the prime to the model on the first and second processing cycles; on the third cycle and following cycles, the target word is presented to the model. A simulation with the BIA model reported by Bijeljac-Babic et al. showed that the model captured the longer average target recognition times for same-language masked primes sharing orthographic similarity to the target (e.g., real–heal) than for cross-language masked primes also bearing orthographic similarity to the target (e.g., beau–beam). As with the empirical data, there was an effect of prime–target relatedness in both prime language conditions.

Bijeljac-Babic et al. (1997) also demonstrated that the size of the cross-language inhibition effect of an orthographically similar masked prime on target recognition increased as a function of the participant's level of proficiency in the prime word's language. Employing the BIA model with a French and an English lexicon and varying the resting activation of the word units in L2 to represent proficiency, Dijkstra, Van Heuven, et al. (1998) successfully simulated the dependence of the cross-language inhibition effect on L2 proficiency. The L2 neighbors have to be sufficiently active to interfere with L1 recognition.

The monolingual results from the control subjects in the study of Bijeljac-Babic et al. (1997) were then simulated with the monolingual IA model. Interestingly, the results of the monolingual simulation deviated from those of the experiment because the model predicted a facilitation effect for the related condition whereas the empirical results produced no priming effect. According to the model, the overlap in several letters between non-word prime and target word should have resulted in faster target recognition. However, the model's predictions were in line with several studies from the monolingual literature (e.g., Ferrand & Grainger, 1992; Forster, Davis, Schoknecht, & Carter, 1987). Dijkstra et al. (1998) discussed possible stimulus confounds that may explain the divergence of empirical and modeling results in Bijeljac-Babic et al.'s monolingual controls. Overall, the simulation results indicated that the BIA model can successfully simulate the effects of different levels of proficiency on cross-language masked priming.

Interlingual Homographs and Cognates   Empirical data from studies employing cognates (e.g., the Dutch and English word *film*, with the same meaning in each language) and interlingual homographs (e.g., the Dutch and English word *room*, which means "cream" in Dutch) constitute a challenge for any model of bilingual word processing. For example, recognition latencies of interlingual homographs appear to be affected by such factors as task demands, list composition, and word characteristics (De Groot, Delmaar, & Lupker, 2000; Dijkstra, Grainger, & Van Heuven, 1999; Dijkstra, Timmermans, & Schriefers, 2000; Dijkstra, Van Jaarsveld, & Ten Brinke, 1998; see Dijkstra & Van Heuven, 2002, for a review). Only models that include components to simulate task demands and strategic modifications of decision criteria depending on list composition will stand a chance of accounting for all experimental effects. However, it is still informative and useful to investigate what an orthographic processing model like the BIA model predicts regarding how these words should be recognized, even without sophisticated task-level processing structures.

Interlingual homographs can be represented in the BIA model in two ways: (a) as a single word node with, for example, a summed frequency of the reading in each language or (b) as separate representations for each language, each with a frequency reflecting its usage in that language (Dijkstra et al., 1999).

Simulations with interlingual homographs represented as a single combined node show that these homographs are always processed faster than control words. However, empirical data (e.g., Dijkstra et al., 1998) indicated that homographs are only faster in a generalized (language-neutral) lexical decision task, in which bilinguals must identify whether the stimulus is a word in either of their languages. In an English lexical decision task, on the other hand, Dijkstra et al. found that homographs were recognized no more quickly than English control words. Thus, the representation of each pair of homographs with a single node in the BIA model cannot account for the data.

However, when the interlingual homograph is represented by two separate word nodes in the BIA, one in each language, the model fails to recognize either of the representations of the homograph (Dijkstra & Van Heuven, 1998). Both word nodes become strongly activated because of bottom up information, but at the same time they inhibit each other as competitors at the word level. Therefore, they will stay below the standard word recognition threshold. Dijkstra and Van Heuven showed that the BIA model with language node to word inhibition can suppress the inappropriate reading of the homograph. Furthermore, they showed that with top-down inhibition from the Dutch language node to all English words, the BIA model could simulate the results of the Dutch go/no go task of Dijkstra et al. (2000), in which subjects only generate a response if the stimulus is a word rather than making a yes/no decision. The BIA model captured the frequency-dependent interference effect observed for homographs when each homograph was represented with a separate node and a resting-level activation based on its within-language frequency.

Other Localist Models

Bilingual Interactive Model of Lexical Access   A localist model has been developed to account for bilingual speech perception. This model is called the Bilingual Interactive Model of Lexical Access (BIMOLA; Léwy & Grosjean, 1997) and is depicted in Fig. 10.2. This model is based on the IA model of auditory word recognition called TRACE (McClelland & Elman, 1986). The BIMOLA has layers of auditory features, phonemes, and words just like TRACE has. However, unlike in TRACE, representations are not duplicated at each time slice. The BIMOLA has a feature level that is common to both languages. On the other hand, the phoneme and word levels are organized by language. This contrasts with the BIA model, for which the languages are not distinguished at the letter and word levels other than by the fact that L1 and L2 words are connected to different language nodes.

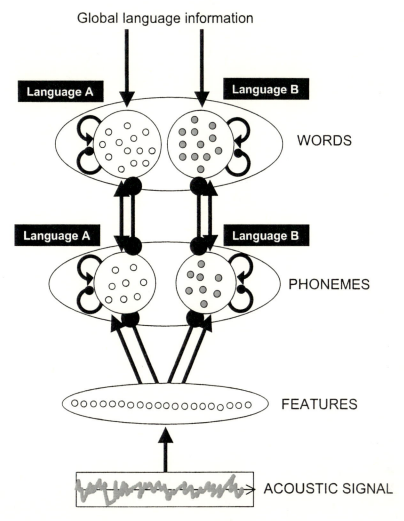

Figure 10.2 The Bilingual Model of Lexical Access (BIMOLA) (Léwy & Grosjean, 1997), a model of bilingual speech perception.

Differences Between the Bilingual Interactive Activation Model and the Bilingual Interactive Model of Lexical Access The BIA model and the BIMOLA are both localist models that share properties like the parallel activation of words of both languages, but there are also some clear differences. Although the BIA model has an integrated lexicon, the BIMOLA has separate lexicons for each language. This means that during recognition in the BIMOLA, L1 words only compete with other L1 words and L2 words only with other L2 words to reach threshold, whereas in BIA, all words compete with all other words through lateral inhibition in a competition that can be biased by top-down activation from the language node level.

The BIA model incorporates competition between words of different languages to account for cross-language interference effects in visual word recognition described in the sections on Neighborhood Effects, Priming Effects, and Interlingual Homographs and Cognates. As a model of speech perception, the BIMOLA has to account for the empirical effects revealed in this different modality, such as the base language effect in guest word recognition (see Grosjean, 2001). To account for language context effects in speech perception, the BIMOLA implements a top-down language activation mechanism that uses global language information to activate words of a particular language.

There are no explicit representations of language nodes in the BIMOLA, but the top-down language activation mechanism included in this model can be seen as an implicit implementation of language nodes. However, the explicit language nodes in the BIA model differ from the top-down language activation mechanism in the BIMOLA because they do not activate the words of the language they represent; rather, the language nodes only inhibit words of the other language. The mechanisms, however, are similar in that they alter the relative activation of the two languages. Here, the different segregation of the lexical units and the different top-down dynamics illustrate the distinctive theoretical assumptions incorporated into visual and speech perception models of bilingual word recognition to account for the different empirical effects of each modality. In other words, the modelers implicitly assume that the different demands of recognition in each modality have led to different functional architectures.

The Semantic, Orthographic, and Phonological Interactive Activation Model Dijkstra and Van Heuven (2002) proposed a new theoretical model called the BIA+ model. This model is an extension of the BIA model to include phonological and semantic representations. Language nodes are also present in the BIA+ model, but they can no longer inhibit words of the other language. The orthographic, phonological, semantic, and language node representations are part of the identification system of the BIA+ model. In addition, the model has a task/decision system that regulates control (see Dijkstra & Van Heuven, 2002).

At this moment, the identification system of the theoretical BIA+ model has been implemented in a localist connectionist model (Van Heuven & Dijkstra, 2003). This implemented model is called the SOPHIA (semantic, orthographic, and phonological interactive activation) model. The architecture of the SOPHIA model is shown in Fig. 10.3. Unique for this model are the sublexical layers of syllables and clusters. The cluster layers consist of onset, nucleus, and coda letter and phoneme representations.

So far, simulations with this model have focused on monolingual, monosyllabic word processing. The SOPHIA model is able to account for a number of effects in monolingual visual word recognition

(priming data, the effects of consistency between orthographic and phonological codes, pseudohomophone effects, and the role of neighborhoods; Van Heuven & Dijkstra, 2001). The model is able to simulate effects that cannot be simulated by other models of visual word recognition that include representations of phonology, such as the dual route cascaded model (Coltheart, Rastle, Perry, Langdon, & Ziegler, 2001) and the MROM-p (Interactive Activation Multiple Read-Out Model of Orthographic and Phonological Processes; Jacobs, Rey, Ziegler, & Grainger, 1998). In particular, SOPHIA can account for the facilitatory effects found for words with many body neighbors in the lexical decision task (Ziegler & Perry, 1998). Body neighbors are those neighbors that share their orthographic rime with the target word. The model is currently applied to bilingual phenomena.

Conclusion

The BIA model, a localist model of bilingual orthographic language processing, has been successful in simulating several empirical data patterns, particularly those involving neighborhood effects in word recognition and in masked priming. A comparison with the BIMOLA, a model of bilingual speech perception, illustrated that different theoretical assumptions may be necessary to capture empirical effects in visual and auditory modalities. The SOPHIA model can already account for several monolingual empirical findings. The model has great potential, especially when it implements all aspects of the BIA+ model to be able to simulate a wide variety of empirical findings in bilingual language processing.

Distributed Approaches

Building a Distributed Model

The construction of distributed models of bilingual language comprehension differs from that of localist models in that it involves two stages. First, the modeler constructs representations (or codes) that will depict the relevant cognitive domains. These domains might include phonological representations of spoken words, orthographic representations of written words, representations of word meaning, or representations of the identity of words appearing in the sequential strings that make up sentences. In addition, the modeler constructs

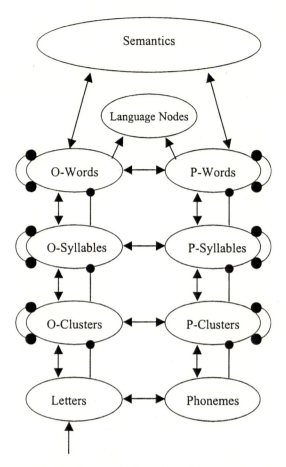

Figure 10.3 The Semantic, Orthographic, and Phonological Interactive Activation (SOPHIA) model (Van Heuven & Dijkstra, 2001, in preparation).

a network architecture that will allow the relevant associations between the domains to be learned. However, connection strengths in the network are initially randomized, so the system begins with no content. In the second stage, the model undergoes training to learn the relevant mappings, for instance, between each word's form and its meaning. It is important to realize that, in distributed models, the modeler's theory is implemented in the way initial representations are constructed and in the architecture that is chosen by the modeler to learn the mappings.

Work in the area of distributed models of bilingual memory is relatively new. In the following sections, we consider three distributed models of bilingual language comprehension. We then examine the potential of distributed models to investigate a range of phenomena of interest in bilingual language processing.

The Bilingual Single Network Model

Thomas (1997a, 1997b, 1998) considered in some depth how distributed models of the monolingual language system, such as Seidenberg and McClelland's (1989) distributed model of word recognition and reading, might be extended to the bilingual case. Two hypotheses were considered: that the bilingual has separate network resources available to learn each language, along with control structures integrating the output of each network, or that the bilingual has a single combined representational resource in which both languages are stored but each language is identified by language-specific contextual information (information that may be based on differences in phonology, on differences in context of acquisition and usage, or simply an abstract language tag). The empirical evidence from visual word recognition contains both indications of the independence of lexical representations for each language (e.g., recognition of interlingual homographs according to within-language frequency [Gerard & Scarborough, 1989], a lack of long-term repetition priming between orthographically dissimilar translation equivalents [Kirsner, Smith, Lockhart, King, & Jain, 1984]) and evidence of interference effects in cases of cross-language similarity, for instance, in the slowed recognition of interlingual homographs compared to cognate homographs under some conditions (Klein & Doctor, 1992) and the speeded recognition of cognate homographs under other conditions (Cristoffanini, Kirsner, & Milech, 1986; Gerard & Scarborough, 1989).

One of the features of distributed networks is that the internal representations they develop depend on similarity patterns within the mappings they must learn (Thomas, 2002). Given that interference between the bilingual's languages occurs when vocabulary items share some degree of similarity, Thomas (1997a, 1997b) decided to explore the single network hypothesis. This is the idea that interference effects are the consequence of attempting to store two languages in a common representational resource. The model therefore sought to capture a combination of empirical effects for independence and for interference as the emergent

product of seeking to learn the form-to-meaning relations for two languages across a single representational resource.

Thomas constructed two artificial languages of 100 items each to examine the interference effects under carefully controlled conditions. Words were constructed around consonant-vowel templates and included both a frequency structure and orthographic patterns that were either shared across the languages or distinct to one. The orthographic representations were similar to those included in the BIA model, involving the position-specific encoding of letters in monosyllabic words. Representations were constructed to encode each word's meaning, based around distributed semantic feature sets (see Plaut, 1995, for a similar monolingual implementation; De Groot, 1992, for a related theoretical proposal). Finally, a binary vector encoded language membership. The network architecture of the BSN model is shown in Fig. 10.4, with the number of units in each layer included in parentheses. This network was trained to learn the relationship between orthography and semantics.

In this model, word recognition begins by turning on the relevant units at input for the letters of the word. The connection weights then carry this activation up to the internal or hidden processing units. Further connections then activate the relevant

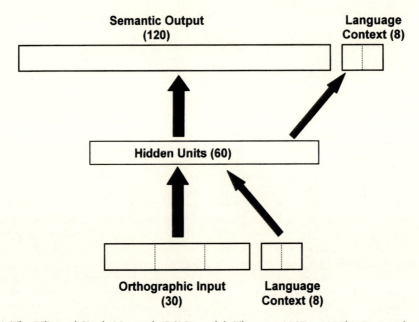

Figure 10.4 The Bilingual Single Network (BSN) model (Thomas, 1997a, 1997b). Rectangles correspond to layers of simple processing units.

semantic features for the target words. In essence, this model transforms an activation pattern for a word's orthography to a pattern for its meaning in two stages.

Examination of the respective activation patterns for each word across the hidden units can give an indication of the representations that the model has developed to recognize the words in two languages. As suggested in the discussion of modeling approaches, this set of distributed representations is less readily interpreted because it is not hand coded but the model's own solution. A statistical technique called principal components analysis allows examination of the latent similarity structure in the representations that the model has learned.

Figure 10.5 depicts the structure of the internal representations plotted on the two most prominent dimensions of a notional similarity space (which in fact has 60 dimensions, capturing decreasing levels of variance). The position of each vocabulary item is plotted in this two-dimensional space. Two versions are shown (a) under conditions of equal training on each language or (b) under conditions in which the network is exposed to one language three times as often as the other. Four pairs of words in each language are linked in the diagram, showing the representation of a cognate homograph in each language, an interlingual homograph, a translation equivalent with a different form but language-common orthography, and a translation equivalent with a different form and language-specific orthography.

This figure illustrates several points. First, the two parallel, vertical bands reveal that the network

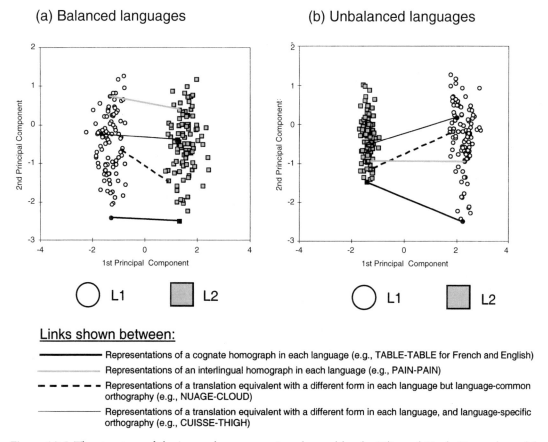

Figure 10.5 The structure of the internal representations learned by the Bilingual Single Network model for balanced and unbalanced networks. Diagrams show the positions of the words in each artificial language on the two most salient dimensions of the 60-dimensional internal similarity space (L1, first language; L2, second language).

has developed distinct representations for each language by virtue of the language membership information included in the input and output. Second, the representations contain a similarity structure that reflects the common set of meanings that the languages share. Thus, in Fig. 10.5a, words with common meanings are roughly at the same vertical level. However, the emergent internal representations also capture common orthographic forms, illustrated by the related positions of homographs. Third, in the balanced network, the orthographic characteristics of the input have been exploited to provide further structure, such that translation equivalents with language-general orthographic patterns are represented more similarly than those without (in Fig. 10.5a, the line linking the translation equivalent in each language cluster is shorter when the two forms have language-general orthography than when they have language-specific orthography). However, this distinction is not apparent in the unbalanced network, Fig. 10.5b, in which the dominance of L1 has not permitted the orthographic distinctions present in L2 to become apparent. Finally, the L2 representations in the unbalanced network are less well delineated, occupying a smaller area of representational space. The L2 has not yet been encoded in sufficient detail.

In functional terms, the model was able to demonstrate behavior illustrating both the independence of lexical representations and interference effects. In terms of independence effects, interlingual homographs showed recognition accuracy that depended on *within-language* frequency effects, and there was an absence of cross-language long-term priming effects for translation equivalents (long-term priming was implemented by giving the network extra training cycles on the prime and then testing the change in recognition accuracy of the target). In terms of interference effects, the model demonstrated a disadvantage for interlingual homographs compared to cognate homographs and, in the unbalanced network, a facilitatory effect for cognate homographs in L2. Finally, the use of the common semantic output layer allowed the model to account for cross-language semantic priming effects.

Despite reconciling effects of independence and interference, this preliminary model has several disadvantages. For example, as discussed in the section Interlingual Homographs and Cognates, interlingual homograph recognition in lexical decision depends on task demands and stimulus list composition; there is no way to achieve such flexibility in the current BSN model. In part this is because lexical decision is a complex task that may

involve the integration of multiple sources of information (see Thomas, 1997a, for a full discussion of lexical decision in the context of monolingual distributed models). Second, the model includes obvious simplifications regarding the use of two small artificial vocabulary sets.

Perhaps most serious, however, this model is able to develop bilingual representations over a single resource because its exposure to each language is simultaneous and intermixed. On the other hand, it is well known that, under conditions of sequential learning, in which training on one set of mappings ceases and another begins, models of this sort are liable to show interference effects, "forgetting" aspects of the first set of knowledge that are inconsistent with the second. This suggests that the BSN model might have difficulty capturing L2 acquisition. Empirically, the commonly held view is that L2 acquisition produces a bilingual lexicon not functionally different from when the two languages are acquired simultaneously, and L2 acquisition does not greatly interfere with L1 performance. Thomas and Plunkett (1995) explored the conditions under which such catastrophic forgetting would occur in networks trained on two (artificial) languages, one after the other. Interference was a genuine problem, although it could be overcome by increasing the salience of the information encoding language membership. We return to the issue of catastrophic forgetting in the section Potential Applications of Distributed Models to Bilingual Phenomena.

The Bilingual Simple Recurrent Network and Self-Organizing Model of Bilingual Processing

Two further distributed models have addressed how the representations for the bilingual's two languages may be acquired within a single representational resource or, more specifically, where the information comes from that allows bilinguals to separate their two languages. The aim of these models was to examine how the implicit structure of the problem faced by the bilingual might lead to the emergence of differentiated internal representations, in the first case through differences in word order in sentences, in the second through differences in word co-occurrence statistics in corpuses of each language and in the third through differences in co-occurrence statistics in the phonology of the words in each language.

French (1998) explored whether word order information would be sufficient to distinguish the two languages in the BSRN shown in Fig. 10.6. The input to the model was a set of sentences in which the language could switch with a certain probability. Each language employed a different vocabulary. French constructed a model in which the input and output representations encoded the identity of all possible words in the vocabulary. A network was used that had cycling activation, such that every word could be processed in the context of the words that had gone before it in a sentence (the so-called simple recurrent network, SRN; Elman, 1990). The network's task was to predict the next word in the sentence. To do so, the network had to acquire representations of sentence structures in each artificial language. French found that, as long as language switches occurred with a sufficiently low probability (0.1%), differences in word order alone were sufficient to develop distinct representations for each language.

Li and Farkaš (2002) developed an ambitious distributed model called the self-organizing model of bilingual processing (SOMBIP), aimed at capturing both bilingual production and comprehension. The model is shown in Fig. 10.7. This work is impressive in that, of all the models, it incorporates most psychological detail in its representation of English and Chinese phonology and in its use of a training set derived from a bilingual child language corpus. The greater the detail incorporated into the model, the more closely it should be able to simulate patterns of empirical data. The model also seeks to include stronger constraints from the neurocomputational level in its use of self-organizing maps and in the learning algorithms employed. *Self-organizing maps* are two-dimensional sheets of simple processing units that, when exposed to a set of training patterns, develop a representation of the similarity structure of the domain across the sheet of units (see Fig. 10.7). Such maps are found in the sensory cortices of the brain, where different areas of the map represent sensations from different areas of the body. In the SOMBIP, two self-organizing maps were learned, one for the representation of the sounds of words in English and Chinese and one for the meanings of words; associative links were then learned between the two maps.

Although the SOMBIP is ambitious in the number of psychological and neurocomputational constraints it incorporates, potentially increasing

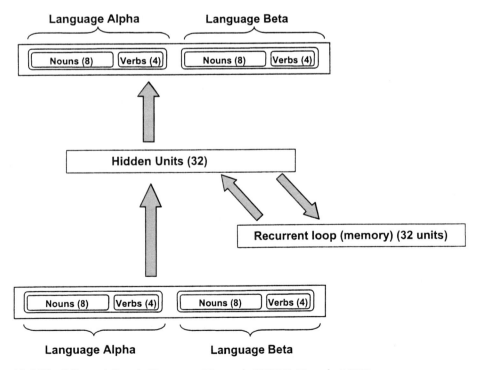

Figure 10.6 The Bilingual Simple Recurrent Network (BSRN) (French, 1998).

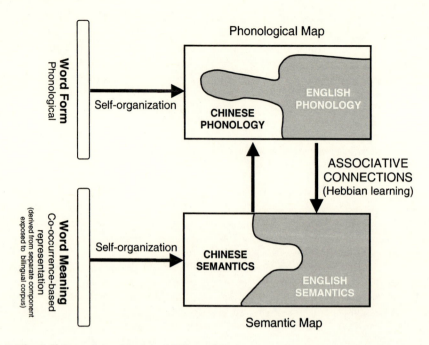

Figure 10.7 The Self-Organizing Model of Bilingual Processing (SOMBIP; Li & Farkaš, 2002).

the validity of subsequent model findings, current results are preliminary and have yet to be compared directly to empirical data. Interestingly, one of the main theoretical claims of the model is that it can account for the language-specific aspects of the bilingual lexicon without recourse to language nodes or language tags. However, some of the design decisions within the model belie this claim.

First, the phonological representations incorporate an additional vector (used to encode tonality) that only Chinese words employ. Such a vector would be sufficient to serve the same role as the language membership information built into the BSN model, information that in that case was sufficient to distinguish two languages within a single set of representations.

Second, the representations of word meaning used in the SOMBIP are based on word co-occurrence statistics (thought to be a valid indicator of meaning in the unilingual case because words with similar meanings tend to occur in similar sentence contexts). However, in the bilingual case, because the words making up the sentences of the two languages are different, this approach has the unfortunate effect of generating two entirely separate meaning systems. This is at odds with the generally held view that the bilingual lexicon has a single, language-common level of semantic representation

(see Francis, chapter 12, this volume; Chen & Ng, 1989; Kirsner et al., 1984; Potter et al., 1984; Smith, 1997). Indeed, the SOMBIP ends up developing representations for the two languages that are so different (both phonologically and semantically) that an additional training procedure has to be included specifically to allow translation equivalents to become associated.

Finally, the use of semantic representations based on word co-occurrence statistics leads to some odd assumptions in the model: One part of the system is used to derive co-occurrence statistics (not shown in Fig. 10.7). To achieve this end, this part of the system is supplied with the identities of all the words in the bilingual's two vocabularies, coded in the structure of their input representations. Yet, it is the very task of another part of the model (the phonological map) to learn these identities. Why is this necessary if the knowledge is already prewired into the system? Despite these difficulties, the SOMBIP is an interesting new model that awaits close evaluation against the empirical data.

Assessment of Existing Distributed Models

These three distributed models explore ways in which bilingual lexical representations may emerge as a consequence of exposing a learning system (construed in broadly neurocomputational terms) to the particular problem that faces the bilingual during language comprehension. The models have in common the assumption that representations will emerge over a shared representational resource. This assumption is driven by parsimony in relating the bilingual system to the unilingual system: We should first explore whether single-resource systems are capable of explaining the behavioral data before adding new assumptions to the models. In addition, the single resource provides a ready explanation for why cross-language interference effects should emerge in bilingual word recognition.

However, the alternate hypothesis that the bilingual's two language systems employ entirely separate representational resources is not quite so easily dismissed because cross-language interference effects could emerge merely from attempts to control and coordinate two competing systems. Drawing an analogy to current debates in research on reading and on inflectional morphology, Thomas (1998) discussed ways in which "single route" and "dual route" hypotheses can be distinguished empirically. In these other debates, there is a question about whether language behavior is generated by a single resource showing differential performance for different stimuli (in this case, regular and irregular items) or whether separate processing mechanisms handle each type of stimulus. Thomas (1998) concluded from this analogy that the question will not be resolved simply on the basis of cross-language interference effects in adult bilinguals, but must appeal to wider evidence concerning acquisition, language loss, and breakdown.

Distributed models of bilingual language comprehension remain at an early stage of development. In the following section, however, we suggest that, together with existing models within the monolingual domain, distributed approaches have the potential to address many of the key issues within bilingual language processing.

Potential Applications of Distributed Models to Bilingual Phenomena

The issue of separate or shared representational resources is one that may be readily examined in distributed modeling, along with interference effects and the possible encoding of language status. However, monolingual models already exist that, if extended to the bilingual domain, would allow

investigation of many of the key issues for bilingual language processing raised in the introduction. In this section, we outline some of the potential extensions.

Certainly in production, perhaps also in comprehension, language processes must be controlled according to language context, for example, to achieve a switch of language in production or to optimize recognition processes during comprehension. Several distributed models have been proposed that examine processes of control (e.g., Cohen, Dunbar, & McClelland, 1990; Gilbert & Shallice, 2002). For instance, Cohen et al. used a distributed model to demonstrate how a naming process could achieve increasing degrees of automaticity and escape from attentional control as it experienced increasing degrees of training. These models could provide a basis for new accounts of the control of bilingual language systems and the relation of control to language proficiency.

Of particular salience in work on L2 acquisition is the question of critical periods, that is, the extent to which the ability to learn an L2 is constrained by the age at which acquisition commences (see Birdsong, chapter 6, and DeKeyser & Larson-Hall, chapter 5, this volume). Assuming that languages employ the same representational resources in the cognitive system, connectionist work has explored how age of acquisition effects can occur in a single network when training on one set of patterns follows that on a first (Ellis & Lambon-Ralph, 2000). The results have demonstrated a reduction in plasticity for the second set of patterns and poorer ultimate performance. This occurred because the first set of patterns had established dominance over the representational resource and optimized it for its own needs. Such a model might provide the basis for a computational exploration of critical period effects in L2 acquisition.

The assumption that languages compete over a single representational resource is of course not a necessary one. Learning an L2 may cause the recruitment of new resources. So-called constructivist distributed networks that recruit hidden units to learn new sets of patterns would provide a profitable framework within which to explore this alternative (see Mareschal & Shultz, 1996).

However, the idea of a common resource provides a ready explanation for the interference and transfer effects during L2 acquisition (see MacWhinney, chapter 3, this volume). Early distributed modeling work examined such transfer effects within several contexts, including the acquisition of pronouns in an L2 (Blackwell & Broeder, 1992), the transfer of word order properties from L1 to L2 (Gasser, 1990), and the acquisition of gender assignment in French (Sokolik & Smith, 1992; see Broeder & Plunkett, 1994, for a review).

The idea that L2 acquisition takes place in a language system with representations that are conditioned by L1 processing may also provide the opportunity to explain other aspects of the bilingual system. For instance, Kroll and Stewart's (1994) revised hierarchical model postulates that, in L2 acquisition, L2 lexical representations initially "hang-off" L1 lexical representations before making direct connections to semantics. It is quite possible that a distributed network system, initially trained on an L1, then trained on L2, would initially adopt the internal representations conditioned by L1 lexical knowledge to drive L2 production and comprehension before undergoing the more laborious reorganization of the internal representational space that would establish direct mappings between semantics and L2 lexical knowledge. In other words, distributed models may be able to produce the revised hierarchical model as an emergent effect of the experience-driven reorganization of language representations within a distributed system.

Of course, L2-induced reorganization of representations implies a consequent effect on the original structure of L1 knowledge. We have already discussed the idea that the assumption of a single representational resource implies that decay of L1 knowledge might occur if immersion in an L2 environment entirely replaced L1 usage. An in-depth consideration of such catastrophic forgetting, including the conditions under which it should and should not occur according to neural network theory, can be found in the work of Thomas (1997a). If these models are correct, a careful study of L1 performance under intense L2 acquisition should reveal systematic (although perhaps subtle) decrements in performance. Although there are anecdotal reports of such decrements, to our knowledge these effects have yet to be studied systematically. (See Seidenberg & Zevin, in press, for a recent discussion of these issues.)

The focus of distributed models on learning mappings between codes provides the potential to account for modality-specific expertise in bilinguals because the visual versus auditory domains and the spoken versus written domains instantiate different types of codes. Expertise in one domain does not necessarily transfer to expertise in another. Plaut (2002) provided a demonstration of how graded, modality-specific specialization can occur in a self-organizing distributed model of (monolingual) naming and gesturing, an approach that is readily extendible to bilingual language processing.

Finally, the ability of distributed systems to capture change over time allows them to address issues of language decay, either when a language is no longer used (language attrition, e.g., Weltens & Grendel, 1993; see Thomas, 1997a, for discussion of insights from computational learning systems) or when a previously working bilingual system experiences deficits following brain damage (see Plaut, 1996, for discussion of distributed approaches in the monolingual domain).

In sum, much of the potential of distributed modeling shown in the monolingual domain remains to be exploited in the study of bilingual language processing.

Advantages and Disadvantages of Localist and Distributed Models

Localist and distributed connectionist models share the property that their behavior is strongly influenced by the structure of the problem domain that they encode. There are three principal dimensions for which the emphasis of these models differs in practice. First, localist networks tend to include both bottom-up and top-down connections, which allows dynamic patterns of activation to cycle through the network. Activation states therefore persist over time, allowing localist models to study the trajectory of activation states while processing a single input, for instance, in terms of "candidates" that are initially activated before the system settles on a final solution or in terms of short-term priming effects as discussed in the BIA model. In addition, alterations in top-down activation, for instance, from language nodes in the BIA model or in the baseline activation of the word units in each language in the BIMOLA, allow localist models to investigate the implications of changes in language context on recognition times. On the other hand, many distributed models have employed only bottom-up or feedforward connections. This means that processing in such distributed models is completed by a single pass through the network. Activation values are computed in a single set of calculations, with no unfolding of activation states over time. However, as the complexity of distributed models increases, this distinction is becoming less salient. So-called attractor networks are trainable distributed networks with both bottom-up and top-down connections (sometimes called *recurrent* connections). Both the bilingual SRN model and the SOMBIP permit cycles of activation in their architecture (see also Thomas, 1997a, for an extension of feedforward networks to modeling short-term priming effects using cascading activation in a feedforward network as proposed by Cohen et al., 1990).

The second, related dimension in which the modeling approaches differ relates to the type of data to which the output of the models is typically compared. Localist models with cycling activation eventually settle to a solution, which is either correct or incorrect given the task. These models therefore generate two types of data: a response time (number of cycles until the network settles into a stable solution) and an accuracy level (the percentage of trials on which the model settles onto the correct solution). Distributed models like the BSN that use a single set of calculations to derive activation values have no temporal component to processing. Although the accuracy of the output can be calculated, there is no equivalent to response time. This restricts the data against which simple distributed models can be compared.

The third difference relates to the predominant use of handwired, fixed connections in localist networks compared to learned connections in distributed models. As discussed, this characteristic makes localist models more amenable to investigating the static structure of the adult bilingual language system, whereas distributed models are more amenable to examining processes of development and change within this system (Thomas, 2002). In principle, localist models can learn their connection strengths (Page, 2000), but this possibility has yet to be exploited in bilingual research.

Although we have seen both localist and distributed models explore the behavior of a bilingual system in which proficiency is greater in one language than in the other, it is nevertheless true that connectionist models of bilingual language comprehension have failed to address the implications of acquiring an L2 when the processing structures for an L1 are already in place. In the localist model, the unbalanced bilingual was simulated by giving the two sets of language nodes different resting activation levels; in the distributed models (both the BSN and the SOMBIP), the unbalanced bilingual was simulated by training the system on two languages simultaneously, but with one language represented in the training set more than the other.

L2 acquisition remains an area to be explored using connectionist models.

In our discussion on approaches to modeling, we highlighted two central issues arising in the way that computational models are related to theory. The first of these was the importance of understanding how a model works so that a successful simulation can be directly related back to the theory that it was evaluating. This characteristic might be referred to as the *semantic transparency* of a model. On this point, note that localist computational models have often been viewed as superior because the activation of each processing node corresponds to the confidence level that a certain concept is present in the input (whether it is a letter feature, a letter, a word, or a language). Every activation state can therefore be readily interpreted. Even unexpected emergent characteristics of IA models that arise from the combination of bottom-up and top-down connections can be recharacterized in theoretical terms.

On the other hand, distributed models in their trained state produce activation patterns across the hidden units without immediate semantic interpretations. Although analytical tools are available to investigate the computational solutions that the distributed network has learned (for instance, the principal components analysis that produced diagrams of the similarity structure of the internal representations in the BSN in Fig. 10.5), the requirement of additional analysis testifies to their reduced semantic transparency. The consequence is increased difficulty in relating particular distributed models back to the theory that generated them.[1]

This brings us to our second issue. Decisions about the particular processing structures chosen in the model may implicitly influence the theoretical hypotheses considered by the modeler. Distributed models are often harder to interpret because, during learning, the network explores a wider range of solutions than the modeler considers when handwiring a localist model. Although the distributed model is potentially less easy to understand, it is also potentially richer.

Two examples suffice. The BIA model includes language nodes that receive activation from the word units in a given language. Each word is effectively given equal membership to a language, an assumption the modeler makes by giving the same value to each connection between a word unit and its language node. However, in a model like the BSN, although language context information is provided with every input, the network is under no obligation to use this information in learning the meaning of each word. The essential point about trainable networks is that they evolve processing structures sufficient to achieve the task. Therefore, it is quite possible that a distributed system will use language context information only to the extent that it is necessary to perform the task (Thomas, 2002). For instance, it may use it to disambiguate interlingual homographs, but not cognate homographs, for the latter have the same status whatever the language context. Thus, the distributed model allows itself the theoretical hypothesis that language membership may not be a universal, uniform representational construct, but a continuum that depends on the specific demands of the task. The flip side is that network solutions embodying such "shades of gray" hypotheses may be harder to understand, but that does not make such hypotheses a priori more unlikely.

Second, representational states adopted by distributed systems may change the way we interpret empirical data. Here, we take an example from monolingual word recognition. Early in the recognition of an ambiguous word like *bank*, priming can be found for both the word's meanings ("money" and "river"). A localist interpretation might encourage the following view: that there are independent, localist representations of each reading of the ambiguous word, and that both readings are initially activated during word recognition, but that subsequently the system settles into a single context-appropriate reading. However, a recurrent distributed network trained to recover the meanings of words from their written forms offers another theoretical possibility.

Kawamoto (1993) used a single representational resource to store the form-meaning mappings for a single language. In this network, the two meanings of an ambiguous word were distinguished by the context in which they were used. When the model was required to recognize the word in one of those two contexts, it went through an intermediate representational state that bore similarity to both meanings before diverging to settle on one of the meanings. This model could account for the empirical data without requiring the simultaneous activation of independent, competing representations because the intermediate, hybrid state could prime words related to either meaning. This model is relevant because the simultaneous activation of independent, subsequently competing representations is a processing assumption that is normally built into localist models, yet a distributed system with a single representational resource may well be able to account for empirical data suggestive of a localist architecture. Again, the implicit assumptions within different models encourage consideration of different theoretical hypotheses.

Finally, connectionist models embody abstract principles of neural computation and, as seen in the Li and Farkaš model, the SOMBIP, a desire to include more constraints from neural processing. This approach encourages us to hope that one day connectionist models of cognitive processing in bilingualism may make contact with functional data gathered from the neural substrate, both under normal circumstances and in breakdown.

What type of data might the more "neurally plausible" bilingual connectionist model attempt to account for? In bilingual aphasia, evidence suggests one or both languages may be impaired by brain damage, and patterns of recovery include the parallel recovery of both languages, selective recovery of one language, antagonistic recovery of one language at the expense of another, or alternate antagonistic recovery in which selective impairment of comprehension/production can alternate between the languages during recovery (see e.g., Green & Price, 2001). Such evidence suggests that bilingual connectionist models will have to be able to simulate selective damage and recovery of a single language as well as selective damage of control structures necessary to account for alternate antagonism (Green, 1986, 1998).

In bilingual brain imaging, data from comprehension studies suggested that early bilinguals, who receive equal practice with their two languages from birth, process both languages with common neural machinery, corresponding to the classical language areas of the brain. In late bilinguals, the degree of language proficiency determines the pattern of neural organization, with highly proficient L2 users showing common areas, but less-proficient subjects showing different patterns of activation for the two languages (Abutalebi, Cappa, & Perani, 2001; see also chapter 24, this volume). Distributed connectionist models embodying increasing neural constraints should aim to reflect the role of language proficiency in determining whether the bilingual comprehension system engages separate or combined computational machinery.

Conclusion

We have argued that the use of computational models is essential for the development of psycholinguistic theories of bilingual language comprehension (and indeed production). We explored localist and distributed networks, examining the bilingual data to which each model has been applied, and the types of bilingual phenomena that each model has the potential to illuminate. Nevertheless, the modeling of bilingual language processing is at an early stage. The localist approach is perhaps more advanced than the distributed approach and, at this stage of theory development, perhaps a more useful research tool. On the other hand, distributed models may have the greater potential given the range of phenomena that have been explored within the unilingual domain that have direct relevance to bilingual language processing. Currently, it is a time for researchers to use different modeling tools to investigate different issues within bilingualism. Eventually, however, these models must come together to generate a (semantically transparent) model that explains how two languages can be acquired, maintained, and controlled in a dynamically changing cognitive system.

Note

1. Interestingly, Li and Farkas (2002) claimed that their model combines the advantages of both localist and distributed models in that it is not only trainable, but also semantically interpretable. Clearly, a model that can address developmental phenomena as well as being easily comprehensible is advantageous. However, the semantic transparency of their model is achieved at some expense to psychological plausibility. The SOMBIP forces not only its words, but also its meanings to be represented over only two dimensions each. It is not clear that this is plausible on psychological grounds, or indeed on neural grounds—the inspiration for cortical maps comes from sensory cortex. Whether the representations of meaning or word forms are driven by the same organizational principles is an open question. However, the depiction of all possible word meanings as $x–y$ coordinates on a two dimensions would seem perhaps too great a simplification for the representation of semantics, compared to the more usual depiction of meaning as a large set of (perhaps hierarchically structured) features.

References

Abutalebi, J., Cappa, S. F., & Perani, D. (2001). The bilingual brain as revealed by functional neuroimaging. *Bilingualism: Language and Cognition, 4*, 179–190.

Baayen, H., Piepenbrock, R., & Van Rijn, H. (1993). *The CELEX lexical database (CD-ROM)*. Philadelphia: University of Pennsylvania, Linguistic Data Consortium.

Bijeljac-Babic, R., Biardeau, A., & Grainger, J. (1997). Masked orthographic priming in bilingual word recognition. *Memory and Cognition, 25*, 447–457.

Blackwell, A., & Broeder, P. (1992, May). *Interference and facilitation in SLA: A connectionist perspective*. Paper presented at Seminar on Parallel Distributed Processing and Natural Language Processing, University of California at San Diego.

Broeder, P., & Plunkett, K. (1994). Connectionism and second language acquisition. In N. C. Ellis (Ed.), *Implicit and explicit learning of languages* (pp. 421–455). London: Academic Press.

Chen, H.-C., and Ng, M. L. (1989). Semantic facilitation and translation priming effects in Chinese-English bilinguals. *Memory and Cognition, 17*, 454–462.

Cohen, J. D., Dunbar, K., & McClelland, J. L. (1990). On the control of automatic processes: A parallel distributed processing account of the Stroop effect. *Psychological Review, 97*, 332–361.

Coltheart, M., Rastle, K., Perry, C., Langdon, R., & Ziegler, J. C. (2001). DRC: A dual cascaded model of visual word recognition and reading aloud, *Psychological Review, 108*, 204–256.

Cristoffanini, P., Kirsner, K., & Milech, D. (1986). Bilingual lexical representation: The status of Spanish-English cognates. *The Quarterly Journal of Experimental Psychology, 38A*, 367–393.

De Groot, A. M. B. (1992). Bilingual lexical representation: A closer look at conceptual representations. In R. Frost & L. Katz (Eds.), *Orthography, phonology, morphology, and meaning* (pp. 389–412). Amsterdam: Elsevier.

De Groot, A. M. B., Delmaar, P., & Lupker, S. J. (2000). The processing of interlexical homographs in translation recognition and lexical decision: support for non-selective access to bilingual memory. *Quarterly Journal of Experimental Psychology, 53A*, 397–428.

Dijkstra, A., De Bruijn, E. R. A., Schriefers, H. J., & Ten Brinke, S. (2000) More on interlingual homograph recognition: Language intermixing versus explicitness of instruction. *Bilingualism: Language and Cognition, 3*, 69–78.

Dijkstra, A., Grainger, J., & Van Heuven, W. J. B. (1999). Recognition of cognates and interlingual homographs: The neglected role of phonology. *Journal of Memory and Language, 41*, 496–518.

Dijkstra, A., Van Jaarsveld, H., & Ten Brinke, S. (1998). Interlingual homograph recognition: Effects of task demands and language intermixing. *Bilingualism, 1*, 51–66.

Dijkstra, A., Timmermans, M., & Schriefers, H. (2000). Cross-language effects on bilingual homograph recognition. *Journal of Memory and Language, 42*, 445–464.

Dijkstra, A., & Van Heuven, W. J. B. (1998). The BIA model and bilingual word recognition. In J. Grainger & A. M. Jacobs (Eds.), *Localist connectionist approaches to human cognition* (pp. 189–225). Mahwah, NJ: Erlbaum.

Dijkstra, A., & Van Heuven, W. J. B. (2002). The architecture of the bilingual word recognition system: From identification to decision. *Bilingualism: Language and Cognition, 5*, 175–197.

Dijkstra, A., Van Heuven, W. J. B., & Grainger, J. (1998). Simulating competitor effects with the bilingual interactive activation model. *Psychologica Belgica, 38*, 177–196.

Ellis, A., & Lambon-Ralph, M. A. (2000). Age of acquisition effects in adult lexical processing reflect loss of plasticity in maturing systems: Insights from connectionist networks. *Journal of Experimental Psychology: Learning, Memory, and Cognition, 26*, 1103–1123.

Elman, J. (1990). Finding structure in time. *Cognitive Science, 14*, 179–211.

Ferrand, L., & Grainger, J. (1992). Phonology and orthography in visual word recognition: Evidence from masked nonword priming. *Quarterly Journal of Experimental Psychology, 42A*, 353–372.

Forster, K. I. (1976). Accessing the mental lexicon. In E. C. J. Walker & R. J. Wales (Eds.), *New approaches to language mechanisms*. Amsterdam: North-Holland.

Forster, K. I., Davis, C., Schoknecht, C., & Carter, R. (1987). Masked priming with graphemically related forms: Repetition or partial activation. *The Quarterly Journal of Experimental Psychology, 39A*, 211–251.

French, R. M. (1998). A simple recurrent network model of bilingual memory. In M. A. Gernsbacher & S. J. Derry (Eds.), *Proceedings of the 20th Annual Conference of the Cognitive Science Society* (pp. 368–373). Mahwah, NJ: Erlbaum.

Gasser, M. (1990). Connectionism and universals of second language acquisition. *Studies in Second Language Acquisition, 12*, 179–199.

Gerard, L. D., & Scarborough, D. L. (1989). Language-specific lexical access of homographs by bilinguals. *Journal of Experimental Psychology: Learning, Memory, and Cognition, 15*, 305–315.

Gilbert, S. J., & Shallice, T. (2002). Task switching: A PDP model. *Cognitive Psychology, 44*, 297–337.

Grainger, J., & Dijkstra, A. (1992). On the representation and use of language information in bilinguals. In R. J. Harris (Ed.), *Cognitive processing in bilinguals* (pp. 207–220). Amsterdam: Elsevier Science.

Grainger, J., & Jacobs, A. M. (1996). Orthographic processing in visual word recognition: A multiple read-out model. *Psychological Review, 103*, 518–565.

Green, D. W. (1986). Control, activation and resource: a framework and a model for the control of speech in bilinguals. *Brain and Language, 27*, 210–223.

Green, D. W. (1998). Mental control of the bilingual lexico-semantic system *Bilingualism: Language and Cognition, 1*, 67–81.

Green, D. W., & Price, C. J. (2001). Functional imaging in the study of recovery patterns in bilingual aphasia. *Bilingualism: Language and Cognition, 4*, 191–201.

Grosjean, F. (2001). The bilingual's language modes. In J. L. Nicol (Ed.), *One mind, two languages: Bilingual language processing*. Oxford: Blackwell.

Jacobs, A. M., & Grainger, J. (1992). Testing a semi-stochastic variant of the interactive activation model in different word recognition experiments. *Journal of Experimental Psychology: Human Perception and Performance, 18*, 1174–1188.

Jacobs, A. M., Rey, A., Ziegler, J. C., & Grainger, J. (1998). MROM-p: An interactive activation, multiple read-out model of orthographic and phonological processes in visual word recognition. In J. Grainger & A. M. Jacobs (Eds.), *Localist connectionist approaches to human cognition* (pp. 147–188). Mahwah, NJ: Erlbaum.

Kawamoto, A. H. (1993). Nonlinear dynamics in the resolution of lexical ambiguity: A parallel distributed processing account. *Journal of Memory and Language, 32*, 474–516.

Kirsner, K., Smith, M. C., Lockhart, R. L. S., King, M. L., & Jain, M. (1984). The bilingual lexicon: Language-specific units in an integrated network. *Journal of Verbal Learning and Verbal Behavior, 23*, 519–539.

Klein, D., & Doctor, E. A. (1992). Homography and polysemy as factors in bilingual word recognition. *South African Journal of Psychology, 22*, 10–16.

Kroll, J. F., & Stewart, E. (1994) Category interference in translation and picture naming: Evidence for asymmetric connections between bilingual memory representations. *Journal of Memory and Language, 33*, 149–174.

Léwy, N., & Grosjean, F. (1997). A computational model of bilingual lexical access. Manuscript in preparation, Neuchâtel Univesity, Switzerland.

Li, P., & Farkas, I. (2002). A self-organizing connectionist model of bilingual processing. In

R. Heredia & J. Altarriba (Eds.), Bilingual sentence processing (pp. 59–85). North-Holland, The Netherlands: Elsevier Science.

Mareschal, D., & Shultz, T. R. (1996). Generative connectionist architectures and constructivist cognitive development. *Cognitive Development, 11,* 571–605.

McClelland, J. L., & Elman, J. L. (1986). The TRACE model of speech perception. *Cognitive Psychology, 18,* 1–86.

McClelland, J. L., & Rumelhart, D. E. (1981). An interactive activation model of context effects in letter perception, Part 1: An account of basic findings. *Psychological Review, 88,* 375–405.

Meyer, D. E., & Ruddy, M. G. (1974, June). *Bilingual word recognition: Organization and retrieval of alternative lexical codes.* Paper presented at the annual meeting of the Eastern Psychological Association, Philadelphia.

Morton, J. (1969). Interaction of information in word recognition. *Psychological Review, 76,* 165–178.

Page, M. (2000). Connectionist modelling in psychology: A localist manifesto. *Behavioral and Brain Sciences, 23,* 443–512.

Plaut, D. C. (1995). Semantic and associative priming in a distributed attractor network. In *Proceedings of the 17th Annual Conference of the Cognitive Science Society* (pp. 37–42). Hillsdale, NJ: Erlbaum.

Plaut, D. C. (1996). Relearning after damage in connectionist networks: Toward a theory of rehabilitation. *Brain and Language, 52,* 25–82.

Plaut, D. C. (2002). Graded modality-specific specialization in semantics: A computational account of optic aphasia. *Cognitive Neuropsychology, 19,* 603–639.

Potter, M. C., So, K-F., Von Eckardt, B., & Feldman, L. B. (1984). Lexical and conceptual representation in beginning and more proficient bilinguals. *Journal of Verbal Learning and Verbal Behavior, 23,* 23–38.

Rumelhart, D. E., & McClelland J. L. (1982). An interactive activation model of context effects in letter perception: Part 2. The contextual enhancement effect and some tests and extensions of the model. *Psychological Review, 89,* 60–94.

Seidenberg, M. S. (1993). Connectionist models and cognitive theory. *Psychological Science, 4,* 228–235.

Seidenberg, M. S., & McClelland, J. L. (1989). A distributed, developmental model of word recognition and naming. *Psychological Review, 96,* 523–568.

Seidenberg, M. S., & Zevin, J. (in press). Computational models in cognitive development: The case of critical periods in language learning. In M. Johnson & Y. Munakata (Eds.), *Attention and Performance 21.* Oxford, U.K.: Oxford University Press.

Smith, M. C. (1997). How do bilinguals access lexical information? In A. M. B. de Groot & J. F. Kroll (Eds.), *Tutorials in bilingualism: Psycholinguistic perspectives* (pp. 145–168). Hillsdale, NJ: Erlbaum.

Sokolik, M., & Smith, M. (1992). Assignment of gender to French nouns in primary and secondary language: A connectionist model. *Second Language Research, 8,* 39–58.

Thomas, M. S. C. (1997a). *Connectionist networks and knowledge representation: The case of bilingual lexical processing.* Unpublished doctoral thesis, Oxford University, England.

Thomas, M. S. C. (1997b). Distributed representations and the bilingual lexicon: One store or two? In J. Bullinaria, D. Glasspool, & G. Houghton (Eds.), *Proceedings of the Fourth Annual Neural Computation and Psychology Workshop* (pp. 240–253). London: Springer.

Thomas, M. S. C. (1998). Bilingualism and the single route/dual route debate. In M. A. Gernsbacher & S. J. Derry (Eds.), *Proceedings of the 20th Annual Conference of the Cognitive Science Society* (pp. 1061–1066). Mahwah, NJ: Erlbaum.

Thomas, M. S. C. (2002). Theories that develop. *Bilingualism: Language and Cognition, 5,* 216–217.

Thomas, M. S. C., & Plunkett, K. (1995). Representing the bilingual's two lexicons. In J. D. Moore & J. F. Lehman (Eds.), *Proceedings of the 17th Annual Cognitive Science Society Conference* (pp. 760–765). Hillsdale, NJ: Erlbaum.

Van Heuven, W. J. B., & Dijkstra, A. (2001, September). *The Semantic, Orthographic, and PHonological Interactive Activation Model.* Poster presented at the 12th Conference of the European Society for Cognitive Psychology, Edinburgh, Scotland.

Van Heuven, W. J. B., & Dijkstra, A. (2003). *The semantic, orthographic, and phonological interactive activation model.* Manuscript in preparation.

Van Heuven, W. J. B., Dijkstra, A., & Grainger, J. (1998). Orthographic neighborhood effects in bilingual word recognition. *Journal of Memory and Language, 39,* 458–483.

Weltens, B., & Grendel, M. (1993). Attrition of vocabulary knowledge. In R. Schreuder & B. Weltens (Eds.), *The bilingual lexicon* (pp. 135–155). Amsterdam: Benjamins.

Ziegler, J. C., & Perry, C. (1998). No more problems in Coltheart's neighborhood: Resolving neighborhood conflicts in the lexical decision task. *Cognition, 68,* B53–B62.

Rosa Sánchez-Casas
José E. García-Albea

11

The Representation of Cognate and Noncognate Words in Bilingual Memory

*Can Cognate Status Be Characterized
as a Special Kind of Morphological Relation?*

ABSTRACT   One of the main issues addressed in bilingual research has been how bilinguals represent and access the words from their two languages. Studies carried out in different languages suggest that the distinction between cognate (words that are similar in form and meaning) and noncognate (words only similar in meaning) translations can be relevant in determining how words are represented in the bilingual lexicon. In the present chapter, we review a program of research in which we examined the visual recognition of these two types of translations in Spanish-English and Catalan-Spanish bilinguals in experiments using the priming paradigm and the lexical decision task. These experiments showed on the one hand that facilitation effects are only obtained with cognate translations and on the other that these effects cannot be the result of mere form and/or meaning similarity. The latter also seems to hold for morphological priming effects within a language. On the other hand, they showed that cognate facilitation effects do not differ from those obtained with morphologically related words both within and between languages. On the basis of this evidence, we propose that cognate words are represented differently from other words related across languages (either by form or meaning), and that this representation can be characterized in morphological terms. The implications of these data for models of bilingual word recognition are discussed.

Current bilingual lexical research focuses on two main questions. One of them is how words from two languages are represented and organized in bilingual memory; the other is how these words are accessed during language processing. The work we present in this chapter concerns the first of these questions, although it is clear that the two are closely related.

Traditionally, there have been two alternative theories concerning bilingual lexical representation: One is the *common memory* theory, which postulates a single integrated memory system for both languages (*compound bilingualism* according to the terminology of Weinreich, 1953/1974). The other is known as the *multiple-memory* theory, and

claims that words from each language are represented separately (*coordinate bilingualism*). Conflicting results regarding these two theories (see Durgunoglu & Roediger, 1987) led to the proposal of mixed hierarchical models (e.g., Kroll, 1993; Kroll & Stewart, 1994; Potter, So, Von Eckardt, & Feldman, 1984) that try to reconcile the former two views by postulating two distinct levels of representation: a (surface) lexical level and a (deep) conceptual level (see Smith, 1997, for evidence on this distinction). A major question that has been asked within the framework of this type of model is not whether there is one bilingual system or two, but how and to what extent the words from the bilingual's two languages are interconnected at both the lexical and conceptual levels (see De Groot, 1993, 2001; Kroll, 1993; and Sánchez-Casas, 1999, for reviews).

The answer to this question appears to depend on two types of variables: variables related to the language user, such as level of proficiency, experience, and learning environment of the second language (L2) (e.g., Chen, 1990; De Groot & Poot, 1997; Kroll, 1993; Kroll & Stewart, 1994; Potter et al., 1984; Talamas, Kroll, & Dufour, 1999); and word type variables, such as "cognate status," concreteness, and word frequency (e.g., Davis, Sánchez-Casas, & García-Albea, 1991; De Groot, 1993; De Groot & Nas, 1991; Dijkstra, Grainger, & Van Heuven, 1999; García-Albea, Sánchez-Casas, & Igoa, 1998; Gollan, Forster, & Frost, 1997; Sánchez-Casas, Davis, & García-Albea, 1992). (See De Groot, 2001, for a general overview of the effects of these variables.) The research reported in this chapter focuses on the role of one word type variable, cognate status. Its general aim is to provide some preliminary evidence that morphological relationships across languages determine the way cognate words are represented in the bilingual lexicon.

The influence of morphology in language processing has attracted increasing attention in psycholinguistic research during the last years, especially in relation to issues concerning lexical representation and processes. This is not surprising if one takes into account that morphological features are considered critical in defining the structure of words, thereby affecting other linguistic levels (semantic, syntactic, and phonological/orthographic) (García-Albea et al., 1998). Many studies in different languages have investigated the role of morphology in the organization of the mental lexicon (e.g., Feldman, 1995; Frost & Katz, 1992; Sandra & Taft, 1994; see the special issue of *Language and Cognitive Processes*, Frost & Grainger, 2000). However, these studies have been restricted to experiments with native speakers of a single language, and very few attempts have been made to explore this issue across languages (but see Cristoffanini, Kirsner, & Milech, 1986; Kirsner, Lalor, & Hird, 1993).

In monolingual research, many studies have attempted to determine whether morphological relations are represented independent of both form (orthographic/phonological) and meaning relationships (see García-Albea et al., 1998, for a review). This question is a critical one because words that are morphologically related share a common root or stem; because of this, they tend to share orthographic/phonological characteristics as well as semantic features. Therefore, morphological relations may in fact have to be reduced to a convergence of semantic, phonological, and orthographic relationships without explicit representation themselves in the lexicon. Generally, these studies have provided evidence that morphological relations are something special and different from form and meaning relationships, and that they can be coded in the lexicon as an independent level of representation (e.g., Drews & Zwitserlood, 1995; Frost, Deutsch, Gilboa, Tannenbaum, & Marslen-Wilson, 2000; Frost, Forster, & Deutsch, 1997; Garcia-Albea et al., 1998; Marslen-Wilson, Tyler, Waksler, & Older, 1994).

In bilingual research, similar questions could be asked, now regarding word relations across languages. In particular, we deal with cognate translations that, similar to morphologically related words, have a common root and are semantically and orthographically (and at times phonologically) similar (e.g., *rico–rich, torre–tower*) or even identical (e.g., *animal–animal*). Given these similarities, it may be the case that a cognate relation between words can be reduced to a mere form or meaning similarity between them. However, it may also be the case that a cognate relation is a special kind of morphological relation, and, as some morphologically related words, they are jointly represented in the bilingual lexicon. These are the two issues addressed in this chapter (see also Friel & Kennison, 2001, for a comparison of methods for operationalizing cognate status).

First, we review some studies that deal with priming effects with cognate and noncognate translations, thus showing the relevance of the distinction between these two types of translations in the study of bilingual lexical representation. Second, we describe a series of experiments carried out with Spanish-English and Catalan-Spanish bilinguals; these experiments investigated the role of form or meaning similarity in lexical representation across languages by contrasting the cognate relation between words with two other types of word relations: those for which the critical words were only similar in meaning (i.e., noncognate words, e.g., *libro–book, hoja–sheet*) and those for which the critical words only shared a similar form (false friends, e.g., *gamo–game, torno–torch*). Third, we review some preliminary evidence from two further experiments using Catalan-Spanish bilinguals and in which morphological effects across languages and within the same language are compared for both cognate and noncognate translations.

Finally, we discuss the implications of these findings for current bilingual lexical models.

The Cognate and Noncognate Distinction: Evidence From Priming Studies

As mentioned, there is evidence to suggest that one of the variables that modulates the way in which words are represented in bilingual memory concerns the characteristics of the word themselves. One of these characteristics examined in a variety of studies and across a variety of languages is the *cognate status* of the translation pair. In these studies, the priming paradigm was one of the procedures most often used. This paradigm tests whether the presentation of a word (the prime) facilitates the recognition of another word (the target), which is subsequently presented. The prime either can be clearly visible (unmasked or standard priming) or presented under conditions in which it is not available for conscious report (masked priming). The response times and error rates on primed target words are compared to those on unprimed words (controls) using tasks such as lexical decision, naming, or semantic categorization. In the bilingual version of this procedure, prime and target belong to different languages, allowing to determine whether priming effects are obtained across languages and thus investigation of the possible connections between words from the two languages in bilingual memory.

The studies that used the standard priming procedure found different patterns of priming effects with cognate and noncognate translations. Some studies showed facilitatory effects with cognate translations (e.g., Cristoffanini et al., 1986; Gerard & Scarborough, 1989; Kerkman, 1984, cited in De Groot, 1993), and others failed to obtain facilitation with noncognate translations (e.g., Cristoffanini et al., 1986; Kirsner, 1986; Kirsner, Brown, Abrol, Chadha, & Sharma, 1980; Kirsner, Smith, Lockhart, King, & Jain, 1984; Scarborough, Gerard, & Cortese, 1984). Yet, other studies, which used shorter SOAs (stimulus onset asynchronies) than those just referred to (less than 300 ms), obtained facilitatory effects with both cognate (De Groot & Nas, 1991) and noncognate translations (e.g., Altarriba, 1992; Chen & Ng, 1989; De Groot & Nas, 1991; Jin, 1990; Schwanenflugel & Rey, 1986).

One of the problems with the standard priming technique used in these studies is that the observed facilitation effects may not be reflecting lexical processing. This may be either because the technique is sensitive to episodic contamination or because of the influences of strategic factors. That is, if the priming technique used allows subjects to consciously identify the priming stimulus, this stimulus will be recorded in episodic memory, and then it would not be possible to separate a lexical priming effect from general memory effects. This will be the case when both long and short SOAs are used (e.g., De Groot, 1983; Feldman & Moskovlijevic, 1987; Feustel, Shiffrin, & Salasoo, 1983; Forster & Davis, 1984; Oliphant, 1983). When the prime presentation is long, subjects will become aware of its relation with the target and can develop a strategy to translate the prime before the target is presented. If this happens, the observed cross-language priming effects could be caused by a reactivation of the episodic trace of the prime's translation and not by residual activation in the reactivated prime's lexical representation. In that case, one would be measuring within-language priming and not cross-language priming (Gollan et al., 1997).

Presenting the prime for a shorter period and following it immediately by the target also is not free of problems because the subjects are still aware of the prime, and the relation between prime and target becomes more transparent. This may encourage the use of certain response strategies. As an example, it is possible that subjects are more inclined to make "yes" responses when the target is preceded by a related word (a translation or a semantically related word) than when it follows an unrelated prime, thus resulting in priming for the related prime–target pairs (for a detailed discussion of the contribution of episodic and strategic factors to priming effects see De Groot & Nas, 1991; Forster, 1998; Forster & Davis, 1984; Tenpenny, 1995).

The influence of these factors can be reduced if the prime is presented under masked conditions (Forster & Davis, 1984; Forster, Davis, Schoknecht, & Carter, 1987). In this procedure, a sequence of visual stimuli is presented in rapid succession, with each stimulus superimposed on the previous one. First, a sequence of hatches (#) is presented for 500 ms, acting as a forward mask. Then, the prime is displayed in lowercase for about 60 ms; finally, the uppercase target is presented for 500 ms. The target also acts as a backward mask. Under these conditions, subjects are not aware of the prime, which reduces the possible influence of episodic and strategic factors. Importantly, there is clear evidence that supports the lexical nature of the masked priming effects, making this procedure more adequate to examine issues related to bilingual lexical memory than the unmasked procedures (e.g., Forster et al., 1987; Forster & Davis, 1984).

Later studies adopted this or a similar priming procedure (e.g., De Groot & Nas, 1991; García-Albea et al., 1998; Gollan et al., 1997; Grainger & Frenck-Mestre, 1998). These studies aimed at investigating the central concern of this chapter: the cognate status of translation pairs. De Groot and Nas (1991) carried out a series of lexical decision experiments (with English-Dutch bilinguals) in which subjects had to decide whether a sequence of letters was a word. Cognate and noncognate prime–target pairs were compared using both masked and unmasked procedures. Both cognate and noncognate translations showed facilitatory effects, but cross-language associative priming (i.e., priming between semantic associates) was only observed in the case of cognate translations (e.g., *baker* will prime *brood* ["bread" in English], but *blanket* will not prime *laken* ["sheet" in English]). On the basis of these findings, the authors suggested that the representation of the words in the two types of translation pairs are connected at the lexical level of representation (as tapped by the translation priming technique), but that only the representations of words in cognate translation pairs, not those of noncognate translations, are linked at the conceptual level of representation (as tapped by the association priming technique).

Like De Groot and Nas (1991), Williams (1994), using the same masking procedure and the lexical decision task, also reported facilitatory effects with noncognate translations. However, other studies have failed to do so (García-Albea et al., 1998; García-Albea, Sánchez-Casas, Bradley, & Forster, 1985; Grainger & Frenck-Mestre, 1998; Sánchez-Casas, Davis, & García-Albea, 1992). This inconsistency may be explained by two factors: the language in which prime and target were presented (either first language L1-L2 or L2-L1) and the exact masking procedure used.

The possible relevance of the languages of the prime and the target was suggested by Grainger and Frenck-Mestre (1998). In particular, the authors proposed that, for priming effects to emerge, the prime has to be in L1 and the target in L2, which is the way that both De Groot and Nas (1991) and Williams (1994) tested their bilingual subjects. As we discuss in the next section later, this suggestion is consistent with the results of other studies that have obtained a pattern of asymmetric

masked priming effects (e.g., Davis & Schoknecht, 1996; Gollan et al., 1997; Jiang, 1999).

The relevance of the exact nature of the masking procedure was pointed out by Davis et al. (1991). Specifically, De Groot and Nas (1991) and Williams (1994) presented the primes in uppercase letters and the targets in lowercase. Furthermore, the prime was longer than the target in number of letters. Consequently, the masking of the prime may not have been complete, and therefore the prime could have been "more available" to the subject than in the display used by Forster and Davis (1984). In fact, reanalyzing the data reported by De Groot and Nas along these lines, it can be observed that the magnitude of the priming effects with noncognate words decreased as a function of prime availability. In particular, when the prime was visible, the reported effect was 113 ms; when the prime and target were not matched in length, the effect was 40 ms; and when Forster and Davis's display was used (lowercase primes and uppercase targets), the effect was reduced to 22 ms. Given these considerations, the results of De Groot and Nas are not necessarily inconsistent with the pattern of results that other authors, using masked priming, reported for cognate and noncognate translations.

Clearer evidence concerning the distinction between cognate and noncognate translations was provided by Davis et al. (1991) in a series of experiments carried out with Spanish-English bilinguals who were competent in both languages. These authors also used a lexical decision task combined with a masked priming procedure (Forster et al., 1987) to compare the pattern of effects of cognate and noncognate translations. But, contrary to previous studies, they tested their bilingual subjects in the two language directions (i.e., Spanish prime–English target and English prime–Spanish target). Three priming conditions were included for each translation type: (a) an identity condition for which prime and target were the same word (e.g., *clear–clear, tail–tail*); (b) a translation condition for which the target was the translation of the prime (e.g., *claro–clear, cola–tail*); and (c) a form control condition for which the target was preceded by a nonword prime with the same orthographic similarity with the target, as in the case of cognate translation pairs (e.g., *clarn–clear, tair–tail*). In addition to this form control, Davis et al. varied the form overlap (in number of letters) between the cognate translation pairs (e.g., *rich–rico, tower–torre*), because some previous unmasked priming results had suggested that the cognate effects may be caused by the cognates' form similarity (Gerard & Scarborough, 1989). The authors also examined the possible influence of language dominance by testing three groups of bilinguals (balanced, Spanish dominant, English dominant) and a fourth group with a low competence in English (that they called semibilinguals).

Davis et al. (1991) found that cognate translations produced a robust facilitatory effect; there was no trend for noncognate priming at all. What is more, the size of the cognate priming effect was the same as of the effect observed with identity prime–target pairs. In addition, the cognate facilitatory effects were not affected by the degree of orthographic similarity. Finally, in contrast to other masked priming studies also examining proficient bilinguals (e.g., Gollan et al., 1997), those effects were obtained regardless of the language of prime and target (i.e., they occurred both when Spanish words were used as primes and English as targets and vice versa) and were of a similar size in the three bilingual groups (balanced, Spanish dominant, and English dominant). In some respects, the pattern of priming effects for the semibilingual group differed from that observed for the bilingual groups. In particular, this group of Spanish speakers, less proficient in their L2 (i.e., English), also did not show noncognate priming effects; priming effects were obtained with cognate words, although only when the prime was in L1 (Spanish) and the target in L2 (English). This suggests that some level of competence is required for cognate priming effects to emerge in both directions (see Mildred, 1986, for similar evidence).

Leaving for the moment the pattern of results for the semibilingual group, the findings reported by Davis et al. (1991) for the proficient bilingual groups clearly demonstrated that cognate and noncognate translations showed different patterns of priming effects. Interestingly, they provided some initial evidence to support the view that the degree of form similarity does not affect the magnitude of the facilitatory effects obtained for cognates, and that meaning similarity by itself (as in noncognate words) does not suffice to produce cross-language priming effects. It should also be stressed that cognate priming effects were not different from identity priming effects and did not change as a function of the language direction of the prime and target and were not affected by the language dominance of the bilingual participants. What do these results suggest?

To answer this question, we first have to ask how masked priming effects arise. One possible interpretation is that such priming effects are the result of persistent activation in the critical memory representations (e.g., Evett & Humphreys, 1981). That is, when the prime is presented, it induces activation in the corresponding word detector in memory. The induced activation is assumed to persist for some time after stimulus offset, so that when the target is subsequently presented, the corresponding word detector will still be in an activated state. Under this interpretation, priming effects should be expected to grade with the degree of prime/target form overlap. However, as shown, cognate priming effects were not smaller than identity priming effects, despite the fact that the words in cognate pairs differed from one another in at least one letter.

An alternative interpretation was suggested by Forster and colleagues (Forster et al., 1987; Forster & Davis, 1984). These authors interpreted the priming effect as a postaccess effect, which they called *entry opening*. Their proposal was based on the idea that visual word recognition can be viewed as a table look-up procedure, for which a stimulus is matched against a stored lexical representation by consulting a table of learned correspondences. Specifically, they suggested that some abstract representation of the stimulus is first used to select a set of compatible lexical candidates. Those candidates are said to be examined in parallel for their congruency with a fuller specification of the stimulus (*postaccess check*); once an appropriate match is found, the corresponding lexical entry needs to be opened for its contents to become available to higher-order language processes (such as parsing). Once an entry is opened, it remains in that state for a few seconds to allow slower processes (such as semantic interpretation) to have continued access to the lexical database. Given that entry opening takes processing time, any reaccess of an already opened entry would save time and thus lead to a facilitation of a response based on information stored in that entry (i.e., priming). Under this interpretation, a priming effect would occur if the priming stimulus resembles the target word sufficiently to open its lexical entry.

Adopting this mechanism of priming, and taking into account the results mentioned above, the cognate priming effects can be explained by assuming that cognate translations are represented jointly in memory. That is, information concerning the words *rico* and *rich* is stored in a common entry. Given such a situation, either word would be able to open the combined entry and so produce a priming effect when that entry is subsequently reaccessed by the target. This interpretation can also explain why no priming effects are found between noncognate translations. These translations are listed separately, so the prime and target open separate entries (Davis et al., 1991; Sánchez-Casas, Davis, et al., 1992).

There is, however, one problem with the opening entry interpretation just described, and this is its difficulty to explain why asymmetrical cognate priming effects are obtained in the semibilingual group. If cognates are jointly represented, the same amount of priming should be expected in both language directions. A possible explanation of the asymmetrical cognate priming effects that would be compatible with the proposal of common lexical representations for cognate translations was suggested by Kim and Davis (2001). These authors carried out an experiment to determine how masked priming effects were affected by processing proficiency in naming Korean words (a logographic writing system) and found only masked priming effects for the practiced logographic processors. To explain the processing proficiency effect, Kim and Davis proposed that priming will only occur when the activation of both prime and target reach a stable state. Specifically, priming will require combined and mutually supportive prime and target activation initially caused by form-based activation and meaning overlap. Such an interpretation could account for the asymmetrical priming effects in the semibilingual group (nonproficient English speakers) by suggesting that the response to L1 targets has probably been made before the prime activation was developed to a sufficient degree, precluding their joint activation.

An alternative processing-based explanation of the asymmetrical cognate priming effects in the semibilingual group might be derived from Kroll and Stewart's model (1994). This model proposes that nonproficient bilinguals interpret words in L2 via activating their translation equivalents in L1. If L2 words are recognized in this indirect way, it is possible that their representations take longer to access than L1 representations, and as a consequence, there might not be enough time for the L2 prime to activate an L1 target (for more details, see Davis, Sánchez-Casas, & García-Albea, 2002). More studies manipulating L2 proficiency are required to test further the processing-based explanations outlined above and to determine their compatibility with an interpretation of the difference between cognate and noncognate words in terms of their representational status based on the open entry model (Forster & Davis, 1984).

Although we are aware of the importance of the role of L2 proficiency in determining masked priming effects, the evidence reviewed in the rest of this chapter considers only the recognition of words involving different cross-language relations in highly proficient bilinguals. In particular, in the next section we examine a series of priming experiments with Catalan-Spanish bilinguals that considers more closely the contribution of form and meaning to cognate priming effects and that provides additional evidence to support the view that cognate and noncognate words are differently represented in the bilingual lexicon.

Can Cognate Relations Be Reduced to Mere Form or Meaning Relationships?

Following the results reported by Davis et al. (1991), García-Albea, Sánchez-Casas, and Valero (1996) carried out several priming experiments in which they investigated more directly the extent that form and meaning contribute to cross-language priming effects. They examined Catalan-Spanish bilinguals with a high proficiency in the two languages. Spanish and Catalan are two Romance languages that share orthography, phonology, and meaning to a large extent. Therefore, they provide a good opportunity to examine in more detail the possible contribution of form or meaning to priming effects across languages.

García-Albea et al. (1996) contrasted three types of word relations. In addition to cognate (e.g., *cotxe–coche*) and noncognate (e.g., *gàbia–jaula*) translations, they included false friends, which, as mentioned, are similar in form but have totally different meanings (e.g., *curta–curva*). These word relations allowed them to determine whether form (false friends), meaning (noncognates), or both (cognates) underlies the priming effects to be observed. They used the same task as Davis et al. (1991) and the same masking procedure, but unlike those authors, they manipulated neither language dominance nor degree of form overlap of cognate translations. Cognate words, noncognates, and false friends were selected and presented under three experimental priming conditions: identity (e.g., *coche–coche, jaula–jaula, curva–curva*), translation (e.g., *cotxe–coche, gàbia–jaula*), an orthographically and phonologically related word in the case of false friends (e.g., *curta–curva*), and a form control (e.g., *corde–coche, prama–jaula, curna–curva*).

Within each prime–target pair, the prime and target had the same number of letters (four or five) and the language of the target could be either Spanish or Catalan. In other words, both language directions were tested.

The results obtained when the target was presented in Catalan are shown in Fig. 11.1. As can be observed, again cognate translations produced a facilitatory priming effect, which was not different statistically from the corresponding identity priming effect. In contrast, noncognate translations did not produce a significant effect. Also, no priming effect was observed for false friends. As illustrated in Fig. 11.2, the general pattern of results was the same when the target was presented in Spanish. Again, only cognate translations produced a facilitatory effect, and as before, identity and cognate primes were equally effective. The effect for noncognates was negligible, and false friends showed a nonsignificant tendency toward inhibition.

The pattern of findings obtained by García-Albea et al. (1996) confirmed the contrast between cognate and noncognate translations found by Davis et al. (1991) with Spanish-English bilinguals. In both studies, only for cognate translations were facilitatory effects observed. These effects were similar in size to those found with identical prime–target pairs, and they were observed in the two language directions (both from L1 to L2 and from L2 to L1). This last finding contrasts with other masked priming studies that have shown asymmetric priming effects

with proficient bilinguals (e.g., Davis & Kim, 2000; Davis & Schoknecht, 1996; Gollan et al., 1997; Jiang, 1999; Jiang & Forster, 2001), a finding that may have resulted from the fact that the language of prime and target had different scripts in the latter set of studies. Gollan et al.'s study is particularly relevant here because these authors compared cognates and noncognates in Hebrew and English (for which cognate translations are similar in meaning and in phonological form, but not in orthography).

Gollan et al. (1997) tested proficient English-Hebrew bilinguals in the two language directions (from L1 to L2 and from L2 to L1) and compared priming effects in the two types of translation, with unrelated word pairs serving as the baseline condition from which priming effects were assessed. Most relevant for the issue addressed here is that the authors observed facilitatory priming effects for cognate and noncognate translations, but only when the prime was in the dominant language and the target in the nondominant language. Gollan et al. suggested that the change in script between prime and target caused the noncognate priming to emerge because this change functions as a powerful orthographic cue that enables the prime to be accessed in time to facilitate the recognition of the target (see, however, Jiang, 1999, for evidence against this account). The authors attributed the asymmetric nature of the cognate priming effect obtained with different scripts to an overreliance on phonology in reading L2 (i.e., Hebrew).

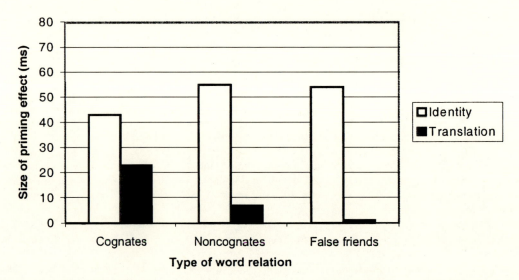

Figure 11.1 Size of priming effect in cognates, noncognates, and false friends as a function of priming condition (identity and translation). The language of the target was Catalan.

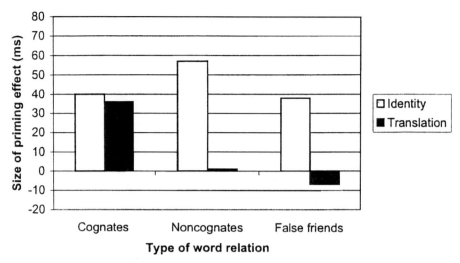

Figure 11.2 Size of priming effect in cognates, noncognates, and false friends as a function of priming condition (identity and translation). The language of the target was Spanish.

Another finding obtained by García-Albea et al. (1996) that contrasts with previous studies is the absence of priming effects for false friends. In particular, Gerard and Scarborough (1989) obtained facilitatory effects for false friends, but these authors used an unmasked priming procedure and identical false friends (that is, words spelled identically, but with different meaning, e.g., "red" in English meaning "net" in Spanish). Moreover, more recent studies have reported inhibitory effects under some conditions (see De Groot, Delmaar, & Lupker, 2000, and Dijkstra et al., 1999, for reviews); however, they used homographs, and this might explain the different pattern of effects. The fact that false friends did not show any effect in García-Albea et al.'s study allows the conclusion that form similarity by itself cannot account for the facilitatory effect in cognate translations. Finally, the consistent lack of facilitation with noncognate translations suggests again that meaning by itself cannot be responsible for the priming effects obtained with cognate translations.

The degree of semantic overlap within cognate and noncognate translations was manipulated by Sánchez-Casas, Suárez-Buratti, and Igoa (1992) in an experiment with Spanish-English bilinguals. Subjects were presented with word pairs and had to decide whether they were translations (this task is called *translation recognition*). The authors selected cognate and noncognate translations that had the same meaning (e.g., *león–lion, vida–life*) and translation pairs that shared their meaning

only partially (e.g., *papel–paper, hoja–sheet*). The experiment clearly showed that there is an asymmetry in the recognition of cognate versus noncognate translations. Only the latter seem to be affected by differences in the meaning relationship between the two words in translation pairs. When noncognate meanings do not neatly map across the two languages, subjects take more time to recognize the translation relation than when they do. However, in recognizing the cognate translations, this factor does not play a role. That is, subjects recognize the cognate translations equally quickly irrespective of the degree of meaning overlap. This same pattern of effects has been obtained when the languages involved are Catalan and Spanish (Guasch, 2001).

Two important conclusions can be derived from the results discussed (Davis et al., 1991; García-Albea et al., 1996). On the one hand, they suggest that cognate relations cannot be reduced to mere form (orthographic and phonological) or meaning relationships, as has also been found in morphologically related words (see García-Albea et al., 1998). On the other hand, they support the claim that cognate translations may be represented jointly in the bilingual lexicon (see details below).

Further evidence for the special representational status of cognate translations was provided by Sánchez-Casas and Almagro (1999). These authors carried out a series of experiments, also with highly competent Catalan-Spanish bilinguals, using the same masked priming procedure and the lexical decision task. In particular, they were interested in determining the time course of priming effects for cognate translations in bilingual word recognition in comparison to those for other types of word relations across languages (i.e., noncognate translations and false friends). To achieve this goal, they manipulated the SOA, selecting three prime durations (30, 60, and 250 ms) that together involved two priming procedures: masked (SOA = 30 ms and 60 ms) and unmasked (SOA = 250 ms).

As in previous studies, Sánchez-Casas and Almagro (1999) compared cognates (e.g., *puño–puny*), noncognates (e.g., *pato–ànec*), and false friends (e.g., *coro–corc*) in three priming conditions: identity, translation (an orthographically and phonologically related word in the case of false friends), and control (an unrelated word). Priming effects were examined for all three of these priming conditions and with each of the three prime durations. On the basis of previous findings with the same languages (García-Albea et al., 1996), only one language direction was tested (Spanish prime and Catalan target). It should be stressed that the words across all three types of word relations had a similar length (four or five letters), and that cognate translations and false friends shared the same degree of form overlap (three letters on average); noncognate translations had on average just one letter in common.

The results obtained with an SOA of 30 ms are presented in Fig. 11.3. It can be observed that identity primes were equally effective in the three word-type conditions. The priming effects were 22, 28, and 28 ms for cognates, noncognates, and false friends, respectively. More interesting, cross-language effects

were observed for cognate translations and false friends, and they were about equal size (19 and 20 ms, respectively) and not different from those obtained with identical prime–target pairs (22 and 28 ms for cognates and false friends, respectively). However, the priming effect for noncognate translations failed to reach significance (5 ms).

Figure 11.4 shows the results with an SOA of 60 ms. In this case, the pattern of priming effects was consistent with previous findings. Cognate translations show facilitation (52 ms), but neither noncognates (10 ms) nor false friends (10 ms) produced reliable effects. Identity priming effects were observed in all three word-type conditions (61, 45, and 48 ms for cognates, noncognates, and false friends, respectively); again, the identity priming and cognate priming conditions did not differ (61 vs. 52 ms, respectively).

Finally, as in some earlier studies (e.g., Altarriba, 1992; Chen & Ng, 1989; De Groot & Nas, 1991; Jin, 1990; Schwanenflugel & Rey, 1986), with an SOA of 250 ms, facilitation was observed both in cognate (101 ms) and in noncognate translations (47 ms). However, again there was no evidence of facilitation for false friends (6 ms). Regarding identity priming, the three types of words produced facilitation (124, 110, and 131 ms for cognates, noncognates, and false friends, respectively). As before, identity and translation effects in the cognate condition were similar in size (101 vs. 124 ms; see Fig. 11.5).

Three aspects of this pattern of results are particularly relevant in view of the issues addressed here. First, cognate translations behaved differently from noncognate translations and false friends,

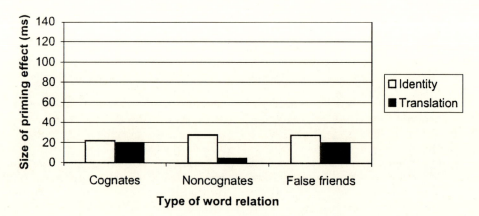

Figure 11.3 Size of priming effect in cognates, noncognates, and false friends as a function of priming condition (identity and translation). The SOA (stimulus onset asynchrony) used was 30 ms.

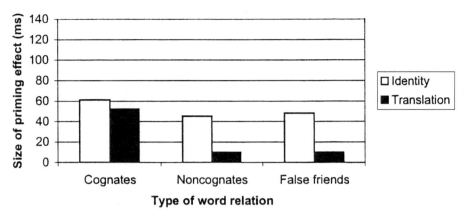

Figure 11.4 Size of priming effect in cognates, noncognates, and false friends as a function of priming condition (identity and translation). The SOA (stimulus onset asynchrony) used was 60 ms.

showing facilitation across all three SOAs. Interestingly, when similar SOAs were used, morphologically related words have been shown to produce a similar pattern of priming. In particular, Dominguez, Seguí, and Cuetos (2002) showed that morphological priming effects are maintained across different SOAs (34, 64, and 250 ms); form and meaning priming effects do not. Both sets of findings provide further evidence that cognate relations, as morphological relations, differ from semantic and orthographic/phonological relationships.

A second noteworthy finding is that, across all three SOAs, cognate relations behave the same as identity relations within a language. This has also been obtained in previous studies (see Davis et al., 1991; García-Albea et al., 1996) and appears to provide further support for the claim that cognate

translations share lexical representations (see Sánchez-Casas, Davis, et al., 1992). Finally, the results clearly showed that both form and meaning contribute to the process of bilingual word recognition, but at different stages. Form seems to play a role early on in the process, as demonstrated by the facilitation observed for false friends at a very short SOA (30 ms). This finding is consistent with a large body of data that supports the view that access to bilingual memory is nonselective (e.g., De Groot et al., 2000; Dijkstra, Van Jaarsveld, & Ten Brinke, 1998; see Dijkstra, chapter 9, this volume). In contrast, meaning similarity by itself seems to exert an influence later in the recognition process, as suggested by the results with noncognates at a longer SOA (250 ms).

The most relevant of these findings is that the pattern of cross-language priming effects with

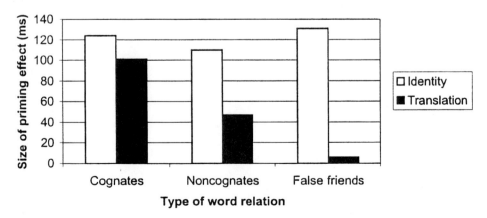

Figure 11.5 Size of priming effect in cognates, noncognates, and false friends as a function of priming condition (identity and translation). The SOA (stimulus onset asynchrony) used was 250 ms.

cognate words resembled closely the pattern obtained, under comparable conditions, with words that were morphologically related within a language. For both types of word relations, it appears that facilitation effects cannot be attributed to just form or meaning similarity. Given this finding, the possibility could be considered that cognate translations involve a special kind of morphological relation. As García-Albea et al. (1998) pointed out, cognate words are indeed morphologically related words, given that they share a common root or stem across languages. Thus, it is possible that they have the same lexical representational status as morphologically related words. This would imply that it is morphology and not language that is critical for lexical organization in bilinguals. Evidence concerning this possibility is presented in the next section.

Can Cognate Relations Be Considered a Special Kind of Morphological Relationship?

The model of word recognition proposed by Kirsner et al. (1993) is the only model that incorporates morphology as an important factor for bilingual lexical organization. In particular, these authors proposed the notion of related words forming a type of morphological "paradigm." The critical idea was that words that share form and meaning will undergo conjoint learning, such that when a word becomes more fluent because of practice, other related words will also benefit. In this model, cognate translations are viewed as a morphological relation of a special kind.

A study by Cristoffanini et al. (1986) with Spanish-English bilinguals provided support for this model. These authors used a lexical decision task and a long-term priming paradigm. In this paradigm, in contrast to those involving short SOAs (for which the interval between prime and target is less than 300 ms, and no other stimuli intervene between the presentation of prime and target), a long time elapses between the presentation of the prime and the target word (several minutes or even longer intervals, and other stimuli intervene between the presentation of the prime and the target).

Specifically, Cristoffanini et al. (1986) designed the experiment in two phases. In the first or study phase, subjects were presented with separate lists of Spanish and English words. In the second or test phase of the experiment, 10 min later, the English words were presented again in English (i.e., repetition priming condition), together with the English translation of the previously presented Spanish words (i.e., translation priming conditions), and a comparable list of English words was presented for the first time. Using this priming procedure, the authors examined priming effects with noncognate translations (e.g., *panadería–bakery*) and with four different types of cognate translations: cognates that were orthographically identical (e.g., *festival-festival*); two types of cognates that shared the same root, followed by different suffixes that are regular in both languages (e.g., *observación-observation, crueldad–cruelty*); and finally cognates with the same root, but with irregular suffixes (e.g., *calamidad–calamity*). The results did not show any priming for noncognate translations, but for cognate translations, priming effects were obtained, and these were of a similar size for the four types of cognates. The authors interpreted these findings as supporting the claim that cognate relations are equivalent to morphological relations.

As far as we know, the only reported studies that have further examined this claim are those carried out by García-Albea et al. (1998) and by Sánchez-Casas, García-Albea, and Igoa (2000) with highly competent Catalan-Spanish bilinguals. In both studies, the authors compared morphological priming effects across languages for cognate and noncognate translations with the effects produced by morphologically related primes within the same language and with the corresponding translation effects.

García-Albea et al. (1998) examined gender and number inflection relations. It should be mentioned that, in Spanish, gender is generally formed by adding the suffix -a (feminine; e.g., *niña*) or -o (masculine; e.g., *niño*) to the stem. Regarding number formation, an -s is added if it ends in a vowel (e.g., *niñas*) and an -es if it ends in a consonant (e.g., *leones*). Only the former was used in this experiment (for more information about these inflections, see García-Albea et al., 1998). The authors used bisyllabic nouns and adjectives with monosyllabic stems that had either a cognate (e.g., *maco-majo*) or a noncognate translation (e.g., *boig-loco*). Half of the prime–target pairs were gender inflections, and the other half were number inflections (in the latter, the prime was always the singular form of the word, and the target was the plural form). The language of the target was always Spanish because previous findings had shown that language direction does not affect the priming effects (Davis et al., 1991; García-Albea et al., 1996). In both cognate and noncognate translation conditions, the Spanish target could be preceded by a morphologically related word in Spanish (e.g., *maja–majo, puerta–puertas, loca–loco, pato–patos*); its translation in Catalan (e.g., *maco–majo, portas–puertas, boig–loco, ànecs–patos*), a morphologically related word in Catalan (e.g., *maca–majo, porta–puertas, boja–loco, ànec–patos*); and an unrelated nonword control.

Figure 11.6 presents the results for the two types of translations. As would be expected if cognate relations are in fact a special case of morphological relations, the size of the priming effect for cognate translations was the same in the within-language morphological condition (56 ms), the cross-language morphological condition (48 ms), and the translation condition (52 ms). However, with noncognate words, only the within-language morphological condition produced significant facilitation (51 ms).

A similar pattern of effects was obtained by Sánchez-Casas et al. (2000), but now with verbal inflections within and across languages. Again, highly proficient Catalan-Spanish bilinguals were tested, and the same masked priming procedure was used. The target was again presented in Spanish and the prime in Catalan. In this case, the authors selected cognate and noncognate Spanish verbs from the three different conjugations that exist in this language (-ar, -er, and -ir; e.g., *olvidar, comer, sufrir*). The cognate and noncognate words

were tested under the same four masked priming conditions: (a) a within-language morphological condition (e.g., *olvida–olvidar, limpio–limpiar*); (b) a translation condition (e.g., *oblidar–olvidar, netejar–limpiar*); (c) a cross-language morphological condition (e.g., *oblida–olvidar, netejo–limpiar*); and (d) an unrelated control condition.

The results of this experiment are shown in Fig. 11.7. As before, cognates showed facilitation when the prime and target were morphologically related within the same language (51 ms), when they were morphologically related across the two languages (36 ms), and when they were translations of one another (38 ms). In contrast, noncognates only showed facilitation when the morphological relation held within the same language (68 ms).

The two experiments just described provide clear evidence that cognate priming effects are the same as priming effects observed with morphologically related words, thus supporting our claim that cognate translations can be considered a special kind of morphological relations. More interesting, the data are consistent with the view that morphology could be the critical principle of organization not only of the monolingual lexicon, as some authors have suggested (e.g., Drews & Zwitserlood, 1995; Frost et al., 1997; Garcia-Albea et al., 1998; Marslen-Wilson et al., 1994), but also of the bilingual lexicon. We now consider the implications of this hypothesis for current models of bilingual lexical memory.

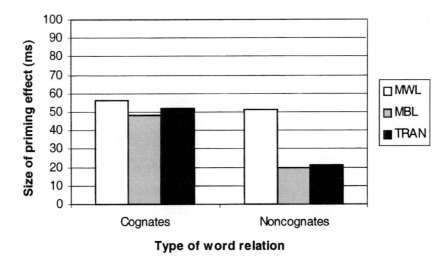

Figure 11.6 Size of priming effect in cognates and noncognates as a function of word relation: gender and number inflections. MWL, morphological relation within language; MBL, morphological relation between languages; TRAN, translation.

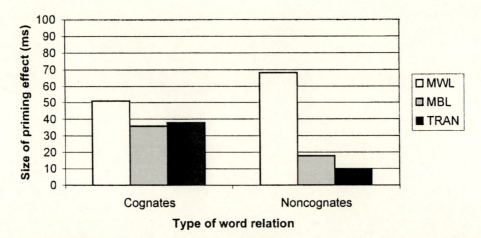

Figure 11.7 Size of priming effect in cognates and noncognates as a function of word relation: verbal inflections. MWL, morphological relation within language; MBL, morphological relation between languages; TRAN, translation.

Implications for Models of Bilingual Memory

We have provided evidence that confirms the idea that the cognate status of a translation is a relevant factor in determining the occurrence of priming effects. In particular, the studies discussed in this chapter have consistently shown that cognate translations produce facilitatory priming effects in bilinguals as long as the bilinguals have a reasonable level of competence in both languages. These effects do not appear to result merely from the form or meaning similarity that characterizes cognate word translations.

Two findings led us to reject the possible contribution of orthographic/phonological similarity: the presence of facilitatory priming effects in cognate translations regardless of their form overlap (e.g., *noche–night*, *torre–tower*; Davis et al., 1991) and the absence of facilitation with false friends, words that are similar in form but not in meaning (e.g., *curta–curva*; García-Albea et al., 1996). Regarding the contribution of meaning to cross-language priming effects, the results clearly showed that noncognate translations, which are only semantically similar to their primes, do not produce any evidence of such effects. This is not to say that form or meaning on their own do not influence bilingual word recognition at all because both false friends and noncognate translations showed facilitatory priming effects, the former with an SOA of 30 ms, and the latter with an SOA of 250 ms.

Moreover, it has been found that the degree of semantic overlap within a translation pair affects the recognition of noncognates, but not that of cognates (e.g., *hoja–sheet*, for which the meaning of the words in this translation pair is not completely identical in the two languages, was recognized as a translation pair slower than *vida–life*, for which the meaning is identical in the two languages; Sánchez-Casas et al., 1992). However, the important finding to stress here is that cognates, in contrast to noncognates and false friends, produced priming effects across all prime durations (30, 60, and 250 ms).

Taken together, this set of findings provides clear evidence to support the claim that cognate priming effects across languages, as seems to be the case for morphological priming within a language, cannot be caused by mere form (false friends) or meaning (noncognate) relations. How then are cognate translations represented in bilingual memory? Several findings suggested that they share a common lexical representation, in contrast to noncognate translations, which presumably are represented separately. On the one hand, the cognate priming effects were equally large as the within-language identity priming effects. This held for both pairs of languages tested, Spanish-English and Catalan-Spanish. On the other hand, as would be expected if cognate translations are indeed represented jointly, language direction did not affect the pattern of priming effects; that is, there were equally large effects in both directions (from L1 to L2 and from L2 to L1).

An alternative proposal regarding the representation of cognate translations in bilingual memory was advanced by De Groot and Nas (1991; see also De Groot, 1992). Assuming a model of bilingual memory in which two levels of representation are distinguished, a lexical (orthographic-phonological) level and a conceptual (meaning) level, these authors have proposed the existence of common representations at the conceptual level for cognate translations, but not for noncognate translations. They based this conclusion on the enhanced priming effects that they observed with cognate translations compared to noncognate translation and on the finding that the cross-language masked priming effects for semantic associates of the primes were only found for cognate translations (e.g., prime *bakery*, target *brood*, meaning "bread") and not for noncognate translations (prime *blanket*, target *laken*, meaning "sheet"). These two accounts of the representation of cognates in memory, however, are not necessarily incompatible. They can, for instance, be reconciled with one another if distributed memory representations are assumed (see De Groot, 1992; Kroll & De Groot, 1997). In this type of representation, cognate translations could share representational nodes or features both at the lexical (form) and at the conceptual (meaning) level. In contrast, noncognate translations might only share features at the conceptual level.

Another set of findings (García-Albea et al., 1998; Sánchez-Casas et al., 2000) led us to move a step further and propose, within the bilingual lexicon, a morphological level of representation in which cognates are jointly represented. This level is different from a pure form level, which contains the word's orthographic and phonological information, and from a concept-representation level, in which the word's meaning is represented. Support for this idea comes from the two final experiments reported in the previous section, which demonstrated that cognate translations produced facilitatory priming effects of equal magnitude as words that were morphologically related within a language and across languages (both noun and verb inflected forms). Further support for the similarity between the cognate and the morphological priming effects was provided by Domínguez et al. (2002), who found that morphological relations showed facilitatory priming across different SOAs, just as cognate relations do.

Returning to the question of how cognate translations are stored in memory, we propose that this type of words is represented on the basis of the common root, as has been suggested for morphologically related words. This would imply, for instance, that words that are morphologically related across languages, such as *porta–puertas*, will be represented under the same root as *puerta–puertas*, words that are morphologically related within the same language. The question now is how such morphological level of representation, which cognate translations share, could be incorporated into models of bilingual word recognition. We refer to two of these models: the distributed lexical/conceptual feature model (Kroll & De Groot, 1997) and the bilingual interactive activation (BIA) model (Dijkstra et al., 1998; Dijkstra & Van Heuven, 1998; see Thomas & Van Heuven, chapter 10, this volume).

The Distributed Lexical/Conceptual Feature Model

Kroll and De Groot (1997) proposed a model that incorporates a language-independent (shared) lexical feature level of representation, containing information regarding the form of words, and a conceptual feature level, for which aspects of meaning are represented. In addition to these two levels of representation, they postulated a level of lemma representations that mediates between the other two (see Fig. 11.8).

The lemma level, which includes some syntactic and semantic characteristics of words, is specific for each language, and it could be considered a means to reflect the activation patterns that result from word form to word meaning mappings. In isolated word recognition, the lemma level would only reflect these form and meaning relationships; however, when contextual information is present, this level could reflect syntactic processes that selectively activate lexical and conceptual features. Proposing language-specific lemmas would not only allow the two languages to function in an autonomous fashion, but also, to the extent that it mediates between the lexical and conceptual levels, it would allow the two languages to influence each other because they share access to common lexical and conceptual features.

As mentioned, within this model, it could be proposed that cognate translations share features at both the lexical (in our case, orthographic and phonological features) and conceptual levels of representation. The greater activation derived from their form and meaning overlap could account for the facilitation effects observed in the three SOAs used (30, 60, and 250 ms). On the contrary, having

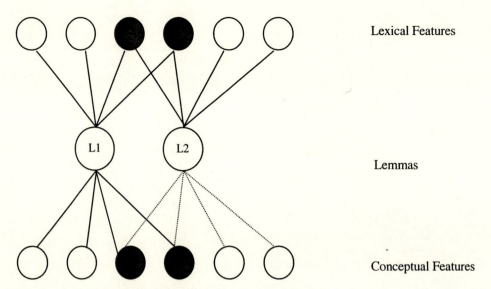

Lexical Features

Lemmas

Conceptual Features

Figure 11.8 The distributed lexical/conceptual feature model. Adapted from Kroll and De Groot, 1997. L1, first language; L2, second language.

only form (false friends) or meaning features (non-cognate translations) in common would not be sufficient for these effects to occur across the different SOAs. False friends priming effects would reflect an early stage in the recognition process, when only word form has been processed; noncognate priming effects could be located at a later stage when the word meaning is taken into account.

A second possibility as to how cognate translations are represented is to postulate a morphological level of representation at which cognate translations would be jointly represented. This additional lexical level could be located, in Kroll and De Groot's (1997) model, between the form level representing orthographic and phonological features and the lemma level. The morphological level would serve two purposes: to represent morphological relations between words from the same family and to provide information to the lemma level not only about the word's form, but also about its morphological structure. Thus, according to this view language-specific lemmas would reflect connections between morphemic-meaning mappings to and from syntax. Figures 11.9 and 11.10 show how this proposal can be implemented into the model in the case of cognate and noncognate words, respectively.[1]

As shown in Fig. 11.9, cognate words (e.g., *porta–puerta*, "door" in English) would share, in

addition to form and meaning features, a common root (*port-*) under which words morphologically related both within and between languages would be represented. In this version of the model, cognate priming effects could be located at the morphological level. Although Kroll and De Groot (1997) did not specify how words are processed in their model, the way these effects occur could be as follows. When one of the cognate words is presented as the prime (in our case, the Catalan word; e.g., *porta*), it will activate its corresponding feature nodes at the form level, most of them shared by its translation (e.g., the Spanish word *puerta*). These nodes will then send activation to the morphological level, at which the cognate's common root is represented (e.g., *port-*). When the cognate word is presented as the target (i.e., *puerta*), both the shared feature nodes and the root node will already be activated, speeding up the target's recognition response. Later in the recognition process, the morphemic level will send activation to the corresponding lemma in the target's language and this in turn to the conceptual level (and possibly back to the morpheme level).

Figure 11.10 shows how noncognate words can be represented in the model. In contrast to cognates, the roots of noncognates would be represented separately. In addition, these words would generally not share form features. Therefore, when a noncognate prime is presented (e.g., the

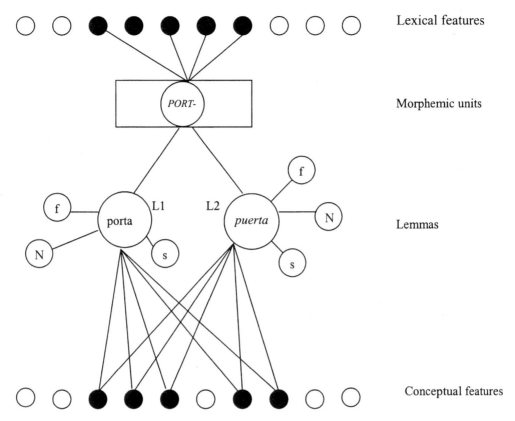

Figure 11.9 The distributed lexical/conceptual feature model for cognate translations. These translations share lexical and conceptual features as well as morphological representations. Lemmas are language specific and reflect connections between the morphological-meaning mappings to and from syntax. The f, s, and N stand for feminine, singular, and noun, respectively. Version adapted from Kroll and De Groot, 1997. L1, first language, L2, second language.

Catalan word *taula*), activation from the form feature nodes will only activate the corresponding root node (i.e., *taul-*), and no activation will reach the root of its translation (i.e., *mes-*). Consequently, no facilitation effects would emerge. The facilitation effects obtained with noncognate words (i.e., when the prime is clearly visible and displayed for 250 ms or longer) would reflect activation at the conceptual level, at which meaning features are shared by this type of translation.

Postulating such a morphological level of representation within Kroll and De Groot's (1997) model would imply, at least in the case of regularly inflected forms,[2] not only that these morphologically complex forms are represented in terms of their roots and affixes, but also that they are morphologically decomposed to access the word's syntactic and semantic information. That is, the model would

require the implementation of a prelexical morphological parsing mechanism that isolates the morphological root without reference to whole-word representations.

The existence of such a mechanism was originally proposed by Taft and Forster (1976) to account for the way polymorphemic words are stored and retrieved, and it has received empirical support from different studies in different languages (e.g., Caramazza, Laudana, & Romani, 1988; Deutsch, Frost, Pollatsek, & Rayner, 2000; Drews & Zwitserlood, 1995; Feldman, 1995; Forster & Azuma, 2000; Frost et al., 1997; Taft, 1985, 1994).

In the domain of visual word recognition in monolinguals, Taft (1994) proposed an implementation of a prelexical morphological parsing mechanism within the framework of an interactive

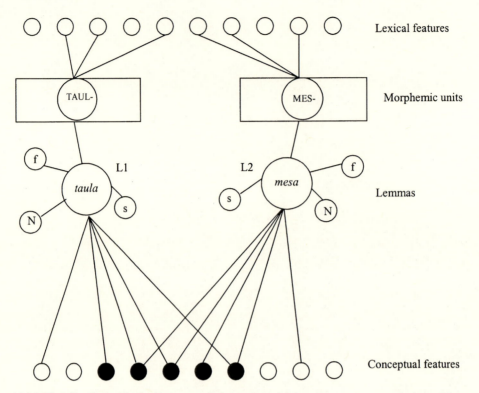

Figure 11.10 The distributed lexical/conceptual feature model for noncognate translations. These translations do not share lexical features or morphological representations, but they do share conceptual features. Lemmas are language specific and reflect the morphological-meaning mappings to and from syntax. The f, s, and N stand for feminine, singular, and noun, respectively. Version adapted from Kroll and De Groot, 1997. L1, first language, L2, second language.

activation model. In this model, Taft distinguished different levels of representations, including letters, bodies, morphemes, words, and concepts. Of relevance here is the morphological level at which only bound morphemes are represented (this would be more clearly the case for transparent prefixed and inflected words; see note 2) and morphological masked priming effects within the same language are located.

Adopting Taft's (1994) approach to bilingual word representation and access, it might be assumed that both cognate and noncognate words are represented in a decomposed format. That is, the root that is shared by cognate words (e.g., *porta–puerta*) and other morphologically related words within and across languages (e.g., *puerta–puertas, porta–puertas*) will be represented at a morphological level together with the corresponding affixes in the two languages (e.g., the root *port-* and the gender morpheme *a* and the plural morpheme *s*).[3] In

contrast, noncognate words (e.g., *taula–mesa*) will have language specific morphological representations, although each of them will be connected to morphologically related words within the same language via a common root (e.g., *taula–taules, mesa–mesas*). The recognition of both cognate and noncognate words will require a prelexical parsing procedure that has to operate on the visual stimulus to extract morphological units that can be matched onto the corresponding lexical representations.

This proposal could in principle be compatible with our version of Kroll and De Groot's (1997) distributed lexical/conceptual feature model for cognate and noncognate words[4] (see Figs. 11.9 and 11.10), although it should be noted that neither our version of the model nor the original model itself incorporates a level at which word units are represented. In our opinion, however, this is not a problem if a form, a lemma, a morphological, and a conceptual level of representation are formulated, as our version of Kroll and De Groot's model does. In fact, to include a word level would be redundant because all the relevant information about the word would already be contained in the four existing levels.

Before considering the BIA model (Dijkstra & Van Heuven, 1998), a final possibility could be suggested for how cognate words can be represented in the framework of Kroll and De Groot's (1997) model. This possibility would be to assimilate the morphological level to the lemma level, that is, to represent lemma entries as morphemic units with information about possible variations. This possibility was considered by Levelt (1989) in the case of inflections for languages with a rich morphology (Catalan and Spanish can be considered morphologically rich languages), for which morphological information has noticeable consequences for syntactic processes (see Cabré, 1994; Varela Ortega, 1992). According to this proposal, in contrast to the language-specific lemmas of noncognate words, the lemmas of cognate words will be shared. This common lemma will contain specifications about the variants in the two languages (e.g., concerning gender or tense) as one more of the diacritic parameters that were proposed by Levelt. Within this model, the translation and morphological masked priming effects obtained with cognate words would emerge at the lemma level, and to access the word information stored at that level, a prelexical morphological decomposition is not necessarily required.

The Bilingual Interactive Activation Model

The BIA model is an extension of the interactive activation model of McClelland and Rumelhart (1981) and was developed to account for bilingual word recognition. The model proposes an integrated lexicon for the two languages of a bilingual and includes four representational levels: letter features, letters, words (their orthographic form), and language nodes. There are connections between the nodes within each level as well as between the nodes of different levels. Letter units can activate or inhibit word units, depending on whether they match or mismatch the input. If there is a match, words send activation to the corresponding language node and back to the letter level. A language node collects activation of all the words that belong to the corresponding language and sends inhibition to all the words belonging to the other language

(Dijkstra & Van Heuven, 1998). (See Fig. 11.11 and Dijkstra, chapter 9, and Thomas & Van Heuven, chapter 10, this volume.)

To account for the facilitation obtained with cognate translations, Dijkstra et al. (1998) extended the model to include a semantic level between the word level and the language node level. In this model, cognate translations are represented separately at the word level, but share their semantic representation. The facilitatory effects obtained for cognate translations could then be attributed to activation at the semantic level and the subsequent feedback from the semantic to the word level.

How could a morphological level be implemented in this tentative extended version of the model? One possibility is to locate the morpheme units between the letter and word levels, as Taft's (1994) interactive activation model suggested. As in the distributed lexical/conceptual feature model, in this case a morphological analysis would be

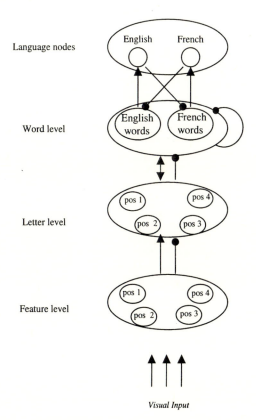

Figure 11.11 Bilingual interactive activation model (BIA) (pos, position). Adapted from Dijkstra and Van Heuven, 1998.

required for access purposes. Another possibility, suggested by one of the authors of the BIA model in the case of monolingual word recognition, is to locate a morphological level between the word level and the semantic level of representation (Giraudo & Grainger, 2000).[5] This morphological level could serve the same functions as we suggested for Kroll and De Groot's (1997) distributed lexical/conceptual feature model, that is, to link all the words that share a common root and to operate as an interface between the word's orthographic information (the current model does not include phonology) and its meaning information. Morphological representations would be linked through excitatory connections to both the word (form) and the meaning levels. Specifically, these representations would receive activation from the word level and send it to the meaning level. This level in turn would send activation back to the morpheme level, and from this it is sent back to the word level (i.e., top-down activation). Within this model, access is assumed to be nonselective; in other words, words from both languages are initially activated.

Figures 11.12 and 11.13 show how morphological representations can be incorporated in the BIA model for cognate and noncognate words, respectively. As can be seen in Figs. 11.12 and 11.13, cognates and noncognates differ in the way their morphological roots are represented. Cognate words share a common root (e.g., *porta–puerta* share the root *port-*); noncognates do not (e.g., *taula–mesa* have different roots, *taul-* and *mes-*). Similar to our proposal concerning Kroll and De Groot's (1997) model, in our version of the BIA model the facilitatory masked priming effects obtained with cognate words (i.e., translation and cross-language morphological effects) would be located at the morphological level.[6]

How then do cross-language facilitatory effects for cognates emerge within the proposed version of the BIA model? In an initial stage of processing, the cognate word presented as the prime (e.g., *porta*) will activate the representation of features and the letters containing these features; the letters that do not correspond to those features will be inhibited. The activated letter nodes will activate the words in the two languages that share these letters; at the same time, the remaining words will be inhibited. At this point in the recognition process, the word node corresponding to the prime becomes activated, sending activation to the morphemic level, which has its root (e.g., *port-*). This morphemic unit will then send activation back not only to the node for the cognate word that has been presented

as the prime, but also to the node for its translation in the other language that shares the same root (e.g., *puerta*). When the target word is presented (e.g., *puerta*), its corresponding root node will be activated already, and this activation state will be sustained by the bottom-up activation from the word level, as well as by the top-down activation from the meaning level. As a consequence of this joint activation at the morphological level, the recognition of the target will be facilitated, and priming effects are observed.

For the cognate priming effects to arise from the morphological level as described above, it is also necessary to assume that the inhibition sent from the relatively highly activated language node (i.e., the Catalan node) to the words in the other language (i.e., Spanish) is not so large that it suppresses entirely the activation sent off by the cognate's shared morphological root to the Spanish word node or alternatively that the inhibitory top-down feedback from the activated Catalan language node arrives too late to cancel the activation reached by the Spanish word node.

It should be noted that, in this version of the model, words are no longer connected directly to the semantic level, and that they can activate but not inhibit their morphological representation. In addition, the model does not postulate direct links from language nodes to morphological nodes. To include such links would on the one hand be redundant because language nodes already modulate lexical activity through cross-language top-down inhibition to word nodes; on the other hand, it would require the assumption that inhibitory connections from language nodes to morphological nodes only exist in the case of noncognate translations because cognate translations share a common node at the morphological level. Thus, we suggest that the only way in which inhibition from the language nodes can affect the activation level of morphological representations would be through the word units. That is, when these word units are inhibited by the language node, they will activate to a lesser degree their corresponding morphemic units.

Cross-language morphological priming effects in cognate words (e.g., *porta–puertas*) can be explained in the same manner as translation priming because they arise from the same shared common root (e.g., *port-*).

Figure 11.13 shows the adapted version of the BIA model for noncognate words. For these words, no facilitation effects would be observed because, with the presentation of the prime (e.g., *taula*), activation will only reach its nonshared

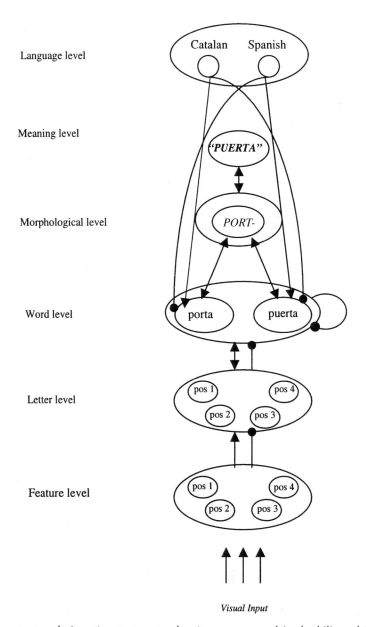

Figure 11.12 Cognate translations (*porta–puerta*; door) as represented in the bilingual interactive activation model (BIA) (pos, position). These translations share a common root. The morphological level is proposed to mediate between meaning and form. Version adapted from Dijkstra and Van Heuven, 1998.

morphological root (e.g., *taul-*). When the target is presented (e.g., *mesa*), its root would not have been previously activated by the prime, receiving initially only form-based activation from the corresponding word unit. This would explain the lack of facilitation effects in noncognate words (at SOAs of 30 and 60 ms). The presence of facilitation effects in these words at a longer SOA (in our case, 250 ms) could be attributed to the later role that meaning-based activation possibly plays in the recognition process given that noncognate words do share a common meaning.

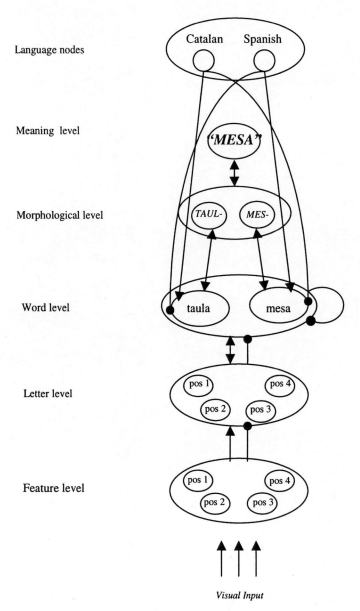

Figure 11.13 Noncognate translations (*taula–mesa*; table) as represented in the bilingual interactive activation model (BIA) (pos, position). These translations do not share a common root. The morphological level is proposed to mediate between meaning and form. Version adapted from Dijkstra and Van Heuven, 1998.

Finally, the facilitation for false friends (e.g., *curta–curva*), that only occurred at a very short SOA (i.e., 30 ms), could be accounted in the following way. Because in the BIA model words from both languages are initially activated, a word presented as the prime (e.g., *curta*) would activate the letters that it has in common with its false friend target (e.g., *curva*). Activation at the word level (i.e., form-based activation) could then be responsible for the presence of facilitation effects at an early stage of processing. Given that false friends, as interlingual homographs, have neither morphological nor semantic overlap, it can be assumed that this form-based initial activation would soon be suppressed by the inhibitory connections postulated in the model. Therefore, at long SOAs (i.e., 60 and 250 ms) no facilitation for false friends occurs.

Conclusion

We began this chapter by proposing that morphology might be a critical factor in modeling the representation of cognates in bilinguals. Throughout this chapter, we have presented experimental evidence that provides preliminary support for this claim, and we have discussed how some of the current models of bilingual memory could incorporate the representation of morphology. However, we appreciate that further work is needed to explain in more detail what is the precise nature of the proposed cross-language morphological representation in the languages tested. Further work is also needed to determine whether the same interpretation applies to other morphologically related words besides inflections (e.g., derived forms) and to find out how the morphological representation relates to both the form representation and the semantic representation of words and what role, if any, it plays in lexical access processes. The present support for a morphological level of representation shared in the case of cognate words between a bilingual's two languages, however, appears to provide the beginning of a promising new research line.

Acknowledgments

The research presented in this chapter was supported by a grant from the Ministry of Science and Technology (BSO2000-1252). We thank Annette de Groot and Judith Kroll for providing many helpful comments on an earlier version of this chapter.

Notes

1. We present versions of the distributed lexical/semantic feature model and the BIA model using Catalan and Spanish words as examples because the majority of experiments reported in the chapter have tested these languages. However, the same interpretations would apply in the case of Spanish-English translations. Nevertheless, it would be interesting to explore whether the morphological characteristics of the language can play a role in the issues we have addressed.

2. In the case of derivational suffixed forms, the results are less clear because factors such as semantic transparency and productivity appear to play a role in determining how these words are represented and accessed (e.g., Drews & Zwitserlood, 1995; Feldman & Larabee, 2001; Marslen-Wilson et al., 1994; Stolz & Feldman, 1995).

3. Although in the example used, *porta–puerta*, the gender and plural morphemes coincide in the two languages (Catalan and Spanish), this is not always the case (e.g., *mito–mite*, "myth" in English) (see Mascaro, 1985, for more details).

4. In our version of this model, we have only represented the word's root, but the representation of affixes (e.g., gender and plural suffixes) could also be included in the case of morphologically complex words. Note, however, that it might be possible that suffixes of regularly inflected forms will not be lexically represented because their use is generally governed by rules.

5. Giraudo and Grainger (2000) referred to their proposal as the supralexical hypothesis to distinguish it from the sublexical hypothesis defended by Taft (1994). Only the latter requires morphological decomposition as a prior stage to access.

6. Giraudo and Grainger (2000) also suggested that the locus of morphological masked priming effects within the same language is the morphological level.

References

Altarriba, J. (1992). The representation of translation equivalents in bilingual memory. In R. J. Harris (Ed.), *Cognitive processing in bilinguals* (pp. 157–174). Amsterdam: Elsevier.

Cabré, M. T. (1994). *Al'entorn de la paraula* (Vols. 1 and 2). Valencia, Spain: Universitat de València. Collecció: Biblioteca Lingüística Catalana.

Caramazza, A., Laudana, A., & Romani, C. (1988). Lexical access in inflectional morphology. *Cognition, 28,* 297–332.

Chen, H.-C. (1990). Lexical processing in a non-native language: Effects of language proficiency and learning strategy. *Memory and Cognition, 18,* 279–288.

Chen, H.-C., & Ng, M.-L. (1989). Semantic facilitation and translation priming in Chinese-English bilinguals. *Memory and Cognition, 17,* 454–462.

Cristoffanini, P. M., Kirsner, K., & Milech, D. (1986). Bilingual lexical representation: The status of Spanish-English cognates. *The Quarterly Journal of Experimental Psychology, 38,* 367–393.

Davis, C. W., & Kim, J. (2000, July). Masked priming by translation and phonological primes in Korean and English. In F. Y. Doré (Ed.), *Abstracts of the XXVII International Congress of Psychology* (p. 405). Hove, U.K.: Psychology Press.

Davis, C. W., Sánchez-Casas, R., & García-Albea, J. E. (1991). *Bilingual lexical representation as revealed using the masked priming procedure.* Unpublished manuscript.

Davis, C. W., Sánchez-Casas, R., & García-Albea, J. E. (2002). *Masked translation priming: Varying language experience and word type with Spanish-English bilinguals.* Manuscript submitted for publication.

Davis, C. W., & Schoknecht, C. (1996). Lexical processing in Thai-English bilinguals. In *Pan-Asiatic Linguistics: Proceedings of the Fourth International Symposium on Language and Linguistics, Thailand* (Vol. 4, pp. 1399–1428).

De Groot, A. M. B. (1983). The range of automatic spreading activation in word priming. *Journal of Verbal Learning and Verbal Behavior, 22,* 417–436.

De Groot, A. M. B. (1992). Bilingual lexical representation: A closer look at conceptual representations. In R. Frost & L. Katz (Eds.), *Orthography, phonology, morphology and meaning* (pp. 389–412). Amsterdam: Elsevier.

De Groot, A. M. B. (1993). Word-type effects in bilingual processing tasks: Support for a mixed representational system. In R. Schreuder & B. Weltens (Eds.), *The bilingual lexicon* (pp. 191–214). Amsterdam: Benjamins.

De Groot, A. M. B. (2001). Lexical representation and lexical processing in the L2 user. In V. Cook (Ed.), *Portraits of the language user* (pp. 32–63). Clevedon, U.K.: Multilingual Matters.

De Groot, A. M. B., Delmaar, P., & Lupker, S. (2000). The processing of interlexical homographs in translation recognition and lexical decision: Support for non-selective access to bilingual memory. *The Quarterly Journal of Experimental Psychology, 53A,* 397–428.

De Groot, A. M. B., & Nas, G. L. J. (1991). Lexical representations of cognate and non-cognates in compound bilinguals. *Journal of Memory and Language, 30,* 90–123.

De Groot, A. M. B., & Poot, R. (1997). Word translation at three levels of proficiency in a second language: The ubiquitous involvement of conceptual memory. *Language Learning, 47,* 215–264.

Deutsch, A., Frost, R., Pollatsek, A., & Rayner, K. (2000). Early morphological effects in word recognition in Hebrew: Evidence from parafoveal preview benefit. *Language and Cognitive Processes, 15,* 487–506.

Dijkstra, A., Grainger, J., & Van Heuven, W. J. B. (1999). Recognition of cognates and interlingual homographs: The neglected role of phonology. *Journal of Memory and Language, 41,* 496–518.

Dijkstra, A., & Van Heuven, W. J. B. (1998). The BIA model and bilingual word recognition. In J. Grainger & A. Jacobs (Eds.), *Localist connectionist approaches to human cognition* (pp. 189–225). Hillsdale, NJ: Erlbaum.

Dijkstra, A., Van Jaarsveld, H., & ten Brinke, S. (1998). Interlingual homograph recognition: Effects of task demands and language intermixing. *Bilingualism: Language and Cognition, 1,* 51–66.

Domínguez, A., Seguí, J., & Cuetos, F. (2002). The time-course of inflectional morphological priming. *Linguistics, 40,* 235–259.

Drews, E., & Zwitserlood, P. (1995). Morphological and orthographic similarity in visual word recognition. *Journal of Experimental Psychology: Human Perception and Performance, 21,* 1098–1116.

Durgunoglu, A. Y., & Roediger, H. L. (1987). Test differences in accessing bilingual memory. *Journal of Memory and Language, 26,* 377–391.

Evett, L. J., & Humphreys, G. W. (1981). The use of abstract graphemic information in lexical access. *The Quarterly Journal of Experimental Psychology, 33A,* 325–350.

Feldman, L. B. (Ed.). (1995). *Morphological aspects of language processing.* Hillsdale, NJ: Erlbaum.

Feldman, L. B., & Larabee, J. (2001). Morphological facilitation following prefixed but not suffixed primes: Lexical architecture or modality-specific processes. *Journal of Experimental Psychology: Human Perception and Performance, 27,* 680–691.

Feldman, L. B., & Moskovlijevic, J. (1987). Repetition priming is not purely episodic in origin. *Journal of Experimental Psychology: Learning, Memory and Cognition, 15,* 1–12.

Feustel, T. C., Shiffrin, R. M., & Salasoo, A. (1983). Episodic and lexical contribution to the repetition effect in word identification. *Journal of Experimental Psychology: General, 112,* 309–346.

Forster, K. I. (1998). The pros and cons of masked priming. *Journal of Psycholinguistic Research, 27,* 203–233.

Forster, K. I., & Azuma, T. (2000). Masked priming for prefixed words with bound stems: Does *submit* prime *permit? Language and Cognitive Processes, 15,* 539–561.

Forster, K. I., & Davis, C. W. (1984). Repetition priming and frequency attenuation in lexical access. *Journal of Experimental*

Psychology: Learning, Memory and Cognition, 10, 680–698.

Forster, K. I., Davis, C. W., Schoknecht, C., & Carter, R. (1987). Masked priming with graphemically related forms: Repetition or activation? *The Quarterly Journal of Experimental Psychology, 39A,* 211–251.

Friel, B., & Kennison, S. (2001). Identifying German-English cognates, false cognates, and non-cognates: Methodological issues and descriptive norms. *Bilingualism: Language and Cognition, 4,* 249–274.

Frost, R., Deutsch, A., Gilboa, O., Tannenbaum, M., & Marslen-Wilson, W. (2000). Morphological priming: Dissociation of phonological, semantic and morphological factors. *Memory and Cognition, 28,* 1277–1288.

Frost, R., Forster, K. I., & Deutsch, A. (1997). What can we learn from the morphology of Hebrew? A masked-priming investigation of morphological representation. *Journal of Experimental Psychology: Learning, Memory, and Cognition, 23,* 829–856.

Frost, R., & Grainger, J. (Eds.). (2000). Cross-linguistic perspective on morphological processing [Special issue]. *Language and Cognitive Processes, 15*(4/5).

Frost, R., & Katz, L. (Eds.). (1992). *Orthography, phonology, morphology and meaning.* Amsterdam: Elsevier.

García-Albea, J. E., Sánchez-Casas, R. M., Bradley, D. C., & Forster, K. I. (1985, November). *Cross-language priming effects in bilingual word recognition.* Paper presented at the meeting of the Fifth Australian Language Conference, Melbourne.

García-Albea, J. E., Sánchez-Casas, R., & Igoa, J. M. (1998). The contribution of word form and meaning to language processing in Spanish: Some evidence from monolingual and bilingual studies. In D. Hillert (Ed.), *Sentence processing: A cross-linguistic perspective* (pp. 183–209). New York: Academic Press.

García-Albea, J. E., Sánchez-Casas, R., & Valero, T. (1996, September). *Form and meaning contribution to word recognition in Catalan-Spanish bilinguals.* Paper presented at the meeting of the Ninth Conference of the European Society for Cognitive Psychology, University of Würzburg, Germany.

Gerard, L. D., & Scarborough, D. L. (1989). Language-specific lexical access of homographs by bilinguals. *Journal of Experimental Psychology: Learning, Memory and Cognition, 15,* 305–315.

Giraudo, H., & Grainger, J. (2000). Effects of prime word frequency and cumulative root frequency in masked morphological priming.

Language and Cognitive Processes, 15, 421–444.

Gollan, T. H., Forster, K. I., & Frost, R. (1997). Translation priming with different scripts: Masked priming with cognates and non-cognates in Hebrew-English bilinguals. *Journal of Experimental Psychology: Learning, Memory and Cognition, 23,* 1122–1139.

Grainger, J., & Frenck-Mestre, C. (1998). Masked priming by translation equivalents in proficient bilinguals. *Language and Cognitive Processes, 13,* 601–623.

Guasch, M. (2001). *Forma y significado en el procesamiento léxico de bilingües del castellano y del catalán.* Unpublished master's thesis, Universitat Rovira i Virgili, Tarragona, Spain.

Jiang, N. (1999). Testing processing explanations for the asymmetry in masked cross-language priming. *Bilingualism: Language and Cognition, 2,* 59–75.

Jiang, N., & Forster, K. I. (2001). Cross-language priming asymmetries in lexical decision and episodic recognition. *Journal of Memory and Language, 44,* 32–51.

Jin, Y.-S. (1990). Effects of concreteness on cross-language priming in lexical decision. *Perceptual and Motor Skills, 70,* 1139–1154.

Kim, J., & Davis, C. W. (2001). Loss of rapid phonological recoding in reading Hanja, the logographic script of Korean. *Psychonomic Bulletin and Review, 8,* 785–790.

Kirsner, K. (1986). Lexical representation: Is a bilingual account necessary? In J. Vaid (Ed.), *Language processing in bilinguals: Psycholinguistic and Neuropsychological perspectives* (pp. 21–45). Hillsdale, NJ: Erlbaum.

Kirsner, K., Brown, H. L., Abrol, S., Chadha, A., & Sharma, N. K. (1980). Bilingualism and lexical representation. *The Quarterly Journal of Experimental Psychology, 32,* 565–574.

Kirsner, K., Lalor, E., & Hird, K. (1993). Exercise, meaning and morphology. In R. Schreuder & B. Weltens (Eds.), *The bilingual lexicon* (pp. 215–248). Amsterdam: Benjamins.

Kirsner, K., Smith. M. C., Lockhart, R. S., King, M. L., & Jain, M. (1984). The bilingual lexicon: Language-specific effects in an integrated network. *Journal of Verbal Learning and Verbal Behavior, 23,* 519–539.

Kroll, J. F. (1993). Accessing conceptual representations for words in a second language. In R. Schreuder & B. Weltens (Eds.), *The bilingual lexicon* (pp. 53–81). Amsterdam: Benjamins.

Kroll, J. F., & De Groot, A. M. B. (1997). Lexical and conceptual memory in the bilingual: mapping form to meaning in two Languages. In A. M. B. de Groot and J. F. Kroll (Eds.), *Tutorials in bilingualism: Psycholinguistic perspectives* (pp. 169–199). Mahwah, NJ: Erlbaum.

Kroll, J. F., & Stewart, E. (1994). Category interference in translation and picture naming:
Evidence for asymmetric connections between
bilingual memory representations. *Journal of
Memory and Language, 33,* 149–174.

Levelt, W. J. M. (1989). *Speaking: From intention
to articulation.* Cambridge, MA: MIT Press.

Marslen-Wilson, W., Tyler, L., Waksler, R., &
Older, L. (1994). Morphology and meaning
in the English mental lexicon. *Psychological
Review, 101,* 3–33.

Mascaro, J. (1985). *Morfologia.* Barcelona, Spain:
Enciclopedia Catalana.

McClelland, J. L., & Rumelhart, D. E. (1981). An
interactive activation model of context effects
in letter perception. Part I: An account of basic
findings. *Psychological Review, 88,* 375–405.

Mildred, H. V. (1986). *Masked priming effects
between and within languages.* Unpublished
honors thesis, Monash University, Melbourne,
Australia.

Oliphant, G. (1983). Repetition and recency effect
in word recognition. *Australian Journal of
Psychology, 35,* 393–403.

Potter, M. C., So, K.-F., Von Eckardt, B., &
Feldman, L. B. (1984). Lexical and conceptual
representations in beginning and proficient
bilinguals. *Journal of Verbal Learning and
Verbal Behavior, 23,* 23–38.

Sánchez-Casas, R. (1999). Una aproximación
psicolingüística al estudio del léxico en el
hablante bilingüe. In M. de Vega & F.
Cuetos (Eds.), *Psicolingüística del español*
(pp. 597–651). Madrid, Spain: Trotta.

Sánchez-Casas, R., & Almagro, Y. (1999, April).
*Efectos de priming entre lenguas utilizando
primes enmascarados y no enmascarados y
diferente asincronía estimular.* Paper presented
at the meeting of the IV Simposium de Psicolingüística, Madrid, Spain.

Sánchez-Casas, R., Davis, C. W., & García-Albea,
J. E. (1992). Bilingual lexical processing:
Exploring the cognate/noncognate distinction.
European Journal of Cognitive Psychology, 4,
293–310.

Sánchez-Casas, R., García-Albea, J. E., & Igoa, J.
M. (2000, July). Can cognate words be char-
acterized as a kind of morphological relations?
In F. Y. Doré (Ed.), *Abstracts of the XXVII
International Congress of Psychology* (pp.
405–406). Hove, U.K.: Psychology Press.

Sánchez-Casas, R., Suárez-Buratti, B., & Igoa,
J. M. (1992, September). *Are bilingual
lexical representations interconnected?* Paper
presented at the meeting of the Fifth
Conference of the European Society for
Cognitive Psychology, Paris, France.

Sandra, D., & Taft, M. (Eds.). (1994). *Morphological structure, lexical representation and
lexical access.* Mahwah, NJ: Erlbaum.

Scarborough, D. L., Gerard, L., & Cortese, C.
(1984). Independence of lexical access in bilingual word recognition. *Journal of Verbal
Learning and Verbal Behavior, 23,* 84–99.

Schwanenflugel, P., & Rey, M. (1986). Interlingual
semantic facilitation: Evidence for a common
representational system in the bilingual lexicon. *Journal of Memory and Language, 25,*
605–618.

Smith, M. C. (1997). How do bilinguals access
lexical information? In A. M. B. de Groot and
J. F. Kroll (Eds.), *Tutorials in bilingualism:
Psycholinguistic perspectives* (pp. 145–168).
Mahwah, NJ: Erlbaum.

Stolz, J. A., & Feldman, L. B. (1995). The role of
orthographic and semantic transparency of the
base morpheme in morphological processing.
In L. B. Feldman (Ed.), *Morphological aspects
of language processing* (pp. 109–129). Hillsdale, NJ: Erlbaum.

Taft, M. (1985). The decoding of words in lexical
access: A review of the morphographic approach. In D. Besner, T. G. Waller, & G. E.
MacKinnon (Eds.), *Reading research: Advances in theory and practice* (pp. 271–294).
New York: Academic Press.

Taft, M. (1994). Interactive activation as a
framework for understanding morphological
processing. *Language and Cognitive
Processes, 9,* 271–294.

Taft, M., & Forster, K. I. (1976). Lexical storage
and retrieval of polymorphemic and poly-
syllabic words. *Journal of Verbal Learning
and Verbal Behavior, 15,* 607–620.

Talamas, A., Kroll, J. F., & Dufour, R. (1999).
From form to meaning: Stages in the
acquisition of second language vocabulary.
*Bilingualism: Language and Cognition,
2,* 45–58.

Tenpenny, P. L. (1995). Abstractionist versus
episodic theories of repetition priming and
word identification. *Psychonomic Bulletin
and Review, 2,* 341–368.

Varela Ortega, S. (1992). *Fundamentos de
morfología.* Madrid, Spain: Síntesis.

Weinreich, U. (1974). *Language in contact:
Findings and problems.* The Hague, The
Netherlands: Mouton. (Original work
published 1953)

Williams, J. N. (1994). The relationship between
word meanings in the first and second
language: Evidence for a common, but restricted, semantic code. *European Journal of
Cognitive Psychology, 6,* 195–220.

Wendy S. Francis

12

Bilingual Semantic and Conceptual Representation

ABSTRACT   The question of whether and to what extent semantic or conceptual representations are integrated across languages in bilinguals has led cognitive psychologists to generate over 100 empirical reports. The terms *semantic* and *conceptual* are compared, contrasted, and distinguished from other levels of representation, and terms used to describe language integration are clarified. The existing literature addressing bilingual episodic and semantic memory at the level of semantic systems and at the level of the translation-equivalent word pair is summarized. This evidence strongly favors shared semantic systems and shared semantic/conceptual representation for translation equivalents. Translation equivalents appear to have a different and closer cognitive status than within-language synonyms. Important directions in future cognitive research on bilingualism include neuroscientific and developmental approaches.

Bilingual semantic and conceptual organization has been a topic of interest to cognitive researchers because of the fundamental cognitive question of redundancy versus efficiency of representation. Solutions to the redundancy/efficiency question will be important, for example, in understanding how two languages can be used competently within a single mind and perhaps in understanding how second languages are acquired. For the purposes of this chapter, bilinguals are considered to be all people who regularly use at least two languages (Grosjean, 1992). This definition implies spoken communicative competence, but encompasses people with a broad range of relative proficiencies in their languages. To pursue this topic, several terminology clarifications are necessary and are discussed in the subsequent sections before turning to the results of research on bilingual representation.

Levels of Representation

The level of representation involved in a task has been a key to understanding results previously thought to be discrepant. Defining these levels has proved somewhat difficult. As pointed out previously (Francis, 1999b, 2000, and see Kroll & Tokowicz, chapter 26, this volume), cognitive research on bilingualism, falling at the intersection of psychology and linguistics and including both language researchers and memory researchers, is inconsistent in the terminology used to address these levels. The example most crucial to the present discussion is that the intended relationship between the terms *semantic* and *conceptual* is ambiguous. In most articles, the relationship assumed by the authors is not specified; in some articles, the terms are used interchangeably, but in others only one term or the other is used exclusively.

To untangle this issue, let us start with something nonlinguistic: the universe of possible ideas or concepts that a human can learn or understand. This must be a systems-level, possibly hardwired aspect of human cognition that ought to be the same across all cultures and languages. However, the concepts actually realized in a given person's experience may vary, with systematic patterns across cultures. Also, in a person who is bicultural, certain concepts may be more relevant or more accessible in one cultural context than in the other.

Now, how is language mapped onto this conceptual system? This is where semantics come into play. Any of the concepts a person can know ought to have the potential to be expressed in any human language. Of course, the concepts actually realized in an individual's language input or output will vary with systematic patterns across languages. Semantic representations may be those concepts that are referred to by particular words or sentences. Thus, semantic representations would be representations of word or sentence meaning. Word meanings, or semantic representations of words, would be a particular type of concept. This view would be consistent with the position of many linguists (e.g., Jackendoff, 1994). A second way to think about this relationship is to consider semantic representations or word meanings as the mappings of verbal labels to their concepts. Although many of the concepts a person knows can be expressed using individual words, there are of course many more concepts that are not associated with any particular word. Such concepts have the potential to be expressed as sentences (or larger units of language), in which case these concepts would be the semantic representations of the sentences that express them.

Across different researchers in this area, some use "conceptual" or "semantic" representation exclusively to describe the focus of their research, and others use both terms interchangeably. If semantic representations are considered as a subset of the set of possible conceptual representations, then all three practices seem reasonable because the conceptual representation associated with a particular word or sentence *is* its semantic representation. Some researchers (e.g., Pavlenko, 1999) have advocated separation of conceptual and semantic levels of representation. In theory, if the constructs are different, they ought to be separable. However, with a subset relationship, the separation is unlikely to be viable in experimental practice, at least with respect to language. To clarify, if a researcher is interested in studying those concepts that also happen to be semantic representations of words, there is no obvious way to separate them. On the other hand, if a researcher is interested in studying concepts that are not semantic representations of words or sentences, then, ironically, it is not clear how to study them using language stimuli.

The central question about bilingual semantic/conceptual representations is the degree to which they are integrated across languages. Here, it is important to talk about systems of possible representations versus representations of specific words. A semantic or conceptual system can be considered to have an innumerable set of possible semantic components, of which any word meaning is identified with a subset or a particular pattern of activation or "connection weights" across the entire system. Within this framework, the degree of integration can be considered at the systems level or at the level of individual word meanings. For both systems and units, this type of distributed or multicomponential representation allows the possibilities of completely shared representations, completely separate representations, and intermediate "partly shared" representations (as explained by De Groot, 1992a, 1992b). However, at the present time, bilingual researchers have not completed the types of studies needed or the analyses necessary for a true connectionist analysis, but some progress is being made in this area (e.g., Thomas & Van Heuven, chapter 10, this volume). We have used primarily the classical information processing approach.

The semantic/conceptual level of representation must also be distinguished from other levels of representation. Concepts can be given verbal labels, sequences of phonemes or graphemes, which are called *words*; *word meanings* are the concepts to which these words refer. In bilinguals, *translation equivalents* are words in different languages that refer to the same concept or have the same meaning. When referring to mental representations of words, cognitive psychologists often call this the *lexical level of representation*. The term *lexical* literally means "having to do with words." Although this term does distinguish the word level from, say, the sentence level, it does not specify what information about words is designated. In linguistics, the term lexical is used rather generally: a *lexical entry* contains several types of knowledge about a word, including phonological, morphological, syntactic, and semantic information, and the *lexicon* is the collection of lexical entries that any person has acquired. In psychology, the lexical level of representation is often meant to refer just to the level of the verbal label, and the lexicon is often meant to refer only to the collection of verbal labels. Less formally, the lexicon is the set of words in a person's vocabulary. This differential usage is often cause for confusion, so it would be advisable to be clear on exactly what the term is intended to mean. Because of this ambiguity, it is tempting to avoid the word lexical altogether, but the term lexical seems appropriate in reference to research that focuses on individual words and their meanings rather than larger units of language such as phrases or full sentences. Such research can be framed in terms of lexical representation, lexical processing, or lexical access.

Terminology Used to Characterize Bilingual Memory and Language Representation

Let us now consider the possible organizations of bilingual semantic representation. In cognitive bilingual research, the organization of bilingual memory and language, specifically the degree of language "integration" in representation, has been a central issue. Terminology in reference to the degree of integration is confusing because some of the terms have different meanings or implications for psycholinguists and memory researchers. In a previous article, the usage patterns for these terms were explained in more detail (Francis, 1999b), but a recapitulation seems useful here. The most integrated and least integrated representations are designated by terms that correspond to the two ends of this continuum. The most general terms are *shared* (alternatively, *common*) and *separate*, and these terms are used to discuss language integration in both memory and language.

Weinreich (1953) adopted the terms *compound* and *coordinate* to describe the mental configurations of the phonological and semantic representations of translation equivalents in bilinguals. In a compound representation, the two phonological forms are identified with a common *semanteme*, whereas in the coordinate representation, each phonological representation is identified with its own separate semanteme. However, Ervin and Osgood (1954) changed the meaning of these terms by applying them to particular language learning histories; compound bilinguals were those who had learned two languages simultaneously in a common context, and coordinate bilinguals were those who had learned the languages at different times or in different contexts. These were the language-learning patterns that they thought would lead to the correspondingly labeled cognitive representations outlined by Weinreich (1953).

In the 1960s and early 1970s, researchers debated whether bilingual memory consists of a single store for information learned in either language or two stores, with one for each language. Later, researchers adopted the terms *single code* and *dual code*, which are used primarily to refer to shared and separate representations, respectively, for the two languages of a bilingual in either language or memory. These terms are also used to refer to the dual-coding theory of bilingual memory proposed by Paivio and Desrochers (1980; Paivio, 1986, 1991), which has a complex configuration of shared and separate representational characteristics. The dual-coding aspect of this theory is the idea that words may be represented cognitively by a verbal code and an imaginal code rather than just a single verbal code. Semantic information about concrete words is located in an imaginal system that is shared by both languages, but some pairs of translation-equivalents are and some are not associated with a common referent. In contrast, abstract words have no referents (and therefore no shared referent) in the image system, are separately represented, and are only connected through translation.

Language independence and language interdependence are contrasting notions of language processing. Here, *independence* means that the two languages operate in relative isolation, so processing verbal items in one language does not affect processing of verbal items in the other language. When two languages operate *interdependently* in a given context, processing in one language is affected by processing in the other language. This distinction can easily be confused with the contrast of language independence versus language dependence in processes and representations. *Language-independent representations* or *processes* are the same (shared) for either language, whereas *language-dependent* ones are different (separate) for each language. Finally, *language-specific* representations or processes are only accessible through one language, whereas *language-general* ones are equally accessible through either language.

All of these terms are meant to refer to cognitive representations or processes that are not directly observable. Researchers often extend the terms to describe situations in which a language match between encoding and retrieval is or is not important, with separate and shared labels, respectively. It should be noted that, although these pairs of terms all refer to the degree of integration and are often used interchangeably, they have subtle differences in their implications and contexts. Implicit in these designations is that an intermediate or mixed representation is also possible.

Evidence of Bilingual Language Integration at the Semantic/Conceptual Level

The following is a brief summary of the important findings in this area. (For a more detailed description and evaluation of each technique and study, along with tables of quantitative comparisons, see Francis, 1999b.) The studies are organized according to the type of representation they address. First, they are classified according to whether they address primarily episodic memory representations or semantic memory representations. This distinction, proposed by Tulving (1972), is one in which the term *episodic memory* is used to refer to memory for events, and the term *semantic memory* is used to refer to information in a person's knowledge base. In the context of this chapter, the episodic memories addressed are primarily for verbal events. The semantic memories addressed are primarily knowledge of language. To determine the type of memory most directly addressed, the main criterion was that experiments on episodic memory typically have a delay between an initial exposure and a retrieval task of some sort, whereas experiments on semantic memory typically deal with simultaneous or immediate sequential processing of stimuli. Of course, studies of episodic memory may shed light on the underlying semantic memory representation of the concepts used as stimuli, but these inferences must be identified as such.

In the following summary, the sets of studies addressing episodic and semantic memory are further divided along a second dimension: studies that address memory systems and studies that address pairwise relationships among corresponding units within these systems. To determine which type of representation was addressed by a particular study, the main criterion was that experiments that address pairwise representations of units typically deal with translation equivalents, whereas studies that address systemwise representation typically deal with associates or influences of items that are not translation equivalents.

Episodic Memory Systems

Studies comparing memory for mixed-language word series to memory for single-language word series have shown that having to remember the language of input in addition to the corresponding concept requires an additional memory load. In these studies, bilingual participants were given a free recall test in which answers were counted as correct only if given in the appropriate language. Recall performance for mixed-language word lists was equivalent (93–100%) to that of single-language word lists when words in the different languages came from different semantic categories (Lambert, Ignatow, & Krauthamer, 1968; McCormack &

Novell, 1975; Nott & Lambert, 1968; Peynircioglu & Durgunoglu, 1993; Saegert, Obermeyer, & Kazarian, 1973). However, performance for mixed-language lists was inferior (68–86%) to that of single-language lists when items from the same semantic category were studied in different languages (Lambert et al., 1968; Nott & Lambert, 1968; Palmer, 1972; Tulving & Colotla, 1970). A single study of recognition memory for unrelated words showed a small but significant enhancement of recognition performance for mixed-language lists relative to single-language lists (McCormack & Colletta, 1975).

Examination of language clustering in recall of mixed-language lists indicates that, although language can be used as an organizer in episodic memory, it is subordinate to semantic organization. In the original reports, there were apparent discrepancies among the results because random sequence was used as a baseline. Because output sequences are strongly influenced by the sequence of the input (e.g., Dalrymple-Alford & Aamiry, 1969), a more appropriate baseline for output clustering is the degree of clustering in the input sequence. A reanalysis using the input sequence clustering as a baseline led to a consistent pattern of results across studies (Francis, 1999b). All five studies showed more clustering in the output sequences than in the input sequences, indicating positive reorganization by language (Dalrymple-Alford & Aamiry, 1969; Lambert et al., 1968; Nott & Lambert, 1968; Saegert, Obermeyer, et al., 1973; Tulving & Colotla, 1970). When compared to semantic category reorganization, which was substantial in the studies that measured it, two studies showed less reorganization by language than by semantic category (Lambert et al., 1968; Nott & Lambert, 1968), and one did not (Dalrymple-Alford & Aamiry, 1969). Thus, language appears not to be as salient an organizing principle as semantic category. The language reorganization observed may be a function of separation at the phonological level.

Several types of interference studies have shown that learning items in one language can adversely affect the learning or retrieval of semantically similar items in the other language. One method has been to examine interference in paired associate learning. *Negative transfer* occurs when a set of paired associates is re-paired after initial learning, and performance on the re-paired list is worse than for a new set of paired associates. Learning the re-paired set also impairs later recall of the original set of pairs relative to a new set, a phenomenon known as *retroactive interference*. Negative transfer (Lopez, Hicks, & Young, 1974; Young & Webber, 1967) and retroactive interference (Lopez et al., 1974; Young & Navar, 1968) occur even if words in the intervening re-paired list are in a different language from the original, showing that associations made in one language carry over to the other language. Therefore, the concepts of the two members of a pair were associated, not just the surface forms, indicating shared conceptual systems for the two languages. In another paired associate learning paradigm, learning to associate translation equivalents with two different cues was more difficult than learning to associate two unrelated different-language words with two different cues (Kintsch & Kintsch, 1969).

Other types of conceptually based interference effects also extend across languages. *Whole–part interference* is shown when learning a set of words interferes with later learning of a subset of those words relative to a new set; *part–whole interference* is shown when the subset is learned first and interferes with learning of the whole set relative to a new set. In a bilingual study of whole–part interference and part–whole interference, the whole lists and part lists were presented either in the same language or in different languages (Saegert, Kazarian, & Young, 1973). Between-language interference was not as strong as within-language interference, but it was substantial in all conditions except that in the part–whole paradigm there was facilitation instead of interference relative to a neutral list when going from the dominant to nondominant language. Misinformation effects induced by presenting misleading information to eyewitnesses between an observed event and questioning (Loftus, 1975) have also been examined in bilinguals. A study with bilingual witnesses showed that the degree of interference was equivalent whether the misleading information was given in the same language or in a different language from the final recall and recognition tests (Shaw, Garcia, & Robles, 1997). Under an extreme separate concept model, encoding and retrieving concepts in one language should not affect encoding and retrieval of concepts in the other language, but these interference results clearly contradict this expectation. Therefore, they support a model in which concepts are at least partly shared.

Analogical transfer in problem solving occurs when a new problem is solved by applying a solution previously learned for a different problem with similar causal structure. Studies using probability problems (Bernardo, 1998) and insight problems

(Francis, 1999a) have shown a high degree of analogical transfer across languages. Directed transfer rates across languages were 89–96% of the corresponding within-language rates. Spontaneous transfer rates across languages ranged from 65% to 95% of the within-language rates. The greatest attenuation was observed as decreased reminding or access to the source problem in spontaneous transfer for pairs of word problems with very high surface similarity, suggesting that reductions in transfer were caused by surface rather than conceptual characteristics of the source and target problems.

Results from other paradigms that addressed episodic memory at the systems level have been interpreted as evidence for separate memory systems, although not necessarily by the researchers who conducted the studies. However, these techniques do not address the semantic/conceptual level of representation. First, when learning and recalling lists of words from the same semantic category, performance declines with each successive list, a phenomenon known as *proactive interference* (or, alternatively, *proactive inhibition*), but if the category changes on a subsequent list, there is a recovery in performance or *release from proactive interference* (Wickens, Born, & Allen, 1963). Performance recovers following a language change as well (Dillon, McCormack, Petrusic, Cook, & Lafleur, 1973; Goggin & Wickens, 1971), but this effect can be explained by phonological differences between words in different languages (O'Neill & Huot, 1984) and therefore is not informative about the semantic level of representation. Second, the tendency when speaking a particular language to recall autobiographical events that occurred in the same language context (Marian & Neisser, 2000; Schrauf & Rubin, 1998, 2000) does not indicate separate memory stores for the two languages, but rather extends the range of known context-related effects on memory.

Episodic Memory Representations of Translation Equivalents

Studies of direct cross-language memory tests such as recall and recognition showed that items learned in one language can be intentionally accessed through the other language as long as the encoding and retrieval conditions encourage conceptual processing, as in free recall or recognition (Durgunoglu & Roediger, 1987; Ervin, 1961; Kintsch, 1970). Similarly, *positive transfer* learning paradigms have shown that learning of a word list (Lambert,

Havelka, & Crosby, 1958; Lopez & Young, 1974; Young & Saegert, 1966) or set of sentences (Opoku, 1992) was enhanced by previous or interpolated learning of the translations relative to previous or interpolated learning of an unrelated list or sentence. These findings provide only weak evidence for shared representation, because the extent to which strategic covert translation contributes to the transfer effects observed is unknown.

To avoid this problem, several studies were designed using less direct measures of memory, including savings and repetition priming paradigms. *Savings* is a phenomenon in which material previously learned but forgotten is relearned more quickly than new material. When nonrecallable number–word paired associates were relearned in a different language, the savings effect (relative to unrelated word sets) was substantial, but this effect was about half the magnitude of the savings observed when the paired associates were relearned in the same language (MacLeod, 1976). *Repetition priming* is a change in speed, accuracy, or bias based on previous experience with an item and typically refers to those effects that last for at least several minutes or after several intervening items. Under a shared-concept model, priming across languages would be expected to the extent that priming within a language is based on conceptual processing. Under a separate concept model, conceptual repetition priming across languages would not be expected.

Three different types of conceptually based priming paradigms have been examined in bilinguals and have yielded substantial cross-language repetition priming. First, *category–exemplar generation priming*, a bias to generate previously studied exemplars to category cues, is substantial even when the exemplars are studied and generated in different languages (Francis, 2001; Francis & Bjork, 1992). Second, *verb generation priming*, a response time advantage for repeated items in generating appropriate verbs to noun cues (e.g., generating "bark" to "dog"), is substantial even when the language changes from the first to second occurrence (Seger, Rabin, Desmond, & Gabrieli, 1999). Third, semantic classification of words is faster for repeated than for new items even when the language changes. This effect has been demonstrated for animate/inanimate decisions (Zeelenberg & Pecher, 2003), natural/manufactured decisions (Zeelenberg & Pecher, 2003), and concrete/abstract decisions (Francis & Goldmann, 2003).

The attenuation of priming across languages in some of these tasks suggests that nonconceptual processes also contribute to the within-language

effects. Semantic processing is not considered the primary basis of repetition priming in *word fragment completion*, a paradigm in which successfully completing a word fragment like "S_N_W_C_" is facilitated by prior presentation of its completion "sandwich." However, within this paradigm, a high degree of repetition priming across languages was observed when the encoding task required deep conceptual processing (Smith, 1991). Substantial but smaller cross-language priming effects occurred when the encoding tasks were less conceptual (Basden, Bonilla-Meeks, & Basden, 1994; Durgunoglu & Roediger, 1987; Heredia & McLaughlin, 1992; Peynircioglu & Durgunoglu, 1993). These studies showing repetition priming across languages indicated that concepts encoded by means of one language are automatically accessible to the other language even when no effort is made to retrieve them.

Studies of recall for bilingual repetitions show a *spacing effect* for translation-equivalent repetitions, in that recall performance is greater when the repetitions occur after several intervening items than when the repetitions occur in immediate succession (Glanzer & Duarte, 1971; Heredia & McLaughlin, 1992; Paivio, Clark, & Lambert, 1988). This result contradicts the expectations of the separate concept model and supports the shared concept model. Under a separate concept model, translation equivalents have different concepts (as would two unrelated words), so their recall probabilities would be independent of each other and therefore not depend on the number of intervening items. However, under a shared concept model, occurrences of translation equivalents involve repetition of the same concept, so the well-established spacing effect for within-language repetitions would be expected to generalize to between-language repetitions of the concept.

The studies on memory for language of input showed that bilinguals often remembered concepts without remembering the language in which the concepts were learned. In a basic study of recognition memory for words, bilinguals were twice as likely to misclassify the language as they were to misrecognize an item (Kintsch, 1970). The phenomenon was more striking in studies designed to increase language confusion, such as using cognates as stimuli (Cristoffanini, Kirsner, & Milech, 1986), having only script to distinguish language (Brown, Sharma, & Kirsner, 1984), or studying mixed language sets of highly related sentences (O'Neill & Dion, 1983; Rosenberg & Simon, 1977). Similarly, in learning successive word lists in which some words were reused in different languages, substantial proactive language confusion was exhibited (Liepmann & Saegert, 1974). Translation intrusions also occurred when mixed-language sets of paired associates were re-paired (Lopez et al., 1974). Translation intrusion errors were exhibited to a lesser degree in a number of free recall experiments not specifically designed to induce confusion (Kolers, 1966; Lambert et al., 1968; Nott & Lambert, 1968; Paivio et al., 1988; Rose & Carroll, 1974). These findings showed that the language of input is not a necessary feature of the episodic memory representation. The finding that memory for language of input for words and sentences can be high under certain experimental circumstances (Cristoffanini et al., 1986; Kintsch, 1970; MacLeod, 1976; O'Neill & Dion, 1983; Rose, Rose, King, & Perez, 1975; Rosenberg & Simon, 1977; Saegert, Hamayan, & Ahmar, 1975; Winograd, Cohen, & Barresi, 1976) and can be attributed to memory for the different phonology or orthography of noncognate translation equivalents in different languages.

Other studies dealing with episodic memory of translation equivalents were not informative about whether the representations are shared at the semantic/conceptual level (for more detail, see Francis, 1999b). In two cases, it was because the basis of the memory phenomenon under investigation was not semantic in nature. First, the finding that word fragments were not good recall cues for words studied in a different language (Watkins & Peynircioglu, 1983) does not bear on the semantic/conceptual level of representation because word fragments constitute cues to orthography and phonology, not meaning. Second, across four studies of repetition priming in *lexical decision* (deciding whether a letter string such as *chair* or *glarb* is a word or not), there was no evidence of facilitation from noncognate translation equivalents (Cristoffanini et al., 1986; Gerard & Scarborough, 1989; Kirsner, Brown, Abrol, Chadha, & Sharma, 1980; Kirsner, Smith, Lockhart, King, & Jain, 1984). Because even the within-language facilitation for repeated items in lexical decision is not thought to be conceptually based, the absence of priming across languages in those studies was not informative on the question of conceptual representation.

In several studies dealing with effects of repetition and generation on recall, there were plausible explanations for the results under either shared or separate models. Some of the observed effects of bilingual repetition on recall could be explained under either a shared or separate concept model.

These effects included the findings that a different language repetition helps free recall relative to a single presentation, a different language massed repetition helps recall more than a same language massed repetition, and same and different language spaced repetitions elicit equivalent recall performance (Durgunoglu & Roediger, 1987; Glanzer & Duarte, 1971; Heredia & McLaughlin, 1992; Kolers, 1966; Kolers & Gonzalez, 1980; Paivio et al., 1988; Winograd et al., 1976).

The advantage for different language repetitions over single presentations is expected under either model, because the joint probability of remembering one of two things with different names is always expected to be higher than the probability of remembering a specific one of those two. The advantage for different language over identical repetitions in massed conditions is expected under either model because the massed between-language repetitions are more distinctive than the identical repetitions because of phonological/orthographical differences. The equivalent performance under spaced conditions for different language and identical repetitions is also plausible under either model because, with increased spacing, identical repetitions approach independence, as would be expected for semantic (e.g., different language) repetitions and even unrelated items. One exception in which between-language spaced repetition of a story led to better recall than a within-language spaced repetition (Hummel, 1986) could be explained under either model by paying more attention to a translated story than to an identical repeated story.

Similarly, findings of *translation-based generation effects*, an advantage in memory for items generated from a translation cue rather than merely read (Arnedt & Gentile, 1986; Basden et al., 1994; Basi, Thomas, & Wang, 1997; O'Neill, Roy, & Tremblay, 1993; Paivio & Lambert, 1981; Potter, So, Von Eckardt, & Feldman, 1984; Vaid, 1988) and the absence of generation effects under some conditions (Durgonoglu & Roediger, 1987; O'Neill et al., 1993; Slamecka & Katsaiti, 1987) were consistent with both shared concept and separate concept models. This is because generation effects are expected based on having to produce a word from a cue rather than simply reading it, regardless of whether the cue is another word in the same language or a translation equivalent. The lack of effect in some cases may be consistent with the single-language literature on the generation effect; the effect appears to be somewhat inconsistent, with positive, null, and even reversed effects across studies. (See Steffens & Erdfelder, 1998, for a review of this literature and evaluation of the conditions under which generation effects occur.)

Semantic/Conceptual Systems

Lexical decisions are faster when a word is immediately preceded by a semantic associate than when it is immediately preceded by an unrelated word or presented in isolation, a phenomenon known as *semantic priming of lexical decision*. Several studies examining this type of semantic priming across languages revealed that the advantage for a related prime held even when it appeared in a different language from the target word (Chen & Ng, 1989; De Groot & Nas, 1991; Frenck & Pynte, 1987; Grainger & Beauvillain, 1988; Jin, 1990; Keatley & De Gelder, 1992; Keatley, Spinks, & De Gelder, 1994; Kirsner et al., 1984; Schwanenflugel & Rey, 1986; Tzelgov & Eben-Ezra, 1992; Williams, 1994). This facilitation was evident whether the control condition was an item with an unrelated prime or an item with no prime. A few discrepant nonsignificant cross-language facilitation effects in these same studies appeared to be Type II errors due to insufficient power. (Although the effect disappeared under response-deadline conditions [Keatley & De Gelder, 1992], it is not clear how this finding might have an impact on the conclusions drawn.)

Noncognate different language associates elicited an effect that was on average 70–80% as large as that of the corresponding within-language associates. Priming effects for cognates were stronger, indistinguishable from within-language priming, but it cannot be determined whether the cognates were processed in the intended language, especially given findings suggesting that lexical access in word reading is nonselective with respect to language (e.g., Dijkstra, Grainger, & Van Heuven, 1999; Jared & Kroll, 2001; Jared & Szucs, 2002). These experiments showed that processing of an item in one language can be facilitated when immediately preceded by a related item in the other language.

Semantic comparisons between words from different languages took no longer than comparisons between words in the same language. The semantic comparisons included verification of category–exemplar relationships (Caramazza & Brones, 1980; Dufour & Kroll, 1995; Potter et al., 1984), choosing the more extreme member of a word pair (Popiel, 1987), and solving analogies (Malakoff, 1988). Producing the name of a superordinate category in response to an exemplar likewise took the same amount of time whether the response was given in the same language or a different language from the exemplar (Shanon, 1982). Other evidence that semantic category is a more dominant organizer of semantic memory than language comes from the finding that language clustering in generating exemplars of two categories from semantic memory (i.e., with no prior study sequence), although substantial, was subordinate to organization by semantic category (Dalrymple-Alford, 1984).

Studies of between-language interference effects have shown that processing in one language can automatically interfere with processing of another. The *Stroop effect* is an interference phenomenon in which the naming of ink colors is slowed when the colors are presented in the form of incongruent color words (e.g., responding "red" when the word *blue* is printed in red ink). The most common variant on this color–word task is a *picture–word* task, in which picture naming is slowed by having an incongruent word superimposed on or presented simultaneously with the target picture (e.g., naming a picture of a goat with the word *sheep* superimposed). Relative to a neutral condition, between-language color–word interference was consistently reliable, ranging from 58% to 95% the magnitude of the within-language effect across studies (Abunuwara, 1992; Chen & Ho, 1986; Dalrymple-Alford, 1968; Dyer, 1971; Fang, Tzeng, & Alva, 1981; Kiyak, 1982; Lee, Wee, Tzeng, & Hung, 1992; Preston & Lambert, 1969; Smith & Kirsner, 1982). Similarly, between-language picture–word interference relative to a neutral control ranged from 75% to 140% of the within-language effect across studies (Costa, Miozzo, & Caramazza, 1999; Ehri & Ryan, 1980; Rusted, 1988; Smith & Kirsner, 1982).

Other Strooplike interference tasks have been examined in bilinguals and have consistently yielded substantial between-language interference for incongruent relative to neutral conditions. The *word–word* interference task requires naming words that have distracter words superimposed on them, which slows performance in bilinguals even if the distracter word is in a different language (Chen & Tsoi, 1990). The *tone–word* interference task requires classification of tones as high, medium, or low, with simultaneous incongruent presentation of the written words high, medium, or low, which slows performance even if responses are to be given in a different language from the distracter words. A *flanker–word* interference task requires classification of a word that is flanked above and below by words that would require a different classification response, which slows responses even if the flanker words are in a different language from the word to be classified (Fox, 1996). In all cases, between-language interference was attenuated relative to within-language interference. In a related translation paradigm, presentation of semantically related distractor words (La Heij, De Bruyn, Elens, Hartsuiker, Helaha, & Van Schelven, 1990; La Heij, Hooglander, Kerling, & Van der Velden, 1996; Miller & Kroll, 2002) or semantically related pictures (La Heij et al., 1996) slowed translation relative to neutral conditions.

Although the standard control for the Stroop interference task is a neutral condition, a number of studies have used a *congruent* condition, in which ink colors and color words match, as a control or comparison condition. The use of congruent trials as a control in Stroop and Stroop-like interference tasks is problematic because it mixes facilitation of the congruent condition relative to the neutral condition and interference of the incongruent condition relative to the neutral condition (MacLeod, 1991). In fact, in bilingual color–word interference studies, a congruent item in a different language has been shown to slow responses relative to neutral items (Abunuwara, 1992; Dalrymple-Alford, 1968), which could have the effect of spuriously reducing the estimate of between-language interference relative to within-language interference. Nevertheless, even relative to the congruent control interference across languages in the color–word task is substantial (Abunuwara, 1992; Altarriba & Mathis, 1997; Dalrymple-Alford, 1968; Tzelgov, Henik, & Leiser, 1990). The net effects of using a congruent condition as a control are less clear for the other Strooplike interference paradigms. For the picture–word task, translation equivalents facilitated picture naming (Costa et al., 1999), but in another study, words phonologically related to the first language translation equivalent slowed second language picture naming (Hermans, Bongaerts, De Bot, & Schreuder, 1998). Interference in incongruent relative to congruent conditions was evident in experiments using the picture–word task (Gerhand, Deregowski, & McAllister, 1995), the tone–word task (Hamers & Lambert, 1972), and the flanker–word task (Guttentag, Haith, Goodman, & Hauch, 1984).

Interference based on automatic processing of the nontarget language has been observed in other paradigms as well. When lexical decisions were made on a word with a translation equivalent, rather than an unrelated word, that was ignored on the previous word-naming trial, response times increased substantially, an effect known as *negative priming* (Neumann, McCloskey, & Felio, 1999).

In a paradigm requiring a decision of whether a phoneme belonged to the name of a picture, rejecting phonemes that were part of the nontarget language name was slower than rejecting phonemes that were not part of the name in either language (Colomé, 2001). In category exemplar generation from semantic memory, *part-set cueing* (auditory presentation of a subset of possible responses) in a different language interfered as much as did cueing in the same language (Peynircioglu & Göksen-Erelcin, 1988). The results of these studies suggested that activation spreads from the nontarget language to the target language by means of the common concept. Together, these studies indicated that the language systems of a bilingual are interdependent and share common elements at the semantic level.

Two types of results that addressed the semantic systems level could be explained with either a shared or a separate semantic system. Differences among associates produced to words in different languages (Dalrymple-Alford & Aamiry, 1970; Kolers, 1963) were not particularly informative about the degree of integration in semantic systems, even when accounting for the likelihood of producing the same associate twice in repeated trials in the same language. Although separate semantic systems would be expected to lead to different associations, several alternative explanations are possible. For example, the co-occurrence frequencies of particular word pairs, frequencies of category exemplars, and word order rules differ across languages, and any of these could lead to differences in the associates generated. Two lexical decision findings were also ambiguous in their implications for semantic representation. Lexical decision times were as fast when bilinguals had to verify words from both languages as in single-language lexical decision (Caramazza & Brones, 1979). Rejecting words from the nontarget language was slower than rejecting items that were nonwords in both languages as long as the words were orthographically legal and pronounceable in the target language (Grainger & Beauvillain, 1987; Nas, 1983; Scarborough, Gerard, & Cortese, 1984; Thomas & Allport, 2000). Both types of lexical decision findings could be attributed to shared semantic systems. However, a plausible alternative is that the letter strings presented were processed by both language systems simultaneously (in parallel), which would not require shared semantic systems. Therefore, these methods did not have clear implications for bilingual semantic representation.

Semantic/Conceptual Representations of Translation Equivalents

Lexical decision studies in which some target words were immediately preceded by presentation of their translation equivalents indicated speeded access relative to items preceded by unrelated primes (Altarriba, 1992; Chen & Ng, 1989; De Groot & Nas, 1991; Frenck-Mestre & Vaid, 1992; Gollan, Forster, & Frost, 1997; Jiang, 1999; Jin, 1990; Keatley & De Gelder, 1992; Keatley et al., 1994; Williams, 1994). Similarly, production of sentences was facilitated when immediately preceded by several practice trials of producing the sentence's translation (MacKay & Bowman, 1969). These studies showed that activation of semantic representations in one language speeds processing of translation equivalents in the other language, which suggests that the semantic representations of translation equivalents in linguistic memory are at least partly shared. An alternative explanation is that the facilitation effects are caused by activation spreading from the semantic representations involved to lower levels of processing, but this would also require shared semantic representation.

Studies of *repetition blindness*, an impairment in encoding or retrieving the second occurrence of a repeated word in a sentence or list (Kanwisher, 1987), showed mixed results when the first occurrence was a translation equivalent. Repetition blindness was observed in one word list study (Sánchez-Casas, Davis, & García-Albea, 1992) and one sentence study (MacKay & Miller, 1994), but not in another sentence study (Altarriba & Soltano, 1996). The positive results support shared representation because the between-language repetition appears to have been treated in the same manner as a within-language repetition. The negative result would support separate representation to the extent that the within-language effect was semantically based, but the results of previous research on this issue suggest that semantic processing does not play an important role in repetition blindness (Kanwisher & Potter, 1990).

Summary of Evidence About Bilingual Episodic and Semantic Memory Integration

For each of the four types of representation addressed, there are experimental studies that clearly contradict extreme separate concept models of bilingual memory. Complementary to these findings, all of the effects showing little or no transfer or interaction between languages could be explained reasonably in nonconceptual terms. Therefore, representation must be at least partly shared in each case. At present, the evidence may not be strong enough to confirm completely shared representation at the semantic level, but it is certainly not ruled out by any of the reviewed studies.

Remaining Issues and Future Directions

The Relationship Between Translation Equivalents and Synonyms

A potential trap that researchers may fall into when using bilingual materials is assuming that translation equivalents have the same cognitive status as within-language synonyms. Intuitively, this idea seems quite compelling because both synonyms and translation equivalents are supposed to "mean the same thing" as the original word. If translation equivalents and synonyms enjoy the same cognitive status, they ought to be processed in a similar manner. However, cognitive experiments involving translation equivalents and synonyms provide convincing evidence that they do not have the same cognitive status because translation equivalents and synonyms elicit different experimental results.

The difference between translation equivalents and synonyms is evident in the way even young children treat words that are intended to refer to the same thing. Children are resistant to giving two different labels to the same object, a phenomenon known as *mutual exclusivity* (Au & Glusman, 1990). This was demonstrated by showing the child a novel object and giving it a novel name, such as *mido*. When the object was put in a group with another kind of novel object, and the child was asked to point out the *theri*, children and adults picked the new object rather than the previously labeled one at a rate higher than chance. In contrast, when bilingual adults, bilingual 4-year-olds, or even monolingual 4-year-olds were told that one of the novel names was a word in another language, they were approximately equally likely to choose the previously labeled or the new object. When asked whether the previously labeled object could be given the new label, the vast majority responded that it could. That is, they did not honor mutual exclusivity across languages (Au & Glusman, 1990). There were no reliable performance differences on either task between monolingual and bilingual children. This study showed that, although children reject synonymy within a language, they accept translation equivalence.

A number of the paradigms used to examine the semantic integration of translation equivalents have also been conducted with synonyms. Several studies of episodic memory show differences between translation equivalents and synonyms in situations of both positive and negative transfer. For example, recall of a word is enhanced more by a translated repetition than by a synonymous repetition (Kolers & Gonzalez, 1980; Paivio et al., 1988). Savings in recall has been demonstrated for nonrecallable translation equivalents (MacLeod, 1976), but not for nonrecallable synonyms (Nelson, 1971). Intrusion rates in free recall (under mixed-language testing conditions) are higher for translation equivalents than for within-language synonyms (Paivio et al., 1988). Studies of semantic memory and language processing yield similar patterns of positive and negative transfer. Transfer of reading speed is 100% for (word-for-word) translated sentences (MacKay & Bowman, 1969), but only partial for synonym-substituted sentences (Levy, Di Persio, & Hollingshead, 1992). Repetition blindness, a decrement in recall performance for second occurrences of words within lists or sentences in rapid serial visual presentation, has been demonstrated for translation repetitions in mixed language word lists and sentences (MacKay & Miller, 1994; Sánchez-Casas et al., 1992; but see Altarriba & Soltano, 1996). In contrast, synonym repetitions did not exhibit repetition blindness (Kanwisher & Potter, 1990).

Because very few of these studies had the explicit purpose of comparing translation-equivalents and synonyms to each other, the individual cross-study comparisons ought to be considered preliminary until controlled comparison studies have been conducted. However, the consistency across paradigms gives strong evidence that translation equivalents are more closely related than are within-language synonyms.

Neuroimaging Studies of Bilingual Conceptual/Semantic Representation

Advances in neuroimaging over the last decade, in particular positron emission tomography (PET) and functional magnetic resonance imaging (MRI), have enabled new methods for examining bilingual cognitive organization. Most relevant to this chapter are studies that focus on bilingual semantic representation, particularly the question of shared versus separate semantic systems. If words in the two languages of a bilingual activate a common semantic system, the same cortical areas ought to be sensitive to semantic relative to nonsemantic processing in both languages, but if the two languages activate separate systems, the localization of activation ought to differ across languages.

Studies addressing semantic representation generally have found no reliable differences in localization of semantic processing across languages (e.g., Chee, Hon, Lee, & Soon, 2001; Illes et al., 1999), which is consistent with the cognitive experimental evidence for shared semantic systems discussed in this chapter. However, studies that also involve phonology, orthography, or processing of whole language, particularly when participants have limited proficiency in one language, often yield different patterns. For a review of the bilingual neuroimaging research with an emphasis on language comprehension and production processes, see Abutalebi, Cappa, and Perani, chapter 24, this volume. A key in this area of research will be for bilingual cognition experts to be involved in focusing studies on questions of maximal theoretical interest, choosing tasks that are appropriate from a cognitive/bilingual perspective, and interpreting results within the context of the bilingual cognition literature.

Developmental Approaches

Researchers have only begun to address the development of conceptual/semantic structures in bilinguals. Developmental models of bilingual language acquisition are likely to be important in the future of bilingual research because they allow for changes in representation with learning. Although cognitive psychologists have studied extensively the organization of bilingual lexical and semantic representation in proficient bilinguals, far less attention has been given to the question of how the representation got to that point (one exception is Kroll's revised hierarchical model; Dufour & Kroll, 1995; Kroll & De Groot, 1997). Surprisingly little is known about what it means cognitively for a person to go from being monolingual to bilingual because data on appropriate cognitive tasks across different levels of learning are sparse. There are very few cross-sectional cognitive studies that examine bilinguals across several different levels of language acquisition in the literature (notable exceptions are the work of Chen, 1990; De Groot & Poot, 1997; Mägiste, 1984, 1985, 1992) and apparently no longitudinal cognitive studies. Therefore, the existing data are insufficient to provide empirical support to build a more comprehensive model of bilingual language development.

As De Groot (2000) pointed out, studying semantic or lexical representation as it exists in a person who is at a particular stage of second language acquisition does not assume that the representation is static, but it instead gives us a window on the acquisition process. It would be informative to capture more windows at different stages of acquisition. Perhaps combining current experimental techniques with the microdevelopmental approach would enable a better understanding of how these representations evolve.

Illustrations of the microdevelopmental approach across a variety of contexts can be found in the edited volume *Microdevelopment: Transition Processes in Development and Learning* (Granott & Parziale, 2002). As an example, Gelman, Romo, and Francis (2002) conducted a microdevelopmental study using notebooks kept by English as a second language students throughout a course to get windows on learning at several different points during their science learning and English language acquisition. Collecting more cognitive measures of bilingual processing or conducting a true experiment addressing semantic or lexical representation on a similar schedule would likely provide new insights on the acquisition process.

A large body of developmental or second language acquisition research *does* describe the patterns of language performance exhibited by second language learners at different levels of proficiency, at different ages, and in different situations. However, these studies shed virtually no light on the cognitive processes underlying the observed effects. For example, many studies have been interpreted as supporting a critical period for second language learning, yet these interpretations rarely explain which cognitive processes or mechanisms might be relatively problematic for older learners. Identification of these cognitive mechanisms would likely be useful in developing more rigorous models of second language acquisition and in developing methods to improve second language learning and instruction.

Acknowledgment

It should be noted that much of the conceptual content of this chapter was also reported in my 1999 *Psychological Bulletin* article (Francis, 1999b).

References

Abunuwara, E. (1992). The structure of the trilingual lexicon. *European Journal of Cognitive Psychology, 4,* 311–322.

Altarriba, J. (1992). The representation of translation equivalents in bilingual memory. In R. J. Harris (Ed.), *Cognitive processing in bilinguals* (pp. 157–174). Amsterdam: Elsevier Science.

Altarriba, J., & Mathis, K. M. (1997). Conceptual and lexical development in second language acquisition. *Journal of Memory and Language, 36,* 550–568.

Altarriba, J., & Soltano, E. G. (1996). Repetition blindness and bilingual memory: Token individuation for translation equivalents. *Memory & Cognition, 24,* 700–711.

Arnedt, C. S., & Gentile, J. R. (1986). A test of dual coding theory for bilingual memory. *Canadian Journal of Psychology, 40,* 290–299.

Au, T. K., & Glusman, M. (1990). The principle of mutual exclusivity in word learning: To honor or not to honor? *Child Development, 61,* 1474–1490.

Basden, B. H., Bonilla-Meeks, J. L., & Basden, D. R. (1994). Cross-language priming in word-fragment completion. *Journal of Memory and Language, 33,* 69–82.

Basi, R. K., Thomas, M. H., & Wang, A. Y. (1997). Bilingual generation effect: Variations in participant bilingual type and list type. *Journal of General Psychology, 124,* 216–222.

Bernardo, A. B. I. (1998). Language format and analogical transfer among bilingual problem solvers in the Philippines. *International Journal of Psychology, 33,* 33–44.

Brown, H., Sharma, N. K., & Kirsner, K. (1984). The role of script and phonology in lexical representation. *The Quarterly Journal of Experimental Psychology, 36A,* 491–505.

Caramazza, A., & Brones, I. (1979). Lexical access in bilinguals. *Bulletin of the Psychonomic Society, 13,* 212–214.

Caramazza, A., & Brones, I. (1980). Semantic classification by bilinguals. *Canadian Journal of Psychology, 34,* 77–81.

Chee, M. W. L., Hon, N., Lee, H. L., & Soon, C. S. (2001). Relative language proficiency modulates BOLD signal change when bilinguals perform semantic judgments. *NeuroImage, 13,* 1155–1163.

Chen, H. C. (1990). Lexical processing in a non-native language: Effects of language proficiency and learning strategy. *Memory & Cognition, 18*, 279–288.

Chen, H. C., & Ho, C. (1986). Development of Stroop interference in Chinese-English Bilinguals. *Journal of Experimental Psychology: Learning, Memory, and Cognition, 12*, 397–401.

Chen, H. C., & Ng, N. L. (1989). Semantic facilitation and translation priming effects in Chinese-English bilinguals. *Memory & Cognition, 17*, 454–462.

Chen, H. C., & Tsoi, K. C. (1990). Symbol-word interference in Chinese and English. *Acta Psychologica, 75*, 123–138.

Colomé, À. (2001). Lexical activation in bilinguals' speech production: Language-specific or language-independent? *Journal of Memory and Language, 45*, 721–736.

Costa, A., Miozzo, M., & Caramazza, A. (1999). Lexical selection in bilinguals: Do words in the bilingual's two languages compete for selection? *Journal of Memory and Language, 41*, 365–397.

Cristoffanini, P., Kirsner, K., & Milech, D. (1986). Bilingual lexical representation: The status of Spanish-English cognates. *Quarterly Journal of Experimental Psychology: Human Experimental Psychology, 38*, 367–393.

Dalrymple-Alford, E. C. (1968). Interlingual interference in a color-naming task. *Psychonomic Science, 10*, 215–216.

Dalrymple-Alford, E. C. (1984). Bilingual retrieval from semantic memory. *Current Psychological Research and Reviews, 3*, 3–13.

Dalrymple-Alford, E. C., & Aamiry, A. (1969). Language and category clustering in bilingual free recall. *Journal of Verbal Learning and Verbal Behavior, 8*, 762–768.

Dalrymple-Alford, E. C., & Aamiry, A. (1970). Word associations of bilinguals. *Psychonomic Science, 21*, 319–320.

De Groot, A. M. B. (1992a). Bilingual lexical representation: A closer look at conceptual representations. In R. Frost & L. Katz (Eds.), *Orthography, phonology, morphology, and meaning* (pp. 389–412). Amsterdam: Elsevier.

De Groot, A. M. B. (1992b). Determinants of word translation. *Journal of Experimental Psychology: Learning, Memory, and Cognition, 18*, 1001–1018.

De Groot, A. M. B. (2000). On the source and nature of semantic and conceptual knowledge. *Bilingualism: Language and Cognition, 3*, 7–9.

De Groot, A. M. B., & Nas, G. L. J. (1991). Lexical representation of cognates and noncognates in compound bilinguals. *Journal of Memory and Language, 30*, 90–123.

De Groot, A. M. B., & Poot, R. (1997). Word translation at three levels of proficiency in a second language: The ubiquitous involvement of conceptual memory. *Language Learning, 47*, 215–264.

Dijkstra, T., Grainger, J., & Van Heuven, W. J. B. (1999). Recognition of cognates and interlingual homographs: The neglected role of phonology. *Journal of Memory and Language, 41*, 496–518.

Dillon, R. F., McCormack, P. D., Petrusic, W. M., Cook, G. M., & Lafleur, L. (1973). Release from proactive interference in compound and coordinate bilinguals. *Bulletin of the Psychonomic Society, 2*, 293–294.

Dufour, R., & Kroll, J. F. (1995). Matching words to concepts in two languages: A test of the concept mediation model of bilingual representation. *Memory & Cognition, 23*, 166–180.

Durgunoglu, A. Y., & Roediger, H. L. (1987). Test differences in accessing bilingual memory. *Journal of Memory and Language, 26*, 377–391.

Dyer, F. N. (1971). Color-naming interference in monolinguals and bilinguals. *Journal of Verbal Learning and Verbal Behavior, 10*, 297–302.

Ehri, L. C., & Ryan, E. B. (1980). Performance of bilinguals in a picture–word interference task. *Journal of Psycholinguistic Research, 9*, 285–302.

Ervin, S. M. (1961). Learning and recall in bilinguals. *The American Journal of Psychology, 74*, 446–451.

Ervin, S. M., & Osgood, C. E. (1954). Second language learning and bilingualism. *Journal of Abnormal and Social Psychology, 49*(Suppl.), 139–146.

Fang, S. P., Tzeng, O. J., & Alva, L. (1981). Intralanguage versus interlanguage Stroop effects in two types of writing systems. *Memory & Cognition, 9*, 609–617.

Fox, E. (1996). Cross-language priming from ignored words: Evidence for a common representational system in bilinguals. *Journal of Memory and Language, 35*, 353–370.

Francis, W. S. (1999a). Analogical transfer of problem solutions within and between languages in English-Spanish bilinguals. *Journal of Memory and Language, 40*, 301–329.

Francis, W. S. (1999b). Cognitive integration of language and memory in bilinguals: Semantic representation. *Psychological Bulletin, 125*, 193–222.

Francis, W. S. (2000). Clarifying the cognitive experimental approach to bilingual research. *Bilingualism: Language and Cognition, 3*, 13–15.

Francis, W. S. (2001). Components of priming in category exemplar generation. *Abstracts of the Psychonomic Society, 6*, 47.

Francis, W. S., & Bjork, R. A. (1992, November). *Cross-language conceptual priming in English-Spanish bilinguals.* Poster presented at the 33rd annual meeting of the Psychonomic Society, St. Louis, MO.

Francis, W. S., & Goldmann, L. (2003). *Priming of semantic judgments within and across languages in Spanish-English bilinguals.* Unpublished manuscript.

Frenck, C., & Pynte, J. (1987). Semantic representation and surface forms: A look at across-language priming in bilinguals. *Journal of Psycholinguistic Research, 16,* 383–396.

Frenck-Mestre, C., & Vaid, J. (1992). Language as a factor in the identification of ordinary words and number words. In R. J. Harris (Ed.), *Cognitive processing in bilinguals* (pp. 265–281). Amsterdam: Elsevier Science.

Gelman, R., Romo, L. F., & Francis, W. S. (2002). Notebooks as windows on learning: The case of a science-into-ESL program. In N. Granott & J. Parziale (Eds.), *Microdevelopment: Transition processes in development and learning* (pp. 269–293). Cambridge, U.K.: Cambridge University Press.

Gerard, L. D., & Scarborough, D. L. (1989). Language-specific lexical access of homographs by bilinguals. *Journal of Experimental Psychology: Learning, Memory, and Cognition, 15,* 305–315.

Gerhand, S. J., Deregowski, J. B., & McAllister, H. (1995). Stroop phenomenon as a measure of cognitive functioning of bilingual (Gaelic/English) subjects. *British Journal of Psychology, 86,* 89–92.

Glanzer, M., & Duarte, A. (1971). Repetition between and within languages in free recall. *Journal of Verbal Learning and Verbal Behavior, 10,* 625–630.

Goggin, J., & Wickens, D. D. (1971). Proactive interference and language change in short-term memory. *Journal of Verbal Learning and Verbal Behavior, 10,* 453–458.

Gollan, T. H., Forster, K. I., & Frost, R. (1997). Translation priming with different scripts: Masked priming with cognates and non-cognates in Hebrew-English bilinguals. *Journal of Experimental Psychology: Learning, Memory, and Cognition, 23,* 1122–1139.

Grainger, J., & Beauvillain, C. (1987). Language blocking and lexical access in bilinguals. *Quarterly Journal of Experimental Psychology: Human Experimental Psychology, 39A,* 295–319.

Grainger, J., & Beauvillain, C. (1988). Associative priming in bilinguals: Some limits of interlingual facilitation effects. *Canadian Journal of Psychology, 42,* 261–273.

Granott, N., & Parziale, J. (2002). *Microdevelopment: Transition processes in development and learning.* Cambridge, U.K.: Cambridge University Press.

Grosjean, F. (1992). Another view of bilingualism. In R. Harris (Ed.), *Cognitive processing in bilinguals* (pp. 51–62). Amsterdam: Elsevier.

Guttentag, R. E., Haith, M. M., Goodman, G. S., & Hauch, J. (1984). Semantic processing of unattended words by bilinguals: A test of the input switch mechanism. *Journal of Verbal Learning and Verbal Behavior, 23,* 178–188.

Hamers, J. F., & Lambert, W. E. (1972). Bilingual interdependencies in auditory perception. *Journal of Verbal Learning and Verbal Behavior, 11,* 303–310.

Heredia, R., & McLaughlin, B. (1992). Bilingual memory revisited. In R. J. Harris (Ed.), *Cognitive processing in bilinguals* (pp. 91–103). Amsterdam: Elsevier Science.

Hermans, D., Bongaerts, T., De Bot, K., & Schreuder, R. (1998). Producing words in a foreign language: Can speakers prevent interference from their first language? *Bilingualism: Language and Cognition, 1,* 213–229.

Hummel, K. M. (1986). Memory for bilingual prose. In J. Vaid (Ed.), *Language processing in bilinguals: Psycholinguistic and neuropsychological perspectives* (pp. 47–64). Hillsdale, NJ: Erlbaum.

Illes, J., Francis, W. S., Desmond, J. E., Gabrieli, J. D. E., Glover, G. H., Poldrack, R. A., et al. (1999). Convergent cortical representation of semantic processing in bilinguals. *Brain and Language, 70,* 347–363.

Jackendoff, R. (1994). Word meanings and what it takes to learn them: Reflections on the Piaget-Chomsky debate. In W. F. Overton & D. S. Palermo (Ed.), *The nature and ontogenesis of meaning* (pp. 129–144). Hillsdale, NJ: Erlbaum.

Jared, D., & Kroll, J. F. (2001). Do bilinguals activate phonological representations in one or both of their languages when naming words? *Journal of Memory and Language, 44,* 2–31.

Jared, D., & Szucs, C. (2002). Phonological activation in bilinguals: Evidence from interlingual homograph naming. *Bilingualism: Language and Cognition, 5,* 225–239.

Jiang, N. (1999). Testing processing explanations for the asymmetry in masked cross-language priming. *Bilingualism: Language and Cognition, 2,* 59–75.

Jin, Y. S. (1990). Effects of concreteness on cross-language priming in lexical decisions. *Perceptual and Motor Skills, 70,* 1139–1154.

Kanwisher, N. G. (1987). Repetition blindness: Type recognition without token individuation. *Cognition, 27,* 117–143.

Kanwisher, N. G., & Potter, M. C. (1990). Repetition blindness: Levels of processing. *Journal of Experimental Psychology: Human Perception and Performance, 16*, 30–47.

Keatley, C., & De Gelder, B. (1992). The bilingual primed lexical decision task: Cross-language priming disappears with speeded responses. *European Journal of Cognitive Psychology, 4*, 273–292.

Keatley, C. W., Spinks, J. A., & De Gelder, B. (1994). Asymmetrical cross-language priming effects. *Memory & Cognition, 22*, 70–84.

Kintsch, W. (1970). Recognition memory in bilingual subjects. *Journal of Verbal Learning and Verbal Behavior, 9*, 405–409.

Kintsch, W., & Kintsch, E. (1969). Interlingual interference and memory processes. *Journal of Verbal Learning and Verbal Behavior, 8*, 16–19.

Kirsner, K., Brown, H. L., Abrol, S., Chadha, N. K., & Sharma, N. K. (1980). Bilingualism and lexical representation. *Quarterly Journal of Experimental Psychology, 32*, 585–594.

Kirsner, K., Smith, M. C., Lockhart, R. S., King, M. L., & Jain, M. (1984). The bilingual lexicon: Language-specific units in an integrated network. *Journal of Verbal Learning and Verbal Behavior, 23*, 519–539.

Kiyak, H. A. (1982). Interlingual interference in naming color words. *Journal of Cross-Cultural Psychology, 13*, 125–135.

Kolers, P. A. (1963). Interlingual word associations. *Journal of Verbal Learning and Verbal Behavior, 2*, 291–300.

Kolers, P. A. (1966). Interlingual facilitation of short-term memory. *Journal of Verbal Learning and Verbal Behavior, 5*, 314–319.

Kolers, P. A., & Gonzalez, E. (1980). Memory for words, synonyms, and translations. *Journal of Experimental Psychology: Human Learning and Memory, 6*, 53–65.

Kroll, J. F., & De Groot, A. M. B. (1997). Lexical and conceptual memory in the bilingual: Mapping form to meaning in two languages. In A. M. B. de Groot & J. F. Kroll (Eds.), *Tutorials in bilingualism: Psycholinguistic perspectives* (pp. 169–199). Mahwah, NJ: Erlbaum.

La Heij, W., De Bruyn, E., Elens, E., Hartsuiker, R., Helaha, D., & Van Schelven, L. (1990). Orthographic facilitation and categorical interference in a word-translation variant of the Stroop task. *Canadian Journal of Psychology, 44*, 76–83.

La Heij, W., Hooglander, A., Kerling, R., & Van der Velden, E. (1996). Nonverbal context effects in forward and backward translation: Evidence for concept mediation. *Journal of Memory and Language, 35*, 648–665.

Lambert, W. E., Havelka, J., & Crosby, C. (1958). The influence of language-acquisition contexts on bilingualism. *Journal of Abnormal and Social Psychology, 56*, 239–244.

Lambert, W. E., Ignatow, M., & Krauthamer, M. (1968). Bilingual organization in free recall. *Journal of Verbal Learning and Verbal Behavior, 7*, 207–214.

Lee, W. L., Wee, G. C., Tzeng, O. J. L., & Hung, D. L. (1992). A study of interlingual and intralingual Stroop effect in three different scripts: logograph, syllabary, and alphabet. In R. J. Harris (Ed.), *Cognitive processing in bilinguals* (pp. 427–442). Amsterdam: Elsevier Science.

Levy, B. A., Di Persio, R., & Hollingshead, A. (1992). Fluent rereading: Repetition, automaticity, and discrepancy. *Journal of Experimental Psychology: Learning, Memory, and Cognition, 18*, 957–971.

Liepmann, D., & Saegert, J. (1974). Language tagging in bilingual free recall. *Journal of Experimental Psychology, 103*, 1137–1141.

Loftus, E. F. (1975). Leading questions and the eyewitness report. *Cognitive Psychology, 7*, 560–572.

Lopez, M., Hicks, R. E., & Young, R. K. (1974). Retroactive inhibition in a bilingual A-B, A-B' paradigm. *Journal of Experimental Psychology, 103*, 85–90.

Lopez, M., & Young, R. K. (1974). The linguistic interdependence of bilinguals. *Journal of Experimental Psychology, 102*, 981–983.

MacKay, D. G., & Bowman, R. W. (1969). On producing the meaning in sentences. *American Journal of Psychology, 82*, 23–39.

MacKay, D. G., & Miller, M. D. (1994). Semantic blindness: Repeated concepts are difficult to encode and recall under time pressure. *Psychological Science, 5*, 52–55.

MacLeod, C. M. (1976). Bilingual episodic memory: Acquisition and forgetting. *Journal of Verbal Learning and Verbal Behavior, 15*, 347–364.

MacLeod, C. M. (1991). Half a century of research on the Stroop effect: An integrative review. *Psychological Bulletin, 109*, 163–203.

Mägiste, E. (1984). Stroop tasks and dichotic translation: The development of interference patterns in bilinguals. *Journal of Experimental Psychology: Learning, Memory, and Cognition, 10*, 304–315.

Mägiste, E. (1985). Development of intra- and interlingual interference in bilinguals. *Journal of Psycholinguistic Research, 14*, 137–154.

Mägiste, E. (1992). Second language learning in elementary and high school students. *European Journal of Cognitive Psychology, 4*, 355–365.

Malakoff, M. E. (1988). The effect of language of instruction on reasoning in bilingual children. *Applied Psycholinguistics, 9,* 17–38.

Marian, V., & Neisser, U. (2000). Language-dependent recall of autobiographical memories. *Journal of Experimental Psychology: General, 129,* 361–368.

McCormack, P. D., & Colletta, P. (1975). Recognition memory for items from unilingual and bilingual lists. *Bulletin of the Psychonomic Society, 6,* 149–151.

McCormack, P. D., & Novell, J. A. (1975). Free recall from unilingual and trilingual lists. *Bulletin of the Psychonomic Society, 6,* 173–174.

Miller, N. A., & Kroll, J. F. (2002). Stroop effects in bilingual translation. *Memory & Cognition, 30,* 614–628.

Nas, G. (1983). Visual word recognition in bilinguals: Evidence for a cooperation between visual and sound based codes during access to a common lexical store. *Journal of Verbal Learning and Verbal Behavior, 22,* 526–534.

Nelson, T. O. (1971). Savings and forgetting from long-term memory. *Journal of Verbal Learning and Verbal Behavior, 10,* 568–576.

Neumann, E., McCloskey, M. S., & Felio, A. C. (1999). Cross-language positive priming disappears, negative priming does not: Evidence for two sources of selective inhibition. *Memory & Cognition, 27,* 1051–1063.

Nott, C. R., & Lambert, W. E. (1968). Free recall of bilinguals. *Journal of Verbal Learning and Verbal Behavior, 7,* 1065–1071.

O'Neill, W., & Dion, A. (1983). Bilingual recognition of concrete and abstract sentences. *Perceptual and Motor Skills, 57,* 839–845.

O'Neill, W., & Huot, R. (1984). Release from proactive inhibition as a function of a language of pronunciation shift in bilinguals. *Canadian Journal of Psychology, 38,* 54–62.

O'Neill, W., Roy, L., & Tremblay, R. (1993). A translation-based generation effect in bilingual recall and recognition. *Memory & Cognition, 21,* 488–495.

Opoku, J. (1992). The influence of semantic cues in learning among bilinguals at different levels of proficiency in English. In R. J. Harris (Ed.), *Cognitive processing in bilinguals* (pp. 175–189). Amsterdam: Elsevier Science.

Paivio, A. (1986). *Mental representations: A dual coding approach* (pp. 239–257). New York: Oxford University Press.

Paivio, A. (1991). Mental representation in bilinguals. In A. G. Reynolds (Ed.), *Bilingualism, multiculturalism, and second language learning* (pp. 113–126). Hillsdale, NJ: Erlbaum.

Paivio, A., Clark, J. M., & Lambert, W. E. (1988). Bilingual dual-coding theory and semantic repetition effects on recall. *Journal of Experimental Psychology: Learning, Memory, and Cognition, 14,* 163–172.

Paivio, A., & Desrochers, A. (1980). A dual-coding approach to bilingual memory. *Canadian Journal of Psychology, 34,* 388–399.

Paivio, A., & Lambert, W. (1981). Dual coding and bilingual memory. *Journal of Verbal Learning and Verbal Behavior, 20,* 532–539.

Palmer, M. B. (1972). Effects of categorization, degree of bilingualism, and language upon recall of select monolinguals and bilinguals. *Journal of Educational Psychology, 63,* 160–164.

Pavlenko, A. (1999). New approaches to concepts in bilingual memory. *Bilingualism: Language and Cognition, 2,* 209–230.

Peynircioglu, Z. F., & Durgunoglu, A. Y. (1993). Effects of a bilingual context on memory performance. In J. Altarriba (Ed.), *Cognition and culture: A cross-cultural approach to psychology* (pp. 57–75). Amsterdam: Elsevier Science.

Peynircioglu, Z. F., & Göksen-Erelcin, F. (1988). Part-set cuing across languages: Evidence for both word- and concept-mediated inhibition depending on language dominance. *Acta Psychologica, 67,* 19–32.

Popiel, S. J. (1987). Bilingual comparative judgments: Evidence against the switch hypothesis. *Journal of Psycholinguistic Research, 16,* 563–576.

Potter, M. C., So, K. F., Von Eckardt, B., & Feldman, L. B. (1984). Lexical and conceptual representation in beginning and proficient bilinguals. *Journal of Verbal Learning and Verbal Behavior, 23,* 23–38.

Preston, M. S., & Lambert, W. E. (1969). Interlingual interference in a bilingual version of the Stroop color–word task. *Journal of Verbal Learning and Verbal Behavior, 8,* 295–301.

Rose, R. G., & Carroll, J. F. (1974). Free recall of a mixed language list. *Bulletin of the Psychonomic Society, 3,* 267–268.

Rose, R. G., Rose, P. R., King, N., & Perez, A. (1975). Bilingual memory for related and unrelated sentences. *Journal of Experimental Psychology: Human Learning and Memory, 1,* 599–606.

Rosenberg, S., & Simon, H. A. (1977). Modeling semantic memory: Effects of presenting semantic information in different modalities. *Cognitive Psychology, 9,* 293–325.

Rusted, J. (1988). Orthographic effects for Chinese-English bilinguals in a picture–word interference task. *Current Psychology: Research and Reviews, 7,* 207–220.

Saegert, J., Hamayan, E., & Ahmar, H. (1975). Memory for language of input in polyglots. *Journal of Experimental Psychology: Human Learning and Memory, 1,* 607–613.

Saegert, J., Kazarian, S., & Young, R. K. (1973). Part/whole transfer with bilinguals. *American Journal of Psychology, 86,* 537–546.

Saegert, J., Obermeyer, J., & Kazarian, S. (1973). Organizational factors in free recall of bilingually mixed lists. *Journal of Experimental Psychology, 97,* 397–399.

Sánchez-Casas, R. M., Davis, C. W., García-Albea, J. E. (1992). Bilingual lexical processing: Exploring the cognate/noncognate distinction. *European Journal of Cognitive Psychology, 4,* 293–310.

Scarborough, D. L., Gerard, L., & Cortese, C. (1984). Independence of lexical access in bilingual word recognition. *Journal of Verbal Learning and Verbal Behavior, 23,* 84–99.

Schrauf, R. W., & Rubin, D. C. (1998). Bilingual autobiographical memory in older adult immigrants: A test of cognitive explanations of the reminiscence bump and the linguistic encoding of memories. *Journal of Memory and Language, 39,* 437–457.

Schrauf, R. W., & Rubin, D. C. (2000). Internal languages of retrieval: The bilingual encoding of memories for the personal past. *Memory & Cognition, 28,* 616–623.

Schwanenflugel, P. J., & Rey, M. (1986). Interlingual semantic facilitation: Evidence for a common representational system in the bilingual lexicon. *Journal of Memory and Language, 25,* 605–618.

Seger, C. A., Rabin, L. A., Desmond, J. E., & Gabrieli, J. D. E. (1999). Verb generation priming involves conceptual implicit memory. *Brain and Cognition, 41,* 150–177.

Shanon, B. (1982). Bilingual identification and classification of words and drawings in two languages. *Quarterly Journal of Experimental Psychology, 34A,* 135–152.

Shaw, J. S., Garcia, L. A., & Robles, B. E. (1997). Cross-language postevent misinformation effects across languages in Spanish-English bilinguals. *Journal of Applied Psychology, 82,* 889–899.

Slamecka, N. J., & Katsaiti, L. R. (1987). The generation effect as an artifact of selective displaced rehearsal. *Journal of Memory and Language, 26,* 589–607.

Smith, M. C. (1991). On the recruitment of semantic information for word fragment completion: Evidence from bilingual priming. *Journal of Experimental Psychology: Learning, Memory, and Cognition, 17,* 234–244.

Smith, M. C., & Kirsner, K. (1982). Language and orthography as irrelevant features in colour-word and picture–word Stroop interference. *Quarterly Journal of Experimental Psychology: Human Experimental Psychology, 34A,* 153–170.

Steffens, M. C., & Erdfelder, E. (1998). Determinants of positive and negative generation effects in free recall. *Quarterly Journal of Experimental Psychology, 51A,* 705–733.

Thomas, M. S. C., & Allport, A. (2000). Language switching costs in bilingual visual word recognition. *Journal of Memory and Language, 43,* 44–66.

Tulving, E. (1972). Episodic and semantic memory. In E. Tulving & W. Donaldson (Eds.), *Organization of memory.* New York: Academic Press.

Tulving, E., & Colotla, V. A. (1970). Free recall of trilingual lists. *Cognitive Psychology, 1,* 86–98.

Tzelgov, J., & Eben-Ezra, S. (1992). Components of the between-language semantic priming effect. *European Journal of Cognitive Psychology, 4,* 253–272.

Tzelgov, J., Henik, A., & Leiser, D. (1990). Controlling Stroop interference: Evidence from a between-language task. *Journal of Experimental Psychology: Learning, Memory, and Cognition, 16,* 760–771.

Vaid, J. (1988). Bilingual memory representation: A further test of dual coding theory. *Canadian Journal of Psychology, 42,* 84–90.

Watkins, M. J., & Peynircioglu, Z. F. (1983). On the nature of word recall: Evidence for linguistic specificity. *Journal of Verbal Learning and Verbal Behavior, 22,* 385–394.

Weinreich, U. (1953). *Languages in contact.* The Hague, The Netherlands: Mouton.

Wickens, D. D., Born, D. G., & Allen, C. K. (1963). Proactive inhibition and item similarity in short-term memory. *Journal of Verbal Learning and Verbal Behavior, 2,* 440–445.

Williams, J. N. (1994). The relationship between word meanings in the first and second language: Evidence for a common, but restricted, semantic code. *European Journal of Cognitive Psychology, 6,* 195–220.

Winograd, E., Cohen, C., & Barresi, J. (1976). Memory for concrete and abstract words in bilingual speakers. *Memory & Cognition, 4,* 323–329.

Young, R. K., & Navar, M. I. (1968). Retroactive inhibition with bilinguals. *Journal of Experimental Psychology, 77,* 109–115.

Young, R. K., & Saegert, J. (1966). Transfer with bilinguals. *Psychonomic Science, 6,* 161–162.

Young, R. K., & Webber, A. (1967). Positive and negative transfer with bilinguals. *Journal of Verbal Learning and Verbal Behavior, 6,* 874–877.

Zeelenberg, R., & Pecher, D. (2003). Evidence for long-term cross-language repetition priming in conceptual implicit memory tasks. *Journal of Memory and Language, 46,* 80–94.

13

Ambiguities and Anomalies

*What Can Eye Movements and Event-Related
Potentials Reveal About Second Language Sentence
Processing?*

ABSTRACT Second language sentence processing is examined here in light of several monolingual psycholinguistic models of parsing, as well as of linguistic theories specifically adapted to account for second language acquisition in adult learners. I first examine studies that have primarily recorded eye movements to trace syntactic processing. Syntactic ambiguity resolution is used in these studies to address various current models of parsing, both in monolinguals and bilinguals. To illustrate how these models can be tested, I discuss a particular type of structural ambiguity: reduced relative clauses. Thereafter, the focus is on studies that have recorded event-related potentials during the processing of spoken and written sentences in bilinguals. In these studies, the emphasis is placed on how semantic and syntactic anomalies, rather than ambiguities, are treated. I conclude with a brief comparison of these two approaches.

White (1997) raised the interesting issue of the relationship between linguistic theory and research on second language (L2) acquisition. As she quite correctly stated, theory is ever changing and subject to sometimes major upheavals. Linguistic theory is no exception. What are the implications for L2 research? The answer to this question is not as immediately apparent as it may seem. As stated by Bialystok (1997):

The field [of second language acquisition] is populated by groups bearing hyphenated allegiances: sociolinguistics, applied linguistics, psycholinguistics, educational linguists, and so on. Although it is clear that each relies in its own way on the parent field of linguistics, it is not at all clear, and certainly not consistent, what role linguistics plays in each research program. (p. 56)

To further complicate matters, within each of these fields there is widespread debate about just which linguistic theory is the best monolingual model

of linguistic achievement (cf. Frazier & Clifton, 1996; MacDonald, Pearlmutter, & Seidenberg, 1994, for two influential and opposing psycholinguistic viewpoints).

In the present chapter, the attention is on the processing of a particular syntactic ambiguity in American-French bilinguals who acquired their L2 (French) past early childhood. The study can be cast in the framework of (at least) three theories, one a largely influential linguistic theory that has undergone several major changes over the years (Chomsky, 1981, 1986, 1993), one a major psycholinguistic theory that has undergone its own upheaval lately (Frazier, 1987; Frazier & Clifton, 1996), and the last an experience-based psycholinguistic model that is facing serious challenges at present from monolingual data (Cuetos, Mitchell, & Corley, 1996; Mitchell, 1994). Indeed, given the numerous reappraisals of monolingual (psycho)linguistic models, any attempt to interpret L2 data in terms of these models can pose quite a challenge.

General Issues of Parsing

In monolingual research, the study of how readers initially resolve structurally ambiguous sentences has proven extremely useful to the understanding of the general processes underlying parsing. Several monolingual studies have used this approach to examine the influence of lexical information on initial parsing decisions. For example, the role of verb argument structure on ambiguity resolution has been examined in numerous studies via the recording of behavioral measures such as eye movements or button presses in self-paced reading (Boland & Boehm-Jernigan, 1998; Ferreira & Henderson, 1990; Frenck-Mestre & Pynte, 1995, 1997; Mitchell, 1989; Mitchell & Holmes, 1985; Trueswell, Tanenhaus, & Kello, 1993) or of event-related potentials (ERPs) of the brain (Osterhout & Holcomb, 1992; Osterhout, Holcomb, & Swinney, 1994; see also Friederici & Frisch, 2000). Other studies have used syntactic ambiguity resolution to determine the role of the relative frequency of syntactic structures associated with a particular lexical element (for various viewpoints, see Holmes, Stowe, & Cupples, 1989; MacDonald et al., 1994; Pickering, Traxler, & Crocker, 2000; Trueswell & Kim, 1998). Yet others have examined the role of thematic information (McRae, Ferretti, & Amyote, 1997; Tanenhaus, Carlson, & Trueswell, 1990; Taraban & McClelland, 1988; Trueswell, Tanenhaus, & Garnsey, 1994) and the use of referential context (Altmann, Garnham, & Dennis, 1992; Clifton, Bock, & Radó, 2000; Ni, Crain, & Shankweiler, 1996) on immediate parsing decisions.

These issues have been examined via the processing of several types of syntactic ambiguities. These are first illustrated via a "classical" syntactic ambiguity, presented in Examples 1 through 3. This particular ambiguity is also of particular interest to the present study given syntactic constraints of the English and French languages, which are discussed in this chapter.

1a. *The student graded by the professor received...*

1b. *The paper graded by the professor received...*

2a. *The businessman loaned money at low interest was...*

2b. *Only the businessman loaned money at low interest was...*

3a. *The shrewd heartless gambler manipulated by the dealer had...*

3b. *The young naïve gambler manipulated by the dealer had...*

This particular structure, involving a reduced relative clause, has been studied extensively in English and, to a lesser degree, in French. Bever (1970) immortalized it for all psycholinguists with the famous example, "The horse raced past the barn fell." First, the monolingual results are outlined as concerns its processing and the models that can account for them and then the way American-French bilinguals process a similar structural ambiguity in their L2 (French) is discussed. The data are discussed in terms of the models that have been appealed to account for them.

According to one theoretical stance, whereby syntax is the predominant factor affecting immediate parsing decisions (Frazier & Clifton, 1996), monolingual (and indeed all) readers should show systematic difficulty on encountering the disambiguating element of this structure (underlined in the examples). This would be caused by readers using an initial heuristic strategy of projecting the simplest syntactic structure, which would be a main verb interpretation of the first verb phrase (VP) (cf. Kimball's seven strategies, 1973). Indeed, it has been shown in some studies that readers do have notorious difficulty with a reduced relative structure compared to an unambiguous control sentence (Ferreira & Clifton, 1986; Rayner, Carlson, & Frazier, 1983). In light of this flavor of "syntax first" model, this difficulty should be experienced quite independent of other factors, such as the relative frequency of the structure, the particular properties of the different lexical items it contains, or the referential context in which it occurs. Any facilitation provided by these extrasyntactic factors would be attributable to the greater ease of reinterpretation of the initially built structure. However, a quick review of some monolingual studies shows this is not a completely resolved issue.

Consider the examples provided in Examples 1 through 3. If readers obey strictly syntactic heuristic principles, they should experience equal difficulty with the first version (a) as with the second (b) of each of these sentence pairs. However, as illustrated by various authors, extrasyntactic factors can in fact influence processing, rendering the second version of each of these pairs easier to process. The animacy of the first noun phrase (illustrated by Examples 1a and 1b) can reduce readers' likelihood to treat this noun as the subject of the initial verb (MacDonald, 1994; Trueswell et al., 1994; but see Ferreira & Clifton, 1986), thus rendering less likely a main clause interpretation in the case of Example 1b than 1a. The lexical properties of the verb itself may also play an important role in determining readers' initial choice of structure, according to some (MacDonald et al., 1994).

In the same vein, the role of the thematic constraints of the first noun phrase (NP) as well as contextual information have been investigated. Under experimental circumstances in which readers are given single thematically independent sentences, difficulty might indeed be predicted, as shown by behavioral measures or electrophysiological evidence, on the reading of the disambiguating region of sentences such as those illustrated in Examples 2 and 3. A quite different result might be expected, however, when readers are given contextual information, such as the focus particle "only" present in Example 2b but not in 2a, or when given more extended referential information when they read sentences in context. Just this effect has been obtained, in various online monolingual studies, showing that Example 2a is in fact harder to process than 2b (Crain & Steedman, 1985; Ni et al., 1996; but see Clifton et al., 2000, for an opposing view). The same result has been obtained when the context is provided by a sentence rather than by a single word (Altmann et al., 1992).

Furthermore, numerous online studies have now provided evidence that semantic and/or thematic information can reduce a reader's likelihood to be "led up the garden path." The examples depicted in Sentences 3a and 3b illustrate this. Readers of English experience less difficulty with sentences such as 3b than with those such as 3a because of the semantic information present in the sentence onset (McRae, Ferretti, & Amyote, 1997; Taraban & McClelland, 1988).

These monolingual studies thus strongly question the hypothesis that readers initially perform a "serial, strictly syntactic" parse of structures and propose, rather, lexically and/or referentially based models of parsing (see MacDonald et al., 1994; but see Clifton et al., 2000, and Pickcring et al., 2000, for contrary viewpoints).

Bilingual Studies of Online Parsing: Evidence From Eye Movements

In the same vein that monolingual models of parsing can be tested via the processing of syntactic ambiguities, so can L2 research gain from this approach. Note first that the same factors that are prone to influence immediate syntactic processing

in the native language will affect L2 processing, provided the reader has sufficient knowledge of the L2 (Dussias, 2001; Frenck-Mestre, 1997, 2002; Frenck-Mestre & Pynte, 1997; Hoover & Dwivedi, 1998; Juffs & Harrington, 1996; see also Fernandez, 1998, for offline L2 studies of syntactic ambiguity resolution). Nonetheless, just what choice the reader will make on encountering a syntactic ambiguity in the L2 can provide valuable information concerning specific L2 issues. This can be illustrated by Examples 4a and 4b.

4a. *Le sous-marin* **détruit** *pendant la guerre* <u>a</u> <u>coulé</u> *en quelques secondes.*
   The submarine **destroyed** *during the war* **sank** *in a few seconds.*
4b. *Le sous-marin* **détruit** *pendant la guerre* <u>un</u> <u>navire</u> *de la marine royale.*
   The submarine **destroys** *during the war* a **ship** *from the royal navy.*

Both of these sentences are syntactically legal in the French language. They are both structurally ambiguous and in the present case equally plausible. They differ, however, concerning readers' initial preference, manifested at the disambiguation point underlined in the examples. The structure presented in Example 4a, involving a reduced relative clause, in which the element following NP1 is not the main verb but a past participle form that is the verb of the reduced relative clause, is known to cause difficulty for readers in the absence of extrasyntactic cues, as discussed in the preceding section. Thus, French native speakers can be expected to experience greater difficulty at the disambiguation of Structure 4a than Structure 4b (i.e., on reading the verb of the main clause [a coulé] than the direct object NP [un navire]), as has indeed been shown with structures similar to these (cf. Pynte & Kennedy, 1993).

This is not, however, as immediately apparent for native English speakers, when reading in French, as outlined next. Although Example 4a may indeed pose some difficulty for native English speakers, Example 4b may pose just as great a problem. Whereas Example 4b is both permissible and plausible in French, it is generally considered an ungrammatical structure in English. Indeed, in English it is generally not permissible to separate the case assigner from the element receiving the case (Haegeman, 1994), that is, to displace the direct object NP from the case-assigning VP.[1] This is not the case for French, as direct object NPs may, but need not, be adjacent to the case-assigning VP.[2] This is elaborated below.

Structure 4a is permissible in both English and French and is both structurally equivalent and equally ambiguous in the two languages. Of the two structures (4a and 4b), Example 4a is the syntactically more complex. For Example 4b, although it is the syntactically simpler structure, it generally violates the constraints of the English language. Which of these considerations will prevail for native English speakers reading in French? Should they find it easier to process Sentence 4a than 4b despite the increased syntactic complexity of the former of these sentences? Might the structural ambiguity of Sentence 4a be blocked for beginning English-French bilinguals if they adopt the parameters of their native language when reading French? Otherwise stated, might they systematically adopt the reduced relative reading of the sentence when they encounter the prepositional phrase, thus rendering the declarative interpretation dispreferred?

Some evidence on this matter has been provided by White (1989a, 1989b, 1991). White argued that French learners of English as a second language should incorrectly assume that Sentence 4b is a licensed structure in English given the syntactic differences across French and English. In line with this, White found that French readers rated structures similar to that presented in Example 4b as grammatically acceptable and found it difficult to distinguish between this structure and the correct English one, for which the object NP is adjacent to the verb (such as "The submarine destroyed a boat during the war."). White's results thus clearly demonstrated the influence of the native language on L2 parsing.

How then might English learners of French be expected to process Structure 4b? White argued that French readers will have difficulty rejecting structures such as Structure 4b, for which there is an intervening element between the case-assigning VP and the object NP because of French having [−strict adjacency], by which it is permissible to displace the object NP. White (1989b, chapter 6) outlined her argument in terms of "parameter setting," by which French learners of English must "reset" the values of this parameter to [+strict adjacency] to accommodate for the more restricted set of sentences possible in English.[3] White accounts for her results in the framework of universal grammar and the inability of adult learners to access Universal Grammar and to properly reset parameters that were set by the properties of the speaker's native language. Indeed, for a French

speaker to consider sentences such as 4b as ungrammatical in English, the speaker would have to revert from a "superset" grammar to a more restricted "subset" in which only one of the two grammatical possibilities is available. This is considered quite difficult.[4]

In light of this line of argumentation, English learners of French should, conversely, experience difficulty with Structure 4b for the mirrored reason. That is, if they apply the strict adjacency principle from English (and the subset principle), they should initially adopt a more restricted grammar of French and should experience difficulty in interpreting Structure 4b. If this principle is applied "blindly," then English native speakers should experience greater difficulty with Structure 4b than 4a, even though the former is the simpler, syntactically speaking. To examine this question, the processing of Structures 4a and 4b was examined with novice English-French bilinguals via the recording of eye movements (Frenck-Mestre, 1998).

The results of this experiment clearly revealed that beginning English-French bilinguals do not treat the ambiguous structures illustrated by Examples 4a and 4b in the same manner that native French readers do. First, it is notable that American readers showed longer reading times compared to French readers at the prepositional phrase region following the first verb (in the examples "during the war") for both sentence structures. This would be expected if the English-dominant bilingual readers projected a main clause structure but then immediately revised this hypothesis because of the absence of a noun phrase following the verb. This interpretation of the data was strengthened by the results obtained at the disambiguation point (underlined in Examples 4a and 4b).

The group of English-French bilinguals experienced considerably more difficulty, as manifested by longer reading times, when the disambiguating element forced a main clause interpretation of the sentence (Example 4b) than a reduced relative structure (Example 4a). Moreover, as compared to French readers, they demonstrated considerably longer reading times for the main clause reading. The data for the group of French readers did not in fact show a difference in processing time for the two structures during the first reading of the sentence, but only in the measure of "total" reading times (i.e., the summation of all fixations in a specified region of the sentence, including the first time the eye entered the region and all subsequent rereadings thereof).

Which Available Theory Best Accounts for the Data?

In view of certain current monolingual models of language processing, it would appear that our data pose some difficulty. In contrast to models that assume a heuristic parser, which will systematically adopt the least complex of two alternative structures, my colleagues and I found that our participants did not show an immediate preference for the syntactically less-complex structure of two alternatives. To the contrary, when our participants were confronted with structurally ambiguous sentences such as illustrated in 4a and 4b, we found that our bilingual readers showed evidence of difficulty with the syntactically less-complex structure when reading in their L2. Moreover, the results from our French monolingual control subjects reading in their native language did not show nearly as strong or as immediate effects of syntactic complexity as has been reported in previous monolingual studies.

Monolingual theories of parsing that posit that the *frequency* of structures (as opposed to the syntactic complexity thereof) is a crucial element in determining the difficulty of processing (cf. Mac-Donald, 1997; MacWhinney, 2001; Mitchell, 1989; Mitchell, Cuetos, Corley, & Brysbaert, 1995) may provide a better framework for understanding the pattern of results we obtained, both in the monolingual group of readers and in the relatively inexperienced bilingual group. Past exposure to and experience with a language and its properties is a key factor in this type of model, which provides quite a different theoretical stance on syntactic processing compared to "syntax-first" accounts.

Consider first the constraint satisfaction model forwarded by MacDonald et al. (1994). From the vantage point of this model, it may be considered quite logical that the reduced relative structures we studied did not produce strong effects in the monolingual group of subjects. Quite a number of the verbs that we selected were frequently used as adjectives (for example "instruit," "maudit," "distrait," among others). In line with MacDonald et al.'s prediction that the frequency of structures will directly affect processing difficulty, this would decrease readers' likelihood to treat this word as the main verb of the phrase and facilitate the processing of a reduced relative structure following a head such a "Le prêtre instruit." Otherwise stated, our French readers may have experienced little difficulty with the reduced relative sentences because of their previous processing of this structure for the particular verbs we chose.[5]

The results obtained in the bilingual group can be explained along similar lines. That is, given that the English language rarely admits the structure presented in Example 4b, in which the direct object complement is separated from its case-assigning verb, our American-French bilingual readers should have had little experience with this structure in their native language (English) and thus be less likely to project it when an alternative structure was available.

Another statistical model of parsing is that known as the linguistic tuning hypothesis and forwarded by Mitchell and colleagues (Mitchell, 1989; Mitchell et al., 1995). The model predicts, in similar fashion to MacDonald et al. (1994), that the amount of difficulty a reader will experience when parsing a structure will be directly related to the amount of prior experience that the reader has had with it. It has been forwarded as an explanatory model of cross-linguistic variation as concerns syntactic ambiguity resolution (cf. Cuetos et al., 1996; Frenck-Mestre & Pynte, 2000a, 2000b, for recent reviews). The model has direct bearing on the results found in our bilingual group of readers.

First, these readers should, in terms of the model, experience greater difficulty with structures such as 4b given that the native language of these bilinguals does not afford them much experience with this structure, and that they were relatively inexperienced in the French language. Second, a prediction can be made as concerns the performance of these bilingual subjects as they gain experience in French. As stated expressly in Cuetos et al. (1996): "The model predicts that parsing preferences will change if, during some period prior to testing, the reader or listener has been exposed to an unusual preponderance of one ambiguity resolution rather than another" (p. 175). From this, we could expect bilingual subjects to show changes in immediate parsing decisions when reading in their L2 if, indeed, they receive linguistic input that differs from that present in their native language (cf. Frenck-Mestre, 2002, for a discussion).

As concerns the ambiguity studied here, we could predict that, with greater experience, English readers of French would accept the [−strict adjacency] criterion in French and subsequently have less difficulty processing structures for which the object NP is displaced from its case-assigning VP. Although we presently only have preliminary data on this question, the results from a small group of more advanced English-French bilinguals suggest that the above prediction holds. The trend in this more advanced group was to behave like their French counterparts when processing the ambiguous structures presented in Sentences 4a and 4b.

It is important to note, nonetheless, that the linguistic tuning hypothesis has not proven capable of accounting for recent monolingual results (cf. Mitchell & Brysbaert, 1998). That is, when online monolingual processing is examined for materials modeled closely on corpora-based sentences, the online preferences are quite the opposite from those that would be predicted by the statistical frequency of structures in the corpora. As such, although attractive, the model appears to be in need of further elaboration prior to acceptance as a general framework.

Then again, we can ask whether the data we report for our bilingual readers can be explained in terms of parameter setting, such as suggested by White (1989a, 1989b). First, refer to a discussion by Fodor (1999) concerning the hypothesis of a "set-and-ready" mechanism that would allow the human parser to determine the correct parameters to describe the grammar of his or her language. In sum, Fodor outlined the impossibility of any such automatic mechanism based on superficially recognizable cues for natural language grammars. She suggested that the only psychologically valid "triggering" mechanism is part and parcel of parsing.

Regarding the acquisition of L2 grammars by adult learners specifically, Fodor (1999) suggested a "processing" account that is not at odds with the frequency-based accounts outlined here. She posited that the increased use or, conversely, disuse of parameter values via parsing will have a direct impact on the "activation" levels of these values (not at all unlike the model forwarded by MacDonald et al., 1994; McRae et al., 1997). The stronger L1 parameter values would be hard to overcome in an initial state, thus producing the type of interference observed by White and as many others and I have observed for various structures (cf. Durgunoglu, 1997; Dussias, 2001; Fernandez, 1999; Frenck-Mestre, 2002; MacWhinney, 1997, for reviews). When the adult learner parses L2 sentences with the incorrect L1 grammar, she or he will eventually be led to disfavor L1 values and apply those parameter values of the L2 that enable a correct parse of the structure, thereby increasing the activation levels of the latter and (perhaps, with a vast amount of exposure) decreasing those of the former.

Hence, through parsing of structures specific to the L2, the adult learner may learn a new set of parameter values along with the L2, which would become increasingly strong with L2 use. Our data from English-dominant readers of French, who had relatively little experience parsing their L2 in comparison to their L1, can easily be accounted for in such terms. Note, however, that the difference between the account proposed here by Fodor (1999) and that proposed by frequency-based models (i.e., Cuetos et al., 1996; MacDonald et al., 1994; MacWhinney, 1997) is not readily apparent.

Robertson and Sorace (1999) provided an interesting discussion of what might be driving the results obtained by White (1989a). They recast White's data in terms of optionality theory. Robertson and Sorace made the parallel between the results they obtained with German adult learners of English concerning verb placement and those obtained by White for French learners of English regarding adverb placement. These authors suggested that rather than assuming an all-or-none mechanism by which native language parameters are reset to those of the L2, that optionality at the level of competence persists in "interlanguage" grammars. This suggestion stems from the observation that residual constructions from the native language grammar (in the case of Robertson & Sorace, V2 constructions from German) are seldom systematically observed. Great variations exist both among learners and within a learner concerning the frequency and manner in which native language constraints are applied. The authors found that the principles and parameters model, although able to broadly explain the pattern of interference from the native language on L2 processing, is inadequate to explain this variation. They appealed therefore to the minimalist program (Chomsky, 1993) in the terms of the model set out by Eubank (1993/1994) of interlanguage grammars. This line of argumentation might also be applied to the data for English-French beginning bilinguals we obtained, although to truly adopt this type of model, individual variation as well as group data need to be examined.

Last, in line with the idea that individual variation need be accounted for, it might be noted that the conclusions I have drawn were based on group results. It goes without saying that there is always considerable variation between participants when any measure of processing is recorded, whether online reading times of various natures (self-paced reading, eye movements) or offline preferences (questionnaires, sentence completion, etc.). It is the intention of experimental psycholinguistics to go beyond this level of individual variation and, through inferential statistics, draw conclusions from group data whenever licensed to do so. This is not always assumed to be a natural choice.

Although much can be learned from the study of individual differences (cf. Segalowitz, 1997, for a review), and although it is a truism to state that adult learners of a language are a heterogeneous group, it is my intention to gain an understanding of the "larger" picture. Theories of sentence processing must indeed take into account changes that occur in parallel to readers' experience with a language, as highlighted by many (MacDonald et al., 1994; MacWhinney, 1997; Mitchell, 1994). Group data can provide as important information in this regard as individual variation, provided one either follows the progress of a particular group or, as we have attempted, are a cross-sectional look at data from learners with more or less "parsing" experience in their L2. This has indeed proven useful in many prior studies of L2 sentence processing.

What Can Other Measures Tell Us About Second Language Sentence Processing? Evidence From Event-Related Potentials

The preceding discussion was of evidence primarily from studies that used eye movements to examine native and L2 sentence processing. Eye movements indeed provide a rich and multidimensional online record of the process(es) in which a reader is engaged. Initial reading of different parts of the sentence can be broken into *first fixation* (i.e., the amount of time spent from when the eyes initially land in a region until a new saccade is engaged) and *gaze duration* (i.e., all fixations in a region prior to the eyes exiting the region). Moreover, the aforementioned "first-pass" measures can be compared to later rereadings. Whereas the initial reading of an element of the sentence is often considered to reveal readers' first choice concerning lexical access and/or parsing, subsequent rereadings are more often equated with reanalysis and/or repair processes.

In addition to these reaction time measures, the pattern and frequency of regressive eye movements can be used to understand how the reader untangles difficult or unexpected structures. I have shown how different theories of parsing can be put to the test by recording readers' eye movement patterns and how comparisons can be made between

bilingual readers' L2 processing and native language processing. There exists, however, another rich, multidimensional, online trace of syntactic processing, which is the recording of event-related scalp potentials during the visual (word-by-word) or auditory presentation of sentences. It is of interest to see whether ERP studies provide complementary information to that provided by eye movement studies. Therefore, a quick look of various ERP studies is given as they relate to sentence processing and bilinguals.

Semantic Anomalies: Variations in the N400 Component

In an early study, Meuter, Donald, and Ardal (1987) compared the ERP trace obtained in the first language (L1; English or French) and L2 (French or English) of two groups of fluent bilinguals while reading sentences. The authors chose to examine variations in the N400 component, as produced by the sentence-final word of semantically anomalous sentences compared to a semantically acceptable ending. The question of interest was whether the "N400 effect" would be obtained in the L2, and whether it would be similar in latency and amplitude to that obtained in the L1. Semantically anomalous sentence-final words produced an N400 effect in both the native language and L2. The authors reported a trend for the N400 effect to be smaller in the L2 than the native language. However, this held true at only one electrode site and for one group of bilinguals only. As such, no firm conclusions can be drawn from this preliminary study about differences in semantic integration processes in the native language and L2 (as indeed none were).

In a subsequent study, Ardal, Donald, Meuter, Muldrew, and Luce (1990) reexamined this question, both in another group of late bilinguals and in a group of "early" bilinguals (mean age of L2 acquisition was 7.3 years). The authors again found an N400 effect in the L2 as well as the native language, that is, a larger N400 to semantically anomalous than semantically acceptable sentence-final words. However, as in the previous study, the N400 effect obtained in the L2 differed from that found in the native language, having a slightly later onset in the L2 than in the L1. Moreover, the bilinguals showed a trend for a later onset of N400 in both languages compared to monolingual controls. No significant differences in the ERP record were found between the early and late bilingual groups. The tentative conclusion from this study was that semantic integration processes are affected by proficiency in a language and will be reflected by the time course of electrophysiological measures of processing. One caveat is nonetheless in order; the native language of the bilinguals in this study varied considerably. As is well known, interactions between the bilingual's native language and L2 are numerous. The conclusions from Ardal et al.'s (1990) study must thus be considered with some caution.

In several more recent studies, ERPs were again used to measure semantic integration processes during sentence processing in the L2 (Hahne, 2001; Hahne & Friederici, 2001; Sanders & Neville, 2003; Weber-Fox & Neville, 1996). These studies also looked at syntactic processing, which is discussed in this section. The general pattern of these studies seems to be that, depending on proficiency in the L2, the N400 effect (as classically produced by semantically anomalous sentence endings or medial words [e.g., "The volcano was *eaten*" or "The scientist criticized Max's *event* of the theorem"] in comparison to semantically acceptable sentences [e.g., "The bread was eaten" or "The scientist criticized Max's *proof* of the theorem"] or, more recently, by sentence-medial nonwords ["bokkers"] compared to real words ["bottles"]) will be equivalent in amplitude and latency in the L2 of bilinguals to that found in the L1 for native speakers. Note that for less-proficient L2 speakers, the amplitude of the N400 effect is often smaller, and its peak is delayed compared to that obtained in the native language (Hahne, 2001; Weber-Fox & Neville, 1996), thus rejoining the results reported in earlier studies.

In sum, those studies that have recorded ERPs (auditory and visual) to examine L1 and L2 sentence processing at the semantic level showed basically indistinguishable patterns for the two languages for proficient bilinguals and relatively minor differences between the L1 and L2 for less-proficient bilinguals.

Syntactic Anomalies

Variations in the N400 Component   The above-mentioned bilingual studies used the N400 component to index the immediate semantic integration of words in visually or auditorily presented sentences. Since the initial finding of Kutas and Hillyard (1980) in monolinguals, this is indeed the most often reported interpretation of variations of the N400. Note, however, that work by Osterhout and

collaborators (McLaughlin, Osterhout, & Kim, 2004; Osterhout, McLaughlin, Kim, Greenwald, & Inoue, 2004) suggested that, in early stages of learning an L2 as an adult, the N400 may not be restricted to the detection of semantic anomalies. Osterhout's group has found that number agreement errors in the L2 (i.e., between the subject of the sentence and the subsequent verb) will initially produce a variation in the ERP trace that has all the characteristics of an N400 effect for young adults who have just begun to learn an L2. With more L2 experience, this effect diminishes, to be replaced by a more canonical syntactic marker in the ERP record. This highly interesting line of work should be followed by any researcher endeavoring to understand the development of L2 sentence processing in adults.

Variations in Early Anterior Negativity and P600   Two major ERP laboratories, one in the United States and one in Germany, have published a series of articles on L2 syntactic anomaly processing (Hahne, 2001; Hahne & Friederici, 2001; Sanders & Neville, 2003; Weber-Fox & Neville, 1996). These articles have all addressed the issue of the critical period hypothesis in one way or another, comparing either early and late bilinguals or the performance of late bilinguals on semantic and syntactic anomaly detection to that of native speakers.

In one of these studies (Weber-Fox & Neville, 1996), direct comparisons were made between five groups of Chinese-English bilinguals, ranging from early (as early as from infancy) to late acquirement of the L2, in relation to the processing of illegal structures in English. Illegalities were of various sorts, including phrase–structure violations and subjacency errors (as in "The scientist criticized Max's of proof the theorem"). The authors found a high level of performance on behavioral tasks for all groups of bilinguals (at least 85% correct). Several different time windows were considered in the electrophysiological trace.

A rather complex pattern of results emerged (Weber-Fox & Neville, 1996). At the earliest window (50–250 ms, or N125), the three groups of early bilinguals did not show a significantly larger response to illegal structures, whereas the two groups of late bilinguals and the monolingual control group did. However, whereas the monolingual participants showed a hemispheric asymmetry, with a larger response at left anterior sites, the late bilinguals showed a bilateral response that was nonetheless larger over the right hemisphere. The latency of the N125 was also delayed in the two groups of late bilinguals compared to monolinguals. As such, the authors concluded that the early negativity found in the late bilingual groups was not the "early anterior negativity" associated with aspects of syntactic processing.

At a later window, often associated with N400 (300–450 or 300–500 ms after word onset), phrase structure violations produced an increased negativity in all bilingual groups as well as in the monolingual controls. Again, however, in the two groups of bilinguals who acquired their L2 after age 11 years, the typical signature of a greater left hemisphere effect was absent. Finally, in the time window associated with the P600 (i.e., 500–700 ms and 700–900 ms; cf. Osterhout & Holcomb, 1992; Osterhout, McKinnon, Bersick, & Corey, 1996), whereas the three groups of early bilinguals showed a response comparable to that found in monolinguals for this type of violation, the two groups of late bilinguals showed greater positivity to illegal structures only in the later time window (700–900 ms), and the amplitude of the P600 was smaller than that found for monolingual controls.

The authors (Weber-Fox & Neville, 1996) suggested that, at least for the types of syntactic anomalies they studied, only very early acquisition of an L2 enables bilinguals to acquire the skills necessary to detect and process them in nativelike fashion. Note, however, that none of the bilingual groups showed a typical early anterior negativity. Moreover, the two groups of late bilinguals did show increased N400 as well as P600 responses to illegal structures, even if the latter effect was delayed in comparison to the early bilinguals and monolinguals. As such, the differences across the bilingual groups were in amplitude and latency rather than in nature.

In a subsequent study (Sanders & Neville, 2003), the ERP trace to auditorily presented materials was compared for monolinguals and Japanese-English late bilinguals. For the bilinguals, no differences in the ERP trace were found between *syntactic* strings (i.e., basically "jabberwocky" sentences in which the syntactic class of elements in the sentence was maintained and that respected English syntax, but that were otherwise meaningless) and *acoustic* strings (which carried neither syntactic nor semantic information). Monolingual controls, however, produced differences across these conditions, both at specific positions in the sentences and across the entire sentence. As such, the authors again concluded that automatic grammatical processing is not acquired by those who learn their L2 later in life (whereas semantic processing is unaffected by age of acquisition).

Another pair of ERP studies (Hahne, 2001; Hahne & Friederici, 2001) suggested a similar yet perhaps more nuanced argument concerning L2 syntactic processing. In these studies, phrase structure violations were employed in German (e.g., "Das Eis wurde im gegessen," literal translation "The ice cream was in the eaten") to determine whether Russian-German and Japanese-German late bilinguals would be sensitive to this type of anomaly. Akin to the study reported by Weber-Fox and Neville (1996), the late bilinguals in these studies did show a difference in the ERP trace to legal and illegal structures, as evidenced by P600, but unlike Weber-Fox and Neville (1996), these studies did not find a "delayed onset" of the P600 in bilinguals.[6]

Two restrictions were nonetheless present. First, the difference in P600 as a function of sentence type was found only in advanced late bilinguals (mean formal learning 6 years; mean residency 5 years), not in less-experienced L2 users (mean formal learning and residency 2.5 years). Second, and most important for the authors' argument, although differences in the P600 were found in the advanced bilinguals as a function of sentence type, no differences were found in either of the late bilingual groups for an earlier left anterior negativity. Monolingual controls showed both effects. This pattern of results led the authors to suggest, in line with their previous monolingual work (Friederici, Hahne, & Mecklinger, 1996), that differences in automatic and more effortful syntactic processing can be indexed by these two components. The absence of an early effect in late bilinguals when encountering illegal structures in their L2 would suggest that they lack automatic processes present in native speakers.

Variations in P600   The ERP studies cited all examined L2 processing for anomalous structures, that is, sentences that contained either a semantic or syntactic anomaly in comparison to semantically/syntactically acceptable sentences or strings that contained only syntactic information compared to complete nonsense strings. Whether the ERP trace will reveal differences for ambiguity resolution is open to debate. In the one study of which I am aware that has used ERPs to examine the processing of ambiguous structures in the L2 (Kotz, 1991), it would appear that perhaps there are indeed differences between anomaly and ambiguity processing.

In the study reported by Kotz (1991), the materials were the same as those used by Osterhout (1990) and Osterhout and Holcomb (1992). The materials played on verb subcategorization information, as illustrated by Examples 1 and 2:

1. *The doctor agreed* **to** *see the patient* **had** *left the hospital.*
2. *The doctor implored* **to** *see the patient* **had** *left the hospital.*

Sentence 1 carries an intransitive verb (agree), whereas Sentence 2 carries a transitive verb (implore) that requires either a direct object or sentential complement. Given that both native and proficient nonnative readers readily use this type of subcategorization information (cf. Frenck-Mestre & Pynte, 1997), it is to be expected that at the preposition "to" the processing of Sentence 1 (in which "agree" is the main verb) will incur less difficulty than that of Sentence 2 (in which implore is the subordinate verb of a reduced relative clause followed by a main clause). This was born out in the ERP data for both monolingual controls and highly proficient Spanish-English bilinguals (mean age of acquisition of English 5.3 years). Both groups showed a significantly larger P600 (time window 600–800 ms[7]) at the preposition "to" when reading sentences containing a transitive verb (as illustrated in Sentence 2) than when reading sentences containing an intransitive verb (as illustrated in Sentence 1). No interaction with group (monolingual vs. bilingual) was observed. Moreover, at the subordinate verb "had," the inverse effect was found: P600 was larger for sentences in which the first verb was intransitive and thus did not entail a subsequent main clause (Example 1) than for those with a transitive verb, in which "had" provided the main verb (Example 2). This obtained for both monolingual and bilingual readers.

The results of this ERP study showed, in line with the eye movement studies reported in this chapter, that proficient L2 readers produce similar results to those obtained for native readers, and that highly specific information, such as the type of construction most commonly associated with a particular verb class, is used by proficient bilinguals in their L2.

What to Conclude Concerning Second Language Syntactic Processing in Late Bilinguals?

In contrast to the ERP data reported for semantic anomaly detection in the L2, which has been found to be basically equivalent in the second and native language, data on syntactic anomaly detection showed discrepancies between native and L2 processing (Hahne, 2001; Hahne & Friederici, 2001; Sanders & Neville, 2003; Weber-Fox & Neville, 1996). Why this should be so when eye movement data have quite often shown that, provided sufficient proficiency, L2 syntactic processing obeys the same principles as native language processing (Dussias, 2001; Frenck-Mestre, 1997, 2002; Frenck-Mestre & Pynte, 1997; Hoover & Dwivedi, 1998; Juffs & Harrington, 1996) is a matter worth contemplating.

As a possible explanation for the differences in results across eye movement and ERP studies, I suggest that there are major differences in the scope of ERP studies on L2 syntactic processing and that of the eye movement studies presented in the first half of this chapter. First, bilingual ERP studies have by and large examined the processing of syntactic anomalies (with the exception of Kotz, 1991). Eye movement studies on syntactic processing, both mono- and bilingual, are dominated by the study of syntactic ambiguities. Second, the main thrust of these ERP studies has been to test the critical period hypothesis; either direct cross-longitudinal comparisons have been made between early and late bilinguals concerning syntactic anomaly detection or, within the late bilinguals, comparisons have been made with monolingual data concerning semantic and syntactic anomaly detection. In the eye movement studies discussed, only the performance of late bilinguals was under scrutiny. Both experienced and beginning bilinguals' data were examined, but nonetheless for late bilinguals (i.e., those who learned their L2 after age 12 years and in almost all cases in a scholastic setting). The debate still rages regarding whether these late bilinguals can ever obtain the same level of automatic processing as native speakers (cf. Birdsong, 1999, and chapter 6, this volume, for a discussion of the question), but such is beyond the scope of the present chapter.

Unlike the ERP studies of anomaly processing, the study of syntactic ambiguities has revealed quite coherent patterns across ERP and eye movement studies. Both measures produce highly similar patterns for native and proficient nonnative speakers. Moreover, there are parallels between the ERP data for anomaly processing and eye movement data on ambiguity resolution. In both, it has been reported that, with increasing L2 experience, late bilinguals' performance resembles that of native readers to a greater or lesser degree. Note, however, that the ERP literature on the processing of syntactic anomalies unanimously found late bilinguals lacking when it comes to early processing decisions in these subjects.[8] This is not the case in the eye movement literature, which clearly reports very detailed and immediate use of grammatical information during parsing in the L2 for highly proficient late bilinguals.

It is my contention that, to understand just where and why the data differ between eye movements and ERPs, direct comparisons must be made between the same subjects and, most important, for the same type of processing. Resolving a syntactic ambiguity may well entail reappraisal of a structure and "repair processes"; however, repair is indeed a possibility. This is not at all immediately apparent for illegal structures, such as have been used in the majority of ERP studies to date. What does the reader "do" when unable to resolve a phrase–structure violation? Whereas the eye movement studies reported showed considerable change in L2 syntactic ambiguity resolution with experience and near-native performance for the most highly skilled bilinguals, it is less evident that improvement would be found for the processing of illegal structures, such as those employed in the bilingual ERP studies. Future research on L2 syntactic parsing is thus faced with an interesting new avenue. Comparisons across techniques (eye movement, ERPs, and functional magnetic resonance) with comparable subject pools and linguistic materials should provide clear advances in the understanding of this most intriguing topic.

Notes

1. Note that this principle can be transgressed in two specific cases: when the direct object is a heavy NP, as illustrated by "The jury will reveal after lunch [the verdict over which they have been debating for almost three weeks.]" and when the direct object is a sentential complement, as illustrated by "The judge said on Monday [that he would refuse to reconsider the case.].

2. In French, sentences such as those illustrated in parentheses are both equally licensed by the grammar ("Jean boit son café lentement" and "Jean boit lentement son café").

3. White (1991) also entertained the hypothesis that the effect observed in French readers of English may be caused by differences across English and French concerning verb raising, as suggested by Pollock (1989).

4. Fodor (1999), as well as Bley-Vroman (1991) and MacWhinney (1997), argued rather strongly against the arguments put forward by White (1989a, 1989b), who situated L2 processing within the greater theory of Universal Grammar.

5. It should be noted that the frequency of structures on its own is most likely not strong enough to reduce all ambiguity, as was clearly outlined by MacDonald and colleagues (MacDonald et al., 1994; MacDonald, 1994, 1997). Stronger constraints would be provided by the culmination of several factors (cf. McRae et al., 1997).

6. In the Hahne (2001) and Hahne and Friederici (2001) studies, the time window for the P600 ranged between 500 and 1,200 ms. Otherwise stated, it was not broken down into several windows, as was the case for the Weber-Fox and Neville (1996) study. Note, nonetheless, that visual inspection of the ERP data does not suggest an earlier onset of P600 in the monolingual control group.

7. An earlier time window, between 500 and 650 ms, revealed no differences as a function of structure for either the monolingual controls or bilingual readers.

8. It is well beyond the scope of this chapter to entertain the current disputes in the literature regarding the exact nature of the different ERP components observed during syntactic anomaly detection. Note, however, that there is presently no clear consensus on this issue (cf. Friederici et al., 1996; Osterhout & Hagoort, 1999; Osterhout et al., 1996).

References

Altmann, G. T. M., Garnham, A., & Dennis, Y. (1992). Avoiding the garden path: Eye movements in context. *Journal of Memory and Language, 31,* 685–712.

Ardal, S., Donald, M. W., Meuter, R., Muldrew, S., & Luce, M. (1990). Brain semantic incongruity in bilinguals. *Brain and Language, 39,* 187–205.

Bever, T. G. (1970). The cognitive basis for linguistic structures. In J. R. Hayes (Ed.), *Cognition and language development* (pp. 277–360). New York: Wiley.

Bialystok, E. (1997). Why we need grammar: Confessions of a cognitive generalist. In L. Eubank, L. Selinker, & M. Sharwood Smith (Eds.), *The current state of interlanguage* (pp. 55–61). Amsterdam: Benjamins.

Birdsong, D. (1999). *Second language acquisition and the critical period hypothesis.* Mahwah, NJ: Erlbaum.

Bley-Vroman, R. (1991). Processing, constraints on acquisition, and the processing of ungrammatical sentences. In L. Eubank (Ed.), *Point counterpoint: Universal grammar in the second language* (pp. 191–197). Amsterdam: Benjamins.

Boland, J. E., & Boehm-Jernigan, H. (1998). Lexical constraints and prepositional phrase attachment. *Journal of Memory and Language, 39,* 684–719.

Chomsky, N. (1981). *Lectures on government and binding.* Dordrecht, The Netherlands: Foris.

Chomsky, N. (1986). *Knowledge of language: Its nature, origin and use.* New York: Praeger.

Chomsky, N. (1993). A minimalist program for linguistic theory. In K. Hale & S. J. Keyser (Eds.), *The view from building 20* (pp. 1–52). Cambridge, MA: MIT Press.

Clifton, C., Jr., Bock, J. K., & Radó, J. (2000). Effects of the focus particle "only" and intrinsic contrast on comprehension of reduced relative clauses. In A. Kennedy, R. Radach, D. Heller, & J. Pynte (Eds.), *Reading as a perceptual process* (pp. 591–620). Amsterdam: Elsevier.

Crain, S., & Steedman, M. (1985). On not being led up the garden path: The use of context by the psychological syntax processor. In D. R. Dowty, L. Kartunnen, & A. M. Zwicky (Eds.), *Natural language parsing: Psychological, computational, and theoretical perspectives* (pp. 320–358). Cambridge, U.K.: Cambridge University Press.

Cuetos, F., Mitchell, D. C., & Corley, M. M. B. (1996). Parsing in different languages. In M. Carreiras, J. García-Albea, & N. Sebastián-Gallés (Eds.), *Language processing in Spanish* (pp. 145–187). Mahwah, NJ: Erlbaum.

Durgunoglu, A. Y. (1997). Bilingual reading: Its components, development, and other issues. In A. M. B. de Groot & J. F. Kroll (Eds.), *Tutorials in bilingualism: Psycholinguistic perspectives* (pp. 225–276). Mahwah, NJ: Erlbaum.

Dussias, P. E. (2001). Sentence parsing in fluent Spanish-English bilinguals. In. J. L. Nicol (Ed.), *One mind, two languages* (pp. 159–176). Oxford, U.K.: Blackwell.

Eubank, L. (1993/1994). On the transfer of parametric values in L2 development. *Language Acquisition, 33,* 183–208.

Fernandez, E. (1998). Language dependency in parsing: Evidence from monolingual and bilingual processing. *Psychologica Belgica, 38,* 197–230.

Fernandez, E. (1999). Processing strategies in second language acquisition: Some preliminary results. In E. C. Klein & G. Martohardjono (Eds.), *The development of second language grammars: A generative approach* (pp. 217–240). Amsterdam: Benjamins.

Ferreira, F., & Clifton, C., Jr. (1986). The independence of syntactic processing. *Journal of Memory and Language, 25,* 348–368.

Ferreira, F., & Henderson, J. M. (1990). Use of verb information in syntactic processing: Evidence from eye movements and word-by-word self-paced reading. *Journal of Experimental Psychology: Learning, Memory and Cognition, 16,* 555–568.

Fodor, J. D. (1999). Learnability theory: Triggers for parsing with. In E. C. Klein & G. Martohardjono (Eds.), *The development of second language grammars: A generative approach* (pp. 363–406). Amsterdam: Benjamins.

Frazier, L. (1987). Sentence processing: A tutorial review. In M. Coltheart (Ed.), *Attention and performance XII: The psychology of reading* (pp. 559–586). Hillsdale, NJ: Erlbaum.

Frazier, L., & Clifton, C., Jr. (1996). *Construal.* Cambridge, MA: MIT Press.

Frenck-Mestre, C. (1997). Examining second language reading: An on-line look. In A. Sorace, C. Heycock, & R. Shillcock (Eds.), *Language acquisition, knowledge representation and processing: GALA 199* (pp. 444–448). Edinburgh, U.K.: HCRC.

Frenck-Mestre, C. (1998, November). *Overcoming parameters: An on-line look at bilingual sentence processing.* Paper presented at the 39th annual meeting of the Psychonomic Society, Dallas, TX.

Frenck-Mestre, C. (2002). An on-line look at sentence processing in the second language. In R. Heredia & J. Altarriba (Eds.), *Bilingual sentence processing* (pp. 217–236). Amsterdam: Elsevier, North-Holland.

Frenck-Mestre, C., & Pynte, J. (1995). Lexical influences on parsing strategies: Evidence from eye movements. In J. M. Findlay, R. W. Kentridge, & R. Walker (Eds.), *Eye movement research: Mechanisms, processes and applications* (pp. 433–444). Amsterdam: Elsevier, North-Holland.

Frenck-Mestre, C., & Pynte, J. (1997). Syntactic ambiguity resolution while reading in second and native languages. *The Quarterly Journal of Experimental Psychology, 50A,* 119–148.

Frenck-Mestre, C., & Pynte, J. (2000a). Resolving syntactic ambiguities: Cross-linguistic differences? In M. DeVincenzi & V. Lombardo (Eds.), *Cross-linguistic perspectives on language processing* (pp. 119–148). Dordrecht, The Netherlands: Kluwer Academic Press.

Frenck-Mestre, C., & Pynte, J. (2000b). Romancing syntactic ambiguity: Why the French and the Italians don't see eye to eye. In A. Kennedy, R. Radach, D. Heller, & J. Pynte (Eds.), *Reading as a perceptual process* (pp. 549–564). Amsterdam: Elsevier, North-Holland.

Friederici, A. D., & Frisch, S. (2000). Verb-argument structure processing: The role of verb-specific and argument-specific information. *Journal of Memory and Language, 43,* 476–507.

Friederici, A. D., Hahne, A., & Mecklinger, A. (1996). Temporal structure of syntactic parsing: Early and late event-related brain potential effects. *Journal of Experimental Psychology: Learning, Memory and Cognition, 5,* 1219–1248.

Haegeman, L. (1994). *Introduction to government and binding theory* (2nd ed.). Cambridge, MA: Blackwell.

Hahne, A. (2001). What's different in second-language processing? Evidence from event-related brain potentials. *Journal of Psycholinguistic Research, 30,* 251–266.

Hahne, A., & Friederici, A. D. (2001). Processing a second language: Late learners' comprehension mechanisms as revealed by event-related brain potentials. *Bilingualism: Language and Cognition, 4,* 123–142.

Holmes, V. M., Stowe, L., & Cupples, L. (1989). Lexical expectations in parsing complement-verb sentences. *Journal of Memory and Language, 28,* 668–689.

Hoover, M. L., & Dwivedi, V. D. (1998). Syntactic processing by skilled bilinguals. *Language Learning, 48,* 1–29.

Juffs, A., & Harrington, M. (1996). Garden path sentences and error data in second language sentence processing. *Language Learning, 46,* 283–326.

Kimball, J. (1973). Seven principles of surface structure parsing in natural language. *Cognition, 2,* 15–47.

Kotz, S. A. (1991). *Event-related brain potentials: A sensitive measurement of bilingual sentence comprehension?* Unpublished master's thesis, Tufts University, Boston, MA.

Kutas, M., & Hillyard, S. A. (1980). Reading senseless sentences: Brain potentials reflect semantic incongruity. *Science, 207,* 203–205.

MacDonald, M. (1994). Probabilistic constraints and syntactic ambiguity resolution. *Language and Cognitive Processes, 9,* 157–201.

MacDonald, M. (1997). Lexical representations and sentence processing. *Language and Cognitive Processes, 12,* 121–136.

MacDonald, M. C., Pearlmutter, N. J., & Seidenberg, M. S. (1994). The lexical nature of syntactic ambiguity resolution. *Psychological Review, 101,* 676–703.

MacWhinney, B. (1997). Second language acquisition and the competition model. In A. M. B. de Groot & J. F. Kroll (Eds.), *Tutorials in bilingualism: Psycholinguistic perspectives* (pp. 113–142). Mahwah, NJ: Erlbaum.

MacWhinney, B. (2001). The competition model: The input, the context and the brain. In P. Robinson (Ed.), *Cognition and second language instruction.* Cambridge: Cambridge University Press.

McLaughlin, J., Osterhout, L., & Kim, A. (2004). Neural correlates of second-language word learning: Minimal instruction produces rapid change. *Nature Neuroscience, 7,* 703–704.

McRae, K., Ferretti, T. R., & Amyote, L. (1997). Thematic roles as verb-specific concepts. *Language and Cognitive Processes, 12,* 137–176.

Meuter, R., Donald, M. W., & Ardal, S. (1987). A comparison of first and second-language ERPs in bilinguals. *Current Trends in Event-Related Potential Research* (EEG Suppl. 40), 412–416.

Mitchell, D. C. (1989). Verb-guidance and other lexical effects in parsing. *Language and Cognitive Processes, 4,* 123–154.

Mitchell, D. C. (1994). Sentence parsing. In M. A. Gernsbacher (Ed.), *Handbook of psycholinguistics* (pp. 375–409). New York: Academic Press.

Mitchell, D. C., & Brysbaert, M. (1998) Challenges to recent theories of language differences in parsing: Evidence from Dutch. In D. Hillert (Ed.), *Sentence processing: A cross-linguistic perspective* (pp. 313–335). New York: Academic Press.

Mitchell, D. C., Cuetos, F., Corley, M. M. B., & Brysbaert, M. (1995). Exposure-based models of human parsing: Evidence for the use of coarse-grained (non-lexical) statistical records. *Journal of Psycholinguistic Research, 24,* 469–488.

Mitchell, D. C., & Holmes, V. M. (1985). The role of specific information about the verb in parsing sentences with local structural ambiguity. *Journal of Memory and Language, 24,* 542-559.

Ni, W., Crain, S., & Shankweiler, D. (1996). Sidestepping garden paths: Assessing the contributions of syntax, semantics and plausibility in resolving ambiguities. *Language and Cognitive Processes, 11,* 283–334.

Osterhout, L. (1990). *Event-related brain potentials elicited during sentence comprehension.* Unpublished doctoral dissertation, Tufts University, Boston, MA.

Osterhout, L., & Hagoort, P. (1999). A superficial resemblance does not necessarily mean you are part of the family: Counterarguments to Coulson, King, and Kutas (1998) in the P600/SPS-P300 debate. *Language and Cognitive Processes, 14,* 1–14.

Osterhout, L., & Holcomb, P. J. (1992). Event-related brain potentials elicited by syntactic anomaly. *Journal of Memory and Language, 31,* 785–806.

Osterhout, L., Holcomb, P. J., & Swinney, D. A. (1994). Brain potentials elicited by garden-path sentences: Evidence of the application of verb information during parsing. *Journal of*

Experimental Psychology: Learning, Memory, and Cognition, 20, 786–803.

Osterhout, L., McLaughlin, J., Kim, A., Greenwald, R., & Inoue, K. (2004). Sentences in the brain: Event-related potentials as real-time reflections of sentence comprehension and language learning. In M. Carreiras & C. Clifton, Jr. (Eds.), *The on-line study of sentence comprehension: Eyetracking, ERP, and beyond* (pp. 271–308). Philadelphia, PA: Psychology Press.

Osterhout, L., McKinnon, R., Bersick, M., & Corey, V. (1996). On the language specificity of the brain response to syntactic anomalies: Is the syntactic positive shift a member of the P300 family? *Journal of Cognitive Neuroscience, 8,* 507–526.

Pickering, M. J., Traxler, M. J., & Crocker, M. W. (2000). Ambiguity resolution in sentence processing: Evidence against frequency-based accounts. *Journal of Memory and Language, 43,* 447–475.

Pollock, J. (1989). Verb movement, universal grammar and the structure of IP. *Linguistic Inquiry, 20,* 365–424.

Pynte, J., & Kennedy, A. (1993). Referential context and within-word refixations: Evidence for "weak interaction." In G. d'Ydewalle & J. van Rensbergen (Eds.), *Perception and cognition: Advances in eye movement research* (pp. 227–238). Amsterdam: North-Holland.

Rayner, K., Carlson, M., & Frazier, L. (1983). The interaction of syntax and semantics during sentence processing: Eye movements in the analysis of semantically biased sentences. *Journal of Verbal Learning and Verbal Behavior, 22,* 358–374.

Robertson, D., & Sorace, A. (1999). Losing the V2 constraint. In E. C. Klein & G. Martohardjono (Eds.), *The development of second language grammars: A generative approach* (pp. 317–362). Amsterdam: Benjamins.

Sanders, L. D., & Neville, H. J. (2003). An ERP study of continuous speech processing II. Segmentation, semantics and syntax in nonnative speakers. *Cognitive Brain Research, 15,* 214–227.

Segalowitz, N. (1997). Individual differences in second language acquisition. In A. M. B. de Groot & J. F. Kroll (Eds.), *Tutorials in bilingualism: Psycholinguistic perspectives* (pp. 85–112). Hillsdale, NJ: Erlbaum.

Tanenhaus, M. K., Carlson, G., & Trueswell, J. C. (1990). The role of thematic structures in interpretation and parsing. *Language and Cognitive Processes, 4,* 1211–1234.

Taraban, R., & McClelland, J. L. (1988). Constituent attachment and thematic role assignment in sentence processing: Influences of content-based expectations. *Journal of Memory and Language, 27,* 597–632.

Trueswell, J. C., & Kim, A. E. (1998). How to prune a garden-path by nipping it in the bud: Fast-priming of verb argument structures. *Journal of Memory and Language, 39,* 102–123.

Trueswell, J. C., Tanenhaus, M. K., & Garnsey, S. M. (1994). Semantic influences on parsing: Use of thematic role information in syntactic ambiguity resolution. *Journal of Memory and Language, 33,* 285–318.

Trueswell, J. C., Tanenhaus, M. K., & Kello, C. (1993). Verb-specific constraints in sentence processing: Separating effects of lexical preference from garden-paths. *Journal of Experimental Psychology: Learning, Memory and Cognition, 19,* 528–553.

Weber-Fox, C., & Neville, H. J. (1996). Maturational constraints on functional specializations for language processing: ERP and behavioral evidence in bilingual speakers. *Journal of Cognitive Neuroscience, 8,* 231–256.

White, L. (1989a). The principle of adjacency in second language acquisition: Do L2 learners obey the subset principle? In S. Gass & J. Schacter (Eds.), *Linguistic perspectives on second language acquisition* (pp. 134–159). Cambridge, U.K.: Cambridge University Press.

White, L. (1989b). *Universal grammar and second language acquisition.* Amsterdam: Benjamins.

White, L. (1991). Adverb placement in second language acquisition: Some effects of positive and negative evidence in the classroom. *Second Language Research, 7,* 133–161.

White, L. (1997). Chasing after linguistic theory: How minimal should we be? In L. Eubank, L. Selinker, & M. Sharwood Smith (Eds.), *The current state of interlanguage* (pp. 63–71). Amsterdam: Benjamins.

PART III

PRODUCTION AND CONTROL

Introduction to Part III
Production and Control

About three decades ago, Fodor, Bever, and Garrett (1974) characterized the state of the art concerning language production as follows: "Practically anything that can be said about language production must be considered speculative even by the standards current in psycholinguistics" (p. 434). The pessimism expressed in this quotation concerning the scientific study of language production can easily be supported by many similar quotations (see also Bock, 1996). However, three decades later, there is good reason to be more optimistic. We have by now a substantial and rapidly growing body of empirical data that allow us to specify the component processes of language production. New experimental procedures and tasks for the study of language production processes have been developed, and at least for some component processes like lexical access and grammatical encoding, explicit computational models have been developed.

The six chapters of the present part show that comparable development is going on in the domain of language production by bilinguals. There is a steadily growing body of empirical research on language production and control in bilinguals, and this section provides an overview of the state of the art in some of the most important domains of bilingual language production. Chapters 14 (by La Heij) and 15 (by Costa) address issues of lexical access in bilinguals. These chapters focus on models primarily developed on the basis of experimental laboratory data, mostly (speeded) picture naming. Chapter 16 (by Myers-Scotton) is also concerned with lexical access; however, it focuses on naturally occurring code switching and its implication for accessing different types of morphemes. Chapters 17 (by Meuter), 18 (by Segalowitz and Hulstijn), and 19 (by Michael and Gollan) cover issues of language selection, language switching, and control from different perspectives.

The chapters not only are of interest to those interested in bilingual language production, but also provide important insights and, perhaps even more important, new directions for thought and future research for those primarily interested in monolingual production. And, it is from the latter perspective that I address two topics that appear to play an important role in bilingual research on language production and control and that have attracted much less attention in monolingual production research.

The first topic concerns the problem of adequate characterization of the conceptual input (or in Levelt's 1989 terms, the preverbal message) to the language production system. At least a large part of monolingual language production research, particularly the experimentally oriented tradition, has tried to bypass this problem. The present chapters suggest that also monolingual research on language production will have to face this topic in future research more explicitly.

The second topic concerns the issues of control, switching, and automaticity, the main focus of the last three chapters of the present section. There appears to be some lack of clarity regarding how to incorporate control processes in a model of language production, and the underlying issues surface much more clearly in bilingual production research, but they will also be of central importance for models of monolingual production. The basic question is: How much of "intelligent" or complex processing is going on in the linguistic formulation modules (like lexical access and selection, grammatical encoding, and phonological encoding) proper and how much should be located outside these modules at other levels, like conceptual preparation or "task schemas."

Before turning to these two topics in more detail, a note on terminology is needed. I use the term (processing) *module* as shorthand for referring to the different processing components of the language production system, like lexical access, grammatical encoding, and the like, but I do not imply by the use of this term that these processing components are necessarily operating in a strict modular fashion.

With respect to the first topic, it appears that in large parts of monolingual language production research, a clear specification of the format and the role of the conceptual input has been avoided more or less systematically. This holds primarily for monolingual production research aiming at uncovering the precise (temporal) details of the working of the respective modules or processing components under investigation. Of course, there are exceptions to this (e.g., Slobin, 1996). But, at least most of the experimental research that tries to uncover the details of the linguistic encoding processes tends to avoid the complexities of the conceptual input.

To understand the potential reasons for this state of affairs, it is useful to realize that language production research has always been in a tenuous position between leaving the input and output sides relatively unconstrained on the one hand and on the other hand trying to have as much (experimental) control over input and output as possible. The following quotations exemplify two extreme positions on this topic. Butterworth (1980) stated: "It would be extraordinarily optimistic to set up manipulations of the input and to expect to find systematic outputs, unless the subject is so limited in what he is allowed to say that generalisations to natural speech become almost impossible" (p. 2). In clear contrast to this position, Rosenberg (1977) stressed the need for experimental approaches of the type used in experimental cognitive psychology:

It should be clear by now that determinants and organisation of the speech production process are not likely to be resolved unless we turn our attention toward the development of manipulative research paradigms which (a) insure adequate control over the input, (b) limit information processing demands, and (c) constrain the speakers responding. (p. 196)

As Bock (1995, 1996) noted, a current practice in monolingual research has been to bypass the difficult problem of an explicit characterization of the conceptual input to language production by keeping the eliciting stimulus the same across experimental manipulations. Typical examples of this approach are implicit priming paradigms, picture word interference experiments, and sentence completion tasks. These approaches try to avoid the difficult and largely unresolved issue of specifying the precise characteristics of the preverbal input representation to language production processes and the more general question about the relation of language and thought. These approaches in monolingual production research have provided important insights into the processing details of the language production process, and they have proven a useful heuristic for experimental research on monolingual language production.

However, the present chapters on bilingual production show that the topic of an adequate characterization of the preverbal input is unavoidable when talking about bilingual language production. For example, La Heij discusses the question whether all necessary information for accessing the appropriate lexical entry should be assumed to be present at the conceptual preverbal message level. If so, we would end up with what La Heij calls "complex access/simple selection." The general approach by La Heij is a very attractive one, but it requires precise specification of the contents and properties of the conceptual input. Costa assumes a somewhat more complex and intelligent selection mechanism that only considers the actual "target" language during the selection process. Also, here we have to assume that some information from the conceptual level plays a role.

Is the need for a sufficiently explicit specification of the conceptual input restricted to bilingual language production, or does it also figure in monolingual production? Despite the success of an experimental approach that keeps the conceptual input constant and thus tries to bypass the problem of a more detailed specification of the conceptual input, it appears that monolingual production research also will be forced to face this problem. Just to name two problems (beyond those provided in the chapter by La Heij): How do speakers choose between levels of specificity for referring to objects depending on the (presumed) expertise of their interlocutors? And, how does context precisely affect the choice between a more or less-specific word? Just to give an example for the latter question, assume you want to refer to a specific fish in a fishpond (e.g., a carp). At what level of processing does a speaker "filter out" the basic level name *fish* and decides to use the more specific name *carp*? From a broader perspective, this is not very different from filtering out the German word for carp, *Karpfen* when you want to refer to a carp in English and not in German. The obvious question is whether this problem is going to be solved in the same way when you are dealing with one language, your first language, or with two languages, your first and second languages.

Put differently, are the mechanisms for filtering out the inappropriate name the same within a language and between two languages? And, more important in the present context, are these mechanisms located at the conceptual level or at a level of the linguistic formulation processes? Thus, in my view, the present chapters strongly suggest that we will not be able to avoid a more detailed characterization of the conceptual input as soon as we start to look at situations that are a bit more complex and a bit more "contextualized" than those currently used in most of research on monolingual production.

Let us now turn to the second topic: control, switching, and automaticity. Although these each can be seen as rather different issues, they have a common underlying basis that plays a role in all chapters of the present section, but is most explicitly present in the last three chapters. When reading the chapters, one is confronted with the question whether control processes and related processes are to be located outside the respective processing module, or whether they are part of the module itself. This issue surfaces much more clearly in bilingual production research, but it is also of central importance for models of monolingual production. As already stated above, one central question in this context is the following: How much of "intelligent" or complex processing is going on in the linguistic formulation modules (like lexical access and selection, grammatical encoding, and phonological encoding) proper, and how much should be located outside these modules at other levels like conceptual preparation, "task schemas," and the like? The proposals range from very simple, highly automatized formulation modules functioning in a ballistic fashion once triggered, with very simple local processing principles, to sophisticated procedures within each module, like verification procedures, selective inhibition, "tags" and "flags," and so on.

It is interesting to look at this issue from a "historical" perspective. In Levelt's (1989) seminal book on language production, the different processing components were highly locally operating devices working in an automatic and ballistic fashion. In the course of time, these modules have become more and more "intelligent," partly as a reaction to new empirical evidence (compare, e.g., Levelt, 1989, with Levelt, Roelofs, & Meyer, 1999). As a consequence, we are now talking about much more complex and intelligent "within-module" processes than we did 10 years ago. However, one might want

to opt for a different solution, namely, keeping the processing modules as local, automatic, and simple as possible while locating control processes and related processes outside the processing modules proper. The present chapters show that this question plays a much more central role in bilingual production than in monolingual production. I hope that the present chapters will bring this topic back to the attention of those primarily interested in monolingual production.

To summarize, the present chapters on bilingual production provide a lot of food for thought, not only for those interested in bilingual language production, but also for those primarily interested in monolingual production. Put differently, bilingual language production is not only an interesting topic by itself, but also (re)introduces topics highly relevant for monolingual production research.

References

Bock, J. K. (1995). Sentence production: From mind to mouth. In J. L. Miller & P. D. Eimas (Eds.), *Handbook of perception and cognition. Volume 11: Speech, language, and communication* (2nd ed., pp. 181–216). San Diego, CA: Academic Press.

Bock, J. K. (1996). Language production: Methods and methodologies. *Psychonomic Bulletin and Review, 3*, 395–421.

Butterworth, B. (1980). Introduction: A brief review of methods of studying language production. In B. Butterworth (Ed.), *Language production* (Vol. 1, pp. 1–17). London: Academic Press.

Fodor, J. A., Bever, T. G., & Garrett, M. F. (1974). *The psychology of language.* New York: Crowell.

Levelt, W. J. M. (1989). *Speaking. From intention to articulation.* Cambridge, MA: MIT Press.

Levelt, W. J. M., Roelofs, A., & Meyer, A. S. (1999). A theory of lexical access in speech production. *Behavioral and Brain Sciences, 22*, 1–75.

Rosenberg, S. (1977). Semantic constraints on sentence production: An experimental approach. In S. Rosenberg (Ed.), *Sentence production: Developments in research and theory* (pp. 195–228). Hillsdale, NJ: Erlbaum.

Slobin, D. I. (1996). From "thought and language" to "thinking for speaking." In J. Gumperz & S. Levinson (Eds.), *Rethinking linguistic relativity* (pp. 70–96). Cambridge, England: Cambridge University Press.

Wido La Heij

14

Selection Processes in Monolingual and Bilingual Lexical Access

ABSTRACT   How do bilinguals selectively retrieve words from either the first or second language when both words express the same conceptual content? Formulated in this way, this problem is very similar to the one faced by monolinguals when a preverbal message does not uniquely specify a single lexical item (the "convergence problem"). In this chapter, I argue that this convergence problem is nonexistent if one assumes that the preverbal message contains all necessary information, including affective and pragmatic features, to uniquely specify a single word. In monolinguals, these features may indicate the intention to use slang, formal language, or a euphemism. In bilinguals, one of these features may indicate that a first or second language word is required. If the preverbal message indeed contains all necessary information, lexical selection can be a simple process based on information that is locally available in the activation levels of words. Like the model proposed by Poulisse and Bongaerts (1994), the resulting model of lexical access can be characterized as "complex access, simple selection." Arguments are provided against recent models of monolingual and bilingual lexical access in which lexical selection is a complex, nonlocal process that needs (a) situational knowledge (about, for instance, the language to be spoken) and (b) knowledge about the activated words (for instance, whether they belong to the first or second language).

Ask a Dutch-English bilingual to name a picture of a dog in English, and sooner or later he or she will come up with the word *dog*. This chapter is about one of the mental processes that are supposed to underlie this seemingly simple task: the process that makes the connection between the "idea" dog and the word *dog*, a step that is often referred to as *lexical access*. Clearly, lexical access is only a small part of bilingual language production, and the question could be asked whether the emphasis on such a small step is warranted.

One answer to this question could be that it seems a very fundamental step. It bridges the gap between two worlds: the world of nonverbal thought and the world of language. Another answer could be that, despite all the research devoted to lexical access, many issues remain to be solved. Finally, one could answer that lexical access is a microcosm of cognitive processing: It involves semantic memory, the representation of words, selective

attention, and other executive functions. If we understand lexical access, we probably know a lot more about cognition in general.

Why study the process of lexical access in bilinguals? Wouldn't it be better to start with the simple case of a monolingual? Investigators of bilingualism often reply to this remark by arguing that, in today's world, bilingualism is the rule rather than the exception. Models of language production should—in that view—be bilingual models with monolingual language production as an option (e.g., De Bot, 1992). Although it is not difficult to agree with that argument, the present chapter takes a different approach. I argue that with respect to lexical access in simple naming tasks, monolinguals face the same problems as bilinguals. So, if you have a satisfactory model of lexical access in monolinguals, you have a satisfactory model of bilingual lexical access as well.

As a consequence of this approach, this chapter is largely devoted to lexical access in the first language (L1). First, I discuss the nature of the conceptual information that the speaker wants to convey (the *preverbal message*) and the problem that this preverbal message may not uniquely specify a single word (the *convergence problem*). Next, two selection processes are discussed that are commonly assumed in language production models: the selection of the conceptual information to be lexicalized (*concept selection*) and the selection of the response word from a set of activated words (*lexical selection*). This discussion leads to a proposal of how words are retrieved in the L1.

The final section discusses the implications of this proposal for bilingual lexical access. In that section, I propose a simple modular account of bilingual lexical access that has two main characteristics. First, the language in which the bilingual intends to speak is—in the form of a "language cue"—part of a complex preverbal message that contains all conceptual, pragmatic, and affective characteristics of the word to be retrieved. Second, the actual selection of a word is a relatively simple process mainly based on the activation levels of lexical representations. In this view, lexical selection does not evaluate the appropriateness of a word that is about to be selected or involve the selective activation or inhibition of words that belong to a particular language. This view, which could be characterized as "complex access, simple selection," is contrasted with recent proposals that could be characterized as "simple access, complex selection."

A Word on Experimental Paradigms, Findings, and Terminology

Since the early 1990s, online research methods have become increasingly popular in language production research. Of these methods, the picture–word interference task—a variant of the color–word Stroop task—is most frequently used. In this task, a target picture and a context word are presented, and the participant is required to name the picture while ignoring the context word. Manipulating the syntactic (Schriefers, 1993), semantic (La Heij, 1988; Underwood, 1976), and phonological (Posnansky & Rayner, 1977; Schriefers, Meyer, & Levelt, 1990) similarity between the context word and the name of the picture has been used to shed light on many aspects of lexical access. Most relevant for the discussion in this chapter is the

semantic interference effect: the observation that pictures are named slower when accompanied by a semantically related context word than when accompanied by an unrelated context word. For example, the naming of the picture of a dog takes more time when the context word *cat* is superimposed than when the word *pen* is superimposed. In the following sections, a small number of experimental results are discussed that were obtained with this picture–word interference paradigm.

In recent years, a discussion has started about what is retrieved on the basis of a preverbal message, an abstract word representation (*lemma*) or a phonological word form (e.g., Caramazza, 1997; Caramazza & Miozzo, 1998; Harley, 1999; Roelofs, Meyer, & Levelt, 1998). In this chapter, I use the theoretically neutral term *lexical representation* or *word*. Finally, I use the following convention: Nonverbal representations (*concepts*) are presented in uppercase letters (e.g., "the picture activates the concept DOG"). When a word denotes a stimulus, verbal response, or lexical representation, italics are used (e.g., "the concept activates the word *dog*," "the word *dog* was presented," and "the speaker produced the word *dog*").

Models: The (Preverbal) Message

In this chapter, only those aspects of models of language production are discussed that are relevant for the retrieval of a single word. Basically, all of these models distinguish two systems, a conceptual system and a lexicon. The conceptual system contains world knowledge in the form of nonverbal representations. In some models, a separate lexical-semantic system is distinguished that contains the meaning of words. However, this difference is not well articulated, and the labels *conceptual system* and *semantic system* are often used interchangeably (see Francis, chapter 12, this volume). The second system is often referred to as the "mental lexicon" or just "lexicon." The lexicon contains representations of words with their syntactic, phonological, and (in some models) semantic characteristics.

At a very general level, the naming of an object with a bare noun is thought to comprise the following steps (see Fig. 14.1 for a simple pictorial representation). First, the visual processing of the object ultimately leads to the activation of a representation in the conceptual system. When that happens, the object is "recognized." That is, information about the object, like function, smell,

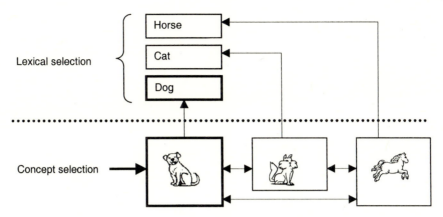

Figure 14.1 A simple model of lexical access. A picture of a dog is presented for naming. At the conceptual level (below the dotted line), the corresponding conceptual representation is selected (concept selection). At the lexical level (above the dotted line), a number of semantically related word candidates become activated. Lexical selection determines which of these words will be produced.

taste, and so on, becomes available. Because other conceptual representations may be activated (e.g., by other stimuli in the speaker's environment), the conceptual information that the speaker wants to express has to be selected. This selection process is referred to as *concept selection*. All current models assume that lexical access does not result in the activation of a single lexical representation. Instead, it is assumed that many words become activated, either because their meaning overlaps with the content of the preverbal message or because not only the selected concept, but also all activated concepts activate their lexical representations. A second selection process (*lexical selection*) is responsible for the selection of one word from this set of candidates. Lexical selection ultimately results in the availability of a phonological word form that can be articulated.

In addition, it is useful to note that Levelt (1989) proposed a monitoring process that uses the word comprehension system to determine whether the meaning of the word about to be articulated matches the content of the preverbal message. If no match is obtained, this may lead to a "covert repair." When the monitor detects a mismatch during or after articulation, an "overt repair" may result.

The Verbal Message

Usually, speakers want to achieve something with their utterances. If they ask a question, they like to hear it answered; if they provide information, they want it to be understood, and if they are in the position to give an order, they want to see the appropriate action taken. In other words, by producing a "verbal message" speakers intend to achieve a "communicative goal" (Levelt, 1989).

Given this goal of a speaker, we may agree on the following, very pragmatic definition of differences in meaning between verbal messages: If an addressee in a particular situation reacts differently to verbal messages A and B, then—for that addressee in that situation—the messages A and B differ in meaning. There are theories that seem to define meaning in such a way that utterances A and B may have the *same* meaning but nevertheless induce *different* reactions on the part of the addressee. As discussed here, these theories of meaning do not seem a very useful starting point for understanding the behavior of speakers.

Because speakers want to achieve a communicative goal, it is evident that in preparing an utterance, they have to anticipate as much as possible how a particular addressee in a particular situation will react. To that end, the speaker should take many aspects into account: the addressee's age, likes and dislikes, intelligence, language skills, sense of humor, social position, occupation, and so on. In addition, the speaker should adjust the utterance to the specific social context. Within sociolinguistics, some of these factors are discussed under the headings *style* and *register*, which refer respectively to the language required in a specific situation and to the language used within specific socioeconomic groups (e.g., occupational groups and teenagers; see also Levelt, 1989).

The following contextual factors that determine our choice of words can be thought of. First, the social context may require a speaker to use formal language (e.g., in a meeting you may address a good friend and colleague as "Mr. Brown" instead of the usual "Jim") or to use slang ("I'm going bonkers between those jerks"). Second, known sensitivities of the addressee may require the use of euphemisms (varying from "rest room" to "collateral damage") or the avoidance of taboo words. Third, limited language skills of the addressee may make you refrain from using low-frequency words (e.g., avoid "eloquent" when talking to a child or to a nonnative speaker). Finally, knowledge about an addressee's familiarity with the conversation topic may determine your choice of category level (to a layperson, you may decide to use the phrase "statistical analysis" instead of the more precise "*t* test").

Even in a laboratory situation, speakers could react to stimuli in very different ways. One and the same stimulus may be called *a line drawing, a picture of an animal, animal, hound, dog, young dog, puppy, whelp, Labrador,* or *pooch* (see also Levelt, Roelofs, & Meyer, 1999). It is mainly because of a contextual factor (the instruction given) that in most experiments participants produce formal, basic category, bare noun utterances (*dog*). Nevertheless, the models discussed in this chapter often simplify matters by assuming that, in naming tasks, the concept activated by a target stimulus (e.g., the concept DOG activated by the picture of a dog) directly activates the corresponding response word in the mental lexicon (e.g., the word *dog*). However, it is probably more realistic to look at the activation and selection of a conceptual representation as a step in the construction of a preverbal message (Levelt, 1989), a process in which contextual factors (including task instructions) also are taken into consideration.

The Convergence Problem

The issue of how word meaning is represented is notoriously difficult, and it is quite understandable that many students of language production have not made it the main focus of their research efforts. One of the aspects of meaning representation that did receive attention, mainly because of the work by Levelt (1989) and Roelofs (1992, 1996), is the so-called convergence problem: the problem that the conceptual information in a preverbal message may not uniquely specify one lexical item. Here,

I discuss two situations in which problems of this sort are argued to arise: the hyperonym problem and the word-to-phrase synonymy problem.

At the basis of Levelt's (1989) and Roelofs's (1992, 1996) discussion of the convergence problem is the feature theory of word meaning. This theory, as presented by Levelt and Roelofs, proposes that the meaning of a word consists of a list of conceptual features, comparable to what is found in a dictionary. For example, the concept MOTHER may be represented by two conceptual features, PARENT and FEMALE. If the speaker wants to express a message containing the concept MOTHER, the conceptual features PARENT and FEMALE will be activated. The hyperonym problem refers to the fact that the activated feature PARENT is a sufficient condition for the retrieval of the word *parent*. So, why not retrieve the hyperonym *parent* instead of the hyponym *mother*? The word-to-phrase synonymy problem refers to the fact that, in this situation, the system seems unable to decide between the word *mother* and the phrase *female parent*.

Levelt (1989) considered the solution of the hyperonym problem a touchstone for theories of lexical access. Indeed, many researchers (e.g., Bierwisch & Schreuder, 1992; Caramazza, 1997; De Bot & Schreuder, 1993; Roelofs, 1992, 1996) made serious efforts to provide a solution. Levelt formulated three principles, including a "principle of specificity" that should prevent the system from producing hyperonyms instead of the intended hyponyms. On the basis of a similar analysis of the convergence problem, Roelofs decided to abandon the feature theory of word meaning altogether. Instead, he proposed a nondecompositional view of word meaning in which lexical concepts like FEMALE, PARENT, and MOTHER are represented by separate nodes. In his view, lemma retrieval starts with the activation of MOTHER and not with activation of the features FEMALE and PARENT.

The proposal to reject a feature theory of word meaning seems in line with developments in the area of concept representation, in which the idea that a concept can be defined by a list of (necessary and sufficient) features is severely criticized. In addition to Wittgenstein's (1953) theoretical point that some concepts (e.g., GAME) do not seem to have a unique defining feature, there are several empirical arguments (see, e.g., Harley, 2001). For example, a simple feature theory has difficulty in accounting for the "typicality effect." Oranges and olives are both fruit and should both possess the feature FRUIT. Nevertheless, it takes much longer to verify the sentence "an olive is a fruit" than to verify the sentence "an orange is a fruit."

Another criticism is that a simple feature model seems to assume that the meaning of a word is fixed. Often, however, word meanings seem "fuzzy." First, speakers may disagree about the category membership of words. McCloskey and Glucksberg (1978) mentioned, for instance, that half of their participants thought that *stroke* was a disease, and half thought that it was not. Second, word meaning seems to depend on the nonverbal or verbal context (see, e.g., Barsalou, 1982). The word *mother* can have a purely technical meaning in one situation ("the one who has given birth to" or "female parent"), but in many other situations *mother* is better characterized as the one who loved and protected you during childhood, irrespective of a biological relation.

Despite these concerns about a feature theory of word meaning, it is questionable whether Levelt's (1989) and Roelofs's (1992) analysis of this theory is adequate and consequently whether Roelofs's rejection of all feature theories on the basis of that analysis is warranted. Let me first examine the word-to-phrase synonymy problem: Why not say *female parent* instead of *mother* despite the fact that "both utterances express the same conceptual content" (Roelofs, 1996, p. 309; see also Fodor, 1980)? Somewhat surprisingly, many psycholinguists seem to take Levelt's and Roelofs's premise that *mother* and *female parent* express the same conceptual content for granted. But what makes them so sure of that? The answer to this question is as simple as it is disconcerting: They are sure of that because they first *define* the conceptual content of MOTHER as FEMALE PARENT. If that definition is incorrect or incomplete, the notorious word-to-phrase synonymy problem is like defining your cat as a dog and then trying to understand why it does not bark.

Defining CAT as DOG does not make it a dog and defining MOTHER as FEMALE PARENT does not make her (just) a female parent. Above, I suggested a simple way of testing whether two utterances differ in meaning. Let us apply this test to the present example: Next time you visit your mother, greet her with a cheerful "Hi, female parent!" and see what happens. Most probably, this test will show that the premise that these two utterances express the same meaning is incorrect. Similar tests of other word-phrase pairs will most probably show that there are very few words that "express the same meaning" as a corresponding phrase. This does not have to surprise us because there is nothing in the feature theory that forces us to assume that all conceptual features of a word have linguistic counterparts (words that express them). For example, it seems very difficult to convey the "mildness" that characterizes a euphemism in any other way than by using the euphemism itself. Clearly, if there is no word-to-phrase synonymy in natural languages, there is no word-to-phrase synonymy problem to be solved.

Levelt's (1989) hyperonym problem seems to be based on a similar logical flaw. Roelofs (1996) presented this problem in the following way: "If the conceptual conditions for the application of a word such as *father* are met, then those of its hyperonyms such as *parent* are automatically satisfied as well" (p. 309). Again, the question is, How can we be so sure about this premise? Surely, fathers belong to the category of parents, but it is not clear whether this implies that "the set of features relevant to a word includes those relevant to its hyperonyms" (p. 314). That is, apart from the definition, no arguments are provided that the *full* meaning of a category name (the word) has to be a subset of the meaning of the names of the category's exemplars. In fact, it is pretty obvious that this is not the case. Category names have a generality or unspecificity that the names of exemplars of a category lack. For example, it could be argued that one important feature of PARENT is GENDER NOT SPECIFIED or GENDER IRRELEVANT. Clearly, that feature cannot be part of the meaning of *mother*. So, when the conceptual conditions for *mother* are met, those for *parent* are not automatically satisfied. Relevant in this context is that, in later developments of the feature theory (e.g., Smith & Medin, 1981), the identification of a word as a member of a category was not based on a complete overlap between the two sets of features but on the amount of overlap. These "probabilistic" feature models can also account for the observation that word meanings seem fuzzy.

In conclusion, there is little we can say with certainty about what comprises the meaning of a word. Clearly, dictionary definitions and simple feature lists do not do any justice to its complexity, fuzziness, and context dependency. Therefore, the only information we can rely on is the speaker's and the addressee's behavior. If an addressee reacts differently to *mother* than to *female parent*, this defines a difference in meaning. In formulating the hyperonym problem, Levelt (1989) may have approached the issue of concept representation from the wrong direction. Instead of looking at the behavior of language users, he—and many others—started with a rather poor and unrealistic feature list representation of word meaning and either wondered how our language production apparatus "repairs" the resulting problems or decided to abandon feature theories altogether.

For the present purposes, the most important conclusion is that if it is assumed that the meaning of a word includes subtle pragmatic and affective aspects, the underlying conceptual representation is so rich and complex that it can only be expressed by using that particular word. That is, natural languages probably do not contain word-to-phrase synonymy pairs or hyperonyms as defined by Levelt (1989). Therefore, there is no convergence problem to be solved.

The Preverbal Message

Possibly, psycholinguists who tried to find solutions for the convergence problem implicitly assumed that the meaning of a word can be decomposed in a set of "core" elements and some paraphernalia that include, for instance, the pragmatic and affective factors discussed in the previous sections. Moreover, the assumption may have been that these two sets of meaning elements play a different role in lexical access. The first step, in which a set of lexical items is activated, may be based on the core meaning, whereas finer selection from this set, on the basis of pragmatic and affective factors, is postponed until later processing levels. With respect to such a view, two questions can be raised. First, is it realistic to assume a "hard" distinction between the core meaning of a word and other aspects of its meaning? Second, how does the more refined selection of words at a later processing level take place? I briefly discuss these two issues in turn.

After what has been said about the complexity and fuzziness of word meaning, it seems very unlikely that nature has endowed us with a system that neatly distinguishes between two sets of meaning components and uses them in different ways. I can refer to Wittgenstein (1953) again: What is the core in the meaning of words like *game* and *art*? Are the strong emotional connotations of the word *mother* part of the core or just paraphernalia, as *female parent* suggests?

Despite these doubts, assume for a moment that word meanings can be subdivided, and that only the core meaning is used in the first step of lexical access. Examine the following example: A speaker

wants to refer to the animal that tries to rip off his pants. In the first stage of lexical access that is only based on core meaning, the words *creature, beast, animal, dog, Doberman,* and somewhat more unlikely, *pooch,* all become active. Next, a selection process has to be assumed that selects the most adequate word from this set. Evidently, this process has to be quite complex. First, it should know about the specific characteristics of the situation and has to consider questions like: Is formal language required? Will a slang word be understood? Does one of these words convincingly express the ferocity of the attacker? Will the addressee understand that I am referring to a dog when I use the word *Dobermann*? Second, to allow for the lexical selection process to make its selection, the activated words have to "carry" these meaning components with them.

In the Lexical Selection section, the probability of such an intelligent selection mechanism is discussed in combination with the idea that word representations contain "tags" that, for instance, represent their pragmatic and affective characteristics. To anticipate the conclusion, this solution is highly unparsimonious given that all information needed to retrieve the appropriate word is available in the conceptual system. The most likely and most parsimonious answer to the issues raised in this section is therefore that the preverbal message contains *all* information necessary to select the appropriate word. This information includes cues as SLANG WORD APPROPRIATE, EUPHEMISM PREFERABLE, and FIRST NAME ALLOWED.

Is Lexicalization Limited to the Preverbal Message?

I proposed that lexical access is based on a complex nonverbal representation that contains all necessary information to arrive at the correct word. It seems reasonable to assume that this complex representation is *all* that we use during the process of lexical access. Indeed, in Levelt's (1989) original "blueprint of the speaker," the preverbal message was the only input to the "formulator." Therefore, it may come as a surprise that current models of lexical access (e.g., Levelt et al., 1999; Starreveld & La Heij, 1996) assume that during lexical access all activated concepts activate lexical representations. These activated concepts may be part of the preverbal message, but could also be activated by other, irrelevant, objects in the speaker's environment or by spreading activation within the conceptual system. For example, if a speaker is asked to name the picture of a dog, spreading activation from the concept DOG to related concepts like CAT and HORSE will result in the activation of the words *cat* and *dog* at the lexical level (see Fig. 14.1 for an illustration).

The main reason for this somewhat counterintuitive assumption seems to be that it realizes in a simple way the activation of a cohort of semantically related words during lexical access. Evidence for the activation of a semantic word cohort comes from a number of observations: the occurrence of semantically related speech errors (*sister* instead of *mother*), the occurrence of blends of semantically related words (e.g., *stummy*, a blend of stomach and tummy; Fromkin, 1973), and the semantic interference effect in word production, discussed at the beginning of this chapter (see Glaser & Glaser, 1989; Roelofs, 1992; and Starreveld & La Heij, 1996, for details). Whereas such a cohort activation may result naturally from a feature-based conceptual representation, models in which holistic conceptual representations are assumed may need the spread of activation in combination with parallel lexical access to arrive at the same result.

Despite these considerations, the idea that during lexical access all activated concepts activate their lexical representations seems rather counterintuitive. Moreover, recent observations in

our laboratory (Bloem & La Heij, 2003) provided strong evidence against this assumption. We used a language production task in which the to-be-named targets were accompanied by either context words or context pictures. As expected, context words induced semantic interference. However, the corresponding context pictures induced semantic facilitation, contrary to the predictions derived from computer implementations of the Levelt et al. (1999) and the Starreveld and La Heij (1996) models. In these models, context pictures automatically activate their names at the lexical level, which renders the situation very similar to the word–context condition. To account for semantic facilitation with picture context, we proposed two modifications of current models: (a) Lexicalization is confined to the preverbal message (as proposed by Levelt, 1989), and (b) this preverbal message activates, in addition to the sought-for word, a cohort of semantically related words (as originally proposed in Morton's 1969 and in Levelt's 1989 models of speech production). These assumptions are illustrated in Fig. 14.2.

Conclusions

The main point that I have tried to make in this section concerns the content of the preverbal message. Arguments were presented in favor of the view that the preverbal message contains all

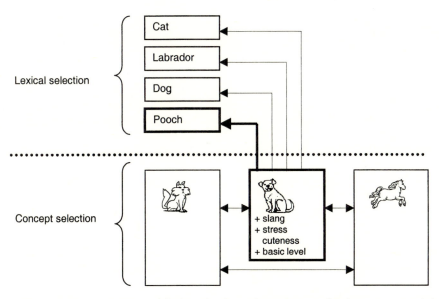

Figure 14.2 The model in Fig. 14.1 modified so that lexicalization is confined to one preverbal message, and the preverbal message contains cues that further specify the sought-for word.

information necessary to retrieve the word that realizes the speaker's communicative goal. To that end, the speaker has to take into account a large amount of information about the context of the conversation and about the characteristics of the addressee. Given the complexity of the preverbal message, it seems unlikely that situations will arise in which this message specifies more than one lexical item. As a consequence, there is no convergence problem to be solved. In addition, I discussed evidence that only the preverbal message is capable of activating words at the lexical level. To account for incidental speech errors, blends, and semantic interference in the picture–word task, it has to be assumed that lexical access is not perfect. That is, in addition to the correct word, other words with meanings that partly overlap the contents of the preverbal message become activated.

Models: Selection and Control Processes

All computer implementations of the models in the previous sections of this chapter consist of processing levels containing nodes that represent conceptual/semantic and lexical representations. These nodes are connected—unidirectionally or bidirectionally—by links. Although the nature of the links differs, they all share the capability to pass "activation" from one node to another, resulting in an increase (excitatory connections) or decrease (inhibitory connections) in activation level of the receiving node. In the implemented models, the presentation of a stimulus picture is simulated by raising the activation level of the nodes either at an early visual level or at the conceptual level. From that moment, activation spreads through the model.

This spread of activation in itself, however, typically does not result in a response. To produce responses, the task instructions (e.g., "name the red picture and ignore the green picture") have to be implemented in the model. This is realized by selection or control processes. In most models, two types of selection or control processes can be distinguished. Under the assumption that all stimuli presented are identified in parallel, the first type of selection process determines what activated conceptual information has to be lexicalized (compare Allport's, 1987, and Van der Heijden's, 1996, notions of "selection for action"). In a task in which, for instance, two pictures are presented, one in red

and one in green (e.g., Humphreys, Lloyd-Jones, & Fias, 1995), this process has to make sure that the conceptual representation of the red picture controls the response. I use the term *concept selection* for this process.

As discussed, during the process of lexicalization not only the intended word, but also semantically related words will become activated to some extent. Lexical selection is the process that selects one word from this set of candidates for further processing (phonological encoding or articulation). Concept selection and lexical selection are discussed in turn.

Concept Selection

Concept selection is discussed with the help of the connectionist Selective Attention Model (SLAM) of Phaf, Van der Heijden, and Hudson (1990). SLAM was developed to simulate tasks in which an aspect of one visual stimulus (its form, color, or position) had to be named and other stimuli in the visual field had to be ignored. So, although the model was not developed to provide an account of lexical access, it does simulate tasks that are very similar to the usual Stroop-like interference tasks used in language production research.

SLAM assumes three processing levels: (a) an early mapping level; (b) a feature level, which consists of three specialized modules: a form (or identity) module, a position module, and a color module; and (c) a response (word) level. Stimulus presentation is simulated by activating the corresponding representations at the mapping level. These representations combine two stimulus features, for example, *red left* and *blue square*. Activation spreads from the mapping level to the identity, position, and color modules at the feature level. Next, activated feature representations in these modules (e.g., RED, BLUE, LEFT, and CIRCLE) send activation to the corresponding names at the response level (e.g., *red, blue, left,* and *circle*).

When a stimulus is presented without instruction, the implemented SLAM model gives no response or a random response. A theoretical analysis of a typical instruction in a filtering task (e.g. "name the color of the figure on the left") revealed—in addition to the "name" instruction that is not further discussed—two essential components. First, the part of the instruction that says that the *color* aspect of the figure (not its position or form) has to be named is supposed to result in a preactivation of all representations in the color module (see Cohen, Dunbar, & McClelland, 1990, for a similar pre-activation by "task demand" nodes).

Suppose that the model is presented with a red square on the left and a blue circle on the right. The processes discussed (stimulus presentation and the instruction to name a color) will result in an equally high activation of the nodes RED and BLUE in the color module. How does the model succeed in naming the correct color? This is not a trivial problem because both in the color module and in the response module all information about position is lost. The model solves this "binding problem" in the following way. The part of the instruction that says ". . . on the left" results in the activation of the representation LEFT in the position module. This representation sends activation back to all activated representations at the mapping level that contain the feature LEFT: RED-LEFT and CIRCLE-LEFT. These representations pass this activation to the representations of RED in the color module and of CIRCLE in the form module (see de Kamps & Van der Velde, 2001, for further elaboration of such a feedback mechanism).

Now the node RED in the color module receives activation from three sources: the activation from the stimulus, the activation that is given to all color representations, and the activation that—via the feedback loop—comes from the LEFT node in the position module. As a consequence, of all feature nodes, the node RED will reach the highest activation level. Because this activation is passed to the response module, the word *red* will become highly activated. Selection of a response word for production (lexical selection) is only based on the activation levels of the words in the response module. That is, the lexical selection process simply selects a "winner" and is completely ignorant of the instructions given.

Not surprisingly, in models of lexical access in language production, much less attention is given to the processes that lead to the selection of the nonverbal representation that has to be lexicalized. These processes are often taken for granted, and only the end result—an increase in activation of the target concept (or preverbal message)—is implemented. In Roelofs's (1992) model "signaling activation" and in Starreveld and La Heij's (1996) model "task activation" are given to the target concept that has to be verbalized. As in SLAM, this extra amount of activation should ultimately lead to a strong activation of the correct name of the target at the lexical level.

Lexical Selection

Whereas models of lexical access in language production generally implement concept selection in very similar ways, they strongly differ in their views on lexical selection. By far the simplest mechanism was proposed by Morton (1969) in his logogen model (see also Dell, 1986). After presentation of the stimulus and the activation of semantic features, logogens (word units) increase their activation proportionally to their degree of semantic similarity to the target concept. When the activation of one of the logogens exceeds a threshold level, the corresponding word is made "available." The solutions in the models of Cohen et al. (1990), SLAM (Phaf et al., 1990), and Starreveld and La Heij (1996) are rather similar. They add to Morton's solution the characteristic that the moment of selection of a particular word is also dependent on the activation levels of the other words. In Starreveld and La Heij's model, this is realized by a simple difference threshold: A word is selected when it exceeds the activation of all other words by a fixed amount δ.

Despite their differences, these three models have one thing in common: Lexical selection is a simple process that is only based on the activation levels of lexical representations. The (often-implicit) rationale behind this approach seems to be an assumption of modularity: Decisions at a certain processing level are taken on the basis of information available at that level. At the lexical level (or "response" level), no information is available about the meaning of words, the task instructions, and the source of the activation of a word (e.g., the red picture or the green picture in the display). Consequently, word meaning and source of activation cannot be used in the selection process. The response word that will be selected is completely determined by the content of the preverbal message and the current activation levels (resting levels) of the lexical representations. Clearly, the content of the preverbal message has to be very specific to ensure that the correct word is selected. In the first section of this chapter, I referred to this approach as complex access, simple selection. The limitations and problems of this approach are discussed further in this section.

This complex access, simple selection approach differs strongly from alternative approaches that could be characterized as "simple access, complex selection." The main assumption of these approaches is that lexical selection cannot be based on activation levels only. Instead, lexical selection is thought to be a rather complex process that uses information about, for instance, the task instructions and the source of activation of words. Roelofs's (1992) original model of lexical access belongs to this class of models. As in Starreveld and La Heij's (1996) model, the conceptual representation of the target concept is given additional activation ("signalling activation"). However, Roelofs also assumed that when activation spreads along the links of the network, it leaves "tags" at each node reached, specifying the source of the activation. So, in a picture–word interference task, there are "picture tags" and "word tags" attached to nodes at the conceptual and lexical level. In addition, permitted response words in an experiment (or all words when no response set is predefined) receive a "flag." In the picture–word task in which the picture has to be named, the lexical selection process determines which word has both a picture tag and a flag. Although this combination uniquely specifies the correct response word, it is assumed that selection cannot take place before a difference threshold in activation has been reached.

In simple object-naming tasks, Roelofs's (1992) and Morton's (1969) lexical selection mechanisms probably perform equally well. That should be reason enough to prefer the simplest solution. But, do these selection processes perform equally well under all conditions? That is the topic of the next section.

Problems in Lexical Selection

In a task in which a number of objects are presented (e.g., two pictures), one of which has to be named aloud, the models discussed in the previous sections probably perform equally well. Concept selection results in an increase in activation of the target concept relative to other activated concepts. Spreading activation to the lexical level will activate a number of words, but ultimately leads to the selection of the correct name, even when selection is only based on an absolute activation threshold, as in Morton's (1969) logogen model. However, there are at least two findings that pose problems for simple threshold models.

First, these models run into problems when they have to account for naming performance in Stroop-like tasks. In these tasks, a nonverbal target is accompanied by an incorrect context word. All current models assume that words activate their lexical representations faster and stronger than

nonverbal stimuli do. As a consequence, shortly after the presentation of, for example, the picture of a dog with the word *cat* superimposed, the incorrect word *cat* will be highly activated. How does the system prevent this word from selection and articulation? Within research on selective attention, this question proved to be one of the most difficult to answer (see, e.g., Keele, 1973; Morton, 1977; Van der Heijden, 1981). Two types of solutions can be distinguished: solutions that maintain the assumption that lexical selection is only based on activation levels and solutions that involve "checking" processes of some sort.

The probably simplest solution was implemented in the connectionist model of lexical access proposed by Starreveld and La Heij (1996; see also Cohen et al., 1990). These authors adjusted the parameters in the model in such a way that—within the stimulus-onset asynchrony range examined—the mere presentation of a word does not suffice to make its lexical representation reach the difference threshold. That is, even when a single word is presented, "task activation" is necessary to make the word reach the difference threshold. This solution is elegant because of its parsimony, but not everyone will be convinced that task activation is necessary to select the lexical representation of a visually presented word.

In SLAM (Phaf et al., 1990), a somewhat different solution is chosen. At the lexical level, a node is assumed that is highly active at the start of a trial and that inhibits the activation of all other lexical representations for a short period after stimulus onset. This inhibition prevents the early selection of the distractor word. By the time the inhibition is released, the name of the target color has received enough activation to compete with the distractor word for selection. This solution produces the desired effect, but also has a strong ad hoc flavor and begs a number of questions. For instance, is the inhibitory node always active, also when it is only detrimental to performance, as in a simple word-reading task?

All other solutions for correct naming performance in Stroop-like tasks assume some sort of "intelligent" checking mechanism. Morton (cited in Van der Heijden, 1981) accounted for the small number of errors in the Stroop task in the following way: "A response is produced, from one or another source, and we then have to check the response against the stimulus to confirm that it is the one we want" (p. 126). This, however, is easier said than done. As emphasized by Van der Heijden (1981), words like *check* and *verify* have to be regarded with great suspicion. One problem is that word representations and color representations are in a completely different format and will never lead to a match when directly compared. This comparison can only be performed by a mechanism that "knows" which word corresponds to which color. The mechanism that possesses that knowledge is our language comprehension system. So, Morton's solution may come down to a simple lexical selection mechanism based on activation thresholds, followed by a checking mechanism that seems identical to Levelt's (1989) "monitor." That is, before articulation, the system determines whether the word that has become available is correct. If not, a new attempt is made.

Roelofs's (1992) original model goes one step further by assuming that the lexical selection process itself performs a "check." In a picture–word interference task, for instance, this process is in some way informed about the instruction "name the picture and ignore the word" and searches for the word that was activated by the picture (the word that has a picture tag). Note that this system has to be highly flexible: To account for lexical selection in the picture–picture task reported by Humphreys et al. (1995), for instance, the assumption has to be that the lexical representations receive red picture tags and green picture tags, and that—on the basis of the instruction—the lexical selection mechanism searches for a word with a red picture tag. Levelt et al. (1999) proposed a somewhat different solution (called *binding by checking*) in which, before lexical selection takes place, a process determines whether the conceptual representation that corresponds to a highly activated word possesses a tag indicating that it is the "message concept."

Four arguments can be raised against these and similar proposals in which lexical selection is a relatively complex and flexible process that uses information from outside the lexicon to arrive at the correct word. A first argument is that the proposed solutions are complex but probably hardly ever needed. In most situations, concept selection suffices to ensure that the lexical representation that reaches the highest activation level is the sought-for word. As argued here, there may be more parsimonious solutions to the problem of preventing incorrect responses under rather unusual conditions, such as those in the Stroop task.

Second, lexical selection in Levelt et al.'s (1999) model seems to serve as yet another monitor that checks whether a word is really the intended one. As a consequence, the model performs such a check at

three levels: before lexical selection, before articulation, and after articulation. Indeed, as noted by Santiago and MacKay (1999), "we need some principle in the theory that limits how many checking mechanisms check checking mechanisms" (p. 55).

Third, in Roelofs's (1992) and Levelt et al.'s (1999) models, lexical selection solves important problems, but its workings are not spelled out in much detail. For example, in Roelofs's original proposal, the lexical selection mechanism can be informed about the task instruction ("name the picture, ignore the word") and can use that information in its search for the word with the correct tag. In Levelt et al.'s proposal, production rules at the lexical level test for the presence of a tag at the conceptual level. Moreover, to account for occasional selection errors, it is argued that these selection mechanisms may suffer from "lapses." It is unclear in these accounts what the nature is of the tags, how tagging is achieved, how tags are read (see also Li, 1998), and how the "lapses" should be interpreted. Given this lack of detail and the difficulty in deriving testable predictions from these accounts, it is not too surprising that concerns have been raised about their practically unconstrained explanatory power (Santiago & MacKay, 1999).

A final argument is that the lexical selection mechanisms proposed by Roelofs (1992) and Levelt et al. (1999) seem to violate Levelt's (1989) original and—in my view—very attractive conceptualization of lexical access. Levelt stressed its speed and proposed that the retrieval of words is in a certain sense automatic: "Formulating and articulating are 'underground processes'...that are probably largely impenetrable to executive control even when one wishes otherwise" (p. 22). And: "the Grammatical Encoder needs only one kind of input: preverbal messages....In order to do its work, *it need not consult with other processing components* [italics added]. The characteristic input is necessary and sufficient for the procedures to apply" (p. 15).[1]

This idea of modularity stands in marked contrast to Levelt et al.'s (1999) proposal in which a production rule at the lexical level does consult other processing components: Before lexical selection takes place, it checks for the presence of a tag at the conceptual level. In Roelofs's (1992) original model, lexical selection seems—at least to some degree—under executive control. First, as discussed, the lexical selection mechanism is informed about the tag it should be looking for (e.g., a picture tag, word tag, or red picture tag). In addition, the erroneous selection of a word that does not possess the correct tag is attributed to a "lapse of attention." This raises the interesting question of whose lapse this is. If it is a lapse of the speaker, lexical selection is evidently under executive control, contrary to Levelt's (1989) proposal. If it is a lapse of attention of the lexical selection mechanism itself, Santiago and MacKay's (1999) "homunculus concern" seems justified.

I conclude that the fact that speakers are able to produce the correct response in Stroop-like tasks poses a problem for simple, activation-based conceptualizations of lexical selection. However, given the strong drawbacks of more complex, "intelligent" selection mechanisms that I discussed, it seems worthwhile to further investigate alternatives, including (a) the idea that a selection threshold can only be reached when there is the intention to produce a naming response (as in Starreveld & La Heij's [1996] model) and (b) the possible role of Levelt's (1989) monitor in preventing the production of erroneous responses (as in Morton's [1977] account).

The second finding that poses a problem for simple activation-based lexical selection models was reported by Glaser and Düngelhoff (1984). These authors asked their participants to name pictures (e.g., the picture of a dog) at a superordinate category level (e.g., *animal*). As distractor words, they used correct basic-level names (*dog*), semantically related basic-level names (e.g., *cat*) and unrelated words (e.g., *pen*). All current models of language production assume that the activated concept DOG will send activation to the lexical representation of the word *dog*, which should make it a stronger competitor in the selection of the correct response word *animal* than the unrelated distractor word *pen*. However, the results showed otherwise. In comparison to the unrelated context word PEN, the context word DOG *facilitated* the naming of the picture of a dog as *animal*.

Starreveld and La Heij's (1996) model is unable to account for this finding. Roelofs (1992) provided an account with the help of the response set mechanism discussed in the Lexical Selection section. The idea is that, in a hyperonym-naming task, only the lexical representations of the permitted category names receive a flag. Because the lexical representation of the context word DOG has no flag, it is simply ignored in the process of lexical selection. However, it does send activation to the concept DOG, and therefore its effect will be facilitatory.

Roelofs's (1992) suggestion that lexical representations can be neatly divided into two sets, one set that is considered by the lexical selection process and one set that is ignored, has been severely challenged. One of the predictions that can be derived from this response set hypothesis is that words that are not part of the response set should not induce semantic interference. Starreveld and La Heij (1999) drew attention to experimental results that contradicted this prediction, and Caramazza and Costa (2000, 2001; but see Roelofs, 2001) provided compelling experimental evidence that contradicted Roelofs's proposal.

In addition, at a theoretical level it could be argued that Roelofs's (1992) response set mechanism is too artificial and too discrete. The all-or-none principle (flag or no flag) may work with a response set of four, but it seems highly unlikely that when 10–20 target pictures are used, all of the picture names are neatly flagged. Data obtained by La Heij and Vermeij (1987) suggested a more realistic account of response set effects. In a picture–word interference task, they used the response set sizes two, four, and eight. *Interference effects*, defined as the difference between context words that were part of the response set and context words that were not, gradually decreased with increasing set size (17 ms, 9 ms, and −3 ms with set sizes of two, four, and eight, respectively). The authors took this finding as support for an activation level account of the response set effect: Words often repeated in an experiment get a higher baseline activation level than words not used as responses. So, instead of an all-or-none flagging solution, a gradual difference in activation level was argued to account for the response set effect (see Cohen et al., 1990, for a similar suggestion).

However, Roelofs's (1992) account of Glaser and Düngelhoff's (1984) facilitation effect completely hinged on a strict dichotomy between acceptable words and unacceptable words. That is, a gradual difference in activation level of lexical representations cannot account for Glaser and Düngelhoff's (1984) observation of the identical-facilitation effect in a category-naming task. So, if we accept that the flagging of words is not a realistic option, the conclusion has to be that current models of language production cannot account for this result. Clearly, this is an important target for future research in the area of language production (see also Vitkovitch & Tyrrell, 1999). I return to Glaser and Düngelhoff's finding in the next section.

In this section, I discussed the processes of concept selection and lexical selection and showed that models of language production strongly differ in their assumptions about lexical selection. I made a case for a simple, activation-based lexical selection mechanism and provided arguments against complex lexical selection mechanisms that use information from outside the mental lexicon. If we stick to Levelt's (1989) original view that only one input—the preverbal message—is necessary and sufficient for retrieving a word in the mental lexicon, there is only one way to ensure that the correct word is retrieved: provide it with the correct input. This is exactly the approach taken in the SLAM model and, in a very simple way, in Starreveld and La Heij's (1996) model. As discussed, in SLAM the task instructions do not affect the workings of the lexical selection mechanism, but only control the input to the lexicalization process.

Models: Extension Toward Bilingualism

Response Language as Cue in the Preverbal Message

One of the central issues in research on bilingual lexical access can be phrased in the following way: How is it possible that an English-French bilingual systematically uses the word *dog* in one situation and *chien* in another situation, despite the fact that both words express the same conceptual content? Formulated this way, the issue is simply another example of the convergence problem discussed in the first section of the chapter. The solution that I proposed there can then be readily applied: *Dog* and *chien* do not express the same meaning. The meaning of *dog* has to contain a feature that it is an English word and the meaning of *chien* that it is a French word. That is, in a bilingual speaker the intention to speak in L1 or a second language (L2) is part of the preverbal message, just as the intention to use formal language, a slang word, a category name, or an euphemism.

This conclusion is completely in line with conclusions reached by a number of researchers in the area of bilingualism. De Bot (1992) concluded that Levelt's (1989) definition of *registers* (e.g., telegraphic speech and motherese) included an L2, and that information about which register to use is present in the preverbal message. De Bot and Schreuder (1993) and Paradis (1987) also assumed that there is no theoretical difference between the different registers used by a monolingual and the languages spoken by a bilingual. These and other authors (e.g., Green, 1993, 1998; Poulisse, 1997; Poulisse & Bongaerts, 1994) all assumed that lan-

guage is indeed one of the cues that is used during lexical access. One question that arises then is whether the cue ensures that only words in the intended language become activated.

Coactivation of Words in the Nonresponse Language

As illustrated in Figs. 14.1 and 14.2, it is generally assumed that during lexical access not only the correct response word, but also semantically related words become somewhat activated. As discussed, this coactivation of semantic neighbors accounts for the observation of semantic errors, blends of semantically related words, and the semantic interference effect in the picture–word task. Given this assumption and the fact that translation equivalents often have an almost perfect match with respect to their semantic content, it seems reasonable to assume that during lexical access also words in the nonresponse language are activated to some extent.

There is also empirical evidence in favor of this view (see also Costa, chapter 15, this volume). First, bilinguals speaking in their L2 may accidentally insert words from their L1. In line with the above argument, Poulisse and Bongaerts (1994) related these "performance switches" to semantic substitutions in L1. Even blends of words from two languages have been observed (e.g., "springling" from English *spring* and German *Frühling*). Second, Colomé (2001) showed that making a phonological decision about the name of a target picture in L2 is affected by the phonological content of the name of the target picture in L1. Third, a number of researchers (Costa, Miozzo, & Caramazza, 1999; Hermans, Bongaerts, De Bot, & Schreuder, 1998) reported a semantic interference effect in picture–word interference tasks in which the pictures had to be named in one language and the context words were presented in the other language of the bilingual. The fact that naming the picture of a dog as *dog* takes longer when the Dutch word *paard* (horse) is superimposed than when the Dutch word *stoel* (chair) is superimposed can be taken as evidence that during the retrieval of the L1 word *dog* also the semantically related L2 word *paard* received some activation.

Lexical Selection in Bilinguals: Language Specific or Nonspecific

I summarized my view on lexical access in monolinguals and bilinguals as complex access, simple selection. Access is complex in the sense that the preverbal message contains all the relevant information, including the intended language. During lexical access, not only the sought-for word, but also many semantically related words become activated, including words in the nonintended language. Lexical selection is a simple, local process that is only based on the activation levels of words. There is only one model of bilingual access that takes this—or at least a very similar—position.

Poulisse and Bongaerts (1994; see also Poulisse, 1997) presented a model in which the presence of a language cue (or "language component") in the preverbal message suffices to produce words in the intended language: "Conceptual information and the language cue work together in activating lemmas of the appropriate meaning and language. In other words, language is one of the features used for selection purposes" (Poulisse, 1997, p. 216). Interestingly, as argued by the authors, this model also provides a satisfactory account of three phenomena pertinent to any model of bilingual access: the ability to separate languages, code switching (rapid switching between the two languages), and accidental intrusions from the nonintended language. The ability to separate languages follows from the use of a language cue at the conceptual level. For example, when the speaker intends to use L2, L2 words receive more activation than the corresponding L1 words. Code switching can be fast because there is no active inhibition of words in one of the two languages, and intrusions may either result from the failure to use the correct language cue or from incidental cases in which the word in the unintended language reaches a higher activation level than the intended word (e.g., because of priming effects).

All other models of bilingual lexical access assume that lexical selection cannot be that simple and propose a selection or control process that (a) completely restricts selection to words in one language (language-selective models; see, e.g., Costa et al., 1999) or (b) selectively activates or inhibits words in one of the languages (most language-nonselective models, e.g., Green, 1993; see Poulisse, 1997, for an overview). Within the latter type of models, inhibition may occur proactively (before lexical access) or reactively (after the activation of words in both languages; see Green, 1998). I discuss language-selective and language-nonselective models in turn.

An important argument in favor of language-selective models is the finding, reported by Costa et al. (1999; see also Hermans, 2000, Experiment 4.1), that picture naming in L2 is facilitated by the presence of the picture's name in L1 (in comparison with an unrelated word in L1). For example, for a English-Dutch bilingual, the naming of a picture of a dog in L2 (*hond*) is facilitated by the presence of the context word *dog* in comparison to the unrelated word *pen*. Costa et al. (1999) concluded from this "translation-facilitation effect" that the word *dog*, which should have been a very strong competitor for the correct word *hond*, is simply not taken into consideration by the lexical selection process (see also Costa, chapter 15, this volume). To allow for language-specific selection, Costa et al. assumed tags that indicate whether a word belongs to L1 or L2.

Interestingly, the translation-facilitation effect bears a clear similarity to Glaser and Düngelhoff's (1984) identical-facilitation effect in category naming discussed in the Problems in Lexical Selection section. Apparently, the distractor word *dog* facilitates both the naming of a picture of a dog as "animal" (Glaser & Düngelhoff) and as "*perro*" (the Spanish word for DOG; Costa et al., 1999). Also, the accounts are somewhat similar. Roelofs (1992) assumed that in naming the picture of a dog as *animal*, the distractor word *dog* can induce facilitation because it is completely ignored by the lexical selection mechanism. Likewise, Costa et al. assumed that in naming the picture of a dog as *perro*, the distractor word *dog* can induce facilitation for the same reason. In Roelofs's account, the distractor word *dog* can be ignored because it is not flagged. In Costa et al.'s account, the distractor word *dog* can be ignored because it does not have a "Spanish word tag."

Caramazza and Costa (2000) rejected Roelofs's account on the basis of their finding that words that do not belong to the set of permitted responses in an experiment (words that do not possess a flag in Roelofs's model) did induce semantic interference. Perhaps somewhat ironically, the same argument can be used against Costa et al.'s language-selective model: Distractor words in the nonintended language do induce semantic interference, which suggests that they are taken into consideration during lexical selection. Costa et al.'s attempt to account for this semantic interference effect by assuming that words in the nonintended language induce this effect via their translation equivalents in the intended language is not entirely convincing.

A second argument against language-selective models is theoretical. As noted, there is a striking similarity between Costa et al.'s (1999) and Hermans's (2000) translation-facilitation effect and

Glaser and Düngelhoff's (1984) identical-facilitation effect in picture categorization. Also, the time courses of both effects are remarkably similar: Hermans (2000, Experiment 4.1) used stimulus-onset asynchrony values of −300 ms, −150 ms, and 0 ms and obtained facilitation effects of 51 ms, 40 ms, and −3 ms, respectively. The corresponding facilitation effects in Glaser and Düngelhoff's (1984) categorization task were 53 ms, 39 ms, and −16 ms, respectively. If Costa et al.'s (1999) idea of language-specific selection (with the help of language tags) is applied to Glaser and Düngelhoff's (1984) finding, it must be concluded that the process of lexical selection can ignore all words that belong to a certain categorization level (e.g., the basic level) with the help of categorization-level tags.

Do two types of tag suffice? Probably not. We can think of quite a number of word sets that might produce between-set facilitation. Imagine, for instance, a picture–word interference experiment in which pictures of famous people have to be named by their first name (e.g., *George*). It does not seem unlikely that naming will be faster when the picture is accompanied by the correct last name of the person (e.g., *Bush*) than when accompanied by an incorrect last name (e.g., *Dylan*), despite the fact that *Bush* could be viewed as a strong competitor in retrieving the correct response *George*. If this prediction would be borne out, the logic that followed above forces the assumption of first-name tags and last-name tags attached to people's names

in the mental lexicon. In addition, a similar facilitation effect obtained in an experiment in which participants respond to pictures by the associated action (e.g., chair–sit, radio–listen) would force the assumption of part-of-speech tags.

I leave it to the reader to think of other sets of words that would show the same effect, but the message will be clear: This approach leads to a proliferation of tags at the lexical level. Clearly, this solution is highly unparsimonious. Many of the semantic features of words that are represented in the conceptual system have to be duplicated in the lexicon in the form of the isolated pieces of information called tags. In combination with the finding discussed above that words from the "ignored" nonresponse language induce semantic interference, the conclusion has to be that language-selective models are difficult to maintain. However, it should be stressed that *all* current models have difficulty in accounting for the facilitation effects reported by Glaser and Düngelhoff (1984) and Costa et al. (1999). Understanding these effects is a challenge for future research in language production.

With the exception of the model of Poulisse and Bongaerts (1994), all language-nonselective models assume that words in one of the two languages of the bilingual can be selectively inhibited or activated to some degree. I have argued that such a process is superfluous when it is assumed that the preverbal message contains a language cue. In the model depicted in Fig. 14.3, this assumption is

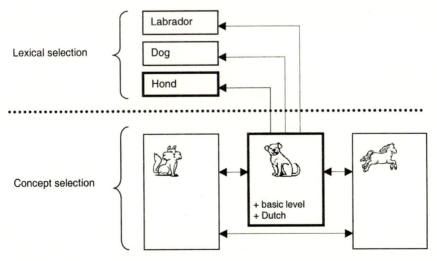

Figure 14.3 The model in Fig. 14.2 is extended for bilingual language production. The language cue is part of the preverbal message, and words in both languages become activated. Because of the language cue, the intended name will reach the highest activation level and will be selected.

incorporated: The language cue that is added to the preverbal message ensures that words in the intended language reach a higher activation level than words in the nonintended language.

One argument that proponents of selective inhibition use is Meuter and Allport's (1999) "paradoxical" asymmetry effect in language switching. Meuter and Allport reported that it takes bilinguals more time to switch from L2 to L1 than to switch from L1 to L2, a finding that is often interpreted as reflecting the strong inhibition of L1 while speaking in L2. Costa (chapter 15, this volume) critically discussed this interpretation of Meuter and Allport's results and concluded that the available evidence does not support the presence of an inhibitory mechanism in proficient bilinguals. Here, I would like to point out that throughout their article Meuter and Allport seemed reluctant to choose between two possible interpretations of their findings: the inhibition of (words within) a language or the inhibition of a "task set." In fact, in their discussion the latter interpretation was given more emphasis: "The 'negative priming' arises from the active inhibition of one of two mutually competing tasks (or languages)" (p. 35). In terms of the model that I propose, the asymmetry effect in language switching may then reflect processes involved in the incorporation of the language cue in the preverbal message.

It should be noted that my arguments do not imply that words in one of the bilingual's languages cannot reach a higher activation level than words in the other language—even on a more permanent basis. We have seen that all models of lexical access assume that each attempt to retrieve a word results in the activation of a set of semantically related words. If we make the assumptions that (a) because of the language cue, semantically related words in the intended language become more strongly activated than semantically related words in the nonintended language; (b) words spread activation to associatively related words within the lexicon (see Alario, Segui, & Ferrand, 2000; La Heij, Dirkx, & Kramer, 1990); and (c) activated words return to a somewhat higher baseline level of activation (as in Morton's 1969 logogen model), then the repeated retrieval of words in one language will ultimately result in relatively high activation levels of the words within that language. Similarly, the nonuse of a language may lower the baseline levels of activation of words in that language, which will make them more difficult to retrieve.

In conclusion, the considerations presented in this section favor the view of bilingual lexical ac-

cess that was advocated by Poulisse and Bongaerts (1994). To summarize that view, the preverbal message contains a language cue that ensures that the word in the intended language reaches the highest activation level; no additional activation or inhibition processes at the lexical level are needed. The only difference between this view and the one depicted in Fig. 14.3 is that Poulisse and Bongaerts assumed that words possess language tags. However, these tags were viewed as part of the word's meaning representation at the lemma level (in Levelt's 1989 original model that was taken as a starting point by Poulisse and Bongaerts, lemmas contained semantic information). If lexical representations do not contain semantic information, as assumed by Levelt et al. (1999), then a language cue at the conceptual level suffices.

Summary

In this chapter, I examined one aspect of language production: the retrieval of a single word on the basis of conceptual information. First, arguments were presented in favor of the view that to achieve a communicative goal, the preverbal message has to contain cues that define the affective and pragmatic characteristics of the sought-for word. Given the resulting complexity of the preverbal message, it was argued to be unlikely that convergence problems as discussed by Levelt (1989) and Roelofs (1992) arise. In addition, I discussed evidence that not all activated concepts, but only the preverbal message is lexicalized. To account for incidental speech errors, blends, and semantic interference in the picture–word task, it must be assumed that lexical access leads to the activation of a set of semantically related words in the mental lexicon. How a preverbal message is constructed and how it gives rise to the activation of a semantic cohort of words at the lexical level is an important issue for further research. Perhaps it is necessary to return to a decompositional (feature-based) view of conceptual representations (see Caramazza, 1997).

In most models of language production, two selection processes are assumed: a first process in which the relevant conceptual information is selected (concept selection) and a second process that selects one word from the set of activated lexical representations (lexical selection). I argued for a model of lexical access that could be characterized as complex access, simple selection. That is, lexical selection is based on a complex preverbal message that contains all relevant information to arrive at the correct word. Lexical selection can then be a simple process that selects one word from the set of activated words on the basis of the activation levels only. An "intelligent" lexical selection process that selects on the basis of (semantic) information instead of activation (e.g., with the help of various tags attached to words) was rejected on the basis of parsimony and of the assumed modularity of the process of lexical access.

The model that results bears striking similarities to Levelt's (1989) original proposal: Lexical access is automatic in the sense that it delivers a "winner" on the basis of the information in the preverbal message (and only on that information). Speakers cannot influence lexical access in any other way than selecting (or perhaps constructing) an adequate preverbal message. This model can be extended to the bilingual situation in a very straightforward way. Intended language is part of the preverbal message. The presence of this language cue ensures that the word in the intended language reaches a higher activation level than the translation equivalent in the nonintended language (Poulisse & Bongaerts, 1994). So, there is no need for a selective activation or selective inhibition of words of a particular language, in the same way as there is no need for selective activation or selective inhibition to account for the production of formal language, slang, taboo words, euphemisms, very high frequency words, and category names by monolinguals.

Finally, I would like to repeat the concerns that were raised by Van der Heijden (1981) and more recently by Santiago and MacKay (1999): We should be extremely reluctant in assuming underspecified control mechanisms that, in combination with convenient tags or flags at convenient places, solve major problems. If there is one thing that this chapter has shown, it is that these mechanisms often induce more problems than they seem to solve.

Acknowledgments

I would like to thank Lex van der Heijden, Patrick Hudson, Gerard Kempen, and Kees de Bot for helpful discussions and comments on an earlier version of this chapter.

Note

1. A nice illustration of this assumed automaticity is the "ugly sister" phenomenon that speakers in a tip-of-the-tongue state may experience (Reason & Lucas, 1984). The attempt to find the correct word sometimes leads to the activation of an incorrect word (the ugly sister) that is immediately rejected by the speaker. However, each new attempt to retrieve the correct word only leads to the reactivation of the ugly sister, which for that reason is also referred to as a *blocking word*. This phenomenon is exactly what may be expected if lexical selection is an automatic process only based on activation levels: Given a certain input (the preverbal message) and the current levels of activation of the lexical representations, the same output will be produced time and time again.

References

Alario, F. X., Segui, J., & Ferrand, L. (2000). Semantic and associative priming in picture naming. *Quarterly Journal of Experimental Psychology, 53A*, 741–764.

Allport, D. A. (1987). Selection for action: Some behavioral and neuropsychological considerations of attention and action. In H. Heuer & A. F. Sanders (Eds.), *Perspectives on perception and action* (pp. 395–419). Hillsdale, NJ: Erlbaum.

Barsalou, L. W. (1982). Context-independent and context-dependent information in concepts. *Memory & Cognition, 10*, 82–93.

Bierwisch, M., & Schreuder, R. (1992). From concepts to lexical items. *Cognition, 42*, 23–60.

Bloem, I., & La Heij, W. (2003). Semantic facilitation and semantic interference in word translation: Implications for models of lexical access in language production. *Journal of Memory and Language, 48*, 468–488.

Caramazza, A. (1997). How many levels of processing are there in lexical access? *Cognitive Neuropsychology, 14*, 177–208.

Caramazza, A., & Costa, A. (2000). The semantic interference effect in the picture–word interference paradigm: Does the response set matter? *Cognition, 75*, 51–64.

Caramazza, A., & Costa, A. (2001). Set size and repetition in the picture–word interference paradigm: implications for models of naming. *Cognition, 80*, 291–298.

Caramazza, A., & Miozzo, M. (1998). More is not always better: A response to Roelofs, Meyer, and Levelt. *Cognition, 69*, 231–241.

Cohen, J. D., Dunbar, K., & McClelland, J. L. (1990). On the control of automatic processes: A parallel distributed processing account of the Stroop effect. *Psychological Review, 97*, 332–361.

Colomé, À. (2001). Lexical activation in bilinguals' speech production: Language-specific or language-independent? *Journal of Memory and Language, 45*, 721–736.

Costa, A., Miozzo, M., & Caramazza, A. (1999). Lexical selection in bilinguals: Do words in the bilingual's two lexicons compete for selection? *Journal of Memory and Language, 41,* 365–397.

De Bot, K. (1992). A bilingual production model: Levelt's "speaking" model adapted. *Applied Linguistics, 13,* 1–24.

De Bot, K., & Schreuder, R. (1993). Word production and the bilingual lexicon. In R. Schreuder & B. Weltens (Eds.), *The bilingual lexicon* (pp. 191–214). Amsterdam: Benjamin.

De Kamps, M., & Van der Velde, F. (2001). Using a recurrent network to bind form, color and position into a unified percept. *Neurocomputing, 38–40,* 523–528.

Dell, G. S. (1986). A spreading activation theory of retrieval in sentence production. *Psychological Review, 93,* 283–321.

Fodor, J. D. (1980). *Semantics.* Cambridge, MA: Harvard University Press.

Fromkin, V. A. (1973). *Speech errors as linguistic evidence.* The Hague, The Netherlands: Mouton.

Glaser, W. R., & Düngelhoff, F.-J. (1984). The time course of picture-word interference. *Journal of Experimental Psychology: Human Perception and Performance, 10,* 640–654.

Glaser, W. R., & Glaser, M. O. (1989). Context effects on Stroop-like word and picture processing. *Journal of Experimental Psychology: General, 118,* 13-42.

Green, D. W. (1993). Toward a model of L2 comprehension and production. In R. Schreuder & B. Weltens (Eds.), *The bilingual lexicon* (pp. 249–277). Amsterdam: Benjamin.

Green, D. W. (1998). Mental control of the bilingual lexico-semantic system. *Bilingualism: Language and Cognition, 1,* 67–81.

Harley, T. A. (1999). Will one stage and no feedback suffice in lexicalization? *Behavioral and Brain Sciences, 22,* 45.

Harley, T. A. (2001). *The psychology of language.* New York: Taylor & Francis.

Hermans, D. (2000). *Word production in a foreign language.* Unpublished doctoral dissertation, University of Nijmegen, The Netherlands.

Hermans, D., Bongaerts, T., De Bot, K., & Schreuder, R. (1998). Producing words in a foreign language: Can speakers prevent interference from their first language? *Bilingualism: Language and Cognition, 1,* 213–229.

Humphreys, G. W., Lloyd-Jones, T. J., & Fias, W. (1995). Semantic interference effects on naming using a postcue procedure: Tapping the links between semantics and phonology with pictures and words. *Journal of Experimental*

Psychology: Learning, Memory, and Cognition, 21, 961–980.

Keele, S. W. (1973). *Attention and human performance.* Pacific Palisades, CA: Goodyear.

La Heij, W. (1988). Components of Stroop-like interference in picture naming. *Memory & Cognition, 16,* 400-410.

La Heij, W., Dirkx, J., & Kramer, P. (1990). Categorical interference and associative priming in picture naming. *British Journal of Psychology, 81,* 511–525.

La Heij, W., & Vermeij, M. (1987). Reading versus naming: The effect of target set size on contextual interference and facilitation. *Perception & Psychophysics, 41,* 355–366.

Levelt, W. J. M. (1989). *Speaking: From intention to articulation.* Cambridge, MA: MIT Press.

Levelt, W. J. M., Roelofs, A., & Meyer, A. S. (1999). A theory of lexical access in speech production. *Behavioral and Brain Sciences, 22,* 1–75.

Li, P. (1998). Mental control, language tags, and language nodes in bilingual lexical processing. *Bilingualism: Language and Cognition, 1,* 92–93.

McCloskey, M., & Glucksberg, S. (1978). Natural categories: Well-defined or fuzzy sets? *Memory & Cognition, 6,* 462–472.

Meuter, R. F. I., & Allport, A. (1999). Bilingual language switching in naming: Asymmetrical costs of language selection. *Journal of Memory and Language, 40,* 25–40.

Morton, J. (1969). The interaction of information in word recognition. *Psychological Review, 76,* 165–178.

Paradis, M. (1987). *The assessment of bilingual aphasia.* Hillsdale, NJ: Erlbaum.

Phaf, R. H., Van der Heijden, A. H. C., & Hudson, P. T. W. (1990). SLAM: A connectionist model for attention in visual selection tasks. *Cognitive Psychology, 22,* 273–341.

Posnansky, C. J., & Rayner, K. (1977). Visual-feature and response components in a picture–word interference task with beginning and skilled readers. *Journal of Experimental Child Psychology, 24,* 440–460.

Poulisse, N. (1997). Language production in bilinguals. In A. M. B. de Groot & J. F. Kroll (Eds.), *Tutorials in bilingualism: Psycholinguistic perspectives* (pp. 201–224). Mahwah, NJ: Erlbaum.

Poulisse, N., & Bongaerts, T. (1994). First language use in second language production. *Applied Linguistics, 15,* 36–57.

Reason, J., & Lucas, D. (1984). Using cognitive diaries to investigate naturally occurring memory blocks. In J. E. Harris & P. E. Morris (Eds.), *Everyday memory, actions and absent-mindedness* (pp. 53–70). London: Academic Press.

Roelofs, A. (1992). A spreading-activation theory of lemma retrieval in speaking. *Cognition, 42,* 107–142.

Roelofs, A. (1996). Computational models of lemma retrieval. In T. Dijkstra & K. de Smedt, (Eds.), *Computational Linguistics* (pp. 308–327). London: Taylor & Francis.

Roelofs, A. (2001). Set size and repetition matter: comment on Caramazza and Costa (2000). *Cognition, 80,* 283–290.

Roelofs, A., Meyer, A. S., & Levelt, W. J. M. (1998). A case for the lemma/lexeme distinction in models of speaking: Comment on Caramazza and Miozzo (1997). *Cognition, 69,* 219–230.

Santiago, J., & MacKay, D. G. (1999). Constraining production theories: Principled motivation, consistency, homunculi, underspecification, failed predictions, and contrary data. *Behavioral and Brain Sciences, 22,* 55–56.

Schriefers, H. (1993). Syntactic processes in the construction of noun phrases. *Journal of Experimental Psychology: Learning, Memory, and Cognition, 19,* 841–850.

Schriefers, H., Meyer, A. S., & Levelt, W. J. M. (1990). Exploring the time course of lexical access in language production: Picture-word interference studies. *Journal of Memory and Language, 29,* 86–102.

Smith, E. E., & Medin, D. L. (1981). *Categories and concepts.* Cambridge, MA: Harvard University Press.

Starreveld, P. A., & La Heij, W. (1996). Time-course analysis of semantic and orthographic context effects in picture naming. *Journal of Experimental Psychology: Learning, Memory, and Cognition, 22,* 896–918.

Starreveld, P. A., & La Heij, W. (1999). What about phonological facilitation, response-set membership, and phonological co-activation? *Behavioral and Brain Sciences, 22,* 56–58.

Underwood, G. (1976). Semantic interference from unattended printed words. *British Journal of Psychology, 67,* 327–338.

Van der Heijden, A. H. C. (1981). *Short-term visual information forgetting.* London: Routledge & Kegan Paul.

Van der Heijden, A. H. C. (1996). Perception for selection, selection for action, and action for perception. *Visual Cognition, 3,* 357–361.

Vitkovitch, M., & Tyrrell, L. (1999). The effects of distractor words on naming pictures at the subordinate level. *Quarterly Journal of Experimental Psychology, 52,* 905–926.

Wittgenstein, L. (1953). *Philosophical investigations.* Oxford, U.K.: Blackwell.

Albert Costa

15

Lexical Access in Bilingual Production

ABSTRACT What is the impact of the lexical and sublexical representations of the language not in use on the bilingual's speech production? Do words from the nonresponse language interfere in language production? In this chapter, I address these issues by comparing two different views of speech production in bilingual speakers: the language-specific and the language-nonspecific views. I focus on how these two views make different claims regarding the extent to which activation flow and selection processes are restricted to one of the two languages of a bilingual. I also discuss the available empirical evidence supporting each hypothesis and propose a tentative explanation that reconciles the seemingly contrasting results. I argue that the available evidence suggests that activation flow is language nonspecific. More controversial are the results regarding the extent to which lexical selection is language specific or nonspecific.

Individuals acquiring a second language (L2) usually report being better able to understand than speak their L2. Although this difference may depend on how the L2 is learned, may be reduced over time, and may eventually disappear when the speaker becomes proficient in both languages, it suggests that the processes engaged in L2 speech production and comprehension involve different types of language competence (Costa & Santesteban, 2004a; French & Jacquet, 2004). This opens the question of the extent to which the organization of lexical knowledge in bilinguals may be addressed independent of the input and output modalities. Most studies of the issue of bilingual language processing have focused on the comprehension (perception) side and therefore have used experimental paradigms that involved mostly processes related to word reading and speech perception. As a result, there has been an important development of models of bilingual word recognition as discussed in other chapters of this handbook (see Dijkstra, chapter 9, and Thomas & Van Heuven, chapter 10, this volume).

Much less research has been devoted to developing models of language production in bilinguals. Perhaps because the current models of language production in monolingual speakers are not very well developed (most of them refer to single-word production) or because of the intrinsic difficulties in developing experimental paradigms in language production, many fundamental questions regarding speech production in bilingual speakers remain unanswered. In this chapter, I focus on various aspects of lexical access in speech production in bilingual speakers, paying special attention to the concepts of "activation flow" and "selection processes" in the context of lexical and sublexical levels of representation. The main question discussed in the chapter concerns the role of the linguistic representations that belong to the language not in use (or the nonresponse language) during speech production in the language in use (the response language). Questions related to code switching and translation are discussed in other chapters in this handbook (see Myers-Scotton, chapter 16, and Meuter, chapter 17) and are only incidentally addressed here.

The chapter has the following structure. First, I review alternative theoretical views about whether activation flow and selection processes are language specific or language nonspecific. Second, the most relevant experimental evidence that speaks to these issues is reviewed. Finally, I discuss the need of postulating inhibitory mechanisms to explain the performance of both highly proficient and low-proficient bilingual speakers.

Before addressing the issue of the language specificity of the activation flow and selection processes, it is important to define these two terms in a broader context of speech production. Speech production entails at least three different levels of representation (e.g., Caramazza, 1997; Dell, 1986; Levelt, 1989; Levelt, Roelofs, & Meyer, 1999). First, at the conceptual (or semantic) level the speaker decides which conceptual information to communicate (see Francis, chapter 12, this volume, for a discussion regarding the differences between the semantic and conceptual levels). Second, a lexical level represents lexical items (or words) along with their grammatical properties.[1] Third, the phonological code of the words is represented. How do the speakers go through all these levels, choosing the concepts they want to express, the words corresponding to those concepts, and finally the phonemes corresponding to those words? This is a central question in speech production (see Fig. 15.1).

Although the types of representations at each level are quite different (e.g., concepts, words, and phonemes), there are two principles that seem to play a role in all of them: activation and selection mechanisms. *Activation* refers to the availability of representations at different levels of processing. When a given representation is more available for production, we say that its level of activation is high; when it is less available, we say that its level of activation is low. Speech production starts with the activation of conceptual representations. It is generally assumed that, during conceptual processing, not only the semantic representation of the intended concept but also those representations of semantically related concepts are activated to some degree. That is, when naming the picture of a dog, the target concept (e.g., dog) along with other related concepts (cat, bark, etc.) become activated. The activation of the semantic representations spreads to the lexical system, activating proportionally the corresponding lexical nodes or

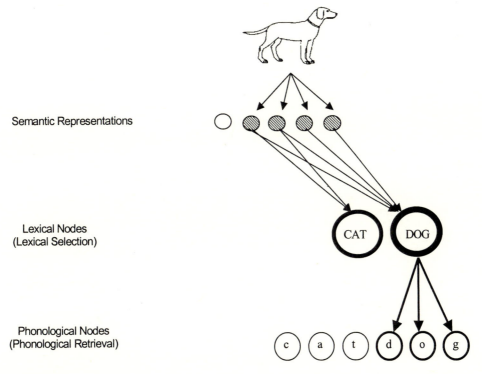

Semantic Representations

Lexical Nodes
(Lexical Selection)

Phonological Nodes
(Phonological Retrieval)

Figure 15.1 Schematic representation of the monolingual system. The arrows represent the flow of activation, and the thickness of the circles indicates the level of activation of the representations.

words. Thus, activation flows from an activated semantic representation to its corresponding lexical node.

Assuming that the conceptual representation of several elements spread activation to their corresponding lexical representations, then the system encounters several word candidates for production (dog, cat, bark, etc.). At this point, a decision has to be made regarding which lexical node to choose among the activated ones for further processing. This decision mechanism is called *lexical selection*. The selection of the intended lexical node will make available its grammatical properties, which in turn will be used to construct the syntactic frame.

There are different views regarding how the lexical selection mechanism works (see La Heij, chapter 14, this volume, for an extended discussion of the different models), but all of them agree that this mechanism is at least sensitive to the level of activation of the intended lexical node. In fact, the dominant view in speech production assumes that the lexical selection mechanism is actually sensitive to the activation of the intended lexical node and to the other lexical nodes that may act as competitors.

Activation from the lexical level also spreads to the sublexical or phonological level. That is, when the lexical node is selected, the next step in the production of speech is the retrieval of its phonological makeup. The issues here regarding activation flow and selection processes are similar to those preceding it. First, is activation flow from the lexical level to the phonological level restricted to the selected lexical node, or is it the case that any activated lexical node spreads some proportional activation to its phonological elements? Second, if activation flow is not restricted to the selected lexical node, the question then is whether the selection of the phonological properties of the target lexical node is affected by the activation of those of other nontarget words.

Given the architecture sketched above, the question in the context of bilingual production is the extent to which activation flow (i.e., how information is passed from level to level) and selection processes (i.e., how the system decides which representation is prioritized for further processing) are restricted to only the language spoken by the bilingual (see Fig. 15.2). More precisely, the first issue refers to whether the lexical and sublexical representations of the nonresponse language are activated concurrent with the corresponding representations of the language intended for production. Assuming

that the representations of the two languages of a bilingual are activated, the second issue is whether the selection processes are affected by the activation levels of representations that do not belong to the response language. Note that the first issue is independent of the second one. In principle, it is possible that activation flow spreads to the two languages of a bilingual (language-nonspecific flow of activation), and that the selection mechanism is not sensitive to the level of activation of representations that do not belong to the intended language (language-specific selection mechanism). This is an important distinction to be kept in mind when discussing the different possible models of bilingual speech production.

Two Words for One Concept

A fundamental question in the study of bilingual speech production concerns the consequences of having a conceptual representation linked to two different lexical items belonging to two different languages (e.g., De Groot, 1992; Gollan & Kroll, 2001; Kroll & Stewart, 1994; La Heij, Hooglander, Kerling, & Van der Velden, 1996; Van Hell & De Groot, 1998; see also Francis's chapter 12 in this volume for a discussion of the organization of the bilingual's memory representations). In other words, is there any effect of having two lexical nodes for almost every word that the speaker is producing? Unlike synonyms, translations are not interchangeable (e.g., communication will not be very much affected if the word *sofa* is produced instead of the word *couch*, but will be disrupted if the speaker says *sillon* [the Spanish name for couch] instead of couch). This is because in many circumstances a bilingual speaker needs to speak only in one language because the interlocutor may not know his or her other language (e.g., Grosjean, 1997, 1998, 2001), and therefore the production of a target's translation may have disastrous consequences for communication.

Thus, the central issue that needs to be addressed is not so much how a lexical node in a given language is selected (see La Heij's chapter 14 in this volume for a discussion of this problem; models of monolingual speech production address this issue as well) but rather how the existence of lexical representations have an impact in the other language of a bilingual. Any approach to this issue requires some assumptions regarding activation flow and selection processes during speech production.

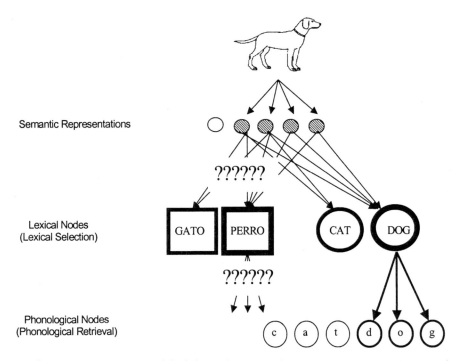

Figure 15.2 Schematic representation of the bilingual system. The squares represent the lexical nodes of the language not-in-use (Spanish) and the circles the lexical nodes of the language in use (English). The arrows represent the flow of activation, and the thickness of the circles indicates the level of activation of the representations. The question marks represent the language-specific and nonspecific activation flow hypotheses. If there is activation flow to the two lexicons of a bilingual individual, then the connections between the semantic representations and the lexical nodes of the language not in use (the squares) will be functional (the language-nonspecific hypothesis); otherwise, they will not (the language-specific hypothesis). The same applies to the connections between the lexical nodes and the phonological nodes.

Activation Flow

In speech comprehension, the listener has no control over the language in which words are presented. In fact, word recognition has a primarily bottom-up component in which some basic properties of the stimulus are automatically processed. Several decades of research have convincingly demonstrated that, during word recognition, activation flow is not language specific. That is, a string of letters would activate lexical items from the two languages of a bilingual regardless of the language to which that string belongs (see Dijkstra, chapter 9, and Thomas & Van Heuven, chapter 10, this volume, for a discussion of the most compelling results in support of nonselective access in bilingual word reading).

However, the directionality of the activation flow is completely different in speech production. For one thing, the processes involved in speech

production are primarily top-down processes. Lexical representations are activated from the conceptual information the speaker wants to convey rather than from the presentation of an external printed (or auditorily presented) stimulus, as in word reading. Furthermore, the speaker has control over many properties of their production, such as which content to communicate, which words and register to use, the rate with which the speech is going to be produced, and certainly the language in which lexicalization is going to take place. That is, the choice of the language in which the words have to be produced depends entirely on the individual who performs the communicative act.

From Concepts to Lexical Nodes

The decision of which language to use to express a given message is based on different types of information (pragmatic, contextual, etc.), information that has little to do with the lexical system (see La Heij, chapter 14, and Meuter, chapter 17, this volume, for a detailed description of how to implement the language selection decision at the conceptual level). Therefore, researchers agree in assuming that the specification of the language output is taken at the conceptual system (De Bot, 1992; Green, 1986, 1998; Poulisse & Bongaerts, 1994). Thus, lexical representations are activated from the conceptual system, and the decision of which language to produce is taken also at that level. In this scenario, it could be postulated that the activation flow from the conceptual system to the lexical system is channeled in such a way that only those words belonging to the response language receive activation (e.g., McNamara, 1967; McNamara & Kushnir, 1972).

Consider the case in which an English-Spanish bilingual is asked to name the picture of a dog in her L2 (e.g., *perro* [dog]). One possible way to achieve a successful selection of the target word *perro* is to assume that the concept DOG only activates its corresponding lexical representation in the selected-for-output language (the Spanish lexicon in the example). Accordingly, lexical selection in the intended language would proceed in a similar way as in the case of monolingual speakers because the lexical entries of English would not be activated. This type of model can be understood as *language specific* in the sense that activation flow from the semantic system is restricted to one language. This may seem the most economical solution. After all, if the speaker wants to say DOG in Spanish (e.g., *perro*) why does the speaker need to bother to activate a "possible" competitor word in the nonresponse language (e.g., *dog*)?

However, current models of lexical access in bilingual speech production favor the idea that activation from the conceptual system flows to lexical representations of both languages of a bilingual (e.g., Costa, Miozzo, & Caramazza, 1999; De Bot, 1992; Dewaele, 2001; Gollan & Acenas, 2000; Green, 1998; Poulisse, 1999). In these models, a given activated semantic representation would automatically spread a proportional amount of activation to any lexical representation to which it is linked. As a consequence, not only the lexical nodes belonging to the response language, but also their corresponding translations would be activated. In other words, activation from the semantic system to the lexical level is language nonspecific.

From Lexical Representations to Phonological Segments

The selection of the to-be-produced lexical node is followed by the retrieval of its corresponding phonological make up. Given that the semantic system spreads activation to the lexical nodes belonging to the two languages of a bilingual, there are two open questions: (a) Do the lexical nodes of the nonresponse language activate their corresponding phonological segments? (b) Does the activation of phonological segments of the nonresponse language affect the target's phonological encoding?

Before going into more detail about this issue, it is important to say a word or two about the locus of language selection. The selection of the lexical node in the proper language has to be done at the lexical level rather than at the sublexical level (phonological level). This is because, among other things, lexical selection makes available the language-specific grammatical properties of the target lexical node. For example, if a Catalan-Spanish bilingual wants to produce the word *fork* in Spanish (*tenedor*), the selection of its corresponding lexical node has to be taken at the lexical level. This is because the speaker needs to have access to the grammatical gender of the word in Spanish (masculine), which happens to be different from that of its translation in Catalan (*forquilla*, feminine). If the decision of which word to produce (*tenedor* or its catalan translation *forquilla*) were to be taken only at the phonological level, it would be a mystery how the speaker ends up choosing the proper grammatical properties (among them gender) because that information is not part of the words' phonological representation.

There are two main views that can be entertained regarding the question of whether lexical nodes that are not selected do nevertheless activate their phonological properties. So-called discrete models of speech production assume that the only phonological information that becomes activated is that of the selected lexical node (Levelt, 1989; Levelt, Schriefers, Vorberg, Meyer, Pechmann, & Havinga, 1991; Schriefers, Meyer, & Levelt, 1990). Thus, the selection process acts as a filter, precluding unwanted activation from the lexical level to spread to the sublexical level. If it is assumed that lexical selection takes place at the lexical level and that the production system honors this discrete processing, then we should expect phonological activation to be restricted to one single lexical node in the response language. Therefore, at the level at which phonological encoding takes place, bilingual and monolingual speakers should be functionally equivalent.

So-called cascaded models of lexical access apply the same activation flow principle through the whole lexical system. In the same way as activated conceptual representations spread proportional activation to their corresponding lexical nodes, any activated lexical representation spreads a proportional amount of activation to its corresponding phonological properties (Caramazza, 1997; Cutting & Ferreira, 1999; Dell, 1986; Goldrick & Rapp, 2002; Griffin & Bock, 1998; Harley, 1993; Humphreys & Riddoch, 1988; Peterson & Savoy, 1998; Rapp & Goldrick, 2000). A reasonable extension of this principle to cases of bilingualism would assume that the phonological properties of any activated lexical node, regardless of the language to which it belongs, are also activated to some degree (e.g., Costa, Caramazza, & Sebastian-Galles, 2000). For example, when a Spanish-English bilingual wants to name a picture in English (*dog*), the phonological properties of *dog* along with those of its translation in Spanish (*perro*) would become activated.

To this point, I have discussed some proposals about the flow of activation in speech production in bilingual speakers. I argued that there is a wide agreement in assuming that the conceptual system activates the two languages of a bilingual simultaneously, supporting the notion that activation flow from the conceptual system to the lexical system is language nonspecific. However, the issue of whether activation from the lexical nodes spreads to their corresponding phonological representations is less clear.

Selection Mechanisms

Given that the semantic system activates both lexicons of a bilingual, there are two questions that become immediately relevant. First, how do bilingual speakers end up selecting words from only one language? Second, which are the effects of having lexical nodes from the nonresponse language activated? Along the same lines, if there is sublexical activation of the words belonging to the nonresponse language, how does such activation affect the target's phonological encoding? Next, I review some theoretical positions regarding the effects that the representations of the nonresponse language may have when selecting information in the response language.

Selecting Lexical Representations

There is wide agreement in assuming that activation level is the basic parameter guiding lexical selection. According to several researchers, the lexical selection mechanism takes into account not only the activation of the target lexical node, but also the activation levels of other lexical items, which act as competitors (e.g., Caramazza, 1997; Levelt, 2001; Roelofs, 1992; see also Dell, 1986, for a model in which lexical competition is implemented in a different way). If the discrepancy in activation levels between the target lexical node and other lexical nodes is large, selection is relatively fast. In contrast, if the level of activation of nontarget lexical nodes is similar to that of the target lexical node, lexical selection is harder (Caramazza & Costa, 2000, 2001; Roelofs, 1992, 2001; Schriefers et al., 1990). What are the effects of having lexical nodes of the nonresponse language activated?

On the assumption that lexical selection involves lexical competition, the issue is the extent to which lexical nodes from the nonresponse language are also considered as competitors. Here, we entertain two hypotheses, which we refer as the language-specific selection hypothesis and the language-nonspecific selection hypothesis.

The language-specific selection hypothesis assumes that the lexical selection mechanism is "blind" to the activation levels of the lexical nodes belonging to the nonresponse language (see Fig. 15.3[a]). That is, the only lexical nodes that are candidates for selection are those of the response language. Therefore, lexical selection in bilingual speakers would proceed in the same way as it does in monolingual speakers, and the presence of a target's translation would have no impact on the ease with which lexical selection is achieved (e.g., the level of activation of the target's translation would be irrelevant for the target's selection).

In contrast, the language-nonspecific selection hypothesis posits that the lexical selection mechanism is sensitive to the activation levels of all lexical nodes regardless of the language to which they belong (see Fig. 15.3[b]). In this view, the selection mechanism simply picks out the lexical node with the highest level of activation in any language. Thus, assuming that lexical selection is a competitive process, then the ease with which the target lexical node is selected would depend on the level of activation of the words of both the response language and the nonresponse language (e.g., Hermans, 2000; Hermans, Bongaerts, De Bot, &

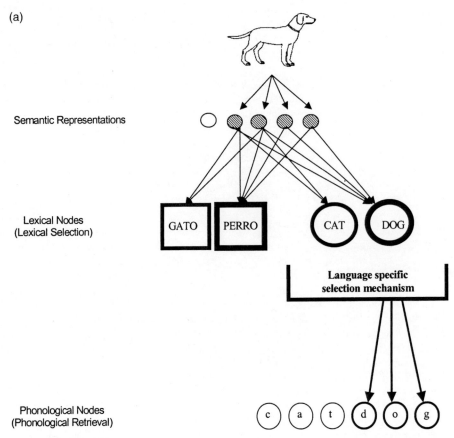

(a)

Semantic Representations

Lexical Nodes
(Lexical Selection)

Language specific
selection mechanism

Phonological Nodes
(Phonological Retrieval)

Figure 15.3 Schematic representation of the bilingual system. The squares represent the lexical nodes of the language not in use (Spanish) and the circles the lexical nodes of the language in use (English). The arrows represent the flow of activation, and the thickness of the circles indicates the level of activation of the representations. The rectangle represents a lexical selection mechanism. In part a, the selection mechanism is language specific; that is, it only considers the activation levels of the lexical nodes belonging to the response language during speech production, rendering any activation of the lexical nodes of the nonresponse language (represented by the squares) irrelevant during the selection process. In part b, the selection mechanism is language nonspecific and therefore considers the level of activation of all lexical nodes irrespective of the language to which they belong.

Schreuder, 1998). That is, words from the nonresponse language also act as competitors.

These two views make different predictions about the role of the nonresponse language during lexical selection. While the language-specific selection hypothesis posits that the existence of another language is irrelevant during lexical selection, the language-nonspecific selection hypothesis assumes that lexical nodes in the nonresponse language may interfere during lexical access. In the section Cross-Language Effects During Selection Processes, I describe some studies that have attempted to provide evidence in favor of one model or the other.

But, before doing so, it should be noted that these two proposals are in many respects underspecified. Language-specific selection models beg a crucial and yet-unanswered question: How does the selection mechanism restrict its search to the lexical nodes of only one language? Likewise, language-nonspecific models must explain the mechanism that prevents words in the nonresponse language from eventual selection (see La Heij, chapter 14, this volume, for a related discussion).

One way to implement the language-specific selection mechanism can be found in the binding-by-checking mechanism proposed by Levelt, Roelofs,

(b)

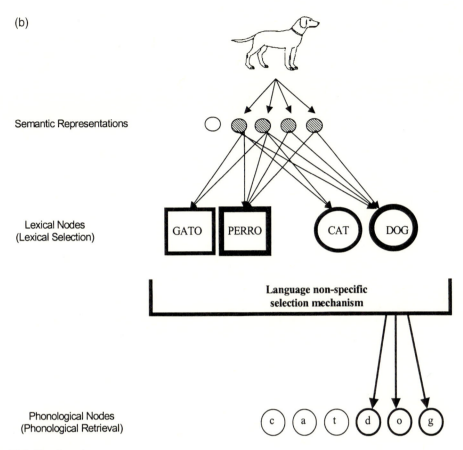

Semantic Representations

Lexical Nodes
(Lexical Selection)

**Language non-specific
selection mechanism**

Phonological Nodes
(Phonological Retrieval)

Figure 15.3 Continued.

and Meyer (1999). This mechanism ensures that the selected word matches the intended meaning of the speaker. Roelofs (1998) extended this mechanism to cases of bilingualism. According to Roelofs, the checking mechanism is sensitive to both the language the speaker wants to use and the language of the selected lexical node. If the language of the selected word does not match that of the intended language, the checking mechanism notes a mismatch, and the selected lexical node is discarded before further processing. In this way, the system ensures that only lexical nodes that belong to the intended language will eventually be produced. For an involuntary intrusion of a word from the nonresponse language to occur, two errors should be present: the selection of a word belonging to the wrong language and a failure in the checking mechanism in charge of binding the intended conceptual representation and the language in which it has to be produced with the

proper lexical node (see La Heij, chapter 14, this volume, for a critical discussion of this position).

Regarding the language-nonspecific hypothesis, there have been two proposals of how to ensure selection in the intended language. The first assumes that the semantic system activates the lexical representations of the response language with more intensity than those of the nonresponse language (e.g., Poulisse, 1999). This differential amount of activation received by the two lexical systems guarantees that the lexical nodes with the higher level of activation correspond to those of the language in use. The second solution appeals to the existence of an inhibitory process acting on the lexical representations that belong to the nonresponse language. In other words, the activation levels of the lexical representations of the language not in use are suppressed. In this way, the lexical nodes of the response language would always be more activated than those of the nonresponse language, ensuring that the word to be selected belongs to the intended language.

Selecting Sublexical Representations

Regarding the stage at which phonological encoding takes place, it is also commonly assumed that the selection of the proper segmental information is determined by the activation levels of the segments that form the target word (Costa & Caramazza, 2002; Meyer, 1996; Meyer & Schriefers, 1991; Roelofs, 2000; Starreveld, 2000). Assuming that the lexical nodes of the nonresponse language activate their corresponding phonological segments, the question is whether such activation interferes with the target's phonological encoding.

An answer to this question depends, in principle, on some assumptions about how the phonological repertoires of the two languages of a bilingual are represented. For example, a language-specific selection mechanism can only be implemented if the bilingual speaker possesses two separate phonological repertoires. In this scenario, it would be possible to postulate a retrieval mechanism sensitive only to the activation levels of one specific phonological repertoire (along the same lines as proposed for the selection of lexical nodes). By contrast, if there is a certain overlap between the phonological systems of the two languages of a bilingual, then the activation of the phonological information corresponding to the translation word would probably have an impact on the ease with which the phonological composition of the target word is retrieved.

Producing Words in One Language: Experimental Evidence

Activation Flow From the Semantic System to the Lexical and Sublexical Systems

The studies reviewed next have explored whether activation flows freely from the semantic system to the two lexical systems of a bilingual irrespective of the language spoken.

The first set of evidence suggesting that the existence of language-nonspecific activation flow comes from the study of spontaneous slips of the tongue in bilingual speakers. Poulisse and Bongaerts (1994; see also Poulisse, 1999) analyzed the L2 production

performance of 45 late Dutch-English bilinguals in different speech production tasks. Of special interest here are those slips of the tongue that ostensibly showed an effect of the first language (L1) system (the so-called L1-based slips). For the 15 relatively proficient bilinguals (speakers who had studied English for at least 7 years) included in the experiment, the number of times that an L1 word was produced involuntarily was very low. These speakers produced an average of 3,361 words in their L2 with only 16 L1 intrusions. However, the 15 "low-proficient" bilinguals, who were exposed to English for only 2 years, produced an average of 2,795 words, with a total of 246 L1 lexical intrusions. These observations suggested that (a) there is concurrent activation of the two languages of a bilingual, and (b) language proficiency correlates negatively with the probability of committing a faulty lexical selection that involves lexical items from the nonresponse language.

Hermans et al. (1998) conducted several picture–word interference experiments in which Dutch-English bilinguals were asked to name pictures in their L2 while ignoring the presentation of distractor words in L1 or L2. In the crucial condition, the distractor word was phonologically related to the target's translation. For example, if the speaker had to name a picture of a mountain in English (*mountain*), the distractor word phonologically related to the target's translation (*berg*) was *berm*. The authors argued that if activation from the semantic system flows to the target's translation in the nonresponse language (*berg*), lexical selection should be harder when the translation word receives extra activation from the distractor word (that is, when the distractor word is phonologically related, e.g., *berm*) than when it does not (when the distractor word is phonologically unrelated, e.g., *kaars*). The results supported this prediction in that naming latencies were slower in the former condition. This result was interpreted as supporting the ideas that (a) the activation flow is not language specific, and (b) the lexical selection mechanism considers the activation levels of words belonging to the response and nonresponse languages (see more later about this claim). That is, the semantic system activates both languages of a bilingual, and the selection mechanism is sensitive to the activation level of any lexical item regardless of the language it belongs to (see also Costa, Colomé, Gómez, & Sebastián-Gallés, 2003, for a different interpretation of these results).

Other studies that have addressed this issue have explored whether there is phonological activation of the target's translation word. For example, Costa et al. (2000) asked whether the cognate status of translation words has an impact on the speed with which they are produced. Cognates are translations with similar phonological/orthographic form (e.g., *guitarra*/guitar). Noncognates are translations with dissimilar phonological/orthographic form (e.g., *pandereta*/tambourine). Costa et al. (2000) hypothesized that if during picture naming the phonological representation of the target's translation is activated, then the retrieval of the' phonological properties of the target word would be easier for cognates than for noncognate words. This is because, for the former set of words, the phonological segments (or features) of the target word (e.g., *guitarra*) would receive activation from two sources, the target lexical representation (e.g., *guitarra*) and its translation in the nonresponse language (e.g., guitar). This situation is different for the noncognate words, for which the target lexical node and its translation would activate different phonological representations. The results confirmed this prediction: Naming latencies were faster for pictures with cognate than with noncognate names. This result was interpreted as supporting the notions that (a) activation flow from the semantic system to the lexical system is language nonspecific, and (b) lexical nodes from the nonresponse language spread activation to their phonological segments (see Kroll, Dijkstra, Janssen, & Schriefers, 2000, for a replication of the cognate effect in picture naming).

Another result indicating that lexical nodes from the nonresponse language activate their phonological properties was reported by Gollan and Acenas (2000), who explored the tip-of-the-tongue (TOT) phenomenon in bilingual speakers (see Gollan & Silverberg, 2001, for a related study). In this study, bilingual speakers tended to fall in TOT states less often with cognate words than with noncognate words. The authors argued that the cognate effect arises because the target's translation (in the case of the cognate words but not in the case of the noncognate words) is sending activation to the phonological elements of the target word. Thus, the phonological elements of a cognate word would be more available than those of a noncognate word. Under the assumption that TOT states arise as a consequence of a failure in retrieving the phonological elements of the target lexical node, then the probability of falling in a TOT state would be higher for noncognates than for cognates. This is because the availability of the phonemes would be higher in the latter than in the former case.

The cognate effects in naming latencies and in TOT rates, along with other convergent experimental evidence (Colomé, 2001), suggest the existence of phonological activation of the target's translation. In other words, the available evidence suggests that activation flow in lexical access—from the semantic system to the lexical level and from the lexical level to the sublexical level—is language nonspecific.

Cross-Language Effects During Selection Processes

The parallel activation of both lexicons of a bilingual during speech production begs the question of how the activation of the representations in the language not in use affects the production process in the response language. As discussed next, such an issue is far from resolved.

Poulisse and Bongaerts (1994) and Poulisse (1999) showed that the retrieval of lexical items in L2 is affected by the existence of L1 words. These authors demonstrated the occurrences of L1 intrusions in L2 speech production, particularly in low-proficient bilinguals. Poulisse and Bongaerts (1994) interpreted these errors as demonstrating that the lexical selection mechanism considers the level of activation of all lexical nodes, irrespective of the language spoken, and that in some cases the mechanism derails and selects the target's translation rather than the intended lexical node.

However, in a more recent study, Poulisse (1999) preferred a different interpretation of the phenomenon. She argued that these errors stem from a deviant behavior in the speech production system called *multiple selection*, in which two lexical nodes are selected for further processing. The unintentional L2 switches arise from two independent errors. First, the lexical selection mechanism erroneously selects two lexical nodes simultaneously (the target and its translation in the nonresponse language). As a consequence of this multiple selection, two word form representations become activated. At that point, another error occurs: Instead of retrieving the phonological representation of the target lexical node in the response language, the corresponding target's translation is retrieved and produced.[2]

Importantly, Levelt et al. (1999) suggested that the selection of two lexical nodes is the source of the slips of the tongue in which the phonological information of two lexical nodes is combined in one single production. In other words, these so-called blend errors are considered to result from having available the phonological information of two previously selected lexical nodes. If multiple selection indeed underlies the L1 intrusions observed by Poulisse (1999), then a considerable number of blend errors across languages would be expected in her corpus, a prediction that was not supported by the data (four errors out of more than 100,000 words produced).

Regardless of the exact locus at which the L1 intrusions take place, it is important to determine whether the results reported by Poulisse (1999) are compelling enough to assume that lexical selection is language nonspecific. And, in fact, the very small number of L1 intrusions produced by the relatively late fluent bilinguals tested by Poulisse may support the notion that this type of bilingual speaker achieves lexical selection by means of a language-specific selection mechanism.

A second result that supports the notion that the activation of lexical nodes belonging to the non-response language affects lexical selection in the response language is that reported by Hermans et al. (1998). As discussed, in this study an increase in the level of activation of the target's translation produced by the presentation of a phonologically similar distractor word led to interference in the production of the picture's name. These results suggested that when speaking in L2, the lexical selection mechanism considers the level of activation of every lexical node, treating the nodes as possible candidates for production, therefore allowing cross-language interference to arise.

Lee and Williams (2001) investigated, by means of a semantic interference paradigm, whether words from the nonresponse language interfere during lexical selection. English-French bilinguals were asked to perform a naming-to-definition task mixed with a picture-naming task. In each trial, the bilinguals were presented with three definitions, and they were asked to produce the word corresponding to each in their L1 (English). After the definitions, two pictures appeared, one after the other, and the participants were asked to name them either in English or in French. Naming latencies were recorded for the second picture (the target picture).

Three critical manipulations were included in the experiment. First, the second definition of a triad was semantically related (e.g., The queen lives at Buckingham...[correct answer "palace"]) or unrelated (e.g., animal that travelers ride on in the desert...[correct answer "camel"]) to the target picture (e.g., "castle"). Second, the target picture (the second picture) was named in L1 (English) or in L2 (French). Third, the first picture was named

either in L1 or on L2. Trials in which the first picture had to be named in French were considered switch trials; those in which the first picture had to be named in English were considered nonswitch trials. The results showed a semantic interference effect. When the second definition was semantically related to the target picture name, naming latencies were slower than when it was unrelated. However, this semantic interference depended on whether the target picture was preceded by a switch trial. If the first picture introduced a language switch (it had to be named in French), then no semantic interference was present. However, if the first picture had to be named in English (no switch condition), then semantic interference effects appeared for the two languages. In other words, if there was a language switch just after the definitions, then no semantic interference was present.

Lee and Williams (2001) interpreted this result as revealing the existence of cross-language competition and inhibitory processes in bilingual language production. They argued that, when producing the name of a target picture in French (*chateau* [castle]), the English lexical node produced in response to the definition of a palace in English (*palace*) interferes with the target selection in French (*chateau*). Crucially, however, such competition disappears if there is a language switch immediately before the target picture. The authors claimed that the language switch leads to the inhibition of lexical nodes in the language in which the definitions have been answered (English), rendering any subsequent interference from English lexical nodes ineffective (e.g., *palace* would not interfere with *chateau* because the English lexical nodes would have been inhibited).[3]

There is, however, another set of results that favors the notion that lexical selection is language specific. Costa et al. (1999) reported a series of picture–word interference experiments in which balanced Catalan-Spanish bilinguals were asked to name pictures in their L1 while ignoring distractor words. Of critical interest is the condition in which the distractor word corresponded to the target's translation (e.g., picture–*taula* [table in Catalan], with the distractor *mesa* [table in Spanish]). In this condition, the target's translation (*mesa*) is supposed to be highly activated (even more than in the case in which the distractor word is phonologically related to the target's translation, as in Hermans et al., 1998) because it receives activation from two sources: the semantic representation of the target picture and the presentation of the distractor word. In such a scenario, if the target's translation is considered a candidate for lexical selection, naming latencies should be slower when the distractor word is the target's translation (*mesa*) than when it is an unrelated word (*perro* [dog in Spanish]).

The results did not support this prediction. In fact, naming latencies were faster in the former than in the latter case. In other words, raising the activation levels of the target's translation did not slow the target's selection, but rather speeded it, suggesting that the lexical selection mechanism does not take into account the activation level of the lexical nodes that belong to the nonresponse language. Importantly, this result has been replicated with two other populations of bilinguals with different degrees of L2 proficiency and with L2 as the language of the response (Costa & Caramazza, 1999; Hermans, 2000).

Thus, there are two seemingly contradictory results. Although a distractor word that partially matches the target's translation (berm) interferes with the selection of the target word (mountain), a distractor word that matches fully the target's translation (berg) facilitates the target production (mountain). At this point, there is no satisfactory explanation for these contrasting results (but see Hermans, 2000, and Costa et al., 2003).

There is also some evidence coming from the TOT study conducted by Gollan and Acenas (2000), suggesting that lexical nodes from the nonresponse language do not interfere during lexical selection. In this study, the probability that a speaker falls in a TOT state depended on whether the speaker knew the target's translation. At first glance, it may be expected that if a TOT state arises in part because of the competition created by the existence of a translation word, target words for which the participant knew the translation would be more likely to produce TOT states. This is because the translation may act as a blocking word, complicating the retrieval of the correct word in the proper language. However, surprisingly bilingual speakers fell in TOT states less often with words for which they knew the translations in the nonresponse language than for words for which they did not know the translation. The authors argued that this result is difficult to explain in terms of models that assume the existence of competing lexical representations across languages.

Integrating the Experimental Results

I have reviewed several studies aimed at finding whether the flow of activation and the selection processes are language specific or language nonspecific. The experimental results regarding the first issue point in the same direction, namely, that during lexical access in speech production the lexical nodes of the two languages of a bilingual are simultaneously activated (Hermans et al., 1998; Poulisse, 1999). Furthermore, there is convergent evidence suggesting that the activation of lexical nodes belonging to the nonresponse language also spreads to their phonological properties (Colomé, 2001; Costa et al., 2000; Kroll, Dijkstra, Janssen, & Schriefers, 2000). Together, these results suggest that activation flow from the semantic system to the lexical and sublexical systems of a bilingual is language nonspecific.

The remaining issue to solve is whether the selection of the lexical and sublexical representations in the response language is affected by the activation of corresponding linguistic representations in the other language. Much less agreement exists regarding this issue. The results of several reaction time studies seemed to favor the notion that lexical selection is language nonspecific (Hermans et al., 1998; Lee & Williams, 2001). However, another set of studies has been interpreted as supporting the notion that lexical nodes belonging to the nonresponse language do not enter the competition process during lexical selection (Costa et al., 1999; Costa & Caramazza, 1999; Hermans, 2000). At this point, it is difficult to adjudicate between these two possibilities. In fact, it is possible that both of them capture the performance of different population of bilingual speakers.

Regarding whether the activation of the sublexical representations of the language not in use affects the selection of the phonological representations in the language in use, the results seem more homogeneous. Evidence from different paradigms, such as phoneme detection (Colomé, 2001), picture naming (Costa et al., 2000; Kroll et al., 2000), and TOT rates (Gollan & Acenas, 2000), suggests that the activation of the phonological properties of the target's translation affects the ease and speed with which the phonological properties of the target in the response language are retrieved. In this sense, phonological encoding seems to follow language-nonspecific processing.

It can be concluded that activation flow and phonological retrieval are two language-nonspecific processes. The extent to which lexical selection is language specific or not remains as an unresolved issue.

However, regardless of which of the two hypotheses turns out to be correct, it may be recalled that neither explains how exactly bilinguals finally select the words in the response language. In the framework of language-nonspecific models, it has been argued that lexical selection in the intended language is achieved by means of the active inhibition of the words in the nonresponse language. In the following section, I discuss the arguments that have been put forward in support of this view.

Does Lexical Selection in Bilinguals Entail Inhibitory Processes?

Some researchers have put forward the notion that lexical selection in the desired language is achieved by suppressing the activation of the lexical nodes that belong to the nontarget language (e.g., Green, 1986, 1998; Meuter & Allport, 1999). Postulating inhibitory mechanisms certainly increases the explanatory power of any given model of lexical access. Interestingly, however, none of the most relevant monolingual speech production models postulates inhibitory processes.

Green (1998) has put forward the most specific implementation of inhibitory control in the language production system. In this (Inhibitory Control) model, there are multiple levels of control. The level at which inhibition is postulated is the lexical level (or lemma level). Lexical nodes are marked with language tags that specify the language to which they belong. During lexical access, those words carrying the tag corresponding to the nontarget language are reactively inhibited, preventing their selection. In other words, the conceptual system activates the lexical nodes of the two languages of a bilingual, but those belonging to the nonresponse language are suppressed later.

There are three important features of the model worth discussing here. First, the inhibition applied to the lexical nodes of the nonresponse language is reactive in the sense that it is only functional after the lexical nodes have been activated. Also, this reactive mechanism assumes that more active lexical nodes will be more inhibited. Second, despite this suppression mechanism, the lexical nodes of the nonresponse language interfere during lexical selection in the response language. Third, there is discrete processing between lexical and sublexical levels, which implies that phonological activation is restricted to the selected lexical node.

The most compelling evidence supporting inhibitory control of the lexical systems of a bilingual

comes from switching experiments. Meuter and Allport (1999) investigated the extent to which a language switch cost is dependent on the direction of the switch (see Meuter, chapter 17, this volume). Bilingual speakers of different languages were asked to name nine digits presented repeatedly in lists, and they were instructed to name a given digit in L1 or L2 depending on the color of the screen of a given trial. The authors measured digit-naming latencies for trials preceded by a same-language response (no-switch trial) or by a different language response (switch trial). Naming latencies for no-switch trials were faster than for switch trials—the switching cost. Interestingly, the magnitude of the switching cost was larger when participants were asked to switch from the less-dominant to the more dominant language than vice versa. That is, to switch from L2 to L1 was more costly than to switch from L1 to L2.

The authors (Meuter & Allport, 1999) interpreted this result as supporting the notion that when speaking one language, the nonresponse language is inhibited. They argued that the magnitude of the inhibition exerted in the lexical nodes is different for L1 than for L2; it is larger for L1. Therefore, after naming in L2 when in a subsequent trial a word in the dominant language (L1) has to be produced, the system needs more time to raise the activation level of its lexical nodes because they have just been strongly inhibited. When a switch in the opposite direction is needed (from L1 to L2), the switching cost is not so large because when speaking in the dominant language, there is no need to inhibit the less dominant language strongly. Therefore, it should be relatively easy to switch to L2. Further support of this differential strength of the suppression mechanism comes from the observation that the magnitude of the asymmetrical switching cost was negatively correlated with the participants' L2 level of proficiency.

These results are consistent with the notion that the reactive inhibition is proportional to the level of activation of the to-be-suppressed lexical nodes: The greater the activation of the lexical nodes of the nonresponse language, the greater the degree of inhibition required. The notion of reactive inhibition leads also to the following prediction: If the bilingual uses the nonresponse language often and is relatively fluent in that language, the bilingual would have to inhibit it greatly. As Green (1998) put it:

Competition between alternative responses should increase with fluency in context where both languages are active. Increased competition should induce greater inhibition of unwanted competitors.... The competitor is more activated for proficient bilinguals and so requires a greater degree of inhibition. (p. 103)

A prediction that follows from this assumption is that when speaking in L1, the degree with which L2 needs to be inhibited correlates positively with its level of activation. Therefore, the amount of inhibition applied to L2 should be larger for proficient bilinguals than for nonproficient bilinguals. In this scenario, the switching cost when switching from L1 to L2 should be larger for proficient than for nonproficient bilinguals given that the former group has to inhibit L2 more strongly when speaking in L1. Note that this prediction is independent of the magnitude of the asymmetrical switching costs. Instead, it is related to how much inhibition is needed to suppress the activation levels of the words belonging to a nonresponse language. A closer look at the Meuter and Allport (1999) results fails to support such a prediction. In fact, an increase in proficiency level correlated with a reduction in the switching costs regardless of the direction of the switch.

Summarizing, the study of Meuter and Allport (1999) revealed three main results: (a) asymmetrical switching cost for less-proficient bilinguals, (b) the magnitude of the asymmetrical switching cost was reduced for more proficient bilinguals, and (c) no increase in switching cost for more proficient bilinguals. One way to reconcile these three results is to assume that reactive inhibitory processes in lexical selection are only functional when the L2 proficiency is low. In this view, the switching cost observed for more fluent bilinguals would not reflect any inhibitory process but just the time to change the task instruction (see Costa & Santesteban, 2004b; Costa, Santesteban, & Felhosi, 2003).

Another important feature of Green's model is the discrete processing between the lexical and sublexical levels of representation. Accordingly, the only phonological information that would be active corresponds to the lexical node that has been selected in the response language. This assumption is at odds with those results that show that the phonological representations of lexical nodes in the nonresponse language are activated during naming in the response language (Colomé, 2001; Costa et al., 2000; Kroll et al., 2000). In fact, the existence of phonological activation of the target's translation is problematic also for the discrete assumption in monolingual models. More important, these effects seem also inconsistent with the notion

of inhibition of the lexical nodes of the nonresponse language. This is because suppressing the activation of lexical nodes would prevent the activation of their phonological properties. Thus, it is not immediately obvious how a model that assumes both discrete processing and reactive inhibition can account for the phonological activation of the nonselected and presumably inhibited target's translation.[4]

However, if inhibitory control is not part of the bilingual speech production system, then how is lexical selection achieved in the intended language? There are several ways in which this can be effected (see, e.g., La Heij, chapter 14, this volume). For example, in Green's (1998) model, lexical selection could be achieved without inhibitory processes. In this model, lexical concepts (those concepts for which a word exists in a given language) are language specific. From this, it would follow that, for instance, a Spanish-English bilingual has two lexical concepts for a given object. Lexicalization starts with the activation of a lexical concept, which in turn activates its corresponding lexical node. The selection of a given lexical node is determined, among other things, by a checking procedure that inspects whether a lexical node corresponds to the intended lexical concept. Thus, in this model lexical concepts are language specific, lexical nodes carry language tags, and there is a checking mechanism that ensures that lexical concepts are linked to appropriate lexical nodes. According to this account, the successful selection of a lexical node in the intended language might be achieved without lexical inhibition. This is because the mechanism that actually guarantees successful selection in the proper language is the checking mechanism that ensures that a given lexical node corresponds to the intended language-specific lexical concept.

Let me illustrate this argument with an example. Assume that the speaker selects the L2 lexical concept DOG (and not the L1 lexical concept *PERRO*). The target conceptual representation (DOG) spreads activation to its lexical representation (*dog*). At the moment of selection, the checking mechanism makes sure that the selected lexical representation (*dog*) is linked to the intended concept (DOG). If such is the case, the retrieval of the phonological properties of the selected lexical node starts. If not, a new selection procedure starts. In other words, lexical nodes from the response language (within-language competitors, *cat* in the example) and nonresponse language (cross-language competitors, *perro* in the example) may be discarded in the same way by the checking mechanism. That is, the same mechanism that prevents the selection of semantically close competitors would be in charge of preventing the selection of the target's translation. Thus, although Green's model assumes the existence of language inhibition, in principle it could account for bilingual lexical selection without such mechanism (see La Heij, chapter 14, this volume, for further discussion).

I reviewed some of the basic claims about the role of inhibitory mechanisms in bilingual speech production. I argued that some results support the notion that lexical access in speech production entails the suppression of the activated lexical nodes belonging to the nonresponse language. However, there are other results that do not seem consistent with such an idea, especially when the production performance of highly proficient bilinguals is addressed. Also, I argued that one of the current models of speech production, of which inhibition is a cornerstone, does not really require such a mechanism to explain how normal speech production proceeds in bilingual speakers. This does not mean to say that inhibitory processes play no role in the production of speech in bilingual speakers. It may very well be that with an increase of L2 proficiency, there is a shift from reliance on inhibitory processes toward language-specific selection mechanisms. Further research needs to be done to determine how inhibitory control is implemented in the speech production system, allowing at the same time the flow of activation to be language nonspecific.

Summary

In this chapter, I focused on two aspects of bilingual speech production: activation flow and selection processes. I contrasted two different views of bilingual lexical access, the language-specific and language-nonspecific views. I argued that there is empirical evidence consistent with the notion that activation flows from the semantic system to the two languages of a bilingual up to the phonological level in a language-nonspecific fashion.

The picture is more complex when the selection mechanisms are concerned. The experimental evidence is mixed in the sense that some results favor the language specificity of the lexical selection mechanism, and others favor the notion of nonspecific lexical selection. A possible way to reconcile the seemingly contradictory data is to assume that, in nonproficient bilinguals, the activation of the lexical nodes of the nonresponse language may affect production performance, but that bilinguals shift from language-nonspecific processing toward language-specific processing when they become more proficient bilinguals. Although this empirical generalization captures some of the current results, it is admittedly rather tentative and requires further research.

Acknowledgments

The work reported here was supported in part by the National Institutes of Health (DC 04542), by the Ramón y Cajal program, and the Spanish government (BSO2001-3492-C04-01), and the McDonnell grant Bridging Mind Brain and Behavior. I thank Antoni Rodríguez-Fornells, Salvador Soto-Faraco, Mikel Santesteban, and Alfonso Caramazza for their helpful comments to earlier versions of this chapter.

Notes

1. There is a debate regarding the functional architecture of the lexical system. According to some models (e.g., Levelt et al., 1999), lexical access would entail the retrieval of two different representations (the lemma and the lexeme). Other authors postulated the existence of only one level of lexical representation (e.g., Caramazza, 1997; Dell, 1986). Here, I adopt this second view, and I refer to the lexical representations with the term *lexical nodes*. Nevertheless, the arguments developed in this chapter are relatively independent of this debate.

2. The reason that led Poulisse to put forward such a new interpretation came from the adoption of the speech production architecture proposed by Levelt et al. (1999), in which frequency effects are located at the level of word form retrieval (Jescheniak & Levelt, 1994). Poulisse (1999) argued that the involuntary selection of L1 elements is to some extent caused by the different frequency values of the L1 and L2 lexical nodes. Thus, if such errors are sensitive to word frequency and this variable affects only the retrieval of word forms, it follows that the level at which such errors are occurring is the phonological level. However, recent results revealed that frequency also exerts its influence at the level at which lexical selection is achieved (Caramazza, Bi, Costa, & Miozzo, 2004; Dell, 1990; Caramazza, Costa, Miozzo, & Bi, 2001; Jescheniak, Meyer, & Levelt, 2003). Thus, the available experimental evidence is not compelling enough to assume that the involuntary L1 intrusions stem from the phonological level.

3. Although these results are interesting, they also show some inconsistencies that may prevent

drawing strong conclusions. Although it is true that naming latencies only revealed semantic interference effects when the target picture was preceded by an English response (nonswitch trials), the scenario is a bit different when paying attention to the error rates. Error rates were larger (in some cases even by a factor of more than 2) whenever the target word had been preceded by a semantically related definition regardless of whether there was a language switch or not. Thus, it is unclear whether lexical competition also occurred for the conditions in which the target picture was preceded by a language switch.

4. Green's model could in part accommodate these results, maintaining the notion of inhibition, but giving up some other assumptions and postulating new ones. First, it could be assumed that there is cascaded processing between the lexical and phonological levels of representation, in such a way that any lexical representation that receives activation spreads a proportional amount of it to the corresponding phonological representation. A further assumption that has to be made is that by the time inhibition reaches the nonresponse lexical nodes, the target's translation has already spread some activation to the nodes representing its phonological properties.

References

Caramazza, A. (1997). How many levels of processing are there in lexical access? *Cognitive Neuropsychology, 14*, 177–208.

Caramazza, A., Bi, Y., Costa, A., & Miozzo, M. (2004).What determines the speed of lexical access: homophone or specific-word frequency? A reply to Jescheniak et al. (2003). *Journal of Experimental Psychology: Learning, Memory, and Cognition, 30*, 278–282.

Caramazza, A., & Costa, A. (2000). The semantic interference effect in the picture-word interference paradigm: Does the response set matter? *Cognition, 75*, 51–64.

Caramazza, A., & Costa, A. (2001). Set size and repetitions are not at the base of the differential effects of semantically related distractors: Implications for models of lexical access. *Cognition, 80*, 291–298.

Caramazza, A., Costa, A., Miozzo, M., & Bi, Y. (2001). The specific-word frequency effect: Implications for the representation of homophones. *Journal of Experimental Psychology: Learning, Memory, and Cognition, 27*, 1430–1450.

Colomé, À. (2001). Lexical activation in bilinguals' speech production: Language-specific or language-independent? *Journal of Memory and Language, 45*, 721–736.

Costa, A., & Caramazza, A. (1999). Is lexical selection in bilingual speech production language-specific? Further evidence from Spanish-English and English-Spanish bilinguals. *Bilingualism: Language, and Cognition, 2*, 231–244.

Costa, A., & Caramazza, A. (2002). The production of noun phrases in English and Spanish: Implications for the scope of phonological encoding in speech production. *Journal of Memory and Language, 46*, 178–198.

Costa, A., Caramazza, A., & Sebastián-Gallés, N. (2000). The cognate facilitation effect: Implications for models of lexical access. *Journal of Experimental Psychology: Learning, Memory, and Cognition, 26*, 1283–1296.

Costa, A., Colomé, A., Gómez, O., & Sebastián-Gallés, N. (2003). Another look at cross-language competition in bilingual speech production: Lexical and phonological factors. *Bilingualism: Language and Cognition, 6*, 167–179.

Costa, A., Miozzo, M., & Caramazza, A. (1999). Lexical selection in bilinguals: Do words in the bilingual's two lexicons compete for selection? *Journal of Memory and Language, 41*, 365–397.

Costa, A., & Santesteban, M. (2004a). Bilingual word perception and production: Two sides of the same coin? *Trends in Cognitive Sciences, 8*, 253.

Costa, A., & Santesteban, M. (2004b). Lexical access in bilingual speech production: Evidence from language switching in highly proficient bilinguals and L2 learners. *Journal of Memory and Language, 50*, 491–511.

Costa, A., Santesteban, M., & Felhosi, G. (2003, September). *Do language-switching costs reveal different degrees of language activation?* Paper presented at the 13th Conference of the European Society for Cognitive Psychology, Granada, Spain.

Cutting, J. C., & Ferreira, V. S. (1999). Semantic and phonological information flow in the production lexicon. *Journal of Experimental Psychology: Learning, Memory, and Cognition, 25*, 318–344.

De Bot, K. (1992). A bilingual production model: Levelt's speaking model adapted. *Applied Linguistics, 13*, 1–24.

De Groot, A. M. B. (1992). Determinants of word translation. *Journal of Experimental Psychology: Learning, Memory, and Cognition, 18*, 1001–1018.

Dell, G. S. (1986). A spreading activation theory of retrieval in sentence production. *Psychological Review, 93*, 283–321.

Dell, G. S. (1990). Effects of frequency and vocabulary type on phonological speech errors.

Language and Cognitive Processes, 5,
313–349.

Dewaele, J. M. (2001). Activation or inhibition?
The interaction of L1, L2 and L3 on the
language mode continuum. In J. Cenoz, B.
Hufeisen, & U. Jessner (Eds.), *Cross-linguistic
influence in third language acquisition:
Psycholinguistic perspectives* (pp. 69–89).
Oxford, U.K.: Oxford University Press.

French, R. M., & Jacquet, M. (2004). Understanding bilingual memory: Models and data.
Trends in Cognitive Sciences, 8, 87–93.

Goldrick, M., & Rapp, B. (2002). A restricted
interaction account (RIA) of spoken word
production: The best of both worlds.
Aphasiology, 16, 20–55.

Gollan, T. H., & Acenas, L. A. (2000, April).
*Tip-of-the-tongue incidence in Spanish-
English and Tagalog-English bilinguals.* Paper
presented at the Third International Symposium on Bilingualism, Bristol, U.K.

Gollan, T. H., & Kroll, J. F. (2001). Bilingual
lexical access. In B. Rapp (Ed.), *The handbook
of cognitive neuropsychology: What deficits
reveal about the human mind* (pp. 321–345).
Philadelphia: Psychology Press.

Gollan, T. H., & Silverberg, N. B. (2001).
Tip-of-the-tongue states in Hebrew-English
bilinguals. *Bilingualism: Language and Cognition, 4,* 63–83.

Green, D. W. (1986). Control, activation and
resource. *Brain and Language, 27,* 210–223.

Green, D. W. (1998). Mental control of the bilingual lexico-semantic system. *Bilingualism:
Language and Cognition, 1,* 67–81.

Griffin, Z. M., & Bock, J. K. (1998). Constraint,
word frequency, and the relationship between
lexical processing levels in spoken word production. *Journal of Memory and Language,
38,* 313–338.

Grosjean, F. (1997). Processing mixed language:
Issues, findings and models. In A. M. B. de
Groot & J. F. Kroll (Eds.), *Tutorials in bilingualism: Psycholinguistic perspectives* (pp.
225–254). Mahwah, NJ: Erlbaum.

Grosjean, F. (1998). Transfer and language mode.
Bilingualism: Language and Cognition, 1,
175–176.

Grosjean, F. (2001). The bilingual's language
modes. In J. Nicol (Ed.), *One mind, two
languages: Bilingual language processing*
(pp. 1–22). Oxford, U.K.: Blackwell.

Harley, T. A. (1993). Phonological activation of
semantic competitors during lexical access in
speech production. *Language and Cognitive
Processes, 8,* 291–309.

Hermans, D. (2000). *Word production in a foreign
language.* Unpublished doctoral thesis,
University of Nijmegen, The Netherlands.

Hermans, D., Bongaerts, T., De Bot, K., &
Schreuder, R. (1998). Producing words in a
foreign language: Can speakers prevent interference from their first language? *Bilingualism:
Language and Cognition, 1,* 213–230.

Humphreys, G. W., & Riddoch, M. J. (1988).
Cascade processes in picture identification.
Cognitive Neuropsychology, 5, 67–104.

Jescheniak, J. D., & Levelt, W. J. M. (1994). Word
frequency effects in speech production:
Retrieval of syntactic information and of
phonological form. *Journal of Experimental
Psychology: Learning, Memory, and Cognition, 20,* 824–843.

Jescheniak, J. D., Meyer, A. S., & Levelt, W. J. M.
(2003). Specific-word frequency is not all that
counts in speech production: Comments on
Caramazza et al. (2001) and new experimental
data. *Journal of Experimental Psychology:
Learning, Memory, and Cognition, 29,*
432–438.

Kroll, J. F., Dijkstra, A., Janssen, N., & Schriefers,
H. (2000, November). *Selecting the language
in which to speak: Experiments on lexical access in bilingual production.* Paper presented
at the 41st Annual Meeting of the Psychonomic Society, New Orleans, LA.

Kroll, J. F., & Stewart, E. (1994). Category interference in translation and picture naming:
Evidence for asymmetric connections between
bilingual memory representations. *Journal of
Memory and Language, 33,* 149–174.

La Heij, W., Hooglander, A., Kerling, R., &
Van der Velden, E. (1996). Nonverbal
context effects in forward and backward
translation: Evidence for concept mediation.
Journal of Memory and Language, 35,
648–665.

Lee, M. W., & Williams, J. N. (2001). Lexical
access in spoken word production by bilinguals: Evidence from the semantic competitor
priming paradigm. *Bilingualism: Language
and Cognition, 4,* 233–248.

Levelt, W. J. M. (1989). *Speaking: From
intention to articulation.* Cambridge, MA:
MIT Press.

Levelt, W. J. M. (2001). Spoken word production:
A theory of lexical access. *Proceedings of the
National Academy of Sciences, 98,*
13, 464–13,471.

Levelt, W. J. M., Roelofs, A., & Meyer, A. (1999).
A theory of lexical access in speech
production. *Behavioral and Brain Sciences,
22,* 1–75.

Levelt, W. J. M., Schriefers, H., Vorberg, D.,
Meyer, A. S., Pechmann, T., & Havinga, J.
(1991). The time course of lexical access in
speech production: A study of picture naming.
Psychological Review, 98, 122–142.

McNamara, J. (1967). The bilingual's linguistic performance: A psychological overview. *Journal of Social Issues, 23*, 59–77.

McNamara, J., & Kushnir, S. L. (1972). Linguistic independence of bilinguals: The input switch. *Journal of Verbal Learning and Verbal Behavior, 10*, 480–487.

Meuter, R. F. I., & Allport, A. (1999). Bilingual language switching in naming: Asymmetrical costs of language selection. *Journal of Memory and Language, 40*, 25–40.

Meyer, A. S. (1996). Lexical access in phrase and sentence production: Results from picture–word interference experiments. *Journal of Memory and Language, 35*, 477–496.

Meyer, A. S., & Schriefers, H. (1991). Phonological facilitation in picture-word interference experiments: Effects of stimulus onset asynchrony and types of interfering stimuli. *Journal of Experimental Psychology: Learning, Memory, and Cognition, 17*, 1146–1160.

Peterson, R. R., & Savoy, P. (1998). Lexical selection and phonological encoding during language production: Evidence for cascaded processing. *Journal of Experimental Psychology: Learning, Memory, and Cognition, 24*, 539–557.

Poulisse, N. (1999). *Slips of the tongue: Speech errors in first and second language production.* Amsterdam, The Netherlands: Benjamins.

Poulisse, N., & Bongaerts, T. (1994). First language use in second language production. *Applied Linguistics, 15*, 36–57.

Rapp, B., & Goldrick, M. (2000). Discreteness and interactivity in spoken word production. *Psychological Review, 107*, 460–499.

Roelofs, A. (1992). A spreading-activation theory of lemma retrieval in speaking. *Cognition, 42*, 107–142.

Roelofs, A. (1998). Lemma selection without inhibition of languages in bilingual speakers. *Bilingualism: Language and Cognition, 1*, 94–95.

Roelofs, A. (2000). WEAVER++ and other computational models of lemma retrieval and word-form encoding. In L. Wheeldon (Ed.), *Aspects of language production* (pp. 71–114). Sussex, U.K.: Psychology Press.

Roelofs, A. (2001). Set size and repetition matter: Comment on Caramazza and Costa (2000). *Cognition, 80*, 283–290.

Schriefers, H., Meyer, A. S., & Levelt, W. J. M. (1990). Exploring the time-course of lexical access in production: Picture-word interference studies. *Journal of Memory and Language, 29*, 86–102.

Starreveld, P. A. (2000). On the interpretation of onsets of auditory context effects in word production. *Journal of Memory and Language, 42*, 497–525.

Van Hell, J. G., & De Groot, A. M. B. (1998). Conceptual representation in bilingual memory: Effects of concreteness and cognate status in word association. *Bilingualism: Language and Cognition, 1*, 193–211.

Carol Myers-Scotton

16

Supporting a Differential Access Hypothesis
Code Switching and Other Contact Data

ABSTRACT This chapter endorses the position of Clahsen (e.g., 1999), Jackendoff (2002), Pinker (1999), inter alia about differences in how words may be accessed in production (i.e., that some lexical words including regular morphology are constructed online while semiproductive or irregular elements are stored as units in the mental lexicon). However, it goes a step in another direction, to argue that not all elements underlying surface-level morphemes are accessed in the same way or at the same point in language production and that this difference is reflected in the distribution patterns of surface-level morphemes in naturally occurring data. Specifically, those elements underlying content morphemes and what are called early system morphemes are salient at the level of the mental lexicon. In contrast, those system morphemes that are structurally assigned (called late system morphemes) are not available to participate in lexical combinations until the level of the formulator. The formulator receives directions from lemmas in the mental lexicon about how to assemble surface-level morphemes, including those late system morphemes that are essential in building larger constituent structures. A Differential Access Hypothesis captures the distinction between morpheme activation, supported by evidence that links variation in data distributions to morpheme type. The evidence this chapter considers comes from language contact phenomena, especially code switching. This hypothesis makes claims related to the two-step retrieval hypothesis of Garrett (1975, 1993, inter alia). Two models relevant to contact data, the Matrix Language Frame (MLF) model and the 4-M model, frame the discussion.

Bilingual data have received little regard when it comes to subjects that most psycholinguists or linguists consider worth studying. First, even though there are more bilinguals than monolinguals in the world, most psycholinguists and linguists choose to study one language or at least one language at a time. They do not seem to consider that how their language of choice occurs with another language could tell them something about either language on its own. Second, among those few in either camp who study bilingualism, empirical bilingual data still lose out. Within psycholinguistics, researchers almost exclusively consider experimental data, not naturally occurring production data. Within linguistics, how language is produced is the poor relation in Chomsky's competence versus performance dichotomy. A notable exception is Jackendoff (2002) and to some extent Clahsen (1999; Clahsen, Eisenbeiss, Hadler, & Sonnenstuhl, 2001). Jackendoff's position is as follows: "Other things being equal, a theory that allows us readily to relate competence to performance ought to be favored over one that creates hard boundaries between the two" (p. 197). I return to this later. And, if all this were not discouraging enough, most of those linguists who do study bilingualism are more interested in describing bilingual data than in indicating how their results might contribute to linguistic theory. The goal of this chapter is to show how contact evidence, available when speakers produce bilingual clauses in a variety of types of contact phenomena, has distinct implications, not only for theories of language production, but also for generative theories of language in general.

The claim is that these data provide a window on how language is organized at the level of the mental lexicon and how it is differentially accessed at the level of the formulator (under a model modified from Levelt, 1989). The model I assume is not fully spelled out here, and it is not compared in detail with other production models simply because discussing such models, as a whole, is not a primary goal for this chapter.

In the model underlying discussion here, production is set in motion well before the projection of surface structures. At the prelinguistic conceptual level, speakers begin to map onto language their intentions about communicating. Bear in mind that speakers are communicating not only referential information, but also information about how they view their own public faces and their relationship with their listeners. This means that they make a number of decisions, largely unconscious, that consider the sociolinguistic and psycholinguistic consequences of potential choices. For monolingual speakers especially, this means considering dialectal and stylistic choices. In fact, all speakers do this as part of weighing the pragmatic implications of how they chose to speak (i.e., how ways of speaking may be interpreted by others).

Bilingual speakers have even more to consider because the decision to produce bilingual speech, especially code switching, entails much more than just selecting a monolingual style/register. (*Bilingual speech* is defined most generally as utterances that include surface-level morphemes from two or more language varieties. Code switching is one type of bilingual speech and comes in several forms, but the only type of interest here includes morphemes from two varieties *in the same clause*.) Before embarking on bilingual speech, bilinguals take into account their own proficiency and that of listeners. They also must answer for themselves a number of questions germane to the linguistic choices they face.

The big question relevant to code switching is, Will engaging in code switching result in sufficient pragmatic and social rewards to make it worth any costs? An example of a cost is that, in some communities, the public view is that code switching is "bad language." (See Myers-Scotton, 1993, and Myers-Scotton & Bolonyai, 2001, for views on why speakers engage in code switching.)

If speakers do engage in code switching, the Matrix Language Frame (MLF) model discussed here argues that speakers select—again unconsciously—what I call a Matrix Language to provide morphosyntactic structure for their bilingual speech. At the same time, speakers consider which of the participating languages is better suited to express specific intentions. According to the MLF model, the way that this decision can be carried out depends on both universal constraints imposed by the grammatical structure of code switching within a clause and on typological features of the specific languages involved. That is, although bilinguals generally can express intentions in any of their languages, the structure of how they do this is structurally constrained (cf. Jake & Myers-Scotton, 1997; Myers-Scotton, 2002a; Myers-Scotton & Jake, 2001).

With these many selections made, speaker intentions access abstract semantic/pragmatic feature bundles that are language specific, but they are not linguistic units. At this point, production becomes relatively simple, and so in some ways, it supports the view of production of La Heij (chapter 14, this volume) as "complex access, simple selection." However, he does not take into account the lemma matching (across participating languages) that Myers-Scotton and Jake (1995) saw as an essential part of selection in code switching when mixed constituents (containing morphemes from both languages) are produced. This is discussed in a later section. The model sketched here has obvious similarities to other models, especially those of Green (1986, 1998) and Poulisse (1997). Also, the approach taken here is compatible with a number of points made by Meuter (chapter 17, this volume), such as that the process of inhibition can operate both locally and globally.

The semantic-pragmatic feature bundles interface with language-specific lemmas in the mental lexicon. Lemmas support surface-level morphemes. Most specifically and in line with the work of Bock and Levelt (1994), features directly elect lemmas supporting what I call *content morphemes* (e.g., nouns and verbs). The information in other lemmas becomes salient in other ways, as will become clear. In this model, lemmas contain all the necessary information that will result in surface-level morphosyntactic structures, not just semantic information. The Abstract Level model developed by Myers-Scotton and Jake assumes that lemmas contain three levels of abstract grammatical information. First, the level of lexical-conceptual structure contains specifications for semantic and pragmatic features. Second, the level of predicate-argument structure refers to mappings of thematic roles (e.g., "agent" and "patient") onto syntactic structures and to specifications for subcategorizations of syntactic predicates (e.g., Can a verb be both transitive and intransitive? Compare *devour* vs. *eat*). The third level, morphological realization patterns, specifies the permissible surface-level configurations of morphemes (e.g., Is case expressed overtly?) as well as word order. (For more details on these levels and the Abstract Level model, see Myers-Scotton, 2002a; Myers-Scotton & Jake, 1995, 2001.) Directions sent to an articulator concerning phonetic surface-level forms are also necessary, of course, but are not discussed here.

Language Contact Studies

Within linguistics, studies of language contact have multiplied in the last 20 years, beginning with heavy interest in code switching (e.g., Pfaff, 1979; Poplack, 1980). The advent of the European Union has stimulated European interest in all forms of contact phenomena; there are many more conferences and workshops on contact languages in Europe than in North America, for example. Also, more articles and books on bilingualism have appeared, thanks as well to the "global economy," with its accompanying rise of bilingualism, especially in languages of wider communication (e.g., not only English, but also languages such as Chinese in Southeast Asia). In addition, this burgeoning interest has meant more studies of long-standing bilingual communities, especially in the third world, as well as of the new bilingual communities created by the huge influx of immigrants to nations from Australia to Norway to Canada.

Yet, many of these studies have been purely descriptive. Some are best considered under the rubric of the sociology of language because their goal was to detail patterns of language use in a bilingual community (e.g., Kropp Dakuba, 1997; Zentella, 1997). Others who considered the social side of language were engaged in theory building; but these theories refer to the psychological and social motivations for producing bilingual speech, not its grammatical nature (e.g., Auer, 1998; Myers-Scotton, 1993).

Many did study the types of grammatical structures found in a bilingual corpus, but their findings may not be of special interest to psycholinguists for two reasons. First, as indicated above, many studies were classifications that were not directed toward supporting any specific hypotheses. Second, they did not necessarily focus on data

within the bilingual clause, the crucial site at which juxtaposing of languages is a grammatical issue. Many of these were studies of code switching (e.g., Meechan & Poplack, 1995; Muysken, 2000) or mixed languages (e.g., Bakker & Mous, 1994; Matras, 2000). Some researchers have attempted to explain some code-switching data within the framework of generative syntactic theories intended to explain monolingual data (e.g., MacSwan, 1999, 2000; Ritchie & Bhatia, 1996). For a critique of such models, largely because they do not consider differing activations of the participating languages (related to the role of a Matrix Language), see Jake, Myers-Scotton, and Gross (2002) and Myers-Scotton (2002a, pp. 157–163).

Little theoretical attention has been directed to other contact phenomena, with the exception of some studies of attrition (e.g., Bolonyai, 2002) and creole formation (Bickerton, 1981, and the collection in DeGraff, 1999, as well as Myers-Scotton, 2001a). A few researchers who are primarily specialists in second language (L2) acquisition have extrapolated from their data to propose speech production models (e.g., Poulisse, 1997; Wei, 2000a, 2000b).

The Matrix Language: Embedded Language Opposition

Starting in 1993 (Myers-Scotton, 1997) and proceeding through publications with Jake (1995, 2000a, 2000b, 2001) and by myself (Myers-Scotton, 2002a), Jake and I have considered code switching within two grammatically oriented frameworks that translate into a model of production, although they are not themselves such a model. These are the MLF model and the newer 4-M (four types of morpheme) model. These models derive from looking at code switching as it actually is present in naturally occurring data. Of course, code switching is of interest to psycholinguists simply because it consists of morphemes from two languages in typically very fluent speech. But, there is a second, perhaps more important reason: There is nothing random about how these morphemes are organized in a clause once it is recognized that the participating languages have different roles and that different types of morpheme have different distribution patterns. That is, these orderly asymmetries have implications for any model of language and its organization in the mind.

The unit of analysis in these models is the bilingual CP (projection of complementizer), commonly used in syntactic theories of various persuasions. The CP is the highest unit projected by lexical elements. It can be defined unambiguously as a complementizer followed by a clause consisting of a subject and predicate. The predicate can be realized as a verb phrase or a predicate adjective phrase. Examples of complementizers are *that* in "I think that I will leave" and *if* in "If it rains, I will leave." (Note that each of these sentences contains two CPs. In the first sentence, the second CP [introduced by *that*] is embedded in the first one.) The complementizer is sometimes replaced by a specifier (e.g., a topicalizer) or a null element (e.g., in so-called independent clauses in many languages, there is no overt complementizer). Also, CPs can contain other null elements, but they are still clauses (i.e., an utterance such as "What?" is a clause with many null elements). In this chapter, I will refer to a bilingual CP simply as a bilingual clause. I will also refer to code switching as if it always occurs only between two languages, but code switching with more than two languages is entirely possible and is frequent.

Of course, there can be larger bilingual units than the bilingual clause when bilinguals speak (i.e., the sentence, the conversational turn, etc.). However, it is only in the bilingual clause that the grammars of both languages are in contact and in which the basic hierarchical opposition of the MLF model between the Matrix Language versus Embedded Language makes any sense. Sentences, of course, may contain more than one clause, and in bilingual speech not all clauses in a sentence have grammatical frames from the same language. This is a reason not to use the sentence as a unit of analysis. (There is good empirical evidence to show that within any bilingual clause the source of the grammatical frame remains the same.)

A critical feature of the MLF model is to recognize that the more important structural role in the bilingual clause goes to only one language; that is, a single language supplies the morphosyntactic frame. The frame itself is called the Matrix Language, but so is the language supplying the frame. This differentiates it from the other participating language, which is called the Embedded Language.

The Matrix Language is structurally identified by the role it plays *within* code switching. It may also be the dominant language in the speaker's community, but that does not figure in identifying the Matrix Language. Often, the Matrix Language is the first language (L1) of the speakers, but this is not always so. Obviously, speakers must be very fluent in the Matrix Language because they use it to frame the bilingual clause. They are often very fluent as well in the Embedded Language; however, depending on the type of embeddings they make in the clause, their fluency can vary. Mixed constituents consist of morphemes from both languages. Sometimes, such a constituent is the entire bilingual clause (see Example 1), but sometimes the clause includes as well monolingual constituents from either language (islands). To embed singly occurring content morphemes in mixed constituents requires less fluency than embedding whole phrasal constituents (Embedded Language Islands, as in Example 2).

Levels of Activation

The structural asymmetry between the participating languages implies that the Matrix Language has a higher level of activation than the Embedded Language. However, because the Embedded Language does supply its own elements, it is also always "on," but at a lower level. But, because of its dominant role in structuring the clause, it follows that the Matrix Language must always be on, even when an Embedded Language element is introduced, even if its level of activation is lowered, as it almost must be when Embedded Language Islands are produced. Of course, bilingual word recognition tasks (e.g., see this volume's chapters 9, 17, and 22 by Dijkstra, Meuter, and Christoffels & De Groot, respectively, for related discussion) also provide implications about differing levels of activation in the bilingual's two languages.

Note that when the Embedded Language supplies full constituents, they are often adjuncts, such as prepositional phrases, and therefore are peripheral to the core thematic grid in the clause; however, the hypothesis is that, even though they are entirely in the Embedded Language, such islands must meet the frame requirements of the Matrix Language. Still, the activation of the Embedded Language may need to be much higher when islands are produced compared with singly occurring words; after all, islands are full constituents with inflections and other functional elements (see Myers-Scotton, 2002a, pp. 139–153 on Embedded Language Islands).

Examples of Code Switching

Example 1, audio-recorded in Oslo, Norway, shows a typical example of the type of bilingual patterning that is found in code switching involving singly occurring elements. A noun from Norwegian (the Embedded Language) is morphosyntactically integrated into a frame supplied by Turkish (the Matrix Language). Note that the Norwegian noun (*skap*) receives a suffix for case from Turkish. The entire bilingual clause is an example of a mixed constituent (because it contains morphemes from two languages). The speaker is a Turkish immigrant in Norway.

Example 1 (Turkish/Norwegian, Türker, 2000, p. 68)

skap-ı	doldur-du-k
cupboard-ACC	fill-PAST-1p1

"We've filled the cupboard."
(Turkish/Norwegian, Türker, 2000, p. 68)

Example 2 illustrates a bilingual clause in Acholi/English audio-recorded in Uganda. It includes an Embedded Language Island from English ("from a good family"). Acholi is a Nilotic language. Such islands not only must be well formed in the Embedded Language, but also must meet Matrix Language requirements for the overall clause structure.

Example 2 (Acholi/English, Myers-Scotton, 2002a, p. 145)

I-ngeyo	en	pe	tye	from a good family	tutwal
2s-know	3s	NEG	COP	from a good family	really

"You know, she is not really from a good family."
(Acholi/English, Myers-Scotton, 2002a, p. 145)

Example 3 is an excerpt from a conversation audio-recorded in Nairobi, Kenya. Two young women were considering the effects of taking a job in a remote area of Kenya. Note that the English verbs *change* and *behave* receive inflections from Swahili. These Swahili prefixes and the Turkish case suffix in Example 1 are the type of system morpheme (called outsider late system morphemes under the 4-M model) that meet the requirements of the System Morpheme Principle of the MLF model. This principle states that only one of the participating languages is the source of these types of morpheme, and that this language is to be called the Matrix Language. Thus, they identify Swahili as the Matrix Language in these two clauses and English as the Embedded Language.

Example 3 (Swahili/English, Myers-Scotton, (1997, p. 103)

...U-ki-kaa huko	u-na-change
Baringo,	
2s-CONDIT-stay there Baringo,	2s-NON-PAST-change

...u-na-anz-a	ku-behave	kama	watu
			wa huko ...
2s-NON-PAST-begin	INF-behave	as	people of there

"If you stay there [in] Baringo, you change ... you begin to behave as people of there."
(Swahili/English, Myers-Scotton, (1997, p. 103)

Contrary to some impressions, speakers generally do not engage in code switching because they cannot express their intentions well enough in the language in which they began speaking. Most bilinguals who use two languages in the same clause are very proficient in the Matrix Language. They switch largely to say something that seems better said in the Embedded Language. Or, in some cases, a phrase must be completed in the Embedded Language, depending on the structures the speaker has initiated (cf. Myers-Scotton, 2002a, pp. 146–147; Myers-Scotton & Jake, 2001, for more on how islands are sometimes motivated by structure, not just pragmatics).

Matching Lemmas

A hypothesis is that when singly occurring Embedded Language elements appear in a mixed constituent, they only appear after their lemmas are matched against Matrix Language lemmas for sufficient congruence at the three levels of abstract grammatical structure (at the level of the mental lexicon). Jake and I (Myers-Scotton & Jake, 1995) developed this argument most extensively. Of course, in all likelihood, Embedded Language nouns, for example, do not match Matrix Language nouns in all ways at these levels. In fact, a main reason for selecting an Embedded Language noun is that its semantic and pragmatic content satisfies the speaker's intentions better than a Matrix Language noun. Results across many corpora show that nouns are the lexical category most often occurring as singly occurring switched elements. Because nouns only receive thematic roles (they do not assign them, as do most verbs and some prepositions), any incongruence they have with a Matrix Language counterpart at the levels of predicate-argument structure seem relatively unimportant in code switching. Further, evidence showed that they easily accept the morphological realization patterns of the Matrix Language frame, even though these may be quite different from frame-building requirements in the language they come from. For example, as in Example 1, an Embedded Language noun, which would not be case marked in the Embedded Language, receives an overt case suffix from the Matrix Language. For this to happen, it follows that not all of the information in an Embedded Language lemma supporting such a noun is activated.

Further, this state of affairs implies that the Matrix Language lemmas remain activated to send frame-building directions to the formulator throughout the bilingual clause. Note that if there is not a Matrix Language lemma to provide a close match for the Embedded Language lemma called, a solution is at hand. In addition to lemmas, the mental lexicon also includes language-specific generalized lexical knowledge that can make the match. This provision solves a number of potential problems. For example, concepts can be expressed in the Embedded Language without matches in the Matrix Language lexicon; or, brand new words for new concepts or objects can occur in either monolingual or bilingual speech. For such words to appear in code switching, they just must be incorporated in phrase structure in ways meeting the levels of predicate-argument structure and morphological realization patterns present in the Matrix Language's generalized lexical knowledge (cf. Myers-Scotton, 2002a, pp. 69, 130–131; Myers-Scotton & Jake, 1995). As a simple example, if nouns occur in an Embedded Language noun phrase with articles but nouns do not occur with articles in the Matrix Language, Embedded Language nouns can—and do—occur in code switching without any article.

Typological Differences

Word order differences, such as that of the order of nouns and their modifiers, do not seem to prevent switching. This noun phrase occurs in Swahili/English code switching: *ina "taste lousy sana,"* literally "it-with taste lousy very," with *sana* "very" from Swahili. Languages, such as Turkish or Hindi, in which verbs occur finally, participate in code switching with languages that have a subject-verb-object order.

However, inflected verbs are not easily switched in many code-switching corpora; still, such switching occurs freely in other data sets, such as in the Swahili/English example in Example 3. A reason for the difficulty in switching verbs is their major role in phrase structure: They assign thematic roles and set subcategorization frames for syntactic complements. Why verbs can be switched in some corpora and not others has largely eluded researchers to date (but, e.g., see Jake & Myers-Scotton, 1997; Myers-Scotton & Jake, 2001, for an argument why English verbs cannot receive Arabic inflections in Palestinian Arabic/English code switching).

The Uniform Structure Principle

Once the asymmetry between what the Matrix Language and the Embedded Language can supply to the bilingual clause is clear, it is obvious that code switching generally proceeds without obstacles across data sets. When there is an obstacle, compromise strategies involving little disruption in the bilingual clause suffice. I say "little disruption" because the clause that results obeys the very same basic constraints as other bilingual clauses. Further, this maintenance of uniformity is the same as that found in monolingual data. This generalization is captured in a simple, but far-reaching, Uniform Structure Principle:

> A given constituent type in any language has a uniform abstract structure and the requirements of well-formedness for this constituent type must be observed whenever the constituent appears. In bilingual speech, the structures of the Matrix Language are always preferred, but some Embedded Language structures are allowed if certain conditions are met. (Myers-Scotton, 2002a, p. 8)

In contact data, the principle explains why the participating languages never have equal roles; for example, one language typically provides the critical elements of morphosyntactic structure (in a clause) in all types of contact phenomena.

The MLF model specifies that the directions that activate frame-building system morphemes for mixed constituents in code switching must come from the Matrix Language, even if these morphemes appear with Embedded Language singly occurring elements. This provision complements the Uniform Structure Principle, which gives preference to one language (the Matrix Language in code switching) in building constituents. The formulator for bilinguals can implement directions from any language with lemmas in the speaker's mental lexicon. In this sense, the formulator is not language specific, although the operations it performs at any one time necessarily are.

Abstract Constraints on Morphology

The main argument of this chapter is that such uniformity, specifically in contact phenomena, reflects more abstract constraints on how different types of morpheme are accessed in language production. That is, I argue that what occurs in naturally occurring code-switching data and other contact data (performance) indicates that recognizing a link between competence and production better explains the nature of language than focusing only on formal models of competence.

Jackendoff: What Is Constructed Online

Now, this particular argument is not part of Jackendoff's (2002) views in his recent, far-reaching claims about a theory of language. However, it is part of Jackendoff's overall claim that what happens in production is "absolutely central in working out the instantiation of language in the mind" (p. 152). In this regard, here is the question he poses: "What aspects of an utterance *must* be stored in long-term memory, and what aspects *can* be constructed online in working memory?" (p. 152). My argument goes a step further in posing another question: Within the set of aspects that can be constructed online in working memory, is it possible that not all the lexical elements that make up these words are salient at the same point in the production process? That is, does the abstract nature of morphological elements and their particular role in phrasal structures affect how and when they are accessed?

Jackendoff's comments about morphological elements largely have to do with how they are stored. After acknowledging that some elements (e.g., content words such as *dog*) must be stored in long-term memory, he argued that morphology is treated in two different ways. First, those inflectional elements involved in productive morphology are stored in a way similar to content words. (Jackendoff referred to the relevant morphological process affecting these affixes as "regular mor-

phology not in terms of rules that add affixes, but rather as free combinations of lexically stored parts"; 2002, p. 180.)

But, the history of other inflectional elements is different for Jackendoff. Other inflection elements are "items in a semi-regular pattern [that is] simply stored" (2002, p. 187). That is, these forms (e.g., the irregular past-tense verb) in some sense are stored as completed forms, not constructed. They contrast with the products of productive morphology that are not "stored," but rather involve procedures that build things of word size or smaller and are constructed online in working memory.

Jackendoff's general conclusion was that we should take "very seriously the question of what is stored and what is computed online" because it justifies "a major reorganization of the theory of grammar" (2002, p. 193).

In this chapter, my goal is to provide evidence for a related argument: Not all of those forms that Jackendoff called grammatical words are built in the lexicon in the same way; some are only built when information on grammatical relations that take account of hierarchical information outside their immediate phrase structure is available.

Clahsen: Combinatorial Operations?

Of course, Jackendoff's position is compatible with that expressed by others, such as Clahsen (1999) and Clahsen et al. (2001). Clahsen and his associates also argued for the "dual structure of the language faculty," but based their claims on experimental findings. The question Clahsen (1999) asked is whether empirical findings "are to be accounted for by combinatorial operations (such as rules of language) or by (access to) lexical entries" (p. 991). In my terms, what he meant is this: Do irregular forms that contain an inflection have their own lemma, or are they part of the same lemma as that for the basic stem?

Clahsen (1999) focused on German noun plurals and participles and amassed evidence comparing various types of responses to regular versus irregular inflected entries. He concluded that, "Lexically restricted (irregular) inflection is not rule-based" (p. 994). Instead, the inflection is part of the lexical item itself. Thus, the argument is that irregular forms are not assembled via rules that join together a base form and an inflection.

Clahsen et al. (2001) reached similar conclusions. They investigated German adjectives and

German strong verbs. These are verbs that change their base form (e.g., *bring-en* [to bring]) to show tense/aspect (e.g., *ge-bracht* [brought] past participle), although they may also take regular tense/aspect inflections as well, as do German weak verbs. The authors had an unsurprising result in lexical decision experiments: Subjects showed shorter response times for high-frequency verb stems than low-frequency ones. But, what was interesting was that response time for the participle forms of strong verbs was related to the frequency of the participles themselves, not to the frequency of the verb stem of these participles. This finding indicated that participles of these verbs were considered as units on their own, not as part of the basic stem of the same verb.

Ullman's Declarative/Procedural Model

The declarative/procedural model of Ullman (2001) is also relevant to the argument about different morpheme types developed in this chapter. Under this model, there are two memory systems, the "declarative" memory system, which contains memorized words, and the "procedural" memory system, which is implicated in the learning of new motor and cognitive "skills," including grammatical information.

Like some other models, Ullman's model posits that the lexicon and grammar are two separate computational systems, but he argued that there are not different components dedicated to each of these capacities. This is important because Ullman argued that differences in performance in late bilinguals in their L2, as compared with their L1, indicate that they process language differently and that the difference is in their use of these two memory systems. He argued that "the processing of linguistic forms that are computed grammatically by procedural memory in L1 is expected to be dependent to a greater extent upon declarative memory in L2" (p. 109). Thus, his argument offers an explanation for why speakers in an L2 do not perform with the same grammatical accuracy that they can in their L1 and may explain why L2 learners have problems with acquiring certain types of grammatical knowledge.

Overall, he cited a wide array of evidence from L2 learning to aphasia to functional neuroimaging about the neural bases of L2 learning. Unfortunately, for the argument I develop here, Ullman was not very specific about what he included under the type of learning that the procedural memory system subserves. However, he did say that "[T]his system may be particularly important in the learning and computation of sequential and hierarchical structures (i.e., in grammatical structure building)" (p. 107).

As will become clear, I indicate that it is important to differentiate types of grammatical morpheme, reflecting the fact that they have different distributions across various types of data. However, especially those morphemes that are most critical in "grammatical structure building" are the ones for which I posit a different route to production. They are also the ones that seem to be hardest to acquire accurately in late L2 learning (cf. Myers-Scotton & Jake, 2000a; Wei, 2000a, 2000b).

The views of Clahsen, Jackendoff, and Ullman, as well as the results of other researchers, such as Marcus, Brinkman, Clahsen, Weise, and Pinker (1995) and Pinker (1999), lead to a particular view of the nature of lemmas in the mental lexicon as it relates to morpheme decomposition. This view is compatible with part of the argument I make here about the nature of different types of grammatical morphemes, how they are organized in the mental lexicon, and how they become salient in production. Data from contact phenomena add strong evidence substantiating the claim that there are lemmas supporting several types of elements. Both content morphemes and regular inflections are supported individually in the mental lexicon (by different lemmas), but there also are holistic lemmas for elements that Jackendoff referred to as "semiproductive."

Code Switching Data as a Window on Combinations

In code switching, regular inflectional elements from one language can join with content morphemes from another language; this is strong evidence that regular inflections are supported as individual elements in the mental lexicon, as just suggested. At the same time, code switching also provides good evidence that Jackendoff's semiproductive elements are based on single units in the mental lexicon; they are not constructed on line. The evidence is that Embedded Language nonfinite verb forms, especially for the participles, from different languages always appear as holistic units in code switching. This is discussed in a later section. However, first the basics of the MLF model are presented more fully.

Predictions of the Matrix Language Frame Model

The MLF model applies specifically to what I have called classic code switching since 1993 (Myers-Scotton, 1997). This is code switching in which the Matrix Language (the source of the abstract morphosyntactic frame for the bilingual clause) is uniformly one of the participating languages for all constituents in the clause. Recall this language is also called the Matrix Language to distinguish it from the other participating language.

Another type of code switching, which I call composite code switching, may well be just as common, if not more so (Myers-Scotton, 1998, 1999, 2002a). In composite code switching, some of the abstract structure underlying the frame comes from more than one of the participating languages—even though one language still dominates in supplying the frame (cf. Myers-Scotton, 2002a, on grammatical convergence and code switching). Such switching occurs when, for a variety of reasons, speakers' proficiency (or related social evaluations and uses) in one participating variety is waning, and it is waxing in the other variety.

Theoretically, the inevitable end point of composite code switching is language shift to the waxing language as the community's dominant language (i.e., monolingual speech would replace code switching). The alternative end point is fossilization of the code-switching patterns at some point (i.e., resulting in a mixed/split language, but there are very few such languages). Only classic code switching is discussed in this chapter, even when the referring term is just *code switching*.

The MLF model is based on two predictions about the asymmetry between the participating languages in structuring bilingual clauses in classic code switching. The first prediction is that only one language supplies the morphosyntactic frame (i.e., can be the Matrix Language). The frame is the set of abstract well-formedness constraints on how the clause is structured. The second asymmetry refers to the source of the surface-level morphemes that indicate syntactic relations across mixed constituents in the frame. The prediction is that, although the Embedded Language contributes content morphemes to mixed constituents, only Matrix Language morphemes indicate grammatical relations within such constituents.

In the MLF model, two testable principles encapsulate details of these predictions, the Morpheme Order Principle and the System Morpheme Principle (Myers-Scotton, 1997, p. 83). The Morpheme Order Principle simply predicts that only one language sets the morpheme order in code switching and identifies that language as the Matrix Language. The System Morpheme Principle also identifies the Matrix Language by making predictions about critical inflections in mixed constituents and is discussed in detail in a later section. Of course, even before 1990, some researchers recognized anecdotally this difference in the roles of the two languages in mixed constituents (e.g., Hasselmo, 1972, Haugen, 1950, and Weinreich, 1953/1967, were among the first, followed by others in the 1980s, e.g., Joshi, 1985, and Sridhar & Sridhar, 1980).

Words With Input From Two Languages

Because the predictions of the model are that the Matrix Language supplies the frame and its frame-building grammatical elements and (implicitly) allows the Embedded Language to supply only content morphemes, the implication is that only inflections from the Matrix Language will appear on Embedded Language content morphemes in mixed constituents in classic code switching. And, this is what happens as far as the frame-building inflections are concerned. Examples abound in code switching of how combinations of Embedded Language content morphemes with inflections from the Matrix Language satisfy the requirements of the Matrix Language morphosyntactic frame. As noted, nouns more readily than verbs accept alien inflectional elements in some language pairs, but examples for both lexical categories are easily found. (There are 91 finite English verb forms with Swahili inflections in the Nairobi corpus of Swahili/English code switching; cf. Myers-Scotton, 1997, p. 88 ff.) Of course, all examples of Embedded Language content morphemes with Matrix Language inflections support the hypothesis that lexical words showing regular morphology are constructed online.

Regular Morphology Across Languages in Code Switching Examples

In addition to the three examples cited above that show how code-switching units are constructed online with input from both languages, I cite two other examples here. Example 4 comes from Ewe, a language in the Akan cluster of language varieties in Ghana. Ewe can be identified as the Matrix Language based on its frame-building features in this clause. The English verb *weed* receives the Ewe inflection for habitual aspect, and the English noun *garden* receives the definite suffix from Ewe. The Ewe suffix for habitual aspect (*-na*) is the type of inflection that identifies Ewe as the Matrix Language under the System Morpheme Principle. This principle does not specify that inflections, such as the definite suffix on *garden*, must come from the language identified as the Matrix Language. However, recall that the Uniform Structure Principle gives preference to maintaining the structure of the Matrix Language. This explains why Ewe also supplies this suffix. Note that *garden* appears in a postpositional phrase headed by Ewe. This phrase follows Ewe order, not that of English, in support of the Morpheme Order Principle.

Example 4 (Ewe/English, Amuzu, 1998, p. 56, cited in Myers-Scotton, 2002a, p. 89)

wo	ts'-na	wo	fe	asi-wo	ts'-na
3PL	take-HAB	3PL	POSS	hand-PL	take-HAB
weed-na	garden-a	me-ε			
weed-HAB	garden-DEF	in-FOC			

"They take [use] their hands to weed in the garden"
(Ewe/English, Amuzu, 1998, p. 56, cited in Myers-Scotton, 2002a, p. 89)

Example 5 comes from Croatian, in contact with English in the speech of Croatian second-generation immigrants in Australia. Croatian is a morphologically rich language with inflections that contain more than one morpheme in one phonological unit. In this case, an English verb (*pack*, transcribed as /pak/ by Hlavac) is inflected with such a Croatian multimorpheme unit. It contains the subject-verb agreement suffix for both first person singular and present tense. The English noun *container* (transcribed as /kontejner/ by Hlavac) receives a suffix for masculine, singular, and accusative. These inflections (subject-verb agreement and accusative case) are the type of frame-building morphemes that, according to the System Morpheme Principle, must come from only one of the languages.

Example 5 (Croatian/English, Hlavac, 2000, p. 392, cited in Myers-Scotton, 2002a, p. 90)

...i tako	one... [kontejner]-e i tako dalje ...	
[pak]-ujem		
and so	those	container- and so on
pack-1S/PRES		M/PL/ACC

"And so [I] pack those...containers and so on ..."
(Croatian/English, Hlavac, 2000, p. 392, cited in Myers-Scotton, 2002a, p. 90)

Code-Switching Evidence for the Holistic Nature of Nonfinite Verb Forms

Depending on the language pair, nonfinite Embedded Language verbs serve a variety of functions in code switching. These verb forms are multimorphemic on their own; that is, they consist of a content morpheme and a so-called inflectional morpheme that fits the type of early system morpheme under the 4-M model. Such system morphemes are defined and exemplified in a following section. However, even though nonfinite verbs are multimorphemic, they always occur as holistic Embedded Language units, even if they receive Matrix Language inflections as well. (For example, in *tuko confused* [we are confused], a clause from Swahili/English code switching, the English past participle is intact, as it would be in a monolingual English clause.)

In contrast, in those language pairs in which the Embedded Language finite verb can receive Matrix Language inflections, the finite verb never occurs in mixed constituents with any Embedded Language inflections as it would have in monolingual data. (For example, recall *u-na-change* [you will change] in Example 3 from Swahili/English code switching; *change* does not appear with any English inflections.) This difference across finite and nonfinite verb forms is evidence that the nonfinite verbs are supported by single lemmas in the mental lexicon.

Recall the statement that, in many language pairs, Embedded Language verbs with agreement or tense/aspect affixes from the Matrix Language do not occur. Instead, in these language pairs, speakers produce the Matrix Language verb for *do* and inflect it with the relevant Matrix Language affixes. This do verb is then followed by a nonfinite (not marked for tense) form of the Embedded Language verb that carries the speaker's intended meaning. In all cases in the literature, no matter what the specific language pairs, the nonfinite verb form appears as the single unit it is in monolingual data. The nonfinite form is typically the infinitive (stem + infinitival affix), but it also can be the present participle in some language pairs. In Example 6, this do construction is illustrated from Turkish/Dutch code switching, with the Dutch infinitive *kijk-en* (watch). There are no examples of Dutch finite verbs receiving Turkish inflections.

ja, maar toch, millet	kijk-en	yap-ıyor
yeah, but still, everybody	watch-INF	do-PROG/3s

"Yeah, but still, everybody is watching you."
(Turkish/Dutch, Backus, 1996, p. 238)

Example 6 (Turkish/Dutch, Backus, 1996, p. 238)
In other language pairs, when inflecting an Embedded Language verb stem with Matrix Language tense/aspect affixes seems blocked, a different compromise strategy is employed (cf. discussion in Jake & Myers-Scotton, 1997; Myers-Scotton, 2002a; Myers-Scotton & Jake, 1995, on congruence). For example, in Acholi/English code switching, a nonfinite Embedded Language verb form occurs very freely and serves several different functions, replacing a finite verb in some constructions. The English present participle is this ubiquitous form. (Acholi, the Matrix Language, is a Nilotic language spoken in Uganda.) Altogether, there are 48 examples in the relatively small corpus studied that show the English present participle functioning in three ways. In only one case does the participle function as a fully inflected verb (with Acholi tense/aspect inflections). Half of the participles (24/48) do receive a subject-verb agreement prefix and then function as part of a reduced relative clause or otherwise subordinate clause (e.g., *gi-doing* [they doing/they who do] as in Example 7).

Example 7 (Acholi/English, Myers-Scotton, 2002a, p. 94)

jo ma-pol	i kom	kare ni	camo	meal	acel
					keken
people	in body/LOC	period	eat	meal	one
COMP-many		this			only
gi-doing	lunch a	gi-camo	supper		
labongo			keken		
3PL-do without	lunch then	3PL-eat	supper only		

"People [who are] many in this period eat only one meal, [people who] do without lunch, then they eat supper only."
(Acholi/English, Myers-Scotton, 2002a, p. 94)

Another 29% (14/48) occur in Acholi infinitive verb positions (i.e., they are equivalent to infinitives), either with or without the Acholi infinitival prefix (as in *ka terrorizing* [to terrorize]). Finally, 21% (10/48) are gerunds or other types of nominals (as in the prepositional phrase *labongo considering life* [without considering life]) or in associative constructions (e.g., *chances me surviving* [chances of surviving] with Acholi *me* as "of").

Some nonfinite verb forms (usually infinitives) also appear as holistic units under the phenomenon that I call *double morphology*. In such a case, an Embedded Language content morpheme (most often a noun) appears with the relevant Matrix Language affix (for plural on nouns, for infinitival marker on infinitive forms). What makes the form noteworthy is that the relevant Embedded Language affix also appears with its Embedded Language head. In examples in which French is the Embedded Language, French infinitives sometimes appear in their holistic (i.e., French) form, but with an infinitival inflection from the Matrix Language. For example, in Congo Swahili/French code switching, the infinitival form *ku-re-nvyoy-er* (to return) appears (Kamwangamalu, 1987, p. 172). Nouns showing double morphology are discussed in the section on early system morphemes.

In addition to the three types of constructions with nonfinite Embedded Language forms that appear holistically in code switching as verb forms, in many language pairs Embedded Language past participles function as predicate adjectives. Again, they always appear as a holistic form. In the Nairobi corpus studied for my work in 1993 (Myers-Scotton, 1997), there are eight examples. One is illustrated in Example 8.

Example 8 (Swahili/English code switching, Nairobi corpus, Myers-Scotton, 1988)

lakini	si	i-ta-ku-w-a	biased?
but	NEG/COP	CL.9-FUT-INF-COP-FV[1]	biased

"But won't it be biased?"
(Swahili/English codeswitching, Nairobi corpus, Myers-Scotton, 1988)

Examples 6 through 8 support the claims (from Jackendoff, Clahsen, and others) discussed here about the differential nature of how surface forms are supported by lemmas in the mental lexicon: Some lemmas support content morphemes, and in combination with lemmas that support regular inflections, they produce inflected words online, even cross-linguistically. But, lemmas that support irregular forms or most nonfinite forms are not productive in this sense. The evidence from code switching is that Embedded Language nonfinite verb forms appear as holistic forms is additional evidence that some words (which contain a so-called inflectional morpheme) are supported as full forms (by lemmas) in the mental lexicon; they are not constructed on line.

Basic Asymmetries in Contact Data

Now, having supported the argument that not all inflected words are accessed in the same way, I return to a related argument and the main goal of this chapter, to argue for differential routes of access from the mental lexicon. Systematic study of naturally occurring data since at least the early 1990s from diverse pairs of languages in contact support two basic asymmetries. Much of this research has been on code switching, but the asymmetries are evident in other language contact phenomena as well. These asymmetries refer to the difference in the roles of content morphemes and what I refer to as system morphemes. The first asymmetry is this: There is a basic split between content morphemes (the lexicon) and the grammar in how they participate in structuring language.

This split is graphically reflected in most contact phenomena. In this chapter, I illustrate that split with code-switching data discussed in terms of the MLF model. How this split is played out differs somewhat across contact phenomena, with variations on the split partly based not only on differences in the proficiency of speakers in the languages involved, but also on the effects of sociopolitical factors. However, I stress that the fact there is a split at all has more to do with the abstract aspects of the types of morpheme than with these external factors, including such psycholinguistic factors as frequency.

As a quick example, in the most prevalent of all contact phenomena—lexical borrowing—how does it happen that nearly 100% of borrowed forms are content words? Content morphemes are the prime candidates for borrowing for two reasons. First, content words signal speaker's intentions (intentions to convey meanings). Second, they are directly accessed at the level of the mental lexicon; this means they are more accessible immediately, and they are more salient than system morphemes (Bock & Levelt, 1994, referred to them as "directly elected").

Further, similar asymmetries between content morphemes and grammatical elements in other contact phenomena become obvious. For example, content morphemes either are modified first (and what is modified most is their lexical-conceptual structure) or are replaced first when speakers show attrition in their L1 and more use of an L2 dominant in the community (cf. Myers-Scotton, 2002a; Schmitt, 2001). In addition, any examination of creoles shows that content morphemes from the superstrate language have quite a different role than superstrate grammatical elements (system morphemes) in shaping the creole (Myers-Scotton 2001b, 2002a). (*Superstrate* refers to the language variety spoken by the overseers/owners present at the time of creole formation.)

The second asymmetry is this: Different types of system morpheme have different patterns of distribution across many contact phenomena. The term *system morpheme* was employed under the MLF model because it captures generalizations not available under other designations. The model distinguishes content morphemes from system morphemes by this criterion: Content morphemes assign or receive thematic roles; system morphemes do not. Note that this criterion does not identify as system morphemes the same morphemes as does a "functional element" (cf. Myers-Scotton 2002a; Myers-Scotton & Jake, 2000b). For example, pronouns in English are content morphemes.

Four Types of Morpheme in the 4-M Model

To motivate a hypothesis that explains differences in distribution, I need to present the basics of the 4-M model. This model differentiates four types of morpheme: content morphemes and three types of system morpheme. (The term *morpheme* is used in the model in two ways: It refers to not only the abstractions underlying surface-level morphemes, but also as the surface-level forms themselves.) In code switching, although Embedded Language content morphemes can occur relatively freely in a mixed constituent, Embedded Language system morphemes cannot. The MLF model captures this notion, but the 4-M model makes further refinements in the category of system morpheme, making possible finer-grained explanations of distributions.

The 4-M classification receives independent motivation from the phrase structure properties of the four morpheme types. *Content morphemes* are defined as those that assign/receive thematic roles and head their immediate maximal projections (e.g., noun phrase). *Prototypical content morphemes* are nouns and verbs. *Thematic roles* refer basically to the semantic roles in any clause (e.g., "agent" or "patient"). *System morphemes* are defined as those inflections and functional elements that do not assign or receive thematic roles. In English, for example, some prepositions are content morphemes (e.g., *for* in "I did it for Stella"; *for* assigns the thematic role of beneficiary to *Stella*). But, some are system morphemes like *at* in "look at that dog."

Early system morphemes are different from late system morphemes in several ways. First, they pattern with content morphemes in sharing the feature of conceptual activation. They can be thought of as fleshing out the meaning of content morphemes. Second, they depend on their content morpheme heads in their immediate maximal projections for their form. (They are what Bock and Levelt, 1994, seemed to have had in mind by referring to some words as "indirectly elected.") However, under the 4-M model, the type of early system morpheme includes not only words (e.g., determiners), but also inflections (e.g., derivational affixes and affixes marking plural).

In contrast with early system morphemes, the two types of late system morpheme do not depend on their heads in syntactic structures. This difference is related to the Differential Hypothesis, which is developed in the next section. In fact, the reason they are called "late" is that they are hypothesized to be projected later than either content morphemes or early system morphemes.

Within the category late system morpheme, bridge late system morphemes are projected when a grammatical configuration (the immediate maximal projection in which they occur) requires them. Thus, *of* in "collar of Bora" is a bridge. Bridges are invariant, at least in all languages examined within the terms of the 4-M model to date. They are called bridges because their role is to join together elements to produce a constituent that is well formed in the relevant language. Thus, in French *il* in "*il pleut chaque jour*" ("It rains each day") is such a bridge (and is different from its homonym, the third person pronoun *il*, which refers to an object).

Outsider late system morphemes are called outsiders because they depend for their form on information from outside their immediate maximal projection. That is, their form is coindexed with elements outside the maximal projection in which they occur. They differ from bridges in this way

and because they have two or more variants. It is not until a larger constituent is assembled that it is clear which variant of their form is to be used. For example, in English, the past tense morpheme is an outsider. Whether past tense is encoded by -*ed* or by the auxiliary verb *do* in its past tense form is not clear until the clause is assembled. With regular verbs in declarative statements, the form is -*ed*. But in interrogative sentences, the verb *do* takes the past tense inflection (as in "Did you go there yesterday?") Subject-verb agreement is also an outsider late system morpheme. Note how subject-verb agreement has two variants in the present tense English; it is marked with -*s* for third-person singular, but with a null element for the other persons and numbers. In languages with overt case, such as German, case also is an outsider late system morpheme. When elements signaling morphology are multimorphemic (e.g., German determiners, which include morphemes for number, gender, and case), the late system morpheme (case) seems to be most salient (cf. Myers-Scotton & Jake, 2000a, 2001, on Italian/Swiss German code switching).

A way to summarize the four types of morpheme is in terms of the abstract oppositions that can separate them. Both content morphemes and early system morphemes have the feature [+ conconceptually activated], but late system morphemes do not. Content morphemes are further differentiated from all system morphemes because they have the feature [+ thematic role assigners/receivers]. Finally, outsider late system morphemes are distinguished from bridge late system morphemes based on phrase-building operations. Late outsiders have the feature [+ requires outside operations], but bridges do not. Across languages, the definitions under the 4-M model do not necessarily put the same lexical categories or types of affix into the same morpheme type. However, the same definitions of morpheme type apply across all languages; therefore, any morphemes across languages that fit the same definition are the same type. (For example, not all the affixes that Hungarian grammarians refer to as case markers are the same morpheme type as what are called case markers in German.)

The Differential Access Hypothesis

The preceding discussion makes it clear that morphemes can be classified under the 4-M model in terms of the different roles that the morphemes have in phrase structure. What is of more interest here is that these four types have different distribution patterns in contact phenomena. (Their differential distribution in monolingual data is also of interest, but not a subject here.) That is, when two languages are present in a clause, the morpheme types do not observe the same restrictions on occurrence. The point has already been made that not all types of morpheme can come from both languages in mixed constituents in code switching. Data presented in the following sections make details of this asymmetry clearer. Limited discussion of data from other contact phenomena also points to asymmetries in how morpheme types can occur. That these asymmetries exist implies differences in the morpheme types, not just in terms of their roles in surface phrase structure, but also at some abstract level. The Differential Access Hypothesis offers an explanation for these differences, referring to how the morphemes are accessed in production. The Differential Access Hypothesis is the following:

> The different types of morpheme under the 4-M model are differentially accessed in the abstract levels of the production process. Specifically, content morphemes and early system morphemes are accessed at the level of the mental lexicon, but late system morphemes do not become salient until the level of the formulator. (Myers-Scotton, 2002a, p. 78)

The hypothesis implies the following scenario for accessing late system morphemes: Lemmas underlying content and early system morphemes send language-specific directions to the formulator to build larger linguistic units. These instructions contain information about assigning late system morphemes to these larger structures. That is, the information in the lemmas supporting late system morphemes does not become salient until the content morphemes that have directions about the syntactic roles (and morphological realizations) of late system morphemes call them.

The Differential Access Hypothesis is similar to Garrett's views (e.g., 1975, 1993, inter alia). He noted that "major and minor grammatical category words behave quite differently" (1993, p. 81). He referred to open class elements as "recruited by direct retrieval processes." For him, the *closed class* elements are "minor category elements that rarely appear in exchanges" and are "recruited as parts of structural frames, most particularly planning frames associated with phonological phrasing" (p. 81). One difference seems to be that Garrett did not

differentiate types of system morpheme and their level of access in relation to content morphemes (and, of course, in my view, not all closed class items are system morphemes).

Note that my hypothesis does not preclude the notion of simultaneous processing; structure at one level does not have to be completed before work at another level begins. Further, the terms "early" and "late" are used more or less metaphorically in the 4-M model. That is, when I say that certain types of morpheme are not activated until later than other types, this simply means their activation depends on salience of the earlier elements, making certain directions and combinations available for procedures at the level of the formulator.

However, note that by separating early system morphemes from late system morphemes, this hypothesis calls into question the implied notion that all constructions with regular morphological elements undergo language production in the same way. True, all system morphemes can be seen as combining with other lexical items to satisfy the variable pattern involved. But, when and where they are assembled is not the same. Thus, my view differs in an important way from the views of Pinker, Clahsen, and others.

Further, in the terms of the 4-M model, my colleagues and I view the English participial forms as necessarily consisting of a content morpheme and an early system morpheme, not a late system morpheme. This difference is relevant to when these forms are accessed.

Even though the participial suffixes often appear on lists of English inflectional suffixes in textbooks, they are more like derivational affixes than other inflectional suffixes in that they change the meaning of the content morpheme that is their head (e.g., present participles can function as gerunds; past participles can function as predicate adjectives, etc.). True, past participles share the same phonetic form with past tense forms for many verbs (e.g., stop, stopped, stopped), but this does not mean that the two verbs are isomorphic in more than form.

Exemplifying Asymmetries in Code Switching With System Morphemes

As indicated, asymmetries in the distribution of system morphemes characterize all contact phenomena, but most dramatically code switching. The MLF model attempts to capture this asymmetry in the System Morpheme Principle. This principle distinguishes among system morphemes by specifying that one type must come from the Matrix Language in mixed constituents, those with "grammatical relations external to their head constituent" (Myers-Scotton, 1997, p. 83). (Unfortunately, many researchers have interpreted the principle as applying to all system morphemes; cf. Myers-Scotton, 2001b.) Because the 4-M model explicitly divides system morphemes into three types, this division should make clearer the limited scope of the System Morpheme Principle. The principle refers only to those morphemes called outsider late system morphemes under the 4-M model. Frame building in the bilingual clause depends on these morphemes because they indicate hierarchical relations beyond those in immediate maximal projections. That is, the role of outsiders is to knit together the clause. For this reason, it is no surprise that they must come from the language from which the morphosyntactic frame is derived.

Outsider Late System Morphemes and the Matrix Language

Examples 9 and 10, as well as the examples cited previously, show that the System Morpheme Principle makes the right predictions for outsider late system morphemes in code switching. In Example 9, even though the verb for *telephone* comes from French, the subject-verb agreement marker (the prefix *na-*) comes from Lingala (the Matrix Language). The reason that this marker is an outsider morpheme is that its form (i.e., which person and number will it refer to?) is not clear until the verb is put in the larger clause with the NP that contains *Ngai* (I).

Example 9 (Lingala/French, Meeuwis & Blommaert, 1998, p. 86; I added the glosses)

Ngai   moto   na-téléphoner.   na-téléphon-aki   na tongo
1s   person   1s-telephone   1s-telephone-PAST   at morning
"I am the one who called. I called this morning."
(Lingala/French, Meeuwis & Blommaert, 1998, p. 86; glosses added by CM-S)

Example 10 came from a Hungarian child who is being raised in the United States and who, at the time of this recording, showed a good deal of code switching between Hungarian and English. (Later, she showed increasing attrition of Hungarian as English became her dominant language.) In this example, she integrated the English noun *caterpillar* into the Hungarian frame by inflecting the noun

with the accusative case suffix that such a direct object would receive in Hungarian. Again, the case that the noun *caterpillar* will receive in this clause is not known until the noun phrase containing it is combined with the verb, which assigns the thematic role of patient to the noun and the case of accusative.

Example 10 (Hungarian/English code switching, Bolonyai, 1998, p. 33)

el-   -enged-t-em   a   caterpillar-t
PREVERB   let- -PST-1s   the   caterpillar-ACC
"I let the caterpillar go."
(Hungarian/English codeswitching, Bolonyai, 1998, p. 33)

Exemplifying Special Distributions for Early System Morphemes

Various researchers have observed that occasionally some system morphemes are doubled in code switching; that is, both the Matrix Language and the Embedded Language versions of the same system morpheme occur with an Embedded Language head. The plural affix is doubled most frequently (e.g., *ma*-ghost-s) in Swahili/English CS, with *ma-*, the prefix marking Swahili noun Class 6 (a plural class). Such instances of double morphology were explained as the result of "mistiming" (Myers-Scotton, 1997). Speakers access an Embedded Language noun that they intend as a plural, and the Embedded Language affix for plural is accessed along with the noun, even though what the morphosytactic frame calls for is the Matrix Language plural affix alone. Doubling of such morphemes is called *double morphology*.

The 4-M model and the Differential Access Hypothesis provide an explanation of why this mistiming happens only with early system morphemes and motivates the following Early System Morpheme Hypothesis: Only early system morphemes may be doubled in classic code switching.

The motivation is as follows: Early system morphemes have a very different relation with the heads in their immediate maximal projection than other system morphemes. Like their heads, early system morphemes are conceptually activated. Under the Differential Access Hypothesis, they are salient at the same time as their content morpheme heads (in the mental lexicon). Thus, they are available for any mistiming to occur. (Evidence that this doubling is a type of "error" is that the doubling only occurs occasionally in code-switching corpora.)

In contrast to early system morphemes, also according to the Differential Access Hypothesis, the structurally assigned system morphemes (late system morphemes) are not available until the level of the formulator. Thus, that double morphology does not affect late system morphemes offers support for this hypothesis.

Examples 11 and 12 show plural affixes from both the Matrix Language and the Embedded Language. Example 11 includes two suffixes, one (-lar) from Turkish (the Matrix Language) and the other (-en) from Dutch (the Embedded Language) on the Dutch noun for *Pole*. Note as well that the Dutch noun receives the Turkish suffix for dative case, in line with the System Morpheme Principle.

Example 11 (Turkish/Dutch, Backus, 1992, p. 90)

Pol-en-lar-a   Holandaca   ders   verdi.
Pole-PL-PL-DAT Dutch   lesson give/PRET-S
"He taught Dutch to Poles."
(Turkish/Dutch, Backus, 1992, p. 90)

Example 12 from Shona/English CS illustrates the English noun *lesson* with the plural noun Class 6 prefix (*ma-*) from Shona for plural and an English suffix (-s) as well. This word also has a Shona prefix for the locative noun Class 18 (*mu-*) that signals the concept of "in." (In effect, *mu-ma-lesson-s*, a noun phrase, is the equivalent of an English prepositional phrase). Nouns in Bantu languages, such as Shona, fall into one of up to 18 or more noun classes and generally have an overt prefix identifying the noun class.

Example 12 (Shona/English, Bernsten & Myers-Scotton, 1988, corpus)

...va-no-nok-a ku-it-a catch-up mu-ma-lesson-s
CL2/PL-hab-be   INF—do-FV   cl.18/LOC-CL.6/PL
late-FV   catch-up   -lesson-PL
"...they are late to catch up in [their] lessons."
(Shona/English, Bernsten & Myers-Scotton, 1988, corpus)

The Uniform Structure Principle Again

Why should the Matrix Language call its own affix in the case of double morphology, as well as in other

cases when only outsider late system morphemes must come from the Matrix Language? For example, why is there a Shona plural marker on the English noun *lesson* in Example 12? Although there is nothing in the MLF model to require that early system morphemes come from the Matrix Language, the Uniform Structure Principle (cited above) gives preference to maintaining the same source of structural elements in any constituent. Under the System Morpheme Principle, outsider morphemes in any mixed constituent in code switching must come from the Matrix Language; thus, to maintain uniformity, the bias is for other system morphemes to come from the Matrix Language as well. And, the code switching literature largely gives evidence of this bias. There are only a few reported examples of early system morphemes and only one bridge system morpheme reported (Arabic *djal* [of] when French is the Matrix Language).

Are Embedded Language Plural Affixes Active?

Embedded Language nouns with their plural suffixes occur in some data sets without the expected Matrix Language marking for plural. Such forms are called *bare forms* because they are not well formed from the standpoint of the Matrix Language. In such cases, researchers are not agreed on the status of this Embedded Language plural marker (cf. Boumans, 1998, for another view). I argue that the Matrix Language marker cannot be accessed because of as yet poorly understood congruence problems between the languages involved. (For example, in Boumans's Moroccan Arabic/Dutch corpus, it is possible that a Dutch noun cannot be inflected with an Arabic plural marker because the Arabic morphosyntactic frame does not "recognize" the Dutch noun as a candidate for Arabic plural inflection; cf. Jake & Myers-Scotton, 1997; Myers-Scotton & Jake, 2001.)

However, there is evidence that the Embedded Language plural marker is in fact accessed *as part of its head* and not as an active system morpheme signaling plural. Some evidence comes from examples found in a Chichewa/English corpus.

In Example 13, the English noun (with plural marking) *apples* occurs, but it is modified by the Chichewa word for "one" (*i-modzi*), which also has a noun class prefix for Class 9, a singular class. The speaker, whose L1 was Chichewa, spoke English fluently, so one cannot explain *apples* in terms of incomplete learning. Rather, again, this seems to be a case of mistiming. (See Myers-Scotton, 2002a, pp. 129–131, for an explanation of how Chichewa Class 9 agreement is spread from the English noun to the Chichewa modifier.)

Example 13 (Chichewa/English CS, Simango, 2000, p. 494)

Ngoni, ta-mu-send-er-a   mw-ana apple-s   i-modzi
IMPER-OBJ/3s-peel-APPL-FV CL1-child apple-PL CL9-one
"Ngoni, peel one apple for the child."
(Chicheîa/English CS, Simango, 2000, p. 494)

Evidence of Asymmetries in Other Contact Data

Naturally occurring data in various types of contact phenomena show how the asymmetry between different types of system morpheme plays out. The most dramatic example may come from classic code switching, in which all outsider late system morphemes (those indicating grammatical relations across phrase structure in the bilingual clause) in mixed constituents must come only from one language, the Matrix Language (the source of the morphosyntactic frame for the bilingual clause). All indications are that this distribution holds across diverse code-switching data sets, although few have been studied quantitatively, and singly occurring exceptions may occur. One quantitative study (Myers-Scotton, 2002b) found that the Matrix Language is the source of all late system morphemes in mixed constituents in all bilingual clauses in the corpus ($N = 229$). Another study (Finlayson, Myers-Scotton, & Calteaux, 1998) reported the same finding for all bilingual clauses ($N = 124$).

Further evidence about asymmetries concerning morpheme type comes from interlanguage (speech produced by L2 learners). Beginners' accuracy is much lower on late system morphemes than other morphemes. For example, English third-person singular -s is less accurately produced by low-level L2 learners than is noun plural -s (an early system morpheme) (Wei, 2000a, 2000b, on Japanese and Chinese learners of English). This finding even applies to advanced L2 learners (Blazquez-Domingo, 2001, on English speakers studying Spanish). They are much less accurate in producing a Spanish preposition that is an outsider morpheme than they are in producing prepositions that are either content morphemes or early system morphemes.

Similar differences apply to other types of contact phenomena. For example, in cases of L1 attrition,

speakers show different patterns of substitution and retention for late system morphemes than they do for the early ones (Bolonyai, 1999, 2002, for Hungarian children living in the United States who were taking on English as their dominant language). Other attrition studies showed that, contrary to some beliefs, outsider morphemes (specifically case markers) are very resistant to loss (Gross, 2000, on long-term German residents in the United States and Hlavac, 2000, on second-generation Croatian speakers in Australia).

More evidence supporting the notion of differential access is available from diverse sources, including monolingual data. For example, the link the 4-M model makes between early system morphemes and content morphemes is borne out in lexical borrowing and in speech errors. Recall that the two morpheme types share the feature of conceptual activation. Speakers of one language sometimes borrow from another language an early system morpheme along with its noun. There are a number of such borrowings from Arabic in various European languages (e.g., *alcohol* from Arabic [*al* + *kuhl*], *al* [the] and *kuhl* [used to make absinthe]). Or, speakers forming a creole sometimes assume an early morpheme preceding a noun is part of the noun (e.g., *lavyan* in Mauritian Creole from French *la viande* [meat]). Also, in speech errors when affixes are "stranded," English plural affixes move with their content morpheme heads more often than is predicted by chance (e.g., "I presume you could get light in poorer picture-s"; Stemberger, 1985, p. 162, cited in Myers-Scotton, 2002a, p. 83). In addition, the asymmetry between the distribution of conceptually activated morphemes (content and early system morphemes) and structurally assigned (late) system morphemes is also evident in the data on speech by Broca's aphasics reanalyzed by Myers-Scotton and Jake (2000a).

Further, I (Myers-Scotton, 2002a) also looked at asymmetries in morpheme distribution in other contact phenomena in relation to the 4-M model and the Differential Access Hypothesis. In the next section, one contact phenomenon, creole development, is discussed in some detail in the terms of the argument of this chapter.

Creole Development and Asymmetries Among Morpheme Types

In creole structure, the contributing languages play different roles as well. A composite of the substrate languages (i.e., the L1s of the slaves/workers developing the creole) is the likely source of most of the abstract morphosyntactic base in any creole. The superstrate or lexifier language (the variety spoken by overseers/owners in the creole scenario) also plays its part. It supplies most of the content morphemes to fill this frame in two ways. First, superstrate content morphemes express most of the intended referential messages. Second, of more interest, these morphemes also appear in reconfigured forms as late system morphemes to meet the requirements of the morphosyntactic frame (Myers-Scotton 2001a, 2002a).

Reconfiguring Content Morphemes as System Morphemes

Creoles develop when workers speaking different L1s are thrown together and need to communicate with each other and their overseers. Attempting to learn the language of the overseers (the superstrate) is often a favored option, but because the workers have limited interactions with superstrate speakers, they have limited possibilities for learning the superstrate language. That is, creole formation is related to L2 acquisition, but it does not have the same structural outcome because the conditions of learning are different. Instead of acquiring an L2 version of what might be called the target language, speakers acquire a new language, the creole.

As just noted, workers develop a language (the creole) that largely has superstrate words. The result is that a creole, such as Gullah, the data source exemplified here, appears to be a version of English. In fact, it is quite different. One reason for the difference is that the morphosyntactic frame for a creole seems to be largely drawn from a composite of the languages of the workers who developed the creole, not from the superstrate language. A second reason, relevant to the 4-M model, is that not all types of English morpheme appear in the creole, and some appear in a reconfigured form.

Jake and I (Myers-Scotton & Jake, 2002) showed that differences in the distribution of English morphemes are predictable based on the 4-M model and the Differential Access Hypothesis. Our reasoning is this: Because content morphemes are conceptually activated (i.e., they convey semantics and pragmatics), they are more accessible to the creole speakers than late system morphemes. Late system morphemes signal grammatical relations, but their uses are not so transparent as are those of content morphemes to the language learner with limited access to hearing the target language used. Also, superstrate late system morphemes do not necessarily meet the requirements of the morphosyntactic frame if we accept the view that this frame comes largely from the substrate languages. Thus, we predicted that English language system morphemes would not occur in a creole with English as its superstrate language.

We (Myers-Scotton & Jake, 2002) tested this Creole System Morpheme Hypothesis by analyzing four texts (108 lines) from Gullah (Turner, 1949/2002). Gullah is a creole spoken on the coast and offshore islands of South Carolina; it has English as its superstrate language. The study concentrated on instances of English regular verb inflections that are outsider late system morphemes (third-person singular present tense -s or past tense -ed). Presumably, verb forms with these morphemes would be assembled online (at the level of the formulator, according to the Differential Access Hypothesis). Results showed that, of all verbal tokens with opportunities for such regular inflections ($N = 26$), English inflection was missing in 100% of the cases. An example of a context for a third-person singular present tense suffix (-s), but with no suffix, is [*i ca fû men (he care[s] for men)*]. There are a few examples of irregular past tense verbs (e.g., *I took*) and six examples of irregular verbs showing either subject-verb agreement (five examples of *is*) or subject-verb agreement and past tense (one example of *was*), but it is likely these are present in the mental lexicon as units and not assembled on line.

Also, creoles give other evidence, in addition to missing verb inflections, that superstrate late system morphemes are not available in creole formation. In both Jamaican Creole (in which one might expect existential *it* from English in "weather clauses" and similar clauses) and in Haitian Creole (in which one would expect the French clitic pronoun *il* to serve this existential role), these superstrate forms are missing. Examples (from Holm, 1988, p. 88) all translate in English as "it's raining." In these cases, the superstrate existential pronoun is a bridge late system morpheme. (In the Gullah texts analyzed by Myers-Scotton & Jake, 2002, the existential *it* was also absent in 27/27 opportunities.)

Example 14a

ren a faal
(Jamaican Creole)
English: *"Rain is falling/It's raining"*

Example 14b

lapli ap tonbe
(Haitian Creole)
French: *"La pluie est tombé"* (Rain is falling)
French: *"Il pleut"* (It is raining)

Yet, to integrate content morphemes into the hierarchical structures that are the defining feature of language, those outsider system morphemes required by the frame must come from somewhere. Reconfigured content morphemes can fill at least some of these roles in creoles. Examples of content morphemes as tense/aspect markers are found in many of the Caribbean creoles. For example, English *been* (as *bin*) signals unmarked (i.e., nonhabitual) anterior tense in many of the English-based creoles, including Gullah. (Anterior tense refers to completed action anterior to the time in focus, not the time of the utterance.) One reason *been*, the past participle of be, may be so accessible is that it is not a lexical word that is assembled online, but is available as a single unit in the mental lexicon. And, in such French-based Caribbean creoles as Haitian Creole, French *aprés* (after) is reconfigured as *ap* to signal progressive aspect.

The hypothesis that content morphemes are available from the superstrate for creole formation because they are conceptually activated implies that early system morphemes, which also are conceptually activated, should be available. And, this is what Jake and I (Myers-Scotton & Jake, 2002) found in the Gullah texts analyzed. The texts showed that at least one type of early system morpheme, verb satellites (particles), occurred along with their head verbs very freely, such as *kʌm tru* (come through) and *tʌk ʋut* (took out). In her two texts, one speaker (Diana) had 14 types of this early system morpheme, with 22 tokens of them, and the other speaker (Rosina) had 11 types and 13 tokens.

Example 15 (Turner, 1949/2002, Rosina text, pp. 280–281)

wɛn dɪ yaŋɪkʌm tru…an i tʌk ʋut ɛwɪtlŋ ʋut dɪ hʋus.
"When the Yankee come through.... And he took out everything out of the house."
(Turner, 2002, Rosina text, p. 280–281)

Creole Development and Two Targets

Clearly, paralleling the code-switching data, the creole development data also illustrate the split between the distribution of conceptually activated morphemes on the one side and structurally assigned ones on the other. In effect, there are two targets in creole development, one for the lexicon and one for the morphosyntactic frame. By implication, both the code-switching data and the creole data support the hypothesis that not all morphemes are accessed in the same way. The fact that the structurally assigned late system morphemes bind together the larger constituents (i.e., the clause), indicating relationships between lower-level phrase structures, indicates that the difference lies at the level of the formulator. This is where directions for larger units are received.

In summary, in creole formation, the outsider system morphemes from the superstrate seem to be inaccessible. One reason is the abstract nature of outsiders; they simply are not as easily learned in limited contact as are the conceptually activated morphemes. A second reason may be how they are accessed. Directions contained in the lemmas supporting English words do not meet the specifications of the creole morphosyntactic frame. Yet, there is a frame (largely from the substrates), and to meet some of that frame's specifications, English content morphemes can be reconfigured as outsider system morphemes. This is what seems to happen across creoles in general. Superstrate content morphemes are reconfigured to serve as outsider late system morphemes; those marking tense and aspect in verbs have been most studied (cf. Myers-Scotton 2001a, 2002a, pp. 277–293). In sum, creole formation proceeds in predictable ways given the 4-M model and the Differential Access Hypothesis.

Summary

Of course, the question that arises regarding the notion that speakers somehow do not treat all morphemes alike in surface-level distributions is this: How do the speakers "know" which types of morphemes go where? Jackendoff (2002) became understandably cautious in answering related questions about universal grammar (UG). He referred to "rules of grammar as lexical constructions of more or less specificity or generality.... They are learned by extracting general variables from previously stored items" (p. 191). Jackendoff's answer to the question, "What guides the extraction?" is UG, but his own version of UG. He said, "Suppose that Universal Grammar consists of a collection of skeletal fragments of l-rules [lexical rules] built into lexical memory" (p. 191).

What about my argument that a basic distinction between types of morpheme is universally evident and in a wide variety of linguistic data? Is this a reason to assume that this distinction is part of UG? Yes and no. I take a different perspective and look instead to production, not UG, as the first line of explanation for these data. This enables me to sidestep the issue of exactly which elements of linguistic structure in humans have a universal basis.

That is, I choose to pay more attention to the production problem than the innateness problem. I try to support two related points that are different sides of the same issue. First, the following important production problem needs to be recognized. To arrive at the surface level, production has to deal with linear input, but we know that language is organized in a hierarchical, not linear, fashion. We need to know that noun A can be the object of verb A without necessarily occurring next to it, or that noun B can be the beneficiary of the action encoded in the verb, but not be next to the verb. How is this hierarchical knowledge introduced into the linear stream?

My second point suggests a solution to this problem, namely, that this vital information about hierarchies and relations among the content morphemes is conveyed from these elements once they arrive at the level of the formulator. Structurally assigned system morphemes (the late system morphemes) that only become available at this point perform these tasks. Therefore, the timing of their salience and the basic conceptually activated versus structurally assigned distinction of the 4-M model are features of the production system. Further, making this distinction is more of an operation than it is a principle, so the issue becomes whether UG includes operations. Jackendoff himself hinted at this idea: "A system of grammatical relations and a system of morphological agreement makes a lot of sense as refinements of a syntax-semantic mapping" (2002, p. 264). He also indicated such a system is part of the interface system between phrasal syntax and meaning. Given that the asymmetries in how morphemes are distributed show every indication of universality, how this interface operates may well be part of UG, admittedly an enlarged sense of UG. Although evidence of these asymmetries is available in monolingual data, the divisions are more obvious in bilingual data. Contact data offer an especially transparent window on production and, necessarily, competence.

Note

1. In examples from Bantu languages (e.g., Swahili, Shona), the morph gloss "FV" in verbs stands for "final vowel." It carries no meaning on its own, but it is part of a meaningful pattern of inflections. Also, words in Bantu languages have a consonant-vowel-consonant-vowel (CVCV) pattern (i.e., they must end in vowels).

References

Amuzu, E. (1998). *Aspects of grammatical structure in Ewe-English codeswitching*. Unpublished master's thesis, University of Oslo, Norway.

Auer, P. (1998). Introduction: Bilingual conversation revisited. In P. Auer (Ed.), *Code-switching in conversation* (pp. 1–24). London: Routledge.

Backus, A. (1992). *Patterns of language mixing: A study of Turkish-Dutch bilingualism*. Wiesbaden, Germany: Harrassowitz.

Backus, A. (1996). *Two in one: Bilingual speech of Turkish immigrants in the Netherlands*. Tilburg, The Netherlands: Tilburg University Press.

Bakker, P., & Mous, M. (Eds.). (1994). *Mixed languages: 15 case studies in language intertwining*. Amsterdam: Institute for Functional Research into Language and Language Use.

Bernsten, J., & Myers-Scotton, C. (1988). [Shona/English corpus]. Unpublished raw data.

Bickerton, D. (1981). *Roots of language*. Ann Arbor, MI: Karoma.

Blazquez-Domingo, R. (2001). Not all prepositions are equal: Differential accuracy by advanced learners of Spanish. *Journal of Spanish Applied Linguistics, 5*, 163–192.

Bock, J. K., & Levelt, W. (1994). Language production: Grammatical encoding. In M. A. Gernsbacher (Ed.), *Handbook of psycholinguistics* (pp. 945–984). New York: Academic Press.

Bolonyai, A. (1998). In-between languages: Language shift/maintenance in childhood bilingualism. *International Journal of Bilingualism 2*, 21–43.

Bolonyai, A. (1999). *The hidden dimensions of language contact: The case of Hungarian-English bilingual children*. Unpublished doctoral dissertation, University of South Carolina, Columbia.

Bolonyai, A. (2002). Case systems in contact: Syntactic and semantic case in bilingual child language. *Southwestern Journal of Linguistics* 21, 1–35.

Boumans, L. (1998). *The syntax of codeswitching: Analysing Moroccan Arabic/Dutch conversations.* Tilburg, The Netherlands: Tilburg University Press.

Clahsen, H. (1999). Lexical entries and rules of language: A multidisciplinary study of German inflection. *Behavioral and Brain Sciences, 22,* 991–1060.

Clahsen, H., Eisenbeiss, S., Hadler, M., & Sonnenstuhl, I. (2001). The mental representation of inflected words: An experimental study of adjectives and verbs in German. *Language, 77,* 510–543.

DeGraff, M. (Ed.). (1999). *Language creation and language change, creolization, diachrony, and development.* Cambridge, MA: MIT Press.

Finlayson, R., Myers-Scotton, C., & Calteaux, K. (1998). Orderly mixing and accommodation in South African codeswitching. *Journal of Sociolinguistics, 2,* 395–420.

Garrett, M. (1975). The analysis of sentence production. In G. Bower (Ed.), *Psychology of learning and motivation* (Vol. 9, pp. 133–177). New York: Academic Press.

Garrett, M. (1993). Errors and their relevance for models of language production. In G. Blanken, J. Dittman, H. Grimm, J. C. Marshall, & C.-W. Wallesch (Eds.), *Linguistic disorders and pathologies* (pp. 72–92). Berlin, Germany: Mouton de Gruyter.

Green, D. W. (1986). Control activation and resource. *Brain and Language, 27,* 210–223.

Green, D. W. (1998). Mental control of the bilingual lexico-semantic system. *Bilingualism: Language, and Cognition, 1,* 67–81.

Gross, S. (2000). *The role of abstract structure in first language attrition: Germans in America.* Unpublished doctoral dissertation, University of South Carolina, Columbia.

Hasselmo, N. (1972). Code-switching as ordered selection. In E. Finchow, K. Guinstad, N. Hasselmo, & W. O'Neil (Eds.), *Studies for Einar Haugen* (pp. 261–280). The Hague, The Netherlands: Mouton.

Haugen, E. (1950). The analysis of linguistic borrowing. *Language, 26,* 210–231.

Hlavac, J. (2000). *Croatian in Melbourne: Lexicon, switching and morphosyntactic features in the speech of second-generation bilinguals.* Unpublished doctoral dissertation, Monash University, Melbourne, Australia.

Holm, J. (1988). *Pidgins and creoles* (Vol. 1). Cambridge, U.K.: Cambridge University Press.

Jackendoff, R. (2002). *Foundations of language.* Oxford, U.K.: Oxford University Press.

Jake, J., & Myers-Scotton, C. (1997). Codeswitching and compromise strategies: Implications for lexical structure. *International Journal of Bilingualism, 1,* 25–39.

Jake, J., Myers-Scotton, C., & Gross, S. (2002). Making a minimalist approach to code-switching work: Adding the Matrix Language. *Bilingualism: Language, and Cognition, 5,* 69–91.

Joshi, A. (1985). Processing of sentences with intrasentential code switching. In D. R. Dowty, L. Karttunen, & A. Zwicky (Eds.), *Natural language parsing* (pp. 190–205). Cambridge, U.K.: Cambridge University Press.

Kamwangamalu, N. M. (1987). French/vernacular code mixing in Zaire: Implications for syntactic constraints on code mixing. *Chicago Linguistic Society Proceedings, 22,* 166–180.

Kropp Dakuba, M. E. K. (1997). *Korle meets the sea, A sociolinguistic history of Accra.* New York: Cambridge University Press.

Levelt, W. J. M. (1989). *Speaking: From intention to articulation.* Cambridge, MA: MIT Press.

MacSwan, J. (1999). *A minimalist approach to intrasentential code switching: Spanish-Nahuatl bilingualism in Central Mexico.* New York: Garland.

MacSwan, J. (2000). The architecture of the bilingual language faculty: Evidence from intrasentential code switching. *Bilingualism, Language, and Cognition, 3,* 37–54.

Marcus, G., Brinkman, F., Clahsen, H., Weise, R., & Pinker, S. (1995). German inflections: The exception that proves the rule. *Cognitive Psychology, 29,* 189–256.

Matras, Y. (2000). Mixed languages: A functional-communicative approach. *Bilingualism, Language, and Cognition, 3,* 79–99.

Meechan, M., & Poplack, S. (1995). Orphan categories in bilingual discourse: Adjectivization strategies in Wolof-French and Fongbe-French. *Language Variation and Change, 7,* 169–194.

Meeuwis, M., & Blommaert, J. (1998). A monolectal view of code-switching: Layered code-switching among Zairians in Belgium. In P. Auer (Ed.), *Code-switching in conversation* (pp. 76–98). London: Routledge.

Muysken, P. (2000). *Bilingual speech: A typology of code-mixing.* Cambridge, U.K.: Cambridge University Press.

Myers-Scotton, C. (1988). [Swahili/English Nairobi corpus]. Unpublished raw data.

Myers-Scotton, C. (1993). *Social motivations for codeswitching: Evidence from Africa.* Oxford, U.K.: Clarendon Press.

Myers-Scotton, C. (1997). *Duelling languages: Grammatical structure in codeswitching* (2nd ed.). Oxford, U.K.: Clarendon Press.

Myers-Scotton, C. (1998). A way to dusty death: The Matrix Language Turnover Hypothesis. In L. Grenoble & L. Whaley (Eds.), *Endangered languages: Language loss and community response* (pp. 289–316). Cambridge, U.K.: Cambridge University Press.

Myers-Scotton, C. (1999). Putting it altogether, the Matrix Language and more. In B. Brendemoen, E. Lanza, & E. Ryen (Eds.), *Language encounters across time and space* (pp. 13–28). Oslo: Novus.

Myers-Scotton, C. (2001a). Implications of abstract grammatical structure: Two targets in Creole formation. *Journal of Pidgin and Creole Languages, 16,* 1–56.

Myers-Scotton, C. (2001b). The Matrix Language Frame Model: Developments and responses. In R. Jacobson (Ed.), *Codeswitching worldwide II* (pp. 23–58). Berlin, Germany: Mouton de Gruyter.

Myers-Scotton, C. (2002a). *Contact linguistics: Bilingual encounters and grammatical outcomes.* Oxford, U.K.: Oxford University Press.

Myers-Scotton, C. (2002b). Frequency and intentionality in (un)marked choices in codeswitching: "This is a 24-hour country." *International Journal of Bilingualism, 6,* 205–219.

Myers-Scotton, C., & Bolonyai, A. (2001). Calculating speakers: Codeswitching in a rational choice model. *Language in Society, 31,* 1–28.

Myers-Scotton, C., & Jake, J. (1995). Matching lemmas in a bilingual language production model: Evidence from intrasentential codeswitching. *Linguistics, 33,* 981–1024.

Myers-Scotton, C., & Jake, J. (2000a). Four types of morpheme: Evidence from aphasia, codeswitching, and second language acquisition. *Linguistics, 38,* 1053–1100.

Myers-Scotton, C., & Jake, J. (Eds.), (2000b). Testing a model of morpheme classification with language contact data. *International Journal of Bilingualism, 4,* 1–8.

Myers-Scotton, C., & Jake, J. (2001). Explaining aspects of codeswitching and their implications. In J. Nicol (Ed.), *One mind, two languages: Bilingual language processing* (pp. 84–116). Oxford, U.K.: Blackwell.

Myers-Scotton, C., & Jake, J. (2002, January). *Sources of inflection: Testing the Creole System Morpheme Hypothesis.* Paper presented at the annual meeting of the Society for Pidgin and Creole Linguistics, San Francisco, CA.

Pfaff, C. (1979). Constraints on language mixing: Intrasentential code-switching and borrowing in Spanish/English. *Language, 55,* 291–318.

Pinker, S. (1999). *Words and rules: The ingredients of language.* New York: Basic Books.

Poplack, S. (1980). Sometimes I'll start a sentence in Spanish y termino Español: Toward a typology of code-switching. *Linguistics, 18,* 581–618.

Poulisse, N. (1997). Language production in bilinguals. In A. M. B. de Groot & J. F. Kroll (Eds.), *Tutorials in bilingualism: Psycholinguistic perspectives* (pp. 201–224). Mahwah, NJ: Erlbaum.

Ritchie, W., & Bhatia, T. (1996). Codeswitching, grammar and sentence production: The problem of light verbs. In E. C. Klein & G. Martoharjono (Eds.), *The development of second language grammars* (pp. 269–287). Amsterdam: Benjamins.

Schmitt, E. (2001). *Beneath the surface: Signs of language attrition in immigrant children from Russia.* Unpublished doctoral dissertation, University of South Carolina, Columbia.

Simango, S. R. (2000). "My madam is fine": The adaption of English loans in Chichewa. *Journal of Multilingual and Multicultural Development, 21,* 487–507.

Sridhar, S. N., & Sridhar, L. (1980). The syntax and psycholinguistics of bilingual codemixing. *Canadian Journal of Psychology, 34,* 407–416.

Stemberger, J. P. (1985). An interactive model of language production. In A. Ellis (Ed.), *Progress in the psychology of language* (Vol. 1, pp. 143–186). London: Erlbaum.

Türker, E. (2000). Turkish-Norwegian codeswitching: Evidence from intermediate and second generation Turkish immigrants in Norway. (Doctoral dissertation, University of Oslo, Norway). Oslo, Norway: Unipub.

Turner, L. (2002). *Africanisms in the Gullah dialect.* Columbia: University of South Carolina Press. (Reissued, with a new introduction by K. W. Mille and M. B. Montgomery) (Original work published 1949, reissued 1967).

Ullman, M. (2001). The neural basis of lexicon and grammar in first and second language: The declarative/procedural model. *Bilingualism, Language, and Cognition, 4,* 105–122.

Wei, L. (2000a). Types of morphemes and their implications for second language morpheme acquisition. *International Journal of Bilingualism, 4,* 29–43.

Wei, L. (2000b). Unequal election of morphemes in adult second language acquisition. *Applied Linguistics, 21,* 106–140.

Weinreich, U. (1967). *Languages in contact.* The Hague, The Netherlands: Mouton. (Original work published 1953)

Zentella, A. C. (1997). *Growing up bilingual, Puerto Rican children in New York.* Malden, MA: Blackwell.

Renata F. I. Meuter

17

Language Selection in Bilinguals
Mechanisms and Processes

ABSTRACT   One fruitful approach to the study of the processes underlying language selection in bilinguals is the analysis of the costs associated with the act of switching from one to the other language. This chapter reviews the experimental findings concerning the cognitive processes that enable the configuration of a switch of language, as well as those that allow a language, once selected, to be maintained. The effects of relative proficiency and language context are evaluated, as is the role of monitoring, and are discussed in the context of current models of bilingual language processing.

Abilities often admired by those who have only limited knowledge (if any) of another language but their own are not only communicating in a foreign tongue, but also the seemingly effortless switching between languages that bilinguals (and polyglots) often display in their communicative interactions. How do bilinguals selectively control the two (or more) languages available to them? How is a switch of language accomplished? This question is even more interesting when one considers nonbalanced bilinguals, for whom it can be assumed that the languages might be asymmetrically established and for whom the selection of a dominant versus a weaker language would require different levels of effort. Most individuals (bilingual or not), when asked, probably would reason that the more proficient, dominant language L1 (typically, but not always, also acquired first) would be the easiest language to use. This intuition is appealing. After all, that at which you are comparably better is easier to do and completed faster.

Although this perception often is true, it is based on performance when already in full flight. Thus, a bilingual might be observed, now conversing fluently in L1, having been overheard commenting—only moments before—in the weaker language (L2). Little attention is paid to the way in which the actual shift between languages is achieved. If speaking the dominant language L1 is easier than speaking the weaker language L2, does it follow

that switching to L1 is easier also? To begin answering this question, we need to consider briefly the architecture of the bilingual lexicon.

Much research focuses on the storage of information pertaining to the different languages, with respect to orthography, conceptual information, and phonology, as well as access to lexical information (for reviews, see Dijkstra, 2001, and chapter 9, this volume; Kroll & De Groot, 1997; Kroll & Dijkstra, 2002; Smith, 1997). Although consensus has not been reached on all fronts as yet, there is considerable evidence in favor of shared or common conceptual representation (e.g., De Groot, 1993), with a variable degree of overlap at the level of orthography (e.g., Bowers, Mimouni, & Arguin, 2000; De Groot & Nas, 1991; Dijkstra & Van Heuven, 1998; Grainger & Dijkstra, 1992; Van Heuven, Dijkstra, & Grainger, 1998; see also Kirsner, Smith, Lockhart, King, & Jain, 1984) and phonology (e.g., Pallier, Colomé, & Sebastián-Gallés, 2001), depending on the extent of similarity between the languages concerned.

Given the complex nature of bilingual language representation, the bilingual's skillful selection of first one, then the other language, often rapidly and intentionally and often within the same conversation or sentence, is even more impressive (see, for example, Clyne, 1980, 1997). These switches of language also occur unintentionally, such as L1 language intrusions in less-proficient L2 speakers

("I have *ook*, I have uh, a brother too" [too]; Poulisse & Bongaerts, 1994, p. 13) or when the speaker is under some stress (Dornic, 1979, 1980; Grosjean, 1982). Other instances of erroneous language selection—as they occur unintentionally and spontaneously in multilingual speakers—were described by Shanon (1991; see also Clyne, 1997, for a discussion of triggered code switches). The sometimes unintentional nature of the phenomenon is suggestive of the cognitive processes and mechanisms that drive language selection. Why does this type of interference occur when at other times the bilingual appears perfectly capable of keeping the two languages separate?

This chapter focuses on the research that has looked at language selection and control experimentally, primarily by studying basic speech production skills such as naming. Typically, bilinguals at varying levels of relative proficiency in their two languages are put in an experimental situation that requires they switch from one to the other language. The focus is on the controlled and willed selection of single responses in a bilingual setting and not on language switching as it occurs spontaneously and (un)intentionally in code switching. Concentrating on individual responses enables the comparative analysis of response latencies under controlled conditions, allowing the evaluation of the role of relative proficiency, language context, and the interplay between the two languages.

Although these tasks (such as the simple naming of pictures in alternate languages) may appear restrictive, there is no a priori reason to assume that the basic processes allowing the occurrence of a—presumably intentional—switch of language in conversation (as motivated by a change of interlocutor or topic) might not be similar, or even identical, to a switch of language occurring in response to task instructions in a naming task. Issues of language selection in conversation and the rules underlying the manner in which different language systems interact in fluent speech are discussed elsewhere in this book (see also Poulisse, 1997, for a recent review). Reference is made to research findings from the monolingual domain as well, in particular those relating to the cognitive processes underlying an individual's ability to switch between different tasks. This is not meant to imply that speaking a Language A (L_A) in favor of a Language B (L_B) is akin to switching, for example, between reading a word (Task A) or naming the color in which it is presented (Task B), but rather to recognize that the nature of the selection processes may be similar.

Four related questions are addressed. First, what are the processes by which interference between multiple languages is prevented? That is, how is a language de-selected? An important issue here is the extent to which, if at all, the de-selection of a language is generalized to that entire language system. Is language selection global or local; that is, do the de-selection or inhibition processes operate on the language as a whole or only on those constituents of the concepts that are relevant?

Second, how might the selection processes be affected by relative proficiency in the respective languages? A reasonable supposition might be that greater proficiency in a language facilitates performance in that language generally.

Third, what are the factors that trigger a language switch, and how effective are they? For example, do language-specific information cues activate the entire language system? Of particular interest here is the type of information that may serve as a cue to determine language choice. External cues, such as occur when the other language is heard, may cause the bilingual to become—if only momentarily—linguistically disoriented and result in a switch of language. Alternatively, such cues may motivate an intentional switch.

The fourth question then becomes, once a language switch has been accomplished successfully, how is the selected language maintained? Here, the role of monitoring is discussed, as is its importance in preventing the bilingual from falling back into the language previously spoken and maintaining the language of choice, particularly if this is the weaker language.

The Selection and De-selection of Languages

It has long been known that switching between languages takes a measurable amount of time (e.g., Dalrymple-Alford, 1967; Kolers, 1966, 1968; Macnamara, Krauthammer, & Bolgar, 1968; Macnamara & Kushnir, 1971). By and large the early experiments aimed at studying intentional language switching in production measured the time taken to read (and comprehend) written monolingual and mixed passages (Kolers, 1966, 1968; Macnamara & Kushnir, 1971). For example, comparisons were made between passages consisting of mixed sentences such as "His horse, followed *de deux bassets, faisait la terre résonner* under its even tread" ("His horse, followed by two hounds, made the earth resound under its even tread"; Kolers, 1966, p. 359) and monolingual passages. The cost associated with a language switch was placed somewhere between 0.2 and 0.5 s. These tangible costs were beautifully consistent with Clyne's (1980) observations that code switches in spontaneous conversation were often preceded by some hesitation, suggesting a time cost as a result of (preparation for) a switch.

The early research was marred by a number of methodological issues, not least of which was the underlying assumption of a fixed time cost, unchanged by the direction of the switch from L1 to L2 or vice versa. (See also Grosjean, 1997, and Paradis, 1980, for further criticisms, including problems with the grammaticality of the code-switched material used, as in the example given.) Typically, a measure of the switch cost was obtained by subtracting the overall response latencies associated with naming/reading monolingual passages, or lists of words, from those associated with the mixed-language presentation and dividing the difference over the number of language switches in the mixed presentation. It was therefore impossible to determine whether (as would be intuitively presupposed) it was easiest to switch to the dominant language. By using averaging procedures, the role of the bilingual's relative proficiency in the two languages was ignored also, as was the possible effect of current language use on the relative ease of switching.

In spite (or perhaps, irrespective) of the limitations of the data, the switch cost thus calculated was striking enough to give rise to a number of theories attempting to explain its origin. One of the most persistent theories held that, at a physiological level, there must be a localizable

> automatic switch that allows each individual to turn from one language to another.... When a child or adult turns to an individual who speaks only English, he speaks English, and turning to a man who speaks French and hearing a word of French, the conditioning signal *turns the switch over* [italics added] and only French words come to mind. (Penfield & Roberts, 1959, p. 253)

This first mention of a language switch mechanism focused on the production of speech, assumed a clear separation between the languages, and assumed that language selection was an externally (exogenously) driven process. I return to the notion of external cueing (e.g., as signaled by a change in interlocutor) implied in this description in the section on language selection and cueing of language choice.

Motivated by the results of an early bilingual Stroop study demonstrating the bilingual's inability to ignore irrelevant and potentially interfering language information at input (Preston, 1965, as cited in Macnamara, 1967a), the idea of a language switch was extended to a model encompassing two switch mechanisms. To account for bilinguals' ability to comprehend their two languages, an automatic switch was postulated, operating at input.[1] Regulating the selection of language in production was a controlled switch at output (Macnamara, 1967a; Macnamara & Kushnir, 1971; see also Caramazza, Yeni-Komshian, & Zurif, 1974; Dornic & Laaksonen, 1990).

The observed switch costs occurred, it was argued, because the *"ease in making a correct response is exactly balanced by difficulty in inhibiting a wrong one* [italics original]" (Macnamara, 1967b, p. 734). In other words, one of the processes underlying the language switch mechanism was that of inhibition, thought to operate such that responses in the dominant language (L1) were harder to suppress, and consequently responses in the weaker language (L2) were more difficult to produce on a switch of language. This difficulty was balanced out by the comparative ease of suppressing responses in the weaker L2 to speak in the stronger L1.

The logical inference is that it should be easier to switch to the dominant L1 than to the weaker L2. Macnamara's (1967b) explanation derived from a study requiring participants to generate—rather than name—words either in one language only or in alternating fashion between their two languages (Irish and English) and was based only on differences in the number of words produced in the different conditions. No response latencies were obtained, thus preventing not only the analysis of the latencies associated with a language switch, but also, more importantly, any comparisons of those latencies with respect to the direction of the switch (from L1 to L2 or vice versa). Macnamara therefore lacked the data (a fact he acknowledged) to verify his theory. Although its constituent assumptions are not incorrect, there is now evidence to suggest that this is not how a switch of language is effected.

Selection and Control: Global or Local Inhibitory Processes?

If the ease with which L_A is suppressed or deselected is not directly commensurate with ease with which the L_B is produced, then what are the processes and mechanisms that allow the bilingual to switch languages, and at what level of selection do these operate? There are various points at which selection can occur and conceivably also degrees to which selection can occur.

On the one hand, it may be that only the possible alternative (same and other-language) responses are suppressed when selecting one language over the other. There is evidence from bilingual word recognition at least that, even on a monolingual task, alternative lexical candidates in the other language are accessed also (e.g., Dijkstra & Van Heuven, 1998; Van Heuven et al., 1998; see also Kroll & Dijkstra, 2002, for a review). The data do not allow the evaluation of whether the entire other language system is activated, but do indicate that all related representations in both lexica are activated and available until fairly late in the selection process (Dijkstra, Grainger, & Van Heuven, 1999; see also Dijkstra, Timmermans, & Schriefers, 2000). For spoken word recognition, similar findings have been reported, suggesting that even in a monolingual setting the irrelevant language is accessed (Spivey & Marian, 1999).

On the other hand, it may be that an entire language system is suppressed to enable error-free use of the other language system appropriate under the circumstances. This latter possibility is one that has been incorporated in a number of recent theories. For example, in bilingual word recognition it has been suggested that language nodes control the degree to which any given language is (more or less) activated through excitatory connections with all word nodes in that language (the Bilingual Interactive Activation model; Dijkstra & Van Heuven, 1998; Grainger, 1993; see also Dijkstra, chapter 9, and Thomas & Van Heuven, chapter 10, this volume; see also Grosjean, 1997, and Li & Farkas, 2002, for arguments against the need to postulate language nodes). A similar proposal was put forward by Green (1986, 1993, 1997, 1998a) to explain the processes underlying the bilingual's ability to control her two languages. To illustrate the way in which such control may be implemented in the system, this model is briefly discussed here.

Green's Inhibitory Control (IC) model (Green, 1993, 1997, 1998a) holds that lemmas are tagged for language-specific information, and these tags are either inhibited or activated by language task schemas. The language task schemas (reminiscent of the schema as proposed originally by Norman & Shallice, 1986, for the control of actions; see also Cooper & Shallice, 2001) are thought to control

language actions (e.g., name a numeral or a picture in L_A rather than L_B). As part of their specified goal, language information is coded also. Competition for output from the lexico-semantic system occurs at the level of the language task schemas, either inhibiting or activating lemmas according to the task relevance of their associated language tags. When the competition is between automatic or routine behaviors (e.g., reading a word aloud, as prompted by its language membership), the winning schema is determined through contention scheduling.

When the competition cannot be resolved easily and selection is willful and deliberate (e.g., when a novel task is carried out, such as naming a picture in a language as cued by a color), contention scheduling is controlled and monitored by the Supervisory Attentional System (SAS; Norman & Shallice, 1986; Shallice, 1988; Shallice & Burgess, 1996). The word, in the correct language, is produced eventually through (a) inhibitory control modulated by the SAS, inhibiting all lemmas with inappropriate language tags; and (b) activation by the SAS of the relevant language task schema. Importantly, lemma selection in L_B—through the inhibition of items in L_A—does not exclude those same items from competing in the selection process. The idea of a supervisory system that monitors language behavior is not a novel one. Obler and Albert (1978) proposed, although not perhaps in as much detail, a bilingual monitor system thought to process, inter alia, linguistic and other cues from the environment and operating continuously to activate the relevant language system.

Implicit in the IC model is the notion that the language as a whole will be affected, because the language task schemas selectively activate or inhibit lemmas according to the task requirements (i.e., to produce L1 or L2) (see also the Bilingual Production model; De Bot, 1992; De Bot & Schreuder, 1993). However, Green (1998b) did suggest that the inhibitory effects are not necessarily global only, but potentially can be selective. For example, translation equivalents and related concepts could be inhibited more strongly than other concepts (as has been shown in bilingual word recognition).

How does the interplay of inhibitory processes affect bilingual language selection in the production of speech? To answer this question, a detailed analysis of the latencies associated with switches of language is required. From this, it emerges that, contrary to early speculations (Macnamara, 1967b), a switch of languages when producing a verbal response is paradoxically slower when switching back to the dominant L1 (Meuter, 1994; Meuter & Allport, 1999). Bilingual participants named numerals rapidly and unpredictably in either L1 or L2, as signaled by a color cue.

As can be seen in Fig. 17.1, the switch costs, although not immediately obvious to a listener, are nevertheless measurable and significant (mean cost for a switch from L2 to the dominant L1 = 143 ms; mean cost for a switch from L1 to the weaker L2 = 85 ms). The switch cost is determined by subtracting from the mean response latency associated with (for example) the first switch to L1, the mean response latency on nonswitch trials in L1 (immediately preceding the first occurrence of L2 switches). The increased response latencies occur on a switch only and are markedly slower in L1 than in L2. When no switches are made, efficiency is once again greater in L1 (i.e., faster response latencies).

Across a series of studies, including numeral naming (Meuter & Allport, 1999), superordinate naming (Meuter, 1994), switching languages in conversation (Meuter, 2001), and picture–word interference (Meuter, 1994), this reverse dominance pattern on a switch of language emerged repeatedly when there was a marked L1/L2 proficiency

disparity: Selecting the stronger L1 was more effortful when the weaker L2 had been used immediately before it. This is consistent with observations of task selection in other domains (Allport & Styles, 1990; Allport, Styles, & Hsieh, 1994; Rogers & Monsell, 1995; see Monsell, 1996, for a comprehensive review). For example, when participants alternated between two versions of the classic Stroop color word task (Stroop, 1935; "name the word" vs. "name the color the word is printed in"), Allport et al. found larger switch costs when switching from the weaker color-naming task to the dominant word-naming task. Similar observations have been made also in other bilingual tasks, such as cued picture naming (Kroll & Peck, 1998, as cited in Kroll & Dijkstra, 2002) and even early bilingual speech recognition (Bosch & Sebastián-Gallés, 1997).

A critical look at the early research on bilingual adaptations of the Stroop task (Stroop, 1935) also showed the same pattern. Meuter (1994) recalculated the data from a number of earlier studies (Albert & Obler, 1978; Dyer, 1971; Kiyak, 1982; Lee, Wee, Tzeng, & Hung, 1992; Preston & Lambert, 1969) using the neutral condition as a baseline measure (cf. Jensen & Rohwer, 1966). In four of the five studies (Albert & Obler, 1978, excepted), while nonbalanced bilinguals did experience relatively

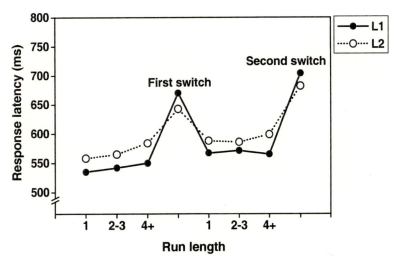

Figure 17.1 Mean response latency (in milliseconds) for both nonswitch and switch trials, indicated in canonical sequence. Nonswitch response trials in L1 and L2 are given as a function of run length (i.e., the number of successive responses in the same language), with run length classified as follows: no more than 1 only, 2–3, or 4 or more successive responses in the same language. The possible sequence of responses is indicated up to and including the second switch in a sequence. A maximum of four switches per sequence was possible (range = [0, 4]). (Adapted from Meuter, 1994; see also Meuter & Allport, 1999.) L1, first language; L2, second language.

greater interference from distractors in the dominant language, greater interference occurred also when *responding* in the dominant language (see Fig. 17.2, top panel). This occurs irrespective of any correspondence between the language of presentation and response. Thus, although the language of the distractor—in relation to the response language—influences the speed of response, of crucial importance also is the language in which the response is given.

How may these paradoxical patterns be explained? Meuter and Allport (1999) argued that the critical components in switching between languages are, first, the establishment of a language set (e.g., to enable a response in L1, competing responses from L2 have to be inhibited) and, second, the inertia this generates in the system. The outcome of the inertia is the tendency to continue responding in the same language. To produce a

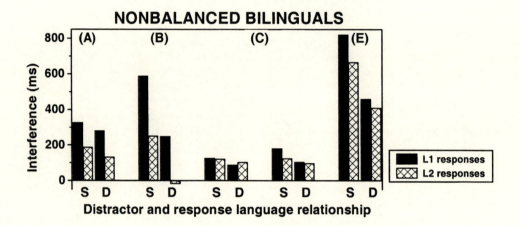

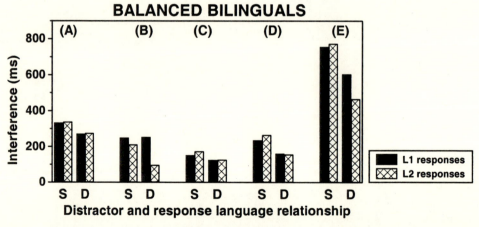

Figure 17.2 Interference per item (in milliseconds) on bilingual color–word Stroop tasks, calculated for five separate studies using a neutral baseline and plotted according to language of response. Language of response is either the same as (S) or different from (D) the language of presentation of the target item. Recalculated data are given for nonbalanced (top panel) as well as balanced participants (lower panel). (A) Preston and Lambert's (1969) Experiment 3 with English-French bilinguals (top panel) and Experiment 1 (lower panel) with English-Spanish bilinguals. (B) Kiyak's (1982) study with Turkish-English bilinguals. (C) Albert and Obler's (1987) study with Hebrew-English bilinguals (two nonbalanced groups and one balanced group). (D) Dyer's (1971) study with Spanish-English bilinguals (combined data). (E) Lee et al.'s (1992) study with Tamil-English bilinguals (lower panel gives combined data). L1, first language; L2, second language.

response in the other language on the next trial, the language set inertia (labeled task set inertia when switching between tasks in other domains; Allport et al., 1994) has to be overcome. It is the language set inertia resulting from responding in the weaker L2 (which required strong suppression of the competing stronger L1) that is the most difficult to conquer. This interpretation is consistent with the idea that the language switch costs represent a conflict effect arising from the persistence of the language response set instituted on the preceding trial. The paradoxical pattern in the bilingual Stroop tasks similarly might be explained by assuming stronger (or earlier) recoding of the distractor item when the intended response language is the dominant L1. It follows that comparatively greater difficulty will be experienced when having to suppress a resulting inappropriate response in L1 (Meuter, 1994).

Within the IC model (Green, 1993, 1997, 1998a), the asymmetrical language switch cost is explained as within-system inhibition. On a switch of language from L2 to L1, the L1 language task schema is selected in favor of the L2 language task schema that dominated language selection on the preceding response. Successful performance in the weaker L2 on the previous trial was due to the inhibition of all lemmas with L1 language tags. Because the inhibition of L1 is especially powerful in nonbalanced bilinguals, the cost that arises from its removal is commensurately large, thus accounting for the larger cost observed.

For a number of reasons, Meuter and Allport (1999) suggested that the suppression of a response in a particular language results in the suppression of that entire language system. First, responses did not become faster with an increase in consecutive responses. Response latencies on switch trials also remained unaffected by this manipulation (see Meuter & Allport, 1999, Fig. 3, p. 32). In other words, longer periods of speaking L_A do not cause L_B to be subjected to increasing inhibition, which would have been reflected in similarly increasing switch costs. Second, a switch cost was observed only on the first response in the other language; the next response was as fast as any others in the same language (see the nonswitch responses in Fig. 17.1). Third, experimentally induced L1-L2 proficiency differences resulted in identical effects in a cued picture-naming task (Loasby, 1998). Fluent bilinguals received selective practice in the naming of line drawings, subsets of which were practiced in L1, others in L2, and the remainder left unpracticed in either language, with the result that

sets of pictures were easier to name in one language than the other. Switch costs were minimal on those switch trials following responses in the practiced language, for which little or no inhibition of a competing response was required. In contrast, switch costs on switch trials following responses in the unpracticed language, requiring strong inhibition of a competing response, were more than four times as large (40 ms and 180 ms, respectively). This pattern of results would obtain only if the suppression of a response competitor (in the other language) resulted in the suppression of the associated language system as a whole. Importantly, the results provided further evidence to support the idea that the critical factor in determining the switch cost is the language set established for the preceding response, that is, the language set *from* which a switch is made.

It may be seen as parsimonious to impose global inhibition on elements belonging to one language L_A to facilitate the use of the other language L_B. It is commonly assumed that the two language systems, more so perhaps when in a bilingual setting, are active to varying degrees (Grainger & Dijkstra, 1992; Green, 1986, 1993, 1998a; Grosjean, 1998). Evidence from code-switching instances also strongly points to the simultaneous activation of the two languages (see Poulisse, 1997). However, if it is assumed that spreading activation is the process by which words in either language are accessed, the question arises regarding the extent to which competing candidates are activated, both within and across languages (see also De Bot, 1992). Consequently, it may well be the case that the suppression effects are more localized, something the paradigms as they were implemented thus far might not have been able to reveal (see also Green, 1998b).

To tease out the possible existence of localized inhibitory effects, Bajo and Green (1999) manipulated the numerical distance in a numeral naming task. German-English bilinguals named numerals (ranging from 1 to 9) in either language, as cued by color. The numerical distance between each successive pair of numerals was either large (e.g., 1–7, a numerical distance of 5) or small (e.g., 1–3, a numerical distance of 1). Numerals were assumed to map onto analogue representations of their magnitude and, once activated, a spread of activation to closely related numeral concepts (i.e., a small numerical distance removed) would result. Moyer and Landauer (1967) first described this effect when they discovered that the larger of a pair of simultaneously presented numerals took measurably longer to name the greater the numerical distance between it and the smaller numeral.

By systematically varying the numerical distance between numeral pairs, Bajo and Green (1999) were able to evaluate any inhibitory effect at the conceptual level, as well as determine the level at which control is effected in selection (i.e., internal to the bilingual lexicon, at the lemma level, or external to it). If global inhibition only operated, then no differences in response latencies would be expected as a function of numerical distance. By contrast, if the inhibitory effects also operated locally, increases in numerical distance should result in increases in response latencies on non-switch trials but concomitant decreases in response latencies on switch trials. The findings were consistent with the operation of local inhibitory effects, indicative—at the conceptual level at least—of an internal locus of control at the lemma level, not necessarily generalized to the entire language. External control was revealed clearly in the asymmetrical switch pattern obtained, larger when switching to the dominant L1.

To recapitulate, a switch of language is enabled through processes of inhibition, affected by the level of proficiency in the to-be-suppressed language. The inhibitory processes can operate both locally and globally, a point discussed in more detail in the next section. The level of proficiency in a given language may differ depending on the particular task (e.g., naming versus comprehension) to be carried out in that language. It is important, therefore, that any calculations aimed at determining relative proficiency and switch costs are carried out with reference to task-specific baselines. It is not only conceivable but highly probable that within-individual, task-specific differences exist that are reflected in differences in ease of processing. Such differences emerge also as a direct consequence of experimental (contextual) demands (see, for example, the practice effects on switch costs described by Meuter & Allport, 1999).

The Role of Relative Proficiency in Language Selection

The pattern of asymmetrical language switch costs that is seen in nonbalanced bilinguals contradicts the intuitive belief that greater proficiency or fluency in a language should be synonymous with greater efficiency. What is critical is not proficiency per se, but rather the extent to which a bilingual is more or less proficient in one language relative to the other. A logical inference from the findings discussed in the previous sections is that, when a bilingual is equally proficient or practiced at the two languages, the resulting switch costs—in either direction—likewise should be equal.

A number of findings support this idea. In one study, a small group of carefully selected balanced English-French bilinguals named the superordinates of common nouns in one or the language, as cued by color (e.g., sparrow–BIRD, carnation–FLEUR [FLOWER]); Meuter, 1994; Meuter & Allport, 1999). They performed under two conditions. In the language-compatible condition, changes in color cues mapped directly onto the actual shifts in language of presentation and cued for a response in that language (e.g., oeillet [carnation]–FLEUR/sparrow–BIRD). In the language-noncompatible condition, changes in color cues instead signaled for a response in the other language (e.g., oeillet–FLOWER/sparrow–OISEAU [BIRD]). In both conditions, large costs of language switching were observed when shifting language of response. More importantly, however, there was no asymmetry in the switch costs. This is in sharp contrast to data obtained from nonbalanced bilinguals in the same task: They showed the expected asymmetry, with larger costs when switching to the dominant L1 in response (Meuter, 1994).

The review of the bilingual Stroop data (Meuter, 1994) also revealed that the asymmetrical interference effect on the response language was reduced or even absent for balanced bilinguals (Fig. 17.2, lower panel). Furthermore, increased practice across 2,000 or so response trials (decreasing the L1-L2 proficiency disparity on the task) significantly reduces the asymmetry in the language switch costs (Meuter & Allport, 1999). Recall also the study by Loasby (1998), in which asymmetries were experimentally induced through additional training on small subsets of pictures. By extension, one could train subsets to equal proficiency in both languages and, it would follow, a reduced or eliminated asymmetry would result.

Much research focusing on the representation of concepts and words in the bilingual lexicon has highlighted the extent to which its architecture and the nature of the selection processes are molded and driven by differences in L1-L2 proficiency (as formulated, for example, in the Revised Hierarchical Model; Kroll & Stewart, 1994; for reviews, see Kroll & De Groot, 1997; Kroll & Tokowicz, 2001). With increased proficiency, a concomitant increase in reliance on conceptual information, as opposed to reliance on lexical information, has been observed, and often an asymmetrical pattern in translation obtains, with backward translation (from L2 to L1) effected faster than forward translation (from L1 to L2). (See De Groot & Poot, 1997, and La Heij, Hooglander, Kerling, & Van der Velden, 1996, for contrasting findings.)

Additional support for the importance of relative proficiency comes from functional imaging studies (see also Abutalebi, Cappa, & Perani, chapter 24, and Hull & Vaid, chapter 23, this volume). Different cortical areas of activation have been found with low proficiency (i.e., nonbalanced) bilinguals (Dehaene et al., 1997; Perani et al., 1996). For example, using functional magnetic resonance imagining, Dehaene et al. looked at auditory story comprehension in late-acquisition (and low-proficiency) French-English bilinguals and found that, although L1 activation was confined to the left temporal lobe, some participants showed additional activation in the left inferior frontal gyrus and the anterior cingulate for L2. This possibly reflected the greater attentional demands made by the processing of a weaker L2. Similar findings were obtained by Perani et al. with low-proficiency Italian-English bilinguals.

In proficient (i.e., balanced) bilinguals, greater overlap between cortical regions subserving processing in both languages has been observed (e.g., Chee et al., 1999; Perani et al., 1998). One positron emission tomographic study of auditory story comprehension (Perani et al., 1998) compared two groups of highly proficient bilinguals, early L2 acquirers and late (after the age of 10 years) L2 acquirers. Bilateral activation in the temporal poles was observed for both L1 and L2, as well as in the hippocampal structures and the lingual gyrus. In addition, again for both languages, there was left hemisphere activation (e.g., in the superior temporal sulcus and the inferior parietal lobule). These patterns were independent of age of L2 acquisition, suggesting that—in language comprehension at least—proficiency rather than age of acquisition determines the brain regions involved in the processing of the two languages.

This finding seemingly contrasts with Kim, Relkin, Kyoung-Min, and Hirsh's (1997) observations, in a silent production task, of activity in non-overlapping regions in the left hemisphere for late bilinguals but marked overlap in Broca's area for early bilinguals. However, different language skills were not evaluated, and no independent measures of language proficiency were reported. Therefore, the possibility that the early and late

bilinguals were equally proficient in both languages cannot be excluded.

The research reviewed thus far has covered paradigms that, by some, may be considered somewhat artificial and far removed from the language behavior that bilinguals engage in when communicating in natural settings. The question invariably arises whether the same observations hold true there. Observations from code-switching data suggest, indirectly, that they do (e.g., Clyne, 1980). Supporting evidence comes from a study in which nonbalanced Spanish-English bilinguals related different personal experiences, unpredictably in one or the other language. Detailed analyses of the monologues (encompassing both response latencies and word counts) revealed that, even though L1 was the more proficient language overall (as evidenced by higher word counts), it took significantly longer to start speaking L1. Not surprisingly, word production in the first 5 s of speech also was markedly reduced. This reflects the asymmetry also found in the naming tasks. The onset asymmetry disappeared about 10 s into the story, re-establishing the normal dominance pattern (Meuter, 2001). The bilinguals were classified further according to self-reported recent use (percentage use on day of testing) of the weaker L2. For the high-usage group (L2 use = 70%), an unexpected pattern emerged: The recent experience of predominant L2 usage resulted in a dominance reversal, such that L2 was now the stronger language.

It appears then, that relative proficiency is a powerful determining factor in the ease with which bilinguals control and regulate their two languages. Moreover, the degree of proficiency can be affected by recent experience, and its relativity applies to a language as a whole. Even training on limited subsets produces generalized effects on responses (cf. Loasby, 1998). Although more localized effects of suppression and activation are possible (see, for example, Bajo & Green, 1999), the paradigms discussed here did not enable an evaluation of them. The conversation analysis did show increasing engagement, on a switch, of the dominant L1, but this may simply reflect an increasingly, globally, active language system.

To uncover any localized effects, if they exist, production paradigms need to incorporate more fine-tuned response latency measures. For example, a language-switching task based on superordinate naming could build into it a measure of semantic relatedness to evaluate the extent to which the lexico-semantic system is affected. In nonbalanced bilinguals, an overall switch cost asymmetry would be predicted, supporting the idea of global suppression. The comparison of switch trials involving a semantic relationship, (e.g., *moineau* [sparrow]–*OISEAU*/robin–BIRD), versus those that do not (e.g., *moineau*–*OISEAU*/church–BUILDING) might reveal greater switch costs on semantically related switch trials. If so, this would demonstrate the operation also of local suppression, affecting conceptually related items more. We remain caught in a dichotomy for now, when in fact the global effect might be masking more subtle local processes, such as those observed in bilingual word recognition (e.g., Dijkstra & Van Heuven, 1998; Van Heuven et al., 1998). What has yet to be established is the extent to which these operate also in bilingual speech production.

There are two caveats to the foregoing discussion. First, Monsell et al. (1997; Monsell, Yeung, & Azuma, 2000) suggested that the switch cost may not always be asymmetrical, but perhaps only when one of the tasks is by far the dominant one. When the difference in relative dominancy between two tasks is not great (i.e., large enough to result in asymmetrical interference effects but too small to result in asymmetrical switch costs) the asymmetry disappears. Although the asymmetry is observed in nonbalanced bilinguals (as a direct consequence of L1-L2 proficiency differences), it remains to be seen how differences in relative proficiency across three languages will affect the switch costs in trilinguals. (See Costa & Santesteban, 2004, for thought-provoking data on highly proficient early bilinguals switching to L3.)

Second, the reduction (or even disappearance) of the asymmetry in language switch cost associated with comparable (balanced) levels of proficiency in the two languages does not imply the disappearance of the language switch cost altogether. Typically, a measurable cost remains. When a negligible cost is observed, it may be that task demands are such that even on nonswitches a cost is experienced. An example of such task demands is given in the next section (cf. Meuter & Shallice, 2001). Expectations of which language to speak, whether anticipated or in response to some external cue (e.g., being spoken to in a particular language), also might affect the ease with which a language is selected.

Language Selection and Cueing of Language Choice

A bilingual individual confronted with information in one or the other language cannot help but pro-cess what is seen or heard. Anecdotal evidence suggests that bilinguals do use, involuntarily, an inappropriate language when cued by something in the environment. They do so also when they appear to cue themselves inadvertently, by producing a trigger word, as in the following utterance: "*Ich habe viele LETTER geschre/geschrieben*" (literal translation: "I have many letters written" [Dutch/German]; Clyne, 1997, p. 108). In this example, the word *LETTER* is both German and Dutch. Its Dutch meaning, while also referring to something that can be written, is confined to a letter of the alphabet and yet triggers—although swiftly corrected—a switch into Dutch. Evidence from bilingual Stroop and picture word interference tasks also demonstrated that bilinguals cannot ignore the language that is irrelevant (and even a hindrance) to the task (see MacLeod, 1991, for a review; see also Fig. 17.1), studies of negative priming have found effects of unattended items (e.g., Fox, 1996), and it has been shown that the irrelevant language is accessed even when in an exclusively monolingual task setting (e.g., Spivey & Marian, 1999). The observation that bilinguals—when using L_A—are affected by the other language L_B, even when it is ignored intentionally or not in active use, suggests that both language systems are active to varying degrees (Grainger & Dijkstra, 1992; Green, 1986; Paradis, 1980), a factor also recognized in models of bilingual speech production (e.g., the Bilingual Production Model; De Bot, 1992; De Bot & Schreuder, 1993). This raises the question of how external language-related information is used to drive language selection.

What constitutes a valid language selection cue in a bilingual setting? In many of the studies discussed in the previous sections, the tasks were cued in some way by a geometrical figure (Macnamara et al., 1968), a color (e.g., Meuter & Allport, 1999), a position on a computer screen (e.g., Rogers & Monsell, 1995), or a variable tone (Kroll & Peck, 1998, as cited in Kroll & Dijkstra, 2002). Such cues are arbitrary and only attain meaning in the experimental context through task instruction. For example, within the IC model (Green, 1998a), language task schemas are formed on the basis of such cues, linking a particular figure, color, position, or tone cue to the production of a specified language (e.g., name a picture in L1, not L2, in response to a high tone). If presented some variable time prior to the presentation of a stimulus (such as a picture), cues can also afford the opportunity to prepare for a response, to some extent at least. However, such arbitrary cues are quite distinct from the cueing validity that a word (whether spoken, heard, or read) directly affords for the language to which it pertains (with the exception of ambiguous lexical items, such as the word *LETTER*, earlier seen to trigger a switch from German to Dutch). An unambiguous cue, as provided by a unique, language-specific word in L_A, unambiguously and directly cues L_A.

Two early studies demonstrated this effect in the monolingual domain. Jersild (1927) and Spector and Biederman (1976) found that the time cost involved in changing between tasks was reduced when cued unambiguously (e.g., when switching between giving the opposite to a written word and subtracting 3 from a digit). In contrast, large costs were observed when switching between adding and subtracting 3 from a digit, costs that were reduced when +3 or −3 next to each digit signaled the operation (Spector & Biederman, 1976). Exactly how these reconfigurations are executed and what the processes underlying the ability to switch between tasks might be has been the subject of increasing research (Allport & Styles, 1990; Allport et al., 1994; Los, 1996; Meiran, 1996, 2000; Meuter, 1994; Meuter & Allport, 1999; Meuter, Humphreys, & Rumiati, 2002; Meuter & Shallice, 2001; Rogers & Monsell, 1995; Rogers, Sahakian, Hodges, Polkey, Kennard, & Robbins, 1998; Rubenstein, Meyer, & Evans, 2001). The observed reduction in switch cost with the presence of a cue suggests that some prior preparation can take place (Meiran, 1996, 2000). The exact nature of the cue is important also. Greater reductions in switch costs were found on an arithmetic switching task when cued by arithmetic symbols as opposed to color. Color cues in turn were more effective than no cues at all (Emerson & Miyake, 2003; see also Baddeley, Chincotta, & Adlam, 2001).

In the bilingual domain, Macnamara et al. (1968) found a reduction in language switch costs when switches occurred in regular alternation, suggesting some preparation as a consequence of predictability. This level of preparation likely is at a global level, preselecting the language required on the next trial, with a cost remaining because the actual response can be selected only on the appearance of the critical stimulus. An earlier study by Dalrymple-Alford (1967) found that direct cueing of a language either was ineffective or else a switch of language could not be triggered by information presented prior to the execution of a switch.

However, Meuter (1994) showed that, when bilinguals have to attend *explicitly* to the language-specific aspects of the stimulus, that particular language is selected for response, even when this is inappropriate. Recall that English-French bilinguals were instructed to label each target word either in the language in which it was presented (the language-compatible condition, e.g., sparrow–BIRD) or in the other language (the language-noncompatible condition, e.g., sparrow–*OISEAU*). In the latter condition, each trial encompasses a within-trial switch of language (e.g., sparrow–*OISEAU*/oeillet–FLOWER), and of particular interest is the pattern of response obtained here. For nonbalanced bilinguals, response latencies on nonswitch and switch trials in mixed lists were equally slow, resulting in a nonexistent switch cost. Furthermore, both types of trials were markedly slower (by an average of 300 and 349 ms, respectively) than nonswitch trials in monolingual lists. This pattern of results (i.e., no measurable switch costs on mixed lists) contrasted with that obtained in the language-compatible condition: A switch cost (measuring 262 ms) was obtained when responding in L1 only.

Consistent with Meiran and colleagues' (Meiran, 2000; Meiran, Chorev, & Sapir, 2000) interpretation of the switch cost, in which one component identified is that of reconfiguration of task set, it appears that attending to the language of presentation L_A—even when the task specifies that the response should not be given in L_A—nonetheless results in its selection. L_A, thus activated, has to be suppressed to respond in the other language, L_B.

Similar findings were obtained in a study comparing switch costs in bilingual picture naming and translation (Kroll, Dietz, & Green, in preparation, as cited in Kroll & Dijkstra, 2002). Bilinguals were asked to switch between languages in a picture-naming and a translation task. In contrast to a picture, a to-be-translated word provides a cue to the response language (albeit in the noncompatible sense described here) and thus may enable earlier language selection. If this occurs, a reduction in (and perhaps even elimination of) switch costs would be expected. As predicted, although asymmetrical switch costs were obtained on the picture-naming task, on the translation task no significant switch costs were obtained. Although this is suggestive of the effectiveness of the language cue provided by the stimulus, it is equally likely that in translation—as in the naming of superordinates in the other language—the word first activates its associated lexicon before the appropriate selection can be made from the lexical candidates in the other language.

Each translation, then, represents an inherent switch between the language of presentation and the language of response. It may be this aspect of the task that makes nonswitch and switch trials appear equally fast. If this is true, it follows that, on an Italian-to-English translation task, for example, increased response latencies would occur on trials in which the critical word is a homographic non-cognate (e.g., *estate* in Italian, meaning "summer") compared to trials in which a language-specific word is to be translated (e.g., *inverno* in Italian, meaning "winter").

There is, of course, something curious about both these tasks: that is, superordinate naming in the other language and translation. In each task, the language of the stimulus, although a valid *task* cue, is not the optimal *language* cue, and the bilingual has to attend explicitly to the language of input (thus generating some internal conflict) to select the appropriate response language. It follows that it should be possible to cue a bilingual more efficiently, in a language-switching setting, by using language-specific cues that correctly and unambiguously cue the associated response language. Also, consistent with the results just described, an incongruent cue would signal (and perhaps initiate preparation for) a response in the inappropriate language, thus resulting in a cost.

Two studies explored the effect of external cues and their validity on the bilingual's response efficiency. The first study assumed that the identity of the interlocutor would be a powerful cue to language selection, and merely attending to this feature might affect language selection (Meuter & Powell, 1997). German-English bilinguals made response language decisions (i.e., in which language would you address this person?) about well-known (German- or English-speaking) individuals whose pictures were interleaved with a bilingual numeral-naming task. Through its associated language, each picture cued the response language required on the next trial unpredictably, either congruently or incongruently. For example, a picture of Freud (German speaker) congruently cued a subsequent trial color cued for response in German. Contrary to predictions, a congruent cue to a switch of language did not reduce the switch cost, and an incongruent cue in a nonswitch context did not result in a significantly increased cost. However, the relevance of the picture to the task (also in terms of its predictive validity) likely was not sufficient.

Accordingly, Meuter and Leisser (2002) incorporated words with language-specific orthography (either English or Spanish) into the basic numeral-naming task because these words would activate directly the associated lexicon. Monolingual and mixed blocks were used, the latter containing both color-cued switches and nonswitches of response language. The numerals were interleaved with neutral letter strings, as well as words for which the language identity either did or did not match the response language required on the next trial (congruent and incongruent cues to the language of response, respectively). Now, incongruent cues did increase responses on nonswitch trials, suggesting some preparation had occurred by way of general activation of the other language. No reduction in switch costs was observed when a switch of language was cued congruently. The cues only appeared for 100 ms, perhaps not sufficient to achieve either complete disengagement from the preceding language set or efficient use of the cue in preparation for a response.

Meuter and Shallice (2001, Experiment 2) observed that, with longer, predictive (color) cue presentations (up to 1000 ms), switch costs did decrease significantly and more so for the weaker L2. However, although a valid cue may facilitate the preparation of a response, the response proper cannot be configured until the stimulus is presented (see also Allport et al., 1994; Los, 1996; Meiran, 2000). Significant reductions in switch costs were found when naming Arabic versus Chinese numerals (Meuter & Tan, 2003). Here, the stimuli unambiguously specified the response language, thus facilitating a switch of language.

The differing effects of cues on nonswitch and switch responses suggest that there may be some fundamental differences in the reconfiguration of language sets depending on whether a switch of response language is required. Support for this notion was found in a study that manipulated both color cue length and switch ratio. Superimposed on the primary numeral-naming task was a secondary vigilance task requiring the suppression of certain (prespecified) responses (cf. Robertson, Manly, Andrade, Baddeley, & Yiend, 1997). In one experiment, Italian-English bilinguals rapidly named numerals in either language, as cued by color, with one important exception. All responses to the numeral 3 (three) were to be suppressed. (See Fig. 17.3 for examples of trial and response sequences.) Not only did the additional task increase the attentional load, but the suppression of a specific response—in a given language—also allowed the precise evaluation of the effect this had on a subsequent response. Suppression trials occurred both

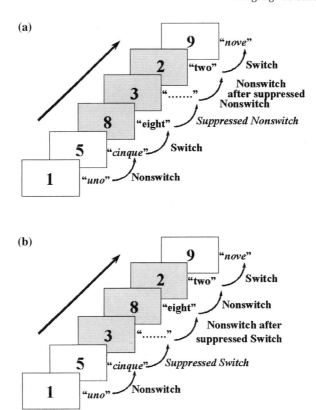

Figure 17.3 Examples of two possible response sequences for the simultaneous appearance of color cue and numeral. (Adapted from Meuter & Shallice, 2001.) (a) A sequence of trials in which the to-be-suppressed numeral "3" (cued for response in English) appears on a nonswitch trial. The subsequent trial is cued for response in the same language (English) and is therefore classified as a nonswitch trial following a suppressed response on a nonswitch. (b) A sequence of trials in which the to-be-suppressed numeral appears on a switch of language (from Italian to English). Accordingly, this type of trial is referred to as a suppressed switch trial. The subsequent trial is cued for response in the same language (English) and is therefore classified as a nonswitch trial following a suppressed switch.

on nonswitches (e.g., an L1 response trial was followed by a suppression trial also cued for response in L1; see Fig. 17.3[a]) and switches of response language (e.g., an L1 response was followed by a suppression trial cued for response in L2; see Fig. 17.3[b]). Of primary interest were those trials immediately following a suppression trial. On both nonswitch and switch trials following a suppressed response, increases in responses latencies were found amounting to costs virtually identical to those observed on regular switch trials (see Fig. 17.4). Most striking was the cost observed on nonswitches following a suppressed response on a switch of language.

An example of such an event is seen in Fig. 17.3(b). Here, the numeral 3 is cued for a switch in response language from the preceding trial (from Italian to English). However, the numeral itself signals that its response is to be withheld, thus resulting in a suppressed switch trial (*nota bene*, only on appearance of the target stimulus could this decision be made). The subsequent trial is cued for response in the same language as just suppressed, effectively a nonswitch trial. The cost incurred on this trial significantly exceeded any other observed cost (see Fig. 17.4; cf. Meuter & Shallice, 2001).

Two dramatic findings emerged from the incorporation of a vigilance component. First, the striking observation of greater cost incurred after a suppressed switch than measured on an actual switch of language suggests that there is something unique about the configuration of a response set associated

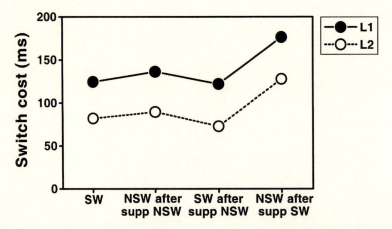

Figure 17.4 Mean switch cost (in milliseconds) for both response languages, for the following trials: (1) regular switches (SW); (2) nonswitches following a suppressed nonswitch (NSW after supp NSW); (3) switches following a suppressed nonswitch (SW after supp NSW); and (4) nonswitches following a suppressed switch (NSW after supp SW). Adapted from Meuter and Shallice (2001).

with a language switch. It appears that the (color) cue is effective in partially reconfiguring the language set, to the extent that the other language is now activated, and some preparatory groundwork has been laid for response (see also Meuter & Shallice, 2001, Experiment 2). This is consistent with Meiran's (2000) postulation that one part of the observed cost in task switching is reflected in the preparation component, effectively consisting of the opportunity to make use of a cue.

Second, the observation that even a nonswitch trial can incur a switchlike cost suggests that the suppression of a response in the same language effectively suppresses that language system. However, these costs do not obtain in a predominantly monolingual context, suggesting that it is the perceived need to use both languages that gives rise to inhibitory processes (Meuter & Shallice, 2001).

Now, two notions need to be reconciled. On the one hand, in a switch context, cueing appears to aid preparation through the global activation of the relevant language system, and response suppression results in the global inhibition of the associated language system. On the other hand, when there is no perceived need to use both languages, the suppression of a response in L_A does not entail the suppression of the entire language system. If global inhibition did occur, then—irrespective of the bilingual's expectations regarding language use—the suppression of a response in L_A should result in the global suppression of L_A.

The critical point here is the type of requirements imposed by the experimental (and by extension the conversational) setting. When in an almost exclusively monolingual setting (strikingly, even when this situation is confined to a block of trials embedded in a bilingual experimental setting), the other language does not appear to affect any selection process. The default value is set to generalized activation of the predominantly required language *for that block only*. Effective strategic behavior on the task requires, on suppression of a response, only minimal suppression of the associated language. When both languages need to be managed, the expectation that a switch of language is likely may give rise to global inhibitory processes.

The reconfiguration of a language switch merits further exploration. Why is the suppression of a response on a switch of language more effortful than that of any other response? What are the component processes executed before the critical stimulus (including the language signal) appears? It would seem that the switch is reconfigured, but preventing its execution—apart from suppressing a response—results in the inhibition of not only the de-selected language but also the response language required on the switch.

Another suggestion put forward is that switching between tasks may involve the operation of inner speech directing the individual by activating the required task instructions. Although inner speech is not an executive control process but one instead associated with the rehearsal and short-term maintenance of phonological information (cf. Baddeley, 1986), some findings in the monolingual task-switching domain suggest that articulatory suppression (e.g., repeating a word over and over while carrying out a language-based task) increases the cost associated with task switching (Baddeley et al., 2001; Emerson & Miyake, 2003). The overt articulation of the task instruction, on the other hand, reduces the switch cost, suggesting that a self-generated reminder serves as an effective cue to the upcoming task (Goschke, 2000).

It is conceivable that, at least for the tasks described thus far, for which arbitrary cues signal the language of response, bilinguals make use of inner speech. If so, concurrent articulatory suppression should increase the cost of switching between languages. However, if the stimuli themselves endogenously cue the response language, inner speech may have no role in facilitating a language switch, and articulatory suppression should not have any effect.

Maintaining the Language of Choice

The selection of a language, whether intentional or inadvertent (as cued by context), is only one aspect of the speech act. What is critical also is the role that monitoring plays, not only in the bilingual's ability to switch effectively between languages but also in the ability to maintain a language for production once it is selected. It has been observed, for example, that on occasion bilinguals may not immediately comprehend what is said to them if they were not expecting to hear the language spoken to them (Taylor, 1976). This could be because there may be a level of monitoring of input required (cf. Macnamara's, 1967a, input switch; Obler and Albert's notion of monitoring, 1978) that does not always function efficiently. Alternatively, a generalized higher level of activation may be associated with one language as compared to the other in the bilingual's lexicon (e.g., Grainger & Dijkstra, 1992; Green, 1986, 1993), preventing immediate recognition. Monitoring might be driven by the Supervisory Attentional System (Green, 1986, 1998a; Norman & Shallice, 1986), but could be operationalized also as the outcome of continual and updated computations following changes in relative activation within an interactive activation network.

From the occurrence of inadvertent code switches (e.g., Clyne, 1997; Shanon, 1991), levels of control can be inferred that normally operate to prevent other language intrusions. It is when errors of language choice occur that a person becomes most aware of the control exerted on a continual basis and the need to monitor the appropriateness of speech output. Unfortunately, the errors are typically too few to be informative, and yet they often provide revealing insights into the functioning of the intact cognitive system.

There are two approaches that have proven useful in accessing error data. One approach involves the study of individuals whose ability to control their everyday behavior has been compromised through neurological damage. This results in a number of errors, of which errors of task selection are most informative. With respect to language switching, those patients who have incurred damage in the frontal lobes are of particular interest. Another approach involves the manipulation of the experimental situation such that higher error rates are elicited (e.g., increasing task difficulty by increasing the attentional load; Meuter & Shallice, 2001). I discuss these two approaches in turn.

Although it is highly unlikely that there exists an isolable on-off language switch mechanism of the type proposed by Penfield and Roberts (1959), the frontal lobes and associated areas could form the possible underlying physiological basis for the bilingual's ability to switch between languages. This suggestion is supported by evidence from various lines of research indicating that the ability to control one's behavior, such as switching tasks successfully, depends on the integrity of the frontal lobes (e.g., Perret, 1974; Sandston & Albert, 1987; Shallice, 1988). Typically, patients with frontal lobe damage exhibit great difficulty in switching between different categories or tasks (e.g., Milner, 1963) and often show a high number of perseverative responses. On other tasks, such as the Stroop task, their performance shows a greater-than-usual inability to suppress unwanted information (Perret, 1974; see also Burgess & Shallice, 1996). If switching between languages is considered another instance of switching between task sets, then it is likely that—given the role of the frontal lobes—language switching also may be subserved by this area. Rogers et al. (1998) suggested that it is specifically the left frontal lobe that is involved in the dynamic reconfiguration of established task sets. Accordingly, a bilingual individual with a frontal lobe injury might experience an inordinate amount of difficulty in switching between the two languages just as would occur with any other form of task switching.

Such a patient was tested recently (Meuter et al., 2002). An Urdu-English bilingual patient with frontal lobe damage, F. K., showed similar response latency patterns to neurologically intact bilinguals (controls) when naming numerals in Urdu and English, with larger costs when switching into the dominant L1. However, unlike the controls, F. K. made numerous errors on this task. In particular, F. K. had great difficulty, once a switch to the weaker L2 was made, to maintain L2 as his response language. He often fell back into an L1 response mode, even after a number of successful, consecutive responses in L2. Also, successful switches into the weaker L2, while reliably faster than switches into the dominant L1, were highly error-prone and frequently resulted in erroneous L1 responses. In other words, F. K. exhibited a strong tendency to perseverate with responses in the dominant L1, even when cued for responses in the weaker L2. The frontal lobe damage and impairment of control processes of F. K. resulted in an inability to modulate inhibitory resources and thus regulate and monitor his language behavior when both languages were required. In particular, F. K.'s monitoring deficiencies targeted his ability both to inhibit his stronger L1 sufficiently and to maintain this inhibition over time.

Another bilingual patient with frontal lobe damage was described whose language mixing behavior, often inappropriate and uncontrollable even when confronted with clear external cues, appeared primarily caused by left frontal lobe damage (Fabbro, Skrap, & Aglioti, 2000). No aphasic symptoms were observed in either language. In each language setting (either Friuli or Italian), the patient would produce at least 40% of his spontaneous utterances in the inappropriate language and lapsed marginally more often into L1 when L2 was required than vice versa, a pattern consistent with the type of monitoring difficulties exhibited by F. K.

Imaging techniques have provided further support for frontal lobe involvement. For example, using functional magnetic resonance imaging, increased activation in the dorsolateral prefrontal cortex was found in Spanish-English bilinguals when switching between languages in a picture-naming task (Hernandez, Dapretto, Mazziotta, & Bookheimer, 2001; Hernandez, Martinez, & Kohnert, 2000). However, Price, Green, and von Studnitz (1999), in a positron emission tomographic study comparing translation and language switching (operationalized as silent reading of alternately presented words in either L1 or L2), found increased activation in Broca's area as well as bilaterally in the supramarginal gyri but no such increase in the frontal lobes. The lack of frontal lobe involvement

may be simply a consequence of task demands because switches were clearly signaled by a change in language of input.

Other evidence suggests that, although the frontal lobes may be involved in holding the known task set rules in mind, the remapping process may well take place elsewhere, in the parietal regions (Meuter, Jackson, Roberts, & Jackson, 1999). Event-related potential responses were measured bilaterally, and although a frontal component was found, it did not distinguish between nonswitch and switch trials. In contrast, such discrimination was observed across the parietal midline. Consistent with the monitoring difficulty found in F. K., this pattern provides further support for frontal lobe involvement in task maintenance, while suggesting that other aspects of language switching (such as remapping color cues to switch requirements) might be driven by the parietal lobes.

The error pattern shown by F. K. suggests that the monitoring of language behavior is critical. Might the role of monitoring be studied also in bilingual individuals without brain damage? Meuter and Shallice's (2001) study attempted to do so by adding a vigilance component to the normal bilingual numeral-naming task. In a series of experiments, the ratio of switch to nonswitch trials in a sequence as well as the ratio of regular to suppressed trials were manipulated (see Fig. 17.3). Increased response latencies occurred with an increase in both the incidence of switch and of suppression trials. Not surprisingly, the added vigilance component increased the error rate substantially. More importantly, more errors were made when L1 was the required response language, both on nonswitch and switch responses.

At first glance, this error pattern appears to contradict that observed in patient F. K., who made many more errors when L2, not L1, was the required response language. However, the juxtaposition of these two patterns, increased in neurologically intact bilinguals when required to speak L1 versus increased errors in a frontal lobe patient when required to speak L2, quickly resolves the contradiction. Taken together, the error patterns suggest strongly that in normal bilinguals the default setting, especially when in a bilingual context, is to inhibit the stronger language (L1) more to allow greater efficiency in L2. That this ability to monitor L1 versus L2 demands in a bilingual context is essential was demonstrated by its evident impairment in the bilingual patient F. K. with frontal lobe damage as well as by Fabbro et al.'s (2000) bilingual Friuli-Italian patient.

To recapitulate, findings from both neurologically damaged and intact bilinguals support the idea that the ability to switch between languages appropriately and then to maintain this selection for as long as the situation demands requires intact monitoring skills. The error patterns also indicate that relative language proficiency plays an important role in the monitoring process: The stronger, dominant language is more difficult both to inhibit and to monitor.

Summary

This chapter provides an overview of the current understanding of the processes that underlie the bilingual's ability to switch (whether consciously or inadvertently) language in production and highlighted some of the factors that affect switching behavior. Language selection is determined by a number of factors, including relative proficiency, contextual cues, and monitoring ability. Although greater proficiency in a language generally is associated with better performance, the opposite is true when a switch of language is made: Switching from the weaker L2 to the dominant L1 is more demanding than switching in the opposite direction. The comparatively greater cost experienced when selecting the dominant language after having just spoken the weaker L2 is one that is carried by the first response only. In conversation, the cost is measurable in terms of time taken to initiate discourse, but superior fluency in L1 quickly reestablishes itself (Meuter, 2001). The asymmetry observed in the switch between languages, larger on a switch to the dominant language, can be accounted for by language set inertia (Meuter & Allport, 1999). Alternatively, inhibition within the system, arising from the need both to select a different language task schema and to inhibit active nontarget lemmas, might account for the asymmetry (Green, 1998a).

It is clear from both patient and normal data that language can be cued exogenously. However, the extent to which cueing is effective remains to be determined. In an experimental setting at least, language cues that are subtle and not explicitly related to task demands do not reliably support language selection, but explicit and unambiguous cues do. When subtle cues do afford some preparation, they appear to do so via a process of global activation. The usefulness of cues is most keenly felt when speaking L2: With increased preparation time, responses are more efficient. The stronger language does not benefit in the same way from advance warning (Meuter & Shallice, 2001). The notion of global activation is consistent with the evident need for response monitoring and maintenance of the response language. When speaking L2, perhaps more so in an L2 setting, there is a continual need to suppress the dominant language. Anecdotal evidence suggests that, even in highly proficient bilinguals, this level of control operates. Inadvertent (and inappropriate) "slips of language" occur under conditions of stress or tiredness.

Last, to facilitate the language selection process, the bilingual has recourse to some useful strategies. One default strategy identified is to inhibit the stronger L1 more, particularly when in a situation that demands the use of both languages. In practice, this strategy has the advantage of increasing the availability of the weaker L2 and thus facilitating its use. At the same time, the bilingual perceives proficiency in the dominant L1 as only marginally compromised, if at all.

The picture is by no means complete, and a number of issues demand further exploration. For example, the relative contribution of local versus global processes needs to be analyzed further. Carefully planned experiments incorporating orthogonal comparisons of practice/relative proficiency, numerical/semantic distance, and language context and/or task demands will allow the evaluation of the contribution of each of these factors as well as their interaction. Also, many bilinguals often have at least a working knowledge of one or more additional languages. Incorporating a third (or even fourth) language into the equation would provide one further means of testing and expanding the validity of the conclusions drawn in this chapter and raises new questions.

First, does the need to monitor and use three or more languages require the same de-selection processes? Some discoveries in the monolingual domain are of relevance here (Arbuthnott & Frank, 2000; Mayr & Keele, 2000; but see also Emerson & Miyake, 2003). Specifically, Task A was easier to select when it was suppressed a few trials before (when switching between three tasks, e.g., C B *A*) as opposed to selecting Task A when it was suppressed more recently (when alternating between two tasks: e.g., A B *A*). By extension, is it easier also to speak L_A when both L_B and L_C are the languages used most recently? The answer to this question will depend, in part, on the relative proficiency in the three (or more) languages. (See Meuter & Binder, 2004, for preliminary data; Costa & Santesteban, 2004.)

Second, how are the selection processes affected by the need to control and manipulate more than two languages at different levels of proficiency? Third, do cues generalize, or are they language specific? Anecdotal evidence suggests that, on occasion, a cue to switch languages (from L_A to L_B) may indeed—correctly—result in a switch of language, but one that—incorrectly—is made to yet another language, L_C. Effective language selection, when selecting from multiple languages, is likely to impose greater processing demands and require more sophisticated monitoring ability, as well as more efficient strategies, to ensure smooth discourse when switching between languages.

Note

1. Although the input switch was described as automatic, this was not synonymous with instantaneous operation: A cost was thought to be associated with a switch both at input and output. The crucial distinction between the selection processes (switches) was based on whether willed purposeful action was required independent of any associated cost (Macnamara & Kushnir, 1971).

References

Albert, M. L., & Obler, L. K. (1978). *The bilingual brain: Neuropsychological and neurolinguistic aspects of bilingualism.* New York: Academic Press.

Allport, A., & Styles, E. A. (1990). *Multiple executive functions, multiple resources? Experiments in shifting attentional control of tasks.* Unpublished manuscript, Oxford University, Oxford, U.K.

Allport, A., Styles, E. A., & Hsieh, S. (1994). Shifting intentional set: Exploring the dynamic control of tasks. In C. Umiltá & M. Moscovitch (Eds.), *Attention and performance 15: Conscious and nonconscious information processing* (pp. 421–452). Hillsdale, NJ: Erlbaum.

Arbuthnott, K., & Frank, J. (2000). Executive control in set switching: Residual switch costs and task set inhibition. *Canadian Journal of Experimental Psychology, 54,* 33–41.

Baddeley, A. D. (1986). *Working memory.* Oxford, U.K.: Oxford University Press.

Baddeley, A. D., Chincotta, D., & Adlam, A. (2001). Working memory and the control of action: Evidence from task switching. *Journal of Experimental Psychology: General, 130,* 641–657.

Bajo, A., & Green, D. (1999, April). *Language switching and symbolic distance effects.*

Paper presented at the Second International Symposium of Bilingualism, Newcastle-upon-Tyne, U.K.

Bosch, L., & Sebastián-Gallés, N. (1997). Native-language recognition abilities in 4-month old infants from monolingual and bilingual environments. *Cognition, 65,* 33–69.

Bowers, J. S., Mimouni, Z., & Arguin, M. (2000). Orthography plays a critical role in cognate priming: Evidence from French/English and Arabic/French cognates. *Memory and Cognition, 28,* 1289–1296.

Burgess, P. W., & Shallice, T. (1996). Response suppression, initiation and strategy use following frontal lobe lesions. *Neuropsychologia, 34,* 263–273.

Caramazza, A., Yeni-Komshian, G., & Zurif, E. B. (1974). Bilingual switching: The phonological level. *Canadian Journal of Psychology, 28,* 310–318.

Chee, M. W. L., Caplan, D., Soon, C. S., Sriram, N., Tan, E. W. L., Thiel, T., et al. (1999). Processing of visually presented sentences in Mandarin and English studied with fMRI. *Neuron, 23,* 127–137.

Clyne, M. G. (1980). Triggering and language processing. *Canadian Journal of Psychology, 34,* 400–406.

Clyne, M. (1997). Some of the things trilinguals do. *International Journal of Bilingualism, 1,* 95–116.

Cooper, R., & Shallice, T. (2001). Contention scheduling and the control of routine activities. *Cognitive Neuropsychology, 17,* 297-338.

Costa, A., & Santesteban, M. (2004). Lexical access in bilingual speech production: Evidence from language switching in highly proficient bilinguals and L2 learners. *Journal of Memory and Language, 50,* 491–511.

Dalrymple-Alford, E. C. (1967). Prestimulus language cueing and speed of identifying Arab and English words. *Psychological Reports, 21,* 27–28.

De Bot, K. (1992). A bilingual production model: Levelt's speaking model adapted. *Applied Linguistics, 13,* 1–24.

De Bot, K., & Schreuder, R. (1993). Word production and the bilingual lexicon. In R. Schreuder & B. Weltens, (Eds.). *The bilingual lexicon* (pp. 191–214). Amsterdam: Benjamins.

De Groot, A. M. B. (1993). Word-type effects in bilingual processing tasks: Support for a mixed-representational system. In R. Schreuder & B. Weltens (Eds.), *The bilingual lexicon* (pp. 27–51). Amsterdam: Benjamins.

De Groot, A. M. B., & Nas, G. L. J. (1991). Lexical representation of cognates and noncognates in compound bilinguals. *Journal of Memory and Language, 30*, 90–123.

De Groot, A. M. B., & Poot, R. (1997). Word translation at three levels of proficiency in a second language: The ubiquitous involvement of conceptual memory. *Language Learning, 47*, 215–264.

Dehaene, S. D., Dupoux, E., Mehler, J., Cohen, L., Paulesu, E., Perani, D., et al. (1997). Anatomical variability in the cortical representation of first and second languages. *Neuroreport, 8*, 3809–3815.

Dijkstra, T. (2001, April). *What we know about bilingual word recognition: A review of studies and results.* Paper presented at the Third International Symposium on Bilingualism, University of the West of England, Bristol, U.K.

Dijkstra, T., Grainger, J., & Van Heuven, W. J. B. (1999). Recognizing cognates and interlingual homographs: The neglected role of phonology. *Journal of Memory and Language, 41*, 496–518.

Dijkstra, T., Timmermans, M., & Schriefers, H. (2000). On being blinded by your other language: Effects of task demands on interlingual homograph recognition. *Journal of Memory and Language, 42*, 445–464.

Dijkstra, T., & Van Heuven, W. J. B. (1998). The BIA model and bilingual word recognition. In. J. Grainger & A. Jacobs (Eds.), *Localist connectionist approaches to human cognition* (pp. 189–225). Hillsdale, NJ: Erlbaum.

Dornic, S. (1979). Information processing in bilinguals: Some selected issues. *Psychological Research, 40*, 329–348.

Dornic, S. (1980). Information processing and language dominance. *International Review of Applied Psychology, 29*, 119–140.

Dornic, S., & Laaksonen, T. (1990, June). *Switching languages in comprehension, naming and translation* (No. 720). Stockholm: Stockholm University, Department of Psychology.

Dyer, F. N. (1971). Color-naming interference in monolinguals and bilinguals. *Journal of Verbal Learning and Verbal Behavior, 10*, 297–302.

Emerson, M. J., & Miyake, A. (2003). The role of inner speech in task switching: A dual-task investigation. *Journal of Memory and Language, 48*, 148–168.

Fabbro, F., Skrap, M., & Aglioti, S. (2000). Pathological switching between languages after frontal lesions in a bilingual patient. *Journal of Neurology, Neurosurgery, and Psychiatry, 68*, 650–652.

Fox, E. (1996). Cross-language priming from ignored words: Evidence for a common

representational system in bilinguals. *Journal of Memory and Language, 35*, 353–370.

Goschke, T. (2000). Intentional reconfiguration and involuntary persistence in task-set switching. In S. Monsell & J. Driver (Eds.), *Attention and performance 18: Control of cognitive processes* (pp. 331–355). Cambridge, MA: MIT Press.

Grainger, J. (1993). Visual word recognition in bilinguals. In R. Schreuder & B. Weltens (Eds.), *The bilingual lexicon* (pp. 11–25). Amsterdam: Benjamins.

Grainger, J., & Dijkstra, T. (1992). On the presentation and use of language information in bilinguals. In R. J. Harris (Ed.), *Cognitive processing in bilinguals* (pp. 207–220). Amsterdam: Elsevier.

Green, D. W. (1986). Control, activation and resource. *Brain and Language, 27*, 210–223.

Green, D. W. (1993). Towards a model of L2 comprehension and production. In R. Schreuder & B. Weltens (Eds.), *The bilingual lexicon* (pp. 249–277). Amsterdam: Benjamins.

Green, D. W. (1997, April). *The bilingual lexico-semantic system: Looping the loop.* Paper presented to the International Symposium of Bilingualism, Newcastle-upon-Tyne.

Green, D. W. (1998a). Mental control of the bilingual lexico-semantic system. *Bilingualism: Language and Cognition, 1*, 67–81.

Green, D. W. (1998b). Schemas, tags and inhibition. *Bilingualism: Language and Cognition, 1*, 100–104.

Grosjean, F. (1982). *Life with two languages: An introduction to bilingualism.* Cambridge, MA: Harvard University Press.

Grosjean, F. (1997). Processing mixed language: Issues, findings, and models. In A. M. B. de Groot & J. F. Kroll (Eds.), *Tutorials in bilingualism: Psycholinguistic perspectives* (pp. 225–254). Mahwah, NJ: Erlbaum.

Grosjean, F. (1998). Studying bilinguals: Methodological and conceptual issues. *Bilingualism: Language and Cognition, 1*, 131–149.

Hernandez, A. E., Dapretto, M., Mazziotta, J., & Bookheimer, S. (2001). Language switching and language representation in Spanish-English bilinguals: An fMRI study. *NeuroImage, 14*, 510–520.

Hernandez, A. E., Martinez, A., & Kohnert, K. (2000). In search of the language switch: An fMRI study of picture naming in Spanish-English bilinguals. *Brain and Language, 73*, 421–431.

Jensen, A. R., & Rohwer, W. D. (1966). The Stroop color-word test: A review. *Acta Psychologia, 25*, 36–93.

Jersild, A. T. (1927). Mental set and shift. *Archives of Psychology, 89.*

Kim, K. H. S., Relkin, N. R., Kyoung-Min, L., & Hirsch, J. (1997). Distinct cortical areas associated with native and second languages. *Nature, 388*, 171–174.

Kirsner, K., Smith, M. C., Lockhart, R. S., King, M. L., & Jain, M. (1984). The bilingual lexicon: Language specific units in an integrated network. *Journal of Verbal Learning and Verbal Behavior, 23*, 519–539.

Kiyak, H. A. (1982). Interlingual interference in naming color words. *Journal of Cross Cultural Psychology, 13*, 125–135.

Kolers, P. A. (1966). Reading and talking bilingually. *American Journal of Psychology, 79*, 357–376.

Kolers, P. A. (1968). Bilingualism and information processing. *Scientific American, 218*, 78–89.

Kroll, J. F., & De Groot, A. M. B. (1997). Lexical and conceptual memory in the bilingual: Mapping form to meaning in two languages. In A. M. B. de Groot & J. F. Kroll (Eds.), *Tutorials in bilingualism: Psycholinguistic perspectives* (pp. 169–199). Mahwah, NJ: Erlbaum.

Kroll, J. F., & Dijkstra, T. (2002). The bilingual lexicon. In R. B. Kaplan (Ed.), *Handbook of applied linguistics* (pp. 301–324). Oxford, U.K.: Oxford University Press.

Kroll, J. F., & Stewart, E. (1994). Category interference in translation and picture naming: Evidence for asymmetric connections between bilingual memory representations. *Journal of Memory and Language, 33*, 149–174.

Kroll, J. F., & Tokowicz, N. (2001). The development of conceptual representation for words in a second language. In J. L. Nicol (Ed.), *One mind, two languages: Bilingual language processing* (pp. 49–71). Cambridge, MA: Blackwell.

La Heij, W., Hooglander, A., Kerling, R., & Van der Velden, E. (1996). Nonverbal context effects in forward and backward word translation: Evidence for concept mediation. *Journal of Memory and Language, 35*, 648–665.

Lee, W. L., Wee, G. C., Tzeng, O. J., & Hung, D. L. (1992). A study of interlingual and intralingual Stroop effect in three different scripts: Logographic, syllabary, and alphabet. In R. J. Harris (Ed.), *Cognitive processing in bilinguals* (pp. 427–442). Amsterdam: North-Holland/Elsevier Science.

Li, P., & Farkas, I. (2002). A self-organizing connectionist model of bilingual processing. In R. Heredia & J. Altarriba (Eds.), *Bilingual sentence processing* (pp. 59–85). Amsterdam: North-Holland/Elsevier Science.

Loasby, H. A. (1998). *A study of the effects of language switching and priming in a picture naming task.* Unpublished manuscript, University of Oxford, Oxford, U.K.

Los, S. (1996). On the origin of mixing costs: Exploring information processing in pure and mixed blocks of trials. *Acta Psychologica, 94*, 145–188.

Macnamara, J. (1967a). The bilingual's linguistic performance: A psychological overview. *Journal of Social Issues, 23*, 59–77.

Macnamara, J. (1967b). The linguistic independence of bilinguals. *Journal of Verbal Learning and Verbal Behavior, 6*, 729–736.

Macnamara, J., Krauthammer, M., & Bolgar, M. (1968). Language switching in bilinguals as a function of stimulus and response uncertainty. *Journal of Experimental Psychology, 78*, 208–215.

Macnamara, J., & Kushnir, S. L. (1971). Linguistic independence of bilinguals: The input switch. *Journal of Verbal Learning and Verbal Behavior, 10*, 480–487.

MacLeod, C. M. (1991). Half a century of research on the Stroop effect: An integrative review. *Psychological Bulletin, 109*, 163-203.

Mayr, U., & Keele, S. W. (2000). Changing internal constraints on action: The role of backward inhibition. *Journal of Experimental Psychology: General, 129*, 4–26.

Meiran, N. (1996). Reconfiguration of processing mode prior to task performance. *Journal of Experimental Psychology: Learning, Memory, and Cognition, 22*, 1–20.

Meiran, N. (2000). Modelling cognitive control in task-switching. *Psychological Research, 63*, 234–249.

Meiran, N., Chorev, Z., & Sapir, A. (2000). Component processes in task switching. *Cognitive Psychology, 41*, 211–253.

Meuter, R. F. I. (1994). *Language switching in naming tasks.* Unpublished doctoral dissertation, University of Oxford, Oxford, U.K.

Meuter, R. F. I. (2001, April). *Switch costs in bilingual discourse: An exploration of relativity in language proficiency.* Poster session presented at the Third International Symposium on Bilingualism, University of the West of England, Bristol, U.K.

Meuter, R. F. I., & Allport, A. (1999). Bilingual language switching in naming: Asymmetrical costs in language selection. *Journal of Memory and Language, 40*, 25–40.

Meuter, R. F. I., & Binder, P. (2004, May). *Language selection in trilingual speakers: L'embarras du choix.* Paper presented at the Annual Conference of the American Association of Applied Linguistics, Portland.

Meuter, R. F. I., Humphreys, G. W., & Rumiati, R. I. (2002). The frontal lobes and bilingual language switching: Modulatory control in language selection. *International Journal of Bilingualism, 6*, 109–124.

Meuter, R. F. I., Jackson, G. M., Roberts, M., & Jackson, S. (1999, April). *Electrophysiological correlates of bilingual language selection.* Poster session presented at the Second International Conference on Bilingualism, Newcastle-upon-Tyne, U.K.

Meuter, R. F. I., & Leisser, R. (2002, April). *Language switching in bilinguals: Effects of context in cueing speech.* Poster session presented at the Experimental Psychology Conference, Adelaide, Australia.

Meuter, R. F. I., & Powell, D. (1997, April). *Language selection in bilinguals: The role of contextual cues.* Poster session presented at the International Symposium on Bilingualism, University of Newcastle-upon-Tyne, Newcastle-upon-Tyne, U.K.

Meuter, R. F. I., & Shallice, T. (2001, April). *Processes underlying language selection in bilingual speakers: Aspects of language set and shift.* Paper presented at the Third International Symposium on Bilingualism, University of the West of England, Bristol, U.K.

Meuter, R. F. I., & Tan, C. (2003, April). *A comparative study on the role of language-specificity and language mode.* Paper presented at the Fourth International Symposium on Bilingualism, Arizona State University, Tempe.

Milner, B. (1963). Effects of different brain lesions on card-sorting. *Archives of Neurology, 9*, 90–100.

Monsell, S. (1996). Control of mental processes. In V. Bruce (Ed.), *Unsolved mysteries of the mind: Tutorial essays on cognition* (pp. 93–148). Hove, U.K.: Taylor & Francis.

Monsell, S., Azuma, R., Yeung, N., Sumner, P., Waters, H., Williams, N., et al. (1997, November). *Are task-switching costs paradoxically asymmetrical?* Paper presented at the 38th Annual Meeting of the Psychonomic Society, Philadelphia.

Monsell, S., Yeung, N., & Azuma, R. (2000). Reconfiguration of task-set: Is it easier to switch to the weaker task? *Psychological Research, 63*, 250–264.

Moyer, R. S., & Landauer, T. K. (1967). Time required for judgements of numerical inequality. *Nature, 215*, 1519–1520.

Norman, D. A., & Shallice, T. (1986). Attention to action: Willed and automatic control of

behavior. In R. J. Davidson, G. E. Schwartz, & D. Shapiro (Eds.), *Consciousness and self-regulation* (Vol. 4, pp. 1–18). New York: Plenum Press.

Obler, L. K., & Albert, M. L. (1978). A monitor system for bilingual language processing. In M. Paradis (Ed.), *Aspects of bilingualism* (pp. 105–113). Columbia, SC: Hornbeam Press.

Pallier, C., Colomé, À., & Sebastián-Gallés, N. (2001). The influence of native-language phonology on lexical access: Exemplar-based versus abstract lexical entries. *Psychological Science, 12*, 445–449.

Paradis, M. (1980). The language switch in bilinguals: Psycholinguistic and neurolinguistic perspectives. In P. H. Nelde (Ed.), *Languages in contact and conflict* (pp. 501–506). Wiesbaden, Germany: Franz Steiner-Verlag.

Penfield, W., & Roberts, L. (1959). *Speech and brain-mechanisms.* Princeton, NJ: Princeton University Press.

Perani, D., Dehaene, S., Grassi, F., Cohen, L., Cappa, S. F., Dupoux, E., et al. (1996). Brain processing of native and foreign languages. *NeuroReport, 7*, 2439–2444.

Perani, D., Paulesu, E., Sebastian-Galles, N., Dupoux, E., Dehaene, S., Bettinardi, V., et al. (1998). The bilingual brain: Proficiency and age of acquisition of the second language. *Brain, 121*, 1841–1852.

Perret, E. (1974). The left frontal lobe of man and the suppression of habitual responses in verbal categorical behavior. *Neuropsychologia, 12*, 323–330.

Poulisse, N. (1997). Language production in bilinguals. In A. M. B. de Groot & J. F. Kroll (Eds.), *Tutorials in bilingualism: Psycholinguistic perspectives* (pp. 201–224). Mahwah, NJ: Erlbaum.

Poulisse, N., & Bongaerts, T. (1994). First language use in second language production. *Applied Linguistics, 15*, 36–57.

Preston, M. S., & Lambert, W. E. (1969). Interlingual interference in a bilingual version of the Stroop color-word task. *Journal of Verbal Learning and Verbal Behavior, 8*, 295–301.

Price, C. J., Green, D. W., & von Studnitz, R. (1999). A functional imaging study of translation and language switching. *Brain, 122*, 2221–2235.

Robertson, I. H., Manly, T., Andrade, J., Baddeley, B. T., & Yiend, J. (1997). "Oops!": Performance correlates of everyday attentional failures in traumatic brain injured and normal subjects. *Neuropsychologia, 35*, 747–758.

Rogers, R. D., & Monsell, S. (1995). The cost of a predictable switch between simple cognitive tasks. *Journal of Experimental Psychology: General, 124*, 207–231.

Rogers, R. D., Sahakian, B. J., Hodges, J. R., Polkey, C. E., Kennard, C., & Robbins, T. W. (1998). Dissociating executive mechanisms of task control following frontal lobe damage and Parkinson's disease. *Brain, 121*, 815–842.

Rubenstein, J. S., Meyer, D. E., & Evans, J. E. (2001). Executive control of cognitive processes in task switching. *Journal of Experimental Psychology: Human Perception and Performance, 27*, 763–797.

Sandston, J., & Albert, M. L. (1987). Perseveration in behavioral neurology. *Neurology, 37*, 1736–1741.

Shallice, T. (1988). *From neuropsychology to mental structure*. Cambridge, U.K.: Cambridge University Press.

Shallice, T., & Burgess, P. (1996). The domain of supervisory processes and temporal organization of behavior. *Philosophical Transactions of the Royal Society London B, 351*, 1405–1412.

Shanon, B. (1991). Faulty language selection in polyglots. *Language and Cognitive Processes, 6*, 339–350.

Smith, M. C. (1997). How do bilinguals access lexical information? In A. M. B. de Groot & J. F. Kroll (Eds.), *Tutorials in bilingualism: Psycholinguistic perspectives* (pp. 145–168). Mahwah, NJ: Erlbaum.

Spector, A., & Biederman, I. (1976). Mental set and mental shift revisited. *American Journal of Psychology, 89*, 669–679.

Spivey, M. J., & Marian, V. (1999). Cross talk between native and second languages: Partial activation of an irrelevant lexicon. *Psychological Science, 10*, 281–284.

Stroop, J. (1935). Studies of interference in serial verbal reactions. *Journal of Experimental Psychology, 18*, 643–662.

Taylor, I. (1976). *Introduction to psycholinguistics*. New York: Holt, Rinehart & Winston.

Van Heuven, W. J. B., Dijkstra, A., & Grainger, J. (1998). Orthographic neighborhood effects in bilingual word recognition. *Journal of Memory and Language, 39*, 458–483.

Norman Segalowitz
Jan Hulstijn

18

Automaticity in Bilingualism and Second Language Learning

ABSTRACT   In this chapter, we examine automaticity in light of the role it might play in second language acquisition and in bilingual functioning. We review various theoretical and operational definitions of automaticity, considering their respective strengths, limitations, and challenges they present to researchers studying automaticity in the context of bilingualism. Studies are reviewed regarding automaticity in grammar acquisition and in lexical access and the connection between automaticity and attention in second language acquisition. The implications of automaticity for second language instruction are also discussed. It is argued that automaticity needs to be carefully defined operationally and always viewed in the larger context of how the control system operates in the acquisition and performance of complex skills.

This chapter examines the role played by automaticity and closely related psychological constructs in bilingual functioning and in second language (L2) acquisition. Why devote a chapter to automaticity in a book about bilingualism? As we show, nearly all psychological approaches to bilingualism and L2 acquisition emphasize the importance, alongside many other factors of course, of *frequency* and practice-based *repetition* involving the mapping of L2 experiences onto their underlying cognitive representations. The prime psychological construct invoked for understanding frequency effects and how repetition leads to improvement in L2 skill (or any skill for that matter) is *automaticity*.

We begin our discussion, therefore, with a review of what automaticity is (and is not) from a general cognitive perspective on skill acquisition, placing automaticity into its larger context and examining different current approaches to its study. This is followed by a discussion of several areas in bilingualism research in which automaticity has received special emphasis. Next, we consider some of the pedagogical implications of research on automaticity for language instruction. Finally, we conclude with a brief discussion of future directions for research on automaticity and bilingualism.

Automaticity

Automaticity has been given both loose theoretical definitions and a number of highly specific operational definitions. Generally, *automaticity* refers to the absence of attentional control in the execution of a cognitive activity, with attentional control understood to imply the involvement, among other things, of intention, possibly awareness, and the consumption of cognitive resources, all in the service of dealing with limited processing capacity (Kahneman, 1973). Some have also associated parallel processing with automatic processing and serial processing with nonautomatic or attention-based processing (Schneider & Shiffrin, 1977; but see Nakayama & Joseph, 1998, for a different interpretation).

A good example of what theorists have in mind by this distinction is what happens when a skilled reader of English recognizes a single letter, say, the letter *A* (Posner & Boies, 1971). Simple, single-letter recognition, it is claimed, requires no conscious effort or effortful attention, is extremely rapid, and cannot be stopped or interfered with by other ongoing activities. When presented with such a stimulus, a fluent reader cannot help recognizing it. It is in this sense that letter recognition is said to be "automatic." In contrast, the recognition of a letter in the Hebrew alphabet by an L1 speaker of English who is only a novice reader of Hebrew might require considerable consciously directed effort, applied slowly over an interval much longer than it takes that same person to recognize a letter of the English alphabet. Thus, the relatively rapid, effortless, and ballistic (unstoppable) activities underlying fluent letter recognition are said to be automatic, standing in contrast to slower, effortful activities that can be interrupted or influenced by other ongoing internal processes (e.g., distractions, competing thoughts).

The characteristics of automaticity mentioned—its rapidity, effortlessness, unconscious nature, and ballistic nature—have each been separately operationalized in various ways in experimental research; some examples are reviewed next. In thinking about these examples, it is important to keep in mind that, in principle, these characteristics do not necessarily always have to bundle together (Bargh, 1992; Neumann, 1984; N. S. Segalowitz, 2003; Tzelgov, 1999). For example, Paap and Ogden (1981) presented evidence showing that fluent letter recognition may be automatic in the sense of being obligatory but nevertheless can consume resources. This illustrates one way in which automaticity does not refer to a unitary construct. It would be an error, therefore, to assume without first doing the requisite empirical research that extensive practice leading to expertise will unfailingly result in performance that has *all* the characteristics typically associated with automaticity.

This distinction between automatic and attention-based processing pervades the cognitive psychological literature on skill acquisition (Ackerman, 1988, 1989; Anderson, 1983; Anderson & Lebiere, 1998; LaBerge & Samuels, 1974; Levelt, 1989; Logan; 1988; Proctor & Dutta, 1995) and is central to many treatments of L2 acquisition (DeKeyser, 2001; N. C. Ellis, 2002; Hulstijn & Hulstijn, 1984; Johnson, 1996; McLaughlin & Heredia, 1996; McLaughlin, Rossman, & McLeod, 1983; and N. S. Segalowitz, 1997, 2003). As will become evident from discussion in this chapter, the idea of automaticity is itself evolving, especially as researchers devise different ways to operationalize what they mean by it.

Broadly speaking, two general theoretical approaches have been followed in attempts to understand the place of automatization during skill development. One approach is typified by Anderson's ACT* (ACT-Star: Adaptive Control of Thought) model of skill acquisition (Anderson, 1983; Anderson & Lebiere, 1998). This approach holds that, in the early phases of skill acquisition, performance largely relies on mechanisms that are under conscious control, often involving declarative knowledge (Anderson, 1983). As the learner gains practice, sequenced components of the new skill that are repeated become routinized or "chunked," rendering them very fast and efficient and unavailable to conscious awareness. The declarative knowledge is said to become proceduralized, and the change is sometimes compared by analogy to the compilation of a computer subroutine that involves converting instructions encoded in a high-level interpreted language into lower-level machine language.

An alternative approach is Logan's (1988) instance theory of automatic processing. Logan proposed that initially performance of a to-be-mastered skill is based on a set of algorithms for executing the desired action. Each time the rule is carried out, there is a new memory trace formed corresponding to the action executed. On subsequent occasions, there is a race between an algorithmic process that constructs the appropriate response and a retrieval process that searches memory for the information needed to perform the action. With increasing practice, more and more representations of the response are stored in memory, so eventually retrieval is accomplished faster than is execution of the algorithm. Logan's theory thus holds that automatization in skill acquisition involves a shift from rule-based to memory-based performance. Logan's theory is able to account very well for the power law (Newell & Rosenbloom, 1981) property of skilled performance, which refers to the frequent observation that response latency decreases as a function of the number of practice instances raised to some power (Logan, 1992).

Theoretical Perspectives and Empirical Studies on Automaticity in Bilingualism

Empirical studies addressing questions about automaticity and bilingualism can be viewed from various perspectives. We review studies that examined (a) automaticity as a characteristic of proficiency, (b) automaticity as a factor in grammar rule acquisition, (c) the relation between automaticity and attention, and (d) bilingualism as a testing ground for learning more about automaticity.

Studies of Automaticity in Second Language Proficiency

The theoretical starting point for studies in this category is the view that accords a central place to automaticity in the development of a complex skill, especially the "compilation" of production units as advocated by Anderson (1983; Anderson & Lebiere, 1998), Ackerman (1988, 1989), and others.

For a specific example related to language skill, consider Levelt's (1989, 1999) "blueprint" of the cognitive architecture of the system responsible for fluent, intentional speech. One component of this architecture is an executive system that he called the conceptualizer, a functional level responsible for generating preverbal messages and monitoring the speaking activity. The work of the conceptualizer is largely an attention-based process in which the speaker is able to attend to the communicative event as it unfolds. Levelt admitted that much of the work of the conceptualizer may become directly or automatically available to the speaker because of a lifetime of practice at generating messages, monitoring the situation for turn-taking cues, selecting sociolinguistically appropriate forms of speech, and so on. Yet, Levelt pointed out that speakers can nevertheless easily attend to these aspects of speech if necessary. In this sense, these aspects of the work of the conceptualizer are not "informationally encapsulated" (nonmodular); that is, they do not function as relatively autonomous cognitive processing modules and so are not automatic.

The three remaining components of the cognitive architecture proposed by Levelt (1989, 1999) are the formulator, responsible for grammatical and phonological encoding; the articulator, responsible for the neuromuscular execution of the phonetic plan; and the speech-comprehension system, responsible for providing the conceptualizer with information required for self-monitoring (see La Heij, chapter 14, and Costa, chapter 15, this volume). In contrast to the conceptualizer, the remaining three components are held to be largely automatic in the sense of being informationally encapsulated (modular). For example, selection of eligible grammatical argument categories permitted by a verb that has been selected, individual word retrieval, or phonological encoding and articulation all occur in an automatic fashion (although Levelt did allow for marginal forms of executive control even here; Levelt, 1989, p. 22).

As for speaking in L2, the issue then becomes whether the scope of automaticity in L2 is the same as in L1. Several authors have followed up on this.

Pienemann (1998) proposed a processability theory using Levelt's model as a starting point for a theory of how procedural, and hence automatized, skills develop in the L2 learner (see Pienemann, Di Biase, Kawaguchi, & Håkansson, chapter 7, this volume). De Bot (1992) also examined how Levelt's model could be applied to the L2 context.

The implications for bilingual development of these ways of thinking about automaticity are clear; later phases of L2 learning must involve automatic processing to a far greater degree than do earlier phases, and this automatic processing will play a significant role in distinguishing fluent from nonfluent abilities. Such an idea may have important consequences for both theory and practice because a role for automaticity in acquiring L2 proficiency could be taken as support for a general skills approach to language learning. Such a skills approach (e.g., Johnson, 1996; McLeod & McLaughlin, 1986) stands in contrast to approaches emphasizing the fine tuning of underlying competence parameters believed to constitute an innate universal grammar (e.g., White, 1989, 1996). Thus, a focus on automaticity in bilingualism may be of significant interest insofar as it has the potential to link a theory of bilingual ability to the broader and more general psychological literature on cognitive skill development.

An early demonstration of the importance of automaticity for understanding L2 proficiency was provided by Favreau and Segalowitz (1983). They compared two groups of relatively fluent L2 readers. One group, here referred to as the stronger bilinguals, comprised people able to read L2 and L1 texts equally fast to achieve the same level of understanding. The other group is referred to here as the weaker bilinguals, although it must be remembered that people in this group still were very strong in an absolute sense. Participants in the weaker group, unlike those in the stronger group, read the L2 more slowly than L1 to achieve comparable levels of comprehension in the two languages. The goal of the study was to see whether the stronger bilinguals possessed more automatic single-word recognition skills than the weaker bilinguals.

To investigate this, Favreau and Segalowitz adapted Neely's (1977) operational definition of automaticity as a ballistic or unstoppable process. This involved a primed lexical decision task in which participants saw a priming stimulus followed by a target stimulus. The prime was either a category name (e.g., FRUIT) or a meaningless string of symbols. The prime signaled the onset of the upcoming target. The target was either a word naming an exemplar from the prime category (e.g., APPLE), an exemplar from another category (e.g., TABLE), or a nonword. The subject had to judge the word/nonword status (lexical decision) of the target. In some conditions, the participants were trained to expect a prime word like FRUIT to be followed by a semantically *unrelated* target word such as TABLE.

Like Neely, Favreau, and Segalowitz (1983) found that, once participants were suitably trained, they showed appropriate facilitation and inhibition effects in L1. For example, with a long interval (1,150 ms) between prime and target, a prime like FRUIT facilitated lexical decision to an *expected* but semantically unrelated target like TABLE or CHAIR, relative to the neutral prime condition. In contrast, a prime like FRUIT inhibited responses to an *unexpected* yet semantically related target like APPLE that was occasionally presented on surprise trials. On the other hand, when the prime–target interval was short (200 ms), lexical decision on these surprise trials was facilitated, indicating that the subject could not suppress the activation of semantically related concepts (APPLE, ORANGE, BANANA, etc., by FRUIT) even though instructions and training indicated that such targets were not predicted by the prime. In this way, the experiment demonstrated the ballistic nature of word meaning activation.

Favreau and Segalowitz (1983) found that in L2 only the stronger group showed this form of automaticity. Interestingly, the evidence also indicated that the weaker bilinguals did not process stimuli more slowly but only less automatically. This research illustrates the important point that subtle cognitive processing differences can exist between groups of relatively highly skilled L2 users (all bilinguals in this study were able to read mature texts to full comprehension), in which for some people (e.g., the stronger bilinguals) certain underlying processes operated in a ballistic fashion; for others, they did not.

Segalowitz and Segalowitz later proposed a somewhat different approach to the study of automaticity (N. S. Segalowitz & Segalowitz, 1993; S. J. Segalowitz, Segalowitz, & Wood, 1998). Practice and experience with a language typically lead to faster processing, which is commonly reflected in various ways, including faster lexical decision times, faster rates of speaking and reading, and better ability to process rapid speech. N. S. Segalowitz (2000; N. S. Segalowitz & Segalowitz, 1993) pointed out, however, that if the construct of

automatic processing is to have explanatory value, then—to avoid circularity—the term *automatic* should be more than a synonym for *fast*.

As a consequence, there is a need to distinguish operationally between the following two situations, each involving a contrast between fast and slow performance. The first is Situation A, in which the faster performance is simply caused by a difference in the run-time speeds of the processes underlying performance and not some difference in the selection of which processes are involved or in the way processes interact with each other. In this case, there is no need to invoke the idea of *automatic processing*, defined now to mean more than fast processing to avoid circularity, to explain the difference in performance.

In contrast, there is Situation B, in which faster performance is caused by more than just a difference in the speed of underlying processes. Here, the difference may lie in the way underlying processes are organized, such as when L2 visual word recognition proceeds directly from the printed stimulus to meaning activation without first passing through a stage of phonological recoding or translation into L1. Or, instead, the difference might lie in the internal organization of a given process without necessarily involving the elimination of one or more stages of processing. Such differences could lead, for example, to more ballistic processing, more parallel processing, and so on, resulting in significantly faster and more efficient performance.

N. S. Segalowitz and Segalowitz (1993) described the fast–slow contrast of Situation A as a case reflecting simple speed-up and the fast–slow contrast in Situation B as a case for which the difference can more appropriately be attributed to automaticity. They proposed that when attempting to determine if automaticity underlies a given case of fast responding, an attempt should be made to reject the null hypothesis that the performance could be caused by merely generalized speed-up.

N. S. Segalowitz and S. J. Segalowitz (1993; S. J. Segalowitz et al., 1998) proposed a way to test—and therefore potentially reject—the speed-up null hypothesis. They argued that, when faster processing is caused only by generalized speed-up of the processes underlying performance, the standard deviation of the reaction time should drop proportional to the reduction in the reaction time. This idea can be understood at an intuitive level by considering the following metaphor. Suppose a videotaped recording of a person making a cup of tea on 50 different occasions is viewed. Each component of the action—putting the water on to boil, pouring the hot water into a cup, inserting the tea bag, and so on—will take a particular length of time. A mean execution time and a standard deviation for this mean can be calculated across the 50 repetitions both for the global action of "making tea" and for each component of this event. Suppose now a new videotape is created by rerecording the original at twice the normal speed. On the new tape, the entire event will appear to be executed in half the time with half the original standard deviation overall; moreover, the mean duration of each component and the standard deviation associated with each component will also be reduced by exactly half. This situation corresponds to what N. S. Segalowitz and Segalowitz (1993) argued to be the null case of generalized speed-up; performance becomes faster because the underlying component processes are executed more quickly and for no other reason. (Of course, this account makes a number of simplifying assumptions about the brain, including that the component processes are organized serially only. They probably are not. However, the scenario described would apply to both the nonoverlapping aspects of the underlying components and to those that are organized serially, which together determine the total time of execution.)

Suppose now we are shown still another videotape in which the mean time for the global action of making tea is again half the original mean time, but the standard deviation for the 50 repetitions is far less than half the original standard deviation. This tape cannot have been produced simply by rerecording the original at twice the normal speed. Instead, there must have been some change in the way the activity of making tea had been carried out, such that some of the slower and more variable components of the action sequence had been dropped or replaced by faster, less-variable components. In other words, there must have been a change that involved more than simple speed-up, namely, some form of restructuring of the underlying processes.

According to this approach, if it is believed that practice and experience have produced some cognitive change other than generalized speed-up—restructuring, more ballistic processing, reduced reliance on decision processes, and so on—then one should try to reject the null hypothesis represented by generalized speed-up. N. S. Segalowitz and Segalowitz (1993) proposed that if faster performance reflects more change than is accounted for by speed-up, then the standard deviation should change by a greater proportion than that seen in

the reaction time. Put another way, if the coefficients of variability—the ratio of the standard deviation to the mean reaction time for each individual—remain the same while reaction times become faster (that is, both standard deviation and reaction time change by the same proportion), then there will be no grounds for rejecting the speed-up null hypothesis, and there will not be a significant correlation between reaction time and coefficient of variability across subjects. If, on the other hand, the coefficient of variability is significantly reduced as reaction time becomes faster, then the null hypothesis can be rejected, and a claim can be made that there has been a change—which N. S. Segalowitz and Segalowitz (1993) called automatization—that must reflect a different recruitment or organization of underlying mechanisms. In this case, as the reaction time reduces, so does the coefficient of variability, and there will be a significant correlation between the two. (See Wingfield, Goodglass, & Lindfield, 1997, for a different approach to dissociating speed of processing from automaticity.)

N. S. Segalowitz and Segalowitz (1993) collected lexical decision data from adults who varied in ability in L2 English or L2 French (S. J. Segalowitz et al., 1998). The results were consistent with their approach for distinguishing automaticity from speed-up. They found that coefficient of variability varied with reaction time in those conditions for which faster responding was logically expected to reflect a change involving more than just speed-up. They also found that coefficient of variability did not vary when faster responding was expected to reflect only speed-up (see also N. S. Segalowitz, Poulsen, & Segalowitz, 1999). These results are interesting for two reasons. Methodologically, they demonstrate how to move beyond merely speculating that an observed case of increased performance speed reflects a higher level of automaticity; it is now possible to assess the degree to which this performance is not solely attributable to generalized speed-up. On a theoretical level, this research demonstrated that higher levels of L2 proficiency, unlike lower levels of L2 proficiency, are associated with more than just differences in processing speed.

Caution must be taken, of course, when using the coefficient of variability analysis just described. Failure to reject the generalized speed-up hypothesis carries with it the usual caveats concerning failure to reject the null hypothesis; it is always wise, therefore, to have convergent evidence to support a generalized speed-up account to conclude from failure to reject that speed-up is what actually occurred. Also, the method of analysis proposed by N. S. Segalowitz and Segalowitz (1993) does not address the many interesting questions that could be asked regarding the kind of change that has taken place when analysis supports a claim for automatization; it only allows concluding that something other than generalized speed-up occurred.

Further research is always required to pinpoint the exact nature of the change; however, analysis of the coefficient of variability may again be useful in that follow-up research. For example, suppose the results of a study indicated that L2 word recognition became faster after some particular form of training, and that a generalized speed-up explanation can be rejected by the coefficient of variability analysis. Follow-up research using a design permitting a coefficient of variability analysis could be useful for looking into whether performance improved because, say, perception of orthographic redundancies (knowledge of spelling pattern frequencies) or phonological recoding had become more automatic.

Automaticity and Grammar Rule Acquisition

Perhaps one of the most hotly debated issues in the field of foreign or L2 learning concerns the learning and subsequent use of explicit grammar rules. Currently, there are three main theoretical positions on this issue, commonly referred to as the strong interface, weak interface, and no interface positions (R. Ellis, 1993; Larsen, Freeman, & Long, 1991, p. 324). Adherents of the strong interface position claim that explicit, declarative knowledge can be transformed or converted into implicit knowledge through practice, as proposed in Anderson's skill acquisition theory (Anderson, 1983; Anderson & Lebiere, 1998). According to the weak interface position, explicit, declarative knowledge may somehow, in a way not yet properly understood, facilitate the acquisition of implicit, procedural knowledge. The no interface position denies a causal role of explicit knowledge in the acquisition of implicit knowledge. In the area of language pedagogy, Krashen (1981) is perhaps the best-known proponent of the no interface position. For a discussion of the theoretical issues involved in the three positions, see the work of R. Ellis (2000), Hulstijn (2002), and Paradis (1994).

Little empirical research has been conducted to test claims made on the basis of these three positions in relation to issues of automatization.

Robinson and Ha (1993) and Robinson (1997) investigated the learning of the so-called dative alternation rule of English by adult speakers of Japanese, Korean, and French (Robinson & Ha, 1993) and Japanese (Robinson, 1997) in a single learning session lasting not longer than 30 min. (*Dative alternation* refers to the fact that, for some monosyllabic verbs in English, the indirect object form can alternate with the direct object form, as in "She gave the book to the boy" and "She gave the boy the book," whereas some bisyllabic verbs only allow the indirect form, as in "She donated the painting to the museum.") In these studies, automaticity was defined as reaction time patterns conforming to the power law. Participants in the 1993 study were presented with the dative alternation rule. Subsequently, in the training phase, they were shown 36 sentences, one at a time. They had to indicate whether the sentence did or did not conform to the rule just presented. Feedback was given on the correctness of each response. There were 8 sentences in the training set. One sentence was presented eight times, one sentence seven times, one six times, and so on, and the 36 sentences were presented in random order. In a subsequent transfer test, participants performed the same task, this time with 32 sentences, 8 of which were identical to the ones used in the training set. Reaction times of responses to old sentences, which had been presented in the previous training phase, were faster than those to new sentences. However, no evidence was found for the hypothesis, based on Logan's instance theory (1988), that reaction times would be faster for sentences presented more often in the training phase than for sentences presented less often.

In interpreting the complex findings of this study, it is important to bear in mind that it was concerned with the application of a rule, explained in advance, in a metalinguistic task (grammaticality judgment) rather than in a functional listening, reading, speaking, or writing task, and that the training phase comprised only 36 trials. We concur with DeKeyser's (2001) interpretation that "neither rule application nor instance retrieval was at work, but a similarity-based item retrieval process" (pp. 142–143). The pattern of results in the 1997 study, which adopted a more complex design and addressed other issues in addition to Logan's instance theory, was similar to that of the 1993 study regarding instance learning. Again, no gradual improvement as a function of number of previous item presentations was found. In summary, the two Robinson studies did not provide evidence for automatization as operationally defined.

Healy and her coworkers (Bourne, Healy, Parker, & Rickard, 1999; Healy, Barshi, Crutcher, et al., 1998) investigated the acquisition of easy and difficult rules by adult native speakers of English. The easy rule required pronunciation of the article *the* as *thuh* or *thee* when preceding nouns beginning with a consonant or a vowel, respectively. The difficult rule required judging the order of letters in meaningless three-letter sequences, such as the invalid LMV and the valid PRQ sequences. PRQ is valid because it can be rearranged to correspond to a sequential string in the alphabet (PQR), whereas LMV cannot. Participants in both experiments were presented with well- and ill-formed stimuli. They judged the stimuli's well-formedness and received feedback on the correctness of their responses. Participants also reported whether their responses were based on a guess, on a rule, on memory of the instance, or on other strategies. In both experiments, response accuracy rose to around 95%, and latencies dropped over the course of 30 learning blocks. Healy et al. (1998) reported that:

> Although all subjects [in the difficult-rule experiment] guessed initially, many subjects soon discovered and started using the rule. However, by block 6, rule use began to give way to an instance strategy so that by the end of 30 blocks of practice, subjects exhibited the instance-based strategy almost exclusively. (p. 26)

In the easy-rule experiment, 40% rule use was reported initially, suggesting that some participants, not surprisingly, were familiar with the *thuh/thee* rule from the start. In Block 30, participants reported using the rule 65% of the time. An interesting finding was that, in the case of the easy rule, rule use resulted in faster response latencies than did use of the instance strategy, whereas the reverse pattern was obtained in the case of the difficult rule. In interpreting these results, one has to bear in mind, as in the case of the Robinson studies reported above, that participants were engaged in a metacognitive judgment task rather than in a speech production task requiring the application of the rules.

N. C. Ellis and Schmidt (1997) and DeKeyser (1997) investigated how adult, literate native speakers of English acquired some rules of grammar of an artificial language in a computer-controlled laboratory setting. These experiments were limited to the written mode for input and output; listening and speaking were not involved.

In all three studies, the participants had to learn patterns in an artificial language that were analogous to grammatical rules. Participants in the first experiment reported in the study of N. C. Ellis and Schmidt (1997) had to learn plural forms in an artificial language (e.g., *bupoon* for the plural of the artificial word *poon*, meaning plane), some of which conformed to frequency criteria that made them "regular" plurals, whereas others did not and hence were "irregular." Participants studied the artificial language names given to 20 picture stimuli in 15 sessions of 1 hour sessions and spanning up to 15 days. Participants in the second experiment were shown meaningless artificial language sentences for a period of 75 min. Participants in DeKeyser's study (1997) were shown artificial language sentences with pictures illustrating their meaning in 22 sessions of an hour or less and spread over an 11-week period. The exposure-learning regimes in these studies differed somewhat, but they had in common that both accuracy and reaction times of participants' responses were measured during the learning. All three studies showed an increase in response accuracy for stimuli conforming to the appropriate grammatical patterns and a concomitant decrease in latency over the course of trials and sessions following a power law of learning. The authors interpreted these results as evidence for automatization of grammar learning. The main focus of these studies, however, was on the issues of implicit versus explicit learning and top-down learning by rule versus bottom-up learning by association and analogy.

N. C. Ellis and Schmidt (1997) argued that the findings of their studies can be accounted for by a simple associative learning mechanism even in the case of the acquisition of regular rule-governed forms. DeKeyser (1997) found that performance in both comprehension practice and production practice followed the same power function learning curve, but that acquisition was skill specific, showing little transfer from comprehension to production and vice versa. DeKeyser argued that L2 rules can be learned in much the same way as learning in other cognitive domains and can be accounted for by Anderson's model of skill acquisition, according to which declarative knowledge, with practice, turns into procedural knowledge.

One of the crucial issues in the debate between proponents of the strong, weak, and no interface positions is concerned with the meaning of the expression *turn into* (*transform* is used as a synonym in this debate) when it is claimed by some and denied by others that explicit knowledge can turn into (or transform into) implicit knowledge. Does this mean that explicit knowledge undergoes a metamorphosis such that, eventually, explicit knowledge has ceased to exist and that, "in its place" implicit knowledge has arisen?

Such a view implicitly rests on the idea that first there is an area in the brain where explicit knowledge resides, and furthermore that, during the process of proceduralization, implicit knowledge is formed, settling itself in the same area, forcing explicit knowledge to dissolve. However, such a strong view of transformation is not supported by brain research. Brain research suggests that declarative knowledge resides in the medial temporal lobe, including the hippocampus, whereas implicit knowledge is distributed over the neocortex (Paradis, 1994; Squire & Knowlton, 2000; Ullman, 2001). Viewed from this neurophysiological perspective, the strong interface position in the L2 acquisition field should be taken to mean that explicit knowledge forms a prerequisite for implicit knowledge to come into existence rather than the claim that explicit knowledge transforms into implicit knowledge.

The evidence of the studies reviewed in this section are consistent with Willingham's (1998) position that, already in the initial phases of learning, implicit knowledge is spontaneously formed, and that explicit processes are simply not used any longer in later phases. The practical relevance of the interface issue remains great: Of course, language teachers and language learners alike want to know to what extent knowledge of grammar rules may foster or hinder the attainment of fluency in language use. In terms of theoretical explanations, however, the interface issue is likely to form part of the much broader neurocognitive issue of explicit and implicit cognition. Empirical evidence may come not only from behavioral data (such as response time and response variability, presented elsewhere in this chapter) but also from neurophysiological data (such as event-related potential and neuroimaging).

Automaticity and Attention in Second Language Proficiency

The research reviewed so far attempted to integrate the concept of automaticity with theories of L2 proficiency and L2 grammar learning. N. S. Segalowitz (1997, 2000) proposed, however, that automaticity addresses just one component of a larger set of issues underlying "cognitive fluency" or processing efficiency that is responsible for the linguistic fluency or proficiency (the rapidity, fluidity, and accuracy) observed in a bilingual individual. Besides automaticity, there is a complementary, nonautomatic aspect involving attention-based processes that are also required for fluent language use. These operate in a close fashion with more automatic processes to determine the overall underlying efficiency of L2 functioning.

Such attention-based processes include focusing on (directing awareness to) the language itself while learning it, such as the noticing and focus-on-form skills that may be necessary for successful learning (Doughty & Williams, 1998; Lightbown & Spada, 1990; Robinson, 1995; Schmidt, 2001). Selective attention is also involved in fluency insofar as the ability to focus on the speech stream as a channel of communication under noisy conditions or focus selectively on phonological cues carrying sociolinguistic messages or on cues to turn taking and the like, as pointed out by Levelt (1989) (see also Eviatar, 1998, and Fischler, 1998, for more on selective attention and language). Finally, there is the attention-directing function of language itself, in which language is used to shape the way a listener or reader builds a mental representation of the message conveyed. This attention-directing function is believed by cognitive linguists to be central to the communicative purpose of language (Langacker, 1987; Talmy, 1996, 2000).

N. S. Segalowitz and Frenkiel-Fishman (in press) found that L2 skills reflecting attention-directing functions of language were significantly related to levels of automaticity of single-word recognition as indexed by the coefficient of variability measure described here. This study involved an attention-shifting task adapted from Rogers and Monsell's (1995) alternating runs paradigm. The stimuli were time adverbials and conjunctions, both good examples of words that serve to direct a person's attention in particular ways while building a mental representation of a message's meaning. Time adverbials direct the listener/reader on how elements of a mental representation should be foregrounded or backgrounded with respect to time. Conjunctions convey the need to form particular links between elements of a mental representation.

Participants were given two tasks (N. S. Segalowitz & Frenkiel-Fishman, in press). In one they had to judge the meaning of a target word belonging to the time adverbial stimulus set. The other task required them to judge a conjunction. For example, in the time adverbial task, subjects judged whether a word (*soon*, *later*, etc.) referred to a moment in time relatively close to or relatively far from the present moment (as an illustration, compare the meanings of "I'll do it *soon*" versus "I'll do it *later*"). In the conjunction task, subjects judged whether a word (*because*, *despite*, etc.) normally indicates the presence or absence of a causal link between the clauses it conjoins (e.g., compare "John passed the exam *because* he studied all night" versus "John passed the exam *despite* partying all night").

In the N. S. Segalowitz and Frenkiel-Fishman (in press) experiment, on each trial either a time adverbial or a conjunction appeared in one of four spatial locations on a screen. This location indicated which task (time adverbial or conjunction judgment) was to be performed. As in the work of Rogers and Monsell (1995), the tasks alternated in a predictable manner according to the sequence "...adverbial adverbial conjunction conjunction..." and thereby requiring a repeat of a given task and a switch to the alternate task on every second trial. This design provided a measure of the switch cost, that is, the cost in response time to switch from one task to the other, compared to repeating a task. Participants performed the experiment in separate L2 and L1 blocks, thus providing a measure of switch cost in each language.

In a separate part of the study (N. S. Segalowitz & Frenkiel-Fishman, in press), subjects' ability to process L2 word meaning was indexed in terms of the coefficient of variability of latency (as discussed in the section Studies of Automaticity in Second Language Proficiency) in a classification task in which nouns were judged as referring to living or nonliving objects. Here also, L1 measures were used as baseline. The results indicated that the switch cost in L2 was significantly correlated with the coefficient of variability of reaction time in the classification task after taking into account performance on the same tasks in L1. The results were interpreted as indicating that attention-focusing skill is related to proficiency as indexed by switch cost and coefficient of variability of reaction time respectively.

Although it is beyond the scope of this chapter to discuss further the role of attention-based processes in L2 functioning and in fluency acquisition (see Schmidt, 2001), it is important to keep in mind that automaticity cannot really be talked about without also talking about attention. Automaticity is recognized only by virtue of its contrast to nonautomatic or less-automatic (attention-based) modes of processing.

Moreover, there are automatic modes of processing that are fully integrated within nonautomatic modes, and it is impossible to fully tease them apart. To illustrate, consider the relatively "simple" case of reading a sentence in L2. One has to process letters, words, and syntactic patterns and integrate all this into the ongoing construction of a representation of the meaning of the sentence and of the larger text. Reading will, of course, be fluent to the extent that many of the mechanisms involved are ballistic and do not consume resources better used for other purposes. However, such a need for automaticity can be identified at *all* levels of processing, from relatively "low-level" letter recognition to aspects of relatively "high-level" attention focusing (see also Tzelgov, Henik, & Leiser, 1990, for a similar point).

This tight relationship between automatic and attention-based mechanisms raises the following interesting question that has yet to be addressed empirically: Do the attention-based and automatic components of proficiency develop independently? If so, can such development account for individual differences in learning success in a given learning context (e.g., a classroom, study abroad, immersion, etc.)? If not, there are at least three alternatives to consider: (a) Do attention-based language skills require a threshold level of automatic processing before they can develop? (b) Does the acquisition of automatic processing abilities require some critical level of supporting attention-based mechanisms in place? (c) Should automatic and attention-based processing be conceived as mutually dependent? These questions have important practical value in addition to theoretical interest because the answers may point in particular directions regarding the most effective way to organize L2 learning experiences.

Studies Using Bilinguals to Investigate Automaticity

The studies reviewed in the previous sections directly addressed questions about the role played by automaticity in bilingualism. Next, we review several related examples of research that made use of the automatic and nonautomatic characteristics of bilingualism to study automaticity itself and related constructs in addition to contributing directly to an understanding of bilingualism as such.

One interesting study in this category is Meuter and Allport's (1999) study of attention. Meuter and Allport were interested in the processes responsible for the shift cost or slowed response time observed when subjects have to perform tasks in two different languages. In their study, bilinguals named numerals shown on the screen using L1 or L2 in a paradigm in which the language of response was cued by color.

Meuter and Allport (1999) found that the cost associated with switching to L1 (that is, the slowing of the L1 response observed after having just responded in L2 compared to having just responded in L1) was greater than the cost associated with switching to L2. This effect is paradoxical because normally it would be expected to be easier to switch to the stronger L1 than to switch to the weaker L2. In fact, however, the authors had predicted this paradoxical effect from their theory of the nature of switch costs. They believe that the cost observed on a given switch trial reflects the need to overcome inhibition activated on the immediately preceding trial. Thus, on a switch trial involving an L2 response, the bilingual has to suppress or inhibit the automatic activation of the competing stimulus name in L1 to respond correctly in L2. If, however, the switch trial requires an L1 response, the bilingual has to do two things: cancel the inhibition to responding in L1 that was activated on the previous trial and overcome any persisting inhibition from that trial.

Meuter and Allport's results were consistent with the idea that there is automatic activation of L1 representations in L1 naming tasks, whereas there is little or no automatic activation of L2 representations in an L2 naming task; this L1 activation may be difficult to overcome when competition between the languages is important. Presumably, their paradigm could be adapted to quantify this automatic activation when it is useful to measure an individual's degree of balance between L1 and L2 in terms of automatic processing and attention flexibility. (See also chapter 17, by Meuter, this volume.)

Bialystok (2001) reported a series of highly original studies on the possible cognitive benefits associated with early bilingualism (also, see Bialystok's chapter 20 in this volume). She investigated what happens when both languages are automatically activated and are always in competition because the individual is growing up bilingual. She compared bilingual children learning their two languages at the same time with monolingual children and found that, in certain nonlinguistic domains, children with strong L2 abilities outperformed monolingual children. The results were consistent with the following idea: Because almost every waking moment involves dealing with language-based cognitive demands, a bilingual with two (or more) equally strong languages at his or her command continually has to inhibit competition from the currently not-to-be-used language(s), competition that arises from the automatic activation of language representations elicited by ongoing thoughts and by stimuli in the environment. For the young bilingual child, this may constitute intensive training of frontal inhibitory systems, training that normally does not occur to the same degree for monolinguals. If correct, this view would then suggest that the automatic activation of language-based representations can, in a bilingual child, have far-reaching consequences by providing sustained training of inhibitory systems that are required even for nonlinguistic cognitive activity (such as those documented by Bialystok). This idea merits further investigation, especially through studies using more direct measures of the automatic nature of language activation and suppression.

Automaticity has also been studied in bilinguals with a view to understand the nature of lexical access. Tzelgov, Henik, Sneg, and Baruch (1996), for example, exploited certain automatic aspects of reading in bilinguals to understand further the nature of lexical access in skilled readers. Some theories of skilled reading hold that readers access meaning from print automatically in a process that is mediated by preassembled phonological representations (Van Orden, 1987) developed during earlier phases of skill acquisition. Other theories suggest that automatization in reading skill acquisition involves a shift from dependence on assembled phonological representations to direct access of meaning from visual input (Waters, Seidenberg, & Bruck, 1984). The mediated access approach characterizes automatic processing as making use of activity-specific "precompiled" productions, as proposed by Anderson (1983) in his process-based ACT* approach.

In contrast, the direct access approach characterizes automatic processing as a memory-based, single-step retrieval process, similar to Logan's (1988) memory-based instance theory of automaticity (i.e., a shift from algorithmic to instance retrieval). Tzelgov et al. examined bilingual readers in a Hebrew-English version of the Stroop paradigm (Stroop, 1935). They used cross-script homophones, such as Hebrew color words written in the Latin (English) alphabet (e.g., *adom*), and English color words written in Hebrew letters that, when sounded out, sound like English words.

Consider now the case in which *adom* is written in green ink, and the correct response is therefore "green." According to the mediated access approach, if the subject is a Hebrew speaker and a skilled reader of English, he or she will automatically access via a phonological route the concept of red because /adom/ in Hebrew means red. According to the direct access approach, however, the phonologically based link between /adom/ and the concept red will be bypassed.

In a series of experiments with Hebrew-English bilinguals, Tzelgov et al. studied whether the automatic processing underlying skilled L2 reading made use of the phonological route (and hence precompiled productions) or the direct route (and hence instance retrieval). They reported finding a strong cross-script Stroop effect, particularly when the stimulus was a transliteration of a color name in Hebrew, the subject's L1 (*adom* activating *red*). The results thus supported the first model described above, namely, that unintentional automatic processing in reading involves precompiled phonological productions and not retrieval of stored instances.

Tzelgov et al. (1996) argued, on the basis of these results and others they obtained, that there is evidence for two different, coexisting forms of automaticity, one involving activity-specific precompiled productions and the other the development of a database for memory retrieval in the execution of the skill in question. The results were also interpreted as support for the asymmetric model of bilingual memory proposed by Kroll (e.g., Kroll & Stewart, 1994) because the Stroop effects were themselves asymmetrical as a function of which language was L1 (see Kroll & Tokowicz, chapter 26, and Dijkstra, chapter 9, this volume, for related discussion).

In sum, it can be seen from these studies that bilingualism can provide a particularly useful situation for studying cognitive mechanisms not only as they relate to L2 processes, but also as they relate to basic, more general cognitive issues such as automaticity.

Instructional Implications

Questions about what role, if any, automaticity plays in L2 acquisition and proficiency will naturally have implications for how to optimize language instruction. Here, the central instructional question is the following: Once language learners have been exposed to new linguistic information, what must they do to be able to achieve later automatic access to that information? As pointed out, the functional, communicative use of language involves the simultaneous manipulation of many linguistic elements at different levels, ranging from the higher levels of content and discourse organization to the lower levels of processing speech sounds and letters (in oral and written communication, respectively). Given the fact that humans have a limited capacity for information processing, it is obvious that language users cannot pay attention to all information at all linguistic levels simultaneously to the same high degree. In most communicative situations, the processing of information at the higher levels—that is, information concerning the content and the course of the communication—consumes much of this limited capacity.

VanPatten (1990), for example, reported a study indicating that, in the early stages of L2 acquisition, learners find it difficult to focus both on message content and various aspects of form (verb form, grammatical functors). Because of the novelty of most communicative acts, the processing of information at the higher levels can hardly be automatized. What can be automatized to a large extent, however, is the processing of information at the intermediate levels of the retrieval of words to express personal thoughts; processing at the lower levels of the planning of the morphosyntactic, phonological, and phonetic aspects of the utterance; and the execution of the planned part of an utterance with the aid of speech organs accompanied by appropriate gestures.

This is what happens during the many years of L1 acquisition and what has turned most adults into fluent speakers of their native tongue. It is therefore important, in the case of L2 instruction, to devise tasks that do not require the allocation of much attention to the higher levels of information, allowing learners to pay attention to information at particular lower levels standing in need of automatization.

The basic principle underlying such tasks is repetition (N. C. Ellis, 2002), but as we discuss in the following sections, simple repetition as such cannot be the whole answer. To the extent learning is promoted through repetition (e.g., in the case of the automatization of the word-by-word understanding of speech), learners should listen to materials that do not contain very many unfamiliar words, preferably several times. Similarly, in the case of reading, learners should be given linguistically "easy" (but yet authentic or quasi-authentic) texts to allow them to increase their reading speed. Teachers and learners alike should make a principled distinction between two types of listening and reading activities: exposure to materials containing new linguistic elements for the purpose of acquiring new knowledge and exposure to materials containing familiar elements for the purpose of automatization.

Research on the Training of Lexical Access

Hulstijn (2001, pp. 283–286) discussed various pedagogical approaches designed, based on the ideas presented in the preceding section, to enhance automatic word recognition. Empirical research on the impact of training for automaticity on subsequent reading and writing skills has only just begun (e.g., Schoonen et al., 2003; Van Gelderen et al., 2004). In a study involving 281 high school students in Grade 8 in the Netherlands, Van Gelderen et al. and Schoonen et al. investigated the relative contribution of three sources of linguistic cognition on reading and writing in Dutch as an L1 and English as an L2 (after approximately 250 hours of instruction). The dependent variables were reading and writing both in L1 (Dutch) and L2 (English). The predictor variables fell into three categories: (a) knowledge of language, measured with tests of receptive vocabulary, grammar, and spelling, in both L1 and L2; (b) speed of access to knowledge of language, measured with computer-based tests of word recognition, lexical retrieval, sentence verification, and sentence building, in both L1 and L2; and (c) metacognitive knowledge, assessed with a questionnaire pertaining to knowledge of text characteristics and strategies of reading and writing in L1 and L2. In analyses using structural equation modeling, significant correlations were found between speed measures and measures for reading and writing skills.

Stronger correlations were found (Van Gelderen et al., 2004) between predictor variables and reading and writing in the case of L2 than in the case of L1. However, no variance in L1 and L2 reading or writing performance was uniquely accounted for by the speed measures when the knowledge of language and metacognitive knowledge measures were also entered into the regression analysis. One plausible interpretation of these findings is that most of these low-intermediate L2 learners could already access their L2 knowledge sufficiently fast to allow processing of semantic and pragmatic information at the text level.

Finally, we review a study that attempted to increase L2 automaticity through explicit training using the latency coefficient of variability as an operational definition of automaticity. Akamatsu (2001) trained 46 Japanese university students, who had at least 6 years of prior instruction in English, in seven weekly sessions to recognize 150 English words quickly. In each session, students had to draw separator lines as quickly and as accurately as possible between words that had been printed with no interword spaces. Before and after training, students took a computer-controlled word recognition test. This test comprised 50 nonwords and 50 high-frequency and 50 low-frequency words that had been part of the training set. Both accuracy and reaction time on correct trials improved significantly from pretest to posttest. More interesting, individuals' latency coefficient of variability and reaction time were highly and significantly correlated in the processing of low-frequency words, but not of high-frequency words, both before and after training. The author speculated that students in this study had already passed the automatization phase for high-frequency words. Training of these words had only resulted in speed-up, whereas training with the low-frequency words had produced a qualitative change, reflecting automatization. The results of this study (and those of N. S. Segalowitz, Watson, & Segalowitz, 1995, reviewed in the section Automaticity and Communicative Approaches to Teaching) support the idea that training activities of a relatively short duration can bring about a qualitative change in the processing of lexical information, indicating a gain in efficiency that reflects more than simple speed-up.

Clearly, research has only begun on the important practical question of how to enhance automatic processing to promote L2 proficiency. Such research is in its infancy because researchers have only just started to identify the learning issues involved and have only recently developed practical performance measures for operationalizing automaticity. There are, of course, ways of bringing L2 materials to the learner and to create repetition conditions in a manner that could promote automaticity beyond those reviewed earlier. For example, some authors have pointed out that, for any task aimed at helping learners gain fluency in oral production, it is essential to provide learners ample time to plan ahead (Robinson, 2001b). In a review of the literature on factors affecting cognitive complexity of L2 production tasks, Skehan and Foster (2001) claimed that "there is considerable agreement that complexity and fluency are enhanced by pre-task planning" (p. 201). They also pointed out that one of the things speakers do when they are given time to plan their oral production well ahead of execution is to bring into working memory elements from long-term memory perceived to be relevant to the task at hand.

Automaticity and Communicative Approaches to Teaching

A fundamental question remains, however, about how to best promote automatization through repetition in real learning situations outside the laboratory. In answering this question, we have to take into account the extensive and essentially negative experience with so-called pattern drills of the audiolingual method in the 1960s and 1970s. This method was used to help L2 learners improve their production skills in language laboratories through the use of equipment to listen to audio recordings and by making recordings of their own speech (Rivers, 1967).

One of the main reasons why many of these drills failed to bring about the desired effect on spontaneous language use is that they required learners to focus on grammatical forms almost exclusively. Many drills did not force learners to process information at the higher levels of discourse. These methods gave way to what are called communicative language teaching (CLT) methods that stress the importance of meaningful communication as part of the learning process. Unfortunately, most CLT methods do not provide sufficient repetition to promote automatization. This is because the openness of typical CLT communication activities cannot guarantee there will be the necessary opportunities for repeating and rehearing language input; efforts by teachers to supplement communicative activities with special repetition exercises are largely unsuccessful for the same reasons earlier audiolingual drill methods were (Johnson, 1996, especially pp. 171–172).

Thus, teachers are faced with the following dilemma: Typical methods that provide the repetition necessary for automaticity to develop ultimately fail to promote learning because of the highly decontextualized nature of the repeated material; at the same time, typical communicative methods that provide opportunities to fully contextualize learning through meaningful communication fail to provide the repetition necessary for automatization. Can this dilemma be overcome?

Gatbonton has addressed this problem by proposing an analysis of L2 learning that focuses on repetition leading to automaticity within highly contextualized learning (Gatbonton & Segalowitz, 1988; in press) and by providing sets of systematically constructed materials for practical applications based on this approach (Gatbonton, 1994). First, Gatbonton agreed with others that a fundamental step in early L2 learning is the automatization of formulaic utterances—chunks of language that are routinized even in the speech of native speakers (N. C. Ellis, 1997, 2002; Pawley & Syder, 1983; Wray, 2002; see chapters in Schmitt, 2004). Second, she advocated selecting the utterances to be automatized from among those expressions and utterance frames useful for a variety of communicative purposes. Third, she proposed ways to create activities systematically that are genuinely communicative (i.e., for which the communication meets a genuinely felt psychological need for information) and the activity is inherently repetitive (i.e., the activities involve, in a way that feels natural, the need to report information to many people, one by one). Thus, Gatbonton advocated repetition to promote automaticity of basic communicative utterances within a context that requires the learner to coordinate these learning activities with the control of attention, decision making, and other higher level aspects of language processing. She called this process *creative automatization* to reflect the idea that the learner achieves automatization through repetition of acts involving the creation of communicatively valuable utterances.

N. S. Segalowitz et al. (1995) provided some preliminary experimental support for this creative automatization proposal in a study using a single case design. In this study, a Greek-speaking psychology student who spoke English as an L2 participated in a psychology tutorial over a 3-week period in which a single article from a psychology journal was analyzed from several different perspectives. Throughout the 3-week period the student performed lexical decision tasks involving a large number of words, including keywords from the studied article and control words matched for frequency but not appearing in the article. The results showed that a measure analogous to the coefficient of variability of the lexical decision reaction time (coefficient of variability could not be used directly because this was a single-subject study) improved significantly for the words contained in the studied article but not for the control words. This result is consistent with the idea that natural and communicatively meaningful activities inherently repetitive can improve automaticity of lexical access. What is not known is how enduring such improved automaticity of lexical access is.

This would be an important question for future research to address.

Summary and Future Directions

We conclude this review by addressing two questions. First, is it possible to have a general theory of automaticity that will apply in a useful way to phenomena of bilingualism? Second, what future directions ought L2 acquisition research on automaticity take?

A General Theory of Automaticity

We have seen that automaticity figures prominently in most accounts of L2 acquisition and proficiency development, just as it does in most accounts of skill acquisition. Nevertheless, the usefulness of studying automaticity cannot to be taken for granted (see, e.g., Pashler's reservations [1998, pp. 357–382]). A major stumbling block to a general theory of automaticity is that the term has either been used in a very broad sense, without clear operational definition, or else has been defined narrowly but in different ways by different authors (e.g., in terms of ballistic processing; as a shift from serial to parallel processing; as restructuring resulting in a significant change in latency coefficient of variability; as latency patterns reflecting the power law). These are exactly the same problems that confront L2 acquisition researchers. They are attempting to distinguish between explicit and implicit learning processes, to understand when awareness is and is not useful in learning, to find ways of determining when language functioning is proceeding in an autonomous versus a monitored manner, and to understand the conditions under which autonomous processing might be acquired and enhanced (N. C. Ellis, 1994; Hulstijn, 2002; Robinson, 2001a). Thus, both cognitive psychologists interested in automaticity in general and L2 acquisition researchers interested specifically in how languages are learned face the common challenge of having to tease apart a complex of deeply intertwined issues. Is progress being made on this, or are we moving around in circles?

We think there is reason for optimism. One interesting example of potential progress in this area was provided by LaBerge (1997, 2000b) in his triangular circuit theory of attention. This theory identifies particular neural circuits as underlying so-called attention-based and automatic phenomena.

These involve neuron clusters in the posterior and anterior cortex for the perception of objects, their attributes, and the organization and execution of action plans; excitatory neurons in the thalamic nuclei that, by virtue of their wide cortical distribution, can selectively enhance cortical activity; and frontal cortex circuitry responsible for control. The linking of these sites forms what LaBerge referred to as "a triangular circuit of attention." Awareness of an object is said to occur when an attentional circuit for that object becomes linked to an attentional circuit related to the self, such as a self-attended representation of a person's spatial or temporal location in relation to the attended object. LaBerge separated automatic processing from attention-based processing in terms of the presence or absence of activity in these triangular circuits.

This theory has generated considerable discussion. For example, Tzelgov (1999), basing his work on LaBerge's theory, proposed that automaticity be used to refer to cases when there is activation of a triangular circuit not involving a self-attended circuit (see also LaBerge, 2000a, for commentary on this). By explicitly proposing neural correlates of attention-based and automatic phenomena, LaBerge raised the bar in the way we talk about automaticity. It is hoped that in time the multiple criteria that have up to now complicated discussion about automaticity will become more precisely defined and distinguishable from one another in terms of underlying neural mechanisms, whether in terms of LaBerge's theory or some other neurobiological approach to attention.

Even prior to the emergence of neural theories of automaticity, there has been a growing consensus that the common element in most automatic phenomena is *ballisticity*, the unstoppable execution of a process once triggered (Bargh, 1992; Favreau & Segalowitz, 1983; Neumann, 1984; Tzelgov, 1999). Although clearly still a work in progress, it appears that it may become possible to provide an account that integrates the neural and behavioral evidence for ballistic processing, thereby allowing more rigorous specification of the relation between automatic and other closely related phenomena.

Future Second Language Research on Automaticity

The developments identified in this chapter should make it possible to address basic questions in L2 acquisition in ways not before possible, using neurophysiological measures (such as event-related potential and neuroimaging) as well as behavioral measures (such as reaction times of responses elicited in a variety of single and dual tasks). Can we monitor the degree of automatic (ballistic) processing in L2 learners at different stages of acquisition? Can we do so for specific aspects of L2 cognition? The current storage-versus-computation debate in linguistics (cf. Nooteboom, Weerman, & Wijnen, 2002) concerning the division of labor between the lexicon (containing chunks of ready-made, stored linguistic information) and the grammar (containing procedures for computing or parsing remaining linguistic information, in language production and reception, respectively) may be highly relevant for the questions of (a) which linguistic phenomena are amenable to automatization and (b) to what extent knowledge of grammar rules can foster or hinder automatization. Perhaps, the success of L2 acquisition that results in increasingly fluent behavior resides, at least partly, in greater availability of ever-larger, preassembled linguistic units and the reduced need to compute information.

As we point out in this chapter, there is reason to believe that it is especially at the intermediate levels of syntactic, morphological, and phonological encoding/decoding, as well as at the lower levels of articulation and perception of acoustic or orthographic signals, that component processes can become automatic to a large extent. Nevertheless, under certain circumstances, the language user can consciously monitor the outcome of these processes and, for instance, decide to repair an error.

A further question that remains to be studied concerns the relationship between the ability to mobilize attentional resources (e.g., noticing) and L2 acquisition. Is noticing a cognitive prerequisite for attaining fluency? If so, for which linguistic phenomena and at which levels of processing might this be the case? How do neurobiological mechanisms of attention and automatic processing determine the cognitive efficiency that underlies high levels of language proficiency? What are the most effective ways to promote proficiency in terms of changing the way attention and automatic processes operate? Can neuroimaging techniques be used to monitor such change (see especially chapters 23 by Hull & Vaid and 24 by Abutalebi, Cappi, & Perani in this volume)?

The acquisition of, and functioning in, an L2 provide paradigmatic examples of the challenges facing cognitive scientists interested in how people acquire the ability to perform complex skills. The availability of the new techniques and the new ways of conceptualizing the issues reviewed here promise to bring important insights to this area.

Acknowledgments

We thank Laura Collin, Elizabeth Gatbonton, Randall Halter, Patsy Lightbown, and Irene O'Brien for helpful comments on earlier versions of this chapter. Support for this chapter came from a grant to Norman Segalowitz from the Natural Sciences and Engineering Research Council of Canada.

References

Ackerman, P. L. (1988). Determinants of individual differences during skill acquisition: Cognitive abilities and information processing. *Journal of Experimental Psychology: General, 117,* 288–318.

Ackerman, P. L. (1989). Individual differences and skill acquisition. In P. L. Ackerman, R. J. Sternberg, & R. Glaser (Eds.), *Learning and individual differences: Advances in theory and research* (pp. 165–217). New York: Freeman.

Akamatsu, N. (2001, February). *Effects of training in word recognition on automatization of word-recognition processing of EFL learners.* Paper presented at the 2001 annual conference of the American Association for Applied Linguistics, St. Louis, MO.

Anderson, J. R. (1983). *The architecture of cognition.* Mahwah, NJ: Erlbaum.

Anderson, J. R., & Lebiere, C. (1998). *The atomic components of thought.* Mahwah, NJ: Erlbaum.

Bargh, J. A. (1992). The ecology of automaticity: Toward establishing the conditions needed to produce automatic processing effects. *American Journal of Psychology, 105,* 181–199.

Bialystok, E. (2001). *Bilingualism in development: Language, literacy, and cognition.* New York: Cambridge University Press.

Bourne, L. E., Jr., Healy, A. F., Parker, J. T., & Rickard, T. C. (1999). The strategic basis of performance in binary classification tasks: Strategy choices and strategy transitions. *Journal of Memory and Language, 41,* 223–252.

De Bot, K. (1992). A bilingual production model: Levelt's speaking model adapted. *Applied Linguistics, 13,* 1–24.

DeKeyser, R. M. (1997). Beyond explicit rule learning: Automatizing second language morphosyntax. *Studies in Second Language Acquisition, 19,* 195–221.

DeKeyser, R. M. (2001). Automaticity and automatization. In P. Robinson (Ed.),

Cognition and second language instruction (pp. 125–151). Cambridge, MA: Cambridge University Press.

Doughty, C., & Williams, J. (Eds.). (1998). *Focus on form in classroom second language acquisition.* Cambridge, U.K.: Cambridge University Press.

Ellis, N. C. (Ed.). (1994). *Implicit and explicit learning of languages.* New York: Academic Press.

Ellis, N. C. (1997). Vocabulary acquisition: word structure, collocation, word-class, and meaning. In N. Schmitt & M. McCarthy (Eds.), *Vocabulary: Description, acquisition and pedagogy* (pp. 122–139). Cambridge, U.K.: Cambridge University Press.

Ellis, N. C. (2002). Frequency effects in language processing: A review with implications for theories of implicit and explicit language acquisition. *Studies in Second Language Acquisition, 24,* 143–188.

Ellis, N. C., & Schmidt, R. (1997). Morphology and longer distance dependencies: Laboratory research illuminating the A in SLA. *Studies in Second Language Acquisition, 19,* 145–171.

Ellis, R. (1993). The structural syllabus and second language acquisition. *TESOL Quarterly, 27,* 91–113.

Ellis, R. (2000, September). *The representation and measurement of L2 explicit knowledge.* Paper presented at the conference on Language in the Mind, National University of Singapore.

Eviatar, Z. (1998). Attention as a psychological entity and its effects on language and communication. In B. Stemmer & H. A. Whitaker (Eds.), *Handbook of neurolinguistics* (pp. 275–287). New York: Academic Press.

Favreau, M., & Segalowitz, N. S. (1983). Automatic and controlled processes in the first- and second-language reading of fluent bilinguals. *Memory & Cognition, 11,* 565–574.

Fischler, I. (1998). Attention and language. In R. Parasuraman (Ed.), *The attentive brain* (pp. 381–399). Cambridge, MA: MIT Press.

Gatbonton, E. (1994). *Bridge to fluency: Speaking.* Scarborough, Ontario: Prentice Hall Canada.

Gatbonton, E., & Segalowitz, N. S. (1988). Creative automatization: Principles for promoting fluency within a communicative framework. *TESOL Quarterly, 22,* 473–492.

Gatbonton, E., & Segalowitz, N. S. (in press). Rethinking communicative language teaching: A focus on access to fluency. *Canadian Modern Language Review.*

Healy, A. F., Barshi, I., Crutcher, R. J., et al. (1998). Toward the improvement of training in foreign languages. In A. F. Healy & L. E. Bourne, Jr. (Eds.), *Foreign language learning* (pp. 3–53). Mahwah, NJ: Erlbaum.

Hulstijn, J. H. (2001). Intentional and incidental second-language vocabulary learning: A reappraisal of elaboration, rehearsal and automaticity. In P. Robinson (Ed.), *Cognition and second language instruction* (pp. 258–286). Cambridge, U.K.: Cambridge University Press.

Hulstijn, J. H. (2002). Towards a unified account of the representation, processing, and acquisition of second-language knowledge. *Second Language Research, 18,* 193–223.

Hulstijn, J. H., & Hulstijn, W. (1984). Grammatical errors as a function of processing constraints and explicit knowledge. *Language Learning, 34,* 23–43.

Johnson, K. (1996). *Language teaching and skill learning.* Oxford, U.K.: Blackwell.

Kahneman, D. (1973). *Attention and effort.* Englewood Cliffs, NJ: Prentice Hall.

Krashen, S. D. (1981). *Second language acquisition and second language learning.* Oxford, U.K.: Pergamon Press.

Kroll, J. F., & Stewart, E. (1994). Category interference in translation and picture naming: Evidence for asymmetric connection between bilingual memory representations. *Journal of Memory and Language, 33,* 149–174.

LaBerge, D. (1997). Attention, awareness, and the triangular circuit. *Consciousness and Cognition, 6,* 149–181.

LaBerge, D. (2000a). Clarifying the triangular circuit theory of attention and its relations to awareness: Replies to seven commentaries. *Psyche, 6.* Retrieved February 20, 2002, from http://psyche.cs.monash.edu.au/v6/psyche-6-06-laberge.html

LaBerge, D. (2000b). Networks of attention. In M. S. Gazzaniga (Ed.), *The new cognitive neurosciences* (pp. 711–724). Cambridge, MA: MIT Press.

LaBerge, D., & Samuels, J. (1974). Toward a theory of automatic information processing in reading. *Cognitive Psychology, 6,* 293–323.

Langacker, R. W. (1987). *Foundations of cognitive grammar, Vol. 1: Theoretical prerequisites.* Stanford, CA: Stanford University Press.

Larsen Freeman, D., & Long, M. H. (1991). *An introduction to second language acquisition research.* London: Longman.

Levelt, W. J. M. (1989). *Speaking: From intention to articulation.* Cambridge, MA: MIT Press.

Levelt, W. J. M. (1999). Producing spoken language: A blueprint of the speaker. In C. M. Brown & P. Hagoort (Eds.), *The neurocognition of language* (pp. 83–122). Oxford, U.K.: Oxford University Press.

Lightbown, P. M., & Spada, N. (1990). Focus-on-form and corrective feedback in communicative language teaching: Effects on second language learning. *Studies in Second Language Acquisition, 12,* 429–448.

Logan, G. D. (1988). Toward an instance theory of automatization. *Psychological Review, 95,* 492–527.

Logan, G. D. (1992). Shapes of reaction-time distributions and shapes of learning curves: A test of the instance theory of automaticity. *Journal of Experimental Psychology: Learning, Memory, and Cognition, 18,* 883–914.

McLaughlin, B., & Heredia, R. (1996). Information-processing approaches to research on second language acquisition and use. In W. C. Ritchie & T. K. Bhatia (Eds.), *Handbook of second language acquisition* (pp. 213–228). New York: Academic Press.

McLaughlin, B., Rossman, T., & McLeod, B. (1983). Second language learning: An information processing perspective. *Language Learning, 33,* 135–158.

McLeod, B., & McLaughlin, B. (1986). Restructuring or automaticity? Reading in a second language. *Language Learning, 36,* 109–123.

Meuter, R. F. I., & Allport, A. (1999). Bilingual language switching in naming: Asymmetrical costs of language selection. *Journal of Memory and Language, 40,* 25–40.

Nakayama, K., & Joseph, J. S. (1998). Attention, pattern recognition, and pop-out in visual search. In R. Parasuraman (Ed.), *The attentive brain* (pp. 279–298). Cambridge, MA: MIT Press.

Neely, J. H. (1977). Semantic priming and retrieval from lexical memory: Roles of inhibitionless spreading activation and limited-capacity attention. *Journal of Experimental Psychology: General, 106,* 226–254.

Neumann, O. (1984). Automatic processing: A review of recent findings and a plea for an old theory. In W. Prinz & A. F. Sanders (Eds.), *Cognition and motor processes* (pp. 255–293). New York: Springer-Verlag.

Newell, A., & Rosenbloom, P. S. (1981). Mechanisms of skill acquisition and the law of practice. In J. R. Anderson (Ed.), *Cognitive skills and their acquisition* (pp. 1–55). Hillsdale, NJ: Erlbaum.

Nooteboom, C., Weerman, F., & Wijnen, F. (Eds.). (2002). *Storage and computation in the language faculty.* Dordrecht, The Netherlands: Kluwer.

Paap, K. R., & Ogden, W. C. (1981). Letter encoding is an obligatory but capacity-demanding operation. *Journal of Experimental Psychology: Human Perception and Performance, 7,* 518–527.

Paradis, M. (1994). Neurolinguistic aspects of implicit and explicit memory: Implications for bilingualism and SLA. In Ellis, N. (Ed.), *Implicit and explicit learning of languages* (pp. 393–419). London: Academic Press.

Pashler, H. E. (1998). *The psychology of attention.* Cambridge, MA: MIT Press.

Pawley, A., & Syder, F. H. (1983). Two puzzles for linguistic theory: Nativelike selection and nativelike fluency. In J. C. Richards & R. W. Schmidt (Eds.), *Language and communication* (pp. 191–225). New York: Longman.

Pienemann, M. (1998). Developmental dynamics in L1 and L2 acquisition: Processability theory and generative entrenchment. *Bilingualism: Language and Cognition, 1,* 1–20.

Posner, M. I., & Boies, S. J. (1971). Components of attention. *Psychological Review, 78,* 391–408.

Proctor, R. W., & Dutta, A. (1995). *Skill acquisition and human performance.* London: Sage.

Rivers, W. M. (1967). *Teaching foreign-language skills.* Chicago: University of Chicago Press.

Robinson, P. (1995). Attention, memory, and the "noticing" hypothesis. *Language Learning, 45,* 283–331.

Robinson, P. (1997). Generalizability and automaticity of second language learning under implicit, incidental, enhanced, and instructed conditions. *Studies in Second Language Acquisition, 19,* 223–247.

Robinson, P. (Ed.). (2001a). *Cognition and second language instruction.* Cambridge, U.K.: Cambridge University Press.

Robinson, P. (2001b). Task complexity, cognitive resources, and syllabus design: A triadic framework for examining task influences on SLA. In P. Robinson (Ed.), *Cognition and second language instruction* (pp. 287–318). Cambridge, U.K.: Cambridge University Press.

Robinson, P., & Ha, M. (1993). Instance theory and second language rule learning under explicit conditions. *Studies in Second Language Acquisition, 15,* 413–438.

Rogers, R. D., & Monsell, S. (1995). Costs of a predictable switch between simple cognitive tasks. *Journal of Experimental Psychology: General, 124,* 207–231.

Schmidt, R. (2001). Attention. In P. Robinson (Ed.), *Cognition and second language instruction* (pp. 3–32). Cambridge, U.K.: Cambridge University Press.

Schmitt, N. (Ed.). (2004). *Formulaic sequences.* Amsterdam: Benjamins.

Schneider, W., & Shiffrin, R. M. (1977). Controlled and automatic human information processing: 1. Detection, search and attention. *Psychological Review, 84,* 1–66.

Schoonen, R., Van Gelderen, A., De Glopper, K., Hulstijn, J., Simis, A., Snellings, P., et al.

(2003). First language and second language writing: The role of linguistic knowledge, speed of processing, and metacognitive knowledge. *Language Learning, 53*, 165–202.

Segalowitz, N. S. (1997). Individual differences in second language acquisition. In A. M. B. de Groot & J. F. Kroll (Eds.), *Tutorials in bilingualism: Psycholinguistic perspectives* (pp. 85–112). Mahwah, NJ: Erlbaum.

Segalowitz, N. S. (2000). Automaticity and attentional skill in fluent performance. In H. Riggenbach (Ed.), *Perspectives on fluency* (pp. 200–219). Ann Arbor: University of Michigan Press.

Segalowitz, N. S. (2003). Automaticity and second languages. In C. Doughty & M. Long (Eds.), *The handbook of second language acquisition* (pp. 382–408). Oxford, U.K.: Blackwell.

Segalowitz, N. S., & Frenkiel-Fishman, S. (in press). Attention control and ability level in a complex cognitive skill: Attention shifting and second language proficiency. *Memory & Cognition.*

Segalowitz, N. S., Poulsen, C., & Segalowitz, S. J. (1999). RT coefficient of variation is differentially sensitive to executive control involvement in an attention switching task. *Brain and Cognition, 38*, 255–258.

Segalowitz, N. S., Watson, V., & Segalowitz, S. J. (1995). Vocabulary skill: Single case assessment of automaticity of word recognition in a timed lexical decision task. *Second Language Research, 11*, 121–136.

Segalowitz, N. S., & Segalowitz, S. J. (1993). Skilled performance, practice, and the differentiation of speed-up from automatization effects: Evidence from second language word recognition. *Applied Psycholinguistics, 14*, 369–385.

Segalowitz, S. J., Segalowitz, N. S., & Wood, A. G. (1998). Assessing the development of automaticity in second language word recognition. *Applied Psycholinguistics, 19*, 53–67.

Skehan, P., & Foster, P. (2001). Cognition and tasks. In P. Robinson (Ed.), *Cognition and second language instruction* (pp. 183–205). Cambridge, U.K.: Cambridge University Press.

Squire, L. R., & Knowlton, B. J. (2000). The medial temporal lobe, the hippocampus, and the memory systems of the brain. In M. S. Gazzaniga (Ed.), *The new cognitive neurosciences* (pp. 765–779). Cambridge, MA: MIT Press.

Stroop, J. R. (1935). Studies of interference in serial and verbal reactions. *Journal of Experimental Psychology, 18*, 643–662.

Talmy, L. (1996). The windowing of attention. In M. Shibatani & S. A. Thompson (Eds.), *Grammatical constructions* (pp. 235–287). Oxford, U.K.: Oxford University Press.

Talmy, L. (2000). *Toward a cognitive semantics* (Vols. 1 & 2). Cambridge, MA: MIT Press.

Tzelgov, J. (1999). Automaticity and processing without awareness. *Psyche, 5.* Retrieved February 20, 2002, from http://psyche.cs.monash.edu.au/v5/psyche-5-05-tzelgov.html

Tzelgov, J., Henik, A., & Leiser, D. (1990). Controlling Stroop interference: Evidence from a bilingual task. *Journal of Experimental Psychology: Learning, Memory, and Cognition, 16*, 760–771.

Tzelgov, J., Henik, A., Sneg, R., & Baruch, O. (1996). Unintentional word reading via the phonological route: The Stroop effect with cross-script homophones. *Journal of Experimental Psychology: Learning, Memory, and Cognition, 22*, 336–349.

Ullman, M. T. (2001). The neural basis of lexicon and grammar in first and second language: The declarative/procedural model. *Bilingualism: Language and Cognition, 4*, 105–122.

Van Gelderen, A., Schoonen, R., De Glopper, K., Hulstijn, J., Simis, A., Snellings, P., et al. (2004). Linguistic knowledge, processing speed and metacognitive knowledge in first- and second-language reading comprehension: A componential analysis. *Journal of Educational Psychology, 96*, 19–30.

Van Orden, G. C. (1987). A ROWS is a ROSE: Spelling, sound and reading. *Memory & Cognition, 15*, 181–198.

VanPatten, B. (1990). Attending to form and content in the input: An experiment in consciousness. *Studies in Second Language Acquisition, 12*, 287–301.

Waters, G., Seidenberg, M. S., & Bruck, M. (1984). Children and adults use of spelling-sound information in three reading tasks. *Memory & Cognition, 12*, 293–305.

White, L. (1989). *Universal grammar and second language acquisition* (Vol. 9). Amsterdam: Benjamins.

White, L. (1996). Universal grammar and second language acquisition: Current trends and new directions. In W. C. Ritchie & T. K. Bhatia (Eds.), *Handbook of second language acquisition* (pp. 85–120). San Diego, CA: Academic Press.

Willingham, D. B. (1998). A neuropsychological theory of motor skill learning. *Psychological Review, 105*, 558–584.

Wingfield, A., Goodglass, H., & Lindfield, K. C. (1997). Separating speed from automaticity in a patient with focal brain atrophy. *Psychological Science, 8*, 247–249.

Wray, A. (2002). *Formulaic language and the lexicon.* Cambridge, U.K.: Cambridge University Press.

Erica B. Michael
Tamar H. Gollan

19

Being and Becoming Bilingual
Individual Differences and Consequences for Language Production

ABSTRACT   The nature of bilingual cognitive processing advantages and disadvantages can be used to constrain models of bilingual language processing and to highlight aspects of cognitive processing that are critical for achieving and maintaining proficient bilingualism. We review some differences between bilinguals and monolinguals and consider whether or not skills known to influence monolingual language fluency, such as working memory capacity and suppression skills, may also be used to explain which individuals are successful in achieving proficiency in a second language and avoiding disadvantages associated with bilingualism. Our focus on working memory is motivated by both practical and theoretical reasons. First, much of the existing literature on individual differences in language processing has focused on working memory. Second, current research on working memory implicates suppression as the variable that underlies the predictive power of working memory measures, and suppression is a mechanism that very naturally relates to current models of bilingual language processing. Specifically, efficient suppression mechanisms may function to limit the amount of interfering information in working memory, thus increasing the apparent capacity of working memory and perhaps also decreasing cross-language interference. This perspective is based on recent developments in research on bilingualism that suggest both languages are always active and thus require the bilingual to use cognitive resources to control the relative levels of activation of the two languages. We suggest that two influential models of bilingual language processing predict a large role for suppression mechanisms in both achieving and maintaining proficient bilingualism.

As long as appropriate input is provided, almost all human beings are capable of becoming proficient in their native language (Segalowitz, 1997). In contrast, many adults have a great deal of difficulty becoming proficient in a second language (L2). There is a wide range of variability in both the speed with which L2 learners progress and the ultimate level of L2 proficiency that they attain, and research suggests that these differences in L2 learning ability are not merely a function of general intelligence (e.g., Ando et al., 1992, as cited in Miyake, 1998). Factors that do appear to influence the ease with which an individual gains proficiency in an L2 include immersion experience, motivation, personality, cognitive strategies, and metalinguistic awareness (Harrington & Sawyer, 1992; Segalowitz, 1997).

In addition to these important factors, mounting evidence suggests that the cognitive abilities that support first language (L1) processing also contribute substantially to successful L2 processing. Recent research has shown that both L1 and L2 processing rely on working memory, a cognitive system considered to store and process information temporarily when cognitive tasks are performed (see Christoffels & De Groot, chapter 22, this volume, for a description of Baddeley's working memory model).

In this chapter, we review some of the literature linking working memory to language processing, and we attempt to elucidate the relationship between working memory capacity and bilingual performance by examining the role of the cognitive mechanism of suppression (or inhibition; we use these terms interchangeably). A number of studies have drawn a connection between working memory and suppression, and we suggest that this link provides a pathway for understanding why working memory capacity is correlated with a variety of measures of bilingual performance. Specifically, we argue that working memory may serve to resolve competing activation across the two languages not only by maintaining task-relevant information, but also by suppressing interfering activation.

We begin by presenting two influential models of bilingualism and argue that both suggest that suppression skills should play a prominent role in determining a learner's rate of acquisition and ultimate L2 proficiency. In addition, before turning to the working memory literature we discuss cognitive processing differences between bilinguals and monolinguals (see also Bialystok, chapter 20, this volume). We highlight this comparison on the assumption that differences between bilinguals and monolinguals are caused at least partly by the greater cognitive demands imposed by bilingualism relative to knowledge and use of just a single language. Critically, we suggest that differences between bilinguals and monolinguals will reflect aspects of cognitive processing that are helpful in achieving and maintaining proficient bilingualism and are therefore also likely be related to individual differences in L2 performance.

Achieving proficiency in an L2 requires mastery of many aspects of the language, including phonology, vocabulary, and syntax. We limit the current discussion primarily to lexical processing, examining early stages of vocabulary acquisition in adult L2 learners as well as later processes involved in single-word translation, production, and comprehension. Although ultimately a bilingual must be able to use and interpret words in a larger context, single-word processing forms the basis for these skills and has been the topic of the majority of psycholinguistic research on bilingualism to date.

Models of Bilingualism

Two models of bilingual language processing, the Inhibitory Control (IC) Model (Green, 1998) and the Revised Hierarchical Model (RHM; Kroll & Stewart, 1994), describe a variety of ways to think about individual differences in bilingual processing at the lexical level. These models do not make explicit predictions about the nature of such individual differences in bilingual processing, but each

offers suggestions regarding which aspects of L2 lexical processing are likely to be most heavily influenced by individual differences in suppression ability.

The Inhibitory Control Model

Considerable experimental evidence suggests that both of a bilingual's languages are always active to some degree (e.g., Colomé, 2001; Hermans, Bongaerts, De Bot, & Schreuder, 1998; Van Hell & Dijkstra, 2002), thus requiring the bilingual to allocate mental resources to control the relative level of activation of each language. As such, an obvious mechanism to consider as potentially quite important for L2 processing is suppression. Although to our knowledge individual differences in suppression ability and L2 processing have not been directly studied to date, several investigators have begun to explore the relationship between suppression and bilingualism. One relatively recent model of bilingualism that assigns a critical role to suppression is Green's (1998) IC Model, which focuses on mechanisms for the control of bilingual performance at the single-word level.

According to the IC Model, bilingual language processing requires multiple levels of control. One type of control allows an individual to execute the target task rather than another of the many possible tasks afforded by the environmental stimuli. Green (1998) called this type of control the *task schema*; it is not unique to bilinguals, and it relies on suppression to allow the individual to inhibit competitor tasks in favor of the intended task. Unlike monolingual processing, bilingual processing requires suppression at the language level as well. In picture naming, for example, the bilingual not only must choose which task to perform (e.g., naming the picture instead of determining its category membership), but also must select a language in which to name.

The IC Model proposes that each lexical item has a language tag, denoting it as either L1 or L2, and word selection is based on which language is more active at any given time. According to the IC Model, inhibition plays a key role in many language tasks, as demonstrated in the following procedural description of picture naming: First, pictures activate concepts, which in turn activate associated lexical items, likely including both L1 and L2 words. Suppression must then occur via language tags. If a bilingual is naming pictures in L2, each picture may activate both L1 and L2 words. Based on the intention to name in L2, the task schema "name in L2" allows the individual to suppress all words with L1 tags.

Suppression of L1 words is predicted to be more difficult than suppression of L2 words because L1 typically has a higher resting level of activation than L2. Support for this hypothesis comes from studies of language switching, which generally show a larger cost for switching from L2 to L1 than vice versa (e.g., Meuter & Allport, 1999; see also Meuter, chapter 17, this volume). According to the IC Model, this phenomenon occurs because the relative difficulty of suppressing L1 leads to subsequent relative difficulty in reactivating that language when required by the task switch.

The IC Model suggests several loci at which individual differences in suppression ability might have consequences for bilingual language processing. In particular, individuals who are unusually good at suppressing irrelevant information might show a larger-than-average cost of switching from a task requiring production in L2 to a task requiring production in L1. In addition, L1-to-L2 translation may be especially affected by individual differences in cognitive skills because this task requires the ability to suppress word forms in L1. During L1-to-L2 translation, L1 words will be highly active for two reasons: (a) as mentioned, the IC Model proposes a higher resting level of activation of L1 compared to L2, and (b) the stimuli themselves (L1 words) provide external cues that continuously boost the activation of the L1 lexicon.

The Revised Hierarchical Model

Another prominent model of bilingual language processing leads to similar predictions, although it proposes that the suppression mechanism plays a less-direct role in leading to proficient bilingualism. In the RHM (Kroll & Stewart, 1994; see Fig. 26.6 in Kroll & Tokowicz, chapter 26, this volume), the increased difficulty of L1-to-L2 (forward) translation as compared to L2-to-L1 (backward) translation is thought to occur primarily because retrieving an L2 word from a concept is especially hard.

In early stages of L2 acquisition, adults appear to have difficulty accessing the meaning of L2 words. Learners thus tend to adopt a strategy of associating L2 words to their L1 translations, forming strong lexical links from L2 to L1. Because L1 is the dominant language, strong bidirectional links also exist between L1 words and concepts (at all stages of L2 proficiency). In contrast, lexical links from L1 to L2 and bidirectional links between L2 words and concepts are initially weak and only become stronger with increasing proficiency. Because L1 words activate their associated concepts so strongly, forward translation begins with an L1 word strongly activating a concept and only subsequently does the relatively weak concept–L2 link provide access to the appropriate translation equivalent. Backward translation, on the other hand, can be accomplished with relative ease using the strong lexical associations from L2 to L1.

Past research supports the claim that L2 learners follow a course in which they initially associate the L2 to the L1 at a lexical level and only later acquire the ability to conceptually mediate L2 words. Talamas, Kroll, and Dufour (1999) showed that less-proficient bilinguals made more errors of lexical form (such as confusing the Spanish word *hombre*, which means "man," with *hambre*, which means "hunger"), whereas more proficient bilinguals made more errors of meaning (such as confusing *hombre* with *mujer*, which means "woman"). These data suggest that with increasing proficiency, L2 words activate semantics more directly. In addition, many studies have suggested that early L2 learners perform backward translation with relatively little activation of concepts relative to forward translation. Backward translation is typically much faster than the reverse and is often unaffected by conceptual manipulations such as presenting stimuli in semantically categorized versus mixed lists (Kroll & Stewart, 1994).

A number of studies have revealed contradictory evidence surrounding the proposal that only forward translation is conceptually mediated. For example, De Groot and Poot (1997) and La Heij, Hooglander, Kerling, and Van der Velden (1996) presented evidence suggesting that both directions of translation are largely conceptually mediated. La Heij et al. did, however, agree with Kroll and Stewart that concept activation is *easier* for L1 words than for L2 words. Thus, many researchers agree that one aspect of L2 learning that is especially difficult is establishing associations between L2 words and concepts. Because this task is thought to be so difficult, it is likely to be a process heavily influenced by individual differences in cognitive skills. In particular, Michael (1998) hypothesized that inhibition of the L1 lexicon is an important component of L2 vocabulary acquisition because it may allow for the development of direct connections between L2 words and concepts. Research examining the precise aspects of L2 lexical processing that are prone to individual differences may ultimately help resolve the controversy about the role of conceptual mediation in backward translation.

To summarize, the IC Model predicts that bilinguals at all stages of proficiency must be able to suppress the activation of L1 words to produce words in L2. In comparison, the RHM suggests that suppression should be especially important for less-proficient bilinguals, partly because of the difficulty of establishing direct connections between concepts and L2 word forms. The two models do not necessarily contradict each other, but instead highlight different roles for suppression at various stages of bilingual processing.

When bilinguals are relatively successful at suppressing the nontarget language, they would be expected to perform language tasks similarly to their monolingual counterparts. The models discussed above, however, illustrate how the presence of the L2 may change the configuration of the entire language system, including processing of L1. In the next section, we consider differences between bilinguals and monolinguals that, under one interpretation, support the view that bilinguals can never completely suppress the nontarget language and thus are never "functionally monolingual."

Bilingual Versus Monolingual Language Processing

Research comparing bilinguals and monolinguals may elucidate some of the necessary cognitive mechanisms for achieving and maintaining proficient bilingualism. The literature on bilingualism is replete with evidence demonstrating that bilinguals perform differently from monolinguals on a broad range of tasks, including both language-based and non-language-based tasks (see also Bialystok, chapter 20, this volume). For example, bilinguals may be slower than monolinguals to identify words in lexical decision (Ransdell & Fischler, 1987). On the other hand, bilinguals may be less affected than monolinguals by concreteness in text recall, perhaps because bilinguals have language-specific retrieval cues that monolinguals do not have (Ransdell & Fischler, 1989). Thus, bilingualism appears to be associated with both cognitive advantages and disadvantages, depending on the type of task used. In contrast to the many observed differences between bilinguals and monolinguals, other studies document a lack of difference between groups (also on a variety of cognitive tasks; e.g., Rosselli et al., 2002). When differences are not found, it may be that bilingualism has no effect on that particular task, or that the task is simply not sensitive enough to detect subtle differences that do exist. Understanding these differences and lack of differences will constrain models of language processing (both mono- and bilingual) by requiring them to specify their underlying cognitive mechanisms.

Perhaps the most intuitively compelling account of differences between bilinguals and monolinguals is the notion of cross-language interference. One of the most obvious things that makes bilinguals different from monolinguals is that, for each concept to be expressed, two very closely matching lexical representations are available (i.e., translation equivalents). If these representations compete for selection, suppression would be quite useful for managing the added interference. Converging justification for predicting that individual differences in suppression ability should be related to bilingual performance comes from studies demonstrating that within-language synonyms (e.g., *sofa* and *couch*, the closest thing to translation equivalents in the monolingual cognitive system) remain active quite late in the process of lexical selection in monolingual language production (Jescheniak & Schriefers, 1998; Peterson & Savoy, 1998). However, a serious challenge for the cross-language interference account comes from a number of experimental findings suggesting that coactive translation equivalents sometimes lead to facilitation (i.e., the opposite of interference). Thus, in addition to the intuitively appealing cross-language interference account, it is important to consider other mechanisms that could account for differences between bilinguals and monolinguals.

A second quite compelling and obvious difference between bilinguals and monolinguals is that, at the level of individual words, bilinguals need to learn and then efficiently retrieve roughly twice as many items as monolinguals. By virtue of speaking two languages, bilinguals necessarily spend less time using words particular to either language. Bilinguals thus may be less able to activate lexical representations specific to each language or may have weaker links in the lexical system relative to monolinguals (Gollan & Acenas, 2004). Vocabulary knowledge and single-word retrieval are quite sensitive to individual differences in cognitive ability and to impairment to the cognitive system. For example, vocabulary measures are highly correlated with verbal IQ, and the inability to name objects (or pictures) is one of the most commonly reported cognitive complaints after even very mild brain damage (Lezak, 1995). Hence, it is reasonable to expect that vocabulary and word retrieval skills should also be sensitive to group differences in experience with language (i.e., mono- vs. bilingualism). Even if translation equivalents do not interfere with (and may even facilitate) one another, it would still be very surprising if the double burden (needing to learn roughly twice as many words) did not lead to both group differences between bilinguals and monolinguals and individual differences within bilinguals.

What follows is a brief review of comparisons between bilinguals and monolinguals in picture naming, proper name retrieval, picture classification, and the verbal fluency task, followed by a discussion of the cognitive mechanisms that these differences suggest are critical for achieving and maintaining proficient bilingualism. We consider two explanations of the differences observed between bilinguals and monolinguals: the cross-language interference account and the weaker links account. The former account most obviously implicates a direct role for suppression in bilingualism, a topic discussed in detail in the Individual Differences section of the chapter. At the end of the section, we consider whether bilingualism leads to differences in suppression skill.

Tip-of-the-Tongue States and Proper Name Retrieval

Research (Gollan & Acenas, 2004; Gollan, Bonanni, & Montoya, in press; Gollan & Silverberg, 2001) suggests that there are robust differences between bilinguals and monolinguals when they are asked to produce very-low-frequency words. Such words are commonly the targets of tip-of-the-tongue states (TOTs). During a TOT, speakers fail to retrieve a word or name that they are sure they know. TOTs are often accompanied by a feeling of imminent recall and the ability to report partial information about the target word form (e.g., the first phoneme; R. Brown & McNeill, 1966).

In several studies comparing bilinguals to age- and education-matched monolinguals, bilinguals (including Hebrew-English, Spanish-English, and Tagalog-English bilinguals) consistently had more TOTs even though they demonstrated equal ability to report the first phoneme of the target word and, in the majority of cases, equal rates of spontaneous TOT resolution. The group difference in number of TOTs remained significant in a variety of conditions, including when the task required retrieval of

words in one language only, when bilinguals retrieved words in their dominant language only, and when the targets were matched for familiarity across groups.

The increased TOT rate in bilingual adults is reminiscent of studies showing that bilingual children have smaller receptive and productive vocabularies in each language relative to their age-matched monolingual counterparts. Most researchers agree that the bilingual vocabulary disadvantage is not found in bilingual adults (for a review, see Hamers & Blanc, 2000); however, the TOT findings suggest that the disadvantage is in fact present if sufficiently sensitive measures are used to detect it.

To date, two manipulations have eliminated the group difference in TOT rate. First, bilinguals had the same number of TOTs as monolinguals when the targets were cognates, which are words that are similar in both form and meaning across languages (e.g., the English word *rhinoceros* and the Spanish word *rinoceronte*, as compared to the noncognate translation equivalents *tweezers* for the Spanish *pinzas*). The group similarity in TOT rates for cognates only held true, however, if bilinguals could produce the word in both languages (i.e., if they translated the target word into their other language correctly; Gollan & Acenas, 2004). Otherwise, cognate targets were just as likely to elicit TOTs in bilinguals as their noncognate counterparts. Importantly, in this study, monolinguals showed no significant cognate facilitations effects on TOT rate, thereby confirming that bilingualism per se (not some characteristic of the cognate materials) produced the reduction in bilingual TOT rate. This finding suggests that, when the materials allow bilinguals to make use of their experience with word forms in both languages, the difference between groups goes away.

A second, and in some ways surprising, variable that eliminated the increased TOT rate in bilinguals was the use of proper name targets (Gollan, Bonanni, et al., in press). In fact, in one study the effect was reversed, and bilinguals had significantly *fewer* TOTs than monolinguals. In a diary study in which participants kept TOT diaries for 4 weeks, bilinguals reported fewer TOTs for proper names relative to their monolingual peers even though (after adjusting for the proportion of time using L1 and L2) bilinguals had more TOTs than monolinguals in L1 and more TOTs in L2 than in L1.

In a second experiment of laboratory-induced TOTs (Gollan, Bonanni, et al., in press), bilinguals and monolinguals had the same number of TOTs for famous names and personal names in which participants attempted to retrieve the names of all the teachers they had from grade school through high school. Importantly, the same bilinguals reported a higher TOT rate relative to the monolinguals in a different condition that required participants to name pictures of objects (thereby replicating the previously reported increased TOT rate). Considered together, these studies showed no consistent bilingual advantage for proper names, but unlike the object-naming findings, neither study produced a bilingual disadvantage in retrieving proper name targets.

The absence of a bilingual disadvantage in these studies is surprising because proper names are the most commonly reported (and often most frustrating and embarrassing) type of TOT target (Cohen & Burke, 1993), and proper name retrieval is notoriously difficult (Burke, Locantore, & Austin, in press). Interestingly, older adults have an increased rate of TOTs relative to younger adults, and the age difference is *most* pronounced for proper name targets (Burke, MacKay, Worthley, & Wade, 1991). This interaction between age and word type suggests that task difficulty influences TOT rate in other comparisons of different participant groups. If bilingual disadvantages (e.g., the increased TOT rate for object names) resulted from a processing overload specific to the language system, then the difference between bilinguals and monolinguals would be expected to be even more robust in the context of a task that is typically most challenging.

Although generally difficult tasks should be especially likely to produce individual differences, these studies indicate that differences between bilinguals and monolinguals also depend on factors quite specific to bilingualism (e.g., that proper names are typically shared across languages). In summary, both the cognate and the proper name findings clearly indicate that bilinguals do exhibit some relative fluency deficits in comparison with monolinguals, but these deficits are quite limited in scope.

Picture Naming Versus Picture Classification

The TOT state is a dramatic type of retrieval failure that occurs relatively infrequently, approximately once or twice a week (A. Brown, 1991). Other evidence for processing costs that may be related to bilingualism comes from response times during

successful picture naming. Gollan, Montoya, Fennema-Notestine, and Morris (in press) demonstrated that Spanish-English bilinguals (even those who reported that English was their strongest language or that they were equally proficient in English and Spanish) were slower to name pictures relative to monolinguals. The same bilinguals, however, were able to classify the same pictures (with counterbalanced presentation of individual pictures between subjects) as "human made" versus "natural" equally quickly relative to their monolingual controls. Importantly, both tasks (i.e., picture naming and picture classification) demonstrated robust repetition effects such that repeated pictures were named and classified more quickly on the second and third presentations. These data indicate that both tasks were sensitive to experimental manipulations, and thus the lack of differences between groups could not be attributed to insensitivity of picture classification to all experimental manipulations.

The presence of robust differences in picture naming in the absence of any differences in picture classification provides evidence that the locus of the bilinguals' relative disadvantage arises after semantic processing during the retrieval of language-specific lexical representations. Moreover, because bilinguals were not at a disadvantage on all tasks, the finding strengthens the claim that the differences between groups in picture naming were caused by bilingualism, not by some other correlated factor, such as culture, that might have also differed between the two groups and affected cognitive processing more generally.

The absence of differences in picture classification does not, however, rule out the possibility that bilinguals and monolinguals carried out the task in different ways; there may be two (or more) different but equally efficient ways of classifying pictures. Furthermore, the absence of differences between groups does not rule out the possibility that differences exist that could not be detected by the task used. These findings, however, do clearly suggest that bilingual disadvantages are not general, and that differences between bilinguals and monolinguals may be more likely to occur in tasks that require a language-specific response.

Category and Phonemic Fluency

The verbal fluency task is another language task that involves intact lexical retrieval and, like picture naming, produces robust differences between bilinguals and monolinguals. In verbal fluency tasks, participants are typically given 60 s to generate as many words as they can that belong to either a given semantic category (e.g., animals, fruits, and vegetables) or a given letter category (e.g., words that begin with the letter F, A, or S; Borkowski, Benton, & Spreen, 1967). In a study comparing Spanish-English bilinguals to English-speaking monolinguals, Gollan, Montoya, and Werner (2002) found that bilinguals (even those who reported their English was as proficient as that of native speakers) produced fewer correct exemplars on 9 of 12 semantic categories and 6 of 10 letter categories tested. Unexpectedly, there was also an interaction between category type and participant type; the bilingual-monolingual difference was larger and more consistent in semantic categories than in letter categories (see Rosselli et al., 2000, for similar findings in older adult bilinguals).

Work in progress by the second author (in collaboration with Victor S. Ferreira) suggests that the group differences may have been reduced on letter fluency because of cognate production (because cognates are easier for bilinguals to produce; see Costa, Caramazza, & Sebastián-Gallés, 2000; Gollan & Acenas, 2004). Relative to their own overall production rates, bilinguals produced more cognates than monolinguals in letter but not semantic categories. These data are shown in Fig. 19.1. Using monolinguals' rate of cognate production as a baseline for how often cognates should occur in letter and semantic fluency in the absence of cross-language facilitation, these data suggest that cross-language facilitation is stronger in the letter fluency task, thereby reducing the fluency difference between groups. This effect may have occurred because letter categories are inherently larger than semantic categories and therefore also contain more cognates. However, other explanations (involving cross-language interference) are possible for the interaction between participant type and category type.

Accounts of Differences Between Bilinguals and Monolinguals

Cross-Language Interference   As noted, one account of the relative bilingual disadvantages in language production tasks is that bilinguals suffer from direct interference between competing lexical representations across languages. Gollan et al. (2002) suggested that the interference account can explain the finding that the bilingual impairment is

larger for semantic fluency than for letter fluency if it is also assumed that cross-language interference is stronger for semantically related words (i.e., translation equivalents) than for words starting with the same letter. This assumption seems reasonable given that translation equivalents would be expected to be coactive during a semantically driven task because of the great overlap in meaning.

According to one instantiation of the interference account, during production in the *Animals* category, semantically related lexical nodes (e.g., the Spanish word for *dog*, which is *perro*, and related words such as the English word *cat*) compete for selection. Because these lexical representations also compete for selection during natural language production, they would be connected by inhibitory links that would be especially strong for translation equivalents that are closest in meaning (see Cutting & Ferreira, 1999, for a discussion of inhibitory links between coactive lexical representations in language production).

In contrast, form-related lexical nodes (e.g., *doll* and the Spanish word *dogal*, which means noose) would only be connected by relatively weak inhibitory links because competition between form-related competitors either does not arise during natural language production (Levelt, Roelofs, & Meyer, 1999) or arises only to the extent that activation from the phonological level (in this case, the phoneme /d/) is allowed to flow back up to the lexical level (e.g., Dell, 1986). In such a model, the impact of bilingualism (or of having twice as many lexical representations active) would be greater for semantic fluency than for letter fluency because, in a semantic fluency task, bilingualism activates lexical representations that strongly interfere with the selection of target lexical nodes.

Interestingly, Rosen and Engle (1997) demonstrated that under a cognitive load, individuals with higher working memory span produced more correct exemplars in semantic fluency and produced fewer perseverations (repeating an exemplar without realizing it) compared to individuals with lower working memory span. These findings suggest a link between suppression mechanisms and semantic fluency and thus seem to provide converging support for the notion that cross-language interference may create a particular problem during semantic fluency. It would be interesting to see if span differences in bilinguals had smaller effects on letter fluency than on semantic fluency, as would be expected if cross-language interference is reduced in letter fluency relative to semantic fluency.

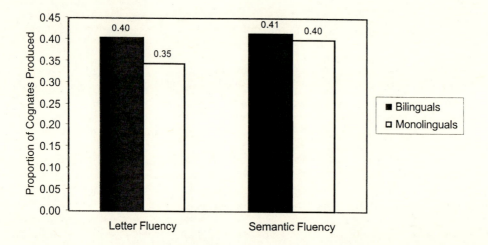

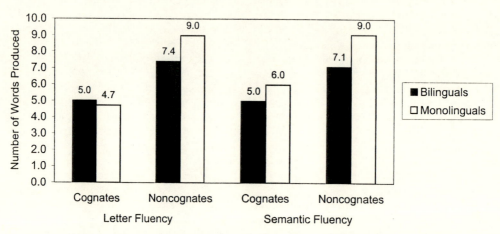

Figure 19.1 The top panel demonstrates bilinguals' greater proportion of cognate production in the letter fluency task relative to monolinguals. The bottom panel shows the raw numbers used to calculate the proportions shown in the top panel. The bottom panel also shows the bilingual group's verbal fluency disadvantage except for the number of cognates produced during letter categories, in which bilinguals actually produced slightly more responses on average (i.e., 5.0 vs. 4.7). These findings suggest that cognate facilitation effects occur during a relatively free language production task (i.e., during category generation), and that cross-language facilitation may explain why the verbal fluency difference between bilinguals and monolinguals was larger on semantic categories. Adapted from Gollan et al. (2002).

To explain bilinguals' greater TOT rate and slower picture-naming times relative to monolinguals, the cross-language interference account would assume that translation equivalents compete for selection. This view is consistent with the finding that bilinguals do *not* have more TOTs than monolinguals for proper name targets (Gollan, Bonanni, et al., in press), possibly because proper name targets simply do not have translation equivalent competitors (i.e., *Tamar* is *Tamar*

both in Hebrew and in English) or because the cross-language translations of proper names are often cognates that also eliminate the difference between groups (e.g., *Dvora* and *Debora*). Thus, it appears that the interference account can explain many of the above-discussed findings (but see Gollan & Acenas, 2004).

The greatest challenge to the interference account comes from data suggesting that the activation of translation equivalents actually facilitates production. Such cross-language facilitation has been reported not only for tasks that explicitly activate both languages (Costa & Caramazza, 1999; Costa, Miozzo, & Caramazza, 1999), but even for tasks in which the activation of translation-equivalent lexical representations is implicit (Gollan & Acenas, 2004; Gollan, Montoya, et al., in press). In the latter studies, target words that bilinguals were able to translate produced fewer TOTs (Gollan & Acenas) and faster picture naming times (Gollan, Montoya, et al.) than target words that bilinguals were not able to translate. Monolinguals' responses to the same stimuli were significantly less affected by the target words' translatability, indicating that translatable words were not simply easier to produce.

Although translation facilitation effects seem to rule out cross-language interference as an account of differences between bilinguals and monolinguals, theoretical and intuitive arguments make us reluctant to abandon cross-language interference entirely until an exact mechanism of the reported translation facilitation effects is identified. Also, it is not entirely unreasonable to assume that interference arises under some conditions and facilitation under others. Moreover, although the translation facilitation effects reported by Gollan et al. primarily involved English-dominant participants failing to show interference effects from Spanish (the less-dominant, and therefore less-active, language), it is important to note that a subset of the participants in each experiment demonstrated the same facilitation effects even though English was their less-dominant language. In other words, for these participants the dominant language not only failed to interfere, it actually facilitated production in the less-dominant language. One possibility is that translation equivalents cause interference during relatively early stages of L2 acquisition and later come to serve as retrieval cues; this hypothesis is consistent with the RHM's above-outlined prediction that suppression should play a greater role in achieving proficient bilingualism than in maintaining it. (See Costa, chapter 15, this volume, and La Heij, chapter 14, this volume, for further discussion of translation facilitation results.)

Weaker Links   As an alternative to the interference account, Gollan and Silverberg (2001) suggested that the reason bilinguals have more TOTs, name pictures more slowly, and have reduced category and letter fluency is that they use words particular to either language less often relative to monolinguals,

thus the connections within the lexical system from semantic to phonological representations are weaker (see also Gollan et al., 2002; Gollan & Acenas, 2004; Gollan, Montoya, et al., in press). The relative weakness arises because links in the lexical system are sensitive to frequency and recency of use (Burke et al., 1991), and links particular to each language are used less often. The weaker links account assumes a very indirect effect of bilingualism on TOTs; use of words in a non-dominant language results in relatively reduced use of words in the dominant language in comparison with monolinguals. It can explain why bilinguals' increased TOT rate is eliminated when the targets are cognates by assuming that translation equivalents facilitate production at the level of phonology (as argued by Costa et al., 2000), and similarly that lexical representations of proper names are unaffected because they do not differ across languages (or because they are cognates). The weaker links account can also use cognate production to explain why semantic fluency is relatively more affected by bilingualism than is letter fluency (see Fig. 19.1). Finally, although strictly speaking the weaker links account does not predict translation facilitation effects, it certainly has an easier time accommodating this finding than the interference account (because the latter specifically predicts the opposite of facilitation).

The weaker links hypothesis predicts that bilinguals who speak twice as much as monolinguals should not be different from monolinguals on language-processing tasks. Consistent with this prediction, 30% or even 70% of individual bilinguals (using 1 or 2 standard deviation cutoffs, respectively) reported a number of TOTs that fell within the range of average monolingual performance (Gollan & Acenas, 2004; Gollan & Silverberg, 2001). However, without direct evidence to support the claim that these bilinguals spoke twice as much as monolinguals, other reasons must be considered. Although highly speculative at this point, an alternative possibility is that some bilinguals may have unusually strong phonological processing skills and therefore may need fewer exposures to word forms to become proficient in retrieving them. In fact, some studies reported stronger phonological processing skills in both bilingual children and adults (e.g., Campbell & Sais, 1995; Papagno & Vallar, 1995). Moreover, phonological short-term memory (STM) seems to be related to vocabulary acquisition in both L1 and L2 (Atkins & Baddeley, 1998; Baddeley, Gathercole, & Papagno, 1998; Cheung, 1996; De Groot &

Van Hell, chapter 1, this volume; Gathercole & Baddeley, 1989; Papagno, Valentine, & Baddeley, 1991; Service, 1992; Service & Kohonen, 1995). That said, however, it would be a mistake to look for improved phonological processing or STM in bilinguals in general; if these advantages existed, then bilinguals (as a group) should not have had more TOTs than monolinguals.

Can Bilingualism Improve Suppression Skills?

Discussions of weaker links and cross-language interference imply that bilingualism imposes drastic processing costs. It is important to note, however, that bilinguals must be viewed under a magnifying glass before such costs can be seen, and in most cases the advantages of bilingualism (whether cognitive, practical, or cultural) far outweigh the costs. To illustrate, most people would prefer occasionally having more difficulty retrieving low-frequency words (i.e., falling into TOTs for words like *carburetor* more often than their monolingual friends, as discussed above; see also Ecke, 1996) to being completely unable to communicate in any language other than their first. Moreover, current research on bilingualism is testing whether bilingualism confers some previously unidentified processing advantages.

On the assumptions that bilinguals must manage cross-language interference and that increased practice controlling interference leads to improved functioning in cognitive control, it would not be surprising if bilinguals were better than monolinguals at carrying out tasks requiring control mechanisms. Importantly, this prediction is based on the assumptions that bilinguals need to manage the activation of both languages, that cross-language interference arises at least at some level of processing, and perhaps most important, that the cognitive mechanism of suppression is subject to practice effects. One confirmation of the predicted bilingual advantage in suppression skills was reported by Ransdell, Arecco, and Levy (2001), who showed that, on a test of writing quality and fluency, monolingual performance suffered in the presence of unattended irrelevant speech, but bilingual performance did not.

The generalizability of these findings, however, may be rather limited. For example, bilinguals do not show better ability to prevent Stroop-like interference (e.g., Sebova & Arochova, 1986). In a typical Stroop task, participants see a list of words written in different colors and must inhibit the automatic response of reading the words and instead name the color of the ink in which each word is printed (Stroop, 1935). On the critical conflict trials, the words are color names that are different from the color of the ink. For example, if the word *red* is written in blue ink, the participant must say "blue." In the section Working Memory and Suppression, we discuss a finding demonstrating that individuals with higher working memory span were better able to prevent Stroop interference than individuals with lower working memory span, but only when the number of conflict trials was high (Long & Prat, 2002). It may be the case that if a bilingual Stroop advantage exists, it also can only be observed under particular circumstances.

For example, in a different, but Stroop-like task, Bialystok (2002) reported that older bilinguals were better than older monolinguals in saying "up" when presented with an arrow that pointed down (and vice versa). A number of studies have shown that the factors related to bilingualism do modulate the Stroop effect (for a review, see Smith, 1997). Specifically, Stroop interference occurs across languages (e.g., when the words are written in one language and color naming is done in the other language) but only with a certain level of proficiency. Further, at very high levels of proficiency, bilinguals become more adept at suppressing the cross-language Stroop effect. In future research, these factors may help to reveal why a bilingual Stroop advantage has not yet been consistently observed (see also Bialystok, chapter 20, this volume).

Future studies comparing bilinguals to monolinguals will no doubt continue to inform research on the cognitive mechanisms that lead to proficient bilingualism. An important consideration in these studies is that selection criteria for both monolinguals and bilinguals will undoubtedly affect the outcome. For example, in the United States monolinguals are quite common. In contrast, in most other parts of the world monolinguals are unusual. In such places, people who remain monolingual may be individuals with cognitive weaknesses for the types of skills important to becoming a proficient bilingual. Similarly, the choice of task will also be important because most tasks tap into multiple cognitive mechanisms, and bilinguals may differ from monolinguals in more than one way. Therefore, interpreting experiments comparing groups will first require breaking down each task into individual components and then generating different predictions regarding how each component should (or should not) be affected by bilingualism.

Individual Differences in Language Processing

The studies reviewed above clearly suggest that bilingualism affects cognitive processing in a number of significant and yet interestingly limited ways. The underlying mechanisms by which bilingualism affects the cognitive system are presently under investigation. We turn now to a discussion of some of the empirical evidence examining individual differences in L1 and L2 processing. These studies provide additional evidence regarding the aspects of bilingual language processing that are most cognitively demanding. The bulk of recent studies on individual differences in language processing have focused on working memory. Two considerations make these studies relevant for discussions of bilingualism. First, several studies suggest that suppression is a central component of working memory (a position discussed in the Working Memory and Suppression section); second, at least some studies show a very direct relationship between working memory measures and bilingual tasks (especially translation).

Working Memory and First Language Processing

Working memory is generally thought of as a system that temporarily stores and processes information during the performance of cognitive tasks. Tests of simple STM capacity typically require only storage and later retrieval of information (e.g., a list of digits or words; for a discussion of several different ways the term *STM* is used, see Delis, Kaplan, Kramer, & Ober, 2000). In contrast, in the context of experimental (rather than clinical) research, tests of working memory capacity usually include additional processing demands (e.g., remembering a sequence of digits and then producing them in reverse order). In more recent measures of working memory capacity, participants are asked to store and later retrieve lists of single words while simultaneously carrying out an additional cognitive task such as reading sentences or solving mathematical operations. These measures are often called *reading span* and *operation span*, respectively.

In a typical operation span task, a participant is presented with math problems in sets ranging in size from two to six. After each mathematical operation, a word is presented for memorization. The participant must solve each equation as it is presented and at the end of the set must recall all of the words from that set. (In a reading span task, the participant would read sentences instead of solving math problems.) The participant's working memory span is then determined by either counting the total number of words correctly recalled or assessing the largest set size at which performance was consistently successful. In many studies measuring working memory span, participants are labeled as "higher" or "lower" working memory span on the basis of a median split or quartile analysis of span scores. Importantly, the designation of an individual as having higher or lower working memory span is relative only to the participants in that particular study and is not an absolute judgment of that individual's working memory capacity. For the purposes of this chapter, the term *span* on its own should be read as working memory span.

Studies using both reading span and operation span show them to be equally correlated with measures of verbal ability, suggesting that individual differences in working memory capacity are independent of task-specific (e.g., language vs. math) processing skill (Engle, Cantor, & Carullo, 1992). The inclusion of some sort of processing component, however, is critical for the predictive power of working memory span tasks. Considerable support exists (summarized in a meta-analysis by Daneman & Merikle, 1996) for the claim that language processing is more highly correlated with measures of dual-task working memory span than with simple storage measures such as word or digit span. This claim does not, however, rule out the possibility that simple STM plays some role in language processing (as noted in the section comparing bilinguals to monolinguals, in which we briefly presented evidence suggesting that phonological STM may be important for vocabulary learning in both L1 and L2).

A now-large body of research supports the idea that working memory is necessary to form and remember an integrated representation of a text. For example, studies have shown that working memory capacity is strongly related to the ability to comprehend written and spoken stories, interpret the intended meaning of an ambiguous word, use context to infer the meaning of an unfamiliar word, and produce category exemplars, synonyms, and sentences from given words (Daneman & Carpenter, 1980, 1983; Daneman & Green, 1986; Gernsbacher & Faust, 1991; Just & Carpenter, 1992; King & Just, 1991; Rosen & Engle, 1997).

In a landmark study by Daneman and Carpenter (1980), participants read a set of passages and answered both comprehension and pronominal reference questions; reading span was highly correlated with performance on both types of question. In a later study, Daneman and Carpenter (1983) assessed the abilities of higher and lower span individuals to detect and recover from semantic ambiguities in passages containing ambiguous words such as *bat*. In each passage, the ambiguity was resolved in a manner that was either consistent or inconsistent with the prior context. All participants spent more time reading the disambiguating word in the inconsistent cases than in the consistent cases, but higher span participants were more likely than lower span participants to resolve the ambiguity correctly. The authors suggested that working memory aids in ambiguity resolution because it allows readers to return to previous information and integrate it with the current representation of the text.

Just and Carpenter (1992) further addressed the issue of ambiguity resolution by recording reading times for garden path sentences. Prior to the ambiguity, disambiguating information was presented in the form of an animate or inanimate noun. For example, the sentence "The evidence examined by the lawyer shocked the jury" should be easier to resolve than the sentence "The defendant examined by the lawyer shocked the jury." Participants with lower working memory span were led down the garden path despite prior disambiguating information, but higher span individuals were successfully able to integrate the pragmatic and syntactic information to avoid being misled.

Working memory is important not only for higher level tasks such as text comprehension, but also for lower level verbal tasks. For example, Daneman and Green (1986) proposed that working memory plays a role in vocabulary acquisition and verbal fluency (two skills that seem obviously important for gaining proficiency in an L2 and, as discussed above, seem to be influenced by bilingualism). In one experiment, participants read a passage containing a novel word and attempted to infer its meaning. The ability to acquire new vocabulary was highly correlated with working memory span. The authors argued that working memory facilitates recall of previous information, thereby better allowing higher span individuals to infer the meanings of unfamiliar words from context. In a second experiment, Daneman and Green showed that working memory span was also correlated with the ability to produce sentences and synonyms from given words.

As mentioned, Rosen and Engle (1997) examined the relationship between working memory span and retrieval of category exemplars. Participants were asked to generate aloud as many animal names as they could in 15 min (the same task used by Gollan et al., 2002, except that in that study participants were given only 1 min to generate exemplars). Individuals with higher working memory span generated more animal names than individuals with lower working memory span. A second experiment used the same paradigm, but included a concurrent digit-tracking task. Under this condition of increased load, individuals with lower working memory span were more likely to perseverate (i.e., to repeat items they had already named) than were individuals with higher working memory span.

Rosen and Engle (1997) suggested that, under increased load, the lower span participants were unable to suppress previously retrieved responses effectively, which contributed to their lower overall retrieval rate (but see Mayr & Kliegl, 2000, who argued that recognition, not suppression, prevents perseverations in semantic fluency). The authors argued that the higher and lower span participants differed not in their category knowledge, but in their ability to control the search process effectively. Given that the ability to retrieve lexical items from memory is an important and potentially challenging skill for bilinguals, Rosen and Engle's hypothesis about the role of suppression in working memory and in word retrieval highlights an important way in which working memory capacity and L2 processing ability may be related. We return to this discussion in a later section.

Working Memory and Second Language Processing

Research on working memory in L1 has shown that as the language task is made more difficult, the effect of span increases (Miyake, Carpenter, & Just, 1994). Given that acquiring an L2 as an adult is usually a more effortful and deliberate process than acquiring a first spoken language as a child (DeKeyser & Larson-Hall, chapter 5, this volume), it seems reasonable to predict that if working memory capacity influences L1 processing, it will have an even stronger impact on L2 processing. Furthermore, the studies discussed in this section support the idea that working memory may be involved in different or additional aspects of L2 processing as compared to L1 processing because L2 acquisition and processing require the integration of a new set of phonemes, labels, and rules into an already-existing linguistic and conceptual system. Finally, the studies in this section indicate that the role of working memory in L2 processing may vary as a function of the relative dominance of L1 over L2 because the particular processes that occur during L2 learning change as an individual gains proficiency (see discussion of RHM).

Miyake (1998) suggested that the vague (but often-discussed) concept of "language aptitude" has working memory capacity as its core. He argued that language comprehension and production consist of processing sequences of symbols over time and thus share many component processes with working memory span tasks. According to Miyake, these types of processes are especially salient in the domain of syntax. Learners initially attempt to use their L1 grammatical structures to interpret and produce L2 sentences (MacWhinney, 1997) and must gradually learn new syntactic distinctions and adjust the relative strengths of various syntactic cues to levels that are more appropriate for the particular language being learned. Overcoming reliance on L1 and adjusting these cue strengths likely make substantial demands on cognitive resources, and in support of this argument, Miyake demonstrated a correlation between working memory span and the acquisition of linguistic cues in Japanese speakers learning English as an L2.

Harrington and Sawyer (1992) also studied native Japanese speakers learning English, focusing on L2 grammar and reading comprehension as measured by the grammar and reading subsections of the Test of English as a Foreign Language (TOEFL). Results showed a significant correlation between working memory span and performance on both subsections of the TOEFL. Participants completed the working memory span task in their L2, thus a possible confound was that the observed correlation was mediated by L2 lexical development and grammatical knowledge. When these factors were statistically partialed out, though, a small effect of working memory span remained, suggesting that working memory does indeed play a role in the acquisition of L2 grammar and reading. It is important to note that participants also completed simple word list memory and forward digit span tasks, and performance on these measures did *not* correlate with L2 grammar and reading.

The studies described thus far included bilinguals and L2 learners who acquired their L2 in classrooms, immersion environments, or other naturally occurring settings. It is also possible to examine the relationship between working memory

capacity and rudimentary L2 learning that takes place in the laboratory. In the work of Kempe, Brooks, and Kharkhurin (1999), adult native English speakers who had never studied Russian were trained on pairs of Russian color adjectives and nouns. After several training sessions, the learners were given each noun and asked to produce the appropriate color adjective. The nouns varied in their gender and transparency, leading to some adjective endings that could be learned by rule and others that required rote memorization. Higher span learners were better than lower span learners at generalizing rules to new items, but differences in working memory span did not predict performance on rote memorization of the endings. In a similar study involving learning of the genitive and dative endings for Russian nouns, working memory span again predicted rule generalization performance, but in this experiment span also predicted the ability to recall the nouns themselves (Kempe & Brooks, 2000). Although the results of these two studies are somewhat contradictory, the line of research suggests that working memory is important in the acquisition of inflectional morphology. In addition, the recall results from Kempe and Brooks suggest that working memory may play a role in vocabulary acquisition, an aspect of L2 processing that is central to the next three studies we discuss.

In a study of proficient English-Spanish and Spanish-English bilinguals, Michael, Tokowicz, and Kroll (2003) compared the magnitude of span differences in translation and L2 picture naming, two single-word production tasks expected to differ in their demands on suppression mechanisms. Both tasks may require suppression of the nontarget language to allow production in the target language, but in translation, as mentioned in our discussion of the IC Model, the nontarget language may have an especially high level of activation because the task explicitly activates both languages, and the language of presentation itself must be suppressed. Michael et al. therefore predicted larger span differences in translation than in L2 picture naming. As predicted, higher span participants performed both directions of translation more quickly and accurately than their lower span counterparts. In contrast, span was not related to L2 picture-naming performance. This pattern of results suggests that high working memory capacity is particularly beneficial for bilingual tasks that necessitate the activation of both languages.

Michael, Dijkstra, and Kroll (2002) and Kroll, Michael, Tokowicz, and Dufour (2002) evaluated individual differences in L2 lexical processing at two different stages of proficiency. In Michael et al.'s (2002) study, highly proficient Dutch-English bilinguals completed a reading span task, word naming (reading aloud) in L1 and L2, and translation in both the forward and backward directions. Because L1 and L2 word naming are fairly automatic tasks for proficient bilinguals, it was predicted that there would be no significant difference between higher and lower span bilinguals on these tasks. Indeed, the results indicated that span had absolutely no effect on word-naming latencies. In contrast to the predictions for word naming, both the IC Model and the RHM predict that translation, particularly forward translation (in which L1 must be suppressed), should place especially large demands on suppression. These predictions were partially confirmed. Higher span participants were significantly faster than lower span participants in *both* forward and backward translation.

These results (Michael et al., 2002) suggest that working memory is critical for controlling the activation of two languages, particularly in a task (like translation) that forces both languages to be active. Interestingly, as predicted, the higher span participants were significantly more accurate than the lower span participants for forward translation, but for backward translation there was no accuracy difference between the two groups. The reason for the lack of interaction between span group and

direction of translation in the reaction time (RT) data remains unclear, but as we discuss next, this pattern appears to be somewhat consistent across studies.

Experiment 2 of Kroll et al.'s (2002) study examined native English speakers who had been studying either French or Spanish for only a short period of time. Participants completed the same set of tasks as in Michael et al.'s (2002) study and similarly were classified as having either higher or lower working memory span. As in the Michael et al. study, there was no relationship between working memory span and word-naming performance. The pattern of results for the translation data, however, demonstrated a complex interaction between span and cognate status, as shown in Fig. 19.2. The results for noncognates were very similar to those observed by Michael et al. Higher span participants were significantly faster than lower span participants to translate in both directions. For cognates, however, the higher span L2 learners in Kroll et al.'s study actually translated *more slowly* than their lower span counterparts. In contrast, among the highly proficient bilinguals studied by Michael et al., the high-span advantage in speed of translation persisted across both noncognates and cognates.

According to Kroll et al. (2002), this remarkable and counterintuitive finding that higher span learners translated cognates more slowly than

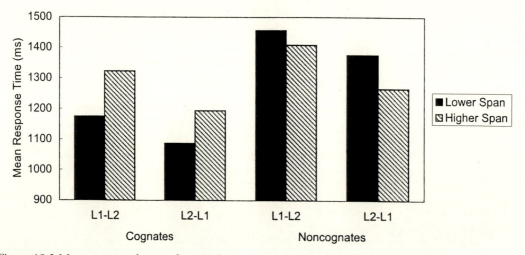

Figure 19.2 Mean response latency for translation (correct responses only) as a function of cognate status and the direction of translation for early second language learners (adapted from Kroll et al., 2002). For cognates, lower span learners were faster than higher span learners in both directions of translation. For noncognates, the higher span learners were faster. L1, first language; L2, second language.

lower span learners may indicate that the higher span learners were attempting to rely less on word form cues and more on conceptual mediation, thereby reducing the cognate facilitation effect and instead producing an added burden of suppressing the tendency to link L2 word forms directly to L1 word forms. Given that the RHM associates concept mediation with increased proficiency, this finding can be taken to indicate that the higher span participants were actually at a more advanced stage of L2 learning. Although the translation performance of the higher span participants appeared to suffer an initial cost in processing time as a result of early attempts at concept mediation, it seems likely that the concept mediation strategy would be beneficial for the longer-term goals associated with attaining L2 proficiency.

Taken together, these studies suggest that there are complex interactions among proficiency level, form similarity across languages (i.e., cognate status), and working memory capacity. At this point, it is difficult to ascertain precisely how these factors interact, but these relationships will no doubt be a topic of investigation in future studies.

Another important topic for future research is the role of immersion experience in L2 learning because the L2 learning environment may interact with working memory capacity in predicting L2 performance. Specifically, preliminary evidence showed that on a comprehension task, L2 learners with some immersion experience showed much smaller effects of span than individuals who were exposed to their L2 only in a classroom (Sunderman, Persaud, & Kroll, 2004). In other words, lower span participants who had immersion experience performed just as well as their higher span immersion peers, whereas lower span participants without immersion experience were generally slower and less accurate at comprehension than their higher span counterparts. These results suggest that immersion experience may provide learners with external resources that allow them to compensate for having relatively low working memory capacity or a poor ability to suppress irrelevant information.

Working Memory and Suppression

The studies reviewed in the section Working Memory and Second Language Processing present a promising new approach to understanding individual differences in achieving and maintaining bilingualism and establish a growing body of support for the proposed link between working memory capacity and bilingual performance. In this section,

we consider whether suppression may mediate the relationship between working memory and bilingualism. We propose that performance on working memory span tasks is correlated with performance on bilingual tasks because both types of tasks may require suppression. Thus far, we have argued that the relationship between bilingualism and suppression is complex; from the standpoint of the IC Model and the RHM, we discussed a number of possible roles for suppression in bilingual processing, and we presented support (albeit limited) for the claim that bilingualism improves suppression skills. We now turn our attention to the final piece of the puzzle, the link between working memory span and suppression ability.

Conway and Engle (1994) were among the first to propose that suppression is an important component of working memory, and that individuals with higher working memory capacity may thus be better at suppressing irrelevant information than individuals with lower working memory capacity. In the last several years, a large amount of empirical evidence from a wide variety of tasks has provided support for the idea that performance on working memory measures involves the ability to maintain activation of multiple representations and inhibit irrelevant information simultaneously. Studies of the relationship between working memory and suppression have generally taken one of two approaches. The first approach is to ask whether the ability to suppress is disrupted by an experimentally imposed working memory load, which would indicate shared resources for the suppression and working memory systems. The second approach is to compare suppression abilities in individuals with higher and lower working memory span.

Engle, Conway, Tuholski, and Shisler (1995) examined the effect of a memory load on negative priming. In a standard priming paradigm, processing of a given stimulus on one trial leads to faster processing of an identical or related stimulus on a subsequent trial. *Negative priming* refers to the phenomenon that ignoring a stimulus on one trial leads to slower processing of an identical or related stimulus on a subsequent trial. Engle and colleagues reasoned that if suppression is a controlled, effortful process requiring resources similar to those involved in working memory, then tying up those resources with a memory load should reduce participants' ability to suppress and thus also reduce negative priming. Indeed, Engle et al. observed that as the memory load increased, the amount of negative priming decreased, and in fact with the largest load, negative priming gave way to facilitation. In a follow-up study, Conway, Tuholski, Shisler, and Engle (1999) provided further support for the idea that negative priming is dependent on working memory, demonstrating that individuals with lower working memory span showed less negative priming than individuals with higher working memory span.

In a similar approach, Conway, Cowan, and Bunting (2001) used the cocktail party phenomenon to examine the relationship between working memory capacity and inhibition. The cocktail party phenomenon refers to the finding that people's attention is often captured by a stimulus with high personal relevance, such as their own name, even when they are actively attending to other input. Using a selective listening procedure in which participants were required to shadow a message presented to their right ear and ignore the words presented to their left ear, Conway et al. found that lower span participants were significantly more likely than higher span participants to report hearing their name in the unattended channel, suggesting that the higher span participants had more resources available to inhibit the distracting information successfully.

As mentioned, the Stroop task is a commonly studied suppression paradigm that has revealed both individual and group differences in cognitive processing under certain circumstances. As we indicated, Long and Prat (2002) found span differences in the magnitude of the Stroop effect, but only in some conditions. When only a small proportion of the trials were conflict trials, all participants experienced a substantial amount of Stroop interference. When conflict trials were relatively frequent, however, higher span participants were able to reduce the amount of Stroop interference greatly, whereas lower span participants were not. This pattern of results is important because it shows that even in a situation that generally leads to interference, individuals with higher working memory span seem to have a greater ability to control that interference, at least when it is particularly useful to do so.

The suppression tasks discussed thus far all involved language processing to some extent. Kane, Bleckley, Conway, and Engle (2001) studied the relationship between working memory and suppression using two visual-orienting tasks that did not require a verbal response. In the prosaccade task, participants had to identify a target letter that appeared in a cued location. In the antisaccade task, the target letter appeared opposite the cued location, requiring the participant to inhibit the reflexive response to look toward the cue. Kane and colleagues found that higher and lower span participants performed similarly on the prosaccade task, but the antisaccade task elicited significant differences between the higher and lower span participants: Higher span participants were both faster and more accurate at identifying target letters than were lower span participants. In addition, Mitchell, Macrae, and Gilchrist (2002) pointed out that there are two components to the antisaccade task: suppressing the reflexive response to look toward the cued location and generating a voluntary eye movement in the direction opposite the cue. They localized the effect of the dual task to the suppression component by demonstrating that a cognitive load interfered equally with a no saccade condition, which required only suppression.

The studies described in this section suggest that working memory capacity and suppression ability are directly related. Both the IC Model and the RHM provide mechanisms for linking suppression to bilingual processing. Although no one to our knowledge has directly tested these claims, the monolingual work described may help explain some of the observed patterns of relationship between working memory span and L2 processing. If working memory span is in part a measure of suppression ability, then the span differences observed in L2 processing may reflect differences in suppression ability that have critical consequences for bilingual language processing.

Summary

We have reviewed experimental evidence and theoretical reasons for considering working memory and suppression as important factors in bilingual language processing. Although the evidence is preliminary and mixed at this point, the reasons for considering these mechanisms are compelling and promise to inform both models of bilingualism as well as models of cognitive processing more generally. As models of suppression, working memory, and bilingualism continue to become more detailed, it will be increasingly possible to predict both how bilingualism may affect these cognitive skills and how these cognitive skills may affect bilingualism.

Acknowledgments

The writing of this chapter was supported in part by a National Research Service Award (NIMH HD41307-02) to Erica B. Michael and by a Career

Development Award (NIDCD DC00191) to Tamar H. Gollan.

References

Atkins, P. W. B., & Baddeley, A. D. (1998). Working memory and distributed vocabulary learning. *Applied Psycholinguistics, 19,* 537–552.

Baddeley, A., Gathercole, S., & Papagno, C. (1998). The phonological loop as a language learning device. *Psychological Review, 105,* 158–173.

Bialystok, E. (2002, April). *Bilingualism: Defense against the decline of executive functions?* Poster presented at the Cognitive Aging Conference, Atlanta, GA.

Borkowski, J. G., Benton, A. L., & Spreen, O. (1967). Word fluency and brain damage. *Neuropsychologia, 5,* 135–140.

Brown, A. (1991). A review of the tip-of-the-tongue experience. *Psychological Bulletin, 109,* 204–223.

Brown, R., & McNeill, D. (1966). The "tip of the tongue" phenomenon. *The Journal of Verbal Learning and Verbal Behavior, 5,* 325–337.

Burke, D. M., Locantore, J. K., & Austin, A. A. (2004). Cherry pit primes Brad Pitt: Homophone priming effects on young and older adults' production of proper names. *Psychological Science, 15,* 164–170.

Burke, D. M., MacKay, D. G., Worthley, J. S., & Wade, E. (1991). On the tip of the tongue: What causes word finding failures in young and older adults? *Journal of Memory and Language, 30,* 542–579.

Campbell, R., & Sais, E. (1995). Accelerated metalinguistic (phonological) awareness in bilingual children. *British Journal of Developmental Psychology, 13,* 61–68.

Cheung, H. (1996). Nonword span as a unique predictor of second-language vocabulary learning. *Developmental Psychology, 32,* 867–873.

Cohen, G., & Burke, D. M. (1993). Memory for proper names: A review. *Memory, 1,* 249–263.

Colomé, À. (2001). Lexical activation in bilinguals' speech production: Language-specific or language-independent? *Journal of Memory and Language, 45,* 721–736.

Conway, A. R. A., Cowan, N., & Bunting, M. F. (2001). The cocktail party phenomenon revisited: The importance of working memory capacity. *Psychonomic Bulletin & Review, 8,* 331–335.

Conway, A. R. A., & Engle, R. W. (1994). Working memory and retrieval: A resource-dependent inhibition model. *Journal of Experimental Psychology: General, 123,* 354–373.

Conway, A. R. A., Tuholski, S. W., Shisler, R. J., & Engle, R. W. (1999). The effect of memory load on negative priming: An individual differences investigation. *Memory & Cognition, 27,* 1042–1050.

Costa, A., & Caramazza, A. (1999). Is lexical selection in bilingual speech production language-specific? Further evidence from Spanish-English and English-Spanish bilinguals. *Bilingualism: Language and Cognition, 2,* 231–244.

Costa, A., Caramazza, A., & Sebastián-Gallés, N. (2000). The cognate facilitation effect: Implications for models of lexical access. *Journal of Experimental Psychology: Learning, Memory, and Cognition, 26,* 1283–1296.

Costa, A., Miozzo, M., & Caramazza, A. (1999). Lexical selection in bilinguals: Do words in the bilingual's two lexicons compete for selection? *Journal of Memory and Language, 41,* 365–397.

Cutting, J. C., & Ferreira, V. S. (1999). Semantic and phonological information flow in the production lexicon. *Journal of Experimental Psychology: Learning, Memory, and Cognition, 25,* 318–344.

Daneman, M., & Carpenter, P. A. (1980). Individual differences in working memory and reading. *Journal of Verbal Learning and Verbal Behavior, 19,* 450–466.

Daneman, M., & Carpenter, P. A. (1983). Individual differences in integrating information between and within sentences. *Journal of Experimental Psychology: Learning, Memory, and Cognition, 9,* 561–584.

Daneman, M., & Green, I. (1986). Individual differences in comprehending and producing words in context. *Journal of Memory and Language, 25,* 1–18.

Daneman, M., & Merikle, P. M. (1996). Working memory and language comprehension: A meta-analysis. *Psychonomic Bulletin & Review, 3,* 422–433.

De Groot, A. M. B., & Poot, R. (1997). Word translation at three levels of proficiency in a second language: The ubiquitous involvement of conceptual memory. *Language Learning, 47,* 215–264.

Delis, D., Kaplan, E., Kramer, J., & Ober, B. (2000). *California Verbal Learning Test-II.* San Antonio, TX: Psychological Corporation.

Dell, G. S. (1986). A spreading-activation model of retrieval in sentence production. *Psychological Review, 93,* 283–321.

Ecke, P. (1996). Cross-language studies of lexical retrieval: Tip-of-the-tongue states in first and foreign languages. *Dissertation Abstracts International Section A: Humanities and Social Sciences, 57(4-A).*

Engle, R. W., Cantor, J., & Carullo, J. J. (1992). Individual differences in working memory and comprehension: A test of four hypotheses. *Journal of Experimental Psychology: Learning, Memory, and Cognition, 18,* 972–992.

Engle, R. W., Conway, A. R. A., Tuholski, S. W., & Shisler, R. J. (1995). A resource account of inhibition. *Psychological Science, 6,* 122–125.

Gathercole, S. E., & Baddeley, A. D. (1989). Evaluation of the role of phonological STM in the development of vocabulary in children: A longitudinal study. *Journal of Memory and Language, 28,* 200–213.

Gernsbacher, M. A., & Faust, M. E. (1991). The mechanism of suppression: A component of general comprehension skill. *Journal of Experimental Psychology: Learning, Memory, and Cognition, 17,* 245–262.

Gollan, T. H., & Acenas, L. A. (2004). What is a TOT? Cognate and translation effects on tip-of-the-tongue states in Spanish-English and Tagalog-English bilinguals. *Journal of Experimental Psychology: Learning, Memory, and Cognition, 30,* 246–269.

Gollan, T. H., Bonanni, M. P., & Montoya, R. I. (in press). Proper names get stuck on bilingual and monolingual speakers tip-of-the-tongue equally often. *Neuropsychology.*

Gollan, T. H., Montoya, R. I., Fennema-Notestine, C., & Morris, S. K. (in press). Bilingualism affects picture naming but not picture classification. *Memory & Cognition.*

Gollan, T. H., Montoya, R., & Werner, G. (2002). Semantic and letter fluency in Spanish-English bilinguals. *Neuropsychology, 16,* 562–576.

Gollan, T. H., & Silverberg, N. B. (2001). Tip-of-the-tongue states in Hebrew-English bilinguals. *Bilingualism: Language and Cognition, 4,* 63–83.

Green, D. W. (1998). Mental control of the bilingual lexico-semantic system. *Bilingualism: Language and Cognition, 1,* 67–81.

Hamers, J. F., & Blanc, M. H. A. (2000). *Bilinguality and bilingualism* (2nd ed.). Cambridge, U.K.: Cambridge University Press.

Harrington, M., & Sawyer, M. (1992). L2 working memory capacity and L2 reading skill. *Studies in Second Language Acquisition, 14,* 25–38.

Hermans, D., Bongaerts, T., De Bot, K., & Schreuder, R. (1998). Producing words in a foreign language: Can speakers prevent interference from their first language? *Bilingualism: Language and Cognition, 1,* 213–229.

Jescheniak, J. D., & Schriefers, K. I. (1998). Discrete serial versus cascading processing in lexical access in speech production: Further evidence from the coactivation of near-synonyms. *Journal of Experimental Psychology: Learning, Memory, and Cognition, 24,* 1256–1274.

Just, M. A., & Carpenter, P. A. (1992). A capacity theory of comprehension: Individual differences in working memory. *Psychological Review, 99,* 122–149.

Kane, M. J., Bleckley, M. K., Conway, A. R. A., & Engle, R. W. (2001). A controlled-attention view of working-memory capacity. *Journal of Experimental Psychology: General, 130,* 169–183.

Kempe, V., & Brooks, P. J. (2000, November). *Learning complex morphological paradigms.* Poster presented at the annual meeting of the Psychonomic Society, New Orleans, LA.

Kempe, V., Brooks, P. J., & Kharkhurin, A. (1999, November). *Multiple determinants of individual differences in language learning.* Poster presented at the annual meeting of the Psychonomic Society, Los Angeles, CA.

King, J., & Just, M. A. (1991). Individual difference in syntactic processing: The role of working memory. *Journal of Memory and Language, 30,* 580–602.

Kroll, J. F., Michael, E., Tokowicz, N., & Dufour, R. (2002). The development of lexical fluency in a second language. *Second Language Research, 18,* 137–171.

Kroll, J. F., & Stewart, E. (1994). Category interference in translation and picture naming: Evidence for asymmetric connections between bilingual memory representations. *Journal of Memory and Language, 33,* 149–174.

La Heij, W., Hooglander, A., Kerling, R., & Van der Velden, E. (1996). Nonverbal context effects in forward and backward word translation: Evidence for concept mediation. *Journal of Memory and Language, 35,* 648–665.

Levelt, W. J. M., Roelofs, A., & Meyer, A. S. (1999). A theory of lexical access in speech production. *Behavioral and Brain Sciences, 22,* 1–75.

Lezak, M. D. (1995). *Neuropsychological assessment* (3rd ed.). New York: Oxford University Press.

Long, D. L., & Prat, C. S. (2002). Working memory and Stroop interference: An individual differences investigation. *Memory & Cognition, 30,* 294–301.

MacWhinney, B. (1997). Second language acquisition and the Competition Model. In A. M. B. de Groot & J. F. Kroll (Eds.), *Tutorials in bilingualism: Psycholinguistic perspectives* (pp. 113–142). Mahwah, NJ: Erlbaum.

Mayr, U., & Kliegl, R. (2000). Complex semantic processing in old age: Does it stay or does it go? *Psychology and Aging, 15,* 29–34.

Meuter, R. F. I., & Allport, A. (1999). Bilingual language switching in naming: Asymmetrical costs of language selection. *Journal of Memory and Language, 40,* 25–40.

Michael, E. B. (1998). *The consequences of individual differences in cognitive abilities for bilingual language processing.* Unpublished doctoral dissertation, The Pennsylvania State University, University Park.

Michael, E. B., Dijkstra, T., & Kroll, J. F. (2002, November). *Individual differences in the degree of language nonselectivity in fluent bilinguals.* Poster presented at the annual meeting of the Psychonomic Society, Kansas City, KS.

Michael, E. B., Tokowicz, N., & Kroll, J. F. (2003, April). *Modulating access to L2 words: The role of individual differences and language immersion experience.* Paper presented at the Fourth International Symposium on Bilingualism, Tempe, AZ.

Mitchell, J. P., Macrae, C. N., & Gilchrist, I. D. (2002). Working memory and the suppression of reflexive saccades. *Journal of Cognitive Neuroscience, 14,* 95–103.

Miyake, A. (1998). Individual differences in second language proficiency: The role of working memory. In A. F. Healy & L. E. Bourne, Jr. (Eds.), *Foreign language learning: Psycholinguistic studies on training and retention* (pp. 339–364). Mahwah, NJ: Erlbaum.

Miyake, A., Carpenter, P. A., & Just, M. A. (1994). A capacity approach to syntactic comprehension disorders: Making normal adults perform like aphasic patients. *Cognitive Neuropsychology, 11,* 671–717.

Papagno, C., Valentine, T., & Baddeley, A. (1991). Phonological short-term memory and foreign-language vocabulary learning. *Journal of Memory and Language, 30,* 331–347.

Papagno, C., & Vallar, G. (1995). Verbal short-term memory and vocabulary learning in polyglots. *The Quarterly Journal of Experimental Psychology, 48A,* 98–107.

Peterson, R. R., & Savoy, P. (1998). Lexical selection and phonological encoding during language production: Evidence for cascaded processing. *Journal of Experimental Psychology: Learning, Memory, and Cognition, 24,* 539–557.

Ransdell, S., Arecco, M. R., & Levy, C. M. (2001). Bilingual long-term working memory: The effects of working memory loads on writing quality and fluency. *Applied Psycholinguistics, 22,* 113–128.

Ransdell, S. E., & Fischler, I. (1987). Memory in a monolingual mode: When are bilinguals at a disadvantage? *Journal of Memory and Language, 26,* 392–405.

Ransdell, S. E., & Fischler, I. (1989). Effects of concreteness and task context on recall of prose among bilingual and monolingual speakers. *Journal of Memory and Language, 28,* 278–291.

Rosen, V. M., & Engle, R. W. (1997). The role of working memory capacity in retrieval. *Journal of Experimental Psychology: General, 126,* 211–227.

Rosselli, M., Ardila, A., Araujo, K., Weekes, V. A., Caracciolo, V., Padilla, M., et al. (2000). Verbal fluency and repetition skills in healthy older Spanish-English bilinguals. *Applied Neuropsychology, 7,* 17–24.

Rosselli, M., Ardila, A., Santisi, M. N., Arecco, M. R., Salvatierra, J., Conde, A., et al. (2002). Stroop-effect in Spanish-English bilinguals. *Journal of the International Neuropsychological Society, 8,* 819–827.

Sebova, E., & Arochova, O. (1986). An attempt at a modification of the Stroop test for preschool age children. *Studia Psychologica, 28,* 179–182.

Segalowitz, N. (1997). Individual differences in second language acquisition. In A. M. B. de Groot & J. F. Kroll (Eds.), *Tutorials in bilingualism: Psycholinguistic perspectives* (pp. 85–112). Mahwah, NJ: Erlbaum.

Service, E. (1992). Phonology, working memory, and foreign-language learning. *Quarterly Journal of Experimental Psychology. A, Human Experimental Psychology, 45A,* 21–50.

Service, E., & Kohonen, V. (1995). Is the relation between phonological memory and foreign language learning accounted for by vocabulary acquisition? *Applied Psycholinguistics, 16,* 155–172.

Smith, M. C. (1997). How do bilinguals access lexical information? In A. M. B. de Groot & J. F. Kroll (Eds.), *Tutorials in bilingualism: Psycholinguistic perspectives* (pp. 145–168). Mahwah, NJ: Erlbaum.

Stroop, J. R. (1935). Studies of interference in serial verbal reactions. *Journal of Experimental Psychology, 18,* 643–662.

Sunderman, G., Persaud, A., & Kroll, J. F. (2004). *When language learning is not a matter of talent alone: The effects of cognitive abilities and study abroad experiences on language processing.* Manuscript in preparation, The Pennsylvania State University, University Park.

Talamas, A., Kroll, J. F., & Dufour, R. (1999). Form related errors in second language learning: A preliminary stage in the acquisition of L2 vocabulary. *Bilingualism: Language and Cognition, 2,* 45–58.

Van Hell, J. G., & Dijkstra, T. (2002). Foreign language knowledge can influence native language performance in exclusively native contexts. *Psychonomic Bulletin & Review, 9,* 780–789.

PART IV

ASPECTS AND IMPLICATIONS OF BILINGUALISM

Introduction to Part IV

Aspects and Implications of Bilingualism

In the *Brain and Language* special issue on the new millennium (Paradis, 2000), it was surmised that in the coming decades the growing awareness of bilingualism in research and clinical settings, bolstered by an increasing number of bilingual speakers in the world coupled with heightened attention to minority rights, would lead to a search for empirical verification of then-current theoretical constructs, with a number of points of focus. In particular, the search for the cerebral structures underlying linguistic competence, metalinguistic knowledge, pragmatic ability, and motivation in the acquisition, learning, and use of verbal communication. We can also expect an exploration of the neuroanatomical and neurophysiological correlates of particular language tasks, such as switching, mixing, and simultaneous interpretation, all with a view to informing language rehabilitation methods. We are today in a better position to integrate a number of what might appear as disparate elements into a theoretical model of the cerebral processing of languages in bilingual speakers than we were some 25 years ago when Albert and Obler (1978) formulated a number of fundamental questions.

The chapters in this part include reviews of contemporary neuroscience approaches to bilingualism. In addition, they consider the cognitive consequences of bilingualism for development, for the relation between language and thought, and for the allocation of mental resources during what is perhaps an uncharacteristically extreme version of bilingualism when skilled interpreters produce translations of spoken discourse in real time. A final chapter considers the state of models of bilingual representation over the past 20 years to identify the elements that are likely to be critical in developing a unified account of representation and processing. Because the chapters themselves effectively represent the topics that they address, I use this

introduction to focus on a set of issues raised primarily by the discussion of the neural basis of bilingualism. I then consider briefly the consequences of bilingualism for language and thought.

Neuroscience Approaches to Bilingualism

The Interpretation of Findings

We have to be extremely cautious in interpreting the results of neuroimaging studies. One finding may hide another. For example, greater left hemisphere activation, as reported in some late bilingual studies and usually interpreted as indicating more left hemisphere dominance for language (implying greater similarity with unilinguals), may in fact reflect greater conscious processing of rules, hence a fundamental dissimilarity with unilinguals (or the first language [L1] of bilingual speakers).

Marian, Spivey, and Hirsch (2003) and Abutalebi, Cappa, and Perani (chapter 24, this volume) compared the Kim, Relkin, Lee, and Hirsch (1997) and Chee, Tan, and Thiel (1999) studies. Because the Kim et al. study reported the activation of separate regions and the Chee et al. study the activation of the same regions for the two languages of bilinguals, they concluded that the two studies are contradictory. Yet, in principle, it is not surprising that a study that uses single words should find similar activations whereas one that uses sentences should find different activation areas for the two languages (even though, admittedly, in the Kim et al. study, it is difficult to know what the subjects were actually doing and whether the baseline and other parameters were valid). Declarative-memory tasks (including those using single words) will yield similar results in both languages; procedural-memory tasks (involving sentences) may be expected to yield different results in late second language (L2) speakers (commensurate with the extent of their lacunae in L2 implicit linguistic competence).

Comparisons between neuroimaging studies that are based on the processing of single words and those that use sentence processing, because they are based on altogether different types of language components of a fundamentally different nature, subserved as they are by different memory systems that rely on different anatomical structures located in different parts of the brain, may only serve to show how the two processes differ from each other.

The effects of single-word processing can be expected to be similar in L1 and L2 by virtue of the declarative-memory support of words in both languages. In contrast, the effects of text processing (sentences and short stories) may differ between L1 and L2 in proportion to bilinguals' greater reliance on pragmatics (and to a lesser extent on some aspects of rote-learned metalinguistic knowledge). Note that both native and L2 speakers use the same cerebral mechanisms in processing verbal communication, but in different proportions (determined by the degree of automatization of L2, extent of metalinguistic knowledge, and degree of reliance on pragmatics).

Also, single words (presented in isolation from any sentential context) do not tap pragmatic aspects of language or the procedural memory system that subserves the language system (implicit linguistic competence; i.e., phonology, morphology, syntax, and semantics other than conscious lexical semantics). Experiments using single words therefore cannot, in my opinion, address questions about the representation of the language system, including questions of the participation of the right hemisphere through pragmatic aspects.

Single words, however, can be expected to activate the right hemisphere to the extent that the conceptual features corresponding to their lexical meanings are connected to right hemisphere sensorimotor and affective representations (the latter through the privileged pathways to subcortical limbic structures). This is true of both uni- and bilinguals.

It is also important not to generalize to language representation or processing from results of experiments that use tasks other than normal language-processing tasks, such as switching on demand in response to a color or a sound clue; deciding whether a word is concrete or abstract, whether it rhymes with another word or not, whether it is a word of L1 or of L2, or whether its meaning is or is not related to another word; memorizing unrelated word pairs; producing on demand words that begin with a certain letter or a three-letter string or that belong to a certain semantic category; deriving a verb from a noun; or counting the number of L2 words in a list of L1 words. In each case, these laboratory tasks, by comparison with appropriate controls, may perhaps allow certain components of processing to be identified. How those components combine in real time may not, however, reflect the events that characterize ordinary language processing outside the laboratory.

Declarative/Procedural Memory

The declarative/procedural (implicit/explicit) distinction has pervasive implications in every neuropsychological domain of bilingualism research and cannot be ignored. It has an impact not only on the interpretation of the results obtained with single words versus those obtained with the rest of language structure (a combination of phonology, morphosyntax, and semantics; i.e., tasks involving sentences and short stories as stimuli), but also on the identification of the cerebral mechanisms used by early and late bilinguals, proficient and nonproficient speakers of an L2.

It is therefore not surprising that it should also be relevant to simultaneous translation (see Christoffels & De Groot, chapter 22, this volume). The declarative knowledge of Patient A. D. (Paradis, Goldblum, & Abidi, 1982) was not affected by her aphasia, as demonstrated by her ability to remember correctly (and state in her available language) which objects she was able to name (and which she could not name) the day before—yet without the ability to recover their names. This might be an explanation for her ability to translate into a language that was not available for spontaneous use: She was probably performing a conscious metalinguistic task (not involving her implicit competence used to produce language automatically). Meaning-based interpreting depends on implicit linguistic competence, whereas transcoding depends on metalinguistic knowledge. The patient must have been transcoding. For a discussion of the cognitive processes involved in simultaneous interpretation, see Christoffels and De Groot's chapter 22 in this volume.

Neuroimaging Evidence and Theory

Neuroimaging studies have so far by and large failed to connect to theoretical debates in the behavioral and clinical literature. The investigation by Price, Green, and von Studnitz (1999) was the first bilingual study actually to test a hypothesis rather than to go on a fishing expedition (i.e., "let's poke here and see what happens," a practice that then leaves researchers in a quandary when it comes to interpreting the data—many of them unexpected). As a result, neuroimaging studies have not provided more answers than previous behavioral and clinical studies. They have at best confirmed some of the clinical findings and have produced a number of unreplicated, contradictory, often-uninterpretable results. For example, it is not known whether the regions showing activation in unexpected areas such as the inferior temporal gyrus and the temporal pole (not to mention right-hemisphere areas) reflect activation or inhibition, and given that there are more inhibitory neurons than activating ones (Chertkow & Murtha, 1999), chances are that some do reflect inhibition. It is also not known whether the observed activation results from some task-related or general problem-solving function.

Paradis (2004) listed over 20 severe problems inherent with neuroimaging techniques that, together with the large number of reported interindividual variables among homogeneous groups of speakers and the number of contradictory findings, should give us serious cause for concern about the reliability and validity of functional neuroimaging techniques applied to cognitive processes in bilingual populations. Current neuroimaging techniques, although extremely useful in detecting infarcts and tumors, are not suited for detecting, let alone measuring, processes that typically last a few milliseconds and occur microns apart within a number of circumscribed areas possibly distributed over large distances cortically and subcortically. The task is made even more difficult considering that some of the processes are not only microanatomical but also biochemical (involving neurotransmitters, hormones, etc.) and may rely on electrical activity (such as firing patterns and Hebb-type cell assemblies). Neuroimaging studies may show that a particular area is active when one or the other of a speaker's languages or both are processed. They do not indicate whether the languages share the same neuronal circuits. At best, they indicate that a gross anatomical area is involved, but say nothing about the microanatomical sites within this region.

Lateralization

It is not so much because the bilingual laterality literature is contradictory that it is considered not worthy of serious attention, but because of the lack of validity of its basic premise, namely, that the percentage of ear, half visual field, or tapping advantage reflects the degree of cerebral lateralization of the language system (Paradis, 2003).

Bilingual laterality studies continue to refer to the age of acquisition variable as pre- and postpuberty (Evans, Workman, Mayer, & Crowley, 2002; Hull & Vaid, chapter 23, this volume). This notion of puberty as a cutoff point of the critical period goes back to Lenneberg's (1967) conjecture that language lateralization is a gradual process that would end at puberty. It was quickly pointed out that the data on which Lenneberg had based his hypothesis did not support it (Krashen, 1973). It has since become apparent that (a) language (qua implicit linguistic competence) lateralization is not gradual, from bilateral to left lateralized, but rather is left lateralized from the start, and (b) that the age for the ability to acquire language like a native speaker is much earlier than the onset of puberty, namely, before 5 years of age (see chapters 5 [DeKeyser & Larson-Hall] and 6 [Birdsong] in this volume for a full discussion of age effects on L2 acquisition).

It should not be surprising that there is right hemisphere involvement in text (stimulus sentence or short story) processing. Semantic and pragmatic features should not be confounded if we are to make sense of event-related potential and neuroimaging experimental findings. *Semantics* (the meaning of a sentence derived from the lexical meaning of its words and its grammatical structure) needs to be distinguished from *pragmatics* (the meaning of an utterance taking various contexts into account, including general knowledge). Every utterance (e.g., a sentence presented as part of a short story or uttered in a natural context) necessarily derives part of its meaning from pragmatics and to that extent can be expected to activate areas of the right hemisphere. To the extent that implicit competence grammatical devices are not available (because they are not provided by the grammar of a particular language, because they have not been internalized by an L2 learner, or because they have been impaired by pathology), speakers will compensate by relying on pragmatics to fill the gap.

At this point, the usefulness of a comparison between experimental laterality studies (problematic because they are based on the invalid premise that the degree of ear or visual half-field advantage is an index of degree of language laterality) and neuroimaging studies (plagued with a lack of consensus on the appropriate parameters to interpret what is observed, such as activation level settings, statistics, etc.) seems extremely limited.

Language and Thought

Contrary to Macnamara's (1970) assumption (see Pavlenko, chapter 21, this volume), bilingual individuals do not need to translate to themselves in L2 what they have heard or said in L1 (or vice versa) to communicate with themselves. Each language is understood directly (Paradis, 2004), just as it is by unilingual native speakers. What this means is that bilinguals are able to organize their mental representations in accordance with the meaning of each language. This ability to adopt two perspectives might account for the results obtained by young bilinguals on intelligence tests. Far from being handicapped, bilingual persons are reported to possess greater cognitive flexibility, which could explain their superior performance not only on metalinguistic tasks and verbal intelligence tests, but also on divergent thinking tasks, on concept formation and general reasoning tests, and in the discovery of underlying rules in the resolution of a problem. The common finding in the disparate cognitive domains investigated by Bialystok (chapter 20, this volume) is that bilingual children are more advanced than unilinguals in solving problems requiring the inhibition of misleading information.

Bilingual persons who speak both languages like natives need not find themselves in any predicament: They may function cognitively differentially without any ill consequences. In fact, their bilingualism is likely to enrich their general mental representations. To the extent that they have native competence in both languages, they are able to organize their representations now in accordance with the patterns of L1, now in accordance with those of L2, thus having more ways of sorting out the same data of experience.

From a neuropsychological viewpoint, bilingual individuals may encode particular concepts in different ways (see Pavlenko, chapter 21, this volume); that is, the conceptual components corresponding to a word and its translation equivalent may sometimes differ considerably, but the cerebral mechanisms that subserve the conceptual representations and the lexical representations are the same, irrespective of the degree of concept–word overlap between languages. (See Francis, chapter 12, this volume, for further discussion of the representation of concepts in the bilingual's two languages.)

The research that is reviewed in the chapters that follow examines distinctions between representation and control (e.g., Bialystok, chapter 20, in the case of bilingual children and Green, chapter 25, in the case of bilingual individuals with aphasia), in the nature of representations and how they are accessed in the two languages, and in the neurocognitive basis of bilingualism. Many of these investigations into the behavioral and neural bases of bilingualism are at an early stage of development. My comments suggest that we be cautious, particularly in generalizing the results of the neuroimaging studies published to date and in interpreting the available evidence on laterality. Despite this caution, there appears to be promise in the convergence of approaches represented by the chapters in this section.

References

Albert, M. L., & Obler, L. K. (1978). *The bilingual brain*. New York: Academic Press.

Chee, M. W. L., Tan, E. W. L., & Thiel, T. (1999). Mandarin and English single word processing studied with functional magnetic resonance imaging. *Journal of Neuroscience, 19,* 3050–3056.

Chertkow, H., & Murtha, S. (1997). PET activation and language. *Clinical Neuroscience, 4,* 78–86.

Evans, J., Workman, L., Mayer, P., & Crowley, P. (2002). Differential bilingual laterality: Mythical monster found in Wales. *Brain and Language, 83,* 291–299.

Kim, K. H., Relkin, N. R., Lee, K.-M., & Hirsch, J. (1997). Distinct cortical areas associated with native and second languages. *Nature, 388,* 171–174.

Krashen, S. (1973). Lateralization, language learning and the critical period: Some new evidence. *Language Learning, 23,* 63–74.

Lenneberg, E. H. (1967). *Biological foundations of language*. New York: Wiley.

Macnamara, J. (1970). Bilingualism and thought. *Monograph Series on Languages and Linguistics, 23,* 25–45.

Marian, V., Spivey, M., & Hirsch, J. (2003). Shared and separate systems in bilingual language processing: Converging evidence from eyetracking and brain imaging. *Brain and Language, 86,* 70–82.

Paradis, M. (2000). The neurolinguistics of bilingualism in the next decades. *Brain and Language, 71,* 178–180.

Paradis, M. (2003). The bilingual Loch Ness monster raises its nonasymmetric head again—or, why bother with such cumbersome notions as validity and reliability? Comments on Evans et al. (2002). *Brain and Language, 87*, 441–448.

Paradis, M. (2004). *Neurolinguistic aspects of bilingualism*. Amsterdam: Benjamins.

Paradis, M., Goldblum, M., & Abidi, R. (1982). Alternate antagonism with paradoxical behavior in two bilingual aphasic patients. *Brain and Language, 15*, 55–69.

Price, C., Green, D., & von Studnitz, R. (1999). A functional imaging study of translation and language switching. *Brain, 122*, 2221–2235.

Ellen Bialystok

20

Consequences of Bilingualism for Cognitive Development

ABSTRACT   Research addressing the possible cognitive consequences of bilingualism for children's development has found mixed results when seeking effects in domains such as language ability and intelligence. The approach in the research reported in this chapter is to investigate the effect that bilingualism might have on specific cognitive processes rather than domains of skill development. Three cognitive domains are examined: concepts of quantity, task switching and concept formation, and theory of mind. The common finding in these disparate domains is that bilingual children are more advanced than monolinguals in solving problems requiring the inhibition of misleading information. The conclusion is that bilingualism accelerates the development of a general cognitive function concerned with attention and inhibition, and that facilitating effects of bilingualism are found on tasks and processes in which this function is most required.

A significant portion of children in the world enter the realm of language learning exposed to multiple languages. These children are required to communicate using different systems and proceed to school where the instructional discourse bears no resemblance to the language at home. Normally, few questions are asked, and few concerns are expressed by parents, teachers, or politicians. In many cultures, this quiet acceptance indicates that the experience is either so common that it is not detected as anomalous or so crucial for survival that it is futile to challenge it. Yet, an experience as broad in its impact as the way in which language is learned and used in the first years may well have an impact on the child's cognitive development. This chapter explores research that has addressed itself to identifying whether childhood bilingualism alters the typical course of cognitive development, either favorably or deleteriously, for children whose language acquisition has proceeded by building two linguistic systems.

The cognitive effect of the linguistic environment in which children are raised appears on the surface to be an issue of psychological and educational relevance, but it conceals an underlying dimension that is explosively political. Children who are recipients of this experience, for better or worse, are neither randomly chosen nor randomly distributed through the population. They tend to belong to specific ethnic groups, occupy particular social positions, and be members of communities of individuals who have recently immigrated.

It is not surprising, then, that historically some attempts to investigate the psychological and educational questions that follow from this situation have failed to meet standards of scientific objectivity. Instead, the judgment about the effect of bilingualism on children's development in early studies was sometimes used to reflect societal attitudes toward such issues as immigration and to reinforce preconceived views of language and its role in education.

In some nontrivial way, bilingual minds cannot resemble the more homogeneous mental landscape of a monolingual. Although there is debate about the precise manner in which languages and concepts are interconnected in bilingual minds, it is uncontroversial that the configuration is more complex than that of a monolingual, for whom concepts and languages ultimately converge in unambiguous and predictable manners. Monolinguals may have multiple names for individual concepts, but the relation among those alternatives (e.g., as synonyms) does not invoke the activation of entire systems of meaning as the alternative names from different languages are likely to do. From the beginning, therefore, bilingualism has consequences. What is *not* inevitable, however, is that one of these consequences is to influence the quality or manner of cognitive development.

Early research on the cognitive consequences of bilingualism paid virtually no attention to such issues as the nature of bilingual populations tested, their facility in the language of testing, or the interpretation of the tests used. As an apparent default, cognitive ability was taken to be determined by performance on IQ tests, at best a questionable measure of intelligence (see Gould, 1981). For example, Saer (1923) used the Stanford-Binet test and compared bilingual Welsh children with monolingual English children and reported the inferiority and "mental confusion" of the bilinguals. Darcy (1963) reviewed many subsequent studies of this type and pointed to their common finding that bilinguals consistently scored lower on verbal tests and were often disadvantaged on performance tests as well. Although Darcy cautioned that multiple factors should be considered, a more salubrious account of this research was offered by Hakuta (1986), who attributed the inferior results of the bilinguals in comparison to their new native-speaking peers to conducting the tests in a language they were only beginning to learn.

The antidote to the pessimistic research was almost as extreme in its claims. In a watershed study, Peal and Lambert (1962) tested a carefully selected group of French-English bilingual children and hypothesized that the linguistic abilities of the bilinguals would be superior to those of the monolinguals but that the nonverbal skills would be the same. Even the expectation of an absence of a bilingual deficit was a radical departure from the existing studies. Not only was the linguistic advantage confirmed in their results, but also an unexpected advantage in some of the nonverbal cognitive measures involving symbolic reorganization was found. Their conclusion was that bilingualism endowed children with enhanced mental flexibility, and this flexibility was evident across all domains of thought.

Subsequent research has supported this notion. Ricciardelli (1992), for example, found that few tests in a large battery of cognitive and metalinguistic measures were solved better by bilinguals, but those that were included tests of creativity and flexible thought. In addition, balanced bilinguals have been found to perform better on concept formation tasks (Bain, 1974), divergent thinking and creativity (Torrance, Wu, Gowan, & Aliotti, 1970), and field independence and Piagetian conservation (Duncan & De Avila, 1979). In a particularly well-designed study, Ben-Zeev (1977) reported bilingual advantages on both verbal and nonverbal measures in spite of a significant bilingual disadvantage in vocabulary. Her explanation was that the mutual interference between languages forces bilinguals to adopt strategies that accelerate cognitive development. Although she did not develop the idea further, it is broadly consistent with the explanation proposed elsewhere (Bialystok, 2001) and below.

Researchers such as Hakuta, Ferdman, and Diaz (1987), MacNab (1979), and Reynolds (1991) challenged the reliability of many of those studies reporting felicitous cognitive consequences for bilingualism and argued that the data were not yet conclusive. MacNab (1979) was the most critical, but conceded that bilinguals consistently outperformed monolinguals in generating original uses for objects, an ability compatible with the claim of Peal and Lambert (1962) for an increase in flexibility of thought. Reynolds's (1991) reservation depended in part on his requirement that evidence for bilingual superiority should be presented in the context of an explanation for why such effects occur.

The purpose of the present review is to describe some selected cognitive processes and evaluate the evidence for bilingual influences on their development and to interpret those effects within an explanatory framework. Peal and Lambert's (1962) idea that bilingualism would foster flexibility of thought has persisted, often accompanied by supporting evidence. Their explanation was that the experience of having two ways to describe the world gave bilinguals the basis for understanding that many things could be seen in two ways, leading to a more flexible approach to perception and interpretation. I return to this idea at the end of the chapter.

The majority of the more recent literature has focused on the consequences of bilingualism for the development of children's linguistic and metalinguistic concepts. It is entirely plausible that learning two languages in childhood could alter the course of these developments, but documenting those abilities has revealed unexpected complexity. Bilingualism is often (but not consistently) found to promote more rapid development of metalinguistic concepts. In contrast, oral language proficiency, particularly in terms of early vocabulary development, is usually delayed for bilingual children.

Reading and the acquisition of literacy is less well studied, but the existing evidence gives little reason to believe that bilingualism itself has a significant impact on the manner or ease with which children learn to read. The effects of bilingualism on all these language-related developments are discussed elsewhere (e.g., Bialystok, 2001, 2002) and are not reviewed here. This chapter examines only the nonverbal cognitive consequences of becoming bilingual in childhood.

The possibility that bilingualism can affect non-verbal cognitive development is steeped in an assumption, namely, that linguistic and nonlinguistic knowledge share resources in a domain-general representational system and can influence each other. In some theoretical conceptions of language, language representations and processes are isolated from other cognitive systems (e.g., Pinker, 1994). Although it may be possible in these views to understand that bilingualism would influence linguistic and metalinguistic development, it is difficult to imagine that the effect of constructing two languages would extend beyond that domain. Therefore, even to pose the possibility that bilingualism influences nonverbal cognitive growth requires accepting that linguistic and nonlinguistic functioning converge on some essential cognitive mechanism. Such cognitive models typically incorporate an executive function, one that includes the limitations of working memory and representational processes and is limited by a central resource responsible for selective attention, inhibition, and planning (e.g., Norman & Shallice, 1986). If bilingualism alters something essential about nonverbal cognitive development, then it might well be through its impact on such a generalized executive function.

In the following discussion, three areas of cognitive development are examined to determine if they are acquired differently, or on a different timescale, by bilingual children. The three areas are concepts of quantity and arithmetic ability, hierarchical classification in a task switch paradigm, and theory of mind. Following this discussion, the common pattern from the three developmental areas is discussed, and a possible explanation for developmental differences between monolingual and bilingual children is proposed.

Quantitative Concepts and Abilities

Quantitative concepts and mathematical abilities were investigated early by researchers interested in determining whether bilingualism had an impact on development. Macnamara (1966, 1967) raised the possibility that bilingualism might interfere with children's competence in these areas. Based on the research available at the time, he concluded that there was no evidence that bilingualism handicapped children's computational ability for mechanical arithmetic, but that it did impair children's ability to solve mathematical word problems. His own large-scale study of English-speaking children in Irish language schools confirmed this pattern. He attributed the deficit to what he considered the inevitable language handicap that followed from bilingualism but did not discount the logical possibility that bilingualism itself was to blame. A simpler explanation, however, is compelling: Children's competence in Irish was inadequate to the task. The culprit was not bilingualism but rather the use of a language for a complex educational purpose that exceeded the children's proficiency in that language. Although bilingualism frequently compromises children's proficiency in one of the languages, the deficit is neither inevitable nor pervasive. Therefore, bilingualism itself may not have been a factor in the performance of the children in that study.

Macnamara concluded that the mechanical abilities to carry out arithmetic operations were equivalent in monolinguals and bilinguals, but others have presented a different view. Some researchers have reported weak but consistent evidence that adult bilinguals take longer to solve mental arithmetic problems than monolinguals, particularly in their weaker language (Magiste, 1980; Marsh & Maki, 1976; McClain & Huang, 1982). Geary, Cormier, Goggin, Estrada, and Lunn (1993) speculated that this difference arose because these mechanical problems were solved verbally by mediating the operations in one of the language, so they developed a task that bypassed the possibility of verbal mediation. They presented arithmetic problems with a solution, and participants only needed to judge whether the solution was correct. If verbal mediation were required, participants would conduct these computations in their stronger language, eliminating the burden of the weak language effect. With the language component of the task removed, they found no overall differences in reaction times to solve these problems. In a more detailed follow-up study, they divided the reaction time between time spent encoding and retrieving and time spent computing the operations. Here, they found no group difference in encoding but a significant monolingual advantage in the computing. Their interpretation was that both groups had the same automated access to the stored arithmetic facts, but that monolinguals could perform computations on these facts more rapidly than bilinguals. They interpreted this as indicating working memory differences between the groups that favored monolinguals.

Frenck-Mestre and Vaid (1993) reported that bilinguals verified simple arithmetic problems most quickly and accurately when the problems were presented as digits, slower when presented in word format in their first language, and slower again in their second language. They pointed to other studies that indicated that number processing itself is not slower in a second language and so concluded that the explanation for their data was that it is arithmetic ability that is compromised for the bilinguals in their second language. This result may reflect the same difference reported by Geary et al. (1993) regarding the computation aspect of solving these problems in a weak language. Frenck-Mestre and Vaid concluded that arithmetic is sensitive to the language in which it is learned, and that the ability to carry out arithmetic operations is impaired in a second language. However, their bilingual participants were late language learners who had weaker proficiency in their second than in their first language, so it is still possible that the effect was signaling a weakness in language competence.

In an interesting study, Spelke and Tsivkin (2001) trained bilinguals to perform new arithmetic operations in each of their languages and then tested them in both languages. For computations involving accurate access to large numbers, performance was better in the language in which that problem was trained, suggesting that the coding of that information was specific to the language. This effect even generalized to numerical information about time and space, indicating a general encoding process for quantities in which language is part of the representation. These results extended the work of Frenck-Mestre and Vaid (1983) regarding the language specificity of these operations. In addition, there was a main effect of language in which participants always performed better in their first language, replicating earlier work on this problem.

The differences reported in these studies can also be found in the simplest numerical procedure, namely, counting. In a small-scale study in our laboratory, we compared the speed with which bilingual adults could count forward and backward in their two languages. The participants were highly fluent speakers of English and Portuguese. They were first asked to recall a list of words in each language to ensure some rough equivalence on a verbal task. Then, they were timed as they counted in both directions in both languages. The relevant measure was the ratio of the time required to count backward over the time required to count forward in the same language. Backward counting would inevitably be slower, and the greater effort required would increase its difference from forward counting. Furthermore, by computing this time as a ratio of the time needed to count forward in each language, possible differences in the time required simply to recite the number sequence in the two languages were eliminated. The results showed no difference between languages on the verbal task but a significant increase in time required to count backward in their weaker language.

These studies indicated that bilingual adults generally take longer to solve mathematical problems than monolingual adults do, particularly when the problems are posed in their weak language. The studies also confirmed, however, that language itself has a role to play in these mathematical operations. Therefore, it is still conceivable that bilingual children who are initially learning these skills may be compromised in their acquisition, and that the deficit may be greater if instruction takes place in the weaker language. This, in fact, was the point that Macnamara was arguing in his early studies on this issue. Therefore, research with children is required to establish whether bilingualism has an impact on the development of mathematical abilities.

Secada (1991) studied Hispanic children solving word problems in both English and Spanish. There were two main findings. First, children could solve the problems equally well in both languages. Second, children who were more balanced in their language abilities for the two languages demonstrated higher overall achievement in the problem-solving tasks. He concluded that the problem-solving ability of the bilingual children was equivalent to that of their monolingual peers. Although his study did not include an explicit comparison with monolingual children solving the same problems, it showed that lower levels of language proficiency did not interfere with the ability of these children to solve the problems in their weaker language. Similarly, Morales, Shute, and Pellegrino (1985) hypothesized that if language proficiency were not an issue, then bilingual children should perform just as well as monolingual children on problem-solving tasks. In their study, there were no differences between monolingual and bilingual groups when math problems were presented to each in the dominant language.

This conclusion is different from the one reached by Mestre (1988). He claimed that bilinguals with mathematical skills comparable to monolinguals tended to solve math word problems incorrectly because of language deficiency. His argument was based on studies with bilingual children who were studying in English but for whom English was their weaker language, a situation similar to that in which Macnamara (1966) predicted grave results for bilinguals. Mestre identified the diverse forms of language proficiency that are required to solve these problems, such as literacy, vocabulary, and syntactic knowledge, and argued that all of them are compromised for bilingual children. These results are different from those reported by Secada, but the children in Mestre's study were not as fully bilingual. In Secada's study, the children were in bilingual education programs with most of their instruction conducted in English, and English was the dominant language for most of the children at the time of the study. In Mestre's study, the children lacked some minimal level of competence in the weaker language to proceed through the process of understanding and solving mathematical word problems.

Comparisons in terms of first and second or stronger and weaker languages help to interpret the results when comparing monolinguals and bilinguals performing arithmetic tasks, but the language itself also contributes importantly to the explanation. In a series of studies examining both children and adults who were Welsh-English bilinguals or English or Welsh monolinguals, Ellis (1992) showed that the longer word names for numbers in Welsh increased working memory demands and reduced the availability of working memory for calculation. This effect of increased time needed to perform in Welsh was independent of the participants' level of bilingualism.

A general result from all these studies is that solving mathematical problems in a weak language is more difficult for bilinguals than it is either for monolinguals or for bilinguals in their strong language. The effect is expressed as longer reaction times in adults and increased errors in children. Some studies have shown that adult bilinguals produce increased reaction time when solving these problems in *both* their languages, so there may also be some costs involved in having two systems to manipulate. But, the main finding is that weakness in language proficiency can affect the ability to carry out problem solving in other domains and interfere with children's ability to master these problems. This is entirely reasonable, but it may

not speak to bilingualism so much as to the necessity for having sufficient language skills to carry out basic cognitive activities in any domain. Studies examining bilingual children in their stronger language generally show no deficit in acquiring mathematical concepts or solving mathematical problems. These results show that bilingualism does not alter children's ability to construct the necessary mental representations for mathematics relative to monolinguals, but that problems framed in a verbal context that exceeds their linguistic sophistication imposes a barrier to accessing those representations and interferes with performance. In that sense, language limitations weaken children's ability to learn concepts and to solve mathematical problems relative to monolinguals.

Prior to the time when arithmetic operations can be carried out, children must establish the concept of invariant quantity as a system of relational meanings. These concepts include understanding various aspects of the number system and its operations, including rules for correspondence and rules for counting. This knowledge develops gradually as children piece together the system and learn the symbolic and notational indicators of that system. The primary principle that children must internalize is cardinality, the idea that numbers have quantitative significance (Fuson, 1988; Gelman & Gallistel, 1978; Wynn, 1992). If this concept is learned differently by bilinguals and monolinguals, then that could set the stage on which further disparities in mathematical ability could be built.

This possibility was tested in a study of children's understanding of cardinality using two problems (Bialystok & Codd, 1997). In the towers task, we showed children piles of Lego blocks and piles of Duplo blocks. The Duplo blocks are identical to the Lego blocks except they are twice as large on each dimension. We told children that each block was an apartment that one family could live in, even though some apartments were big and some were small. We were going to build apartment buildings out of the blocks, and they had to count the apartments (blocks) and tell us which building had more families living in it. Children were shown pairs of towers and were reminded each time to count the blocks. The relevant trials were those that compared a Lego tower and a Duplo tower, but in which the higher Duplo tower had fewer blocks. Height was a compelling, although misleading, cue, and children needed to ignore the height and report that the tower that resulted in a higher number when counting was the tower with more blocks. Children found this difficult, but the bilingual children performed significantly better than the monolinguals in their ability to resist focusing on the height of the tower and attend only to the counting operation.

The second problem was the sharing task. Children were shown two identical dolls and a set of candies that they were asked to divide equally between them. When the candies had been divided and the child agreed that both dolls had the same number of candies, they were asked to count the candies in the pile of the first doll and then to say, without counting, how many candies were in the second doll's pile. Like the towers task, the problem required counting a small set of items and making a statement about quantity based on the counting procedure. The difference was that the towers task contained misleading information that appeared to give them the answer, but the sharing task did not. The sharing task was difficult, but both groups performed to the same level. Although these were the same children solving similar problems, the bilingual advantage was found only for the towers task.

Both the towers task and the sharing task are based on the cardinal principle that the last number counted indicates the quantity of the set. The difference between the problems is that the towers task assesses this principle in the context of misleading information specifically designed to distract the child by presenting a plausible but incorrect alternative to the cardinal principle. Bilingual children were better able than monolinguals to focus on the counting operation and not attend to the irrelevant height.

In both these domains, bilingual children (and adults) were equivalent to monolinguals on direct assessments of mathematical ability. For problem solving, bilinguals were sometimes hampered by inadequate linguistic competence and performed less well or less efficiently, especially when tested in their weaker language. For children learning basic arithmetic concepts, however, bilinguals performed better than monolinguals when the problem was presented in a misleading context. In this case, the bilingual children demonstrated superiority in their ability to focus attention and ignore misleading cues. These attentional abilities translated into superior performance on a test of basic quantitative concepts.

Task Switching and Concept Formation

A surprising but consistent deficit in young children's performance has been shown on a task that requires children to follow a simple rule to sort a set of cards and then reverse that rule to sort the same cards in a different way. In a series of studies, Zelazo and his colleagues (Frye, Zelazo, & Palfai, 1995; Jacques, Zelazo, Kirkham, & Semcesen, 1999; Zelazo & Frye, 1997; Zelazo, Frye, & Rapus, 1996) have demonstrated children's failure to reverse a rule that has been established for a particular set. In the task, children are shown a container consisting of two sorting compartments, each indicated by a target stimulus, for example, a red square and a blue circle. They are then given a set of cards containing instances of shape–color combinations that reverse the pairings, in this case, blue squares and red circles. Children are first told to sort by one dimension, for example, color, and place all the blue squares in the compartment indicated by the blue circle and all the red circles in the compartment indicated by the red square. Children can perform this classification essentially without errors. When they have completed that phase, they are asked to re-sort the same cards by the opposite dimension, shape. In this case, the blue squares must be placed in the box indicated by the red square and the red circles must be placed in the box indicated by the blue circle. The finding is that preschool children persist in sorting by the first dimension (color), continuing to place the blue squares with the blue circle, even though they are reminded of the new rule on each trial. Bilingual children, however, adapt to the new rule and solve this problem earlier than monolinguals (Bialystok, 1999; Bialystok & Martin, 2004).

There are different possibilities for why children perseverate on the first set of rules. The explanation proposed by Zelazo and Frye (1997) is called the cognitive complexity and control theory. They argue that children cannot solve the problem until they acquire sufficiently complex rule systems and reflective awareness of those rules. According to this interpretation, the task requires children to construct complex embedded representations of rules in which instructions concerning specific dimensions are embedded under a more general representation that classifies the stimuli. The ability to switch the sorting criterion depends on representing the relation between the dimensions in terms of the higher order rule that unifies the specific lower order rules. Young children are unable to do this, and because they represent only the individual rules, they fail the task. By 5 years old, children have the ability to represent a hierarchical structure and can pass the task, seeing the cards as, for example, simultaneously a red thing and a round thing.

There is no doubt that the representational demands of this task are difficult. Children must appreciate the dual nature of the sorting task and recognize that either dimension can be used as a classification criterion. This explanation places much of the burden on the development of adequate representations of the problem. However, the task also imposes high demands on children's ability to control selective attention: Children must inhibit attention to a perceptual dimension that was previously valid and refocus on a different aspect of the same stimulus display.

Our explanation for the difficulty presented by the problem and for the reason for the bilingual advantage comes from the need to selectively attend to and recode specific display features. Children code the target stimuli according to the first rule system, in this case, the red thing and the blue thing. When the second rule system is explained, those descriptions become obsolete and must be revised, recoding the targets as the square thing and the round thing. Having already represented the targets in one way, however, it is difficult for children now to think of the items as a square thing and a round thing. This reinterpretation of the targets requires inhibition of their original values, and that is difficult because the colors remain perceptually present even though they are now irrelevant.

Two studies provided converging support for this interpretation of the primary source of difficulty in this task. Typically, the experimenter names each card when passing it to the child to be sorted, but children persist in sorting it according to the obsolete dimension. Kirkham, Cruess, and Diamond (2003) revised the procedure by requiring the child to name each card before placing it into the sorting box. The modification produced significantly better performance, presumably by redirecting children's attention to the new relevant feature. Furthermore, instructing children to place the cards in the container face up instead of face down as in the standard version made the task more difficult as it increased children's distraction to the obsolete feature. Similarly, Towse, Redbond, Houston-Price, and Cook (2000) presented a test card to children who had made postswitch errors and asked them to name the card. More than half of these children described the card by naming the preswitch dimension; they continued to see the card as a blue thing even though they had just been taught the shape game. Both these studies indicate that children persist in mentally encoding the cards according to the description relevant in the preswitch phase. Correct performance in the postswitch phase requires that they inhibit those descriptions so they can reinterpret the card in terms of the postswitch feature.

The conclusion from these studies is that the primary difficulty children face in the postswitch phase of the card sort task is in ignoring the continued presence of the cue that indicated the rule for the preswitch sorting and reinterpreting that target stimulus in a new way. If the obsolete feature from that target stimulus is removed, children easily reassign the values and sort correctly on the postswitch phase (Bialystok & Martin, 2004, Study 2). In the standard version, however, the problem is difficult because of its demands on control of attention, and bilingual children consistently solve this problem earlier than comparable monolinguals.

Theory of Mind

The final example of a cognitive achievement that may be differentially developed in monolingual and bilingual children is one that has been intensively investigated in the past several years. Researchers have been interested in the emergence of children's understanding of theory of mind, the knowledge that beliefs, attitudes, and perceptions are constructed by individual minds that have a particular (literal or metaphorical) point of view (e.g., review in Wellman, 1990). The breadth and pervasiveness of this understanding across cognitive domains makes its development central to children's intellectual growth.

Explanations for children's success on theory of mind tasks at the age of about 4 years have varied. One view, called the *theory theory*, considers that theory of mind is a holistic construct that exists independent of other cognitive achievements and emerges with maturation (Astington, 1993; Perner, 1991). Other explanations take a more processing view by considering the memory and executive functioning demands built into these tasks and demonstrate a correlation between success on these executive tasks and theory of mind problems (Carlson & Moses, 2001; Carlson, Moses, & Hix, 1998; Hala & Russell, 2001; Hughes, 1998). In a reversal of that position, Perner, Stummer, and Lang (1998) argued that it is competence with theory of mind that brings children to higher levels of executive functioning, thereby reversing the direction of putative causality.

In the standard paradigms for assessing theory of mind, children are given information about a situation or an object, the information is then modified, and the child is required to predict whether another person, not present when the amendments were described, would know the updated information. In situation-based tasks, a toy is hidden in a location and then moved; in false contents task, a container that is assumed to hold one kind of item actually holds another; in appearance-reality tasks, an object that looks to be one thing turns out to be a different kind of thing. The question asked of the child is whether another child who was not shown the truth about the location, contents, or identity would know what the correct values were. Children who fail the theory of mind task respond by saying that the novice child would have full access to the information that the experimental child had and be able to answer the questions properly.

Although the modularized view of these abilities is compelling and consistent with much evidence, the tasks nonetheless incorporate complex processing demands. If bilingual children were precocious in the development of at least one of these component processes, then it is possible that they would solve theory of mind tasks earlier than monolinguals. The kinds of tasks for which bilingual children have shown an advantage are those that include misleading information, a situation characteristic as well of these theory of mind tasks. The tasks are based on conflict between two states—real and altered, appearance and reality—and the child must understand which possible configuration will provide the correct answer. The difficulty is that the original state of the display, namely, the appearance of the object or the initial hiding place, remains visible during the questioning, potentially misleading the child into the original response. Therefore, children must resist basing their answers on these previously correct and now-obsolete cues.

Senman and I (Bialystok & Senman, 2004) examined this possibility in a study in progress using appearance-reality tasks. Four items that appeared to be one thing but were found on inspection to be something else were shown to monolingual and bilingual children who were 4 years old. The four items were an object that looked like a rock but was actually a sponge, a crayon box that had Legos inside instead of crayons, a plastic whale that was really a pen, and a plastic snowman that opened up and was really a book. Following the standard procedure for these tasks, the experimenter showed the child each item and discussed what it looked like. When children agreed on the appearance of each object, the experimenter revealed the actual identity (or contents) of the item.

The testing phase consisted of three questions. The first two questions are called the appearance questions because they are based on the original expectation of the object from first looking at it: What did you think this was when you first saw it? What will Tigger (a stuffed toy participating in the initial interaction but hidden during the revelation) think it is when we bring him back? The third question is called the reality question because it assesses the actual identity of the item that is not revealed by its outward appearance: What is it really? There was no difference between responses to the two appearance questions, so they were combined into a single score for appearance questions that was compared to performance on the reality question.

Monolingual and bilingual children exhibited different patterns for the two questions. Both groups performed the same on the appearance question, but the bilingual children outperformed the monolinguals on the reality question. The answers to the appearance question are supported by the continued presence of the objects during questioning. The reality question, in contrast, requires children to go beyond the appearance of the display and state the actual identity or function of the object. Because the appearance conflicts with the correct answer to the reality question, the solution requires children to ignore that appearance actively and to state what it is in spite of that misleading perceptual exterior.

On the theory of mind task used in this study, bilingual children outperformed monolinguals on questions that place high demands on the ability to control attention and inhibit misleading perceptual information. Consistently, this is the kind of process that bilingual children master earlier than their monolingual peers.

Bilingualism: What's the Difference?

In the three examples of cognitive performance described, there is no overall advantage that comes to children who are bilingual. They do not display mathematical precocity and are compromised on certain mathematical computations and problems presented in their weaker language, they do not demonstrate superior skill in monitoring and updating classification problems, and they are not consistently more advanced than monolinguals in establishing the basic concepts for theory of mind. However, in all three domains, problems in which conflicting information, especially perceptual information, interferes with the correct solution and requires attention and effort to evaluate and ultimately ignore one of the options are solved better by bilinguals.

This ability to inhibit attention to misleading information constitutes a significant processing advantage, but other aspects of cognitive development are impaired for bilingual children. One prime area of consistent bilingual *disadvantage* is in receptive vocabulary. Bilingual children generally score lower than respective monolinguals in each of their languages. This result has been replicated in almost every study that has compared monolingual and bilingual children in the preschool and sometimes early school years (review in Bialystok, 2001). It is this weak competence in the language of schooling that led Macnamara (1966) to caution that bilingual children were disadvantaged both educationally and cognitively, and it was undoubtedly this compromised verbal proficiency that was responsible for his conclusion that bilingualism impaired children's ability to solve mathematical word problems.

However, as subsequent research showed, bilingual and monolingual children who were equated for language ability solved mathematical problems to exactly the *same* level of competence. In many domains, therefore, bilingual children develop cognitive skills in the same manner and on the same schedule as do monolinguals. Although this may not seem to be newsworthy, early proclamations of the debilitating effect of bilingualism on children's development are safely eradicated by the declaration that the bilingualism might instead have no effect at all on children's development.

What is significant about the bilingual advantage in resolving conflicting information is its persistence across verbal and nonverbal domains of problem solving. This selectivity of attention is an aspect of executive functioning that develops gradually through childhood. Tipper and his colleagues (Tipper, Bourque, Anderson, & Brehaut, 1989; Tipper & McLaren, 1990) argued that attention is comprised of independent and independently developing components. Three of these components are inhibition, selection, and habituation. Two of them, selection and habituation, are as well formed in childhood and function for children essentially the same as they do for adults. In contrast, inhibition develops slowly, changing children's performance as it emerges and imposing a measure of selectivity on their behavior. Other researchers also have documented the development

of inhibition in young children and connected it to important changes in problem solving (Dagenbach & Carr, 1994; Dempster, 1992; Diamond, 2002; Diamond & Taylor, 1996; Harnishfeger & Bjorklund, 1993). Inhibition is the essential factor in distinguishing the performance of the bilingual children, so it may be that bilingualism exerts its effect primarily on the inhibition component of attention.

Inhibition and control of attention are carried out in the frontal lobes (Stuss, 1992). Patients with damage to the frontal lobes experience difficulty in tasks that require switching attention (e.g., Wisconsin Card Sorting Test) and selecting relevant features in the presence of distracting information (e.g., Tower of London) (Burgess & Shallice, 1996; Kimberg, D'Esposito, & Farah, 1997; Luria, 1966; Perrett, 1974). Even automated tasks, like Stroop tests, are difficult for these patients because they have inadequate control over their attention to the irrelevant features of the Stroop stimuli, normally the color word. This performance profile is the reverse of that obtained with bilingual children: What is difficult for frontal patients develops early for bilingual children.

Cognitive control of attention declines in healthy older adults with normal aging. Hasher and Zacks (1988) elaborated a model of attention that includes both the excitatory mechanisms that are triggered by environmental stimuli and the inhibitory mechanisms that are required to suppress the activation of extraneous information. Without adequate inhibition, working memory becomes cluttered with irrelevant information and decreases the efficiency of cognitive processing (Hasher, Zacks, & May, 1999). Dempster (1992) proposed a similar description but described the rise and fall of these inhibitory processes over the entire lifespan rather than just their decline with aging. The consequence of aging in these views is that older adults have less control over the contents of working memory than do younger adults, a situation that is functionally similar to the difference between monolingual and bilingual children solving problems based on selective attention.

Duncan (1996) used selective attention and inhibitory control to integrate research from several areas of cognitive processing. He demonstrated that the effects of frontal lobe lesions, differences in intelligence (defined by g, the measure of general intelligence proposed by Spearman, 1927), and divided attention are evidence of the same processes that distinguish between active or passive control of attention. These processes are situated in the frontal lobes, making the frontal structures the seat of highly generalized forms of intelligence. This analysis supports the association between the processes that are enhanced for bilingual children and the processes that are damaged through frontal lobe injury and decline with normal aging. Moreover, these processes are central to general concepts of intelligence as measured by standardized tests. This line of reasoning that includes intelligence, or g, in the equation potentially carries profound implications for claims about the effect of bilingualism on intelligence, but such conclusions are vastly premature because any relevant or detailed research examining the logical steps in this argument does not exist. But, bilingualism clearly alters specific cognitive processes that are part of the underpinnings to this broader view of intelligence. Why would bilingualism have this effect?

Current research on the organization of two languages in the mind of adult bilinguals shows convincingly that both languages remain active during language processing in either language. This view is in contrast to earlier models that posited a "switch" that activated only the relevant language (Macnamara & Kushnir, 1971). Evidence for shared processing comes from both psycholinguistic and neuroimaging studies. Psycholinguistic models differ on whether the word level of representation for the two languages is separate (Brauer, 1998; Durgunoglu & Roediger, 1987; Van Hell & de Groot, 1998) or common (Chen & Ng, 1989; Francis, 1999a; Grainger, 1993; Guttentag, Haith, Goodman, & Hauch, 1984; Hermans, Bongaerts, de Bot, & Schreuder, 1998) but agree that these lexical representations are connected through a common conceptual system (review in Smith, 1997). Some of the contradiction between the positions on how words are represented is resolved when proficiency levels are included in the analysis (Francis, 1999b; Kroll & De Groot, 1997; Kroll & Stewart, 1994). Higher levels of proficiency in the second language produce lexical-semantic (conceptual) configurations that more closely resemble those constructed in the first language, whereas second languages with low proficiency levels require mediation of the first language. In fact, below some threshold of proficiency, it becomes debatable whether the individuals are bilinguals or second language learners. The research described above examining cognitive consequences of bilingualism considers only bilinguals who are reasonably proficient in both languages, thereby assuming some approach to balanced proficiency. This is the situation, then, for bilinguals in studies that have demonstrated shared representations that are mutually active during language processing in either language.

Neuroimaging studies of language processing in bilinguals provide a unique perspective on this issue by attempting to identify the regions of cortical activation. Studies by Chee, Tan, and Thiel (1999) and Illes et al. (1999) using functional magnetic resonance imaging (fMRI), Klein and colleagues (Klein, Milner, Zatorre, Zhao, & Nikelski, 1999; Klein, Zatorre, Milner, Meyer, & Evans, 1995) using positron emission tomography, and Pouratian et al. (2000) using intraoperative optical imaging of intrinsic signals found no disparity in the activated regions when performing tasks in either the first or second language (although Pouratian et al. did also find some areas unique to each language in a naming task). Conversely, studies by Kim, Relkin, Lee, and Hirsch (1997) and Dehaene et al. (1997) using fMRI found some evidence of separate activation when using each of the languages, at least for some bilinguals on some kinds of tasks. Again, part of the conflict can be attributed to the level of proficiency in the second language (e.g., Perani et al., 1998). As in the behavioral studies, high proficiency in both languages was associated with more complete overlap in the processing regions.

If two languages are mutually active (psycholinguistic evidence) and share common representational regions (neuroimaging evidence), then a mechanism is required to keep them functionally distinct. Without procedures for separating the languages, any use of one language would evoke unwanted intrusions from the other. Green (1998) addressed this question with a model based on inhibitory control, an executive system for activating or inhibiting linguistic representations (lemmas). The model has three components: a hierarchy of language task schemas, lexical representations, and a selection mechanism based on inhibition. A regulatory system, modeled after Shallice's (1988) supervisory attentional system, controls levels of activation by regulating the language task schemas. This makes the model responsive to the demands of each individual situation. The task schemas determine output by controlling the activation levels of the competing responses from the two languages and inhibiting the lemmas that belong to the language incorrect for that situation. The basic notion is that each of a bilingual's two languages can be described on a continuum of activation in a specific context (cf., Grosjean, 1997; Paradis, 1997) and not through a binary switch as earlier models had posited.

The central mechanism of this model is inhibition of competing lexical representations. Green (1998) cited evidence showing that positron emission tomographic studies of translation indicated increased activity in the anterior cingulate, an area activated during Stroop tasks and associated with the inhibition of prepotent responses (Posner & DiGirolamo, 2000), whereas comparable scans of performance while reading (but not translating) did not invoke activity in this area. This pattern was confirmed in a study by Price, Green, and von Studnitz (1999), who showed separate brain activation patterns for switching and translating, with translating again activating the anterior cingulate.

Green's explanation depends on accepting inhibition as the primary mechanism for negotiating the language used in specific contexts, and independent evidence has supported the plausibility of this interpretation. Juncos-Rabadan (1994) and Juncos-Rabadan and Iglesias (1994) showed that language deterioration in the elderly is attributable to declines in attentional abilities, and that bilinguals suffer loss in attentional processing on both their languages. They attributed the changes to problems with inhibition mechanisms and demonstrated these processing changes occurred equally with both languages in bilinguals.

Studies by Hernandez and colleagues, also examining aging and bilingualism, provided further evidence for the role of inhibitory control mechanisms in language processing for bilinguals (Hernandez, Dapretto, Mazziotta, & Bookheimer, 2001; Hernandez & Kohnert, 1999; Hernandez, Martinez, & Kohnert, 2000). They presented older and younger Spanish-English bilinguals with a switching task in which the participant was required to name simple line drawings in one or the other language. A cue preceding each trial indicated the language in which the response was required. The interesting results came from mixed block presentations in which the two languages were combined into a single block, requiring rapid monitoring and switching between languages. These conditions were more difficult for the older bilinguals than the younger ones, as evidenced by a significant increase in the reaction time. More interesting, however, is that an fMRI study of a small number of (young) bilingual individuals performing this task showed that switching between languages was accompanied by activation in the dorsolateral prefrontal cortex, an area involved in task switching and control of attention. Finally, a study by Rodriguez-Fornells, Rotte, Heinze, Nösselt, and Münte (2002) used fMRI to locate the ability of bilinguals to prevent interference from the other language through an inhibition mechanism in regions of the frontal lobes.

If the inhibitory control model of Green is correct, then bilingualism by its very nature results in greater use of inhibitory control because it is invoked every time language is used. Bilingual children therefore experience extensive practice of this executive function in the first few years of life, at least once both languages are known to a sufficient level of proficiency to offer viable processing systems. If this practice in inhibiting linguistic processing carries over to processing in disparate cognitive domains, then bilinguals should be more able than monolinguals to perform tasks that require the inhibition of irrelevant information (see Meuter, chapter 17, and Michael & Gollan, chapter 19, this volume, for related discussion concerning adult bilingual performance).

The prefrontal cortex is the last brain area to mature in development, a possible reason that many of the tasks that require switching attention or ignoring conflicting information are difficult for young children to solve. The bilingual experience of negotiating two language representations, switching attention between them on a constant basis, and selecting subtle features of linguistic input to guide performance in choosing the correct response language may accelerate the development of the responsible cortical areas. Thus, bilingualism may provide the occasion for a more rapid development of an essential cortical center, and the consequence of that development influences a wide range of cognitive activities.

This explanation is based on the assumption that cortical organization is plastic and that it can be altered with experience. Both presumptions are supported in neuroscience research. Studies by Recanzone, Merzenich, Jenkins, Grajski, and Dinse (1992) comparing finger sensitivity in monkeys that did or did not receive a stimulating learning experience and by Ebert, Pantev, Wienbruch, Rockstroh, and Taub (1995) comparing finger sensitivity in violin players and nonmusicians reported cortical reorganization and enhancement in the representation area responsible for those fingers. In both cases, an environmental experience that offered massive practice in an activity resulted in a reorganization of a significant cortical region.

In rehabilitation research, Taub (2001) has been successful in reestablishing motor control in areas paralyzed through stroke. Patients who lose control over some area, for example, an arm, have the spared arm immobilized and are trained to use the paralyzed arm through massive practice, an experience that results in the transfer of motor control for that arm to an undamaged cortical region. Bilingualism may provide another example of this kind of reorganizational process. The environmental experience of using two languages from childhood provides massive practice in the attention and inhibition centers of the prefrontal cortex and promotes their development.

The Bilingual Impact

Speculations about the manner in which bilingualism may influence cognitive functioning are rarely couched in terms of detailed processes like control of attention and inhibition. Instead, the descriptions are pitched at the level of overall intelligence, claiming enhancements (e.g., Peal & Lambert, 1962) or deficits (e.g., Saer, 1923), but broad in their implications. How can the processing descriptions proposed here be reconciled with the claims made by these more global views?

In an early description of intelligence, Cattell (1963) distinguished between fluid and crystallized forms. Fluid intelligence declines with aging and is correlated with a range of frontal tasks (Kray & Lindenberger, 2000; Salthouse, Fristoe, McGuthry, & Hambrick, 1998). In contrast, crystallized intelligence remains relatively stable across the lifespan, if anything increasing with the accretion of knowledge and experience, and does not correlate with those tasks that demand online processing and attention. In Duncan's (1996) model, described in the section Bilingualism: What's the Difference?, he posits a relation between g and performance in a variety of frontal tasks, but it is possible that his equation could be made more precise by considering only fluid intelligence rather than the commonality across all forms of intellectual assessment. If bilingualism has an impact on a general form of intelligence, then based on the performance on specific tasks, it is likely that the impact is confined to fluid intelligence, those aspects of performance most dependent on executive control. There is, of course, no evidence that bilingualism *does* affect intelligence. The claim here is more simply that the specific cognitive processes that do appear to be enhanced by bilingualism would most likely have an impact on only one aspect of general intelligence, namely, fluid intelligence.

The most general aspect of cognition that Peal and Lambert (1962) identified as the locus of bilingual influence was creative thinking and

flexibility of thought, a conclusion shared by others as well (cf. MacNab, 1979). The usual explanation for this advantage is that having two linguistic systems and two names for things endows bilinguals with the capacity to see things from different perspectives, in both aspects, and switch between these designations. For example, creativity tasks, such as requiring the participant to generate unusual uses for common objects, requires individuals to suppress the usual use or appearance of these objects, freeing oneself to entertain alternatives. The nonverbal tests in which Peal and Lambert's (1962) bilinguals excelled all required a degree of manipulation as opposed to more straightforward concept formation or computation. These measures are aspects of fluid intelligence. Moreover, they frequently require the ability to ignore misleading information, such as the usual use of a common object, to attend to a subtler feature and propose a novel function. If indeed bilinguals perform these tasks better than monolinguals, it would be attributable to precisely the same processes that ensured their advantage in the other executive function tasks described throughout. In that sense, creativity may indeed be an indirect beneficiary of bilingualism, at least in the way it is assessed on psychological tests.

Bilingualism changes something fundamental about the way cognitive processes are shaped by young children. How extensive these changes are in either cognitive space or developmental time are questions that are still under investigation. Even if these advantages prove to be more transient or more fragile than some of the more optimistic data suggest they are, their role in discarding old fears that bilingualism confuses children and retards their intellectual growth has been a worthy outcome.

Acknowledgment

The preparation of this chapter and the research reported in it was supported by a grant from the Natural Sciences and Engineering Research Council of Canada.

References

Astington, J. W. (1993). *The child's discovery of the mind*. Cambridge, MA: Harvard University Press.

Bain, B. C. (1974). Bilingualism and cognition: Toward a general theory. In S. T. Carey (Ed.), *Bilingualism, biculturalism, and education: Proceedings from the conference at College*

Universitaire Saint Jean (pp. 119–128). Edmonton, Canada: University of Alberta.

Ben-Zeev, S. (1977). The influence of bilingualism on cognitive strategy and cognitive development. *Child Development, 48*, 1009–1018.

Bialystok, E. (1999). Cognitive complexity and attentional control in the bilingual mind. *Child Development, 70*, 636–644.

Bialystok, E. (2001). *Bilingualism in development: Language, literacy, and cognition.* New York: Cambridge University Press.

Bialystok, E. (2002). Acquisition of literacy in bilingual children: A framework for research. *Language Learning, 52*, 159–199.

Bialystok, E., & Codd, J. (1997). Cardinal limits evidence from language awareness and bilingualism for developing concepts of number. *Cognitive Development, 12*, 85–106.

Bialystok, E., & Martin, M. (2004). Attention and inhibition in bilingual children: Evidence from the dimensional change card sort task. *Developmental Science, 7*, 325–339.

Bialystok, E., & Senman, L. (2004). Executive processes in appearance–reality tasks: The role of inhibition of attention and symbolic representation. *Child Development, 75*, 562–579.

Brauer, M. (1998). Stroop interference in bilinguals: The role of similarity between the two languages. In A. F. Healy & L. E. Bourne, Jr. (Eds.), *Foreign language learning: Psycholinguistic studies on training and retention* (pp. 317–337). Mahwah, NJ: Erlbaum.

Burgess, P. W., & Shallice, T. (1996). Response suppression, initiation and strategy use following frontal lobe lesions. *Neuropsychologia, 34*, 263–272.

Carlson, S. M., & Moses, L. J. (2001). Individual differences in inhibitory control and children's theory of mind. *Child Development, 72*, 1032–1053.

Carlson, S. M., Moses, L. J., & Hix, H. R. (1998). The role of inhibitory control in young children's difficulties with deception and false belief. *Child Development, 69*, 672–691.

Cattell, R. B. (1963). Theory of fluid and crystallized intelligence: A critical experiment. *Journal of Educational Psychology, 54*, 1–22.

Chee, M. W. L., Tan, E. W. L., & Thiel, T. (1999). Mandarin and English single word processing studied with functional magnetic resonance imaging. *Journal of Neuroscience, 19*, 3050–3056.

Chen, H. C., & Ng, N. L. (1989). Semantic facilitation and translation priming effects in Chinese-English bilinguals. *Memory and Cognition, 18*, 279–288.

Dagenbach, D., & Carr, T. (1994). *Inhibitory processes in attention, memory, and language.* New York: Academic Press.

Darcy, N. T. (1963). Bilingualism and the measurement of intelligence: A review of a decade of research. *Journal of Genetic Psychology, 103*, 259–282.

Dehaene, S., Dupoux, E., Mehler, J., Cohen, L., Paulesu, E., Perani, D., et al. (1997). Anatomical variability in the cortical representation of first and second language. *NeuroReport, 8*, 3809–3815.

Dempster, F. N. (1992). The rise and fall of the inhibitory mechanism: Toward a unified theory of cognitive development and aging. *Developmental Review, 12*, 45–75.

Diamond, A. (2002). Normal development of prefrontal cortex from birth to young adulthood: Cognitive functions, anatomy, and biochemistry. In D. T. Stuss & R. T. Knight (Eds.), *Principles of frontal lobe function* (pp. 466–503). London: Oxford University Press.

Diamond, A., & Taylor, C. (1996). Development of an aspect of executive control: Development of the abilities to remember what I said and to "do as I say, not as I do." *Developmental Psychology, 29*, 315–334.

Duncan, J. (1996). Attention, intelligence, and the frontal lobes. In M. Gazzaniga (Ed.), *The cognitive neurosciences* (pp. 721–733). Cambridge, MA: MIT Press.

Duncan, S. E., & De Avila, E. A. (1979). Bilingualism and cognition: Some recent findings. *Journal of the National Association for Bilingual Education, 4*, 15–50.

Durgunoglu, A. Y., & Roediger, H. L. (1987). Test differences in accessing bilingual memory. *Journal of Memory and Language, 26*, 377–391.

Ebert, T., Pantev, C., Wienbruch, C., Rockstroh, B., & Taub, E. (1995). Increased cortical representation of the fingers of the left hand in string players. *Science, 270*, 305–306.

Ellis, N. C. (1992). Linguistic relativity revisited: The bilingual word-length effect in working memory during counting, remembering numbers, and mental calculation. In R. J. Harris (Ed.), *Cognitive processing in bilinguals* (pp. 137–155). Amsterdam: North-Holland.

Francis, W. S. (1999a). Analogical transfer of problem solutions within and between languages in Spanish-English bilinguals. *Journal of Memory and language, 40*, 301–329.

Francis, W. S. (1999b). Cognitive integration of language and memory in bilinguals; semantic representation. *Psychological Bulletin, 125*, 193–222.

Frenck-Mestre, C., & Vaid, J. (1993). Activation of number facts in bilinguals. *Memory and Cognition, 21*, 809–818.

Frye, D., Zelazo, P. D., & Palfai, T. (1995). Theory of mind and rule based reasoning. *Cognitive Development, 10*, 483–527.

Fuson, K. C. (1988). *Children's counting and concepts of number*. New York: Springer-Verlag.

Geary, D. C., Cormier, P., Goggin, J. P., Estrada, P., & Lunn, M. C. E. (1993). Mental arithmetic: A componential analysis of speed-of-processing across monolingual, weak bilingual, and strong bilingual adults. *International Journal of Psychology, 28*, 185–201.

Gelman, R., & Gallistel, C. R. (1978). *The child's understanding of number*. Cambridge, MA: Harvard University Press.

Gould, S. J. (1981). *The mismeasure of man*. New York: Norton.

Grainger, J. (1993). Visual word recognition in bilinguals. In R. Schreuder & B. Weltens (Eds.), *The bilingual lexicon* (pp. 11–25). Amsterdam: Benjamins.

Green, D. W. (1998). Mental control of the bilingual lexico-semantic system. *Bilingualism: Language and Cognition, 1*, 67–81.

Grosjean, F. (1997). Processing mixed languages: Issues, findings, and models. In A. M. B. de Groot & J. F. Kroll (Eds.), *Tutorials in bilingualism: Psycholinguistic perspectives* (pp. 225–254). Mahwah, NJ: Erlbaum.

Guttentag, R. E., Haith, M. M., Goodman, G. S., & Hauch, J. (1984). Semantic processing of unattended words in bilinguals: A test of the input switch mechanism. *Journal of Verbal Learning and Verbal Behavior, 23*, 178–188.

Hakuta, K. (1986). *Mirror of language: The debate on bilingualism*. New York: Basic Books.

Hakuta, K., Ferdman, B. M., & Diaz, R. (1987). Bilingualism and cognitive development: three perspectives. In S. Rosenberg (Ed.), *Advances in applied psycholinguistics: Reading, writing, and language learning* (Vol. 2, pp. 284–319). New York: Cambridge University Press.

Hala, S., & Russell, J. (2001). Executive control with strategic deception: A window on early cognitive development? *Journal of Experimental Child Psychology, 80*, 112–141.

Harnishfeger, K. K., & Bjorklund, D. F. (1993). The ontogeny of inhibition mechanisms: A renewed approach to cognitive development. In R. Pasnak & M. Howe (Eds.), *Emerging themes in cognitive development* (Vol. 1, pp. 28–49). New York: Springer-Verlag.

Hasher, L., & Zacks, R. T. (1988). Working memory, comprehension, and aging: A review and a new view. In G. H. Bower (Ed.), *The psychology of learning and motivation* (Vol. 22, pp. 193–225). San Diego, CA: Academic Press.

Hasher, L., Zacks, R. T., & May, C. P. (1999). Inhibitory control, circadian arousal, and age. In D. Gopher & A. Koriat (Eds.), *Attention and performance, 17: Cognitive regulation of performance: Interaction of theory and application* (pp. 653–675). Cambridge, MA: MIT Press.

Hermans, D., Bongaerts, T., De Bot K., & Schreuder, R. (1998). Producing words in a foreign language: Can speakers prevent interference from their first language? *Bilingualism: Language and Cognition, 1*, 213–229.

Hernandez, A. E., Dapretto, M., Mazziotta, J., & Bookheimer, S. (2001). Language switching and language representation in Spanish-English bilinguals: An fMRI study. *NeuroImage, 14*, 510–520.

Hernandez, A. E., & Kohnert, K. J. (1999). Aging and language switching in bilinguals. *Aging, Neuropsychology, and Cognition, 6*, 69–83.

Hernandez, A. E., Martinez, A., & Kohnert, K. (2000). In search of the language switch: An fMRI study of picture naming in Spanish-English bilinguals. *Brain and Language, 73*, 421–431.

Hughes, C. (1998). Executive function in preschoolers: Links with theory of mind and verbal ability. *British Journal of Developmental Psychology, 16*, 233–253.

Illes, J., Francis, W. S., Desmond, J. E., Gabrieli, J. D. E., Glover, G. H., Poldrack, R., et al. (1999). Convergent cortical representation of semantic processing in bilinguals. *Brain and language, 70*, 347–363.

Jacques, S., Zelazo, P. D., Kirkham, N. Z., & Semcesen, T. K. (1999). Rule selection versus rule execution in preschoolers: An error-detection approach. *Developmental Psychology, 35*, 770–780.

Juncos-Rabadan, O. (1994). The assessment of bilingualism in normal aging with the Bilingual Aphasia Test. *Journal of Neurolinguistics, 8*, 67–73.

Juncos-Rabadan, O., & Iglesias, F. J. (1994). Decline in the elderly's language: Evidence from cross-linguistic data. *Journal of Neurolinguistics, 8*, 183–190.

Kim, K. H. S., Relkin, N., Lee, K., & Hirsch, J. (1997). Distinct cortical areas associated with native and second languages. *Nature, 388*, 171–174.

Kimberg, D. Y., D'Esposito, M., & Farah, M. J. (1997). Effects of bromocriptine on human subjects depend on working memory capacity. *Neuroreport, 8*, 3581–3585.

Kirkham, N., Cruess, L., & Diamond, A. (2003). Helping children apply their knowledge to their behavior on a dimension-switching task. *Developmental Science, 6*, 449–476.

Klein, D., Milner, B., Zatorre, R. J., Zhao, V., & Nikelski, J. (1999). Cerebral organization in bilinguals: A PET study of Chinese-English verb generation. *NeuroReport, 10*, 2841–2846.

Klein, D., Zatorre, R. J., Milner, B., Meyer, E., & Evans, A. C. (1995). The neural substrates of bilingual language processing: evidence from positron emission tomography. In M. Paradis (Ed.), *Aspects of bilingual aphasia* (pp. 23–36). Oxford, U.K.: Pergamon.

Kray, J., & Lindenberger, U. (2000). Adult age differences in task switching. *Psychology and Aging, 15*, 126–147.

Kroll, J. F., & De Groot, A. M. B. (1997). Lexical and conceptual memory in the bilingual: Mapping form to meaning in two languages. In A. M. B. de Groot & J. F. Kroll (Eds.), *Tutorials in bilingualism* (pp. 169–199). Mahwah, NJ: Erlbaum.

Kroll, J. F., & Stewart, E. (1994). Category interference in translation and picture naming: Evidence for asymmetric connections between bilingual memory representations. *Journal of Memory and Language, 33*, 149–174.

Luria, A. R. (1966). *Higher cortical functions in man.* London: Tavistock.

MacNab, G. L. (1979). Cognition and bilingualism: A reanalysis of studies. *Linguistics, 17*, 231–255.

Macnamara, J. (1966). *Bilingualism and primary education.* Edinburgh, U.K.: Edinburgh University Press.

Macnamara, J. (1967). The effect of instruction in a weaker language. *Journal of Social Issues, 23*, 121–135.

Macnamara, J., & Kushnir, S. (1971). Linguistic independence of bilinguals: The input switch. *Journal of Verbal Learning and Verbal Behavior, 10*, 480–487.

Magiste, E. (1980). Arithmetical calculations in monolinguals and bilinguals. *Psychological Research, 42*, 363–373.

Marsh, L. G., & Maki, R. H. (1976). Efficiency of arithmetic operations in bilinguals as a function of language. *Memory and Cognition, 4*, 459–464.

McClain, L., & Huang, J. Y. S. (1982). Speed of simple arithmetic in bilinguals. *Memory and Cognition, 10*, 591–596.

Mestre, J. P. (1988). The role of language comprehension in mathematics and problem solving. In R. R. Cocking & J. P. Mestre (Eds.), *Linguistic and cultural influences on learning mathematics* (pp. 201–220). Hillsdale, NJ: Erlbaum.

Morales, R. V., Shute, V. J., & Pellegrino, J. W. (1985). Developmental differences in understanding and solving simple mathematics word problems. *Cognition and Instruction, 2*, 41–57.

Norman, D. A., & Shallice, T. (1986). Attention in action: Willed and automatic control of behavior. In R. J. Davidson, G. E. Schwartz, & D. Shapiro (Eds.), *Consciousness and self-regulation* (Vol. 4, pp. 1–18). New York: Plenum Press.

Paradis, M. (1997). The cognitive neuropsychology of bilingualism. In A. M. B. de Groot & J. F. Kroll (Eds.), *Tutorials in bilingualism: Psycholinguistic perspectives* (pp. 331–354). Mahwah, NJ: Erlbaum.

Peal, E., & Lambert, W. (1962). The relation of bilingualism to intelligence. *Psychological Monographs, 76*(546), 1–23.

Perani, D., Paulesu, E., Galles, N. S., Dupoux, E., Dehaene, S., Bettinardi, V., et al. (1998). The bilingual brain: Proficiency and age of acquisition of the second language. *Brain, 121*, 1841–1852.

Perner, J. (1991). *Understanding the representational mind.* Cambridge, MA: MIT Press.

Perner, J., Stummer, S., & Lang, B. (1998). Executive functions and theory of mind: Cognitive complexity or functional dependence? In P. D. Zelazo, J. W. Astington, & D. R. Olson (Eds.), *Developing theories of intention: Social understanding and self-control* (pp. 133–152). Mahwah, NJ: Erlbaum.

Perrett, E. (1974). The left frontal lobe of man and the suppression of habitual responses in verbal categorical behavior. *Neuropsychologia, 12*, 323–330.

Pinker, S. (1994). *The language instinct.* New York: Morrow.

Posner, M. I., & DiGirolamo, G. J. (2000). Executive attention: Conflict, target detection, and cognitive control. In R. Parasuraman (Ed.), *The attentive brain* (pp. 401–423). Cambridge, MA: MIT Press.

Pouratian, N., Bookheimer, S. Y., O'Farrell, A. M., Sicotte, N. L., Cannestra, A. F., Becker, D., et al. (2000). Optical imaging of bilingual cortical representations. *Journal of Neurosurgery, 93*, 676–681.

Price, C. J., Green, D. W., & von Studnitz, R. (1999). A functional imaging study of translation and language switching. *Brain, 122*, 2221–2235.

Recanzone, G. H., Merzenich, M. M., Jenkins, W. M., Grajski, K. A., & Dinse, H. R. (1992). Topographic reorganization of the hand representation in cortical area 3b of owl monkeys trained in a frequency-discrimination task. *Journal of Neurophysiology, 67*, 1031–1056.

Reynolds, A. G. (1991). The cognitive consequences of bilingualism. In A. G. Reynolds (Ed.), *Bilingualism, multiculturalism, and second language learning: The McGill conference in honour of Wallace E. Lambert* (pp. 145–182). Hillsdale, NJ: Erlbaum.

Ricciardelli, L. A. (1992). Bilingualism and cognitive development in relation to threshold theory. *Journal of Psycholinguistic Research, 21*, 301–316.

Rodriguez-Fornells, A., Rotte, M., Heinze, H.-J., Nösselt, T. M., & Münte, T. F. (2002). Brain potential and functional MRI evidence for how to handle two languages with one brain. *Nature, 415*, 1026–1029.

Saer, D. J. (1923). The effects of bilingualism on intelligence. *British Journal of Psychology, 14*, 25–38.

Salthouse, T. A., Fristoe, N. M., McGuthry, K. E., & Hambrick, D. Z. (1998). Relation of task switching to speed, age, and fluid intelligence. *Psychology and Aging, 13*, 445–461.

Secada, W. G. (1991). Degree of bilingualism and arithmetic problem solving in Hispanic first graders. *The Elementary School Journal, 92*, 213-231.

Shallice, T. (1988). *From neuropsychology to mental structure*. Cambridge, U.K.: Cambridge University Press.

Smith, M. C. (1997). How do bilinguals access lexical information? In A. M. B. de Groot & J. F. Kroll (Eds.), *Tutorials in bilingualism* (pp. 145–168). Mahwah, NJ: Erlbaum.

Spearman, C. (1927). *The abilities of man*. New York: Macmillan.

Spelke, E. S., & Tsivkin, S. (2001). Language and number: A bilingual training study. *Cognition, 78*, 45–88.

Stuss, D. T. (1992). Biological and psychological development of executive functions. *Brain and Cognition, 20*, 8–23.

Taub, E. (2001, April). *Adult brain plasticity: Unlearning paralysis*. Paper presented at the symposium Beyond the Myth: Experience Expectant and Experience Dependent Brain Plasticity at the biennial meeting of the Society for Research in Child Development, Minneapolis, MN.

Tipper, S. P., Bourque, T. A., Anderson, S. H., & Brehaut, J. C. (1989). Mechanisms of attention: A developmental study. *Journal of Experimental Child Psychology, 48*, 353–378.

Tipper, S. P., & McLaren, J. (1990). Evidence for efficient visual selectivity in children. In J. T. Enns (Ed.), *The development of attention: Research and theory* (pp. 197–210). New York: North-Holland.

Torrance, E. P., Wu, J. J., Gowan, J. C., & Aliotti, N. C. (1970). Creative functioning of monolingual and bilingual children in Singapore. *Journal of Educational Psychology, 61*, 72–75.

Towse, J. N., Redbond, J., Houston-Price, C. M. T., & Cook, S. (2000). Understanding the dimensional change card sort: Perspectives from task success and failure. *Cognitive Development, 15*, 347–365.

Van Hell, J. G., & De Groot, A. M. B. (1998). Conceptual representation in bilingual memory: Effects of concreteness and cognate status in word association. *Bilingualism: Language and Cognition, 1*, 193–211.

Wellman, H. M. (1990). *Child's theory of mind*. Cambridge, MA: MIT Press.

Wynn, K. (1992). Children's acquisition of the number words and the counting system. *Cognitive Psychology, 24*, 220–251.

Zelazo, P. D., & Frye, D. (1997). Cognitive complexity and control: A theory of the development of deliberate reasoning and intentional action. In M. Stamenov (Ed.), *Language structure, discourse, and the access to consciousness* (pp. 113–153). Amsterdam: Benjamins.

Zelazo, P. D., Frye, D., & Rapus, T. (1996). An age-related dissociation between knowing rules and using them. *Cognitive Development, 11*, 37–63.

Aneta Pavlenko

21

Bilingualism and Thought

ABSTRACT   This chapter discusses the implications of recent theoretical and empirical investigations in linguistic relativity for the study of bilingualism. It starts with a discussion of new developments in the study of the Sapir-Whorf hypothesis and then offers a framework for the study of bilingualism and thought from a neo-Whorfian perspective. Subsequently, it outlines nine areas in which current empirical inquiry either illuminates thought processes of adult bi- and multilingual individuals or offers productive directions for future studies of bilingualism and thought. The chapter ends with a discussion of ways in which research with bilingual individuals can offer unique contributions to the study of linguistic relativity and to the understanding of the interaction between language and thought.

Traditionally, research on bilingualism and cognition has focused on the implications of bilingualism for individual cognitive processes (cf. Bialystok, chapter 20, this volume). The goal of this type of inquiry is to show the impact of bilingualism per se rather than to examine how particular languages—and combinations of languages—may influence the thought processes of their speakers. Studies of the bilingual mental lexicon have commonly focused on lexical processing, rarely touching on linguistic and cultural specificity of conceptual representation. As a result, research in bilingualism has accumulated an impressive amount of knowledge on lexical and cognitive processing in bilingual individuals but tells us little about the impact of cross-linguistic and cross-cultural differences on thought processes (Pavlenko, 1999). In turn, cross-linguistic studies of conceptual representation have established numerous differences in conceptualization of space, time, or motion across speakers of different languages but do not clarify how divergent concepts may be represented in bi- or multilingual speakers.

The goal of the present chapter is twofold. On the one hand, it aims to illuminate thought processes of bilingual individuals whose languages encode particular concepts in different ways. On the other, it aims to write bilingualism into the inquiry on linguistic relativity and to argue that an in-depth understanding of the relationship between language and thought is impossible without close attention to ways in which multiple languages and forms of thought interact in the minds of bi- and multilingual individuals.

I start with a brief discussion of new approaches to the study of linguistic relativity, paying particular attention to recent reformulations of the terms *language* and *thought*. Then, I critically survey existing proposals on the implications of the Sapir-Whorf hypothesis for users of more than one language and offer a framework for future studies of bilingualism and thought. Subsequently, I outline nine areas in which current empirical investigations either illuminate thought processes of adult bi- and multilinguals or offer productive directions for future inquiry. I end by pointing to ways in which research with bilingual individuals can offer unique contributions to the study of linguistic relativity and, more generally, to the understanding of the interaction between language and thought. Throughout the discussion, I use the terms *bilingualism* and *multilingualism* interchangeably to refer to the use of two or more languages by individual speakers and groups of speakers, as is common in the literature in the field.

Contemporary Approaches to Linguistic Relativity

Since 1992, there has been a new surge of interest in the theory of linguistic relativity, otherwise known as the Sapir-Whorf hypothesis. For Whorf (1956),

> The "linguistic relativity principle"...means, in informal terms, that users of markedly different grammars are pointed by their grammars toward different types of observations and different evaluations of externally similar acts of observation, and hence are not equivalent as observers but must arrive at somewhat different views of the world. (p. 221)

The debates on linguistic relativity and on the writings of Benjamin Lee Whorf (1956) and his teacher and mentor Edward Sapir (1921, 1929) have waxed and waned throughout the 20th century. The 1960s and the 1970s, dominated by Chomskian generative linguistics, witnessed a profound disillusionment with the theory. Only a few staunch supporters, most notably Dell Hymes, weathered the storm; "most 'responsible' scholars have steered clear of relativism. It has become a bête noire, identified with scholarly irresponsibility, fuzzy thinking, lack of rigor, and even immorality" (Lakoff, 1987, p. 304). The current impetus for investigations in linguistic relativity came from the groundbreaking work of George Lakoff (1987), John Lucy (1992a, 1992b, 1997a), Dan Slobin (1996, 2000, 2001), and Stephen Levinson and associates (Bowerman & Levinson, 2001; Gumperz & Levinson, 1996; Levinson, 1996, 1997, 2003). Although I refer to these scholars as neo-Whorfians, this label does not imply that these scholars share a common view of linguistic relativity or the relationship between language and thought. Rather, they share a common interest in the ramifications of the Sapir-Whorf hypothesis and a desire to abandon the traditional debate about the merits of linguistic determinism versus linguistic relativity, a dichotomy that oversimplifies and misinterprets Sapir and Whorf's original arguments. Instead, neo-Whorfians forge new, complex, and nuanced approaches to the study of ways in which different aspects of language may influence distinct modes of thought. They also acknowledge that some cognitive processes and modes of thought may not be affected by language at all. As a result of these changes, recent years saw both new, sophisticated theoretical proposals and empirical advances in the study of the relationship between language and thought (Bowerman & Levinson, 2001; Gentner & Goldin-Meadow, 2003; Gumperz & Levinson, 1996; Lakoff, 1987; Levinson, 2003; Lucy, 1992a, 1992b, 1997a; Niemeier & Dirven, 2000; Nuyts & Pederson, 1997; Pütz & Verspoor, 2000).

How are language and thought conceptualized in this inquiry? Although traditional approaches to the study of linguistic relativity focus on structural differences between languages, some contemporary scholars argue that language cannot be neatly reduced to structure, and that structure should be considered as an intrinsic and constitutive, but not necessarily privileged, part of socially significant communicative practices (Duranti, 1994, 1997; Edwards, 1997; Hill & Mannheim, 1992; Rumsey, 1990; Sherzer, 1987). Consequently, rather than limiting themselves to the study of ways in which grammars of different languages may influence the thought of their speakers, these scholars transcend the boundaries of the traditional understanding of the Sapir-Whorf hypothesis and envision multiple ways in which language can influence thought on a variety of levels.

Lucy (1996) identifies three levels of interaction between language and thought: (a) the *semiotic* level, on which we can see the general impact of the use of any natural language; (b) the *structural* level, on which we can see the influence of lexical and morphosyntactic categories (this is the level traditionally connected to the Sapir-Whorf hypothesis); and (c) the *functional* level, which entails the influence of particular ways of speaking. To reflect current interest in discourses, Lucy (1996, 2000) proposes to refer to the functional level as *discursive relativity*, with discourses as social practices, rather than language structures alone, playing the key part in constituting speakers' worlds.

The present discussion pays attention to both structural and functional, or discursive, levels of interaction between language and thought. The term *discourse* refers to a way of organizing knowledge through linguistic resources and practices or, in other words, to a concatenation of terms and metaphors drawn on systematically to characterize and evaluate actions and events from a particular perspective (Potter & Wetherell, 1987, p. 138). Unlike the traditional view of linguistic relativity, the functional approach is sensitive to alternative discursive constructions of reality that may be found within speech communities, influenced by age, gender, ethnicity, or socioeducational background of the speakers. In this view, two different languages are no longer alternative ways of describing the "same reality": They not only differ from each other, but also consist of multiple discourses associated with various contexts.

This approach was found to be productive in the study of language and space, previously explored exclusively through the lenses of structural relativity. Pederson (1995) found that rural and urban speakers of Tamil in South India differed systematically in their verbal and nonverbal performance on three problem-solving spatial tasks (a memory task, a route completion task, and inferencing) because of differences in habitual linguistic encoding of spatial information: Absolute references were more typical of Tamils from rural settings, and relative references were more typical for those from urban settings. His study suggests that even in areas such as spatial terminology, usually seen as uniform within a particular language, differences in discursive practices may result in differences in verbal and nonverbal performance.

Undoubtedly, different neo-Whorfian scholars espouse distinct views of language and of the relationship between language and thought. What is important for the present chapter is the shared acknowledgment that speakers' construction of the world may be influenced by the structural patterns of their languages, as well as by their discourses, and that it may be changed through participation in alternative discourses, such as schooling, or through additional language learning. This perspective builds on Whorf's (1956) original assumption that second language (L2) learning—just like socialization into new discourses—may result in assimilation of new perspectives and conceptual restructuring.

The goal of neo-Whorfian inquiry is to examine the influence of language, conceived of either as structures or as discourses, on thought. Thought is typically defined in two ways: Some scholars focus on the contents of thought, that is, speakers' conceptualizations of the world; others examine the processes of thinking, such as attending, remembering, or reasoning (Lucy, 1992b). More often than not, the two foci are combined, and the scholarly inquiry examines ways in which differences in linguistic encodings correspond to different conceptualizations and lead to differences in cognitive processes. Consequently, in what follows I see *concepts* as mental representations that affect individuals' immediate perception, attention, and recall and allow members of specific language and culture groups to conduct identification, comprehension, inferencing, and categorization along similar lines (Pavlenko, 1999).

This approach to conceptual representation recognizes that concepts are based on linguistic and perceptual bases and distinguishes between language-based (or language-related) concepts and concepts not immediately linked to language, for which language users may have a mental representation but no specific linguistic means of encoding. The latter possibility was also recognized by Whorf (1956), who emphasized his interest in "linguistic thinking" or "thought insofar as it is linguistic" (pp. 67–68).

Language-based concepts in turn are subdivided into lexicalized and grammaticized concepts. *Lexicalized* concepts entail lexical encodings of natural objects, artifacts, substances, events, or actions, and *grammaticized* concepts entail morphosyntactically encoded notions, such as number, gender, tense, or aspect (Slobin, 2001). Bruner (1996), Chafe (2000), Hill and Mannheim (1992), and Lucy (1992a, 1992b, 1996, 1997a) also argue for an expansion of the scope of the study of mental representations from lexicalized and grammaticized concepts to narrative structures, discourses, and discursive indexing of identities.

In addition to defining what one understands as language and thought, it is crucial to define what is considered as evidence of influence of language on thought. In the present chapter, I adopt Lucy's (1992a, 1996, 1997a, 2000) view that, to avoid showing the influence of "language on language," one needs to consider (whenever possible) evidence from both verbal and nonverbal behaviors. *Nonverbal* behaviors refer to those elicited through classification, categorization, sorting, matching, memory, and role-playing tasks; *verbal* behaviors include elicitation, inferencing, and picture description, as well as interviews, storytelling, and other conversational activities (of particular importance here is the speakers' selection of aspects of reality for subsequent description and memorization). In this view, the influence of language on thought will be seen as the case where "the particular language interpretation guides or supports cognitive activity and hence the beliefs and behaviors dependent on it" (Lucy, 1997b, p. 295). Some scholars also argue that early psychological studies of linguistic relativity oversimplified the Sapir-Whorf hypothesis "to make it fit experimental paradigms" (Lee, 1997, p. 454) and, as a result, "effectively side-stepped looking at what people mean by what they say, and what they do, interactionally, with words" (Edwards, 1997, p. 22). Consequently, underscoring Whorf's original interest in "habitual thought," neo-Whorfians aim to combine experimental research with the study of thought in context, that is, in daily activities and practices, at the intersection of linguistics, psychology, and anthropology (Edwards, 1997; Hunt & Agnoli, 1991; Lucy, 1992b, 1996, 1997a).

In sum, neo-Whorfians acknowledge that different language levels may affect distinct cognitive processes and activities to varying degrees or not at all. Contemporary investigations of linguistic relativity, conducted both in experimental and naturalistic contexts, aim at uncovering ways in which cross-linguistic differences in lexical and morpho-syntactic categories, as well as in discourses, correspond to different conceptual representations of objects, actions, events, time, or space and lead to differences in thought processes.

Bilingualism and Linguistic Relativity

Over the years, bilingualism rarely entered into debates about language and thought: Current collections of work on linguistic relativity are devoted exclusively to explorations in monolingual contexts (for an exception, see a chapter by Gomez-Imbert in Gumperz & Levinson, 1996). This monolingual bias does not, however, come from Whorf (1956), one of the first to champion the importance of "multilingual awareness" and to argue that "to restrict thinking to the patterns merely of English, and especially to those patterns which represent the acme of plainness in English, is to lose a power of thought which, once lost, can never be regained" (p. 244).

Whorf's writings clearly show his belief that additional language learning has the power of transforming or enhancing the speaker's world-view. It is, therefore, ironic, that later on his work was misinterpreted as an argument for linguistic determinism, a view according to which the language one speaks determines one's view of the world once and forever. Clearly, Whorf, an avid language learner committed to comparative linguistics, did not and could not entertain such a possibility; rather, he argued for the benefits of linguistic pluralism (Fishman, 1980). His early supporters expressed a similar interest in implications of linguistic relativity for L2 learning and use (J. Carroll, 1963) as well as an awareness that bilingualism of their research participants may have an impact on their findings (J. Carroll, 1963; J. Carroll & Casagrande, 1958). At times, they even expressed a belief that "whoever learns a new

language becomes a new person" (Rossi-Landi, 1973, p. 33).

Eventually, however, the phenomena of bilingualism and translation were co-opted to refute linguistic relativity in a way succinctly summarized by Stubbs (1997): "But languages are not incompatible. We can translate between them. And bilinguals speak different languages, but they do not perceive the world differently when they switch from one language to another" (p. 359). In the field of bilingualism, this thesis was espoused by Macnamara (1970, 1991), who repeatedly argued that if the Whorfian hypothesis were true, bilinguals would be doomed, having to conform to one of the three patterns: (a) "think" in Language A when speaking either A or B, that is, employ the semantic framework appropriate to Language A; as a result, the speakers' attempts to understand Language B or to make themselves understood "would be quite futile" (Macnamara, 1991, p. 48); (b) "think" in a "hybrid" manner, appropriate to neither language, that is, employ a hybrid semantic system and risk "understanding no one and being understood by no one" (Macnamara, 1991, p. 48); (c) have two semantic systems, appropriate to their two languages. The third possibility, according to Macnamara (1970), means that bilinguals will think differently depending on which language is used and consequently will have difficulties (a) "communicating" with themselves and (b) translating into one language what was said in another. In a later paper, Macnamara (1991) took a less radical view and suggested that in the third case bilinguals would be able to translate and to communicate with speakers of either language. Yet, he claimed that these implications ran afoul of the guiding principles of natural language semantics—whatever can be expressed in one language, can be translated into another—and quipped that if linguistic relativity on the scale proposed by Whorf were true, then Whorf's own learning of Hopi and Navaho would be "extremely mysterious" (Macnamara, 1991, p. 49), if not impossible.

Not surprisingly, other scholars in bilingualism, many of them bi- and multilingual themselves, tried to counter Macnamara's (1970, 1991) and other similar arguments. Paradis (1979), in his reply to Macnamara (1970), argued that the first two options and difficulties with translation are indeed the case, and that none of the three cases described could be used to refute the Whorfian hypothesis *ad absurdo*. In fact, Macnamara's first option closely describes the phenomenon of first language (L1) transfer, well established in the field of second language acquisition (SLA) and indeed known to impede intercultural communication. His second option is reminiscent of a language contact situation in which speakers of a contact variety may develop new linguistic repertoires and new conceptualizations distinct from those employed by members of their L1 and L2 communities. And the third option well describes bicultural bilinguals who adjust their linguistic and conceptual repertoires depending on the interlocutor.

Interestingly, some bicultural bilinguals do indeed experience difficulties in translating from one language to another (cf. Todorov, 1994). These difficulties are often commented on by bilingual writers who view translation as an approximation at best (for an in-depth discussion of the work of bilingual writers, see Beaujour, 1989; Kellman, 2000; Pavlenko, 1998). Some of these individuals, particularly those who had learned a second language later in life, see themselves as living in two different and often incompatible worlds; others view L2 socialization as a means of an intense personal transformation (Beaujour, 1989; E. Hoffman, 1989; Kellman, 2000; Pavlenko, 1998; Wierzbicka, 1985). What emerges from these testimonies is a far more nuanced picture of linguistic effects than could ever be imagined within a monolingual perspective. This picture deserves further examination, if only because it directly contradicts facile statements about bilinguals not seeing the world differently through the lenses of their two languages. Consider, for instance, a statement by the well-known linguist Anna Wierzbicka (1985):

> It is not impossible (though very difficult) to leave the experiential world of one's native language for that of another language, or stretching the metaphor to the limit, to inhabit two different worlds at once. But when one switches from one language to another it is not just the form that changes but also the content. (p. 187)

In fact, it is quite possible that bilinguals are the only ones to experience directly the effects of linguistic relativity, and to fully understand these effects, we need to pay more attention to linguistic transitions. Yet, many researchers continue to see bilingualism as a challenge for the Sapir-Whorf hypothesis and bilinguals as undesirable and "messy" subjects who should be excluded from experimental research to eliminate intervening variables. Clearly, initial empirical studies, such as Lucy's (1992a), had to be carried out with monolingual

speakers to establish baseline cross-linguistic differences. What is unfortunate is that once such differences have been established for particular languages or concepts, further research was rarely if ever conducted with bilingual speakers.

Several reasons explain this lack of attention to bilingualism. To begin, many linguists and psychologists, particularly in North America, are still reluctant to acknowledge that more than half of the world's population is bi- and multilingual (Romaine, 1995); thus, if we are to grapple with the Sapir-Whorf hypothesis or any other cognitive theory, we have to understand how it plays out with multilingual speakers. The research with bilingual subjects is further compromised by the lack of understanding of bilingualism in mainstream psychology. Some researchers treat bilingualism as a monolithic phenomenon and thus do not pay much attention to linguistic trajectories of their study participants; others consider it possible to use bilingual subjects as if they were monolingual, either completely discounting their bilingualism (Berlin & Kay, 1969, p. 12) or assuming that because the subjects had learned the L2 postpuberty, it would not affect their L1 (cf. Munnich, Landau, & Dosher, 2001).

These researchers are clearly unaware of two facts. First, the critical period is no longer a given in the field of SLA (Birdsong, 1999; Ioup, Boustagui, El Tigi, & Mosel, 1994), and even if it were, it had been posited (and explored) regarding phonological and syntactic but not conceptual competence. Furthermore, research has demonstrated that regardless of the age of acquisition, L2 learners' L1 competence in a variety of domains, including conceptual representation, is subject to L2 influence (Cook, 2003; Pavlenko, 2000).

Several scholars have pointed to the pervasive monolingual bias of explorations in cognitive psychology and linguistics. Hunt and Agnoli (1991) expressed concern over ways in which the scholarly community had ignored experiences of bilingual individuals, who may perceive their two worlds as untranslatable and incommensurable. Green (1998) cautioned against approaching all bilinguals in the same way because they may have different levels of expertise and different competences in their two languages. Ochs (1993) and Lee (1997) advocated a view of L2 socialization as enculturation into new ways of thinking and speaking.

Building on these proposals, I suggest that research on linguistic relativity can and should incorporate bilingualism as a test case rather than as an argument against the Whorfian hypothesis. The context-sensitive view advocated here sees bilinguals as members of multiple discursive communities with linguistic repertoires that are not necessarily identical to those of monolingual speakers. Consequently, individual bilingualism is seen (a) as a conglomerate of linguistic and social trajectories, whereby differences in age and history of language acquisition, as well as in language proficiency, may lead to distinct effects of language on thought; (b) as a dynamic process whereby L2 socialization is viewed as a productive site of possible cognitive transformations and enrichment, in accordance with Whorf's (1956) original arguments. This perspective allows me to offer a framework (see also Pavlenko, 1999, 2000, 2002a) that incorporates seven possible relationships between language and thought in individual bi- and multilinguals:

1. *Coexistence of L1 and L2 conceptual domains* is directly implied by the Sapir-Whorf hypothesis and suggests that bicultural bilinguals using different languages may draw on distinct conceptual representations and index distinct discursive identities.
2. *L1-based conceptual transfer* refers to the L1-based conceptual system guiding L2 language learning and use, at least in the beginning and intermediate stages of L2 acquisition.
3. *Internalization of new concepts* entails adoption of L2 words—and underlying concepts—into the L1 of immigrant bilinguals and learners in language contact situations who perceive the need to emphasize distinctions nonexistent in the L1 or to refer to new objects and notions specific to the L2 community.
4. *Shift from L1 to L2 conceptual domain* refers to a shift of category prototypes or boundaries in the process of L2 socialization.
5. *Convergence of L1 and L2 conceptual domains* entails creation of a unitary concept, domain, or system distinct from both the L1 and L2 based, which may occur in simultaneous bilingualism or arise as a result of language contact.
6. *Restructuring of a conceptual domain* refers to a case where a shift is not complete but certain elements may be deleted from or incorporated in a concept or a conceptual domain.
7. *Attrition of previously learned concepts* involves a loss of previously learned concepts, classification schemas, categorical distinctions, or narrative conventions, evidenced in deviation from L1-based categorization patterns.

I will now review the evidence for these and other possible effects from the studies of linguistic relativity. Despite the fact that neo-Whorfian theorizing made requirements for convincing evidence more rigorous and the terms of debate more complex, several studies forged exciting new directions in the study of language and thought. I discuss this research in terms of cross-linguistic differences in nine basic concepts, which allow us to talk about our surroundings and experiences: color, objects and substances, number, space, motion, time, emotions, and personhood. I also discuss the findings in the inquiry on discursive relativity and autobiographical memory, paying particular attention to work that either illuminates bilinguals' thought processes or offers new directions for research in bilingualism.

Color

The domain of color reference has been at the center of debates on linguistic relativity for more than 50 years. This interest stems from the fact that different languages treat the notion of "color" differently by encoding varying numbers of colors in different ways (e.g., nominally, verbally, adjectivally) and making different semantic distinctions between hues. For instance, classic Greek did not distinguish between the colors English speakers call *blue* and *black*; contemporary Russian and Italian offer, respectively, two and four terms corresponding to the English *blue* (Hunt & Agnoli, 1991). Some languages, such as Fon (Benin) or Ngbaka-ma'bo (Central Africa), do not even conceptualize color as a dimension independent of other parameters of colored objects (Dubois, 1997; Lucy, 1997b).

Initial color studies offered some evidence that color codability (i.e., availability of a verbal label) makes colors more distinct and therefore more memorable (cf. Brown & Lenneberg, 1954; J. Carroll & Casagrande, 1958). In contrast, later studies argued that color perception is subject to universal, physiologically based constraints, and that it is perceptual salience, not language, that may cause differences in memory (Berlin & Kay, 1969; Heider, 1972). The split between proponents and opponents of universal constraints on color cognition is still characteristic of the field (cf. Hardin & Maffi, 1997). At the same time, the field has come closer to acknowledging both biological and cultural/linguistic influences on color cognition.

The proponents of relativity acknowledge the physiological basis of color vision but argue that earlier studies were compromised because of the lack of attention to linguistic status of color terms and because of their reliance on focal colors, on the basic color terms of American English, on the Western concept of color, on bilingual informants (in Berlin & Kay, 1969), and on methodologies at odds with the researchers' own objectives (Dubois, 1997; Hardin & Banaji, 1993; Hunt & Agnoli, 1991; Lucy, 1992b, 1997b; Saunders & van Brakel, 1997a, 1997b). In turn, the supporters of universal constraints on color cognition agree that such influences may be moderated by language (cf. Davies & Corbett, 1997; Davies, Sowden, Jerrett, Jerrett, & Corbett, 1998). Studies show that, in some contexts, perception of and memory for colors may be influenced by their codability in the speaker's language, as seen on sorting, categorization, and memory tasks (Davidoff, Davies, & Roberson, 1999; Davies & Corbett, 1997; Davies et al., 1998; Kay & Kempton, 1984; Lucy, 1997b). For instance, speakers of Setswana (a Bantu language spoken in Botswana), a language that has a single term *botala* for *blue* and *green*, were more likely than speakers of English and Russian to group the two colors together (Davies & Corbett, 1997).

To date, only a few studies have addressed bilinguals' color concepts. Ervin-Tripp (1961/1973) demonstrated that Navaho-English bilinguals' color categories differ from those of monolingual speakers of English and Navaho and form one underlying system. In turn, bilingual speakers of Kwakwa'la (spoken on Vancouver Island) and English differentiate between *yellow* and *green* when speaking English but in Kwakwa'la stick to the composite term *lhenxa* (yellow-with-green) (Saunders & van Brakel, 1997a). Saunders and van Brakel (1997b) note that several informants in Kay and Berlin's subsequent research (Kay, Berlin, Maffi, & Merrifield, 1997; Kay, Berlin, & Merrifield, 1991) appeal to L2 loans from English and Spanish when discussing colors.

The L2 influence was also found in a study by Caskey-Sirmons and Hickerson (1977) that examined color boundaries of native speakers of Korean, Japanese, Hindi, Cantonese, and Mandarin who had learned English as adults. The researchers found that the boundaries for nonoverlapping color terms had shifted in the process of L2 socialization and were no longer comparable to the areas mapped by monolingual speakers of these languages. For instance, in Hindi there is no word for *gray*. Not surprisingly, in the achromatic series monolingual Hindi speakers did not map the gray area. In contrast, three of five Hindi-English bilinguals did map such an area, showing sensitivity to the new distinction acquired in English.

In sum, it appears that, in the case of divergent color systems, bilinguals' conceptual representations and consequently patterns of verbal and nonverbal categorization may differ from those of monolingual speakers. These representations may be unified or language dependent and may incorporate new concepts and distinctions internalized in the process of L2 socialization.

Objects and Substances

The second prominent area of research involves linguistic and conceptual differences in representation of objects and substances. This line of inquiry derives from cross-linguistic differences in number marking. The majority of European languages are known as noun class languages and mark most nouns for number. These languages encode a count/mass distinction morphosyntactically; that is, they include the notion of "unit" or "form" as a part of a basic meaning of a noun, directing attention to number. Other languages, such as Yucatec, Japanese, or Mandarin, are known as classifier languages and lack a morphosyntactic count/mass distinction. In these languages, nouns commonly refer to substances, rather than objects, and must be accompanied by a numeral classifier that provides information about material properties of the referent (Foley, 1997; Lucy, 1992a). Because classifier languages provide no syntactic support for the object/substance distinction, they offer a natural arena in which to investigate cognitive behaviors of both children and adults.

Studies have established that children learning English show preference for shape-based classification of various objects as early as 2 years of age; similar preferences are shown by English-speaking adults. In contrast, Yucatec- and Japanese-speaking children and adults show preference for material-based classification on verbal and nonverbal tasks, with Yucatec adults exhibiting it also in their everyday activities (Gentner & Boroditsky, 2001; Imai, 2000; Imai & Gentner, 1997; Lucy, 1992a; Lucy & Gaskins, 2001). Zhang and Schmitt (1998) also investigated effects that particular types of classifiers have on conceptualization and categorization of objects. Speakers of Mandarin in their studies perceived objects that share a classifier as more similar to each other than did speakers of English; in recall tasks, they were more likely than speakers of English to recall classifier-sharing objects in clusters.

To date, I know of no studies that address shape- versus material-based object categorization preferences of bilingual subjects to see whether, for instance, the learning of English modifies categorization preferences of Japanese speakers or vice versa. Other interesting questions in this area arise regarding childhood bilinguals: When does language start influencing categorization preferences in different domains? How do children reconcile incompatible patterns? Lucy and Gaskins (2001) suggest that in the area of object categorization such influence occurs in later childhood; work on motion patterns and spatial cognition shows that in these areas the influence starts early on (Bowerman & Choi, 2001; Gentner & Boroditsky, 2001; Gopnik, 2001).

In addition to number marking, languages may differ in ways they encode even such everyday objects as shoes and boots or cups and glasses. For instance, both English and Russian have translation equivalents of *cups/chashki* and *glasses/stakany*, but objects that English-speakers consider to be paper cups are seen as *stakanchiki* (small glasses) in Russian, a language in which "glassness" is defined through shape and the absence of handles rather than through material. As a result, speakers of languages that encode objects differently perform differently on sorting and categorization tasks (Kronenfeld, 1996; Malt, Sloman, & Gennari, 2003; Malt, Sloman, Gennari, Shi, & Wang, 1999).

A few studies also throw light on the bilinguals' performance. Graham and Belnap (1986) showed that intermediate and advanced Spanish learners of English who had resided in the United States less than a year exhibited L1-based categorization patterns in cases where boundary differences in English did not correspond to those in Spanish (e.g., in the case of *chair*, *stool*, and *bench* vs. *silla* and *banco*). Malt and Sloman (2003) asked three groups of L2 users of English to name common household objects in English. The stimuli consisted of 60 pictures of storage containers (bottles, jars, etc.) and 60 pictures of housewares (dishes, plates, bowls, etc.). The researchers reported that even the most advanced speakers in their study, ones who had been in the United States for 8 or more years and had 10 or more years of formal English instruction, exhibited some discrepancies from mono-

lingual naming patterns, especially when it came to the housewares.

Together, these findings point to a pervasive influence of L1-based categorization patterns and to difficulties in acquiring full conceptual representations in the L2. Future studies of object categorization will need to pay closer attention to similarities and differences in L1 and L2 categorization patterns and consider the possibility of L2 influence on L1, as well as the interaction between three or more languages with distinct patterns.

Number and Numeric Systems

The third line of inquiry also draws on differences in number marking, as well as on those in number encoding. As discussed, languages differ significantly in grammatical number marking: Classifier languages, such as Indonesian or Japanese, lack the category altogether; noun class languages, such as English, allow their speakers to differentiate one *basket* from two or more *baskets*; and some languages, like Yimas, differentiate among one *impram* (basket), two *impraml* (baskets), and more than two *impramat* (baskets) (Foley, 1997). Lucy's (1992a) work showed that, because objects are marked for number in English but not in Yucatec, speakers of the two languages differ systematically in memory for objects.

Languages also differ in number encoding, using a variety of systems. Most languages have a base number and number names that are often a contraction of smaller units. English, for instance, is a base 10 language in which 21 could be expressed as "two tens and one." Although base 10 system has now taken over most languages, numerical encoding remains highly variable, with base 2 used in some aboriginal languages in Australia and base 20 in Eskimo and Yoruba (Dehaene, 1997). The most transparent reflection of the decimal structure is found in the grammar of Asian languages with roots in ancient Chinese (Chinese, Japanese, and Korean among them), in which number names are fully congruent with the base 10 numeration system. When speakers of these languages learn numeracy, all they have to learn are the digits from 0 to 9 and the notion of place value; then they can generate numbers without any further memorization (e.g., 17 is represented as *seventeen* in English but as *ten-seven* in Korean or Japanese). In contrast, children learning English or French have to learn by rote not only the numerals from 0 to 10, but also those from 11 to 19, and the tens numbers from 20 to 90. What are the cognitive consequences of these linguistic differences?

In a series of studies, Miura and associates (Miura, 1987; Miura, Kim, Chang, & Okamoto, 1988; Miura & Okamoto, 1989) compared cognitive representation of number of American, Chinese, Japanese, and Korean first graders by asking the children to construct various numbers with two types of rods, short ones that represented 1 unit, and longer ones that represented 10 units. They found that Chinese, Japanese, and Korean children preferred to use a combination of 10-unit and 1-unit rods, while American children were more likely to represent numbers through a collection of 1-unit rods. The researchers explained the difference through the fact that the notion of place value is an inherent component of linguistic encoding of number in Asian languages, but needs to be understood and internalized by English-speaking children. They also found that more Asian children than American children were able to construct each number in two ways, which suggests greater flexibility of mental number manipulation.

In turn, Miller and Stigler (1987) showed that Chinese children between 4 and 6 years of age outperformed English-speaking American children of the same age on abstract counting and on counting sets of objects varying in size and arrangement; Chinese children could also count higher than their American peers. The "teens" created a particular stumbling block for American children; they were also more likely to skip numbers and were the only ones to produce nonstandard numbers such as "forty-twelve."

Together, these studies suggest that number encoding in Asian languages facilitates understanding of basic mathematical concepts such as place value, numerical relations such as part-whole, and the mental manipulation of number quantities required for numerical reasoning. At the same time, it is also possible that dramatic differences between populations are enhanced by social and cultural factors (cf. Towse & Saxton, 1997). Furthermore, the early differences in understanding of the place value concept, mental flexibility, or counting skill may be strictly developmental; it remains to be determined what role, if any, they play in later mathematical performance.

Little is known at this point about implications of grammatical number marking differences for bilinguals' verbal and nonverbal performance, even though numerous studies have addressed mathematical performance of bilingual children and adults (for a discussion, see Bialystok, chapter 20, this volume). These studies have established that some areas of numerical cognition are language-independent (Spelke & Tsivkin, 2001), that there is an advantage in calculation speed for the preferred language (Noel & Fias, 1998), that the preferred language is not necessarily the first one but may be the language of schooling (Vaid & Menon, 2000) or training (Spelke & Tsivkin, 2001), and that L1 dominance for mental computation may decrease with the length of residence in the L2 context (Tamamaki, 1993). These studies, however, focused on bilingualism per se, rather than on the effects of having two diverging numeric systems. Future studies could examine numeracy development in bilingual children who are learning two distinct numerical systems and see, for instance, whether there is transfer of skills and concepts, such as place value, from one language into another.

Space

The fourth area in which both lexicosemantic and morphosyntactic differences may be important involves conceptualization of space and memory for spatial arrangements. Cross-linguistic differences in conceptualization of space are commonly discussed in terms of three frames of reference. An *absolute* frame uses information external to both the speech participants and the figure-ground scene, such as north, south, east, or west; this frame is commonly used by the speakers of Tzeltal, a Mayan language, spoken in Mexico. An *intrinsic* frame uses the features of the object in question as the point of departure, and the *relative* or *deictic* frame is based on projections from the human body, such as "in front (of me)" or "to the left." The latter frames are commonly used by speakers of English or Dutch to describe small layouts for which absolute systems are not appropriate. Studies have shown that different speech communities may favor different reference frames. As a result, members of these speech communities differ systematically in their performance on verbal and nonverbal problem-solving, memory, role-playing, and description elicitation tasks, with Tzeltal speakers, for instance, favoring an absolute frame of reference for tabletop arrangements, and Dutch speakers opting for the relative one (Bowerman, 1996a, 1996b; M. Carroll, 1993, 1997; Choi & Bowerman, 1991; Levinson, 1996, 1997, 2003; Pederson, Danziger, Wilkins, Levinson, Kita, & Senft, 1998).

Munnich, Landau, and Dosher (2001) hypothesized that, because the distinction between immediate support (typically expressed with the preposition *on*) and nonsupport (typically expressed with the prepositions *above* or *over*) is obligatory in English but not in Japanese or Korean, speakers of these languages may differ in remembering contact information regarding specific spatial arrangements. Although speakers of Japanese and Korean did indeed differ from speakers of English on a linguistic task, there were no significant differences among the groups on a spatial memory task. These results may indicate that language does not influence this area of spatial cognition (as argued by the authors) or, alternatively, they may stem from the logic of the experiment or the nature of the stimuli. It is also possible that they are caused by the subject selection criteria. All of the Japanese and Korean participants in the study were undergraduate and graduate students in U.S. universities. The authors argued that, because the participants had learned their English after the age of 12, they would not be expected to have nativelike proficiency in English. In fact, their English proficiency is irrelevant (even though we can expect it to be relatively high). What is crucial here is the possibility that 10 or more years of English learning and subsequent residence in an English-speaking environment with high linguistic demands may have had an impact on the participants' L1 competence (Cook, 2003; Pavlenko, 2000). It is thus entirely possible that both the Japanese and Korean participants performed as bilinguals and not in a manner representative of monolingual speakers of the two languages.

To date, it is not yet clear how spatial information is represented in the memory of different types of bilinguals. Studies in SLA suggest that, at least in the initial and intermediate stages, L1-based spatial categories aid in the process of L2 learning, at times resulting in L1 transfer (Becker & Carroll, 1997; Jarvis & Odlin, 2000). In contrast, acculturated Russian L2 users of English were shown to transform their conceptualization of public space under the influence of the English concept of "personal space," which does not exist in Russian (Pavlenko, 2003). All of these studies, however, relied exclusively on verbal tasks. It is therefore critical to see how bilinguals whose languages favor different frames of reference would behave on nonverbal tasks of the kind used in the study by Pederson et al. (1998).

Motion

The fifth area, also influenced by both lexico-semantic and morphosyntactic differences, involves conceptualization of motion and thus memory for states and actions. Here, following Talmy (1991), researchers distinguish between two types of languages. *Satellite-framed* languages, such as English, favor constructions in which main verbs refer to the manner of motion and verb satellites indicate its path (e.g., come in, run in, dash in). These languages have an elaborate domain of manner of movement, presumably because it is obligatorily marked syntactically (Slobin, 2000). *Verb-framed* languages, such as French or Spanish, favor constructions in which the main verb refers to the path of motion and the marking of manner may require an additional verb (e.g., *entrar corriendo*/to enter by running). (Clearly, most languages have both types of constructions, and this classification refers to the preferred construction rather than to the only one available.)

A series of large-scale cross-linguistic empirical studies conducted by Slobin and associates (Berman & Slobin, 1994; Slobin, 1996, 2000) convincingly demonstrated that speakers of satellite-framed languages represent manner and directed motion as a single conceptual event, while users of verb-framed languages build mental images of physical scenes with minimal focus on the manner of movement. Speakers of satellite-framed languages also tend to pay more attention to motor patterns, rate, and quality of movement than speakers of verb-framed languages and experience more mental imagery related to manner of movement in naturalistic contexts (Slobin, 2000). The work of Bowerman and Choi (Bowerman, 1996a, 1996b; Bowerman & Choi, 2001; Choi & Bowerman, 1991) demonstrated that children learning English, a satellite-framed language, and Korean, a verb-framed language, exhibit sensitivity to language-specific categorization principles before their second birthday and use these principles for non-linguistic cognitive purposes in categorization tasks and in everyday activities.

Again, little is known to date about ways in which motion categories are represented by bilingual speakers. Slobin (2000) found that, after reading a passage from Isabel Allende's *The House of Spirits*, Spanish-English bilinguals reported distinctly different imagery in the two languages, with more manner of motion imagery in English (but still much less than reported by monolingual speakers of English). A series of empirical studies by Jarvis (1994, 2000) demonstrated that beginning and intermediate learners of English who described collisions appealed to L1 transfer in their use of motion verbs and produced strikingly different descriptions. In future studies, it is important to use a combination of verbal and nonverbal tasks to examine how motion is represented in bilinguals who speak a satellite-framed and a verb-framed language.

Time

Yet another concept intrinsically linked to both space and motion is time. Explorations of cross-linguistic differences in encoding and conceptualization of time are rooted in Whorf's (1956) original arguments about the lack of the time concept in Hopi. Several critics, most notably Gipper (1976) and Malotki (1983), argued against Whorf, pointing out that Hopi has a rich and extended temporal system. At the same time, both Gipper (1976) and Malotki (1983) admitted that, although their work rejects the notion of Hopi as a "timeless" language, it supports the idea that the Hopi sense of time and the role time plays in their lives and culture do not correspond to Western notions. Gipper (1976) described the Hopi time experience as cyclic rather than linear, and Malotki (1983) emphasized that "for a good many Hopi who are living on their ancestral land and are clinging to what is left of their ancient traditions, time is basically an organic experience which unfolds in harmony with the cyclic rhythms of their social, agricultural, or religious events" (p. 633). Lucy (1996) pointed out that Malotki (1983) and others, who look for a "concept of time" in Hopi, completely miss Whorf's crucial point about distinct structuration of the time words in English and Hopi grammars. In other words, the issue is the difference between conceptualizations of time rather than the lack or existence of an abstract time concept in Hopi.

The debate about the concept of time was so heated that not until recently did scholars dare to approach the issue again from a Whorfian perspective. To date, Boroditsky's (2001) study is the only one explicitly engaged with bilingual subjects. The researcher shows that English and Mandarin use different spatiotemporal metaphors when talking about time: English favors horizontal metaphors (e.g., *ahead* of time, *behind* schedule, looking

forward); Mandarin typically describes time as vertical, using spatial morphemes *shàng* (up) and *xià* (down) (notably, each language has a handful of the opposite metaphors as well). In her study, Boroditsky (2001) compared performance of native speakers of English and Mandarin-English bilinguals on a series of psycholinguistic tasks, all conducted in English. The subjects were first exposed to visual stimuli that served as either horizontal or vertical spatial primes. Then, they were asked to answer a true/false question about time, with half of the questions using a horizontal metaphor (March comes *before* April) and half using purely temporal terms (March comes *earlier* than April). She found that both English-speaking and Mandarin-speaking subjects answered the before/after questions faster after horizontal primes than after vertical primes. They did differ, however, on the purely temporal questions: English speakers answered them faster after horizontal primes and bilinguals after vertical primes. These differences were taken to signify differences in the temporal thought in the two speech communities, English and Mandarin.

Boroditsky (2001) also examined the effects of age of acquisition and length of exposure on reaction time. She found that age of acquisition—but not the overall length of exposure—was a reliable predictor of patterns of response: The later in life did the participants learn English, the more likely they were to show the vertical bias in their responses. It is unfortunate, however, that the researcher did not examine the effects of exposure to the L2 context, which are likely to differ from the effects of overall length of exposure (i.e., participants who had studied English for 10 years, 5 of them in the United States, may be much more competent and acculturated than those who studied English for 15 years, with only 1 or 2 of them in an English-speaking context). In future studies, it would be important to pay more attention to this variable and to conceptualizations of time on which speakers draw in daily language use and thus in "habitual thought."

Emotions

The next area of investigation, emotion terms and discourses, has produced a wealth of studies that explored cross-linguistic differences and their implications for how emotions are constructed—and experienced—in different cultures (Athanasiadou

& Tabakowska, 1998; Edwards, 1997; Enfield & Wierzbicka, 2002; Harkins & Wierzbicka, 2001; Harré, 1986; Heelas, 1986; Kövecses, 2000; Lutz, 1988; Lutz & White, 1986; Markus & Kitayama, 1991, 1994; Wierzbicka, 1999). This work has been extended to an empirical context with both monolingual and bilingual subjects. Pavlenko's (2002c) study showed that speakers of Russian and American English exhibited systematic differences in their description of two short films portraying emotional situations. English encodes emotions through adjectives; as a result, American narrators discussed emotions as states. In contrast, Russian favors emotion verbs, particularly imperfective and reflexive verbs (it also contains some emotion adjectives and adverbs). Consequently, Russian narrators discussed emotions as actions and processes and paid more attention to the body language and movements of the film characters.

In a study in which the same visual stimuli were used with Russian-English bilinguals, Pavlenko (2002b) found that these bilinguals may be in the process of restructuring their basic concepts of emotion from process to state. In the Russian narratives, this restructuring resulted in instances of L2 influence on L1, such as incorporation of perception copulas and change-of-state verbs. Some bilinguals also seemed to have lost categorical distinctions between various emotions required by Russian. In turn, Rintell (1984) examined emotion identification by L2 users of English. The researcher found that intermediate learners of English, familiar with emotion vocabulary but not with emotion scripts (which include prosodic and pragmatic aspects of emotion performance), failed to identify some of the emotions when listening to tape-recorded conversations in English.

Together, the studies above suggest that different languages may rely on different means of linguistic encoding of emotions and on different conceptualizations. L2 learners, at least in the early stages, may be unfamiliar with culture-specific emotion scripts and conceptualizations and instead appeal to L1-based representations in comprehension and production. In the process of L2 socialization, bilinguals may transform their conceptualizations of emotions and possibly form two distinct emotion repertoires in their two languages. In the future, it would be advisable to look at areas in which emotion conceptualizations diverge and see how bi- and multilingual speakers categorize and express these emotions in their two languages.

Personhood

The eighth area of inquiry examines cross-linguistic differences in conceptualization of personhood. This notion is expressed both in lexicalized (e.g., forms of address, kinship terms) and grammaticized concepts (e.g., verbal marking). Most importantly, it is expressed in personal pronouns, which combine properties of both lexicalized and grammaticized concepts and encode complex relationships between selves and societies. Pronominal systems differ widely across languages, with some languages encoding only a few pronouns and others as many as 200 (Mühlhäusler & Harré, 1990). Studies in linguistic anthropology that examine pronominal systems, terms of address, and discourses of personhood suggest that "selves" and "persons" are differently conceptualized, encoded, and performed around the world (Becker, 1995; Foley, 1997; Markus & Kitayama, 1991, 1994; Mühlhäusler & Harré, 1990; Rosaldo, 1980; Shweder & Bourne, 1984). Some scholars view these differences in terms of the opposition between the egocentric, individualistic, and autonomous Western concept of self and the sociocentric, context-embedded conception espoused in many traditional societies (Foley, 1997; Shweder & Bourne, 1984). Others argue that this dichotomous view oversimplifies the issues, and that even within the same speech community selves may be constructed differently in distinct contexts (Hollan, 1992).

To date, only a few studies have attempted to examine some aspects of bilinguals' representations of personhood. C. Hoffman, Lau, and Johnson (1986) presented Chinese-English bilinguals with four character descriptions. Two contained lexical labels in English (*artistic type* and *liberal type*) but not Chinese, and the other two did the reverse. When the language of description did not offer a convenient lexical label, several sentences were used to describe the character in question. The analysis of the participants' performance on four tasks (free impression elicitation, free recall, recognition, and inference) demonstrated the effects of concept codability, that is, availability of lexical labels. When character traits were lexicalized, the participants exhibited superior performance on impression and recall tasks, while subjects without the benefit of a label exhibited superior memory on recognition tasks, which required close attention to presented information. These results suggest that bicultural bilinguals may possess two sets of language- and culture-specific personhood concepts that are activated in interactions in the language in question and facilitate comprehension, recognition, and recall.

In turn, Heyman and Diesendruck (2002) explored how the distinction between the verb *to be* and its Spanish counterparts *ser* and *estar* influences the reasoning of Spanish-English bilingual children about human psychological characteristics. *Ser* commonly refers to permanent characteristics and properties; *estar* refers to temporary states and properties. The study showed that bilingual children had formed distinct conceptual representations of these verbs: They treated *ser* and *to be* as more likely to convey the stability of psychological characteristics than *estar*. In view of the difficulties experienced by native speakers of English in internalizing conceptual distinctions between *ser* and *estar*, this and similar contrasts (e.g., English *to know* versus Spanish *saber/conocer* or French *savoir/connaître*) could be productively explored in future research with bilinguals at different proficiency levels.

Future studies could also explore how bi- and multilinguals at different proficiency and cultural competence levels conceptualize and perform selves in relations to other persons. For instance, cultural competence in Japanese involves the ability to evaluate one's own status with regard to that of one's interlocutor(s) and to mark the differences linguistically in an appropriate manner without appearing either rude or exaggeratedly polite. Cultural competence in French or Russian involves the ability to differentiate appropriately between the informal and formal you (*tu/vous* or *ty/vy*). A nativelike conceptual representation of these lexicalized and grammaticized concepts would involve not only the knowledge of and about such distinctions, but also the knowledge of links between these categories and linguistic practices, namely, in which contexts particular personal pronouns, honorifics, forms of address, or caste terms are likely to be used.

Discourse

The next line of inquiry focuses on discourses, showing that members of different speech communities may rely on different interpretive stances, frames, and scripts to decide on the tellability of events and to reconstruct worlds in stories (Berman & Slobin, 1994; Chafe, 1980, 2000; Liebes & Katz, 1990; McCabe & Bliss, 2003; Sherzer, 1987; Slobin, 1996, 2000; Tannen, 1980). Ervin-Tripp's

(1954/1973, 1964/1973, 1967/1973) pioneering explorations have shown that bicultural bilinguals often draw on different cultural themes when responding to visual prompts in their respective languages. In a somewhat different format, her work has been followed up by Koven (1998), who examined ways in which simultaneous Portuguese-French bilinguals talked about the same personal experience in their two languages. She found that these children of Portuguese immigrants drew on different linguistic repertoires when telling their stories: In Portuguese, they resorted to colloquial discourses they had learned from their peasant parents and relatives; in French, they drew on discourses of urban youth. As a result, the stories in French exhibited a more critical stance and indexed the storytellers as tough Parisian youths, while the stories in Portuguese took a less empowered stance, linked to the speakers' rural and immigrant origins. Together, these studies point to the possibility of bilingual speakers indexing different identities in their two or more languages through the use of distinct linguistic repertoires.

Cross-linguistic studies of storytelling also suggest that different speech communities may rely on different narrative conventions and structures, the latter seen by Bruner (1996) as evidence of narrative thought. Western stories typically have a problem resolution part, while in some other cultures, the conflict is created but not necessarily resolved in the story; this in turn influences comprehensibility by interlocutors raised in different narrative traditions (Holmes, 1997; McCabe & Bliss, 2003; Mistry, 1993). Moreover, while most European languages favor temporal—and often chronological—narrative sequencing, stories told in the American Indian language Kuna focus much more on location, direction, and ways in which actions are performed, so that Western listeners and readers have difficulty following these narratives in translation (Sherzer, 1987). Here, future studies could build on previous inquiry identifying speech communities in which narratives are constructed differently and examining ways in which bi- or multilingual speakers construct stories about "the same" event in the languages in question.

Autobiographical Memory

The last line of inquiry to be discussed is investigation of bilingual autobiographic memory. Several studies, most notably the work of Schrauf and associates, suggest that bilinguals tend to retrieve memories in the same language in which they were encoded or at least to report them more vividly and in more detail if reporting in the language of the event (Javier, Barroso, & Muñoz, 1993; Marian & Neisser, 2000; Schrauf, 2000; Schrauf & Rubin, 1998, 2003). The stories told in the language of the event are more elaborate, detailed, and emotional; they include more idea and thought units and evoke a higher level of imagery and emotional texture (Javier et al., 1993). At the same time, it is clear that most memories, like any other inner speech activities, can be translated according to the needs of the context, even though some aspects may be transformed or deleted in translation (cf. Pavlenko, 1998).

Interesting evidence regarding such transformations comes from memoirs of bilingual writers (Pavlenko, 1998, 2001; Todorov, 1994). These personal testimonies suggest that autobiographical tellings in the writers' two or more languages are often quite distinct and incompatible because the languages and the discourses associated with them shape the stories in distinct ways. This intriguing intersection between narrative conventions and autobiographic memory awaits further exploration with bilingual participants. Future inquiry will allow us to assess the impact of cross-linguistic differences in narrative structure and conventions on verbal recalls of events that took place in distinct linguistic contexts.

The studies of autobiographic memory also suggest that the metaphor of two—or more—different worlds is not simply a poetic affordance but an apt description of the lives of bicultural bilinguals. As Schrauf and Rubin (2003) state regarding bilingual immigrants, these bilinguals are people with dual sociocultural worlds or associational networks that consist of "an innumerable concatenation of forgotten, half-remembered, and vividly remembered contexts in which [they] came to communicative and cultural competence, learning where and when and how to be unconsciously 'native'" (p. 134).

Interaction Between Languages and Thought in Bilingual Individuals

In sum, while recognizing that concepts not encoded in a particular language may nevertheless be imagined by its speakers, research has convincingly demonstrated that lexically and morphosyntactically encoded concepts sensitize speakers of a particular language to specific distinctions and ensure the ease and uniformity of everyday processes of encoding and decoding. In this, salient mental representations facilitate recall, categorization, and comprehension along the lines of habitual modes of thought and may complicate communication with members of other speech communities. We can also see that outcomes of the few studies with bilingual subjects are quite different from those with monolinguals. While the studies with monolingual participants show systematic intergroup differences (or lack thereof) in verbal and nonverbal performances, bilinguals may exhibit the seven—and possibly more—different performance patterns outlined in the beginning of the chapter.

To begin, some bilinguals draw on distinct conceptual representations when speaking their respective languages (Saunders & van Brakel, 1997a), experience different imagery related to the L1- and L2-based concepts (Slobin, 2000), draw on distinct discourses and linguistic repertoires, and index distinct discursive identities in their two languages (Ervin-Tripp, 1954/1973, 1964/1973, 1967/1973; Koven, 1998; Pavlenko, 1998, 2001). These verbal behaviors suggest coexistence of L1- and L2-based conceptual domains. Strong evidence has accumulated in support of the second pattern, L1-based conceptual transfer experienced by beginning and intermediate L2 learners (Becker & Carroll, 1997; Boroditsky, 2001; Graham & Belnap, 1986; Jarvis, 1994, 2000; Jarvis & Odlin, 2000; Pavlenko & Jarvis, 2002). The third pattern, internalization of new concepts, is well documented in the study of conceptually driven lexical borrowing, loan translation, and code switching in immigrant bilingualism (Pavlenko, 2002a; Romaine, 1995). Limited evidence is also available for processes such as shift (Caskey-Sirmons & Hickerson, 1977), convergence (Ervin-Tripp, 1961/1973), restructuring (Caskey-Sirmons & Hickerson, 1977; Pavlenko, 2002b), and attrition (Pavlenko, 2002b) of language-based concepts in the process of L2 socialization (for an in-depth discussion, see Pavlenko, 2002a).

Different types of bilinguals behave differently in experimental and natural contexts. Simultaneous bicultural bilinguals may develop representations different from those of sequential or late bilinguals; among late bilinguals, foreign language users and speakers with minimal exposure to the target language may differ from L2 users socialized into the target language community. Overall, language-influenced conceptual changes appear to be affected by eight factors (for an in-depth discussion, see Pavlenko, 1999, 2000). *Individual* factors include (a) the speakers' language learning histories; (b) their language dominance and proficiency; (c) the degree of biculturalism and acculturation; and (d) expertise in the domain in question. *Interactional* factors include (e) the context of language interaction and (f) the linguistic status of the interlocutor (i.e., familiarity with the speaker's languages). *Linguistic* and *psycholinguistic* factors include (g) the degree of relatedness between the mental representations in the languages in question (concept comparability) and (h) the degree to which the concept of one language could be expressed in the other language and the means with which it is expressed (type of encoding).

Together, investigations of bilingual performance on verbal and nonverbal tasks and in natural contexts show that conceptual representations may be transformed in adulthood in the process of L2 socialization. These findings have important implications for the study of the bilingual mental lexicon. To date, most studies in this area have engaged with the lexical level of processing and representation. Conceptual processing, if included, was tested through naming and recognition tasks. The present discussion suggests that conceptual representations of bilingual individuals are complex and dynamic phenomena, and that to create a full picture of how specific concepts are represented in the memory of particular bilingual individuals or groups of individuals, a variety of verbal and nonverbal tasks will need to be used, including but not limited to naming, categorization, matching, inferencing, memory tasks, role playing, elicited storytelling, and most importantly, the study of habitual thought (i.e., spontaneous behavior in naturalistic contexts). Further research in this area has enormous potential for discovery of new effects of language on cognition that would be distinct from what we see in cross-linguistic explorations with monolingual speakers.

While I have outlined some directions for future inquiry in the respective sections, three more general comments need to be made. First, to date there are only a few studies that explore cross-linguistic differences in conceptual representation in bilingual individuals. None of these studies offers a rigorous combination of verbal and nonverbal tasks with extensive investigation of habitual modes of thought. In the future, it would be preferable to conduct studies that combine different types of evidence and explore effects in different kinds of bilingual individuals. Second, while at

least a few studies were conducted with bilingual individuals, none were conducted with other types of multilinguals; this lacuna is still awaiting to be filled. Finally, because recent inquiry suggests that sign language use may enhance individuals' face memory (Arnold & Mills, 2001), future inquiry also needs to consider possible cross-modal linguistic effects on the thought processes of hearing and deaf sign language users.

Conclusion

As Duranti (1997, p. 60) points out, the fact that our notions of language and worldview have changed means that some of the assumptions on which Sapir and Whorf's work was based are no longer taken for granted, and that the range of the phenomena investigated under the rubric of "linguistic relativity" has been modified and expanded. This chapter proposed a number of ways in which research on linguistic relativity could benefit from including bilingual subjects and, conversely, has shown how the study of the bilingual lexicon, memory, and cognition could gain from new directions offered in neo-Whorfian inquiry. Current empirical and phenomenological studies with bilingual subjects strongly suggest that languages may indeed create different worlds for their speakers, and that participation in discursive practices of a new target language community may transform these worlds. Together, these studies convincingly demonstrate that bilingualism could be extremely beneficial for enriching the speakers' linguistic repertoires and offering them alternative conceptualizations crucial for flexible and critical thinking. No one understood this better than Benjamin Lee Whorf, who more than 60 years ago argued that "those who envision a future world speaking only one tongue, whether English, German, Russian, or any other, hold a misguided ideal and would do the evolution of the human mind the greatest disservice" (1941/1956, p. 244).

Acknowledgments

This chapter has benefited tremendously from the generous and thoughtful comments on earlier drafts offered by David Green, Scott Jarvis, Michele Koven, Terry Odlin, Sanna Reynolds, and Bob Schrauf and by the editors of the volume, Judy Kroll and Annette de Groot. All remaining errors or inaccuracies are strictly my own.

References

Arnold, P., & Mills, M. (2001). Memory for faces, shoes, and objects by deaf and hearing signers and hearing nonsigners. *Journal of Psycholinguistic Research, 30*, 185–195.

Athanasiadou, A., & Tabakowska, E. (Eds.). (1998). *Speaking of emotions: Conceptualisation and expression.* Berlin, Germany: Mouton de Gruyter.

Beaujour, E. (1989). *Alien tongues: Bilingual Russian writers of the 'first' emigration.* Ithaca, NY: Cornell University Press.

Becker, A. (1995). *Body, self, and society: The view from Fiji.* Philadelphia: University of Pennsylvania Press.

Becker, A., & Carroll, M. (1997). *The acquisition of spatial relations in a second language.* Amsterdam: Benjamins.

Berlin, B., & Kay, P. (1969). *Basic color terms: Their universality and evolution.* Berkeley, CA: University of California Press.

Berman, R., & Slobin, D. (1994). *Relating events in narrative: A crosslinguistic developmental study.* Hillsdale, NJ: Erlbaum.

Birdsong, D. (1999). *Second language acquisition and the critical period hypothesis.* Mahwah, NJ: Erlbaum.

Boroditsky, L. (2001). Does language shape thought? Mandarin and English speakers' conceptions of time. *Cognitive Psychology, 43*, 1–22.

Bowerman, M. (1996a). Learning how to structure space for language: A crosslinguistic perspective. In P. Bloom, M. Peterson, L. Nadel, & M. Garrett (Eds.), *Language and space* (pp. 385–436). Cambridge, MA: MIT Press.

Bowerman, M. (1996b). The origins of children's spatial semantic categories: Cognitive versus linguistic determinants. In J. Gumperz & S. Levinson (Eds.), *Rethinking linguistic relativity* (pp. 145–176). Cambridge, U.K.: Cambridge University Press.

Bowerman, M., & Choi, S. (2001). Shaping meanings for language: Universal and language-specific in the acquisition of spatial semantic categories. In M. Bowerman & S. Levinson (Eds.), *Language acquisition and conceptual development* (pp. 475–511). Cambridge, U.K.: Cambridge University Press.

Bowerman, M., & Levinson, S. (Eds.). (2001). *Language acquisition and conceptual development.* Cambridge, U.K.: Cambridge University Press.

Brown, R., & Lenneberg, E. (1954). A study in language and cognition. *Journal of Abnormal and Social Psychology, 49*, 454–462.

Bruner, J. (1996). Frames for thinking: Ways of making meaning. In D. Olson & N. Torrance (Eds.), *Modes of thought: Explorations in culture and cognition* (pp. 93–105). Cambridge, U.K.: Cambridge University Press.

Carroll, J. (1963) Linguistic relativity, contrastive linguistics, and language learning. *International Review of Applied Linguistics, 1*, 1–20.

Carroll, J., & Casagrande, J. (1958). The function of language classifications in behavior. In Maccoby, E., Newcomb, Th., & E. Hartley (Eds.), *Readings in social psychology* (pp. 18–31). New York: Holt.

Carroll, M. (1993). Deictic and intrinsic orientation in spatial descriptions: A comparison between English and German. In J. Altarriba (Ed.), *Cognition and culture* (pp. 23–44). Amsterdam: Elsevier.

Carroll, M. (1997). Changing place in English and German: Language-specific preferences in the conceptualization of spatial relations. In J. Nuyts & E. Pederson (Eds.), *Language and conceptualization* (pp. 137–161). Cambridge, U.K.: Cambridge University Press.

Caskey-Sirmons, L., & Hickerson, N. (1977). Semantic shift and bilingualism: Variation in color terms of five languages. *Anthropological Linguistics, 19*, 358–367.

Chafe, W. (Ed.). (1980). *The Pear Stories: Cognitive, cultural, and linguistic aspects of narrative production.* Norwood, NJ: Ablex.

Chafe, W. (2000). Loci of diversity and convergence in thought and language. In M. Pütz & M. Verspoor (Eds.), *Explorations in linguistic relativity* (pp. 101–123). Amsterdam: Benjamins.

Choi, S., & Bowerman, M. (1991). Learning to express motion events in English and Korean: The influence of language-specific lexicalization patterns. *Cognition, 41*, 83–121.

Cook, V. (2003). *Effects of the second language on the first.* Clevedon, U.K.: Multilingual Matters.

Davidoff, J., Davies, I., & Roberson, D. (1999). Color categories in a stone-age tribe. *Nature, 402*, 604–605.

Davies, I., & Corbett, G. (1997). A cross-cultural study of color grouping: Evidence for weak linguistic relativity. *British Journal of Psychology, 88*, 493–517.

Davies, I., Sowden, P., Jerrett, D., Jerrett, T., & Corbett, G. (1998). A cross-cultural study of English and Setswana speakers on a color triads task: A test of the Sapir-Whorf hypothesis. *British Journal of Psychology, 89*, 1–15.

Dehaene, S. (1997). *The number sense: How the mind creates mathematics.* New York: Oxford University Press.

Dubois, D. (1997). Cultural beliefs as nontrivial constraints on categorization: Evidence from colors and odors. *Behavioral and Brain Sciences, 20,* 188.

Duranti, A. (1994). *From grammar to politics: Linguistic anthropology in a Western Samoan village.* Berkeley: University of California Press.

Duranti, A. (1997). *Linguistic anthropology.* Cambridge, U.K.: Cambridge University Press.

Edwards, D. (1997). *Discourse and cognition.* London, England: Sage.

Enfield, N., & Wierzbicka, A. (Eds.). (2002). The body in description of emotion: Cross-linguistic studies. Special issue. *Pragmatics and Cognition, 10,* 1–25.

Ervin, S. (1973). Identification and bilingualism. In A. Dil (Ed.), *Language acquisition and communicative choice. Essays by Susan M. Ervin-Tripp* (pp. 1–14). Stanford, CA: Stanford University Press. (Original work published 1954)

Ervin-Tripp, S. (1973). Semantic shift in bilinguals. In A. Dil (Ed.), *Language acquisition and communicative choice. Essays by Susan M. Ervin-Tripp* (pp. 33–44). Stanford, CA: Stanford University Press. (Original work published 1961)

Ervin-Tripp, S. (1973). Language and TAT content in bilinguals. In A. Dil (Ed.), *Language acquisition and communicative choice. Essays by Susan M. Ervin-Tripp,* (pp. 45–61). Stanford, CA: Stanford University Press. (Original work published 1964)

Ervin-Tripp, S. (1973). An issei learns English. In A. Dil (Ed.), *Language acquisition and communicative choice. Essays by Susan M. Ervin-Tripp* (pp. 62–77). Stanford, CA: Stanford University Press. (Original work published 1967)

Fishman, J. (1980). The Whorfian hypothesis: Varieties of valuation, confirmation and disconfirmation: I. *International Journal of the Sociology of Language, 26,* 25–40.

Foley, W. (1997). *Anthropological linguistics.* Oxford, U.K.: Blackwell.

Gentner, D., & Boroditsky, L. (2001). Individuation, relativity, and early word learning. In M. Bowerman & S. Levinson (Eds.), *Language acquisition and conceptual development* (pp. 215–256). Cambridge, U.K.: Cambridge University Press.

Gentner, D., & Goldin-Meadow, S. (Eds.). (2003). *Language in mind: Advances in the study of language and thought.* Cambridge, MA: MIT Press.

Gipper, H. (1976). Is there a linguistic relativity principle? In R. Pinxten (Ed.) *Universalism versus relativism in language and thought. Proceedings of a colloquium on the Sapir-Whorf hypothesis* (pp. 217–228). The Hague, The Netherlands: Mouton.

Gopnik, A. (2001). Theories, language, and culture: Whorf without wincing. In M. Bowerman & S. Levinson (Eds.), *Language acquisition and conceptual development* (pp. 45–69). Cambridge, U.K.: Cambridge University Press.

Graham, R., & Belnap, K. (1986). The acquisition of lexical boundaries in English by native speakers of Spanish. *International Review of Applied Linguistics in Language Teaching, 24,* 275–286.

Green, D. W. (1998). Bilingualism and thought. *Psychologica Belgica, 38,* 251–276.

Gumperz, J., & Levinson, S. (Eds.). (1996). *Rethinking linguistic relativity.* Cambridge, U.K.: Cambridge University Press.

Hardin, C., & Banaji, M. (1993). The influence of language on thought. *Social Cognition, 11,* 277–308.

Hardin, C., & Maffi, L. (Eds.). (1997). *Color categories in thought and language.* Cambridge, U.K.: Cambridge University Press.

Harkins, J., & Wierzbicka, A. (Eds.). (2001). *Emotions in crosslinguistic perspective.* Berlin, Germany: Mouton de Gruyter.

Harré, R. (Ed.). (1986). *The social construction of emotions.* Oxford, U.K.: Blackwell.

Heelas, P. (1986). Emotion talk across cultures. In R. Harré (Ed.), *The social construction of emotions* (pp. 234–266). Oxford, U.K.: Blackwell.

Heider, E. (1972). Universals in color naming and memory. *Journal of Experimental Psychology, 93,* 10–20.

Heyman, G., & Diesendruck, G. (2002). The Spanish *ser/estar* distinction in bilingual children's reasoning about human psychological characteristics. *Developmental Psychology, 38,* 407–417.

Hill, J., & Mannheim, B. (1992). Language and world view. *Annual Review of Anthropology, 21,* 381–406.

Hoffman, C., Lau, I., & Johnson, D. (1986). The linguistic relativity of person cognition: An English-Chinese comparison. *Journal of Personality and Social Psychology, 51,* 1097–1105.

Hoffman, E. (1989). *Lost in translation. A life in a new language.* New York: Penguin Books.

Hollan, D. (1992). Cross-cultural differences in the self. *Journal of Anthropological Research, 48,* 283–300.

Holmes, J. (1997). Struggling beyond Labov and Waletzky. *Journal of Narrative and Life History, 7,* 91–96.

Hunt, E., & Agnoli, F. (1991). The Whorfian hypothesis: A cognitive psychology perspective. *Psychological Review, 98,* 377–389.

Imai, M. (2000). Universal ontological knowledge and a bias toward language-specific categories in the construal of individuation. In S. Niemeier & R. Dirven (Eds.), *Evidence for linguistic relativity* (pp. 139–160). Amsterdam: Benjamins.

Imai, M., & Gentner, D. (1997). A crosslinguistic study of early word meaning: Universal ontology and linguistic influence. *Cognition, 62*, 169–200.

Ioup, G., Boustagui, E., El Tigi, M., & Mosel, M. (1994). Reexamining the critical period hypothesis: A case study of successful adult SLA in a naturalistic environment. *Studies in Second Language Acquisition, 16*, 73–98.

Jarvis, S. (1994). *L1 influence on interlanguage lexical reference*. Unpublished manuscript, Indiana University, Bloomington.

Jarvis, S. (2000). Methodological rigor in the study of transfer: Identifying L1 influence in the interlanguage lexicon. *Language Learning, 50*, 245–309.

Jarvis, S., & Odlin, T. (2000). Morphological type, spatial reference, and language transfer. *Studies in Second Language Acquisition, 22*, 535–556.

Javier, R., Barroso, F., & Muñoz, M. (1993). Autobiographical memory in bilinguals. *Journal of Psycholinguistic Research, 22*, 319–338.

Kay, P., Berlin, B., Maffi, L., & Merrifield, W. (1997). Color naming across languages. In C. Hardin & L. Maffi (Eds.), *Color categories in thought and language*. Cambridge, U.K.: Cambridge University Press.

Kay, P., Berlin, B., & Merrifield, W. (1991). Biocultural implications of systems of color naming. *Journal of Linguistic Anthropology, 1*, 12–25.

Kay, P., & Kempton, W. (1984). What is the Sapir-Whorf hypothesis? *American Anthropologist, 86*, 65–79.

Kellman, S. (2000). *The translingual imagination*. Lincoln: University of Nebraska Press.

Kövecses, Z. (2000). *Metaphor and emotion: Language, culture, and body in human feeling*. Cambridge, U.K./Paris: Cambridge University Press/Editions de la Maison des Sciences de l'Homme.

Koven, M. (1998). Two languages in the self/the self in two languages: French-Portuguese bilinguals' verbal enactments and experiences of self in narrative discourse. *Ethos, 26*, 410–455.

Kronenfeld, D. (1996). *Plastic glasses and church fathers: Semantic extensions from the ethnoscience tradition*. New York: Oxford University Press.

Lakoff, G. (1987). *Women, fire, and dangerous things. What categories reveal about the mind*. Chicago: University of Chicago Press.

Lee, P. (1997). Language in thinking and learning: Pedagogy and the new Whorfian framework. *Harvard Educational Review, 67*, 430–471.

Levinson, S. (1996). Language and space. *Annual Review of Anthropology, 25*, 353–382.

Levinson, S. (1997). From outer to inner space: Linguistic categories and non-linguistic thinking. In J. Nuyts & E. Pederson (Eds.), *Language and conceptualization* (pp. 13–45). Cambridge, U.K.: Cambridge University Press.

Levinson, S. (2003). *Space in language and cognition*. Cambridge, U.K.: Cambridge University Press.

Liebes, T., & Katz, E. (1990). *The export of meaning: Cross-cultural readings of Dallas*. New York: Oxford University Press.

Lucy, J. (1992a). *Grammatical categories and cognition. A case study of the linguistic relativity hypothesis*. Cambridge, U.K.: Cambridge University Press.

Lucy, J. (1992b). *Language diversity and thought. A reformulation of the linguistic relativity hypothesis*. Cambridge, U.K.: Cambridge University Press.

Lucy, J. (1996). The scope of linguistic relativity: An analysis and review of empirical research. In J. Gumperz & S. Levinson (Eds.), *Rethinking linguistic relativity* (pp. 37–69). Cambridge, U.K.: Cambridge University Press.

Lucy, J. (1997a). Linguistic relativity. *Annual Review of Anthropology, 26*, 291–312.

Lucy, J. (1997b). The linguistics of "color." In C. Hardin & L. Maffi (Eds.), *Color categories in thought and language* (pp. 320–346). Cambridge, U.K.: Cambridge University Press.

Lucy, J. (2000). Introductory comments. In S. Niemeier & R. Dirven (Eds.), *Evidence for linguistic relativity* (pp. ix–xxi). Amsterdam: Benjamins.

Lucy, J., & Gaskins, S. (2001). Grammatical categories and the development of classification preferences: A comparative approach. In M. Bowerman & S. Levinson (Eds.), *Language acquisition and conceptual development* (pp. 257–283). Cambridge, U.K.: Cambridge University Press.

Lutz, C. (1988). *Unnatural emotions: Everyday sentiments on a Micronesian atoll and their challenge to Western theory*. Chicago: University of Chicago Press.

Lutz, C., & White, G. (1986). The anthropology of emotions. *Annual Review of Anthropology, 15*, 405–436.

Macnamara, J. (1970). Bilingualism and thought. In J. Alatis (Ed.), *Georgetown University 21st Annual Round Table* (Vol. 23, pp. 25–40). Washington, DC: Georgetown University Press.

Macnamara, J. (1991). Linguistic relativity revisited. In R. Cooper & B. Spolsky (Eds.), *The influence of language on culture and thought: Essays in honor of Joshua A. Fishman's 65th birthday* (pp. 45–60). Berlin, Germany: Mouton de Gruyter.

Malotki, E. (1983). *Hopi time. A linguistic analysis of the temporal concepts in the Hopi language.* Berlin, Germany: Mouton de Gruyter.

Malt, B., & Sloman, S. (2003). Linguistic diversity and object naming by non-native speakers of English. *Bilingualism: Language and Cognition, 6,* 47–67.

Malt, B., Sloman, S., & Gennari, S. (2003). Universality and language specificity in object naming. *Journal of Memory and Language, 49,* 20–42.

Malt, B., Sloman, S., Gennari, S., Shi, M., & Wang, Y. (1999). Knowing versus naming: Similarity and the linguistic categorization of artifacts. *Journal of Memory and Language, 40,* 230–262.

Marian, V., & Neisser, U. (2000). Language-dependent recall of autobiographical memories. *Journal of Experimental Psychology: General, 129,* 361–368.

Markus, H., & Kitayama, S. (1991). Culture and the self: Implications for cognition, emotion, and motivation. *Psychological Review, 98,* 224–253.

Markus, H., & Kitayama, S. (1994). The cultural construction of self and emotion: Implications for social behavior. In S. Kitayama & H. Markus (Eds.), *Emotion and culture: Empirical studies of mutual influence* (pp. 89–130). Washington, DC: American Psychological Association.

McCabe, A., & Bliss, L. (2003). *Patterns of narrative discourse: A multicultural, life-span approach.* Boston: Allyn & Bacon.

Miller, K., & Stigler, J. (1987). Counting in Chinese: Cultural variation in a basic cognitive skill. *Cognitive Development, 2,* 279–305.

Mistry, J. (1993). Cultural context in the development of children's narratives. In J. Altarriba (Ed.), *Cognition and culture: A cross-cultural approach to psychology* (pp. 207–228). Amsterdam: Elsevier Science.

Miura, I. (1987). Mathematics achievement as a function of language. *Journal of Educational Psychology, 79,* 79–82.

Miura, I., Kim, C., Chang, C., & Okamoto, Y. (1988). Effects of language characteristics on children's cognitive representation of number: Cross-national comparisons. *Child Development, 59,* 1445–1450.

Miura, I., & Okamoto, Y. (1989). Comparisons of U.S. and Japanese first graders' cognitive representation of number and understanding of place value. *Journal of Educational Psychology, 81,* 109–113.

Mühlhäusler, P., & Harré, R. (1990). *Pronouns and people: The linguistic construction of social and personal identity.* Oxford, U.K.: Blackwell.

Munnich, E., Landau, B., & Dosher, B. (2001). Spatial language and spatial representation: A cross-linguistic comparison. *Cognition, 81,* 171–207.

Niemeier, S., & Dirven, R. (Eds.). (2000). *Evidence for linguistic relativity.* Amsterdam: Benjamins.

Noel, M., & Fias, W. (1998). Bilingualism and numeric cognition. *Psychologica Belgica, 38,* 231–250.

Nuyts, J., & Pederson, E. (Eds.). (1997). *Language and conceptualization.* Cambridge, UK: Cambridge University Press.

Ochs, E. (1993). Constructing social identity: A language socialization perspective. *Research on Language and Social Interaction, 26,* 287–306.

Paradis, M. (1979). Language and thought in bilinguals. In W. McCormack & H. Izzo (Eds.), *The Sixth LACUS Forum* (pp. 420–431). Columbia, SC: Hornbeam Press.

Pavlenko, A. (1998). Second language learning by adults: Testimonies of bilingual writers. *Issues in Applied Linguistics, 9,* 3–19.

Pavlenko, A. (1999). New approaches to concepts in bilingual memory. *Bilingualism: Language and Cognition, 2,* 209–230.

Pavlenko, A. (2000). L2 influence on L1 in late bilingualism. *Issues in Applied Linguistics, 11,* 175–205.

Pavlenko, A. (2001). "In the world of the tradition I was unimagined": Negotiation of identities in cross-cultural autobiographies. *The International Journal of Bilingualism, 5,* 317–344.

Pavlenko, A. (2002a). Conceptual change in bilingual memory: A neo-Whorfian approach. In F. Fabbro (Ed.), *Advances in the neurolinguistics of bilingualism* (pp. 69–94). Udine, Italy: Udine University Press.

Pavlenko, A. (2002b). Bilingualism and emotions. *Multilingua, 21,* 45–78.

Pavlenko, A. (2002c). Emotions and the body in Russian and English. *Pragmatics and Cognition, 10,* 201–236.

Pavlenko, A. (2003). Eyewitness memory in late bilinguals: Evidence for discursive relativity. *The International Journal of Bilingualism, 7, 3,* 257–281.

Pavlenko, A., & Jarvis, S. (2002). Bidirectional transfer. *Applied Linguistics, 23,* 190–214.

Pederson, E. (1995). Language as context, language as means: Spatial cognition and habitual language use. *Cognitive Linguistics, 6,* 33–62.

Pederson, E., Danziger, E., Wilkins, D., Levinson, S., Kita, S., & Senft, G. (1998). Semantic typology and spatial conceptualization. *Language, 74*, 557–589.

Potter, J., & Wetherell, M. (1987). *Discourse and social psychology: Beyond attitudes and behavior.* London: Sage.

Pütz, M., & Verspoor, M. (Eds.). (2000). *Explorations in linguistic relativity.* Amsterdam: Benjamins.

Rintell, E. (1984). But how did you *feel* about that? The learner's perception of emotion in speech. *Applied Linguistics, 5*, 255–264.

Romaine, S. (1995). *Bilingualism* (2nd ed.). Oxford, U.K.: Blackwell.

Rosaldo, M. (1980). *Knowledge and passion: Ilongot notions of self and social life.* Cambridge, U.K.: Cambridge University Press.

Rossi-Landi, F. (1973). *Ideologies of linguistic relativity.* The Hague, The Netherlands: Mouton.

Rumsey, A. (1990). Wording, meaning, and linguistic ideology. *American Anthropologist, 92*, 346–361.

Sapir, E. (1921). *Language: An introduction to the study of speech.* New York: Harcourt, Brace, & Company.

Sapir, E. (1929). The status of linguistics as a science. *Language, 5*, 207–14.

Saunders, B., & Van Brakel, J. (1997a). Are there nontrivial constraints on color categorization? *Behavioral and Brain Sciences, 20*, 167–179.

Saunders, B, & Van Brakel, J. (1997b). Color: An exosomatic organ? *Behavioral and Brain Sciences, 20*, 212–220.

Schrauf, R. (2000). Bilingual autobiographical memory: Experimental studies and clinical cases. *Culture and Psychology, 6*, 387–417.

Schrauf, R., & Rubin, D. (1998). Bilingual autobiographical memory in older adult immigrants: A test of cognitive explanations of the reminiscence bump and the linguistic encoding of memories. *Journal of Memory and Language, 39*, 437–457.

Schrauf, R., & Rubin, D. (2003). On the bilingual's two sets of memories. In R. Fivush & C. Haden (Eds.), *Autobiographical memory and the construction of a narrative self: Developmental and cultural perspectives* (pp. 121–145). Mahwah, NJ: Erlbaum.

Sherzer, J. (1987). A discourse-centered approach to language and culture. *American Anthropologist, 89*, 295–309.

Shweder, R., & Bourne, E. (1984). Does the concept of the person vary cross-culturally? In R. Shweder & R. LeVine (Eds.), *Culture theory: Essays on mind, self, and emotion* (pp. 158–199). Cambridge, MA: Harvard University Press.

Slobin, D. (1996). From "thought and language" to "thinking for speaking." In J. Gumperz & S. Levinson (Eds.), *Rethinking linguistic relativity* (pp. 70–96). Cambridge, U.K.: Cambridge University Press.

Slobin, D. (2000). Verbalized events: A dynamic approach to linguistic relativity and determinism. In S. Niemeier & R. Dirven (Eds.), *Evidence for linguistic relativity* (pp. 107–138). Amsterdam: Benjamins.

Slobin, D. (2001). Form-function relations: How do children find out what they are? In M. Bowerman & S. Levinson (Eds.), *Language acquisition and conceptual development* (pp. 406–449). Cambridge, U.K.: Cambridge University Press.

Spelke, E., & Tsivkin, S. (2001). Initial knowledge and conceptual change: Space and number. In M. Bowerman & S. Levinson (Eds.), *Language acquisition and conceptual development* (pp. 70–97). Cambridge, U.K.: Cambridge University Press.

Stubbs, M. (1997). Language and the mediation of experience: Linguistic representation and cognitive orientation. In F. Coulmas (Ed.), *The handbook of sociolinguistics* (pp. 358–373). Oxford, U.K.: Blackwell.

Talmy, L. (1991). Path to realization: A typology of event conflation. *Proceedings of the 17th Annual Meeting of the Berkeley Linguistics Society*, 480–519.

Tamamaki, K. (1993). Language dominance in bilinguals' arithmetic operations according to their language use. *Language Learning, 43*, 239–262.

Tannen, D. (1980). A comparative analysis of oral narrative strategies: Greek and American English. In W. Chafe (Ed.), *The Pear Stories: Cognitive, cultural, and linguistic aspects of narrative production* (pp. 51–87). Norwood, NJ: Ablex.

Todorov, T. (1994). Dialogism and schizophrenia. In A. Arteaga (Ed.), *An other tongue. Nation and ethnicity in the linguistic borderlands* (pp. 203–214). Durham, NC: Duke University Press.

Towse, J., & Saxton, M. (1997). Linguistic influences on children's number concepts: Methodological and theoretical considerations. *Journal of Experimental Child Psychology, 66*, 362–375.

Vaid, J., & Menon, R. (2000). Correlates of bilinguals' preferred language for mental computations. *Spanish Applied Linguistics, 4*, 325–342.

Whorf, B. (1956). *Language, thought, and reality* (J. B. Carroll, Ed.). New York: Wiley.

Wierzbicka, A. (1985). The double life of a bilingual. In R. Sussex & J. Zubrzycki (Eds.), *Polish people and culture in Australia* (pp. 187–223). Canberra: Australian National University.

Wierzbicka, A. (1999). *Emotions across languages and cultures: Diversity and universals.* Cambridge, U.K./Paris: Cambridge University Press/Editions de la Maison des Sciences de l'Homme.

Zhang, S., & Schmitt, B. (1998). Language-dependent classification: The mental representation of classifiers in cognition, memory, and ad evaluations. *Journal of Experimental Psychology: Applied, 4,* 375–385.

Ingrid K. Christoffels
Annette M. B. de Groot

22

Simultaneous Interpreting
A Cognitive Perspective

ABSTRACT   Simultaneous interpreting (SI) is one of the most complex language tasks imaginable. During SI, one has to listen to and comprehend the input utterance in one language, keep it in working memory until it has been recoded and can be produced in the other language, and produce the translation of an earlier part of the input, all of this at the same time. Thus, language comprehension and production take place simultaneously in different languages. In this chapter, we discuss SI from a cognitive perspective. The unique characteristics of this task and comparisons with other, similar, tasks illustrate the demanding nature of SI. Several factors influence SI performance, including the listening conditions and the language combination involved. We discuss some processing aspects of SI, such as the control of languages and language recoding. We ask whether experience in interpreting is related to some special capabilities and discuss possible cognitive subskills of SI, such as exceptional memory skills. Finally, we discuss the implications of SI for theories of language production.

When people are faced with a foreign language barrier, the usual way around it is to find someone who speaks both languages to translate for them. Translation involves rephrasing a message expressed in one language (the *source* language) into another language (the *target* language). The term *translation* is often used in a broad sense to refer to any way in which a fragment of source language can be turned into the analogous target language fragment, irrespective of input and output modality. To distinguish explicitly between different types of translation, in this chapter the term is generally used in its narrow sense. It then refers to text-to-text translation and contrasts with *interpreting*, which typically involves the verbal rephrasing of a source language utterance into a target language utterance. From a cognitive perspective, it is important to distinguish between translation and interpreting because they are likely to engage different cognitive processes (De Groot, 1997, 2000; Gile, 1997).

Simultaneous interpreting (SI), sometimes called conference interpreting, can be argued to be one of the most complex language tasks imaginable because many processes take place at the same time. New input is continuously presented while the interpreter is involved simultaneously in comprehending that input and storing segments of it in memory. At the same time, an earlier segment has to be reformulated mentally into the target language, and an even earlier segment has to be articulated (e.g., Gerver, 1976; Lambert, 1992; Padilla, Bajo, Cañas, & Padilla, 1995). This complexity makes the study of SI a challenging enterprise. If we are to understand fully how this task is performed, the separate research areas of language comprehension and language production, bilingualism, discourse processing, memory, attention, expertise, and complex skill performance may all provide relevant insights and should therefore ideally all be taken into account (De Groot, 2000). On the other hand, the process of SI itself may inform theories and models within all these separate research fields (De Groot, 2000; Frauenfelder & Schriefers, 1997; Lonsdale, 1997; MacWhinney, 1997; see also MacWhinney, chapter 3, this volume). Models of bilingualism, for example, need to accommodate the fact that in interpreting two languages must be activated and controlled simultaneously (Grosjean, 1997), and theories of speech perception that assign articulation a crucial role in comprehension (e.g., Liberman & Mattingly, 1985) should be reconciled with the fact that in SI production and comprehension are performed simultaneously.

The Experimental Study of Simultaneous Interpreting

In trying to understand SI, researchers have generally taken three different approaches. The first approach concerns the detailed study of the output of the interpreting process under varying circumstances. The second approach is to regard SI as a complex *task* and as such to compare it with other tasks to gain more insight about the relevant processing components. For example, interpreting is often compared with *shadowing*, which involves the immediate verbatim repetition of what is heard. Interpreting and shadowing are similar in that both tasks involve simultaneous listening and speaking, but they are different in that shadowing does not require the input to be transformed.

The third approach regards SI as a complex *skill* and compares experienced professional interpreters with students learning SI or with untrained but proficient bilinguals. The hypothesis underlying this approach is that interpreters may possess specific task-relevant subskills. Superior processing in particular cognitive subskills would suggest that the interpreting experience itself may boost these skills, or that interpreters are self-selected on the specific abilities required for performing the task adequately.

Research on interpreting has its own methodological problems (e.g., Massaro & Shlesinger, 1997). A critical issue is that professional interpreters do not abound, so an adequate sample for any given study cannot always be obtained, especially if a specific language combination is required. Many studies are therefore prone to a lack of statistical power, making it hard to draw general conclusions from the data. Other methodological problems concern a lack of ecological validity of the experimental setting and the stimulus materials (e.g., Gile, 2000; but see Frauenfelder & Schriefers, 1997).

In the remainder of this chapter, we first discuss a number of essential characteristics and processing aspects of SI that together illustrate its cognitive complexity. We then examine a set of factors that are known to influence interpreting performance. Next, we review research that compares SI with similar tasks. Finally, we consider SI as a manifestation of expertise and address some issues that need to be resolved before SI can be modeled. But, before beginning our review of SI research, we describe briefly the different forms of interpreting and compare interpreting with translating to show that cognitively they should be regarded as distinct tasks.

Forms of Interpreting

In professional practice, two kinds of interpreting are common: *simultaneous* interpreting and *consecutive* interpreting. The main difference between these two forms of interpreting is the timing between input and output. In consecutive interpreting, an interpreter starts to interpret when the speaker stops speaking, either in breaks in the source speech (discontinuous interpreting) or after the entire speech is finished (continuous interpreting) (see also, Gerver, 1976). The consecutive interpreter usually takes notes while the source speech is delivered. SI contrasts with consecutive interpreting in that the interpreter is required to listen and speak at the same time instead of alternating between listening and speaking. As a consequence, the cognitive demands of SI and consecutive interpreting are likely to be different. Consecutive interpreting puts large demands on long-term memory because it requires reciting a message into another language on the basis of memory and a few notes, whereas in SI constraints in online information processing are likely to constitute the main challenge to acceptable performance.

Mixtures of text-to-text translation and interpreting also exist. For example, in so-called sight interpreting, the interpreter produces a verbal translation of a written text (Moser-Mercer, 1995). SI from or into sign language is especially interesting because the two languages involved are in a different modality.

Interpreting Versus Translating

In many respects, translating and interpreting are very similar tasks. Both are modes of bilingually mediated communication for a third party (see also Neubert, 1997). These forms of language use are unique in the sense that interpreters and translators are not supposed to contribute to the content of the message that they have to transfer. In addition to monitoring what they say or write, as normal speakers or writers would do, interpreters and translators have to match the content of what they say or write to the content of a source text.

The typical differences between translating and interpreting concern the modes of input and output. These are the visual and written mode in the case of translating and the auditory and verbal mode in the case of interpreting. There are other obvious differences between the two (see Gile, 1995; Padilla & Martin, 1992), some of which are likely to influence the language comprehension process. In SI, the input rate is determined by the speaker of the source text. The rate will usually be comparable to that in normal speech, that is, about 100 to 200 words per min. Speech is transient; any information missed is irretrievable. The clarity of input in interpreting can vary widely because of the variability of the speakers or because of variability of the quality of technical equipment and environmental circumstances. In translating, the source text is static and permanently available. It can be consulted and reread at a rate that suits the translator.

Regarding language production, there is a noticeable difference in the amount of output produced by interpreters and translators within a given time span. Interpreters usually work in pairs, taking turns approximately every 30 min. The speed of delivery is speaking rate. This amounts to up to approximately 4,000 words on average in a 30-min turn. Translators usually produce that amount of translated text in an entire day.

More important, there is only one "go" to produce a good interpretation, whereas iterative improvement of the target text is an essential component of the translation process (Gile, 1995; Moser-Mercer, Künzli, & Korac, 1998). When translating, there is also an opportunity to use dictionaries and to consult experts and colleagues. In contrast, interpreters have to acquire the relevant knowledge in advance. Moreover, unlike translating, interpreting always takes place directly in front of an audience. An advantageous consequence of this is that interpreters usually share the communicative context with the source speaker and the listeners. Also, just as the audience, the interpreter has access to extralinguistic information to aid comprehension (e.g., nonverbal communication and slides). In contrast, in translating, the translated text is typically the only source of information available to its readers.

A translated text is generally of a higher quality than an interpreted text, a fact that relates, in addition to cognitive demand differences between the tasks, to differences in the goals that need to be achieved in the two tasks. The readers of a translation expect a well-written text; therefore, the linguistic acceptability requirements are very high in translating. For interpreters, it is especially important to deliver clear target language, but the stylistic demands are those of ordinary speech, which implies that grammatically less-well-formed utterances are acceptable. A final noteworthy difference is that an interpreted text is usually shorter than the original source text, whereas a translated text is usually longer (Chernov, 1994; Padilla & Martin, 1992). The latter difference implies that interpreting involves a loss of information.

Characteristics of Simultaneous Interpreting

The Simultaneity of Comprehension and Production

One of the most salient features of SI is that two streams of speech have to be processed simultaneously: The input has to be understood, and the output has to be produced. Note that this implies that interpreters have a split conceptual attention (MacWhinney, 1997, and chapter 3, this volume). One conceptual focus is directed to understanding the input; the other focus is on conceptualizing and producing an earlier part of the message. Past research suggests that interpreters exploit natural pauses and hesitations in the source speech to reduce simultaneous processing to a minimum (Barik, 1973; Goldman-Eisler, 1972, 1980).

In an analysis of the temporal characteristics of source and target delivery patterns, Barik (1973) confirmed that interpreters proportionally speak more during pauses in the input than would be expected if the input and output patterns were independent (but see Gerver, 1976). When taking this into account, about 70% of the time that interpreters are speaking, they are simultaneously listening to input (Chernov, 1994). In other words, most of the time interpreters have to cope with simultaneous comprehension and production of language (see also Goldman-Eisler, 1972).

The Lag Between Source and Target Message

The production of the target message usually lags behind that of the source message by a few seconds.

Before being able to produce an adequate interpreting output, a certain amount of input has to be available. This lag, the so-called ear–voice span, is measured as the number of words or seconds between the input and the corresponding output.

Average lags reported for interpreting are longer than for shadowing. For interpreting, the average lag varies between 4 and 5.7 words (Gerver, 1976; Goldman-Eisler, 1972; Treisman, 1965), whereas for shadowing it varies between 2 and 3 words (Gerver, 1976; Treisman, 1965). Consistent with Barik's study (1973), who reported lags of 2 to 3 s for interpreting, in our laboratory we observed average lags of about 2 s for interpreting and 1 s for shadowing. We estimated this to be equivalent to about 5 words for interpreting and between 2 and 3 words for shadowing (Christoffels & De Groot, 2004).

The ear–voice span is likely to be influenced by a number of factors, such as the language of input (Goldman-Eisler, 1972). Even so, the reported average span across the various studies seems consistent. In fact, as discussed in the section on determinants of interpreting output, some input manipulations do not influence the ear–voice span. The span appears to result from an interplay between two contrasting factors. The first is that there is an advantage in waiting as long as possible before starting to produce the translation. The longer the actual production is delayed, the more information about the intended meaning of the input is available (see also Barik, 1975; Kade & Claus, 1971) and the lower the chance of misinterpretation because ambiguities may be resolved.

In support of this, in a study on sign language interpreting Cokely (1986) observed that the number of errors was negatively correlated with time lag. Furthermore, Barik (1975) suggested that specific difficulties observed in SI with function words (e.g., to, for, as) are caused by misinterpretation because of too short an ear–voice span. Because these words are highly ambiguous without sufficient context, they may lead to interpreting errors when translated before the intended meaning is fully resolved.

In contrast, there is also an advantage in keeping the lag as short as possible because a short lag taxes memory less than a long lag. With a long lag, the interpreter runs the risk of loss of information from working memory, with the effect of losing the thread of the input speech. Barik (1975) reported that the longer the interpreter lagged behind, the greater the likelihood that source text content was omitted.

To conclude, there appears to be an optimal ear–voice span that is a compromise between the length of the stretches of input required for full understanding and the limits of working memory. The result of these opposing demands settles on an average lag of four to five words (see also Anderson, 1994; Goldman-Eisler, 1980).

The Unit of Interpreting

Closely related to the issue of an optimal ear–voice span is the question of what constitutes the unit ("chunk") from which SI output is built. The interpreting unit is probably larger than a single word because the span consists of several words on average. Moreover, literal word-by-word translation would render an unintelligible interpretation, if only because languages often differ in word order, and single words do not always have an exact translation equivalent. So, rather than translating each incoming word separately, interpreting usually involves rephrasing at a higher level (Goldman-Eisler, 1980; Schweda-Nicholson, 1987).

In an analysis of a large number of translation chunks, Goldman-Eisler (1972) found that for about 92% of these chunks the ear–voice span consisted of at least a complete noun phrase plus verb phrase, from which she concluded that the verb phrase is an especially crucial part of the input chunk. Apparently, grammatical information is needed before interpreting is possible, and the clause may be the favored unit in interpreting. This is also indicated by the tendency of interpreters to postpone the translation when the verb is uttered late in the input clause. Furthermore, Goldman-Eisler found that in 90% of the cases interpreters started to translate before a natural pause in the source speech occurred, which suggested that interpreters do not merely mirror the input chunking of the speaker but impose their own segmentation of the text. Nevertheless, Barik (1975) found that the more the speaker of the source text paused at grammatical junctions, the better the performance. The usefulness of such input parsing again converges with the idea of the clause as the unit of processing in interpreting.

In an eye-tracking study involving sight interpreting of ambiguous phrases presented in context, McDonald and Carpenter (1981) reported that during the first "pass," parsing was very similar to parsing in ordinary reading. The interpretation was typically produced during a time-consuming second pass of a chunk, when phrases were reread. They concluded that parsing or chunking in (sight) translation is initially very similar to the analogous processes in reading comprehension.

It thus seems that a good candidate for the preferred unit of interpreting is the clause. Interpreting strategies, which may also influence the size of the chunking unit, are discussed in a later section.

Processing Aspects of Simultaneous Interpreting

Control of Languages

It is a basic requirement of SI to produce "pure" target language, that is, language that does not contain any language switches. Yet, the nature of the task demands that both languages are simultaneously activated while performing the task. Therefore, control of languages is crucial to SI. To explain how languages are kept separate and interference of the nontarget language is prevented in common speech of bilinguals, a number of theories propose a mechanism of external global inhibition or deactivation of activity in the nontarget language system or global activation of the target language (De Bot & Schreuder, 1993; Dijkstra & Van Heuven, 1998; D. W. Green, 1986, 1998, and chapter 25, this volume; Grosjean, 1997; Paradis, 1994). Experiments on language switching provide evidence for a general inhibitory control mechanism (e.g., Meuter & Allport, 1999). That the control of languages may be especially important in SI was suggested by the results of a positron emission tomographic (PET) study by Price, Green, and Von Studnitz (1999). These authors reported that word translation in comparison to reading in the first language (L1) and second language (L2) increased the activity of the areas in the brain believed to control action.

The inhibitory control model proposed by D. W. Green (1986, 1998) addresses the issue of language control most directly. In this model, the bilingual avoids speaking in the unintended language by suppressing activity in the nontarget language system. So-called language task schemas compete to determine the output. Top-down control is achieved by an executive system that boosts the activation of the target task schema (and suppresses activation of the competing task schemas). Translation is given as an example task in which an alternative schema must be suppressed. According to D. W. Green (1998, and chapter 25, this volume), presentation of a word in the L1 that has to

be translated in the L2 will, in addition to a translation schema, also trigger the "naming-in-L1" task. To translate from L1 to L2, an L1 production schema must be inhibited, and the schema for L2 must be activated; that schema in turn inhibits lemmas that are tagged to belong to L1. If word translation is a task that already involves high levels of control, then the control demands imposed by SI on the cognitive system must be very high indeed.

SI may be problematic for any activation-inhibition account because, unlike common language production by bilinguals, SI requires activation of both languages simultaneously. A number of authors have considered ways in which SI might be integrated into existing theoretical frameworks and the implications for language selection and control.

In a framework toward a neurolinguistic theory of SI, Paradis (1994, 2000) proposed the subset and the activation threshold hypotheses (see also Paradis, 1997). The subset hypothesis states that all the elements of one language are strongly associated into a subset that behaves like a separate network that can be separately activated or inhibited. The activation threshold hypothesis holds that an item is selected when its activation exceeds that of its competitors, which are simultaneously inhibited (their activation thresholds are raised). More impulses are required to self-activate a trace (in production) voluntarily than to have it activated by external stimuli (in comprehension). When a bilingual speaks in one language only, the activation threshold of the nonselected language is raised sufficiently to prevent interference during production (cf. the notion of global inhibition). Paradis (1994, 2000) suggested that in SI the threshold of the source language is higher than the threshold of the target language because production requires more activation than comprehension. It is not clear whether such an activation pattern allows for the production of target language only, without interference from the source language, or what the consequences are of higher activation of the target language for comprehension of the source language.

De Bot (2000) discussed a bilingual version of Levelt's model for language production in relation to interpreting (see De Bot & Schreuder, 1993).[1] Like Paradis, De Bot assumed that language-specific subsets develop, that spreading activation is the main mechanism of selection of elements and rules, and that languages can be separately activated as a whole. In the bilingual counterpart of Levelt's model, all linguistic elements are labeled for language. At the conceptual level (the preverbal message), it is specified what the language of a particular output chunk should be. To prevent the selection of source language elements, De Bot (2000) suggested that in SI the target language cue has a high value, so that only elements from that particular language are selected.

Finally, Grosjean (1997) attempted to integrate SI within the theoretical concept of the language mode continuum, which entails that bilinguals may find themselves on a continuum with the extreme points of being in a completely monolingual mode (complete deactivation of the other language) or in a completely bilingual mode (both languages are activated, and language switches can occur). To allow for SI, Grosjean added input and output components to the continuum and suggested that the activation of these two components, rather than the level of activation of each language, varies. At the input side, both languages are activated to allow for comprehension of input and monitoring of output. At the output side, the source language output mechanism is inhibited (in the monolingual mode). Grosjean acknowledged that, even with the addition of these two components to his model, unanswered questions remain, such as how the interpreter is able to switch occasionally from target to source language while for production the source language should be strongly inhibited.

To our knowledge, no past studies have examined language control in SI. Nevertheless, it should be clear that the control of languages is an important aspect of processing in SI. In the final part of this chapter, this issue, and specifically the issue of selectively producing target language in SI, is discussed further.

Language Recoding

What exactly happens when the source language is recoded in the target language? Theoretically, two interpreting strategies have been distinguished: a *meaning-based* strategy and a *transcoding* strategy (e.g., Anderson, 1994; Fabbro & Gran, 1994; Fabbro, Gran, Basso, & Bava, 1990; Isham, 1994; Isham & Lane, 1994; Massaro & Shlesinger, 1997). These strategies have also been referred to as vertical and horizontal translation (De Groot, 1997, 2000) or Strategy I and Strategy II, respectively (Paradis, 1994).

Meaning-based interpreting is conceptually mediated interpretation. The interpreter is thought to retain the meaning of chunks of information and to recode the meaning of these chunks in the target language (Fabbro & Gran, 1994). In other words, according to this strategy, interpreting involves full comprehension of the source language in a way similar to common comprehension of speech. From the representation of the inferred meaning, production takes place in the target language.

The transcoding strategy involves the literal transposition of words or multiword units. The interpreter supposedly translates the smallest possible meaningful units of the source language that have an equivalent in the target language. Transcoding is often called a *word-based* or *word-for-word* strategy (e.g., Fabbro et al., 1990), but if this strategy strictly involved replacing single words by their translation equivalents, its role has to be limited because the resulting interpretation would be unintelligible. Paradis (1994) proposed that transcoding can take place at different levels of the language system (phonology, morphology, syntax, and semantics) by automatic application of rules. One linguistic element is directly replaced by its structural equivalent in the target language. Figure 22.1 depicts the two alternative strategies. They are usually not considered mutually exclusive; both strategies can be available to the experienced interpreter.

The important difference between these two strategies is that, in transcoding, small translation units are transposed into the other language without necessarily first being fully comprehended and integrated into the discourse representation, whereas the meaning-based strategy clearly involves full comprehension, including grasping the pragmatic intention of the input, after which the constructed meaning is produced in the target language.

According to Paradis (1994), translation-specific systems subserve the transcoding strategy. Connections between equivalent items in the two languages may function independently of those that subserve each of the separate languages: Patients showing "paradoxical translation" after brain damage were able to translate into a language that was not available for spontaneous production, but comprehension of both languages was normal at all times (Paradis, Goldblum, & Abidi, 1984, in Paradis, 1994; see also D. W. Green, chapter 25, this volume). According to Paradis, this shows that there are four neurofunctionally independent systems: one underlying L1, one underlying L2, and two translation-specific systems involving connections between the two languages, both from L1 to L2 and vice versa. The meaning-based strategy does not appeal to these systems. Meaning-based interpreting depends on implicit linguistic competence,

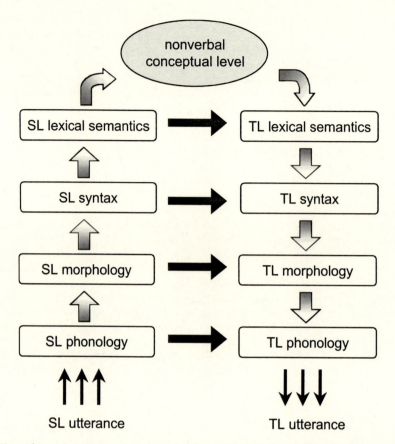

Figure 22.1 Two alternative interpreting strategies (based on Paradis, 1994). The light arrows depict the meaning-based strategy. The source language (SL) utterance is fully comprehended and represented at a nonverbal conceptual level before its meaning is produced as an utterance in the target language (TL). The dark arrows depict the transcoding strategy, according to which particular parts of the utterance (e.g., a certain word or grammatical construction) are directly transcoded into their equivalent in the target language.

acquired incidentally and used automatically, whereas transcoding depends on metalinguistic knowledge that is learned consciously and that is available to conscious recall.

Transcoding, or more specifically, word-based interpreting, is often regarded as an inferior interpreting procedure and is associated with unacceptable output (e.g., Shreve & Diamond, 1997). It is supposedly used relatively often by inexperienced interpreters, in the case of difficult source text (e.g., highly technical text), or under stress (Fabbro & Gran, 1994). In contrast, Paradis (1994) argued that beginning interpreters often employ the meaning-based strategy, whereas skilled interpreters may use transcoding because the rules underlying transcoding presumably have to be learned.

Transcoding at the lexical level does not necessarily imply that words are translated via direct lexical links between the form representations of the corresponding source language and target language words, as in the word association model for word translation (Potter, So, Von Eckardt, & Feldman, 1984). Translation of individual words can be semantically mediated, and there is evidence that even at an early stage of learning an L2, this is indeed what happens (De Groot, 2002; but see Kroll & Stewart, 1994). If the semantic level is distinguished from a conceptual level of representation, with the former storing the lexical meaning of words and the latter containing multimodal, nonlinguistic representation structures (Pavlenko, 1999; see also Francis, chapter 12, this volume) transcoding at the word level can be regarded as implicating the semantic level of representation, whereas in meaning-based interpreting the non-linguistic conceptual level is involved.

Theoretical Accounts of Recoding   Theoretical accounts of the processes involved in SI seem to assume, albeit implicitly, that all interpreting is meaning-based interpreting. In the bilingual language production model discussed by De Bot (2000), all incoming speech is parsed, delexicalized, and turned into a nonverbal conceptual code that serves as input to the production mechanism. Therefore, input speech and output speech are not connected; consequently, all interpreting is conceptually mediated.

The two earlier models of Gerver (1976) and Moser (1978) were developed as extensions of the information processing models common in the 1970s (see De Bot, 2000, and Moser-Mercer, Lambert, Darò, & Williams, 1997). Gerver's model focuses on how chunks of information are stored temporarily to achieve a continuous stream of input and output. Decoding and storage of source language are represented by one component, which is connected to a component representing encoding and storage of target language. This arrangement suggests that this model considers interpretation to be exclusively conceptually mediated. Similarly, in Moser's (1978) model, the input is fully comprehended before production of the target language is set in motion.

Finally, although Paradis (1994) postulated the existence of transcoding (see above), in the flowchart of the events in SI that he presented again only meaning-based interpreting seems to be represented: After a phrase has been decoded, the words' forms are discarded from short-term memory, and only their meaning is retained in long-term memory. Subsequently, the chunk is encoded in the target language and produced. The idea that the form of the input is discarded during SI, which is referred to as *deverbalization*, is discussed next.

Deverbalization   It is often assumed that, in meaning-based SI, the source language is completely deverbalized: The linguistic forms are lost, and only the meaning of the message remains. In other words, the message is encoded nonverbally before it is produced in the target language. In fact, Seleskovitch (1976) claimed that skilled interpreting has nothing to do with finding linguistic equivalents of the source language in the target language at all, but only with understanding the meaning of the input. According to this strong view

of deverbalization, interpreting is only possible when the interpreter completely understands what is said; once a fragment of the source language is understood, the form is lost and only the meaning remains (*théorie du sens*).

Both these aspects of the deverbalization view have been questioned. According to Darò (1994), the idea that a good interpretation necessarily implies complete understanding of the input is a "consolidated professional ideology" (p. 265). An interpreter often may not understand the content of a message completely but nevertheless succeed in translating the "surface structure" of the input (Darò, 1994). Gile (1991) stated that there is not much evidence in favor of the idea that the source message form is lost.

Looking at memory for sentence form, Isham (1994) provided evidence against the idea that the form of the input is lost in SI. Isham (1993; as cited in 1994) found similar recall of sentence form in sign language interpreters who interpreted passages from English to American Sign Language as in a control group of noninterpreters who just listened to these passages. In a similar study, Isham (1994) found that spoken language interpreters recalled less of the sentence form than bilingual listeners. However, the interpreters showed two different patterns of recall: One group of interpreters showed form recall similar to that of the listeners, and the other group showed almost no such recall. Nevertheless, systematic deverbalization does not seem to occur; in both of Isham's experiments, most of the interpreters still had some information on the sentence form available. Isham's (1994) results also suggest that the spoken language interpreters' relatively low form recall performance may not be caused by SI as such but by working in two spoken languages. This possibility is discussed further in the next section.

To conclude this section, we are not aware of the existence of any experimental data evidencing the existence of two qualitatively different interpreting strategies, and none of the theoretical accounts of SI discussed have incorporated the transcoding strategy. Nevertheless, it seems plausible that both transcoding and meaning-based interpreting occur, but complete deverbalization seems unlikely. The two strategies may, however, be difficult to disentangle experimentally because they may result in similar output. On the one hand, it is possible that in meaning-based interpreting the exact form of the input still resides in an input buffer. In that case, this form may still influence the target language output, even though no transcoding occurs. On the other hand, while the input is being transcoded into matched output, it is likely that this input is simultaneously processed further, up to full comprehension, resulting in a level of comprehension that matches comprehension resulting from pure meaning-based interpreting.

Self-Monitoring

Speakers are assumed to monitor their own speech, and the self-monitoring system involved is thought to employ the comprehension system (Levelt, 1989). However, in SI the comprehension system is already occupied with understanding the source text (Frauenfelder & Schriefers, 1997). This raises the question how monitoring in SI comes about. That interpreters indeed monitor whether the produced translation is correct has been suggested by several authors (Gerver, 1976; Isham, 2000; Lonsdale, 1997) and is evident from the self-corrections that we have observed in our own data and that were reported by others (e.g., Gerver, 1976).

Most of the theoretical accounts of SI discussed in previous sections have incorporated some form of output monitoring. In both Gerver's (1976) and Moser's (1978) model, the monitoring of output is performed by comparing the meanings of the source message (retained in the input buffer) and the target message before production takes place. In Paradis's account (1994), it occurs after production has taken place. Paradis himself noted that the comparison between the meaning of the source and target messages is not specified in his model and there is no consideration to what happens when the output is not satisfactory.

The issue of output monitoring in SI is particularly interesting because apparently three speech streams in two languages reside simultaneously in the language system: the comprehension of input, the production of output, and the monitoring of output. Especially for the comprehension system, the situation is complicated because it needs to handle source language input and target language output simultaneously. How these speech streams can all cooccur at the same time and how they are kept separate from one another are questions that still have to be resolved.

Memory Processes

SI poses a great burden on working memory because interpreters simultaneously have to store information and perform all sorts of mental operations to comprehend, translate, and produce speech. In addition, because interpreters monitor their output, it may be necessary to keep some sort of representation of the input phrase available until after production in the target language.

One of the best-known models of working memory is that of Baddeley and colleagues (see e.g., Baddeley & Logie, 1999; Gathercole & Baddeley, 1993). This multiple-component model consists of a *central executive* and two "slave" systems, specialized for the temporary storage of phonologically based material and of visuospatial material. These subsidiary systems are called the *phonological loop* and the *visuospatial sketchpad*, respectively. A fourth component has been proposed, the *episodic buffer*, which is a limited-capacity store capable of integrating information from different sources in a multidimensional code (Baddeley, 2000). The central executive is seen as a mechanism controlling processes in working memory, including the coordination of the subsidiary systems, the manipulation of material held in these systems, and the control of encoding and retrieval strategies. The phonological loop is specialized in maintaining verbally coded information and is therefore the most relevant slave system for SI. It consists of two parts: the phonological store and the subvocal rehearsal process. The phonological store retains material in a phonological code, which decays over time. The subvocal rehearsal process serves to refresh the decaying representations in the store.

Short-term recall for lists of words is disrupted when participants continuously articulate irrelevant syllables during the presentation of these words, a technique called *articulatory suppression* (e.g., Baddeley, Lewis, & Vallar, 1984). Articulatory suppression also leads to reduced recall of auditorily presented short discourse (Christoffels, 2004). The requirement to maintain information during speech production may be an important aspect of the task difficulty of SI because producing speech during SI resembles articulatory suppression. In fact, one may expect reduced recall because of the disruption of the rehearsal process in all tasks in which comprehension and verbal production are involved simultaneously (see also Darò & Fabbro, 1994; Isham, 2000).

After interpreting, text recall is indeed worse than after listening to it (e.g., Christoffels, 2004; Darò & Fabbro, 1994; Gerver, 1974b; Isham, 1994). Two possible causes for the reduced recall after SI can be deduced from the articulatory loop model. First, production of the target speech may prevent subvocal rehearsal. Second, apart from the incoming source language, the interpreter's own voice enters the phonological store, possibly causing interference.

Isham (2000) found that verbatim recall after articulatory suppression was worse than recall after both common listening and dichotomously listening (listening to two speech streams, one of them presented to each ear). He concluded that reduced recall after SI is mainly caused by the actual production of speech and not by the fact that two speech streams enter the phonological store simultaneously. Another reason for the reduced recall after SI may be the higher cognitive demands of simultaneous comprehension and production.

The pattern of results found when comparing recall following interpreting with recall following other, similar tasks is not consistent, however: Recall after interpreting was found to be better than after shadowing (Gerver, 1974b), but digit span performance was found to be worse in an interpreting condition than in any of the remaining conditions, including shadowing (Darò & Fabbro, 1994). Note however, that shadowing involved verbal repetition of digits presented 1 s apart; these circumstances may actually support recall. Finally, no differences in recall whatsoever were obtained between conditions of SI, shadowing, articulatory suppression (Christoffels, 2004), or paraphrasing (Christoffels & De Groot, 2004). (Paraphrasing in this context involved rephrasing the meaning of a sentence in the same language but in different words or using an alternative grammatical construction; see Moser, 1978.) These inconsistent results are likely to be caused by differences in the relevance of long- and short-term memory in recall performance across these studies.

In conclusion, the relevant studies disagree on whether interpreting and shadowing lead to different memory performance, but clearly memory performance after interpreting is worse than after just listening to a text. Interference from articulatory activity during interpreting forms at least a partial explanation for this differential memory performance. This explanation is supported by the better sentence recall of sign language interpreters in comparison to spoken language interpreters (Isham, 1994).

Working memory is important in ordinary language processing (see Gathercole & Baddeley, 1993). It remains to be seen whether working memory has a role in interpreting beyond its role in ordinary language processing. That such is the case is suggested by studies that indicated that professional interpreters possess outstanding memory skills (see the section on cognitive skills). Apart from the phonological loop, the central executive and the episodic store are bound to be important. They are presumably involved in the activation of relevant information in long-term memory, the suppression of irrelevant information, the integration of information, and the coordination of the different processes during SI (see also Bajo, 2002).

Determinants of Interpreting Output

Listening Conditions: Input Rate, Information Density, and Sound Quality of Input

Input rate influences the rate at which information has to be processed. Consequently, it also influences interpreting performance. It is not always the case, however, that the faster the input rate is, the harder interpreting becomes. Slow, monotonous delivery of the source message can be as stressful as a speeded presentation (Gerver, 1976). According to Gerver, rates between 100 and 120 words per min are comfortable for the interpreter. When comparing the effect of increasing the input rate in shadowing and interpreting (from 95 up to 164 words per min), he found that the proportion of correctly shadowed text decreased only at the two highest rates, whereas in SI, performance decreased further with each increase in input rate. Moreover, shadowers maintained a steady ear-voice span of 2 to 3 words at all input rates and increased their articulation rates as input rate increased. In contrast, the interpreters' span increased from 5 to 8.5 words, and their output rate remained the same, indicating that they paused more and spoke less the higher the input rate (Gerver, 1969, in Gerver, 1976).

Shadowing performance is more accurate than SI performance, both for bilinguals not trained in SI (Treisman, 1965) and for SI professionals (Gerver, 1974a). Treisman investigated the effect of information density rather than input rate on accuracy of performance. Interpreting suffered more than shadowing from increasing information density. No effect of information density on the ear–voice span was found. The last result, however, was based on six participants only, so this null effect can be caused by lack of statistical power. Gerver manipulated the amount of noise in the input and found that this manipulation had a larger effect on the number or errors in interpreting than in shadowing. The ear–voice span again remained constant irrespective of the amount of noise. Both findings suggest that interpreters sacrifice accuracy to keep a constant ear–voice span (Gerver, 1976). Alternatively, the participants may already have performed at their maximum lag in the relatively easy conditions and were therefore unable to increase their ear–voice span any further when the amount of noise or the information density increased (see the discussion on the lag between source and target language).

To summarize, these findings indicated that interpreting is more difficult and more sensitive to factors influencing task difficulty than shadowing. Furthermore, they showed that not all factors that increase task difficulty also affect the ear–voice span.

Translation Direction and Language Combination

A recurring question concerns the role of the direction of translation in interpreting. It is often claimed that interpreting is easier into than from one's native language, which is typically the interpreters' dominant language (see Barik, 1975; Gerver, 1976; Gile, 1997; Treisman, 1965). In word translation studies, such a directional effect has been observed by some authors, who have shown that translating from L1 into L2 is slower and more prone to errors than translating from L2 into L1 (e.g., Kroll, Michael, Tokowicz, & Dufour, 2002; Kroll & Stewart, 1994), but others have reported null effects or even the opposite effect (e.g., De Groot & Poot, 1997; La Heij, Hooglander, Kerling, & Van der Velden, 1996; see for discussion, Kroll & De Groot, 1997).

In interpreting studies, there is little experimental evidence in support of any directional effect. Rinne et al. (2000) compared, using PET, interpreting from and into the native language, among other things. They found more extensive activation during translation into L2, possibly reflecting differences in difficulty between the two translation directions. Treisman (1965) found that both French-dominant and English-dominant bilinguals (without interpreting experience) were better when interpreting from English into French than when interpreting in the reverse direction. In a study on allocation of attention and text type, Darò, Lambert, and Fabbro (1996) found no effect of translation direction. Finally, Barik (1973, 1994) provided a detailed analysis of translation direction

data of three professional interpreters and three inexperienced participants. For the professionals, the number of errors and omissions were the same for the two directions. Interestingly, the participants without experience in SI performed better when interpreting from L1 into L2 than vice versa. To conclude, so far no consistent effect of translation direction has been obtained.

It is possible that the particular language combination involved influences the difficulty of interpreting: The more the two languages involved deviate from one another on the lexical, morphological, syntactic, semantic, and pragmatic levels, the more difficult SI is likely to be. For example, Barik (1975) observed that syntactic differences between source and target language might cause problems. If, for instance, certain grammatical constructions specific to a (source) language are transferred into the target language, awkward or ungrammatical target language may result. Note that such an influence of the source language on the target language may indicate a role for the transcoding strategy in SI discussed in the section on language recoding.

Goldman-Eisler (1972) found a longer ear–voice span for interpreting from German to English than from English to French or French to English. The author attributed this finding to the fact that, in German but not in English and French, the verb frequently follows the object (subject-object-verb order). Because the minimal translation unit is likely to be a clause (as discussed earlier), when interpreting from German into English the interpreter may have to wait for the verb in the input, causing lengthening of the ear–voice span. Similar problems may arise when interpreting from languages with occasional verb-subject-object order, such as Arabic (Gile, 1997; MacWhinney, 1997, and chapter 3, this volume). It seems, then, that language combinations differ in the extent to which they pose demands on working memory. As a consequence, they may differ in the ease with which an interpretation can be produced.

The effort model of SI (Gile, 1995, 1997) provides a capacity account of why effects of language combination may arise. This model discusses SI in terms of a limited capacity system. Three basic concurrent, conscious, and deliberate "efforts" are presented: the listening and analysis effort, the production effort, and the memory effort. Each effort represents all the different processes involved in comprehension, production, and memory, respectively. Moreover, a separate coordination effort is postulated. At any point in time, the three basic efforts are processing different speech segments. The total capacity requirement is the sum of all four efforts. It varies depending on the specific information segments that are processed and therefore fluctuates in accordance with the incoming speech flow. As a consequence, errors may even occur with relatively easy source segments because of a sequential failure originating from an upstream difficulty in the source message.

For example, when capacity needed to produce a difficult chunk is not immediately available, this causes an increased memory load because incoming input has to be stored until production is possible. The additional capacity required for memory may diminish capacity for comprehension, which in turn may lead to problems in the comprehension of the next speech segment. Specific difficulties with certain language combinations can be expected for similar reasons. For example, syntactic differences between source and target language that force an interpreter to wait before formulating the target utterance tend to increase the load on the memory effort.

To summarize, the sparse experimental data suggest that, of the two variables discussed in this section, that is, translation direction and language combination, the latter may be the more important determinant of interpreting performance.

Source Text Characteristics

Redundancy and the Possibility of Anticipation
The characteristics of the source text, especially the degree to which it is redundant, are likely to have an effect on interpreting performance. Chernov (1994) stated that, given the large processing load involved, SI of nonredundant speech (e.g., poetry or legal papers) should be impossible. He assumed that speech redundancy normally enables the anticipation of subsequent input.

Other authors have acknowledged the importance of anticipation in SI as well (e.g., De Bot, 2000; Moser-Mercer, 1997). In Moser's model of SI (1978), a decision point is included that allows for anticipation. On a decision that prediction of input is possible, current input is discarded. That interpreters indeed anticipate subsequent input is evidenced by the fact that they sometimes produce a translation of a part of the source text that has not yet been produced by the speaker (e.g., Besien, 1999; Gernsbacher & Shlesinger, 1997). In fact, a certain amount of anticipation is always involved in interpreting because the interpreter usually does not await the entire sentence before starting to interpret (Moser-Mercer, Frauenfelder, Casado, & Künzli, 2000).

If at discourse level a text is highly structured according to a familiar schema, this may help predict what comes next. In a pilot study, Adamowicz (1989) presented SI students with a prepared, structured text and a spontaneous text. Adamowicz argued that the prepared text was more predictable than a spontaneous text, and that the difference in predictability between the two text types should influence the ear–voice span because anticipation allows for a shorter lag between speaker and interpreter in the case of prepared text. This prediction was substantiated by the data. Note, however, that Adamowicz's line of argument and her data are contrary to the commonly held belief that interpreting is only feasible in the case of spontaneous speech because it is more redundant, has a lower information density, and contains more hesitations than a prepared text (e.g., Anderson, 1994; Chernov, 1994; Gile, 1997).

Finally, the context of a source text and prior knowledge of the topic may make the text more predictable, help activate relevant "registers" in memory, and help select the most salient units of meaning from memory (see De Bot, 2000). Anderson (1994) tested two factors that interpreters traditionally believe to be sources of contextual information that are important for interpreting: the amount of text-relevant knowledge the interpreter has prior to the interpreting event and the presence of visual information while interpreting (e.g., the speaker). She found no difference in quality of SI when professional interpreters received a complete text of the speech beforehand, a summary of the speech, or no information other than its title. Anderson also obtained no difference between conditions with and without visual information of the speaker on video. Similarly, Jesse, Vrignaud, Cohen, and Massaro (2001) found no superior SI performance when presenting visual information on speech lip movements together with auditory speech. Clearly, further research is needed to establish what role these types of contextual information play in SI, if any.

Manipulation of Texts Darò et al. (1996) studied, among other things, the role of text difficulty in SI. They found that the number of errors was larger for the difficult texts, which were more syntactically complex and contained more low-frequency words than the easy texts.

Barik (1975) observed difficulties not only for function words and grammatical structures that differ between source and target language, but also for some relatively common, notably abstract words. He suggested these words might be problematic because they may have different translation equivalents depending on the context. It would be interesting to determine whether these observations hold up experimentally and whether factors known to influence single-word translation (e.g., word frequency and word concreteness) affect SI performance as well.

Van Hell (1998) found that, for single-word translation in a highly constrained sentence context, the effects of word concreteness and cognate status were attenuated as compared to these effects on word translation in isolation (the variable cognate status is a measure of the orthographic and phonological overlap between the words in a pair of translation equivalents; compare the noncognate word pair *bike* and its Dutch equivalent *fiets* with the cognate word pair *cat* and its equivalent *kat*).

Incidentally, an effect of word manipulations such as cognate status would point at the use of the transcoding strategy in SI because, according to the meaning-based interpreting strategy, the interpreting output is produced from relatively large chunks of input coded in a nonverbal conceptual form. It should therefore not matter whether word equivalents in source and target language are cognates.

Shlesinger (2000b) examined the effect of some of these word-type manipulations on interpreting. She embedded different types of strings containing adjective modifiers (e.g., *delicate, immature, fractured, vulnerable ego*) in six text segments and looked, among other things, at the effect of the length of the input strings and whether they contained true or false cognates. False cognates, or interlingual homographs, are orthographically similar (or identical) words that belong to two different languages but that do not share meaning across these languages (for example, the English word *slim* means clever in Dutch). Suppressing a false cognate presumably requires effort; the interpreter must assess whether a cognate orthographic form involves a true or a false cognate and must then access the appropriate target language replacement (Gernsbacher & Shlesinger, 1997). Therefore, the presence of false cognates was expected to influence performance. However, Shlesinger found better performance for short than for long words in the input strings (i.e., a word length effect), but no effect of false cognates was found. This null effect was qualified by another finding:

Only a surprisingly small part of the manipulated strings was actually interpreted (only one of four modifiers), reducing the chance of a false-cognate effect to materialize. It is likely that the modifiers may have been regarded as redundant information that can be easily skipped, whether automatically or deliberately (Schlesinger, 2000b).

To summarize, text type and text difficulty are likely to influence SI, and there is some evidence that corroborates this suggestion. Although it is not clear which text characteristics play the largest role in SI, an important variable may be whether parts of the input can be easily anticipated. Specific word properties, like word length, may influence interpreting output as well.

Simultaneous Interpretation Versus Similar Tasks

Mental Load and Stress

Several studies have considered the role of mental load and stress in interpreting in comparison to other, similar tasks. A number of these studies used the finger-tapping version of a verbal-manual interference paradigm. Finger tapping is interrupted by the processing demands of another (cognitive) task, and this interference is larger the more demanding this other task is, thus indicating the cognitive load that is involved. A. Green, Sweda-Nicholson, Vaid, White, and Steiner (1990) found that interference on tapping was larger for interpreting (and paraphrasing) than for shadowing, indicating that the former is a cognitively more demanding task.

The finger-tapping paradigm has also been used to infer lateralization of language. Concerning SI, the question posed in this type of research was whether interpreters, bilinguals, and monolinguals showed different lateralization patterns in L1 and L2 (see, e.g., Corina & Vaid, 1994; Fabbro et al., 1990; A. Green et al., 1990). Results have not been consistent across the different studies, but lately the differences in lateralization data have been taken to indicate larger involvement of pragmatic strategies to compensate for low L2 proficiency rather than differential brain representation of language processes (Fabbro, 2001; Fabbro & Gran, 1997; Paradis, 2000).

Hyönä, Tommolo, and Alaja (1995) took pupil dilation as a measure of processing load. Students of interpreting listened to, shadowed, and interpreted an auditorily presented text. In shadowing, the pupil diameter was larger than in listening, but interpreting yielded an even larger average pupil diameter than shadowing, again suggesting that processing load is largest in interpreting.

Studies using other physiological measures also indicated that mental load during SI is high, and that coping with the difficulties of SI induces stress in interpreters. Klonowicz (1990) found an elevated heart rate for both shadowing and interpreting in comparison to just listening, suggesting an equally large mental effort on these tasks. In a second study, Klonowicz (1994) studied the development of systolic blood pressure, diastolic blood pressure, and heart rate during four successive turns in interpreting. At the beginning of each turn, systolic and diastolic blood pressures increased immediately. During the turn, systolic blood pressure dropped to normal levels, whereas diastolic blood pressure remained elevated. Heart rate only normalized in the first two turns, after which it also remained elevated. According to Klonowicz (1994), these results point to systematically increased arousal in SI that mimics the arousal leading to the development of essential hypertension.

Moser-Mercer et al. (1998) investigated the effect of prolonged interpreting turns (i.e., longer than 30 min) on both the quality of output and psychological and physiological stress experienced by the interpreters. Rather interesting trends occurred, similar to findings for air traffic control, which is known to be an extremely demanding task (Zeier, 1997). After an initial rise of the level of stress hormones, it decreased with further time on task. The decrease may be caused by decreased motivation to perform well. Mental overload caused by increased time on task appears to change the interpreter's attitude to the job: Less effort is expended and carelessness may set in. This interpretation corresponds to the finding that the number of serious meaning errors increases during the second 30 min on task, even though the interpreters were apparently not aware of this performance drop (see also Zeier, 1997). To summarize, these studies indicate that SI involves a high mental load and can induce physiological stress.

Sources of Difficulty in Simultaneous Interpreting

In the studies described in the previous sections, SI and shadowing were often contrasted. Worse performance in SI, larger pupil dilation, longer ear–voice span, and relatively large effects of information density and noise on SI indicate that interpreting is more sensitive than shadowing to factors that increase task difficulty. The combined results of these studies suggest that interpreting is a more demanding and more complex task than shadowing is. Using PET, Rinne et al. (2000) also contrasted SI and shadowing. The brain areas that were selectively activated in SI (i.e., after subtraction of the areas that were activated in shadowing) were those that are typically associated with lexical retrieval, working memory, and semantic processing. This suggests that these cognitive processes play a larger role in interpreting than in shadowing.

Shadowing and interpreting share one source of task difficulty in SI, namely, the simultaneity of comprehension and production. The tasks differ in that interpreting, not shadowing, involves the recoding of source into target language, which may account for the observed differences between the two tasks. Recoding may consist of two subcomponents: First, in SI the message has to be reformulated. Second, SI involves the simultaneous activation of two languages (e.g., Anderson, 1994; De Groot, 1997). It is possible that not all of these task (sub)components contribute equally to task difficulty.

Anderson (1994) compared performance on shadowing, interpreting, and paraphrasing. In contrast to shadowing, in both paraphrasing and interpreting reformulation is required, but only in interpreting two languages are involved. By exploiting these task characteristics, it is possible to disentangle the subcomponent of reformulating a message from the subcomponent of doing so in another language. Twelve professional interpreters performed poorer in interpreting than in shadowing on two quality measures, but interpreting differed from paraphrasing only according to one of the two quality measures. The ear–voice span was smaller in shadowing than in interpreting and paraphrasing, but it did not differ between the last two tasks. In other words, Anderson replicated the difference between shadowing and interpreting, but the results did not clearly indicate that the involvement of two languages instead of just one is an important additional subcomponent in SI on top of the reformulation subcomponent.

In a study mentioned earlier, we attempted to disentangle all three proposed sources of cognitive complexity in SI by comparing the shadowing of sentences with paraphrasing and interpreting them (Christoffels & De Groot, 2004). Bilinguals without interpreting experience performed these tasks simultaneously and in a delayed condition, that is, immediately after presentation of each sentence. By including this condition, the effect of simultaneity of comprehension and production as a source of difficulty in SI could be tested. The quality of the shadowing output was better in the delayed than in the simultaneous condition, but the difference was small, suggesting that simultaneity of input and output on its own adds somewhat to the complexity of SI but is not a major source of complexity. Also, the difference in output quality between the three tasks in the delayed condition was small, suggesting that having to rephrase a sentence per se—even into a different language—may also not be a major source of difficulty on its own. However, in the simultaneous condition, interpreting and paraphrasing performance were notably poorer than in the delayed condition, whereas shadowing performance was much more similar in these two conditions. These findings showed that especially the combined requirements of simultaneity and rephrasing have a detrimental effect on the quality of performance in SI.

There was no difference between paraphrasing and interpreting in the quality of performance, which may suggest that the additional demand of activating two languages on top of reformulation is not substantial. However, the ear–voice span was significantly larger in paraphrasing than in interpreting. The paraphrasing task has been considered as "unilingual interpreting" or "intralanguage translating" (Anderson, 1994; Malakoff & Hakuta, 1991). For this reason, the task is often used as an exercise or assessment task in the training of interpreters (Moser-Mercer, 1994), and interpreting in bilinguals has been compared directly to paraphrasing by monolinguals (Green et al., 1990). In support of this view, interpreters sometimes accidentally "translate" into the same language (Anderson, 1994; De Bot, 2000).

However, the larger ear–voice span for paraphrasing than for interpreting suggests that paraphrasing is more demanding than interpreting. The reason may be that the vocabulary demands in paraphrasing are likely to be larger than in interpreting because the latter only may require a basic vocabulary in both languages, whereas paraphrasing requires a large vocabulary in the one language concerned (Malakoff & Hakuta, 1991). Moreover, changing the grammatical structure, as is typically required in paraphrasing, may be more demanding than finding a grammatical equivalent of an input segment in the output language, as required in interpreting.

A final, perhaps critical, difficulty in paraphrasing may be that, despite the fact that the input message is already properly formulated, an alternative wording has to be found. In paraphrasing, it may therefore be necessary to inhibit the original sentence form and to monitor output rigidly to avoid literal repetition. All in all, there is reason to believe that paraphrasing may involve higher demands than interpreting.

In conclusion, it seems that both requirements (of simultaneity of comprehension and production and of reformulation) contribute to the complexity of SI, but that especially the combination of these two components taxes the limited mental resources.

Novices Versus Experts

Are Interpreters Special?

Is there anything that distinguishes experienced interpreters from novices? If so, are the differences qualitative or quantitative, and are they caused by a difference in talent or training? Neubert (1997) claimed that untrained or "natural" translation is distinctly different from professional translation and interpreting. Harris and Sherwood (1978), however, argued that translation in general is an innate skill. According to them, translation is coextensive with bilingualism, and therefore all bilinguals are able to translate (see also Malakoff, 1992; Malakoff & Hakuta, 1991).

Dillinger (1994) compared professional interpreters and balanced bilinguals on comprehension during interpreting, as measured by a wealth of different variables. He found only small quantitative differences and no qualitative differences between the two groups and argued that interpreting is not a special, acquired skill but the application of an existing skill that accompanies bilingualism naturally. Of course, it is still an open question whether any differences may be found for language production.

Studies in which only nonprofessional interpreters participate are sometimes criticized for not being informative about professional interpreting (e.g., Setton, 1999; see also Gile, 1991, 1994). But research with professionals also can have potential drawbacks. As Shlesinger (2000a) pointed out, it may be difficult to distinguish between idiosyncratic strategies applied by the experienced interpreter and other, more general cognitive processes involved in the process. When novices perform the

SI task, presumably no such strategies have developed yet. It is therefore both theoretically and methodologically important to learn whether interpreting in trained professionals and untrained bilinguals involves similar processes or is fundamentally different.

Cognitive Subskills

By comparing novices and professionals on tasks that are supposed to tap into possibly relevant subskills, we can gain more insight into what cognitive subskills are in fact important for SI. In the next section, we discuss memory skills, verbal fluency, basic language processes, and other subskills in relation to SI.

Memory Skills   A number of studies indicated that interpreting is associated with efficient working memory skills. Padilla, Bajo, Cañas, and Padilla (1995) compared experienced interpreters with student interpreters and noninterpreters on a standard digit span test and a reading span test, which is thought to tap into both the processing and storage aspects of working memory (Daneman & Carpenter, 1980). They found that the average performance of the interpreters was higher than that of the other two participant groups (see also Bajo, Padilla, & Padilla, 2000). In our laboratory, we found that, for unbalanced bilinguals, interpreting performance was significantly correlated with both the digit span and the reading span in the two languages concerned, although only marginally so for L1 (Christoffels, De Groot, & Waldorp, 2003), indicating a relation between SI performance and working memory capacity in this group. Moreover, memory performance in L1 and L2 of professional interpreters was superior to that of bilinguals who had no SI experience but were similarly proficient in L2 (Christoffels, De Groot, & Kroll, 2003).

Padilla et al. (1995) compared recall of words in conditions with and without articulatory suppression during presentation. For the articulatory suppression condition, a significant group effect was obtained. This was caused by a decrement in the recall scores of all groups except the experienced interpreters, who apparently were resistant to the effect of articulatory suppression (see also Bajo et al., 2000). This finding suggests that the ability to cope with concurrent articulation is important in SI. This conclusion is also supported by the association that occurs between retention under conditions of articulatory suppression on the one hand and SI performance in bilinguals without previous SI experience on the other hand (Christoffels, 2003).

In contrast, Chincotta and Underwood (1998) did not find a difference in digit span between English-Finish interpreters and Finish students majoring in English, neither in a condition with articulatory suppression nor in one without such suppression. However, consistent with earlier findings, differences in memory processes between the two groups were suggested by the finding that the standard language effect in the digit span task (a larger digit span in the language in which one can articulate faster) disappeared for the students in an articulatory suppression condition, whereas for the interpreters it persisted.

Finally, Bajo (2002) reported that word recall in interpreters, participants with a similarly large reading span, and noninterpreters alike was disrupted by divided attention manipulations that tapped into the visual spatial sketchpad and the central executive components of working memory. The finding that the interpreters did not outperform other groups on these working memory tasks suggests that the ability to cope with simultaneity of verbalization and recall in SI may not reflect a general ability of the executive to coordinate multiple tasks and processes, but instead involves a specific skill to coordinate the verbal processes implicated in SI.

To summarize, findings of superior or qualitatively different performance on several verbal memory tasks for professional interpreters than for other groups of participants suggest the importance of efficient working memory skills for SI.

Verbal Fluency   Fabbro and Darò (1995) observed greater resistance to the detrimental effects of delayed auditory feedback in students of SI than in monolingual controls. In a delayed auditory feedback condition, the speakers' own voice is amplified and delayed for a few hundred milliseconds, a situation that in general causes speech disruption. The student interpreters showed less speech disruption than the controls. Fabbro and Darò suggested that the students were more resistant to the interfering effects of delayed auditory feedback because they had developed a high general verbal fluency as well as an ability to pay less attention to their own verbal output.

Moser-Mercer et al. (2000) reported a number of pilot studies comparing five students of interpreting with five experienced interpreters, all native speakers of French. In line with the results of

Fabbro and Darò (1995), they obtained a smaller detrimental effect of delayed auditory feedback for the professionals than for the students on reading a French text but not on reading an English text. No differences were found between professionals and students on tasks involving semantics, free association, spelling, morphology, and phonology. Finally, in a shadowing task, the interpreters' ear–voice span was similar to that of the students in their native French language, whereas the students were *faster* in shadowing in English. Moreover, in both languages, the interpreters made more errors than the students did. Moser-Mercer et al. (2000) explained these remarkable results by suggesting that professionals are used to processing larger chunks of input than those required in shadowing, which might make it harder for them to respect the instruction of immediate repetition imposed by the shadowing task. If this explanation holds, then we should be cautious in using the shadowing task in studies that test interpreters (see also Frauenfelder & Schriefers, 1997).

To summarize, none of the differences between professionals and students observed by Moser-Mercer et al. (2000) clearly supports the idea that professionals have special verbal fluency skills. Perhaps the two groups compared in this study performed similarly because the students were already enrolled in an SI training program and were therefore possibly (self-) selected on verbal fluency skills. The additional interpreting experience of the professionals may not exert a notable effect on some of the subskills involved in SI. However, given the small sample size, we cannot draw any firm conclusions from the results of this study.

Basic Language Processes   Efficient language processing may be especially important for SI. The more the language processes that are involved in SI are automated, the more processing capacity will be available for other relevant processes and the faster the outcome of these processes will be available for further processing. For example, the ability to access and retrieve words quickly may be an important subskill. Bajo et al. (2000) presented a categorization task to four groups of participants: interpreters, interpreting students, bilinguals, and monolinguals. On each trial, the participants had to decide whether a word was a member of the category to which another word referred. Especially for atypical exemplars of categories, the interpreters were faster than all other groups, indicating faster semantic access. In a lexical decision task, no difference was found between the

groups on the words, but on the nonwords the interpreters were faster than the bilingual participants. The relevance of quick lexical access is also indicated by the positive correlation between interpreting performance on the one hand and word naming and word translation in the two languages involved (English and Dutch) on the other hand, a result that we obtained for unbalanced bilinguals untrained in SI (Christoffels et al., 2003). However, when comparing the performance of interpreters and other highly proficient bilinguals (teachers of L2) on these same tasks, we obtained no differences between groups. This finding suggests that efficient lexical retrieval may not be uniquely related to SI, but to high L2 proficiency instead (Christoffels, De Groot, & Kroll, 2004).

Finally, in a dichotic listening task, Fabbro, Gran, and Gran (1991) compared students of interpreting with professionals in how well they detected errors in translations of sentences. The participants simultaneously received the source sentence to one ear and its translation to the other ear. Professional and student interpreters did not differ from one another in recognizing correct translations. However, an interesting difference between the two groups was that the students recognized more syntactic errors than the professionals, whereas the professionals recognized more semantic errors. This suggests that the groups differed in the level at which they processed the input.

To summarize, although it is not altogether clear which language subprocesses are most critical for skilled SI performance, there is some evidence to suggest that interpreters are relatively efficient in processing meaning.

Other Subskills   A number of other potentially relevant subskills of SI are worth mentioning. Gernsbacher and Shlesinger (1997) pointed out that people differ in how efficiently they can suppress interfering information, such as the inappropriate meanings of homonyms, recently processed (but currently inappropriate) syntactic form, and the literal interpretation of metaphors. They suggested that, in interpreting, resources required for suppression are diminished because the system is already involved in simultaneous comprehension and production. Because, nevertheless, interfering information will have to be suppressed, the ability to do so effectively is likely to be another important subskill of interpreting.

Similarly, Tijus (1997) argued that the most important subskill of SI is to be able to detect inconsistencies resulting from incorrect assignment of meaning to polysemous phrases and to resolve them immediately. Detecting and quickly resolving such inconsistencies requires a large memory capacity for input processing (Tijus, 1997), which again points to the relevance of efficient memory processes for interpreting.

Training or Selection?

It is not clear whether the differences found between interpreters and other groups of participants concern qualitative or quantitative differences in underlying processes. Another relevant question that needs to be answered is whether the skills required for SI have developed as a consequence of training and experience in SI or whether successful interpreters chose a career in SI because they possess certain talents that make them well suited to the task.

Bajo et al. (2000) presented evidence suggesting that training in interpreting can improve performance on basic language skills. They compared students of interpreting who received a year of training with an untrained control group on three tasks: comprehension, categorization, and lexical decision. Both groups were tested twice, once at the beginning of that year and once at the end. The student interpreters, but not the controls, showed improved performance on the second test.

The most likely answer to the question of what causes differences between novices and experienced interpreters is that both certain language and memory abilities are required for a high performance level, and that certain skills develop with practice. It is, therefore, of great practical interest to find out which aspects of SI can and should be learned on the one hand and what determines aptitude and which tests can predict aptitude on the other hand (Moser-Mercer, 1994).

Gerver, Longley, Long, and Lambert (1984) addressed the latter issues. They developed a set of psychometric tests to select trainees for a course in simultaneous and consecutive interpreting. At the beginning of this course, they administered tests based on text materials (recall, "cloze," and error detection); linguistic subskills (synonym generation, sentence paraphrasing, and comprehension); and a nonlinguistic speed stress test. The tests correlated with final examination ratings, and students passing the course had a higher score on all tests than the students who failed, albeit the difference was not significant for each of the tests. The text-based tests were more predictive for passing the course than the linguistic subskills and speed

tests, suggesting that especially rather general verbal abilities and the processing of text are predictive for SI and consecutive interpreting. Prediction of pass/fail rates was better on the basis of these tests than on the existing selection procedures, showing that aptitude testing can be useful in practice (see Hoffman, 1997, for a discussion of interpreting regarded as a skill from the perspective of the psychology of expertise, and see Arjona-Tseng, 1994; Lambert, 1991; and Moser-Mercer, 1994, for discussions of aptitude tests used in training programs).

Relevant Issues and Concluding Remarks

In this chapter, we presented an overview of experimental research into SI from a cognitive perspective. In the final part of this chapter, we briefly review a number of the most important issues that need to be addressed in developing a complete model of SI.

The Locus of Recoding

An important issue to resolve is where and how in the system actual recoding of language (translation) takes place. Two alternative theoretical views on this issue were discussed: meaning-based interpreting and transcoding. Although little direct experimental data exist to support either of these two recoding strategies, there is some evidence to suggest that, in addition to meaning-based interpreting, transcoding also takes place. This issue of how translation takes place has to be taken into account by models of bilingual processing. For example, if transcoding occurs, it may take place at a number of different levels in the bilingual system: phonological, morphological, syntactic, and semantic (Paradis, 1994). This implies the existence of direct links between representations of the linguistic elements of one language and the corresponding representations in the other language. The existence of such links constrains current models of bilingual memory.

Resource-Consuming Subcomponents of Simultaneous Interpreting

A further question is which subcomponents of the full interpreting task appeal to the limited mental resources of the interpreter and how these resources are allocated. In fact, it is not yet clear which subcomponents should be distinguished in SI in the first place and whether they share resources. Both Gerver (1976) and Gile (1997) assumed that resources are limited and shared between the various components in their models. As a consequence, the monitoring of output, for instance, might suffer if the listening conditions are suboptimal. It is as yet unclear whether language recoding, the switch of language itself, should be regarded as an additional resource-consuming processing step in SI in addition to the steps required for comprehending and producing language, or whether instead the nonverbal meaning is derived from the source language and the target message is subsequently simply produced from this meaning representation (Anderson, 1994; De Groot, 1997; Isham & Lane, 1994). If only meaning-based translation holds—and not transcoding—it may not be necessary to assume an additional translation stage.

Representation, Selection, Access, and Control

An issue that has received little attention so far is how the language system(s) are represented and specifically whether language comprehension and production are subserved by one and the same system or by two functionally independent systems instead. Yet, to model SI it is necessary to make choices regarding the basic architecture of the language system(s). Considering monolingual language processing, we may ask which parts, representations, or processes are shared between the language comprehension and production systems. Kempen (1999), for example, assumed that grammatical encoding and decoding are performed by the same system, an assumption that may be difficult to reconcile with the simultaneity of comprehension and production in SI, and Frauenfelder and Schriefers (1997) and De Bot (2000) suggested that comprehension and production processes may share the lexical and grammatical knowledge systems (but see Harley, 2001).

With respect to bilingual language processing, common questions are how the two languages are represented in the bilingual mind and how lexical access to bilingual memory comes about. Most of the relevant research on bilingual memory representation focuses on the lexicon and converges on the conclusion that word forms are represented in language-specific memory stores, whereas word meanings are stored in memory representations

that are shared between the two languages (for reviews, see De Groot, 2002; Kroll & Dijkstra, 2002). The research on access to bilingual memory mainly supports the idea that lexical access is nonselective, that is, that both during comprehension and during production, words from both languages are initially activated (e.g., Colomé, 2001; Dijkstra, Van Jaarsveld, & Ten Brinke, 1998; Hermans, Bongaerts, De Bot, & Schreuder, 1998; Jared & Kroll, 2001; Van Heuven, Dijkstra, & Grainger, 1998, but see Costa, chapter 15, this volume, for language-specific *selection*).

As mentioned (see The Control of Languages), in a framework in which control of languages is exercised by global inhibition of the nontarget language, presumably two languages must be active simultaneously in SI. The ensuing question is how it is possible that during SI only the target language is produced.

Figure 22.2 illustrates two alternative proposals that allow target language production in SI within a framework of global inhibition of the nontarget language; in addition, it illustrates a third proposal that does not assume global inhibition of a language. To simplify matters, only lexical activation is considered. According to all three solutions, lexical items belonging to the source language must be separated from those of the target language. The items of different languages may form independent subsets, or they are somehow labeled for language (e.g., using language tags or by connections to language nodes; De Bot, 2000; Dijkstra & Van Heuven, 1998; D. W. Green, 1986, 1998; Poulisse, 1997).

The important difference between the first two alternatives (Figs. 22.2[a] and 22.2[b]) is whether separate input and output lexicons exist. If the parsimonious solution is chosen, with just one lexicon for both comprehension and production (Fig. 22.2[a]), the problem is to explain why source language elements are *not* being selected for production even though both languages are activated. One possibility is that, irrespective of activation in the lexicon, the source target elements are not considered for selection at all (e.g., Costa, Miozzo, & Caramazza, 1999) (see Fig. 22.2[a]). In other words, this alternative assumes language-specific selection. Indeed, Costa (chapter 15, this volume) argues that in highly proficient bilinguals (such as interpreters), lexical selection may be language specific. The mechanism for such "filtering" of language is as yet unclear. Perhaps only items with a target language label can be selected when certain language schemas are adopted.

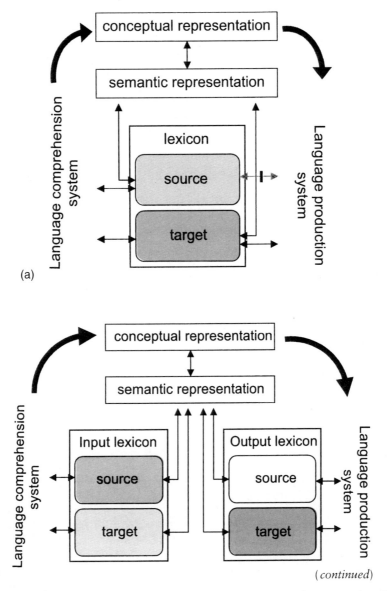

Figure 22.2 The conceptual and semantic levels of representation are separated. Meaning-based translation is illustrated by the route from the language comprehension system via the conceptual level of representation to the language production system. Transcoding at the lexical level takes the shortcut from the source language lexicon via the semantic level to the target language lexicon. (a) The lexicon is integrated for input and output. Both source language and target language lexicons are highly activated (gray in the figure), but selection of source lexicon items for production is not possible. (b) The input and output lexicons are separated. The input lexicons for both languages are activated (gray) to allow for comprehension of the source language and monitoring the produced output. There is (almost) no activation of the source language in the output system, so production only takes place in the target language. Selection of lexical items may be language nonspecific and based solely on the level of activation; source language items are hardly activated and therefore not selected. (c) The input and output lexicons are separated. There is no global activation/inhibition of languages, but a subset of appropriate items is activated instead (gray). Language is one of the elements contained by the conceptual message that determines what lexical items are activated. Selection is language nonspecific and based on the level of activation; the intended item in the target language is selected because it was activated more than semantically related items in both languages.

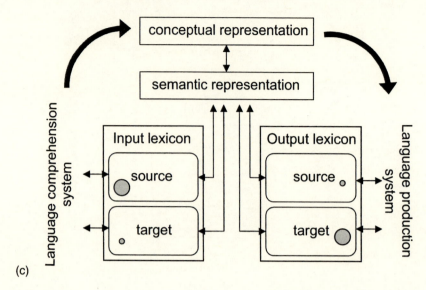

conceptual representation

semantic representation

Language comprehension system

Input lexicon

source

target

Output lexicon

source

target

Language production system

(c)

Figure 22.2 Continued.

SI performance may also be explained in terms of an inhibition account by assuming separate input and output lexicons that can be separately activated or inhibited (see Fig. 22.2[b]). According to this scheme, the output lexicon for the source language is strongly inhibited in SI, so that usually only target language elements will be selected. On the input side, both languages are active, but not to the same degree, to allow for comprehension of the input and monitoring of the produced output (see also Grosjean, 1997).

Finally, a third option is not to assume that global activation or inhibition of language systems controls language output, but that only specific activation of the relevant elements in the lexicon occurs. Language is one of the properties embedded in the conceptual message that selectively activates a number of relevant semantically related lexical elements in both languages. However, because of this language cue, the appropriate element in the target language will receive the most activation and will therefore be selected.

Such a proposal, based on a model by Poulisse and Bongaerts (1994, in Poulisse, 1997), is discussed in detail by La Heij (chapter 14, this volume). This option is presented in Fig. 22.2(c) in a model that assumes (functionally) separate input and output lexicons. If integrated input and output lexicons were assumed instead, the elements of the source language that received a lot of activation by the input might be inadvertently selected for

production. Whatever the solution to be chosen, any model of SI, but also models of common bilingual language processing, should ultimately be able to explain the language control that is exercised during SI.

The selection of topics that we addressed in this chapter has been dictated primarily by the available research. It is clear that SI is an extremely complex task, and that many of its intricacies are yet to be resolved. The fact that SI, despite its complexity, is at all possible may help to constrain models of (bilingual) language processing because it requires these models to account for simultaneous language comprehension and production, for the simultaneous use and control of two languages, for translation processes, and for monitoring in SI. Although SI is complex, we hope to have demonstrated that there are ways to study it successfully. This fact, combined with the recognition that no account of the bilingual mind and bilingual language processing can be complete without the inclusion of a satisfactory explanation of SI performance, may challenge other researchers to take up the study of SI as well.

Acknowledgments

The Netherlands Organization for Scientific Research is gratefully acknowledged for funding this project. This chapter was written while I. K. Christoffels was supported by a grant from this organization awarded to A. M. B. de Groot. We thank Judith Kroll, Susanne Borgwaldt, and Lourens Waldorp for their valuable comments on earlier versions of this chapter.

Note

1. In Levelt's model (Levelt, 1989; Levelt, Roelofs, & Meyer, 1999), three subcomponents are proposed. The first component, the *conceptualizer*, formulates the intended message in a preverbal, nonlinguistic form. This preverbal message contains all the information required for the second component, the *formulator*, to convert the message in a speech plan by applying grammatical and phonological rules and selecting the appropriate lexical items. Lexical items consist of two parts, the *lemma* (representing syntax) and the *lexeme* (representing morphophonological form). The third component, the *articulator*, subsequently converts the speech plan into sounds.

References

Adamowicz, A. (1989). The role of anticipation in discourse: Text processing in simultaneous interpreting. *Polish Psychological Bulletin, 20,* 153–160.

Anderson, L. (1994). Simultaneous interpretation: Contextual and translational aspects. In S. Lambert & B. Moser-Mercer (Eds.), *Bridging the gap: Empirical research in simultaneous interpretation* (pp. 101–120). Amsterdam: Benjamins.

Arjona-Tseng, E. (1994). A psychometric approach to the selection of translation and interpreting students in Taiwan. In S. Lambert & B. Moser-Mercer (Eds.), *Bridging the gap: Empirical research in simultaneous interpretation* (pp. 69–86). Amsterdam: Benjamins.

Baddeley, A. (2000). The episodic buffer: A new component of working memory. *Trends in Cognitive Sciences, 4,* 417–423.

Baddeley, A. D., Lewis, V., & Vallar, G. (1984). Exploring the articulatory loop. *Quarterly Journal of Experimental Psychology, 36A,* 233–252.

Baddeley, A. D., & Logie, R. H. (1999). Working memory: The multiple-component model. In A. Miyake & P. Shah (Eds.), *Models of working memory: Mechanisms of active maintenance and executive control* (pp. 28–61). Cambridge, U.K.: Cambridge University Press.

Bajo, M. T. (2002, March). *Working memory in translation and language interpretation.* Paper presented at the Workshop on Processing and Storage of Linguistic Information in Bilinguals, Amsterdam.

Bajo, M. T., Padilla, F., & Padilla, P. (2000). Comprehension processes in simultaneous interpreting. In A. Chesterman, N. Gallardo San Salvador, & Y. Gambier (Eds.), *Translation in context* (pp. 127–142). Amsterdam: Benjamins.

Barik, H. C. (1973). Simultaneous interpretation: Temporal and quantitative data. *Language and Speech, 16,* 237–270.

Barik, H. C. (1975). Simultaneous interpretation: Qualitative and linguistic data. *Language and Speech, 18,* 272–297.

Barik, H. C. (1994). A description of the various types of omissions, additions and errors of translation encountered in simultaneous interpretation. In S. Lambert & B. Moser-Mercer (Eds.), *Bridging the gap: Empirical research in simultaneous interpretation* (pp. 121–137). Amsterdam: Benjamins.

Besien, V. (1999). Anticipation in simultaneous interpretation. *Meta, 14,* 250–259.

Chernov, G. V. (1994). Message redundancy and message anticipation in simultaneous interpretation. In S. Lambert & B. Moser-Mercer (Eds.), *Bridging the gap: Empirical research in simultaneous interpretation* (pp. 139–153). Amsterdam: Benjamins.

Chincotta, D., & Underwood, G. (1998). Simultaneous interpreters and the effect of concurrent articulation on immediate memory. *Interpreting, 3,* 1–20.

Christoffels, I. K. (2003). *Listening while talking: The retention of prose under articulatory suppression in relation to simultaneous interpreting.* Manuscript submitted for publication, University of Amsterdam, The Netherlands.

Christoffels, I. K. (2004). *Cognitive studies in simultaneous interpreting.* Unpublished doctoral dissertation, University of Amsterdam, The Netherlands.

Christoffels, I. K., & De Groot, A. M. B. (2004). Components of simultaneous interpreting: A comparison with shadowing and paraphrasing. *Bilingualism: Language and Cognition, 7,* 1–14.

Christoffels, I. K., De Groot, A. M. B., & Kroll, J. F. (2004). *Memory and language skills in simultaneous interpreting: Expertise and language proficiency.* Manuscript in preparation.

Christoffels, I. K., De Groot, A. M. B., & Waldorp, L. J. (2003). Basic skills in a complex task: A graphical model relating memory and lexical retrieval to simultaneous interpreting. *Bilingualism: Language and Cognition, 6,* 201–211.

Cokely, D. (1986). The effects of lag time on interpreters' errors. *Sign Language Studies, 53,* 341–375.

Colomé, À. (2001). Lexical activation in bilinguals' speech production: Language-specific or language-independent? *Journal of Memory and Language, 45*, 721–736.

Corina, D. P., & Vaid, J. (1994). Lateralization for shadowing words versus signs. In S. Lambert & B. Moser-Mercer (Eds.), *Bridging the gap: Empirical research in simultaneous interpretation* (pp. 237–248). Amsterdam: Benjamins.

Costa, A., Miozzo, M., & Caramazza, A. (1999). Lexical selection in bilinguals: Do words in the bilingual's two lexicons compete for selection? *Journal of Memory and Language, 41*, 365–397.

Daneman, M., & Carpenter, P. A. (1980). Individual differences in working memory and reading. *Journal of Verbal Learning and Verbal Behavior, 19*, 450–466.

Darò, V. (1994). Non-linguistic factors influencing simultaneous interpretation. In S. Lambert & B. Moser-Mercer (Eds.), *Bridging the gap: Empirical research in simultaneous interpretation* (pp. 249–269). Amsterdam: Benjamins.

Darò, V., & Fabbro, F. (1994). Verbal memory during simultaneous interpretation: Effects of phonological interference. *Applied Linguistics, 15*, 365–381.

Darò, V., Lambert, S., & Fabbro, F. (1996). Conscious monitoring of attention during simultaneous interpretation. *Interpreting, 1*, 101–124.

De Bot, K. (2000). Simultaneous interpreting as language production. In B. Englund Dimitrova & K. Hyltenstam (Eds.), *Language processing and simultaneous interpreting* (pp. 65–88). Amsterdam: Benjamins.

De Bot, K., & Schreuder, R. (1993). Word production and the bilingual lexicon. In R. Schreuder & B. Weltens (Eds.), *The bilingual lexicon* (pp. 191–214). Amsterdam: Benjamins.

De Groot, A. M. B. (1997). The cognitive study of translation and interpretation: Three approaches. In J. H. Danks, G. M. Shreve, S. B. Fountain, & M. K. McBeath (Eds.), *Cognitive processes in translation and interpreting* (pp. 25–56). Thousand Oaks, CA: Sage.

De Groot, A. M. B. (2000). A complex-skill approach to translation and interpreting. In S. Tirkkonen-Condit & R. Jääskeläinen (Eds.), *Tapping and mapping the processes of translation and interpreting* (pp. 53–68). Amsterdam: Benjamins.

De Groot, A. M. B. (2002). Lexical representation and lexical processing in the L2 user. In V. Cook (Ed.), *Portraits of the L2 user* (pp. 32–63). Clevedon, U.K.: Multilingual Matters.

De Groot, A. M. B., & Poot, R. (1997). Word translation at three levels of proficiency in a second language: The ubiquitous involvement of conceptual memory. *Language Learning, 47*, 215–264.

Dijkstra, A., & Van Heuven, W. J. B. (1998). The BIA model and bilingual word recognition. In J. Grainger & A. Jacobs (Eds.), *Localist connectionist approaches to human cognition* (pp. 189–225). Mahwah, NJ: Erlbaum.

Dijkstra, T., Van Jaarsveld, H., & Ten Brinke, S. (1998). Interlingual homograph recognition: Effects of task demands and language intermixing. *Bilingualism: Language and Cognition, 1*, 51–66.

Dillinger, M. (1994). Comprehension during interpreting: What do interpreters know that bilinguals don't? In S. Lambert & B. Moser-Mercer (Eds.), *Bridging the gap: Empirical research in simultaneous interpretation* (pp. 155–189). Amsterdam: Benjamins.

Fabbro, F. (2001). The bilingual brain: Cerebral representation of languages. *Brain and Language, 79*, 211–222.

Fabbro, F., & Darò, V. (1995). Delayed auditory feedback in polyglot simultaneous interpreters. *Brain and Language, 48*, 309–319.

Fabbro, F., & Gran, L. (1994). Neurological and neuropsychological aspects of polyglossia and simultaneous interpretation. In S. Lambert & B. Moser-Mercer (Eds.), *Bridging the gap: Empirical research in simultaneous interpretation* (pp. 273–317). Amsterdam: Benjamins.

Fabbro, F., & Gran, L. (1997). Neurolinguistic research in simultaneous interpretation. In Y. Gambier, D. Gile, & C. Taylor (Eds.), *Conference interpreting: Current trends in research* (pp. 9–27). Amsterdam: Benjamins.

Fabbro, F., Gran, L., Basso, G., & Bava, A. (1990). Cerebral lateralization in simultaneous interpretation. *Brain and Language, 39*, 69–89.

Fabbro, F., Gran, B., & Gran, L. (1991). Hemispheric specialization for semantic and syntactic components of language in simultaneous interpreters. *Brain and Language, 41*, 1–42.

Frauenfelder, U. H., & Schriefers, H. (1997). A psycholinguistic perspective on simultaneous interpretation. *Interpreting, 2*, 55–89.

Gathercole, S. E., & Baddeley, A. D. (1993). *Working memory and language*. Hove, U.K.: Erlbaum.

Gernsbacher, M. A., & Shlesinger, M. (1997). The proposed role of suppression in simultaneous interpretation. *Interpreting, 2*, 119–140.

Gerver, D. (1974a). The effect of noise on the performance of simultaneous interpreters: accuracy of performance. *Acta Psychologica, 38*, 159–167.

Gerver, D. (1974b). Simultaneous listening and speaking and the retention of prose. *Quarterly*

Journal of Experimental Psychology, 26, 337–341.

Gerver, D. (1976). Empirical studies of simultaneous interpretation: A review and a model. In R. W. Briskin (Ed.), *Translation: Applications and research* (pp. 165–207). New York: Gardner Press.

Gerver, D., Longley, P., Long, J., & Lambert, S. (1984). Selecting trainee conference interpreters: A preliminary study. *Journal of Occupational Psychology, 57,* 17–31.

Gile, D. (1991). Methodological aspects of interpretation (and translation) research. *Target, 3,* 153–174.

Gile, D. (1994). Methodological aspects of interpretation and translation research. In S. Lambert & B. Moser-Mercer (Eds.), *Bridging the gap: Empirical research in simultaneous interpretation* (pp. 39–56). Amsterdam: Benjamins.

Gile, D. (1995). *Basic concepts and models for interpreter and translator training.* Amsterdam: Benjamins.

Gile, D. (1997). Conference interpreting as a cognitive management problem. In J. H. Danks, G. M. Shreve, S. B. Fountain, & M. K. McBeath (Eds.), *Cognitive processes in translation and interpreting* (pp. 196–214). Thousand Oaks, CA: Sage.

Gile, D. (2000). Issues in interdisciplinary research into conference interpreting. In B. Englund Dimitrova & K. Hyltenstam (Eds.), *Language processing and simultaneous interpreting* (pp. 89–106). Amsterdam: Benjamins.

Goldman-Eisler, F. (1972). Segmentation of input in simultaneous translation. *Journal of Psycholinguistic Research, 1,* 127–140.

Goldman-Eisler, F. (1980). Psychological mechanisms of speech production as studied through the analysis of simultaneous translations. In B. Butterworth (Ed.), *Language production. Vol. 1: Speech and talk* (pp. 143–153). London: Academic Press.

Green, A., Sweda-Nicholson, N., Vaid, J., White, N., & Steiner, R. (1990). Hemispheric involvement in shadowing vs. interpretation: A time-sharing study of simultaneous interpreters with matched bilingual and monolingual controls. *Brain and Language, 39,* 107–133.

Green, D. W. (1986). Control, activation, and resource: A framework and a model for the control of speech in bilinguals. *Brain and Language, 27,* 210–223.

Green, D. W. (1998). Mental control of the bilingual lexico-semantic system. *Bilingualism, Language and Cognition, 1,* 67–81.

Grosjean, F. (1997). The bilingual individual. *Interpreting, 2,* 163–187.

Harley, T. A. (2001). *The psychology of language: From data to theory* (2nd ed.). Hove, U.K.: Psychology Press.

Harris, B., & Sherwood, B. (1978). Translating as an innate skill. In D. Gerver & H. W. Sinaiko (Eds.), *Language interpretation and communication* (pp. 155–170). New York: Plenum Press.

Hermans, D., Bongaerts, T., De Bot, K., & Schreuder, R. (1998). Producing words in a foreign language: Can speakers prevent interference from their first language? *Bilingualism: Language and Cognition, 1,* 213–229.

Hoffman, R. R. (1997). The cognitive psychology of expertise and the domain of interpreting. *Interpreting, 2,* 189–230.

Hyönä, J., Tommola, J., & Alaja, A.-M. (1995). Pupil dilation as a measure of processing load in simultaneous interpretation and other language tasks. *Quarterly Journal of Experimental Psychology, 48A,* 598–612.

Isham, W. P. (1994). Memory for sentence form after simultaneous interpretation: Evidence both for and against deverbalization. In S. Lambert & B. Moser-Mercer (Eds.), *Bridging the gap: Empirical research in simultaneous interpretation* (pp. 191–211). Amsterdam: Benjamins.

Isham, W. P. (2000). Phonological interference in interpreters of spoken-languages: An issue of storage or process? In B. Englund Dimitrova & K. Hyltenstam (Eds.), *Language processing and simultaneous interpreting* (pp. 133–149). Amsterdam: Benjamins.

Isham, W. P., & Lane, H. (1994). A common conceptual code in bilinguals: Evidence from simultaneous interpreting. *Sign Language Studies, 85,* 291–316.

Jared, D., & Kroll, J. F. (2001). Do bilinguals activate phonological representations in one or both of their languages when naming words. *Journal of Memory and Language, 44,* 2–31.

Jesse, A., Vrignaud, N., Cohen, M., & Massaro, D. W. (2001). The processing of information from multiple sources in simultaneous interpreting. *Interpreting, 5,* 95–115.

Kade, O., & Claus, C. (1971). Some methodological aspects of simultaneous interpreting. *Babel, 17,* 12–16.

Kempen, G. (1999). *Human grammatical coding.* Unpublished manuscript, Leiden University, The Netherlands.

Klonowicz, T. (1990). A psychophysiological assessment of simultaneous interpreting: The interaction of individual differences and mental workload. *Polish Psychological Bulletin, 21,* 37–48.

Klonowicz, T. (1994). Putting one's heart into simultaneous interpretation. In S. Lambert &

B. Moser-Mercer (Eds.), *Bridging the gap: Empirical research in simultaneous interpretation* (pp. 213–224). Amsterdam: Benjamins.

Kroll, J. F., & De Groot, A. M. B. (1997). Lexical and conceptual memory in the bilingual: Mapping form to meaning in two languages. In A. M. B. de Groot & J. F. Kroll (Eds.), *Tutorials in bilingualism* (pp. 169–199). Mahwah, NJ: Erlbaum.

Kroll, J. F., & Dijkstra, A. (2002). The bilingual lexicon. In R. Kaplan (Ed.), *Handbook of applied linguistics* (pp. 301–321). New York: Oxford University Press.

Kroll, J. F., Michael, E., Tokowicz, N., & Dufour, R. (2002). The development of lexical fluency in a second language. *Second Language Research, 18*, 137–171.

Kroll, J. F., & Stewart, E. (1994). Category interference in translation and picture naming: Evidence for asymmetric connections between bilingual memory representations. *Journal of Memory and Language, 33*, 149–174.

La Heij, W., Hooglander, A., Kerling, R., & Van der Velden, E. (1996). Nonverbal context effects in forward and backward word translation: Evidence for concept mediation. *Journal of Memory and Language, 35*, 648–665.

Lambert, S. (1991). Aptitude testing for simultaneous interpretation at the University of Ottawa. *Méta, 36*, 586–594.

Lambert, S. (1992). Shadowing. *Méta, 37*, 263–273.

Levelt, W. J. M. (1989). *Speaking: From intention to articulation*. Cambridge, MA: MIT Press.

Levelt, W. J. M., Roelofs, A., & Meyer, A. S. (1999). A theory of lexical access in speech production. *Behavioural and Brain Sciences, 22*, 1–75.

Liberman, A. M., & Mattingly, I. G. (1985). The motor theory of speech perception revised. *Cognition, 74*, 431–461.

Lonsdale, D. (1997). Modeling cognition in SI: Methodological issues. *Interpreting, 2*, 91–117.

MacWhinney, B. (1997). Simultaneous interpretation and the competition model. In J. H. Danks, G. M. Shreve, S. B. Fountain, & M. K. McBeath (Eds.), *Cognitive processes in translation and interpreting* (pp. 215–232). Thousand Oaks, CA: Sage.

Malakoff, M., & Hakuta, K. (1991). Translation skill and metalinguistic awareness in bilinguals. In E. Bialystok (Ed.), *Language processing and language awareness* (pp. 141–166). New York: Oxford University Press.

Malakoff, M. E. (1992). Translation ability: A natural bilingual and metalinguistic skill. In R. J. Harris (Ed.), *Cognitive processing in bilinguals* (pp. 515–529). Amsterdam: North Holland.

Massaro, D. W., & Shlesinger, M. (1997). Information processing and a computational approach to the study of simultaneous interpretation. *Interpreting, 2*, 13–53.

McDonald, J. L., & Carpenter, P. A. (1981). Simultaneous translation: Idiom interpretation and parsing heuristics. *Journal of Verbal Learning and Verbal Behaviour, 20*, 231–247.

Meuter, R. F. I., & Allport, A. (1999). Bilingual language switching in naming: Asymmetrical costs of language selection. *Journal of Memory and Language, 40*, 25–40.

Moser, B. (1978). Simultaneous interpretation: A hypothetical model and its practical application. In D. Gerver & H. W. Sinaiko (Eds.), *Language Interpretation and Communication* (pp. 353–368). New York: Plenum.

Moser-Mercer, B. (1994). Aptitude testing for conference interpreting: Why, when and how. In S. Lambert & B. Moser-Mercer (Eds.), *Bridging the gap: Empirical research in simultaneous interpretation* (pp. 57–68). Amsterdam: Benjamins.

Moser-Mercer, B. (1995). Sight translation and human information processing. In A. Neubert & G. M. Shreve (Eds.), *Basic issues in translation studies: Proceedings of the Fifth International Conference* (Vol. 2, pp. 159–166). Kent, OH: Kent State University.

Moser-Mercer, B. (1997). Beyond curiosity: Can interpreting research meet the challenge? In J. H. Danks, G. M. Shreve, S. B. Fountain, & M. K. McBeath (Eds.), *Cognitive processes in translation and interpreting* (pp. 176–195). Thousand Oaks, CA: Sage.

Moser-Mercer, B., Frauenfelder, U. H., Casado, B., & Künzli, A. (2000). Searching to define expertise in interpreting. In B. Englund Dimitrova & K. Hyltenstam (Eds.), *Language processing and simultaneous interpreting* (pp. 107–131). Amsterdam: Benjamins.

Moser-Mercer, B., Künzli, A., & Korac, M. (1998). Prolonged turns in interpreting: Effect on quality, physiological and psychological stress (pilot study). *Interpreting, 3*, 47–64.

Moser-Mercer, B., Lambert, S., Darò, V., & Williams, D. (1997). Skill components in simultaneous interpreting. In Y. Gambier, D. Gile, & C. Taylor (Eds.), *Conference interpreting: Current trends in research* (pp. 133–148). Amsterdam: Benjamins.

Neubert, A. (1997). Postulates for a theory of translation. In J. H. Danks, G. M. Shreve, S. B. Fountain, & M. K. McBeath (Eds.), *Cognitive processes in translation and interpreting* (pp. 1–24). Thousand Oaks, CA: Sage.

Padilla, P., Bajo, M. T., Cañas, J. J., & Padilla, F. (1995). Cognitive processes of memory in simultaneous interpretation. In J. Tommola

(Ed.), *Topics in interpreting research* (pp. 61–72). Turku, Finland: University of Turku.

Padilla, P., & Martin, A. (1992). Similarities and differences between interpreting and translation: Implications for teaching. In C. Dollerup & A. Loddegaard (Eds.), *Teaching translation and interpreting: Training, talent and experience* (pp. 195–204). Amsterdam: Benjamins.

Paradis, M. (1994). Toward a neurolinguistic theory of simultaneous translation: The framework. *International Journal of Psycholinguistics, 10*, 319–335.

Paradis, M. (1997). The cognitive neuropsychology of bilingualism. In A. M. B. de Groot & J. F. Kroll (Eds.), *Tutorials in bilingualism* (pp. 331–354). Mahwah, NJ: Erlbaum.

Paradis, M. (2000). Prerequisites to a study of neurolinguistic processes involved in simultaneous interpreting: A synopsis. In B. Englund Dimitrova & K. Hyltenstam (Eds.), *Language processing and simultaneous interpreting* (pp. 17–24). Amsterdam: Benjamins.

Pavlenko, A. (1999). New approaches to concepts in bilingual memory. *Bilingualism: Language and Cognition, 2*, 209–230.

Potter, M. C., So, K. F., Von Eckardt, B., & Feldman, L. B. (1984). Lexical and contextual representation in beginning and more proficient bilinguals. *Journal of Verbal Learning and Verbal Behavior, 23*, 23–28.

Poulisse, N. (1997). Language production in bilinguals. In A. M. B. de Groot & J. F. Kroll (Eds.), *Tutorials in bilingualism* (pp. 201–224). Mahwah, NJ: Erlbaum.

Price, C. J., Green, D. W., & Von Studnitz, R. (1999). A functional imaging study of translation and language switching. *Brain, 122*, 2221–2235.

Rinne, J. O., Tommola, J., Laine, M., Krause, B. J., Schmidt, D., Kaasinen, V., et al. (2000). The translating brain: Cerebral activation patterns during simultaneous interpreting. *Neuroscience Letters, 294*, 85–88.

Schweda-Nicholson, N. (1987). Linguistic and extralinguistic aspects of simultaneous interpretation. *Applied Linguistics, 8*, 194–205.

Seleskovitch, D. (1976). Interpretation: A psychological approach to translating. In R. W. Brislin (Ed.), *Translation: Application and research* (pp. 92–116). New York: Gardner.

Setton, R. (1999). *Simultaneous interpretation: A cognitive pragmatic analysis.* Amsterdam: Benjamins.

Shlesinger, M. (2000a). Interpreting as a cognitive process: How can we know what really happens? In S. Tirkkonen-Condit & R. Jääskeläinen (Eds.), *Tapping and mapping the processes of translation and interpreting* (pp. 4–15). Amsterdam: Benjamins.

Shlesinger, M. (2000b). *Strategic allocation of working memory and other attentional resources in simultaneous interpreting.* Unpublished doctoral dissertation, Bar Ilan University, Ramat Gan, Israel.

Shreve, G. M., & Diamond, B. J. (1997). Cognitive processes in translation and interpreting: Critical issues. In J. H. Danks, G. M. Shreve, S. B. Fountain, & M. K. McBeath (Eds.), *Cognitive processes in translation and interpreting* (pp. 233–251). Thousand Oaks, CA: Sage.

Tijus, C. A. (1997). Understanding for interpreting, interpreting for understanding. In Y. Gambier, D. Gile, & C. Taylor (Eds.), *Conference interpreting: Current trends in research* (pp. 29–48). Amsterdam: Benjamins.

Treisman, A. M. (1965). The effects of redundancy and familiarity on translating and repeating back a foreign and a native language. *British Journal of Psychology, 56*, 369–379.

Van Hell, J. G. (1998). *Cross-language processing and bilingual memory organization.* Unpublished doctoral dissertation, University of Amsterdam, The Netherlands.

Van Heuven, W. J. B., Dijkstra, T., & Grainger, J. (1998). Orthographic neighborhood effects in bilingual word recognition. *Journal of Memory and Language, 39*, 458–483.

Zeier, H. (1997). Psychophysiological stress research. *Interpreting, 2*, 231–249.

Rachel Hull
Jyotsna Vaid

23

Clearing the Cobwebs From the Study of the Bilingual Brain
Converging Evidence From Laterality and Electrophysiological Research

ABSTRACT   Investigations of neuropsychological functioning in multiple language users offer much promise in answering questions originating from cognitive as well as biological approaches to language. These include questions about the neural concomitants of bilingual lexical functioning, age of onset of bilingualism, degree of proficiency, and degree of overlap in language structure. There is by now a sizable body of experimental literature on the bilingual brain, including studies that have employed laterality procedures, electrophysiological measures, and hemodynamic measures. To date, few systematic attempts have been made to integrate findings from these different sources of evidence. This chapter summarizes findings from a meta-analysis of laterality studies that compared bilinguals with monolinguals, and the chapter presents converging evidence drawn from recent electrophysiological studies of bilinguals.

From early accounts of selective language loss and recovery in polyglot aphasia to recent laterality, electrophysiological, and functional neuroimaging studies of brain-intact bilinguals, questions inspired by the "bilingual brain" (Albert & Obler, 1978; Goral, Levy, & Obler, 2002) have fascinated researchers and theorists for over a century. The subject has engaged not only those whose main focus has been bilingualism, but also those for whom bilingualism has provided a research tool for probing deeper questions about the nature of language and of brain functional organization. Questions posed by research with bi- and multilinguals extend the scope of inquiry beyond monolingualism and get at the core of what the human capacity for language might be (Genesee, 2003).

Some of the questions that have been examined to date include whether the cortical substrate for language (particularly the role of the right hemisphere [RH]) as observed in single-language users is the same for individuals who acquired two (or more) languages simultaneously (Vaid & Genesee, 1980) and whether cerebral representation of a later-acquired language differs from that of one acquired earlier or from one that is of a lesser proficiency (Ullman, 2001). In contrast to the variables of age of onset of bilingualism (e.g., pre- or postpuberty) and the extent of mastery attained in the two languages at the time of testing, less-frequently studied context variables include the manner in which each language was acquired (formal vs. informal) and the predominant mode of bilingual interaction (i.e., involving single-language use or frequent switching between languages; see Grosjean, 2000).

Other research has focused on language structure variables, seeking to determine whether cerebral representation of language (in bilinguals and monolinguals alike) is influenced by the particular computational requirements of such language-specific characteristics as the nature of the writing system (e.g., Liu & Perfetti, 2003; Nakada, Fujii, & Kwee, 2001) or the phonemic versus nonphonemic status of tone in the language (e.g., Klein, Zatorre, Milner, & Zhao, 2001).

For linguists and psycholinguists interested in issues of how two (or more) languages are organized, accessed, and produced, the neuropsychological study of the brain offers an additional level at which to test, and eventually perhaps to constrain, cognitive models of bilingual lexical memory or language processing (e.g., Green, 1998; Kroll & Dijkstra, 2002). For example, neurobehavioral investigations could be used to address current debates about whether words in the bilingual's languages are accessed selectively or nonselectively.

For cognitive neuroscientists, bilingualism is of interest insofar as it allows for a study of the influence of early experience on brain plasticity for language. In contrast to monolinguals, who do not show much variation in age of first exposure to language or in language mastery, bilinguals differ considerably on these dimensions and thereby offer cognitive neuroscientists a way of studying neural correlates of early versus delayed exposure to language and degree of language competence attained. In short, the study of bilinguals allows for a test of the neural basis, if any, of the notion of a critical or sensitive period for language acquisition (Johnson & Newport, 1989; Newport, Bavelier, & Neville, 2001). Studies of the effects of early sensory experience (e.g., Burton, Snyder, Conturo, Akbudak, Ollinger, & Raichle, 2002; Neville, Coffey, Lawson, Fischer, Emmorey, & Bellugi, 1997) have shown variability in the degree of brain plasticity for different functions. It may be reasonable to expect variations in the degree of plasticity for different language functions as well (Newport et al., 2001).

Clinical Sources of Evidence

Our current understanding of neural bases of language functioning in bilinguals is based on accumulated evidence and hypotheses derived from a variety of sources, clinical and normative. Clinical sources are largely in the form of case reports of language loss or recovery in bilingual (or polyglot) aphasics following unilateral brain injury (see Fabbro, 2001; Green & Price, 2001). Paradis (2001) documented a variety of patterns of language recovery or impairment, including parallel and nonparallel patterns. However, as the vast majority of the early clinical literature and a good proportion of even recent studies consisted of single or selected cases rather than unselected group samples, the actual incidence of parallel versus nonparallel patterns of language impairment or recovery cannot be reliably determined because of possible sampling bias, that is, the overinclusion of

atypical cases that were included precisely because they were unusual.

A similar problem clouds the interpretation of another aspect of the clinical evidence, namely, crossed aphasia, which has a direct bearing on the question of whether bi- or multilingualism alters the canonical pattern of left hemispheric (LH) dominance for language. Although some researchers have argued for a greater role for the RH in bilingual language functioning relative to that in monolinguals, primarily on the basis of a larger incidence of crossed aphasia among polyglots relative to the low estimate observed in monolinguals, here again the overinclusion of possibly unrepresentative cases may have contributed to this effect. There do exist a few recent group studies of unselected cases; however, these have yielded mixed results with respect to the question of a higher incidence of crossed aphasia in polyglots versus single-language users (see Vaid, 2002, for further discussion of this issue).

Quite apart from the problem of sampling bias, clinical studies also suffer from extreme variability in how the patients' languages were assessed postmorbidly (and they typically have precluded premorbid assessment). Although the work of Michel Paradis and his associates in particular has sought to ameliorate this situation through the use of an extensive array of standardized measures across a variety of language pairs, there still remains a paucity of comparative observations using these standardized measures.

Finally, what is particularly problematic in interpreting studies derived from clinical populations is the issue of compensatory function: Whenever there is injury to the brain, there is the possibility of subsequent reorganization of brain function. Thus, even if clinical data were to point reliably to greater RH participation in (certain subgroups of) bilinguals, it would be difficult to disentangle postmorbid reorganization of brain functions from the situation characterizing brain functioning prior to the brain injury. Ultimately, to fully understand language organization in the healthy brain, studies involving brain-intact individuals must be considered.

Experimental Sources of Evidence

There are, in fact, quite a number of studies of language organization in brain-intact bilinguals. These may be classified into three types: studies involving lateralized presentation of visual or auditory input, studies involving event-related potential (ERP) recordings from LH and RHs during language tasks, and those involving functional imaging using hemodynamic measures (see also Kochunov et al., 2003, for an anatomic study of brain shape differences between bilingual groups). Although laterality studies are the most numerous, electrophysiological and imaging studies of bilinguals are on the rise.

In terms of the issues they have addressed, neuroimaging studies with bilinguals have largely focused on whether there are overlapping or distinct cortical (or, in some cases, subcortical) regions activated during first language (L1) versus second language (L2) processing or during the processing of a proficient versus a less-proficient language (see Abutalebi, Cappa, & Perani, chapter 24, this volume, for a review). Evidence on this question is mixed, with some studies suggesting an overlapping representation and others a distinct representation, particularly in less-fluent bilinguals. Consequently, only tentative conclusions about the nature of individual differences in bilingual cortical activation patterns may be drawn from the evidence to date, especially given that very few of the studies actually compared different bilingual subgroups, such as proficient versus nonproficient users of a given language.

Furthermore, only a handful of the imaging studies have addressed the question of whether and how the two languages of bilinguals may differ at the interhemispheric level. Indeed, of the 40-plus bilingual imaging studies that have appeared, we were able to identify only 6 that specifically measured and reported quantitative data regarding functional asymmetry of the bilinguals' languages. We summarize these briefly in the section Electrophysiology and Imaging Research With Bilinguals.

Researchers using imaging technologies often make an implicit (and sometimes explicit) claim that imaging as a source of evidence about neural functioning is somehow more direct and informative than other sources because imaging captures the workings of the brain in vivo. This claim is accompanied by a tendency on the part of some neuroimaging researchers, as well as others who cite imaging findings, to discredit and dismiss other sources of evidence, such as the bilingual aphasia literature or the behavioral laterality literature, as unreliable, indirect, and ultimately uninformative.[1] It should be pointed out, however, that neuroimaging studies of language in general, and of bilingual language processing in particular, have

themselves been subjected to criticism on a number of methodological and interpretive grounds (see Paradis, 1999; Vaid & Hull, 2002, for further discussion).

Toward Convergence

We suggest that, instead of dismissing entire bodies of literature, a more fruitful approach would be one that recognizes that each methodological perspective has something to offer—even as it may have specific limitations—and that therefore each body of literature should be given due consideration. Specifically, we wish to argue that the behavioral laterality literature, rather than being viewed as unreliable, may be a particularly informative source of evidence and should also be acknowledged for its historical and heuristic contribution to theorizing about brain/language relationships.

As the earliest experimental source of evidence on brain functioning in brain-intact individuals, laterality studies with bilinguals provided the first empirical challenge to the view that the LH is always dominant for language. This body of work also provided the earliest hints that the RH may contribute to language processing in bilinguals to a greater degree than had previously been considered. There has been a resurgence of interest within mainstream cognitive neuroscience research (by which is usually implicitly meant research on monolinguals) on the RH's contribution to language processing (e.g., Chiarello, 2003; Federmeier & Kutas, 1999). It would be appropriate to consider how this work interfaces with what has already been studied with bilinguals in this regard.

We feel that revisiting the bilingual laterality literature would be instructive on several counts. First, it would serve to place neurobehavioral investigations of language processing and the brain in a historical context. Indeed, what is sometimes forgotten is that hypotheses about proficiency or age-related effects on bilingual neural organization discussed in current electrophysiological and neuroimaging studies have their intellectual roots in hypotheses initially formulated and tested in a behavioral laterality context (e.g., Vaid & Genesee, 1980). Second, an examination of bilingual laterality studies would serve as a cautionary reminder of the methodological and interpretive challenges that confront any empirical investigation of individual differences in brain functioning. Third, and most important, such an examination would make it possible for converging findings to be uncovered across different methods or research techniques.

To date, there has been no systematic attempt to seek convergence between laterality findings from behavioral methodologies and those from neuro-behavioral ones. This, then, was one aim of the present overview. To draw connections between the behavioral laterality literature and other sources of normative evidence, it is necessary to establish just what the laterality literature has found. To this end, an additional aim was to present the outcome of a meta-analytic review of bilingual laterality studies.

In what follows, we first discuss the behavioral literature at large and suggest why it has resisted summary. We next present five hypotheses that have been examined in the bilingual laterality literature. Then, we briefly describe a meta-analytic review of studies within this literature in which bilinguals and monolinguals were directly compared. Next, we consider how the findings from the meta-analysis of individual differences in language lateralization fit with analogous findings from recent event-related brain potential studies of bilinguals. We conclude with general remarks about the importance of converging evidence and an indication of some variables that remain to be teased apart in future experimental research on brain lateralization of language in bilinguals.

Bilingual Laterality Studies: An Overview

The sheer size and complexity of the bilingual laterality literature have hindered previous attempts to render the findings coherent. Although modest in comparison to the number of laterality studies conducted with monolinguals, the total number of laterality studies with bilinguals of which we are aware is currently around 150. The studies differ from each other in a number of respects: languages or language pairings of the bilingual participants, language acquisition histories, contexts of language use, testing paradigms, response measures, language components studied, and tasks used. For example, dichotic listening studies typically use word-level stimuli and measure response accuracy, whereas visual half-field studies use words, word pairs, or sentences and measure response latency to speeded judgments on the basis of visual, phonetic, semantic, or syntactic dimensions of the stimuli. Dual-task studies in turn measure interference in motoric performance (finger tapping) while par-

ticipants concurrently perform a variety of verbal comprehension or production tasks.

The behavioral laterality studies also vary in their degree of methodological rigor. Many of the early studies did not systematically screen bilinguals on proficiency or other relevant parameters (e.g., L2 acquisition age). Others did not match stimuli across the two languages in terms of frequency, length, or other germane criteria. Still others did not use appropriate statistical analyses (see Obler, Zatorre, Galloway, & Vaid, 1982). In the face of these sources of variability, the challenge for students of this (as any experimental) literature has been to attend carefully to methodological aspects of individual studies to evaluate their internal validity.

In light of the methodological differences in the literature, it is perhaps not surprising that studies have also differed in their outcomes, with some reporting greater RH involvement in one or both languages of bilinguals as compared to that in monolinguals; others report no differences, and still others report greater LH involvement. This multiplicity of findings has prompted some scholars to conclude that the bilingual laterality literature is contradictory and hence not worthy of serious attention (Paradis, 2003; Sussman & Simon, 1988). Nevertheless, others have viewed the complexity of this literature as an inevitable reflection of the multifaceted nature of the topic and various approaches to it (Vaid, 2002).

Indeed, several integrative reviews (e.g., Ullman, 2001; Vaid, 1983, 2002; Zatorre, 1989) have tried to make some sense of the literature and relate bilingual laterality findings to more general theoretical formulations about language and about the brain. Although many of these reviews sought to be comprehensive and thorough, qualitative reviews are open to the possibility of bias in terms of which studies get included and how they are discussed. To get a more accurate picture, all relevant studies should be considered, and the effects of possible variables moderating the outcomes should be systematically assessed.

What we are advocating here is a quantitative rather than a narrative review. Meta-analysis, which provides a quantitative assessment of a body of work, would seem to be particularly useful in answering whether or how bilingualism affects brain lateralization for language. The results of a meta-analytic investigation of laterality studies comparing bilinguals with monolinguals could in turn inform questions of broader theoretical interest in the cerebral lateralization literature at large, that is, the role played by the RH in mediating linguistic function and the extent of variation in cerebral lateralization for language in neurologically healthy monolingual participants. In other words, meta-analysis offers an opportunity not only to summarize patterns of language lateralization in bilinguals, but also to arrive at a clearer understanding of language lateralization in monolinguals. Before discussing the results from a meta-analysis of lateralization in bilinguals versus monolinguals (Hull & Vaid, 2003b), we review existing hypotheses about language lateralization in bilinguals.

Hypotheses About Language Lateralization in Bilinguals

Although it is generally accepted that the left cerebral hemisphere is the dominant hemisphere for language, and particularly for grammar, a number of studies have questioned the degree to which this pattern is altered by gender, handedness, and various experiential factors, such as bilinguality. Indeed, several different hypotheses have been proposed with respect to how bilingualism, as a source of differences in language experience, might influence brain functioning (see Genesee, 1982; Vaid & Hall, 1991). Some of these hypotheses developed in response to suggestions first made by early neurologists reporting cases of selective loss and recovery of language in polyglots; others developed from psychological investigations of individual differences in cognitive functioning in relation to language acquisition history.

In the following list, the first two hypotheses focus on comparisons between bilinguals and monolinguals and the remainder address differences between bilingual subgroups.

1. *The L2 hypothesis.* This hypothesis predicts that the RH is more involved in the processing of the L2 relative to the L1 of bilinguals. As such, when comparing bilinguals (particularly on the L2) with monolinguals, more LH involvement in the latter relative to the former may be expected.
2. *Balanced bilingual hypothesis.* This hypothesis posits that the incidence of nativelike proficiency in two (or more) languages alters hemispheric involvement such that RH activation for both languages of fluent bilinguals is predicted to be greater than that of monolinguals.
3. *Stage of L2 acquisition hypothesis.* The stage of L2 acquisition hypothesis (Obler, 1981) predicts that initial stages of L2 (and perhaps also L1) acquisition are associated with greater RH involvement than are later stages of mastery in the language. Thus, the hypothesis predicts more RH involvement among beginning learners of an L2 relative to advanced learners, with fluent bilinguals presumably showing a shift to growing LH involvement.
4. *Manner of L2 acquisition hypothesis.* The manner of L2 acquisition hypothesis (see Galloway & Krashen, 1980) was initially proposed as an extension of the stage hypothesis as it applies mainly to late L2 acquisition. According to the manner hypothesis, if the L2 was acquired primarily in an informal manner (e.g., in a natural context and with emphasis on actual communication and daily interaction with other interlocutors), there should be greater RH involvement compared to an L2 acquired in a formal setting. In the latter case, a predominant emphasis on the rules of grammar or spelling or language usage restricted to visual rather than combined visual and auditory modes should be associated with greater LH involvement. Thus, the manner hypothesis leads to the interesting prediction that, if the mode of L2 acquisition and use is predominantly a formal one, there may be greater LH involvement in the L2 than in the L1.
5. *Age of L2 acquisition hypothesis.* The age of L2 acquisition hypothesis (Genesee, Hamers, Lambert, Mononen, Seitz, & Starck, 1978) posits that the earlier the acquisition of an L2 relative to the L1, the closer the pattern of lateralization should be for the two languages. Thus, early bilinguals should show no differential lateralization patterns in their two languages, whereas late bilinguals should show more discrepancy. In the original framing of the hypothesis (Vaid & Genesee, 1980), it was assumed that early bilinguals would behave like monolinguals (both groups showing LH dominance), whereas late bilinguals would show a different pattern from that of early bilinguals, the precise nature of which would in turn reflect other variables such as proficiency and manner of acquisition. Given that neither the cerebral cortex nor the corpus callosum are

fully developed at least through the age of 5 years (see Joseph, 1982), the age hypothesis allows for the possibility that languages acquired after the brain is relatively mature may be functionally organized in distinct ways from those learned earlier.

Toward a Demystification of the Laterality Literature: Our Meta-analysis

An early meta-analysis of the bilingual laterality literature (Vaid & Hall, 1991) examined a total of 59 studies that had appeared as of December 1989. All five hypotheses summarized above were tested. The findings showed support for the existence of differences in lateralization between monolinguals and certain bilingual subgroups. One particularly salient outcome of the Vaid and Hall (1991) meta-analysis was that, contrary to the expectation that hemispheric involvement in early bilinguals would resemble that of monolinguals, early bilinguals instead showed bilateral involvement for both languages and significantly differed in lateralization from late bilinguals. Trends were also observed for differential laterality related to the experimental paradigm employed (e.g., tachistoscopic viewing showed less left lateralization than dichotic listening); other trends failed to reach significance owing, perhaps, to the small cell sizes in many cases. Finally, although there were hints of task-related effects, many of the studies had not been designed to consider task-related processing effects, thus task was not coded as a moderator variable in the Vaid and Hall meta-analysis.

Our meta-analysis of the bilingual laterality literature (Hull & Vaid, 2003b) included studies that appeared up to December 2001. This meta-analysis specifically focused on studies assessing lateralization in bilinguals versus monolinguals. In addition, unlike the previous meta-analysis, our meta-analysis kept the languages spoken by monolinguals and bilinguals in any given study constant; thus, bilinguals' data on their L1 only (in the case of late bilinguals and on both languages in the case of early bilinguals) was compared with that of monolingual speakers of that language. Finally, we coded for the effects of task-related processing demands in hemispheric functioning.

As noted, our meta-analysis (Hull & Vaid, 2003b) included only those behavioral language lateralization studies of brain-intact individuals that provided quantitative data concerning direct comparisons of monolinguals and bilinguals on the *same L1*. As a result, no neuroimaging studies qualified for this meta-analysis. Excluded as well were all studies that failed to use identical lateralized presentation conditions for bilinguals and monolinguals (e.g., stimulus exposure differed between groups). The stringent criteria resulted in a total of 23 studies, all of which directly compared linguistic function in monolinguals with that of bilinguals, and many also evaluated hemispheric specialization for language within bilingual subgroups.

The primary goal of our meta-analysis (Hull & Vaid, 2003b) was to establish whether and under what experimental conditions systematic differences might exist in the lateralization of language between monolinguals and bilinguals. Thus, the results of the meta-analysis have direct bearing on the balanced bilingual and the L2 hypotheses. An additional goal was to determine, for those studies in the sample for which within-bilingual comparisons were also possible, whether L2 fluency or age of L2 acquisition moderated language lateralization. The outcomes of the analysis thus have bearing on the age and the stage hypotheses as well.[2] (It should be remembered that data from the late bilinguals in this meta-analysis were limited to performance in the L1 only.)

The main experimental variable in our meta-analysis (Hull & Vaid, 2003b) was that of group, that is, bilinguals versus monolinguals. This variable was operationalized as follows: *bilinguals*, persons who were able to communicate in at least two languages (regardless of fluency level); *monolinguals*, persons with very little or no exposure to a language other than the native one. In addition, bilinguals were classified according to age of onset of L2 exposure and by L2 proficiency. *Early bilinguals* were defined as bilinguals whose exposure to the L2 occurred by age 6 years; *late bilinguals* were defined as bilinguals whose exposure to the L2 occurred after age 6 years.

In addition to the moderator variables of L2 acquisition age and L2 fluency, three other moderator variables were examined (Hull & Vaid, 2003b): participant gender, testing paradigm, and task demands. Criteria for *task demands* were difficult to establish, but what we finally selected were the following: *visual* demands, when the verbal material was presented to visual half-fields or visual aspects of the verbal stimuli were highlighted (e.g., orthographic judgments); *auditory*, when the verbal material was typically presented dichotically or auditory aspects of the stimuli were highlighted (e.g., rhyme judgments); *semantic*, when participants were to process the meaning of the verbal input (e.g., synonym or semantic category judgments, paraphrasing, or translation); *surface*, which referred to tasks tapping syntactic properties of words and sentences (e.g., part of speech judgments); and *global*, which referred to general verbal tasks that did not isolate an individual sensory modality or language component (e.g., reading/listening to a story).

Meta-analytic Outcomes

The main outcomes of this meta-analysis were as follows (for further details, see Hull & Vaid, 2003b):

- Monolinguals as a group were LH dominant overall when collapsed across paradigms and tasks. However, monolinguals showed bilateral involvement on tachistoscopic viewing paradigms and bilateral involvement on tasks with visual demands.[3]
- Early bilinguals showed bilateral activation (all were fluent bilinguals).
- Late fluent bilinguals showed LH dominance overall and did not differ from monolinguals.
- Collapsed across acquisition age, bilinguals showed bilateral involvement for tachistoscopic viewing, dichotic listening, and verbal-manual interference testing paradigms; they showed LH dominance for tasks with auditory demands and bilateral involvement for tasks with visual and global demands.
- Bilingual and monolingual women did not differ; they were relatively more LH lateralized than bilingual men, but less LH lateralized than monolingual men.
- Bilingual men showed bilateral hemispheric involvement; monolingual men showed LH dominance. This group difference was significant.

Discussion of Meta-analytic Outcomes

Overall, our findings (Hull and Vaid, 2003b) clearly showed that monolinguals and (early) bilinguals do indeed differ in hemispheric specialization for the processing of the native language. Furthermore, a difference was obtained between early and late bilinguals. Specifically, early bilinguals showed evidence for bilateral hemispheric involvement compared to monolinguals and late bilinguals, who showed LH dominance overall. The consistency of differential lateralization in language users with distinct language acquisition histories lends support to the notion of some form of a "sensitive period" for language acquisition. What is not clear is whether this sensitive period reflects strictly neurological (e.g., brain maturational) parameters or other parameters (e.g., situational or cognitive changes in language experience and use over a lifetime).

In addition to the findings with respect to language acquisition history, interesting interactions of gender with group were also revealed. In particular, bilaterality was more pronounced in bilingual than in monolingual men, but despite similar trends for women, differences in laterality failed to reach significance between monolingual and bilingual women. There may be speculation as to why women do not show marked differences in lateralization as a function of the number of languages learned. Is it because women simply make greater use of both hemispheres during language tasks in general? This possibility was suggested by an additional finding in the meta-analysis: Monolingual and bilingual women showed greater RH involvement than monolingual and bilingual men during dichotic listening tasks. Another possibility is that women as a group are more sensitive to emotional or pragmatic aspects of language than are men (see Voyer, 1996) and thus may recruit the RH more than men when processing spoken language. Both these possibilities need to be explored more directly in future research.

Our meta-analytic findings (Hull & Vaid, 2003b) offer a descriptive summary of language lateralization effects across a variety of linguistic tasks and language acquisition histories and as such can be used to inform models of the functional organization of language in the bilingual brain and to suggest areas for further research in bilingualism. For example, given that early bilinguals evidenced greater RH involvement during language processing than either late bilinguals or monolinguals, further research may be directed at what this difference might reflect in terms of language-processing mechanisms.

One view has been that the RH is particularly associated with pragmatic or metalinguistic strategies (Paradis, 2000); an increased reliance on RH-mediated strategies for language processing could thus be interpreted as compensation for relatively weaker linguistic skills. However, our results showing greater RH involvement only in bilinguals who acquired proficiency in both languages early in life argues against a "compensation" explanation.

An alternative possibility is that young children growing up in a multilingual environment may need to employ a holistic monitoring strategy to identify the appropriate language to use in a specific situation (e.g., with school friends vs. with grandparents). Such a strategy could conceivably stimulate increased RH activation, in line with the suggestion that the RH is preferentially involved with holistic or Gestalt-like processing (e.g., Fabbro, Gran, Basso, & Bava, 1990).

Still other interpretations of early bilinguals' apparent bilateral hemispheric involvement in language could be proposed and tested in the context of models of the bilingual mental lexicon and bilingual conceptual organization, most of which so far have drawn their evidence primarily from studies of late bilinguals (see, e.g., De Groot, 1993; Kroll, 1993; Kroll & De Groot, 1997).

Another matter of theoretical interest concerns how the patterns of hemispheric activity revealed by our meta-analysis (Hull & Vaid, 2003b) fit with what is known about the involvement of the two hemispheres in areas of cognitive functioning outside of language use. A particularly compelling comparison can be made between our results and an integrative perspective that relates neural differences to differences in declarative and procedural memory systems (Paradis, 1994; Ullman, 2001). According to the declarative/procedural model developed by Ullman (2001) on the basis of an examination of lesion, neuroimaging, and electrophysiological studies, lexical knowledge makes use of declarative memory, which is thought to be housed in temporal lobe structures. Declarative memory has been implicated in the explicit learning and use of facts and of event knowledge. In contrast, grammatical knowledge is thought to be subserved by implicit, procedural memory thought to be housed in left frontal and basal ganglia structures. Procedural memory has been implicated in the development of motor and cognitive skills in the L1. With respect to L2s acquired subsequent to an L1, Ullman proposed that linguistic forms with grammatical computation that is thought to depend on procedural systems in L1 are more dependent on declarative and lexical memory in L2, either by memorization or construction by explicit rules. As such, Ullman argued that linguistic forms in L2 should be more reliant on declarative than procedural memory than those in L1. This reliance should be greater in earlier stages of L2 acquisition

than in later L2 acquisition. With increasing practice in the L2, there should presumably be an improvement in the processing of grammatical rules by procedural memory; this would be reflected in an increasing reliance on the LH for L2 processing. Consistent with Ullman's prediction, fluent late bilinguals in our meta-analysis showed LH dominance for language processing, whereas nonfluent late bilinguals showed significantly greater RH involvement, although it must be noted that our nonfluent sample was relatively small (comprised of seven comparison groups).

Bilingual studies concerning cognitive processes other than language are limited, but there is at least one recent study that compared monolinguals and bilinguals on a face discrimination task (Hausmann, Durmusoglu, Yazgan, & Güntürkün, 2004). The experiment showed that early fluent bilinguals displayed a reduced RH advantage on face discrimination tasks relative to monolinguals. The authors proposed that the neuronal space available for nonlinguistic functions in bilinguals is "crowded" by the demand for additional cortical space needed to process the two languages, and thus less space is available for nonlinguistic functions. Whereas caution must be used in generalizing from the results of a single study, the results of Hausmann et al. provided at least some support for the notion that early multiple language experience may affect not only the organization of language, but also that of nonlinguistic functions.

Taken together, the lateralization differences revealed by the meta-analysis (Hull & Vaid, 2003b) and the studies discussed in this section make clear that particular differences in language acquisition history (e.g., early vs. late L2 acquisition) may give rise to functional differences in language processing. In a broader sense, the present meta-analytic results also explicate a range of language skills, which any person can develop, that have a measurable impact on the functional organization of the brain for language and perhaps even for other aspects of human cognition.

An important caveat that must be kept in mind is that our (Hull & Vaid, 2003b) meta-analysis covered only a subset of the extant bilingual laterality literature, focusing as it did only on those studies in which bilinguals and monolinguals were directly compared and in which monolinguals' language matched bilinguals' L1. Thus, a good proportion of the overall bilingual laterality literature had to be excluded. Fortunately, the results of a comprehensive meta-analysis that considered the full set of bilingual laterality studies, including those without monolingual controls (see Hull, 2003; Hull & Vaid, 2003a), corroborated the bilingual group differences noted in our meta-analysis.

A critical interpretive issue that our (Hull & Vaid, 2003b) meta-analysis brought to light is the importance of distinguishing proficiency effects from age of L2 acquisition effects when designing studies or interpreting conclusions. Because early bilinguals are generally highly proficient in both languages whereas late bilinguals tend to vary in their L2 proficiency, care must be taken to avoid interpreting proficiency effects as age effects or vice versa. In our analysis, we separately examined high versus moderately proficient late bilinguals (all early bilinguals were highly proficient) and found that most of the bilingual within-group variance was explained in terms of early versus late L2 acquisition, whereas degree of L2 fluency explained only about one third of the variance.

Our (Hull & Vaid, 2003b) review also indicated a need for caution when considering the use of language tasks involving global demands because groups tested with such tasks yielded by far the greatest levels of unexplained variance, even after the application of all combinations of the moderators (e.g., L2 acquisition age, L2 fluency, participant sex). Thus, tasks that tap global demands, such as listening to a story, appear to be inadequate for eliciting consistent lateralization patterns across participants. Given the lack of moderating influence associated with global task demands, it is suggested that future efforts aimed at finding reliable relationships between specific language tasks and hemisphericity will be more fruitful if they make use of behavioral tasks that study specific linguistic subcomponents (e.g., semantic, syntactic, phonetic, orthographic, or pragmatic) in isolation.

In general, the explanatory value of the laterality literature would be enhanced by inclusion of greater numbers of specific kinds of controlled studies. The majority of bilinguals included in our (Hull & Vaid, 2003b) meta-analysis were fluent in the L2; therefore, the results are relatively less informative on the question of effects of degree of L2 competence. More studies are needed that compare fluent bilinguals versus those with differing levels of mastery of the L2. Studies examining proficiency effects should ideally use a common standard for judging L2 fluency (Grosjean, 1998). More studies are also needed that systematically include sex as a variable and that examine late bilinguals varying in their manner of L2 acquisition. Finally, more studies that specifically look at task-related processing effects are needed. Although the meta-analysis found support for task effects, in many cases the cell sizes were too small to permit useful conclusions about the interaction of group and task effects.

Electrophysiological and Imaging Research with Bilinguals: Lessons From Behavioral Laterality Research

The findings from our (Hull & Vaid, 2003b) meta-analysis underscore the importance of including monolingual participants in any study that seeks to address whether the state of being bilingual uniquely affects cerebral representation of language. The meta-analysis showed that, when bilinguals and monolinguals are directly compared in a given experiment, *something* in the processing of language in bilinguals appears to be different from that in monolinguals, and that something likewise differentiates language processing in early bilinguals from individuals who acquire an L2 later in life. Moreover, the meta-analysis indicated that language processing in monolinguals may reflect more recruitment of the RH than has been expected; furthermore, it was found that RH involvement is especially evident on certain tasks and in certain subgroups (e.g., women more so than men for auditory tasks).

What we cannot conclude from this literature are answers to questions about *intrahemispheric* differences in the neural regions subserving various components of language or the time course of neural processing of language. Such questions are, of course, readily addressed by positron emission tomographic, functional magnetic resonance imaging (fMRI), and event-related brain potential studies (see Kutas, 1997; Hagoort, Brown, & Osterhout, 1999; and Price, 1998, for reviews). An additional question that imaging techniques can perhaps better address is how differences in cerebral representation for language interact with those for other cognitive functions, such as memory or executive control (Jackson, Swainson, Cunnington, & Jackson, 2001; Price, Green, & von Studnitz, 1999).

Although it is not our intention here to discuss in great detail the imaging literature concerning bilinguals, particularly because most such studies do not speak to lateralization differences, it may be worthwhile to describe the findings of those few that did provide some information about hemispheric differences. One fMRI study that compared fluent English-Spanish and Spanish-English bilinguals who had acquired their L2 at around 12 years of age showed spatially overlapping frontal lobe activation patterns on a semantic processing task (Illes et al., 1999). An effect size analysis of frontal lobe laterality in these findings revealed that left frontal activation exceeded right frontal activation for both languages of the late bilinguals and more so for the L2 relative to the L1 (although the latter trend did not reach significance). Conversely, an fMRI study with moderately fluent French-English bilinguals who acquired the L2 during late childhood showed increased RH participation during L2 (relative to L1) processing on a global language comprehension task; laterality effect size analysis revealed activation differences between the two languages were significant (Dehaene et al., 1997).

An additional finding of interest derives from the laterality effect size analysis of the fMRI results of a word stem completion (i.e., production) task that involved fluent Chinese-English bilinguals with late L2 acquisition (Chee, Tan, & Thiel, 1999). In this case, the analysis showed a nonsignificant trend for greater *left* frontal activation during L1 production relative to L2, a finding in direct contrast with that of the semantic comprehension tasks of Illes et al. (1999). Interestingly, comparisons of laterality effect sizes for frontal lobe activation patterns of early and late bilinguals in the Chee et al. study showed a nonsignificant trend for increased RH participation on both languages of early bilinguals relative to participants with late L2 acquisition.

Imaging studies that evaluate overall laterality patterns across a variety of linguistic tasks performed by participant groups that vary in language acquisition history and the specific languages learned could provide a new tool for investigating the conditions under which cerebral lateralization differences may emerge. However, to date, imaging studies as a whole have not contributed much to this question. As noted, of the approximately 40 bilingual functional imaging studies that have appeared thus far, only 6 specifically measured and reported data regarding the overall laterality of native and nonnative languages in bilinguals.

Bilingual Event-Related Potential and Laterality Studies: Converging Evidence

The number of ERP studies with bilinguals or L2 learners was at the time of this writing around 36.

Although a separate review of ERP evidence is clearly needed, it is beyond the scope of the present overview. Instead, we draw certain connections between findings observed in the laterality literature, as revealed in our (Hull & Vaid, 2003b) meta-analysis, and those noted in selected ERP studies in which relevant comparisons were undertaken.

The ERP technique is used to identify averaged evoked brain potentials or components elicited by specific sensory, motor, or cognitive "events" (Kutas, 1997). ERP component signatures are comprised of a series of peaks (positive voltage) and valleys (negative voltage) described in terms of their polarity, peak onset, and peak amplitude and their scalp distribution. During a given cognitive task, the systematic variations in the amplitude of electrical activity in the brain (i.e., signature forms) and deviations in the latencies of their onset are termed *ERP effects* (Hahne & Friederici, 2001). These allow researchers to infer the degree and timing of electrical activity in the brain during a specific cognitive activity (for a review of language-related effects, see Hagoort et al., 1999; Kutas & Van Petten, 1994). The most studied of the language-related components, the N400 effect, is thought to reflect an unexpected semantic event; the N280 and P600 components in turn have been hypothesized to correlate with automatic and controlled aspects of syntactic processing, respectively (see Hahne & Friederici, 1999).

Given the high temporal resolution of the ERP technique, studies using this method allow fine-grained analysis of the temporal unfolding of events, whether these are events that normally last milliseconds, seconds, or minutes. As such, ERP studies provide an ideal opportunity to study linguistic processing in real time. Moreover, unlike traditional behavioral online methodologies, which use reaction time measures for some ancillary task on which judgments are required (e.g., lexical decision), ERP techniques do not require participants to engage in some other task but provide a more unobtrusive measure of participants' responses while they are simply reading or listening to words or sentences for comprehension.

Role of Timing of Language Exposure

Recent electrophysiological research suggests the importance of early sensory and language experience in influencing how neural subsystems subserving language will develop and function. One claim currently under study is that delayed acquisition of an L2 (e.g., L2 acquired after puberty) is associated with deficits in grammatical processing and in the processing of certain phonological tasks, whereas semantic processing and the processing of other phonological judgments are hypothesized as unaffected by age of L2 acquisition (Ullman, 2001; Weber-Fox & Neville, 2001). Next, we briefly summarize findings of bilingual ERP studies relevant to this claim and discuss them in relation to the laterality evidence.

Semantic Processing

The typical ERP study of semantic processing employs a sentence comprehension task in which a context-anomalous versus a context-congruent word is presented, usually at the end of the sentence. Meuter, Donald, and Ardal (1987) used such a procedure to study semantic processing in fluent bilinguals, tested separately in each language, across left and right frontal and parietal sites. They compared the N400 effect elicited during L1 versus L2 sentence presentation for groups differing in the temporal order in which French and English were learned (i.e., acquisition order) and in their age of L2 acquisition (i.e., early vs. late).

Meuter et al. (1987) found that fluent bilingual groups exhibited bilateral N400 effects that were similar across L1s regardless of whether the L1s were the same or different languages. This result accorded with the meta-analytic findings for early and late fluent bilinguals performing language tasks that involved semantic demands (Hull & Vaid, 2003b). Specifically, we found that fluent bilinguals *as a group* (i.e., including those with early and late L2 acquisition) consistently showed a bilateral pattern of hemispheric involvement across different L1s during tasks that tapped semantic features of language, such as the sentence comprehension tasks used by Meuter et al. Furthermore, Meuter et al. noted that their French-English bilinguals (i.e., the "late" L2 group) tended to show a larger N400 effect for left parietal sites when reading incongruent sentence endings and more so in the L2 than in the L1. This finding may also have some support from the meta-analytic findings in that, when the set of fluent bilinguals was partitioned by age of L2 acquisition, the subset of *late* bilinguals was relatively more LH dominant for language as compared to *early* bilinguals, who showed more bilateral hemispheric involvement overall.

Another ERP study of semantic processing (Ardal, Donald, Meuter, Muldrew, & Luce, 1990) also found evidence consistent with outcomes of our meta-analysis (Hull & Vaid, 2003b). In this study, ERP recordings were compared in monolinguals and late bilinguals while they read semantically anomalous sentences in either English or French. Although much of the bilingual data were collapsed across language acquisition order, comparisons of the results when bilinguals read sentences only in the L1 revealed "considerable overlap between the distributions" of monolinguals and late bilinguals (Ardal et al., 1990, p. 199). Ardal et al. further reported that, regardless of acquisition order, bilinguals with a high degree of L2 proficiency displayed patterns of brain activity that correlated with those of L1 use. Our meta-analysis also found very similar patterns of (LH) brain involvement for monolinguals and late bilinguals overall on the L1.

Weber-Fox and Neville (1996, 2001) also found that late bilinguals and monolinguals showed comparable ERPs, in this case to open class words on tasks involving semantic anomaly detection and on tasks that involved the reading of correct sentences (Neville, Mills, & Lawson, 1992). These ERP results were generally consistent with the meta-analytic (Hull & Vaid, 2003b) laterality finding that, on semantic processing tasks, late fluent bilinguals and monolinguals showed similar patterns of lateralization.

Syntactic Processing

Semantic investigations have found that overall ERP patterns during L2 use increasingly overlap with those of the native language and/or of monolinguals as proficiency in the L2 increases and diverge more with decreased proficiency (Hahne & Friederici, 2001; Hahne, Jescheniak, & Friederici, 2001; Weber-Fox & Neville, 2001). Other work suggests that syntactic processing may be more vulnerable to proficiency and age of exposure effects.

Hahne and Friederici (2001) conducted a study of sentence comprehension in Japanese-German bilinguals who had acquired the L2 after puberty. The participants listened to German sentences with or without syntactic and/or semantic violations and judged them for linguistic integrity. The authors reported overlapping bilateral patterns of electrical activity for monolinguals and bilinguals in the N400 effect, although in certain cases the degree of bilateral activation was greater in the bilingual group. However, the bilinguals' ERP components for syntactic violations were quite different from those of monolinguals. Specifically, syntactic violations elicited *less* LH activation in late bilinguals relative to monolinguals both at early processing stages (left anterior component, or LAN) and later ones (P600). Whereas the laterality results were based on a relatively small data set evaluating syntactic processing as such, the meta-analytic results indicated that bilinguals as a group (i.e., collapsed across early and late L2 acquisition age) showed relatively less LH lateralization than did monolinguals. More behavioral laterality studies are needed to determine whether this pattern will be supported in a larger data set.

To test whether there is electrophysiological support for a "sensitive period" view that late L2 users process language, particularly grammar, in a different way from native speakers, Friederici, Steinhauer, and Pfeifer (2002) trained adult participants on a miniature artificial language complete with its own vocabulary and grammatical rules distinct from those in the participants' native language. One group of participants was trained in both the lexicon and the syntax of the L2 and was termed the fluent group, whereas a second set, designated nonfluent, was trained only in the lexicon. After training, both groups were exposed to syntax violations in the (artificial) L2.

In native speakers of a single language, syntactic violations elicit a biphasic response consisting of an early negativity (which is interpreted to reflect the interruption of an automatic parsing process) and a late positivity (which is thought to reflect structural reanalysis and repair processes) (Hahne & Friederici, 1999). In previous studies of detection of syntactic anomalies involving phrase structure violations (e.g., Hahne & Friederici, 2001; Weber-Fox & Neville, 1996), late L2 learners did not show the early negativity but showed a reduced late positivity (P600) in the RH, suggesting the use of compensatory or alternative conceptual-semantic processes.

For the artificial grammar stimuli, Friederici et al. (2002) found that the fluent group exhibited brain activity patterns that "correspond precisely to the biphasic ERP pattern that is commonly thought to reflect automatic syntax parsing in healthy native speakers of natural languages" (p. 531). From these findings, Friederici et al. concluded that there was no support for the notion that late acquisition of an L2 dictates the recruitment of neural substrates for language that are in addition to or distinct from those of monolinguals. Quite the reverse, they interpreted their findings as evidence for an overlap in neural activity for late L2 learners and native speakers.

Similarly, in a recent study by Weber-Fox and Neville (2001) that extended a previous one and used mostly the same participants (Weber-Fox & Neville, 1996), English-speaking monolinguals and Chinese-English users varying in their age of L2 exposure showed no group differences in the processing of closed class words. Instead, the N280 component was largest over left anterior electrode sites for all groups. This finding was in opposition to a prediction (supported in a previous study with American Sign Language [ASL]-English users; see Neville et al., 1992) that ERPs elicited by closed class words would be more sensitive to delays in L2 immersion relative to ERPs elicited by open class words and semantic anomalies. The divergence between the performance of the ASL (Neville et al., 1992) and the Chinese learners of English (Weber-Fox & Neville, 2001) was interpreted to reflect differences in English grammar proficiency rather than L1 differences. To account for a discrepancy in results for syntactic judgments between the earlier Chinese-English study (1996) and the later one, Weber-Fox and Neville (2001) proposed that "the decreased asymmetry found previously could have been in part related to differences in the specific language functions tested, i.e., detection of grammatical anomalies vs. reading appropriately used closed-class words" (p. 1350). In other words, tasks involving syntactic anomaly detection (which typically rely on anomalous uses of closed class words) may have called on different kinds of processes than tasks involving correctly used closed class words.

Although our (Hull & Vaid, 2003b) meta-analysis had an insufficient number of data points to permit reliable conclusions about laterality differences in syntactic processing between language groups (there were only three comparison sets), we did find that late (fluent) L2 learners exhibited lateralization patterns for language processing that were identical to those of monolinguals, as was found by Friederici et al. (2002) and Weber-Fox and Neville (2001).

Notably, Friederici et al. (2002) found that the nonfluent late bilinguals in their sample failed to show patterns of brain activity similar to those of native speakers. Similarly, Neville et al. (1992) noted that longer peak latencies in deaf ASL-English users were associated with less-proficient knowledge of English grammar, as measured by a standardized test. Whereas the meta-analysis was unable to provide reliable data on the laterality patterns of nonfluent (late) L2 learners because of the small sample size (seven comparison groups, in this case), the data we did have showed a trend toward less LH lateralization for nonfluent L2 users compared with monolinguals. Taken together, our findings and those of Friederici et al. (2002) with respect to L2 proficiency suggest that it may have a moderating effect on the organization of an L2 for those who acquire the L2 later in life.

Finally, with respect to our meta-analytic finding of differential organization for language in early L2 acquirers relative to late L2 learners, supportive evidence was found in an ERP study conducted by Neville et al. (1997). The study recorded ERPs from proficient early and late bilinguals during a sentence-reading task. The results indicated that the patterns of neural activity in early bilinguals, at least as related to the syntactic processing of sentences, involved more symmetrical participation of the two hemispheres relative to proficient late bilinguals. The finding prompted Neville et al. to conclude "marked effects of age of acquisition of language" (p. 305) because this relatively large RH involvement found in early bilinguals was not evident in the late L2 learners. That is, late bilinguals in this study showed relatively more LH dominance than early bilinguals, a finding that corroborated our own results concerning the directionality of differential lateralization of language in early and late bilinguals.

Conclusion

The earliest source of evidence on the neural mediation of language in brain-intact bilingual users, namely, cerebral laterality research, has been supplemented by two additional sources of evidence: hemodynamic neuroimaging and electrophysiological research on language. These more recent sources offer increased spatial and temporal precision in the mapping of language phenomena and as such show great promise in deepening and refining our understanding of neural correlates of language processing. Nevertheless, we believe that the newer methodologies stand to benefit from greater consideration of the potential relevance in terms of the hypotheses posed, the variables addressed, and the outcomes obtained from the earlier laterality literature.

The laterality literature provided the earliest articulation of experimental hypotheses of neural underpinnings of cognitive differences between monolinguals and bilinguals and among different bilingual subgroups. It is promising that the trends observed in our meta-analytic findings in the laterality literature (Hull & Vaid, 2003b) are generally supported by the findings of ERP studies with

bilinguals and late L2 learners. Specifically, both sources of evidence suggest that semantic processing may be relatively less altered than syntactic processing by differences in language experience (e.g., monolingual vs. delayed L2 exposure in bilinguals). The ERP evidence further shows that syntactic processing may be vulnerable to delayed L2 exposure, particularly when the individuals are not proficient in the L2 (Friederici et al., 2002). The evidence from ERP and laterality studies also converges in suggesting that acquisition of an L2 very early in life (i.e., by the age of 6 years) appears to influence cerebral organization of language in ways that are distinct from those of late L2 learners (Neville et al., 1997). Specifically, early bilinguals tend to exhibit bilateral patterns of brain activation, whereas late bilinguals show LH dominance for language overall. The laterality data also point to RH participation in language processing even in monolinguals, at least for certain tasks (see Federmeier & Kutas, 2002, for relevant ERP data on the RH's contribution).

One lesson from the laterality literature is the importance of including relevant comparison groups in the research design. Two critical ones we identified were monolinguals and early bilinguals. In an earlier meta-analysis of the language laterality literature with bilinguals (Vaid & Hall, 1991), only 11 of the 59 studies that were included had monolingual counterparts, the assumption in the literature at that time apparently was that monolinguals' performance indices need not be specifically studied as they were presumed to show the canonical pattern of LH dominance. Yet, as revealed in the more recent meta-analysis that considered 23 monolingual comparison groups (Hull & Vaid, 2003b), this assumption is unwarranted given that monolinguals also may show bilateral hemispheric involvement, at least on certain tasks and procedures. Thus, the main question implicitly raised when individual differences in laterality first came under study (i.e., is there more RH involvement in bilinguals relative to monolinguals?) must be replaced with more fine-grained investigations that acknowledge the role of the RH in both bilingual and monolingual language processing, and that look for relative differences in RH involvement across groups and in interaction with stimulus and task conditions.

So far, only a small subset of the electrophysiological and neuroimaging studies with bilinguals has included monolingual or early bilingual controls. This should be redressed in future research using such techniques. In addition, L2 fluency and age of acquisition of the L2 have tended to be confounded in recent neuroimaging and ERP research. These variables also require disentangling in future research.

Finally, what is particularly intriguing from the earliest laterality studies to the most recent ERP ones is the finding that early acquisition of bilingualism appears to result in bilateral involvement for language processing. More research needs to be done to explore how early simultaneous exposure to two languages may alter metalinguistic processing strategies, either at the executive control level (Bialystok, 2001) or at the level of early functional differentiation of linguistic structures (see Genesee, 2003).

Although studies on the bilingual brain using imaging technologies have revived interest in long-standing questions about hemispheric differences associated with bilinguality, the research is still in its infancy. It is our belief that progress in understanding the complexities and the specificities of the bilingual brain using these newer technologies will require that all available sources of evidence be consulted when formulating hypotheses and interpreting findings. Stronger links need to be forged, we feel, with the cognitive literature on bilingualism (see De Bruijn, Dijkstra, Chwilla, & Schriefers, 2001; Gollan & Kroll, 2001), with bilingual aphasia research (Green & Price, 2001; Paradis, 2001), and last, but not least, with the bilingual laterality literature..

Acknowledgments

This research was supported by a Texas A&M University Academic Excellence Award to the first author and by a Texas A&M University Honors' Teacher/Scholar Award to the second author. Portions of this research were presented at the Third International Symposium on Bilingualism held in Bristol, United Kingdom, in 2001 and at the annual meeting of the Southwest Cognition Conference held in Dallas, Texas, in 2001. We thank Renata Meuter and Michel Paradis for comments on the chapter and Judy Kroll and Annette de Groot for their thorough editing.

Notes

1. Segalowitz (1986) provided a concise review of relevant findings in the aphasia literature, as well as useful discussion of reliability and validity issues with respect to behavioral measures of brain lateralization for language.

2. In light of the fact that only one study involved in our meta-analysis included data on the manner of L2 acquisition, we were unable to meta-analytically evaluate the manner hypothesis.

3. Semantic demands also indicated bilateral activation in monolinguals, but these data were drawn from only seven comparison groups; all other moderators and interactions not reported were also too small to provide reliable data.

References

Albert, M., & Obler, L. K. (1978). Experimental neuropsychology. In M. Albert & L. K. Obler (Eds.), *The bilingual brain: Neurolinguistic aspects of bilingualism* (pp. 158–201). New York: Academic Press.

Ardal, S., Donald, M., Meuter, R., Muldrew, S., & Luce, M. (1990). Brain responses to semantic incongruity in bilinguals. *Brain and Language, 39*, 187–205.

Bialystok, E. (2001). *Bilingualism in development: Language, literacy and cognition*. New York: Cambridge University Press.

Burton, H., Snyder, A., Conturo, T., Akbudak, E., Ollinger, J., & Raichle, M. (2002). Adaptive changes in early and late blind: A fMRI study of Braille reading. *Journal of Neurophysiology, 87*, 589–607.

Chee, M., Tan, E., & Thiel, T. (1999). Mandarin and English single word processing studied with functional magnetic resonance imaging. *Journal of Cognitive Neuroscience, 19*, 3050–3056.

Chiarello, C. (2003). Parallel systems for processing language: Hemispheric complementarity in the normal brain. In M. Banich & M. Mack (Eds.), *Mind, brain and language: Multidisciplinary perspectives* (pp. 229–247). Mahwah, NJ: Erlbaum.

De Bruijn, E., Dijkstra, T., Chwilla, D., & Schriefers, H. (2001). Language context effects on interlingual homograph recognition: evidence from event-related potentials and response times in semantic priming. *Bilingualism: Language and Cognition, 4*, 155–168.

De Groot, A. M. B. (1993). Word type effects in bilingual processing tasks: Support for a mixed-representational system. In R. Schreuder & B. Weltens (Eds.), *The bilingual lexicon* (pp. 27–51). Amsterdam: Benjamins.

Dehaene, S., Dupoux, E., Mehler, J., Cohen, L., Paulesu, E., Perani, D., et al. (1997). Anatomical variability in the cortical representation of first and second language. *NeuroReport, 8*, 3809–3815.

Fabbro, F. (2001). The bilingual brain: Bilingual aphasia. *Brain and Language, 79*, 201–210.

Fabbro, F., Gran, L., Basso, G., & Bava, A. (1990). Cerebral lateralization in simultaneous interpretation. *Brain and Language, 39*, 69–89.

Federmeier, K., & Kutas, M. (1999). Right words and left words: Electrophysiological evidence for hemispheric differences in meaning processing. *Cognitive Brain Research, 8*, 373–392.

Federmeier, K., & Kutas, M. (2002). Picture the difference: Electrophysiological investigations of picture processing in the cerebral hemispheres. *Neuropsychologia, 40*, 730–747.

Friederici, A., Steinhauer, K., & Pfeifer, E. (2002). Brain signatures of artificial language processing: Evidence challenging the critical period hypothesis. *Proceedings of the National Academy of Sciences, 99*, 529–534.

Galloway, L., & Krashen, S. (1980). Cerebral organization in bilingualism and second language. In R. Scarcella & S. Krashen (Eds.), *Research in second language acquisition* (pp. 74–80). Rowley, MA: Newbury.

Genesee, F. (1982). Experimental neuropsychological research on second language processing. *TESOL Quarterly, 16*, 315–321.

Genesee, F. (2003, April). *Bilingual acquisition: Exploring the limits of the language faculty.* Keynote address, Fourth International Symposium on Bilingualism, Arizona State University, Tempe.

Genesee, F., Hamers, J., Lambert, W. E., Mononen, L., Seitz, M., & Starck, R. (1978). Language processing strategies in bilinguals: A neuropsychological study. *Brain and Language, 5*, 1–12.

Gollan, T., & Kroll, J. F. (2001). Bilingual lexical access. In B. Rapp (Ed.). *The handbook of cognitive neuropsychology* (pp. 321–345). Philadelphia: Psychology Press.

Goral, M., Levy, E., & Obler, L. K. (2002). Neurolinguistic aspects of bilingualism. *The International Journal of Bilingualism, 6*, 411–440.

Green, D. (1998). Mental control of the bilingual lexico-semantic system. *Bilingualism: Language and Cognition, 1*, 67–81.

Green, D., & Price, C. (2001). Functional imaging in the study of recovery patterns in bilingual aphasia. *Bilingualism: Language and Cognition, 4*, 191–201.

Grosjean, F. (1998). Studying bilinguals: Methodological and conceptual issues. *Bilingualism: Language and Cognition, 1*, 131–149.

Grosjean, F. (2000). The bilingual's language modes. In J. Nicol (Ed.), *One mind, two languages: Bilingual language processing* (pp. 1–22). Oxford, U.K.: Blackwell.

Hagoort, P., Brown, C., & Osterhout, L. (1999). The neurocognition of syntactic processing. In C. Brown & P. Hagoort (Eds.), *The neurocognition of language* (pp. 273–315). Oxford, U.K.: Oxford University Press.

Hahne, A., & Friederici, A. (1999). Electrophysiological evidence for two steps in syntactic analysis: Early automatic and late controlled processes. *Journal of Cognitive Neuroscience, 11*, 194–205.

Hahne, A., & Friederici, A. (2001). Processing a second language: Late learners' comprehension mechanisms as revealed by event-related potentials. *Bilingualism: Language and Cognition, 4*, 123–141.

Hahne, A., Jescheniak, J., & Friederici, A. (2001, November). *Processing a foreign language: Sentence comprehension mechanisms as revealed by ERPs.* Poster presented at the annual meeting of the Psychonomic Society, Orlando, FL.

Hausmann, M., Durmusoglu, G., Yazgan, Y., & Güntürkün, O. (2004). Evidence for reduced hemispheric asymmetries in non-verbal functions in bilinguals. *Journal of Neurolinguistics, 17*, 285–299.

Hull, R. (2003). *How does bilingualism matter? A meta-analytic tale of two hemispheres.* Unpublished doctoral dissertation, Texas A&M University, College Station.

Hull, R., & Vaid, J. (2003a, May). *A (continuing) tale of two hemispheres.* Paper presented at the Fourth International Symposium on Bilingualism, Arizona State University, Tempe.

Hull, R., & Vaid, J. (2003b). *What is right? A meta-analysis of bilingual vs. monolingual language lateralization.* Manuscript submitted for publication.

Illes, J., Francis, W., Desmond, J., Gabrieli, J., Glover, G., Poldrack, R., et al. (1999). Convergent cortical representation of semantic processing in bilinguals. *Brain and Language, 70*, 347–363.

Jackson, G., Swainson, R., Cunnington, R., & Jackson, S. (2001). ERP correlates of executive control during repeated language switching. *Bilingualism: Language and Cognition, 4*, 169–178.

Johnson, J., & Newport, E. (1989). Critical period effects in second language learning: The influence of maturational state on the acquisition of English as a second language. *Cognitive Psychology, 21*, 60–99.

Joseph, R. (1982). The neuropsychology of development: Hemispheric laterality, limbic language, and the origin of thought. *Journal of Clinical Psychology, 44*, 3–34.

Klein, D., Zatorre, R., Milner, B., & Zhao, V. (2001). A cross-linguistic PET study of tone perception in Mandarin Chinese and English speakers. *NeuroImage, 13*, 646–653.

Kochunov, P., Fox, P., Lancaster, J., Tan, L.H., Amunts, K., Zilles, K., et al. (2003). Localized morphological brain differences between

English-speaking Caucasians and Chinese-speaking Asians. *Developmental Neuroscience, 14*, 1–4.

Kroll, J. F. (1993). Accessing conceptual representation for words in a second language. In R. Schreuder & B. Weltens (Eds.), *The bilingual lexicon* (pp. 53–81). Amsterdam: Benjamins.

Kroll, J. F., & De Groot, A. M. B. (1997). Lexical and conceptual memory in the bilingual: Mapping form to meaning in two languages. In A. M. B. de Groot & J. F. Kroll (Eds.), *Tutorials in bilingualism* (pp. 169–199). Mahwah, NJ: Erlbaum.

Kroll, J. F., & Dijkstra, T. (2002). The bilingual lexicon. In R. Kaplan (Ed.), *Handbook of applied linguistics* (pp. 301–321). Oxford, U.K.: Oxford University Press.

Kutas, M. (1997). Views on how the electrical activity that the brain generates reflects the functions of different language structures. *Psychophysiology, 34*, 383–398.

Kutas, M., & Van Petten, C. (1994). Psycholinguistics electrified: Event-related brain potential investigations. In M. A. Gernsbacher (Ed.), *Handbook of psycholinguistics* (pp. 83–143). San Diego, CA: Academic Press.

Liu, Y., & Perfetti, C. A. (2003). The time course of brain activity in reading English and Chinese: An ERP study of Chinese bilinguals. *Human Brain Mapping, 18*, 167–175.

Meuter, R., Donald, M., & Ardal, S. (1987). A comparison of first- and second-language ERPs in bilinguals. *Current Trends in Event-Related Potential Research, (S40)*, 412–416.

Nakada, T., Fujii, Y., & Kwee, I. (2001). Brain strategies for reading in the second language are determined by the first language. *Neuroscience Research, 40*, 351–358.

Neville, H., Coffey, S., Lawson, D., Fischer, A., Emmorey, K., & Bellugi, U. (1997). Neural systems mediating American Sign Language: Effects of sensory experience and age of acquisition. *Brain and Language, 57*, 285–308.

Neville, H., Mills, D., & Lawson, D. (1992). Fractionating language: Different neural subsystems with different sensitive periods. *Cerebral Cortex, 2*, 244–258.

Newport, E., Bavelier, D., & Neville, H. (2001). Critical thinking about critical periods: Perspectives on a critical period for language acquisition. In E. Dupoux (Ed.), *Language, brain and cognitive development: Essays in honor of Jacques Mehler* (pp. 481–502). Cambridge, MA: MIT Press.

Obler, L. K. (1981). Right hemisphere participation in second language acquisition. In K. Diller (Ed.), *Individual differences and universals in language learning aptitude* (pp. 53–64). Rowley, MA: Newbury.

Obler, L. K., Zatorre, R., Galloway, L., & Vaid, J. (1982). Cerebral lateralization in bilinguals: Methodological issues. *Brain and Language, 15*, 40–54.

Paradis, M. (1994). Neurolinguistic aspects of implicit and explicit memory: Implications for bilingualism. In N. Ellis (Ed.), *Implicit and explicit learning of first and second languages* (pp. 393–419). San Diego, CA: Academic Press.

Paradis, M. (1999). *Neuroimaging studies of the bilingual brain: Some words of caution.* Paper presented at 25th Lacus Forum, University of Alberta, Edmonton.

Paradis, M. (2000). The cerebral division of labor in verbal communication. *Brain and Cognition, 43*, 13.

Paradis, M. (2001). Bilingual and polyglot aphasia. In R. S. Berndt (Ed.), *Handbook of neuropsychology* (pp. 69–91). Oxford, U.K.: Elsevier Science.

Paradis, M. (2003). The bilingual Loch Ness monster raises its nonasymmetric head again—or, Why bother with such cumbersome notions as validity and reliability? Comments on Evans et al. (2002). *Brain and Language, 87*, 441–448.

Price, C. (1998). The functional anatomy of word comprehension and production. *Trends in Cognitive Science, 2*, 281–288.

Price, C., Green, D., & von Studnitz, R. (1999). A functional imaging study of translation and language switching. *Brain, 122*, 2221–2236.

Segalowitz, S. (1986). Validity and reliability of noninvasive lateralization measures. *Child Neuropsychology, 1*, 191–208.

Sussman, H., & Simon, T. (1988). The effects of gender, handedness, L1/L2 and baseline tapping rate on language lateralization: An assessment of the time-sharing paradigm. *Journal of Clinical and Experimental Psychology, 10*, 69.

Ullman, M. (2001). The neural basis of lexicon and grammar in first and second language: The declarative/procedural model. *Bilingualism: Language and Cognition, 4*, 105–122.

Vaid, J. (1983). Bilingualism and brain lateralization. In S. Segalowitz (Ed.), *Language functions and brain organization* (pp. 315-339). New York: Academic Press.

Vaid, J. (2002). Bilingualism. In V. S. Ramachandran (Ed.), *Encyclopedia of the human brain* (Vol. 1, pp. 417–434). San Diego, CA: Academic Press.

Vaid, J., & Genesee, F. (1980). Neuropsychological approaches to bilingualism. *Canadian Journal of Psychology, 34*, 417–445.

Vaid, J., & Hall, D. G. (1991). Neuropsychological perspectives on bilingualism: Right, left and center. In A. Reynolds (Ed.), *Bilingualism, multiculturalism, and second language learning: The McGill conference in honor of Wallace E. Lambert*, (pp. 81–112). Hillsdale, NJ: Erlbaum.

Vaid, J., & Hull, R. (2002). Re-envisioning the bilingual brain using functional neuroimaging: Methodological and interpretive issues. In F. Fabbro (Ed.), *Advances in the neurolinguistics of bilingualism: A festschrift for Michel Paradis* (pp. 315–355). Udine, Italy: Udine University Press.

Voyer, D. (1996). On the magnitude of laterality effects and sex differences in functional literalities. *Laterality, 1*, 51–83.

Weber-Fox, C., & Neville, H. (1996). Maturational constraints on functional specializations for language processing: ERP and behavioral evidence in bilingual speakers. *Journal of Cognitive Neuroscience, 8*, 231–256.

Weber-Fox, C., & Neville, H. (2001). Sensitive periods differentiate processing of open- and closed-class words: An ERP study of bilinguals. *Journal of Speech, Language, and Hearing Research, 44*, 1338–1353.

Zatorre, R. (1989). On the representation of multiple languages in the brain: Old problems and new directions. *Brain and Language, 36*, 127–147.

Jubin Abutalebi
Stefano F. Cappa
Daniela Perani

24

What Can Functional Neuroimaging Tell Us About the Bilingual Brain?

ABSTRACT   Over the past decade, functional neuroimaging technologies such as positron emission tomography and functional magnetic resonance imaging have enabled neuroscientists to examine the spatial and temporal mechanisms of cognitive functioning and to probe online the close relationship between brain and mind. The advent of these noninvasive neuroimaging techniques opened a new era in the investigation of language organization in healthy individuals. The main focus of the present chapter is to provide an overview of the most relevant results that have so far been achieved in the field of the exploration of the cerebral basis of bilingualism using functional neuroimaging techniques and to discuss which conclusions may be drawn from these studies. In particular, this chapter focuses on the potential role of a number of variables suggested to play a role on the shaping of language representations in the bilingual brain. Consistent results indicate that attained second language (L2) proficiency and perhaps language exposure are more important than the age of L2 acquisition as a determinant of the cerebral representation of languages in bilinguals/polyglots. Indeed, increasing L2 proficiency appears to be associated at the neural level with the engagement of the same network subserving the first language (L1) within the dedicated language areas, but it has also been shown that age of L2 acquisition may specifically affect the cortical representation of grammatical processing.

Although philosophers have for centuries pondered the relationship between mind and brain, neuroscientists have only recently been able to investigate this issue analytically. This possibility stems largely from developments in neuroimaging technologies, among them most notably positron emission tomography (PET) and functional magnetic resonance imaging (fMRI). These techniques can now capture "in vivo" images of the physiology of mind processes. For instance, they show us how specific regions of the brain "light up" when subjects are engaged in linguistic activities, such as listening to stories or producing words. Hence, they provide us with a powerful tool for mapping the language faculty in the human brain.

The issue of language and brain mechanism becomes more intriguing if we consider the unique capacity of the human brain to acquire, store, and use more than one language. Actually, more than half of the population of the earth speak more than one language. Hence, the phenomenon of bilingualism is expected to grow in future years (adopting the definition of bilingualism that covers not only the so-called balanced bilinguals, of which there may be relatively few, but also unbalanced forms, in which one of the languages dominates over the other; De Groot & Kroll, 1997). It becomes clear that related questions, whether theoretical or practical, deserve serious attention. How do bilinguals understand and produce language? Are there fundamental differences with monolingual speakers? How do people learn and acquire a second language (L2)? How does the human brain represent and organize multiple languages? Are there different or overlapping brain areas responsible for the processing of different languages? And, in the case of differential cerebral organization of languages, is this caused by the age of L2 acquisition or rather the degree of L2 proficiency? These are just a few of the many questions that can be raised in this respect. The last three issues are of a particular interest to neuroscientists and may be well addressed with the advances of functional neuroimaging techniques.

The main focus of the present chapter is to provide an overview of the most relevant results that have so far been achieved in the field of the cerebral basis of bilingualism using functional neuroimaging techniques and to discuss which conclusions may be drawn from these studies. We start with a brief introduction about the history of mapping language in the human brain; this discussion is followed by an elementary overview of PET and fMRI techniques and of their contribution to the field of neurolinguistics. We then consider those neuroimaging studies that have been specifically addressed to enlighten the cerebral organization of multiple languages. In particular, this chapter focuses on the potential role of a number of variables been suggested to play a role in the shaping of language representations in the bilingual brain.

The Brain and Language Relationship

Since the mid-18th century, brain scientists have proposed that several different parts of the brain are involved with language. Indeed, in the 19th century there was a rapid expansion of knowledge because of the systematic investigation of the effects of localized brain damage on language processing (the anatomoclinical method). This marked the beginning of an era of attempts to localize mental functions within the brain. Although earlier authors had appreciated, for example, that the substance of the brain, as opposed to the ventricles, had specific functions, the main localization theories began with the phrenologists. Gall speculated (1815, as cited in Leischner, 1987, p. 133) that the human brain was composed of many organs in which various human faculties resided. In those theories, an essential duality of the brain was assumed; that is, both sides were considered equipotential.

The duality theories were soon superseded by more discrete localization theories, closely related to the observations of the French surgeon Paul Broca (1861, 1865), who pointed out that there was an area in the brain especially devoted to speech. The story of Broca's achievements has been well recorded, and the subsequent designation of the foot of the third frontal convolution of the

dominant hemisphere as Broca's area is widely known. However, it was Wernicke, in his monograph (1874) on aphasia, who attempted to create a comprehensive model based on anatomoclinical localization principles.

Within the next dozen or so years, many different cerebral centers for various functions were defined, comprising centers for writing, reading, calculating, and so on. In general, these implicated the left side of the brain. Moreover, these discoveries gave scientists the first glimpses of the distributed nature of language function in the brain. The brain seemed to have no single location where language is created or stored. Instead, it looked as if different parts of the brain control different aspects of speech and language.

Interest in aphasia in bilinguals developed concurrently with the discovery of these various language centers and reflected the numerous controversies about the representation of language in the brain. In particular, it was observed that, if a bilingual subject was affected by an aphasia-producing left hemispheric lesion, both languages were not always affected to the same degree. Moreover, the recovery of language, which could follow, was not always parallel for both languages. Many different language recovery patterns have been described (for a classification, see Paradis, 1983): To account in bilingual aphasia for patterns of recovery of languages that could be labeled as differential, selective, successive, and antagonistic, neurologists invoked differential cerebral localization for each language.

For example, Scoresby-Jackson (1867) postulated that the foot of the third frontal convolution (Broca's area) should be a sort of language organ only for native languages, whereas the remaining part of the convolution might be responsible for L2s. He gave this explanation to account for an aphasic patient who selectively lost the use of his L2 after brain damage.

Pitres (1895) strongly argued against this view of different cerebral localization for different languages. Pitres founded his criticism on Charcot's theory, which assumed the existence of four independent speech centers (articulatory, auditory, graphic, and reading). Pitres indicated that, to recognize one center for each language, for each language the existence of four centers must be admitted. The impairment of one language would then presuppose the existence of four lesion foci, which is unlikely.

From that time, the debate of a hypothetical differential localization of multiple languages in the

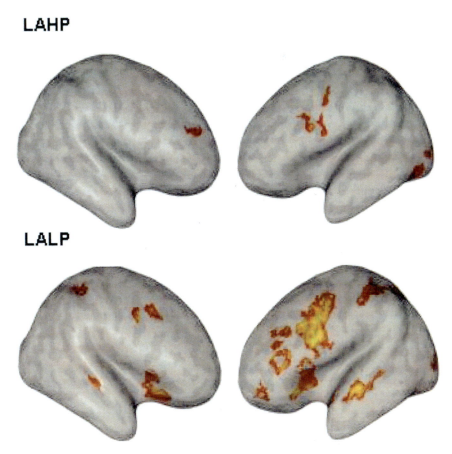

LAHP

LALP

Figure 24.1 Brain templates of the cerebral activation patterns of subjects judging the semantic content of sentences in their second language (L2) compared to that in their first language (L1). Two groups of Italian-German bilinguals are displayed: late acquisition and high proficiency (LAHP, top row), and late acquisition and low proficiency (LALP, bottom row). Brain activity patterns are displayed on the lateral surfaces of both hemispheres. The activation patterns of the LAHP group entailed a similar neural system and did not differ essentially in extension to that of an early acquisition and high proficiency Italian-German group (data not shown). On the other hand, as shown in the figure, the group of LALP bilinguals significantly engaged more extended brain areas. These results underline the crucial role of proficiency in the cerebral organization of the bilingual brain.

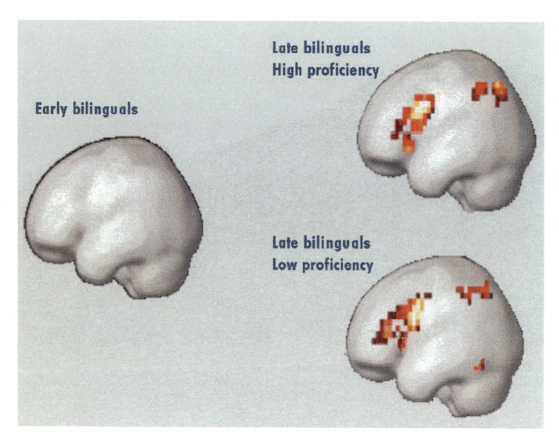

Figure 24.2 Brain activity patterns of bilinguals judging the grammatical content of sentences in their second language as compared to that in their first language. Three groups of Italian-German bilinguals are displayed: early bilinguals; late but high-proficiency bilinguals; late but low-proficiency bilinguals. Brain activity patterns are displayed on the lateral surfaces of the left hemisphere. Although early bilinguals engaged for both languages the same identical neural structures, this did not apply for late bilinguals. Both groups of late bilinguals engaged more extended brain areas for grammatical processing in their second language (L2). These results underline the age of acquisition effect on the neural underpinnings of grammatical processing.

same brain has invigorated discussion (for review, see Paradis, 1998; Fabbro, 1999). Some authors argued against an anatomic segregation for multiple languages within the language areas (Penfield, 1965). The majority of researchers were inclined to consider various kinds of differential representation, including distinct neuroanatomic localization. Segalowitz (1983) argued that it would be surprising if bilingualism had no effect on brain organization, and that there are numerous reasons to believe that cerebral representation of language is not entirely the same in polyglots as in monolinguals. Others have proposed that bilinguals are somewhat less lateralized than monolingual speakers, with the right hemisphere prevalently subserving one of the languages of the bilingual (Albert & Obler, 1978).

The "aphasiological panorama" was enriched in the late 1970s by studies with electrical cortical stimulation of language representation in bilinguals; the result was the temporary inactivation of a brain region (Ojemann & Whitaker, 1978). With these techniques, Ojemann and Whitaker mapped naming sites in the lateral cortex of the dominant cerebral hemisphere in bilingual epileptic patients chosen for neurosurgical treatment. In all patients studied, each language involved some "common" sites of naming interference and some "specific" area in which naming was interrupted only for one language. In the series of studies carried out by his group, Ojemann postulated that L2s should be organized in a somewhat different manner because their naming areas were generally larger than those for first languages (L1s).

It is noteworthy that both aphasiological studies and electrical cortical stimulation in bilinguals have provided evidence for heterogeneous patterns of localization. At the same time, they may have actually hampered the effort to define the general rules and the determinants of language organization in the bilingual brain. Indeed, although clinical studies have enhanced our knowledge about language recovery patterns in bilingual aphasics, they were not successful in defining the differential architecture of the bilingual brain and in identifying the variables that may be responsible for the heterogeneous patterns of language localization.

More than a century ago, Pitres (1895) theorized that greater exposure to a given language prior to disease onset may be a crucial factor for the differential recovery of languages, and Calvin and Ojemann (1994) questioned if the occurrence of larger naming sites for the L2 were caused by decreased knowledge or rather later acquisition.

In psycholinguistics, it is well known that several factors may influence the bilinguals' performance, among them the age of L2 acquisition, the degree of proficiency in each language, the modality of language learning, and the differential exposure to languages. In general, it was quite difficult to address these issues in clinical studies, mainly because of the well-known limitations of the anatomoclinical method.

Functional neuroimaging offers a number of advantages over patient studies, and lesion-based neuropsychology in general, regarding understanding the functional organization of the bilingual brain. First, aphasiological studies deal with "experiments of nature" in which it is, of course, impossible to control for the linguistic variables that may affect language representation. Second, aphasiological study may demonstrate whether a certain brain region is necessary for a given language component, but not usually the broader system of which that region may form a part. Third, the kind of anatomic information that can be derived from clinical studies is limited, with lesions that often differ markedly in size and location across different patients. PET and fMRI allow more precise spatial characterization of the areas of activation during language tasks. Thus, the advent of noninvasive neuroimaging techniques, as well as the application of electrophysiological techniques such as event-related brain potentials and magnetoencepalography, makes it more feasible to address crucial questions related to the cerebral organization of multiple languages. With these techniques, we can focus on healthy bilingual subjects with well-defined language backgrounds, and by using well-designed paradigms, we can attempt to characterize the neural architecture of the bilingual brain.

Functional Neuroimaging Techniques and Their Application in Neurolinguistics

Functional neuroimaging technologies such as PET and fMRI have enabled neuroscientists to examine the spatial and temporal mechanisms of cognitive functioning and to probe online the close relationship between brain and mind. The application of these technologies to address appropriate research issues may enable us to localize the components of cognitive processing in the human brain and to image their orchestration as humans perform a variety of cognitive tasks. If a cognitive process can be sustained for only a few seconds, the snapshot revealed by PET or fMRI can show which parts of the brain are active and to what degree (see Perani & Cappa, 1998, for a review).

It is generally accepted that regional cerebral blood flow (rCBF) reflects synaptic activity. Local increases in blood flow are necessary to replace the energy consumed by neurons. These changes in rCBF have been demonstrated to be closely related to changes in neural activity in both space and time. In functional neuroimaging studies, images of blood flow are collected in at least two different conditions (e.g., while generating words and while at rest). The perfusion data are then compared to find areas in which the experimental task is associated with increased cerebral blood flow in comparison with the control task. These areas of increased perfusion are typically referred to as *activations*.

PET measures blood flow employing radioactive labeled water, specifically hydrogen combined with oxygen (^{15}O), a radioactive isotope of oxygen. The labeled water, which is administered into a vein in the arm, emits copious numbers of positrons as it decays. In just over a minute, the radioactive water accumulates in the brain, providing an image of blood flow. The fast decay of ^{15}O and the small amounts permit many measurements of blood flow to be performed in a single session. Each picture serves as a snapshot that provides information about the momentary activity of the brain. Typically, images of blood flow are collected before a task is begun, thus providing a baseline condition (control task) to compare with those obtained when the brain is engaged in the experimental task. Subtracting blood flow measurements collected during the control task from those associated with the experimental task indicates the parts of the brain active during the latter.

Thus, PET allows assay of biological systems in vivo, providing information about brain function that is complementary to the anatomic information portrayed by structural imaging techniques, such as computed tomography and magnetic resonance imaging (MRI). Indeed, combining functional PET data with the high-resolution anatomic maps produced by MRI provides powerful data sets to investigate structure/function relationships in the brain.

Compared to PET, fMRI is a more recent non-invasive technique based on the measurement of MRI signal changes associated with alterations in local blood oxygenation levels. The fundamentals of fMRI are well established and are based on a phenomenon known as blood oxygenation level dependence (BOLD). In response to the activation, the rCBF increases to the relevant region, but for reasons that are still not well understood, the rCBF increases far more than the expected increase in oxygen demand (Ogawa, Lee, Kay, & Tank, 1990). The BOLD effect is particularly manifested in the venous compartment, which is only 60–70% saturated with oxygen at rest and hence has the capacity to get more oxygenated during the activation state, with a corresponding increase in MRI signal intensity. Using this totally noninvasive method, it is possible to localize functional brain activation with an accuracy of millimeters and a temporal resolution of about 3 s.

Besides these advantages in spatial and temporal resolution when compared to the PET technique, the fact that no radionuclides are used makes it feasible to repeat experiments several times on the same subject. Using fMRI, it is therefore possible to take advantage of more complex experimental designs.

However, fMRI imaging has some limits. For instance, crucial structures of the brain (in particular, orbitofrontal and inferior temporal regions and the temporal pole) may not be visualized because of interference with the magnetic field. This is mainly because the air enclosed in adjacent structures (the middle ear and the mastoid bone) creates serious interference with the magnetic field, resulting in a loss of their visualization.

A large body of functional neuroimaging studies has been devoted to the investigation of language organization in the intact human brain. Briefly, imaging studies employing these techniques have not only largely confirmed the anatomic knowledge gained from neuropsychological lesion studies, but also opened a number of new perspectives in our understanding of the brain–language relationship. Indeed, most imaging studies underline the importance of classical language-related areas within the perisylvian cortex of the left hemisphere, such as Broca's area. However, functional neuroimaging studies have considerably enlarged and redefined the scope of its participation in language processing: The left frontal convexity is involved in many tasks, such as word generation (Martin, Wiggs, Ungerleider, & Haxby, 1996), semantic and phonemic fluency (Mummery, Patterson, Hodges, & Wise, 1996; Paulesu et al., 1997), semantic monitoring (Thompson-Schill, D'Esposito, Aguirre, & Farah, 1997), and verbal working memory (Smith, Jonides, & Koeppe, 1996). Moreover, language-related activation has been reported also outside the classical language areas, such as in the inferior temporal gyrus and in the temporal pole, in the lingual and fusiform gyri (see reviews in Price, 1998, and Indefrey & Levelt, 2000). Furthermore, right hemispheric activation in mirror regions is observed during the performance of most language tasks.

These language-related areas located outside the classical language zone appear to be specialized for specific components of language processing, such as lexical semantics. Noteworthy, the functional role of the language-related areas as revealed by neuroimaging techniques appears to be characterized in terms of linguistically relevant systems, such as phonology, syntax, and lexical semantics, rather than in terms of activities, such as speaking, repeating, reading, and listening (Neville & Bavelier, 1998). For instance, a neuroimaging experiment of syntax error detection in monolinguals (Moro, Tettamanti, Perani, Donati, Cappa, & Fazio, 2001) detected the involvement of a selective deep component of Broca's area and a right inferior frontal region in addition to the left caudate nucleus and insula activated only during syntactic processing, indicating their role in syntactic computation. These findings provide original in vivo evidence that these brain structures in fact constitute an integrated neural network selectively engaged in morphological and syntactic computation.

Functional neuroimaging has also taught us that areas related to linguistic processing in the normal human brain appear not only more extended, but also less fixed than previously thought. For example, even when the task and experimental design are held constant, changes in language-related brain activation can be observed as a consequence of increased familiarity with the task. Striking evidence was provided by Petersen, Van Mier, Fiez, and Raichle (1998), who investigated the effects of practice on a verbal task using PET. The neural differences putatively related to processing differences between a high and a low practice performance of verb generation were highlighted by this study, in which decreasing brain activity in the left frontal convexity was reported following practice.

Visualizing the Bilingual Brain

As illustrated in the discussion here, some aphasiological investigations in bilinguals have provided evidence that a bilingual may selectively lose one of his or her languages while the other is spared, suggesting that multiple languages in the same brain may be somewhat differentially organized. The current research is focused on the degree of functional integration or separation of the languages in the polyglot brain. Several environmental factors have been considered to affect the neural organization of language, such as age of language acquisition and degree of proficiency attained in each of the spoken languages.

Regarding the first factor, a large body of literature suggests that linguistic abilities are sensitive to the age of exposure to language. People who learn a language at later ages, particularly after late infancy or puberty, do not generally achieve the same level of proficiency as young learners (Birdsong, 1999; Johnson & Newport, 1989). The causes of these age effects on language performance are controversial (see also Birdsong, chapter 6, this volume). Explanations range from the postulation of biologically based "critical periods" to differences between infant and adult learning contexts (Lenneberg, 1967; for extensive discussion about the "critical period," see also DeKeyser & Larson-Hall, chapter 5, this volume). In particular, the phonological and morphosyntactical components seem particularly deficient when L2 is learned later in life, whereas the lexicon seems to be acquired with less difficulty after puberty. This fact may entail the hypothesis that the neural representation of an L2 differs as a function of its age of acquisition.

On the other hand, proficiency also appears to play an important role in L2 organization. Several psycholinguistic studies indicated that processing the L2 changes during the acquisition in late language learners. For instance, in early stages of language learning, lexical items of the L2 are processed through association with their translation equivalents in the L1, whereas in later learning stages (and with increased proficiency), processing of L2 words is more directly conceptually mediated (Kroll & Dufour, 1995; Kroll & Stewart, 1994). In other words, L1 and L2 lexical items are both thought to access a common semantic system directly as a bilingual becomes more proficient in the L2. Thus, it may be asked if the increasing proficiency of late learners also entails a reorganization of language areas in the bilingual brain. Similarly, it could be asked if a hypothetical segregation of language areas is only a function of different ages of L2 acquisition. These interesting issues have been addressed by functional neuroimaging studies in normal adult bilinguals.

Here, we review these investigations with the specific aim to detect the factors that may have a major impact on the cerebral organization of two languages. The studies are here divided in two groups: those investigating language production (including word repetition) and those investigating language comprehension in bilinguals. As we described elsewhere (Abutalebi, Cappa, & Perani, 2001), this broad subdivision is only based on the experimental paradigms used for the imaging studies, which include a number of diverse behavioral tasks, ranging from sentence comprehension to lexical retrieval. Although some of these can be clearly considered to focus, respectively, on input processes or output processes (word generation), the distinction is not directly applicable to other language domains, such as word repetition and judgment tasks. Nonetheless, this atheoretical and to a certain degree arbitrary subdivision appears to have interesting implications for the interpretation of language-specific differences of brain activity patterns. A third section considers those studies investigating the neural basis of translation.

Language Production Studies in Bilinguals

Various functional neuroimaging studies investigated the neural correlates of language production in bilinguals (Table 24.1; Chee, Tan, & Thiel, 1999; Illes et al., 1999; Kim, Relkin, Lee, & Hirsch, 1997; Klein, Milner, Zatorre, Meyer, & Evans, 1995; Klein, Zatorre, Milner, Meyer, & Evans, 1994; Perani et al., 2003; Yetkin, Yetkin, Haughton, & Cox, 1996). These studies differ from a methodological point of view because several authors did not formally investigate the level of proficiency in the L2 but divided subjects only on the basis of their age of L2 acquisition (see Table 24.1 for details). A further important variable is that different experimental paradigms and modalities have been used to study language production in bilinguals.

The first two studies that opened this interesting field were carried out by Klein and coworkers (Klein et al., 1994, 1995). PET was used to elucidate whether production in an L2 involved the same neural substrates as production in the L1. The subjects of both studies were 12 Canadian late bilinguals with a high degree of proficiency as established by a screening language examination. In their first study, the authors used a word repetition task for L1 (English) and L2 (French) and reported that the pattern of brain activity was similar across the two languages. In particular, both languages commonly engaged brain activity in

overlapping areas of the left frontal lobe. However, when subjects repeated words by using their L2, a selective activation was also found in the left putamen, a subcortical structure belonging to the basal ganglia. The authors suggested that the left putamen may be involved in articulation processes when producing an L2 learned late in life. This hypothesis may be supported by lesion studies of the so-called foreign accent syndrome (Blumstein, Alexander, Ryalls, Katz, & Dworetzky, 1987; Gurd, Bessel, Bladon, & Bamford, 1988), in which monolingual patients acquired a so-called foreign accent when speaking after left subcortical damage. We should, however, underline that, with the exception of the second study of Klein and coworkers, in which the same experimental group of highly proficient bilinguals was used (Klein et al., 1995), none of the successive studies demonstrated the selective activation of the left putamen for L2. Moreover, the kind of task used in Klein et al.'s experiment (Klein et al., 1994) allows us to draw only limited conclusions about the cerebral organization of bilinguals because lexical-semantic access is not necessarily involved during repetition tasks.

In their second experiment, the authors (Klein et al., 1995) used several word generation tasks: rhyme generation, based on phonological cues; synonym generation, requiring semantic search; and translation, requiring lexical access in the other language. Irrespective of task requirements (rhymes or synonyms) and language used, a considerable overlap of activation was observed in frontal areas (left dorsolateral frontal cortex, particularly Brodmann areas [Ba] 9, 45, 46, and 47). Within the activated system, the left inferotemporal regions (Ba 20/37) and the left superior parietal cortex (Ba 7) were always involved irrespective of language and task, with the only exception rhyme generation in L2. Because no evidence of a differential neural substrate subserving language processing was found, the authors concluded that a similar distributed network of brain areas is engaged irrespective of task requirement in language production in highly proficient bilinguals despite the late acquisition of L2 (subjects in this study were late L2 learners).

Contrasting results to the studies of Klein and coworkers were provided by Yetkin and colleagues (1996). In an fMRI experiment based on word generation (phonemic verbal fluency) in multilinguals, larger foci of brain activation were reported for the "less-fluent" languages. *Fluent* was defined as speaking the language currently and for at least 5 years, whereas *nonfluent* was used for languages

Table 24.1 Neuroimaging Studies Investigating Language Production in Bilinguals

Study	Task and Methods	Group of Study	Main Results
Klein et al., 1994	Repetition of words in L2 compared to that in L1 studied by PET	Homogeneous group of 12 high-proficiency bilinguals who learned L2 after age 5 years	Increasing activity in the left putamen when repeating words in L2
Klein et al., 1995	PET investigation of phonological and semantic word generation in L1 and L2	Homogeneous group of 12 high-proficiency bilinguals who learned L2 after age 5 years	No evidence that a language learned later in life may be differently represented from the native language
Yetkin et al., 1996	Word generation in L1, L2, and L3 investigated by fMRI	Noncontrolled group of 5 multilinguals fluent in L2 but not in L3	Greater activity for languages in which subjects were least fluent
Kim et al., 1997	fMRI investigation of sentence generation task in L1 and L2	Noncontrolled group of 6 early bilinguals and 6 late bilinguals	Common areas of left frontal lobe activation for L1 and L2 in early bilinguals and spatially separated areas for late bilinguals
Chee, Tan et al., 1999a	fMRI study of cued word generation in L1 and L2	Controlled group of 15 early bilinguals and 9 late bilinguals, all highly proficient	Similar pattern of brain activations for early and late bilinguals
Illes et al., 1999	fMRI investigation of semantic and nonsemantic decisions in L1 and L2	Group of 8 late bilinguals (except Subject 8) with high degree of proficiency	No differences in brain activity for L1 and L2 during the semantic task
Perani et al., 2003	fMRI investigation of phonologically cued verbal fluency in L1 and L2	Homogeneous group of early and high-proficiency bilinguals but exposed differentially to languages	More extensive brain activity for the language to which subjects are less exposed, even when highly proficient for that language
De Bleser et al., 2003	Cognates and noncognate naming in L1 and L2 investigated with PET	Eleven late bilinguals (Dutch/French) with good but not nativelike proficiency for L2	More extended brain activity for noncognate naming in L2
Briellmann et al., 2004	fMRI during noun–verb generation	Six heterogeneous quadrilinguals	More extended left-side brain activity, mostly prefrontal cortex, for languages with lower proficiency

fMRI, functional magnetic resonance imaging; L1, L2, L3, first, second, third language, respectively; PET, positron emission tomography.

studied for 2 to 4 years and without regular use in the everyday life. The experimental group was composed of heterogeneous subjects, fluent in at least two languages and nonfluent in a third language. The languages ranged from Indo-European (English, German, Russian, Norwegian, French, Spanish) to Ural-Altaic (Turkish, Japanese, and Chinese).

Activations were primarily observed in the left prefrontal cortex (Yetkin et al., 1996), irrespective of language used, particularly in the inferior frontal, middle frontal, and precentral gyri. Additional foci of brain activation were reported, such as in the supplementary motor area and parietal lobe, but the precise localizations in terms of stereotactical coordinates of these activations were not specified. It is interesting that in all subjects the extension of focal brain activation was greater for a third language (L3) than for L2 and L1. Whereas the average activation was less for L1 than for L2, the difference did not reach statistical significance. Unfortunately, these findings are difficult to interpret given the lack of control of important variables such as the age of language acquisition and proficiency, which cannot be equated with language fluency. Classifying a bilingual as fluent only on empirical basis (subjects in the study were only asked how well they spoke each language) is far from a detailed psycholinguistic language proficiency evaluation. Moreover, the authors labeled English always as L1 despite the fact that the native language was Turkish in Subject 2 and Chinese in Subject 5.

The fMRI study performed by Kim and coworkers (1997) also used a very inhomogeneous group of bilinguals. The studied 12 bilinguals; of these, 6 had been exposed to L1 and L2 during early infancy; 6 began learning L2 after puberty. Again, the volunteers were bilinguals for widely different pairs of languages, ranging from Indo-European to languages from the Far East. In the experiment, they had to describe, using covert language production during fMRI scanning, what they had done at different times of the previous day. The brain activity in the left inferior frontal cortex (i.e., Broca's area) in this study was differentially activated for the two groups: There were overlapping activations for both languages in early learners; there were spatially segregated activations in the case of late learners. On the other hand, the regions activated by L1 and L2 within Wernicke's area overlapped in both groups of subjects, regardless of the age of L2 acquisition.

The authors' (Kim et al., 1997) conclusion was that age of acquisition is a major factor in the cortical organization of L2 processing. However, it must be underlined that the production of extended speech relies heavily on lexical-semantic and conceptual processing; in contrast, most of the linguistic processing limitations observed in bilinguals are related to phonological tasks or to morpho-syntactic processing. The subtle differences in activation in Broca's area may reflect these differences at the phonological and syntactic level. A further major problem for the interpretation of this study, as mentioned, is that no formal assessment of language proficiency was conducted. Because there is a general negative correlation between age of acquisition and proficiency (Johnson & Newport, 1989), these two variables were confounded in this experiment.

This issue was addressed by Chee, Tan, and their group (1999) using fMRI. These authors found no difference within the left prefrontal cortex when comparing word generation in early bilinguals and late bilinguals when the degree of language proficiency was kept constant. They compared 15 early bilinguals (L2 acquisition before age 6 years) to 9 late bilinguals (L2 acquisition after age 12 years). All subjects were native speakers of Mandarin, with English as L2, and were studied when producing words cued by a word stem presented visually on a screen. Brain activity was mainly located in the left prefrontal cortex, along the inferior and middle frontal gyri (Ba 44/45 and Ba 9/46). The authors predicted that the processing of Mandarin would require neural resources distinct from English because Mandarin has an ideographic writing system. However, the pattern of brain activation in response to Mandarin words was similar to that observed for English, and this was true for both early and late bilinguals with high proficiency.

The discrepancy between the studies of Kim and colleagues (1997; extended language production) and Chee, Tan, and colleagues (1999; word stem completion) might be related to the subjects' *different level of proficiency in each language*. As mentioned, in Kim's study the differential activation in Broca's area for the L2 in late bilinguals could have been caused by inferior proficiency in the L2. On the other hand, Chee, Tan, et al.'s subjects came from Singapore, which has a really integrated bilingual society in which bilingual speakers can be expected to be highly proficient in each language. In other words, these studies leave open the possibility that language proficiency, rather than age of acquisition, may be the crucial factor in determining the neural organization of language processing in bilinguals, as highlighted from the study of Perani and coworkers (1998) in language comprehension tasks (discussed separately in this section).

Along similar lines, the fMRI study of Illes and coworkers (1999) also included only subjects with a controlled degree of language proficiency. All were English-Spanish bilinguals recruited from Stanford University (Stanford, CA) and performed two kinds of task: semantic decisions about visually presented words (concrete or abstract) and non-semantic decisions (upper- or lowercase type). This study confirmed previous findings (Chee, Tan, et al., 1999; Perani et al., 1998): When the degree of proficiency in bilinguals is very high, a common neural network is activated independent of age of acquisition. Indeed, no differences were found when directly comparing both languages. The main activation foci were found in the left inferior frontal gyrus (Ba 44, 45, 47), with some activation in corresponding areas of the right hemisphere in a few subjects. Interestingly, semantic judgments led to a more extensive pattern of brain activity within those areas than did nonsemantic judgments. Unfortunately, the brain regions scanned in this fMRI experiment were too limited to allow further conclusions. The scanned area extended from the stereotactical coordinates $Z = -10$ to $Z = +46$ and therefore did not include brain regions, such as the middle and inferior temporal gyri, that may be important for semantic judgment tasks (Perani et al., 1999; Price, 1998).

The role of proficiency was addressed also by De Bleser and coworkers (2003). The authors investigated with PET lexical retrieval by means of naming visually presented cognate and noncognate items in L1 (Dutch) and L2 (French) in a group of Belgian late bilinguals with good, but not native-like, proficiency in their L2. Comparisons of cognate naming in L1 and L2 and noncognate naming in L1 showed overlapping brain activation patterns in the left hemisphere. Conversely, naming of noncognates in L2 entailed an additional selective activation of left prefrontal areas along the left inferior frontal gyrus. The authors suggested a relation between activation in left prefrontal areas and effortful lexical retrieval, as may be the case of retrieval of noncognates in an L2 for which subjects have a lower proficiency.

A further factor that may be responsible for differential cerebral organization of languages in bilinguals was investigated by Perani et al. (2003) in a study that attempted to assess the effect of "environmental exposure" to one language. This was addressed by examining two groups of early bilinguals with a high degree of proficiency divided on the basis of their language dominance, referred to as the language acquired first in life (6 Spanish-born versus 5 Catalan-born individuals). All of these subjects were living in Catalonia (Spain), and Catalan was prevalent in their everyday language exposure, as assessed by detailed psycholinguistic investigations. This study showed first that the language acquired first in life, irrespective of language proficiency and age of L2 acquisition, may be an important factor for differences in the bilingual brain, resulting in some differences in brain activation even in early bilinguals. In particular, the L1 engaged fewer brain areas for the generation of words. One explanation may be that the generation of words in the L1 is a more automatic task and is reflected, at the cerebral level, by the engagement of

fewer neural resources. This is in agreement with previous results (Raichle et al., 1994; Thompson-Shill et al., 1997; Thompson-Shill, D'Esposito, & Kan, 1999) in which a less-automatic cognitive task engages more cerebral resources, as is the case for the generation of words in the L2 in bilinguals.

Another finding from the study of Perani et al. (2003) concerned the role of differential exposure to a given language. More extensive brain activation in the left dorsolateral frontal cortex was found for the group of Catalans when generating words in Spanish when compared to the group of Spaniards generating words in Catalan. These findings suggest that an L2 associated with lower environmental exposure is in need of additional neural resources in comparison to L1 (i.e., Spanish language in Catalans). On the other hand, the group of Spaniards, well exposed to Catalan, had a reduced area of brain activation for word generation in L2. The authors hypothesized that the brain activations were related to exposure and practice. The brain might then eventually support the generation of words with less or more recruitment of cerebral structures.

Before attempting to draw some conclusions from the results of production studies, several limitations of the available evidence must be acknowledged. The majority of the production experiments in bilinguals were based on single-word processing, particularly in word generation (fluency) tasks. With the exception of Kim et al.'s (1997) study, all imaging investigations focused on tasks expected to involve only single-word lexical processing with no grammatical processing.

Fluency tasks are associated with the same pattern of brain activation found previously in monolinguals, namely, involvement of the left dorsolateral frontal cortex (Poline, Vandenberghe, Holmes, Friston, & Frackowiak, 1996). The generation of words according to a cue is a complex task that involves multiple cognitive processes, such as lexical search, lexical retrieval, and speech production. Anatomo-functional differences have been reported between fluency tasks, for example, between phonemic verbal fluency and semantic verbal fluency (Mummery et al., 1996; Paulesu et al., 1997). Functional studies of brain representation of different languages should take carefully into account these cognitive aspects.

Considering these limitations, which conclusions may be drawn? Are we now able to answer the initial question whether there are anatomically segregated brain areas subserving two (or multiple) languages in the human brain? And, if so, are there general rules determining a spatial segregation of language areas for bilinguals?

From the reported results, we may outline the following conclusions: There are no differences in brain activity for very early bilinguals (we might assume that these subjects were highly proficient for both languages) and, similarly, no differences for late bilinguals if they are highly proficient in both languages (Chee, Tan, et al., 1999; Illes et al., 1999; Klein et al., 1995). Contrasting to this assumption is the study of Kim and coworkers (1997) in which spatially separated regions were activated within Broca's area for L1 and L2. However, as this study lacked any information about the degree of proficiency in L2 of the subjects, we do not know whether this differential cerebral organization was a consequence of the age of L2 acquisition or rather of reduced proficiency. This critique is also applicable to Yetkin et al.'s study (1996), even if they provided evidence that when a language is spoken less fluently, a larger cerebral activation can be observed in comparison with more fluent languages. We do not know, however, if this result must be ascribed to high/low proficiency or high/low exposure. In terms of proficiency, as addressed with psycholinguistic testing, a recent fMRI study carried out in a group of quadrilinguals (Briellmann et al., 2004) provided further evidence that larger foci of brain activity, mostly within the left prefrontal cortex, are related to the less-proficient languages (such as L3 or L4).

Overall, these findings appear to indicate that attained proficiency might be more important than age of acquisition as a determinant of the cerebral representation of languages in bilinguals/polyglots. Moreover, the results of the study by Perani et al. (2003) underline that differences in environmental exposure to a language may also account for functional modulation in the cerebral representation of languages, even when age of L2 acquisition and proficiency are kept constant.

Further investigations, taking into appropriate consideration at least these three important linguistic criteria (age of L2 acquisition, degree of language proficiency, and preferential exposure to a language), are necessary to draw stronger conclusions.

Language Comprehension Studies in Bilinguals

Many studies have investigated the brain correlates of language comprehension in bilinguals. These studies are listed in Table 24.2. Perani and colleagues carried out several PET studies in which they investigated the receptive sentence processing of late low-proficiency bilinguals (Perani et al., 1996), early high-proficiency bilinguals, and late high-proficiency bilinguals (Perani et al., 1998). In the first, Perani and coworkers (1996) studied with PET nine late acquisition bilinguals (Italian-English) who had low proficiency in their L2, English, which they had studied at school for at least 5 years. None of the subjects had spent more than 1 month in an English-speaking environment, and they therefore mastered L2 poorly. Partially different cerebral substrates were active for the L1 and L2 when compared to the baseline condition (attentive rest condition). Areas activated by the L1 comprised left perisylvian areas, including the angular gyrus (Ba 39), the superior and middle temporal gyri (Ba 21 and 22), the inferior frontal gyrus (Ba 45), and the temporal pole (Ba 38). Several homologous areas (Ba 21, 22, and 38) were also activated in the right hemisphere. In contrast, the set of active language areas was considerably reduced when applying the same analysis to the L2. Specifically, only the left and right superior and middle temporal areas remained active.

One of the crucial areas of differential activation was, rather unexpectedly, the temporal pole. Activation of this region has been seldom reported in the functional imaging studies on language and memory. However, some studies have shown that the anterior part of the temporal lobe is activated by tasks requiring listening or reading sentences or a continuous text (Bottini et al., 1994; Fletcher et al., 1995; Mazoyer, et al., 1993; Perani et al., 1996) rather than unconnected verbal material. Perani and coworkers (1996) suggested that these regions might be involved in processes associated with the sentence or even the discourse level, such as integration with prior knowledge, inference, and anaphoric reference. In addition, the temporal poles might be recruited on the basis of increasing memory demands when the subjects are engaged in the natural task of listening to some simple narrative.

In the second experiment (Perani et al., 1998), the authors tested Italian native speakers who learned English after age 10 years, who had spent 1 to 6 years in an English-speaking country, and who currently used English in their daily activities. These late bilinguals were scanned during experimental conditions such as listening to Italian, English, or Japanese stories (unknown to all subjects) or attentive silence. In the second part of the same experiment, the authors examined early acquisition and high-proficiency Spanish and Catalan bilinguals. These early bilinguals were scanned while

Table 24.2 Neuroimaging Studies Investigating Language Comprehension in Bilinguals

Study	Task and Methods	Group of Study	Main Results
Perani et al., 1996	Passive listening to stories in L1, L2, and a third unknown language as studied by PET	Homogeneous group of 9 low-proficiency late bilinguals	Greater activations when processing the native language in comparison to L2
Dehaene et al., 1997	fMRI single-subject study of listening to stories in L1 and L2	Homogeneous group of 8 low-proficiency late bilinguals	Differential brain activation for late L2 learners (including the right hemisphere)
Perani et al., 1998	Two PET studies of two groups of subjects listening to stories in L1 and L2	Two homogeneous groups of bilinguals: 9 high-proficiency but late bilinguals and 12 high-proficiency but early bilinguals	Overlapping patterns of brain activity in all high-proficiency bilinguals, underlining the crucial role of proficiency
Chee, Caplan, et al., 1999	fMRI investigation of visually presented sentence comprehension in L1 and L2	Homogeneous group of 14 early bilinguals	Common patterns of brain activity for L1 and L2
Price et al., 1999	Single-word comprehension in L1 and L2 studied by PET	Homogenous group formed by 6 late bilinguals	Greater activity in the left temporal lobe for L1
Chee et al., 2001	fMRI scanning while bilinguals perform semantic judgments	Two homogenous groups of low-proficiency and high-proficiency bilinguals	Reduced brain activity in left prefrontal and parietal regions when subjects were highly proficient
Wartenburger et al., 2003	fMRI investigation of grammatical and semantic judgment in bilinguals	Three controlled groups of bilinguals divided on the basis of age of L2 acquisition and proficiency	Age of acquisition dependency of grammar and proficiency dependency of semantic judgments

fMRI, functional magnetic resonance imaging; L1, and L2 indicate first and second language, respectively; PET, positron emission tomography.

listening to Spanish and Catalan stories. In both groups of bilinguals (early and late high-proficiency bilinguals), L1 and L2 yielded highly similar cerebral activation patterns. In fact, both groups showed brain activity located mainly in the left superior and middle temporal gyrus and in the left temporal pole.

The overlapping pattern of activation for L1 and L2 in Perani et al.'s 1998 study contrasted to the considerable differences in L1-L2 activations found in low-proficiency speakers (Perani et al., 1996). The combined results of these studies provided the first in vivo evidence for a different functional representation of L1 and L2 in comprehension when a crucial variable such as language proficiency is taken into account.

Dehaene et al. (1997) performed a similar experiment using fMRI in a comparable group of

experimental subjects (eight late bilinguals, with French the L1 and English the L2) scanned while listening to short stories alternatively in French and English. Listening to the stories in L1 engaged a set of left-sided brain areas, with additional similar, although much weaker, activation in the right hemisphere, whereas this pattern radically changed when subjects processed their L2. It is noteworthy that a single-subject analysis showed a quite disparate pattern of brain activity for L2, indicating large intersubject variability. Indeed, listening to L2 engaged a highly variable network of left and right temporal and frontal areas among the subjects, in some individuals restricted only to the right hemisphere. On the basis of these results, the authors confirmed that, although the processing of the L1 essentially relies on a dedicated left hemispheric cerebral network, the processing of an L2 acquired late in life and mastered with reduced proficiency may be differentially organized.

This series of experiments (Dehaene et al., 1997; Perani et al., 1996, 1998) provided evidence of functional modulation in the network that mediates language comprehension in the bilingual brain. The main result is that, although listening to stories in L1 and in L2 yields very different patterns of cortical activity in low-proficiency subjects, no major differences are present in highly proficient subjects, even with later L2 acquisition. The languages spoken by the low- and high-proficiency volunteers were identical and so was the procedure. Hence, we must conclude that the degree of mastery of L2 is responsible for the observed differences between the groups: Auditory language comprehension in proficient bilinguals who have learned L2 after the age of 10 years relies on a macroscopic network of areas that is similar for L1 and L2 groups.

It is noteworthy that these results were also confirmed by two further studies (Chee, Caplan, et al., 1999b; Price, Green, & von Studnitz, 1999). In the first, fMRI was used to investigate a very homogeneous group of 14 early bilinguals, using two orthographically and phonologically distant languages (English and Mandarin), while they evaluated sentence meaning. A comparable set of brain areas was activated for L1 and L2, among them the left inferior and middle frontal gyri, the left superior and middle temporal gyri, the left temporal pole, the anterior supplementary motor area, and, bilaterally, superior parietal regions and occipital regions. Thus, also with these two orthographically and phonologically distant languages, a strikingly overlapping brain activity pattern was present for both languages, as indicated by the direct contrasts (English vs. Mandarin and vice versa) that yielded no significant differences.

The study of Price et al. (1999), in which six late bilinguals were investigated using PET, provided results at the single-word level. The language areas in the left temporal lobe were more activated when processing the L1 compared to a less-known language. Indeed, comprehension of words in L1 yielded greater activation in the temporal pole than comprehension of the words in L2. This is in agreement with Perani et al.'s (1996) results in late bilinguals with a low degree of proficiency.

Chee, Hon, Lee, and Soon (2001) used a different task (semantic judgment) to evaluate with fMRI the effect of the language proficiency on cerebral language representation in bilinguals. Two different groups of Mandarin-English bilinguals who differed in language proficiency were studied. Higher language proficiency was associated with smaller activation foci within the left prefrontal and parietal areas, whereas lower proficiency was associated with a more extended network of activations, including foci in the right hemisphere. The results are apparently different from those of Perani et al.'s (1996, 1998). However, the nature of the task should be considered: passive listening to stories in the studies of Perani and coworkers and active judging of the semantic contents in the study of Chee and coworkers. The latter seems to require the engagement of additional neural resources when the language is mastered poorly.

In conclusion, in early bilinguals who received equal practice with their two languages from birth a single and common language system appears to be responsible for the processing of both languages (Chee, Caplan, et al., 1999; Perani et al., 1998). This system extends along a left-sided network comprising all the classical language areas. In the temporal lobe, these include the superior and middle temporal gyri, the angular gyrus, and the temporal pole, a structure that seems specifically engaged by sentence- and discourse-level processing. In the case of late bilinguals, the degree of language proficiency seems to be a critical factor in shaping the functional brain organization of languages because high-proficiency late bilinguals activated strikingly similar left hemispheric areas for L1 and L2 (Chee, Caplan, et al., 1999; Perani et al., 1998), whereas less-proficient subjects had different patterns of activation for their two languages (Chee et al., 2001; Dehaene et al., 1997; Perani et al., 1996; Price et al., 1999). In the case of comprehension of extended text (but not semantic judgment), the activation was more limited in the case of L2. This may reflect a less-consistent pattern of activation (as suggested by the results of Dehaene's study) or more limited processing, focusing on a superficial analysis of the less-proficient language. Also, in the case of comprehension, increasing language proficiency appears to be a crucial factor for language representation in bilinguals.

We should at this point underline that the paradigms employed so far with functional imaging in language studies do not allow a clear differentiation of the various language components (semantic, morphological, and syntactic) as traditionally defined within linguistic theory. For instance, there is an ongoing discussion whether there is a critical period in L2 acquisition (Johnson & Newport, 1989) and whether this period concerns only the phonological and morphosyntactic domains of language processing. Using ERPs, Weber-Fox and Neville (1996) found that different aspects of language (i.e., semantic and syntax) are differentially affected by the age of L2 acquisition.

To address this issue, an fMRI study investigated the neural correlates of grammatical and semantic judgments in three groups of Italian-German bilinguals. The subjects acquired the L1 and L2 from birth (first group) or after the age of 6 years, but with different proficiency levels (second and third group) (Wartenburger, Heekeren, Abutalebi, Cappa, Villringer, & Perani, 2003). This study demonstrated

that age of acquisition specifically affects the cortical representation of grammatical processes. Only in the case of the L2 acquired very early in life do overlapping neural substrates for L1 and L2 grammar result. In addition, in late bilinguals proficiency is the main determinant of the cerebral organization of both grammar and semantics. This is illustrated in Fig. 24.1, which reports the brain activity patterns in two of the three groups of late bilinguals with different levels of proficiency of Wartenburger et al.'s study during semantic judgment.

These findings are in agreement with the existence of a 'critical period' for language acquisition

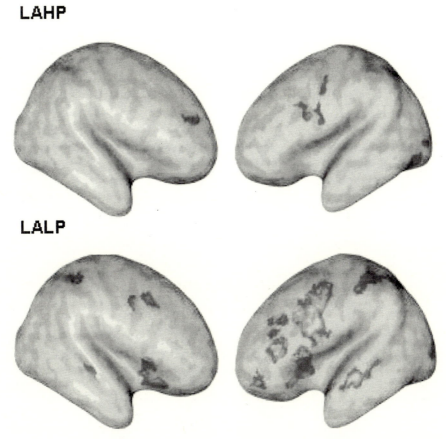

Figure 24.1 Brain templates of the cerebral activation patterns of subjects judging the semantic content of sentences in their second language (L2) compared to that in their first language (L1). Two groups of Italian-German bilinguals are displayed: late acquisition and high proficiency (LAHP, top row), and late acquisition and low proficiency (LALP, bottom row). Brain activity patterns are displayed on the lateral surfaces of both hemispheres. The activation patterns of the LAHP group entailed a similar neural system and did not differ essentially in extension to that of an early acquisition and high proficiency Italian-German group (data not shown). On the other hand, as shown in the figure, the group of LALP bilinguals significantly engaged more extended brain areas. These results underline the crucial role of proficiency in the cerebral organization of the bilingual brain.

and suggest that grammatical processing, given its dependence on age of acquisition, is based on competence which should be neurologically "wired-in" (see Fig. 24.2).

Neuroimaging Studies of Translation and the Language Selection Mechanism

Three studies (Table 24.3) addressed the neural basis of the translation and language selection mechanisms with functional neuroimaging (Hernandez, Dapretto, Mazziotta, & Bookheimer, 2001;

Price et al., 1999; Rodriguez-Fornells, Rotte, Heinze, Nösselt, & Münte, 2002).

Price and coworkers (1999) studied six subjects whose L1 was German and who became fluent in their L2 (English) late, after infancy. Subjects were studied with PET while they read or translated written words, one at a time, from L1 to L2 and vice versa. In distinct blocks, the words were presented only in German, only in English, or in alternation between the two languages. Noteworthy, the regions most active during translation were located outside the classical language areas. Translating, when compared to reading, activated mainly the anterior cingulate and bilateral subcortical

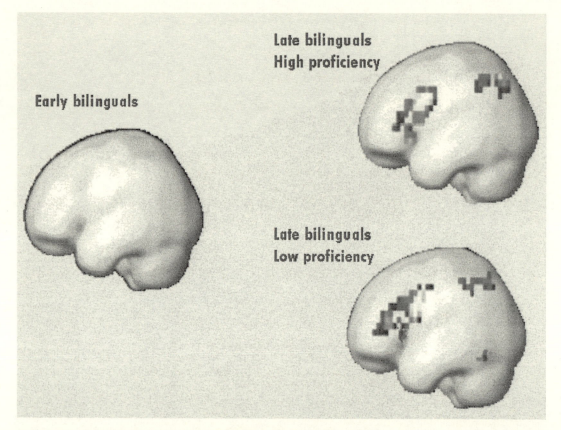

Figure 24.2 Brain activity patterns of bilinguals judging the grammatical content of sentences in their second language as compared to that in their first language. Three groups of Italian-German bilinguals are displayed: early bilinguals; late but high-proficiency bilinguals; late but low-proficiency bilinguals. Brain activity patterns are displayed on the lateral surfaces of the left hemisphere. Although early bilinguals engaged for both languages the same identical neural structures, this did not apply for late bilinguals. Both groups of late bilinguals engaged more extended brain areas for grammatical processing in their second language (L2). These results underline the age of acquisition effect on the neural underpinnings of grammatical processing.

Table 24.3 Neuroimaging Studies Investigating Language Translation and Language Selection Mechanism

Study	Task and Methods	Group of Study	Main Results
Price et al., 1999	PET investigation of written word translation from L1 to L2 and vice versa	Homogenous group of six late bilinguals	Activation of the anterior cingulate and bilateral subcortical structures while translating
Hernandez et al., 2001	Language naming and switching investigated by fMRI	Homogenous group of six early bilinguals more fluent in English than in Spanish	Overlapping brain areas when naming in either L1 and L2, increasing brain activity in the left frontal lobe when switching
Rodriguez-Fornells et al., 2002	fMRI study of language selection between Spanish-Catalan visually presented words	Homogenous group of seven high-proficiency early bilinguals compared to a group of seven monolinguals	Bilinguals, in comparison to monolinguals, showed a selective activation of a prefrontal area that may be implicated in inhibiting the nontarget language

fMRI, functional magnetic resonance imaging; L1, and L2 indicate first and second language, respectively; PET, positron emission tomography.

structures (the putamen and the head of the caudate nucleus). Price and colleagues attributed this to the need for greater coordination of mental operations for translation, during which the direct cerebral pathways for naming words must be inhibited in favor of less-automated circuits.

This hypothesis was also raised in neuropsychological lesion studies in bilinguals, indicating that damage to subcortical structures may interfere with the complex mechanism implicated in the selection of languages. Aglioti and coworkers described the case of a bilingual suffering left subcortical damage (capsulo-putaminal lesion) that inhibited language changes when speaking (Aglioti, Beltramello, Girardi, & Fabbro, 1996; Aglioti & Fabbro, 1993). Abutalebi, Miozzo, and Cappa (2000) also reported the case of a polyglot who was no longer able to speak in one language, showing pathological language mixing caused by a lesion located in the head of the caudate nucleus in the left hemisphere. It has thus been theorized that the bilinguals'/polyglots' lexical representations may be selectively accessed under the control of neural routes involving a cortical-subcortical circuit in which the left basal ganglia may represent the "supervisor" of language output in bilinguals. A further interesting finding of Price et al.'s study (1999) was the activation of Broca's area and supramarginal gyrus during language switching. It is noteworthy that Poetzl (1925, 1930) and Leischner (1943) had suggested, on the basis of defective

switching performance by patients with supramarginal lesions, a central role for this region in language switching.

The second study (Hernandez et al., 2001) was carried out with Spanish-English early and supposedly high-proficiency bilinguals who were more fluent in English as formally tested. To examine the neural correlates of language switching, subjects named objects in one language or switched between languages. When confronting the pattern of brain activity for each language, overlapping patterns resulted in the left dorsolateral prefrontal cortex (Ba 46 and 6) and Broca's area (Ba 44 and 45). It is noteworthy that the authors reported increasing activity in the dorsolateral prefrontal cortex for the switching condition relative to the nonswitching conditions, suggesting that the left dorsolateral prefrontal is implicated in the mechanism of language switching and language selection. Unfortunately, the whole switching condition was pooled together so that we do not know whether there are differences when switching from L1 to L2 or rather from L2 to L1.

The intriguing issue of how bilinguals select languages was further addressed by the study of Rodriguez-Fornells et al. (2002). The main aim of their study was to enlighten how bilinguals inhibit the nontarget language (Catalan in the study) during lexical access of visually presented words in the target language (Spanish in the study). This was addressed by studying with ERPs and fMRI a group of early bilinguals (Catalan-Spanish) reporting a high degree of language proficiency for both languages. The results were compared to a group of Spanish monolinguals selecting visually presented real Spanish words intermixed with pseudowords. Interestingly, only in the group of bilinguals a selective activation of a left anterior prefrontal region (Ba 45 and 9) was reported, which the authors correlated to the inhibition of the nontarget language.

A further intriguing finding of Rodriguez-Fornells et al.'s study (2002) was that ERPs showed a typical sensitivity to word frequency only for words in the target language and not for words in the nontarget language. It may be hypothesized that words from the nontarget language are not accessed through a direct "lexical route," but rather they are discarded through a "sublexical" route.

In conclusion, these three neuroimaging investigations underline the role of left subcortical and dorsolateral prefrontal brain regions in the mechanism of language selection, supporting neuropsychological lesion findings in bilinguals (Abutalebi et al., 2000; Aglioti et al., 1993, 1996).

Conclusions

A number of important functional neuroimaging studies addressing the cerebral representation of bilingualism have been performed. In the present chapter, we reviewed these studies, emphasizing how several factors shown to be crucial in psycholinguistics may affect the neural basis of the bilingual language system. These factors are mainly represented by the age of L2 acquisition, the degree of proficiency for languages, and the degree of usage/exposure to languages. The available evidence suggests that proficiency is the most relevant factor. In the case of language production tasks in general and in tasks of language comprehension, there are differences that appear to be in opposite directions: more extensive cerebral activations associated with production in the less-proficient language and smaller activations with comprehending the less-proficient language. Hence, it may be speculated that this puzzling result may reflect the inherent differences of these aspects of linguistic processing. In the case of "effortful" tasks such as word generation, this difference may be attributed to the recruitment of additional resources.

On the other hand, in the case of sentence comprehension, the automatic nature of the processing may be reflected in a more limited elaboration of the linguistic material in the less-proficient language. Another possibility, suggested by the single-subject study of Dehaene et al. (1997), is the large intersubject variability in the activation pattern for comprehension of L2. It must be underlined that the neuroimaging data do not question the claim that age of acquisition is a major determinant of proficiency in L2. Many linguistic and neurophysiological studies have found that late learners are typically less proficient than early learners (Flege, Munro, & MacKay, 1995; Johnson & Newport, 1989; Weber-Fox & Neville, 1996). The role of age of acquisition seems to have crucial implications for particular domains of language, such as grammar, as shown by the study of Wartenburger and coworkers (2003).

The specific role of practice and exposure, in terms of frequency of usage, has to be investigated further and should not be confounded with proficiency (in terms of absolute level of fluency). The finding that language exposure may be an additional crucial factor for the neural representation of multiple languages (Perani et al., 2003) may provide important inputs either to educational fields, such as in the case of L2 learning, or to language rehabilitation in bilingual aphasia.

In our opinion, the most important contribution of imaging studies of bilingualism to our understanding of language representation in the brain is the observation of aspects of invariance and plasticity. We can conclude from the available evidence that the patterns of brain activation associated with tasks that engage specific aspects of linguistic processing are remarkably consistent across different languages and different speakers. These relatively fixed patterns, however, are clearly modulated by a number of factors analytically addressed in this review. Proficiency, age of acquisition, and exposure can affect brain activity, interacting in a complex way with the levels of language representation and the modalities of language performance. Future studies are expected to disentangle the specificity and selectivity of these interactions. In general, the imaging study of multilingual subjects appears to be a promising model for the study of the interactions between a prewired neurobiological substrate and environmental, time-locked influences.

References

Abutalebi, J., Cappa, S. F., & Perani, D. (2001). The bilingual brain as revealed by functional neuroimaging. *Bilingualism: Language and Cognition, 4,* 179–190.

Abutalebi, J., Miozzo, A., & Cappa, S. F. (2000). Do subcortical structures control language selection in bilinguals? Evidence from pathological language mixing. *Neurocase, 6,* 101–106.

Aglioti, S., Beltramello, A., Girardi, F., & Fabbro, F. (1996). Neurolinguistic and follow-up study of an unusual pattern of recovery from bilingual subcortical aphasia. *Brain, 119,* 1551–1564.

Aglioti, S., & Fabbro, F. (1993). Paradoxical selective recovery in a bilingual aphasic following subcortical lesion. *Neuroreport, 4,* 1359–1362.

Albert, M. L., & Obler, L. K. (1978). *The bilingual brain.* New York: Academic Press.

Birdsong, D. (1999). *Second language acquisition and the critical period hypothesis.* Mahwah, NJ: Erlbaum.

Blumstein, S. E., Alexander, M. P., Ryalls, J. H., Katz, W., & Dworetzky, B. (1987). On the nature of foreign accent syndrome: A case study. *Brain and Language, 31,* 215–244.

Bottini, G., Corcoran, R., Sterzi, R., Paulesu, E., Schenone, P., Scarpa, P., et al. (1994). The role of the right hemisphere in the interpretation of figurative aspects of language. A positron emission tomography activation study. *Brain, 117,* 1231–1253.

Briellmann, R. S., Saling, M. M., Connell, A. B., Waites, A. B., Abbott, D. F., & Jackson, G. D. (2004). A high-field functional MRI study of quadrilingual subjects. *Brain and Language, 89,* 531–542.

Broca, P. (1861). Perte de la parole, ramolissement chronique et destruction partielle du lobe antérieur gauche du cerveau. *Bulletin de la Societé d' Anthropologie, 11,* 235–237.

Broca, P. (1865). Sur le siège de la faculté du langage articulé. *Bulletin de la Société d'Anthropologie, 6,* 337–393.

Calvin, W. H., & Ojemann, G. A. (1994). *Conversation with Neil's brain.* New York: Addison-Wesley.

Chee, M. W. L., Caplan, D., Soon, C. S., Sriram, N., Tan, E. W. L., Thiel, T., et al. (1999). Processing of visually presented sentences in Mandarin and English studied with fMRI. *Neuron, 23,* 127–137.

Chee, M. W. L., Hon, N., Lee, H. L., & Soon, C. S. (2001). Relative language proficiency modulates BOLD signal change when Bilinguals perform semantic judgments. *Neuroimage, 13,* 1155–1163.

Chee, M. W. L., Tan, E. W. L., & Thiel, T. (1999). Mandarin and English single word processing studied with functional magnetic resonance

imaging. *Journal of Neuroscience, 19,* 3050–3056.

De Bleser, R., Dupont, P., Postler, J., Bormans, G., Speelman, D., Mortelmans, L., et al. (2003). The organisation of the bilingual lexicon: A PET study. *Journal of Neurolinguistics, 16,* 439–456.

De Groot, A. M. B., & Kroll, J. F. (Eds.). (1997). *Tutorials in bilingualism: Psycholinguistic perspectives.* Mahwah, NJ: Erlbaum.

Dehaene, S. D., Dupoux, E., Mehler, J., Cohen, L., Paulesu, E., Perani, D., et al. (1997). Anatomical variability in the cortical representation of first and second languages. *Neuroreport, 8,* 3809–3815.

Dufour, R., & Kroll, J. F. (1995). Matching words to concepts in two languages: A test of the concept mediation model of bilingual representation. *Memory & Cognition, 23,* 166–180.

Fabbro, F. (1999). *The neurolinguistics of bilingualism. An introduction.* Hove, U.K.: Psychology Press.

Flege, J. E., Munro, M. J., & MacKay, I. R. A. (1995). Effects of age of second-language learning on the production of English consonants. *Speech Communication, 16,* 1–26.

Fletcher, P. C., Happé, F., Frith, U., Baker, S. C., Dolan, R. J., Frachowiak, R. S. J., et al. (1995). Other minds in the brain: A functional imaging study of "theory of mind" in story comprehension. *Cognition, 57,* 109–128.

Gurd, J. M., Bessel, N. J., Bladon, R. A. W., & Bamford, J. M. (1988). *Neuropsychologia, 26,* 237–251.

Hernandez, A. E., Dapretto, M., Mazziotta, J., & Bookheimer, S. (2001). Language switching and language representation in Spanish-English Bilinguals: An fMRI study. *Neuroimage, 14,* 510–520.

Illes, J., Francis, W. S., Desmond, J. E., Gabrieli, J. D. E., Glover, G. H., Poldrack, R., et al. (1999). Convergent cortical representation of semantic processing in bilinguals. *Brain and Language, 70,* 347–363.

Indefrey, P., & Levelt, W. J. M. (2000). The neural correlates of language production. In M. S. Gazzaniga (Ed.), *The new cognitive neurosciences.* Cambridge, MA: MIT Press.

Johnson, J., & Newport, E. (1989). Critical period effects in second language learning: the influence of maturational state on the acquisition of English as a second language. *Cognitive Psychology, 21,* 60–99.

Kim, K. H. S., Relkin, N. R., Lee, K. M., & Hirsch, J. (1997). Distinct cortical areas associated with native and second languages. *Nature, 388,* 171–174.

Klein, D., Milner, B., Zatorre, R., Meyer, E., & Evans, A. (1995). The neural substrates underlying word generation: A bilingual functional-imaging study. *Proceedings of the National Academy of Sciences U.S.A., 92,* 2899–2903.

Klein, D., Zatorre, R., Milner, B., Meyer, E., & Evans, A. (1994). Left putaminal activation when speaking a second language: evidence from PET. *Neuroreport, 5,* 2295–2297.

Kroll, J. F., & Stewart, E. (1994) Category interference in translation and picture naming: Evidence for asymmetric connections between bilingual memory representations. *Journal of Language and Memory, 33,* 149–174.

Leischner, A. (1943). Die Aphasien der Taubstummen. Ein Beitrag zur Lehre der Asymbolie. *Archiv fuer Psychiatrie und Nervenkrankheiten, 115,* 469–548.

Leischner, A. (1987). *Aphasien und Sprachentwicklungsstoerungen.* Stuttgart, Germany: Thieme Verlag.

Lenneberg, E. H. (1967). *Biological foundations of language.* New York: Wiley.

Martin, A., Wiggs, C. L., Ungerleider, L. G., & Haxby, E. (1996). Neural correlates of category-specific knowledge. *Nature, 379,* 649–652.

Mazoyer, B. M., Tzourio, N., Frank, V., Syrota, A., Murayama, N., Levrier, O., et al. (1993). The cortical representation of speech. *Journal of Cognitive Neuroscience, 5,* 467–479.

Moro, A., Tettamanti, M., Perani, D., Donati, C., Cappa, S. F., & Fazio, F. (2001). Syntax and the brain: Disentangling grammar by selective anomalies. *Neuroimage, 13,* 110–118.

Mummery, C. J., Patterson, K., Hodges, J. R., & Wise, R. J. S. (1996). Generating a "tiger" as an animal name or a word beginning with T: Differences in brain activations. *Proceedings of the Royal Society London B., 263,* 989–995.

Neville, H. J., & Bavelier, D. (1998). Neural organization and plasticity of language. *Current Opinion in Neurobiology, 8,* 254–258.

Ogawa, S., Lee, T. M., Kay, A. R., & Tank, D. W. (1990). Brain magnetic resonance imaging with contrast dependent on blood oxygenation. *Proceedings of the National Academy of Sciences U.S.A., 87,* 9868–9872.

Ojemann, G. A., & Whitaker, H. A. (1978). The bilingual brain. *Archives of Neurology, 35,* 409–412.

Paradis, M. (1983). *Readings on aphasia in bilinguals and polyglots.* Montreal, Canada: Didier.

Paradis, M. (1998). Language and communication in multilinguals. In B. Stemmer & H. Whitaker (Eds.), *Handbook of neurolinguistics* (pp. 417–430). San Diego, CA: Academic Press.

Paulesu, E., Goldacre, B., Scifo, P., Cappa, S. F., Gilardi, M. C., Castiglioni, I., et al. (1997) Functional heterogeneity of left inferior frontal cortex as revealed by fMRI. *NeuroReport, 8,* 2011–2016.

Penfield, W. (1965). Conditioning the uncommitted cortex for language learning. *Brain, 88,* 787–798.

Perani, D., Abutalebi, J., Paulesu, E., Brambati, S., Scifo, P, Cappa S. F., et al. (2003). The role of age of acquisition and language usage in early, high-proficient bilinguals: A fMRI study during verbal fluency. *Human Brain Mapping, 19,* 179–182.

Perani, D., & Cappa, S. F. (1998). Neuroimaging methods in neuropsychology. In G. Denes & L. Pizzamiglio (Eds.), *Handbook of clinical and experimental neuropsychology* (pp. 69–94). London: Psychology Press.

Perani, D., Cappa, S. F., Schnur, T., Tettamanti, M., Collina, S., Rosa, M. M., et al. (1999). The neural correlates of verb and noun processing: A PET study. *Brain, 122,* 2337–2344.

Perani, D., Dehaene, S., Grassi, F., Cohen, L., Cappa, S. F., Dupoux, E., et al. (1996). Brain processing of native and foreign languages. *NeuroReport, 7,* 2439–2444.

Perani, D., Paulesu, E., Sebastian-Galles, N., Dupoux, E., Dehaene, S., Bettinardi, V., et al. (1998). The bilingual brain: Proficiency and age of acquisition of the second language. *Brain, 121,* 1841–1852.

Petersen, S. E., Van Mier, H., Fiez, J. A., & Raichle, M. E. (1998). The effects of practice on the functional anatomy of task performance. *Proceedings of the National Academy of Sciences U.S.A., 95,* 853–860.

Pitres, A. (1895). Etude sur l'aphasie chez les polyglottes. *Revue de médecine, 15,* 873–899.

Poetzl, O. (1925). Ueber die parietal bedingte Aphasie und ihren Einfluss auf das Sprechen mehrerer Sprachen. *Zeitschrift fuer die gesamte Neurologie und Psychiatrie, 99,* 100–124.

Poetzl, O. (1930). Aphasie und Mehrsprachigkeit. *Zeitschrift fuer die gesamte Neurologie und Psychiatrie, 124,* 145–162.

Poline, J. B., Vandenberghe, R., Holmes, A. P., Friston, K. J., & Frackowiak, R. S. J. (1996). Reproducibility of PET activation studies: lessons from a multi centre European experiment. *Neuroimage, 4,* 34–54.

Price, C. J. (1998). The functional anatomy of word comprehension and production. *Trends in Cognitive Science, 2,* 281–288.

Price, C. J., Green, D., & von Studnitz, R. (1999). A functional imaging study of translation and language switching. *Brain, 122,* 2221–2236.

Raichle, M. E., Fiez, J. A., Videen, T. O., MacLeod, A. M., Pardo, J. V., Fox, P. T., et al. (1994). Practice related changes in human brain functional anatomy during nonmotor learning. *Cerebral Cortex, 4,* 8–26.

Rodriguez-Fornells, A., Rotte, M., Heinze, H. J., Nösselt, T., & Münte, T. F. (2002). Brain potential and functional MRI evidence for how to handle two languages with one brain. *Nature, 415,* 1026–1029.

Scoresby-Jackson, R. (1867). Case of aphasia with right hemiplegia. *Edinburgh Medical Journal, 12,* 696–706.

Segalowitz, S. J. (1983). *Two sides of the brain.* Englewood Cliffs, NJ: Prentice Hall.

Smith, E. E., Jonides, J., & Koeppe, R. A. (1996). Dissociating verbal and spatial working memory using PET. *Cerebral Cortex, 6,* 11–20.

Thompson-Schill, S. L., D'Esposito, M., Aguirre, G. K., & Farah, M. J. (1997). Role of left inferior prefrontal cortex in retrieval of semantic knowledge: A reevaluation.

Proceedings of the National Academy of Sciences U.S.A., 94, 14,792–14,797.

Thompson-Schill, S. L., D'Esposito, M., & Kan, I. P. (1999). Effects of repetition and competition on activity in left prefrontal cortex during word generation. *Neuron, 23,* 513–522.

Wartenburger, I., Heekeren, H. R., Abutalebi, J., Cappa, S. F., Villringer, A., & Perani, D. (2003). Early setting of grammatical processing in the bilingual brain. *Neuron, 37,* 159–170.

Weber-Fox, C. M., & Neville, H. J. (1996). Maturational constraints on functional specialization for language processing: ERP and behavioral evidence in bilingual speakers. *Journal of Cognitive Neuroscience, 8,* 231–256.

Wernicke, C. (1874). *Der aphasische Symptomenkomplex.* Breslau: Cohn & Weigert.

Yetkin, O., Yetkin, F. Z., Haughton, V. M., & Cox, R. W. (1996). Use of functional MR to map language in multilingual volunteers. *American Journal of Neuroradiology, 17,* 473–477.

David W. Green

25

The Neurocognition of Recovery Patterns in Bilingual Aphasics

ABSTRACT   We have yet to explain the variety of recovery patterns in bilingual aphasics despite the practical and theoretical importance of doing so. I consider the reasons for this state of affairs and identify what is needed to achieve a causal understanding. Theoretically, I distinguish the issue of the representation of a linguistic system from its control and explore the neuroanatomic bases of representation and control. Methodologically, I argue for the importance of neuroimaging studies (positron emission tomography, functional magnetic resonance imaging) to complement psycholinguistic and neuropsychological data and propose a number of psycholinguistic and neuroimaging studies aimed at clarifying the causal basis of recovery patterns. A final section briefly considers the implications for rehabilitation.

There are two related reasons for seeking to understand the nature of recovery patterns in bilingual aphasics. First, a principled basis for specifying rehabilitation programs is needed. As a result of migration patterns and intermarriage, the number of bilingual and polyglot speakers will increase and with it, as a result of stroke, closed head injury, or neurodegenerative disease, the incidence of bilingual aphasia. In the case of the United States, for example, Paradis (2001) estimated, on the basis of census data, that there will be well over 45,000 new cases per annum. Second, the patterns of recovery in bilingual aphasics challenge accounts of the representation and control of language in the brain. This challenge will drive the theoretical and empirical innovations necessary to achieve a principled basis for rehabilitation.

A key requirement is a causal account of recovery patterns that can provide predictors of recovery and guidance for rehabilitation. At present, we lack such a causal account and cannot predict clinical outcomes. The following quotation (Paradis, 1995) indicates the scale of the task:

No correlation has been found between the pattern of recovery and neurological, etiologi-
cal, experiential or linguistic parameters: not site, size or origin of lesion, type or severity of aphasia, type of bilingualism, language structure type or factors related to acquisition or habitual use. (p. 211)

This chapter outlines a blueprint for tackling the problem. The first section identifies the basic patterns of recovery and discusses why we lack a causal account. A key factor is the need for a neurocognitive approach, informed by neuroimaging studies of patients, to the representation and control of language in the brain. The second section describes such an approach, and the third section applies it to some key patterns of recovery. Before concluding, a final section briefly considers the implications for rehabilitation.

The Nature of the Problem

Patterns of Loss and Recovery

Different patterns of recovery can be identified in terms of the relative impairment of two or more languages (first language [L1], second language [L2], etc.) and the course of recovery. I describe these patterns and then consider their incidence and practical impact.

Paradis (1977) identified six basic recovery patterns. Languages can be affected equally, differentially, or selectively. *Parallel* recovery occurs when both languages are impaired and restored at the same rate; *differential* recovery occurs when languages recover differentially relative to their premorbid levels; *selective* recovery occurs when at least one language is not recovered at all. In *blended* recovery, patients mix their languages inappropriately.

There are different trajectories to a particular "end state." Two or more languages may eventually recover, but the second language may only begin to recover when the first has (fully) recovered. This is termed *successive* recovery. A special case of selective recovery, *antagonistic* recovery, occurs when as one language recovers, a second language becomes impaired.

Two further patterns, *alternating antagonism* and *selective aphasia*, may be considered variants of antagonistic and selective recovery, respectively (Paradis, 2001). In alternating antagonism, patients can access only one of their languages in spontaneous speech for alternating periods of time (Nilipour & Ashayeri, 1989; Paradis, Goldblum, & Abidi, 1982). In the case of selective aphasia (Paradis & Goldblum, 1989), in contrast to selective recovery, there are aphasic problems in one language with no obvious deficits in the other.

These basic patterns do not exhaust the set of possibilities. A language may be recovered in an antagonistic fashion, and a third never recover at all. Or, in the case of alternating antagonism, there may be a temporary inability to translate into the language that the patient can use spontaneously (Patient A. D., Paradis et al., 1982). There are also other rare, but important, cases involving a selective deficit, such as the loss of the ability to avoid switching between languages (Patient S. J., Fabbro, Skrap, & Agliotti, 2000; see Ansaldo & Joanette, 2002, for a review and interpretation of reported cases of pathological language switching and language mixing).

Incidence and Impact

The true incidence of the basic patterns of recovery is unknown. Fabbro (1999; see Paradis, 1977), estimated, on the basis of published cases, that the typical pattern of recovery is one in which both languages recover in parallel (40% of cases). Better recovery of the mother tongue (L1) occurs in 32%

of the cases, and better recovery of the L2 occurs in 28% of the cases. In a review of cases reported between 1990 and 2000 and that did include reports of unselected cases, Paradis (2001) found that the majority exhibited parallel recovery (81/132, 61%), 24 (18%) showed differential recovery, 12 (9%) showed a blended recovery pattern, 9 (7%) had selective recovery, and 6 (5%) had successive recovery, but he rightly cautioned against inferring population values from these figures.

The communicative impact of these different patterns of recovery varies. Parallel recovery allows an individual eventually to achieve premorbid levels of communication with family, peers, and the wider public. In contrast, other patterns, such as antagonistic or selective recovery, can create severe communication problems. A person may be unable to communicate linguistically with their immediate family and friends or be unable to work.

Why Don't We Have a Causal Account of Recovery Patterns?

Paradis (2001) argued that we have the theoretical tools to account for the patterns but do not understand what determines a particular type of recovery or, in the case of nonparallel recovery, what determines the language that is preferentially recovered. The argument in this section is that two key ingredients are lacking to answer these questions: critical data and explicit neurocognitive accounts that specify the relevant causal parameters. This argument is pursued by considering three aspects of the problem: the nature of language, individual differences in recovery processes, and the lesion deficit methodology.

Abstract Characterization of Language Languages differ, and myriad language combinations are possible. Languages must be considered at a suitable level of abstractness to find unity among the diversity of outcomes. At an abstract level, there are four linguistic means for communicating experience (see, e.g., Tomasello, 1995): individual symbols (lexical items), markers on symbols (grammatical morphology), ordering patterns of symbols (word order), and prosodic variations of speech (e.g., stress, intonation, timing).

Languages differ in the weight they attach to these different means. In some languages, word order is basically free, and information on "who did what to whom" is conveyed by word endings or by prosody in tone languages. By contrast, in

English, such information is conveyed by word order, and this is relatively rigid. These different linguistic means require different processes. A given lesion can therefore give rise to different outcomes in different languages because one process is relatively more important in one language than another, so there can be more opportunities for errors of a certain type to reveal themselves in one language than another (e.g., Paradis, 2001). Damage to a device implementing that process will exert greater effect in one language than another and so underlie differential recovery in one instance and selective recovery in another.

Individual Differences in Recovery Recent years have seen a number of developments that have improved the quality and validity of data. Standardized instruments for assessing language performance in different languages (e.g., the Bilingual Aphasia test; see Paradis, 2001) are vital to establishing valid data sets. Further, records of unselected cases of bilingual aphasia (see Paradis, 2001, p. 71) help overcome any bias in published case reports toward the unusual. These developments are welcome, but they do not go far enough. Individuals differ in their ability to recover from damage.

A lesion at a given site and extent may yield different effects (e.g., parallel recovery vs. differential recovery) because of a more effective repair process in one individual compared to another. A number of factors are known to affect the likelihood of recovery from a focal lesion. These factors include age, premorbid IQ/education level, and the integrity of the frontal lobes (see, e.g., Robertson & Murre, 1999). It follows that neuropsychological assessments that focus only on language tasks may fail to detect dimensions critical to recovery.

Lesion Deficit Approach The patterns of recovery provide evidence of potentially dissociable cognitive systems underlying different languages (e.g., Gollan & Kroll, 2001; Paradis, 2001). Consider, for instance, cases of the preferential recovery of one language over another. In some cases, the mother tongue is recovered better than a language acquired second. In other cases, the converse obtains. Case reports also indicate that the devices involved in translation from one language to another are cognitively distinct from those mediating picture naming or spontaneous speech production. A neurocognitive account must take the further step of identifying the neuroanatomical bases of these devices and systems. Until recently, the primary means for establishing the neuroanatomical representation of such devices was the lesion deficit approach.

This approach is important because it indicates the cortical regions necessary for performance of a linguistic task (e.g., speaking in L1), but it cannot establish whether a given deficit reflects damage to a specialized device at the site of the lesion or to a distributed network with connections that pass through the lesion site. More seriously from the point of view of correlating lesion site and extent to recovery patterns, it cannot establish whether there is residual capacity in the damaged tissue. It also leaves open other possible mechanisms of recovery (e.g., the use of a duplicate but previously inhibited mechanism) or cognitive changes in the way a given task is performed. This lesion deficit approach needs to be complemented by one involving neuroimaging (see Price & Friston, 1999; Green & Price, 2001).

In the normal brain, positron emission tomography (PET) and functional magnetic imaging (fMRI) can identify the complete set of regions associated with one task relative to another and, critically, how one region interacts with another. However, such methods (described in the Exploring Recovery Patterns section) also have inherent limitations. One limitation is pertinent here: These methods (along with other physiological measures such as single- and multiunit electrophysiology or electroencephalography [EEG]) tell us about the activation or engagement of a system in the performance of a task but not about its necessity (e.g., Brown & Hagoort, 2000; Sarter, Bernston, & Cacioppo, 1996). A combination of neuropsychological assessment, data on lesion site, and neuroimaging data (together with other techniques such as transcranial magnetic stimulation) can help identify regions that are both necessary and sufficient for task performance. Critical to such an endeavor is a view of how the processes that mediate language use map onto the neuroanatomical substrate. The next section addresses this question.

A Neurocognitive Approach: Representation and Control

A neurocognitive approach must characterize the bilingual system at a cognitive level, state how the devices at this level map onto the neuroanatomical networks, and show how damage at the neuroanatomical level can give rise to the observed behavior (see Morton & Frith, 1995, for an insightful account of causal modeling). It must also state how damaged networks and circuits recover function.

The first part of this section considers the cognitive devices comprising the bilingual system. I presuppose a distinction between thought and language (Clark, 1996; Johnson-Laird, 1983) but grant that in thinking for speaking (Slobin, 1996) bilinguals formulate their messages in terms of the concepts of the language (Black & Chiat, 2000; Green, 1998a; Levelt, Roelofs, & Meyer, 1999). The second part specifies how these devices and their properties may be implemented in the neural system.

Cognitive-Level Description

The devices used to perform different tasks refer to actual neurocomputational machines, so an adequate cognitive description needs to include parameters relevant to the working of real devices. The focus in what follows is on the types of device, but keep in mind that each device is not only dedicated to processing information of a certain type, but also is both capacity constrained (that is, it processes inputs of a certain type at a limited rate) and resource constrained. It will fail to operate, for example, without the metabolic means to do so. Although the concepts of capacity and resource are distinct and, as discussed, can be identified with distinct neural properties, there is a relation between the two concepts. As resources decline, the "functional capacity" of the system will decrease, although the precise nature of the decline is an open question.

I distinguish between a device representing the meanings of words, their syntactic properties, and the word forms (the bilingual lexico-semantic system) and devices involved in controlling the outputs from that system. This contrast leads to the expectation that certain patterns of recovery may arise from problems in controlling the bilingual lexico-semantic system rather than from damage to it. Damage to different components of the control system may yield different outcomes. Alternatively, the same broad clinical outcome may arise for different reasons (e.g., damage to the lexico-semantic system or to components of the control system).

To appreciate the problem of control, consider the task of naming a picture in L1. To perform this task, individuals must avoid performing other tasks, such as free-associating to the picture or assessing its aesthetic qualities. Following Green (1998b), I say that individuals must activate a particular task schema that coordinates relevant devices (see also Monsell, 1996). In the case of picture naming, the schema pairs a picture name in L1 (say) with the output of a picture recognition device that has activated a set of lexical concepts. The schema for producing a name in L1 may be in competition with the other schemas, particularly with one to name the picture in L2. Top-down control is achieved in the normal case by a higher level, or executive, system that boosts the relative activation of the target schema (Shallice, 1988). On this account, language control is part of a system for the control of action in general (e.g., Green, 1986, 1998b; Meuter & Allport, 1999; Paradis, 1981), although such a claim does not preclude circuits specialized for the control of linguistic actions (e.g., Paradis, 2001). Problems in production can arise because of difficulty in ensuring that the intended schema is dominant.

For bilingual speakers to name the picture in the intended language, the lexical representations of words also need to be coded or tagged for language in some way (Albert & Obler, 1978) to allow their selection by the task schemas (Green, 1998b; see also De Bot & Schreuder, 1993; Dijkstra & Van Heuven, 1998, for various views on such tagging). Comparable tags (or units coding for language) are also part of the monolingual speaker's repertoire, allowing the selection of vocabulary suited for different registers. Disconnection, or noisy transmission, between schemas and tags or between the representation of lexical concepts and tags provides ways in which a selective pattern of recovery could arise.

How is selection actually achieved? Given a requirement to speak in only one language, selection could be achieved at a late stage by filtering or by inhibiting "lemmas" or lexical nodes that lack the requisite tag (Green, 1998b). Individuals, of course, must select appropriate words in other tasks. Neuroimaging studies indicate that such selection involves inhibitory processes both in the standard Stroop color–word task (Peterson, Skudlarski, Gatenby, Zhang, Anderson, & Gore, 1999) and, more significantly, in a picture–word interference task (De Zubicarary, McMahon, Eastburn, & Wilson, 2002). In the case of selecting between words in different languages, selection may be biased against the nontarget language by selectively deactivating entire language systems or parts of such systems (De Bot & Schreuder, 1993; Grosjean, 1998, 2001; Paradis, 1981, 2001; see also Rodriguez-Fornells, Rotte, Heinze, Nösselt, & Münte, 2002, for evidence of selection in visual word recognition) or by inhibiting such systems or their components (Dijkstra & Van Heuven, 1998; Green, 1986). In pathological cases, such a mechanism explains the temporary loss, or permanent inaccessibility, of a language—it is not destroyed but inhibited—a conjecture first proposed by Pitres (1895/1983; see Paradis, 2001).

There is debate on the extent, or the conditions under which, naming in one language rather than another involves selection among lexical candidates from both languages or from just one language (e.g., Costa, Miozzo, & Caramazza, 1999; see also Costa, chapter 15, this volume). A detailed analysis of the relevant normal data is outside the scope of this chapter, but current evidence suggests that words in L1 invariably compete for selection when individuals are naming pictures in L2 (Hermans, Bongaerts, De Bot, & Schreuder, 1999). L2 names for pictures also compete for selection when individuals are naming in L1 when individuals are required also to name in L2 within the same block of trials (Kroll & Peck, 1998, cited in Gollan & Kroll, 2001). Unfortunately, there appear to be no experimental studies examining competition in grammatical encoding.

Competitive costs can be reduced by differentiating lexical concepts in the two languages. MacWhinney (1997, p. 120) commented that individuals can limit competition by directly linking the L2 term to its concept rather than by linking it to the L1 lexical item (as in the lexical route in the Revised Hierarchical Model of bilingual memory representations; see Kroll & De Groot, 1997). The extent of such differentiation will presumably depend on the type of concept (e.g., whether it is language specific). It may also depend on proficiency and usage.

Fluency within a language may be viewed as an outcome of tightening within-language links over between-language links. Over time, the two systems achieve a quasi-independent status equivalent to the subset hypothesis (Paradis, 1981, 2001). Usage may also be important. For instance, when individuals are required to translate between languages, selection may rely less on concept differentiation and more on selection via language tags. Computational modeling of systems evolving under different circumstances would be helpful as a means to explore these conjectures.

Neuroanatomical Description and the Convergence Hypothesis

An important question concerns the extent to which an L2 is processed differently from the L1. In the normal brain, language functions in monolingual, right-handed individuals are typically represented in a distributed left hemisphere network (Loring et al., 1990; Springer et al., 1999). In principle, different languages might be represented in a different neuroanatomical substrate (e.g., in homologous areas of the right hemisphere).

However, Rapport, Tan, and Whitaker (1983), in a study of right-handed polyglot aphasics prior to surgery, found no evidence of the disruption of picture naming following intracarotid injection of sodium amytal into the right hemisphere. In contrast, naming was massively disrupted following injection into the left hemisphere. Further, in a study of 88 reported cases of right-handed bilingual aphasics, Fabbro (1999, pp. 210–211) found that only 8% had a lesion to the right hemisphere. Taking into account reporting biases, he concluded that the incidence of aphasia in bilinguals with right hemisphere lesions is not in fact higher than that shown by monolingual aphasics. In sum, current data indicate that although languages form distinct subsets (see Paradis, 1981, 2001), they are represented in a common substrate.

I suppose, more specifically, the convergence hypothesis (see Green, 2003). According to this hypothesis, as proficiency in L2 increases, the representation of L2 and its processing profile (i.e., event-related potential [ERP] and neuroimaging data) converge with those of native speakers of that language (see also Abutalebi, Cappa, & Perani, chapter 24, this volume, for related discussion). That is, any qualitative differences between native speakers of a language and L2 speakers of that language disappear as proficiency increases (for rather different views see, e.g., Paradis, 1994, and Ullman, 2001). Current ERP and neuroimaging data are consistent with this hypothesis (e.g., Abutalebi, Cappa, & Perani, 2001; Osterhout & McLaughlin, 2000; Weber-Fox & Neville, 2001; but see also Hahne & Friederici, 2001, and Vaid & Hull, 2002, for a critical review of the neuroimaging data and Kroll & Dussias, 2004, for an assessment of the ERP and psycholinguistic data on syntactic processing in L2). Notice that the convergence hypothesis is a claim about neural representation and processing profiles and not a claim about whether an L2 speaker of a language can simulate or pass as a native speaker of that language.

Unfortunately, there is a dearth of longitudinal online psycholinguistic or functional imaging studies specifically on L2 grammatical processing and encoding, so the robustness of this hypothesis is open to question. For the present, the convergence hypothesis allows simplification of the problem of mapping devices to neuroanatomical structures. I suppose an identity, at least at the broad anatomic level, with the representations of monolingual speakers and differentiation at the microanatomic level (Paradis, 1977, 2001).

In the following paragraphs, I propose a series of identifications (Green & Price, 2001). First, I consider how the bilingual lexico-semantic system and its control system map onto neural structures. Conceivably, a given device maps onto a specific neural mechanism in a restricted neuroanatomical area, but this appears not to be the case with language. Second, I consider the neural identifications of capacity and resource.

The Bilingual Lexico-Semantic System Regions sustaining word production can be divided into those involved in articulation (including the premotor cortex, the supplementary motor area, and the cerebellum) and those involved in retrieving phonology. Phonological retrieval (Price, 2000) involves the left anterior insula and the left frontal operculum (part of Broca's area). In the case of reading, the bilateral supramarginal gyri are implicated in the mapping of orthography to phonology (see discussion of the claim that they are the site of a language "switch").

Both neuropsychological and neuroimaging studies indicate that there is a degree of specialization within monolingual speakers for syntactic and semantic processes. Breedin and Saffran (1999) reported a patient, D. M., who was good at detecting grammatical violations despite a pervasive loss of semantic knowledge. ERP data from normal individuals indicated that there are distinct mechanisms mediating at least postlexical syntactic and semantic processes (Hagoort, Brown, & Osterhout, 2000). For instance, N400 (found 400 ms after an event) is sensitive to violations of semantic expectancy, whereas P600 (found 600 ms after an event) is sensitive to syntactic violations.

ERP data cannot provide direct evidence of the neural sources of such effects. However, functional imaging studies on grammatical processing and encoding in native speakers (Hagoort et al., 2000) indicated a common syntactic component subserved by the left frontal area (a dorsal part of Broca's area and adjacent parts of the middle frontal gyrus). Finally, research on semantic representation of words identified regions in the temporo-parietal region—the left extrasylvian temporal cortex and the left anterior inferior frontal cortex. A possible area associated with the integration of syntax and semantics lies in the anterior temporal pole (e.g.,

Dronkers, Redfern, & Knight, 2000; Noppeney & Price, 2004).

Neurocognitive Level of Control The devices for controlling language tasks are likely to be implemented by control circuits involving both frontal attentional and subcortical mechanisms (see, e.g., Price, Green, & Von Studnitz, 1999). For instance, language task schemas may be mediated partly by subcortical neural mechanisms (e.g., in the basal ganglia; see also Crosson, Novack, & Trenerry, 1988), with the level of activation modulated both by external input and by frontal systems, including the anterior cingulate (but cf. Carter et al., 2000). If production in one language rather than another requires suppression of the schema for producing utterances in the nonselected language, it follows that there must be an executive input when individuals are required to switch languages on a designated cue (see Jackson, Swainson, Cunnington, & Jackson, 2001, for ERP evidence in a numeral naming task and Hernandez, Dapretto, Mazziotta, & Bookheimer, 2001, for functional magnetic resonance imaging [fMRI] evidence in a picture-naming task). It follows that damage to frontal structures should impair the ability either to maintain a given language or to avoid switching between languages.

Fabbro, Skrap, and Aglioti (2000) reported the case of S. J. (a Friulian-Italian speaker) with a lesion to the left prefrontal cortex and part of anterior cingulate. The speaker S. J. showed normal comprehension in both Italian and Friulian and intact clausal processing in both languages. However, S. J. was unable to avoid switching into Friulian even when addressing an Italian speaker S. J. knew spoke no Friulian. Likewise, when required to speak Friulian only, S. J. would switch into Italian. Switching can only be considered problematic when it arises inappropriately, as in the case of S. J. (see Grosjean, 2001). I infer that this selective deficit in preventing a language switch, or in maintaining a monolingual output, was a consequence of a lesion in the anterior cingulate that precluded one language schema maintaining dominance over the other, although this outcome may also partly reflect an inability to maintain the communicative goal of speaking in the target language.

The need to suppress an alternate schema should also arise in the case of translation. Presentation of a word in L1, say, will also trigger naming. Translation in this sense is analogous to a Stroop task in which a habitual response must be suppressed. To translate from L1 to L2, for instance, individuals must inhibit an L1 production schema and activate the schema for L2. This schema-level process can then modulate output from the lexico-semantic system. Functional imaging studies of performance in Stroop-like tasks all showed increased activation in the anterior cingulate, which may serve to modulate task schemas. Price et al. (1999; see also Klein, Milner, Zatorre, Meyer, & Evans, 1995) confirmed such an increase for translation.

If subcortical mechanisms in the basal ganglia are also implicated in selecting the relevant action, then translation should also increase activation in these regions. The study by Price et al. (1999) confirmed increases in the relevant areas (the bilateral putamen and the head of caudate). Increases also were observed in the areas associated with articulation (the supplementary motor area, a ventral region of the left anterior insula and the cerebellum), consistent with the notion that during translation responses associated with the input orthography must be inhibited.

Left subcortical lesions also lead to outcomes compatible with the present proposal. The individual E. M. (Aglioti, Beltramello, Girardi, & Fabbro, 1996) suffered damage to the caudate nucleus and the putamen and had difficulty maintaining her native Venetan but would constantly switch into Italian, a language learned only at school and rarely spoken. Damage to the basal ganglia could have limited her ability to activate the production schema in L1 in competition with that for L2. Such a difficulty would also lead to problems in naming even in the absence of lexical deficits in L1. Lesions located at the head of caudate nucleus in the left hemisphere can also elicit pathological language mixing in which no one language dominates (Abutalebi, Miozzo, & Cappa, 2000). Such cases are consistent with the idea that lexical representations are accessed under the control of frontal-basal ganglia circuits (see also Abutalebi et al., 2001).

Lesions in other areas can result in bilinguals displaying good comprehension in both languages but with an ability to speak in just one of them. Pötzl (1925) supposed that the left parietal area played a central role in language switching, and that damage to it prevented switching from one language to another. However, there are patients with lesions in that area who showed no such difficulties (see Paradis, 2001, p. 81).

The precise role of the parietal regions in language switching still needs to be determined. Price et al. (1999) found increased activation during language switching not only in a region of Broca's area (Brodmann area [Ba] 44) but also in the bilateral supramarginal gyri. The former region has been associated with phonemic segmentation and the latter with mapping orthography to phonology (see discussion of the claim that they are the site of a language "switch"), but because a given region may subserve a number of functions, it is preferable to claim that both regions are activated in phonological processing tasks. Jackson et al. (2001) reported a sustained increase in the size of an ERP component (the late positive complex) over the parietal region in a numeral-naming task when individuals had to switch from naming in one language to naming in another. One interpretation of these two sets of data, consistent with the present proposal, is that the parietal region is involved in implementing a change in stimulus–response mapping driven by the task schema.

Capacity and Resource

We can identify the capacity of a cognitive device with the average number of functionally intact neural units in the relevant neural mechanism (see Shallice, 1988, p. 233). The capacity of the device for retrieving the phonology of words, for instance, may relate to the number of functioning cells in specific regions such as the posterior inferior frontal cortex (Broca's area). Alternatively, a better index of capacity may be the interconnectivity of neural units. In contrast, the resources can be identified with the metabolites, neurotransmitters, or neuromodulators needed to operate the neural mechanism. These two identifications lead to the expectation that restricting the number of neural units (e.g., via a stroke) reduces capacity and so may impair performance.

Likewise, reducing resource (e.g., through the loss of the cells producing a resource) to a given neural mechanism in the absence of any change in its capacity may impair performance. One line of support for this claim comes from unmedicated patients with Parkinson's disease. They have reduced dopamine levels in the prefrontal cortex (caused by damage of the cells in the substantia nigra) and show deficits in working memory (e.g., Levin, Labre, & Weiner, 1989). Conversely, healthy adults given a dopamine agonist show working memory improvements (e.g., Muller, Von Cramon, & Pollmann, 1998).

Exploring Recovery Patterns

The key aim of this section is to consider how neuroimaging studies can be used to examine the causal basis of different patterns of recovery. I first review different possible mechanisms of recovery. I argue for the importance of Hebbian learning as a primary mechanism for the restitution of function and point to how different mechanisms of recovery might be distinguished in terms of their activation patterns. PET and fMRI allow assessment of such patterns. I describe these methods briefly and discuss some of the methodological prerequisites for using these methods to study patients. The final part outlines possible studies of patients with different patterns of recovery with a view to determine their causal basis.

Mechanisms of Recovery

Recovery may be achieved via different mechanisms (e.g., Code, 2001; Papathanasiou & Whurr, 2000; Rickard, 2000), yielding recovery based on normal cognitive processes or not. Individuals might compensate for loss of function by developing a new strategy and so deploy different cognitive processes involving different neural regions. In other cases, there may be restitution of function within the same, or neighboring, neural networks using learning processes identical to those that led to the formation of the network. Following Robertson and Murre (1999), I suppose that recovery from brain damage involves a process of Hebbian learning (Hebb, 1949).

In Hebbian learning, two neurons or neuronal groups or circuits can reconnect if they are activated at the same time. Spontaneous recovery can arise by random activation of one of the groups in the case of well-connected networks with small lesions. Activation spreads through the network, and any currently activated groups become reconnected. At the other extreme, neural self-repair is impossible if circuits are too disconnected or lack neurones, and only compensation is possible. At some intermediate point, restitution is possible given suitable input. Intuitively, a network less well connected may be more sensitive to the precise nature of the inputs, and simulations discussed by Robertson and Murre (1999, pp. 553–557) showed that when an intermediate number of connections is lost, restitution does depend on the partially disconnected network receiving targeted (patterned) stimulation that allows appropriate reconnection (see Harley, 1996, and Plaut, 1996, for existence proofs of recovery of function in other types of networks).

Hebbian learning may be important in allowing function to be restored in areas surrounding the lesion site. Restitution of function may also be achieved by creating patterns of connectivity in neighboring neural networks (neural plasticity). Neuroimaging can differentiate these alternatives, given the tasks are performed normally, by determining whether the regions activated are identical to those in normal bilingual controls. When different regions are involved, neuroimaging will reveal activity in different areas for patients relative to normal controls.

What further factors (specific or general) may affect recovery of function? Damage to an area can sometimes suppress activity in a relatively remote undamaged area (*diaschisis*), thereby temporarily impairing performance in tasks in which the functionality of that area is required. Restitution of function occurs when diaschisis is reversed and yields normal activity in that region. Behaviorally, recovery because of the reversal of diaschisis is also likely to occur earlier than recovery because of compensation.

Damaged circuits may also fail to recover function because of suppression from undamaged circuits that compete to control output. In this case, new lesions that reduce the activation of intact networks can lead to enhanced functioning by allowing Hebbian learning to take place in the network that was damaged initially (see Kapur, 1996, for a review of "paradoxical facilitation").

More generally, recovery may also reflect attentional factors. Deficits in attentional control (specifically, sustained attention) are strong predictors of recovery from brain damage. Attentional control may be important not only because it is a factor in providing suitable input to the damaged areas, but also because of its connection to the arousal system. Neurotransmitters (e.g., noradrenaline) associated with the arousal system are also strongly implicated in cortical plasticity. Hence, the importance of wider cognitive, and pharmacological, assessments of bilingual aphasics in the study of recovery patterns.

Neuroimaging

Hemodynamic methods (PET and fMRI) rely on close coupling between changes in the activation of a population of neurons and change in blood supply. A hemodynamic effect arises only when there is a change in the overall metabolic demand in a neuronal population. PET and fMRI track different signals. PET measures the decay of a short-lived isotope, which accumulates in a neural region in proportion to the amount of blood flowing through that region. The most typical fMRI method indexes metabolic demand, and hence relative neural activity, by assessing the ratio of deoxyhemoglobin to oxyhemoglobin in the blood.

Each method has advantages and disadvantages. Minimally, PET studies examine changes in patterns of activation by contrasting conditions that differ in the cognitive operation of interest. Trials of a certain type have to be blocked, and the number of observations is restricted because PET involves the administration of ionizing radiation. There are no such constraints in the case of fMRI. However, PET has the advantage that it is more or less equally sensitive to activity in all brain regions, whereas fMRI signals are not. The magnetic signal is susceptible to factors other than blood oxygenation levels, making it difficult to record from certain regions (e.g., the orbitofrontal region).

PET and fMRI offer important advantages for the study of recovery patterns. To explore recovery, we need to be able to chart changes. At a minimum, performance needs to be assessed after the acute phase and at some later time. Because both methods track changes in the whole brain, neural activity can be measured in the absence of overt manual or vocal response (Price & Friston, 2002). In consequence, processing can be assessed even when there is no ability to speak a language or even, apparently, to understand it. There may also be normal effects in one region but abnormal effects in another. So, for example, in listening to a story in a nonrecovered language, activity in the auditory regions may be normal, but there may be abnormal effects in regions associated with semantics. At a later point in recovery, both regions may show normal response.

Neuroimaging also allows consideration of how areas work together. In the normal case, there is a functional integration of different areas. If control is normal, then the anterior cingulate will modulate activity in the basal ganglia normally. This circuit will provide a normal modulatory influence on the systems mediating word production. In contrast, diaschisis, for example, will yield abnormal patterns of activation. Büchel, Frith, and Friston (2000) described methods for examining effective connectivity ("the influence one neuronal system exerts on another," p. 339) using structural equation modeling of the patterns of activation in different regions of interest.

Methodological Cautions

Functional imaging studies of patients require that the performance level of the patient and normal controls is matched (Price & Friston, 1999). If the patient cannot perform the task, for instance, the corresponding neuronal responses will not be elicited. Further, if the patient performs the task but does so in a way different from normal bilinguals, the neuronal abnormality will covary with the cognitive abnormality, and it is not possible to distinguish the cause of the neuronal abnormality (see Green & Price, 2001, for elaboration within the bilingual context). Differences in the way a task is performed may be detectable in the patterns of reaction time or error to stimuli of different types or in individuals' verbal protocols of what they are doing (Rickard, 2000).

Differences in activation pattern may also reflect differences in the relative difficulty of the task for the patient compared to a matched control even when the overt performance level is closely matched. One check here is to examine changes in activation patterns with variations in task difficulty. If restitution of function is occurring within normally activated regions, then as relative difficulty decreases for the patient, there will be convergence with the patterns shown by normal controls. In contrast, if patients and controls show different stable patterns over variations in task difficulty, then it is reasonable to infer that restitution is an outcome of neural plasticity (Rickard, 2000, p. 308).

Neuroimaging Bilingual Aphasics

Problems of control seem to offer a ready account of certain recovery patterns. The case of S. J. (Fabbro et al., 2000), mentioned in the Patterns of Loss and Recovery section, offers a clear instance. Lexical representations were intact, but there was a problem in ensuring that one language schema continued to dominate another. I attribute this difficulty to the lesion in the area of the anterior cingulate. Drugs (e.g., dopamine agonists) that modulate activity in the anterior cingulate, and so alter the resources available to it, may improve the ability of patients like S. J. to speak just one of their languages. It follows that the effective connectivity of regions associated with language control and regions associated with word production should again be normal when the individual is switching between languages.

Alternating antagonism also seems suited to a pure control explanation (Green, 1986). The subject A. D. (Paradis et al., 1982) was a French-Arabic speaker with a lesion in the temporo-parietal region of the left hemisphere who presented with a specific form of alternating antagonism during the course of recovery. On one day, she was able to speak French spontaneously but not Arabic. On the following day, she was able to speak Arabic spontaneously but not French. However, on the day, for instance, when she was unable to speak Arabic spontaneously but could speak French spontaneously, she was able to translate into Arabic, suggesting that the lexical representations of that language were available for production. By contrast, on the same day that she could speak French spontaneously, she could not translate into it. This pattern of performance suggests that part of her problem lay in selecting between competing language task schemas of a given type (e.g., translating into L1 vs. translating into L2) once one had become dominant or perhaps in linking a nondominant schema to the relevant lexical concepts.

An exploration of the control problem might begin by considering the patients' ability to handle conflict tasks. For instance, with standard Stroop stimuli, the patient must suppress the normal reading response to name the hue in which a color word is printed. Compared to normal bilingual controls, patients with alternating antagonism might show an abnormal pattern of correlated activity in the anterior cingulate when required to process such stimuli. As in the case of S. J., if resource constraints underlie the problem, impaired performance should improve with the administration of a dopamine agonist.

These patterns of recovery are rare, so it is important to examine whether other, more common patterns reflect problems with the control mechanism. In the next section, we consider how neuroimaging studies may contribute to better understanding of four such recovery patterns.

Parallel Recovery   If control processes are intact, then the regions associated with control and those associated with word production should modulate normally in both languages (i.e., there should be the normal pattern of effective connectivity) during word production and conflict tasks. Recovery will then primarily reflect restitution in the lexico-semantic system. Hebbian mechanisms provide more complete recovery when the network connections are better preserved, so the extent of perilesional activation is likely to be critical to the recovery of function (see Warburton, Price, Swinburn, & Wise, 1999, for evidence of perilesional activation in monolingual aphasic patients). If this is so, the link between the amount of preserved functional capacity in the perilesional tissue and

different recovery patterns can be explored. Perilesional activity might initially be greater for both L1 and L2 in patients showing parallel recovery of both their languages compared to patients showing either selective or antagonistic recovery.

Parallel recovery does not entail that both languages are recovered in the same manner. If there is restitution of function in one case but compensation in the other, then only the former language will show activation patterns during task performance (e.g., picture naming) indistinguishable from those of normal bilingual controls.

Differential, Selective, and Antagonistic Patterns of Recovery   Viewed dynamically, a differential pattern may arise because use of one language rather than the other during the initial phase of recovery leads to greater restitution of its network via Hebbian learning. Selective recovery, in contrast, may arise because progressive use of just one language consolidates its network and progressively isolates it from the other.

An alternative possibility is that both patterns reflect problems of control. For instance, there could be damage to the mechanism that selects the intended language or a disconnection or disruption of the link connecting the representation of the meanings of words and the units coding for language (or alternatively between the units coding for language and the schema). Selective recovery, as opposed to differential recovery, reflects greater difficulty in selecting one language over another. A third possibility is that the lexico-semantic system of one language is marginally more impaired than that of the other language, and this impairment leads to a problem in controlling that language. This lack of control blocks its recovery via Hebbian mechanisms and isolates it from the other language. One way of advancing research in this area is to determine the nature of the representations accessible under these patterns of recovery.

Consider a selective pattern of recovery. Under a strong control hypothesis, there is access to meaning but an inability to select lexical concepts in the nonrecovered language. If there is access to the meaning of words but an inability to select lexical concepts in the nonrecovered language, then individuals should still show semantic interference. Consider a Spanish-English bilingual with selective recovery of Spanish performing the following task. Individuals are required to press one key provided an arrow points in one direction and another key if the arrow points in the opposite direction. Pairing the arrow with an incongruent direction word in

English (e.g., ← RIGHT) as contrasted with a row of X's should slow reaction time, reflecting an increase in response conflict. Such a conflict might also be detectable in specific brain regions such as the anterior cingulate. In the recovered or better-recovered language, for which semantic access is preserved as assessed by this online task, neuronal activity in bilingual aphasics should pattern in the same way as bilingual controls. In contrast, when there is evidence of semantic access but an inability to select the lexical concept for production, the regions associated with language control will activate abnormally, an example of "differential" diaschisis (cf. Price, Warburton, Moore, Frackowiak, & Friston, 2001).

If there is access to meaning, is there also access to word form? Consider the task of determining whether a predesignated phoneme (e.g., "t") is present in the Spanish name of a pictured object such as a table (*mesa* in Spanish; Colomé, 2001; Hermans, 2000). Normal bilinguals are slower to reject the target phoneme if it is present in the translation equivalent compared to control trials in which it is not. If segments of the word form of the nonrecovered language are activated, then patients also should show this phoneme interference effect. Further, there will be increased activation in the anterior cingulate on incongruent trials compared to control trials. If, on the other hand, there is no access to the word form, then bilingual aphasics will react similarly to monolingual controls.

Antagonistic recovery may be construed as a special case of selective recovery. Why should the recovery of one language be impaired when a second language improves (e.g., Paradis & Goldblum, 1989)? A control explanation of the antagonistic pattern of recovery might be as follows. Initial language use is probabilistically determined and does not directly reflect the rate at which recovery will occur for the two languages. A small difference in the rates of recovery, reflecting perhaps different degrees of damage to the lexico-semantic system, will be sufficient to induce different end states in the course of language use. An initially less-dominant language schema becomes more and more dominant (via Hebbian learning), inhibiting use of the other language schemas and increasing the connectivity within the lexico-semantic system for the selected (and initially less-well-recovered) language. Such an account presumes that, after an initial phase in which competition between languages is weak, inhibiting the schemas for the better-recovered language becomes more difficult.

As in the case of selective recovery, what information is available for the less-recovered language can be assessed. The arrow task described in this section offers a partial test. At an early stage of recovery, the patient would be tested in the most-recovered language, and we would look for evidence for response conflict from the less-recovered language. At a later stage, the patient would be tested in the other language, and we would look for the reverse effects. Comparable studies are possible for examining access to word form.

Implications for Rehabilitation

Understanding recovery patterns has the practical goal of developing a principled basis for rehabilitation. The argument is that understanding the causal basis permits a targeted intervention. Rehabilitation in aphasia is a complex topic (see, e.g., Code, 2000), so my illustrations here are not intended as clinical prescriptions. Consider a pure control problem, as in the case of S. J. (Fabbro et al., 2000; discussed in the first paragraph of the Neuroimaging Bilingual Aphasics section), a pharmacological intervention might be appropriate. But, to the extent inappropriate switching stems from a failure to maintain the communicative goal (e.g., speak in L1), an appropriate intervention might seek to increase the person's capacity to sustain attention (see Robertson & Murre, 1999, for relevant techniques) and so maintain the communicative goal.

As indicated, different patterns of recovery may reflect the consequences of random stimulation to a damaged network. Such stimulation, at least for small lesions, can lead not only to an adaptive outcome (e.g., parallel recovery of both languages), but also to maladaptive outcomes for larger lesions: A given circuit may become connected to a formerly distinct circuit. One relevant factor here may be the extent to which individuals are aware of their speech output (Robertson & Murre, 1999). Shuren, Hammond, Maher, Rothi, and Heilman (1995) reported the case of a jargon aphasic who was unaware of his errors in the normal course of events but recognized error when listening to a tape recording of his own speech. This suggests that part of his problem was attentional; when the attentional load (involved in planning and in producing speech) was reduced, he was able to recognize problems.

Recognition of error is important because in its absence circuits involved in flawed production may become connected. In the case of bilingual aphasics, pathological mixing may arise from an initial problem of control becoming entrenched. A possible intervention might then be to record, and to play back, the mixed speech and to create conditions, with short utterances at first, during which the same language is maintained. Training individuals to overcome interference (e.g., in the standard Stroop task) may also be helpful.

One possible cause of selective recovery is difficulty in binding lexical concepts to a language tag. Associating various kinds of language-specific contextual cues (e.g., music or scenes) to lexical items may help re-create the units coding for language and allow these to be linked to set an initial set of lexical concepts.

It is reasonable to expect that treatments that work for monolingual aphasics may be helpful for bilingual/polyglot aphasics (Juncos-Rabadan, Pereiro, & Rodríguez, 2002), but there is one possibility potentially available for the bilingual aphasic that is used quite spontaneously. Bilingual aphasics with parallel recovery frequently self-cue and produce the correct word in the nontarget language to retrieve the intended word (e.g., Juncos-Rabadán et al., 2002; Roberts & Le Dorze, 1998). One important area for future research will be to explore the benefits of implicit techniques such as priming. Can priming in a language that is accessible affect access to representations in a language previously inaccessible? What are the conditions for such an effect to occur?

Summary

Paradis (2001) asked: What determines the particular type of recovery? In the case of nonparallel recovery, what selects a particular language for preferential recovery over another? My answer is a call to action. We need to gain a more complete neurocognitive picture of patients to construct an adequate causal theory. With this aim in mind, this chapter emphasized the usefulness of the contrast between representation and control.

In terms of the studies required, neuroimaging research on normal bilinguals, guided by adequate theory, is a critical prerequisite. Given the goal, we must develop tests that are maximally general; they should be readily convertible to different pairs of languages and be capable of being carried out at different stages in the recovery process.

Conjectures on the causal basis of recovery patterns will also be usefully complemented by simulation studies examining the conditions under which different patterns of recovery may arise. Such studies provide existence proofs and need to be constrained by data from neuroimaging studies to ensure their neurological plausibility.

Finally, the project to understand the patterns of recovery requires suitable databases. Reports of unselected cases of bilingual aphasics are rare. Ideally, we need to create researchable databases in which relevant data (lesion site, language background, performance on standardized tests, cognitive test performance, and functional imaging data) can be used to test and explore different models. In the short term, the most tractable way forward is through intensive studies of single cases combined with psycholinguistic and neuroimaging studies of normal bilinguals.

Acknowledgments

I am grateful to the editors and to Cathy Price for helpful comments and suggestions. I thank the Wellcome Trust (grant 074735) for support.

References

Abutalebi, J., Cappa, S. F., & Perani, D. (2001). The bilingual brain as revealed by functional imaging. *Bilingualism: Language and Cognition, 4,* 179–190.

Abutalebi, J., Miozzo, A., & Cappa, S. F. (2000). Do subcortical structures control language selection in bilinguals? Evidence from pathological language mixing. *Neurocase, 6,* 101–106.

Aglioti, S., Beltramello, A., Girardi, F., & Fabbro, F. (1996). Neurolinguistic follow-up study of an unusual pattern of recovery from bilingual subcortical aphasia. *Brain, 119,* 1551–1564.

Albert, M. L., & Obler, L. K. (1978). *The bilingual brain: Neuropsychological and neurolinguistic aspects of bilingualism.* New York: Academic Press.

Ansaldo, A. I., & Joanette, Y. (2002). Language mixing and language switching. In F. Fabbro (Ed.), *Advances in the neurolinguistics of bilingualism* (pp. 261–274). Udine, Italy: Forum.

Black, M., & Chiat, S. (2000). Putting thoughts into verbs: Developmental and acquired impairments. In W. Best, K. Bryan, & L. Maxim (Eds.), *Semantic processing: Theory and practice* (pp. 52–79). London: Whurr.

Breedin, S. D., & Saffran, E. M. (1999). Sentence processing in the face of semantic loss: A case study. *Journal of Experimental Psychology: General, 128,* 547–562.

Brown, C. M., & Hagoort, P. (2000). The cognitive neuroscience of language: Challenges and future directions. In C. M. Brown & P. Hagoort (Eds.), *The neurocognition of language* (pp. 3–14). Oxford, U.K.: Oxford University Press.

Büchel, C., Frith, C., & Friston, K. (2000). Functional integration: Methods for assessing interactions amongst neuronal systems. In C. M. Brown & P. Hagoort (Eds.), *The neurocognition of language* (pp. 337–355). Oxford, U.K.: Oxford University Press.

Carter, C. S., Macdonald, A. M., Botvinick, M., Ross, L. L., Stenger, A. V., Noll, D., et al. (2000). Parsing executive processes: Strategic vs. evaluative functions of the anterior cingulate cortex. *Proceedings of the National Academy of Sciences, 97,* 1944–1948.

Clark, H. H. (1996). Communities, commonalities and communication. In J. J. Gumperz & S. C. Levinson (Eds.), *Rethinking linguistic relativity* (pp. 324–355). Cambridge, U.K.: Cambridge University Press.

Code, C. (2000). Multifactorial processes in recovery from aphasia: Developing the foundations for a multi-level framework. *Brain and Language, 77,* 25–44.

Colomé, À. (2001). Lexical activation in bilinguals' speech production: Language-specific or language independent? *Journal of Memory and Language, 45,* 721–736.

Costa, A., Miozzo, M., & Caramazza, A. (1999). Lexical selection in bilinguals: Do words in the bilingual's lexicons compete for selection? *Journal of Memory and Language, 41,* 365–397.

Crosson, B., Novack, T. A., & Trenerry, M. R. (1988). Subcortical language mechanisms: Windows on a new frontier. In H. A. Whitaker (Ed.), *Phonological processes and brain mechanisms* (pp. 24–58). New York: Springer.

De Bot, K., & Schreuder, R. (1993). Word production and the bilingual lexicon. In R. Schreuder & B. Weltens (Eds.), *The bilingual lexicon* (pp. 191–214). Amsterdam: Benjamins.

De Zubicaray, G. I., McMahon, K. L., Eastburn, M. M., & Wilson, S. J. (2002). Orthographic/phonological facilitation of naming responses in the picture-word task: An event-related fMRI study using overt vocal responding. *NeuroImage, 16,* 1084–1093.

Dijkstra, A., & Van Heuven, W. J. B. (1998). The BIA model and bilingual word recognition. In J. Grainger & A. Jacobs (Eds.), *Localist connectionist approaches to human cognition* (pp. 189–225). Mahwah, NJ: Erlbaum.

Dronkers, N. F., Redfern, B. B., & Knight, R. T. (2000). The neural architecture of language disorders. In M. S. Gazzaniga (Ed.), *The new cognitive neurosciences* (pp. 949–960). Cambridge, MA: MIT Press.

Fabbro, F. (1999). *The neurolinguistics of bilingualism: An introduction.* Hove, U.K.: Psychology Press.

Fabbro, F., Skrap, M., & Aglioti, S. (2000). Pathological switching between languages following frontal lesions in a bilingual patient. *Journal of Neurology, Neurosurgery and Psychiatry, 68,* 650–652.

Gollan, T. H., & Kroll, J. F. (2001). Lexical access in bilinguals. In B. Rapp (Ed.), *A handbook of cognitive neuropsychology: What deficits reveal about the human mind* (pp. 321–345). New York: Psychology Press.

Green, D. W. (1986). Control, activation and resource. *Brain and Language, 27,* 210–223.

Green, D. W. (1998a). Bilingualism and thought. *Psychologica Belgica, 38,* 253–278.

Green, D. W. (1998b). Mental control of the bilingual lexico-semantic system. *Bilingualism: Language and Cognition, 1,* 67–81.

Green, D. W. (2003). The neural basis of the lexicon and the grammar in L2 acquisition. In R. van Hout, A. Hulk, F. Kuiken, & R. Towell (Eds.), *The interface between syntax and the lexicon in second language acquisition* (pp. 197–218). Amsterdam: Benjamins.

Green, D. W., & Price, C. (2001). Functional imaging in the study of recovery patterns in bilingual aphasics. *Bilingualism: Language and Cognition, 4,* 191–201.

Grosjean, F. (1998). Studying bilinguals: Methodological and conceptual issues. *Bilingualism: Language and Cognition, 1,* 131–149.

Grosjean, F. (2001). The bilingual's language modes. In J. Nicol (Ed.), *One mind, two languages: Bilingual language processing* (pp. 1–22). Oxford, U.K.: Blackwell.

Hagoort, P., Brown, C. M., & Osterhout, L. (2000). The neurocognition of syntactic processing. In C. M. Brown & P. Hagoort (Eds.), *The neurocognition of language* (pp. 273–316). Oxford, U.K.: Oxford University Press.

Hahne, A., & Friederici, A. D. (2001). Processing a second language: Late learners' comprehension mechanisms as revealed by event-related brain potentials. *Bilingualism: Language and Cognition, 4,* 123–141.

Harley, T. A. (1996). Connectionist model of the recovery of language functions following brain damage. *Brain and Language, 52,* 7–24.

Hebb, D. O. (1949). *The organization of behaviour: A neuropsychological theory.* New York: Wiley.

Hermans, D. (2000). *Word production in a foreign language.* Unpublished doctoral dissertation, University of Nijmegen, The Netherlands.

Hermans, D., Bongaerts, T., De Bot, K., & Schreuder, R. (1999). Producing words in a foreign language: Can speakers prevent interference from their first language? *Bilingualism: Language and Cognition, 1*, 213–229.

Hernandez, A. E., Dapretto, M., Mazziotta, J., & Bookheimer, S. (2001). Language switching and language representation in Spanish-English bilinguals: An fMRI study. *NeuroImage, 14*, 510–520.

Jackson, G. M., Swainson, R., Cunnington, R., & Jackson, S. R. (2001). ERP correlates of executive control during repeated language switching. *Bilingualism: Language and Cognition, 4*, 169–178.

Johnson-Laird, P. N. (1983). *Mental models: Towards a cognitive science of language, inference and consciousness.* Cambridge, U.K.: Cambridge University Press.

Juncos-Rabadán, O., Pereiro, A. X., & Rodríguez, M. J. (2002). Treatment of aphasia in bilingual subjects. In F. Fabbro (Ed.), *Advances in the neurolinguistics of bilingualism* (pp. 275–298). Udine, Italy: Forum.

Kapur, N. (1996). Paradoxical functional facilitation in brain-behaviour research. *Brain, 19*, 1775–1990.

Klein, D., Milner, B., Zatorre, R., Meyer, E., & Evans, A. (1995). The neural substrates underlying word generation: A bilingual functional-imaging study. *Proceedings of the National Academy of Sciences U.S.A., 92*, 2899–2903.

Kroll, J. F., & De Groot, A. M. B. (1997). Lexical and conceptual memory in bilinguals: Mapping form to meaning in two languages. In A. M. B. de Groot & J. F. Kroll (Eds.), *Tutorials in bilingualism: Psycholinguistic perspectives* (pp. 169–199). Mahwah, NJ: Erlbaum.

Kroll, J. F., & Dussias, P. E. (2004). The comprehension of words and sentences in two languages. In T. K. Bhatia & W. C. Ritchie (Eds.), *The handbook of bilingualism* (pp. 169–200). Oxford, U.K.: Blackwell.

Levelt, W. J. M., Roelofs, A., & Meyer, A. S. (1999). A theory of lexical access in speech production. *Behavioral and Brain Sciences, 22*, 1–75.

Levin, B. E., Labre, M. M., & Weiner, W. J. (1989). Cognitive impairments associated with early Parkinson's disease. *Neurology, 39*, 557–561.

Loring, D. W., Meador, K. J., Lee, G. P., Murro, A. M., Smith, J. R., Flanigin, H. F., et al. (1990). Cerebral language lateralization: Evidence from intracarotid amobarbital testing. *Neuropsychologica, 28*, 831–838.

MacWhinney, B. (1997). Second language acquisition and the competition model. In A. M. B. de Groot & J. F. Kroll (Eds.), *Tutorials in bilingualism: Psycholinguistic perspectives* (pp. 113–142). Mahwah, NJ: Erlbaum.

Meuter, R. F. I., & Allport, A. (1999). Bilingual language switching in naming: Asymmetrical costs of language selection. *Journal of Memory and Language, 40*, 25–40.

Monsell, S. (1996). Control of mental processes. In V. Bruce (Ed.), *Unsolved mysteries of the mind: Tutorial essays on cognition* (pp. 93–148). Hove, U.K.: Taylor & Francis.

Morton, J., & Frith, U. (1995). Causal modelling: A structural approach to developmental psychopathology. In D. Cicchetti & D. J. Cohen (Eds.), *Manual of developmental psychopathology* (pp. 357–390). New York: Wiley.

Muller, U., Von Cramon, D. Y., & Pollmann, S. (1998). D1—versus D2—receptor modulation of visuo-spatial working memory in humans. *Journal of Neuroscience, 18*, 2720–2728.

Nilipour, R., & Ashayeri, H. (1989). Alternating antagonism between two languages with successive recovery of a third in a trilingual aphasic patient. *Brain and Language, 36*, 23–48.

Noppeney, U., & Price, C. J. (2004). An fMRI study of syntactic adaptation. *Journal of Cognitive Neuroscience, 16*, 702–713.

Osterhout, L., & McLaughlin, J. (2000, April). *What brain activity can tell us about second-language learning.* Paper presented at the 13th Annual CUNY Conference on Human Sentence Processing, San Diego, CA.

Papathanasiou, I., & Whurr, R. (2000). Recovery of function in aphasia. In I. Papathanasiou (Ed.), *Acquired neurogenic disorders: A clinical perspective* (pp. 28–48). London: Whurr.

Paradis, M. (1977). Bilingualism and aphasia. In H. Whitaker & H. A. Whitaker (Eds.), *Studies in neurolinguistics* (Vol. 3, pp. 65–121). New York: Academic Press.

Paradis, M. (1981). Neurolinguistic organization of the bilingual's two languages. In J. E. Copeland & P. W. Davis (Eds.), *The Seventh LACUS Forum* (pp. 486–494). Columbia, SC: Hornbeam Press.

Paradis, M. (1994). Neurolinguistic aspects of implicit and explicit memory: Implications for bilingualism and second language acquisition. In N. Ellis (Ed.), *Implicit and explicit language learning* (pp. 393–419). London: Academic Press.

Paradis, M. (1995). Epilogue. In M. Paradis (Ed.), *Aspects of bilingual aphasia* (pp. 211–223). New York: Pergamon/Elsevier Science.

Paradis, M. (2001). Bilingual and polyglot aphasia. In R. S. Berndt (Ed.), *Handbook of neuropsychology*, 2nd ed. *Vol. 3: Language and aphasia* (pp. 69–91). Amsterdam: Elsevier Science.

Paradis, M., & Goldblum, M. C. (1989). Selected crossed aphasia in a trilingual patient followed by reciprocal antagonism. *Brain and Language, 36*, 62–75.

Paradis, M., Goldblum, M. C., & Abidi, R. (1982). Alternate antagonism with paradoxical translation behaviour in two bilingual aphasic patients. *Brain and Language, 15*, 55–69.

Peterson, B. S., Skudlarski, P., Gatenby, J. C., Zhang, H., Anderson, A. W., & Gore, J. C. (1999). An fMRI study of Stroop word-color interference: Evidence for cingulate subregions subserving multiple distributed attentional systems. *Biological Psychiatry, 45*, 1237–1258.

Pitres, A. (1895). Etude sur l'aphasie chez les polyglottes. *Revue de medicine, 15*, 873–899. Translation in M. Paradis (Ed.), *Readings on aphasia in bilinguals and polyglots* (pp. 26–49). Montreal, Canada: Didier, 1983.

Plaut, D. C. (1996). Relearning after damage in connectionist networks: Towards a theory of rehabilitation. *Brain and Language, 52*, 25–82.

Pötzl, O. (1925). Über die parietal bedingte Aphasie und ihren Einfluss auf das sprechen mehrer sprachen. *Zeitschrift für die gesamte Neurologie und Psychiatrie, 12*, 145–162.

Price, C. J. (2000). The anatomy of language: Contributions from functional neuroimaging. *Journal of Anatomy, 197*, 335–359.

Price, C. J., & Friston, K. J. (1999). Scanning patients with tasks they can perform. *Human Brain Mapping, 8*, 102–108.

Price, C. J., & Friston, K. J. (2002). Functional imaging studies of neuropsychological patients: Applications and limitations. *Neurocase, 8*, 345–354.

Price, C. J., Green, D., & Von Studnitz, R. (1999). A functional imaging study of translation and language switching. *Brain, 122*, 2221–2236.

Price, C. J., Warburton, E. A., Moore, C. J., Frackowiak, R. S. J., & Friston, K. J. (2001). Dynamic diaschisis: Anatomically remote and context-sensitive human brain lesions. *Journal of Cognitive Neuroscience, 13*, 419–429.

Rapport, R. L., Tan, C. T., & Whitaker, H. A. (1983). Language function and dysfunction among Chinese and English speaking polyglots: Cortical stimulation, Wada testing, and clinical studies. *Brain and Language, 18*, 342–366.

Rickard, T. C. (2000). Methodological issues in functional magnetic resonance imaging studies of plasticity following brain injury. In H. S. Levin & J. G. Grafman (Eds.), *Cerebral reorganization of function after brain damage* (pp. 304–317). Oxford, U.K.: Oxford University Press.

Roberts, P. M., & Le Dorze, G. (1998). Bilingual aphasia: Semantic organization, strategy use, and productivity in semantic verbal fluency. *Brain and Language, 65*, 287–312.

Robertson, I. H., & Murre, J. M. (1999). Rehabilitation of brain damage: Brain plasticity and principles of guided recovery. *Psychological Bulletin, 125*, 544–575.

Rodriguez-Fornells, A., Rotte, M., Heinze, H-J., Nösselt, T., & Münte, T. F. (2002). Brain potential and functional MRI evidence for how to handle two languages with one brain. *Nature, 415*, 1026–1029.

Sarter, M., Bernston, G., & Cacioppo, J. (1996). Brain imaging and cognitive neuroscience: Towards strong inference in attributing function to structure. *American Psychologist, 51*, 13–21.

Shallice, T. (1988). *From neuropsychology to mental structure*. Cambridge, U.K.: Cambridge University Press.

Shuren, J. E., Hammond, C. S., Maher, L. M., Rothi, L. J. G., & Heilman, K. M. (1995). Attention and anosognosia: The case of a jargon aphasic patient with unawareness of language deficit. *Neurology, 45*, 376–378.

Slobin, D. I. (1996). From "thought and language" to "thinking for speaking." In J. J. Gumperz & S. C. Levinson (Eds.), *Rethinking linguistic relativity* (pp. 177–202). Cambridge, U.K.: Cambridge University Press.

Springer, J. A., Binder, J. R., Hammeke, T. A., Thomas, A., Swanson, S. J., Bellgowan, P. S. F., et al. (1999). Language dominance in neurologically normal and epilepsy subjects: A functional MRI study. *Brain, 122*, 2033–2046.

Tomasello, M. (1995). Language is not an instinct. *Cognitive Development, 10*, 131–156.

Ullman, M. T. (2001). The neural basis of lexicon and grammar in first and second language: The declarative/procedural model. *Bilingualism: Language and Cognition, 4*, 105–122.

Vaid, J., & Hull, R. (2002). Re-envisioning the bilingual brain using functional neuroimaging: Methodological and interpretive issues. In F. Fabbro (Ed.), *Advances in the neurolinguistics of bilingualism* (pp. 315–355). Udine, Italy: Forum.

Warburton, E. A., Price, C. J., Swinburn, K., & Wise, K. J. (1999). Mechanisms of recovery from aphasia: Evidence from positron emission tomography studies. *Journal of Neurology, Neurosurgery and Psychiatry, 66*, 155–161.

Weber-Fox, C. M., & Neville, H. J. (2001). Sensitive periods differentiate processing for open and closed class words: An ERP study in bilinguals. *Journal of Speech, Language, and Hearing Research, 44*, 1338–1353.

Judith F. Kroll
Natasha Tokowicz

26

Models of Bilingual Representation and Processing
Looking Back and to the Future

ABSTRACT   Early research on the representation and processing of information in bilingual memory debated whether the two languages were stored and accessed together or separately in memory. In this chapter, we argue that the question that motivated the initial research and model development on this topic failed to address a set of critical issues. These include distinctions between levels of language representation, differences in components of processing associated with unique task goals in comprehension versus production, and the consequences of developmental aspects of language experience. We examine the legacy of the debate about shared versus separate representations in a review of models that focus on each of the issues we have identified. Finally, in the course of our review, if the evidence was available, we consider the implications of recent neuroimaging research for constraining models of bilingual representation and processing.

Perhaps the most enduring question in psycholinguistic studies of bilingualism is whether bilinguals have a single system of memory representation and processing devoted to all of the languages they use or separate systems, one for each language (e.g., Kolers, 1963; McCormack, 1977; Weinreich, 1953). Life experience offers ample support for each alternative. Bilinguals appear to be able to function in each of their languages when required to do so, without frequent or random intrusions of the other language, yet they can also code switch with other bilingual speakers in a manner that suggests simultaneous activity of both languages. In the early literature on this topic, an answer to the question of whether the languages were functionally independent failed to emerge despite an increasing number of empirical studies that tested predictions based on the two alternatives. With hindsight, it is easy to see why the question was ill formed, how the models proposed were underspecified, and why the resulting evidence was difficult to interpret.

The question of whether bilinguals have shared or separate language representations requires that assumptions be made about a number of features of the cognitive architecture. These features include levels of representation, the distinction between representation and process, the manner in which cognitive representations and processes are recruited to perform different tasks, and the ways in which representations and processes change at different stages of learning and in response to different learning contexts.

The first problem with early bilingual models is that they failed to consider distinctions among levels of representation. A priori, there is no reason why the answer to the question of how the two languages are represented needs to be the same for orthography, phonology, semantics, and syntax. Indeed, the question may be answered differently for different aspects of language representation and for bilinguals whose particular languages constrain the possibilities of shared representation and whose language learning histories determine the context in which the two languages are acquired.

A second issue is that the questions of what is represented and how that information is processed were conflated in much of the early research. Thus, the assumption that the two languages were stored in independent memory systems was generally associated with a selective view of language processing that suggested that there might be a language switch that effectively enabled one language and shut the other down as needed (e.g., Macnamara & Kushnir, 1971). As Van Heuven, Dijkstra, and Grainger (1998) pointed out, these questions can be viewed independently of one another. It is possible to have shared memory representations with selective access or separate representations with parallel and nonselective access. One question is about the representation or code; the other is about the process of accessing that information.

A third respect in which the early bilingual models failed to characterize cognitive activity adequately concerns their scope. Few distinctions were made to address the distinct demands of comprehension, production, or memory. Models were considered general, and predictions were tested for comprehension, production, and memory as if they were the same. Tests of particular models might therefore succeed or fail depending on the relation of the nature of evidence to the hypothesized mechanism.

Finally, although early research focused on different types of bilingualism (e.g., Weinreich, 1953), later models for the most part did not consider the consequences of the bilingual's learning history or the developmental changes associated with increasing skill in the second language (L2; see De Groot & Poot, 1997; Kroll & Stewart, 1994; MacWhinney, 1997; Mägiste, 1984; and Potter, So, Von Eckardt, & Feldman, 1984, for exceptions).

We can illustrate the problem in the early models using an example drawn from an often-cited article by Kirsner, Smith, Lockhart, King, and Jain (1984). Our example is not intended to single out these authors. To the contrary, this paper made an important contribution by demonstrating that it was possible to obtain cross-language semantic priming even when the two languages are mixed and orthographically distinct. Kirsner et al. contrasted five models of the bilingual lexicon using a scheme initially proposed by Meyer and Ruddy (1974). These models are shown in Fig. 26.1. In each of the five configurations, words in the bilingual's two languages have separate representations or share the same representation. The grouping of words vertically reflects their semantic relations, whereas the horizontal connections depict lexical connections across translation equivalents. In Model A, there are separate representations for words in each language and lexical connections only within, but not across, languages. Kirsner et al. rejected this extreme version of the separate model

on the grounds that it would prevent translation. Model B maintains separate lexical nodes for words in each language but includes translation links across languages. Model D, like Models A and B, assumes separate lexical representations. However, now there are not only the translation links of Model B, but also cross-language connections to associated words. Model C is an extreme version of the integrated model, with shared lexical nodes and therefore shared semantic relations within and across languages. The final alternative, Model E, assumes shared conceptual representations but separate lexical representations for each language.

Model E has been taken by some (e.g., Kroll & Sholl, 1992; Potter et al., 1984) as a solution to the apparent controversy surrounding the issue of separate versus shared language representation. If only semantic, but not lexical, representations are shared, then tasks that reflect lexical-level processing will tend to support independence across the two languages, whereas tasks that reflect semantic processing will tend to support the common interdependent alternative.

The pattern of cross-language priming results obtained by Kirsner et al. (1984) allowed them to reject all but Models D and E, which they were unable to distinguish on the basis of the observed data. But, the point of this example for present purposes is that the family of models shown in Fig. 26.1 fails to address each of the issues identified above. Although lexical and semantic representations are distinguished, no information is specified concerning the form of those representations. The models do not identify orthographic and phonological aspects of lexical form or provide adequate detail that might allow the models to handle cases in which precise translation equivalents do not exist.

Likewise, no assumptions are made about the selectivity of lexical access, although the arrangement of separated versus integrated lexical representations would appear to suggest selective versus nonselective access. The priming focus of the Kirsner et al. (1984) article suggests that the models are intended to capture aspects of comprehension, but the arrangement in Model E was initially proposed by Potter et al. (1984) to account for bilingual performance in language production tasks. Thus, distinctions are not drawn between initial access from word to concept in comprehension and later lexicalization from concept to word in production.

Finally, the architecture and processing within the lexicon in this family of alternatives appears to

SEGREGATED MEMORIES

INTEGRATED MEMORIES

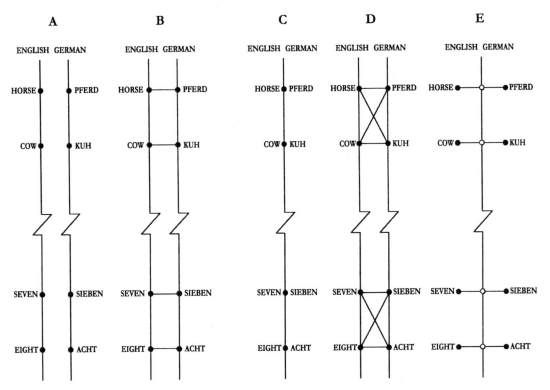

Figure 26.1 Five models of the bilingual lexicon. Adapted from Kirsner et al. (1984).

reflect an ultimate arrangement for proficient bilinguals that ignores their learning history, structural differences between their two languages, and their relative language dominance. How the relations between word and concept develop as L2 learners become more proficient in the L2 and how the proficient state of the lexicon may reflect dynamic changes in language use and activity are not addressed.

In response to the problems described, contemporary models have become more specialized, focusing on particular aspects of the codes that may be shared across languages; on the way in which lexical or grammatical information is accessed in bilinguals under specific task conditions such as reading, listening, speaking, or remembering; and on the processes that characterize the cognitive changes that enable L2 learners to become proficient bilinguals. These cognitive changes include the component processes that allow the development of skilled performance in the L2 (e.g., see Segalowitz & Hulstijn, chapter 18, this volume) as

well as the control mechanisms that permit attention to be allocated appropriately to the desired language and language task (e.g., Bialystok, chapter 20, this volume; Green, 1986, 1998; Michael & Gollan, chapter 19, this volume). In this context, the issue of independence or interdependence of bilingual language systems has not been abandoned but instead recast to accommodate what we now know about language processing and the cognitive mechanisms that support it.

In this chapter, we provide an overview of models that have brought research on the representation and processing of two languages to its contemporary state. Our review is necessarily selective because of the length limitations of the present text and the availability of other recent reviews of related material in this volume (e.g., Costa, chapter 15; Dijkstra, chapter 9; La Heij, chapter 14; Sánchez-Casas & García-Albea, chapter 11; and Thomas & Van Heuven, chapter 10) and others (e.g., De Groot, 2002; Dijkstra & Van Heuven, 2002; Gollan & Kroll, 2001; Kroll & De

Groot, 1997; Kroll & Dijkstra, 2002; Kroll & Dussias, 2004; Kroll & Sunderman, 2003; Kroll & Tokowicz, 2001). We focus specifically on models that address the issues raised in this section, namely, which aspects of representation are shared and to what extent access to them is selective, how cross-language interactions change in the face of different task demands, and how the course of L2 acquisition affects the form of representations and connections across the two languages.

Furthermore, we restrict our discussion to models of lexical representation and to accounts of online processing because a disproportionate number of studies have addressed the bilingual lexicon. (For a review of models and evidence regarding syntactic processes, see Frenck-Mestre, chapter 13, this volume; Kroll & Dussias, 2004; MacWhinney, 1997, and chapter 3, this volume; Pienemann, Di Biase, Kawaguchi, & Håkansson, chapter 7, this volume). Questions about memory retrieval outside the time frame of initial comprehension or production are also of interest but beyond the scope of the present review. (For a review of research on bilingual memory, see Durgunoglu & Roediger, 1987; Francis, chapter 12, this volume; Marian & Neisser, 2000; Paivio, 1991; Schrauf & Rubin, 1998).

Finally, where there are available data, we consider the theoretical implications of recent neuroimaging evidence for models of bilingual representation and processing (see Abutalebi, Cappa, & Perani, chapter 24, this volume, for a comprehensive review of the imaging research). Interestingly, cognitive neuroscience approaches to bilingualism have returned to the question of whether the bilingual's two languages are represented in a separate or integrated memory system by asking whether and where there is distinct neural activity associated with each language. In some respects, the theoretical implications of this approach are potentially regressive with respect to model development. However, the new imaging evidence has also served the important function of reviving interest in how the timing and context of L2 learning has an impact on the organization of the two languages in the brain. We briefly consider the implications of this new approach in our review.

A Review of Models: Levels of Representation, Processing Tasks, and Development

We now turn to a review of specific models. Our review is organized into three sections. The first considers models that illustrate the ways in which assumptions have been made about different levels of representation. The second examines models proposed to address particular language-processing tasks, such as comprehension or production. The final section focuses on developmental issues and their consequences for proficient bilingual performance.

Levels of Representation

An advance in modeling the bilingual lexicon came from the recognition that different aspects of the lexical code may distinctly constrain the form of cross-language interactions. The development of computational models of word recognition in the monolingual domain (e.g., Grainger & Jacobs, 1996; McClelland & Rumelhart, 1981; Seidenberg & McClelland, 1989) generated a number of alternative candidates that, with some modification, appeared to provide a reasonable extension to the bilingual case. Grainger and Dijkstra (1992) and Dijkstra and Van Heuven (1998) first proposed such an extension of the Interactive Activation Model, called the BIA or Bilingual Interactive Activation model. The BIA model, a localist connectionist model, is at present the bilingual model of word form that has been studied most extensively. We describe it only briefly because two chapters in the present volume examine the model, its associated evidence, recent extensions, and its relation to distributed models (Dijkstra, chapter 9; Thomas & Van Heuven, chapter 10). We then examine the Distributed Feature Model (De Groot, 1992a), a model focused specifically on semantic representation.

Word Form   The BIA model (see Fig. 10.1 in Thomas & Van Heuven, chapter 10, this volume) borrows the basic architecture of McClelland and Rumelhart's (1981) Interactive Activation model, such that processing is initiated by visual input from text and proceeds in a bottom-up manner from letter features to letters to words. The BIA model assumes that the lexicon is integrated across languages, and that lexical access is parallel and nonselective. Thus, during early stages of word recognition, patterns of activation and inhibition within and across levels of representation are hypothesized to be language blind. However, unlike models of word recognition for monolinguals, the bilingual model requires that there be a basis on which words can eventually be correctly selected in the intended language. In the BIA model, the mechanism introduced to achieve language selection is the layer of language nodes. The language nodes, as represented in the original BIA model, inhibit words in the nontarget language. Their top-down influence is not thought to alter the early activation of words in each of the two languages but to increase the later likelihood of selecting a word from the intended language (see Dijkstra & Van Heuven, 2002, for a revision of this mechanism in the BIA+ model).

Unlike earlier bilingual models, the BIA model proposes a precise mechanism for the way in which orthographic forms are activated in two languages when a bilingual recognizes visually presented words. For languages with orthographies that are similar, there will be parallel activation that results in competition at the lexical and sublexical levels. This property of the model has been investigated by exploiting the presence of words with a form that overlaps across languages. These include *cognates*, translation pairs that share word form and meaning; *interlingual homographs*, words that are similar in form in both languages but not translation equivalents; and *orthographic neighbors*, words in each language with a lexical form that is only slightly different from the target word. If lexical access is nonselective across languages, then the consequences of cross-language activity should influence recognition performance. If lexical access is selective, then the presence of other-language form relatives should be irrelevant, and processing should proceed in the same way as for a monolingual reader.

Thus, according to the selective view, a word like *room*, which is an interlingual homograph in English and Dutch (in which the word *room* means cream), would be processed in each language as if it were an unambiguous word. In contrast, according to the nonselective view, both language senses of the word would be active and compete, similar to the competition observed for lexically ambiguous words within a language.

Over a large number of studies and using a range of experimental paradigms, convincing support for the nonselective alternative has been reported (see Dijkstra, chapter 9, this volume, for details and Thomas & Van Heuven, chapter 10, this volume, for a description of how the model has been implemented). A particularly compelling aspect of the evidence on word recognition is that the activity of the L2 influences the native language even when the task is performed in the native language alone (e.g., Van Hell & Dijkstra, 2002).

Although the initial evidence for the BIA model focused on orthographic interactions across languages, more recent evidence on phonology suggests that phonological codes are also active in both languages during word recognition (e.g., Brysbaert, Van Dyck, & Van de Poel, 1999; Dijkstra, Grainger, & Van Heuven, 1999; Jared & Kroll, 2001; Jared & Szucs, 2002; Marian & Spivey, 1999; Schwartz, Kroll, & Diaz, 2003). For example, Schwartz et al. showed that the time for English-Spanish bilinguals to name cognates was a function of the match between the orthographic and phonological similarity of their forms in the two languages. These findings and others suggest that it is not orthography alone but the interaction between orthography and phonology across the bilingual's two languages that determines the course of visual word recognition.

The inclusion of cross-language phonological activity requires an extension to the BIA model that was described by Dijkstra and Van Heuven (2002) in a model now called the BIA+ and by Van Heuven (2000) (see the semantic, orthographic, and phonological interactive activation [SOPHIA] model in Fig. 10.3, chapter 10, this volume). The new models introduce both lexical and sublexical phonology to account for the observed patterns of orthographic and phonological interaction. Finding cross-language phonological interactions also accommodates the observation that nonselectivity is not restricted to languages with a visual form that is similar (e.g., see Gollan, Forster, & Frost, 1997, for an example of priming between Hebrew and English).

The specificity of the BIA model allows clear predictions to be tested about the form of cross-language interactions during visual word recognition. However, by accounting for only one aspect of lexical form, the model fails to fully characterize word recognition in and out of meaningful context. Just as the new extensions in the BIA+ and SOPHIA models include phonological representations, they also now include semantic representations to address this issue.

Only a few studies have investigated the effects of semantic and syntactic context on cross-language activation during lexical access (e.g., Altarriba, Kroll, Sholl, & Rayner, 1996; Elston-Güttler, 2000; Schwartz, 2003; Van Hell, 1998). The answer to the question of whether context can modulate the parallel activation of information about words in both languages and, if so, at what level in the system will be critical to the development of the next generation of models. The preliminary evidence on this issue suggests that, at least under some circumstances, it is possible to modulate the presence of cross-language interactions. Both Van Hell (1998) and Schwartz (2003) found evidence that, in the context of a highly constrained sentence, cross-language activity was reduced. However, for the same materials, in low-constraint sentences and out of context, there was clear evidence for cross-language influences. An intriguing aspect of these results is that the language of the context itself does not appear to determine selectivity. If lexical access was fundamentally selective, then we might expect that the language of the sentence would be an effective cue to selection. Yet, in each of these studies, the low-constraint sentence context did not override nonselectivity. Like cross-language semantic priming studies in which the language of the prime has been manipulated (e.g., De Bruijn, Dijkstra, Chwilla, & Schriefers, 2001), these results suggest a limited role for language-specific cues per se, at least in comprehension.

Although most of the evidence for language nonselectivity has been based on behavioral measures, a few studies have examined neural activity during bilingual word recognition. De Bruijn et al. (2001) found similar N400 effects in an event-related potential (ERP) study for target words semantically related to an interlingual homograph regardless of the language bias preceding the homograph. In ERP research, the N400 has been taken as an index of lexical and semantic processing. Finding similar results regardless of language context would appear to support the nonselective account provided by the BIA model. In contrast, an ERP and functional magnetic resonance imaging (fMRI) study by Rodriquez-Fornells, Rotte, Heinze, Nösselt, and Münte (2002) claimed that selectivity was possible in a language decision task in which bilingual participants could use phonological information to avoid cross-language interference (but see Grosjean, Li, Münte, & Rodriquez-Fornells, 2003, for a critique of these results).

Marian, Spivey, and Hirsch (2003) also examined the parallel activation of the two languages by comparing cross-language interactions in an eye movement paradigm and using fMRI measures. Their results fall somewhere between the two alternatives, with some evidence for shared areas of brain activation and other evidence for differences. They suggested that the presence of both similarities and differences is consistent with a time course account in which the same cortical mechanisms are likely to be activated for both languages during early stages of processing, but as processing proceeds, patterns of activation may become more distinct. It will remain to be seen how well the developing body of neuroimaging evidence fits with the nonselective account that appears so compelling on the basis of the behavioral data.

Meaning   We turn now to the representation of meaning because a complete model of the bilingual lexicon will require that the semantics be specified (see Francis, 1999, and chapter 12, this volume, for a comprehensive review of research on semantic and conceptual representation in bilinguals). Much of the research on language processing in bilinguals has assumed that the same semantic representations are accessed for both languages (e.g., Costa, Miozzo, & Caramazza, 1999; La Heij et al., 1990; Potter et al., 1984) because past research has appeared to support that assumption. For example, in a bilingual variant of primed lexical decision, semantically related words prime each other even when the prime and target appear in different languages (e.g., Altarriba, 1990; Chen & Ng, 1989; Keatley, Spinks, & De Gelder, 1994; Meyer & Ruddy, 1974; Schwanenflugel & Rey, 1986; Tzelgov & Eben-Ezra, 1992). Although the pattern of cross-language priming often reveals an asymmetry, with more priming from the first language (L1) to L2, the presence of cross-language priming at all, especially under conditions that minimize the likelihood of translation, suggests that some shared meaning is accessed across languages. Similarly, in a Stroop-type picture–word production task, interference is observed when a distractor word is semantically related to the picture's name regardless of the language in which it appears (e.g., Costa et al., 1999; Hermans, 2000; Hermans, Bongaerts, De Bot, & Schreuder, 1998).

The reliance on out-of-context tasks in which participants translate concrete nouns or name pictured objects may have contributed to the assumption of shared semantics because these circumstances may be the most likely to evoke the same meaning in each of the bilingual's languages. It also made it reasonable to ignore distinctions between semantic and conceptual representations and the more general implications of lexical semantics that would be relevant in ordinary sentence contexts. In contrast, research on linguistic relativity focuses on just those circumstances that are most likely to evoke different meanings across languages, for example, when there are no precise translation equivalents or when the linguistic or cultural context biases the appropriate sense of meaning (see Pavlenko, 1999, and chapter 21, this volume, for a discussion of linguistic relativity).

To accommodate the possibility of both shared and separate semantics under different circumstances, De Groot and colleagues (De Groot, 1992a, 1992b, 1995; De Groot, Dannenburg, & Van Hell, 1994; Van Hell, 1998; Van Hell & De Groot, 1998) proposed a model of bilingual semantics called the Distributed Feature Model (see Fig. 26.2). A key assumption in the model is that the degree to which semantic representations are shared across languages is a consequence of the word's lexical category. Representations for concrete nouns and cognates are assumed to be quite similar across languages, whereas representations for abstract nouns and noncognates are assumed to be more distinct. In some respects, the Distributed Feature Model uses word type to model lexico-semantic representations in a manner that resembles the way in which older models used the learning history of the bilingual to model compound versus coordinate representations (e.g., Lambert, 1969). In one case, attributes of the language representation determine the architecture of the system. In the other, attributes of the language user constrain the nature of the representations and their relations (see the discussion of compound vs. coordinate bilingualism in a later section of this chapter).

The Distributed Feature Model predicts that the degree of overlap across translation equivalents will determine the time it takes speakers to translate from one language to the other or to recognize whether two words are the correct translation equivalents of one another. To the extent that translation requires semantic processing (De Groot et al., 1994; La Heij, Kerling, & Van der Velden; 1996; but see Kroll & Stewart, 1994), then the speed of access to semantic representations should influence performance. In a series of studies, De Groot and colleagues (De Groot, 1992a, 1992b, 1995; De Groot et al., 1994; Van Hell, 1998; Van Hell & De Groot, 1998) confirmed these predictions. Using a range of tasks that included translation production, translation recognition, lexical decision, and word association, these experiments showed that the time to recognize and produce translation equivalents is faster when the word pairs are concrete nouns or cognates. Van Hell and De Groot also demonstrated that word associations were more similar across languages for concrete words and cognates than for abstract words and noncognates.

The Distributed Feature Model assumes that the semantic system itself is shared across the bilingual's two languages. The features that comprise the pool of semantic primitives are hypothesized to be

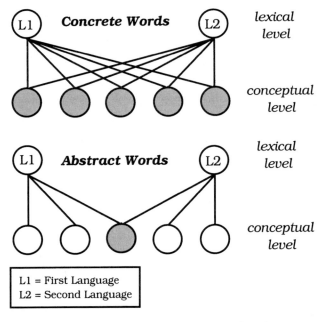

Figure 26.2 The Distributed Feature Model. Adapted from Van Hell and De Groot (1998).

available to either language (see Illes et al., 1999, for neuroimaging evidence that the same areas of the brain are active when bilinguals make concreteness judgments about words in each of their languages). How those features combine within a language then determines the similarity of particular concepts. Earlier research on concreteness effects within a single language showed that concrete words have higher contextual availability than abstract words (e.g., Schwanenflugel & Shoben, 1983). Abstract words appear to depend more on provided context for their meaning than concrete words. The Distributed Feature Model extends this idea to the bilingual case. If the context in which words are processed differs across languages and cultures, then the meaning of abstract words will depend more on the context in which their sense is instantiated than the meaning of concrete words.

In a study with Dutch-English bilinguals who performed a semantic rating task on translation pairs (i.e., how similar are these two words?), Tokowicz, Kroll, De Groot, and Van Hell (2002) found that indeed concrete translation equivalents were more likely to share meaning than abstract translation equivalents, although no distinction between cognate and noncognate translations was found. A further difference reported by Tokowicz et al. was that words with more than one translation equivalent were rated as less semantically similar to their translation equivalents than words with only one translation equivalent. This finding suggests that the existence of alternate translations influences how adequate each individual translation is considered. Indeed, Tokowicz (2000) found that the time to produce translation equivalents in a translation production task was slower for words considered to have multiple translation equivalents than for words with only a single dominant translation. These results suggest that bilinguals can have (nearly) identical concepts for some words and different concepts for other words. The consequence of differences in the degree of overlap in meaning for the nature of cross-language processing will depend on the nature of the task, the bilingual's level of proficiency, and the context of acquisition (e.g., Dufour & Kroll, 1995; Finkbeiner, Forster, Nicol, & Nakamura, 2004; Jiang, 2000; Silverberg & Samuel, 2004).

Processing Tasks

Even with a model of bilingual representation that provides an adequate characterization of lexical form and meaning, we would need to make additional assumptions about the ways in which the goals associated with different tasks utilize those representations. The same lexicon may underlie word recognition and word production, but the manner in which lexical processes are initiated and the demands on processing resources associated with each task may differentially constrain performance (see Kroll & Dijkstra, 2002, for a comparison of bilingual comprehension and production). Here, we consider two models that address the issue of how the task determines the nature of the information that is retrieved and the manner in which processing is controlled. One is a model of lexical production to account for the way in which a bilingual initiates a spoken word in response to the requirement to name a picture, translate a word, or speak a thought. The other is a model of the control processes that are hypothesized to be recruited so that only the intended language is selected for comprehension or production.

Production   Far less research on the bilingual lexicon has examined production relative to comprehension. Although code switching has been studied extensively by linguists and sociolinguists (see Myers-Scotton, chapter 16, this volume), it is only recently that the methods developed by psycholinguists to study speech production within the native language (e.g., Levelt, 1989; Levelt, Roelofs, & Meyer, 1999; Peterson & Savoy, 1998) have been extended to the bilingual case (e.g., Colomé, 2001; Costa & Caramazza, 1999; Costa et al., 1999; De Bot & Schreuder, 1993; Gollan & Silverberg, 2001; Hermans et al., 1998; Miller & Kroll, 2002). Our purpose in the present discussion is not to provide a comprehensive review of this work (see Costa, chapter 15, and La Heij, chapter 14, in this volume). Rather, we hope to illustrate how the components of a model of lexical access in production will necessarily address some different issues than a model of comprehension.

We adopt a model of spoken production proposed first by Poulisse and Bongaerts (1994) and later extended by Hermans (2000) (see Fig. 26.3). The model characterizes the bilingual lexicon in the face of the requirement to speak a word in one language or the other. Like models in the monolingual domain (e.g., Levelt et al., 1999), the production model shown in Fig. 26.3 assumes that there are three levels of representation engaged in translating an idea into a spoken word. First, the idea must be represented conceptually. If the event that initiates speaking is a pictured object, as shown in the model, then this first step will involve

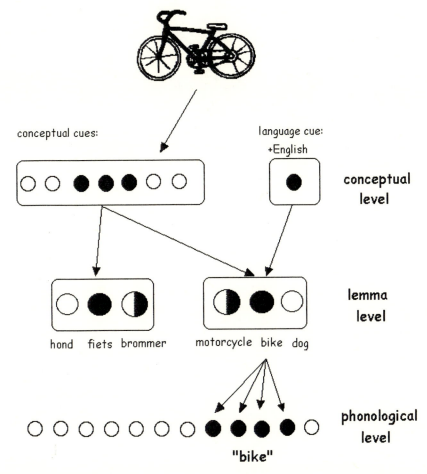

Figure 26.3 A model of bilingual language production. Adapted from Poulisse and Bongaerts (1994) and Hermans (2000).

recognizing the object and accessing its meaning. In this model, there is also a language cue represented at the conceptual level. The language cue signals information about the language in which the utterance is to be spoken. If lexical access in production is language selective, then the intention to speak a word in one of the bilingual's languages rather than the other might suffice to turn the remaining steps in the production process into the monolingual case. However, experiments suggest that even when bilinguals know that they will be speaking only one of their two languages, that knowledge is not sufficient to effectively switch off the activation of other language alternatives (e.g., Colomé, 2001; Costa, Caramazza, & Sebastián-Gallés, 2000; Kroll, Dijkstra, Janssen, & Schriefers, in preparation).

Following conceptual processing, a set of lemmas is hypothesized to be activated in each of the bilingual's two languages. Although there is some debate about what information is stored at the lemma level, particularly regarding grammatical category, there is general agreement that at this level abstract lexical representations for words in each language are activated. Unlike the assumptions of an integrated lexicon in comprehension models such as BIA or BIA+, the assumption here is that the syntactic constraints specified at the lemma level will require that lemmas are necessarily distinct for words in each of the bilingual's languages. At the final level depicted in the model, the phonology of the spoken word is specified. Like the assumption of the Distributed Feature Model for semantics, the production model assumes that each language draws on a common pool of phonological features. Thus, although there may be distinct aspects of the phonology associated with each language, the assumption is that the phonological system itself is shared so that common phonological elements in each language will activate the same or similar representations.

A key question about production concerns the sequencing of these representations prior to the production of a spoken word or sentence. In research on monolingual production, this issue has been at the center of a debate about the nature of lexical access and the interactions between syntax and semantics (e.g., Dell, 1986; Levelt et al., 1999; Vigliocco & Hartsuiker, 2002). In the bilingual domain, the issue is potentially even more complicated because the language of speaking also has to be determined. If representations are activated for both languages in parallel, then the question of whether they compete for selection is critical because proficient bilinguals will have at least two words available for each concept. In the model shown in Fig. 26.3, there is activation of candidates in both languages at the lemma level, but the assumption is that selection occurs at this level (e.g., see Hermans et al., 1998) and that phonology is specified only for the language the person intends to speak. The evidence suggests that there is in fact activation to the level of the phonology for words in both languages (e.g., Colomé, 2001; Costa et al., 2000; Kroll et al., in preparation). The theoretically difficult question is whether all activated information competes for selection or whether the language cue can effectively guide the selection process. In this volume, consult Costa (chapter 15), La Heij (chapter 14), and Meuter (chapter 17) for an indepth discussion of this particular issue.

The point for present purposes is that how the very same representations may be engaged will differ depending on whether the task requires comprehension or production. In production, the initiating event consists of conceptual activity. The corresponding sequence of processing from concepts to words will necessarily engage feedback from semantics that may or may not be available during comprehension, for which the sequence from words to concepts is more likely to be driven by properties of the stimulus input rather than its meaning. In the production model illustrated here, the language cue is hypothesized to be encoded as part of the conceptual representation of the event that initiates production. In a comprehension model such as BIA or BIA+, the language nodes are not activated until relatively late in the processing se-

quence. Given these differences, it is perhaps surprising that the empirical evidence suggests that lexical access is language nonselective for both comprehension and production. However, it is important not to conclude that the apparent similarities arise from the same mechanism. Particularly in production, it should be possible in theory to use context and available cues to bias selection. A number of studies suggest that this may be the case (e.g., Bloem & La Heij, 2003; Miller & Kroll, 2002).

Control   Like many cognitive models, those that characterize the bilingual lexicon have been designed without much concern for how the cognitive system actually manages to produce actions in response to task goals. The problem is especially acute in light of the evidence for language nonselectivity in both comprehension and production. If candidates in both of the bilingual's languages are routinely available in comprehension and in production regardless of the intention to use one language only, then a mechanism must be in place to modulate the resulting competition and to control performance. A number of models have addressed the control problem by finding solutions within the lexicon itself (e.g., the language nodes served this purpose in the original BIA model) or by positing a mechanism that falls outside the lexicon but uses the output of the lexical system to achieve proficient performance. Green (1998) proposed the Inhibitory Control (IC) Model, shown in Fig. 26.4, to accomplish this goal. The model is described in some detail by Meuter (chapter 17, this volume), so our review touches only on its central points.

Like other models of production, the IC model assumes that a conceptual representation is generated at the onset of planning. That conceptual activity in turn activates both the lexico-semantic system and the supervisory attentional system (SAS). The role of the SAS is to control the activation of task schemas for particular language processing goals. Thus, the task schema for naming a picture in the L1 would differ from the schema for naming a picture in L2 or translating a word from L1 to L2. The IC model further assumes that lemmas are tagged for language membership. A critical function of the task schemas is to activate lemmas in the intended language and to inhibit lemmas in the unintended language. Because the level of competition created by this process will require attentional resources, the degree of inhibitory control required for a bilingual to perform a particular task will be related to the relative

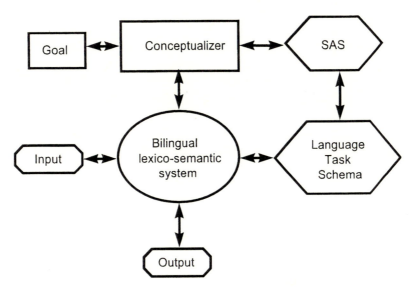

Figure 26.4 The Inhibitory Control Model. Adapted from Green (1998). SAS, supervisory attentional system.

activation of lemmas in each language. For example, if lexical candidates in the more dominant L1 are active when a bilingual is attempting to name a picture in L2, then the inhibitory processes required to modulate the competition from L1 to L2 will be greater than those required when the task is performed in the L1 itself.

An important source of evidence regarding inhibitory control comes from experiments on deliberate language switching (see Meuter, chapter 17, this volume, for a review of this literature). Research on language switching has shown that switch costs are greater when bilinguals are required to switch into L1 relative to L2 (e.g., Meuter & Allport, 1999). The asymmetry in switch costs appears at first counterintuitive because it might be thought that the more dominant L1 will always be automatically available. However, from the perspective of the IC model, the result makes a good deal of sense because switch costs will be greatest when the processing on the trial just prior to the switch induces a great deal of competition and therefore requires significant inhibition. It is precisely this mechanism that is hypothesized to occur when a bilingual performs a task such as picture naming or number naming in the L2. If L1 lemmas compete prior to the selection of the word to be produced in L2, then the inhibition of the L1 lemmas will produce a cost when L1 is the target language to produce on the subsequent trial.

A complete understanding of how attentional and task processes influence performance will be an important feature of the next generation of models of the bilingual lexicon (see Dijkstra & Van Heuven, 2002, and Von Studnitz & Green, 2002, for an illustration of how this mechanism might work in comprehension). As Meuter (chapter 17, this volume) notes, it is not entirely clear how to think about the scope of the inhibitory mechanism proposed within the IC model. Identifying the factors that determine the range of inhibition will be critical as it seems unreasonable to think that the entire language is inhibited at once. Furthermore, the IC model, as depicted in Fig. 26.4, makes few assumptions about the architecture of the lexicon itself, an issue that we considered in some detail in the previous sections of this chapter. It will be important to understand how assumptions about representation and processing within the lexicon constrain, and are constrained by, the attentional mechanisms that serve as an interface to the more general cognitive system and to action.

An aspect of the IC model that has only recently been investigated concerns the implications of inhibitory control for the achievement of L2 proficiency. If the mental juggling that appears to be required by using two languages can only be effectively controlled by the allocation of sufficient attentional resources, then individuals who already possess high memory capacity may be advantaged

L2 learners. A number of studies investigating individual differences in memory and attentional resources for L2 acquisition suggest that this may be the case (see Michael & Gollan, chapter 19, this volume). Furthermore, in the case of highly skilled translators and interpreters, it seems clear that they possess extraordinary cognitive resources that enable their remarkable performance (see Christoffels & De Groot, chapter 22, this volume).

What is less clear is the direction of causality. We do not yet know whether individuals with enhanced cognitive abilities are more likely to become skilled bilinguals or whether the process of becoming bilingual has the positive consequences of enhancing cognitive skills more generally. The evidence on young bilingual children (see Bialystok, chapter 20, this volume) provides compelling support for the view that bilingualism itself may confer a set of cognitive benefits that extend beyond language processing to executive control functions. However, little is known about whether the advantages observed in early childhood endure into adulthood or whether late acquisition of an L2 has similar consequences.

What is evident in this discussion is that models of bilingual processing and its control will require an account that considers not only representation and control, but also developmental aspects of language acquisition. In the final section of our review, we turn to models of bilingual representation and processing that have focused on these developmental issues.

Developing Second Language Proficiency

Early Versus Late Acquisition: Compound Versus Coordinate Bilingualism   We now consider how the context in which L2 is acquired may affect semantic and lexical representations and their interconnections. Although some researchers have viewed L2 acquisition from the perspective of the critical period hypothesis (e.g., Lambert, 1972), our review considers aspects of L2 acquisition that are not typically the focus of research on that topic (see Birdsong, chapter 6, and DeKeyser & Larson-Hall, chapter 5, this volume, for current reviews of the critical period hypothesis). Depending on the acquisition context of the bilingual, a distinction has been made between *compound* and *coordinate* bilinguals. Generally defined, compound bilinguals are individuals who learn two languages simultaneously, in the same context, whereas coordinate

bilinguals are individuals who learn their two languages in succession, in separate contexts. However, it should be noted that there has been disagreement in past research concerning the definitions of compound and coordinate bilingualism and whether this distinction is a continuum or rather a dichotomy (Lambert, 1969).

One of the hypothesized differences between compound and coordinate bilinguals regards the similarity of concepts referred to by L1 and L2 words. It was believed that compound bilinguals had one set of concepts that could be referenced by either language, whereas coordinate bilinguals had two sets of concepts, each set uniquely available to one of the two languages. This distinction has been applied not only to semantic aspects of the language, but also to syntactic, phonological, and cultural aspects (e.g., Lambert, Havelka, & Crosby, 1958).

To test the compound/coordinate distinction, Lambert (1961) used the semantic differential to determine whether translation equivalents shared meaning in the two languages. In this task, the bilingual rates a word relative to adjectives (e.g., how cold is a house?) and then does the same for the translation equivalent. The theoretical prediction was that compound bilinguals would rate translation equivalents more similarly than coordinate bilinguals. Lambert found that compound bilinguals did give similar ratings to translation equivalents, but that the ratings of coordinate bilinguals depended on their particular acquisition context—coordinates who learned L1 and L2 in the same cultural context rated translations similarly, whereas coordinates who learned the two languages in different cultural contexts rated translations dissimilarly. These findings showed that the experience of the learner is important above and beyond the manner of learning. Although the evidence on the semantic differential revealed differences between compound and coordinate bilinguals, there were also questions whether these differences reflected the most critical aspects of the learning context.

More recent research has examined the neural consequences of the language-learning context. Whereas psycholinguistic research has moved away from the question of whether the two languages are stored together or separately in favor of asking what circumstances elicit behavior that appears similar or different, neuroimaging studies of bilingualism have returned to the question to ask whether the same neural tissue is activated during processing of the two languages. In some instances, the diffusion of activation as well as the activated areas are considered important.

A number of studies have reported that early bilinguals are more likely than late bilinguals to activate the same brain regions when processing L1 and L2 (e.g., Kim, Relkin, Lee, & Hirsch, 1997). However, because early/late bilingualism is often confounded with proficiency, Abutalebi et al. (chapter 24, this volume) concluded that age of acquisition (AoA) is not as important as the degree of proficiency attained for determining whether the same neural substrates serve the two languages: When individuals are highly proficient in their two languages, the languages appear to use the same neural networks, whereas distinct networks are used when bilinguals are not very proficient in L2, at least when tested using language production tasks (e.g., Chee, Tan, & Thiel, 1999; Illes et al., 1999; Klein, Milner, Zatorre, Meyer, & Evans, 1995; but see Perani et al., 2003, for evidence that the language acquired first may be associated with reduced brain activation during lexical retrieval tasks).

In contrast to the conclusion of neuroimaging studies suggesting that proficiency may be more important than the context of acquisition, studies of brain laterality show that early bilinguals have more bilateral hemispheric involvement for the native language than monolinguals and late bilinguals, even when the late bilinguals are proficient in L2 (see Hull & Vaid, chapter 23, this volume, for the results of a meta-analysis including a large number of bilingual laterality studies). This finding suggests that learning an L2 early in life leads to a qualitative difference in how language is processed by the brain above and beyond language proficiency. Note that although the conclusions of the imaging and laterality studies may seem contradictory on the surface, they are not necessarily at odds with one another because the neuroimaging evidence concerns similarity between areas used by the two languages, whereas the laterality evidence concerns the areas used by the brain to process L1.

Another factor that may be critical in determining the nature of meaning representations for words in the two languages is age of acquisition (AoA). There is ample evidence suggesting that, even when word frequency is controlled, words that are learned earlier in life have a processing advantage over words that are learned later in life (e.g., Gerhand & Berry, 1998; Morrison & Ellis, 1995; Morrison, Ellis, & Chappell, 1997). Izura and Ellis (2002) reported a similar finding for the effect of AoA in L2. Regardless of L1 AoA, L2 words that were learned early have a processing advantage over L2 words learned later. This result

suggests that the age at which a word is acquired will influence the connections between that word and its corresponding meaning. It also suggests that, for late L2 learning, the AoA of an L2 word does not simply inherit the AoA of its translation equivalent. The implication for bilinguals who learn their languages later than early childhood is that L2 words will not be as strongly connected to their meanings as L1 words.

Some support for that conclusion was reported in a study by Silverberg and Samuel (2004) in which they compared semantic priming effects in bilinguals who differed in both the context of acquisition and in their proficiency in L2. Only early bilinguals who were highly proficient in the L2 produced significant semantic priming, whereas late bilinguals failed to show these effects regardless of their L2 proficiency. The consequences of both factors, context of acquisition and degree of L2 proficiency, will be important foci in future research on this topic.

Developing Lexical and Conceptual Representations in the Second Language   In the final portion of our review, we consider how the connections between words and their meanings develop with increasing proficiency in the L2. Results from several studies in the cognitive literature led to the conclusion that words were likely stored separately from concepts in memory (e.g., Anderson & Bower, 1973; Potter, 1979; Snodgrass, 1980). One particularly important finding was that it takes around 200–300 ms longer to name a picture than to read a word aloud (e.g., Cattell, 1886; Fraisse, 1960; Potter & Faulconer, 1975). In a classic study, Potter et al. (1984) used this empirical observation as a means to evaluate two models of bilingual memory representation—the Word Association and Concept Mediation Models.

According to the Word Association Model (see Fig. 26.5[a]), an L1 word is directly associated to its L2 equivalent. To gain access to concepts, L2 words must first activate their L1 equivalents. By comparison, the Concept Mediation Model (see Fig. 26.5[b]) hypothesizes that words in each language are directly associated to concepts, but that translation equivalents are not directly connected to each other. The concepts in both models are proposed to be amodal, and it is further assumed that pictures have direct access to the same concepts.

To test these models, Potter et al. (1984) compared the time it took bilinguals to translate words from L1 to L2 and to name pictures in L2. The logic Potter et al. used assumed that picture naming

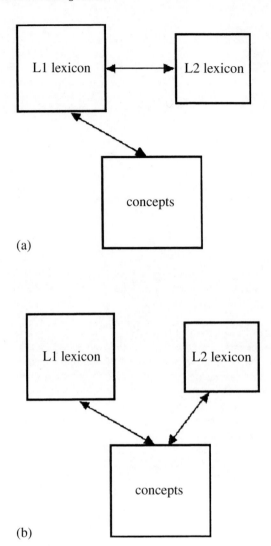

Figure 26.5 The (a) Word Association and (b) Concept Mediation Models. Adapted from Potter et al. (1984). L1, first language; L2, second language.

always requires conceptual processing. If translation from L1 to L2 resembles picture naming, then it can be concluded that translation is also conceptually mediated. Of interest is that the two models make different predictions about the relation between picture naming in L2 and translation from L1 to L2. The Word Association Model predicts that L2 picture naming should take more time than translation because two additional steps are necessary (concept retrieval and L1 word retrieval). Potter et al. reasoned that these two extra steps are also responsible for the difference in the amount of time it takes to name pictures and words in L1.

Therefore, they estimated the magnitude of the difference between picture naming and translation time predicted by the Word Association Model to be in the range of 200–300 ms. In contrast, the Concept Mediation Model predicts that the two tasks should take approximately the same amount of time because they involve similar component processes.

The results of a first experiment with highly proficient Chinese-English bilinguals showed that L2 picture naming took about the same amount of time to perform as L1-to-L2 translation and therefore favored the Concept Mediation Model. The surprising result was that, in a second experiment, a group of less-proficient English-French bilinguals produced the same pattern, suggesting that they also conceptually mediated the L2. Potter et al. (1984) concluded that the Concept Mediation Model more accurately characterized the memory representations of both less- and more proficient bilinguals than the Word Association Model.

The results of the Potter et al. (1984) study are counterintuitive because we might have expected that the less-proficient bilinguals would be more likely to rely on translation equivalents than the more proficient bilinguals. However, two aspects of the design may have inadvertently affected the conclusions. First, the items used in the experiment with the less-proficient English-French participants were intentionally selected to be well known by novices in the L2, and items that were not known by half of the participants were removed from the analyses. As we later discuss, this selection criterion may have biased the results in favor of the concept mediation pattern.

A second critical aspect of the Potter et al. (1984) study concerns the selection of the less-proficient bilinguals. In this study, they were a group of highly motivated students about to go to France on a study abroad program. Although the data showed clearly that this group was far less proficient than the English-Chinese bilinguals to whom they were compared (e.g., they were slower and more error prone), it is possible that they were beyond an initial stage of lexical acquisition that is characterized by reliance on word-to-word associations across the two languages.

To determine whether the Word Association Model characterizes L2 learners at the earliest stages of acquisition, Kroll and Curley (1988) and Chen and Leung (1989) used a methodology similar to the one used by Potter et al. (1984), but included participants who were of lower proficiency in L2 than Potter et al.'s less-proficient group. These studies showed that, for learners at early stages of acquisition, translation from L1 to L2 was indeed performed more quickly than L2 picture naming, confirming the prediction of the Word Association Model. Both studies also replicated the results of the Potter et al. study for more proficient bilinguals. Therefore, these data suggest that there is a transition from a stage of acquisition in which there is reliance on translation equivalents between L1 and L2 to a stage in which direct concept mediation is possible.

To account for this developmental sequence, Kroll and Stewart (1994) proposed the Revised Hierarchical Model. The model (see Fig. 26.6) integrates the connections depicted in the Word

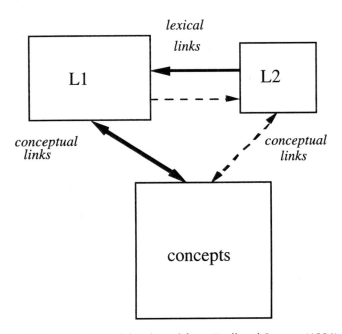

Figure 26.6 The Revised Hierarchical Model. Adapted from Kroll and Stewart (1994). L1, first language; L2, second language.

Association and Concept Mediation Models. Unlike the earlier models, the Revised Hierarchical Model makes two critical assumptions about the strength of connections between words and concepts in bilingual memory. The first is that L1 words are assumed to be more strongly connected to concepts than are L2 words. The second is that L2 words are assumed to be more strongly connected to their corresponding translation equivalents in L1 than the reverse. The resulting asymmetries are thought to reflect the consequences of L2 acquisition in late learners who possess a fully developed lexicon for words in L1 and their associated concepts. Like other claims about transfer from the L2 to L1 (e.g., MacWhinney, 1997), the Revised Hierarchical Model proposes that, during early stages of L2 acquisition, the learner exploits the existing word-to-concept connections in L1 to access meaning for new words in L2. Thus, a strong lexical connection from L2 to L1 will be established during learning. Over time, there may be feedback that establishes L1-to-L2 connections at this level, but they will be weaker than those for L2 to L1 because the learner does not need to use L2 in the same way. As learners become more proficient in L2, they will begin to develop the ability to conceptually process L2 words directly, but the connections between words and concepts are assumed to remain stronger for L1 than for L2 for all but the most balanced bilinguals.

One consequence of the asymmetries represented within the Revised Hierarchical Model is a predicted asymmetry in translation performance, such that translation from L1 to L2 in the forward direction of translation will be conceptually mediated, whereas translation from L2 to L1 in the backward translation can proceed directly via the lexical connections from L2 words to their translation equivalents. Therefore, forward translation will take longer to perform than backward translation and will be more likely to engage semantics. As L2 proficiency increases, the connection from L2 words to concepts will strengthen, resulting in a decrease in the magnitude of the translation asymmetry and a corresponding increase in the degree to which backward translation is also conceptually mediated.

To test the hypothesis that only forward translation involves conceptual mediation, Kroll and Stewart (1994) had relatively proficient Dutch-English bilinguals translate words from L1 to L2 and L2 to L1. They manipulated the semantic context of the translation lists. One list was semantically mixed, whereas the other list was semantically

categorized (e.g., all fruits, all animals, etc.). Only translation from L1 to L2 was affected by the semantic context in which translation was performed. Translation from L1 to L2 was slower for words presented in semantically categorized lists than for the same words presented in semantically mixed lists; translation from L2 to L1 was unaffected by this manipulation. These findings provided initial support for the claim that only L1-to-L2 translation necessarily involves concept mediation.

A number of studies have examined the developmental predictions of the Revised Hierarchical Model. Talamas, Kroll, and Dufour (1999) had more and less-proficient bilinguals perform a translation recognition task (De Groot, 1992b) in which a pair of words was presented and participants indicated whether the two words were translations of each other. The critical items were nontranslation foils that were related to one another by virtue of being form related (e.g., man–hambre [hunger] instead of man–hombre [man]) or meaning related (e.g., man–mujer [woman] instead of man–hombre [man]) to the correct translation. The results showed that the less-proficient bilinguals suffered more form than meaning interference, whereas the reverse was true for the more proficient bilinguals. The results are thus consistent with a developmental shift from form to meaning with increasing proficiency in the L2.

In a study similar to that of Talamas et al. (1999), Sunderman (2002) also used a translation recognition task to investigate the development of L2 in a group of native English speakers learning Spanish as adults. In that study, three types of "no" trials were compared: form related (man–mano [hand]), meaning related (man–mujer [woman]), and form related to the translation (man–hambre [hunger]). The results showed that all participants, regardless of proficiency, were slower to reject word pairs that were form or meaning related relative to unrelated controls. However, only the less-proficient participants were slower to respond to the foils that were form related to the correct translation (e.g., man–hambre). Although the presence of semantic effects for all groups failed to replicate the results of Talamas et al. (see also Altarriba & Mathis, 1997), the differential effect of the form-related translation foil suggests, as the Revised Hierarchical Model predicts, that access to the translation equivalent may play a particularly important role early in L2 learning (see MacWhinney, chapter 3, this volume, for related arguments about the scope of transfer during L2 acquisition).

Additional support for the developmental predictions of the Revised Hierarchical Model comes from a study by Kroll, Michael, Tokowicz, and Dufour (2002). In that study, learners in a summer intensive language program and proficient bilinguals performed the same bilingual tasks. The results showed that L1-to-L2 translation generally took longer to perform than L2-to-L1 translation, but that the asymmetry was smaller for the more proficient group than for the learners, supporting the prediction of the Revised Hierarchical Model that the two directions of translation become more similar with increased L2 proficiency.

There have also been a number of studies in which results contrary to the predictions of the Revised Hierarchical Model have been found. In one such study, De Groot and Poot (1997) tested learners at three proficiency levels (low, average, and high) on a translation production task. The concreteness or imageability of the translated words was manipulated such that some items were *concrete* (i.e., represented entities that were perceptible; e.g., table), whereas other items were *abstract* (i.e., represented entities that were imperceptible; e.g., beauty). Because the hypothesized difference between these two word types is in meaning, any difference in translation time was taken to indicate conceptually mediated translation. De Groot and Poot found that there was a concrete–abstract difference for bilinguals in all three proficiency groups and therefore concluded that translation is always conceptually mediated and bilinguals do not need to rely on L1 for access to meaning. Furthermore, the results showed that translation in both directions was influenced by concreteness to a similar extent, and they therefore concluded that both directions of translation are conceptually mediated, inconsistent with the predictions of the Revised Hierarchical Model.

De Groot and Poot's (1997) results are important because the performance of learners of different proficiency levels was directly compared. However, because the results of this study are counter to much of the research on language production, we must interpret them carefully. In particular, more recent research has revealed that concrete words are likely to have fewer translations across languages than abstract words (Schönpflug, 1997; Tokowicz & Kroll, 2003; Tokowicz et al., 2002). Furthermore, Tokowicz and Kroll reported that the existence of an alternate translation slows translation speed considerably. Therefore, the effects of concreteness on translation may come from multiple sources and must be interpreted carefully.

Altarriba and Mathis (1997) reported another study that found results counter to the predictions of the Revised Hierarchical Model. In this study, naïve learners were trained on four color words in Spanish. After scoring 100% accuracy on several quizzes testing their knowledge of the Spanish color words, they were tested on a Stroop-type interference task using the color words they had just learned. The findings showed that the learners indeed showed interference in L2. Because they were at the very earliest stages of learning a new language (they had learned only a few words), these results were contrary to the predictions of the Revised Hierarchical Model. However, it is not clear that these results are representative of what would be found with L2 learners in a more typical learning situation (i.e., with more word pairs studied over a longer period of time). What is interesting about these results is that they demonstrate the capabilities of the language-learning situation under unique circumstances: When a small number of items are learned with extensive training, the results mimic those of proficient bilinguals. This finding provides evidence that individual items can become conceptually mediated; the bounds of this learning have yet to be demonstrated.

Perhaps the most compelling evidence supporting the prediction of the Revised Hierarchical Model that L1-to-L2 translation is conceptually mediated but L2-to-L1 translation is not comes from a study that examined transfer from picture naming to translation (Sholl, Sankaranarayanan, & Kroll, 1995). If only translation from L1 to L2 is conceptually mediated, then only L1-to-L2 translation should benefit from prior study during which concepts are named as pictures, a task also believed to be conceptually mediated (e.g., Potter & Faulconer, 1975). This is precisely the result reported by Sholl et al. Translation from L1 to L2 was facilitated when concepts had been named previously as pictures in L2 or L1. In contrast, translation from L2 to L1 was unaffected by prior picture naming.

The conclusions of Sholl et al. (1995) were subsequently challenged by a study reported by La Heij et al. (1996) in which Dutch-English bilinguals were asked to translate words in each direction and to name words in each language. The critical conditions of the La Heij et al. study consisted of picture primes that were related to the target word to be translated or named. Like the results of Kroll and Stewart (1994), there was little effect of the semantic context on word naming. However, unlike the results of Kroll and Stewart and Sholl et al., there were significant semantic effects of picture primes in both directions of translation, suggesting that both directions of translation are conceptually mediated. Because the Dutch-English bilinguals in the La Heij et al. study were very similar to the Dutch-English participants in the Kroll and Stewart study, it seems unlikely that the nature of the participants' bilingualism was responsible for the different pattern of results across these studies.

In a study similar to the one by Sholl et al. (1995), Francis, Tokowicz, and Kroll (2003) showed that translation from L1 to L2 was facilitated by previous translation only in the *same* direction, whereas translation from L2 to L1 was facilitated by previous translation in *either* direction, further suggesting that the two directions of translation may engage different component processes. The results of the Francis et al. study also suggest that, as bilinguals become more proficient, the two directions of translation become more similar because the asymmetrical priming disappears, and both directions of translation are primed by previous translation in either direction. Finally, the results suggest that, within an individual, there may be some words that are conceptually mediated and others that are not. The "easier" items in the Francis et al. study, as defined by relatively higher word frequency, showed symmetrical priming regardless of the bilingual group's proficiency.

This result may help to explain some of the apparently conflicting results in the studies reviewed here. In the La Heij et al. (1996) experiments, items were chosen intentionally to be high frequency, and therefore likely to be known by all participants, and were repeated throughout the experiment. In the Kroll and Stewart (1994) study, the items were generally much lower in frequency and presented only once to a given participant. The pattern of results reported by Francis et al. (2003) suggests that both the proficiency of the bilingual participants and the nature of the items will determine the likelihood of observing asymmetries in performance. These findings highlight the developmental nature of becoming bilingual: Transitions from less to more proficient are not limited to the individual bilingual but also are relevant for individual words.

Summary

In this chapter, we provided a review of the state of bilingual models of representation and processing. Although our review was limited to the lexicon, a topic on which there has been a disproportionate amount of research in recent years, many of the issues covered will also apply to other domains of language processing. Early models of the bilingual lexicon were general and largely failed to provide an adequate characterization of how information in each language might be represented. Later models responded to that criticism by providing a more specific account but within a relatively narrow focus. Concerns about control mechanisms, about the manner in which processing changes in the face of task demands, and about the consequences of the ways in which proficiency develops in the L2 will all be crucial to the next stages of model development.

With the exception of the BIA model (see also Grosjean, 1997; Thomas, 1997), few models have been implemented computationally. Likewise, it is only recently that a range of evidence has been available to test behavioral predictions of bilingual models and then to assess their neurocognitive underpinnings. We anticipate that the next period of research and model construction will be informed by all of these perspectives. Although in the future it may become more difficult to answer the question of whether the bilingual's two languages are maintained in separate or shared memory systems, we are confident that research on bilingual representation and processing will provide important insights not only into the nature of bilingualism, but also more fundamentally into the relation between language and cognition.

Acknowledgments

The writing of this chapter was supported in part by National Science Foundation Grant BCS-0111734 and National Institute of Mental Health grant RO1MH62479 to Judith F. Kroll and by a National Research Service Award NIMH HD-42948-01 to Natasha Tokowicz. We thank Erica Michael for helpful comments on an earlier version of the chapter and Nora Kroll-Rosenbaum for assistance in graphic design.

References

Altarriba, J. (1990). *Constraints on interlingual facilitation effects in priming in Spanish-English bilinguals.* Unpublished doctoral dissertation, Vanderbilt University, Nashville, TN.

Altarriba, J., Kroll, J. F., Sholl, A., & Rayner, K. (1996). The influence of lexical and conceptual constraints on reading mixed-language sentences: Evidence from eye-fixation and naming times. *Memory & Cognition, 24,* 477–492.

Altarriba, J., & Mathis, K. M. (1997). Conceptual and lexical development in second language acquisition. *Journal of Memory and Language, 36,* 550–568.

Anderson, J. R., & Bower, G. H. (1973). *Human associative memory.* New York: Wiley.

Bloem, I., & La Heij, W. (2003). Semantic facilitation and semantic interference in word translation: Implications for models of lexical access in language production. *Journal of Memory and Language, 48,* 468–488.

Brysbaert, M., Van Dyck, G., & Van de Poel, M. (1999). Visual word recognition in bilinguals: Evidence from masked phonological priming. *Journal of Experimental Psychology: Human Perception and Performance, 25,* 137–148.

Cattell, J. M. (1886). The time it takes to see and name objects. *Mind, 11,* 63–65.

Chee, M. W. L., Tan, E. W. L., & Thiel, T. (1999). Mandarin and English single word processing studied with functional magnetic resonance imaging. *Journal of Neuroscience, 19,* 3050–3056.

Chen, H.-C., & Leung, Y.-S. (1989). Patterns of lexical processing in a nonnative language. *Journal of Experimental Psychology: Learning, Memory, and Cognition, 15,* 316–325.

Chen, H.-C., & Ng, M.-L. (1989). Semantic facilitation and translation priming effects in Chinese-English bilinguals. *Memory & Cognition, 17,* 454–462.

Colomé, À. (2001). Lexical activation in bilinguals' speech production: language-specific or language independent? *Journal of Memory and Language, 45,* 721–736.

Costa, A., & Caramazza, A. (1999). Is lexical selection language specific? Further evidence from Spanish-English bilinguals. *Bilingualism: Language and Cognition, 2,* 231–244.

Costa, A., Caramazza, A., & Sebastián-Gallés, N. (2000). The cognate facilitation effect: Implications for models of lexical access. *Journal of Experimental Psychology: Learning, Memory, and Cognition, 26,* 1283–1296.

Costa, A., Miozzo, M., & Caramazza, A. (1999). Lexical selection in bilinguals: Do words in the bilingual's two lexicons compete for selection? *Journal of Memory and Language, 41,* 365–397.

De Bot, K., & Schreuder, R. (1993). Word production and the bilingual lexicon. In R. Schreuder & B. Weltens (Eds.), *The bilingual lexicon* (pp. 191–214). Amsterdam: Benjamins.

De Bruijn, E. R. A., Dijkstra, A., Chwilla, D. J., & Schriefers, H. J. (2001). Language context effects on interlingual homograph recognition: Evidence from event-related potentials and response times in semantic priming.

Bilingualism: Language and Cognition, 4, 155–168.

De Groot, A. M. B. (1992a). Bilingual lexical representation: A closer look at conceptual representations. In R. Frost & L. Katz (Eds.), *Orthography, phonology, morphology, and meaning* (pp. 389–412). Amsterdam: Elsevier Science.

De Groot, A. M. B. (1992b). Determinants of word translation. *Journal of Experimental Psychology: Learning, Memory, and Cognition, 18,* 1001–1018.

De Groot, A. M. B. (1995). Determinants of bilingual lexicosemantic organization. *Computer Assisted Language Learning, 8,* 151–180.

De Groot, A. M. B. (2002). Lexical representation and lexical processing in the L2 user. In V. Cook (Ed.), *Portraits of the L2 user* (pp. 32–63). Clevedon, U.K.: Multilingual Matters.

De Groot, A. M. B., Dannenburg, L., & Van Hell, J. G. (1994). Forward and backward word translation by bilinguals. *Journal of Memory and Language, 33,* 600–629.

De Groot, A. M. B., & Poot, R. (1997). Word translation at three levels of proficiency in a second language: The ubiquitous involvement of conceptual memory. *Language Learning, 47,* 215–264.

Dell, G. S. (1986). A spreading-activation theory of retrieval in sentence production. *Psychological Review, 93,* 283–321.

Dijkstra, A., Grainger, J., & Van Heuven, W. J. B. (1999). Recognizing cognates and interlingual homographs: The neglected role of phonology. *Journal of Memory and Language, 41,* 496–518.

Dijkstra, A., & Van Heuven, W. J. B. (1998). The BIA model and bilingual word recognition. In J. Grainger & A. M. Jacobs (Eds.), *Localist connectionist approaches to human cognition* (pp. 189–225). Mahwah, NJ: Erlbaum.

Dijkstra, A., & Van Heuven, W. J. B. (2002). The architecture of the bilingual word recognition system: From identification to decision. *Bilingualism: Language and Cognition, 5,* 175–197.

Dufour, R., & Kroll, J. F. (1995). Matching words to concepts in two languages: A test of the concept mediation model of bilingual representation. *Memory & Cognition, 23,* 166–180.

Durgunoglu, A. Y., & Roediger, H. L. (1987). Test differences in accessing bilingual memory. *Journal of Memory and Language, 26,* 377–391.

Elston-Güttler, K. E. (2000). *An inquiry into cross-language differences in lexical-conceptual relationships and their effect on L2 lexical processing.* Unpublished doctoral dissertation, University of Cambridge, Cambridge, U.K.

Finkbeiner, M., Forster, K., Nicol, J., & Nakamura, K. (2004). The role of polysemy in masked semantic and translation priming. *Journal of Memory and Language, 51,* 1–22.

Fraisse, P. (1960). Recognition time measured by verbal reaction to figures and words. *Perceptual and Motor Skills, 11,* 204.

Francis, W. S. (1999). Cognitive integration of language and memory in bilinguals: Semantic representation. *Psychological Bulletin, 125,* 193–222.

Francis, W. S., Tokowicz, N., & Kroll, J. F. (2003, April). *Translation priming as a function of bilingual proficiency and item difficulty.* Poster presented at the Fourth International Symposium on Bilingualism, Tempe, AZ.

Gerhand, S., & Berry, C. (1998). Word frequency effects in oral reading are not merely age of acquisition effects in disguise. *Journal of Experimental Psychology: Learning, Memory and Cognition, 24,* 267–283.

Gollan, T. H., Forster, K. I., & Frost, R. (1997). Translation priming with different scripts: Masked priming with cognates and non-cognates in Hebrew-English bilinguals. *Journal of Experimental Psychology: Learning, Memory, and Cognition, 23,* 1122–1139.

Gollan, T., & Kroll, J. F. (2001). Bilingual lexical access. In B. Rapp (Ed.), *The handbook of cognitive neuropsychology: What deficits reveal about the human mind* (pp. 321–345). Philadelphia: Psychology Press.

Gollan, T. H., & Silverberg, N. (2001). Tip-of-the-tongue states in Hebrew-English bilinguals. *Bilingualism: Language and Cognition, 4,* 63–84.

Grainger, J., & Dijkstra, A. (1992). On the representation and use of language information in bilinguals. In R. Harris (Ed.), *Cognitive processing in bilinguals* (pp. 207–220). Amsterdam: Elsevier.

Grainger, J., & Jacobs, A. M. (1996). Orthographic processing in visual word recognition: A multiple read-out model. *Psychological Review, 103,* 518–565.

Green, D. W. (1986). Control, activation, and resource: A framework and a model for the control of speech in bilinguals. *Brain and Language, 27,* 210–223.

Green, D. W. (1998). Mental control of the bilingual lexico-semantic system. *Bilingualism: Language and Cognition, 1,* 67–81.

Grosjean, F. (1997). Processing mixed language: Issues, findings, and models. In A. M. B. de Groot & J. F. Kroll (Eds.), *Tutorials in bilingualism: Psycholinguistic perspectives* (pp. 225–254). Mahwah, NJ: Erlbaum.

Grosjean, F., Li, P., Münte, T., & Rodriquez-Fornells, A. (2003). Imaging bilinguals: When the neurosciences meet the language sciences. *Bilingualism: Language and Cognition, 6,* 159–165.

Hermans, D. (2000). *Word production in a foreign language.* Unpublished doctoral dissertation, University of Nijmegen, Nijmegen, The Netherlands.

Hermans, D., Bongaerts, T., De Bot, K., & Schreuder, R. (1998). Producing words in a foreign language: Can speakers prevent interference from their first language? *Bilingualism: Language and Cognition, 1,* 213–229.

Illes, J., Francis, W. S., Desmond, J. E., Gabrieli, J. D. E., Glover, G. H., Poldrack, R., et al. (1999). Convergent cortical representation of semantic processing in bilinguals. *Brain and Language, 70,* 347–363.

Izura, C., & Ellis, A. W. (2002). Age of acquisition effects in word recognition and production in first and second languages. *Psicológica, 23,* 245–281.

Jared, D., & Kroll, J. F. (2001). Do bilinguals activate phonological representations in one or both of their languages when naming words? *Journal of Memory and Language, 44,* 2–31.

Jared, D., & Szucs, C. (2002). Phonological activation in bilinguals: Evidence from interlingual homograph recognition. *Bilingualism, Language and Cognition, 5,* 225–239.

Jiang, N. (2000). Lexical representation and development in a second language. *Applied Linguistics, 21,* 47–77.

Keatley, C., Spinks, J., & De Gelder, B. (1994). Asymmetrical semantic facilitation between languages. *Memory & Cognition, 22,* 70–84.

Kim, K. H. S., Relkin, N. R., Lee, K. M., & Hirsch, J. (1997). Distinct cortical areas associated with native and second languages. *Nature, 388,* 171–174.

Kirsner, K., Smith, M. C., Lockhart, R. L. S., King, M. L., & Jain, M. (1984). The bilingual lexicon: Language-specific units in an integrated network. *Journal of Verbal Learning and Verbal Behavior, 23,* 519–539.

Klein, D., Milner, B., Zatorre, R., Meyer, E., & Evans, A. (1995). The neural substrates underlying word generation: A bilingual functional-imaging study. *Proceedings of the National Academy of Sciences U.S.A., 92,* 2899–2903.

Kolers, P. A. (1963). Interlingual word associations. *Journal of Verbal Memory and Verbal Behavior, 2,* 291–300.

Kroll, J. F., & Curley, J. (1988). Lexical memory in novice bilinguals: The role of concepts in retrieving second language words. In M. Gruneberg, P. Morris, & R. Sykes (Eds.),

Practical aspects of memory (Vol. 2, pp. 389–395). London: Wiley.

Kroll, J. F., & De Groot, A. M. B. (1997). Lexical and conceptual memory in the bilingual: Mapping form to meaning in two languages. In A. M. B. de Groot & J. F. Kroll (Eds.), *Tutorials in bilingualism: Psycholinguistic perspectives* (pp. 169–199). Mahwah, NJ: Erlbaum.

Kroll, J. F., & Dijkstra, A. (2002). The bilingual lexicon. In R. Kaplan (Ed.), *Handbook of applied linguistics* (pp. 301–321). Oxford, U.K.: Oxford University Press.

Kroll, J. F., Dijkstra, A., Janssen, N., & Schriefers, H. (in preparation). *Selecting the language in which to speak: Cued-picture naming experiments on lexical access in bilingual production.* Unpublished manuscript, The Pennsylvania State University, University Park.

Kroll, J. F., & Dussias, P. (2004). The comprehension of words and sentences in two languages. In T. Bhatia & W. Ritchie (Eds.), *Handbook of bilingualism* (169–200). Cambridge, MA: Blackwell.

Kroll, J. F., Michael, E., Tokowicz, N., & Dufour, R. (2002). The development of lexical fluency in a second language. *Second Language Research, 18,* 137–171.

Kroll, J. F., & Sholl, A. (1992). Lexical and conceptual memory in fluent and nonfluent bilinguals. In R. Harris (Ed.), *Cognitive processing in bilinguals* (pp. 191–204). Amsterdam: Elsevier.

Kroll, J. F., & Stewart, E. (1994). Category interference in translation and picture naming: Evidence for asymmetric connections between bilingual memory representations. *Journal of Memory and Language, 33,* 149–174.

Kroll, J. F., & Sunderman, G. (2003). Cognitive processes in second language acquisition: The development of lexical and conceptual representations. In C. Doughty & M. Long (Eds.), *Handbook of second language acquisition* (pp. 104–129). Cambridge, MA: Blackwell.

Kroll, J. F., & Tokowicz, N. (2001). The development of conceptual representation for words in a second language. In J. L. Nicol (Ed.), *One mind, two languages: Bilingual language processing* (pp. 49–71). Cambridge, MA: Blackwell.

La Heij, W., De Bruyn, E., Elens, E., Hartsuiker, R., Helaha, D., & Van Schelven, L. (1990). Orthographic facilitation and categorical interference in a word-translation variant of the Stroop task. *Canadian Journal of Psychology, 44,* 76–83.

La Heij, W., Kerling, R., & Van der Velden, E. (1996). Nonverbal context effects in forward and backward translation: Evidence for concept mediation. *Journal of Memory and Language, 35,* 648–665.

Lambert, W. E. (1961). Behavioral evidence for contrasting forms of bilingualism. In M. Zarechnak (Ed.), *Report of the 12th Annual Round Table Meeting on Linguistics and Language Studies.* Washington, DC: Georgetown University Press.

Lambert, W. E. (1969). Psychological studies of the inter-dependencies of the bilingual's two languages. In J. Puhvel (Ed.), *Substance and structure of language* (pp. 99–126). Berkeley: University of California Press.

Lambert, W. E. (1972). *Language, psychology, and culture.* Stanford, CA: Stanford University Press.

Lambert, W. E., Havelka, J., & Crosby, C. (1958). The influence of language acquisition contexts on bilingualism. *Journal of Abnormal and Social Psychology, 56,* 239–244.

Levelt, W. J. M. (1989). *Speaking: From intention to articulation.* Cambridge, MA: MIT Press.

Levelt, W. J. M., Roelofs, A., & Meyer, A. S. (1999). A theory of lexical access in speech production. *Behavioral and Brain Sciences, 22,* 1–75.

Macnamara, J., & Kushnir, S. L. (1971). Linguistic independence of bilinguals: The input switch. *Journal of Verbal Learning and Verbal Behavior, 10,* 480–487.

MacWhinney, B. (1997). Second language acquisition and the competition model. In A. M. B. de Groot & J. F. Kroll (Eds.), *Tutorials in bilingualism: Psycholinguistic perspectives* (pp. 113–142). Mahwah, NJ: Erlbaum.

Mägiste, E. (1984). Stroop tasks and dichotic translation: The development of interference patterns in bilinguals. *Journal of Experimental Psychology: Learning, Memory, and Cognition, 10,* 304–315.

Marian, V., & Neisser, U. (2000). Language-dependent recall of autobiographical memories. *Journal of Experimental Psychology: General, 129,* 361–368.

Marian, V., & Spivey, M. (1999). Activation of Russian and English cohorts during bilingual spoken word recognition. In M. Hahn & S. C. Stoness (Eds.), *Proceedings of the 21st Annual Conference of the Cognitive Science Society* (pp. 349–354). Mahwah, NJ: Erlbaum.

Marian, V., Spivey, M., & Hirsch, J. (2003). Shared and separate systems in bilingual language processing: Converging evidence from eyetracking and brain imaging. *Brain and Language, 86,* 70–82.

McClelland, J. L., & Rumelhart, D. E. (1981). An interactive activation model of context effects in letter perception, Part 1: An account of basic findings. *Psychological Review, 88,* 375–405.

McCormack, P. D. (1977). Bilingual linguistic memory: The independence-interdependence issue revisited. In P. A. Hornby (Ed.), *Bilingualism: Psychological, social, educational implications* (pp. 57–66). New York: Academic Press.

Meuter, R. F. I., & Allport, A. (1999). Bilingual language switching in naming: Asymmetrical costs of language selection. *Journal of Memory and Language, 40,* 25–40.

Meyer, D. E., & Ruddy, M. G. (1974). *Bilingual word recognition: Organization and retrieval of alternative lexical codes.* Paper presented at the annual meeting of the Eastern Psychological Association, Philadelphia.

Miller, N. A., & Kroll, J. F. (2002). Stroop effects in bilingual translation. *Memory & Cognition, 30,* 614–628.

Morrison, C. M., & Ellis, A. W. (1995). Roles of word frequency and age of acquisition in word naming and lexical decision. *Journal of Experimental Psychology: Learning, Memory and Cognition, 21,* 116–153.

Morrison, C. M., Ellis, A. W., & Chappell, T. D. (1997). Age of acquisition norms for a large set of object names and their relation to adult estimates and other variables. *Quarterly Journal of Experimental Psychology: Human Experimental Psychology, 50A,* 528–559.

Paivio, A. (1991). Mental representation in bilinguals. In A. G. Reynolds (Ed.), *Bilingualism, multiculturalism, and second language learning: The McGill conference in honour of Wallace E. Lambert* (pp. 113–126). Hillsdale, NJ: Erlbaum.

Pavlenko, A. (1999). New approaches to concepts in bilingual memory. *Bilingualism: Language and Cognition, 2,* 209–230.

Perani, D., Abutalebi, J., Paulesu, E., Brambati, S., Scifo, P., Cappa, S. F., et al. (2003). The role of age of acquisition and language usage in early, high-proficient bilinguals: An fMRI study during verbal fluency. *Human Brain Mapping, 19,* 170–182.

Peterson, R. R., & Savoy, P. (1998). Lexical selection and phonological encoding during language production: Evidence for cascaded processing. *Journal of Experimental Psychology: Learning, Memory, and Cognition, 24,* 539–557.

Potter, M. C. (1979). Mundane symbolism: The relations among objects, names, and ideas. In N. R. Smith & M. B. Franklin (Eds.), *Symbolic functioning in childhood* (pp. 41–65). Hillsdale, NJ: Erlbaum.

Potter, M. C., & Faulconer, B. A. (1975). Time to understand pictures and words. *Nature (London), 253,* 437–438.

Potter, M. C., So, K.-F., Von Eckardt, B., & Feldman, L. B. (1984). Lexical and conceptual representation in beginning and more proficient bilinguals. *Journal of Verbal Learning and Verbal Behavior, 23,* 23–38.

Poulisse, N., & Bongaerts T. (1994). First language use in second language production. *Applied Linguistics, 15,* 36–57.

Rodriquez-Fornells, A., Rotte, M., Heinze, H.-J., Nösselt, T., & Münte, T. (2002). Brain potential and functional MRI evidence for how to handle two languages with one brain. *Nature, 415,* 1026–1029.

Schönpflug, U. (1997, April). *Bilingualism and memory.* Paper presented at the First International Symposium on Bilingualism, Newcastle-upon-Tyne, U.K.

Schrauf, R. W., & Rubin, D. C. (1998). Bilingual autobiographical memory in older adult immigrants: A test of cognitive explanations of the reminiscence bump and the linguistic encoding of memories. *Journal of Memory and Language, 39,* 437–457.

Schwanenflugel, P. J., & Rey, M. (1986). Interlingual semantic facilitation: Evidence for a common representational system in the bilingual. *Journal of Memory and Language, 25,* 605–618.

Schwanenflugel, P. J., & Shoben, E. J. (1983). Differential context effects in the comprehension of abstract and concrete verbal materials. *Journal of Experimental Psychology: Learning, Memory, and Cognition, 9,* 82–102.

Schwartz, A. (2003). *Word and sentence-based processes in second language reading.* Unpublished doctoral dissertation, The Pennsylvania State University, University Park.

Schwartz, A., Kroll, J. F., & Diaz, M. (2003). *Reading words in Spanish and English: Mapping orthography to phonology in two languages.* Unpublished manuscript, The Pennsylvania State University, University Park.

Seidenberg, M. S., & McClelland, J. L. (1989). A distributed, developmental model of word recognition and naming. *Psychological Review, 96,* 523–568.

Shaffer, D. (1976). Is bilingualism compound or coordinate? *Lingua, 40,* 69–77.

Sholl, A., Sankaranarayanan, A., & Kroll, J. F. (1995). Transfer between picture naming and translation: A test of asymmetries in bilingual memory. *Psychological Science, 6,* 45–49.

Silverberg, S., & Samuel, A. G. (2004). The effect of age of second language acquisition on the representation and processing of second language words. *Journal of Memory and Language, 51,* 381–398.

Snodgrass, J. G. (1980). Towards a model for picture-word processing. In P. A. Kolers, M. E.

Wrolstad, & H. Bouma (Eds.), *Processing of visible language* (Vol. 2, pp. 565–584). New York: Plenum.

Sunderman, G. (2002). *Lexical development in a second language: Can the first language be suppressed?* Unpublished doctoral dissertation, The Pennsylvania State University, University Park.

Talamas, A., Kroll, J. F., & Dufour, R. (1999). Form related errors in second language learning: A preliminary stage in the acquisition of L2 vocabulary. *Bilingualism: Language and Cognition, 2*, 45–58.

Thomas, M. S. C. (1997). *Connectionist networks and knowledge representation: The case of bilingual lexical processing.* Unpublished doctoral dissertation, Oxford University, Oxford, U.K.

Tokowicz, N. (2000). *Meaning representation within and across languages.* Unpublished doctoral dissertation, The Pennsylvania State University, University Park.

Tokowicz, N., & Kroll, J. F. (2003). *Accessing meaning for words in two languages: The effects of lexical and semantic ambiguity in bilingual production.* Unpublished manuscript, The Pennsylvania State University, University Park.

Tokowicz, N., Kroll, J. F., De Groot, A. M. B., & Van Hell, J. G. (2002). Number of translation norms for Dutch-English translation pairs: A new tool for examining language production. *Behavior Research Methods, Instruments, & Computers, 34*, 435–451.

Tzelgov, J., & Eben-Ezra, S. (1992). Components of the between-language semantic priming effect. *European Journal of Cognitive Psychology, 4*, 253–272.

Van Hell, J. G. (1998). *Cross-language processing and bilingual memory organization.* Unpublished doctoral dissertation, University of Amsterdam, Amsterdam.

Van Hell, J. G., & De Groot, A. M. B. (1998). Conceptual representation in bilingual memory: Effects of concreteness and cognate status in word association. *Bilingualism: Language and Cognition, 1*, 193–211.

Van Hell, J., & Dijkstra, T. (2002). Foreign language knowledge can influence native language performance: Evidence from trilinguals. *Psychonomic Bulletin & Review, 9*, 780–789.

Van Heuven, W. J. B. (2000). *Visual word recognition in monolingual and bilingual readers: Experiments and computational modeling.* Doctoral thesis, University of Nijmegen, Nijmegen, The Netherlands. NICI Technical Report 20-01.

Van Heuven, W. J. B., Dijkstra, A., & Grainger, J. (1998). Orthographic neighborhood effects in bilingual word recognition. *Journal of Memory and Language, 39*, 458–483.

Von Studnitz, R., & Green, D. W. (2002). Interlingual homograph interference in German-English bilinguals: Its modulation and locus of control. *Bilingualism: Language and Cognition, 5*, 1–23.

Vigliocco, G., & Hartsuiker, R. J. (2002). The interplay of meaning, sound, and syntax in sentence production. *Psychological Bulletin, 128*, 442–472.

Weinreich, U. (1953). *Languages in contact.* New York: The Linguistics Circle of New York.

Author Index

Subject Index